MICHELIN

Road Atlas

USA CANADA MEXICO

NORTH AMERICA

Legend .... **Cover flap**

Key to Map Pages .... **Inside front cover**

How to Use this Atlas **2**

Listing of State and City Maps **3**

United States Interstate Map **4–5**

Canada Highway Map **6–7**

Michelin Scenic Drives **8–11, 301–302**

Maps **12–187**

United States 12–155

BONUS MAPS! *Washington DC to Boston*

Large-Scale Northeast Corridor Maps 144–151

Canada 156–183

Mexico 184–187

Index with City and Local Maps **188–283**

United States 188–276

Canada 277–282

Mexico 283

City to City Distance Chart **284–285**

Distances and Driving Times across North America **286–287**

Tourism and Border Crossing Information **288**

Parks Index with GPS Coordinates **289–300**

United States 289–297

Canada 298–300

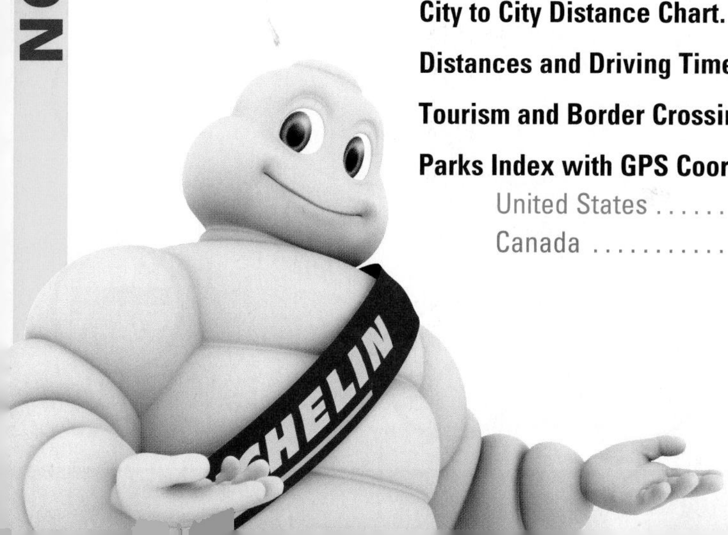

ROAD MAPS are organized geographically. *United States, Canada, and Mexico road maps are organized in a grid layout, starting in the northwest of each country. To find your way, use either the* ***Key to Map Pages*** *inside the front cover, the* ***Listing of State and City Maps*** *on page 3, or the* ***index*** *in the back of the atlas.*

COUNTRY COLORS
Colors represent countries throughout the atlas.
Red → Canada
Green → Mexico
Blue → United States
Purple → United States (Northeast Corridor)

MAP SCALES
Scale bars are shown at a constant length throughout the atlas for quick and easy scale comparison between regions.

DRIVING DISTANCES
Use this chart to check driving distances between major cities within each map. Refer to distance and driving time information at the back of the atlas for travel over greater distances.

LOCATOR MAPS
A quick glance at this miniature map lets you check which states and/or provinces are shown on each page.

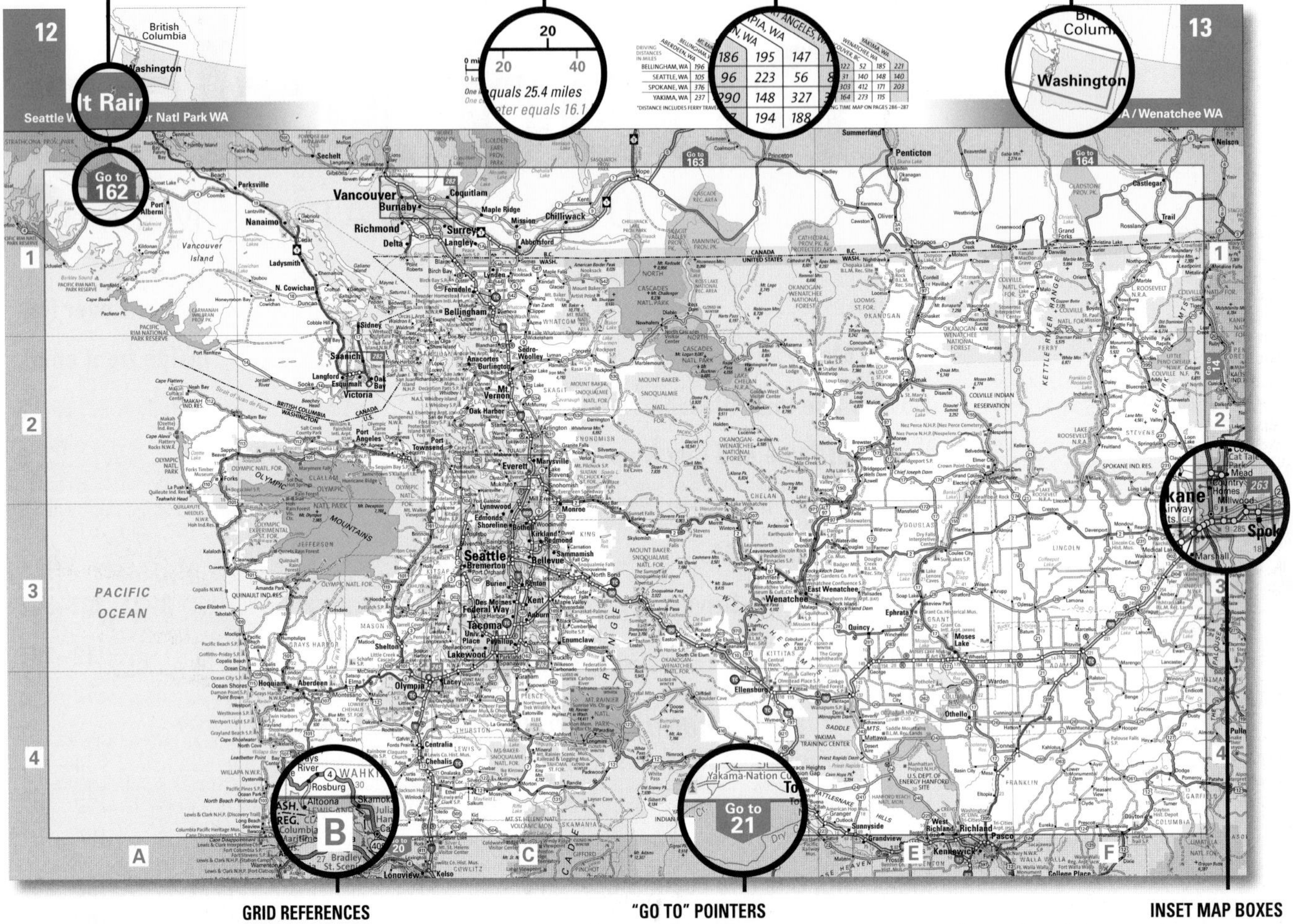

GRID REFERENCES
Use grid references to locate places listed in the index. For instance, Rosburg WA is listed in the index with "12" and "B4", indicating that the town may be found on page 12 in grid square B4.

"GO TO" POINTERS
Handy page tabs point the way to the next map, making navigation a breeze.

INSET MAP BOXES
These color-coded boxes outline areas that are featured in greater detail in the index section. The tab with "263" (above) indicates that a detailed map of Spokane may be found on page 263 (below).

HOW THE INDEX WORKS
Cities and towns are listed alphabetically, with separate indexes for the United States, Canada, and Mexico. Figures after entries indicate population, page number, and grid reference. Entries in bold color indicate cities with detailed inset maps. The U.S. index also includes counties and parishes, which are shown in bold black type.

INSET MAP INDEXES
Many inset maps have their own indexes. Metro area inset map indexes list cities and towns; downtown inset map indexes list points of interest.

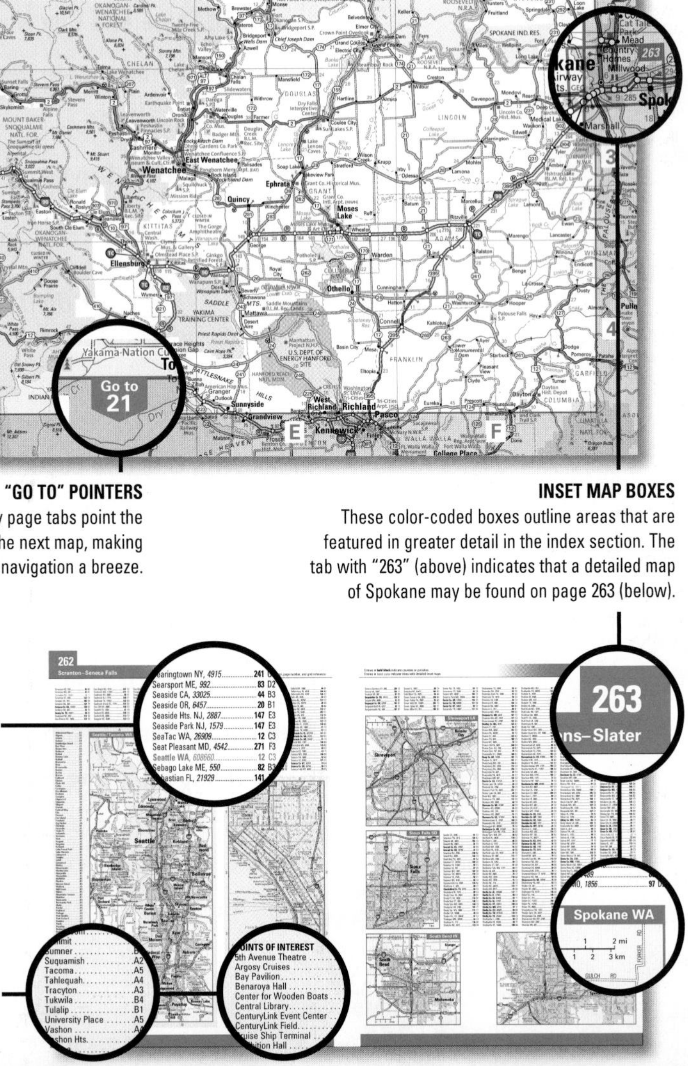

UNITED STATES pages 12–155

ALABAMA (AL) 119–120, 127–128, 135–137
- Birmingham 195
- Huntsville 221
- Mobile 236
- Montgomery 236

ALASKA (AK) 154–155
- Anchorage 189
- Juneau 223

ARIZONA (AZ) 46–48, 53–55
- Flagstaff 213
- Phoenix 249
- Phoenix Downtown 249
- Tucson 268
- Yuma 276

ARKANSAS (AR) 106–108, 116–118, 124–126
- Fayetteville 212
- Hot Springs 219
- Little Rock 227

CALIFORNIA (CA) 28–29, 36–37, 44–46, 52–54
- Bakersfield 192
- Fresno 214
- Los Angeles 228
- Los Angeles Downtown 230
- Monterey Bay 236
- Oxnard/Ventura 247
- Palm Springs 247
- Sacramento 255
- San Diego 258
- San Diego Downtown 258
- San Francisco Bay Area 259
- San Francisco Downtown 260
- Santa Barbara 260
- Stockton 265

COLORADO (CO) 32–34, 40–42, 48–50
- Colorado Springs 205
- Denver 209
- Denver Downtown 209
- Fort Collins 213
- Pueblo 252

CONNECTICUT (CT) 94–95, 148–150
- Hartford 218
- New Haven/Bridgeport 238
- Stamford 264
- Waterbury 273

DELAWARE (DE) 103–104, 114, 145–146
- Dover 211
- Wilmington 274

DISTRICT OF COLUMBIA (DC) 103–104, 114, 144
- Washington 270
- Washington Downtown 272

FLORIDA (FL) 135–143
- Daytona Beach 208
- Fort Myers 214
- Jacksonville 222
- Key West 224
- Melbourne/Titusville 232
- Miami/Fort Lauderdale 233
- Miami Downtown 233
- Orlando 246
- Panama City 247
- Pensacola 247
- Tallahassee 265
- Tampa/St. Petersburg 266

GEORGIA (GA) 120–121, 128–130, 137–139
- Atlanta 190
- Atlanta Downtown 191
- Augusta 191
- Columbus 205
- Macon 231
- Savannah 261

HAWAII (HI) 152–153
- Honolulu 219

IDAHO (ID) 14–15, 22–24, 30–31
- Boise 196
- Idaho Falls 221
- Pocatello 250

ILLINOIS (IL) 73–75, 87–89, 97–99, 108–109
- Chicago 203
- Chicago Downtown 202
- Peoria 247
- Quad Cities (Davenport IA) 208
- Rockford 255
- Springfield 264

INDIANA (IN) 89–90, 99–100, 109
- Evansville 212
- Fort Wayne 214
- Indianapolis 221
- Indianapolis Downtown 222
- South Bend 263

IOWA (IA) 27, 35, 72–74, 86–88
- Cedar Rapids 200
- Davenport/Quad Cities 208
- Des Moines 210

KANSAS (KS) 42–43, 50–51, 96, 106
- Kansas City 224
- Topeka 267
- Wichita 273

KENTUCKY (KY) 99–101, 108–111
- Frankfort 214
- Lexington 227
- Louisville 230

LOUISIANA (LA) 124–126. 132–135
- Baton Rouge 194
- Lafayette 225
- New Orleans 239
- New Orleans Downtown 239
- Shreveport 263

MAINE (ME) 81–85
- Augusta 191
- Portland 251

MARYLAND (MD) 102–104, 114, 144–146
- Annapolis 189
- Baltimore 193
- Baltimore Downtown 194
- Washington DC 270

MASSACHUSETTS (MA) 94–95, 150–151
- Boston 197
- Boston Downtown 197
- New Bedford/Fall River 238
- Springfield 264
- Worcester 275

MICHIGAN (MI) 65, 68–71, 75–77, 89–90
- Ann Arbor 190
- Detroit 210
- Detroit Downtown 210
- Flint 213
- Grand Rapids 215
- Kalamazoo 223
- Lansing 225

MINNESOTA (MN) 19, 27, 64–67, 72–73
- Duluth 211
- Minneapolis/St. Paul 235
- Minneapolis Downtown 236

MISSISSIPPI (MS) 118–119, 125–127, 133–135
- Biloxi/Gulfport 195
- Jackson 222
- Vicksburg 269

MISSOURI (MO) 86–87, 96–98, 106–108
- Branson 198
- Jefferson City 223
- Kansas City 224
- St. Louis 256
- St. Louis Downtown 256
- Springfield 264

MONTANA (MT) 14–17, 22–25
- Billings 194
- Great Falls 215
- Helena 218
- Missoula 236

NEBRASKA (NE) 33–35, 42–43, 86, 96
- Lincoln 227
- Omaha 245

NEVADA (NV) 29–31, 37–38, 45–46, 53
- Carson City 199
- Las Vegas 226
- Las Vegas Strip 226
- Reno 253

NEW HAMPSHIRE (NH) 81–82, 84, 94–95
- Concord 206
- Manchester 231

NEW JERSEY (NJ) 93–94, 104–105, 145–148
- Atlantic City 191
- Newark (New York NY) 240
- Trenton 268

NEW MEXICO (NM) 48–49, 55–57
- Albuquerque 189
- Las Cruces 226
- Santa Fe 260

NEW YORK (NY) 78–81, 92–95, 105, 147–149
- Albany/Schenectady/Troy 188
- Buffalo/Niagara Falls 198
- New York 240
- Manhattan/New York 242
- Rochester 254
- Syracuse 265

NORTH CAROLINA (NC) 111–113, 115, 120–123
- Asheville 190
- Charlotte 201
- Fayetteville 213
- Greensboro/Winston-Salem 216
- Raleigh/Durham/Chapel Hill 253
- Wilmington 275

NORTH DAKOTA (ND) 17–19, 25–27
- Bismarck 196
- Fargo 212

OHIO (OH) 90–91, 100–102
- Akron 188
- Canton 199
- Cincinnati 204
- Cleveland 204
- Cleveland Downtown 205
- Columbus 206
- Dayton 208
- Toledo 267
- Youngstown/Warren 276

OKLAHOMA (OK) 49–51, 59, 106, 116
- Oklahoma City 244
- Tulsa 269

OREGON (OR) 20–22, 28–30
- Eugene 212
- Portland 251
- Salem 257

PENNSYLVANIA (PA) 91–94, 102–104, 146–147
- Allentown/Bethlehem 189
- Erie 212
- Harrisburg 218
- Lancaster 225
- Philadelphia 248
- Philadelphia Downtown 248
- Pittsburgh 250
- Pittsburgh Downtown 250
- Scranton/Wilkes-Barre 261
- York 275

RHODE ISLAND (RI) 95, 149–151
- Newport 239
- Providence 251

SOUTH CAROLINA (SC) 121–123, 130–131
- Charleston 200
- Columbia 205
- Greenville/Spartanburg 217
- Myrtle Beach 237

SOUTH DAKOTA (SD) 25–27, 33–35
- Pierre 249
- Rapid City 253
- Sioux Falls 263

TENNESSEE (TN) 108–111, 118–121
- Chattanooga 201
- Knoxville 225
- Memphis 232
- Nashville 237

TEXAS (TX) 49–51, 56–63, 116, 124, 132–133
- Amarillo 189
- Austin 192
- Corpus Christi 206
- Dallas/Fort Worth 207
- Dallas Downtown 207
- El Paso 211
- Houston 220
- Houston Downtown 220
- Lubbock 231
- McAllen 232
- San Antonio 257
- San Antonio Downtown 257
- Waco 269

UTAH (UT) 31–32, 38–40, 46–48
- Ogden 244
- Provo 252
- Salt Lake City 257

VERMONT (VT) 81–82, 94
- Burlington 199
- Montpelier 237

VIRGINIA (VA) 102–104, 110–115, 144
- Charlottesville 201
- Norfolk/Hampton Roads 243
- Richmond 254
- Roanoke 254
- Washington DC 270
- Williamsburg 274

WASHINGTON (WA) 12–14, 20–22
- Olympia 245
- Seattle/Tacoma 262
- Seattle Downtown 262
- Spokane 263
- Yakima 275

WEST VIRGINIA (WV) 91, 101–103, 111–112, 144
- Charleston 200
- Huntington 221

WISCONSIN (WI) 64–65, 67–69, 73–75
- Green Bay 216
- Madison 231
- Milwaukee 234
- Milwaukee Downtown 234
- Racine/Kenosha 252

WYOMING (WY) 23–25, 31–33
- Casper 199
- Cheyenne 202

PUERTO RICO (PR) 187
- San Juan 276

CANADA pages 155–183

ALBERTA (AB) 155, 157–160, 164–165
- Calgary 277
- Edmonton 277

BRITISH COLUMBIA (BC) 155–158, 162–164
- Vancouver 282
- Victoria 282

MANITOBA (MB) 161, 166–168
- Winnipeg 282

NEW BRUNSWICK (NB) 177–181
- Fredericton 277
- Saint John 280

NEWFOUNDLAND & LABRADOR (NL) 182–183
- St. John's 280

NORTHWEST TERRITORIES (NT) 155

NOVA SCOTIA (NS) 180–182
- Halifax 277

NUNAVUT (NU) 6–7

ONTARIO (ON) 167–174
- Hamilton 278
- London 278
- Niagara Falls (Buffalo NY) 198
- Ottawa 279
- Sudbury 281
- Toronto 281
- Toronto Downtown 281
- Windsor (Detroit MI) 210

PRINCE EDWARD ISLAND (PE) 179–182
- Charlottetown 277

QUÉBEC (QC) 171, 174–179, 182–183
- Gatineau (Ottawa ON) 279
- Montréal 279
- Québec 280
- Sherbrooke 281

SASKATCHEWAN (SK) 159–161, 165–166
- Regina 280
- Saskatoon 280

YUKON (YT) 155

MEXICO pages 184–187

- Cancún 283
- Guadalajara 283
- México 283
- Monterrey 283

United States Interstate Map

0 mi 125 250 375
0 km 125 250 375 500

One inch equals 217 miles
One centimeter equals 138 kilometers

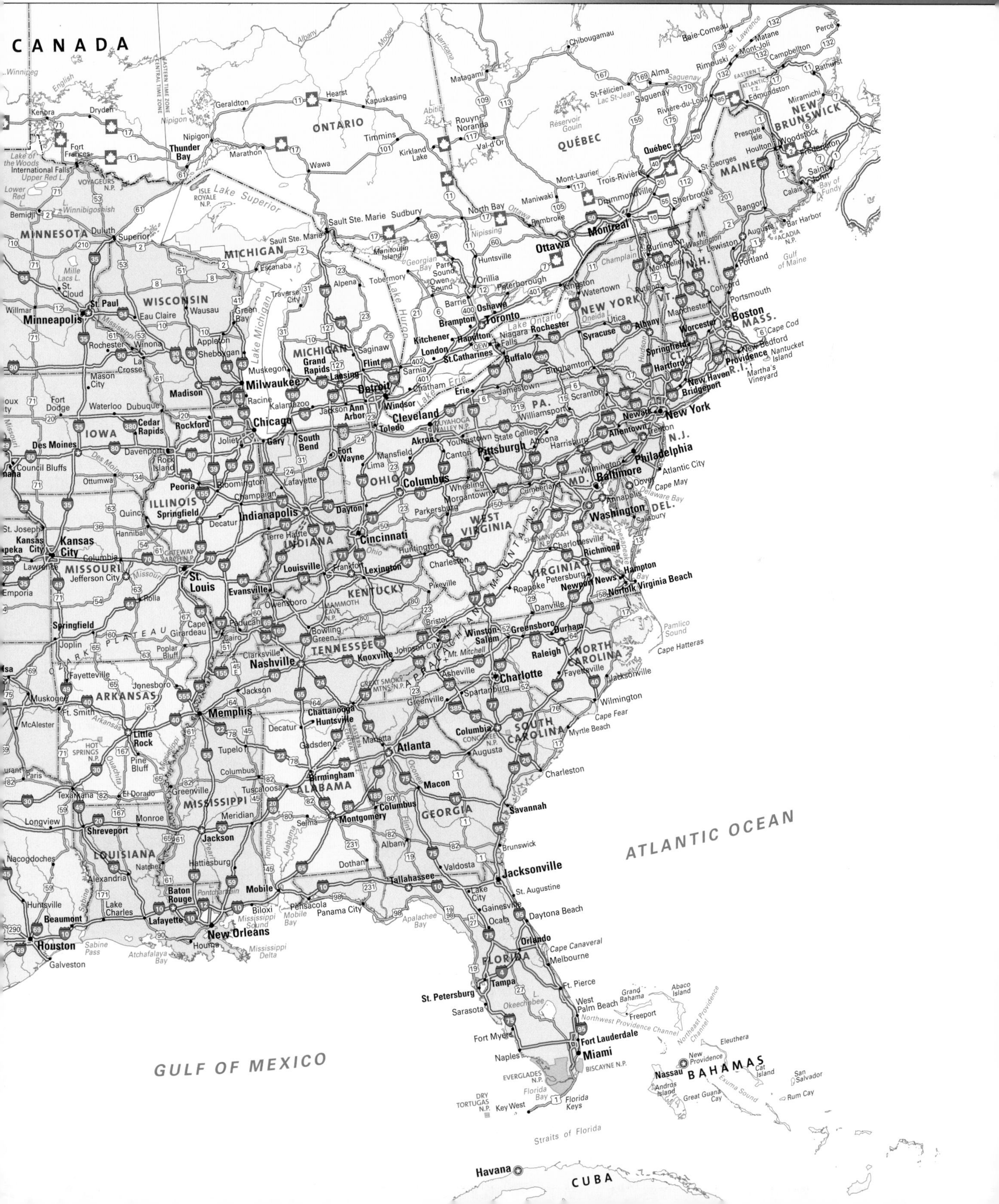
CANADA
ONTARIO
QUÉBEC
NEW BRUNSWICK
MINNESOTA
WISCONSIN
MICHIGAN
IOWA
ILLINOIS
INDIANA
OHIO
PA.
NEW YORK
VT.
N.H.
MAINE
MASS.
CT.
R.I.
N.J.
DEL.
MD.
WEST VIRGINIA
VIRGINIA
KENTUCKY
TENNESSEE
NORTH CAROLINA
SOUTH CAROLINA
GEORGIA
FLORIDA
ALABAMA
MISSISSIPPI
LOUISIANA
ARKANSAS
MISSOURI
BAHAMAS
CUBA
ATLANTIC OCEAN
GULF OF MEXICO
Lake Superior
Lake Michigan
Lake Huron
Lake Erie
Lake Ontario
Straits of Florida
Minneapolis
St. Paul
Duluth
Milwaukee
Madison
Chicago
Detroit
Toronto
Ottawa
Montreal
Québec
Buffalo
Cleveland
Columbus
Cincinnati
Indianapolis
Louisville
St. Louis
Kansas City
Des Moines
Pittsburgh
Philadelphia
New York
Boston
Baltimore
Washington
Richmond
Norfolk
Virginia Beach
Raleigh
Charlotte
Nashville
Memphis
Knoxville
Atlanta
Birmingham
Montgomery
Jackson
New Orleans
Houston
Mobile
Jacksonville
Orlando
Tampa
St. Petersburg
Miami
Fort Lauderdale
Savannah
Charleston
Columbia
Havana
Nassau

Canada Highway Map

0 mi 200 400
0 km 200 400 600

One inch equals 250 miles/Un pouce équivaut à 250 milles
One cm equals 159 km/Un cm équivaut à 159 km

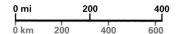

BAFFIN BAY
GREENLAND
(KALAALLIT NUNAAT)
(Denmark)
Devon Island
Lancaster Sound
SIRMILIK NATL. PARK
Bylot Island
Arctic Bay
Borden Peninsula
Pond Inlet
Brodeur Peninsula
Prince Regent Inlet
Clyde River
BAFFIN ISLAND
Davis Strait
Qikiqtarjuaq
AUYUITTUQ NATL. PARK
Gulf of Boothia
Igloolik
Cumberland Peninsula
Nettilling Lake
Prince Charles Island
Foxe Basin
Kugaaruk
MELVILLE PENINSULA
Pangnirtung
Cumberland Sound
Amadjuak Lake
Repulse Bay
NUNAVUT
UKKUSIKSALIK NATL. PARK
Hall Peninsula
EASTERN TIME ZONE
Iqaluit
Foxe Peninsula
Cape Dorset
Foxe Channel
Southampton Island
Coral Harbour
Salisbury Island
Kimmirut
Meta Incognita Peninsula
Resolution Island
LABRADOR SEA
Détroit d'Hudson / Hudson Strait
Evans Str.
Nottingham Island
Cape Chidley
TORNGAT MOUNTAINS NATL. PARK
Mt. Caubvik / Mont d'Iberville 1,652 m
Akpatok Island
Chesterfield Inlet
Fisher Str.
Coats Island
Ivujivik
Salluit
Kangiqsujuaq
Rankin Inlet
Whale Cove
Mansel Island
CENTRAL TIME ZONE
EASTERN TIME ZONE
PÉNINSULE D'UNGAVA
Kangirsuk
Baie d'Ungava / Ungava Bay
TORNGAT MOUNTAINS
Nain
Natuashish
Hopedale
AKAMI-UAPISHKU-KAKKASUAK-MEALY MOUNTAINS NATL. PARK RES.
Ottawa Islands
Puvirnituq
Kuujjuaq
George
BAIE D'HUDSON / HUDSON BAY
Feuilles
Caniapiscau
NEWFOUNDLAND AND LABRADOR
LABRADOR
Cartwright
Red Bay
St. Anthony
NEWFOUNDLAND TIME ZONE
Smallwood Res.
Happy Valley-Goose Bay
Churchill Falls
Churchill
Schefferville
Umiujaq
Lac à l'Eau Claire
Blanc-Sablon
St. Barbe
TERRA NOVA NATL. PARK
Bonavista
Gander
St. John's
Belcher Islands
Sanikiluaq
Lac Bienville
Caniapiscau
Labrador City
Wabush
Fermont
Atikonak Lake
GROS MORNE NATL. PARK
Grand Falls-Windsor
NEWFOUNDLAND ISLAND
Argentia
Corner Brook
Kuujjuarapik
Rés. de Caniapiscau
Fort Severn
Lac Burton
Rés. de la Grande-Deux
Rés. de la Grande-Trois
Peawanuck
Natashquan
Havre-St-Pierre
RÉS. DE PARC NAT. DE L'ARCHIPEL-DE-MINGAN
Île d'Anticosti
Stephenville
Grand Bank
Channel-Port aux Basques
St-Pierre
ST-PIERRE AND MIQUELON (France)
Baie James / James Bay
Chisasibi
Radisson
Lac Sakami
QUÉBEC
Réservoir Manicouagan
Sept-Îles
Port-Menier
Severn
Akimiski I.
Wemindji
Big Trout Lake
Webequie
Attawapiskat
Kashechewan
Mt. Jacques-Cartier 1,268 m
PARC NAT. FORILLON
Gaspé
Golfe du St-Laurent / Gulf of St. Lawrence
Îles-de-la-Madeleine
Cap-aux-Meules
CAPE BRETON HIGHLANDS NATL. PARK
Sydney
SABLE I. NATL. PARK RES.
Sable I. (Nova Scotia)
Waskaganish
Lac Mistassini
Lac Manouane
Baie-Comeau
Matane
St. Lawrence
ONTARIO
Albany
Moosonee
Moose Factory
Chibougamau
Chapais
Réservoir Pipmuacan
Rimouski
Campbellton
Bathurst
KOUCHIBOUGUAC NATL. PARK
PRINCE EDWARD I.
P.E.I.
Charlottetown
Souris
Central Patricia
Lac Evans
Matagami
Lac St-Jean
Saguenay
Edmundston
Grand Falls
Miramichi
NEW BRUNSWICK
Summerside
Moncton
FUNDY N.P.
Truro
Lake St. Joseph
Sioux Lookout
Savant Lake
Armstrong
Réservoir Gouin
St-Félicien
Jonquière
Hearst
Kapuskasing
Lake Abitibi
Rouyn-Noranda
Val-d'Or
Québec
MAINE
Fredericton
Saint John
Calais
Halifax
Dartmouth
Lunenburg
NOVA SCOTIA
Dryden
Silver Dollar
Rainy L.
Lake Nipigon
Marathon
Timmins
Kirkland Lake
PARC NAT. DE LA MAURICIE
Trois-Rivières
Drummondville
Sherbrooke
Bangor
Digby
KEJIMKUJIK NATL. PARK
Yarmouth
Fort Frances
International Falls
Thunder Bay
PUKASKWA N.P.
Lake Superior
Sault Ste. Marie
Elliot Lake
Sudbury
North Bay
Ottawa
Pembroke
Gatineau
Montréal
Cornwall
Augusta
Duluth
Espanola
Lake Champlain
Burlington
Montpelier
Portland
Sault Ste. Marie
MICHIGAN
Parry Sound
GEORGIAN BAY ISLANDS N.P.
BRUCE PENINSULA N.P.
Huntsville
Midland
Orillia
Peterborough
Kingston
Watertown
N.H.
VT.
Concord
Escanaba
Alpena
Lake Huron
Owen Sound
Barrie
Oshawa
Lake Ontario
Boston
MASS.
Providence
ATLANTIC OCEAN
Minneapolis
St. Paul
Eau Claire
WISCONSIN
Green Bay
Toronto
Kitchener
Hamilton
Rochester
Syracuse
Albany
Springfield
Hartford
CT.
R.I.
Rochester
Sarnia
London
Brantford
Niagara Falls
Buffalo
NEW YORK
La Crosse
Milwaukee
Lake Michigan
Madison
Lansing
Detroit
Windsor
Lake Erie
Erie
PENNSYLVANIA
Scranton
New Haven
New York
NEW JERSEY
Mississippi
Waterloo
Dubuque
Chicago
POINT PELEE N.P.
Cleveland
Allentown
Trenton
Philadelphia
NOTE: Legislated standard time zone boundaries shown; observed time may differ locally.

Experience the thrill of the open roads of North America with these great Scenic Drives from Michelin. The famous star ratings highlight natural and cultural attractions along the way.

- ★★★ **Worth a special journey**
- ★★ **Worth a detour**
- ★ **Interesting**

Michelin Scenic Drives are indicated by a green and yellow dashed line (▬▬▬) on corresponding atlas maps for easy reference. The following 17 drives are also plotted for your use.

North Coast/Mendocino★★ .... Maps 259, 36
Napa Valley/Sonoma★★ .... Map 36
Willamette Valley★ .... Maps 251, 20, 257, 212
Florida Panhandle★ .... Maps 265, 137, 136, 247
Coastal Carolinas★★ .... Maps 115, 123, 275, 237, 131, 200, 261
San Juan Country★★ .... Map 40
Snake River Valley★ .... Maps 221, 23, 22, 196, 30
Hill Country★★ .... Maps 192, 61, 60, 257
Southern New Mexico★ .... Maps 211, 56, 226, 48, 49, 57
New Jersey Pine Barrens★ .... Maps 191, 147, (105, 104)
Litchfield Hills★★ .... Maps 148, 94
Hudson River Valley★★★ .... Maps 240, 148, 94
Thompson Canyon★ .... Maps 282, 163
Alberta Badlands★★★ .... Maps 277, 164, 165
Saint John River Valley★★ .... Maps 277, 180, 178
Annapolis Valley/Atlantic Shore★★ . Maps 180, 181, 277
Blue Heron Drive★★ .... Maps 277, 181

ABBREVIATIONS

N	North	**NL**	National Lakeshore
E	East	**NM**	National Memorial/ National Monument
S	South	**NMP**	National Military Park
W	West	**NP**	National Park
NE	Northeast	**NPR**	National Park Reserve
NW	Northwest	**NRA**	National Recreation Area
SE	Southeast	**NWR**	National Wildlife Refuge
SW	Southwest	**PP**	Provincial Park
Hwy.	Highway	**SHP**	State Historical Park
Pkwy.	Parkway	**SHS**	State Historic Site
Rte.	Route	**SP**	State Park
Mi	Miles	**SR**	State Reserve
Km	Kilometers	**VC**	Visitor Center
Sq Ft	Square Feet		
NHS	National Historic Site		

For detailed coverage of the attractions, and for suggestions of places to dine and stay overnight, see Michelin's North America **Regional Atlas Series**, designed for the way you drive, and Michelin's **Green Guide Collection**, the ultimate guidebooks for the independent traveler.

NORTHWEST

Anchorage/Fairbanks/Denali★★★

892 miles/1,436 kilometers

Maps 189, 154, 155

From **Anchorage★**, Alaska's largest city, take Rte. 1 (Glenn Hwy. and Tok Cutoff) N and then E through the broad Matanuska Valley to the small town of **Tok**. The route passes agricultural communities, the **Matanuska Glacier** and the Wrangell Mountains before heading up the Copper River Basin. From Tok, take the Alaska Hwy. (Rte. 2) NW to **Fairbanks★**, a friendly town with a frontier feel. The road passes the **Trans-Alaska Pipeline** and **Big Delta SHP** then parallels the Tanana River. From Fairbanks, opt for Rte. 3 W that crosses the river at Nenana, then veers S to **Denali NP★★★**, home of spruce forests, grassy tundra, grizzlies,moose and North America's highest peak, **Mount McKinley** (20,320ft). Return S to Anchorage via Rtes. 3 and 1.

Alaska Range, Denali NP

© Alaska Stock/age fotostock

Badlands★★

164 miles/264 kilometers

Maps 253, 26

From **Rapid City★**, South Dakota, drive SE on Rte. 44 through Farmingdale and Scenic, then east to Interior to enter **Badlands NP★★**. Take Rte. 377 NE 2mi to Cedar Pass and stop at the park's Ben Reifel VC. From there, Cliff **Shelf Nature Trail★★** (.5mi) is popular for its shady junper trees and **Castle Trail★★★** (4.5mi) is spectacular in early morning when the moonscape valley and pointed spires get first light. Turn left onto Rte. 240, **Badlands Loop Road★★★**, along the northern rim, where prairie grasslands give way to buttes and hoodoos. **Pinnacles Overlook★★** is a sweeping viewpoint to the south. Drive N to I-90, and cross the Interstate N to Wall. On Main St. visit **Wall Drug★**, a "drug store" with over 20 shops filled with historical photos, 6,000 pairs of cowboy boots, wildlife exhibits and Western art displayed in five dining rooms. In the backyard a roaring, 80ft **Tyrannosaurus** sends toddlers running. Leave Wall on I-90, driving W. Take Exit 67 to Ellsworth Air Force Base, where the **South Dakota Air** and **Space Museum** displays stealth bombers and other aircraft. Continue W on I-90 back to Rapid City to conclude the tour.

Badlands NP

© kwiktor/iStockphoto.com

Black Hills★★

244 miles/393 kilometers

Maps 253, 26, 25

From **Rapid City★**, drive S on US-16 then US-16A S past Keystone. Take Rte. 244 W to **Mount Rushmore NM★★★**. Continue W on Rte 244 to the junction of US-16/385. Enroute S to Custer, **Crazy Horse Memorial★** honors the famous Sioux chief. From Custer, head S on US-385through Pringle to the junction of Rte. 87. Take Rte. 87 N through **Wind Cave NP★★** and into **Custer SP★★**. Follow **Wildlife Loop Road★★** (access S of Blue Bell, across from Rte. 342 junction) E and N to US-16A. Then travel W to join scenic **Needles Highway★★** (Rte. 87) NW to US-16/385 N. Where US-16 separates, continue N on US-385 to **Deadwood★★**, a former gold camp. Turn left onto US-14A, driving SW through **Lead★**, site of the former **Homestake Gold Mine★★**, to Cheyenne Crossing. Drive N on US-14A to I-90, turning SE back to Rapid City.

Mount Rushmore NM

Columbia River Gorge★★

83 miles/134 kilometers

Maps 251, 20, 21

From **Portland★★**, Oregon's largest city, take I-84 E to Exit 17 in Troutdale. There, head E on the winding **Historic Columbia River Highway★★** (US-30), which skirts the steep cliffs above the river. For great **views★★**, stop at **Vista House at Crown Point**. You'll pass the 620ft **Multnomah Falls★★** and moss-draped **Oneonta Gorge**. At Ainsworth State Park (Exit 35), rejoin I-84 and travel E to Mosier (Exit 69), where US-30, with its hairpin turns, begins again. Continue E on US-30, stopping at **Rowena Crest Viewpoint★★** for grand vistas—and wildflowers. Just past the Western-style town called The Dalles, take US-197 N to conclude the tour at **The Dalles Lock** and **Dam VC★★**.

Grand Tetons/Yellowstone★★★

224 miles/361 kilometers

Map 24

Note: parts of this tour are closed in winter.

From **Jackson★★**, drive N on US-26/191/89 to Moose. Turn left onto Teton Park Rd. to access **Grand Teton NP★★★** and **Jenny Lake Scenic Drive★★★**. From Teton Park Rd., drive N to the junction of US-89/191/287 (**John D. Rockefeller Jr. Memorial Pkwy.**) and follow the parkway N into **Yellowstone NP★★★** to **West Thumb**. Take Grand Loop Rd. W to **Old Faithful★★★**, the world's most famous geyser. Continue N on the Grand Loop Rd., passing **Norris Geyser Basin★★** en route to **Mammoth Hot Springs★★★**. Turn E on Grand Loop Rd. to Tower Junction, then S into **Grand Canyon of the Yellowstone★★★**. Continue S from Canyon Village through **Hayden Valley★★** to Lake. Head SW, back to West Thumb, to conclude to tour.

Grand Teton NP

© Jason Langley/Getty Images

Pacific Coast/Olympic Peninsula★★★

419 miles/675 kilometers

Maps 245, 12

From the state capital of **Olympia**, drive N on US-101 to Discovery Bay. Detour on Rte. 20 NE to **Port Townsend★★**, a well-preserved Victorian seaport. From Discovery Bay, head W on US-101 through **Port Angeles** to the **Heart O' the Hills** park entrance for **Olympic NP★★★** to see **Hurricane Ridge★★★**. Back on US-101, head E then S to the park entrance that leads to **Hoh Rain Forest★★★**. Follow US-101 S, then E after Queets to **Lake Quinaulte**, home to bald eagles, trumpeter swans and loons. Continue S on US-101 to Aberdeen, taking Rte. 105 to the coast. At Raymond, return to US-101 heading S to **Long Beach**. Follow Rte. 103 N past the former cannery town of **Oysterville** to **Leadbetter Point★** on Willapa Bay, where oysters are still harvested. Return S to **Ilwaco** and drive E and S on US-101 to Astoria, Oregon, to end the tour.

The Oregon Coast★★

368 miles/592 kilometers

Maps 20, 28

Leave **Astoria★**, Oregon's first settlement, via US-101, heading SW. **Fort Clatsop National Memorial★★** recalls Lewis and Clark's historic stay. **Cannon Beach★** boasts a sandy beach and tall coastal rock. At the farming community of **Tillamook★**, go west on 3rd

Cannon Beach, Oregon Coast

© Craig Tuttle/Getty Images

St. to **Cape Meares** to begin **Three Capes Scenic Drive★★**. Continue S, rejoining US-101 just beyond Pacific City. Drive S on US-101 through **Newport★**, then **Yachats★**, which neighbors **Cape Perpetua Scenic Area★★**. From **Florence** to **Coos Bay★** stretches **Oregon Dunes National Recreation Area★★**. At Coos Bay, take Cape Arago Hwy. W to tour the gardens of **Shore Acres State Park★**. Drive S on the highway to rejoin US-101. Pass **Bandon★**, known for its cheese factory, and Port Orford, with its fishing fleet. Farther S, **Boardman State Park★** shelters Sitka spruce, Douglas fir and **Natural Bridge Cove**. End the tour at **Brookings**.

SOUTHWEST

Big Bend Area★★

581 miles/935 kilometers

Maps 211, 56, 57, 62, 60

Head S from **El Paso★** via I-10, then E to Kent. Take Rte. 118 S to Alpine, passing **McDonald Observatory★** (telescope tours) and **Fort Davis NHS★★**. Continue S to Study Butte to enter **Big Bend NP★★★**, edged by the Rio Grande River and spanning 1,252sq mi of spectacular canyons, lush bottomlands, sprawling desert and mountain woodlands. The park has more species of migratory and resident birds than any other national park. Travel E to the main VC at Panther Junction in the heart of the park (US-385 and Rio Grande Village Dr.). Then take US-385 N to Marathon. Turn E on US-90 to Langtry, site of **Judge Roy Bean VC★**. Continue E to **Seminole Canyon SP★★**, with its 4,000-year-old pictographs. Farther E, **Amistad NRA★** is popular for water sports. Continue on US-90 to conclude the tour in Del Rio.

Canyonlands of Utah★★★

481 miles/774 kilometers

Maps 39, 40

From **St. George★**, drive NE on I-15 to Exit 16. Take Rte. 9 E to Springdale, gateway to **Zion NP★★★**, with its sandstone canyon, waterfalls and hanging gardens. Continue E on Rte. 9 to Mt. Carmel Junction, turn left onto US-89 and head N to the junction with Rte. 12. Take Rte. 12 SE to **Bryce Canyon NP★★★**, with its colored rock formations. Continue SE on Rte. 12 to Cannonville, then S to **Kodachrome Basin SP★★**, where sandstone chimneys rise from the desert floor. Return to Cannonville, and drive NE on Rte. 12 through Boulder to Torrey. Take Rte. 24 E through **Capitol Reef NP★★**—with its unpaved driving roads and trails—then N to I-70. Travel E on I-70 to Exit 182, then S on US-191 to Rte. 313 into **Canyonlands NP★★★** to **Grand View Point Overlook**. Return to US-191, turning S to access **Arches NP★★★**—the greatest concentration of natural stone arches in the country. Continue S on US-191 to **Moab★** to end the tour.

Canyonlands NP

© Alan Copson/Getty Images

Central Coast/Big Sur★★★

118 miles/190 kilometers

Maps 236, 44

From **Cannery Row★** in **Monterey★★**, take Prescott Ave. to Rte. 68. Turn right and continue to Pacific Grove Gate (on your left) to begin scenic **17-Mile Drive★★**, a private toll road. Exit at Carmel Gate to reach the upscale artists' colony of **Carmel★★**, site of Carmel **mission★★★**. The town's Scenic Road winds S along the beachfront. Leave Carmel by Hwy. 1 S. Short, easy trails at **Point Lobos SR★★** line the shore. Enjoy the wild beauty of the **Big Sur★★★** coastline en route to San Simeon, where **Hearst Castle★★★**, the magnificent estate of a former newspaper magnate, overlooks the Pacific Ocean. Continue S on Hwy. 1 to **Morro Bay**, where the tour ends.

Bixby Creek Bridge, Big Sur

© Michele Falzone/Getty Images

Colorado Rockies★★★

499 miles/803 kilometers

Maps 209, 41, 33, 40

Note: Rte. 82 S of Leadville to Aspen is closed mid-Oct to Memorial Day due to snow.

From **Golden★★**, **W of Denver★★★**, drive W on US-6 along Clear Creek to Rte. 119, heading N on the Peak to **Peak Highway★★** to **Nederland★**. Continue N on Rte. 72, then follow Rte. 7 N to the town of **Estes Park★★**. Take US-36 W to enter **Rocky Mountain NP★★★**. Drive **Trail Ridge Road★★★** (US-34) S to the town of **Grand Lake★**. Continue

Aspen, Colorado Rockies
© Aurora/hemis.fr

S to Granby, turn left on US-40 to I-70 at Empire. Head W on I-70 past **Georgetown**★ and through **Eisenhower Tunnel**. You'll pass ski areas Arapahoe Basin, **Keystone Resort**★ and **Breckenridge**★★. At Exit 195 for **Copper Mountain Resort**★, take Rte. 91 S to **Leadville**★★, Colorado's former silver capital. Then travel S on US-24 to Rte. 82 W over **Independence Pass**★★ to **Aspen**★★★. Head NW to I-70, passing **Glenwood Springs**★★ with its **Hot Springs Pool**★★. Drive E on I-70 along **Glenwood Canyon**★★ and the Colorado River to **Vail**★★. Continue E on I-70 to the old mining town of **Idaho Springs** to return to Golden via Rte. 119.

Lake Tahoe Loop★★

71 miles/114 kilometers

Map 37

Begin in **Tahoe City** at the intersection of Rtes. 89 and 28. Drive S on Rte. 89. **Ed Z'berg-Sugar Pine Point State Park**★ encompasses a promontory topped by **Ehrman Mansion**★ and other historic buildings. Farther S, **Emerald Bay State Park**★★ surrounds beautiful **Emerald Bay**★★. At the bay's tip stands **Vikingsholm**★★, a mansion that resembles an ancient Nordic castle. At **Tallac Historic Site**★★, preserved summer estates recall Tahoe's turn-of-the-19C opulence. From Tahoe Valley, take Rte. 50 NE. **South Lake Tahoe**, the lake's largest town, offers lodging, dining and shopping. High-rise hotel-casinos characterize neighboring **Stateline** in Nevada. Continue N to Spooner Junction. Then follow Nevada Rte. 28 N to **Sand Harbor** (7mi), where picnic tables and a sandy beach fringe a sheltered cove. Continue through Kings Beach to end the tour at Tahoe City.

Emerald Bay, Lake Tahoe
© Donyanedomam/iStockphoto.com

Maui's Hana Highway★★

62 miles/100 kilometers

Map 153

Leave **Kahului** on Rte. 36 E toward **Paia**, an old sugar-plantation town. Continue E on Rte. 36, which becomes Rte. 360, the **Hana Highway**★★. The road passes **Ho'okipa Beach Park**, famous for windsurfing, and **Puohokamoa Falls**, a good picnic stop, before arriving in **Hana**, a little village on an attractive bay. If adventurous, continue S on the Pulaui Highway to **Ohe'o Gulch**★★ in **Haleakala NP**★★★, where small waterfalls tumble from the SE flank of the dormant volcano Haleakala. Past the gulch the grave of aviator **Charles Lindbergh** can be found in the churchyard at Palapala Hoomau Hawaiian Church. End the tour at Kipahulu.

Haleakala NP, Maui
© Brigitta L. House/Michelin

Redwood Empire★★

182 miles/293 kilometers

Maps 36, 28

In **Leggett**, S of the junction of Hwy. 1 and US-101, go N on US-101 to pass through a massive redwood trunk at **Chandelier Drive-Thru Tree Park**. To the N, see breathtaking groves along 31mi **Avenue of the Giants**★★★.

Avenue of the Giants, Redwood Empire
© GaryRBenson/iStockphoto.com

Humboldt Redwoods SP★★ contains Rockefeller Forest★★, the world's largest virgin redwood forest. From US-101, detour 4mi to **Ferndale**★, a quaint Victorian village. N. along US-101, **Eureka**★ preserves a logging camp cookhouse and other historic sites. The sleepy fishing town of **Trinidad**★ is home to a marine research lab. **Patrick's Point SP**★★ offers dense forests, agate-strewn beaches and clifftop **view**★★. At **Orick**, enter the **Redwood National and State Parks**★★, which protect a 379ft-high, 750-year-old **tree**★. The tour ends in Crescent City.

Santa Fe Area★★★

267 miles/430 kilometers

Maps 189, 48, 260, 49

From **Albuquerque**★, drive E on I-40 to Exit 175 and take Rte. 14, the **Turquoise Trail**★★, N to **Santa Fe**★★★. This 52mi back road runs along the scenic Sandia Mountains and passes dry washes, arroyos and a series of revived "ghost towns." Continue N on US-84/285, turning NE onto Rte. 76, the **High Road to Taos**★★. East of Vadito, take Rte. 518 N to Rte. 68 N into the rustic Spanish colonial town of **Taos**★★, a center for the arts. Head N on US-64 to the junction of Rte. 522. Continue W on US-64 for an 18mi round-trip detour to see the 1,200ft-long, three-span **Rio Grande Gorge Bridge** over the river. Return to Rte. 522 and take this route, part of the **Enchanted Circle**★★ Scenic Byway, N to **Questa**, starting point for white-water trips on the Rio Grande. Turn onto Rte. 38, heading E to the old mining town of **Eagle Nest**. There, detour 23mi E on US-64 to **Cimarron**, a Wild West haunt. Back at Eagle Nest, travel SW on US-64, detouring on Rte. 434 S to tiny **Angel Fire**. Return to Taos on US-64 W to end the tour.

Taos Pueblo, Santa Fe Area

Sedona/Grand Canyon NP★★★

482 miles/776 kilometers

Maps 249, 54, 47, 213

Drive N from **Phoenix**★ on I-17 to Exit 298 and take Rte. 179 N toward **Sedona**★★ in the heart of **Red Rock Country**★★★. The red-rock formations are best accessed by four-wheel-drive vehicle via 12mi **Schnebly Hill Road**★ (off Rte. 179, across Oak Creek bridge from US-89A "Y" junction), which offers splendid **views**★★★. Then head N on Rte. 89A through Sedona to begin 14mi drive of **Oak Creek Canyon**★★. Continue N on Rte. 89A and I-17 to **Flagstaff**★, commercial hub for the region. Take US-180 NW to Rte. 64, which leads N to the **South Rim**★★★ of **Grand Canyon NP**★★★. Take the shuttle (or drive, if permitted) along **West Rim Drive**★★ to **Hermits Rest**★. Then travel **East Rim Drive**★★★ (Rte. 64 E) to **Desert View Watchtower**★ for **views**★★★ of the canyon. Continue to the junction with US-89 at Cameron. Return S to Flagstaff, then S to Phoenix via I-17.

Grand Canyon NP

NORTHEAST

The Berkshires★★★

57 miles/92 kilometers
Map 94

From **Great Barrington**, take US-23 E to Monterey, turning left onto Tyringham Rd., which becomes Monterey Rd., to experience scenic **Tyringham Valley★**. Continue N on Main Rd. to Tyringham Rd., which leads to **Lee**, famous for its marble. Then go NW on US-20 to **Lenox★**, with its inviting inns and restaurants. Detour on Rte. 183 W to **Tanglewood★**, site of a popular summer music festival. Return to Lenox and drive N on US-7 to **Pittsfield**, the commercial capital of the region. Head W on US-20 to enjoy **Hancock Shaker Village★★★**, a museum village that relates the history of a Shaker community established here in 1790. Rte. 41 S passes West Stockbridge, then opt for Rte. 102 SE to **Stockbridge★★** and its picturesque **Main Street★**. Follow US-7 S to the junction with Rte. 23, passing **Monument Mountain★** en route. Return to Great Barrington.

Cape Cod★★★

164 miles/264 kilometers
Maps 151, 95

At US-6 and Rte. 3, cross **Cape Cod Canal** via Sagamore Bridge and turn onto Rte. 6A to tour the Cape's **North Shore★★**. Bear right onto Rte. 130 to reach **Sandwich★**, famous for glass manufacture. Continue on Rte. 6A E to Orleans. Take US-6 N along **Cape Cod National Seashore★★★**, with its wooded and marshland trails, to reach **Provincetown★★**, a resort town offering **dune tours★★** and summer theater. Return to Orleans and take Rte. 28 S through **Chatham★**, then W to Hyannis, where ferries depart for **Nantucket★★★**. Continue to quaint **Falmouth★**. Take Surf Dr., which becomes Oyster Pond Rd. to nearby **Woods Hole**, a world center for marine research and departure point for ferries to **Martha's Vineyard★★**. Take Woods Hole Rd. N to Rte. 28. Cross the canal via Bourne Bridge and head E on US-6 to end the tour at Rte. 3.

Maine Coast★★

238 miles/383 kilometers
Maps 82, 251, 83

From **Kittery**, drive N on US-1 to **York★**, then along US-1A to see the 18C buildings of **Colonial York★★**. Continue N on coastal US-1A to **Ogunquit★**. Rejoin US-1 and head N to Rte. 9, turn right, and drive to **Kennebunkport**, with its colorful shops. Take Rte. 9A/35 to **Kennebunk**. Then travel N on US-1 to **Portland★★**, Maine's largest city,

Brant Point Light, Nantucket, Cape Cod
© grantreig/iStockphoto.com

where the **Old Port★★** brims with galleries and boutiques. Take US-1 N through the outlet town of **Freeport**, then on to **Brunswick**, home of **Bowdoin College**. Turn NE through **Bath★**, **Wiscasset**, **Rockland**, **Camden★★**, **Searsport** and **Bucksport**. At Ellsworth, take Rt. 3 S to enter **Acadia NP★★★** on **Mount Desert Island★★★**, where **Park Loop Road★★★** (closed in winter) parallels open coast. From the top of **Cadillac Mountain★★★**, the **views★★★** are breathtaking. The tour ends at **Bar Harbor★**, a popular resort village.

Acadia NP, Maine Coast
© Chris Murray/Getty Images

Mohawk Valley★

114 miles/184 kilometers
Maps 188, 94, 80

From the state capital of **Albany★**, take I-90 NW to Exit 25 for I-890 into **Schenectady**, founded by Dutch settlers in 1661. Then follow Rte. 5 W along the Mohawk River. In Fort Hunter, **Schoharie Crossing SHS★** stretches along a canal towpath. Near Little Falls, **Herkimer Home SHS** (Rte. 169 at Thruway Exit 29A) interprets colonial farm life. Rte. 5 continues W along the Erie Canal to Utica. From Utica, drive W on Rte. 49 to Rome, where the river turns N and peters out. The tour ends in Rome, site of **Fort Stanwix NM★**.

South Shore Lake Superior★

530 miles/853 kilometers
Maps 211, 64, 65, 69

From **Duluth★**, drive SE on I-535/US-53 to the junction of Rte. 13 at Parkland. Follow Rte. 13 E to quaint Bayfield, gateway to **Apostle Islands NL★★**, accessible by boat. Head S to the junction of US-2, and E through Ashland, Ironwood and Wakefield. There, turn left onto Rte. 28, heading NE to Bergland, and turning left onto Rte. 64. Drive N to Silver City and take Rte. M-107 W into **Porcupine Mountains Wilderness SP★**. Return to Rte. 64 and go E to Ontonagon. Take Rte. 38 SE to Greenland, then follow Rte. 26 NE to Houghton. Cross to Hancock on US-41 and continue NE to Phoenix. Turn left onto Rte. 26 to Eagle River and on to Copper Harbor via **Brockway Mountain Drive★★**. Return S to Houghton via US-41, then travel S and E past Marquette, turning left onto Rte. 28. Head E to Munising, then take County Road H-58 E and N through **Pictured Rocks NL★**. End the tour at Grand Marais.

Villages of Southern Vermont★★

118 miles/190 kilometers
Map 81

Head N from the resort town of **Manchester★** by Rte. 7A. At Manchester Center, take Rte. 11 E past **Bromley Mountain**, a popular ski area, to Peru. Turn left on the backroad to **Weston★**, a favorite tourist stop along Rte. 100. Continue to **Chester**, turning right onto Rte. 35 S to reach **Grafton★**, with its **Old Tavern**. Farther S, Rte. 30 S from Townshend leads to **Newfane** and its lovely **village green★**. Return to Townshend, then travel W, following Rte. 30 through West Townshend, passing **Stratton Mountain** en route to Manchester. S of Manchester by Rte. 7A, the crest of Mt. Equinox is accessible via **Equinox Skyline Drive** (fee). Then continue S on Rte. 7A to end the tour at **Arlington**, known for its trout fishing.

The White Mountains★★★

127 miles/204 kilometers
Map 81

From the all-season resort of **Conway**, drive N on Rte. 16 to **North Conway★**, abundant with tourist facilities. Continue N on US-302/ Rte. 16 through **Glen**, passing **Glen Ellis Falls★** and **Pinkham Notch★★** en route to Glen House. There, drive the Auto Road to the top of **Mount Washington★★★** (or take guided van tour). Head N on Rte. 16 to Gorham, near the Androscoggin River, then W on US-2 to Jefferson Highlands. Travel SW on Rte. 115 to Carroll, then S on US-3 to Twin Mountain. Go SW on US-3 to join I-93. Head S on I-93/ Rte.3, passing scenic **Franconia Notch★★★** and **Profile Lake★★**. Bear E on Rte. 3 where it separates from the interstate to visit **The Flume★★**, a natural gorge 90ft deep. Rejoin I-93 S to the intersection with Rte. 112. Head E on Rte. 112 through Lincoln on the **Kancamagus Highway★★★** until it joins Rte. 16 back to Conway.

White Mountain National Forest
© Peter Unger/Getty Images

Michelin Scenic Drives - continues on page 301

British Columbia

Washington

0 mi   20   40
0 km   20   40   60
One inch equals 25.4 miles
One centimeter equals 16.1 kilometers

1
2
3
4

A   **B**   **C**

STRATHCONA PROV. PARK

Go to 162

PACIFIC RIM NATL. PARK RESERVE

Tofino
Ucluelet
Kennedy Lake
Great Central Lake
Henderson Lake
Sproat Lake
Port Alberni
Alberni Inlet
Bamfield
Cape Beale
Pachena Pt.
Barkley Sound
Sarita
Kildonan
Green Cove

Vancouver Island

PACIFIC RIM NATIONAL PARK RESERVE

CARMANAH WALBRAN PROV. PK.

Cape Flattery
Neah Bay
Makah Cultural Center
MAKAH IND. RES.
Makah (Ozette) Ind. Res.
Cape Alava
Ozette Lake
Sekiu
Clallam Bay
Sappho
Beaver

OLYMPIC NATL. PARK

Forks
Forks Timber Museum
La Push
Quileute Ind. Res.
Teahwhit Head
QUILLAYUTE NEEDLES N.W.R.
Hoh Ind. Res.

OLYMPIC EXPERIMENTAL ST. FOR.

PACIFIC OCEAN

Kalaloch
Clearwater
Queets
QUINAULT IND. RES.
Quinault Rain Forest
L. Quinault
Amanda Park
Neilton
Copalis N.W.R.
Cape Elizabeth
Taholah
Moclips
Pacific Beach S.P.
Pacific Beach
Carlisle
Griffiths-Priday S.P.
Copalis Beach
Ocean City
Ocean City S.P.
Ocean Shores
Damon Point S.P.
Point Brown
Westport
Westhaven S.P.
Westport Light S.P.
Twin Harbors
Grayland
Grayland Beach S.P.
Cape Shoalwater
North Cove
Tokeland
Leadbetter Point
WILLAPA N.W.R.
Oysterville
Ocean Park
Pacific Pines S.P.
North Beach Peninsula
Long Beach
Seaview
Ilwaco
Cape Disappointment
Lewis & Clark N.H.P. (Discovery Trail)
Columbia Pacific Heritage Mus.
Cape Disappointment S.P.
Fort Columbia S.P.
Lewis & Clark Interpretive Ctr.
Fort Stevens S.P.
Lewis & Clark N.H.P. (Station Camp)
Warrenton
Lewis & Clark N.H.P. (Fort Clatsop)
Astoria

Denman I.
Hornby Island
Buckley Bay
Fanny Bay
Halfmoon Bay
False Bay
Elsie Lake
Qualicum Beach
Coombs
Parksville
Lantzville
Nanaimo
Gabriola Island
Cedar
Nanaimo Lakes
Cowichan Lake
Youbou
Honeymoon Bay
Lake Cowichan
Ladysmith
Chemainus
N. Cowichan
Crofton
Duncan
Galiano Island
Saltspring Island
Ganges
Cobble Hill
Mill Bay
Sidney
Saanich
Langford
Esquimalt
Victoria
Oak Bay
Sooke
Jordan River
Port Renfrew

Sechelt
Gibsons
Langdale
Horseshoe Bay
Bowen Island
Port Mellon
Lions Bay
CYPRESS PROV. PARK

PORPOISE BAY PROV. PARK

BURKE PROV. PK.
GOLDEN EARS PROV. PARK
SASQUATCH PROV. PARK
Harrison Lake
Pitt Lake
Alouette Lake
Chehalis Lake
Coquitlam Lake
Kent

Vancouver
Burnaby
Coquitlam
Maple Ridge
Mission
Chilliwack
Richmond
Surrey
Langley
Abbotsford
Delta
Blaine
Birch Bay
Point Roberts
Peace Arch S.P.
Boundary Bay
Sumas
WASH.
B.C.
Lynden
Ferndale
Everson
Maple Falls
Kendall
Deming
Mt. Baker
Glacier
Clipper
Van Zandt
Acme
Bellingham
Western Wash. Univ.
Lummi Island
San Juan Islands
Orcas I.
Waldron I.
Friday Harbor
Lopez I.
Anacortes
Burlington
Sedro-Woolley
Lyman
Concrete
Rockport
Rasar S.P.
Sumas
American Border Peak
Nooksack Falls
Artist Point
Mt. Shuksan 9,131
Mt. Baker 10,778
MT. BAKER NATL. REC. AREA
Baker Lake
Lake Shannon
WHATCOM
SKAGIT
MOUNT BAKER-SNOQUALMIE NATL. FOR.
Mt. Vernon
Oak Harbor
Coupeville
Whidbey Island
Deception Pass S.P.
N.A.S. Whidbey Island
Fort Casey S.P.
Fort Ebey S.P.
Stanwood
Silvana
Arlington
Darrington
Whitehorse Mtn. 6,852
SNOHOMISH
Granite Falls
Robe
Verlot
Silverton
Marysville
Lake Stevens
Everett
Mukilteo
Mill Creek
Snohomish
Monroe
Sultan
Startup
Index
Gold Bar
Lynnwood
Edmonds
Shoreline
Bothell
Woodinville
Kirkland
Redmond
Duvall
Carnation
Sammamish
Fall City
Snoqualmie Falls
North Bend
Bellevue
Seattle
Bremerton
Port Orchard
Bainbridge Island
Silverdale
Poulsbo
Kingston
Edmonds
KITSAP
Seabeck
Belfair
Burien
Renton
Issaquah
Des Moines
Federal Way
Kent
Maple Valley
Ravensdale
Black Diamond
Auburn
Sumner
Tacoma
Univ. Place
Puyallup
Enumclaw
Buckley
Wilkeson
Carbonado
Lakewood
Parkland
Spanaway
Steilacoom
Gig Harbor
Vaughn
PIERCE
Orting
Graham
Eatonville
Greenwater
Mineral
Ashford
Packwood
Randle
Morton
Glenoma
Olympia
Lacey
Yelm
Rainier
Tenino
Roy
McKenna
Tumwater
THURSTON
MASON
Shelton
Aberdeen
Hoquiam
Cosmopolis
Montesano
Elma
McCleary
Satsop
Central Park
Malone
GRAYS HARBOR
Centralia
Chehalis
Napavine
Winlock
Toledo
Vader
Castle Rock
Onalaska
Mossyrock
Morton
LEWIS
Rochester
Oakville
Brooklyn
Raymond
South Bend
Menlo
Willapa
Lebam
Frances
Pe Ell
Doty
Adna
PACIFIC
WAHKIAKUM
Naselle
Rosburg
Skamokawa
Cathlamet
COWLITZ
SKAMANIA
MT. ST. HELENS NATL. VOLCANIC MON.
GIFFORD PINCHOT
LEWIS AND CLARK
WASH.
OREG.
Go to 20

Go to 20

Strait of Juan de Fuca

BRITISH COLUMBIA
WASHINGTON
CANADA
U.S.

Port Angeles
Port Townsend
Sequim
Dungeness
Carlsborg
Agnew
Joyce
Salt Creek County Park
Olympic Game Farm
Protection Island N.W.R.
Dungeness N.W.R.
Fort Flagler S.P.
Fort Worden S.P.
Marrowstone
Hood Canal
Quilcene
Brinnon
Dosewallips S.P.
Seabeck
Holly
Eldon
Lilliwaup
Hoodsport
Potlatch S.P.
Tahuya
Union
Allyn
Grapeview
Vaughn
PUGET SOUND

OLYMPIC NATL. FOR.

OLYMPIC MOUNTAINS
Mt. Olympus 7,965
Mt. Deception 7,788
Mt. Walker Viewpoint
Hurricane Ridge
Hoh Rain Forest Vis. Ctr.
Sol Duc Hot Springs
Marymere Falls
L. Crescent
Soleduck
Bogachiel S.P.
Queets Rain Forest
Quinault Rain Forest
JEFFERSON

MT. RAINIER NATL. PARK
Mt. Rainier 14,411
Highest Pt. in Wash.
Paradise
Longmire
Sunrise Vis. Ctr.
TATOOSH RANGE
Ohanapecosh
CASCADE RANGE

Astoria

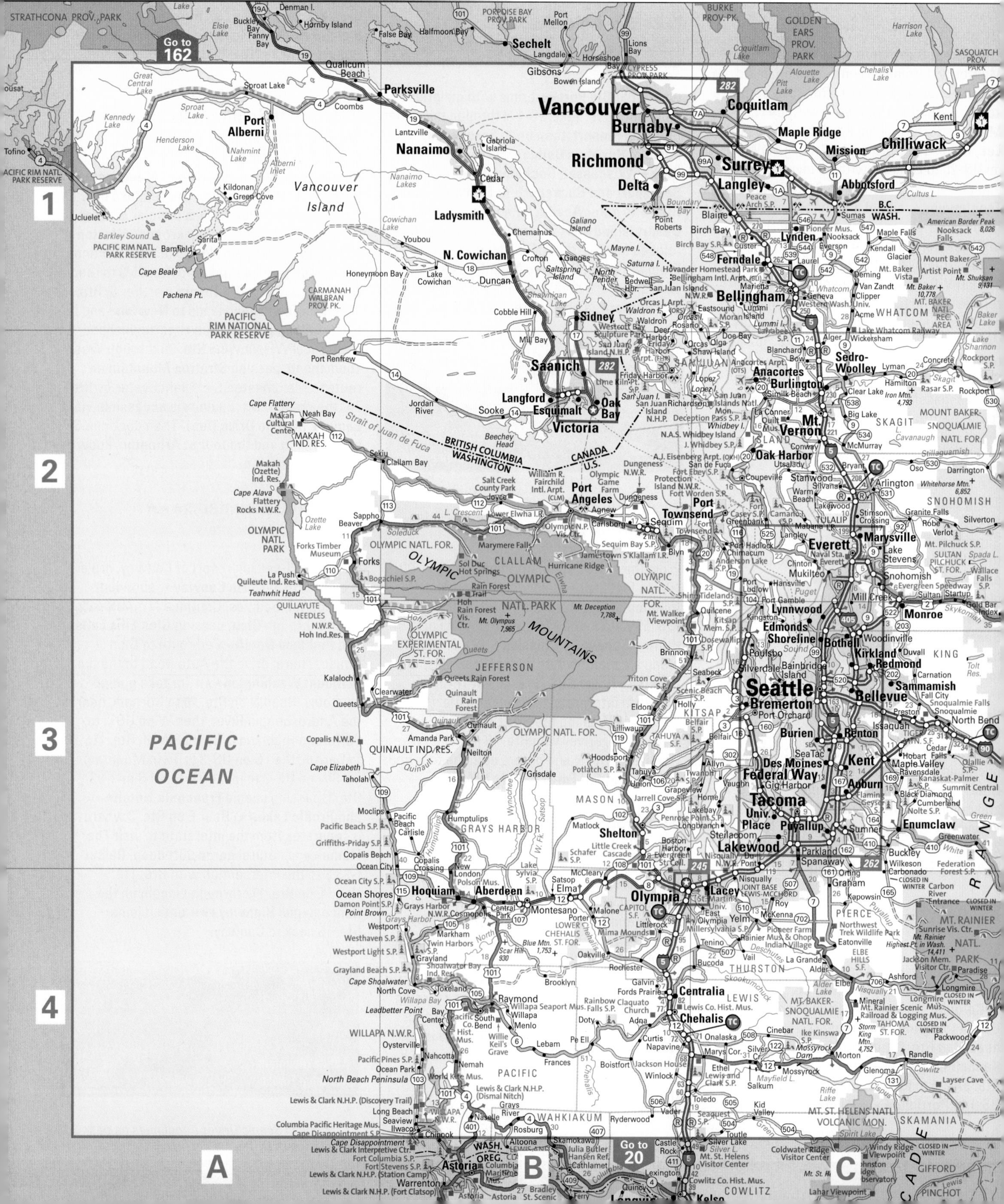

DRIVING DISTANCES IN MILES	ABERDEEN, WA	BELLINGHAM, WA	MT. RAINIER NP, WA	OKANOGAN, WA	OLYMPIA, WA	PORT ANGELES, WA	SEATTLE, WA	SPOKANE, WA	TACOMA, WA	VANCOUVER, BC	WENATCHEE, WA	YAKIMA, WA
BELLINGHAM, WA	196		186	195	147	127*	88	360	122	52	185	221
SEATTLE, WA	105	88	96	223	56	83*		278	31	140	148	140
SPOKANE, WA	376	360	290	148	327	362*	278		303	412	171	203
YAKIMA, WA	237	221	87	194	188	223*	140	203	164	273	115	

*DISTANCE INCLUDES FERRY TRAVEL

SEE ALSO DISTANCE AND DRIVING TIME MAP ON PAGES 286–287

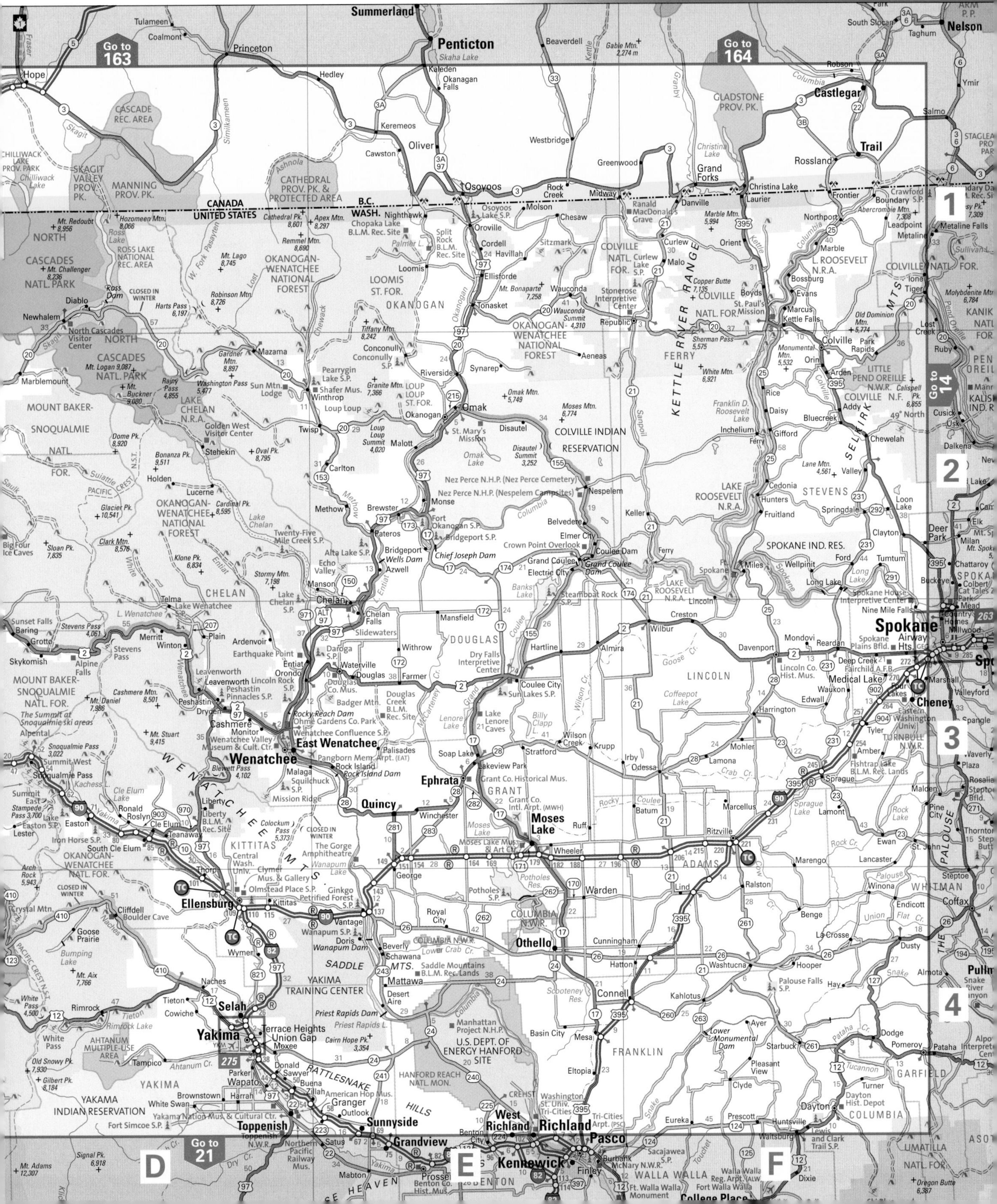

0 mi 20 40

0 km 20 40 60

One inch equals 25.4 miles

One centimeter equals 16.1 kilometers

Spokane WA / Coeur d'Alene ID

DRIVING DISTANCES IN MILES	BONNERS FERRY, ID	BROWNING, MT	COEUR D'ALENE, ID	COLVILLE, WA	GREAT FALLS, MT	HELENA, MT	KALISPELL, MT	LEWISTON, ID	MISSOULA, MT	SHELBY, MT	SPOKANE, WA	WEST GLACIER, MT
GREAT FALLS, MT	369	124	364	471		85	222	420	199	82	398	192
LEWISTON, ID	196	413	118	176	420	334	315		221	448	103	348
MISSOULA, MT	244	201	167	274	199	114	116	221		227	201	136
SPOKANE, WA	110	336	34	73	398	313	238	103	201	426		271

SEE ALSO DISTANCE AND DRIVING TIME MAP ON PAGES 286–287

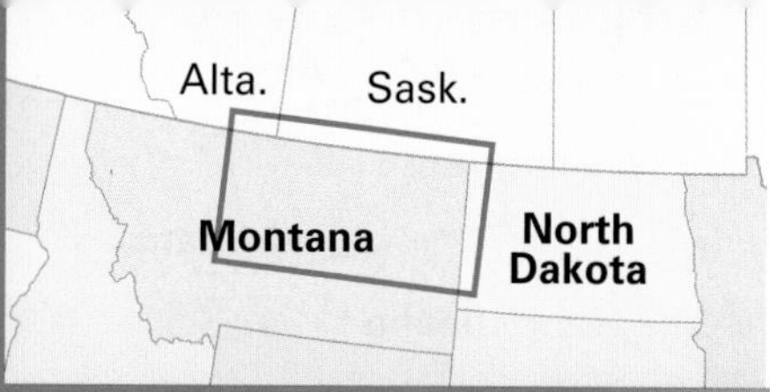

0 mi 20 40
0 km 20 40 60
One inch equals 25.4 miles
One centimeter equals 16.1 kilometers

Great Falls MT / Havre MT

DRIVING DISTANCES IN MILES

	GLASGOW, MT	GLENDIVE, MT	GREAT FALLS, MT	HARLOWTON, MT	HAVRE, MT	LEWISTOWN, MT	MALTA, MT	MILES CITY, MT	ROUNDUP, MT	SHELBY, MT	WILLISTON, ND	WOLF POINT, MT
GLENDIVE, MT	147		351	309	306	242	217	74	219	408	106	98
GREAT FALLS, MT	277	351		133	118	109	207	329	183	82	422	326
HAVRE, MT	159	306	118	210		175	89	345	198	102	304	208
WILLISTON, ND	145	106	422	415	304	324	215	180	325	406		96

SEE ALSO DISTANCE AND DRIVING TIME MAP ON PAGES 286–287

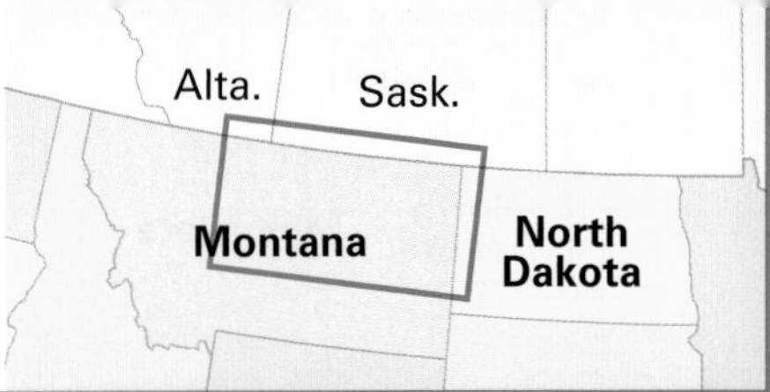

0 mi 20 40
0 km 20 40 60

One inch equals 25.4 miles
One centimeter equals 16.1 kilometers

Bismarck ND / Minot ND

DRIVING DISTANCES IN MILES	BISMARCK, ND	BOTTINEAU, ND	DETROIT LAKES, MN	DICKINSON, ND	FARGO, ND	GRAND FORKS, ND	JAMESTOWN, ND	MINOT, ND	PEMBINA, ND	RUGBY, ND	THIEF RIVER FALLS, MN	WILLISTON, ND
BISMARCK, ND		189	244	97	199	274	105	116	347	153	319	229
FARGO, ND	199	271	45	291		79	97	268	152	221	113	424
GRAND FORKS, ND	274	198	125	367	79		173	212	77	148	61	340
MINOT, ND	116	76	313	178	268	212	171		238	64	276	128

SEE ALSO DISTANCE AND DRIVING TIME MAP ON PAGES 286–287

0 mi   20   40
0 km   20   40   60
One inch equals 25.4 miles
One centimeter equals 16.1 kilometers

1
2
3
4

A   **B**   **C**

Go to **12**

Go to **28**

PACIFIC OCEAN

WASHINGTON

OREGON

Portland
Vancouver
Salem
Eugene
Springfield
Corvallis
Albany
Newport
Lincoln City
Astoria
Seaside
Tillamook
McMinnville
Hillsboro
Beaverton
Tigard
Forest Grove
Gresham
Lake Oswego
Oregon City
Damascus
Canby
Woodburn
Molalla
Silverton
Keizer
Dallas
Monmouth
Stayton
Lebanon
Sweet Home
Junction City
Cottage Grove
Florence
Reedsport
North Bend
Coos Bay
Roseburg
Sutherlin
Longview
Kelso
St. Helens
Battle Ground
Camas
Washougal

PACIFIC

CASCADE RANGE

COAST RANGES

CALAPOOYA MTS.

SKAMANIA

COWLITZ

CLATSOP

COLUMBIA

TILLAMOOK

YAMHILL

POLK

MARION

LINN

BENTON

LINCOLN

LANE

DOUGLAS

COOS

CLACKAMAS

MULTNOMAH

WASHINGTON

CLARK

LEWIS

WAHKIAKUM

HOOD RIVER

WARM SPRING IND. RES.

Mt. Hood – Highest Pt. in Oregon 11,229

Mt. Jefferson 10,497

DRIVING DISTANCES IN MILES

	ASTORIA, OR	BEND, OR	BURNS, OR	COOS BAY, OR	EUGENE, OR	KENNEWICK, WA	LA GRANDE, OR	NEWPORT, OR	PORTLAND, OR	SALEM, OR	THE DALLES, OR	WALLA WALLA, WA
BEND, OR	252		142	227	115	245	295	183	158	134	137	276
EUGENE, OR	216	115	257	105		328	377	101	112	65	198	359
KENNEWICK, WA	306	245	256	440	328		111	328	212	264	131	49
PORTLAND, OR	97	158	299	224	112	212	261	116		48	82	243

SEE ALSO DISTANCE AND DRIVING TIME MAP ON PAGES 286–287

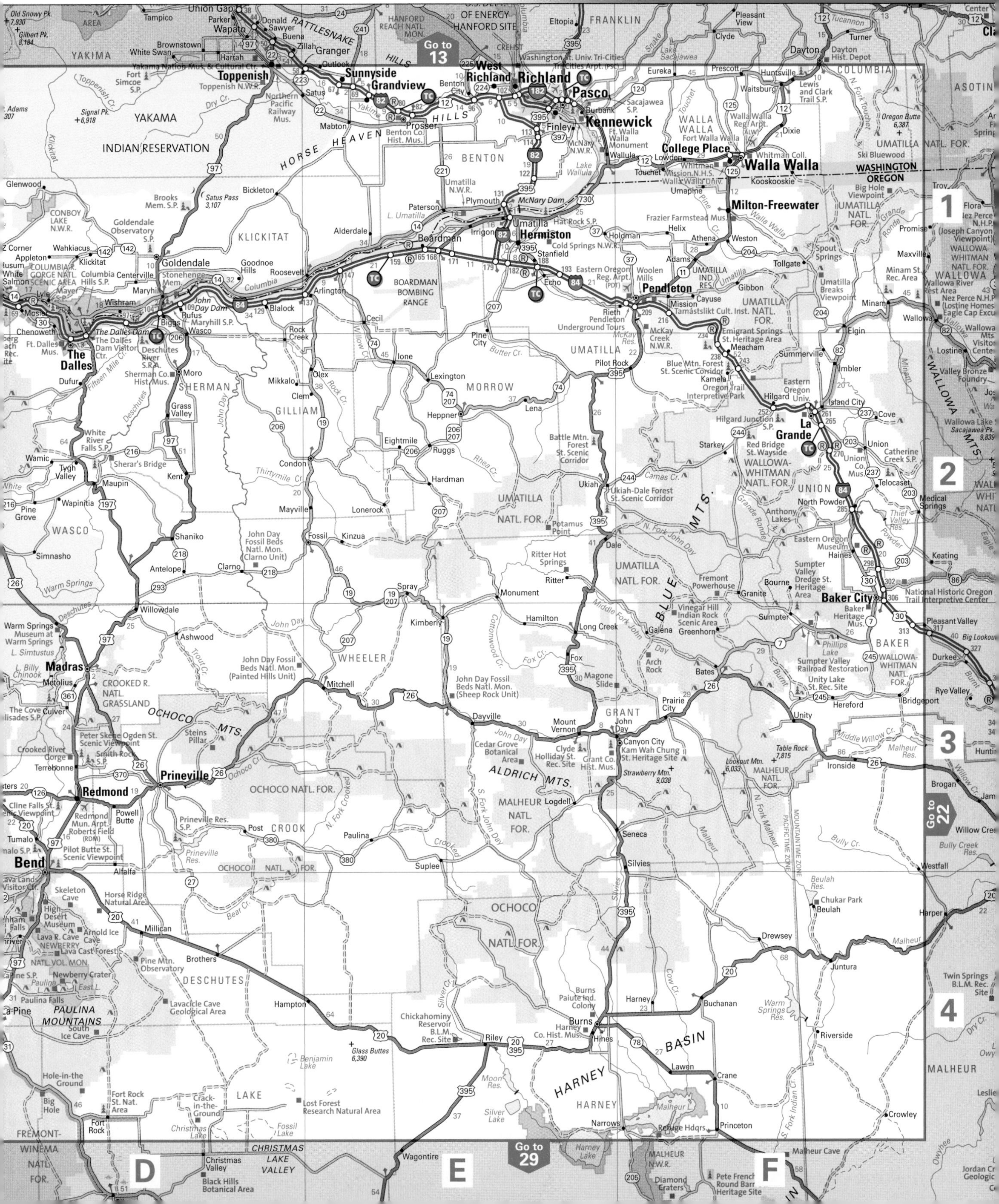

0 mi 20 40
0 km 20 40 60
One inch equals 25.4 miles
One centimeter equals 16.1 kilometers

Boise ID / La Grande OR

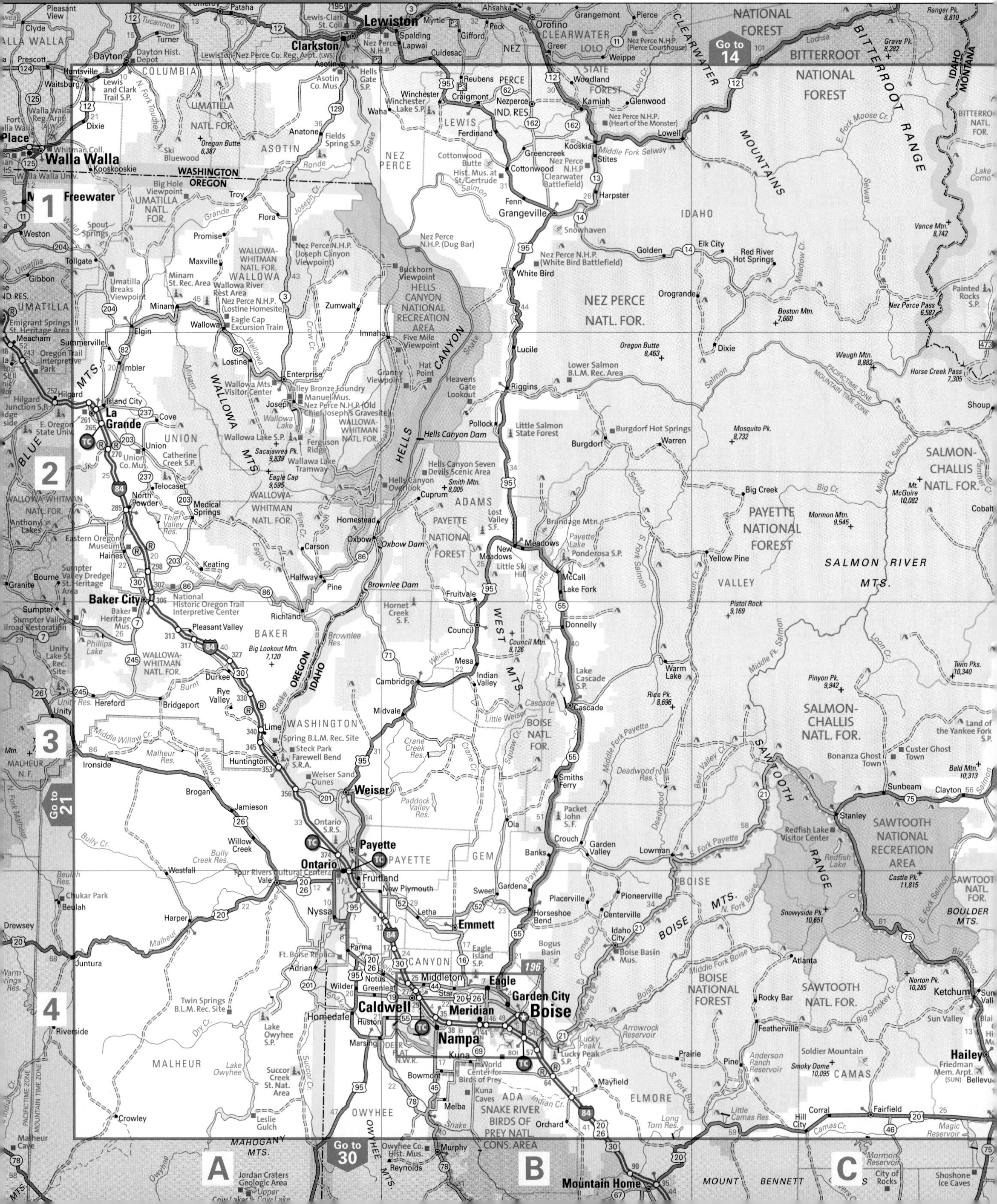

DRIVING DISTANCES IN MILES

	BOISE, ID	BOZEMAN, MT	BUTTE, MT	GRANGEVILLE, ID	HAMILTON, MT	IDAHO FALLS, ID	JACKSON, WY	LA GRANDE, OR	ONTARIO, OR	SALMON, ID	SUN VALLEY, ID	W. YELLOWSTONE, MT
BOISE, ID		485	486	202	339	288	378	170	58	247	163	395
BUTTE, MT	486	81		290	103	203	275	566	541	150	312	162
IDAHO FALLS, ID	288	199	203	483	272		92	455	342	168	153	109
W. YELLOWSTONE, MT	395	90	162	451	264	109	128	562	449	244	252	

SEE ALSO DISTANCE AND DRIVING TIME MAP ON PAGES 286–287

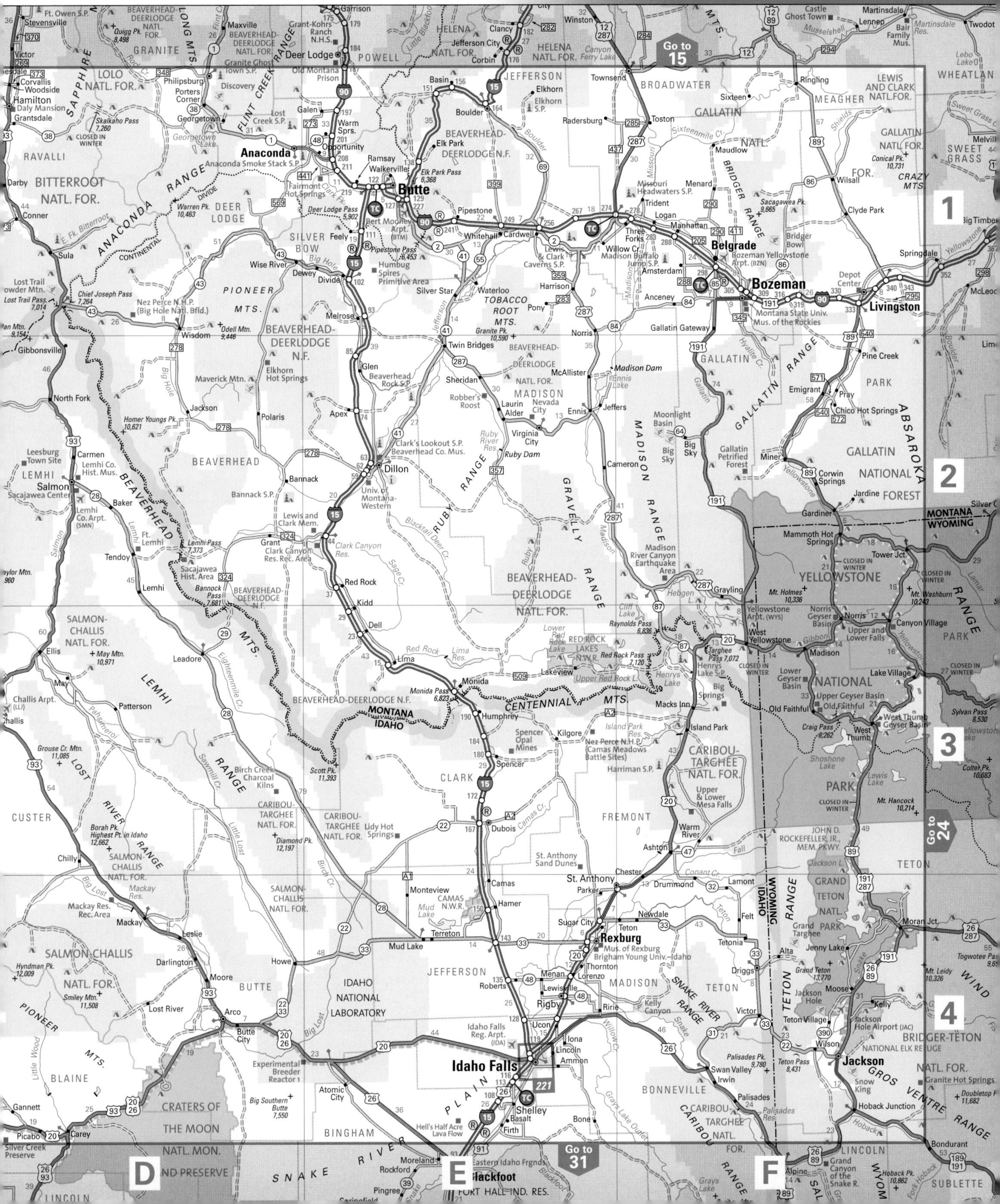

Billings MT / Yellowstone Natl Park WY

0 mi 20 40
0 km 20 40 60

One inch equals 25.4 miles
One centimeter equals 16.1 kilometers

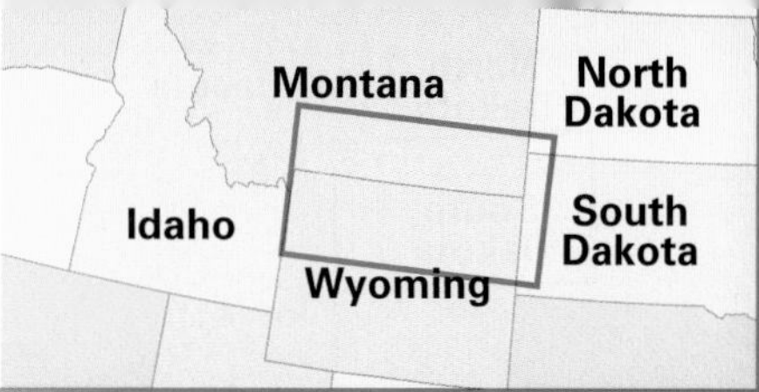

DRIVING DISTANCES IN MILES	BILLINGS, MT	BOZEMAN, MT	BUFFALO, WY	CODY, WY	GILLETTE, WY	JACKSON, WY	MILES CITY, MT	RAPID CITY, SD	SHERIDAN, WY	SPEARFISH, SD	W. YELLOWSTONE, MT	WORLAND, WY
BILLINGS, MT		141	165	111	233	287	144	379	131	333	232	161
BUFFALO, WY	165	306		180	70	342	237	216	34	170	396	91
SPEARFISH, SD	333	474	170	350	100	512	186	53	202		564	261
W. YELLOWSTONE, MT	232	90	396	147	464	128	376	610	363	564		236

SEE ALSO DISTANCE AND DRIVING TIME MAP ON PAGES 286–287

0 mi 20 40
0 km 20 40 60
One inch equals 25.4 miles
One centimeter equals 16.1 kilometers

Go to 18
Go to 25
Go to 34

MISSOURI NATIONAL GRASSLAND
SLOPE
Pretty Butte 3,182
Black Butte 3,465
White Butte Highest Pt. in N. Dak. 3,506
Stewart Lake N.W.R.
Amidon · White Lake N.W.R.
Havelock
North Star Butte 2,818
Mott · Regent
Carson · Lark · Flasher
Lake Patricia N.W.R.
Fort Rice St. Hist. Site
Hazelton · Appert Lake N.W.R. · Round Lake
Marmarth
Fort Dilts St. Hist. Site
Rhame
Bowman · Pioneer Trails Reg. Mus.
Scranton · Reeder
Gascoyne · Bucyrus
Hettinger · Haynes
HETTINGER
Bentley · Pretty Rock N.W.R. · Leipzig
Elgin · Heil · Leith · Raleigh
GRANT
Breien · Solen
Cannon Ball
Shields · St. Gertrude · Cannonball Stage Station St. Hist. Site
CENTRAL TZ / MOUNTAIN TZ
EMMONS
Linton · Springwater
Welk Homestead
Strasburg
Sunburst Lake N.W.R. · Burnt Creek
Westfield · Hague · Zeeland
Rice Lake

NORTH DAKOTA
SOUTH DAKOTA

BOWMAN
CUSTER NATL. FOR.
Ladner · Ludlow
Buffalo
Camp Crook · Harding
HARDING
Reva · Reva Gap · Slim Buttes
Sorum · Redig
Zeona · Hoover
Castle Rock
Geographic Center of the U.S.
Castle Rock Buttes 3,741
BUTTE

ADAMS
Lodgepole · Ralph
Prairie City · Bison · Meadow
PERKINS
Glad Valley · Firesteel · Isabel
Thunder Butte 2755
Iron Lightning
Red Elm · Faith · Dupree · Lantry
GRAND RIVER NATIONAL GRASSLAND
White Butte · Lemmon · Morristown · Watauga · McIntosh · Walker
Petrified Wood Park · Thunder Hawk · Keldron
Shadehill Res. · Shadehill · Hugh Glass Mon. · Shadehill Rec. Area
Llewellyn Johns Rec. Area
New Leipzig

CEDAR RIVER NATL. GRASSLAND
PAMPLIN HILLS
SIOUX
St. Gertrude Shields
Selfridge
PORCUPINE HILLS
Fort Yates
McLaughlin · Mahto
Bullhead · Little Eagle
Kenel · West Pollock Rec. Area
STANDING ROCK IND. RES.
CORSON
Rattlesnake Butte 2,284
Wakpala
Trail City
Mobridge · Glenham · Selby
CAMPBELL
Pollock · Herreid · Mound City
Lake Hiddenwood Rec. Area
Salt Lake
WALWORTH
Akaska · Lowry
Swan Lake
Swan Creek R.A.
Indian Creek R.A.
Sitting Bull Monument

CHEYENNE RIVER IND. RES.
Timber Lake · Glencross · Whitehorse · Green Grass
Little Moreau Rec. Area
DEWEY
La Plant · Ridgeview · Parade
Eagle Butte
ZIEBACH
Red Scaffold · Red Owl · Howes
Cherry Creek · Bridger · Kirley
Maurine · Mud Butte · Ben Ash Monument · Opal
Stoneville · Fairpoint
Newell · Nisland · Vale · Arpan
Belle Fourche Dam · Belle Fourche Res.
Rocky Point Rec. Area · Fruitdale
MEADE
Union Center · Enning · Plainview
White Owl · Marcus
Milesville · Pedro · Hereford
Bear Butte S.P.
Sturgis · Whitewood · Tilford · Piedmont · Summerset · Black Hawk
Ft. Meade B.L.M. Rec. Area
Black Hills Natl. Cem.
Deadwood · Central City · Lead · Terry Peak · Deer Mtn.
Nemo · Silver City · Rochford · Deerfield
BLACK HILLS NATL. FOR.
Ellsworth A.F.B.
Box Elder · Rapid City
New Underwood · Owanka · Wasta · Wall · Quinn
Natl. Grasslands Vis. Ctr. · Wall Drug Store
HAAKON
Ottumwa · Creighton · Midland · Philip · Nowlin
Rapid City Reg. Arpt. (RAP) · Farmingdale · Caputa
Rockerville · Hill City · Mt. Rushmore Natl. Mem. · Keystone · Hayward · Hermosa
PENNINGTON
Black Elk Pk. Highest Pt. in S.D. 7,242
Crazy Horse Mem. · Custer
WIND CAVE NATL. PARK · CUSTER S.P.
Pringle · Fairburn · Buffalo Gap · Red Shirt
Jewel Cave Natl. Mon.
Mammoth Site · Hot Springs · Oral · Smithwick
Hay Canyon Butte 3,440
BADLANDS NATL. PARK
Scenic · Imlay · Interior · White River Vis. Ctr.
Cottonwood · Minuteman Missile N.H.S.
Minuteman Missile N.H.S.
Badlands Petrified Gardens
Cactus Flat · Kadoka · Belvidere
Prairie Homestead Hist. Site · Pinnacles Overlook
BUFFALO GAP NATL. GRASSLAND
Ben Reifel Visitor Center
JACKSON
Wanblee · Cedar Butte
PINE RIDGE IND. RES.
Kyle · Hisle · Allen · Potato Creek
Oglala Lakota Coll.
OGLALA LAKOTA
Wounded Knee · Manderson · Porcupine · Oglala
BENNETT
Patricia · Vetal · Martin
Longvalley · Eagle Nest Butte 3410 · Norris
Hermosa
White River
MELLETTE
Wood · Mosher
Cedar Butte

STANLEY
Hayes · Fort Pierre
Pierre · Oahe Dam · Oahe Chapel · Oahe Downstream Rec. Area · Fort Pierre Chouteau
La Verendrye Monument
Fort Sully Game Refuge
Sutton Bay Rec. Area · Agar · Onida
SULLY
Mission Ridge · Cedar Butte 2053 · Triple U Buffalo Ranch · Okobojo Pt. Rec. Area · Cow Creek Rec. Area
FORT PIERRE NATIONAL GRASSLAND
Wendte · Van Metre · Capa
HUGHES · Canning · Blunt
Farm Island Rec. Area
LOWER BRULE I.R.
JONES
Draper · Vivian · Kennebec · Presho
Murdo · Okaton · Stamford · Draper
Pioneer Auto Mus. · 1880 Town
LYMAN
Kennebec · Presho
ROSEBUD IND. RES.
Winner · White River · Ideal · Carter · Witten
TRIPP
Okreek · Mission · Parmelee · Antelope · Hidden Timber
Sinte Gleska Univ.
TODD
Rosebud · St. Francis · Buechel Mem. Lakota Mus. · Spring Creek · Clearfield
Olsonville

Go to 34

A · B · C
1 · 2 · 3 · 4

DRIVING DISTANCES IN MILES	ABERDEEN, SD	BROOKINGS, SD	HOT SPRINGS, SD	HURON, SD	MITCHELL, SD	MOBRIDGE, SD	PIERRE, SD	RAPID CITY, SD	SIOUX FALLS, SD	WAHPETON, ND	WALL, SD	WATERTOWN, SD
ABERDEEN, SD		150	412	90	146	99	160	357	204	154	303	98
PIERRE, SD	160	188	247	115	155	107		193	226	301	138	189
RAPID CITY, SD	357	390	56	313	275	243	193		346	543	55	436
SIOUX FALLS, SD	204	57	401	127	73	303	226	346		210	292	103

SEE ALSO DISTANCE AND DRIVING TIME MAP ON PAGES 286–287

0 mi 20 40
0 km 20 40 60
One inch equals 25.4 miles
One centimeter equals 16.1 kilometers

Medford OR / Redding CA

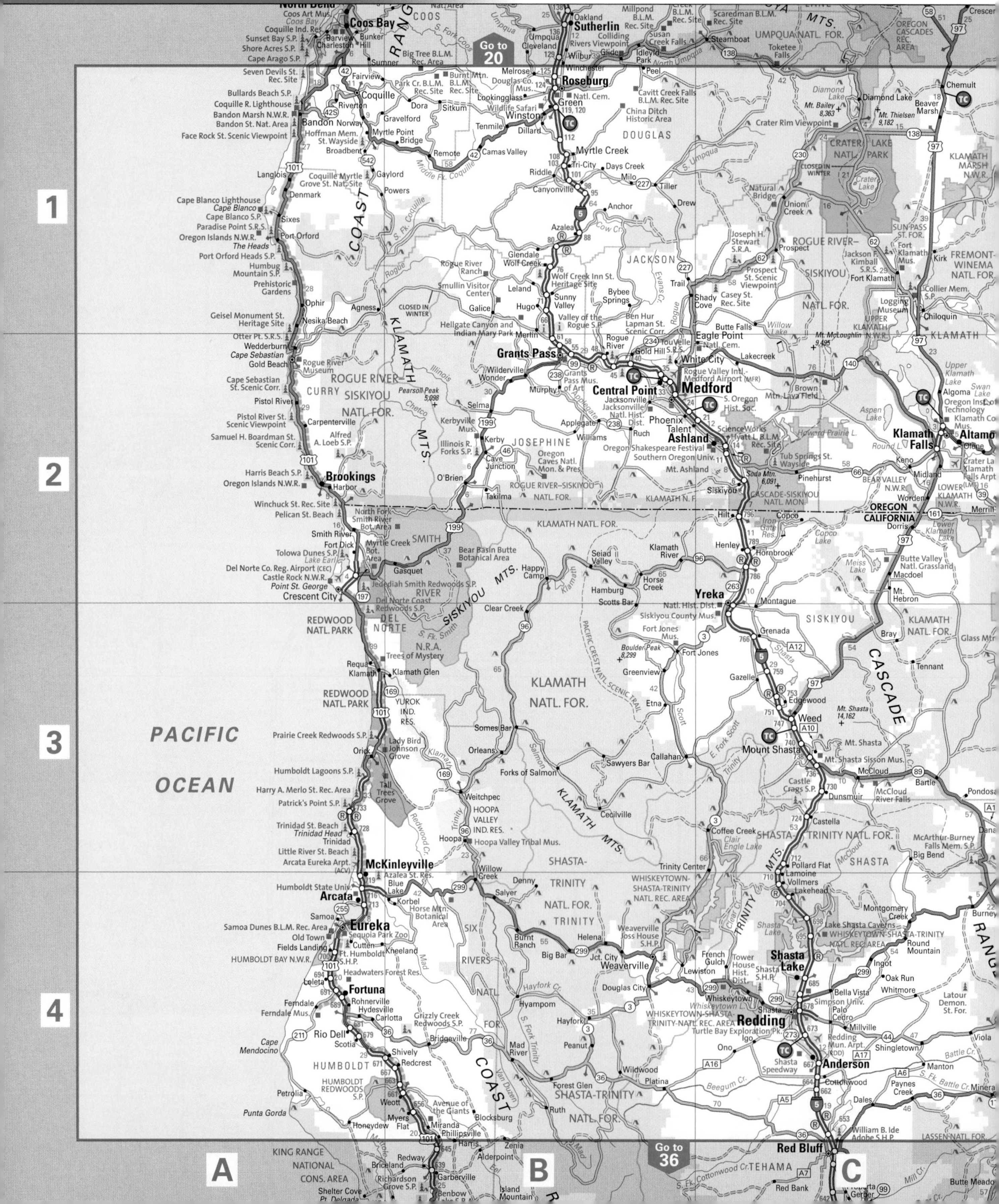

DRIVING DISTANCES IN MILES	ALTURAS, CA	CRATER LAKE NP, OR	CRESCENT CITY, CA	EUREKA, CA	KLAMATH FALLS, OR	LAKEVIEW, OR	LASSEN VOLCANIC NP, CA	MEDFORD, OR	REDDING, CA	ROSEBURG, OR	SUSANVILLE, CA	WINNEMUCCA, NV
LAKEVIEW, OR	56	153	282	332	98		192	171	199	265	161	212
MEDFORD, OR	176	80	111	192	76	171	208		148	94	221	383
REDDING, CA	143	198	189	133	141	199	63	148		242	114	364
SUSANVILLE, CA	105	226	303	247	170	161	74	221	114	315		250

SEE ALSO DISTANCE AND DRIVING TIME MAP ON PAGES 286–287

0 mi 20 40
0 km 20 40 60
One inch equals 25.4 miles
One centimeter equals 16.1 kilometers

Twin Falls ID / Elko NV

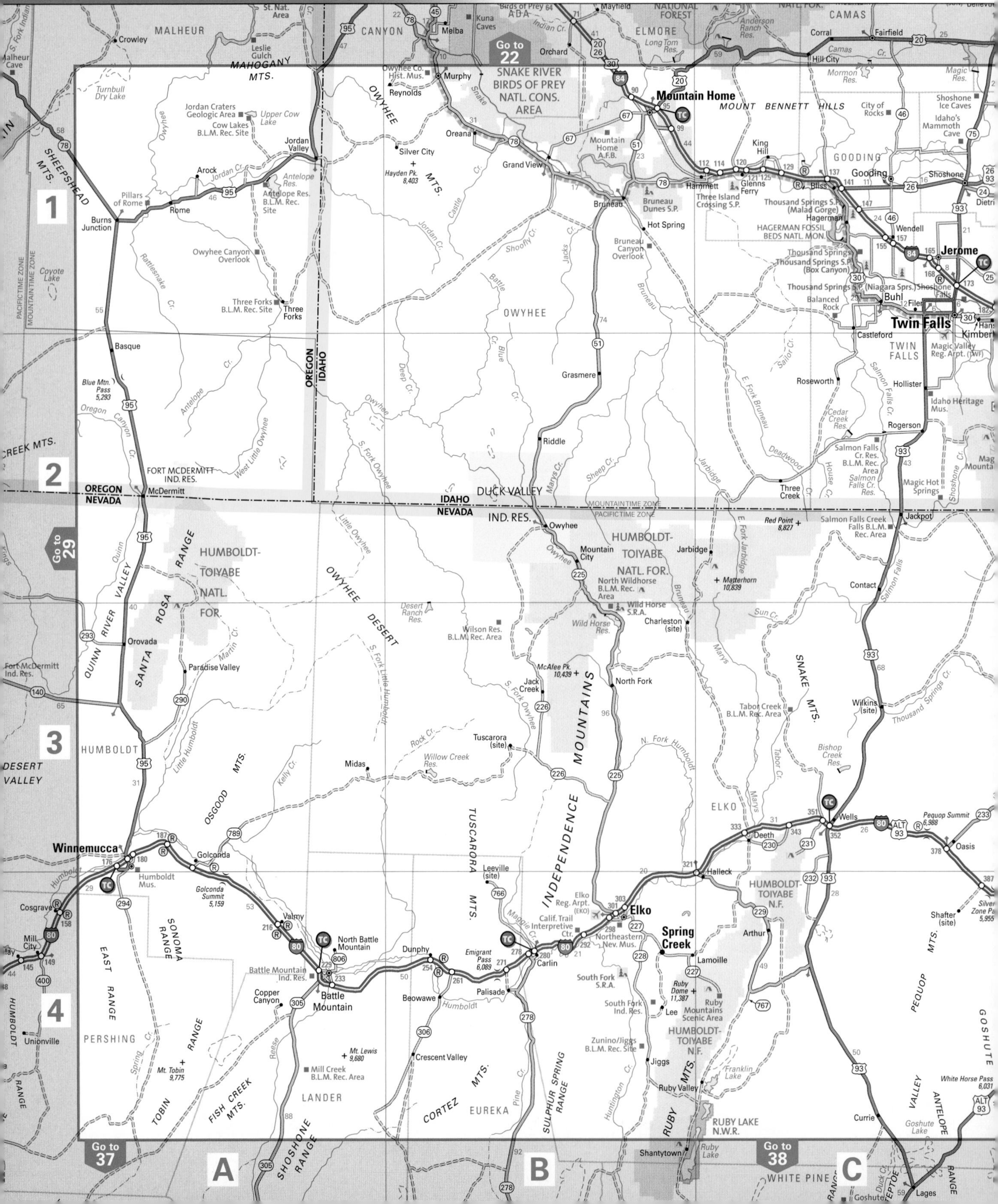

DRIVING DISTANCES IN MILES

	BRIGHAM CITY, UT	ELKO, NV	EVANSTON, WY	MONTPELIER, ID	MOUNTAIN HOME, ID	OGDEN, UT	POCATELLO, ID	PROVO, UT	SALT LAKE CITY, UT	TWIN FALLS, ID	WELLS, NV	WINNEMUCCA, NV
ELKO, NV	286		314	375	194	267	283	279	232	167	50	127
POCATELLO, ID	107	283	200	87	193	127		205	159	116	233	410
SALT LAKE CITY, UT	56	232	82	145	295	37	159	47		217	182	359
TWIN FALLS, ID	165	167	259	204	86	185	116	264	217		117	294

SEE ALSO DISTANCE AND DRIVING TIME MAP ON PAGES 286–287

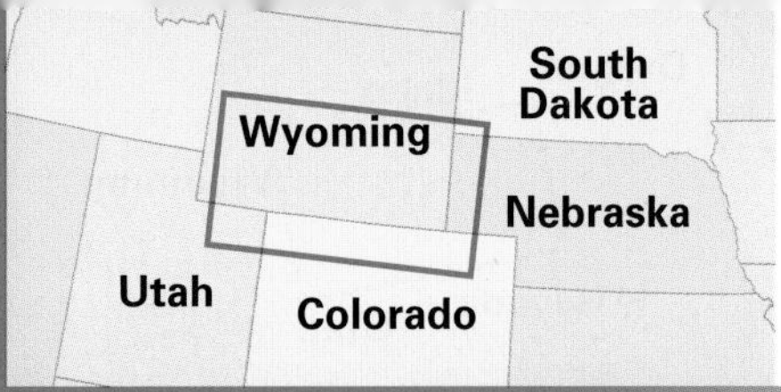

0 mi 20 40
0 km 20 40 60
One inch equals 25.4 miles
One centimeter equals 16.1 kilometers

Rock Springs WY / Craig CO

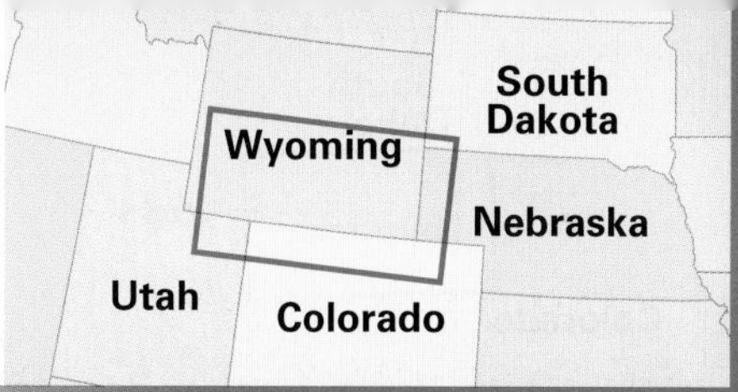

DRIVING DISTANCES IN MILES

	CASPER, WY	CHEYENNE, WY	CRAIG, CO	FORT COLLINS, CO	KEMMERER, WY	LANDER, WY	LARAMIE, WY	PINEDALE, WY	RAWLINS, WY	ROCK SPRINGS, WY	SCOTTSBLUFF, NE	VERNAL, UT
CASPER, WY		175	234	217	297	144	148	271	117	214	173	322
CHEYENNE, WY	175		221	44	342	276	52	355	151	260	111	367
CRAIG, CO	234	221		194	257	221	171	269	117	149	331	123
ROCK SPRINGS, WY	214	260	149	273	86	118	210	98	110		370	111

SEE ALSO DISTANCE AND DRIVING TIME MAP ON PAGES 286–287

0 mi   20   40

0 km 20 40 60

One inch equals 25.4 miles
One centimeter equals 16.1 kilometers

PINE RIDGE IND. RES.

SHANNON

Go to 26

MELLETTE

TRIPP

BENNETT

TODD

ROSEBUD IND. RES.

BUFFALO GAP NATL GRASSLAND

FALL RIVER

SOUTH DAKOTA / NEBRASKA

OGLALA NATL GRASSLAND

Chadron

DAWES

P I N E   R I D G E

SIOUX

Ft. Robinson

FORT ROBINSON S.H.P.

NEBRASKA NATL. FOR.

CHERRY

Valentine

VALENTINE N.W.R.

SAMUEL R. McKELVIE NATL. FOR.

BROWN

BOX BUTTE

SHERIDAN

Alliance

SURVEY VALLEY

S A N D   H I L L S

HOOKER

THOMAS

BLAINE

NEBRASKA NATL. FOR.

Scottsbluff

MORRILL

GRANT

CRESCENT LAKE N.W.R.

McPHERSON

LOGAN

CUSTER

BANNER

GARDEN

ARTHUR

Arthur

KEITH

LINCOLN

North Platte

Mountain Time Zone / Central Time Zone

CHEYENNE

Sidney

DEUEL

Ogallala

Lake McConaughy

KIMBALL

NEBRASKA / COLORADO

Julesburg

SEDGWICK

PERKINS

Sterling

LOGAN

WASHINGTON

PHILLIPS

CHASE

HAYES

FRONTIER

GOSPER

YUMA

COLORADO / NEBRASKA

Go to 42

DUNDY

HITCHCOCK

RED WILLOW

McCook

FURNAS

Lexington

Gothenburg

Cozad

A   B   C

1   2   3   4

DRIVING DISTANCES IN MILES

	CHADRON, NE	GRAND ISLAND, NE	LINCOLN, NE	MCCOOK, NE	NORFOLK, NE	NORTH PLATTE, NE	OGALLALA, NE	OMAHA, NE	SCOTTSBLUFF, NE	SIOUX CITY, IA	STERLING, CO	YANKTON, SD
GRAND ISLAND, NE	373		95	147	105	143	196	150	318	180	281	167
LINCOLN, NE	453	95		226	119	223	275	58	397	153	361	218
NORTH PLATTE, NE	230	143	223	67	248		53	278	175	373	138	310
OMAHA, NE	508	150	58	281	115	278	330		452	99	416	163

SEE ALSO DISTANCE AND DRIVING TIME MAP ON PAGES 286–287

0 mi 20 40
0 km 20 40 60

One inch equals 25.4 miles
One centimeter equals 16.1 kilometers

San Francisco CA / Sacramento CA

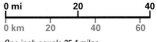

One inch equals 25.4 miles.

DRIVING DISTANCES IN MILES	AUSTIN, NV	CHICO, CA	MERCED, CA	RENO, NV	SACRAMENTO, CA	SAN FRANCISCO, CA	SAN JOSE, CA	S. LAKE TAHOE, CA	STOCKTON, CA	TONOPAH, NV	UKIAH, CA	YOSEMITE VIL., CA
RENO, NV	171	164	243		132	217	245	59	177	237	261	199
SACRAMENTO, CA	302	88	118	132		87	115	100	48	329	153	170
SAN FRANCISCO, CA	387	182	131	217	87		43	185	82	352	116	183
YOSEMITE VIL., CA	280	257	79	199	170	183	168	180	123	199	289	

SEE ALSO DISTANCE AND DRIVING TIME MAP ON PAGES 286–287

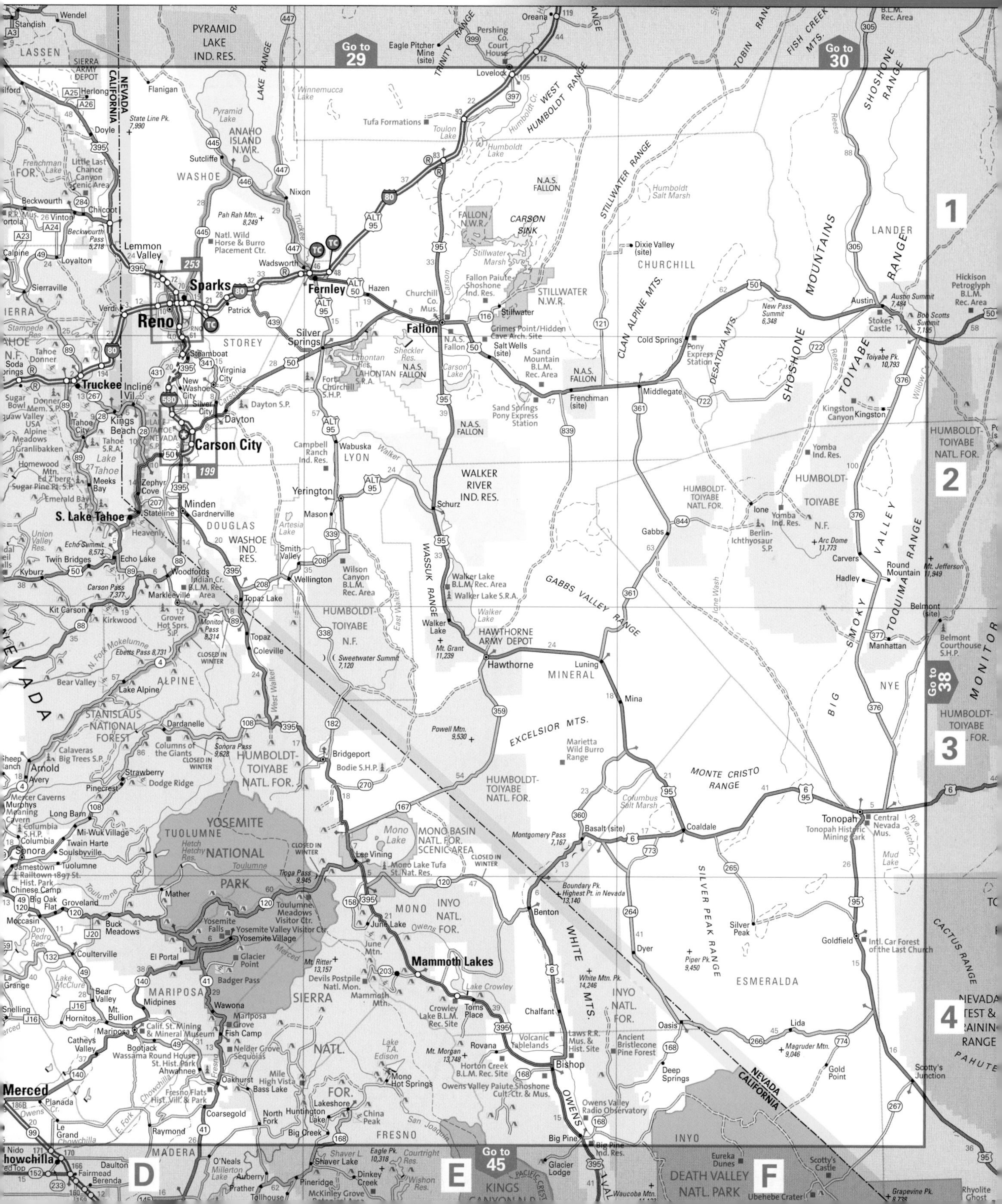

0 mi   20   40
0 km   20   40   60
One inch equals 25.4 miles
One centimeter equals 16.1 kilometers

Go to 30

Go to 37

Go to 45

Go to 46

A   B   C

1   2   3   4

SHOSHONE RANGE
CORTEZ MTS.
RUBY LAKE N.W.R.
Ruby Valley
Shantytown
Ruby Lake
ELKO
Currie
White Horse Pass 6,031
Gold Hill Ghost Town
Dutch Mtn. 7,794
Ibapah
Callao
Goshute IND. RES.
Goshute
DEEP CREEK RANGE
Ibapah Pk. 12,087
Trout Creek
Blue Mass Scenic Area
Salt Marsh Lake
Gandy
CONFUSION RANGE
Eskdale
NEVADA UTAH
Mt. Moriah 12,050
Sacramento Pass 7,136
Baker
Garrison
Pruess Lake
DESERT EXPERIMENTAL RANGE

LANDER
EUREKA
Tonkin Spring B.L.M. Rec. Area
SULPHUR SPRING RANGE
HUMBOLDT-TOIYABE NATL. FOR.
DIAMOND MTS.
Newark Lake
Diamond Pk. 10,614
WHITE PINE
BUTTE MOUNTAINS
CHERRY CREEK RANGE
Goshute Canyon and Cave
Cherry Creek
STEPTOE RANGE
ANTELOPE RANGE
Goshute Lake
Lages
Tippett
SCHELL CREEK RANGE
SPRING VALLEY
HUMBOLDT-TOIYABE NATL. FOR.
North Schell Pk. 11,883

TOIYABE RANGE
Austin
Austin Summit 7,484
Stokes Castle
Bob Scotts Summit 7,195
Hickison Petroglyph B.L.M. Rec. Area
Eureka
Eureka Sentinel Mus.
Eureka Opera House
Robinson Summit 7,539
Little Antelope Summit 7,438
Steptoe (site)
McGill
Ely Arpt. (ELY)
Ruth Lane Ely E. Ely
Nev. Northern Railway Mus.
Garnet Hill
Mt. Moriah

Summit Mtn. 10,461
Toiyabe Pk. 10,793
FISH CREEK RANGE
Mt. Hamilton 10,745
Illipah Res. B.L.M. Rec. Area
Ward Mtn. B.L.M. Rec. Area
EGAN RANGE
Ward Charcoal Ovens S.H.P.
Cleve Creek B.L.M. Rec. Site
Cave Lake S.P.
Connors Pass 7,733
Majors Place
Wheeler Pk. 13,063
Lehman Caves
GREAT BASIN NATL. PARK
Shoshone
Minerva (site)
HUMBOLDT-TOIYABE NATL. FOR.

Kingston
Kingston Canyon
HUMBOLDT-TOIYABE NATL. FOR.
Potts (site)
Duckwater
Duckwater Ind. Res.
Currant Mtn. 11,513
Currant Summit 6,999
Preston
Lund
Currant
SNAKE RANGE
LAKE VALLEY
WILSON CREEK RANGE
Mt. Wilson 9,296
INDIAN PEAK RANGE

BIG SMOKY VALLEY
TOQUIMA RANGE
Arc Dome 11,773
Carvers
Hadley
Round Mountain
Mt. Jefferson 11,949
Belmont (site)
Belmont Courthouse S.H.P.
Manhattan
MONITOR RANGE
HUMBOLDT-TOIYABE NATL. FOR.
HOT CREEK RANGE
Lunar Crater Volcanic Field Natl. Natural Landmark
PANCAKE RANGE
RAILROAD VALLEY
Adams-McGill Res.
Sunnyside
White
318
Spring Valley S.P.
Meadow Valley B.L.M. Rec. Site
Hamlin Valley
Ursine

Tonopah
Central Nev. Mus.
Tonopah Hist. Mining Park
Warm Springs Summit 6,293
Warm Springs (site)
NYE
REVEILLE RANGE
Nyala (site)
Troy Pk. 11,298
GRANT RANGE
HUMBOLDT-TOIYABE NATL. FOR.
Michael Heizer's City
BASIN & RANGE NATIONAL MONUMENT
SEAMAN RANGE
Pioche
Caselton
Echo Canyon S.P.
Cathedral Gorge S.P.
Panaca
Modena
Uvada
Zane
Beryl

Goldfield
Intl. Car Forest of the Last Church
CACTUS RANGE
KAWICH RANGE
EXTRATERRESTRIAL HIGHWAY
TONOPAH TEST RANGE
Queen City Summit 5,935
Tempiute (site)
Rachel
Hiko
LINCOLN
Caliente
Caliente Railroad Depot
Kershaw-Ryan S.P.
Rainbow Canyon
Elgin
CLOVER MTS.
Beaver Dam S.P.
Lost Pk. 7,514
DIXIE NATL. FOR.
Enterprise
Mountain Meadows Monument
Newcastle
Pinto

Scotty's Junction
PAHUTE MESA
BELTED RANGE
NEVADA TEST & TRAINING RANGE
GROOM RANGE
Groom Lake
PAHRANAGAT RANGE
Ash Springs
Alamo
PAHRANAGAT N.W.R.
DELAMAR MTS.
Delamar Lake
Caliente
Carp
WASHINGTON
Baker Dam B.L.M. Rec. Site
Veyo
Snow Canyon S.P.
Gunlock
Gunlock S.P.
PAIUTE IND. RES.
Shivwits
Santa Clara
Jacob Hamblin Home
Ivins
St. George
Dixie State Univ.
Joshua Tree Natural Area

Grapevine Pk. 8,738
NEVADA NATIONAL SECURITY SITE
DESERT NATL. WILDLIFE RANGE

PACIFIC TIME ZONE
MOUNTAIN TIME ZONE

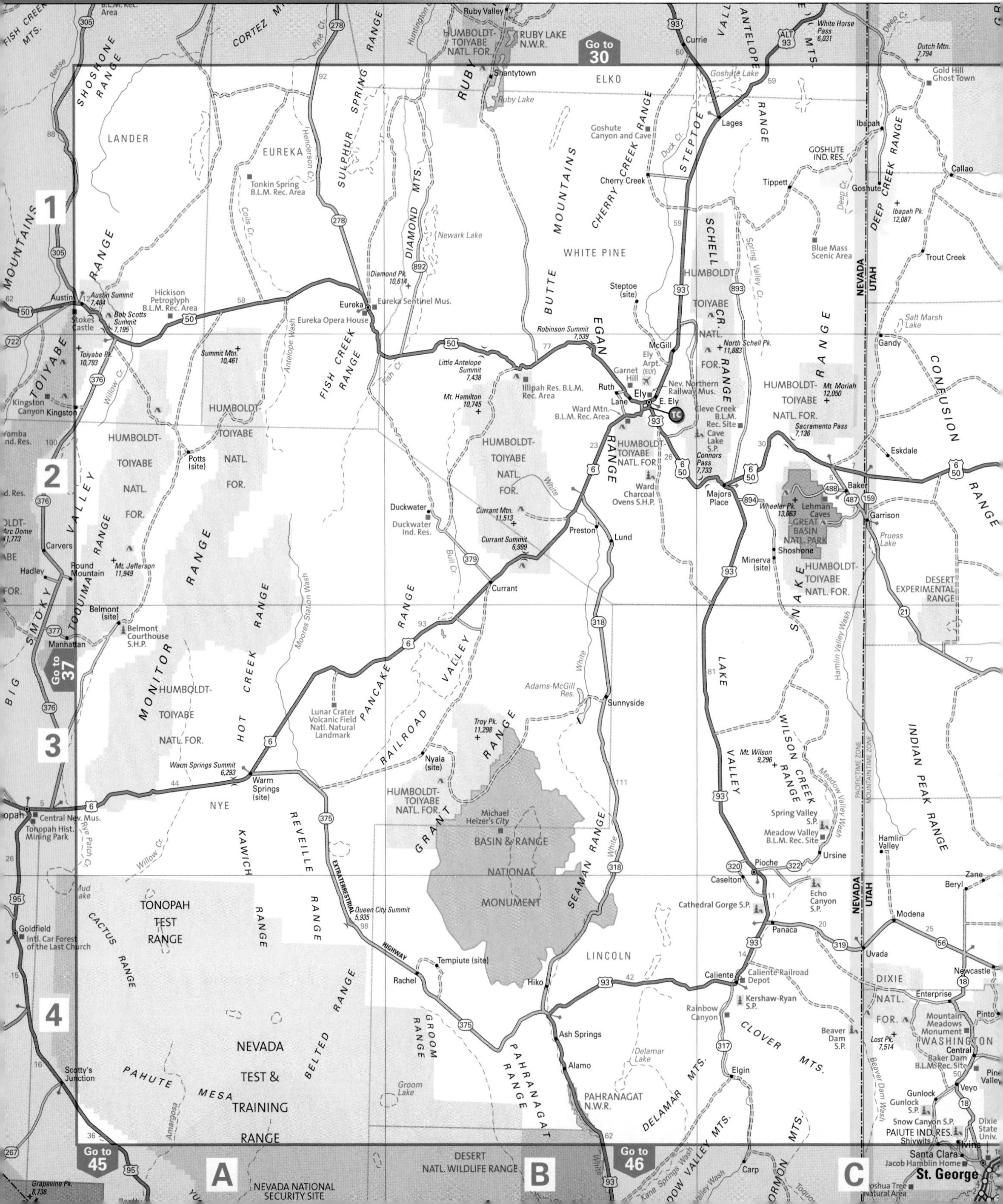

DRIVING DISTANCES IN MILES

	AUSTIN, NV	BAKER, NV	CEDAR CITY, UT	DELTA, UT	ELY, NV	GREEN RIVER, UT	PROVO, UT	ST. GEORGE, UT	SALINA, UT	SPRINGDALE, UT	TONOPAH, NV	TORREY, UT
ELY, NV	147	68	198	156		332	243	216	224	261	167	307
PROVO, UT	426	193	204	88	243	137		256	94	266	410	172
SALINA, UT	371	187	128	68	224	108	94	180		190	411	78
SPRINGDALE (ZION), UT	408	193	64	205	261	297	266	45	190		339	191

SEE ALSO DISTANCE AND DRIVING TIME MAP ON PAGES 286–287

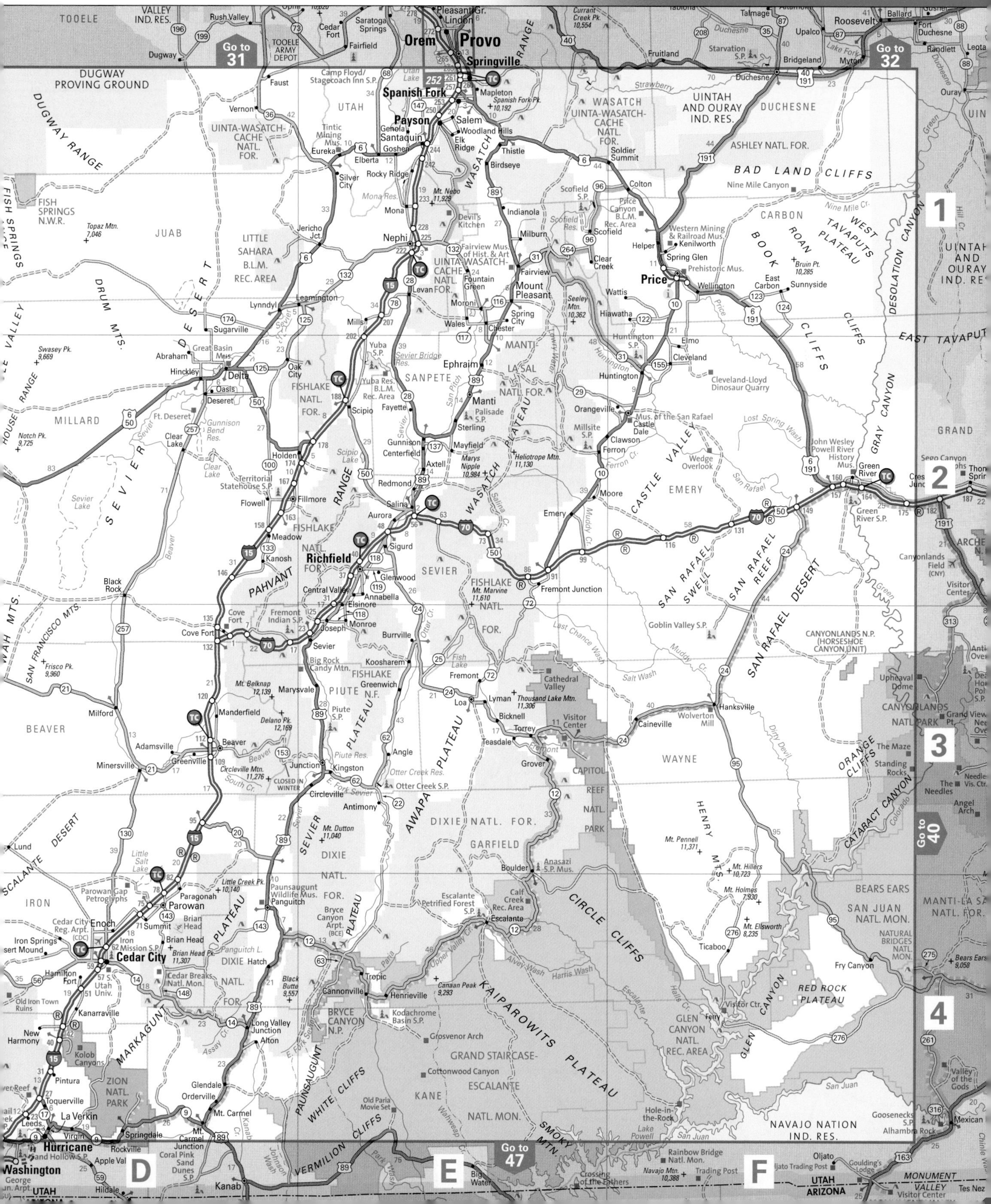

Utah | Colorado

0 mi 20 40
0 km 20 40 60
One inch equals 25.4 miles
One centimeter equals 16.1 kilometers

Grid references: 1, 2, 3, 4 (left side); A, B, C (bottom)

Go to 32
Go to 39
Go to 48

Selected places and features:

Roosevelt, Ballard, Gusher, Fort Duchesne, Randlett, Leota, Myton, Bridgeland, Upalco, Bonanza, Ouray N.W.R., UINTAH, OURAY, UINTAH AND OURAY INDIAN RESERVATION, Dinosaur, Massadona, Blue Mountain, Elk Springs, Rangely, Hamilton, Axial, Pagoda, MOFFAT, ROUTT, Oak Creek, Phippsburg, Stagecoach, Muddy Pass 8,772, ARAPAHO NATL. FOR.

UINTAH, Ouray, White, LAND CLIFFS, TAVAPUTS PLATEAU, Bruin Pt. 10,285, Sunnyside, East Carbon, CARBON, DESOLATION CANYON, EAST TAVAPUTS PLATEAU, CATHEDRAL BLUFFS, RIO BLANCO, White River Mus., Meeker, Buford, WHITE RIVER NATL. FOR., Ripple Creek Pass 10,343, Devil's Causeway, Yampa, Toponas, MEDICINE BOW-ROUTT NATL. FOR., Sheep Mtn. 12,241, Radium, McCoy, Burns, Bond, State Bridge, UPPER COLORADO RIVER B.L.M. REC. AREA, EAGLE, Gore Pass 9,527, Wolcott, Edwards, Avon

GRAY CANYON, ROAN CLIFFS, ROAN PLATEAU, GARFIELD, NAVAL OIL SHALE RES., Rifle, Rifle Falls S.P., Rifle Gap S.P., Rio Blanco, Parachute, Rulison, Battlement Mesa, De Beque, Glenwood Springs, Glenwood Caverns, Hot Springs Pool, Carbondale, El Jebel, Basalt, Meredith, Snowmass, Woody Creek, Aspen, Aspen Mtn., Aspen Highlands, Buttermilk Mtn., PITKIN, Marble, Redstone, Crystal, Paonia, Somerset, Bowie, Crested Butte, Mount Crested Butte, Kebler Pass 9,980, Ohio Pass 10,033, RUBY RANGE, ELK MTS., Maroon Bells, Independence Pass 12,093, Ashcroft, Ghost Town, Castle Peak 14,265

BOOK CLIFFS, GRAND, Mack, Loma, Fruita, Grand Junction, COLORADO NATL. MON., Glade Park, Clifton, Palisade, Cameo, Mesa, Molina, Collbran, Vega S.P., Powderhorn, GRAND MESA NATL. FOR., Grand Mesa, Cedaredge, Paonia, DELTA, Hotchkiss, Crawford, Crawford S.P., Maher, WEST ELK MTS., Mt. Gunnison 12,719, GUNNISON NATL. FOR., Almont, Gunnison, Western State Colorado University, Parlin, Ohio, Doyleville

Crescent Junction, Thompson Springs, Westwater, Cisco, John Wesley Powell River History Mus., Green River S.P., ARCHES NATL. PARK, Delicate Arch, The Windows, Fisher Towers, Castle Valley, Castleton Tower, Moab, Gateway, DOMINGUEZ CANYON B.L.M. REC. AREA, MESA, GRAND MESA NATL. FOR., Orchard City, Ft. Uncompahgre Living Hist. Mus., Delta, Austin, Sweitzer Lake S.P., Lazear, BLACK CANYON OF THE GUNNISON NATL. PARK, Olathe, Montrose Regional Arpt. (MTJ), Curecanti Needle, Blue Mesa Res., Sapinero, CURECANTI NATL. REC. AREA, Cochetopa Canyon B.L.M. REC. AREA, Gunnison-Crested Butte Reg. Arpt. (GUC), Cochetopa Pass 10,032

Canyonlands Field (CNY), CANYONLANDS NATL. PARK, The Maze, The Needles, Standing Rocks, Needles Overlook, Upheaval Dome, Dead Horse Point S.P., Grand View Pt., Looking Glass Rock, Wilson Arch, La Sal, La Sal Junction, Paradox, Bedrock, Uravan, Nucla, Naturita, Redvale, Vancorum, Norwood, Redstone, MANTI-LA SAL NATL. FOR., Mt. Waas 12,311, Mt. Peale 12,721, LA SAL MTS., Hanging Flume, Columbine Pass 9,120, UNCOMPAHGRE PLATEAU, MONTROSE, Montrose, Cimarron, Colona, Ridgway, Ridgway S.P., OURAY, Dallas Divide, Ouray, Uncompahgre Pk. 14,309, UNCOMPAHGRE NATL. FOR., Lake City, San Luis Pk. 14,014, HINSDALE, Powderhorn, North Pass 10,149, COCHETOPA

BEARS EARS NATL. MON., GLEN CANYON NATL. REC. AREA, CATARACT CANYON, Angel Arch, Church Rock, Newspaper Rock St. Hist. Mon., Summit Point, Shay Mtn. 9,988, Monticello, Ucolo, Slick Rock, Egnar, Gypsum Gap 6,100, SAN MIGUEL, DOLORES RIVER B.L.M. REC. AREA, UNCOMPAHGRE NATL. FOR., Placerville, Sawpit, Telluride Regional Arpt. (TEX), Mountain Village, Telluride, Pandora, Ophir, Lizard Head Pass 10,222, Mt. Wilson 14,246, Camp Bird, Ouray Hot Springs, Bridal Veil Falls, Red Mtn. Pass 11,008, Silverton, Molas Pass 10,910, Coal Bank Pass 10,640, Rico, Dunton, SAN JUAN MOUNTAINS, Spring Creek Pass 10,901, Creede, Wagon Wheel Gap, RIO GRANDE, LA GARITA, Wheeler Geologic Area

MANTI-LA SAL NATL. FOR., Mt. Linnaeus 10,961, Abajo Pk. 11,360, Blanding, Dinosaur Mus., Eastland, Edge of the Cedars S.P., Bears Ears 9,058, SAN JUAN, Dove Creek, Cahone, Pleasant View, Lowry Pueblo Ruins, Yellow Jacket, McPhee Res., Lewis, Lebanon, Arriola, Dolores, Anasazi Heritage Center, CANYONS OF THE ANCIENTS NATL. MON., Stoner, TAYLOR MESA, Rockwood, Hermosa, Trimble, Vallecito, Vallecito Res., Purgatory Resort, Mt. Eolus 14,083, Montezuma Pk. 13,150, Summit Peak 13,300, SAN JUAN NATL. FOR., WEMINUCHE WILDERNESS, MINERAL NATL. FOR., South Fork, Wolf Creek Pass, Wolf Creek, Spar City

GLEN CANYON NATL. REC. AREA, Goosenecks S.P., Alhambra Rock, Mexican Hat, Goulding's Trading Lodge, Valley of the Gods, Bluff, Montezuma Creek, Aneth, NAVAJO NATION IND. RES., Cortez, Yucca House Natl. Mon., Towaoc, Hovenweep Natl. Mon., MESA VERDE NATL. PARK, Mancos, Mayday, Hesperus, Breen, Durango, Fort Lewis Coll., Durango-Silverton Narrow Gauge RR, Grandview, Bayfield, Gem Village, Oxford, Chimney Rock, Nutria, Lonetree, Pagosa Springs, ARCHULETA

MONUMENT VALLEY, Tes Nez Iah, UTAH / ARIZONA, Four Corners Mon. & Navajo Tribal Park, Red Mesa, UTE MOUNTAIN UTE IND. RES., Ute Mountain Tribal Park Visitor Center, MONTEZUMA, COLORADO / NEW MEXICO, SOUTHERN UTE IND. RES., Ignacio, Bondad, Tiffany, Allison, Arboles, Chromo

Go to 48

DRIVING DISTANCES IN MILES	ALAMOSA, CO	ASPEN, CO	COLORADO SPRS., CO	CORTEZ, CO	DENVER, CO	DURANGO, CO	GRAND JUNCTION, CO	GREEN RIVER, UT	MOAB, UT	MONTROSE, CO	PUEBLO, CO	TRINIDAD, CO
COLORADO SPRS., CO	162	157		359	70	314	318	418	404	236	43	127
DENVER, CO	230	164	70	452		337	250	350	337	277	111	196
DURANGO, CO	152	244	314	45	337		169	214	160	107	271	260
GRAND JUNCTION, CO	261	135	318	203	250	169		102	88	62	360	444

SEE ALSO DISTANCE AND DRIVING TIME MAP ON PAGES 286–287

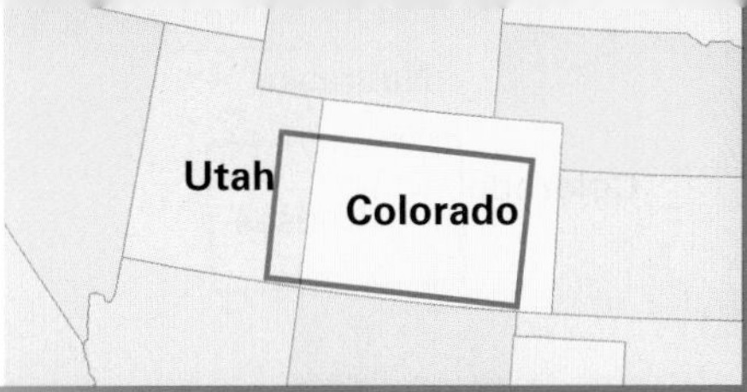

0 mi 20 40
0 km 20 40 60
One inch equals 25.4 miles
One centimeter equals 16.1 kilometers

Garden City KS / Dodge City KS

DRIVING DISTANCES IN MILES

	BURLINGTON, CO	DODGE CITY, KS	EMPORIA, KS	GARDEN CITY, KS	HAYS, KS	LAMAR, CO	MANHATTAN, KS	MCCOOK, NE	OAKLEY, KS	SALINA, KS	TOPEKA, KS	WICHITA, KS
GARDEN CITY, KS	167	52	290		139	98	272	167	79	204	311	205
OAKLEY, KS	88	136	293	79	87	156	247	88		179	286	268
SALINA, KS	266	164	118	204	93	335	72	240	179		111	92
WICHITA, KS	354	153	85	205	181	303	131	329	268	92	137	

SEE ALSO DISTANCE AND DRIVING TIME MAP ON PAGES 286–287

0 mi 20 40
0 km 20 40 60

One inch equals 25.4 miles
One centimeter equals 16.1 kilometers

DRIVING DISTANCES IN MILES

	BAKERSFIELD, CA	BISHOP, CA	DEATH VALLEY, CA	FRESNO, CA	RIDGECREST, CA	SALINAS, CA	SAN FRANCISCO, CA	SAN JOSE, CA	SAN LUIS OBISPO, CA	STOCKTON, CA	TONOPAH, NV	YOSEMITE VIL, CA
BAKERSFIELD, CA		215	236	111	99	209	287	245	119	243	318	200
BISHOP, CA	215		169	219	141	302	283	269	333	223	119	130
FRESNO, CA	111	219	333		196	145	190	153	134	130	288	90
SAN JOSE, CA	245	269	437	153	344	61	43		191	68	338	168

SEE ALSO DISTANCE AND DRIVING TIME MAP ON PAGES 286–287

Bakersfield CA / Death Valley Natl Park CA

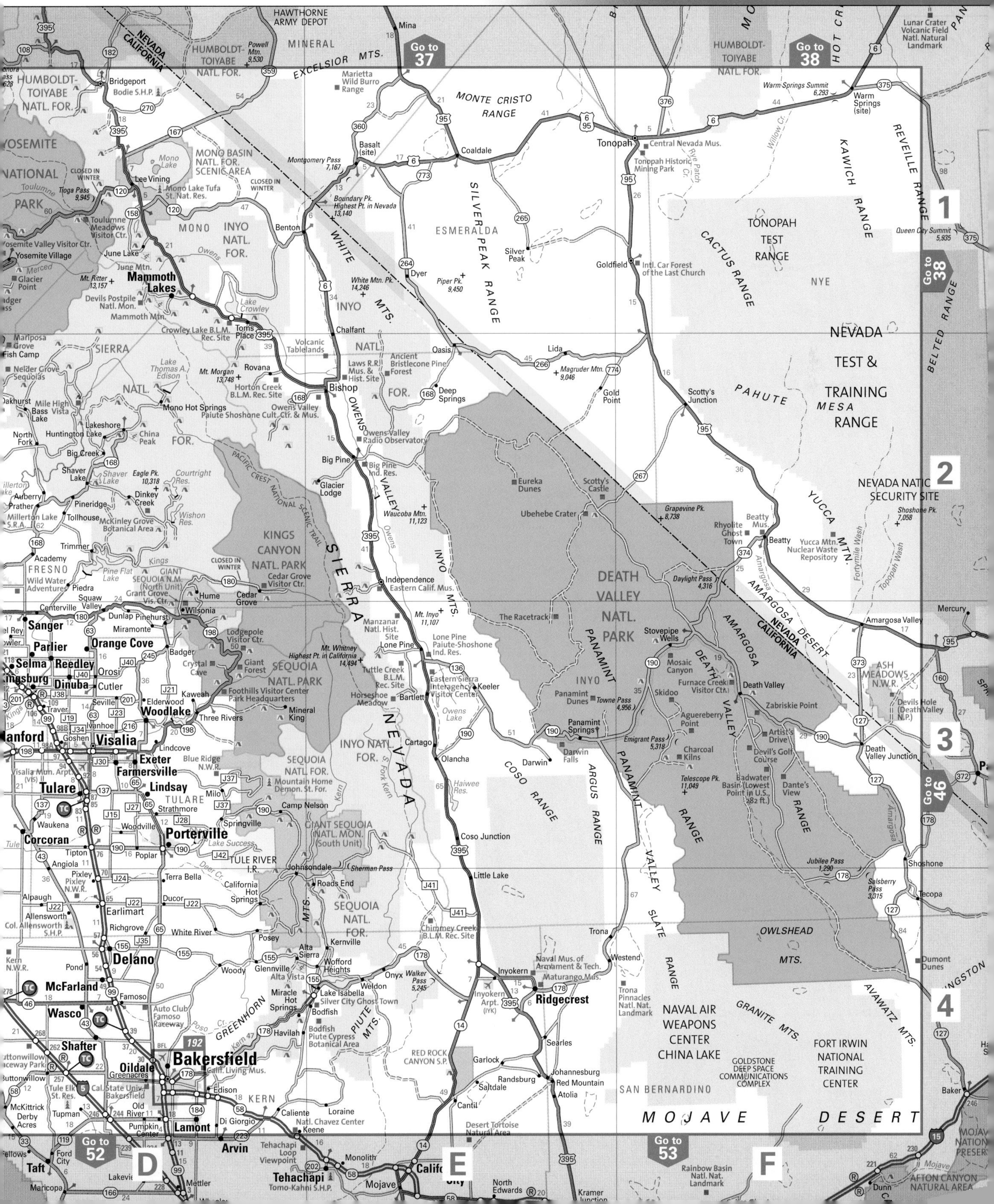

Nevada Utah
California
Arizona

0 mi   20   40
0 km   20   40   60
One inch equals 25.4 miles
One centimeter equals 16.1 kilometers

NEVADA TEST & TRAINING RANGE
NEVADA NATIONAL SECURITY SITE
Shoshone Pk. 7,058
Yucca Lake
NYE
Dog Bone Lake
Desert Lake
DESERT RANGE
Groom Lake
PAHRANAGAT N.W.R.
DELAMAR MTS.
LINCOLN
Lake
MEADOW VALLEY MTS.
MORMON MTS.
Go to 38
NEVADA UTAH
WASHINGTON
ZION NATL. PARK
Veyo
Gunlock
Silver Reef S.P.
Snow Canyon S.P.
Dixie State Univ.
Leeds
Toquerville
La Verkin
Rockville
Springdale
PAIUTE IND. RES.
Shivwits
Santa Clara
Ivins
Jacob Hamblin Home
Joshua Tree Natural Area
St. George
St. George Mun. Arpt. (SGU)
Washington
Hurricane
Sand Hollow S.P.
Apple Valley
Hildale
UTAH
ARIZONA
Colorado City
Cane Beds

Amargosa Valley
Mercury
ASH MEADOWS N.W.R.
Creech A.F.B.
Indian Springs
NATL. WILDLIFE RANGE
Hayford Pk. 9,912
SHEEP RANGE
CLARK
Carp
Kane Springs Wash
Mormon Pk. 7,411
Glendale
Moapa
MOAPA RIVER IND. RES.
Logandale
Overton
Beaver Dam
Littlefield
Mt. Bangs 8,012
Mesquite
Bunkerville
Virgin River Rec. Area
Virgin River Canyon B.L.M. Rec. Area
VIRGIN MTS.
HURRICANE CLIFFS
UINKARET PLATEAU

Death Valley Junction
Devils Hole (Death Valley N.P.)
Pahrump
Charleston Pk. 11,918
Lee Canyon
Floyd Lamb Park
SPRING MOUNTAINS N.R.A.
TULE SPRINGS FOSSIL BEDS NATL. MON.
NELLIS AIR FORCE RANGE COMPLEX
Las Vegas
North Las Vegas
Henderson
MUDDY MTS.
VALLEY OF FIRE S.P.
Lost City Mus.
Fortification Hill 3,718
Temple Bar
Meadview
GOLD BUTTE NATL. MONUMENT
LAKE MEAD NATL. REC. AREA
Lake Mead
GRAND CANYON-PARASHANT NATL. MONUMENT
SHIVWITS PLATEAU
Poverty Mtn. 6,791
Mt. Trumbull
Mt. Trumbull 8,028
Ranger Station
Toroweap Overlook
Grand Wash Cliffs
Colorado

Pahrump
SPRING MOUNTAINS
RED ROCK CANYON N.C.A.
Spring Mtn. Ranch S.P.
Blue Diamond
Sloan
SLOAN CANYON N.C.A.
Boulder City
Hoover Dam
Willow Beach
WHITE HILLS
Joshua Tree Forest
Garnet Mtn. 8,440
Grand Canyon West & Skywalk
Grand Canyon West Arpt. (GCW)
GRAND CANYON NATL. PARK
Natural Bridge

Shoshone
Tecopa
INYO
Goodsprings
Sandy Valley
Jean
Nelson
Nelson
Roach Lake
Primm
Buffalo Bill's
Ivanpah Lake
Mesquite Lake
Searchlight
Cottonwood Cove
Lake Mohave
Mt. Perkins 5,456
Mt. Tipton 7,148
Dolan Springs
Red Lake
Chloride
Windy Point B.L.M. Rec. Site
Peach Springs
Nelson
Yampai
Grand Canyon Caverns
AUBREY CLIFFS
HUALAPAI IND. RES.

Dumont Dunes
KINGSTON RANGE
SHADOW VALLEY
Clark Mtn. 7,929
Mountain Pass
Mountain Pass 4,730
Nipton
NEVADA CALIFORNIA
Cal-Nev-Ari
SACRAMENTO MTS.
CERBAT MTS.
Truxton
Truxton Wash
Hackberry
Valentine
Seligman
Halloran Springs
Baker
Silver Lake
Cima Dome
Cima
Cinder Cones
Soda Lake
Ivanpah
NEW YORK MTS.
MOJAVE NATIONAL PRESERVE
Providence Mountains St. Rec. Area
CASTLE MTS. NATL. MON.
LANFAIR VALLEY
Davis Dam
Laughlin
McConnico
Kingman
Kingman Arpt. (IGM)
Mohave Mus. of History & Arts and Historic Rt. 66 Mus.
Hualapai Mtn. Park
Hualapai Pk. 8,417
Snow Mtn. 5,879
Cross Mtn. 6,463
Mohon Pk. 7,499
Mt. Hope 7,263
JUNIPER MTS.
PRESCOTT NATL. FOR.
AQUARIUS MOUNTAINS
Hyde Creek Mtn. 7,272

DESERT
DEVILS PLAYGROUND
Kelso
Kelso Dunes
Mitchell Caverns
SAN BERNARDINO
Goffs
Big Bend of the Colorado S.R.A.
Oatman
Bullhead City
Laughlin/Bullhead Intl. Arpt. (IFP)
Colorado River Museum
BLACK MESA
Yucca
Wild Cow Springs B.L.M. Rec. Site
Wikieup
Aubrey Pk. 5,078
Granite Pk. 7,069
Burro Creek B.L.M. Rec. Site
Bagdad
Cypress Mtn. 8,251

Ludlow
Pisgah Crater
Go to 53
BRISTOL MTS.
Bagdad
OLD NATIONAL TRAIL HWY.
Amboy Crater Natl. Nat. Landmark
Amboy
Cadiz
Danby
Fenner
Essex
South Pass 2,750
Needles
Mohave Valley
FORT MOJAVE IND. RES.
Golden Shores
HAVASU
Topock
HAVASU N.W.R.
Moabi Reg. Park
Lake Havasu City
Lake Havasu City Arpt. (HII)
Lake Havasu S.P.
MOHAVE MTS.
DUTCH FLAT
MC CRACKEN MTS.
POACHIE RANGE
JOSHUA FOREST PARKWAY
Burro Creek
Hillside
WEAVER MTS.
Date
Congress

MARINE CORPS AIR GROUND COMBAT CENTER TWENTYNINE PALMS
Landers
Twentynine Palms
Twentynine Palms Ind. Res.
MOJAVE TRAILS NATL. MON.
OLD WOMAN MTS.
Cadiz Lake
Danby Lake
Bristol Lake
PIUTE MTS.
CHEMEHUEVI VALLEY
TURTLE MTS.
Havasu Lake
London Bridge
CHEMEHUEVI IND. RES.
Cattail Cove S.P.
WHIPPLE MTS.
Parker Dam
Bill Williams River N.W.R.
Parker Strip B.L.M. Rec. Area
Buckskin Mountain S.P.
Alamo Lake
Alamo Lake S.P.
Tres Alamos 4,293
Alamo Lake
Santa Maria River
BUCKSKIN MTS.
Swansea Ghost Town
LA PAZ

Joshua Tree
Yucca Valley
Hidden Valley
Quail Mtn. 5,814
JOSHUA TREE NATL. PARK
Oasis Visitor Ctr.
Twentynine Palms
SHEEP HOLE MTS.
COXCOMB MT
RIVERSIDE
Vidal Jct.
Earp
Big River
Vidal
Rice
Parker
CACTUS PLAIN
Colorado River Indian Tribes Mus.
Poston
Bouse
Bouse Wash
Forepaugh

Go to 54
A   B   C
1 2 3 4

DRIVING DISTANCES IN MILES

	CHINLE, AZ	FLAGSTAFF, AZ	GRAND CANYON, AZ	HOLBROOK, AZ	KAYENTA, AZ	KINGMAN, AZ	LAKE HAVASU CITY, AZ	LAS VEGAS, NV	LAUGHLIN, NV	PAGE, AZ	PRESCOTT, AZ	ST. GEORGE, UT
FLAGSTAFF, AZ	216		89	93	152	148	209	249	182	135	89	271
GRAND CANYON, AZ	232	89		182	153	175	236	276	209	136	131	272
LAS VEGAS, NV	465	249	276	341	374	103	154		94	277	251	118
ST. GEORGE, UT	358	271	272	353	255	221	272	118	212	159	369	

SEE ALSO DISTANCE AND DRIVING TIME MAP ON PAGES 286–287

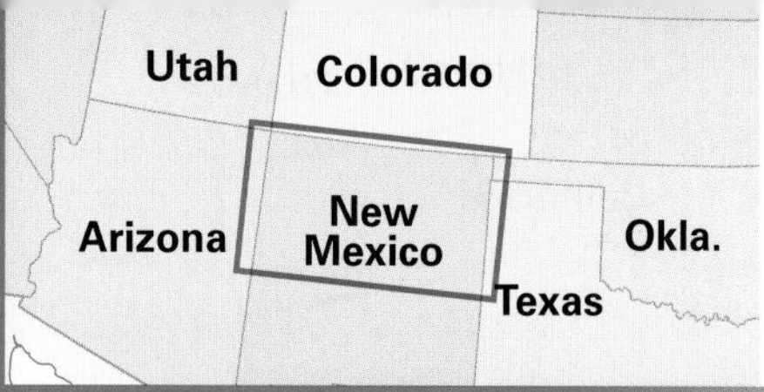

0 mi   20   40
0 km   20   40   60
One inch equals 25.4 miles
One centimeter equals 16.1 kilometers

Major places: Durango, Shiprock, Aztec, Farmington, Bloomfield, Kirtland, Fruitland, Bloomfield, Gallup, Grants, Milan, Bernalillo, Rio Rancho, Albuquerque, Los Lunas, Belen, Socorro, Espanola, Los Alamos, White Rock, Cuba, Chama, Dulce, St. Johns, Springerville, Eagar, Chinle, Fort Defiance, Window Rock, Zuni Pueblo, Acoma Pueblo, Laguna Pueblo

Counties / regions: SAN JUAN, MONTEZUMA, LA PLATA, ARCHULETA, CONEJOS, CARSON NATL. FOR., RIO ARRIBA, JICARILLA APACHE IND. RES., NAVAJO NATION INDIAN RES., MCKINLEY, CIBOLA, CIBOLA NATL. FOR., SANDOVAL, BERNALILLO, VALENCIA, SOCORRO, CATRON, APACHE, ZUNI IND. RES., ZUNI (RAMAH) IND. RES., SANTA FE NATL. FOR., JEMEZ MTS., JEMEZ NATL. REC. AREA, SAN MATEO MTS., MANZANO MTS., SEVILLETA N.W.R., CHACO MESA, SAN JUAN BASIN, CHINLE ALLEY, CARRIZO MTS., CHUSKA MTS., DEFIANCE PLATEAU, ZUNI MTS., DATIL MTS., GALLINAS MTS., NORTH PLAINS

Parks / monuments: MESA VERDE NATL. PARK, Four Corners Mon. & Navajo Tribal Park, Ute Mountain Tribal Park, Aztec Ruins N.M., Chaco Culture N.H.P., Pueblo Bonito Ruins, De-Na-Zin Wilderness Area, Bisti Wilderness Area, Canyon de Chelly Natl. Mon., El Morro Natl. Mon., El Malpais Natl. Mon., El Malpais Natl. Cons. Area, Bandera Crater & Ice Caves, Petrified Forest Natl. Park, Painted Desert Visitor Ctr., Petroglyph Natl. Mon., Kasha-Katuwe Tent Rocks Natl. Mon., Bandelier Natl. Mon., Salinas Pueblo Missions N.M., Ghost Ranch Ed. & Retreat Ctr., Echo Amphitheater, Cumbres and Toltec Scenic R.R., Durango & Silverton Narrow Gauge Railroad, Salmon Ruins Mus. & Heritage Park, Angel Peak B.L.M. Rec. Area, Bluewater Lake S.P., New Mex. Mining Museum, Red Rock State Park

Go to 40
Go to 47
Go to 40
Go to 56

Grid references: 1, 2, 3, 4 (rows) — A, B, C (columns)

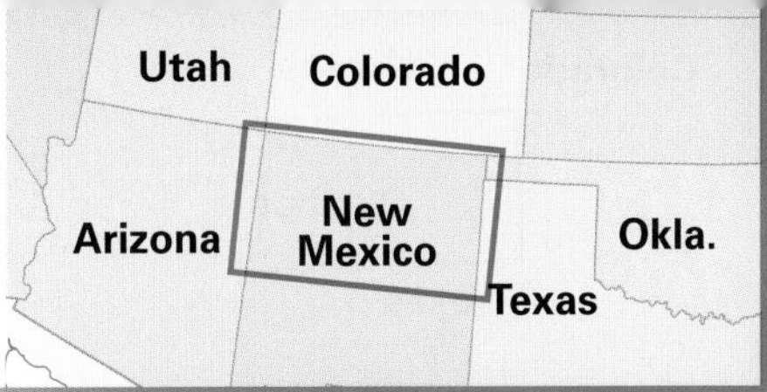

DRIVING DISTANCES IN MILES	ALBUQUERQUE, NM	CLAYTON, NM	CLOVIS, NM	DURANGO, CO	FARMINGTON, NM	GALLUP, NM	SANTA FE, NM	SOCORRO, NM	TAOS, NM	TRINIDAD, CO	TUCUMCARI, NM	VAUGHN, NM
ALBUQUERQUE, NM		266	220	212	181	141	55	77	123	242	174	104
FARMINGTON, NM	181	368	401	50		120	205	263	211	300	355	284
SANTA FE, NM	55	216	213	207	205	197		132	68	192	167	96
TUCUMCARI, NM	174	111	82	386	355	316	167	251	195	198		98

SEE ALSO DISTANCE AND DRIVING TIME MAP ON PAGES 286–287

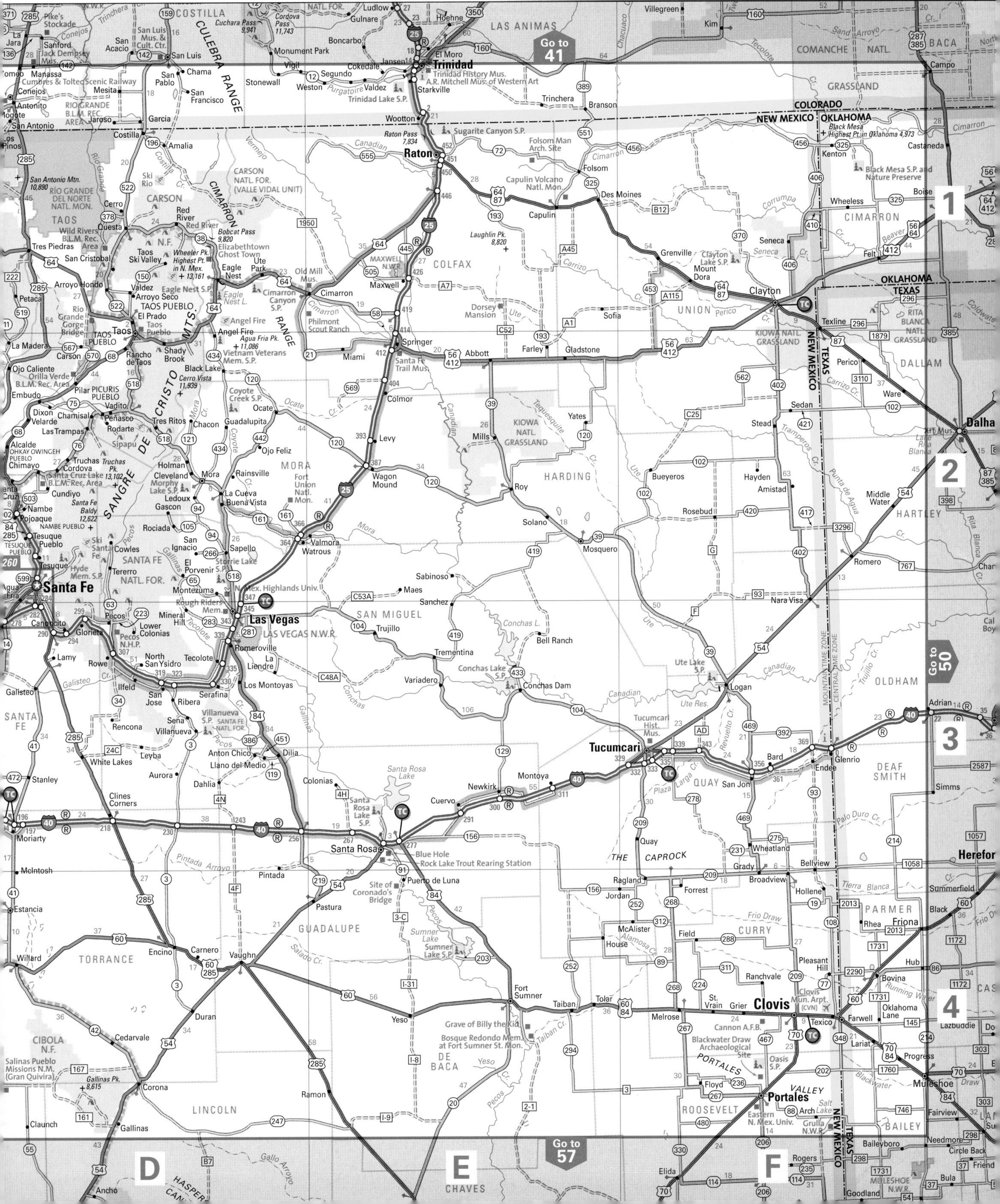

0 mi 20 40
0 km 20 40 60
One inch equals 25.4 miles
One centimeter equals 16.1 kilometers

Amarillo TX / Liberal KS

DRIVING DISTANCES IN MILES

	AMARILLO, TX	ARDMORE, OK	BARTLESVILLE, OK	CHILDRESS, TX	CLINTON, OK	ENID, OK	LAWTON, OK	LIBERAL, KS	OKLAHOMA CITY, OK	STILLWATER, OK	TULSA, OK	WOODWARD, OK
AMARILLO, TX		361	419	118	177	298	240	165	262	329	371	177
LAWTON, OK	240	103	243	124	98	142		287	85	152	194	175
OKLAHOMA CITY, OK	262	99	157	225	85	84	85	259		67	109	143
TULSA, OK	371	206	48	334	194	117	194	321	109	71		205

SEE ALSO DISTANCE AND DRIVING TIME MAP ON PAGES 286–287

0 mi 20 40
0 km 20 40 60
One inch equals 25.4 miles
One centimeter equals 16.1 kilometers

Los Angeles CA / Santa Barbara CA

DRIVING DISTANCES IN MILES	BAKERSFIELD, CA	BARSTOW, CA	BLYTHE, CA	EL CENTRO, CA	LOS ANGELES, CA	NEEDLES, CA	PALM SPRINGS, CA	SAN BERNARDINO, CA	SAN DIEGO, CA	SAN LUIS OBISPO, CA	SANTA BARBARA, CA	YUMA, AZ
LOS ANGELES, CA	111	118	230	234		263	110	62	124	190	97	294
SAN DIEGO, CA	234	181	211	117	124	326	143	111		314	221	177
SANTA BARBARA, CA	150	213	325	330	97	358	205	157	221	93		391
YUMA, AZ	403	294	103	65	294	187	171	225	177	483	391	

SEE ALSO DISTANCE AND DRIVING TIME MAP ON PAGES 286–287

0 mi 20 40
0 km 20 40 60
One inch equals 25.4 miles
One centimeter equals 16.1 kilometers

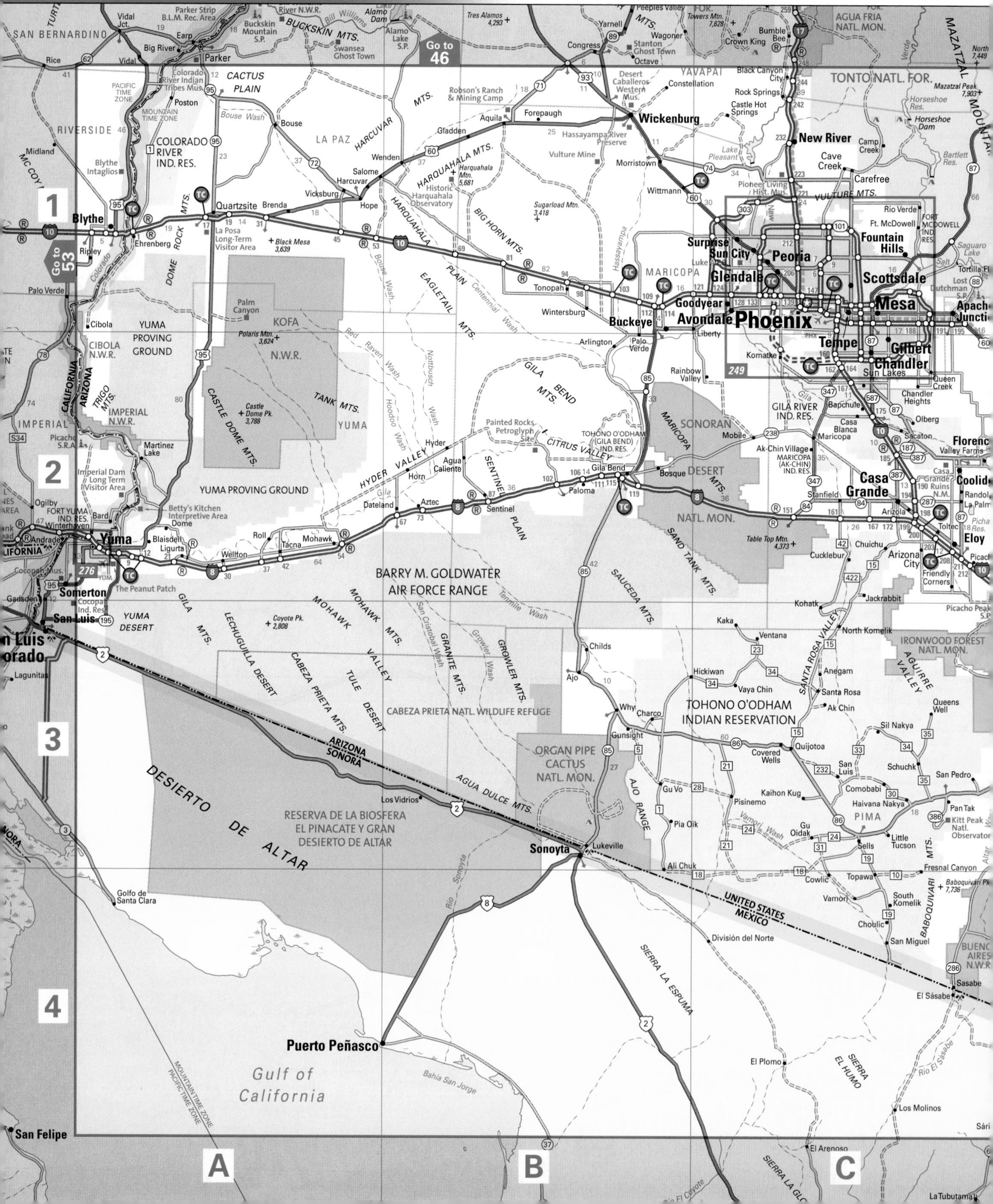

DRIVING DISTANCES IN MILES

	BLYTHE, CA	CASA GRANDE, AZ	DOUGLAS, AZ	EAGAR, AZ	GLOBE, AZ	LORDSBURG, NM	NOGALES, AZ	PHOENIX, AZ	SAFFORD, AZ	SILVER CITY, NM	TUCSON, AZ	YUMA, AZ
LORDSBURG, NM	417	228	101	184	155		185	278	77	45	161	401
PHOENIX, AZ	140	50	237	227	92	278	181		169	322	118	183
TUCSON, AZ	258	68	120	242	106	161	65	118	128	205		241
YUMA, AZ	103	179	360	401	265	401	304	183	368	446	241	

SEE ALSO DISTANCE AND DRIVING TIME MAP ON PAGES 286–287

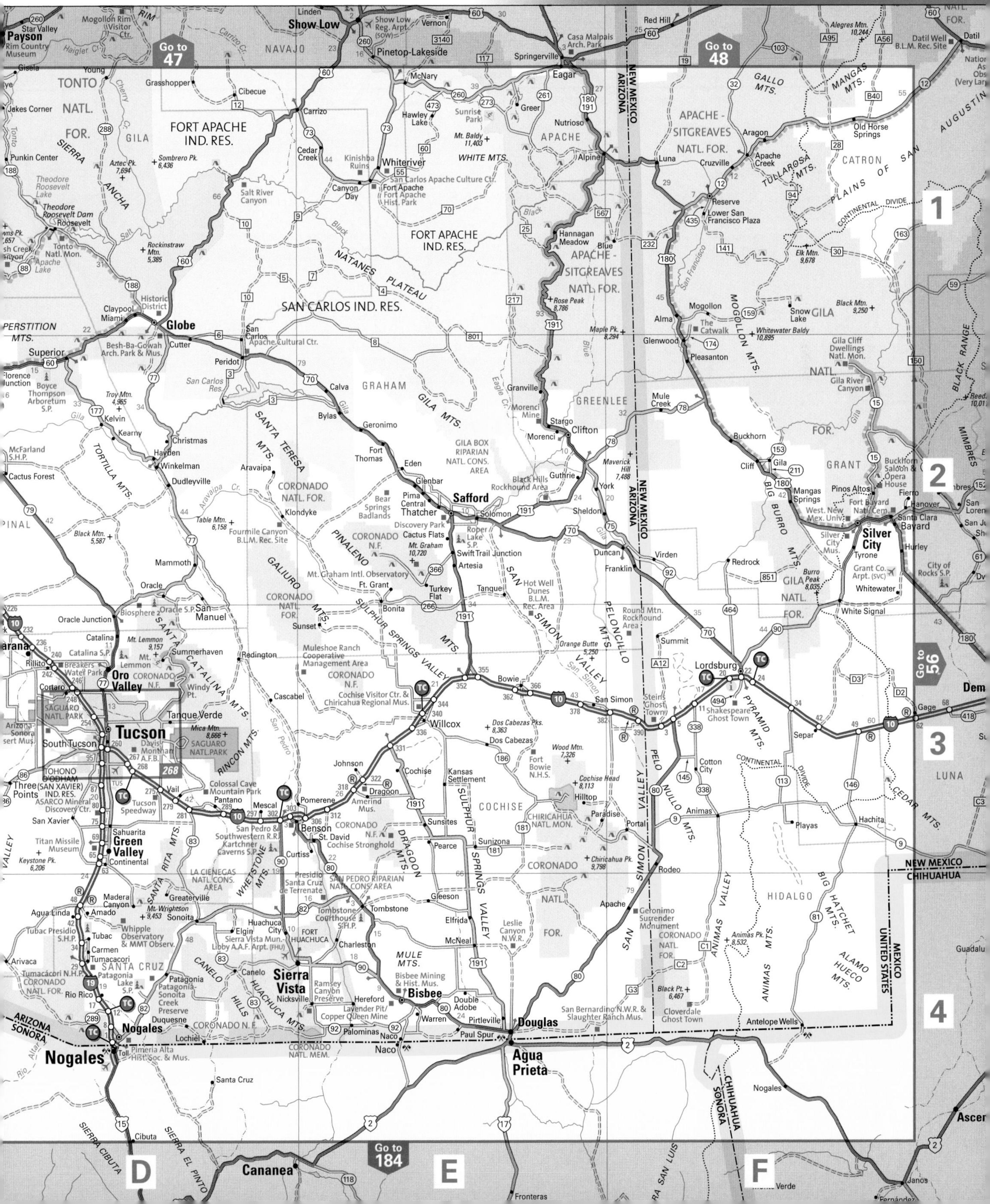

El Paso TX / Las Cruces NM

0 mi 20 40
0 km 20 40 60

One inch equals 25.4 miles
One centimeter equals 16.1 kilometers

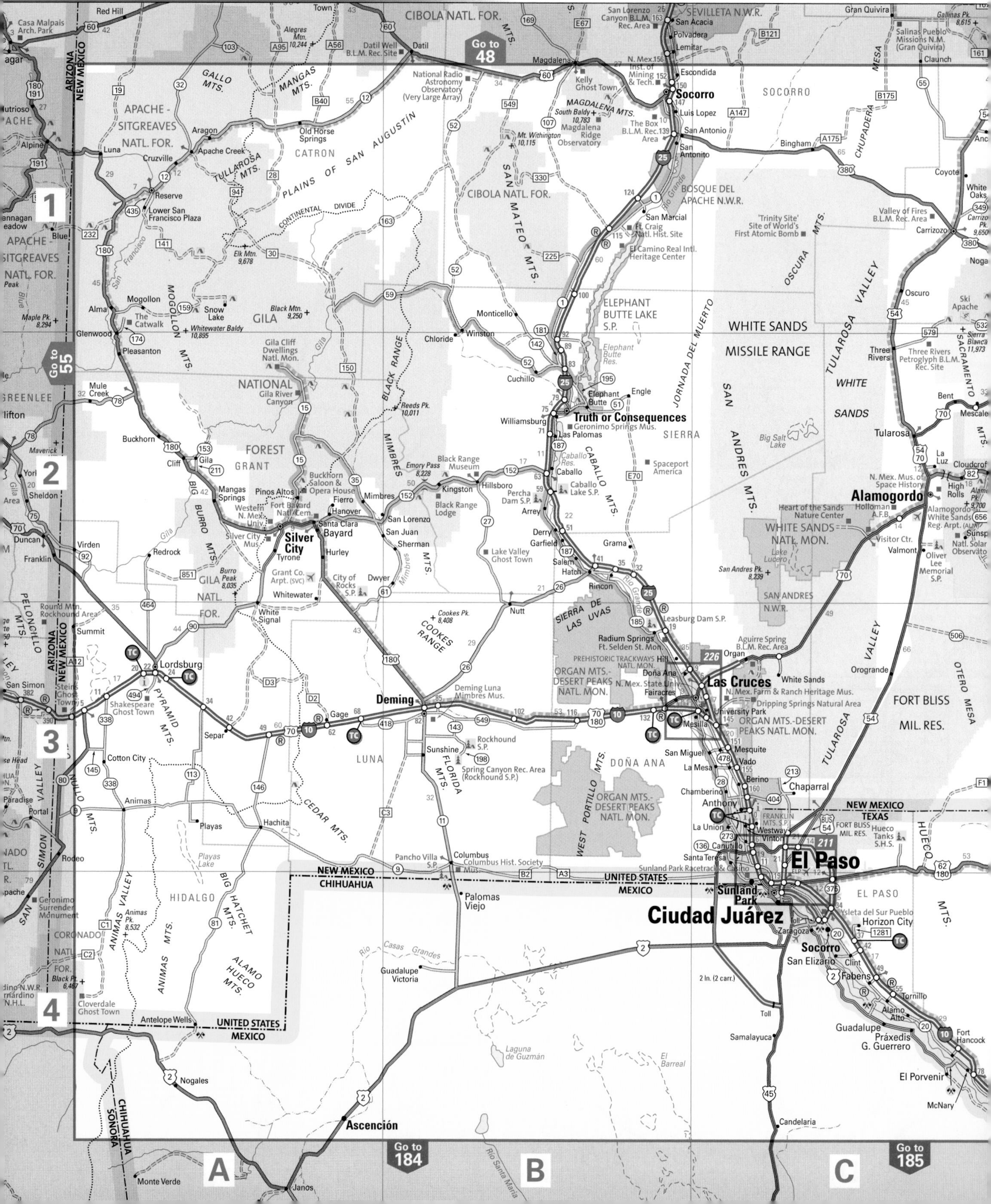

DRIVING DISTANCES IN MILES

	ALAMOGORDO, NM	CARLSBAD, NM	EL PASO, TX	HOBBS, NM	LAS CRUCES, NM	LORDSBURG, NM	ODESSA, TX	PECOS, TX	PORTALES, NM	ROSWELL, NM	SILVER CITY, NM	SOCORRO, NM
CARLSBAD, NM	144		162	70	203	321	137	87	168	76	311	241
EL PASO, TX	86	162		232	42	160	285	209	295	203	150	190
LAS CRUCES, NM	65	203	42	250		122	325	250	274	182	111	146
ROSWELL, NM	117	76	203	117	182	304	201	163	92		293	164

SEE ALSO DISTANCE AND DRIVING TIME MAP ON PAGES 286–287

Roswell NM / Carlsbad Caverns Natl Park NM

0 mi · 20 · 40
0 km · 20 · 40 · 60
One inch equals 25.4 miles
One centimeter equals 16.1 kilometers

Major cities and places:

Plainview, Littlefield, Levelland, Lubbock, Slaton, Brownfield, Seminole, Lamesa, Andrews, Midland, Odessa, West Odessa, Big Spring, Stanton, Snyder, Colorado City, Sweetwater, Abilene, San Angelo, Coleman, Ballinger, Brady, Vernon

Go to 50
Go to 57
Go to 62
Go to 60

Grid references: 1, 2, 3, 4 (rows); A, B, C (columns)

Counties: LAMB, HALE, FLOYD, MOTLEY, COTTLE, HARDEMAN, WILBARGER, FOARD, KING, KNOX, DICKENS, CROSBY, LUBBOCK, HOCKLEY, COCHRAN, TERRY, LYNN, GARZA, KENT, STONEWALL, HASKELL, YOAKUM, GAINES, DAWSON, BORDEN, SCURRY, FISHER, JONES, SHACKELFORD, MARTIN, HOWARD, MITCHELL, NOLAN, TAYLOR, CALLAHAN, ECTOR, MIDLAND, GLASSCOCK, STERLING, COKE, RUNNELS, COLEMAN, CRANE, UPTON, REAGAN, IRION, TOM GREEN, CONCHO, McCULLOCH, PECOS, CROCKETT, SCHLEICHER, MENARD, EDWARDS

Plainview, Wayland Baptist Univ., Llano Estacado Mus., Floydada, Matador, Paducah, Crowell, Thalia, Vernon, Chillicothe, Tolbert

Littlefield, Anton, Abernathy, New Deal, Idalou, Lorenzo, Ralls, Crosbyton, Dickens, Guthrie, Benjamin, Munday, Goree, Seymour, Red Springs

Levelland, Wolfforth, Slaton, Post, Southland, Spur, Jayton, Rochester, Haskell, Stamford

Brownfield, Tahoka, O'Donnell, Lamesa, Gail, Snyder, Hermleigh, Roby, Anson, Stamford, Avoca, Albany

Seminole, Andrews, Midland, Odessa, West Odessa, Stanton, Big Spring, Coahoma, Colorado City, Loraine, Roscoe, Sweetwater, Merkel, Abilene, Clyde, Baird

San Angelo, O.C. Fisher Lake, Angelo State Univ., Goodfellow A.F.B., Sterling City, Garden City, Water Valley, Carlsbad, Robert Lee, Bronte, Winters, Ballinger, Coleman, Santa Anna

Big Lake, McCamey, Rankin, Big Lake, Mertzon, Christoval, Eldorado, Menard, Brady

DRIVING DISTANCES IN MILES

	ABILENE, TX	BIG SPRING, TX	BROWNWOOD, TX	DALLAS, TX	FORT WORTH, TX	LUBBOCK, TX	ODESSA, TX	SAN ANGELO, TX	SHERMAN, TX	TEMPLE, TX	WACO, TX	WICHITA FALLS, TX
ABILENE, TX		110	78	191	153	166	176	91	249	194	235	144
DALLAS, TX	191	298	190		32	354	364	265	64	130	94	141
LUBBOCK, TX	166	106	247	354	317		142	185	322	358	399	207
WACO, TX	235	343	124	94	87	399	409	219	159	40		201

SEE ALSO DISTANCE AND DRIVING TIME MAP ON PAGES 286–287

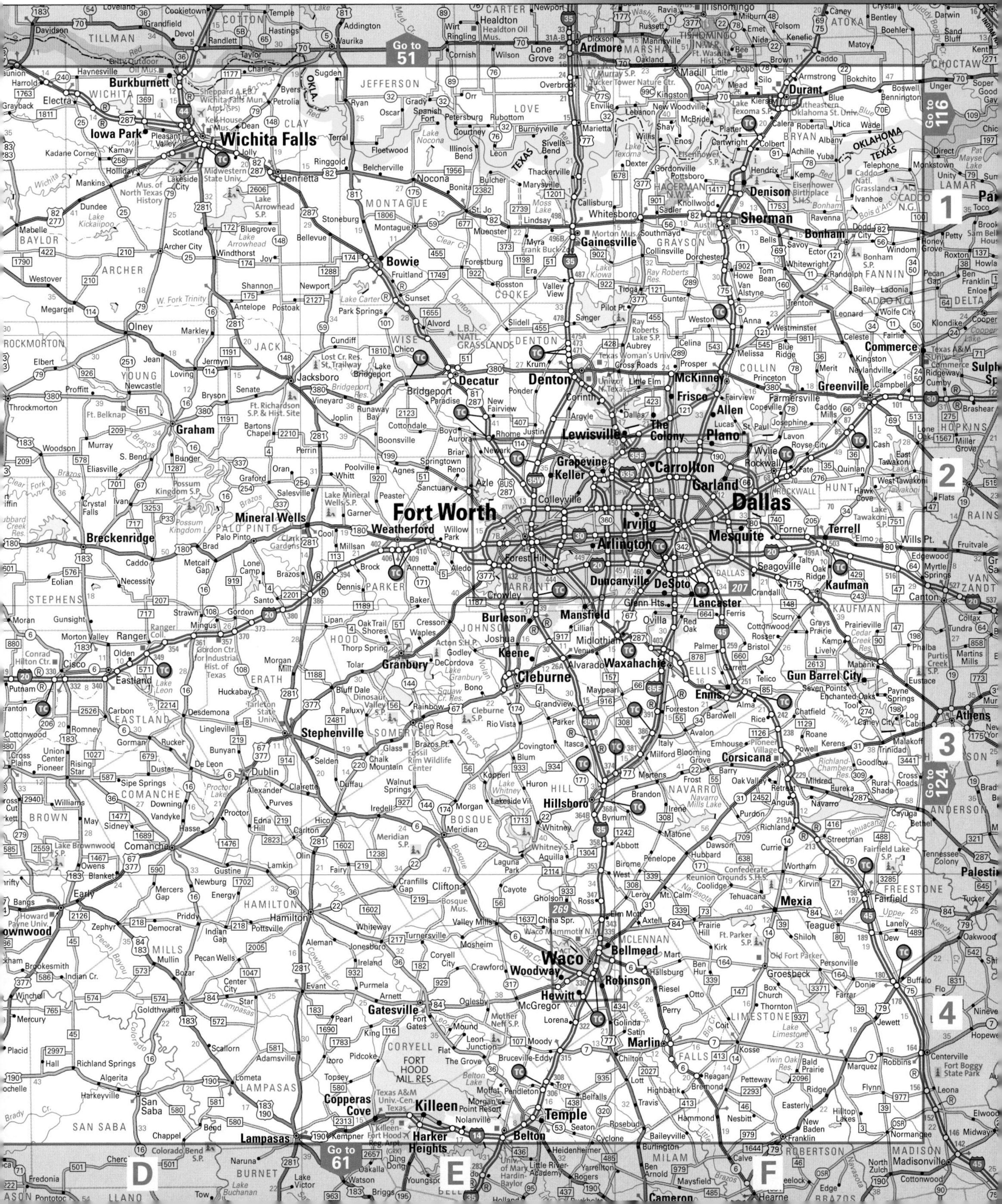

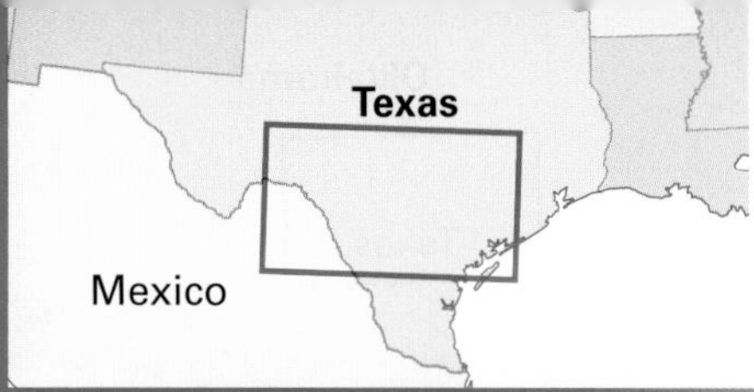

Del Rio TX / Eagle Pass TX

0 mi 20 40
0 km 20 40 60

One inch equals 25.4 miles
One centimeter equals 16.1 kilometers

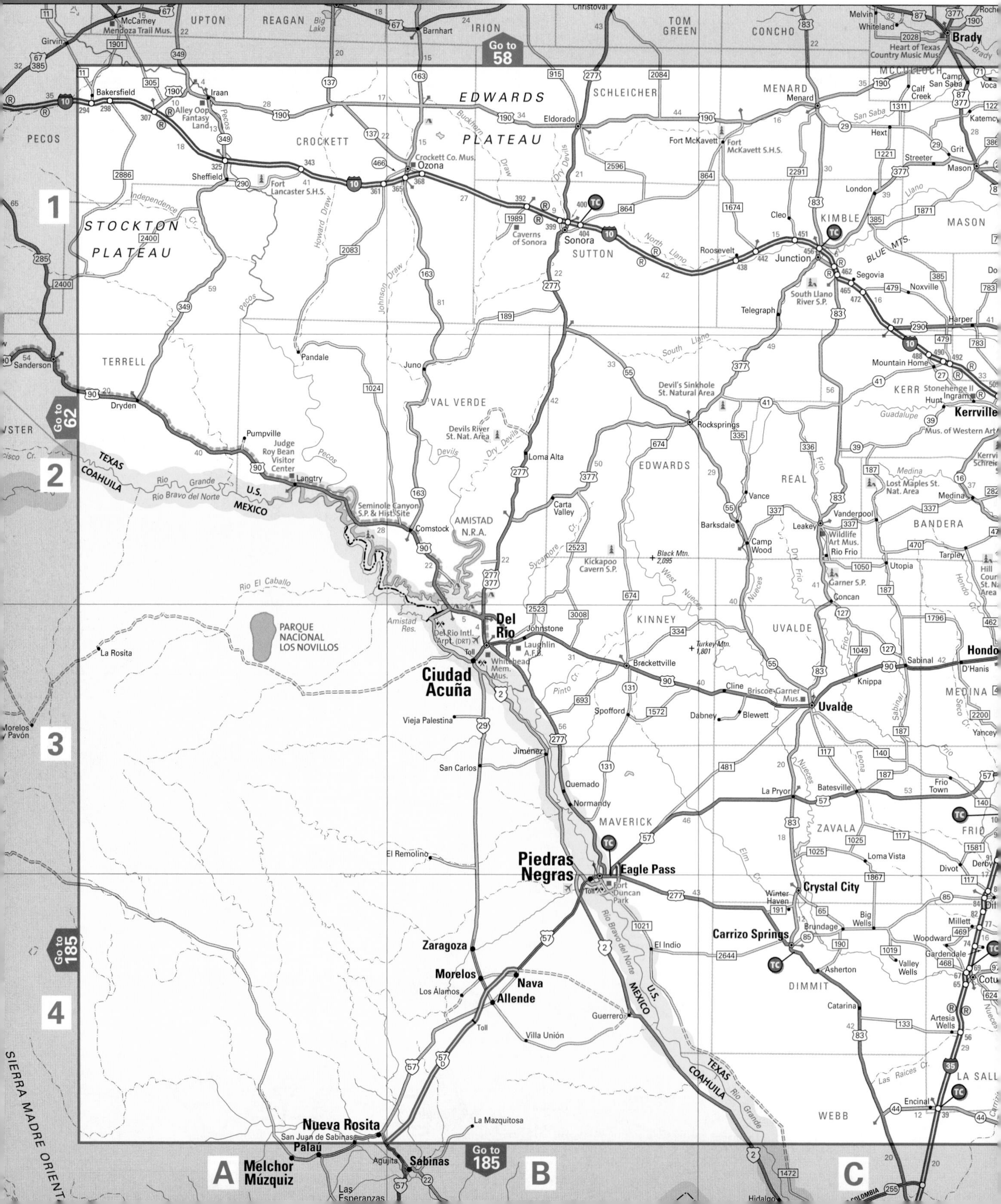

DRIVING DISTANCES IN MILES	AUSTIN, TX	BEEVILLE, TX	COLLEGE STATION, TX	COLUMBUS, TX	DEL RIO, TX	EAGLE PASS, TX	FREDERICKSBURG, TX	SAN ANTONIO, TX	SONORA, TX	TEMPLE, TX	UVALDE, TX	VICTORIA, TX
AUSTIN, TX		136	108	92	229	226	78	78	244	67	159	123
DEL RIO, TX	229	235	322	277		55	178	152	89	295	70	268
SAN ANTONIO, TX	78	110	171	128	152	145	67		172	144	82	118
VICTORIA, TX	123	56	160	87	268	254	186	118	292	187	198	

SEE ALSO DISTANCE AND DRIVING TIME MAP ON PAGES 286–287

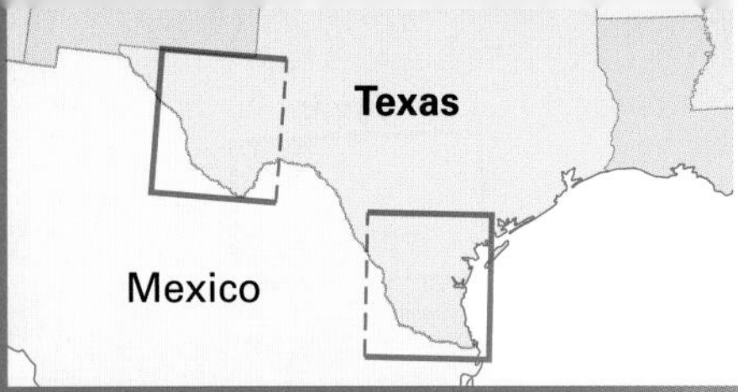

Odessa TX / Big Bend Natl Park TX

DRIVING DISTANCES IN MILES

	ALPINE, TX	BIG BEND NP, TX	FORT STOCKTON, TX	ODESSA, TX	PECOS, TX	VAN HORN, TX
ALPINE, TX		97	65	151	96	110
FORT STOCKTON, TX	65	123		86	58	119
ODESSA, TX	151	209	86		76	163
VAN HORN, TX	110	207	119	163	87	

SEE ALSO DISTANCE AND DRIVING TIME MAP ON PAGES 286–287

0 mi 10 20 30
0 km 20 40
One inch equals 25.4 miles
One centimeter equals 16.1 kilometers

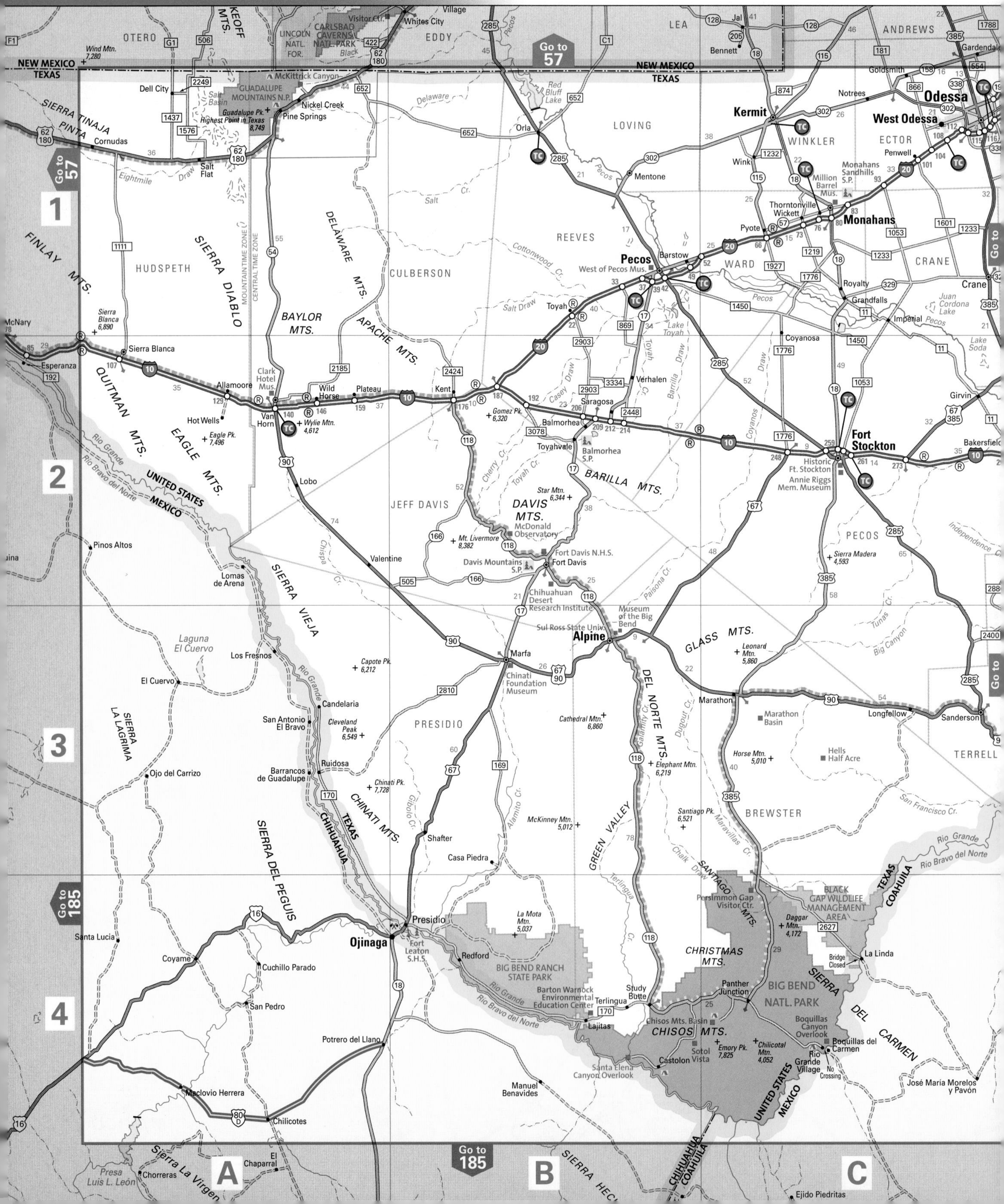

DRIVING DISTANCES IN MILES

	BEEVILLE, TX	BROWNSVILLE, TX	CARRIZO SPRS, TX	CORPUS CHRISTI, TX	HARLINGEN, TX	KINGSVILLE, TX	LAREDO, TX	MCALLEN, TX	VICTORIA, TX
BROWNSVILLE, TX	192		282	157	27	119	202	61	226
CORPUS CHRISTI, TX	59	157	199		131	38	141	152	94
LAREDO, TX	130	202	79	141	176	124		144	186
MCALLEN, TX	168	61	223	152	35	114	144		221

SEE ALSO DISTANCE AND DRIVING TIME MAP ON PAGES 286–287

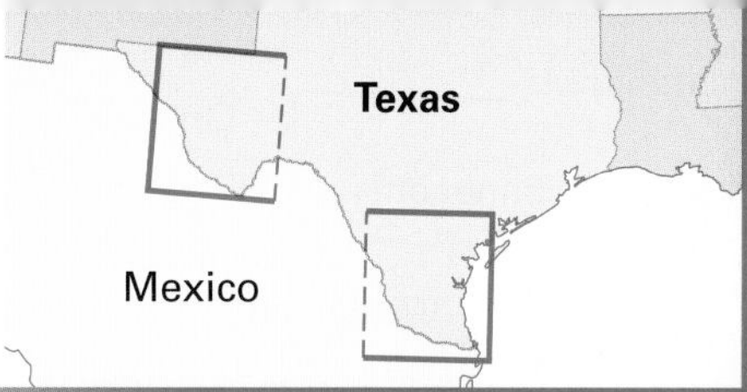

Manitoba Ontario

Minnesota

Michigan

Wisconsin

0 mi   20   40

0 km   20   40   60

One inch equals 25.4 miles
One centimeter equals 16.1 kilometers

Duluth MN / International Falls MN

Go to 168

Go to 19

Go to 66

Go to 67

Go to 211

International Falls

Fort Frances

Bemidji

Hibbing

Virginia

Grand Rapids

Duluth

Superior

Brainerd

Baxter

Detroit Lakes

Park Rapids

Cloquet

Hermantown

Two Harbors

Ely

Eveleth

Mountain Iron

Chisholm

VOYAGEURS NATL. PARK

QUETICO PROVINCIAL PARK

LAKE OF THE WOODS

BELTRAMI ISLAND STATE FOREST

RED LAKE IND. RES.

SUPERIOR NATIONAL FOREST

CHIPPEWA N.F.

MESABI RANGE

CANADA / U.S.

MANITOBA / ONTARIO

ONTARIO / MINNESOTA

MINNESOTA / WISCONSIN

DRIVING DISTANCES IN MILES

	ASHLAND, WI	BEMIDJI, MN	BRAINERD, MN	DETROIT LAKES, MN	DULUTH, MN	GRAND PORTAGE, MN	HOUGHTON, MI	INTERNAT'L FALLS, MN	IRONWOOD, MI	ISHPEMING, MI	THUNDER BAY, ON	VIRGINIA, MN
BEMIDJI, MN	239		96	91	153	295	362	109	254	384	314	124
DULUTH, MN	92	153	116	202		143	215	157	107	238	183	61
HOUGHTON, MI	132	362	325	412	215	358		370	108	87	654	274
INTERNAT'L FALLS, MN	247	109	190	200	157	245	370		262	393	205	97

SEE ALSO DISTANCE AND DRIVING TIME MAP ON PAGES 286–287

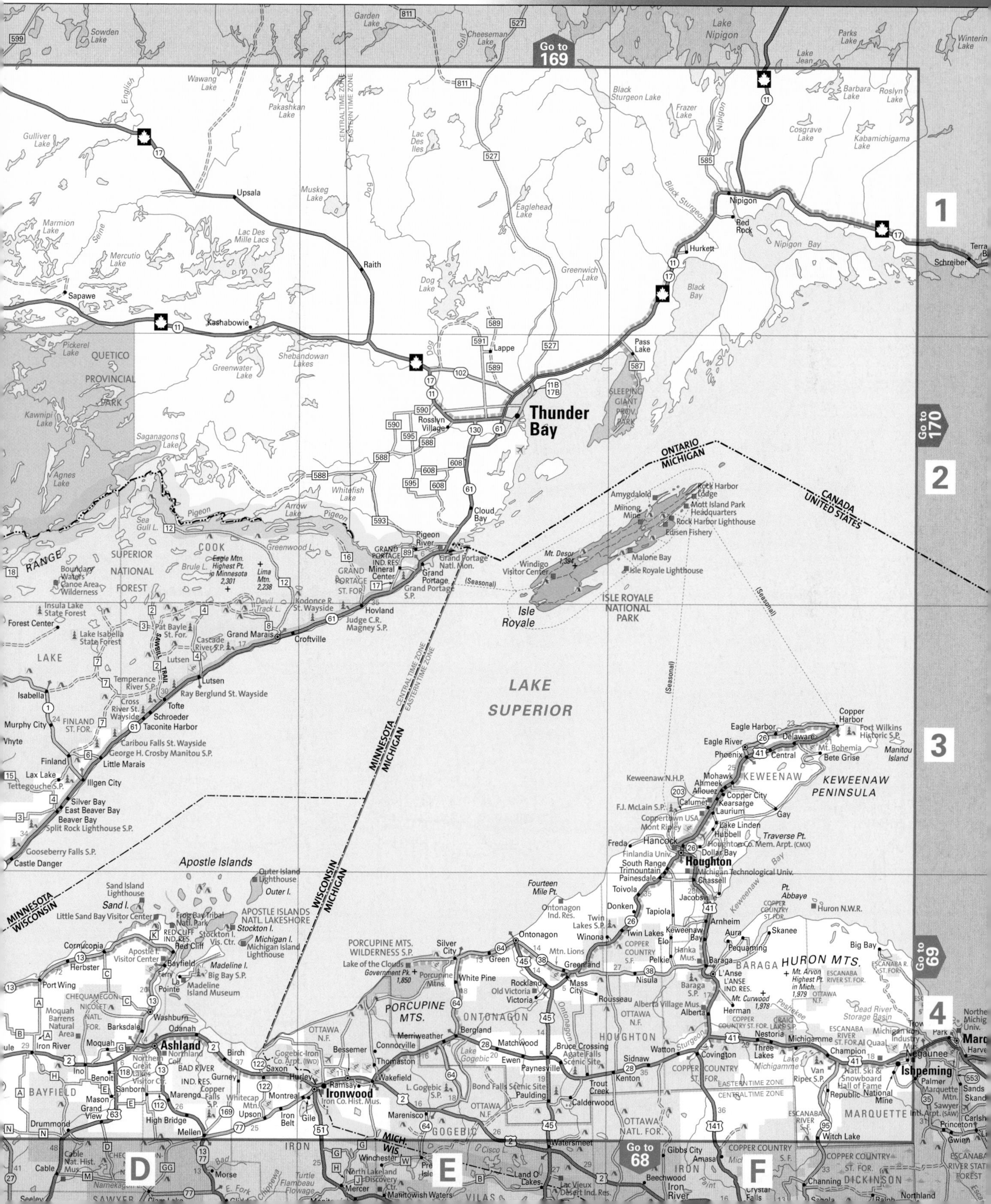

St Cloud MN / Willmar MN

0 mi 10 20 30 40
0 km 10 20 30 40 50 60

One inch equals 18.4 miles
One centimeter equals 11.7 kilometers

DRIVING DISTANCES IN MILES

	ASHLAND, WI	BRAINERD, MN	DULUTH, MN	EAU CLAIRE, WI	FERGUS FALLS, MN	MARSHALL, MN	MINNEAPOLIS, MN	MORRIS, MN	RICE LAKE, WI	ST. CLOUD, MN	ST. PAUL, MN	WILLMAR, MN
EAU CLAIRE, WI	167	220	155		267	236	93	247	57	156	83	193
MINNEAPOLIS, MN	196	129	158	93	176	148		156	103	64	10	92
ST. CLOUD, MN	205	62	149	156	117	131	64	98	155		73	63
WILLMAR, MN	263	112	206	193	113	68	92	57	196	63	102	

SEE ALSO DISTANCE AND DRIVING TIME MAP ON PAGES 286–287

0 mi 10 20 30 40
0 km 10 20 30 40 50 60

One inch equals 18.4 miles
One centimeter equals 11.7 kilometers

DRIVING DISTANCES IN MILES

	ESCANABA, MI	GREEN BAY, WI	IRON MOUNTAIN, MI	IRONWOOD, MI	L'ANSE, MI	MANISTIQUE, MI	MARINETTE, WI	MARQUETTE, MI	RHINELANDER, WI	STEVENS POINT, WI	TRAVERSE CITY, MI	WAUSAU, WI
ESCANABA, MI		111	52	178	134	54	57	65	132	185	252	171
GREEN BAY, WI	111		96	202	178	165	54	175	124	87	363	93
MARQUETTE, MI	65	175	79	145	70	86	122		147	238	269	204
WAUSAU, WI	171	93	133	121	176	225	112	204	58	35	423	

SEE ALSO DISTANCE AND DRIVING TIME MAP ON PAGES 286–287

Marquette MI / Sturgeon Bay WI

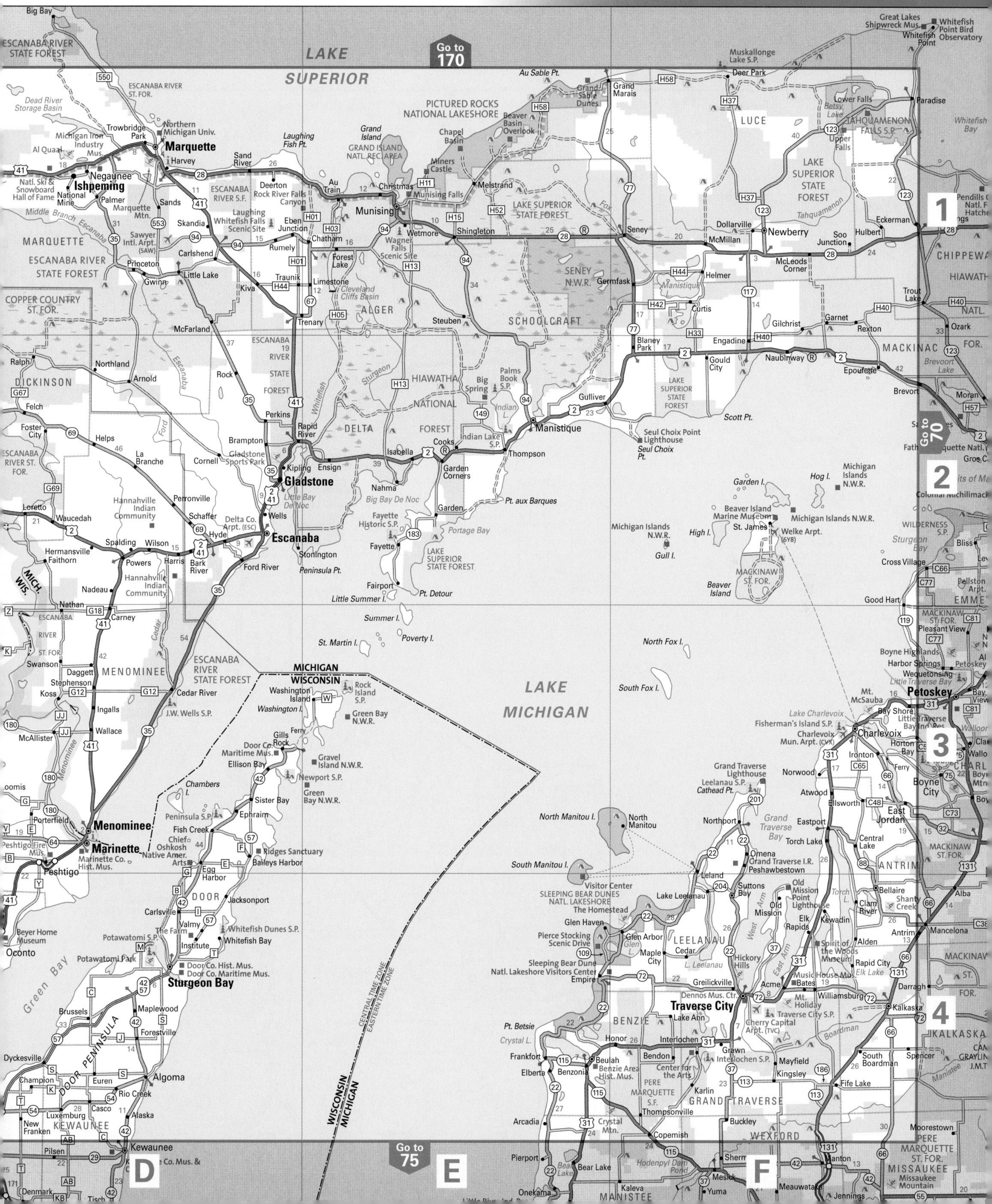

0 mi 10 20 30 40
0 km 10 20 30 40 50 60
One inch equals 18.4 miles
One centimeter equals 11.7 kilometers

LAKE SUPERIOR

Great Lakes Shipwreck Museum
Whitefish Pt. Bird Observatory
Whitefish Point
Searchmont
CANADA U.S.
ONTARIO MICHIGAN

Go to 170

Sault Ste. Marie
Sault Ste. Marie
Soo Locks
Lake Superior State Univ.
Heyden

Au Sable Pt.
Grand Island
Grand Island Natl. Rec. Area
PICTURED ROCKS NATIONAL LAKESHORE
Miners Castle
Beaver Basin Overlook
Chapel Basin
Grand Sable Dunes
Grand Marais
Muskallonge Lake S.P.
Deer Park
Lower Falls
Upper Falls
TAHQUAMENON FALLS S.P.
Paradise
Point Iroquois Light
Gros Cap
Bay Mills Community
Brimley S.P.
Sugar I.
Echo Lake
Echo Bay

Au Train
Christmas
Munising Falls
Munising
Wetmore
Shingleton
Wagner Falls Scenic Site
Forest Lake
Limestone
Traunik
Cleveland Cliffs Basin

SENEY N.W.R.
Germfask
SCHOOLCRAFT
HIAWATHA NATIONAL FOREST
Steuben
Big Spring
Palms Book S.P.
Indian Lake
Gulliver
Manistique
Indian Lake S.P.
Cooks
Isabella
Thompson
Garden Corners
Nahma
Garden
Fayette Historic S.P.
Fayette
Portage Bay
Pt. aux Barques

Seney
McMillan
Helmer
Curtis
Blaney Park
Gould City
Naubinway
Epoufette
Brevort
Gilchrist
Garnet
Engadine
Scott Pt.
Seul Choix Point Lighthouse
Seul Choix Pt.
Sand Dunes

LUCE
LAKE SUPERIOR STATE FOREST
Dollarville
Newberry
Soo Junction
Hulbert
McLeods Corner
Strongs
Eckerman
Pendills Creek Natl. Fish Hatchery
Raco
Brimley
Dafter
Barbeau
Neebish
Richards Landing
Hilton Beach
Kentvale

CHIPPEWA
HIAWATHA
Trout Lake
Rexton
Ozark
Rudyard
Fibre
Kinross
Chippewa Co. Intl. Arpt. (CIU)
Pickford
Stalwart
Goetzville
Cedarville
Hessel
Les Cheneaux Islands
Desbarais
DeTour Village

MACKINAC NATIONAL FOREST
Brevoort Lake
St. Martin Bay
Moran
Allenville
St. Ignace
Fort Mackinac
Mackinac Island S.P.
Mackinac Island
Bois Blanc I.
MACKINAC ST. FOR.

Father Marquette Natl. Mem.
Straits of Mackinac
Straits State Toll
Colonial Michilimackinac
Mackinaw City
Historic Mill Creek
Pointe Aux Pins

LAKE HURON

Garden I.
Hog I.
Beaver Island Marine Museum
Michigan Islands N.W.R.
High I.
St. James
Welke Arpt. (6Y8)
Michigan Islands N.W.R.
Gull I.
MACKINAW ST. FOR.
Beaver Island

LAKE SUPERIOR STATE FOREST
Fairport
Pt. Detour
Little Summer I.
Summer I.
Go to 69

St. Martin I.
Poverty I.
North Fox I.
South Fox I.

LAKE MICHIGAN

Rock Island S.P.
Washington Island
Green Bay N.W.R.
Washington I.
Gravel Island N.W.R.
St. Martin Island N.W.R.

MICHIGAN WISCONSIN

North Manitou I.
North Manitou
South Manitou I.
Visitor Center
SLEEPING BEAR DUNES NATL. LAKESHORE
The Homestead
Pierce Stocking Scenic Drive
Glen Haven
Glen Arbor
Maple City
Sleeping Bear Dunes Natl. Lakeshore Visitors Center
Empire

Cheboygan
Cheboygan S.P.
Mullett Lake
Alverno
Aloha S.P.
Grace
Hammond Bay
Huron Beach
Onaway S.P.
Ocqueoc Falls
Ocqueoc
PRESQUE ISLE
Millersburg
Hawks

EMMET
Pellston Reg. Arpt. (PLN)
Pellston
Brutus
Burt Lake
Burt Lake S.P.
Topinabee
Indian River
Afton
Tower
Onaway
MACKINAW STATE FOREST
Good Hart
WILDERNESS S.P.
Sturgeon Bay
Bliss
Levering
Carp Lake
Cross Village
Pleasant View
Nub's Nob
Boyne Highlands
Harbor Springs
Wequetonsing
Petoskey S.P.
Conway
Oden
Bay View
Epsilon

Mt. McSauba
Petoskey
Bay Shore
Little Traverse Bay
Fisherman's Island S.P.
Charlevoix Mun. Arpt. (CVX)
Charlevoix
Horton Bay
Walloon Lake
Clarion
Wolverine
Vanderbilt

Lake Charlevoix
Ironton
Norwood
Boyne City
East Jordan
Boyne Falls
Boyne Mtn.
Elmira
OTSEGO
Otsego Club
Treetops Resort
Hillman

CHARLEVOIX
Atwood
Ellsworth
Gaylord
Johannesburg
Vienna
Atlanta
MONTMORENCY
Lewiston

Grand Traverse Lighthouse
Leelanau S.P.
Cathead Pt.
Northport
Omena
Peshawbestown
Leland
Grand Traverse I.R.
Lake Leelanau
Suttons Bay
Old Mission
Old Mission Point Lighthouse
Northport
LEELANAU
Cedar
Greilickville
Glen Lake
ANTRIM
Eastport
Torch Lake
Central Lake
Bellaire
Alba
Oak Grove
Waters
CAMP GRAYLING JOINT MANEUVER TRAINING CTR.

West Arm
East Arm
Elk Rapids
Kewadin
Clam River
Shanty Creek
Mancelona
Alden
Rapid City
Antrim
Spirit of the Woods Museum
Music House Mus.
Hickory Hills
Acme
Bates
Williamsburg
Mt. Holiday
Kalkaska
Frederic
Lovells
MACKINAW ST. FOR.
Comins
Fairview
OSCODA
Kirtlands Warbler Wildlife Management Area
Red Oak
Luzerne
Mio
McKinley

Traverse City
Cherry Capital Arpt. (TVC)
Lake Ann
Interlochen
Interlochen S.P.
Grawn
Mayfield
Fife Lake
South Boardman
Darragh
GRAND TRAVERSE
Kingsley
Spencer
Hanson Hills
Grayling
CAMP GRAYLING J.M.T.C.
North Higgins Lake S.P.
Higgins Lake
CRAWFORD
HURON NATL. FOR.

BENZIE
Frankfort
Elberta
Beulah
Benzonia
Benzie Area Hist. Mus.
Honor
Bendon
Center for the Arts
PERE MARQUETTE S.F.
Karlin
Crystal Mtn.
Thompsonville
Copemish
MANISTEE
Arcadia
Pierport
Bear L.
Crystal L.
Pt. Betsie

KALKASKA
Civilian Conservation Corps Museum
Roscommon
HURON NATL. FOR.
South Higgins Lake S.P.
St. Helen
OGEMAW

WEXFORD
Mesick
Harrietta
Yuma
Meauwataka
Buckley
Manton
Sherman
MISSAUKEE
Missaukee Mountain
Moorestown
Houghton Lake
ROSCOMMON
Rose City
Rifle River Rec. Area
South Branch

Go to 75
Go to 75
Go to 76

A B C
1 2 3 4

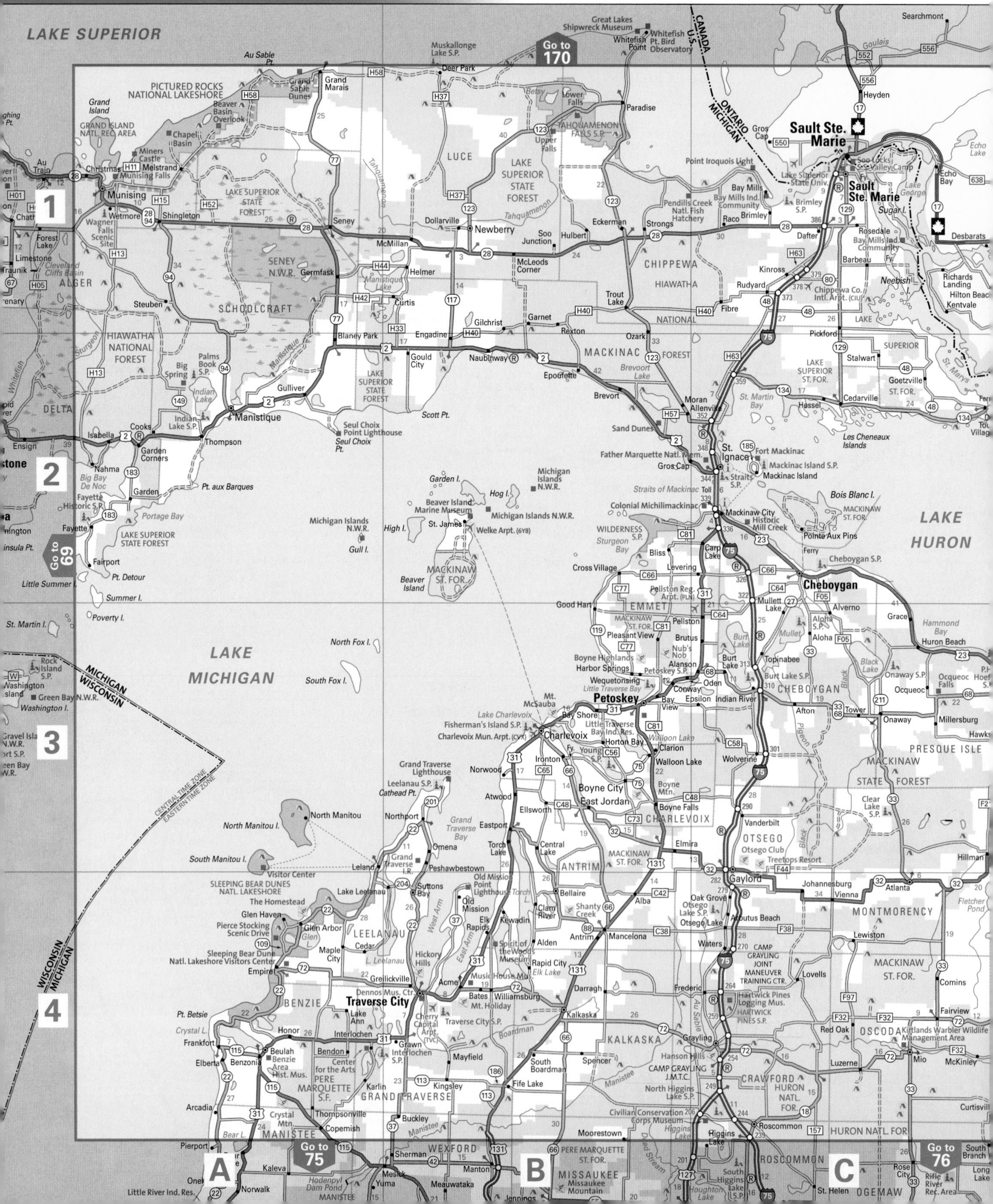

DRIVING DISTANCES IN MILES	ALPENA, MI	CHEBOYGAN, MI	GAYLORD, MI	GRAYLING, MI	MACKINAW CITY, MI	MANISTIQUE, MI	MUNISING, MI	PETOSKEY, MI	ROGERS CITY, MI	SAULT STE. MARIE, MI	SUDBURY, ON	TRAVERSE CITY, MI
ALPENA, MI		78	76	95	94	187	215	101	38	148	334	141
MACKINAW CITY, MI	94	16	60	87		95	123	38	58	57	242	106
SAULT STE. MARIE, MI	148	71	114	142	57	120	120	93	112		186	160
TRAVERSE CITY, MI	141	115	65	52	106	198	226	67	135	160	346	

SEE ALSO DISTANCE AND DRIVING TIME MAP ON PAGES 286–287

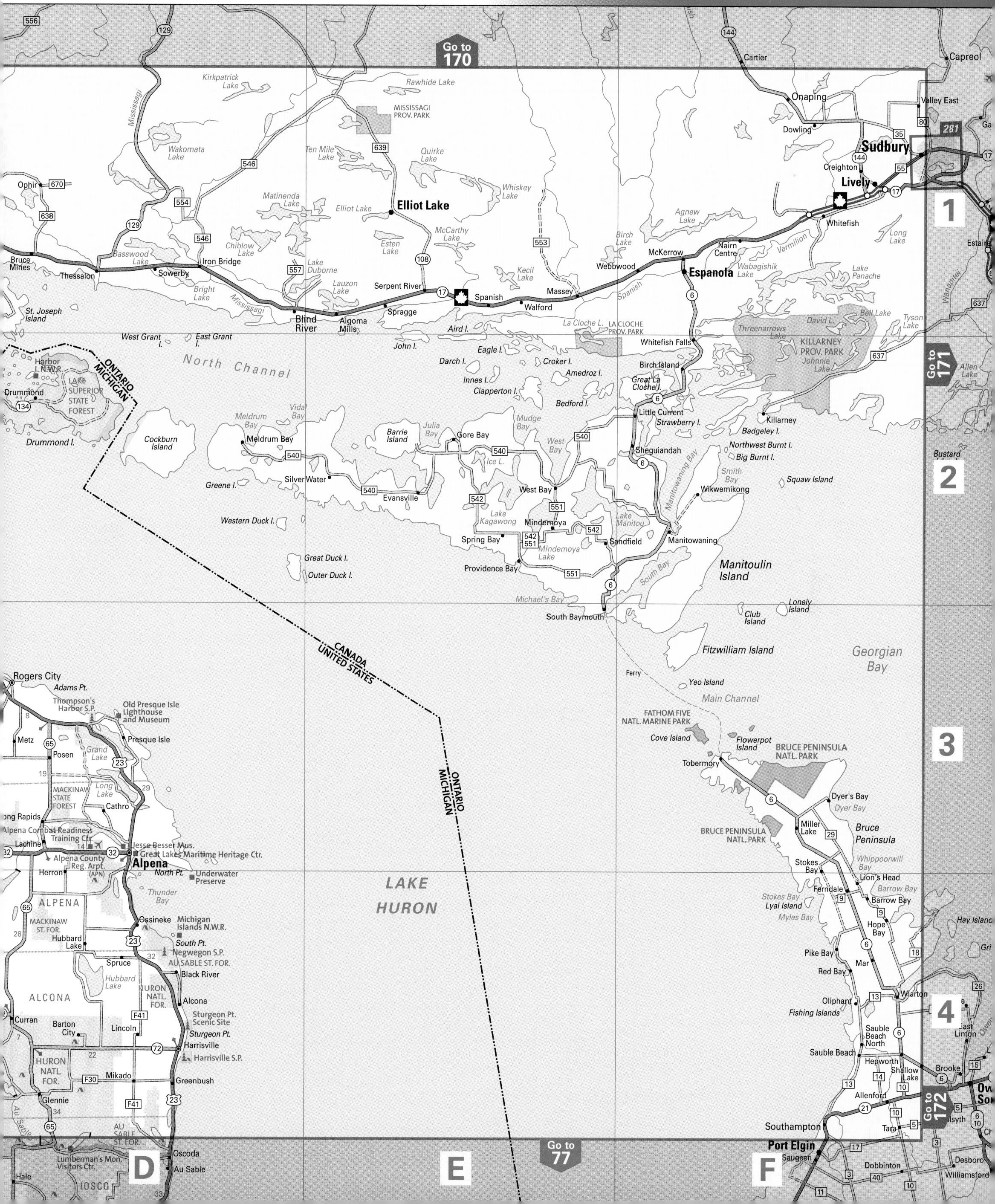

0 mi 10 20 30 40
0 km 10 20 30 40 50 60

One inch equals 18.4 miles
One centimeter equals 11.7 kilometers

Mankato MN / Fort Dodge IA

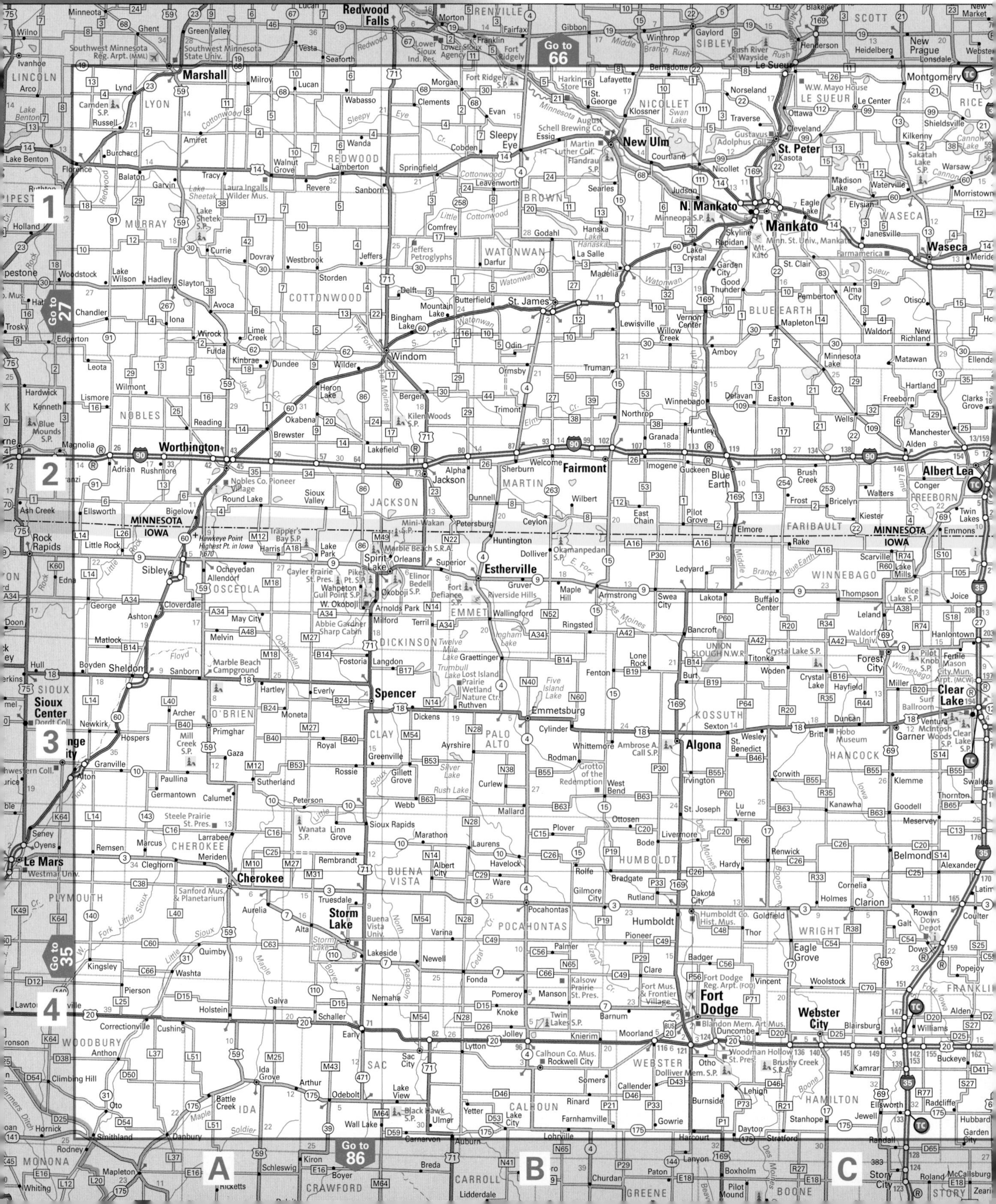

DRIVING DISTANCES IN MILES	ALBERT LEA, MN	DECORAH, IA	DUBUQUE, IA	FORT DODGE, IA	LA CROSSE, WI	MANKATO, MN	MASON CITY, IA	ROCHESTER, MN	SPENCER, IA	WATERLOO, IA	WINONA, MN	WORTHINGTON, MN
FORT DODGE, IA	124	186	200		245	138	97	183	95	108	225	148
MANKATO, MN	56	151	253	138	149		100	80	123	186	128	108
ROCHESTER, MN	62	68	170	183	71	80	103		189	116	51	174
WATERLOO, IA	130	79	93	108	138	186	79	116	189		144	244

SEE ALSO DISTANCE AND DRIVING TIME MAP ON PAGES 286–287

Milwaukee WI / Madison WI

0 mi 10 20 30 40
0 km 10 20 30 40 50 60

One inch equals 18.4 miles
One centimeter equals 11.7 kilometers

DRIVING DISTANCES IN MILES

	CADILLAC, MI	DUBUQUE, IA	GRAND RAPIDS, MI	GREEN BAY, WI	KALAMAZOO, MI	MADISON, WI	MILWAUKEE, WI	MUSKEGON, MI	OSHKOSH, WI	ROCKFORD, IL	SHEBOYGAN, WI	TOMAH, WI
GRAND RAPIDS, MI	99	364		393	53	335	277	40	363	271	332	424
GREEN BAY, WI	492	229	393		362	135	115	400	50	211	61	162
MADISON, WI	434	93	335	135	304		78	341	86	78	132	98
MILWAUKEE, WI	377	167	277	115	247	78		285	87	95	54	168

SEE ALSO DISTANCE AND DRIVING TIME MAP ON PAGES 286–287

0 mi 10 20 30 40
0 km 10 20 30 40 50 60
One inch equals 18.4 miles
One centimeter equals 11.7 kilometers

Detroit MI / Lansing MI

DRIVING DISTANCES IN MILES

	ANN ARBOR, MI	BAD AXE, MI	BATTLE CREEK, MI	CADILLAC, MI	DETROIT, MI	FLINT, MI	HAMILTON, ON	LANSING, MI	LONDON, ON	MT. PLEASANT, MI	PORT HURON, MI	SAGINAW, MI
DETROIT, MI	42	107	116	209		62	203	86	128	149	58	97
LANSING, MI	63	140	56	131	86	53	270		191	67	117	86
PORT HURON, MI	101	81	175	211	58	64	154	117	75	155		100
SAGINAW, MI	87	64	142	116	97	36	253	86	174	60	100	

SEE ALSO DISTANCE AND DRIVING TIME MAP ON PAGES 286–287

0 mi 10 20 30 40
0 km 10 20 30 40 50 60

One inch equals 18.4 miles
One centimeter equals 11.7 kilometers

Buffalo NY / Rochester NY

DRIVING DISTANCES IN MILES	BATH, NY	BUFFALO, NY	ITHACA, NY	NIAGARA FALLS, NY	ONEONTA, NY	OSWEGO, NY	ROCHESTER, NY	SYRACUSE, NY	TORONTO, ON	TUPPER LAKE, NY	UTICA, NY	WATERTOWN, NY
BUFFALO, NY	113		153	20	263	158	74	152	106	321	199	210
ROCHESTER, NY	78	74	89	88	200	73		88	181	257	135	146
SYRACUSE, NY	105	152	59	166	118	38	88		260	176	53	65
UTICA, NY	152	199	108	213	65	81	135	53	307	131		86

SEE ALSO DISTANCE AND DRIVING TIME MAP ON PAGES 286–287

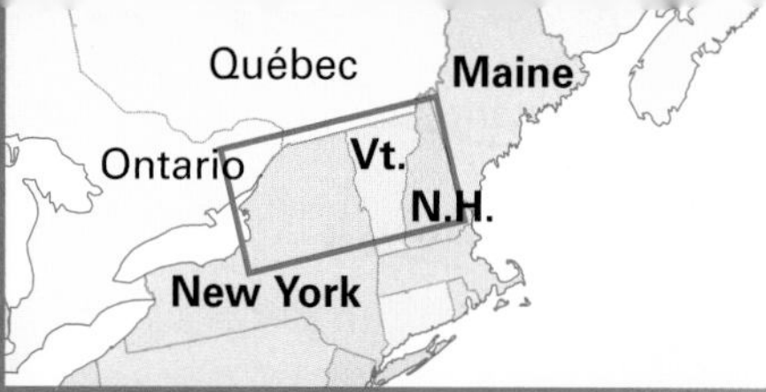

0 mi 10 20 30 40
0 km 10 20 30 40 50 60

One inch equals 18.4 miles
One centimeter equals 11.7 kilometers

Watertown NY / Lake Placid NY

DRIVING DISTANCES IN MILES	BURLINGTON, VT	CONCORD, NH	LAKE PLACID, NY	OGDENSBURG, NY	PLATTSBURGH, NY	RUTLAND, VT	ST. JOHNSBURY, VT	SARATOGA SPRS., NY	SYRACUSE, NY	UTICA, NY	WATERTOWN, NY	WHITE RIVER JCT., VT
BURLINGTON, VT		150	68	208	51	69	76	115	230	183	195	91
CONCORD, NH	150		215	357	198	104	104	173	280	228	312	59
LAKE PLACID, NY	68	215		96	49	133	141	106	192	148	126	156
WATERTOWN, NY	195	312	126	68	167	244	319	179	65	86		289

SEE ALSO DISTANCE AND DRIVING TIME MAP ON PAGES 286–287

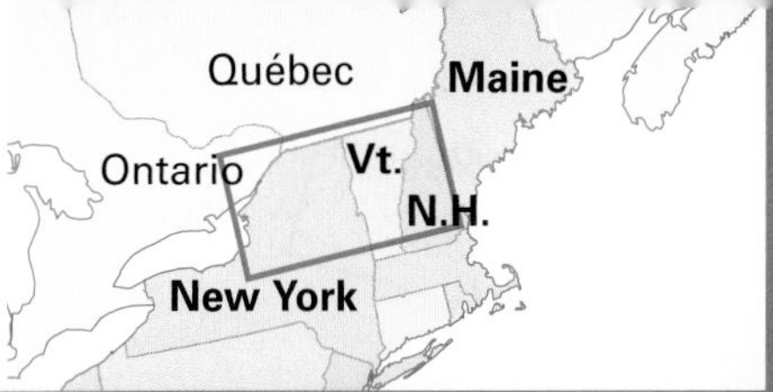

0 mi 10 20 30 40
0 km 10 20 30 40 50 60

One inch equals 18.4 miles
One centimeter equals 11.7 kilometers

Portland ME / Augusta ME

DRIVING DISTANCES IN MILES

	AUGUSTA, ME	BANGOR, ME	BAR HARBOR, ME	BERLIN, NH	CALAIS, ME	CONCORD, NH	CONWAY, NH	LEWISTON, ME	MACHIAS, ME	PORTLAND, ME	PORTSMOUTH, NH	WATERVILLE, ME
AUGUSTA, ME		77	120	110	173	141	97	35	158	58	110	20
BANGOR, ME	77		45	160	97	214	170	108	83	131	184	56
BAR HARBOR, ME	120	45		204	112	257	214	151	71	175	227	100
PORTLAND, ME	58	131	175	93	228	83	62	36	213		53	84

SEE ALSO DISTANCE AND DRIVING TIME MAP ON PAGES 286–287

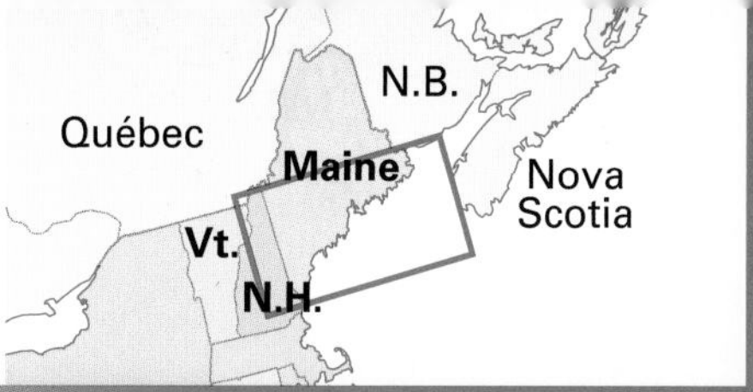

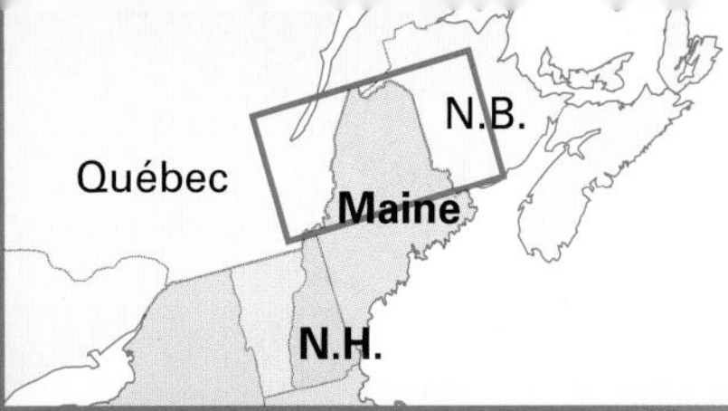

0 mi 10 20 30 40
0 km 10 20 30 40 50 60

One inch equals 18.4 miles
One centimeter equals 11.7 kilometers

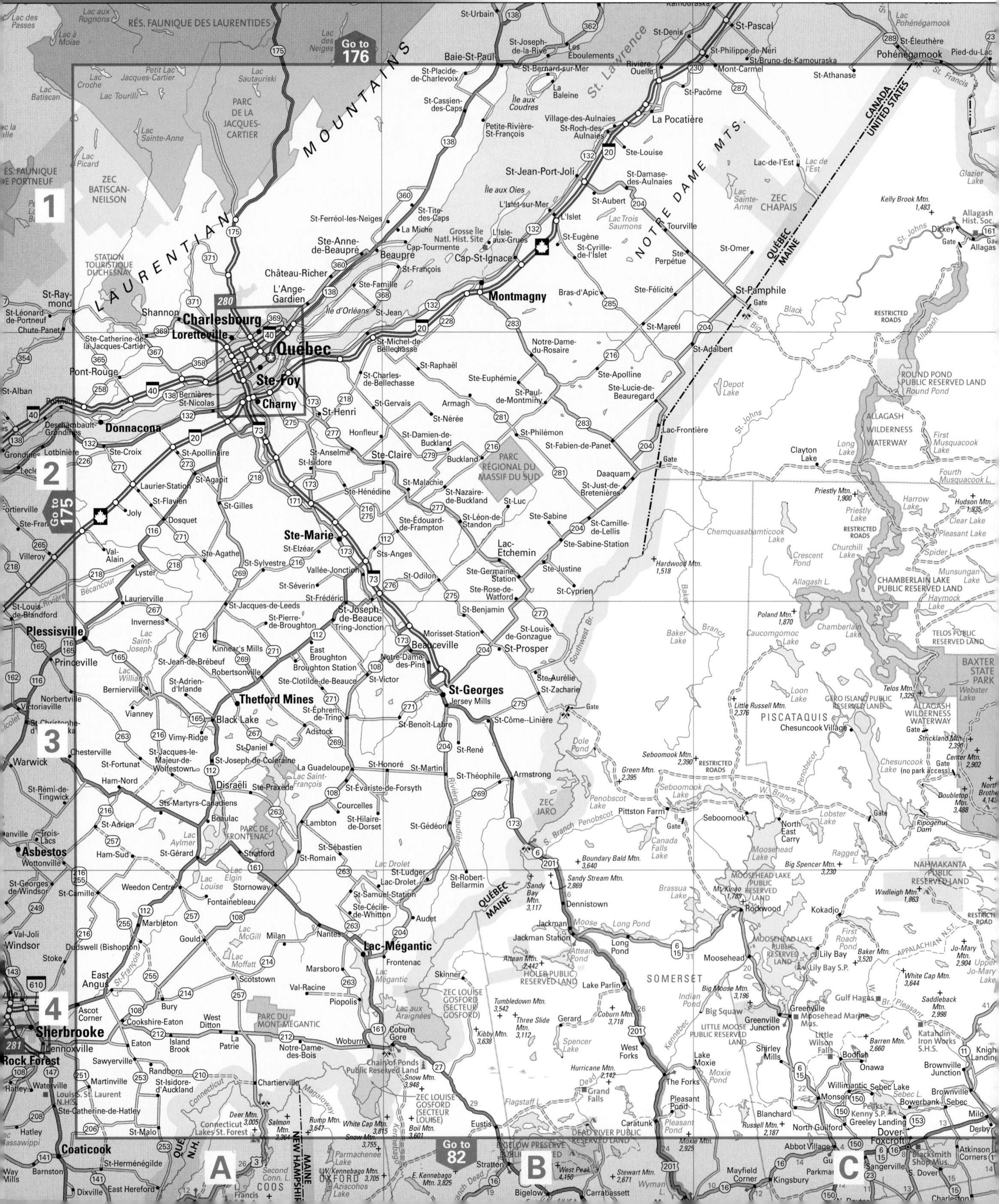

DRIVING DISTANCES IN MILES

	BANGOR, ME	CALAIS, ME	CARIBOU, ME	FREDERICTON, NB	GREENVILLE, ME	HOULTON, ME	JACKMAN, ME	LINCOLN, ME	MADAWASKA, ME	MILLINOCKET, ME	PRESQUE ISLE, ME	QUÉBEC, QC
HOULTON, ME	122	91	55	73	155		204	83	102	73	42	286
LINCOLN, ME	51	77	135	114	83	83	132		174	35	122	231
MADAWASKA, ME	214	207	50	167	212	102	269	174		164	62	182
PRESQUE ISLE, ME	162	133	13	113	166	42	215	122	62	113		246

SEE ALSO DISTANCE AND DRIVING TIME MAP ON PAGES 286–287

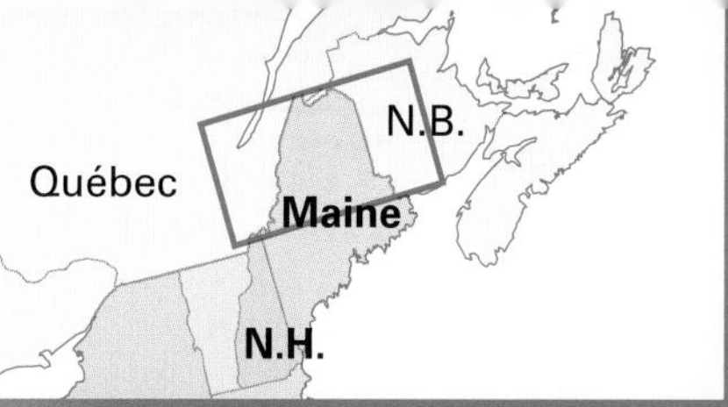

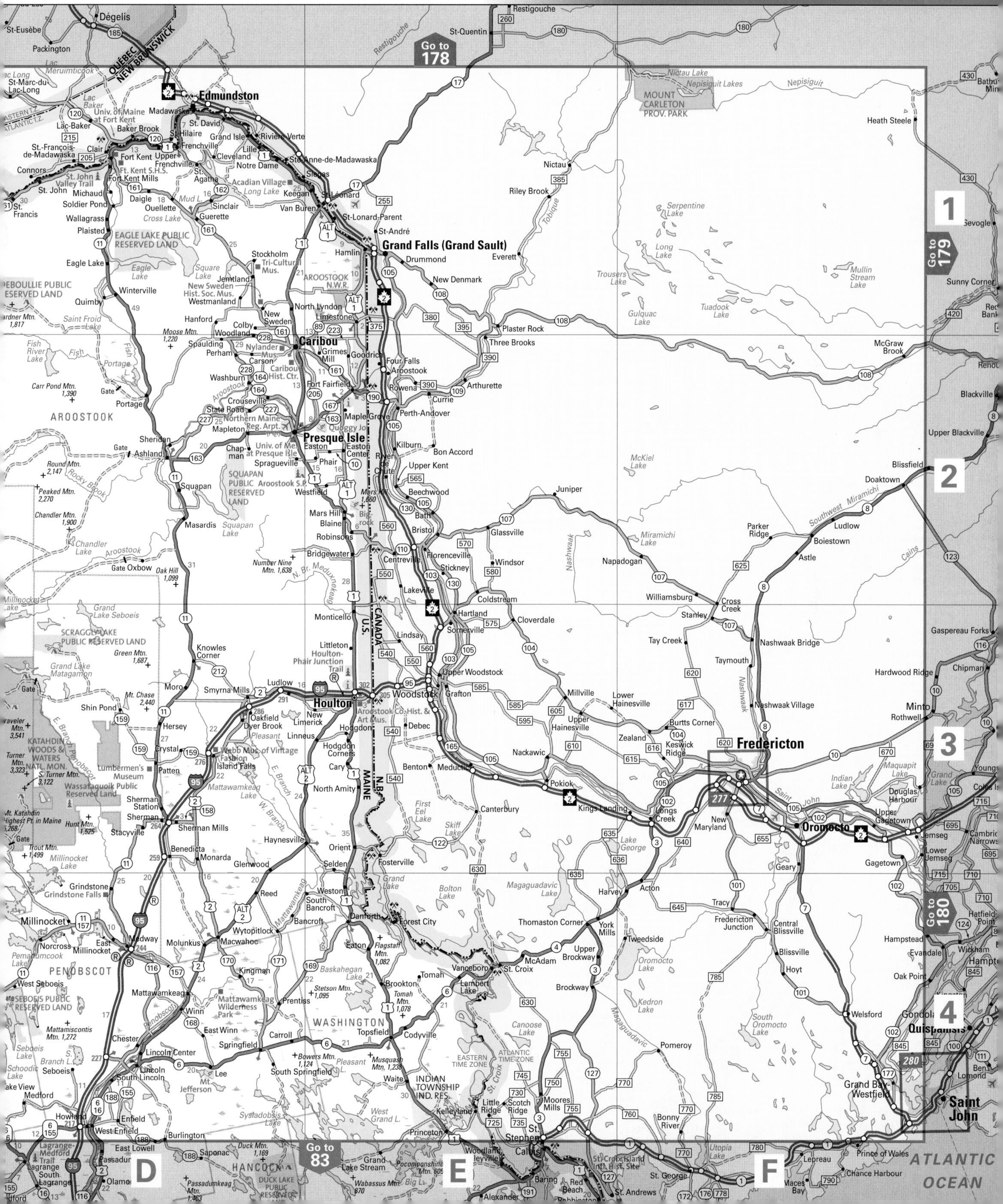

Des Moines IA / Omaha NE

0 mi 10 20 30 40
0 km 10 20 30 40 50 60

One inch equals 18.4 miles
One centimeter equals 11.7 kilometers

DRIVING DISTANCES IN MILES

	AMES, IA	BURLINGTON, IA	CARROLL, IA	CEDAR RAPIDS, IA	CRESTON, IA	DAVENPORT, IA	DES MOINES, IA	IOWA CITY, IA	KIRKSVILLE, MO	MARYVILLE, MO	OMAHA, NE	OTTUMWA, IA
CEDAR RAPIDS, IA	108	106	173		211	87	129	28	170	276	266	111
DES MOINES, IA	34	157	90	129	81	171		113	145	146	136	86
IOWA CITY, IA	136	82	195	28	195	59	113		143	260	250	83
OMAHA, NE	171	328	97	266	98	308	136	250	275	112		221

SEE ALSO DISTANCE AND DRIVING TIME MAP ON PAGES 286–287

Davenport IA / Peoria IL

0 mi 10 20 30 40
0 km 10 20 30 40 50 60

One inch equals 18.4 miles
One centimeter equals 11.7 kilometers

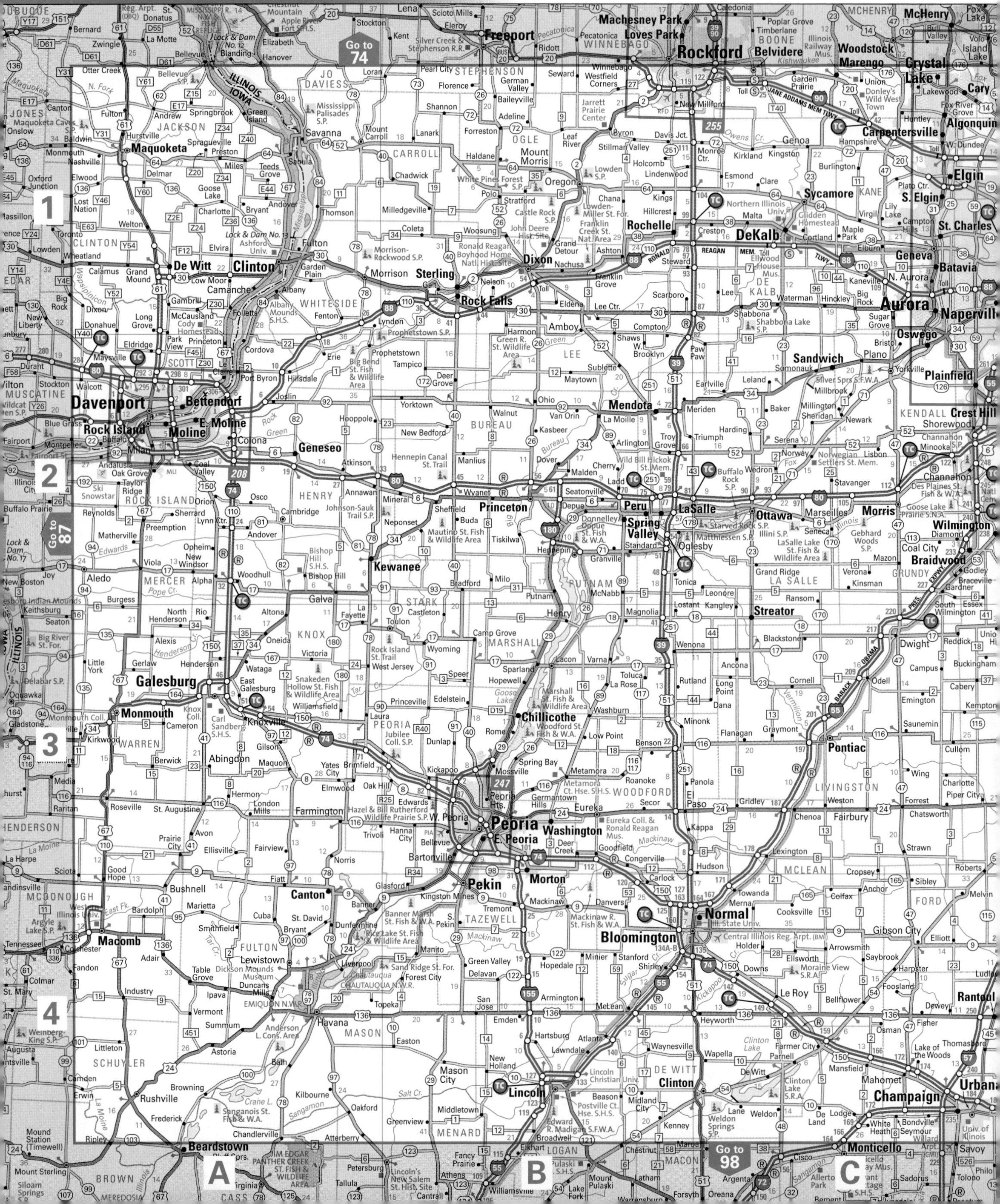

DRIVING DISTANCES IN MILES	BLOOMINGTON, IL	CHAMPAIGN, IL	CHICAGO, IL	DAVENPORT, IA	JOLIET, IL	KALAMAZOO, MI	KOKOMO, IN	LAFAYETTE, IN	LA SALLE, IL	PEORIA, IL	ROCKFORD, IL	SOUTH BEND, IN
CHAMPAIGN, IL	54		141	192	115	255	145	94	117	94	189	198
CHICAGO, IL	135	141		170	40	150	158	121	98	168	86	93
PEORIA, IL	41	94	168	99	132	291	235	184	63		135	234
SOUTH BEND, IN	201	198	93	248	105	76	86	104	164	234	183	

SEE ALSO DISTANCE AND DRIVING TIME MAP ON PAGES 286–287

0 mi 10 20 30 40
0 km 10 20 30 40 50 60
One inch equals 18.4 miles
One centimeter equals 11.7 kilometers

Fort Wayne IN / Toledo OH

DRIVING DISTANCES IN MILES	AKRON, OH	CLEVELAND, OH	COLUMBUS, OH	DETROIT, MI	ERIE, PA	FORT WAYNE, IN	LIMA, OH	MANSFIELD, OH	MUNCIE, IN	TOLEDO, OH	WHEELING, WV	YOUNGSTOWN, OH
CLEVELAND, OH	38		144	171	106	214	163	81	287	119	16	275
FORT WAYNE, IN	237	214	186	170	322		66	151	75	109	290	274
MANSFIELD, OH	66	81	67	156	179	151	93		209	105	141	112
TOLEDO, OH	142	119	148	60	227	109	83	105	180		261	179

SEE ALSO DISTANCE AND DRIVING TIME MAP ON PAGES 286–287

0 mi 10 20 30 40
0 km 10 20 30 40 50 60

One inch equals 18.4 miles
One centimeter equals 11.7 kilometers

Pittsburgh PA / Erie PA

DRIVING DISTANCES IN MILES	ALLENTOWN, PA	ALTOONA, PA	BINGHAMTON, NY	ELMIRA, NY	ERIE, PA	HARRISBURG, PA	JOHNSTOWN, PA	PITTSBURGH, PA	READING, PA	SCRANTON, PA	STATE COLLEGE, PA	WILLIAMSPORT, PA
ALLENTOWN, PA		218	132	188	361	82	217	284	37	76	165	116
HARRISBURG, PA	82	140	181	157	298		138	205	65	119	88	83
PITTSBURGH, PA	284	99	363	284	126	205	73		262	301	139	215
SCRANTON, PA	76	185	61	117	317	119	233	301	103		149	83

SEE ALSO DISTANCE AND DRIVING TIME MAP ON PAGES 286–287

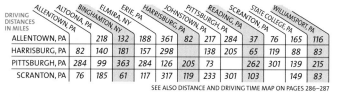

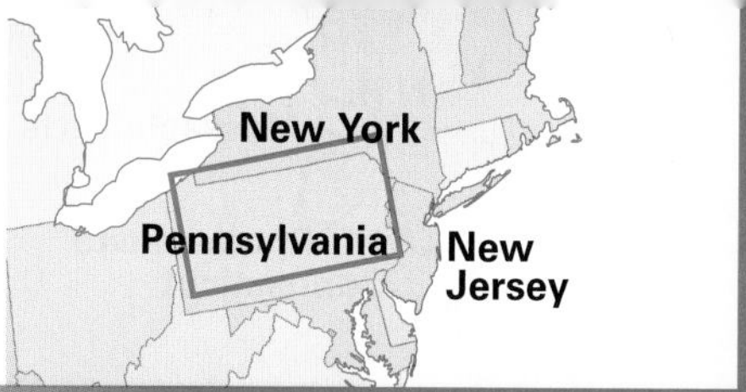

Vt. N.H
Massachusetts
New York
Rhode Island
Pa. Connecticut
N.J.

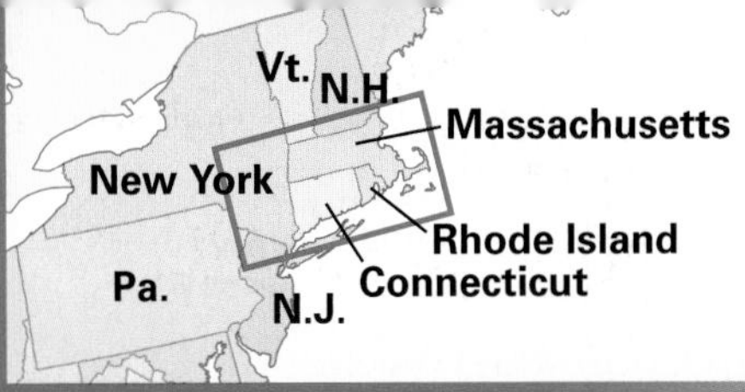

0 mi   10   20   30   40
0 km 10 20 30 40 50 60
One inch equals 18.4 miles
One centimeter equals 11.7 kilometers

Hartford CT / Albany NY

Go to 80

Go to 81

Go to 79

Go to 150

Go to 93

Go to 148

Go to 105

1

2

3

4

A   B   C

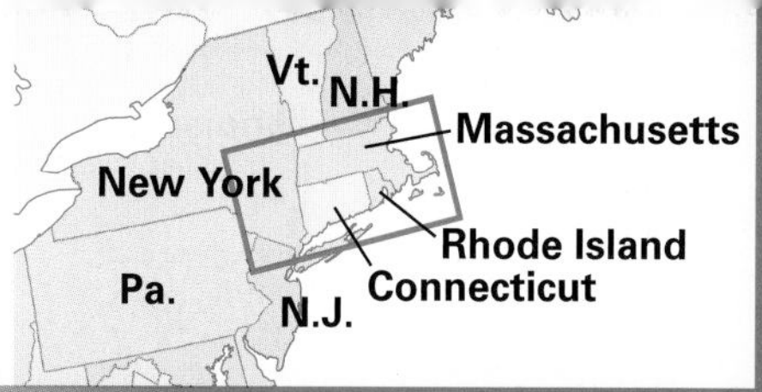

DRIVING DISTANCES IN MILES

	ALBANY, NY	BOSTON, MA	HARTFORD, CT	MANCHESTER, NH	NEWBURGH, NY	NEW HAVEN, CT	NEW YORK, NY	ONEONTA, NY	PROVIDENCE, RI	PROVINCETOWN, MA	SPRINGFIELD, MA	WORCESTER, MA
ALBANY, NY		172	111	145	89	150	151	81	170	271	86	133
BOSTON, MA	172		102	54	201	139	215	251	52	117	95	46
HARTFORD, CT	111	102		131	99	39	115	190	73	200	25	62
NEW YORK, NY	151	215	115	245	56	78		193	177	292	141	176

SEE ALSO DISTANCE AND DRIVING TIME MAP ON PAGES 286–287

0 mi 10 20 30 40
0 km 10 20 30 40 50 60

One inch equals 18.4 miles
One centimeter equals 11.7 kilometers

Kansas City MO / Topeka KS

DRIVING DISTANCES IN MILES

	COLUMBIA, MO	IOLA, KS	JEFFERSON CITY, MO	KANSAS CITY, MO	LAWRENCE, KS	MACON, MO	OSAGE BEACH, MO	QUINCY, IL	ROLLA, MO	ST. JOSEPH, MO	SEDALIA, MO	TOPEKA, KS
JEFFERSON CITY, MO	32	263		161	198	88	44	131	65	217	64	225
KANSAS CITY, MO	129	106	161		37	148	173	251	226	56	97	63
ST. JOSEPH, MO	185	154	217	56	76	131	229	210	282		153	71
TOPEKA, KS	193	100	225	63	26	209	236	314	289	71	161	

SEE ALSO DISTANCE AND DRIVING TIME MAP ON PAGES 286–287

0 mi 10 20 30 40
0 km 10 20 30 40 50 60

One inch equals 18.4 miles
One centimeter equals 11.7 kilometers

St Louis MO / Springfield IL

DRIVING DISTANCES IN MILES

	BLOOMINGTON, IN	CHAMPAIGN, IL	DECATUR, IL	EFFINGHAM, IL	EVANSVILLE, IN	INDIANAPOLIS, IN	LOUISVILLE, KY	MT. VERNON, IL	ST. LOUIS, MO	SPRINGFIELD, IL	TERRE HAUTE, IN	VINCENNES, IN
EVANSVILLE, IN	117	192	184	117		166	114	90	170	247	107	51
INDIANAPOLIS, IN	47	123	177	137	166		112	205	239	212	77	123
ST. LOUIS, MO	223	179	116	103	170	239	264	81		97	169	185
SPRINGFIELD, IL	209	87	40	89	247	212	326	158	97		155	169

SEE ALSO DISTANCE AND DRIVING TIME MAP ON PAGES 286–287

Cincinnati OH / Louisville KY

0 mi 10 20 30 40
0 km 10 20 30 40 50 60

One inch equals 18.4 miles
One centimeter equals 11.7 kilometers

Columbus OH / Charleston WV

DRIVING DISTANCES IN MILES

	CHARLESTON, WV	CHILLICOTHE, OH	CINCINNATI, OH	COLUMBUS, OH	DAYTON, OH	HUNTINGTON, WV	LEXINGTON, KY	LOUISVILLE, KY	MAYSVILLE, KY	PARKERSBURG, WV	WHEELING, WV	ZANESVILLE, OH
CHARLESTON, WV		121	202	168	198	52	176	251	155	73	176	155
CINCINNATI, OH	202	108		109	52	150	85	100	63	191	235	164
COLUMBUS, OH	168	47	109		70	135	193	207	114	108	130	58
LEXINGTON, KY	176	191	85	193	135	126		80	67	249	319	247

SEE ALSO DISTANCE AND DRIVING TIME MAP ON PAGES 286–287

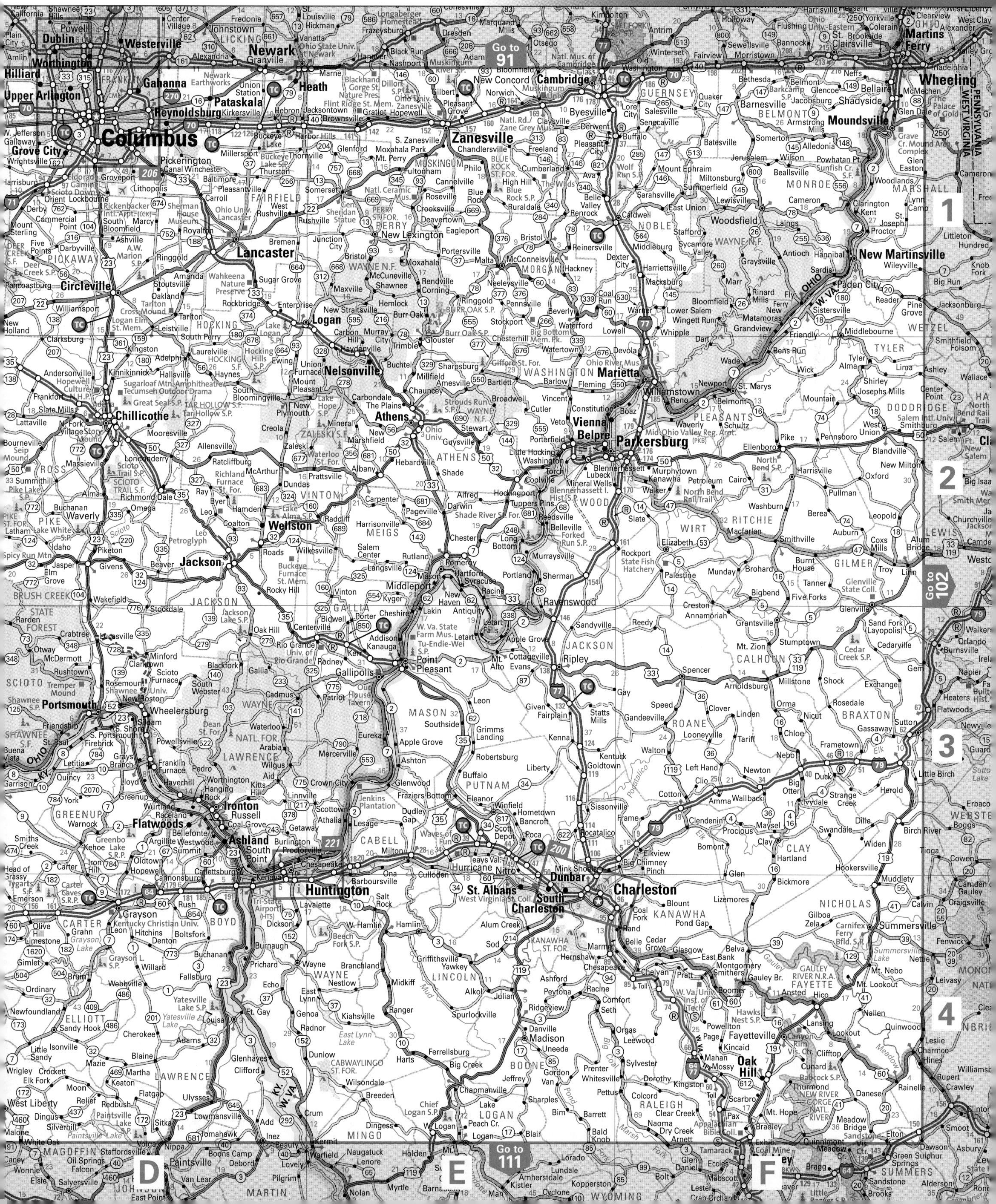

0 mi 10 20 30 40
0 km 10 20 30 40 50 60

One inch equals 18.4 miles
One centimeter equals 11.7 kilometers

Charlottesville VA / Morgantown WV

DRIVING DISTANCES IN MILES

	BALTIMORE, MD	CHARLOTTESVILLE, VA	CUMBERLAND, MD	ELKINS, WV	FREDERICKSBURG, VA	FRONT ROYAL, VA	GETTYSBURG, PA	HAGERSTOWN, MD	MORGANTOWN, WV	SALISBURY, MD	WASHINGTON, DC	WHEELING, WV
BALTIMORE, MD		161	140	229	98	110	62	76	211	106	38	290
CHARLOTTESVILLE, VA	161		163	142	70	74	190	141	204	235	118	279
MORGANTOWN, WV	211	204	71	62	252	161	181	138		317	205	76
WASHINGTON, DC	38	118	134	192	54	73	80	70	205	115		284

SEE ALSO DISTANCE AND DRIVING TIME MAP ON PAGES 286–287

0 mi 10 20 30 40

0 km 10 20 30 40 50 60

One inch equals 18.4 miles

One centimeter equals 11.7 kilometers

Philadelphia PA / Harrisburg PA

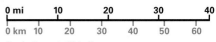

DRIVING DISTANCES IN MILES

	ALLENTOWN, PA	ATLANTIC CITY, NJ	BALTIMORE, MD	DOVER, DE	HARRISBURG, PA	LANCASTER, PA	NEWARK, NJ	NEW YORK, NY	PHILADELPHIA, PA	TRENTON, NJ	WASHINGTON, DC	WILMINGTON, DE
HARRISBURG, PA	82	171	83	126		44	154	165	109	135	123	102
NEW YORK, NY	84	125	192	160	165	165	11		91	55	228	120
PHILADELPHIA, PA	63	62	104	74	109	79	80	91		34	140	30
WASHINGTON, DC	188	186	38	94	123	123	218	228	140	179		110

SEE ALSO DISTANCE AND DRIVING TIME MAP ON PAGES 286–287

0 mi 10 20 30 40
0 km 10 20 30 40 50 60

One inch equals 18.4 miles
One centimeter equals 11.7 kilometers

Tulsa OK / Fayetteville AR

DRIVING DISTANCES IN MILES	BARTLESVILLE, OK	BRANSON, MO	FAYETTEVILLE, AR	INDEPENDENCE, KS	JOPLIN, MO	MOUNTAIN HOME, AR	MUSKOGEE, OK	NEWPORT, AR	ROLLA, MO	SPRINGFIELD, MO	TULSA, OK	WEST PLAINS, MO
BRANSON, MO	213		95	188	111	84	181	178	147	41	225	109
FAYETTEVILLE, AR	154	95		165	88	127	86	241	227	121	113	182
SPRINGFIELD, MO	177	41	121	153	70	112	193	219	110		189	109
TULSA, OK	48	225	113	86	116	237	52	344	295	189		293

SEE ALSO DISTANCE AND DRIVING TIME MAP ON PAGES 286–287

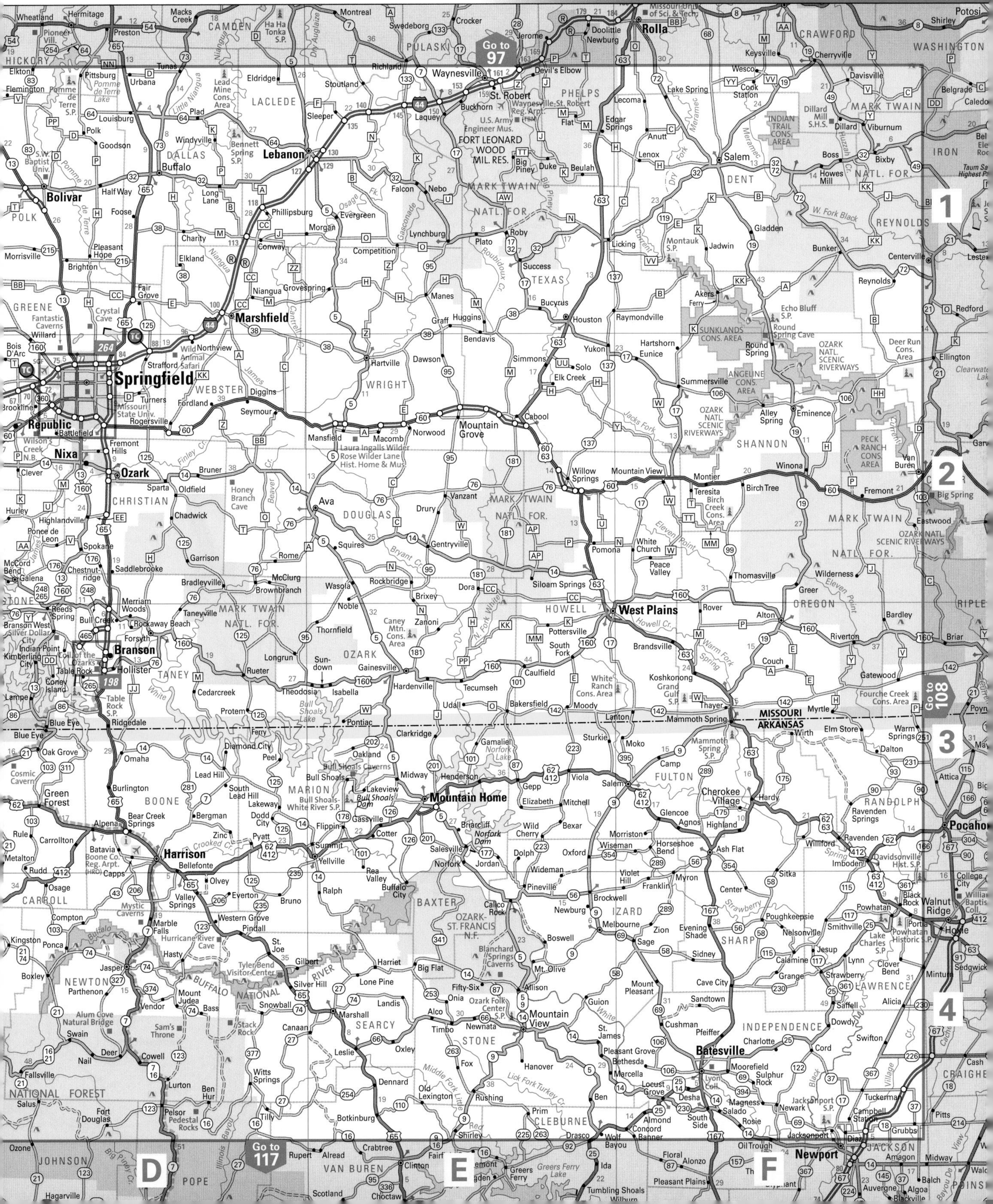

0 mi 10 20 30 40
0 km 10 20 30 40 50 60

One inch equals 18.4 miles
One centimeter equals 11.7 kilometers

Jonesboro AR / Cape Girardeau MO

DRIVING DISTANCES IN MILES

	BOWLING GREEN, KY	CAPE GIRARDEAU, MO	CARBONDALE, IL	CLARKSVILLE, TN	DYERSBURG, TN	HOPKINSVILLE, KY	JACKSON, TN	JONESBORO, AR	NASHVILLE, TN	OWENSBORO, KY	PADUCAH, KY	POPLAR BLUFF, MO
BOWLING GREEN, KY		199	206	63	217	63	196	349	68	76	135	239
CAPE GIRARDEAU, MO	199		46	155	112	136	161	155	197	168	67	75
JONESBORO, AR	349	155	199	268	101	249	160		285	304	178	81
NASHVILLE, TN	68	197	204	46	178	68	132	285		141	133	237

SEE ALSO DISTANCE AND DRIVING TIME MAP ON PAGES 286–287

0 mi 10 20 30 40
0 km 10 20 30 40 50 60

One inch equals 18.4 miles
One centimeter equals 11.7 kilometers

Knoxville TN / Richmond KY

DRIVING DISTANCES IN MILES

	ASHEVILLE, NC	BECKLEY, WV	BRISTOL, TN/VA	COOKEVILLE, TN	GATLINBURG, TN	HICKORY, NC	JOHNSON CITY, TN	KNOXVILLE, TN	LONDON, KY	MAMMOTH CAVE NP, KY	PIKEVILLE, KY	RICHMOND, KY
BRISTOL, TN/VA	83	140		224	118	98	24	117	213	348	116	265
HICKORY, NC	78	196	98	291	147		98	185	280	415	214	332
KNOXVILLE, TN	109	256	117	107	40	185	107		100	234	202	151
LONDON, KY	205	287	213	129	136	280	203	100		136	121	53

SEE ALSO DISTANCE AND DRIVING TIME MAP ON PAGES 286–287

0 mi 10 20 30 40
0 km 10 20 30 40 50 60

One inch equals 18.4 miles
One centimeter equals 11.7 kilometers

Greensboro NC / Roanoke VA

DRIVING DISTANCES IN MILES

	DANVILLE, VA	GREENSBORO, NC	LYNCHBURG, VA	NORFOLK, VA	RALEIGH, NC	RICHMOND, VA	ROANOKE, VA	ROANOKE RAPIDS, NC	ROCKY MOUNT, NC	WILLIAMSBURG, VA	WINSTON-SALEM, NC	WYTHEVILLE, VA
GREENSBORO, NC	46		106	230	69	200	101	132	124	237	30	120
RALEIGH, NC	89	69	140	179		157	156	84	54	204	96	186
RICHMOND, VA	160	200	114	91	157		192	91	127	49	228	256
ROANOKE, VA	83	101	55	285	156	192		190	211	243	107	78

SEE ALSO DISTANCE AND DRIVING TIME MAP ON PAGES 286–287

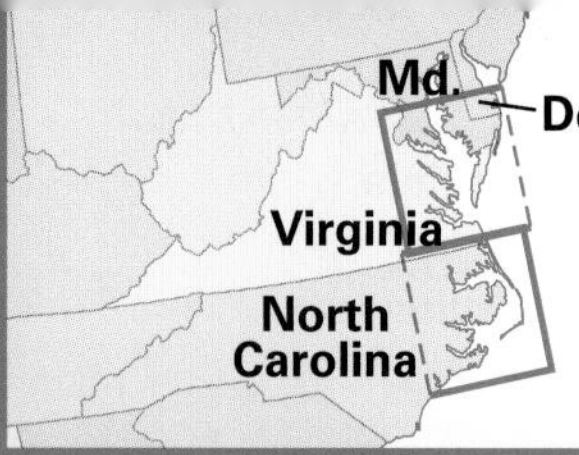

0 mi 10 20 30 40
0 km 10 20 30 40 50 60

One inch equals 18.4 miles
One centimeter equals 11.7 kilometers

DRIVING DISTANCES IN MILES	ELIZABETH CITY, NC	GREENVILLE, NC	MOREHEAD CITY, NC	NAGS HEAD, NC	NEW BERN, NC	NORFOLK, VA	OCEAN CITY, MD	RICHMOND, VA	SALISBURY, MD	VIRGINIA BEACH, VA	WASHINGTON, DC	WILLIAMSBURG, VA
MOREHEAD CITY, NC	150	82		184	35	185	326	241	321	206	352	221
NAGS HEAD, NC	59	135	184		149	82	214	179	209	94	284	131
NORFOLK, VA	50	130	185	82	151		138	91	133	18	196	43
WASHINGTON, DC	243	270	352	284	317	196	139	108	115	212		153

SEE ALSO DISTANCE AND DRIVING TIME MAP ON PAGES 286–287

0 mi 10 20 30 40
0 km 10 20 30 40 50 60

One inch equals 18.4 miles
One centimeter equals 11.7 kilometers

Fort Smith AR / Texarkana AR–TX

DRIVING DISTANCES IN MILES

	ARKADELPHIA, AR	FORT SMITH, AR	HENRYETTA, OK	HOT SPRINGS, AR	LITTLE ROCK, AR	MCALESTER, OK	MENA, AR	NEWPORT, AR	PARIS, TX	PINE BLUFF, AR	RUSSELLVILLE, AR	TEXARKANA, AR/TX
FORT SMITH, AR	152		100	126	165	114	81	220	214	210	87	180
HOT SPRINGS, AR	37	126	224		65	193	75	154	207	76	67	117
LITTLE ROCK, AR	72	165	263	65		278	141	89	242	45	81	153
TEXARKANA, AR/TX	83	180	227	117	153	188	99	241	92	163	180	

SEE ALSO DISTANCE AND DRIVING TIME MAP ON PAGES 286–287

0 mi 10 20 30 40
0 km 10 20 30 40 50 60

One inch equals 18.4 miles
One centimeter equals 11.7 kilometers

Memphis TN / Oxford MS

DRIVING DISTANCES IN MILES

	BIRMINGHAM, AL	CLARKSDALE, MS	COLUMBIA, TN	COLUMBUS, MS	DECATUR, AL	FLORENCE, AL	GREENVILLE, MS	HUNTSVILLE, AL	JACKSON, TN	MEMPHIS, TN	OXFORD, MS	TUPELO, MS
BIRMINGHAM, AL		248	161	122	83	121	286	101	223	241	185	136
HUNTSVILLE, AL	101	260	79	163	25	65	318		205	216	196	148
MEMPHIS, TN	241	76	210	175	191	156	148	216	91		85	109
TUPELO, MS	136	113	159	66	123	92	172	148	107	109	50	

SEE ALSO DISTANCE AND DRIVING TIME MAP ON PAGES 286–287

0 mi 10 20 30 40
0 km 10 20 30 40 50 60

One inch equals 18.4 miles
One centimeter equals 11.7 kilometers

Atlanta GA / Chattanooga TN

DRIVING DISTANCES IN MILES

	ANNISTON, AL	ASHEVILLE, NC	ATHENS, GA	ATLANTA, GA	AUGUSTA, GA	CHATTANOOGA, TN	GADSDEN, AL	GATLINBURG, TN	GREENVILLE, SC	HUNTSVILLE, AL	MANCHESTER, TN	SPARTANBURG, SC
ATLANTA, GA	91	207	70		149	113	117	187	146	191	180	173
AUGUSTA, GA	240	179	97	149		266	266	240	110	334	333	118
CHATTANOOGA, TN	120	225	170	113	266		94	156	245	109	69	272
GREENVILLE, SC	238	64	104	146	110	245	264	125		313	311	30

SEE ALSO DISTANCE AND DRIVING TIME MAP ON PAGES 286–287

North Carolina
South Carolina

0 mi 10 20 30 40
0 km 10 20 30 40 50 60
One inch equals 18.4 miles
One centimeter equals 11.7 kilometers

Charlotte NC / Columbia SC

Go to 111
Go to 112
Go to 121
Go to 130
Go to 131

U.S. DEPT. OF ENERGY SAVANNAH RIVER SITE

Major cities and towns shown on map include: Hickory, Conover, Newton, Salisbury, Asheboro, Siler City, Mooresville, Davidson, Cornelius, Kannapolis, Concord, Huntersville, Charlotte, Mint Hill, Matthews, Lincolnton, Gastonia, Shelby, Kings Mtn., Gaffney, York, Rock Hill, Fort Mill, Indian Trail, Monroe, Albemarle, Wadesboro, Rockingham, Hamlet, Pinehurst, Southern Pines, Aberdeen, Laurinburg, Cheraw, Bennettsville, Dillon, Marion, Chester, Lancaster, Chesterfield, Darlington, Florence, Lake City, Winnsboro, Camden, Bishopville, Hartsville, Sumter, Manning, Newberry, Lexington, Columbia, Cayce, Irmo, Batesburg-Leesville, Aiken, Orangeburg, Georgetown, Kingstree

CONGAREE NATL. PARK
FORT JACKSON MIL. RES.
CAROLINA SANDHILLS N.W.R.
SAND HILLS S.F.
FRANCIS MARION NATL. FOR.

DRIVING DISTANCES IN MILES

	CHARLOTTE, NC	COLUMBIA, SC	FAYETTEVILLE, NC	FLORENCE, SC	GOLDSBORO, NC	HICKORY, NC	LUMBERTON, NC	MOREHEAD CITY, NC	MYRTLE BEACH, SC	ROCK HILL, SC	SUMTER, SC	WILMINGTON, NC
CHARLOTTE, NC		91	139	107	208	47	128	298	173	26	115	205
COLUMBIA, SC	91		170	80	240	139	139	289	146	70	45	199
MYRTLE BEACH, SC	173	146	116	66	170	220	83	165		181	93	71
WILMINGTON, NC	205	199	92	120	100	292	77	95	71	220	158	

SEE ALSO DISTANCE AND DRIVING TIME MAP ON PAGES 286–287

0 mi 10 20 30 40
0 km 10 20 30 40 50 60
One inch equals 18.4 miles
One centimeter equals 11.7 kilometers

Shreveport LA / Tyler TX

DRIVING DISTANCES IN MILES

	ALEXANDRIA, LA	EL DORADO, AR	GREENVILLE, TX	LONGVIEW, TX	LUFKIN, TX	MONROE, LA	NACOGDOCHES, TX	NATCHEZ, MS	NATCHITOCHES, LA	SHREVEPORT, LA	TEXARKANA, AR/TX	TYLER, TX
ALEXANDRIA, LA		147	276	179	160	96	167	76	55	121	190	213
MONROE, LA	96	86	267	170	223		203	95	100	103	172	204
SHREVEPORT, LA	121	96	165	68	121	103	101	198	73		69	102
TYLER, TX	213	196	77	42	82	204	76	288	164	102	118	

SEE ALSO DISTANCE AND DRIVING TIME MAP ON PAGES 286–287

0 mi 10 20 30 40
0 km 10 20 30 40 50 60

One inch equals 18.4 miles
One centimeter equals 11.7 kilometers

Jackson MS / Hattiesburg MS

DRIVING DISTANCES IN MILES

	BIRMINGHAM, AL	EVERGREEN, AL	GREENVILLE, MS	HATTIESBURG, MS	JACKSON, MS	MCCOMB, MS	MERIDIAN, MS	NATCHEZ, MS	SELMA, AL	TUSCALOOSA, AL	VICKSBURG, MS	WINONA, MS
HATTIESBURG, MS	239	184	215		90	75	89	142	193	183	132	180
JACKSON, MS	241	243	125	90		76	91	102	195	185	42	94
MERIDIAN, MS	149	152	216	89	91	167		194	104	94	133	113
TUSCALOOSA, AL	61	211	225	183	185	261	94	287	82		227	144

SEE ALSO DISTANCE AND DRIVING TIME MAP ON PAGES 286–287

Alabama Georgia

0 mi   10   20   30   40
0 km 10 20 30 40 50 60
One inch equals 18.4 miles
One centimeter equals 11.7 kilometers

Go to 120

Go to 127

Go to 136   Go to 137

Birmingham Leeds Fairfield Homewood Mountain Brook Vandiver New London Wolf Creek Mumford Crossroads Hightower Ranburne Univ. of West Georgia Clem Whitesburg Palmetto Roscoe Madras Jonesboro
Pelham Columbiana Talladega Curry Pyriton Newell Graham Roopville Lowell Tyus Centralhatchee Newnan East Newnan Turin Peachtree City
Sylacauga Alexander City Roanoke LaGrange West Point Lanett Valley Opelika Auburn Tuskegee Phenix City Columbus
Clanton Wetumpka Millbrook Montgomery Tallassee Prattville
Greenville Troy Union Springs Eufaula Cuthbert Dawson
Andalusia Opp Enterprise Ozark Dothan Blakely

TALLADEGA NATL. FOR. CLAY RANDOLPH HEARD COWETA FAYETTE MERIWETHER SPALDING PIKE
SHELBY COOSA TALLAPOOSA CHAMBERS TROUP HARRIS TALBOT
CHILTON AUTAUGA ELMORE LEE MUSCOGEE CHATTAHOOCHEE
LOWNDES MONTGOMERY MACON RUSSELL MARION WEBSTER STEWART QUITMAN RANDOLPH TERRELL
BUTLER CRENSHAW BULLOCK BARBOUR HENRY CLAY CALHOUN DOUGHERTY
COVINGTON COFFEE DALE EARLY MILLER BAKER GENEVA HOUSTON

Fort Rucker U.S. Army Aviation Center
Ft. Benning U.S. Army Maneuver Ctr.
Maxwell A.F.B.
Tuskegee Airmen N.H.S.
Horseshoe Bend Natl. Mil. Park

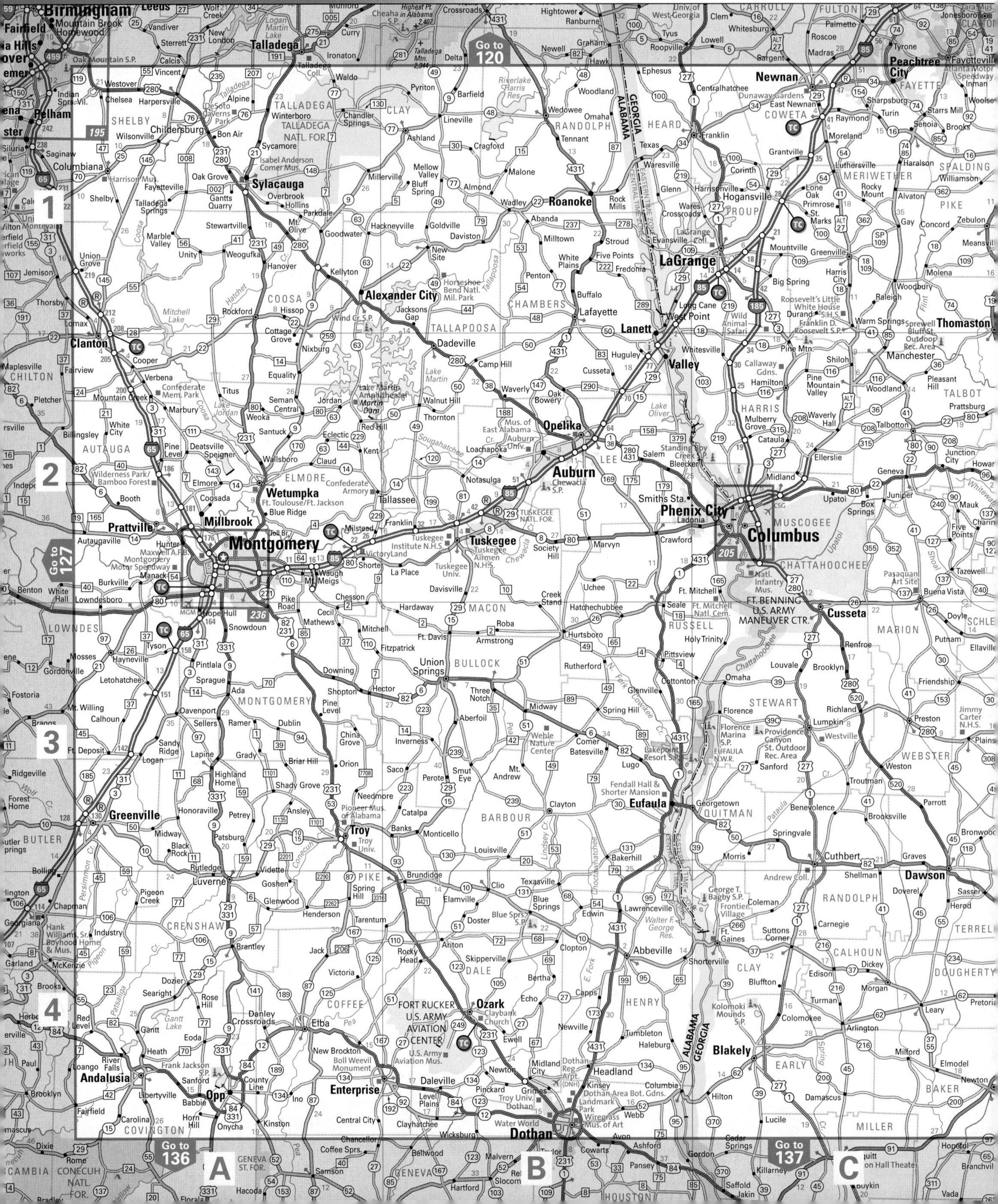

DRIVING DISTANCES IN MILES	ALBANY, GA	ATLANTA, GA	AUBURN, AL	AUGUSTA, GA	BIRMINGHAM, AL	COLUMBUS, GA	DOTHAN, AL	LA GRANGE, GA	MACON, GA	MONTGOMERY, AL	TIFTON, GA	WAYCROSS, GA
ALBANY, GA		180	121	226	253	86	83	129	102	165	43	116
COLUMBUS, GA	86	106	34	249	167		97	46	95	79	135	208
MACON, GA	102	84	151	123	234	95	186	114		203	102	159
MONTGOMERY, AL	165	158	54	301	88	79	103	95	203		214	287

SEE ALSO DISTANCE AND DRIVING TIME MAP ON PAGES 286–287

0 mi 10 20 30 40
0 km 10 20 30 40 50 60

One inch equals 18.4 miles
One centimeter equals 11.7 kilometers

Savannah GA / Hilton Head Island SC

DRIVING DISTANCES IN MILES

	AUGUSTA, GA	BEAUFORT, SC	BRUNSWICK, GA	CHARLESTON, SC	GEORGETOWN, SC	HILTON HEAD I., SC	HINESVILLE, GA	ORANGEBURG, SC	SAVANNAH, GA	STATESBORO, GA	WALTERBORO, SC	WAYCROSS, GA
AUGUSTA, GA		126	194	142	181	127	157	74	135	81	111	184
CHARLESTON, SC	142	66	175		58	95	138	73	107	150	51	203
HILTON HEAD I., SC	127	32	113	95	157		75	116	35	88	64	141
SAVANNAH, GA	135	42	78	107	163	35	41	123		53	71	106

SEE ALSO DISTANCE AND DRIVING TIME MAP ON PAGES 286–287

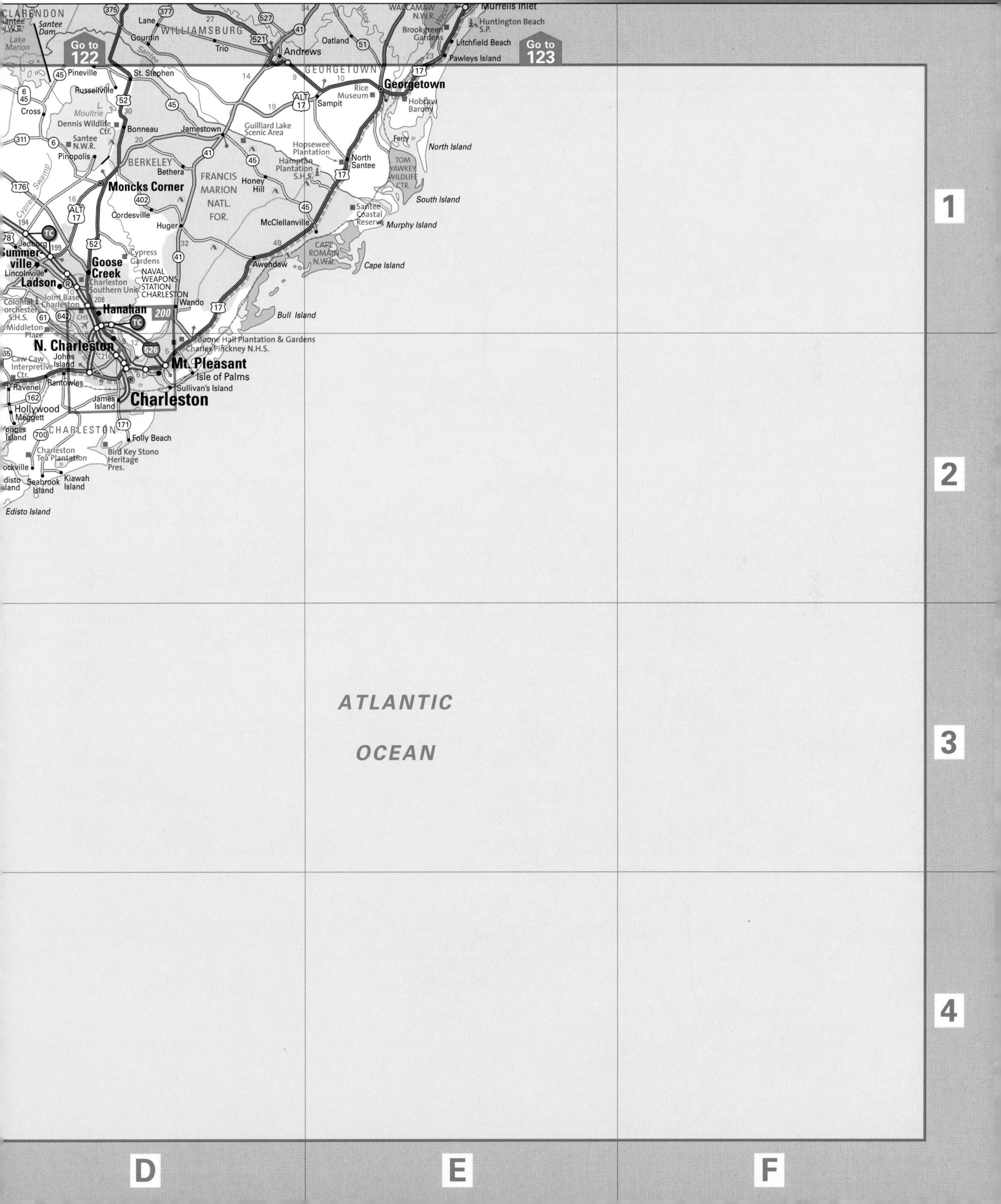

Houston TX / Beaumont TX

0 mi 10 20 30 40
0 km 10 20 30 40 50 60

One inch equals 18.4 miles
One centimeter equals 11.7 kilometers

DRIVING DISTANCES IN MILES	ALEXANDRIA, LA	BEAUMONT, TX	DE RIDDER, LA	FREEPORT, TX	GALVESTON, TX	HOUSTON, TX	HUNTSVILLE, TX	LAFAYETTE, LA	LAKE CHARLES, LA	LUFKIN, TX	OPELOUSAS, LA	PORT ARTHUR, TX
BEAUMONT, TX	157		82	143	75	84	157	133	57	112	144	18
HOUSTON, TX	241	84	166	61	53		75	217	141	121	228	93
LAFAYETTE, LA	87	133	119	276	208	217	290		76	216	27	130
LAKE CHARLES, LA	100	57	49	200	132	141	214	76		140	87	54

SEE ALSO DISTANCE AND DRIVING TIME MAP ON PAGES 286–287

0 mi 10 20 30 40
0 km 10 20 30 40 50 60

One inch equals 18.4 miles
One centimeter equals 11.7 kilometers

New Orleans LA / Baton Rouge LA

DRIVING DISTANCES IN MILES

	BATON ROUGE, LA	BILOXI, MS	GULFPORT, MS	GULF SHORES, AL	HAMMOND, LA	HATTIESBURG, MS	HOUMA, LA	MCCOMB, MS	MOBILE, AL	NEW ORLEANS, LA	PASCAGOULA, MS	PENSACOLA, FL
BATON ROUGE, LA		151	140	254	51	174	101	102	205	91	170	264
BILOXI, MS	151		12	110	106	82	148	161	61	93	20	120
MOBILE, AL	205	61	75	48	159	97	201	215		146	41	58
NEW ORLEANS, LA	91	93	81	195	57	115	57	111	146		112	205

SEE ALSO DISTANCE AND DRIVING TIME MAP ON PAGES 286–287

0 mi 10 20 30 40
0 km 10 20 30 40 50 60
One inch equals 18.4 miles
One centimeter equals 11.7 kilometers

Pensacola FL / Panama City FL

DRIVING DISTANCES IN MILES

	BREWTON, AL	DE FUNIAK SPRS., FL	DOTHAN, AL	FT. WALTON BEACH, FL	MARIANNA, FL	MOBILE, AL	PANAMA CITY, FL	PENSACOLA, FL	PERRY, FL	TALLAHASSEE, FL	THOMASVILLE, GA	VALDOSTA, GA
PANAMA CITY, FL	143	65	82	64	61	160		102	160	104	134	186
PENSACOLA, FL	57	82	152	39	138	58	102		256	200	230	282
TALLAHASSEE, FL	201	123	110	166	68	247	104	200	52		35	85
VALDOSTA, GA	283	204	133	247	149	329	186	282	66	85	42	

SEE ALSO DISTANCE AND DRIVING TIME MAP ON PAGES 286–287

Georgia

Florida

0 mi   10   20   30   40
0 km 10   20   30   40   50   60
One inch equals 18.4 miles
One centimeter equals 11.7 kilometers

Go to 129

Go to 137

Go to 140

GULF

OF

MEXICO

Tallahassee

Gainesville

Ocala

Valdosta

Thomasville

Moultrie

Perry

Live Oak

Lake City

Starke

Waycross

OKEFENOKEE

N.W.R.

A   B   C

1

2

3

4

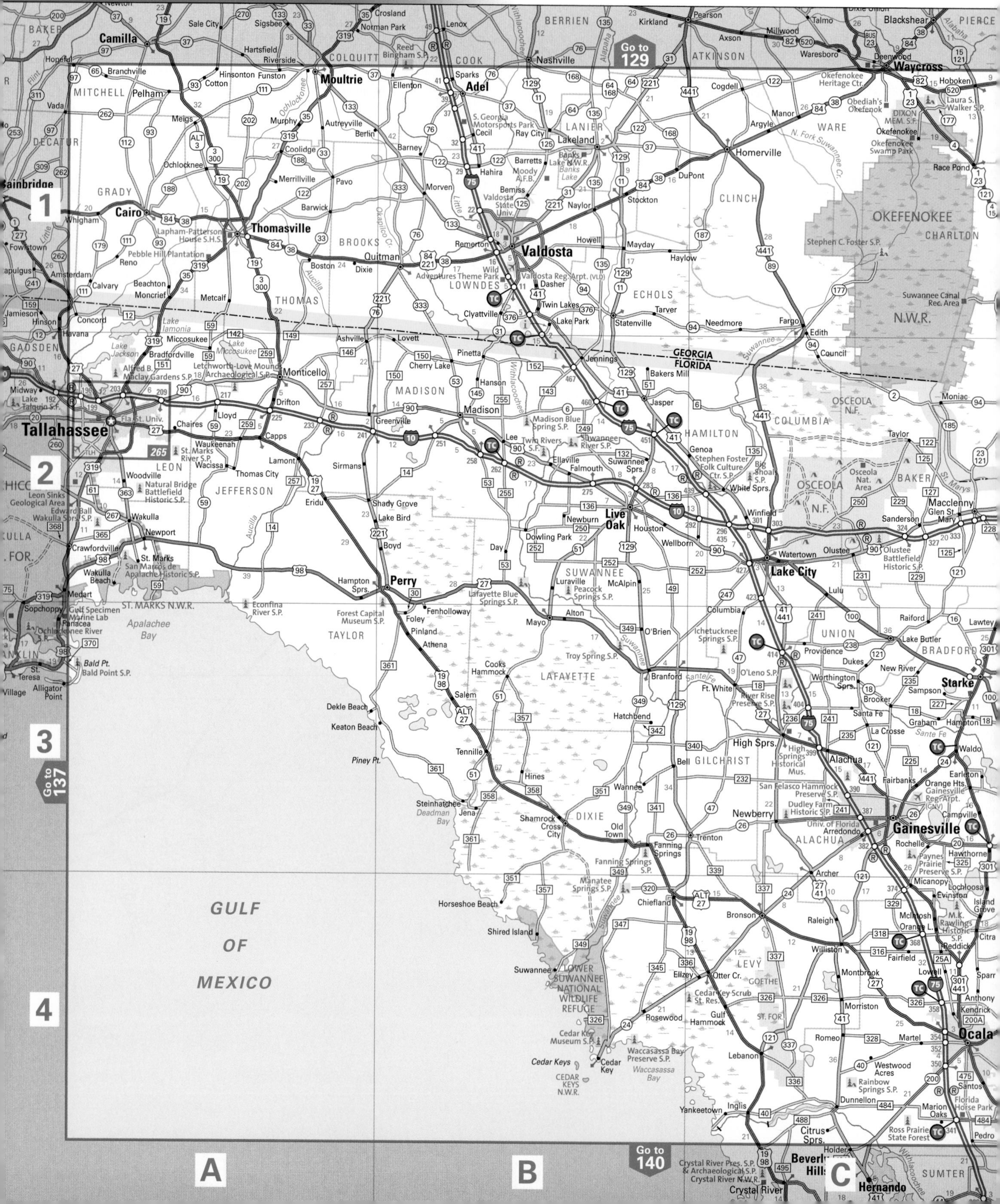

DRIVING DISTANCES IN MILES

	BRUNSWICK, GA	DAYTONA BEACH, FL	GAINESVILLE, FL	JACKSONVILLE, FL	LAKE CITY, FL	OCALA, FL	PERRY, FL	ST. AUGUSTINE, FL	STARKE, FL	TALLAHASSEE, FL	VALDOSTA, GA	WAYCROSS, GA
DAYTONA BEACH, FL	160		99	91	154	77	225	53	92	258	209	173
JACKSONVILLE, FL	69	91	70		62	101	133	41	45	166	117	78
OCALA, FL	171	77	40	101	80		120	81	57	186	137	170
TALLAHASSEE, FL	235	258	152	166	109	186	52	207	145		85	146

SEE ALSO DISTANCE AND DRIVING TIME MAP ON PAGES 286–287

0 mi 10 20 30 40
0 km 10 20 30 40 50 60
One inch equals 18.4 miles
One centimeter equals 11.7 kilometers

Tampa FL / Sarasota FL

DRIVING DISTANCES IN MILES	FORT MYERS, FL	FORT PIERCE, FL	LAKELAND, FL	MELBOURNE, FL	OKEECHOBEE, FL	ORLANDO, FL	PUNTA GORDA, FL	ST. PETERSBURG, FL	SARASOTA, FL	TAMPA, FL	TITUSVILLE, FL	W. PALM BEACH, FL
FORT PIERCE, FL	126		122	57	36	120	127	197	150	172	95	57
ORLANDO, FL	155	120	56	72	108		131	107	130	82	40	169
SARASOTA, FL	74	150	85	190	114	130	50	35		60	170	184
TAMPA, FL	123	172	37	142	162	82	99	25	60		121	223

SEE ALSO DISTANCE AND DRIVING TIME MAP ON PAGES 286–287

Florida

One inch equals 18.4 miles
One centimeter equals 11.7 kilometers

0 mi 10 20 30 40
0 km 10 20 30 40 50 60

Go to
140

1

Don Pedro Island S.P.
775
771
Placida
Island Bay
Charlotte
Harbor
Pres. S.P.
158
Gasparilla
Island
765
41
23
Pirate
Harbor
31
75
31
Babcock
Wilderness
Adventures
Gasparilla
N.W.R.
Charlotte
Harbor
Gasparilla Island S.P.
Boca Grande
Old Port Boca Grande Lighthouse
Pine
Island
N.W.R.
Bokeelia
Pineland
765
41
143
N. Ft. Myers
Tice
80
78
141
138
**Ft. Myer
Shores**
TC
Cayo Costa S.P.
Matlacha
78
Fort Myers
TC
Captiva I.
Captiva
767
St. James City
767
Cape Coral
884
136
Ft. Myers Villas
131
82
RSW
Punta
Rassa
Iona
869
128
**San
Carlos
Park**
LEE
Sanibel
Sanibel I.
Toll
Ft. Myers
Beach
865
41
123
39
Estero
Lovers Key S.P.
Evergade
Wonder
Gardens
214
116
Bonita Springs
865
75
Delnor-Wiggins
Pass S.P.
846
111
Naples Park
951
Golden Gate
North Naples
31
107
Artis-Naples
Naples Zoo at Caribbean Gardens
7
105
Naples Municipal Arpt. (APF)
84
Naples
951
Naples Botanical Garden
8
E. Naples
**Naples
Manor**
8
951

2

GULF

OF

MEXICO

Marco Island
Marco Island
Marco I. Trolley Tours

Cape
Romano

3

4

DRY TORTUGAS
NATL. PARK
Fort
Jefferson

224
KEY WEST
N.W.R.
Stock Island
1
Key West
Naval
Air
Station
Key West
Marquesas
Keys

A   **B**   **C**

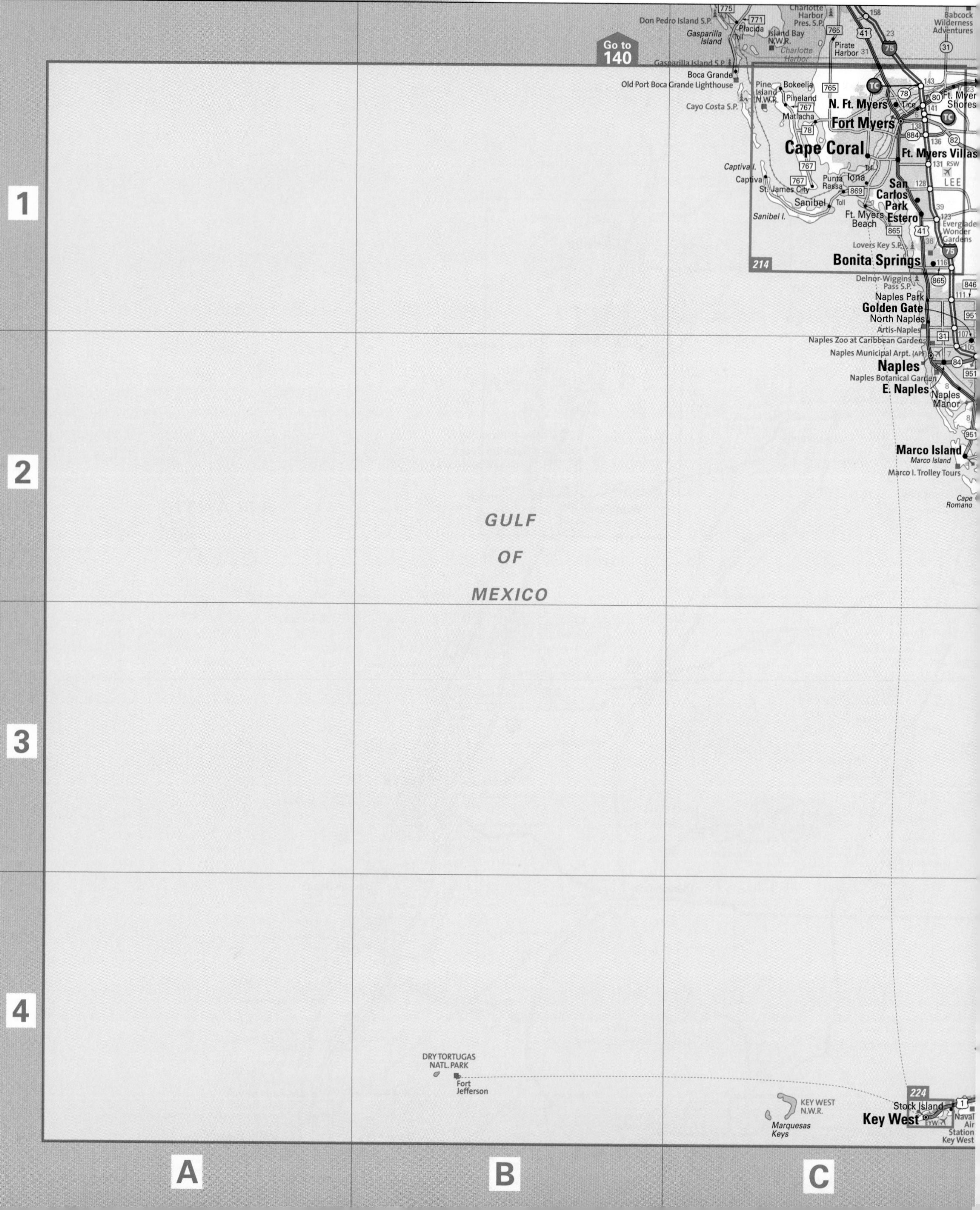

DRIVING DISTANCES IN MILES

	BELLE GLADE, FL	BOCA RATON, FL	FLAMINGO, FL	FORT LAUDERDALE, FL	FORT MYERS, FL	HOMESTEAD, FL	KEY LARGO, FL	KEY WEST, FL	MARATHON, FL	MIAMI, FL	NAPLES, FL	W. PALM BEACH, FL
FORT MYERS, FL	84	155	227	139		174	195	308	260	155	36	125
KEY WEST, FL	235	211	181	190	308	133	113		48	168	273	234
MIAMI, FL	83	44	87	23	155	34	55	168	120		121	67
W. PALM BEACH, FL	41	28	153	48	125	100	121	234	186	67	144	

SEE ALSO DISTANCE AND DRIVING TIME MAP ON PAGES 286–287

BONUS MAPS!

0 mi 5 10 15 20
0 km 5 10 15 20 25 30

One inch equals 9.85 miles
One centimeter equals 6.25 kilometers

Northeast Corridor / Washington DC

BONUS MAPS!

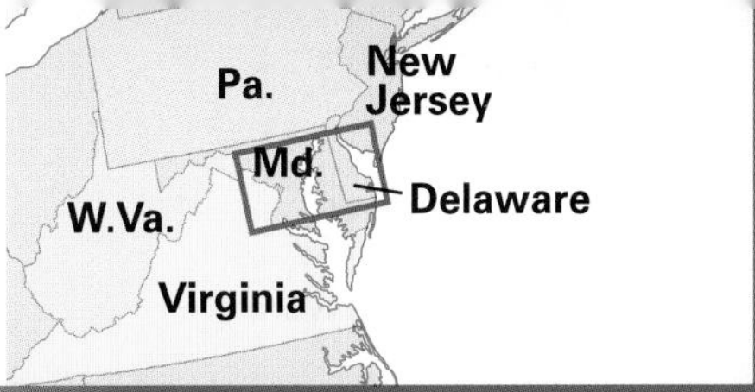

DRIVING DISTANCES IN MILES

	ANNAPOLIS, MD	BALTIMORE, MD	CAMBRIDGE, MD	DOVER, DE	ELKTON, MD	FREDERICK, MD	HAGERSTOWN, MD	LEESBURG, VA	MANASSAS, VA	REHOBOTH BEACH, DE	VINELAND, NJ	WASHINGTON, DC
BALTIMORE, MD	25		78	98	58	51	76	71	67	111	109	38
DOVER, DE	62	98	64		40	135	160	135	131	43	77	94
FREDERICK, MD	73	51	128	135	106		28	25	61	161	158	44
WASHINGTON, DC	31	38	87	94	94	44	70	38	31	120	145	

SEE ALSO DISTANCE AND DRIVING TIME MAP ON PAGES 286–287

BONUS MAPS!

0 mi 5 10 15 20
0 km 5 10 15 20 25 30
One inch equals 9.85 miles
One centimeter equals 6.25 kilometers

Northeast Corridor / Philadelphia PA

BONUS MAPS!

DRIVING DISTANCES IN MILES

	ALLENTOWN, PA	ATLANTIC CITY, NJ	ELKTON, MD	LANCASTER, PA	LONG BRANCH, NJ	NEW BRUNSWICK, NJ	NEW YORK, NY	PHILADELPHIA, PA	READING, PA	TOMS RIVER, NJ	TRENTON, NJ	WILMINGTON, DE
NEW YORK, NY	84	125	137	165	55	34		91	118	75	55	120
PHILADELPHIA, PA	63	62	50	79	77	55	91		63	58	34	30
TRENTON, NJ	66	77	88	105	53	22	55	34	89	48		68
WILMINGTON, DE	77	86	20	53	106	90	120	30	56	85	68	

SEE ALSO DISTANCE AND DRIVING TIME MAP ON PAGES 286–287

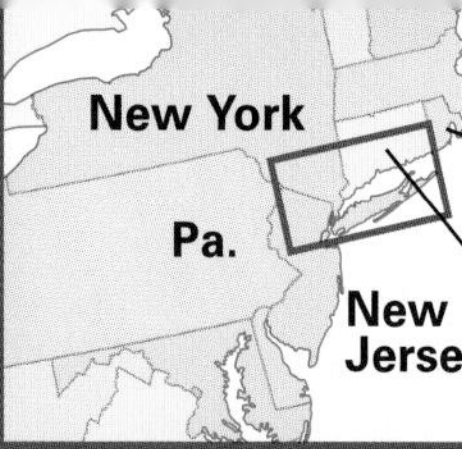

BONUS MAPS!

0 mi 5 10 15 20
0 km 5 10 15 20 25 30

One inch equals 9.85 miles
One centimeter equals 6.25 kilometers

Northeast Corridor / New York NY

DRIVING DISTANCES IN MILES	BRIDGEPORT, CT	DANBURY, CT	HARTFORD, CT	NEWARK, NJ	NEWBURGH, NY	NEW HAVEN, CT	NEW LONDON, CT	NEW YORK, NY	PATERSON, NJ	RIVERHEAD, NY	STAMFORD, CT	WATERBURY, CT
BRIDGEPORT, CT		31	56	69	73	19	64	60	71	115	21	33
NEWARK, NJ	69	79	125		66	88	134	11	18	88	48	108
NEW HAVEN, CT	19	35	39	88	78		46	78	89	133	40	30
NEW YORK, NY	60	69	115	11	56	78	124		16	78	38	99

SEE ALSO DISTANCE AND DRIVING TIME MAP ON PAGES 286–287

BONUS MAPS!

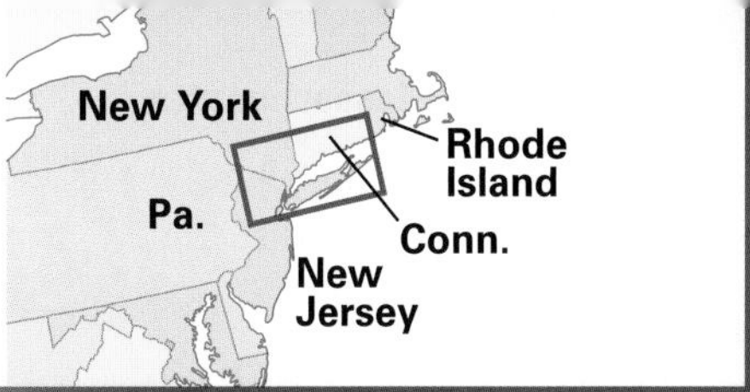

Massachusetts
Rhode Island
Connecticut

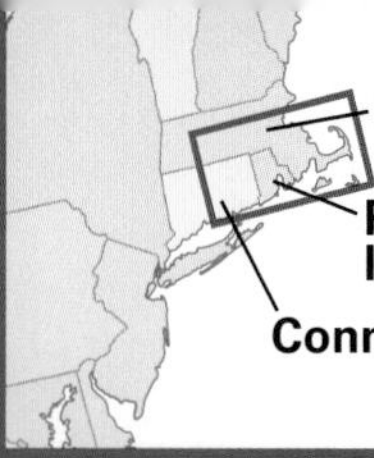

BONUS MAPS!

0 mi   5   10   15   20
0 km 5 10 15 20 25 30
One inch equals 9.85 miles
One centimeter equals 6.25 kilometers

Go to 94
Go to 95
Go to 94
Go to 149

Major cities and towns:

Greenfield, Gardner, Fitchburg, Leominster, Chelmsford, Amherst, Northampton, Easthampton, Holyoke, Chicopee, Westfield, West Springfield, Springfield, Agawam, Longmeadow, Worcester, Shrewsbury, Auburn, Southbridge, Webster, Framingham, Natick, Marlborough, Milford, Woonsocket, N. Attleboro, Central Falls, Pawtucket, North Providence, Providence, Johnson, E. Providence, Cranston, West Warwick, Warwick, Putnam, Willimantic, Storrs, Vernon, Manchester, East Hartford, West Hartford, Hartford, Wethersfield, Newington, New Britain, Southington, Middletown, Meriden, Wallingford, North Haven, Norwich, New London, Groton, Westerly, Wakefield, Pawcatuck, Mystic

WORCESTER

HAMPSHIRE

FRANKLIN

HAMPDEN

TOLLAND

WINDHAM

MIDDLESEX

KENT

WASHINGTON

MASS. / CONN.

R.I. / CONN.

MASS. TURNPIKE

DRIVING DISTANCES IN MILES	BOSTON, MA	GLOUCESTER, MA	HARTFORD, CT	HYANNIS, MA	NEW BEDFORD, MA	NEW LONDON, CT	NEWPORT, RI	PLYMOUTH, MA	PROVIDENCE, RI	PROVINCETOWN, MA	SPRINGFIELD, MA	WORCESTER, MA
BOSTON, MA		35	102	72	60	109	73	41	52	117	95	46
HARTFORD, CT	102	136		155	104	46	85	127	73	200	25	62
PROVIDENCE, RI	52	92	73	71	33	58	33	41		117	75	43
SPRINGFIELD, MA	95	129	25	148	127	71	111	120	75	193		55

SEE ALSO DISTANCE AND DRIVING TIME MAP ON PAGES 286–287

BONUS MAPS!

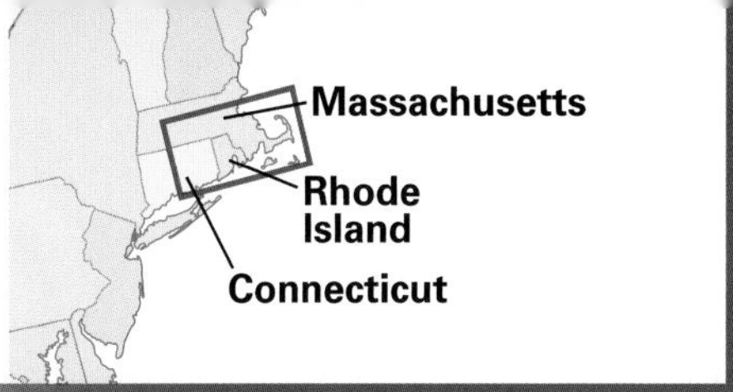

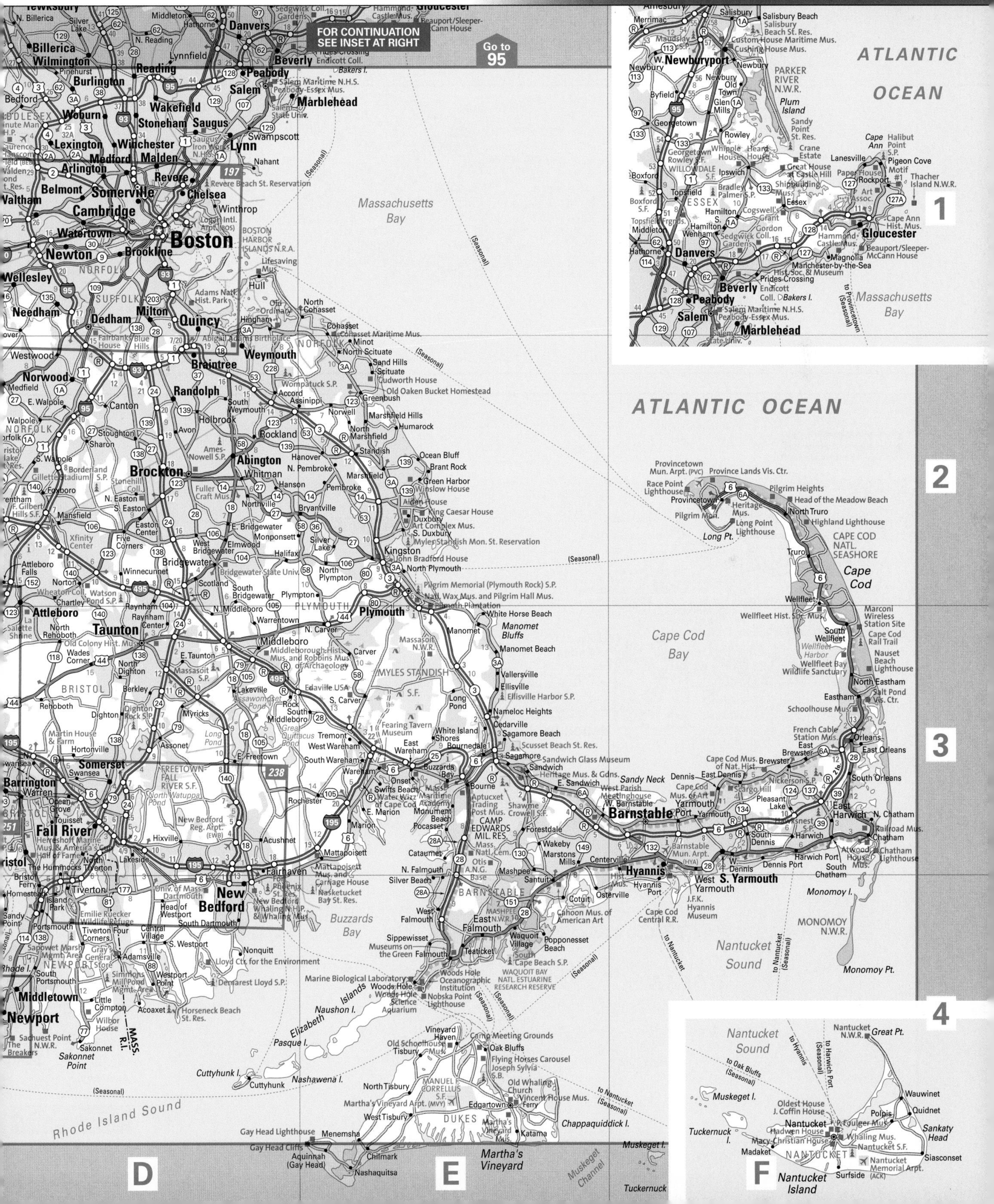

CANADA
UNITED STATES
MEXICO
HAWAII

0 mi   10   20   30   40
0 km 10   20   30   40   50   60
One inch equals 18.4 miles
One centimeter equals 11.7 kilometers

Map 1

PACIFIC OCEAN

Kaua'i

Hā'ena S.P.   Princeville   Kīlauea Pt.
              Hanalei   N.W.R.
NĀPALI COAST N.W.R.   Hā'ena   Kīlauea Pt.
STATE WILDERNESS PARK Hanalei Kalihiwai N.W.R.
  NĀPALI NAT. AREA RES.   560   Kīlauea
  HONO'O   Pu'u okila Lookout   56   Anahola
  NĀPALI NAT. AREA RES.   15
KU'IA NAT. AREA RES.   Wai'ale'ale MAKALEHA MTS.
PU'UKAPELE FOR. RES. (World's   KEALIA
Polihale S.P.   KŌKE'E Rainiest Spot) NONOU Keālia
Nohili Pt.   550   5,148   FOR. RES.
PACIFIC WAIMEA Waimea   Kawaikini 580   Kapa'a
MISSILE CANYON Canyon 5,243 Wailua River S.P. 56
RANGE   S.P. lookout   583 Hanamā'ulu
FACILITY Māna 12   Ahukini St. Rec. Pier
BARKING   550   Līhu'e   Lihu'e Arpt. (LIH)
SANDS 50   Waimea   50 Puhi 51
Kekaha   Kalāheo   Oma'o 58
  Pākālā Village 11 Kōloa   Hulē'ia
  Kaumakani Hanapēpē 'Ele'ele Kukui'ula N.W.R.
  Numila Lāwa'i Po'ipū
  Spouting KAUA'I
  Horn   COUNTY

FOR CONTINUATION SEE MAP BELOW

Map 2

FOR CONTINUATION SEE MAP ABOVE

O'ahu

Kahuku   James C. Campbell
Kawela Bay Pt.   N.W.R.
Waiale'e   Kahuku
Sunset Beach   Mālaekahana S.R.A.
Waimea   83   Lā'ie
Kawailoa Beach Polynesian Cultural Center
Pūpūkea   Hau'ula
Kawailoa   Pu'u Ka'inapua'a SACRED FALLS S.P.
Mokulē'ia   Hale'iwa 2,360 Punalu'u
Ka'ena Pt. S.P.   Kamo'oloa   83
Ka'ena Pt.   930   99   Kahana   Ka'a'awa
  21   Waialua   11   Whitmore   Ka'a'awa Beach Park
MĀKUA MIL. RES.   8   Village   KUALOA REG. PARK
  Wahiawā   Waikāne
CLOSED TO   H2   83   Kahalu'u
PUBLIC   Mililani   'Ahuimanu
  93   Town OʻAHU FOREST He'eia
Mākaha   NAVAL Pearl N.W.R. MARINE CORPS BASE HAWAII
Wai'anae   MAGAZINE City   750 Kāne'ohe
Mā'ili   PEARL HARBOR H3   Kailua
  93   99   Waipahu   63
Nānākuli   Honouliuli Natl.   Maunawili
Makakilo City   Mon. H1 76 Waimānalo
Honokai Hale NAVAL 61 Waimānalo Bay Park
  RES.   Waimānalo Beach
Kapolei   'Ewa Villages Sea Life Park
  'Ewa Beach Makapu'u Pt.
  Waimalu   72 Blow Hole
  HNL   Hanauma Bay St. Underwater Park
HONOLULU 219 H1
COUNTY   Honolulu

PACIFIC OCEAN

Map 3

Kaiwi Channel

Kalaupapa Airport (LUP)
Kahi'u KALAWAO
Pālā'au Pt. COUNTY
Pālā'au KALAUPAPA
'Īlio Pt. S.P. NATL. HIST. PARK Hīpuapua Hālawa Bay
Pāpōhaku Ho'olehua Kalaupapa Falls Hālawa
Beach Molokai 470 Pu'u 'Ali'i MOLOKA'I Cape Hālawa
  Airport (MKK) 480 Kualapu'u FOR. RES.
Maunaloa 460 Pu'u Nānā Pu'u 'Ali'i 'Ili'ili'ōpae Waialua
Molokai Ranch Nat. Area Res. 460 Kamakou Heiau
Headquarters Kaunakakai 4,970 Pūko'o
Lā'au Pt. 'Ualapu'e
  450 Kakaha'i 24 Honolua
  N.W.R. Kamalō Bay Nākālele Pt.
Moloka'i MAUI Honokōhau
  COUNTY Honokahua Haleki'i-Pihana
Kalohi Channel Honokōwai Kahakuloa Heiau St. Mon.
  Kā'anapali 30 Waihe'e 340 36
Shipwreck WEST MAUI Kahului
Beach NAT. AREA Waiehu Kahului
Keanapapa Pt. Garden of RES. Pu'u Kukui Waihe'e Bay
  the Gods Lāna'i 5,788 Wailuku
  Lahaina WEST MAUI Waikapū 380 Pu'unēnē
  Hist. Dist. FOR. RES. Pā'ia 311 Kealia Pond
Lāna'i City Keōmuku 16 30 Kāheki N.W.R.
  Village Olowalu Māʻalaea 310 Kahului
  440 Lāna'ihale Papawai Pt. Maui Māʻalaea Kīhei
Kaumalapau 3,370 Maui Bay Kama'ole
  Lāna'i Airport (LNY) 440 Ocean Ctr. 31 Kēōkea
Kaunolū Village Pu'u Pehe Pu'u Moa'ulanui 'Ulupalakua 37
  Palaoa Hulopo'e Beach Park 1,483 Mākena
  Pt. Lao o Kukui Mākena Beach
PACIFIC Kaho'olawe Mākena S.P.
OCEAN Lao o Lao o Molokini
  Kealaikahiki Kākā 'ĀHIHI-KĪNA'U
  Kealaikahiki Channel NAT. AREA 26
    Alalākeiki Channel RES.

FOR CONTINUATION SEE MAP AT RIGHT

Ni'ihau inset (Map 1 / left)

Lehua
Kīkepa Pt.
Keawanui Bay
Pu'uwai
Pāni'au
1,281
Pueo Pt.
Ni'ihau
(RESTRICTED PUBLIC ACCESS)
Kawaihoa

Kaulakahi Channel

Kaua'i Channel

A   B   C

1   2   3   4

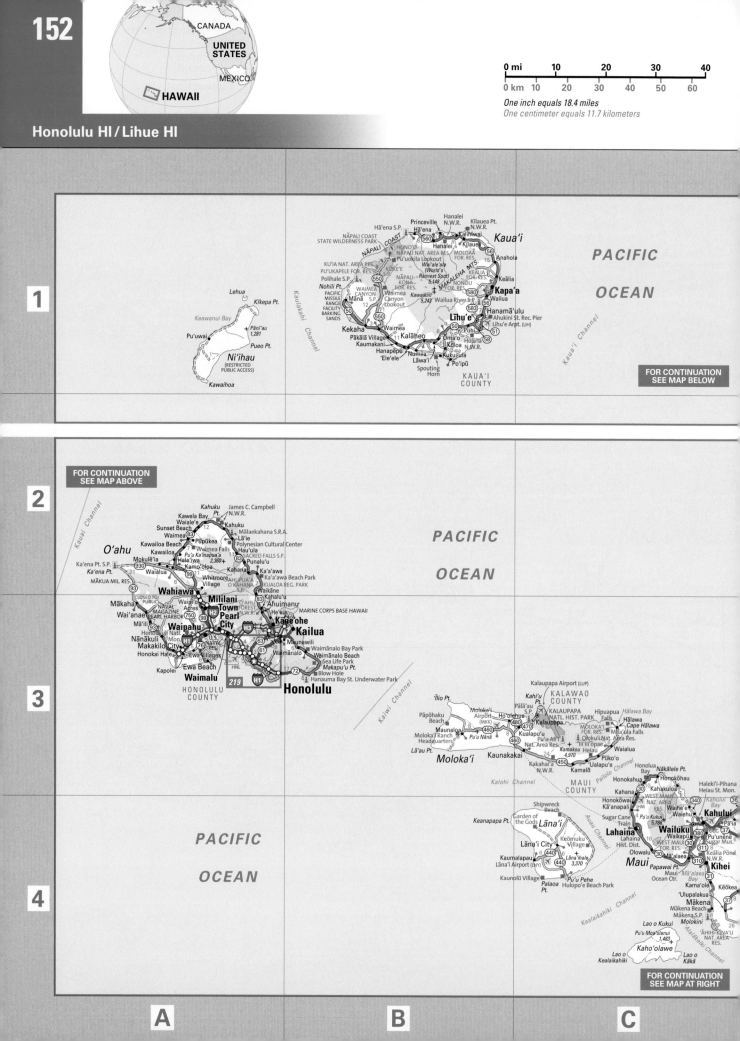

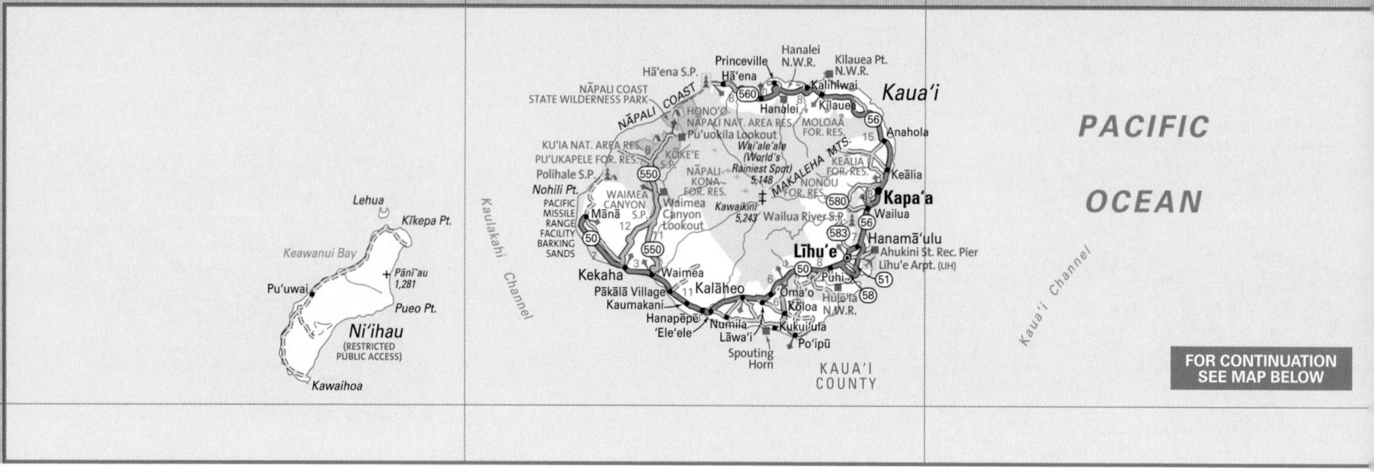

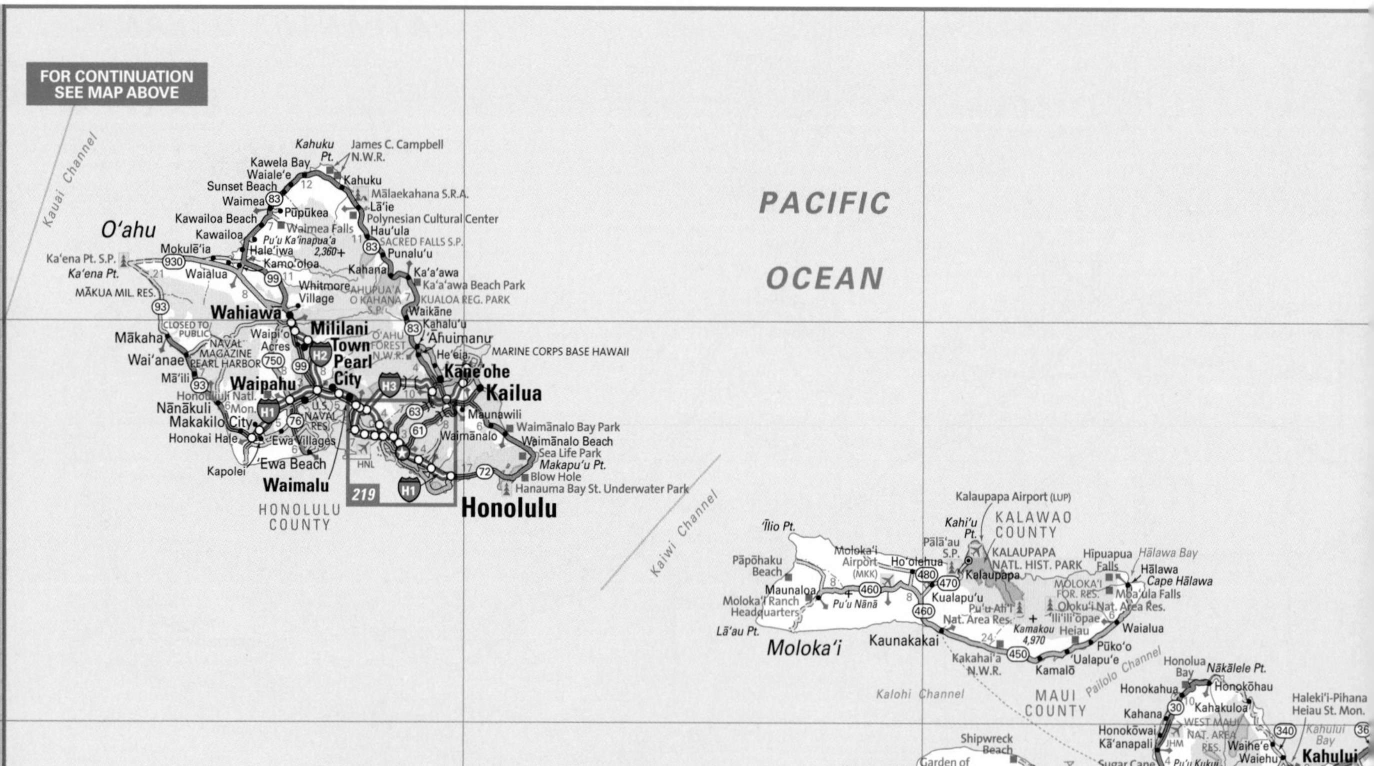

DRIVING DISTANCES IN MILES

	HĀNA	HILO	HONOLULU	HO'OLEHUA	KAHULUI	KAILUA	KAILUA-KONA	LAHAINA	LANAI CITY	LIHUE	WAHIAWĀ	WAIMEA
HILO	149*		217*	169*	121*	235*	88	142*	155*	319*	234*	54
HONOLULU	129*	217*		54*	101*	14	185*	92*	74*	102*	23	172*
KAHULUI	42	121*	101*	76*		119*	109*	23	57*	202*	118*	79*
LIHUE	230*	319*	102*	156*	202*	120*	285*	225*	176*		119*	174*

*DISTANCE INCLUDES AIR TRAVEL

SEE ALSO DISTANCE AND DRIVING TIME MAP ON PAGES 286–287

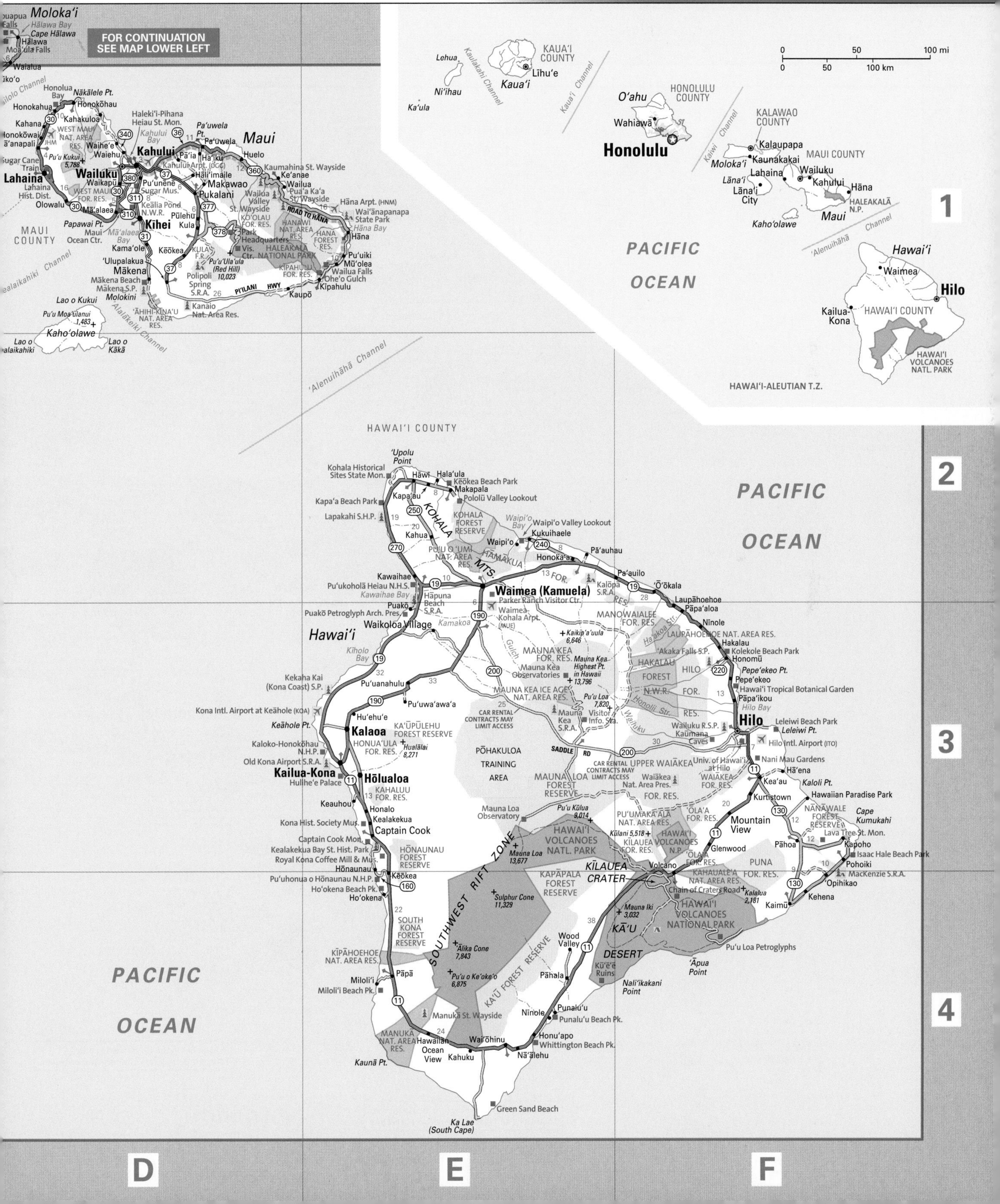

154

Alaska
Yukon Nunavut
N.W.T.
B.C.
Alta.

Anchorage AK / Fairbanks AK

0 mi   100   200
0 km   100   200   300

One inch equals 142 miles
One centimeter equals 90 kilometers

ARCTIC OCEAN

KOLYMA RANGE

CHUKCHI RANGE

CHUKCHI SEA

Mys Schmidta

Vankaren

Egvekinot

Anadyr

CHUKCHI PENINSULA

Gulf of Anadyr

Beringovsky

Cape Navarin

YAK RANGE

(Barrow) Utqiaġvik   Point Barrow
Wiley Post-Will Rogers   Iñupiat Heritage Ctr.
Memorial Airport (BRW)
Icy Cape   Wainwright
Alaska Maritime   Atqasuk   Smith Bay
N.W.R.   Teshekpuk L.   Harrison   RESTRICTED
Point   Bay   ACCESS   Prudhoe Bay
Lay   ARCTIC   PLAINS   Nuiqsut   Prudhoe Bay
Cape Lisburne   Colville   Deadhorse
ALASKA   Colville   Sagwon
MARITIME   Ikkillik   ARCTIC
N.W.R.   LISBURNE   DE LONG MTS.   11   N.W.R.
Point   PENINSULA   NOATAK NATL. PRES.   BROOKS   RANGE
Hope   Noatak   BAIRD MTS.   Simon Paneak   Arctic
Kivalina   KOBUK   Memorial   Anaktuvuk Pass   Village
CAPE KRUSENSTERN   VALLEY   Museum   GATES OF THE ARCTIC   PHILIP SMITH MTS.
NATL. MON.   Noorvik   NATL   N.P. AND PRESERVE
Cape Krusenstern   Kiana   PARK   ENDICOTT MTS.
Cape   Kotzebue   Ambler   Bettles   Coldfoot   Venetie
Espenberg   OTZ   Kobuk   YUKON FLATS
Shishmaref   Kotzebue   Selawik   Shungnak   Allakaket   N.W.R.   Fort Yukon
Emmytagyn   Sound   Deering   SELAWIK   KANUTI   Beaver   Dinjik Zhit
Uelen   Diomede   N.W.R.   KOYUKUK   N.W.R.   Emit Zit
Mechigmen   Wales   Taylor   BERING   N.W.R.   Hughes   Stevens   11
Nunyagmo   Brevig   LAND   Huslia   Koyukuk   Village   WHITE MTS.
Providenyia   Mission   BRIDGE   Buckland   Koyukuk   STEESE   NATL. REC.
Teller   NATL. PRES.   CONTINENTAL   TAL   Rampart   AREA   Chena
RUSSIA   Council   DIVIDE   Tanana   ELLIOT HWY   Chena River
Gambell   UNITED STATES   White   Koyuk   Koyukuk   Manley   Minto   Univ. of   6   S.R.A.
SEWARD PENINSULA   Mountain   Hot   Alaska   Fox   Chena Hot
KAMCHATKA TIME ZONE   Golovin   Nulato   NOWITNA   Springs   Fairbanks   Fairbanks
ALASKA TIME ZONE   OME   Elim   N.W.R.   Nenana   North Pole   Big De
Savoonga   Nome   Shaktoolik   Galena   Ruby   Anderson   FORT   ALASKA
St. Lawrence   Alaska   Koyukuk   GAL   WAINWRIGHT   3   Big Delta
Island   Maritime   Unalakleet   Yukon   MIL. RES.   Delta Junction
N.W.R.   IDITAROD TRAIL   Poorman   Lake   DENALI N.P.   FORT GREELY
Norton   UNK   Minchumina   AND PRESERVE   MIL. RES.
Sound   Stebbins   St. Michael   Innoko   Denali   Visitor   CLOSED IN
ALASKA MARITIME   Kaltag   Ophir   (Iditarod years)   (Mount McKinley)   Ctr.   WINTER   4
N.W.R.   Emmonak   INNOKO   Takotna   TCT   Highest Point in   Healy
Nunam Iqua   Kotlik   N.W.R.   MTS.   North America   Lignite   RICHARDSON
St. Matthew   Alakanuk   Grayling   McGrath   20,310 ft.   Cantwell   Denali   HWY
Island   Scammon   Anvik   Shageluk   Nikolai   Summit   81
ALASKA   Bay   Mountain   KSM   Denali S.P.   Paxson
MARITIME   Cape Romanzof   Village   St. Mary's   Iditarod   Chase   RANGE   Gakor
N.W.R.   Hooper Bay   Chevak   Pilot Station   Flat   KUSKOKWIM   Petersville   Lake
Marshall   Holy Cross   Crooked   Talkeetna   Louise   Gulkana
Newtok   Russian   Upper Kalskag   Creek   Sleetmute   Lime   Talkeetna Hist. Mus.   S.R.A.
Cape Mohican   Tununak   Mission   Lower Kalskag   Red Devil   Village   Independence Mine   Glennallen
Mekoryuk   Toksook   Yukon   Chuathbaluk   S.H.P.   GLENN   Copper
Nunivak   Bay   ANI   Aniak   Trapper Creek   HWY   Center
Island   Nightmute   Kasigluk   Akiachak   Skwentna   Willow   1
YUKON DELTA   Chefornak   Napakiak   Kwethluk   KILBUCK   Houston   Palmer   Mount Marcus
N.W.R.   Kipnuk   Napaskiak   Bethel   MTS.   Sutton   Baker   116
Eek   Tuntutuliak   Anchorage   Wasilla   13,176 ft.   Valdez
BERING SEA   Kwigillingok   Quinhagak   Captain Cook S.R.A.   LAKE   Nikiski   CHUGACH S.P.   VDZ
Kuskokwim   Redoubt Volcano   CLARK   Hope   Alyeska   Fairtlek
Bay   Goodnews Bay   TOGIAK   10,197 ft.   N.P. & PRES.   Kenai   Whittier   Cordova
St. Paul I.   Platinum   N.W.R.   Lake   Soldotna   Moose Pass
SNP   Togiak   AHKLUN MTS.   WOOD-   Clark   Nondalton   KENAI   1
St. Paul   Pribilof   Cape Newenham   TIKCHIK S.P.   Koliganek   Iliamna   N.W.R.   Seward
PRIBILOF ISLAND   Islands   Togiak Bay   New   Port   STERLING HWY   9
SEAL AND OTTER   Goodnews   Aleknagik   Stuyahok   Alsworth   Newhalen   Anchor Point   Alaska SeaLife Ctr.
PRES.   St. George   ALASKA   Manokotak   Ekwok   Iliamna L.   Homer   KENAI   twice-monthly service
PBV   St. George I.   MARITIME   Dillingham   Levelock   Kohanok   Anchor River S.R.A.   PEN.   June-Sept.
N.W.R.   Clarks   Kvichak   Seldovia   Caines Head
Togiak Bay   Point   South   Naknek   KENAI FJORDS   S.R.A.
Cape Constantine   Egegik   Naknek   King   Visitor   Montague
Bristol   Ten Thousand Smokes   Salmon   Center   Island
Bay   Becharof L.   KATMAI N.P.   Mount Katmai   Shuyak Island S.P.
Pilot Point   BECHAROF   AND PRES.   6,715 ft.   Afognak Island S.P.
N.W.R.   Valley of   Kodiak   Ft. Abercrombie
Port   ALASKA   Ten Thousand Smokes   Ouzinkie   St. Hist. Pk.   Gulf of
ALEUTIAN   ISLANDS   Heiden   PENINSULA   ANIAKCHAK   Karluk   Port Lions   ADQ
NATL. MON.   Kodiak   Kodiak
Seguam I.   Umnak   Dutch Harbor   & PRES.   Larsen Bay   KODIAK   Pasagshak S.R.S.
Island   Unalaska   Mount   Chignik   N.W.R.   Alutiiq   Island
ALASKA MARITIME   Nikolski   Fox   Akutan   IZEMBEK   Veniaminof   Lake   Akhiok   Mus.   Old Harbor
N.W.R.   Islands   Unalaska   N.W.R.   7,075 ft.   Chignik   KODIAK
Island   Cold   Perryville   Trinity Islands   N.W.R.
Krenitzen   Bay   King   ALASKA   Chirikof I.
False Pass   Cove   Unga   PENINSULA
Islands   Sanak I.   Island   Sand Point   N.W.R.
HAWAII-ALEUTIAN TIME ZONE   Unimak Island   Shumagin Islands   ALASKA
Aleutian WWII   CDB   MARITIME
Natl. Hist.   N.W.R.
Area   ALASKA MARITIME N.W.R.

BERING SEA

ARCTIC CIRCLE

INTERNATIONAL DATE LINE

Bering Strait

2

Bethel

Fairbank

Anchorage **Wasilla**

Kenai

Kodiak

Distances in the U.S. shown in miles.
Aux États-Unis, les distances sont en milles.

TRAVEL NOTE: Always inquire locally for road
conditions and closures, especially in winter.

PACIFIC OCEAN

Gulf of

1   **2**   **3**   **4**

A   **B**   **C**

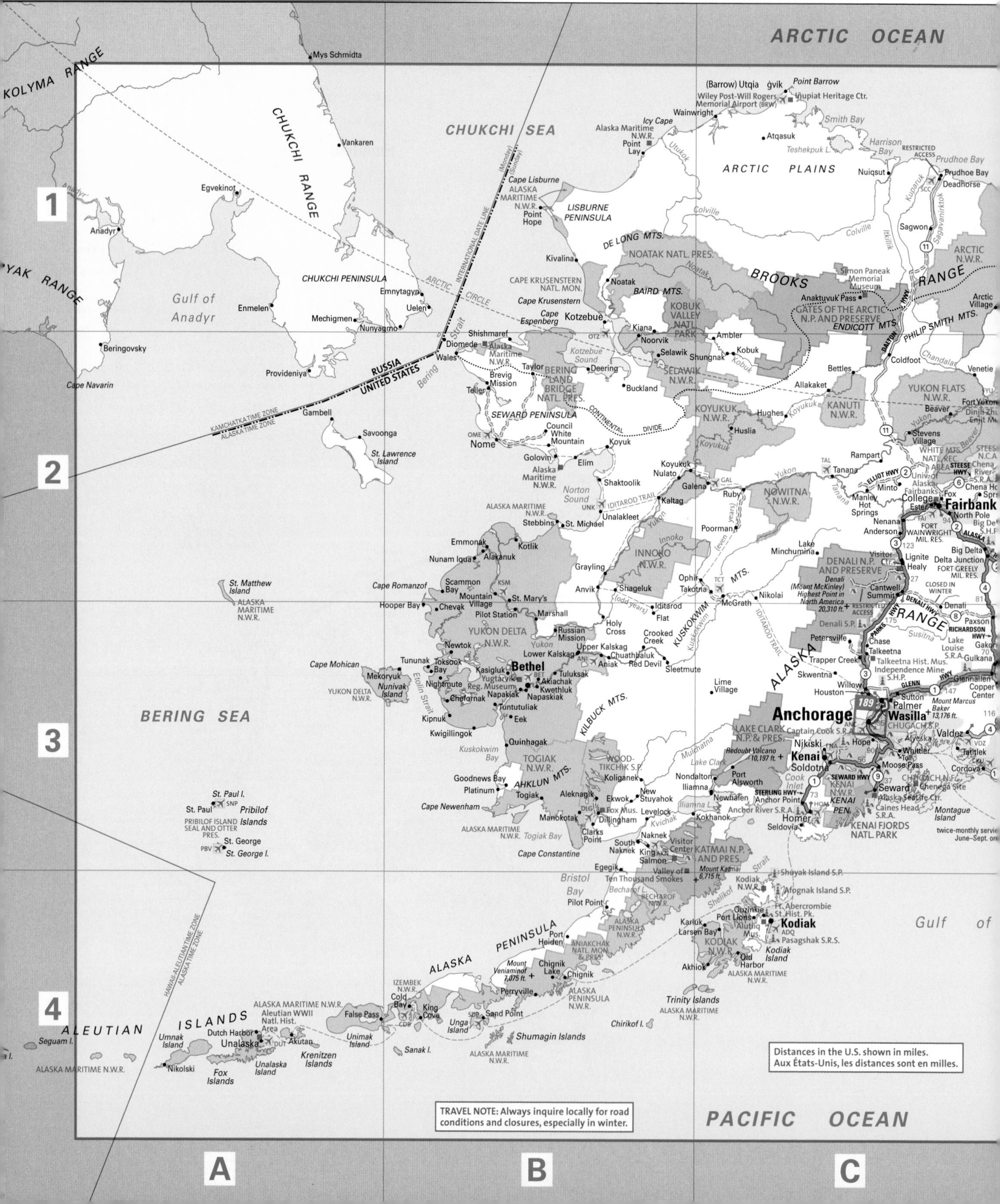

DRIVING DISTANCES IN MILES	ANCHORAGE, AK	DAWSON CREEK, BC	DENALI NP, AK	FAIRBANKS, AK	HOMER, AK	JUNEAU, AK	PRINCE GEORGE, BC	PRINCE RUPERT, BC	SKAGWAY, AK	TOK, AK	WHITEHORSE, YT	YELLOWKNIFE, NT
ANCHORAGE, AK		1516	275	378	225	841*	1679	1514	807	323	697	1844
DAWSON CREEK, BC	1516		1503	1400	1740	963*	224	625	862	1193	819	741
FAIRBANKS, AK	378	1400	103		603	726*	1564	1398	691	207	581	1729
WHITEHORSE, YT	697	819	684	581	921	211*	982	817	110	374		1147

*DISTANCE INCLUDES FERRY TRAVEL   SEE ALSO DISTANCE AND DRIVING TIME MAP ON PAGES 286–287

Alaska
Yukon   Nunavut
N.W.T.
B.C.
Alta.

The Alaska Marine Highway—with ferry service to
30 communities in Alaska, plus Bellingham WA and
Prince Rupert BC—is an All-American Road

Distances in Canada shown in kilometers.
Au Canada, les distances sont en kilomètres.

Go to 158
Go to 164
Go to 156
Go to 157

Alaska

British Columbia Alberta

0 mi · 20 · 40 · 60
0 km 20 · 40 · 60 · 80
One inch equals 40.3 miles/Un pouce équivaut à 40.3 milles
One centimeter equals 25.4 km/Un cm équivaut à 25.4 km

Go to 155

Mt. Pattullo 2,729 m
Meziadin Lake
Meziadin Junction
Stewart
Hyder
Meziadin Lake Provincial Park
Motase Pk. 2,411 m
Bear Lake
SUSTUT PROVINCIAL PARK
CONTINENTAL DIVIDE

CASSIAR HWY

Coffman Cove

Go to 155

TONGASS
Heceta I.
Noyes I.
Klawock
AKW
Thorne Bay
Craig
Hollis
Kasaan
Baker I.
Waterfall
Suemez I.
Hydaburg
Sukkwan
Dall I.
Forrester I.
Long I.
Cordova Bay
ALASKA MARITIME N.W.R.

Meyers Chuck
Cleveland Peninsula
Revillagigedo Island
Ketchikan
Saxman
Gravina Island
ANNETTE ISLAND IND. RES.
Metlakatla
KTN
NATIONAL
FOREST
Prince of Wales Island
Clarence Strait
Duke I.

MISTY
FIORDS
NATIONAL
MONUMENT

ALASKA B.C.

SWAN LAKE-KISPIOX RIVER PROVINCIAL PARK

BABINE RIVER CORRIDOR PROVINCIAL PARK

Kinskuch Lake
Lavender Pk. 2,323 m
Alice Arm
Cranberry Junction
Cutoff Mtn. 1,649 m
Mt. Weber 2,007 m
Kitwancool Lake
Shelagyote Pk. 2,466 m
Kisgegas Pk. 2,347 m
Centre Pk. 1,990 m
Mt. Lovell 1,995 m

New Aiyansh
Gitwinksihlkw
Nass Camp
NISGA'A MEMORIAL LAVA BED PROVINCIAL PARK
Gitanyow
Gitwangals Battle Hill N.H.S.
Kispiox
New Hazelton
'Ksan Hist. Village & Mus.
Hazelton
Seeley Lake Prov. Pk.
Ross Lake Prov. Pk.
South Hazelton
Mt. Thomlinson 2,591 m
Fort Babine
Nilkitkwa L.
Blunt Mtn. 2,286 m
Babine Lake-Smithers Landing Marine Prov. Park

Laxgalts'ap
Gingolx
Alder Pk. 2,220 m
Oscar Pk. 2,304 m
Lava Lake
Cedarvale
Kitwanga
Kitseguecla
Moricetown
Smithers Landing
Red Bluff Prov. Pk.
Granisle
Fulto Lake

Nass Bay
Nasoga Gulf

SEVEN SISTERS PROV. PARK
Rosswood
Smithers Arpt. (YYD)
BABINE MOUNTAINS PROV. PARK

KHUTZEYMATEEN GRIZZLY BEAR SANCTUARY
Mt. Kenney 2,073 m
Shames Mountain
Heritage Park Mus.
Usk
Kleanza Creek Prov. Park
Smithers
Telkwa
Ski Smithers
Tyhee Lake Provincial Park
Topley

U.S. CANADA
ALASKA TIME ZONE
PACIFIC TIME ZONE
Dixon Entrance

Chatham Sound
Lax Kw'alaams
Dundas I.
Exchamsiks River Prov. Pk.
Terrace
N.W. Reg. Arpt.-Terrace-Kitimat (YXT)
Lakelse Lake Prov. Park
Lakelse Lake
Eagle Pk. 2,093 m
Houston

Masset Arpt. (ZMT)
Masset
Graham Island
NAIKOON PROV. PARK
Ian Lake
Port Clements
Juskatla
Tlell
McBride
Mus. of Northern B.C.
Prudhomme Lake Prov. Park
Prince Rupert
Prince Rupert Arpt. (YPR)
North Pacific Hist. Fishing Village
Port Edward
Stephens I.
Diana Lake Prov. Park
Port Essington
Porcher Island
Oona River
Kitkatla
Khtada Lake
GITNADOIKS RIVER PROVINCIAL PARK
Kitimat
Kitamaat Village
Morice Lake
Kidprice Lake
Nadina Lake
Nanika Lake
Tagetochlain Lake
Noralee
Wistaria Prov. Park
Little Andrews Bay Marine Prov. Park
Tahtsa L.
Tweedsmuir Pk. 2,182 m
Ootsa Lake

Haida Gwaii (Queen Charlotte Islands)
Yakoun L.
Queen Charlotte
Moresby Camp
Qay'llnagaay Heritage Center
Skidegate
Alliford Bay
Sandspit
Sandspit Arpt. (YZP)

Hecate Strait

McCauley I.
Pitt Island
Banks Island
Klewnuggit Inlet Marine Prov. Park
Lowe Inlet Marine Prov. Park
Hawkesbury Island
Hartley Bay
Gribbell Island
Powell Pk. 2,012 m
Kemano
Troitsa L.
Whtesail Lake
Glatheli Lake
Michel Pk. 2,252 m
Eutsuk Lake
Oppy L.

COAST

Sewell Inlet
GWAII HAANAS NATIONAL PARK RESERVE & HAIDA HERITAGE SITE
Moresby Island

Gil I.
Campania I.
Anchor I.
Princess Royal Island
Green Inlet Marine Prov. Park
Mussel Inlet
TWEEDSMUIR NORTH PROVINCIAL PARK
Surel L.
Pondosy L.
Blanchet L.
HUCHSDUWACHSDU NUYEM JEES/KITLOPE HERITAGE CONSERVANCY
Sigutlat L.
Kimsquit

Aristazabal Island
Price I.
Klemtu
Swindle I.
Jackson Narrows Marine Prov. Park
Roderick I.
Pooley I.
Ocean Falls
Link Lake
Sir Alexander Mackenzie Provincial Park
Kalone Pk. 2,557 m
Thunder Mtn. 2,681 m
Firvale
QBC
Bella Coola
Hagensbor
Bella Bella
Shearwater
Oliver Cove Marine Prov. Pk.
Cascade Inlet
Dean Channel
King I.
Mt. Saugsta 2,972 m

MOUNTAINS

PACIFIC
OCEAN

Distances in Canada shown in kilometers.
Au Canada, les distances sont en kilomètres.

HAKAI LUXVBALIS CONSERVANCY
Goose I.
Namu
Hunter I.
Burke Channel
Rivers Inlet
Oweikeno Lake
Mt. Buxton 1,045 m
Calvert I.
Dowsons Landing
Good Hope
Draney Inlet
Penrose Island Marine Prov. Pk.
Rivers Inlet
Long L.
Smith Sound
Belize Inlet

Go to 162

LANZ & COX ISLANDS PROV. PK.
Lanz I.
Cox I.
CAPE SCOTT PROV. PARK
Hope I.
Nigei I.
To Port Hardy
God's Pocket Marine Prov. Pk.
Sullivan Bay
Seymour Inlet

A
B
C

1
2
3
4

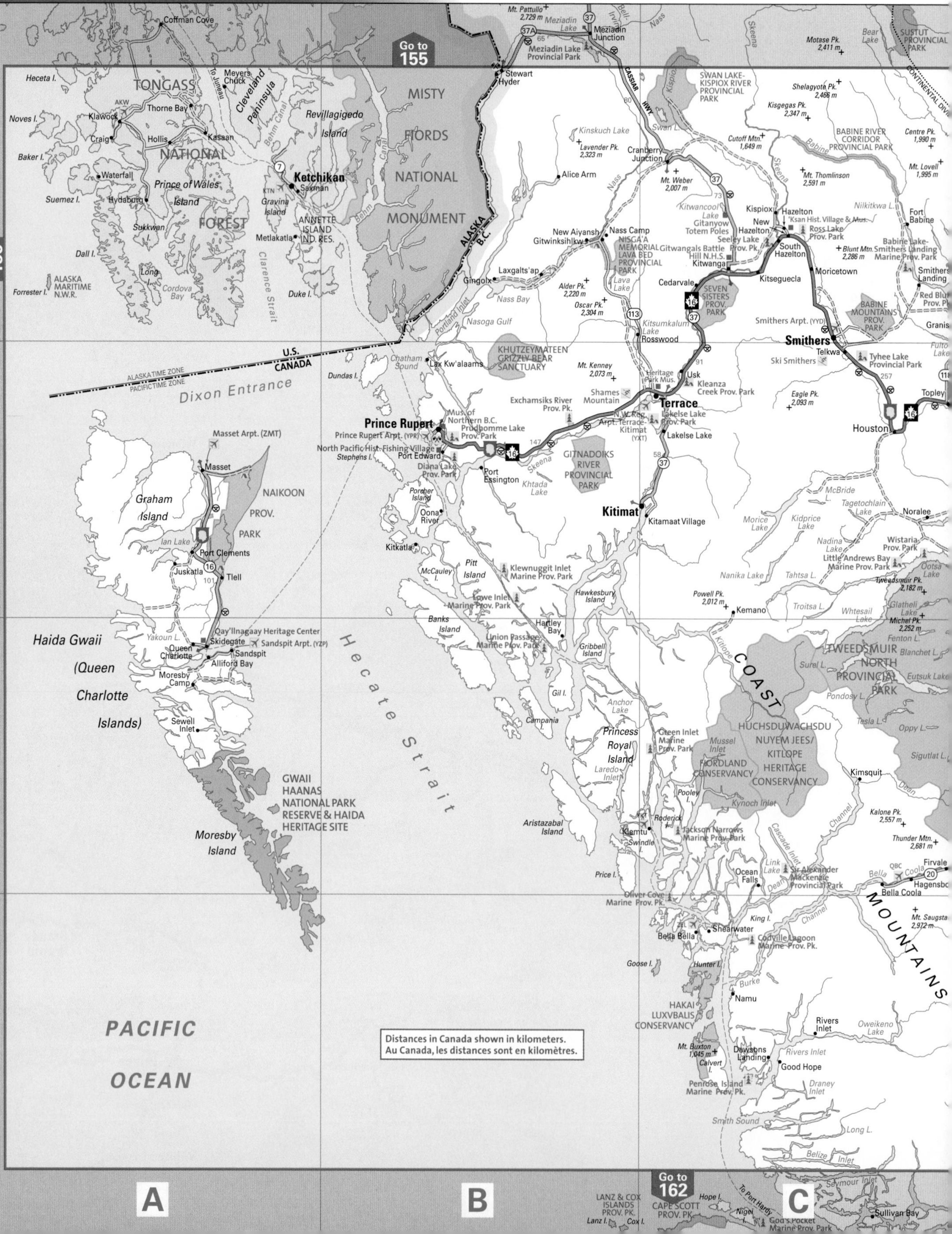

DRIVING DISTANCES IN KM / DISTANCES ROUTIÈRES EN KM

	DAWSON CREEK, BC	GRANDE PRAIRIE, AB	KAMLOOPS, BC	KITIMAT, BC	100 MILE HOUSE, BC	PRINCE GEORGE, BC	PRINCE RUPERT, BC	SMITHERS, BC	STEWART, BC	TERRACE, BC	VALEMOUNT, BC	WILLIAMS LAKE, BC
DAWSON CREEK, BC		124	931	1041	734	406	1130	777	1109	983	642	644
PRINCE GEORGE, BC	406	530	525	635	328		724	371	703	577	295	238
PRINCE RUPERT, BC	1130	1254	1249	205	1052	724		353	463	147	1019	962
WILLIAMS LAKE, BC	644	768	287	873	90	238	962	609	941	815	332	

SEE ALSO DISTANCE AND DRIVING TIME MAP ON PAGES 286–287 / VOIR AUSSI CARTE DES DISTANCES ET DES TEMPS DE PARCOURS PAGES 286–287

0 mi 20 40 60
0 km 20 40 60 80

One inch equals 40.3 miles/Un pouce équivaut à 40.3 milles
One centimeter equals 25.4 km/Un cm équivaut à 25.4 km

Grande Prairie AB / Jasper AB

DRIVING DISTANCES IN KM / DISTANCES ROUTIÈRES EN KM

	DAWSON CREEK, BC	EDMONTON, AB	FORT McMURRAY, AB	GRANDE PRAIRIE, AB	JASPER, AB	LLOYDMINSTER, AB/SK	MEADOW LAKE, SK	N. BATTLEFORD, SK	PEACE RIVER, AB	SLAVE LAKE, AB	VALEMOUNT, BC	WHITECOURT, AB
EDMONTON, AB	597		439	462	367	238	415	375	484	251	488	177
GRANDE PRAIRIE, AB	124	462	756		397	700	824	837	197	318	518	279
JASPER, AB	521	367	796	397		605	782	742	578	464	121	271
N. BATTLEFORD, SK	972	375	814	837	742	137	158		866	633	863	559

SEE ALSO DISTANCE AND DRIVING TIME MAP ON PAGES 286–287 / VOIR AUSSI CARTE DES DISTANCES ET DES TEMPS DE PARCOURS PAGES 286–287

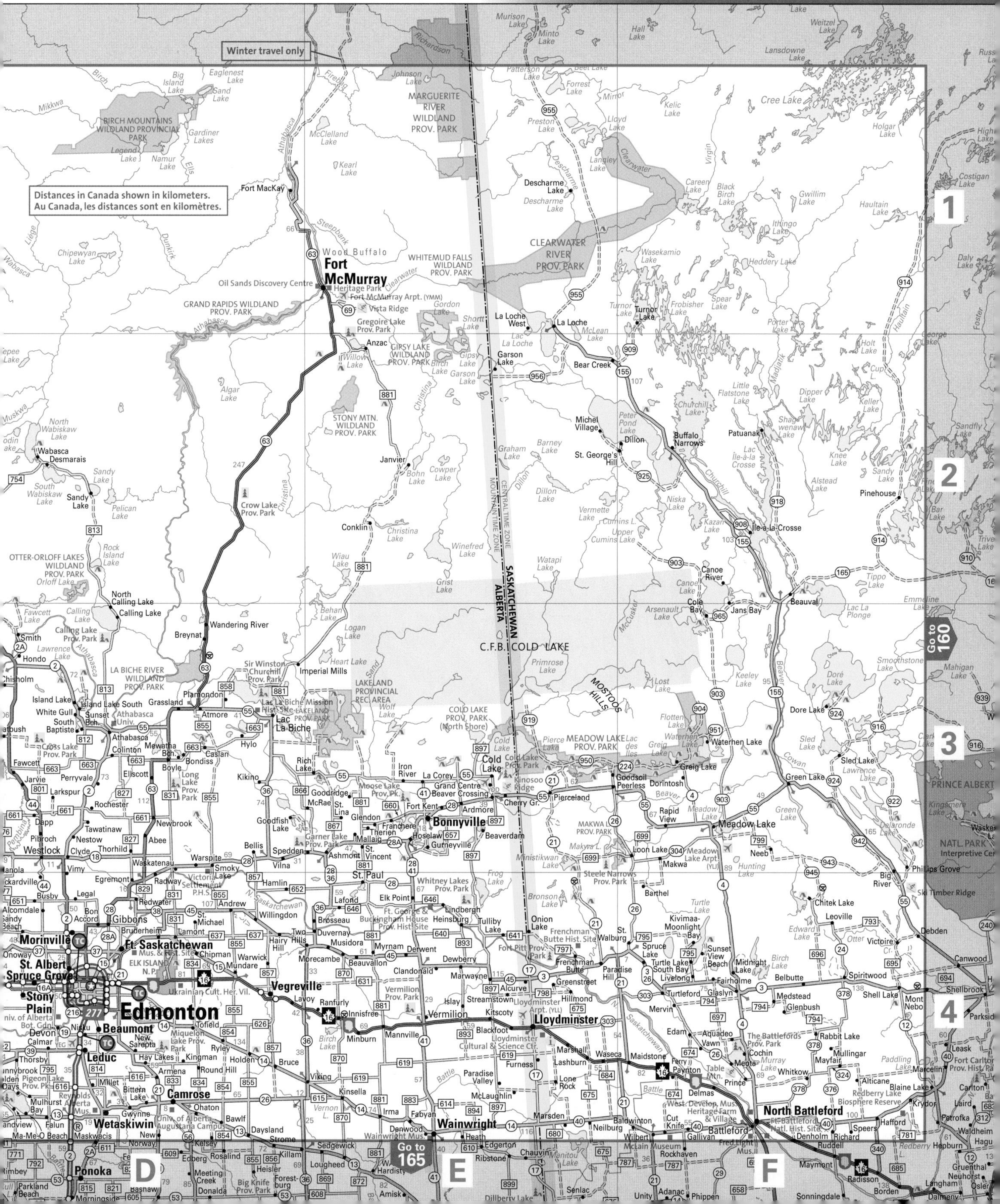

Alberta · Sask. · Manitoba · Ontario

0 mi 20 40 60
0 km 20 40 60 80
One inch equals 40.3 miles/Un pouce équivaut à 40.3 milles
One centimeter equals 25.4 km/Un cm équivaut à 25.4 km

MARGUERITE RIVER WILDLAND PROV. PARK

WHITEMUD FALLS WILDLAND PROV. PARK

CLEARWATER RIVER PROV. PARK

GYPSY LAKE WILDLAND PROV. PARK

Go to 159

ALBERTA / SASKATCHEWAN

C.F.B. COLD LAKE

COLD LAKE PROV. PARK (North Shore)

MEADOW LAKE PROV. PARK

MAKWA LAKE PROV. PARK

MOSTOOS HILLS

Steele Narrows Prov. Park

The Battlefords Prov. Park

Lloydminster

Go to 165

North Battleford

PRINCE ALBERT NATL. PARK

CLARENCE STEEPBANK LAKES PROV. WIDERNESS PARK

NARROW HILLS PROV. PARK

CANDLE LAKE PROV. PARK

LAC LA RONGE PROV. PARK

WAPANEKA HILLS

La Ronge

Missinipe

Stanley Mission

Southend Reindeer

Brabant Lake

Pelican Narrows

Deschambault Lake

Sandy Bay

Prince Albert

Melfort

Nipawin

Tisdale

WILDCAT HILL PROV. PARK

PASQUIA HILLS

Cumberland House Prov. Hist. Park

Go to 166

La Loche
La Loche West
Bear Creek
Buffalo Narrows
Ile-à-la-Crosse
Pinehouse
Beauval
Green Lake
Big River
Meadow Lake
Goodsoil
Pierceland
Canoe Lake
Cole Bay
Dore Lake
Waterhen Lake
Loon Lake
Turtleford
Spiritwood
Shellbrook
Canwood
Leask
Blaine Lake
Rosthern
Duck Lake
St. Louis
Birch Hills
Kinistino
Weldon
Star City
Carrot River
White Fox
Choiceland
Candle Lake
Montreal Lake
Weyakwin
Molanosa

DRIVING DISTANCES IN KM /
DISTANCES ROUTIÈRES EN KM

	FLIN FLON, MB	GILLAM, MB	GRAND RAPIDS, MB	LA LOCHE, SK	LA RONGE, SK	LYNN LAKE, MB	MEADOW LAKE, SK	NIPAWIN, SK	N. BATTLEFORD, SK	PRINCE ALBERT, SK	THE PAS, MB	THOMPSON, MB
FLIN FLON, MB		676	402	889	613	703	633	388	571	375	141	380
MEADOW LAKE, SK	633	1309	867	305	496	1336		399	158	258	569	1013
PRINCE ALBERT, SK	375	1051	609	514	238	1078	258	141	196		311	781
THOMPSON, MB	380	296	328	1269	697	323	1013	640	977	781	470	

SEE ALSO DISTANCE AND DRIVING TIME MAP ON PAGES 286–287 / VOIR AUSSI CARTE DES DISTANCES ET DES TEMPS DE PARCOURS PAGES 286–287

Alberta
Sask. Manitoba
Ontario

Distances in Canada shown in kilometers.
Au Canada, les distances sont en kilomètres.

Go to 167

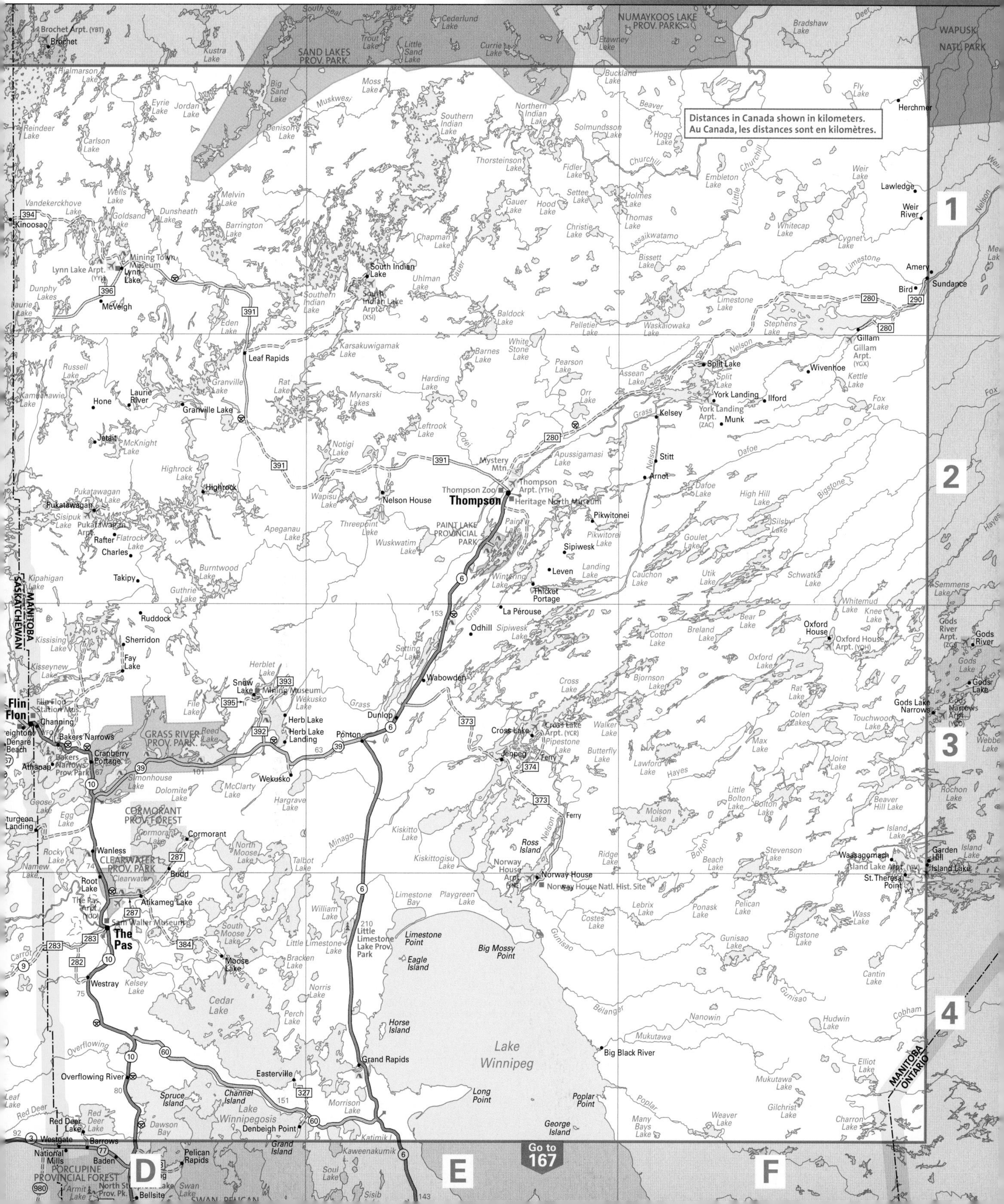

British Columbia
Washington

0 mi 20 40
0 km 20 40 60
One inch equals 25.4 miles/Un pouce équivaut à 25.4 milles
One cm equals 16.1 km/Un cm équivaut à 16.1 km

Go to 156

COAST MOUNTAINS

Long Lake
Belize Inlet
Seymour Inlet
MacKenzie Sound
Kingcome Inlet
Mt. Everard 2,182 m
Costello Peak 1,713 m
Mt. Rodell 2,187 m
Mt. Cridge 1,795 m
Mt. Grenville 3,109 m
Mt. Raleigh 3,078 m
Good Hope Mtn. 3,240 m
Mt. Queen Bess 3,298 m
Chilko Lake
Mt. Tatlow 3,066 m
Yohetta Lake
TS'IL-OS PROV. PARK
Monmouth Mtn. 3,194 m
BISHOP RIVER PROV. PK.
Toba Inlet
Mt. Gilbert 3,109 m
Toba 2,896 m
HOMATHKO RIVER - TATLAYOKO PROTECTED AREA
Homathko
Southgate
Bishop
Superb Mtn. 2,469 m
Mt. Smith 2,299 m
UPPER LILLOOET PROV. PARK
CLENDINNING PROV. PARK
Granite Pk. 2,048 m
Bute Inlet

Hope I.
Nigei I.
William Lake
CAPE SCOTT PROV. PARK
God's Pocket Marine Prov. Pk.
Queen Charlotte Strait
Port Hardy
Bear Cove
Holberg
Port Hardy Arpt. (YZT)
Coal Harbour
Holberg Inlet
Winter Harbour
Quatsino Prov. Park
Quatsino
Marble River Prov. Park
Neroutsos Inlet
Port Alice
Quatsino Sound
Lawn Point Prov. Park
Brooks Bay
BROOKS PENINSULA PROV. PARK
Big Bunsby Marine Prov. Pk.
Checleset Bay
Kyuquot
Kyuquot Sound
Rugged Point Marine Prov. Park
Catala Island Marine Prov. Pk.
Esperanza Inlet
Nuchatlitz Prov. Park
Nootka Island
Nootka Sound
Yuquot

Sullivan Bay
Broughton Archipelago Marine Prov. Park
Broughton I.
Cormorant Channel Marine Prov. Pk.
Simoom Sound
Gilford I.
Tribune Ch.
Thompson Sound
Knight Inlet
Mt. Kennedy 2,028 m
Loughborough Inlet
Phillips Arm

Sointula
Malcolm I.
Alert Bay
Port McNeill
Telegraph Cove
Beaver Cove
U'Mista Cult. Ctr.
Kokish
Nimpkish Lake
Minstrel Island
Port Neville
Turnour I.
Cracroft Is.
Call Inlet
Hardwicke I.
Hardwicke Island
W. Thurlow I.
Blind Channel
Big Bay
Stuart Island
Sonora I.
Walsh Cove Prov. Park
Princess Louisa Marine Prov. Pk.

Nimpkish Lake Prov. Park
Bonanza Lake
Sayward
Thurston Bay Marine Prov. Park
Rock Bay
Rock Bay Marine Prov. Park
Octopus Is. Marine Prov. Park
Surge Narrows Prov. Park
Surge Narrows
Ha'thayim Marine Prov. Pk.
Refuge Cove
DESOLATION SOUND MARINE PROV. PK.

Woss
Mt. Cain
SCHOEN LAKE PROV. PARK
Victoria Pk. 2,163 m
VANCOUVER ISLAND
Granite
Quadra I.
Maud I. Prov. Park
Morton Lake Prov. Park
Loveland Bay Prov. Park
Elk Falls Prov. Park
Mus. at Campbell River
Heriot Bay
Mansons Land. Prov. Park
Whaletown
Mansons Landing
Okeover Arm Prov. Park
Inland Lake Prov. Park
Jervis Inlet
Harmony Islands Marine Prov. Park

Tahsish-Kwois Prov. Park
Tahsish Inlet
Woss Lake
Woss Lake Prov. Park
Vernon Lake
Zeballos
Tahsis
Campbell River
Campbell River Arpt. (YBL)
Quathiaski Cove
Kwagiulth Mus.
Smelt Bay Prov. Park
Lund
Powell River
Powell River Arpt. (YPW)
Westview
Saltery Bay
Saltery Bay Prov. Park
Earls Cove
Skookumchuck Narrows Prov. Park
Nelson I.
Garden Bay

Upper Campbell Lake
STRATHCONA PROV. PARK
Butte Lake
Mt. Washington
Gold River
Miracle Beach
Saratoga Beach
Black Creek
Miracle Beach Prov. Park
Merville
Little River
Lazo
Comox Valley Arpt. (YCB)
Van Anda
Blubber Bay
Texada I.
Gillies Bay
Seche
Earls Cove
Irvines Landing
Madeira Park
Halfmoon Bay
Simson Prov. Park
Squitty Bay Prov. Park

Bligh Island Marine Prov. Pk.
Muchalet Inlet
Courtenay
Comox
Royston
Cumberland
Comox L.
Union Bay
Sandy I.
Denman I.
Fillongley Prov. Park
Hornby I.
Jedediah Island Marine Prov. Park
Lasqueti I.
False Bay
Sargeant Bay Prov. Park
Robert Creek Prov. Park

Hesquiat Lake Prov. Park
Sydney Inlet Prov. Park
Boat Basin
Stewardson Inlet
Sulphur Passage Prov. Park
Herbert Inlet
Bedwell Sound
Great Central L.
Buckley Bay
Fanny Bay
Rosewall Creek Prov. Park
Bowser
Horne Lake Caves Prov. Park
Stamp River Prov. Park
MacMillan Prov. Park
Qualicum Beach
French Creek
Parksville
Rathtrevor Beach Prov. Park
Nanoose Bay
Gabriola Island
Lantzville

HESQUIAT PEN. PROV. PARK
Maquinna Marine Prov. Park
Flores Island Prov. Park
Gibson Marine Prov. Pk.
Flores I.
Ahousat
Clayoquot Sound
Vargas Island Prov. Park
Whale Centre Museum
Tofino
Epper Passage Prov. Park
Dawley Passage Prov. Park
Tofino Arpt. (YAZ)
Clayoquot Plateau Prov. Park
Sproat Lake
Clayoquot Arm Prov. Park
Taylor Arm Prov. Park
Sproat L.
Sproat Lake Prov. Park
Port Alberni
Coombs
Errington
Little Qualicum
Englishman River Falls Prov. Park
Nanaimo
Cedar

Kennedy L.
Alberni Valley Falls Prov. Park
Alberni Inlet
Nahmint
PACIFIC RIM NATIONAL PARK RESERVE (Long Beach Unit)
Ucluelet
Kildonan
Green Cove
Cassidy
Ladysmith
Nanaimo Arpt. (YCD)
Thet

PACIFIC OCEAN

Barkley Sound
PACIFIC RIM NATIONAL PARK RESERVE (Broken Group Islands Unit)
Bamfield
Sarita
Hitchie Creek Prov. Park
Cowichan Lake
Youbou
Chemainus
Quw'utsun' Cult. Ctr.
N. Cowichan
Gordon Bay Prov. Park
Honeymoon Bay
Mesachie L.
Lake Cowichan
Duncan
Glenora
Cowichan River Prov. Park

Nitinat Lake
Clo-oose
PACIFIC RIM NATIONAL PARK RESERVE (West Coast Trail Unit)
CARMANAH WALBRAN PROV. PARK
RESTRICTED ROAD
Port Renfrew
Sooke Lake

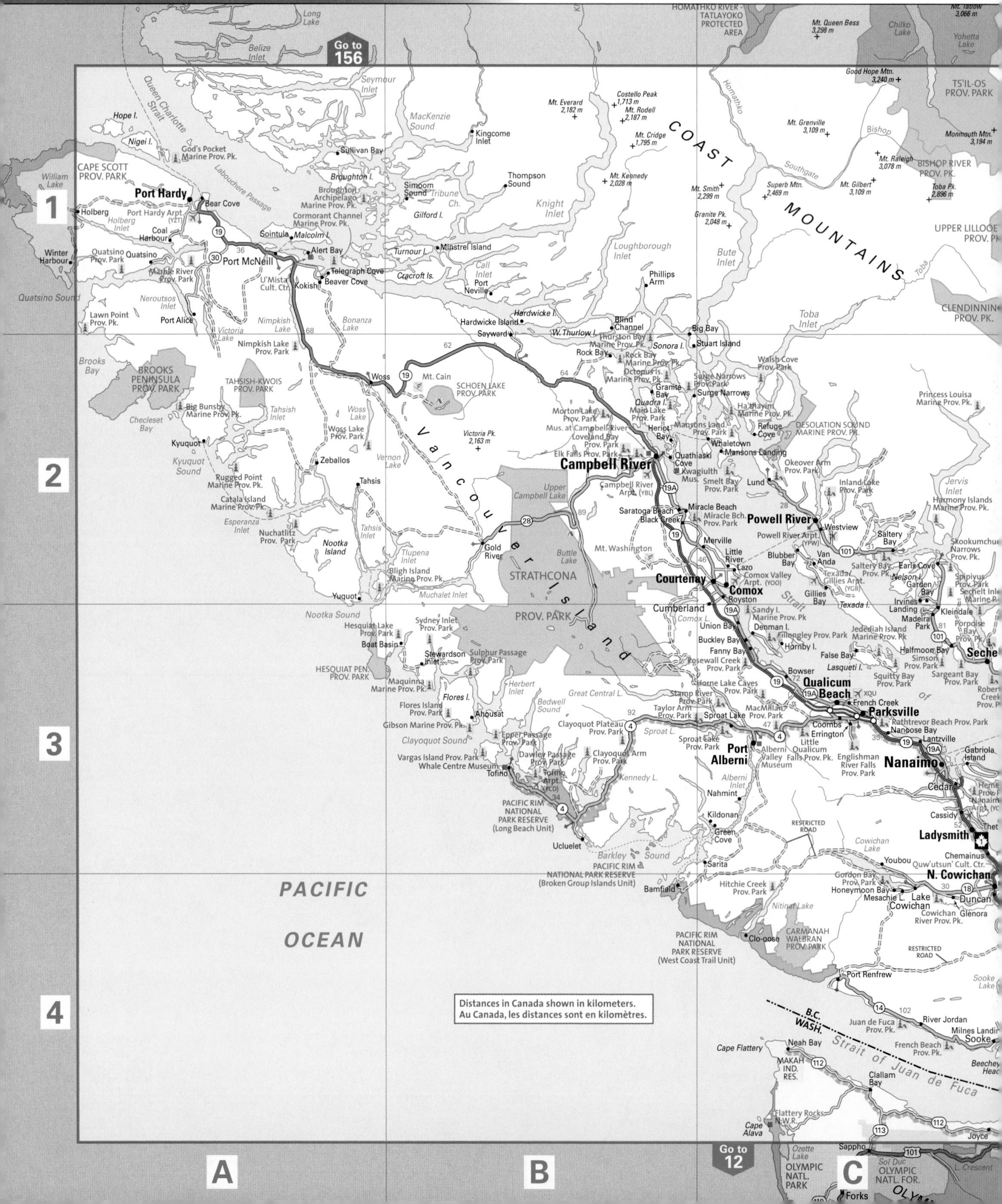

Distances in Canada shown in kilometers.
Au Canada, les distances sont en kilomètres.

B.C. WASH.
Strait of Juan de Fuca
River Jordan
Milnes Landing
Sooke
Cape Flattery
Neah Bay
French Beach Prov. Park
Beechey Head
MAKAH IND. RES.
Clallam Bay
Flattery Rocks N.W.R.
Cape Alava
Ozette Lake
Cape Alava
Sappho
Joyce
OLYMPIC NATL. PARK
OLYMPIC NATL. FOR.
Forks

Go to 12

DRIVING DISTANCES IN KM / DISTANCES ROUTIÈRES EN KM

	CAMPBELL RIVER, BC	KAMLOOPS, BC	KELOWNA, BC	MERRITT, BC	NANAIMO, BC	OSOYOOS, BC	PORT ALBERNI, BC	PORT HARDY, BC	SALMON ARM, BC	VANCOUVER, BC	VICTORIA, BC	WHISTLER, BC
KAMLOOPS, BC	512		163	87	363	231	441	750	108	355	393	475
NANAIMO, BC	153	363	403	279		404	82	391	471	23	113	104
VANCOUVER, BC	172	355	395	271	23	396	101	410	463		69	123
VICTORIA, BC	266	393	433	309	113	434	195	504	501	69		192

SEE ALSO DISTANCE AND DRIVING TIME MAP ON PAGES 286–287 / VOIR AUSSI CARTE DES DISTANCES ET DES TEMPS DE PARCOURS PAGES 286–287

0 mi 20 40 60
0 km 20 40 60 80

One inch equals 40.3 miles/Un pouce équivaut à 40.3 milles
One centimeter equals 25.4 km/Un cm équivaut à 25.4 km

Calgary AB / Banff AB

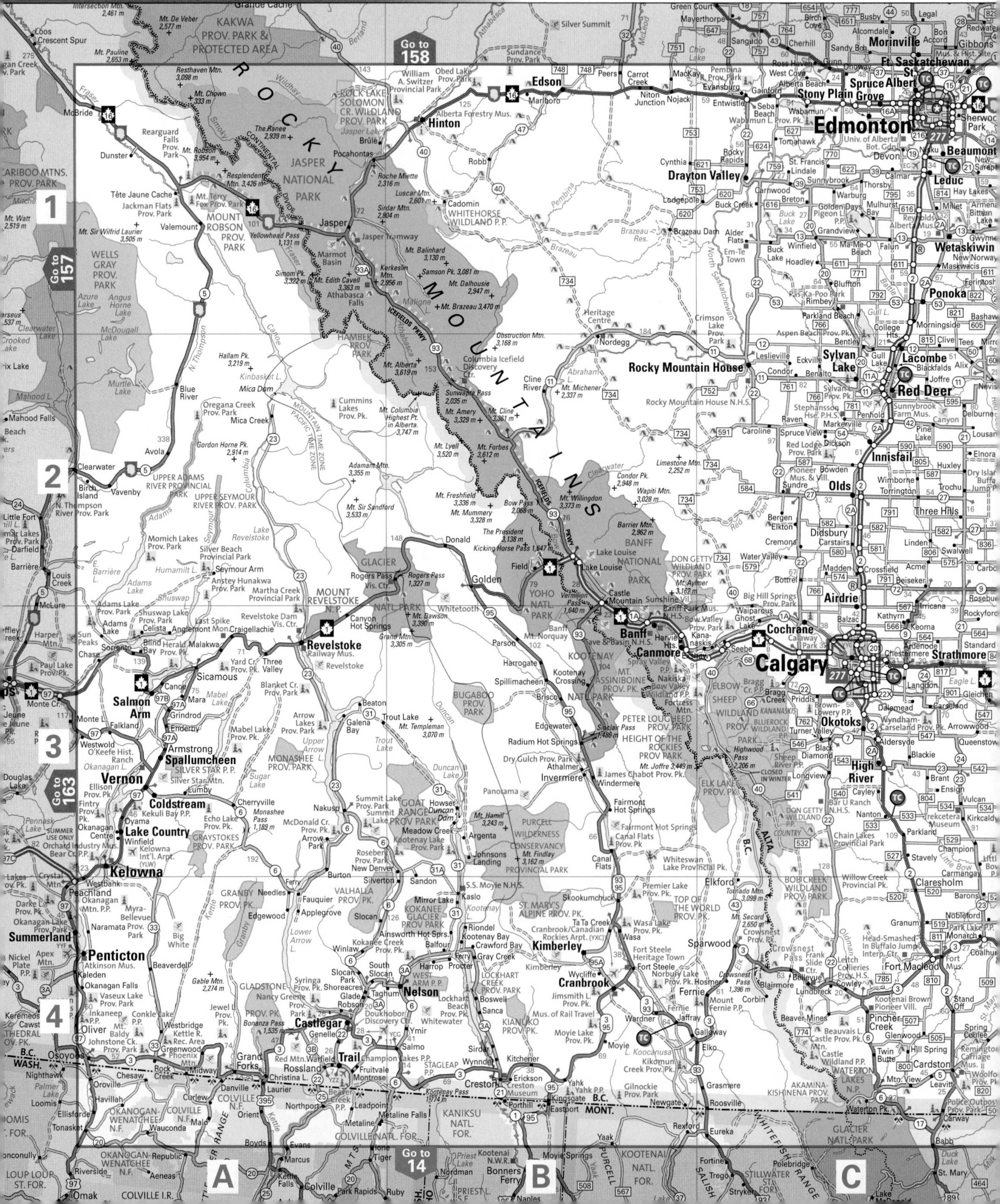

DRIVING DISTANCES IN KM / DISTANCES ROUTIÈRES EN KM

	BANFF, AB	CALGARY, AB	CRANBROOK, BC	EDMONTON, AB	JASPER, AB	KELOWNA, BC	LETHBRIDGE, AB	LLOYDMINSTER AB/SK	MEDICINE HAT, AB	RED DEER, AB	SASKATOON, SK	SWIFT CURRENT, SK
CALGARY, AB	128		383	296	396	638	216	534	285	145	620	503
EDMONTON, AB	412	296	679		367	934	512	238	579	150	513	676
LETHBRIDGE, AB	344	216	306	512	612	809		605	164	360	650	382
SASKATOON, SK	748	620	969	513	880	1255	650	275	486	639		267

SEE ALSO DISTANCE AND DRIVING TIME MAP ON PAGES 286–287 / VOIR AUSSI CARTE DES DISTANCES ET DES TEMPS DE PARCOURS PAGES 286–287

Distances in Canada shown in kilometers.
Au Canada, les distances sont en kilomètres.

Go to 159
Go to 160
Go to 166
Go to 15
Go to 16

0 mi 20 40 60
0 km 20 40 60 80

One inch equals 40.3 miles/Un pouce équivaut à 40.3 milles
One centimeter equals 25.4 km/Un cm équivaut à 25.4 km

Saskatoon SK / Regina SK

Sask. Manitoba
Ontario
Montana N.D. Minn.

DRIVING DISTANCES IN KM / DISTANCES ROUTIÈRES EN KM	BRANDON, MB	DAUPHIN, MB	GRAND RAPIDS, MB	MOOSE JAW, SK	PORTAGE LA PRAIRIE, MB	PRINCE ALBERT, SK	REGINA, SK	SASKATOON, SK	SWIFT CURRENT, SK	THE PAS, MB	WINNIPEG, MB	YORKTON, SK
BRANDON, MB		166	525	448	134	745	377	639	618	570	216	270
REGINA, SK	377	366	787	68	511	368		261	241	557	593	195
SASKATOON, SK	639	502	689	224	691	141	261		267	578	773	331
WINNIPEG, MB	216	322	430	664	82	819	593	773	834	611		442

SEE ALSO DISTANCE AND DRIVING TIME MAP ON PAGES 286–287 / VOIR AUSSI CARTE DES DISTANCES ET DES TEMPS DE PARCOURS PAGES 286–287

Distances in Canada shown in kilometers.
Au Canada, les distances sont en kilomètres.

0 mi 20 40 60
0 km 20 40 60 80
One inch equals 40.3 miles/Un pouce équivaut à 40.3 milles
One centimeter equals 25.4 km/Un cm équivaut à 25.4 km

Kenora ON / Fort Frances ON

DRIVING DISTANCES IN KM / DISTANCES ROUTIÈRES EN KM

	DRYDEN, ON	FORT FRANCES, ON	GERALDTON, ON	GRAND FORKS, ND	HEARST, ON	KENORA, ON	MARATHON, ON	NIPIGON, ON	STEINBACH, MB	THUNDER BAY, ON	WAWA, ON	WINNIPEG, MB
FORT FRANCES, ON	190		627	315	845	215	641	445	310	335	805	420
KENORA, ON	140	215	772	429	990		786	585	184	480	950	205
THUNDER BAY, ON	340	335	292	650	510	480	306	110	664		470	685
WINNIPEG, MB	345	420	977	228	1195	205	991	790	55	685	1155	

SEE ALSO DISTANCE AND DRIVING TIME MAP ON PAGES 286–287 / VOIR AUSSI CARTE DES DISTANCES ET DES TEMPS DE PARCOURS PAGES 286–287

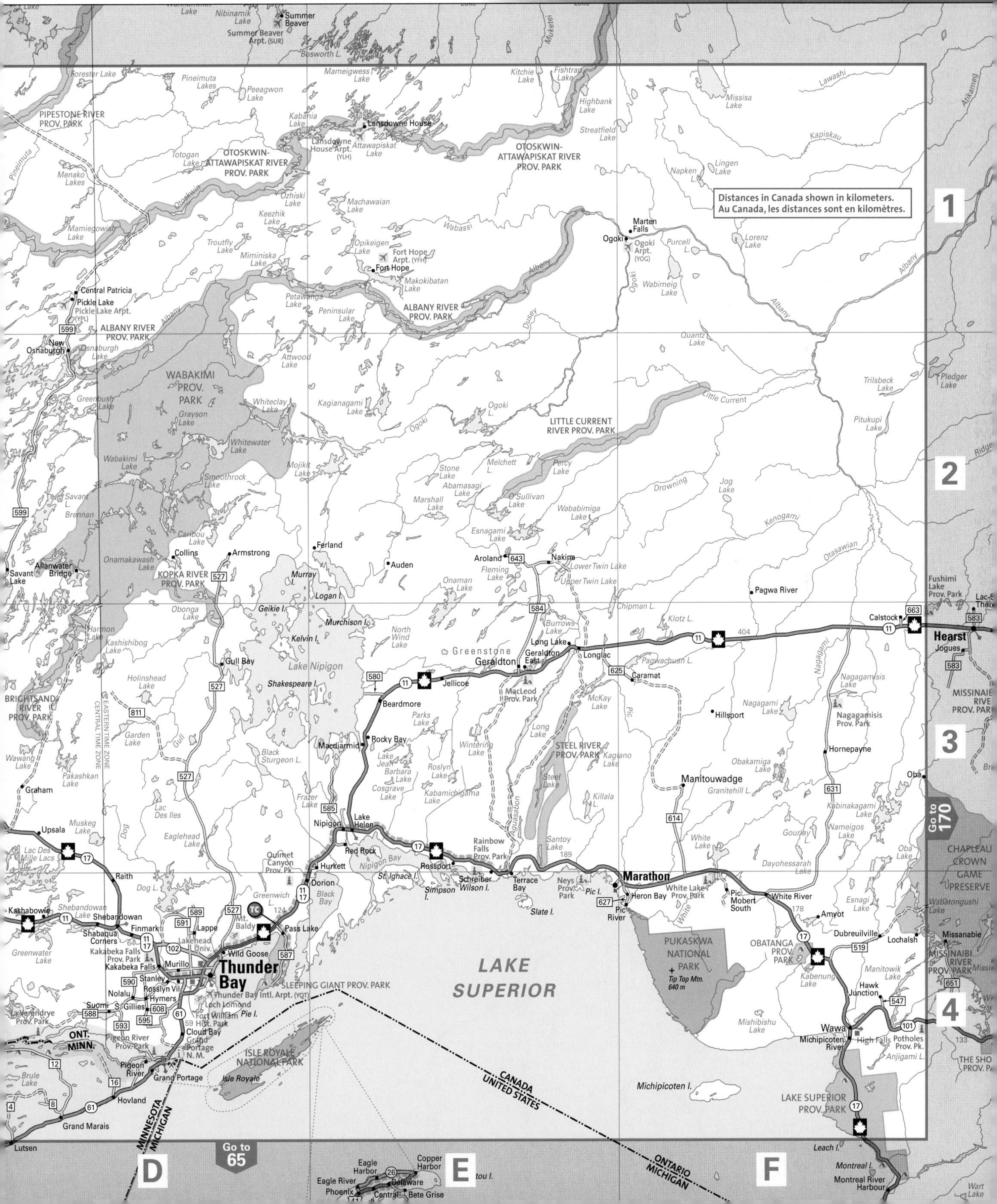

Ontario   Québec

Mich.   N.Y.

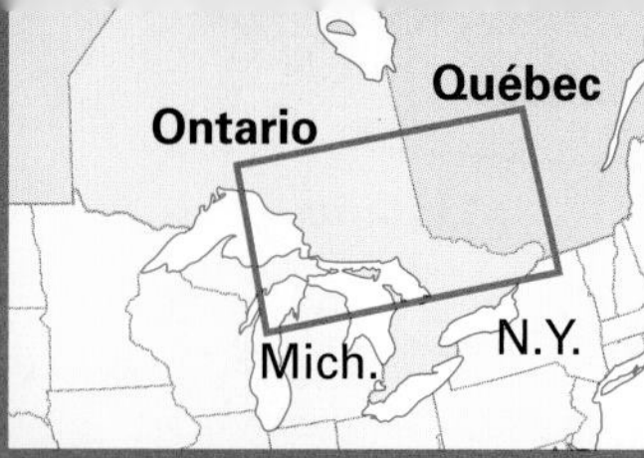

0 mi   20   40   60
0 km 20   40   60   80

One inch equals 40.3 miles/Un pouce équivaut à 40.3 milles
One centimeter equals 25.4 km/Un cm équivaut à 25.4 km

Distances in Canada shown in kilometers.
Au Canada, les distances sont en kilomètres.

Go to 169

Go to 169

Go to 65

Go to 69

Go to 70

Go to 172

LAKE SUPERIOR

LAKE MICHIGAN

LAKE HURON

Georgian Bay

North Channel

ONTARIO / MICHIGAN

CANADA / UNITED STATES

CENTRAL TIME ZONE / EASTERN TIME ZONE

WISCONSIN / MICHIGAN

Selected place names

Jellicoe, MacLeod Prov. Park, Caramat, Calstock, Hearst, Hallebourg, Lac-Ste-Thérèse, Fraserdale, Schreiber, Terrace Bay, Marathon, Heron Bay, Pic River, Pic Mobert South, White River, Manitouwadge, Hornepayne, Oba, Jogues, Mattice, Opasatika, Harty, Kapuskasing, Moonbeam, Fauquier, Smooth Rock Falls, Driftwood, Clute, Hunta, Cochrane, Tunis, Iroquois Falls, Porquis Jct., Connaught, Hoyle, Porcupine, S. Porcupine, Timmins, Matachewan, Foleyet, Gogama, Shining Tree, Westree, Sudbury, Lively, Chelmsford, Capreol, Espanola, Elliot Lake, Blind River, Thessalon, Iron Bridge, Spanish, Massey, Whitefish Falls, Little Current, Manitowaning, Killarney, Wikwemikong, Gore Bay, Providence Bay, South Baymouth, Tobermory, Lion's Head, Wiarton, Sault Ste. Marie, Searchmont, Ranger Lake, Echo Bay, Bruce Mines, Desbarats, St. Joseph, Dunns Valley, Wawa, Michipicoten River, Chapleau, Missanabie, Dubreuilville, Lochalsh, Hawk Junction, Sultan, Biscotasing, Gowganda, Batchawana Bay, Pancake Bay, Paradise, Whitefish Point, Grand Marais, Munising, Newberry, McMillan, Seney, Germfask, Curtis, Manistique, Gulliver, Naubinway, Engadine, Trout Lake, St. Ignace, Mackinaw City, Cheboygan, Pellston, Petoskey, Charlevoix, Boyne City, East Jordan, Gaylord, Atlanta, Alpena, Rogers City, Onaway, Hillman, Traverse City, Kalkaska, Grayling, Mio, Lincoln, Harrisville, Escanaba, Gladstone, Marquette, Christmas

PUKASKWA NATIONAL PARK
LAKE SUPERIOR PROV. PARK
PICTURED ROCKS NATIONAL LAKESHORE
HIAWATHA NATL. FOR.
LAKE SUPERIOR STATE FOREST
SENEY N.W.R.
MACKINAW STATE FOREST
SLEEPING BEAR DUNES NATL. LAKESHORE
BRUCE PENINSULA NATL. PARK
FATHOM FIVE NATL. MARINE PARK
KILLARNEY PROV. PARK
FRENCH RIVER PROV. PARK
CHAPLEAU CROWN GAME PRESERVE
MISSINAIBI RIVER PROV. PARK
STEEL RIVER PROV. PARK
NEYS PROV. PARK
OBATANGA PROV. PARK
POTHOLES PROV. PK.
THE SHOALS PROV. PARK
WAKAMI LAKE PROV. PARK
CHAPLEAU-NEMEGOSENDA RIVER PROV. PARK
MISSISSAGI PROV. PARK

DRIVING DISTANCES IN KM / DISTANCES ROUTIÈRES EN KM

	HEARST, ON	HUNTSVILLE, ON	KIRKLAND LAKE, ON	MONT-LAURIER, QC	NORTH BAY, ON	ORILLIA, ON	OTTAWA, ON	ROUYN-NORANDA, QC	SAULT STE. MARIE, ON	SUDBURY, ON	TIMMINS, ON	WAWA, ON
KIRKLAND LAKE, ON	370	370		505	250	578	610	154	580	315	140	475
OTTAWA, ON	955	350	610	209	364	415		456	787	488	730	1015
SAULT STE. MARIE, ON	545	560	580	1004	430	562	787	734		305	440	225
SUDBURY, ON	550	250	315	699	124	263	488	469	305		290	530

SEE ALSO DISTANCE AND DRIVING TIME MAP ON PAGES 286–287 / VOIR AUSSI CARTE DES DISTANCES ET DES TEMPS DE PARCOURS PAGES 286–287

172

Ontario
Mich.   N.Y.
Pa.
Ohio

London ON / Windsor ON

0 mi   20   40
0 km   20   40   60
One inch equals 25.4 miles/Un pouce équivaut à 25.4 milles
One cm equals 16.1 km/Un cm équivaut à 16.1 km

Distances in Canada shown in kilometers.
Au Canada, les distances sont en kilomètres.

LAKE HURON

Georgian Bay

LAKE ERIE

Lake St. Clair

Detroit

Windsor

Toledo

London

Sarnia

Goderich

Owen Sound

Kitchener

Hamilton

Erie

DRIVING DISTANCES IN KM / DISTANCES ROUTIÈRES EN KM

	BARRIE, ON	HAMILTON, ON	KINGSTON, ON	KITCHENER, ON	LONDON, ON	NIAGARA FALLS, ON	ORILLIA, ON	OWEN SOUND, ON	PETERBOROUGH, ON	SARNIA, ON	TORONTO, ON	WINDSOR, ON
KINGSTON, ON	350	330		430	430	390	317	430	180	530	260	620
NIAGARA FALLS, ON	200	68	390	130	190		237	260	260	290	130	380
TORONTO, ON	90	70	260	105	185	130	127	190	135	280		370
WINDSOR, ON	430	310	620	285	190	380	467	390	490	160	370	

SEE ALSO DISTANCE AND DRIVING TIME MAP ON PAGES 286–287 / VOIR AUSSI CARTE DES DISTANCES ET DES TEMPS DE PARCOURS PAGES 286–287

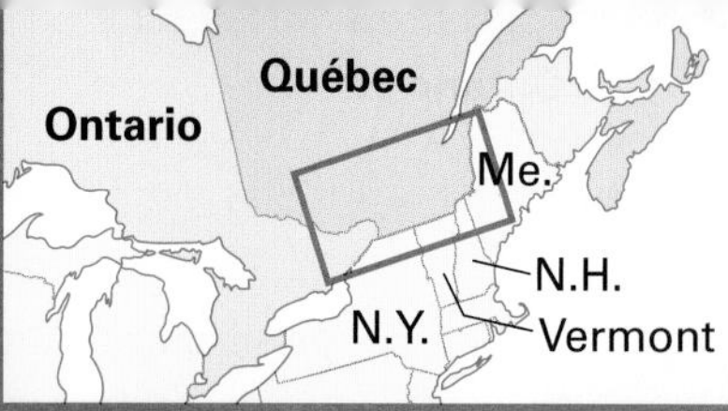

174

Ontario   Québec
Me.
N.H.
N.Y.   Vermont

Ottawa ON / Montréal QC

One inch equals 25.4 miles/Un pouce équivaut à 25.4 milles
One cm equals 16.1 km/Un cm équivaut à 16.1 km

Go to 171

Go to 176

Distances in Canada shown in kilometers.
Au Canada, les distances sont en kilomètres.

Go to 171

Go to 173

Go to 80

Go to 176

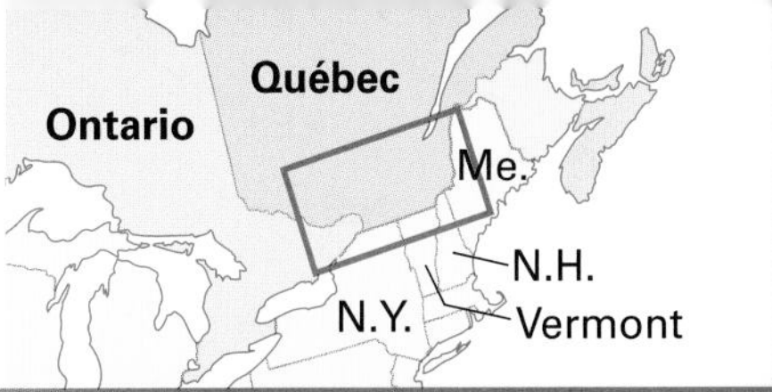

DRIVING DISTANCES IN KM / DISTANCES ROUTIÈRES EN KM

	BURLINGTON, VT	CORNWALL, ON	DRUMMONDVILLE, QC	KINGSTON, ON	MONT-LAURIER, QC	MONTRÉAL, QC	MONT-TREMBLANT, QC	OTTAWA, ON	QUÉBEC, QC	ST-GEORGES, QC	SHERBROOKE, QC	TROIS-RIVIÈRES, QC
MONTRÉAL, QC	153	103	116	283	230		126	194	250	325	143	146
OTTAWA, ON	360	97	310	175	209	194	208		444	485	337	340
QUÉBEC, QC	394	353	151	533	445	250	298	444		102	233	135
SHERBROOKE, QC	174	246	82	426	402	143	269	337	233	148		158

SEE ALSO DISTANCE AND DRIVING TIME MAP ON PAGES 286–287 / VOIR AUSSI CARTE DES DISTANCES ET DES TEMPS DE PARCOURS PAGES 286–287

Québec
P.E.I.
N.B.
Maine

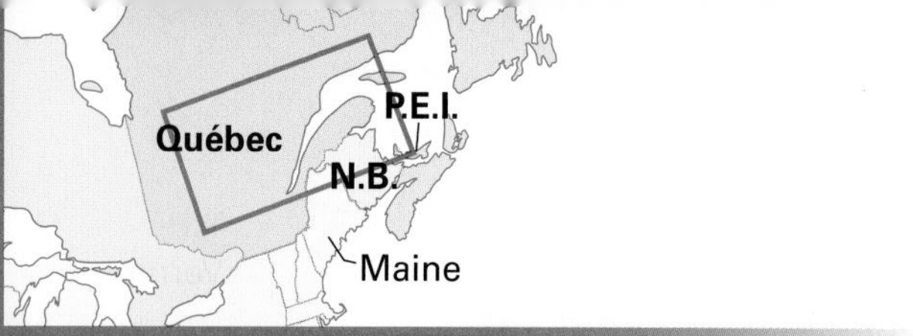

0 mi 20 40 60
0 km 20 40 60 80
One inch equals 40.3 miles/Un pouce équivaut à 40.3 milles
One centimeter equals 25.4 km/Un cm équivaut à 25.4 km

Distances in Canada shown in kilometers.
Au Canada, les distances sont en kilomètres.

RÉSERVE FAUNIQUE ASSINICA

RÉSERVE FAUNIQUE DES LACS-ALBANEL-MISTASSINI-ETWACONICHI

Chibougamau
Chapais
Chibougamau-Chapais (YMT)
Waswanipi

Mistissini

Dolbeau-Mistassini
Normandin
St-Félicien
St-Prime
Roberval
Alma
Saguenay
Chicoutimi
Jonquière

RÉSERVE FAUNIQUE ASHUAPMUSHUAN

RÉSERVE FAUNIQUE MASTIGOUCHE

La Tuque

Parent

PARC DE LA JACQUES-CARTIER

RÉS. FAUNIQUE DES LAURENTIDES

Mont-Laurier

Québec
Lévis
Montmagny

St-Raymond

Shawinigan
Ste-Marie
Donnacona

La Malbaie
Clermont
Baie-St-Paul

Go to 171
Go to 174
Go to 174

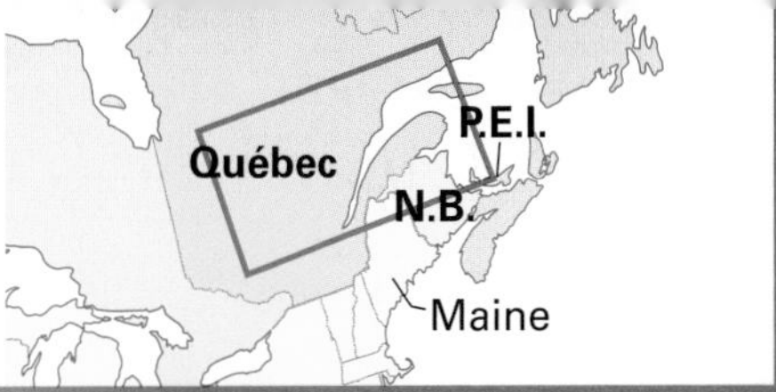

DRIVING DISTANCES IN KM / DISTANCES ROUTIÈRES EN KM

	BAIE-COMEAU, QC	CAMPBELLTON, NB	CHIBOUGAMAU, QC	CHICOUTIMI, QC	EDMUNDSTON, NB	GASPÉ, QC	HAVRE-ST-PIERRE, QC	MATANE, QC	MIRAMICHI, NB	QUÉBEC, QC	RIMOUSKI, QC	SEPT-ÎLES, QC
CHICOUTIMI, QC	435	444	359		269	771	884	348	622	211	253	667
EDMUNDSTON, NB	368	188	628	269		534	817	249	268	317	180	600
GASPÉ, QC	287	340	1130	771	534		743	294	518	706	389	526
QUÉBEC, QC	408	508	570	211	317	706	857	412	582		507	640

SEE ALSO DISTANCE AND DRIVING TIME MAP ON PAGES 286–287 / VOIR AUSSI CARTE DES DISTANCES ET DES TEMPS DE PARCOURS PAGES 286–287

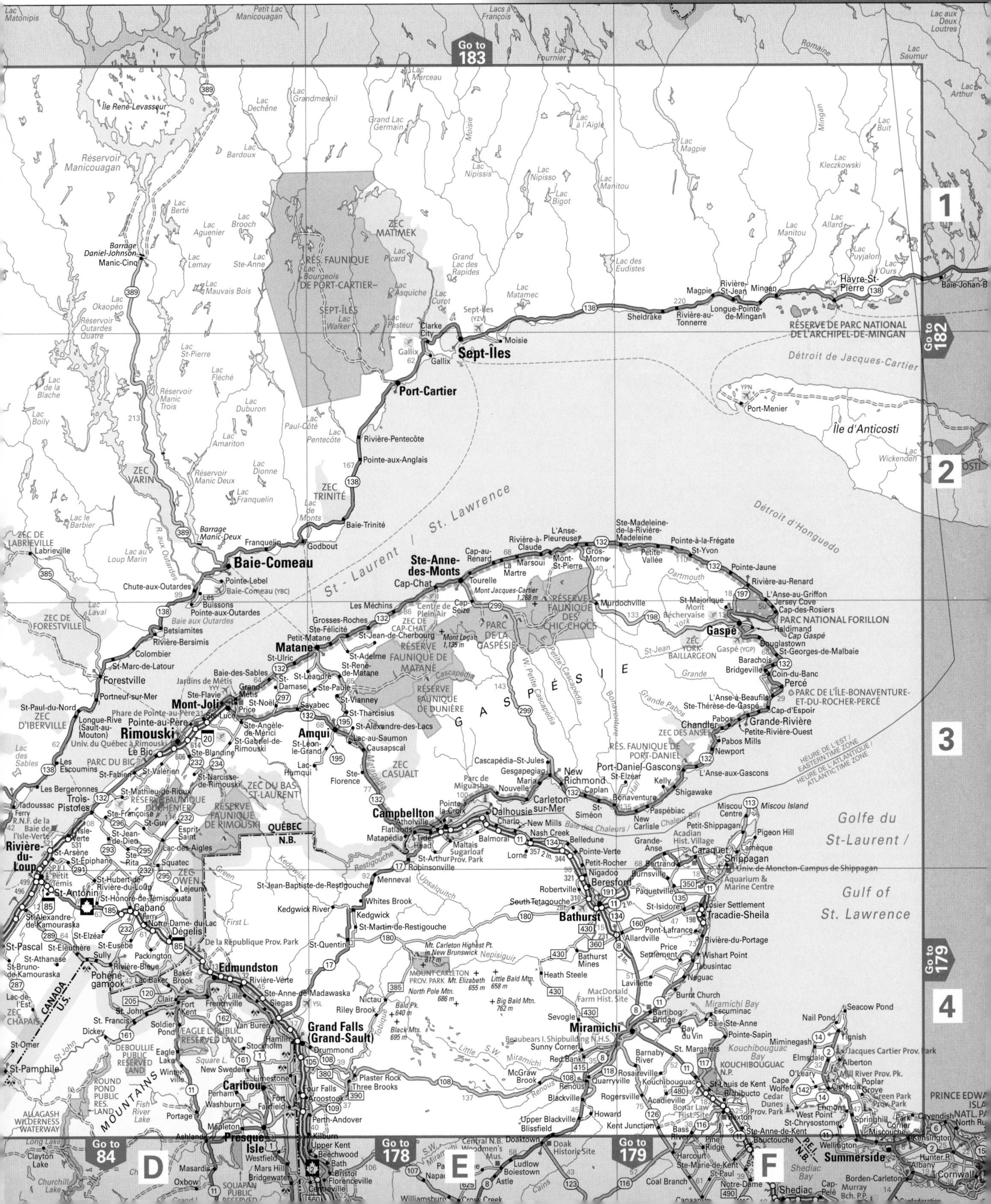

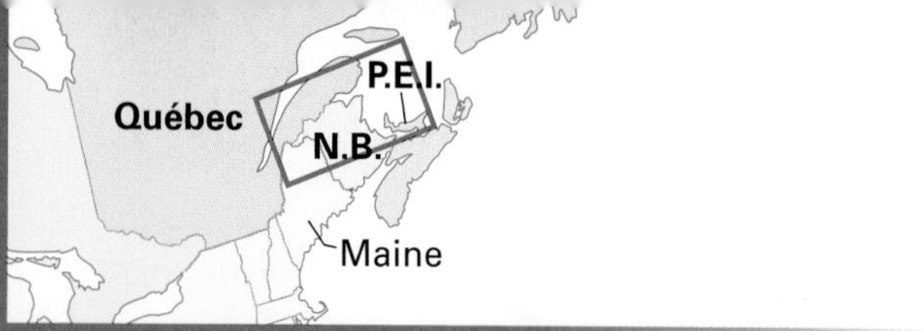

0 mi 20 40
0 km 20 40 60
One inch equals 25.4 miles/Un pouce équivaut à 25.4 milles
One cm equals 16.1 km/Un cm équivaut à 16.1 km

Rimouski QC / Edmundston NB

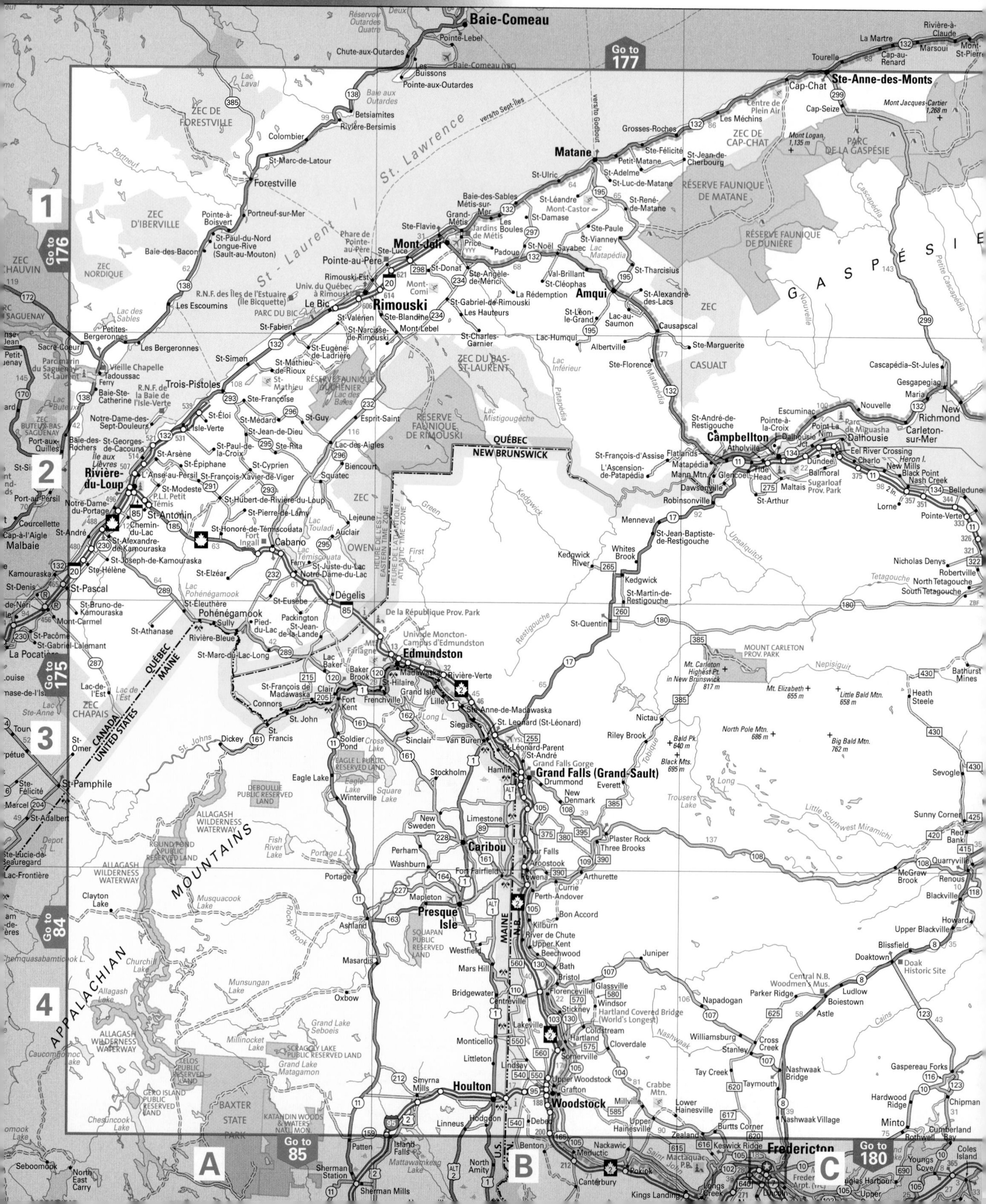

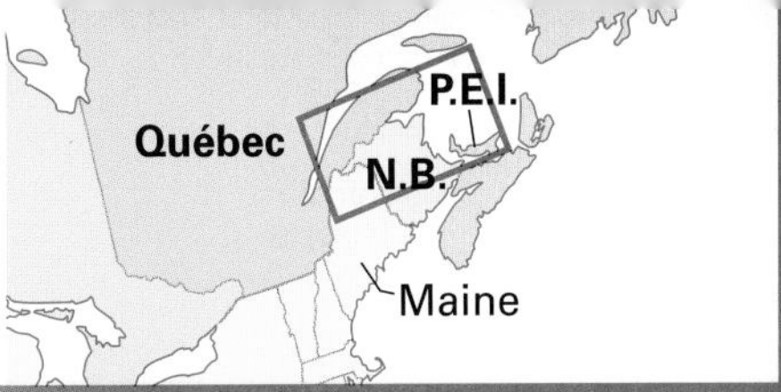

DRIVING DISTANCES IN KM / DISTANCES ROUTIÈRES EN KM

	BATHURST, NB	BORDEN-CARLETON, PE	CAMPBELLTON, NB	CHARLOTTETOWN, PE	EDMUNDSTON, NB	FREDERICTON, NB	GASPÉ, QC	GRAND FALLS, NB	MATANE, QC	MIRAMICHI, NB	MONCTON, NB	RIMOUSKI, QC
CHARLOTTETOWN, PE	338	56	438		629	362	791	581	562	273	164	596
EDMUNDSTON, NB	189	428	188	638		279	534	57	249	268	447	180
MATANE, QC	262	506	168	562	249	553	294	331		346	487	95
MONCTON, NB	206	108	306	164	447	170	659	390	487	141		502

SEE ALSO DISTANCE AND DRIVING TIME MAP ON PAGES 286–287 / VOIR AUSSI CARTE DES DISTANCES ET DES TEMPS DE PARCOURS PAGES 286–287

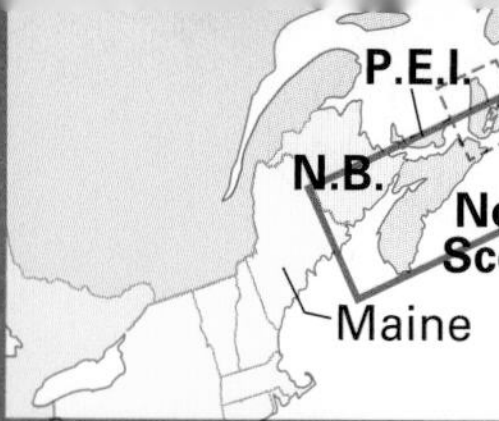

0 mi 20 40
0 km 20 40 60

One inch equals 25.4 miles/Un pouce équivaut à 25.4 milles
One cm equals 16.1 km/Un cm équivaut à 16.1 km

Saint John NB / Yarmouth NS

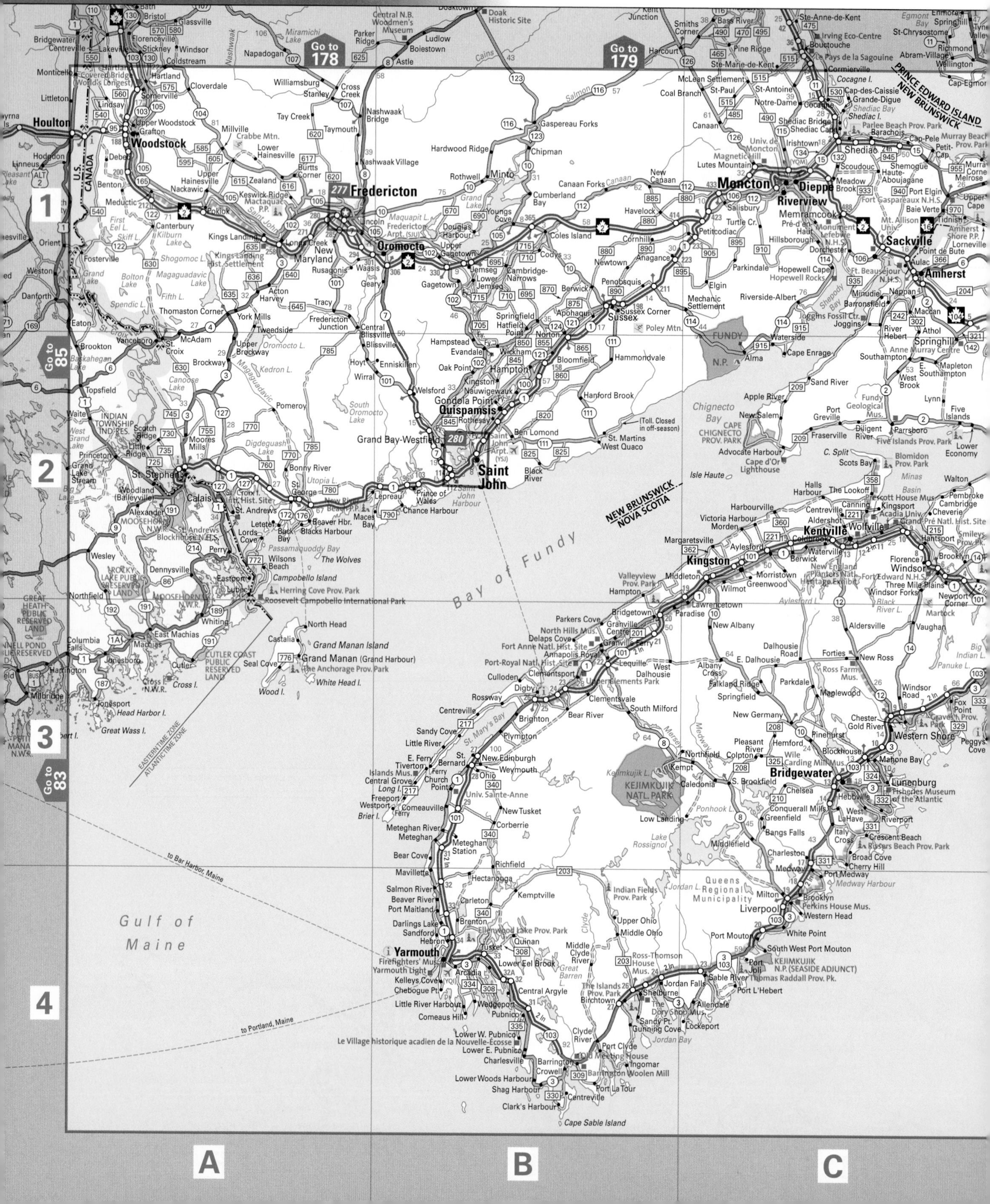

DRIVING DISTANCES IN KM / DISTANCES ROUTIÈRES EN KM

	CHARLOTTETOWN, PE	CHÉTICAMP, NS	DIGBY, NS	FREDERICTON, NB	HALIFAX, NS	MONCTON, NB	PORT HAWKESBURY, NS	SAINT JOHN, NB	ST. STEPHEN, NB	SYDNEY, NS	TRURO, NS	YARMOUTH, NS
HALIFAX, NS	322	425	235	462		260	265	410	515	415	89	339
MONCTON, NB	164	481	231	170	260		374	150	278	497	182	599
SAINT JOHN, NB	350	640	72	114	410	150	497		119	647	321	176
SYDNEY, NS	374	173	623	689	415	497	123	647	766		326	727

SEE ALSO DISTANCE AND DRIVING TIME MAP ON PAGES 286–287 / VOIR AUSSI CARTE DES DISTANCES ET DES TEMPS DE PARCOURS PAGES 286–287

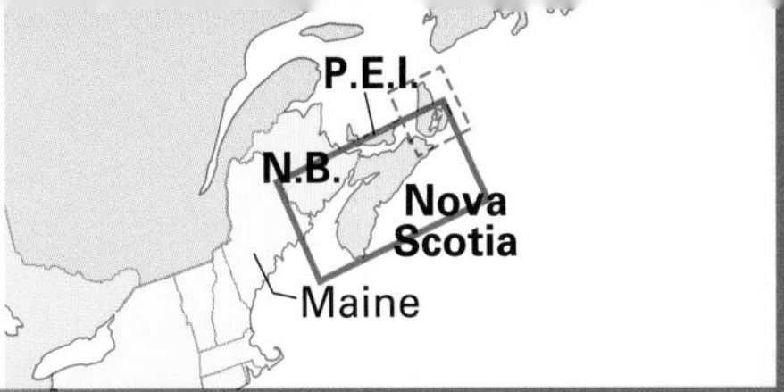

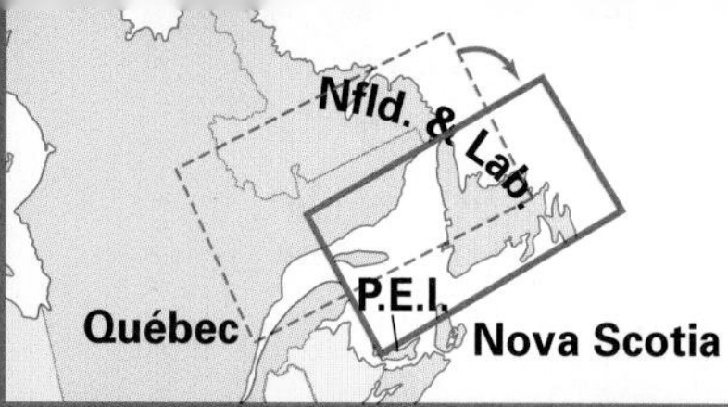

Nfld. & Lab

Québec

P.E.I.

Nova Scotia

0 mi 20 40 60
0 km 20 40 60 80
One inch equals 40.3 miles/Un pouce équivaut à 40.3 milles
One centimeter equals 25.4 km/Un cm équivaut à 25.4 km

FOR CONTINUATION SEE INSET AT RIGHT
POUR CONTINUER VOIR À DROITE

Distances in Canada shown in kilometers.
Au Canada, les distances sont en kilomètres.

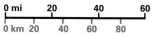

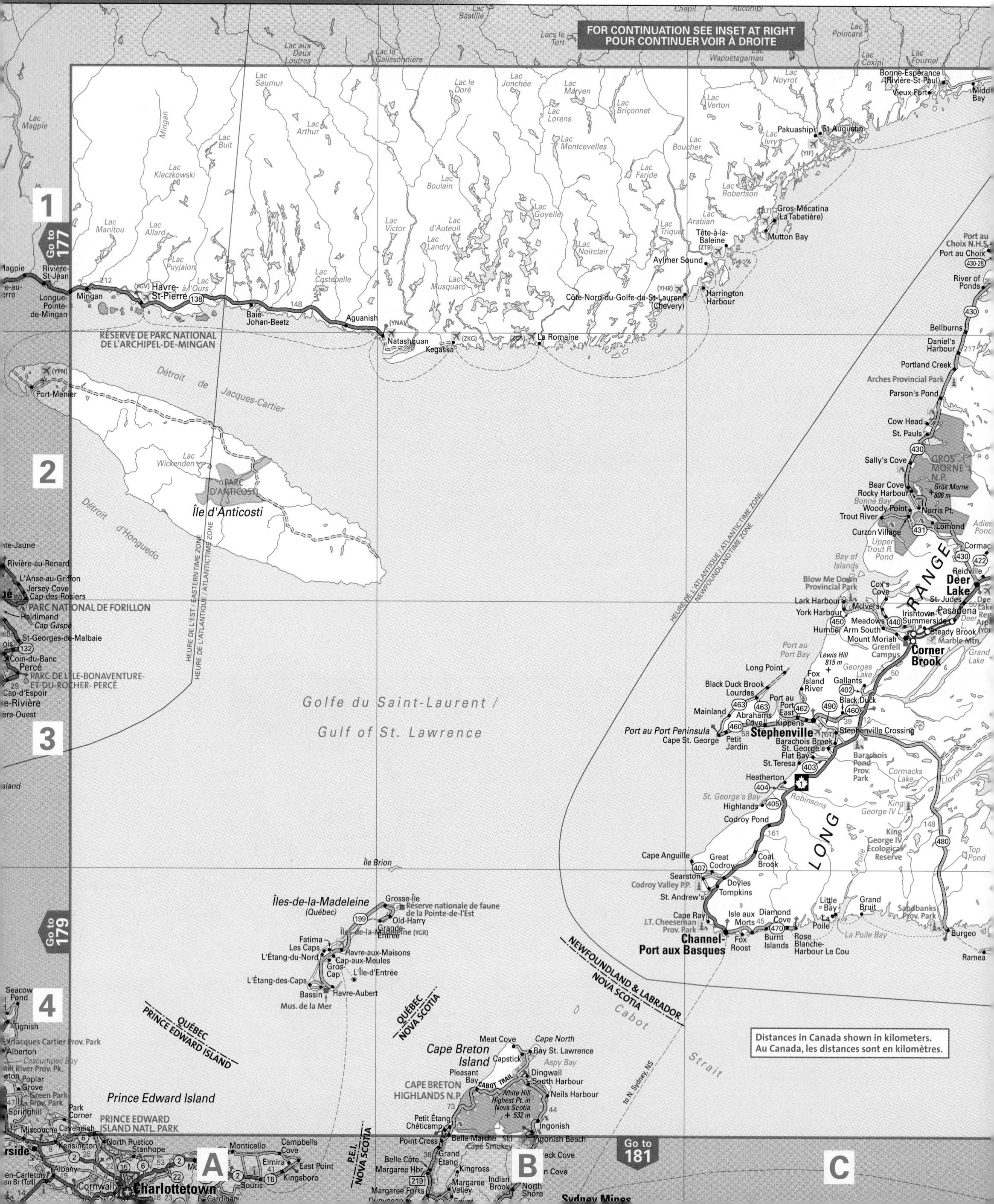

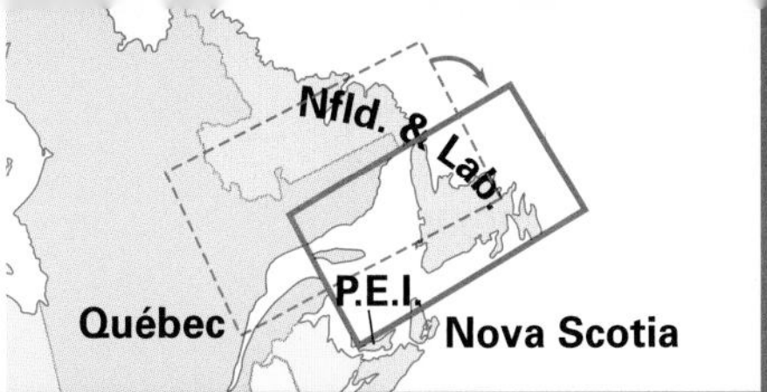

DRIVING DISTANCES IN KM / DISTANCES ROUTIÈRES EN KM

	ARGENTIA, NL	BISHOP'S FALLS, NL	BONAVISTA, NL	CHAN.-PT. AUX BASQUES, NL	CORNER BROOK, NL	DEER LAKE, NL	GANDER, NL	GRAND FALLS-WINDSOR, NL	MARYSTOWN, NL	ST. ANTHONY, NL	ST. JOHN'S, NL	STEPHENVILLE, NL
BISHOP'S FALLS, NL	363		307	482	280	225	72	18	384	628	393	339
CHAN.-PT. AUX BASQUES, NL	845	482	789		202	257	554	464	866	660	875	151
CORNER BROOK, NL	643	280	587	202		55	352	262	664	458	673	59
ST. JOHN'S, NL	134	393	296	875	673	618	321	411	293	1021		732

SEE ALSO DISTANCE AND DRIVING TIME MAP ON PAGES 286–287 / VOIR AUSSI CARTE DES DISTANCES ET DES TEMPS DE PARCOURS PAGES 286–287

NOTE: Legislated standard time zone boundaries are shown; however, Labrador—except for the coastal area from L'Anse-au-Clair to Cartwright—operates on Atlantic Standard Time.

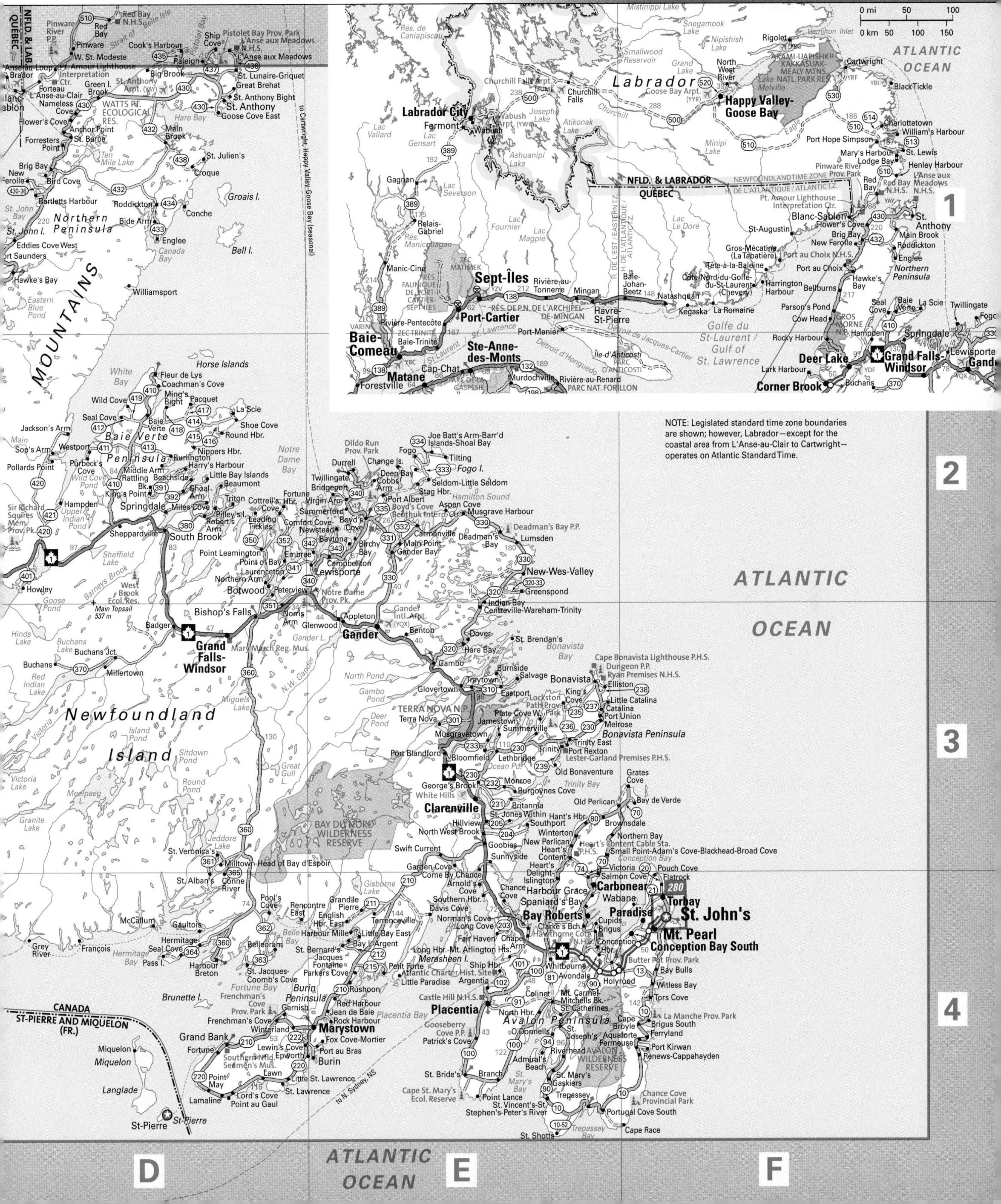

0 mi 50 100 150
0 km 50 100 150 200

One inch equals 83.75 miles/Una pulgada igual a 83.75 millas
One centimeter equals 53 km/Un centímetro igual a 53 km

1
2
3
4

A B C

RIVING ISTANCES IN KM / ISTANCIAS DE MANEJO EN KM	CHIHUAHUA	CIUDAD JUÁREZ	CIUDAD VICTORIA	CULIACÁN	DURANGO	HERMOSILLO	MAZATLÁN	MÉXICO	MONTERREY	SAN LUIS POTOSÍ	TIJUANA	TORREÓN
CHIHUAHUA		385	1086	919	686	579	1209	1538	808	1155	1456	449
HERMOSILLO	579	795	1666	706	941		729	1810	1387	1416	884	1028
MONTERREY	808	1236	288	924	689	1387	901	892		509	2362	359
TORREÓN	449	834	637	914	266	1028	892	1089	359	706	1905	

SEE ALSO DISTANCE AND DRIVING TIME MAP ON PAGES 286–287 / CONSULTE, PARA DISTANCIAS Y TIEMPO DE MANEJO, EN LAS PÁGINAS 286-287

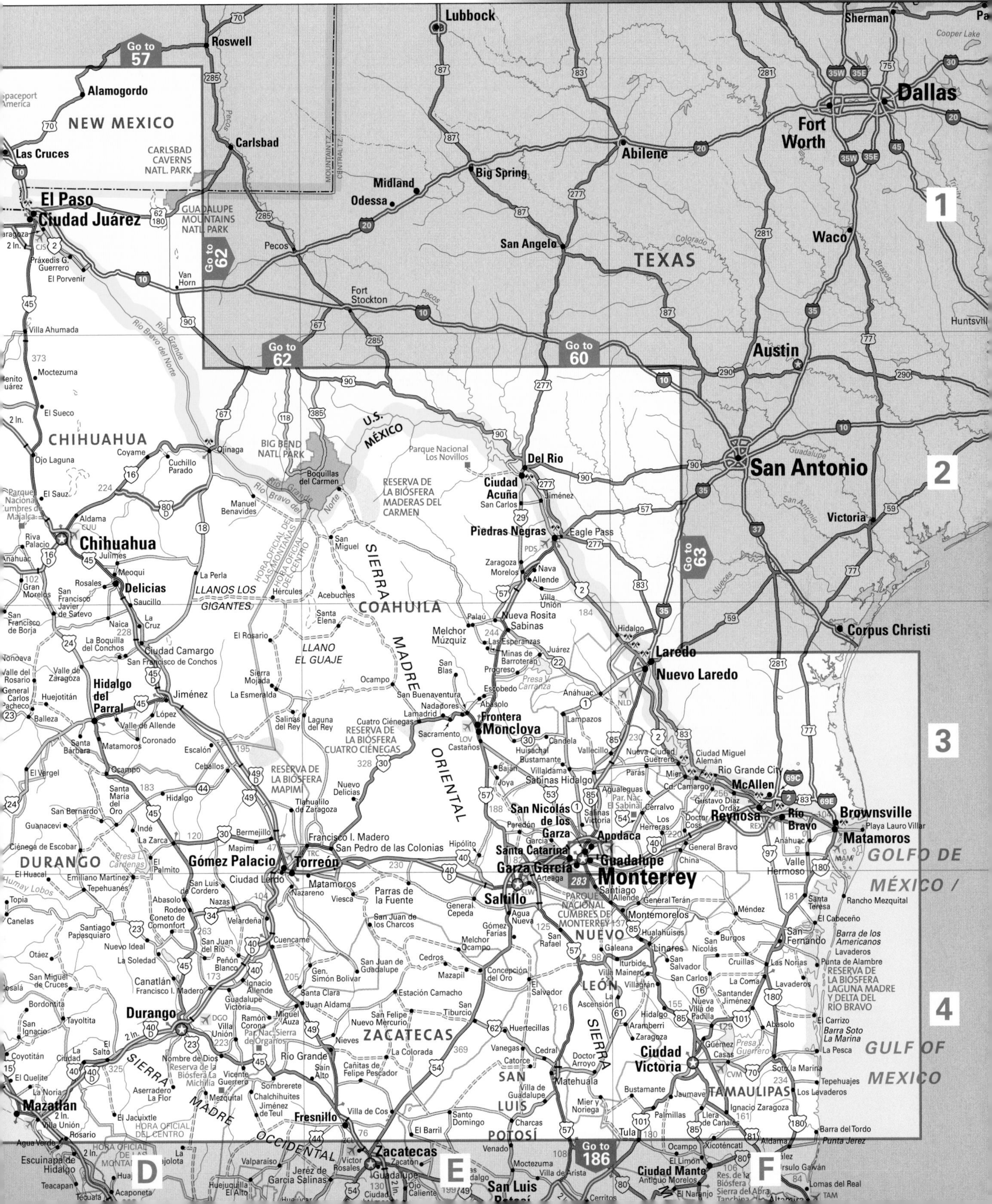

0 mi 50 100 150
0 km 50 100 150 200
One inch equals 83.75 miles/Una pulgada igual a 83.75 millas
One centimeter equals 53 km/Un centímetro igual a 53 km

DRIVING DISTANCES IN KM / DISTANCIAS DE MANEJO EN KM

	ACAPULCO	CANCÚN	CIUDAD VICTORIA	DURANGO	GUADALAJARA	MAZATLÁN	MÉRIDA	MÉXICO	PUEBLA	SAN LUIS POTOSÍ	TUXTLA GUTIÉRREZ	VERACRUZ
GUADALAJARA	897	2275	774	599		523	1904	578	691	336	1510	943
MÉRIDA	1777	321	1725	2182	1904	2408		1326	1282	1707	786	995
MÉXICO	422	1736	682	856	578	1081	1326		133	381	932	365
SAN LUIS POTOSÍ	834	2161	438	475	336	687	1707	381	496		1313	747

SEE ALSO DISTANCE AND DRIVING TIME MAP ON PAGES 286–287 / CONSULTE, PARA DISTANCIAS Y TIEMPO DE MANEJO, EN LAS PÁGINAS 286-287

PUERTO RICO

Distances in Puerto Rico shown in kilometers. / Distancias en Puerto Rico constan en kilómetros.

OCÉANO ATLÁNTICO / ATLANTIC OCEAN

MAR CARIBE / CARIBBEAN SEA

GOLFO DE MÉXICO / GULF OF MEXICO

PENÍNSULA DE YUCATÁN

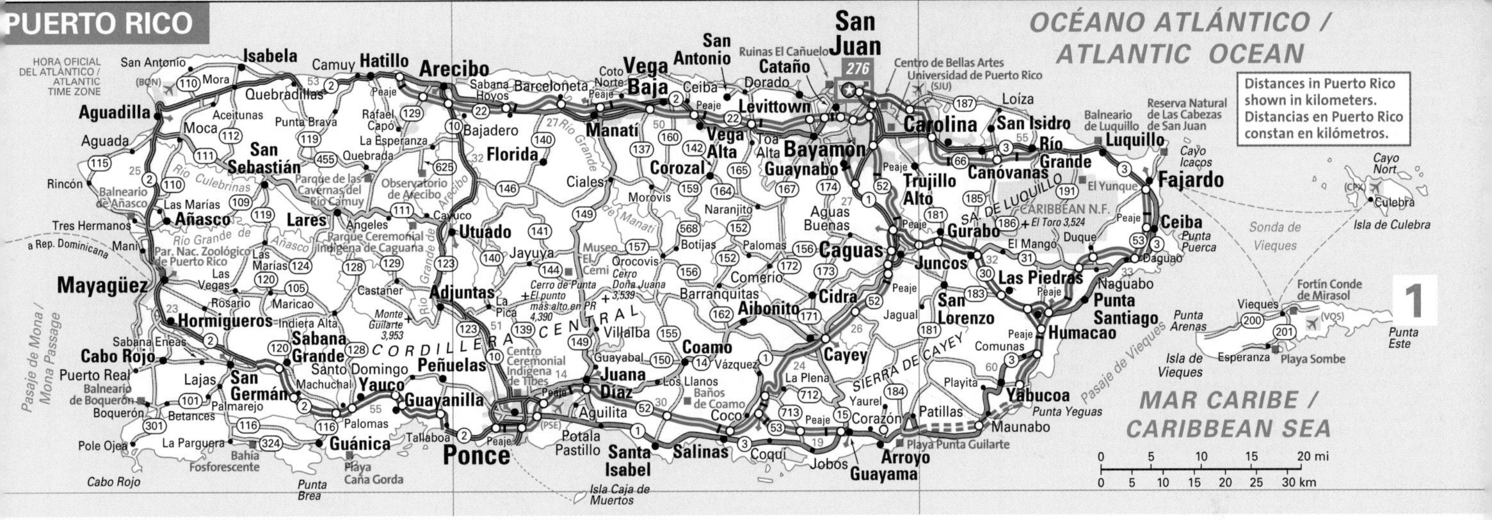

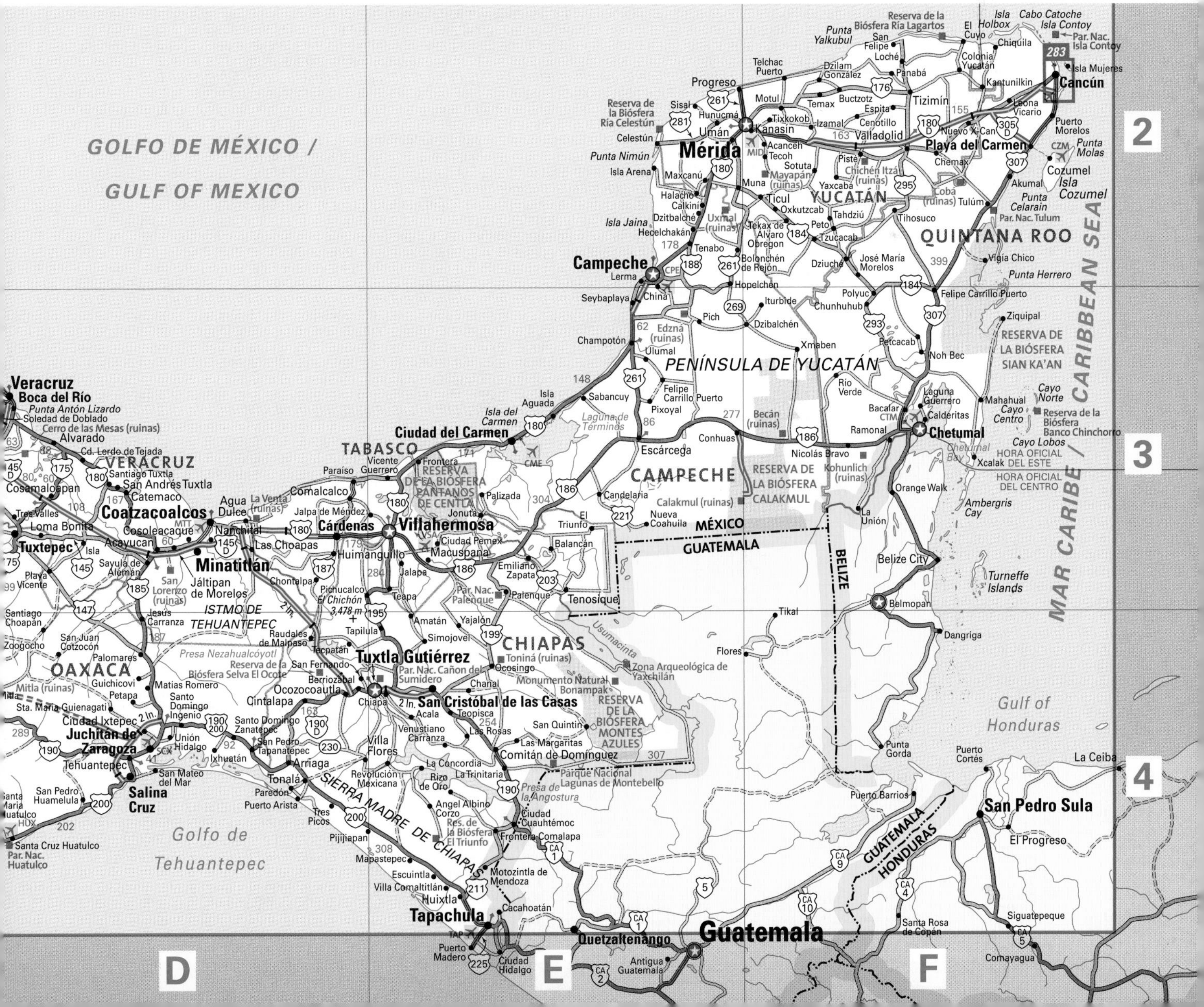

Figures after entries indicate population, page number, and grid reference.

UNITED STATES

A

Abbeville AL, *2688* 128 B4
Abbeville GA, *2908* 129 E3
Abbeville LA, *12257* 133 F3
Abbeville MS, *419* 118 C3
Abbeville SC, *5237* 121 E3
Abbeville Co. SC, *25417* 121 E3
Abbotsford WI, *2310* 68 A4
Abbottstown PA, *1011* 103 E1
Abercrombie ND, *263* 19 F4
Aberdeen ID, *1994* 31 E1
Aberdeen MD, *14959* 145 D1
Aberdeen MS, *5612* 119 D4
Aberdeen NC, *6350* 122 C1
Aberdeen OH, *1638* 100 C3
Aberdeen SD, *26091* 27 E2
Aberdeen WA, *16896* 12 B4
Abernathy TX, *2805* 58 A1
Abilene KS, *6844* 43 E2
Abilene TX, *117063* 58 C3
Abingdon IL, *3319* 88 A3
Abingdon MD, *950* 145 D1
Abingdon VA, *8191* 111 E3
Abington MA, *15985* 151 D2
Abita Sprs. LA, *2365* 134 B2
Absarokee MT, *1150* 24 B2
Absecon NJ, *8411* 147 F4
Acadia Par. LA, *61773* 133 E2
Accokeek MD, *10573* 144 B4
Accokeek Acres MD, *1500* 144 B4
Accomac VA, *519* 114 C3
Accomack Co. VA, *33164* 114 C3
Accord MA, *2300* 151 D2
Accord NY, *562* 94 A3
Achille OK, *492* 59 F1
Achilles VA, *650* 113 F2
Ackerman MS, *1510* 126 C1
Ackley IA, *1589* 73 D4
Acme MI, *650* 69 F4
Acomita Lake NM, *416* 48 B3
Acton CA, *7596* 52 C2
Acton MA, *21924* 150 C1
Acushnet MA, *3073* 151 D3
Acworth GA, *20425* 120 C3
Ada MN, *1707* 19 F3
Ada OH, *5952* 90 B3
Ada OK, *16810* 51 F4
Ada Co. ID, *392365* 22 B4
Adair IA, *781* 86 B2
Adair OK, *790* 106 A3
Adair Co. IA, *7682* 86 B2
Adair Co. KY, *18656* 110 B2
Adair Co. MO, *25607* 87 D4
Adair Co. OK, *22683* 106 B4
Adairsville GA, *4648* 120 B3
Adair Vil. OR, *840* 20 B3
Adairville KY, *852* 109 F3
Adams MA, *5515* 94 C1
Adams MN, *787* 73 D2
Adams NE, *573* 35 F4
Adams NY, *1775* 79 E2
Adams OR, *350* 21 F1
Adams TN, *633* 109 E3
Adams WI, *1967* 74 A1
Adams Ctr. NY, *1568* 79 E2
Adams Co. CO, *441603* 41 F1
Adams Co. ID, *3976* 22 B2
Adams Co. IL, *67103* 87 F4
Adams Co. IN, *34387* 90 A3
Adams Co. IA, *4029* 86 B3
Adams Co. MS, *32297* 126 A4
Adams Co. NE, *31364* 35 D4
Adams Co. ND, *2343* 26 A1
Adams Co. OH, *28550* 100 C3
Adams Co. PA, *101407* 103 E1
Adams Co. WA, *18728* 13 F4
Adams Co. WI, *20875* 74 A2
Adamston NJ, *4900* 147 E3
Adamstown MD, *2372* 144 A2
Adamstown PA, *1789* 146 A2
Adamsville AL, *4522* 119 F4
Adamsville RI, *550* 151 D4
Adamsville TN, *2207* 119 D1
Addis LA, *3593* 134 A2
Addison AL, *758* 119 E3
Addison IL, *36942* 203 C4
Addison ME, *300* 83 E2
Addison MI, *605* 90 B1
Addison NY, *1763* 93 D1
Addison TX, *13056* 207 D1
Addison Co. VT, *36821* 81 D3
Adel GA, *5334* 137 F1
Adel IA, *3682* 86 C2
Adelanto CA, *31765* 53 D2
Adelphi MD, *15086* 270 E1
Adelphia NJ, *700* 147 E2
Adena OH, *759* 91 F4
Adrian GA, *664* 129 F2
Adrian MI, *21133* 90 B1
Adrian MN, *1209* 72 A2
Adrian MO, *1677* 96 B4
Advance IN, *477* 99 E1
Advance MO, *1347* 108 B2
Adwolf VA, *1530* 111 F2
Affton MO, *20307* 256 B3
Afton IA, *845* 86 C3
Afton NY, *822* 93 F1
Afton OK, *1049* 106 B3
Afton WY, *1911* 31 F1
Agawam MA, *28438* 150 A2
Agency IA, *638* 87 E3
Agency MO, *684* 96 B1
Agoura Hills CA, *20330* 228 A2
Agua Dulce TX, *3014* 63 E2
Agua Fria NM, *2800* 49 D2
Aguilar CO, *538* 41 E4
Ahoskie NC, *5039* 113 F3
Ahsahka ID, *600* 14 B4
Ahuimanu HI, *8810* 152 A3
Aiken SC, *29524* 121 F4
Aiken Co. SC, *160099* 122 A4
Ainsworth IA, *567* 87 F2
Ainsworth NE, *1728* 34 C1
Airmont NY, *8628* 148 B3
Airport Drive MO, *698* 106 B2
Airway Hts. WA, *6114* 13 F3
Aitkin MN, *2165* 64 B4
Aitkin Co. MN, *16202* 64 B4
Ajo AZ, *3304* 54 B3
Ak-Chin Vil. AZ, *862* 54 C2
Akiachak AK, *627* 154 B3
Akins OK, *493* 116 B1
Akron AL, *356* 127 E1
Akron CO, *1702* 41 F1
Akron IN, *1167* 89 F3
Akron IA, *1486* 35 F1
Akron MI, *402* 76 B2
Akron NY, *2868* 78 B3

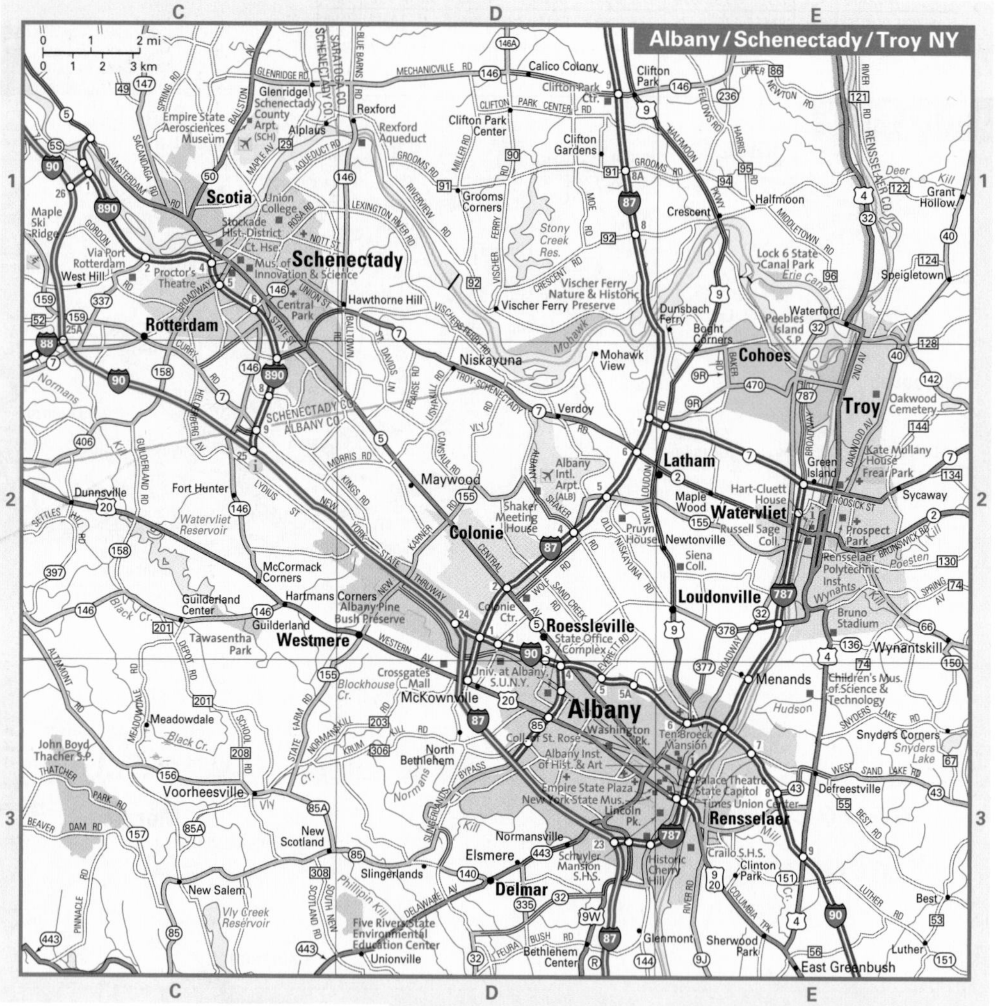

Albany	D3	E. Greenbush	E3	Maywood	D2	Scotia	C1
Alplaus	C1	Elsmere	D3	McCormack Corners	C2	Sherwood Park	E3
Best	E3	Ft. Hunter	C2	McKownville	D3	Slingerlands	D3
Bethlehem Ctr.	D3	Glenmont	D3	Meadowdale	C3	Snyders Corners	E3
Boght Corners	E1	Glenridge	C1	Menands	E3	Speigletown	E1
Calico Colony	D1	Grant Hollow	E1	Mohawk View	D2	Sycaway	E2
Clifton Gardens	D1	Green Island	E2	New Salem	C3	Troy	E2
Clifton Park	D1	Grooms Corners	D1	New Scotland	C3	Unionville	D3
Clifton Park Ctr.	D1	Guilderland	C2	Newtonville	E2	Verdoy	D2
Clinton Park	E3	Guilderland Ctr.	C2	Niskayuna	D2	Vischer Ferry	D1
Cohoes	E2	Halfmoon	E1	Normanville	D3	Voorheesville	C3
Colonie	D2	Hartmans Corners	C2	N. Bethlehem	D3	Waterford	E1
Crescent	E1	Hawthorne Hill	D1	Rensselaer	E3	Watervliet	E2
Defreestville	E3	Latham	E2	Rexford	D1	W. Hill	C1
Delmar	D3	Loudonville	E2	Roessleville	D2	Westmere	D2
Dunnsville	C2	Luther	E3	Rotterdam	C1	Wynantskill	E2
Dunsbach Ferry	E1	Maple Wood	E2	Schenectady	C1		

Akron OH, *199110* 91 E3
Akron PA, *3876* 146 A2
Akutan AK, *1027* 154 A4
Alabaster AL, *30352* 127 F1
Alachua FL, *9059* 138 C3
Alachua Co. FL, *247336* 138 C3
Alakanuk AK, *677* 154 B2
Alamance Co. NC, *151131* 112 C4
Alameda CA, *73812* 259 C3
Alameda NM, *4200* 48 C3
Alameda Co. CA, *1510271* 36 B4
Alamo CA, *14570* 259 D2
Alamo GA, *2797* 129 E3
Alamo NM, *1085* 48 B4
Alamo TN, *2461* 108 C4
Alamo TX, *18353* 63 E4
Alamogordo NM, *30403* 56 C2
Alamo Hts. TX, *7031* 257 E2
Alamosa CO, *8780* 41 D4
Alamosa Co. CO, *15445* 41 D4
Alanson MI, *738* 70 C3
Alapaha GA, *668* 129 E4
Alba MO, *555* 106 B2
Albany CA, *18539* 259 C2
Albany GA, *77434* 129 D4
Albany IL, *891* 88 A1
Albany IN, *2165* 90 A4
Albany KY, *2033* 110 B3
Albany LA, *1088* 134 B2
Albany MN, *2561* 66 B2
Albany MO, *1730* 86 B4
Albany NY, *97856* 94 B1
Albany OH, *828* 101 E2
Albany OR, *50158* 20 B3
Albany TX, *2034* 58 C2
Albany WI, *1018* 74 B4
Albany Co. NY, *304204* 94 B1
Albany Co. WY, *36299* 33 E2
Albemarle NC, *15903* 122 B1
Albemarle Co. VA, *98970* 102 C4
Albers IL, *1190* 98 B3
Albert City IA, *699* 72 B4
Albert Lea MN, *18016* 72 C2
Alberton MT, *420* 15 D4
Albertville AL, *21160* 120 A3
Albertville MN, *7044* 66 C3
Albia IA, *3766* 87 D3
Albin VA, *700* 102 C2
Albion ID, *267* 31 D2
Albion IL, *1988* 99 D4
Albion IN, *2349* 90 A2
Albion IA, *505* 87 D1
Albion MI, *8616* 76 A4
Albion NE, *1650* 35 E3
Albion NY, *6056* 78 B3
Albion PA, *1516* 91 F1
Albion WA, *579* 14 A4
Albuquerque NM, *545852* 48 C3
Alburg VT, *497* 81 D1
Alburnett IA, *673* 87 E1
Alburtis PA, *2361* 146 B1
Alcalde NM, *285* 49 D2
Alcester SD, *807* 35 F1
Alcoa TN, *8449* 110 C4
Alcona Co. MI, *10942* 71 D4
Alcorn MS, *1017* 126 A3
Alcorn Co. MS, *37057* 119 D2
Alda NE, *642* 35 D4
Aldan PA, *4152* 248 B4
Alden IA, *787* 72 C4
Alden MN, *661* 72 C2
Alden NY, *2605* 78 B3
Alderson WV, *1184* 112 A1
Alderwood Manor WA, *8442* 262 B2
Aldine TX, *15869* 220 C1
Aledo IL, *3640* 87 F2
Aledo TX, *2716* 59 E2
Alex OK, *550* 51 E3
Alexander AR, *2901* 117 E2
Alexander ND, *223* 17 F2
Alexander City AL, *14875* 128 A1
Alexander Co. IL, *8238* 108 C2
Alexander Co. NC, *37198* 112 A4
Alexandria AL, *3917* 120 A4
Alexandria IN, *5145* 89 F4
Alexandria KY, *8477* 100 B3
Alexandria LA, *47723* 125 E4
Alexandria MN, *11070* 66 B2
Alexandria SD, *615* 27 E4
Alexandria TN, *966* 110 A4
Alexandria VA, *139966* 144 B3
Alexandria Bay NY, *1078* 79 E1
Alexis IL, *831* 88 A3
Alfalfa Co. OK, *5642* 51 D1
Alford FL, *489* 136 C1
Alfred ME, *2497* 82 B4
Alfred NY, *4174* 92 C1
Alger OH, *860* 90 B3
Alger Co. MI, *9601* 69 E1
Algoa TX, *900* 132 B4
Algodones NM, *814* 48 C3
Algoma MS, *590* 118 C3
Algoma WI, *3167* 69 D4
Algona IA, *5560* 72 B3
Algona WA, *3014* 262 B5
Algonac MI, *4110* 76 C4
Algonquin IL, *30046* 88 C1
Algood TN, *3495* 110 A3
Alhambra CA, *83089* 228 D2
Alhambra IL, *681* 98 B3
Alice TX, *19104* 63 E2
Aliceville AL, *2486* 127 E1
Ali Chuk AZ, *161* 54 B3
Aliquippa PA, *9438* 91 F3
Aliso Viejo CA, *47823* 229 G6
Allamakee Co. IA, *14330* 73 F3
Allamuchy NJ, *78* 94 A4
Allardt TN, *634* 110 B3
Allegan MI, *4998* 75 F4
Allegan Co. MI, *111408* 75 F4
Allegany NY, *1816* 92 C1
Allegany Co. MD, *75087* 102 C1
Allegany Co. NY, *48946* 78 C4
Alleghany Co. NC, *11155* 111 F3
Alleghany Co. VA, *16250* 102 A4
Allegheny Co. PA, *1223348* 92 A4
Allen NE, *377* 35 F2
Allen OK, *932* 51 F3
Allen SD, *420* 26 B4
Allen TX, *84246* 59 F2
Allen Co. IN, *355329* 90 A3
Allen Co. KS, *13371* 96 A4
Allen Co. KY, *19956* 109 F2
Allen Co. OH, *106331* 90 B3
Allendale MI, *17579* 75 F3
Allendale NJ, *6505* 148 B3
Allendale SC, *3482* 130 B1
Allendale Co. SC, *10419* 130 B1
Allenhurst GA, *695* 130 B3
Allenhurst NJ, *496* 147 F2
Allen Par. LA, *25764* 133 E1
Allen Park MI, *28210* 210 B4
Allenspark CO, *528* 41 D1
Allenton RI, *1400* 150 C4
Allenton WI, *823* 74 C2
Allentown NJ, *1828* 147 D2
Allentown PA, *118032* 146 B1
Allenwood NJ, *925* 147 E2
Allerton IA, *501* 87 D3

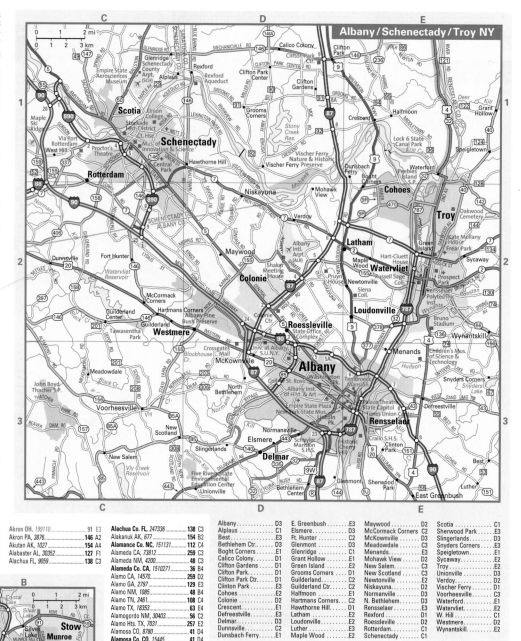

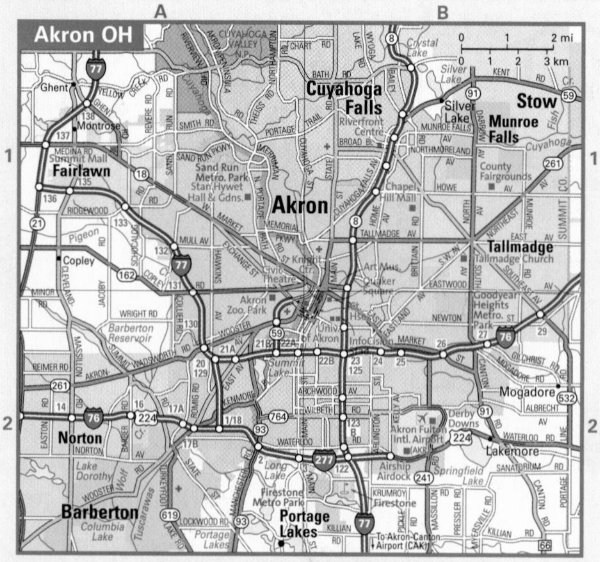

Akron	A1	Fairlawn	A1	Montrose	A1	Silver Lake	B1
Barberton	A2	Ghent	A1	Munroe Falls	B1	Stow	B1
Copley	A1	Lakemore	B2	Norton	A2	Tallmadge	B1
Cuyahoga Falls	B1	Mogadore	B2	Portage Lakes	A2		

Entries in **bold black** indicate counties or parishes.
Entries in **bold color** indicate cities with detailed inset maps.

Allgood AL, 622 .... 119 F4
Alliance NE, 8491 .... 34 A2
Alliance NC, 776 .... 115 D3
Alliance OH, 22322 .... 91 E3
Allison IA, 1029 .... 73 D4
Allison Gap VA, 900 .... 111 F2
Alloway NJ, 1402 .... 145 F1
Alpine CA, 14236 .... 53 D4
Alpine NJ, 1849 .... 148 B3
Alpine TX, 5905 .... 62 B3
Alpine UT, 9555 .... 31 F4
Alpine WY, 828 .... 31 F1
Alpine Co. CA, 1175 .... 37 D3
Alsen LA, 950 .... 134 A2
Alton MO, 871 .... 107 F3
Alton NH, 501 .... 81 F4
Altona IL, 531 .... 88 A3
Altona NY, 730 .... 81 D1
Alton Bay NH, 400 .... 81 F4
Altoona AL, 933 .... 120 A3
Altoona IA, 14541 .... 86 C2
Amber OK, 419 .... 51 E3
Amberley OH, 3585 .... 204 B2
Ambler PA, 6417 .... 146 C2
Amboy IL, 2500 .... 88 B1
Amboy MN, 534 .... 72 C2
Amboy WA, 1608 .... 20 C1
Ambridge PA, 7050 .... 92 A3
Amidon ND, 20 .... 18 A4
Amissville VA, 550 .... 103 D3
Amite LA, 4141 .... 134 B1
Amite Co. MS, 13131 .... 126 A4
Amity AR, 723 .... 117 D3
Amity OR, 1614 .... 20 B2
Amityville NY, 9523 .... 148 C4
Anahuac TX, 2243 .... 132 B3
Anamoose ND, 227 .... 18 C2
Anamosa IA, 5533 .... 87 F1
Anchorage AK, 291826 .... 154 C3
Anchorage KY, 2348 .... 230 F1
Anchor Pt. AK, 1930 .... 154 C3
Anchorville MI, 3200 .... 76 C4
Anderson Co. TN, 75129 .... 110 C4
Anderson Co. TX, 58458 .... 124 A4
Andersonville OH, 779 .... 101 D2
Andover CT, 3303 .... 150 A3
Andover IL, 578 .... 88 A2
Andover KS, 11791 .... 43 F4
Andover MA, 8762 .... 95 E1
Andover MN, 30598 .... 67 D3
Andover NJ, 606 .... 94 A4
Andover NY, 1042 .... 92 C1
Andover OH, 1145 .... 91 F2
Andrew Co. MO, 17291 .... 96 B1
Andrews IN, 1149 .... 89 F3
Andrews NC, 1781 .... 121 D1
Andrews SC, 2861 .... 122 C4
Andrews TX, 11088 .... 57 F3
Andrews Co. TX, 14786 .... 57 F3
Androscoggin Co. ME, 107702 .... 82 B2
Aneta ND, 222 .... 19 E3
Aneth UT, 501 .... 40 A4
Angel Fire NM, 1216 .... 49 D2
Angelica NY, 869 .... 78 B4
Angelina Co. TX, 86771 .... 124 B4
Angels Camp CA, 3836 .... 36 C3
Angier NC, 4350 .... 123 D1
Angleton TX, 18862 .... 132 A4
Angola IN, 8612 .... 90 A2
Angola NY, 2127 .... 78 A4
Angola on the Lake NY, 1675 .... 78 A4
Angoon AK, 459 .... 155 E4
Anguilla MS, 726 .... 126 A1
Angwin CA, 3051 .... 36 B3
Aniak AK, 501 .... 154 B3
Anita IA, 972 .... 86 B2
Ankeny IA, 45582 .... 86 C1
Anmoore WV, 770 .... 102 A2
Anna IL, 4442 .... 108 C1
Anna OH, 1567 .... 90 B4
Anna TX, 8249 .... 59 F1
Annabella UT, 795 .... 39 E2
Anna Maria FL, 1503 .... 140 B3
Annandale MN, 3228 .... 66 C3
Annandale NJ, 1695 .... 147 D1
Annandale VA, 41008 .... 144 B3
Annapolis MD, 38394 .... 144 C3
Ann Arbor MI, 113934 .... 76 B4
Anne Arundel Co. MD, 537656 .... 144 C3
Annetta TX, 1288 .... 59 E2
Anniston AL, 23106 .... 120 A4
Annsville NY, 2956 .... 148 B2
Annville KY, 1095 .... 110 C1
Annville PA, 4767 .... 93 E4
Anoka MN, 17142 .... 67 D3

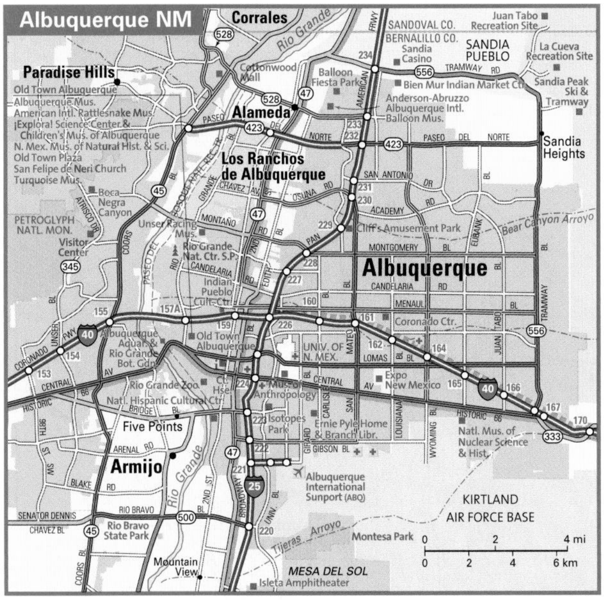

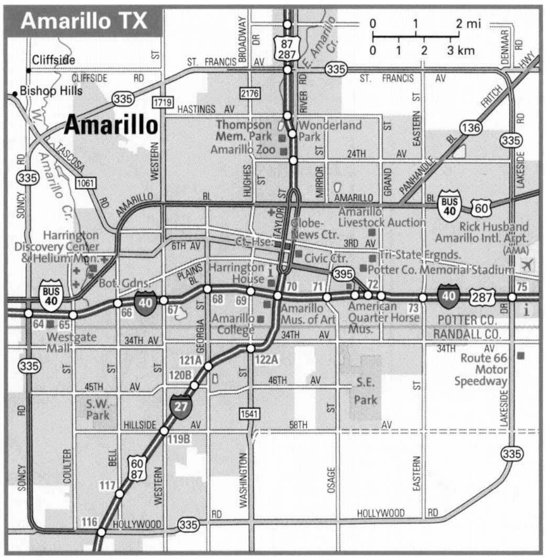

Amelia LA, 2459 .... 134 A3
Amelia OH, 4801 .... 100 B2
Amelia City FL, 1300 .... 139 D2
Amelia Co. VA, 12690 .... 113 D2
Amelia C.H. VA, 1099 .... 113 D1
Amenia NY, 955 .... 94 B3
American Beach FL, 800 .... 139 D2
American Canyon CA, 19454 .... 36 B3
American Falls ID, 4457 .... 31 E1
American Fork UT, 26263 .... 31 F4
Americus GA, 17041 .... 129 D3
Americus KS, 894 .... 43 F3
Amery WI, 2902 .... 67 E3
Ames IA, 58965 .... 86 C1
Ames TX, 1003 .... 132 B3
Amesbury MA, 16283 .... 95 E1
Amherst MA, 19065 .... 150 A1
Amherst NH, 613 .... 95 D1
Amherst NY, 122366 .... 78 B3
Amherst OH, 12021 .... 91 D2
Amherst TX, 721 .... 57 F1
Amherst VA, 2231 .... 112 C1
Amherst WI, 1035 .... 74 B1
Amherst Co. VA, 32353 .... 112 C1
Amherstdale WV, 350 .... 111 F1
Ammon ID, 13816 .... 23 E4
Amory MS, 7316 .... 119 D4
Amsterdam MT, 180 .... 23 F1
Amsterdam NY, 18620 .... 94 A1
Amsterdam OH, 511 .... 91 F4
Anacoco LA, 869 .... 125 D4
Anaconda MT, 9298 .... 23 D1
Anacortes WA, 15778 .... 12 C2
Anadarko OK, 6762 .... 51 D3
Anaheim CA, 336265 .... 52 C3
Anahola HI, 2223 .... 152 B1
Andale KS, 928 .... 43 E4
Andalusia AL, 9015 .... 128 A4
Andalusia IL, 1178 .... 87 F2
Anderson CA, 9932 .... 28 C4
Anderson IN, 56129 .... 89 F4
Anderson MO, 1961 .... 106 B3
Anderson SC, 26686 .... 121 E3
Anderson TX, 222 .... 61 F1
Anderson Co. KS, 8102 .... 96 A4
Anderson Co. KY, 21421 .... 100 A4
Anderson Co. SC, 187126 .... 121 E2

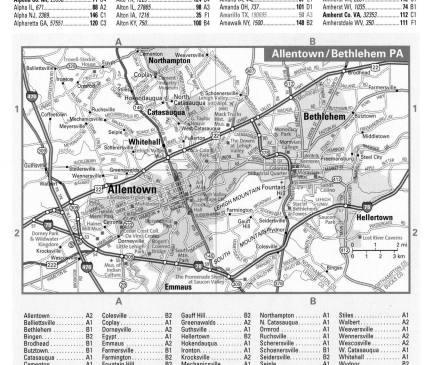

Allyn WA, 1963 .... 12 C3
Alma AR, 5419 .... 116 C1
Alma GA, 3466 .... 129 F4
Alma KS, 832 .... 43 F2
Alma MI, 9383 .... 76 A2
Alma NE, 1133 .... 43 D1
Alma WI, 781 .... 73 E1
Almena KS, 408 .... 42 C1
Almena WI, 677 .... 67 E3
Almon GA, 1000 .... 121 D4
Almont MI, 2674 .... 76 C3
Aloe TX, 850 .... 61 E3
Aloha OR, 49425 .... 20 B2
Alorton IL, 2002 .... 256 C3
Alpaugh CA, 1026 .... 45 D4
Alpena MI, 10483 .... 71 D3
Alpena SD, 286 .... 27 E3
Alpena Co. MI, 29598 .... 71 D4
Alpha IL, 671 .... 88 A2
Alpha NJ, 2369 .... 146 C1
Alpharetta GA, 57551 .... 120 C3
Alsip IL, 19277 .... 203 D6
Alta IA, 1883 .... 72 A4
Alta UT, 383 .... 31 F4
Alta WY, 394 .... 23 F4
Altadena CA, 42777 .... 228 D1
Altamahaw NC, 347 .... 112 B4
Altamont IL, 2319 .... 98 C2
Altamont KS, 1080 .... 106 A2
Altamont NY, 1720 .... 94 B1
Altamont OR, 19257 .... 28 C2
Altamont TN, 1045 .... 120 A1
Altamonte Sprs. FL, 41496 .... 141 D1
Alta Vista KS, 444 .... 43 F2
Altavista VA, 3450 .... 112 C2
Altha FL, 536 .... 137 D2
Altheimer AR, 984 .... 117 F3
Alto GA, 1172 .... 121 D3
Alto TX, 1225 .... 124 B4
Alton IL, 27865 .... 98 A3
Alton IA, 1216 .... 35 F1
Alton KY, 750 .... 100 B4
Altoona KS, 414 .... 106 A1
Altoona PA, 46320 .... 92 C4
Altoona WI, 6706 .... 67 F4
Alturas CA, 2827 .... 29 D3
Altus AR, 758 .... 116 C1
Altus OK, 19813 .... 51 D4
Alum Creek WV, 1749 .... 101 E4
Alva FL, 2596 .... 143 D1
Alva OK, 4945 .... 51 D1
Alvarado TX, 3785 .... 59 E3
Alvin TX, 24236 .... 132 B4
Alvord TX, 1334 .... 59 E1
Ama LA, 1316 .... 239 B2
Amado AZ, 295 .... 55 D4
Amador Co. CA, 38091 .... 36 C3
Amagansett NY, 1165 .... 149 F3
Amalga UT, 488 .... 31 E2
Amana IA, 442 .... 87 E1
Amanda OH, 737 .... 101 D1
Amarillo TX, 190695 .... 50 A3
Amawalk NY, 1500 .... 148 B2

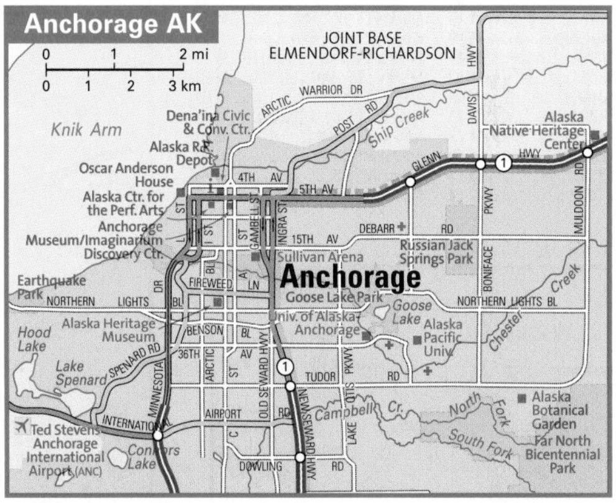

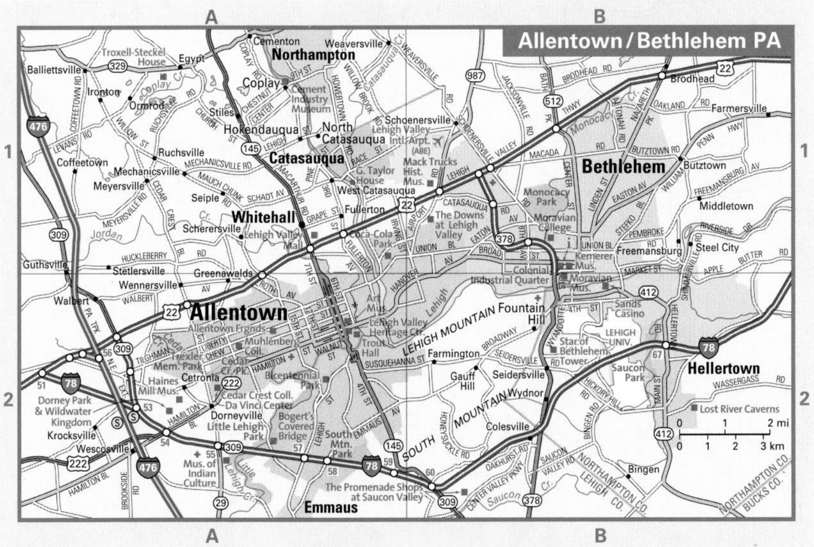

Allentown A2	Colesville B2	Gauff Hill B2	Northampton A1	Stiles A1
Balliettsville A1	Coplay A1	Greenawalds A2	N. Catasauqua A1	Walbert A2
Bethlehem B1	Dorneyville A2	Guthsville A1	Ormrod A1	Weaversville A1
Bingen B2	Egypt A1	Hellertown B2	Ruchsville A1	Wennersville A2
Brodhead B1	Emmaus A2	Hokendauqua A1	Schererville A1	Wescosville A2
Butztown B1	Farmersville B1	Ironton A1	Schoenersville B1	W. Catasauqua A1
Catasauqua A1	Farmington B2	Krocksville A2	Seidersville B2	Whitehall A1
Cementon A1	Fountain Hill B2	Mechanicsville A1	Seiple A1	Wydnor B2
Cetronia A2	Freemansburg B1	Meyersville A1	Steel City B1	
Coffeetown A1	Fullerton A1	Middletown B1	Stetlersville A1	

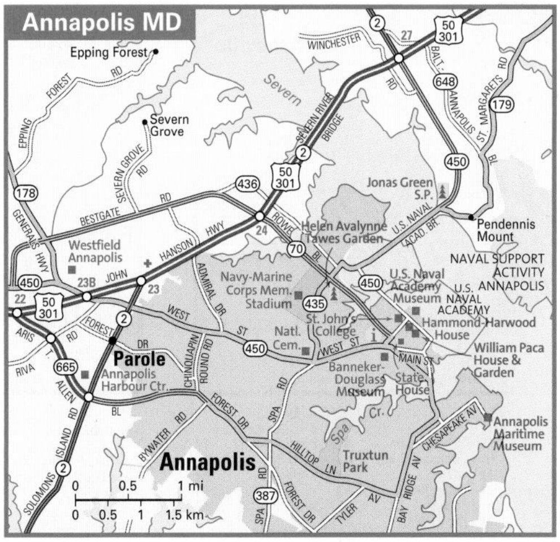

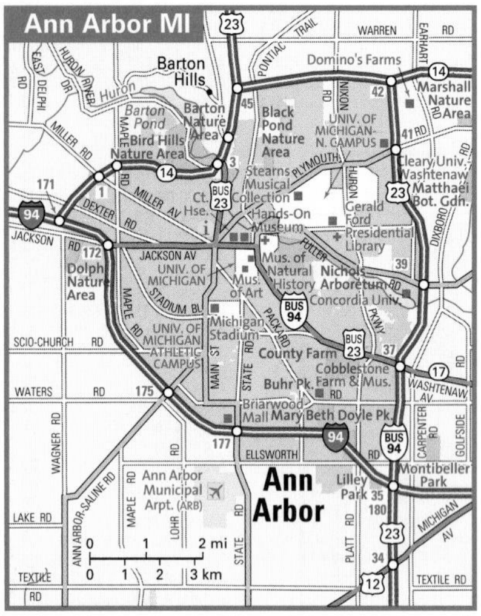

Anoka Co. MN, *330844* **67** D3
Ansley NE, *441* **35** D3
Anson ME, *752* **82** B1
Anson TX, *2430* **58** C2
Anson Co. NC, *26948* **122** B2
Ansonia CT, *19249* **149** D2
Ansonia OH, *1174* **90** A4
Ansonville NC, *631* **122** B1
Ansted WV, *1404* **101** F4
Antelope SD, *826* **26** C4
Antelope Acres CA, *1000* **52** C1
Antelope Co. NE, *6685* **35** E2
Anthon IA, *565* **72** A4
Anthony FL, *1600* **138** C4
Anthony KS, *2269* **43** E4
Anthony NM, *9360* **56** C3
Anthony TX, *5011* **56** C3
Antigo WI, *8234* **68** B3
Antioch CA, *102372* **36** B3
Antioch IL, *14430* **74** C4
Antlers OK, *2453* **116** A3
Anton TX, *1126* **58** A1
Antonito CO, *781* **49** D1
Antrim NH, *1397* **81** E4
Antrim Co. MI, *23580* **70** B3
Antwerp NY, *686* **79** E1
Antwerp OH, *1736* **90** A2
Apache OK, *1444* **51** D3
Apache Co. AZ, *71518* **47** F3
Apache Jct. AZ, *35840* **54** C1
Apalachicola FL, *2231* **137** D3
Apalachin NY, *1131* **93** E1
Apex NC, *37476* **112** C4
Aplington IA, *1128* **73** D4
Apollo PA, *1647* **92** A4
Apollo Beach FL, *14055* **266** C3
Apopka FL, *41542* **141** D1
Appalachia VA, *1754* **111** E2
Appanoose Co. IA, *12887* **87** D3
Apple Creek OH, *1173* **91** E3
Applegate CA, *800* **36** C2
Appleton MN, *1412* **27** F2
Appleton WI, *72623* **74** C1
Appleton City MO, *1127* **96** C4
Apple Valley CA, *69135* **53** D2
Apple Valley MN, *49084* **67** D4
Applewood CO, *7160* **209** B3
Appling GA, *225* **121** F4
Appling Co. GA, *18236* **129** F3
Appomattox VA, *1733* **112** C1
Appomattox Co. VA, *14973* **112** C1
Aptos CA, *6220* **44** B2
Aquebogue NY, *2438* **149** E3
Arab AL, *8050* **119** F3
Arabi LA, *3635* **239** C1
Aragon GA, *1249* **120** B3
Aransas Co. TX, *23158* **61** F4
Aransas Pass TX, *8204* **63** F2
Arapaho OK, *796* **51** D3
Arapahoe NE, *1026* **34** C4
Arapahoe WY, *1656* **32** B1
Arapahoe Co. CO, *572003* **41** E1
Arbuckle CA, *3028* **36** B2
Arbutus MD, *20483* **193** B3
Arbyrd MO, *509* **108** B4
Arcade CA, *96025* **255** B2

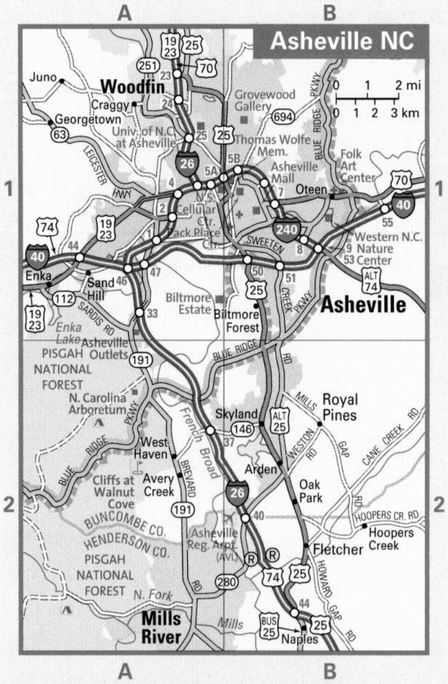

Arden B2
Asheville B1
Avery Creek A2
Biltmore Forest B1
Craggy A1
Enka A1
Fletcher B2
Georgetown A1
Hoopers Creek B2
Juno A1
Mills River A2
Naples B2
Oak Park B2
Oteen B1
Royal Pines B2
Sand Hill A1
Skyland B2
W. Haven A2
Woodfin A1

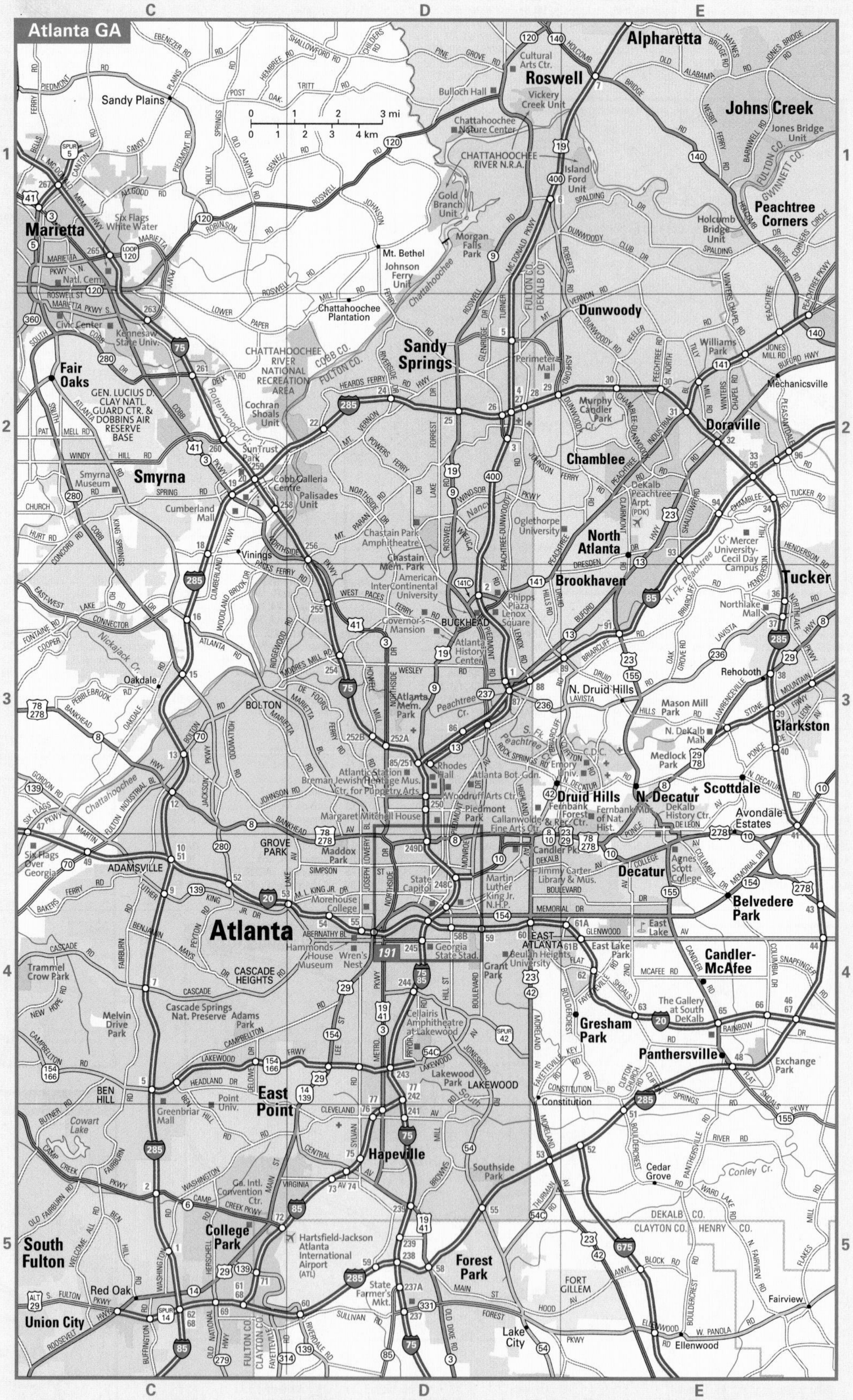

Alpharetta E1
Atlanta C4
Avondale Estates E3
Belvedere Park E4
Brookhaven D3
Cedar Grove E5
Chamblee E2
Chattahoochee Plantation D2
Clarkston E3
College Park C5
Constitution D4
Decatur E4
Doraville E2
Druid Hills D3
Dunwoody E2
E. Point C4
Ellenwood E5
Fair Oaks C2
Fairview E5
Forest Park D5
Gresham Park E4
Hapeville D5
Johns Creek E1
Lake City D5
Marietta C1
Mechanicsville E2
Mount Bethel D1
N. Atlanta E2
N. Decatur E3
N. Druid Hills E3
Oakdale C3
Panthersville E4
Peachtree Corners E1
Red Oak C5
Rehoboth E3
Roswell D1
Sandy Plains C1
Sandy Sprs. D2
Scottdale E3
Smyrna C2
S. Fulton C5
Tucker E2
Union City C5
Vinings C2

Entries in **bold black** indicate counties or parishes.
Entries in **bold color** indicate cities with detailed inset maps.

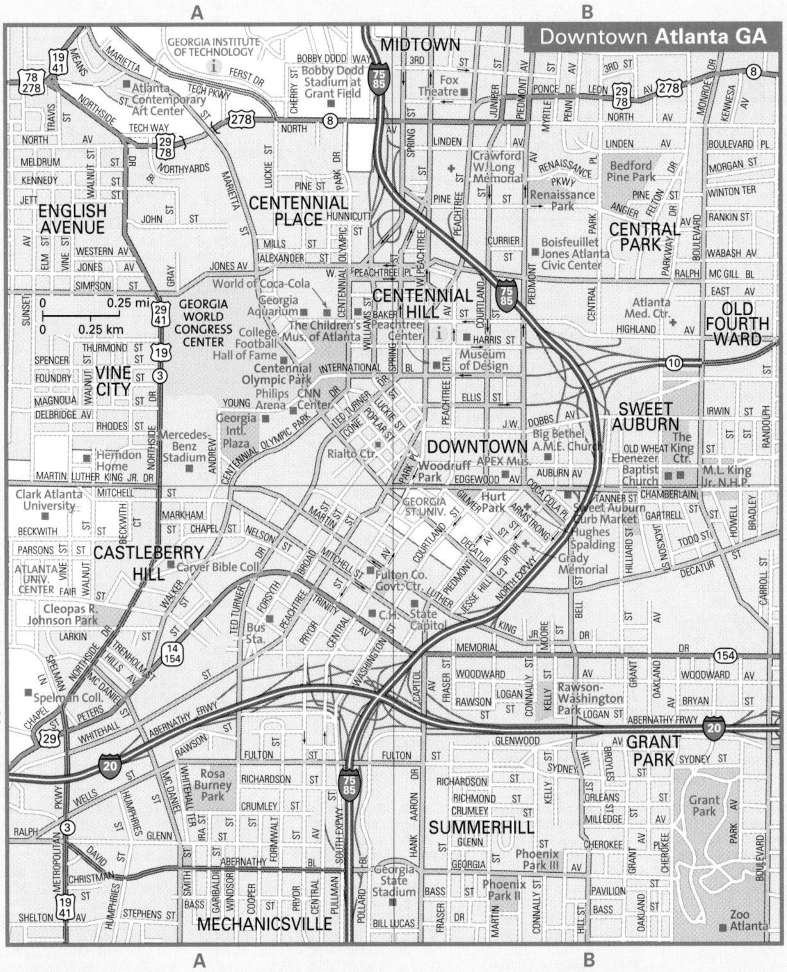

POINTS OF INTEREST

APEX Museum.......B1
Atlanta Contemporary Art Center.......A1
Atlanta University Center.......A2
Big Bethel African Meth. Episcopal Church.......B1
Bobby Dodd Stadium at Grant Field.......A1
Boisfeuillet Jones Atlanta Civic Center.......B1
Bus Station.......A2
Carver Bible College.......A2
City Hall.......A2
Clark Atlanta University.......A2
CNN Center.......A1
Ebenezer Baptist Church.......B1
Fox Theatre.......B1
Fulton County Government Center.......A2
Georgia Aquarium.......A1
Georgia Institute of Technology.......A1
Georgia State Stadium.......A2
Georgia State University.......B2
Georgia World Congress Center.......A1
Herndon Home.......A1
The King Center.......B1
Martin Luther King, Jr. Natl. Hist. Park.......B1
Mercedes-Benz Stadium.......A1
Museum of Design.......B1
Peachtree Center.......B1
Philips Arena.......A1
Rialto Center.......A1
Spelman College.......A2
State Capitol.......B2
Sweet Auburn Curb Market.......B2
The Children's Mus. of Atlanta.......A1
World of Coca-Cola.......A1
Zoo Atlanta.......B2

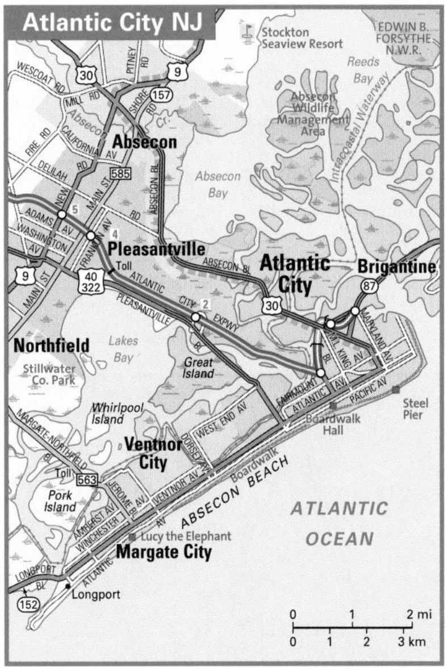

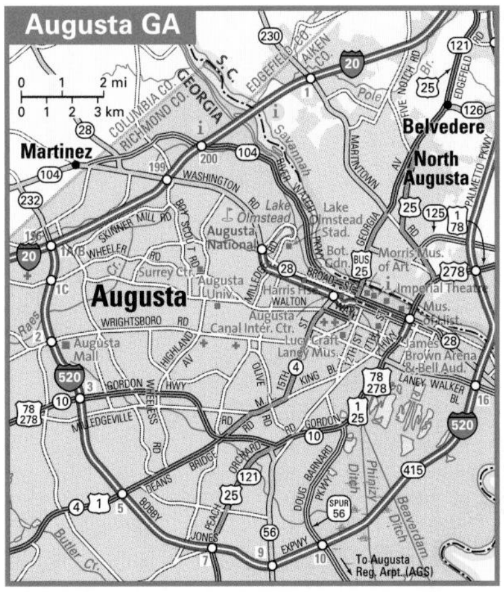

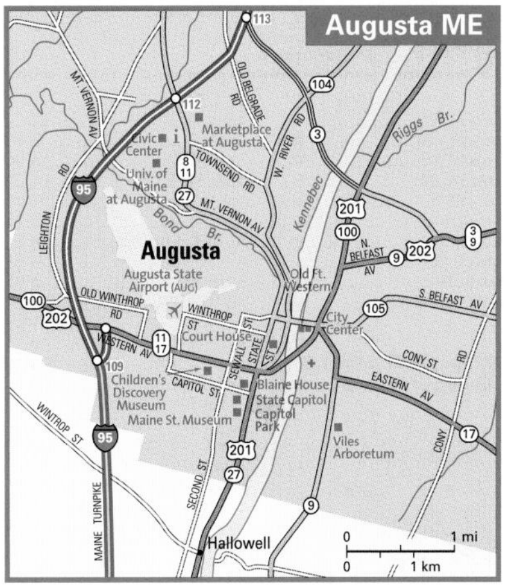

Arcade GA, *1786* **121** D3
Arcade NY, *2071* **78** B4
Arcadia CA, *56364* **228** E2
Arcadia FL, *7637* **140** C4
Arcadia IN, *1666* **89** F4
Arcadia KS, *310* **106** B1
Arcadia LA, *2919* **125** D2
Arcadia MO, *608* **108** A1
Arcadia OH, *590* **90** C3
Arcadia WI, *2925* **73** E1
Arcadia Lakes SC, *861* **205** F1
Arcanum OH, *2129* **100** B1
Arcata CA, *17231* **28** A4
Archbald PA, *6984* **93** F2
Archbold OH, *4346* **90** B2
Archdale NC, *11415* **112** B4
Archer FL, *1118* **138** C3
Archer City TX, *1834* **59** D1
Archer Co. TX, *9054* **59** D1
Archie MO, *1170* **96** B3
Archuleta Co. CO, *12084* **40** C4
Arco ID, *995* **23** D4
Arcola IL, *2916* **99** D1
Arcola MS, *361* **126** A1
Arcola TX, *1642* **132** A4
Arden CA, *96025* **255** B2
Arden DE, *439* **146** B3
Ardencroft DE, *231* **274** E1
Arden Hills MN, *9552* **235** C1
Ardentown DE, *264* **274** E1
Ardmore AL, *1194* **119** F2
Ardmore OK, *24283* **51** F4
Ardmore PA, *12455* **146** C3
Ardmore TN, *1213* **119** F2
Ardonia NY, *950* **148** B1
Arena WI, *834* **74** A3
Arenac Co. MI, *15899* **76** B1
Arendtsville PA, *952* **103** E1
Argenta IL, *947* **98** C1
Argentine MI, *2525* **76** B4
Argo AL, *4071* **119** F4
Argonia KS, *501* **43** E4
Argos IN, *1691* **89** F2
Argos Corner DE, *550* **145** F3
Argyle MN, *639* **19** F2
Argyle TX, *3282* **59** E2
Argyle WI, *857* **74** A4
Arimo ID, *355* **31** E1
Aripeka FL, *308* **140** B1
Ariton AL, *764* **128** B4
Arizola AZ, *550* **54** C2
Arizona City AZ, *10475* **54** C2
Arkadelphia AR, *10714* **117** D3
Arkansas City AR, *366* **117** F4
Arkansas City KS, *12415* **51** E1
Arkansas Co. AR, *19019* **117** F3
Arkoma OK, *1989* **116** B1
Arkport NY, *844* **78** C4
Arlee MT, *636* **15** D3
Arlington GA, *1479* **128** C4
Arlington IA, *429* **73** E4
Arlington KS, *473* **43** E4
Arlington KY, *324* **108** C2
Arlington MA, *42844* **151** D1
Arlington MN, *2233* **66** C4
Arlington NE, *1243* **35** F3
Arlington NY, *4061* **148** B1
Arlington OH, *1455* **90** C3
Arlington OR, *586* **21** E1
Arlington SD, *915* **27** F3
Arlington TN, *11517* **118** B1
Arlington TX, *365438* **59** E2
Arlington VT, *1213* **81** D4
Arlington VA, *207627* **144** B3
Arlington WA, *17926* **12** C2
Arlington Co. VA, *207627* **144** B3
Arlington Hts. IL, *75101* **89** D1
Arlington Hts. OH, *745* **204** B2
Arma KS, *1481* **106** B1
Armada MI, *1730* **76** C3
Armijo NM, *9500* **48** C3
Armona CA, *4156* **44** C3
Armonk NY, *4330* **148** C2
Armour SD, *699* **27** E4
Armstrong IA, *926* **72** B2
Armstrong Co. PA, *68941* **92** A3
Armstrong Co. TX, *1901* **50** B3
Arnaudville LA, *1057* **133** F2
Arnett OK, *524* **50** C2
Arnold CA, *3843* **37** D3
Arnold MD, *23106* **144** C3
Arnold MN, *2960* **64** C4
Arnold MO, *20808* **98** A3
Arnold NE, *597* **34** C3
Arnold PA, *5157* **92** A4
Arnolds Park IA, *1126* **72** A3
Aroma Park IL, *743* **89** D3
Aromas CA, *2650* **44** B2
Aroostook Co. ME, *71870* **85** D2
Arp TX, *970* **124** B3
Arredondo FL, *1400* **138** C3
Arroyo Grande CA, *17252* **52** A1
Arroyo Hondo NM, *474* **49** D1
Arroyo Seco NM, *1785* **49** D1
Artesia CA, *16522* **228** E4
Artesia MS, *440* **127** D1
Artesia NM, *11301* **57** E2
Arthur IL, *2288* **98** C1
Arthur NE, *117* **34** B3
Arthur ND, *337* **19** E3
Arthur TN, *1100* **110** C3
Arthur Co. NE, *460* **34** B3
Arthurdale WV, *950* **102** B2
Arundel on the Bay MD, *1000* **144** C3
Arundel Vil. MD, *8000* **193** C4
Arvada CO, *106433* **41** E1
Arvin CA, *19304* **52** B1
Asbury IA, *4170* **73** F4
Asbury Park NJ, *16116* **147** F2
Ascension Par. LA, *107215* **134** A2
Ascutney VT, *540* **81** E4
Asharoken NY, *654* **148** C3
Ashaway RI, *1485* **150** C4
Ashburn GA, *4152* **129** D4
Ashburn VA, *43511* **144** A3
Ashburnham MA, *6081* **95** D1
Ashdown AR, *4723* **116** C4
Asheboro NC, *25012* **112** B4
Ashe Co. NC, *27281* **111** F3
Asherton TX, *1084* **60** C4
Asheville NC, *83393* 121 E1
Ashfield MA, *550* **94** C1
Ash Flat AR, *1082* **107** F3
Ashford AL, *2148* **137** D1
Ash Fork AZ, *396* **47** D3
Ash Grove MO, *1472* **106** C1
Ashkum IL, *761* **89** D3
Ashland AL, *2037* **128** B1
Ashland CA, *21925* **259** D3
Ashland IL, *1333* **98** B1
Ashland KS, *867* **42** C4
Ashland KY, *21684* **101** D3
Ashland ME, *709* **85** D2
Ashland MA, *16593* **150** C1
Ashland MS, *569* **118** C2
Ashland MO, *3707* **97** E3
Ashland MT, *824* **25** D1
Ashland NE, *2453* **35** F3
Ashland NH, *1244* **81** F3
Ashland OH, *20362* **91** D3
Ashland OR, *20078* **28** C2
Ashland PA, *2817* **93** E3
Ashland VA, *7225* **113** E1
Ashland WI, *8216* **65** D4
Ashland City TN, *4541* **109** E3
Ashland Co. OH, *53139* **91** D3
Ashland Co. WI, *16157* **67** F1
Ashley IL, *536* **98** C4
Ashley IN, *983* **90** A2
Ashley MI, *563* **76** A3
Ashley ND, *749* **27** D1
Ashley PA, *2790* **261** A2
Ashley Co. AR, *21853* **125** F1
Ashmore IL, *785* **99** D1
Ashtabula OH, *19124* **91** F1
Ashtabula Co. OH, *101497* **91** F1
Ashton ID, *1127* **23** F3
Ashton IL, *972* **88** B1
Ashton RI, *2600* **150** C3
Ashuelot NH, *375* **94** C1
Ashville AL, *2212* **120** A4
Ashville OH, *4097* **101** D1
Ashwaubenon WI, *16963* **68** C4
Asotin WA, *1251* **14** B4
Asotin Co. WA, *21623* **22** A1
Aspen CO, *6658* **40** C2
Aspen Hill MD, *48759* **144** B2
Aspen Park CO, *882* **209** A4
Aspermont TX, *919* **58** C2
Aspinwall PA, *2801* **250** C1
Assaria KS, *413* **43** E3
Assinippi MA, *2700* **151** E2
Assonet MA, *1200* **151** D3
Assumption IL, *1168* **98** C1
Assumption Par. LA, *23421* **134** A3
Astatula FL, *1810* **140** C1
Astor FL, *1556* **139** D4
Astoria IL, *1141* **88** A4
Astoria OR, *9477* **20** B1
Atascadero CA, *28310* **44** C4
Atascosa Co. TX, *44911* **61** D3
Atchison KS, *11021* **96** B1
Atchison Co. KS, *16924* **96** A2
Atchison Co. MO, *5685* **86** A4
Atco NJ, *4500* **147** D4
Atglen PA, *1406* **146** A3
Athena OR, *1126* **21** F1
Athens AL, *21897* **119** F2
Athens GA, *115452* **121** D4
Athens IL, *1988* **98** B1
Athens ME, *847* **82** C1
Athens MI, *1024* **90** A1
Athens NY, *1668* **94** B2
Athens OH, *23832* **101** E2
Athens PA, *3367* **93** E1
Athens TN, *13458* **120** C1
Athens TX, *12710* **124** A3
Athens WV, *1048* **112** A1
Athens WI, *1105* **68** A3
Athens Co. OH, *64757* **101** E2
Atherton CA, *6914* **259** C5
Athol ID, *692* **14** B2
Athol MA, *8265* **95** D1
Atkins AR, *3016* **117** D1
Atkins IA, *1670* **87** E1
Atkins VA, *1143* **111** F2
Atkinson IL, *972* **88** A2
Atkinson NE, *1245* **35** D1
Atkinson NH, *6751* **95** E1
Atkinson Co. GA, *8375* **129** E4
Atlanta GA, *420003* 120 C4
Atlanta IL, *1692* **88** B4
Atlanta IN, *725* **89** F4
Atlanta MI, *827* **70** C4
Atlanta NY, *650* **78** C4
Atlanta TX, *5675* **124** C1
Atlantic IA, *7112* **86** B2
Atlantic Beach FL, *12655* **139** D2
Atlantic Beach NY, *1891* **147** F1
Atlantic Beach NC, *1495* **115** D4
Atlantic City NJ, *39558* 147 F4
Atlantic Co. NJ, *274549* **147** D4
Atlantic Highlands NJ, *4385* **147** E1
Atlantis FL, *2005* **143** F1
Atmore AL, *10194* **135** F1
Atoka OK, *3107* **51** F4
Atoka TN, *8387* **118** B1
Atoka Co. OK, *14182* **51** F4
Attala Co. MS, *19564* **126** C1
Attalla AL, *6048* **120** A3
Attapulgus GA, *449* **137** E1
Attawaugan CT, *950* **150** B3
Attica IN, *3245* **89** D4
Attica KS, *626* **43** E4
Attica MI, *994* **76** C3
Attica NY, *2547* **78** B3
Attica OH, *899* **90** C3
Attleboro MA, *43593* **151** D2
Atwater CA, *28168* **36** C4
Atwater MN, *1133* **66** B3
Atwater OH, *758* **91** E3
Atwood IL, *1224* **98** C1
Atwood KS, *1194* **42** B1
Atwood TN, *938* **108** C4
Auberry CA, *2369* **45** D2
Aubrey TX, *2595* **59** F2
Auburn AL, *53380* **128** B2
Auburn CA, *13330* **36** C2
Auburn GA, *6887* **121** D3
Auburn IL, *4771* **98** B1
Auburn IN, *12731* **90** A2
Auburn KS, *1227* **96** A3
Auburn KY, *1340* **109** F2
Auburn ME, *23055* **82** B3
Auburn MA, *16188* **150** B2
Auburn MI, *2087* **76** B2
Auburn NE, *3460* **86** A4
Auburn NY, *27687* **79** D3
Auburn PA, *741* **146** A1
Auburn WA, *70180* **12** C3
Auburn WY, *328* **31** F1
Auburndale FL, *13507* **140** C2
Auburndale WI, *703* **68** A4
Auburn Hills MI, *21412* **210** B1
Audrain Co. MO, *25529* **97** E2
Audubon IA, *2176* **86** B1
Audubon NJ, *8819* **248** D4
Audubon PA, *8433* **248** A1
Audubon Co. IA, *6119* **86** B2
Audubon Park KY, *1473* **230** D2
Audubon Park NJ, *1023* **248** D4
Auglaize Co. OH, *45949* **90** B4
Au Gres MI, *889* **76** B1
Augusta AR, *2199* **117** F1
Augusta GA, *195844* 121 F4
Augusta IL, *587* **87** F4
Augusta KS, *9274* **43** F4
Augusta KY, *1190* **100** C3
Augusta ME, *19136* 82 C2
Augusta MI, *885* **75** F4
Augusta MT, *309* **15** E3
Augusta WI, *1550* **67** F4
Augusta Co. VA, *73750* **102** B4

Figures after entries indicate population, page number, and grid reference.

Aulander NC, 895 ... 113 E3
Ault CO, 1519 ... 33 E4
Aumsville OR, 3584 ... 20 B2
Aurelia IA, 1036 ... 72 A4
Aurora CO, 325078 ... 41 E1
Aurora IL, 197899 ... 88 C1
Aurora IN, 3750 ... 100 B2
Aurora MN, 1682 ... 64 C3
Aurora MO, 7508 ... 106 C2
Aurora NE, 4479 ... 35 E4
Aurora NY, 724 ... 79 D4
Aurora NC, 520 ... 115 D3
Aurora OH, 15548 ... 91 E2
Aurora OR, 918 ... 20 C2
Aurora SD, 532 ... 27 F3
Aurora TX, 1220 ... 59 E2
Aurora UT, 1016 ... 39 E2
Aurora Co. SD, 2710 ... 27 D4
Au Sable MI, 1404 ... 76 C1
Autaugaville AL, 870 ... 127 F2
Auxvasse MO, 983 ... 97 E2
Ava IL, 654 ... 98 B4
Ava MO, 2993 ... 107 E2
Avalon CA, 3728 ... 52 C3
Avalon NJ, 1334 ... 105 D4
Avalon PA, 4705 ... 250 A1
Avawam KY, 450 ... 111 D2
Avella PA, 804 ... 91 F4
Avenal CA, 15505 ... 44 C3
Avenel NJ, 17011 ... 147 E1
Aventura FL, 35762 ... 143 F2
Averill Park NY, 1693 ... 94 B1
Avery CA, 646 ... 37 D3
Avery Co. NC, 17797 ... 111 F4
Avery Creek NC, 1950 ... 121 E1
Avilla IN, 2401 ... 90 A2
Avis PA, 1484 ... 93 D2
Aviston IL, 1945 ... 98 B3
Avon MN, 1396 ... 66 C2
Avon NY, 3394 ... 78 C3
Avon NC, 776 ... 115 F3
Avon OH, 21193 ... 91 D2
Avon PA, 1667 ... 146 A2
Avon SD, 590 ... 35 E1
Avon-by-the-Sea NJ, 1901 ... 147 F2
Avondale AZ, 76238 ... 54 C1
Avondale CO, 674 ... 41 E3
Avondale LA, 4954 ... 134 B3
Avondale MO, 440 ... 224 C2
Avondale PA, 1265 ... 146 B3
Avondale RI, 425 ... 149 F2
Avondale Estates GA, 2960 ... 190 E3
Avonia PA, 1205 ... 91 F1
Avon Lake OH, 22581 ... 91 D2
Avonmore PA, 1011 ... 92 A4
Avon Park FL, 8836 ... 141 D3
Avoyelles Par. LA, 42073 ... 125 F4

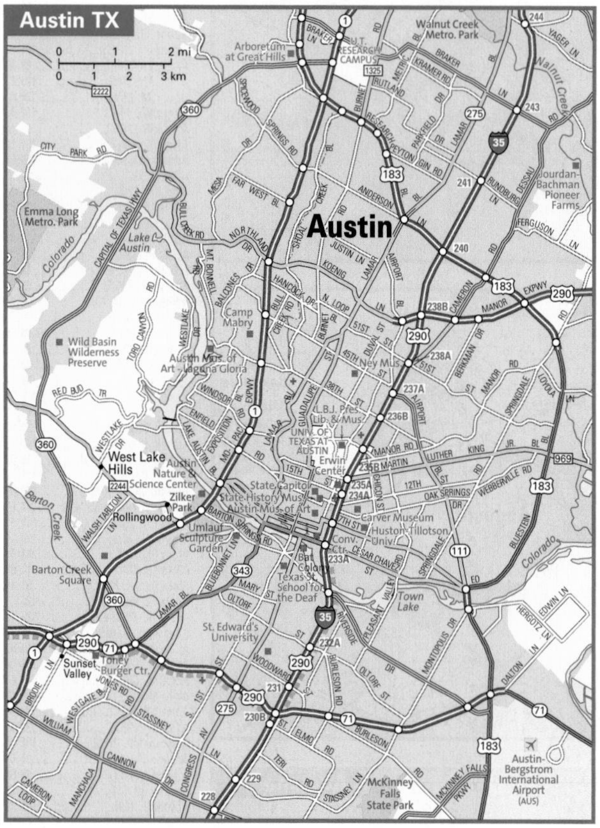

Au Sable Forks NY, 559 ... 81 D2
Austin AR, 2038 ... 117 E2
Austin IN, 4295 ... 99 F3
Austin MN, 24718 ... 73 D2
Austin NV, 192 ... 37 F1
Austin PA, 562 ... 92 C2
Austin TX, 790390 ... 61 E1
Austin Co. TX, 28417 ... 61 F2
Austintown OH, 29677 ... 91 F3
Autauga Co. AL, 54571 ... 127 F2
Avoca AR, 488 ... 106 C3
Avoca IA, 1506 ... 86 A2
Avoca NY, 946 ... 78 C4
Avoca PA, 2661 ... 261 C2
Avoca WI, 637 ... 74 A3
Avon AL, 543 ... 137 D1
Avon CO, 6447 ... 40 C1
Avon CT, 18098 ... 94 C3
Avon IL, 799 ... 88 A3
Avon IN, 12446 ... 99 F1
Awendaw SC, 1294 ... 131 D1
Axtell KS, 406 ... 43 F1
Axtell NE, 726 ... 35 D4
Ayden NC, 4932 ... 115 D3
Ayer MA, 2868 ... 95 D1
Aynor SC, 560 ... 122 C3
Azalea Park FL, 12556 ... 246 D2
Azle TX, 10947 ... 59 E2
Aztec NM, 6763 ... 48 B1
Azusa CA, 46361 ... 228 E2

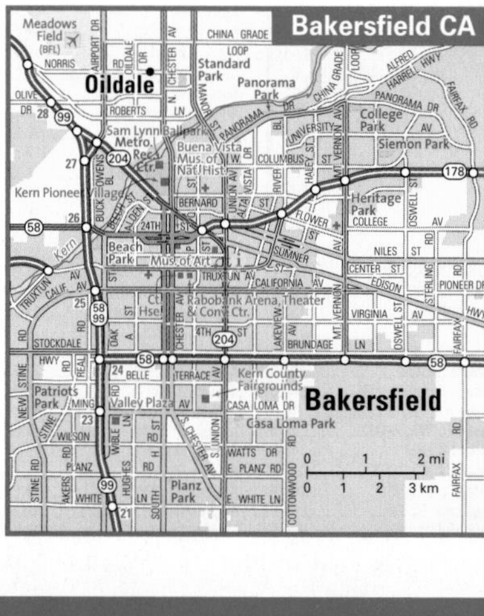

B

Babbie AL, 603 ... 128 A4
Babbitt MN, 1475 ... 64 C3
Babson Park FL, 1356 ... 141 D3
Babylon NY, 12166 ... 148 C4
Baca Co. CO, 3788 ... 42 A4
Bacon Co. GA, 11096 ... 129 F4
Baconton GA, 915 ... 129 D4
Bad Axe MI, 3129 ... 76 C2
Baden PA, 4135 ... 92 A3
Badger IA, 561 ... 72 C4
Badin NC, 1974 ... 122 B1
Bagdad AZ, 1876 ... 46 C4
Bagdad FL, 3761 ... 135 F2
Baggs WY, 440 ... 32 C3
Bagley MN, 1392 ... 64 A3
Bahama NC, 550 ... 112 C4
Bailey NC, 569 ... 113 D4
Bailey Co. TX, 7165 ... 49 F4
Bailey Island ME, 400 ... 82 B3
Bailey's Crossroads VA, 23643 ... 270 B4
Bailey's Prairie TX, 727 ... 132 A4
Baileyton AL, 610 ... 119 F3
Baileyton TN, 431 ... 111 D3
Bainbridge GA, 12697 ... 137 D1
Bainbridge IN, 746 ... 99 E1
Bainbridge NY, 1355 ... 79 E4
Bainbridge OH, 3267 ... 101 D2
Bainbridge Island WA, 23025 ... 12 C3
Baird TX, 1496 ... 58 C3
Baiting Hollow NY, 1642 ... 149 E3
Baker LA, 13895 ... 134 A2
Baker MT, 1741 ... 17 F4
Baker City OR, 9828 ... 21 F2
Baker Co. FL, 27115 ... 138 C2
Baker Co. GA, 3451 ... 128 C4
Baker Co. OR, 16134 ... 21 F3
Bakersfield CA, 347483 ... 45 D4
Bakersville NC, 464 ... 111 E4
Bala-Cynwyd PA, 10300 ... 146 C3
Balaton MN, 643 ... 72 A1
Balch Sprs. TX, 23728 ... 207 E3
Balcones Hts. TX, 2941 ... 257 E2
Bald Knob AR, 2897 ... 117 F1
Baldwin FL, 1425 ... 139 D2
Baldwin GA, 3279 ... 121 D3
Baldwin IL, 373 ... 98 B4
Baldwin LA, 2436 ... 133 F3
Baldwin MD, 850 ... 144 C1
Baldwin MI, 1208 ... 75 F2
Baldwin PA, 19767 ... 250 C3
Baldwin WI, 3957 ... 67 E4
Baldwin City KS, 4515 ... 96 A3
Baldwin Co. AL, 182265 ... 135 E1
Baldwin Co. GA, 45720 ... 129 E1
Baldwin Harbor NY, 8102 ... 147 F1
Baldwin Park CA, 75390 ... 228 E2
Baldwinsville NY, 7378 ... 79 D3
Baldwinville MA, 2028 ... 95 D1
Baldwyn MS, 3297 ... 119 D3
Balfour NC, 1187 ... 121 E1
Bal Harbour FL, 2513 ... 233 B3
Ball LA, 4000 ... 125 E4
Ballantine MT, 320 ... 24 C1
Ballard UT, 801 ... 32 A4
Ballard Co. KY, 8249 ... 108 C2
Ballentine SC, 850 ... 122 A3
Ball Ground GA, 1433 ... 120 C3
Ballinger TX, 3767 ... 58 C4
Ballouville CT, 950 ... 150 B3
Ballston Spa NY, 5409 ... 80 C4
Ballville OH, 2976 ... 90 C2
Ballwin MO, 30404 ... 98 A3
Bally PA, 1090 ... 146 B1
Balmorhea TX, 479 ... 62 B2
Balmville NY, 3178 ... 148 B1
Balsam Lake WI, 1009 ... 67 E3
Baltic CT, 1250 ... 149 F1
Baltic OH, 795 ... 91 E4
Baltic SD, 1089 ... 27 F4
Baltimore MD, 620961 ... 144 C2
Baltimore OH, 2966 ... 101 D1
Baltimore Co. MD, 805029 ... 144 C1
Baltimore Highlands MD, 7019 ... 193 C4
Bamberg SC, 3607 ... 130 C1
Bamberg Co. SC, 15987 ... 130 B1
Bancroft ID, 377 ... 31 E1
Bancroft IA, 732 ... 72 B3
Bancroft KY, 494 ... 230 F1
Bancroft MI, 545 ... 76 B3
Bancroft NE, 495 ... 35 F2
Bancroft WV, 587 ... 101 E3
Bandera TX, 857 ... 61 D2
Bandera Co. TX, 20485 ... 60 C2
Bandon OR, 3066 ... 28 A1
Bangor ME, 33039 ... 83 D1
Bangor MI, 1885 ... 75 E4
Bangor PA, 5273 ... 93 F3
Bangor WI, 1459 ... 73 F2
Bangs TX, 1603 ... 59 D4
Banks OR, 1777 ... 20 B1
Banks Co. GA, 18395 ... 121 D3
Banner Co. NE, 690 ... 33 F3
Banner Elk NC, 1028 ... 111 F4
Banner Hill TN, 1497 ... 111 E4
Bannertown NC, 950 ... 112 A3
Banning CA, 29603 ... 53 D2
Bannockburn IL, 1583 ... 203 C2
Bannock Co. ID, 82839 ... 31 E1
Banquete TX, 726 ... 63 F2
Bantam CT, 759 ... 94 C3
Baraboo WI, 12048 ... 74 A2
Baraga MI, 2053 ... 65 F4
Baraga Co. MI, 8860 ... 65 F4
Barataria LA, 1109 ... 134 B3
Barber Co. KS, 4861 ... 43 D4
Barberton OH, 26550 ... 91 E3
Barbour Co. AL, 27457 ... 128 B3
Barbour Co. WV, 16589 ... 102 A2
Barbourmeade KY, 1218 ... 230 F1
Barboursville WV, 3964 ... 101 E4
Barbourville KY, 3165 ... 110 C2
Bardstown KY, 11700 ... 110 A1
Bardwell KY, 723 ... 108 C2
Bardwell TX, 649 ... 59 F3
Bareville PA, 6625 ... 146 A2
Bargersville IN, 4013 ... 99 F1
Bar Harbor ME, 2552 ... 83 D2
Barker NY, 533 ... 78 B3
Barling AR, 4649 ... 116 C1
Barlow KY, 675 ... 108 C2
Bar Mills ME, 800 ... 82 B3
Barnegat NJ, 2817 ... 147 E4
Barnegat Light NJ, 574 ... 147 E4
Barnegat Pines NJ, 1300 ... 147 E3
Barnes Co. ND, 11066 ... 19 D4
Barnesville GA, 6755 ... 129 D1
Barnesville MN, 2563 ... 19 F4
Barnesville OH, 4193 ... 101 F1
Barneveld WI, 1231 ... 74 A3
Barnhart MO, 5682 ... 98 A4
Barnsboro NJ, 2500 ... 146 C4
Barnsdall OK, 1243 ... 51 F1
Barnstable MA, 45193 ... 151 F3
Barnstable Co. MA, 215888 ... 151 E4
Barnum MN, 613 ... 64 C4
Bar Nunn WY, 2213 ... 33 D1
Barnwell SC, 4750 ... 130 B1
Barnwell Co. SC, 22621 ... 130 B1
Baroda MI, 873 ... 89 E1
Barrackville WV, 1302 ... 102 A1
Barre MA, 1009 ... 150 B1
Barre VT, 9052 ... 81 E2
Barren Co. KY, 42173 ... 110 A2
Barre Plains MA, 1200 ... 150 B1
Barrett TX, 3199 ... 132 B3
Barrington IL, 10327 ... 203 B2
Barrington NH, 8576 ... 81 F4
Barrington NJ, 6983 ... 248 D4
Barrington RI, 16310 ... 151 D3
Barrington Hills IL, 4209 ... 203 A2
Barron WI, 3423 ... 67 E3
Barron Co. WI, 45870 ... 67 E3
Barrow AK, 4212 ... 154 C1
Barrow Co. GA, 69367 ... 121 D3
Barry IL, 1318 ... 97 F1
Barry Co. MI, 59173 ... 75 F4
Barry Co. MO, 35597 ... 106 C2
Barstow CA, 22639 ... 53 D1
Barstow MD, 750 ... 144 C4
Bartelso IL, 595 ... 98 B3
Bartholomew Co. IN, 76794 ... 99 F2
Bartlesville OK, 35750 ... 51 F1
Bartlett IL, 41208 ... 203 A3
Bartlett NE, 117 ... 35 D2
Bartlett NH, 373 ... 81 F2
Bartlett TN, 54613 ... 118 B1
Bartlett TX, 1623 ... 61 E1
Barton MD, 457 ... 102 C1
Barton VT, 737 ... 81 E1
Barton Co. KS, 27674 ... 43 D3
Barton Co. MO, 12402 ... 106 B1
Bartonsville MD, 1451 ... 144 A1
Bartonville IL, 6471 ... 88 B3
Bartow FL, 17298 ... 140 C2
Bartow Co. GA, 100157 ... 120 B3
Barview OR, 1844 ... 20 A4
Basalt CO, 3857 ... 40 C2
Basalt ID, 394 ... 23 E4
Basehor KS, 4613 ... 96 B2
Basile LA, 1821 ... 133 E2
Basin MT, 212 ... 15 E4
Basin WY, 1285 ... 24 C3
Basin City WA, 1092 ... 13 E4
Baskett KY, 550 ... 99 E4
Basking Ridge NJ, 3600 ... 148 A4
Bassett NE, 619 ... 35 D1
Bassett VA, 1100 ... 112 B2
Bass Harbor ME, 600 ... 83 D2
Bass Lake IN, 1195 ... 89 E2
Bastrop LA, 11365 ... 125 F2
Bastrop TX, 7218 ... 61 E2
Bastrop Co. TX, 74171 ... 61 E2
Basye VA, 1253 ... 102 C3
Batavia IL, 26045 ... 88 C1
Batavia IA, 499 ... 87 E3
Batavia NY, 15465 ... 78 B3
Batavia OH, 1509 ... 100 B2
Batesburg-Leesville SC, 5362 ... 122 A4
Bates Co. MO, 17049 ... 96 B4
Batesville AR, 10248 ... 107 F4
Batesville IN, 6520 ... 100 A2
Batesville MS, 7463 ... 118 B3
Batesville TX, 1068 ... 60 C3
Bath ME, 8514 ... 82 C3
Bath MI, 2083 ... 76 A3
Bath NY, 5786 ... 78 C4
Bath PA, 2693 ... 93 F3
Bath Co. KY, 11591 ... 100 C4
Bath Co. VA, 4731 ... 102 B4
Baton Rouge LA, 229493 ... 134 A2
Battle Creek IA, 713 ... 72 A4
Battle Creek MI, 52347 ... 75 F4
Battle Creek NE, 1207 ... 35 E2
Battlefield MO, 5590 ... 107 D2
Battle Ground IN, 1334 ... 89 E4
Battle Ground WA, 17571 ... 20 C1
Battle Lake MN, 875 ... 19 F4
Battlement Mesa CO, 4471 ... 40 B2
Battle Mtn. NV, 3635 ... 30 A4
Baudette MN, 1106 ... 64 A1
Baumstown PA, 422 ... 146 B2
Bauxite AR, 487 ... 117 E2
Bawcomville LA, 3588 ... 125 E2
Baxley GA, 4400 ... 129 F3
Baxter IA, 1101 ... 87 D1
Baxter MN, 7610 ... 64 A4
Baxter TN, 1365 ... 110 A4
Baxter Co. AR, 41513 ... 107 E4
Baxter Estates NY, 999 ... 241 G2
Baxter Sprs. KS, 4238 ... 106 B2
Bay AR, 1801 ... 108 A4
Bayard IA, 471 ... 86 B1
Bayard NE, 1209 ... 33 F2
Bayard NM, 2328 ... 55 F2
Bayboro NC, 1263 ... 115 D3
Bay City MI, 34932 ... 76 B2
Bay City OR, 1286 ... 20 B2
Bay City TX, 17614 ... 61 F3
Bay Co. FL, 168852 ... 136 C2
Bay Co. MI, 107771 ... 76 B2
Bayfield CO, 2333 ... 40 C4
Bayfield WI, 487 ... 65 D4
Bayfield Co. WI, 15014 ... 65 D4
Bay Harbor Islands FL, 5628 ... 233 C4
Bay Head NJ, 968 ... 147 E3
Bay Hill FL, 4884 ... 246 B3
Baylor Co. TX, 3726 ... 59 D1
Bay Minette AL, 8044 ... 135 E1
Bayonet Pt. FL, 23467 ... 140 B2
Bayonne NJ, 63024 ... 148 B4
Bayou Cane LA, 19355 ... 134 A3
Bayou George FL, 800 ... 136 C2
Bayou Goula LA, 612 ... 134 A2
Bayou La Batre AL, 2558 ... 135 E2
Bayou Vista LA, 4652 ... 134 A3
Bayou Vista TX, 1537 ... 132 B4
Bay Park NY, 2212 ... 241 G5
Bay Pines FL, 2931 ... 266 A3
Bay Pt. CA, 21349 ... 259 D1
Bayport MN, 3471 ... 67 D4
Bayport NY, 8896 ... 149 D4
Bay Ridge MD, 2300 ... 144 C3
Bay St. Louis MS, 9260 ... 134 C2
Bay Shore NY, 26337 ... 149 D4
Bayshore Gardens FL, 16323 ... 266 B5
Bay Side NJ, 1800 ... 147 E4
Bayside WI, 4389 ... 234 D1
Bay Sprs. MS, 1786 ... 126 C3
Baytown TX, 71802 ... 132 B3
Bay View OH, 632 ... 91 D2
Bay Vil. OH, 15651 ... 204 D2
Bayville NJ, 4700 ... 147 E3
Bayville NY, 6669 ... 148 C3
Beach ND, 1019 ... 17 F4
Beach City OH, 1033 ... 91 E3
Beach City TX, 2198 ... 132 B3
Beach Haven NJ, 1170 ... 147 E4
Beach Haven Gardens NJ, 1200 ... 147 E4
Beach Haven Terrace NJ, 1100 ... 147 E4
Beachwood NJ, 11045 ... 147 E3
Beachwood OH, 11953 ... 204 G2
Beacon IA, 494 ... 87 D2
Beacon NY, 15541 ... 148 B1
Beacon Falls CT, 5596 ... 149 D1
Beadle Co. SD, 17398 ... 27 D3
Bealeton VA, 4435 ... 103 D3
Beals ME, 618 ... 83 E2
Bean Sta. TN, 2826 ... 111 D3
Bear DE, 19371 ... 145 E1
Bear Creek AL, 1070 ... 119 E3
Bearden AR, 966 ... 117 E4
Beardstown IL, 6123 ... 98 A1
Bear Lake Co. ID, 5986 ... 31 F2
Bear River City UT, 853 ... 31 E3
Beasley TX, 641 ... 132 A4
Beatrice AL, 301 ... 127 F4
Beatrice NE, 12459 ... 35 F4
Beatty NV, 1010 ... 45 F2
Beattyville KY, 1307 ... 110 C1
Beatyestown NJ, 3223 ... 94 A4
Beaufort NC, 4039 ... 115 E4
Beaufort SC, 12361 ... 130 C2
Beaufort Co. NC, 47759 ... 113 F4
Beaufort Co. SC, 162233 ... 130 C3
Beaumont CA, 36877 ... 53 D2
Beaumont MS, 951 ... 135 D1
Beaumont TX, 118296 ... 132 C3
Beaumont Place TX, 4500 ... 220 D2
Beauregard Par. LA, 35654 ... 133 D2
Beaver OK, 1515 ... 50 C1
Beaver PA, 4531 ... 91 F3
Beaver UT, 3112 ... 39 D3
Beaver WV, 1308 ... 111 F1
Beaver City NE, 609 ... 42 C1
Beaver Co. OK, 5636 ... 50 C1
Beaver Co. PA, 170539 ... 91 F3
Beaver Co. UT, 6629 ... 39 D3
Beavercreek OH, 45193 ... 100 C1
Beaver Crossing NE, 403 ... 35 E4
Beaverdale PA, 1035 ... 92 B4
Beaver Dam KY, 3409 ... 109 E1
Beaver Dam WI, 16214 ... 74 B2
Beaver Falls PA, 8987 ... 91 F3
Beaverhead Co. MT, 9246 ... 23 D2
Beaver Meadows PA, 869 ... 93 E3
Beaver Sprs. PA, 674 ... 93 D3
Beaverton MI, 1071 ... 76 A2
Beaverton OR, 89803 ... 20 C2
Beavertown PA, 965 ... 93 D3
Bechtelsville PA, 942 ... 146 B1
Beckemeyer IL, 1040 ... 98 B3
Becker MN, 4538 ... 66 C3
Becker Co. MN, 32504 ... 19 F3
Beckett NJ, 4847 ... 146 C4
Beckham Co. OK, 22119 ... 50 C3
Beckley WV, 17614 ... 111 F1
Beckville TX, 847 ... 124 C3
Bedford IN, 13413 ... 99 F3
Bedford IA, 1440 ... 86 B3
Bedford KY, 599 ... 100 A3
Bedford MA, 13320 ... 151 D1
Bedford NH, 21203 ... 95 D1
Bedford NY, 1834 ... 148 C2
Bedford OH, 13074 ... 204 G3
Bedford PA, 2841 ... 102 C1
Bedford TX, 46979 ... 207 B2
Bedford VA, 6222 ... 112 B1
Bedford Co. PA, 49762 ... 92 C4
Bedford Co. TN, 45058 ... 120 A1
Bedford Co. VA, 68676 ... 112 B1
Bedford Hts. OH, 10751 ... 204 G3
Bedford Hills NY, 3001 ... 148 C2
Bedford Park IL, 580 ... 203 D5
Beebe AR, 7315 ... 117 F2
Bee Cave TX, 3925 ... 61 E1
Beech Bottom WV, 523 ... 91 F4
Beech Creek PA, 701 ... 93 D3
Beecher IL, 4359 ... 89 D2
Beech Grove IN, 14192 ... 99 F1
Beechwood Vil. KY, 1324 ... 230 E1
Bee Co. TX, 31861 ... 61 E4
Beemer NE, 678 ... 35 F2
Bee Ridge FL, 9598 ... 140 B4
Beersheba Sprs. TN, 477 ... 120 A1
Beesleys Pt. NJ, 1400 ... 147 F4
Beeville TX, 12863 ... 61 E4
Beggs OK, 1321 ... 51 F2
Bel Air MD, 1258 ... 145 D1
Belcamp MD, 1900 ... 145 D1
Belchertown MA, 2899 ... 150 A1
Belcourt ND, 2078 ... 18 C1
Belding MI, 5757 ... 75 F3
Belen NM, 7269 ... 48 C4
Belfair WA, 3931 ... 12 C3
Belfast ME, 6668 ... 82 C2
Belfast NY, 837 ... 78 B4
Belfast PA, 1257 ... 93 F3
Belfield ND, 800 ... 18 A4
Belford NJ, 1768 ... 147 E1
Belfry MT, 218 ... 24 B2
Belgium WI, 2245 ... 75 D2
Belgrade MN, 740 ... 66 B3
Belgrade MT, 7389 ... 23 F1
Belgrade Lakes ME, 350 ... 82 B2
Belhaven NC, 1688 ... 115 E3
Belinda City TN, 2100 ... 109 F4
Belington WV, 1921 ... 102 A2
Belknap Co. NH, 60088 ... 81 F4
Bell CA, 35477 ... 228 D3
Bellair FL, 16539 ... 222 C4
Bellaire MI, 1086 ... 69 F4
Bellaire OH, 4278 ... 101 F1
Bellaire TX, 16855 ... 132 A3
Bellamy AL, 543 ... 127 E2
Bella Villa MO, 729 ... 256 B3
Bella Vista AR, 26461 ... 106 C3
Bella Vista CA, 2781 ... 28 C4
Bellbrook OH, 6943 ... 100 C1
Bell Buckle TN, 500 ... 119 F1
Bell Co. KY, 28691 ... 110 C3
Bell Co. TX, 310235 ... 61 E1
Belle MO, 1545 ... 97 F4
Belle WV, 1260 ... 101 F4
Belleair FL, 3869 ... 140 B2
Belleair Beach FL, 1560 ... 140 B2
Belleair Bluffs FL, 2031 ... 266 A2
Belle Ctr. OH, 813 ... 90 C4
Belle Chasse LA, 12679 ... 134 B3
Bellefontaine OH, 13370 ... 90 B4
Bellefontaine Neighbors MO, 10860 ... 256 C1
Bellefonte AR, 454 ... 107 D3
Bellefonte DE, 1193 ... 146 B4
Bellefonte KY, 888 ... 101 D3
Bellefonte PA, 6187 ... 92 C3
Belle Fourche SD, 5594 ... 25 F3
Belle Glade FL, 17467 ... 143 E1
Belle Haven VA, 532 ... 114 B3
Belle Isle FL, 5988 ... 141 D1
Bellemeade KY, 865 ... 230 F2
Belle Plaine IA, 2534 ... 87 E1
Belle Plaine KS, 1681 ... 43 E4
Belle Plaine MN, 6661 ... 66 C4
Belle Rose LA, 1902 ... 134 A3
Bellerose NY, 1193 ... 241 G3
Bellerose Terrace NY, 2198 ... 241 G3
Belle Terre NY, 792 ... 149 D3
Belle Vernon PA, 1093 ... 92 A4
Belleview FL, 4492 ... 139 D4
Belleville IL, 44478 ... 98 B3
Belleville KS, 1991 ... 43 E1
Belleville MI, 3991 ... 90 C1
Belleville NJ, 35926 ... 148 B4
Belleville PA, 1827 ... 92 C4
Belleville WI, 2385 ... 74 B3
Bellevue ID, 2287 ... 22 C4
Bellevue IL, 1978 ... 88 B3
Bellevue IA, 2191 ... 74 A4
Bellevue KY, 5955 ... 204 B3
Bellevue MI, 1282 ... 76 A4
Bellevue NE, 50137 ... 86 A2
Bellevue OH, 8202 ... 204 B3
Bellevue PA, 8370 ... 92 A4
Bellevue WA, 122363 ... 12 C3
Bellevue WI, 14570 ... 74 C1
Bellflower CA, 76616 ... 228 D3
Bell Gardens CA, 42072 ... 228 D3
Bellingham MA, 4854 ... 150 C2
Bellingham WA, 80885 ... 12 C1
Bellmawr NJ, 11583 ... 146 C3
Bellmead TX, 9901 ... 59 E4
Bellows Falls VT, 3148 ... 81 E4
Bellport NY, 2084 ... 149 D4
Bells TN, 2437 ... 108 C4
Bells TX, 1392 ... 59 F1
Bellview FL, 23355 ... 247 A1
Bellville OH, 1918 ... 91 D3
Bellville TX, 4097 ... 61 F2
Bellwood IL, 19071 ... 203 C4
Bellwood NE, 435 ... 35 E3
Bellwood PA, 1828 ... 92 C4
Bellwood VA, 6352 ... 254 B3
Belmar NJ, 5794 ... 147 F2
Belmond IA, 2376 ... 72 C3
Belmont CA, 25835 ... 259 B5
Belmont MA, 24729 ... 151 D1
Belmont MS, 2021 ... 119 D3
Belmont NH, 1301 ... 81 F4

Entries in **bold black** indicate counties or parishes.
Entries in **bold color** indicate cities with detailed inset maps.

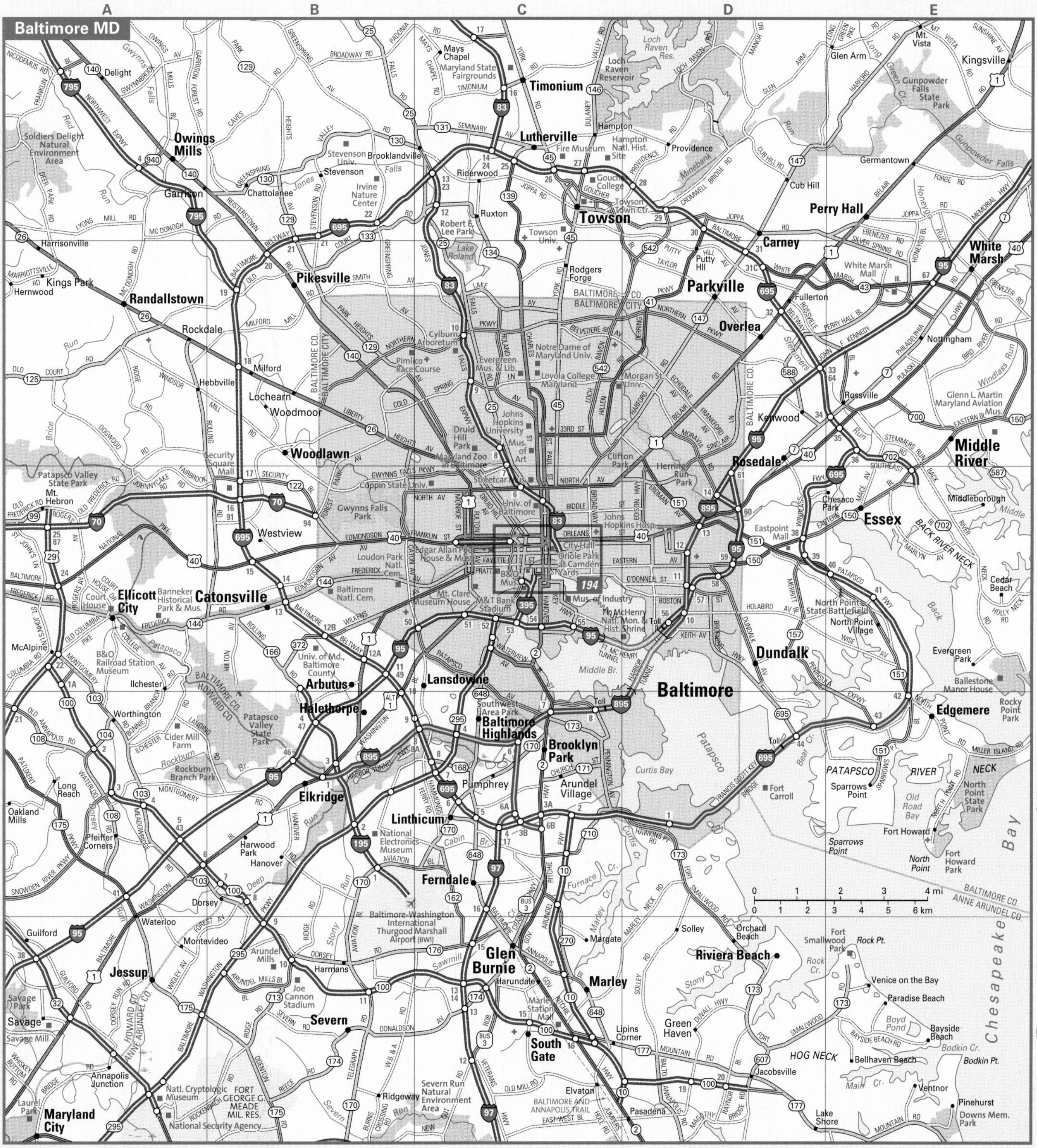

Annapolis Jct. A5
Arbutus B3
Arundel Vil. C4
Baltimore D3
Baltimore Highlands ...C4
Bayside Beach E5
Bellhaven Beach E5
Brooklandville C1
Brooklyn Park C4
Carney D1
Catonsville B3
Cedar Beach E3
Chattolanee B1
Chesaco Park E3
Cub Hill D1
Delight A1
Dorsey B4
Dundalk D3
Edgemere E4
Elkridge B4
Ellicott City A3
Elvaton C5
Essex E3
Evergreen Park E3
Ferndale C4
Ft. Howard E4
Fullerton D2
Garrison A1
Germantown E1
Glen Arm E1
Glen Burnie C5
Green Haven D5
Guilford A5
Halethorpe B4
Hampton C1
Hanover B4
Harmans B5
Harrisonville A2
Harundale C5
Harwood Park B4
Hebbville A2
Hernwood A2
Ilchester A3
Jacobsville D5
Jessup A5
Kenwood D2
Kings Park A2
Kingsville E1
Lake Shore D5
Lansdowne C3
Linthicum C4
Lipins Corner C5
Lochearn B2
Long Reach A4
Lutherville C1
Margate C5
Marley C5
Maryland City A5
Mays Chapel C1
McAlpine A3
Middleborough E3
Middle River E2
Milford B2
Montevideo A5
Mt. Hebron A3
Mt. Vista E1
N. Point Vil. E3
Nottingham E2
Oakland Mills A4
Orchard Beach D5
Overlea D2
Owings Mills A1
Paradise Beach E5
Parkville D2
Pasadena D5
Perry Hall E1
Pfeiffer Corners A4
Pikesville B2
Pinehurst E5
Providence D1
Pumphrey C4
Putty Hll D2
Randallstown A2
Riderwood C1
Ridgeway B5
Riviera Beach D5
Rockdale A2
Rodgers Forge C2
Rosedale D2
Rossville E2
Ruxton C1
Savage A5
Severn B5
Solley D5
S. Gate C5
Sparrows Pt. E4
Stevenson B1
Timonium C1
Towson C1
Venice on the Bay E5
Ventnor E5
Waterloo A5
Westview B3
White Marsh E2
Woodlawn B2
Woodmoor B2
Worthington A4

Figures after entries indicate population, page number, and grid reference.

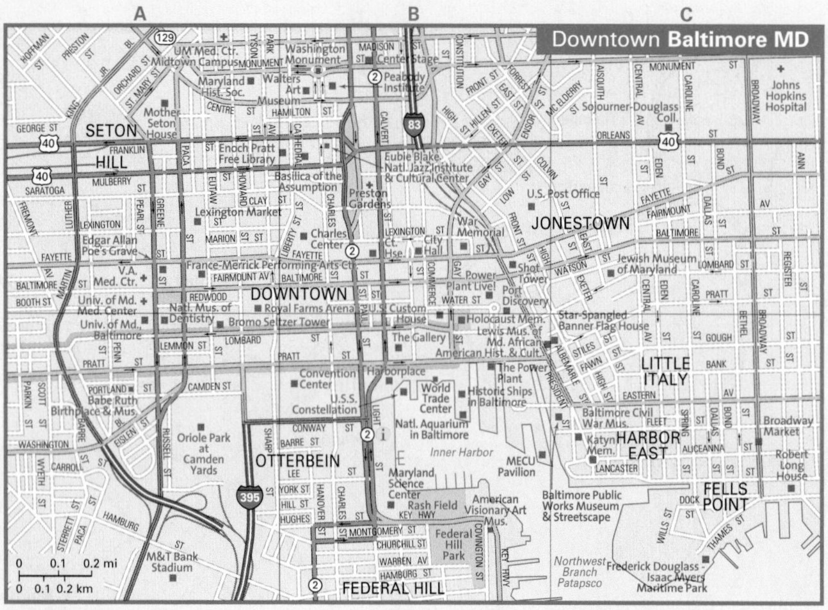

POINTS OF INTEREST

American Visionary Art Museum B2
Babe Ruth Birthplace & Museum A2
Baltimore Civil War Museum C2
Baltimore Public Works Mus. & Streetscape .. C2
Basilica of the Assumption B1
Broadway Market C2
Bromo Seltzer Tower A2
Charles Center B1
Convention Center B2
Edgar Allan Poe's Grave A1
Enoch Pratt Free Library A1
Eubie Blake Natl. Jazz Institute & Cult. Ctr. B1
France-Merrick Performing Arts Center A1
Frederick Douglass-Isaac Myers Maritime Pk.. C2
The Gallery B2
Harborplace B2
Historic Ships in Baltimore B2
Jewish Mus. of Maryland C1
Katyn Memorial C2
Lewis Mus. of MD. African-American History & Culture B2
Lexington Market A1
M&T Bank Stadium A2
Maryland Historical Society A1
Maryland Science Center B2
MECU Pavilion B2
Mother Seton House A1
National Aquarium in Baltimore B2
National Museum of Dentistry A2
Oriole Park at Camden Yards A2
Peabody Institute B1
Port Discovery B1
The Power Plant B2
Power Plant Live B1
Robert Long House C2
Royal Farms Arena A1
Shot Tower B1
Sojourner-Douglas College C1
Star-Spangled Banner Flag House C2
U.S. Custom House B2
Univ. of Maryland, Baltimore A2
U.S.S. Constellation B2
Walters Art Museum B1
War Memorial B1
Washington Monument B1
World Trade Center B2

Belmont NY, *969* **92** C1
Belmont NC, *10076* **122** A1
Belmont WV, *903* **101** F2
Belmont WI, *986* **74** A4
Belmont Corner ME, *375* **82** C2
Belmont Co. OH, *70400* **101** F1
Bel-Nor MO, *1499* **256** B2
Beloit KS, *3835* **43** E1
Beloit OH, *978* **91** F3
Beloit WI, *36966* **74** B4
Belpre OH, *6441* **101** E2
Bel-Ridge MO, *2737* **256** B2
Belt MT, *597* **15** F3
Belton KY, *500* **109** E2
Belton MO, *23116* **96** B3
Belton SC, *4134* **121** E3
Belton TX, *18216* **59** E4
Beltrami Co. MN, *44442* **64** A2
Beltsville MD, *16772* **144** B3
Belvedere CA, *2068* **259** B2
Belvedere SC, *5792* **121** F4
Belvedere Park GA, *15152* **190** E4
Belvidere IL, *25585* **74** B4
Belvidere NJ, *2681* **93** F3
Belwood NC, *950* **121** F1
Belzoni MS, *2235* **126** B1
Bement IL, *1730* **98** C1
Bemidji MN, *13431* **64** A3
Bemiss GA, *1500* **137** F1
Benavides TX, *1362* **63** E2
Ben Avon PA, *1781* **250** A1
Benbrook TX, *21234* **207** A3
Bend OR, *76639* **21** D3
Bendersville PA, *641* **103** E1
Benewah Co. ID, *9285* **14** B3
Benham KY, *500* **111** D2
Ben Hill Co. GA, *17634* **129** E3
Benicia CA, *26997* **36** B3
Benjamin TX, *258* **58** C1
Benkelman NE, *953* **42** B1
Benld IL, *1556* **98** B2
Ben Lomond CA, *6234* **44** A2
Bennet NE, *719* **35** F4
Bennett CO, *2308* **41** E1
Bennett Co. SD, *3431* **26** B4
Bennettsville SC, *9069* **122** C2
Bennington KS, *672* **43** E2
Bennington NE, *1458* **35** F3
Bennington NH, *381* **81** E4
Bennington VT, *9074* **94** C1
Bennington Co. VT, *37125* **81** D4
Benoit MS, *477* **118** A4
Bensenville IL, *18352* **203** C4
Bensley VA, *5819* **113** E1

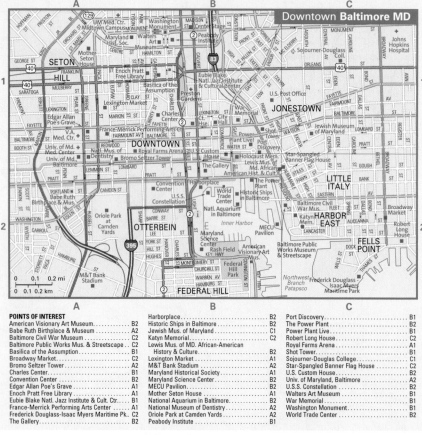

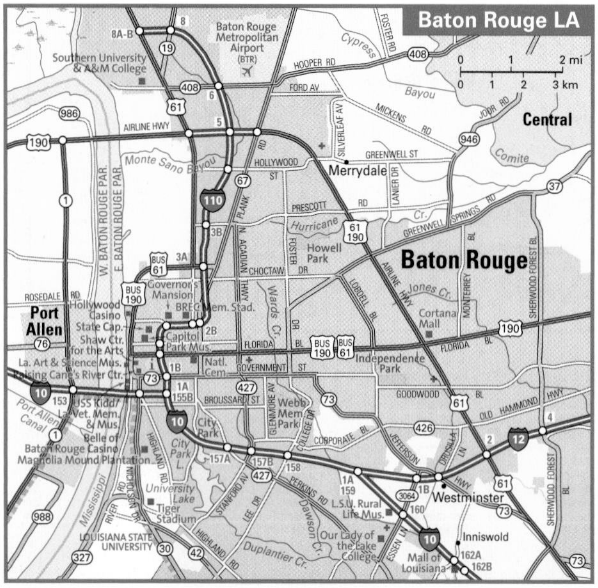

Benson AZ, *5105* **55** D3
Benson MD, *950* **144** C1
Benson MN, *3240* **66** A3
Benson NC, *3311* **123** D1
Benson Co. ND, *6660* **19** D2
Bent Co. CO, *6499* **41** F3
Bent Creek NC, *1287* **121** E1
Bentleyville OH, *864* **204** G3
Bentleyville PA, *2581* **92** A4
Benton AR, *30681* **117** E2
Benton IL, *7087* **98** C4
Benton KS, *880* **43** F4
Benton KY, *4349* **109** D2
Benton LA, *1948* **124** C2
Benton ME, *2557* **82** C2
Benton MO, *863* **108** B2
Benton PA, *824* **93** E2
Benton TN, *1385* **120** C1
Benton WI, *973* **74** A4
Benton City WA, *3038* **21** E1
Benton Co. AR, *221339* **106** B3
Benton Co. IN, *8854* **89** D3
Benton Co. IA, *26076* **87** E1
Benton Co. MN, *38451* **66** C2
Benton Co. MS, *8729* **118** C2
Benton Co. MO, *19056* **97** D4
Benton Co. OR, *85579* **20** B3
Benton Co. TN, *16489* **109** D4
Benton Co. WA, *175177* **21** E1
Benton Harbor MI, *10038* **89** E1
Bentonia MS, *440* **126** B2
Bentonville AR, *35301* **106** C3
Benzie Co. MI, *17525* **69** F4
Benzonia MI, *497* **69** E4
Berea KY, *13561* **110** C1
Berea OH, *19093* **91** E2
Berea SC, *14295* **217** A2
Beresford SD, *2005* **35** F1
Bergen NY, *1176* **78** B3
Bergen Co. NJ, *905116* **148** B3
Bergenfield NJ, *26764* **148** B3
Bergholz OH, *664* **91** F4
Bergman AR, *439* **107** D3
Berino NM, *1441* **56** C3
Berkeley CA, *112580* **36** B4
Berkeley IL, *5209* **203** C4
Berkeley MO, *8978* **256** B1
Berkeley RI, *2800* **150** C3
Berkeley Co. SC, *177843* **131** D1
Berkeley Co. WV, *104169* **103** D2
Berkeley Hts. NJ, *13183* **148** A4
Berkeley Sprs. WV, *624* **102** C1
Berkley MA, *5749* **151** D3
Berkley MI, *14970* **210** B2
Berks Co. PA, *411442* **146** B1
Berkshire CT, *950* **149** D2
Berkshire Co. MA, *131219* **94** C2
Berlin CT, *19590* **149** E1
Berlin GA, *551* **137** F1
Berlin MD, *4485* **114** C2
Berlin MA, *2866* **150** C1
Berlin NH, *10051* **81** F2
Berlin NJ, *7588* **147** D3
Berlin OH, *898* **91** E4
Berlin PA, *2104* **102** C1
Berlin WI, *5524* **74** B1
Berlin Hts. OH, *714* **91** D2
Bermuda Run NC, *1725* **112** A4
Bernalillo NM, *8320* **48** C3
Bernalillo Co. NM, *662564* **48** C3
Bernardston MA, *2155* **94** C1
Bernardsville NJ, *7707* **148** A4
Berne IN, *3999* **90** A3
Bernice LA, *1689* **125** E2
Bernice OK, *562* **106** B3
Bernie MO, *1958* **108** B3
Bernstadt KY, *475* **110** C2
Bernville PA, *955* **146** A1
Berrien Co. GA, *19286* **129** E4
Berrien Co. MI, *156813* **89** E1
Berrien Sprs. MI, *1800* **89** E1
Berry AL, *1148* **119** E4
Berryville AR, *5356* **106** C3
Berryville TX, *975* **124** A3
Berryville VA, *4185* **103** D2
Berthold ND, *454* **18** B2
Berthoud CO, *5105* **33** E4
Bertie Co. NC, *21282* **113** F4
Bertram IA, *294* **87** F1
Bertram TX, *1353* **61** D1
Bertrand MI, *1700* **89** F1
Bertrand MO, *821* **108** B2
Bertrand NE, *750* **35** D4
Berwick LA, *4946* **134** A3
Berwick ME, *2187* **82** A4
Berwick PA, *10477* **93** E3
Berwyn IL, *56657* **89** D1
Berwyn PA, *3631* **146** B3
Berwyn Hts. MD, *3123* **270** E2
Bessemer AL, *27456* **127** F1
Bessemer MI, *1905* **65** E4
Bessemer PA, *1111* **91** F3
Bessemer City NC, *5340* **122** A1
Bethalto IL, *9521* **98** B3
Bethany CT, *5473* **149** D1
Bethany IL, *1352* **98** C1
Bethany MO, *3292* **86** C4
Bethany OK, *19051* **51** E3
Bethany WV, *1036* **91** F4
Bethany Beach DE, *1060* **145** F4
Bethel AK, *6080* **154** B3
Bethel CT, *9549* **148** C2
Bethel DE, *171* **145** E4
Bethel ME, *2411* **82** B2
Bethel NC, *1577* **113** E4
Bethel OH, *2711* **100** C2
Bethel VT, *569* **81** E3
Bethel VA, *500* **103** D3
Bethel Acres OK, *2895* **51** F3
Bethel Hts. AR, *2372* **106** C3
Bethel Park PA, *32313* **92** A4
Bethel Sprs. TN, *718* **119** D1
Bethesda MD, *60858* **144** B3
Bethesda OH, *1256* **101** F1
Bethlehem CT, *3596* **149** D1
Bethlehem GA, *601* **121** D4
Bethlehem MD, *600* **145** D4
Bethlehem NH, *972* **81** F2
Bethlehem NC, *4214* **111** F4
Bethlehem PA, *74982* **146** C1
Bethlehem Ctr. NY, *2500* **188** D3
Bethpage NY, *16429* **148** C4
Betmar Acres FL, *4000* **140** C2
Bettendorf IA, *33217* **88** A2
Bettsville OH, *661* **90** C2
Beulah CO, *1164* **41** E3
Beulah MI, *342* **69** E4
Beulah MS, *348* **118** A4
Beulah ND, *3121* **18** B3
Beulaville NC, *1296* **123** E2
Beverly MA, *39502* **151** F1
Beverly NJ, *2577* **147** D3
Beverly OH, *1313* **101** E1
Beverly WV, *702* **102** B3
Beverly Beach FL, *338* **139** E4
Beverly Beach MD, *1600* **144** C3
Beverly Hills CA, *34109* **52** C2
Beverly Hills FL, *8445* **140** B1
Beverly Hills MI, *10267* **210** B2
Beverly Hills MO, *574* **256** B2
Beverly Shores IN, *613* **89** E2
Bevier MO, *718* **97** E1
Bevil Oaks TX, *1274* **132** C2
Bevis OH, *5700* **204** A1
Bexar Co. TX, *1714773* **61** D2
Bexley OH, *13057* **206** C2
Bibb Co. AL, *22915* **127** F1
Bibb Co. GA, *155547* **129** D2
Bicknell IN, *2915* **99** E3
Bicknell UT, *327* **39** E3
Biddeford ME, *21277* **82** B4
Bienville Par. LA, *14353* **125** D2
Big Bear City CA, *12304* **53** D2
Big Bear Lake CA, *5019* **53** D2
Big Beaver PA, *1970* **91** F3
Big Bend WI, *1290* **74** C3
Big Chimney WV, *627* **101** F3
Big Coppitt Key FL, *2458* **143** D4
Big Delta AK, *591* **154** C2
Big Flats NY, *5277* **93** D1
Bigfork MT, *4270* **15** D2
Biggs CA, *1707* **36** B2
Big Horn Co. MT, *12865* **24** C2
Big Horn Co. WY, *11668* **24** C3
Big Lake MN, *443* **66** C3
Big Lake TX, *2936* **58** A4
Big Lake WA, *1835* **12** C2
Biglerville PA, *1200* **103** E1
Big Oak Flat CA, *3388* **37** D4
Big Pine CA, *1756* **37** E4
Big Pine Key FL, *4252* **143** D4
Big Piney WY, *552* **32** A1
Big Rapids MI, *10601* **75** F2
Big River CA, *1327* **46** B4
Big Run PA, *624* **92** B3
Big Sandy MT, *598* **16** B2
Big Sandy TN, *557* **109** D3
Big Sandy TX, *1343* **124** B2
Big Sky MT, *2308* **23** F2
Big Spr. TX, *27282* **58** A3
Big Sprs. NE, *400* **34** B3
Big Stone City SD, *467* **27** F2
Big Stone Co. MN, *5269* **27** F2
Big Stone Gap VA, *5614* **111** E2
Big Timber MT, *1641* **24** A1
Big Water UT, *475* **47** D1
Big Wells TX, *697* **60** C4
Billerica MA, *40243* **95** E1
Billings MO, *1035* **106** C2
Billings MT, *104170* **24** C1
Billings NY, *800* **148** B1
Billings OK, *509* **51** E1
Billings Co. ND, *783* **18** A3
Billington Hts. NY, *1685* **78** B4
Biloxi MS, *44054* **135** D2
Biltmore Forest NC, *1343* **121** E1
Bingen PA, *1300* **189** B2
Binger OK, *672* **51** D3
Bingham ME, *758* **82** B1
Bingham Co. ID, *45607* **23** E4
Bingham Farms MI, *1111* **210** B2
Binghamton NY, *47376* **93** E1
Biola CA, *1623* **44** C2
Birch Bay WA, *8413* **12** C1
Birch Run MI, *1555* **76** B3
Birch Tree MO, *679* **107** F2
Birchwood Vil. MN, *870* **235** E1
Bird City KS, *447* **42** B1
Bird Island MN, *1042* **66** B4
Birdsboro PA, *5163* **146** B2
Birmingham AL, *212237* **119** F4
Birmingham MI, *20103* **76** C4
Birnamwood WI, *818* **68** B4
Biron WI, *839* **74** A1
Bisbee AZ, *5575* **55** E4
Biscayne Park FL, *3055* **233** B4
Biscoe AR, *476* **117** F2
Biscoe NC, *1700* **122** C1
Bishop CA, *3879* **37** E4
Bishop TX, *3134* **63** F2
Bishopville SC, *3471* **122** B3
Bismarck MO, *1546* **108** A1
Bismarck ND, *61272* **18** C4
Bison SD, *333* **26** A2
Bithlo FL, *8268* **141** D1
Bitter Sprs. AZ, *452* **47** D1
Biwabik MN, *969* **64** C3
Bixby OK, *20884* **106** A4
Blackbird DE, *700* **145** E1
Black Canyon City AZ, *2837* **47** D4
Black Creek NC, *769* **123** E1
Black Creek WI, *1316* **68** C4
Black Diamond WA, *4151* **12** C3
Blackduck MN, *785* **64** A3
Black Eagle MT, *904* **15** F3
Black Earth WI, *1338* **74** A3
Blackfoot ID, *11899* **31** E1
Blackford Co. IN, *12766* **90** A4
Black Forest CO, *13116* **41** E2
Blackhawk SD, *2892* **26** A3
Black Hawk Co. IA, *131090* **73** E4
Black Jack MO, *6929* **256** B1
Black Lick PA, *1462* **92** B4
Blacklick Estates OH, *8682* **206** C3
Black Mtn. NC, *7848* **121** E1
Black River NY, *1348* **79** E1
Black River Falls WI, *3622* **73** F1
Black Rock AR, *662* **107** F4
Black Rock NM, *1323* **48** A3
Blacksburg SC, *1848* **122** A1
Blacksburg VA, *42620* **112** A2
Blackshear GA, *3445* **129** F4
Blackstone MA, *9026* **150** C2
Blackstone VA, *3621* **113** D2
Blackville SC, *2406* **130** B1
Blackwell OK, *7092* **51** E1
Blackwells GA, *2200* **120** C3
Blackwood NJ, *4545* **146** C3
Bladenboro NC, *1750* **123** D3
Bladen Co. NC, *35190* **123** D2
Bladensburg MD, *9148* **270** E3
Blades DE, *1241* **145** E4
Blaine ME, *301* **85** E2
Blaine MN, *57186* **67** D3
Blaine TN, *1856* **110** C4
Blaine WA, *4684* **12** C1
Blaine Co. ID, *21376* **23** D4
Blaine Co. MT, *6491* **16** B2
Blaine Co. NE, *478* **34** C2
Blaine Co. OK, *11943* **51** D2
Blair NE, *7990* **35** F3
Blair OK, *818* **51** D4
Blair WI, *1366* **73** F1
Blair Co. PA, *127089* **92** C4
Blairs VA, *916* **112** C3
Blairstown IA, *692* **87** E1

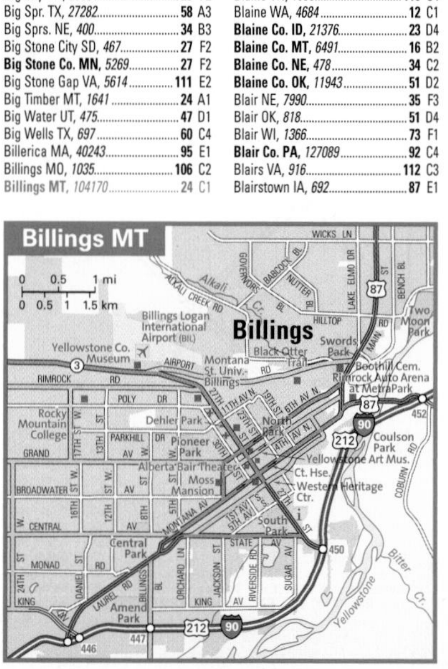

Entries in **bold black** indicate counties or parishes.
Entries in **bold color** indicate cities with detailed inset maps.

Blairstown NJ, *515* **93** F3
Blairsville GA, *652* **121** D2
Blairsville PA, *3412* **92** B4
Blakely GA, *5068* **128** C4
Blakely PA, *6564* **93** F2
Blakes VA, *550* **113** F1
Blanca CO, *385* **41** D4
Blanchard LA, *2899* **124** C2
Blanchard OK, *7670* **51** E3
Blanchard PA, *740* **93** D3
Blanchardville WI, *825* **74** A3
Blanchester OH, *4243* **100** C2
Blanco TX, *1739* **61** D2
Blanco Co. TX, *10497* **61** D1
Bland MO, *539* **97** F4
Bland VA, *409* **112** A2
Bland Co. VA, *6824* **111** F2
Blanding UT, *3375* **40** A4
Blandinsville IL, *651* **87** F4
Blandon PA, *7152* **146** B1
Blasdell NY, *2553* **78** B3
Blauvelt NY, *5689* **148** B3
Blawenburg NJ, *280* **147** D1
Blawnox PA, *1432* **250** C1
Bleckley Co. GA, *13063* **129** E2
Bledsoe Co. TN, *12876* **110** B4
Blennerhassett WV, *3089* **101** E2
Blessing TX, *927* **61** F3
Bliss ID, *318* **30** C1
Bliss Corner MA, *5280* **238** C2
Blissfield MI, *3340* **90** B1
Blocher IN, *600* **100** A3
Bloomdale OH, *678* **90** C2
Bloomer WI, *3539* **67** F3
Bloomfield CT, *20626* **150** A3
Bloomfield IN, *2405* **99** E2
Bloomfield IA, *2640* **87** E3
Bloomfield KY, *838* **100** A4
Bloomfield MO, *1933* **108** B2
Bloomfield NE, *1028* **35** E1
Bloomfield NJ, *47315* **148** B4
Bloomfield NM, *8112* **48** B1
Bloomfield NY, *1361* **78** C3
Bloomfield WI, *3722* **74** C4
Bloomfield Hills MI, *3869* **210** B1
Bloomingburg OH, *938* **100** C1
Bloomingdale FL, *22711* **266** D2
Bloomingdale IL, *22018* **203** B3
Bloomingdale NJ, *7656* **148** A3
Bloomingdale TN, *9888* **111** E3
Blooming Grove NY, *17351* **148** B1
Blooming Grove TX, *821* **59** F3
Blooming Prairie MN, *1996* **73** D2
Bloomington CA, *23851* **229** H2
Bloomington ID, *206* **31** F2
Bloomington IL, *76610* **88** C4
Bloomington IN, *80405* **99** F2
Bloomington MN, *82893* **67** D4
Bloomington TX, *2459* **61** F4
Bloomington WI, *735* **73** F3
Bloomsburg PA, *14855* **93** E3
Bloomsbury NJ, *870* **146** C1
Bloomville OH, *956* **90** C3
Blossburg PA, *1538* **93** D2
Blossom TX, *1494* **116** A4
Blount Co. AL, *57322* **119** F3
Blount Co. TN, *123010* **110** C4
Blountstown FL, *2514* **137** D2
Blountsville AL, *1684* **119** F3
Blountville TN, *3074* **111** E3
Blowing Rock NC, *1241* **111** F4
Bloxom VA, *387* **114** C2
Blue Anchor NJ, *1500* **147** D4
Blue Ash OH, *12114* **100** B2
Blue Bell PA, *6067* **146** C2
Blue Diamond NV, *290* **46** A2
Blue Earth MN, *3353* **72** C2
Blue Earth Co. MN, *64013* **72** C1
Bluefield VA, *5444* **111** F2
Bluefield WV, *10447* **111** F2
Blue Grass IA, *1452* **87** F2
Blue Hill ME, *943* **83** D2
Blue Hill NE, *936* **35** D4
Blue Hills CT, *2901* **150** A3

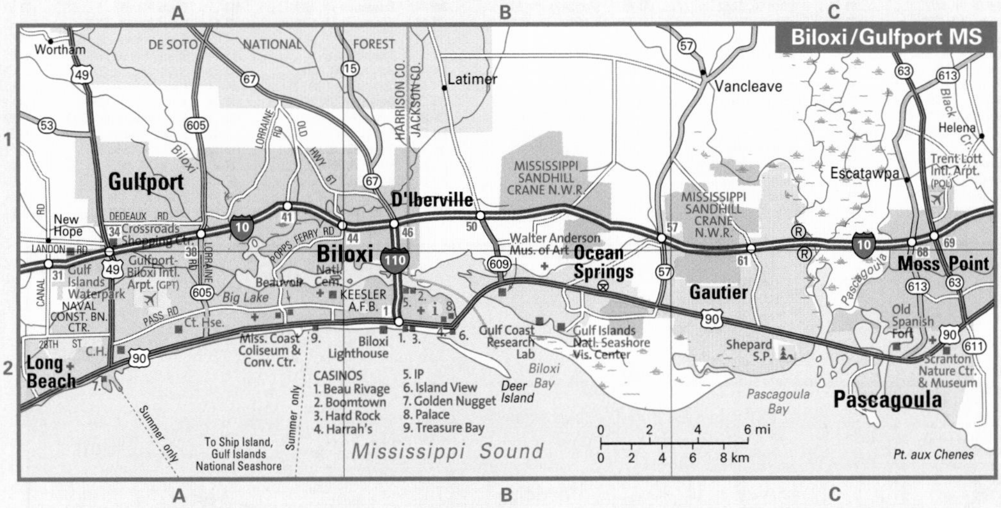

Biloxi A2
D'Iberville B1
Escatawpa C1
Fontainebleau B2
Gautier C2
Gulfport A1
Helena C1
Latimer B1
Long Beach A2
Moss Pt. C2
New Hope A1
Ocean Sprs. B2
Pascagoula C2
Vancleave C1
Wortham A1

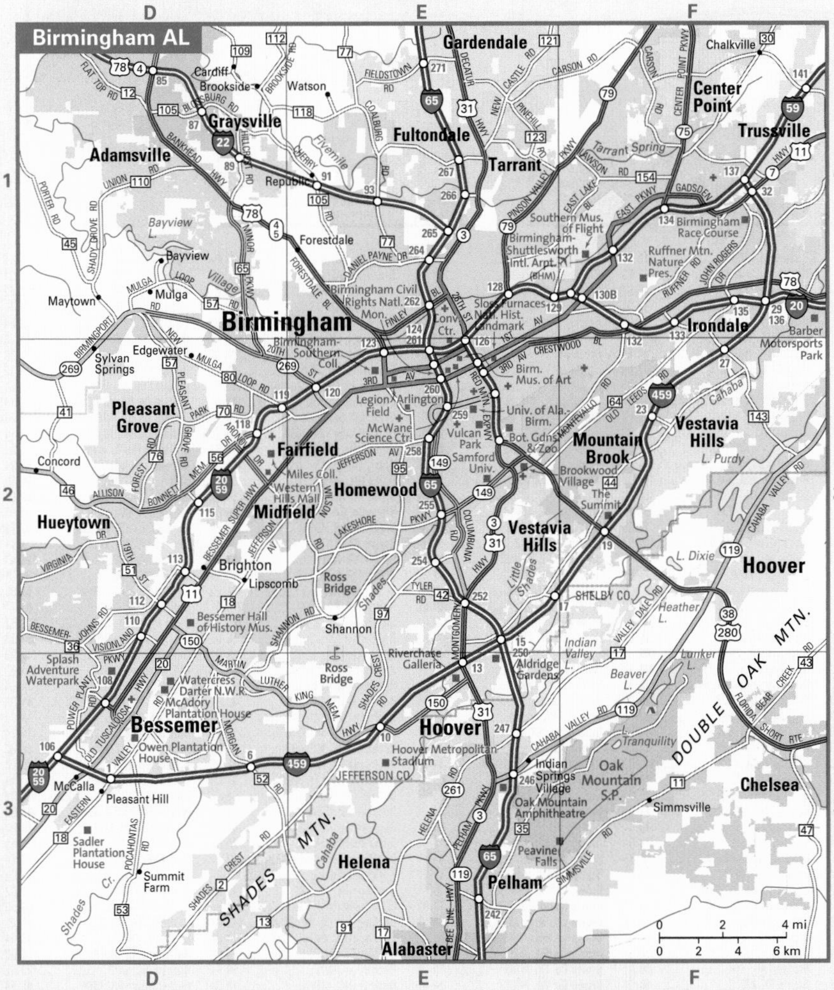

Adamsville D1
Alabaster E3
Bayview D1
Bessemer D3
Birmingham E1
Brighton D2
Brookside D1
Cardiff D1
Center Pt. F1
Chalkville F1
Chelsea F3
Concord D2
Edgewater D2
Fairfield D2
Forestdale E1
Fultondale E1
Gardendale E1
Graysville D1
Helena E3
Homewood E2
Hoover E3
Hueytown D2
Indian Sprs. Vil. E3
Irondale F1
Lipscomb D2
Maytown D1
McCalla D3
Midfield D2
Mtn. Brook F2
Mulga D1
Pelham E3
Pleasant Grove D2
Pleasant Hill D3
Republic E1
Shannon E2
Simmsville F3
Summit Farm D3
Sylvan Sprs. D2
Tarrant City E1
Trussville F1
Vestavia Hills E2
Watson E1

Blue Island IL, *23706* **203** D6
Blue Lake CA, *1253* **28** B4
Blue Mound IL, *1158* **98** C1
Blue Mound TX, *2394* **207** A2
Blue Mounds WI, *855* **74** A3
Blue Mtn. MS, *920* **118** C2
Blue Pt. NY, *4773* **149** D4
Blue Rapids KS, *1019* **43** F1
Blue Ridge AL, *1341* **128** A2
Blue Ridge GA, *1290* **120** C2
Blue Ridge TX, *822* **59** F2
Blue Ridge VA, *3084* **112** B1
Blue Ridge Manor KY, *767* **230** F2
Blue River CO, *849* **41** D2
Blue Sprs. MO, *52575* **96** C2
Bluff UT, *258* **40** A4
Bluff City TN, *1733* **111** E3
Bluffdale UT, *7598* **31** E4
Bluffs IL, *715* **98** A1
Bluffton IN, *9897* **90** A3
Bluffton OH, *4125* **90** B3
Bluffton SC, *12530* **130** C3
Bluford IL, *688* **98** C4
Blunt SD, *354* **26** C3
Blythe CA, *20817* **53** F3
Blythe GA, *721* **129** F1
Blytheville AR, *15620* **108** B4
Boalsburg PA, *3722* **92** C3
Boardman OH, *35376* **91** F3
Boardman OR, *3220* **21** E1
Boardman Bridge CT, *600* **148** C1
Boaz AL, *9551* **120** A3
Boaz WV, *1297* **101** F2
Bobtown PA, *757* **102** A1
Boca Grande FL, *700* **140** C4
Boca Raton FL, *84392* **143** F1
Bodega Bay CA, *1077* **36** A3
Bodfish CA, *1956* **45** E4
Boerne TX, *10471* **61** D2
Bogalusa LA, *12232* **134** C1
Bogart GA, *1034* **121** D4
Bogata TX, *1153* **116** A4
Boger City NC, *554* **122** A1
Bogota NJ, *8187* **240** D1
Bogue NC, *684* **115** D4
Bogue Chitto MS, *887* **127** D2
Bohners Lake WI, *2444* **74** C4
Boiling Spr. Lakes NC, *5372* **123** E3
Boiling Sprs. NC, *4647* **121** F1
Boiling Sprs. PA, *3225* **93** D4
Boiling Sprs. SC, *8219* **121** F2
Boise ID, *205671* **22** B4
Boise City OK, *1266* **50** A1
Boise Co. ID, *7028* **22** C4
Bokchito OK, *632* **59** F1
Bokeelia FL, *1780* **142** C1
Bokoshe OK, *512* **116** B1
Boley OK, *1184* **51** F3
Boling TX, *1122* **61** F3
Bolingbrook IL, *73366* **89** D2
Bolivar MO, *10325* **107** D1
Bolivar NY, *1047* **92** C1
Bolivar OH, *994* **91** E3
Bolivar TN, *5417* **118** C1
Bolivar WV, *1045* **144** A2
Bolivar Co. MS, *34145* **118** A4
Bolivia NC, *143* **123** E3
Bollinger Co. MO, *12363* **108** B2
Bolton CT, *5170* **150** A3
Bolton MS, *567* **126** B2
Bolton NC, *691* **123** D3
Bolton Landing NY, *513* **81** D3
Bon Air VA, *16366* **113** E1
Bonaire GA, *800* **129** D2
Bonanza AR, *575* **116** C1
Bonanza OR, *415* **29** D2
Bonaparte IA, *433* **87** E3
Bond Co. IL, *17768* **98** B3
Bondsville MA, *1876* **150** A2
Bonduel WI, *1478* **68** C4
Bondurant IA, *3860* **86** C2
Bonesteel SD, *275* **35** D1
Bonham TX, *10127* **59** F1
Bon Homme Co. SD, *7070* **35** E1
Bonifay FL, *2793* **136** C1
Bonita CA, *12538* **258** C2
Bonita Sprs. FL, *43914* **142** C1
Bonneauville PA, *1800* **103** E1
Bonner MT, *1663* **15** D4
Bonner Co. ID, *40877* **14** B2
Bonners Ferry ID, *2543* **14** B1
Bonner Sprs. KS, *7314* **96** B2
Bonne Terre MO, *6864* **98** A4
Bonnet Shores RI, *2200* **150** C4
Bonneville Co. ID, *104234* **23** F4
Bonney Lake WA, *17374* **262** B5
Bonnieville KY, *255* **110** A1
Bono AR, *2131* **108** A4
Bonsall CA, *3982* **53** D3
Booker TX, *1516* **50** B1
Boomer WV, *615* **101** F4
Boone CO, *339* **41** E3
Boone IA, *12661* **86** C1
Boone NC, *17122* **111** F3
Boone Co. AR, *36903* **107** D3
Boone Co. IL, *54165* **74** B4
Boone Co. IN, *56640* **99** F1
Boone Co. IA, *26306* **86** C1
Boone Co. KY, *118811* **100** B2
Boone Co. MO, *162642* **97** E2
Boone Co. NE, *5505* **35** E3
Boone Co. WV, *24629* **101** E4
Booneville AR, *3990* **116** C1
Booneville KY, *81* **110** C1
Booneville MS, *8743* **119** D2
Boonsboro MD, *3336* **144** A1
Boonton NJ, *8347* **148** A3
Boonville CA, *1035* **36** A2
Boonville IN, *6246* **99** E4
Boonville MO, *8319* **97** D2
Boonville NY, *2072* **79** E2
Boonville NC, *1222* **112** A3
Boothbay ME, *550* **82** C3
Boothbay Harbor ME, *1086* **82** C3
Boothville LA, *854* **134** C4
Bootjack CA, *960* **37** D4
Borden IN, *808* **99** F3
Borden Co. TX, *641* **58** B2
Bordentown NJ, *3924* **147** D2
Borger TX, *13251* **50** B2
Boron CA, *2253* **52** C1
Borrego Sprs. CA, *3429* **53** E3
Boscobel WI, *3231* **73** F3
Bosque Co. TX, *18212* **59** E3
Bosque Farms NM, *3904* **48** C4
Bossier City LA, *61315* **124** C2
Bossier Par. LA, *116979* **125** D1
Boston GA, *1315* **137** E1
Boston MA, *617594* **151** D1
Boswell IN, *778* **89** D4
Boswell OK, *709* **59** F1
Boswell PA, *1277* **92** B4
Botetourt Co. VA, *33148* **112** B1
Bothell WA, *33505* **12** C3
Botkins OH, *1155* **90** B4
Botsford CT, *1000* **149** D2
Bottineau ND, *2211* **18** C1
Bottineau Co. ND, *6429* **18** C1
Botto KY, *550* **110** C2
Boulder CO, *97385* **41** E1
Boulder MT, *1183* **23** E1
Boulder City NV, *15023* **46** B2
Boulder Co. CO, *294567* **41** D1
Boulder Creek CA, *4923* **44** A2
Boundary Co. ID, *10972* **14** B1
Bound Brook NJ, *10402* **147** D1
Bountiful UT, *42552* **31** E4
Bourbon IN, *1810* **89** F2
Bourbon MO, *1632* **97** F4
Bourbon Co. KS, *15173* **96** B4
Bourbon Co. KY, *19985* **100** B4
Bourbonnais IL, *18631* **89** D2
Bourne MA, *1418* **151** E3
Bouse AZ, *996* **54** A1
Boutte LA, *3075* **134** B3
Bovey MN, *804* **64** B3
Bovill ID, *260* **14** B4
Bovina TX, *1868* **49** F4
Bowbells ND, *336* **18** B1
Bow Ctr. NH, *7519* **81** F4
Bowdle SD, *502* **27** D2
Bowdoin Ctr. ME, *425* **82** B3
Bowdoinham ME, *722* **82** B3
Bowdon GA, *2040* **120** B4
Bowen IL, *494* **87** F4

Figures after entries indicate population, page number, and grid reference.

Bowers DE, 335 145 F3
Bowie AZ, 449 55 E3
Bowie MD, 54727 144 C3
Bowie TX, 5218 59 E1
Bowie Co. TX, 92565 116 B4
Bowleys Quarters MD, 6755 144 C2
Bowling Green FL, 2930 140 C3
Bowling Green KY, 58067 109 F2
Bowling Green MO, 5334 97 F2
Bowling Green OH, 30028 90 C2
Bowling Green VA, 1111 103 D4
Bowman GA, 862 121 E3
Bowman ND, 1650 25 F1
Bowman SC, 968 130 C1
Bowman Co. ND, 3151 25 F1
Bow Mar CO, 866 209 B4
Boxborough MA, 4996 150 C1
Box Butte Co. NE, 11308 34 A2
Box Elder MT, 87 16 B2
Box Elder SD, 7800 26 A3
Box Elder Co. UT, 49975 31 D3
Boxford MA, 2339 151 F1
Boyce LA, 1004 125 E4
Boyce VA, 589 103 D2
Boyceville WI, 1086 67 E3
Boyd TX, 1207 59 E2
Boyd WI, 552 67 F4
Boyd Co. KY, 49542 101 D4
Boyd Co. NE, 2099 35 D1
Boyden IA, 707 35 F1
Boydton VA, 431 113 D3
Boyertown PA, 4055 146 B2
Boyette FL, 5895 140 C3
Boykins VA, 564 113 E3
Boyle MS, 650 118 A4
Boyle Co. KY, 28432 110 B1
Boyne City MI, 3735 70 B3
Boynton Beach FL, 68217 143 F1
Boys Town NE, 745 245 A2
Bozeman MT, 37280 23 F1
Braceville IL, 793 88 C2
Bracken Co. KY, 8488 100 C3
Brackettville TX, 1688 60 B3
Bradbury CA, 1048 228 E2
Braddock PA, 2159 250 C2
Braddock Hts. MD, 2608 144 A1
Braddock Hills PA, 1880 250 C2
Bradenton FL, 49546 140 B3
Bradenton Beach FL, 1171 140 B3
Bradford AR, 759 117 F1
Bradford IL, 768 88 B2
Bradford NH, 356 81 E4
Bradford OH, 1842 90 B4
Bradford PA, 8770 92 B1
Bradford RI, 1406 150 C4
Bradford TN, 1048 108 C4
Bradford VT, 788 81 E3
Bradford Co. FL, 28520 138 C3
Bradford Co. PA, 62622 93 E2
Bradfordville FL, 1100 137 E2
Bradford Woods PA, 1171 92 A3
Bradley AR, 628 125 D1
Bradley IL, 15895 89 D3
Bradley ME, 1242 83 D1
Bradley WV, 2040 101 F4
Bradley Beach NJ, 4298 147 F2
Bradley Co. AR, 11508 117 E4
Bradley Co. TN, 98963 120 C1
Bradley Jct. FL, 686 140 C3
Bradner OH, 985 90 C2
Brady TX, 5528 58 C4
Braham MN, 1793 67 D2
Braidwood IL, 6191 88 C2
Brainerd MN, 13590 64 B4
Braintree MA, 35744 151 D2
Bramwell WV, 364 111 F1
Branch Co. MI, 45248 90 A1
Branchville AL, 825 119 F4
Branchville NJ, 841 94 A4
Branchville SC, 1024 130 C1
Brandenburg KY, 2643 99 F4
Brandon FL, 103483 140 C2
Brandon MS, 21705 126 B3
Brandon SD, 8785 27 F4
Brandon VT, 1648 81 D3
Brandon WI, 879 74 C2
Brandywine MD, 6719 144 B4
Brandywine Manor PA, 1200 146 B3
Branford CT, 29089 149 D2
Branford FL, 712 138 B3
Branson MO, 10520 107 D3
Brant Beach NJ, 800 147 E4
Brantley AL, 809 128 A4
Brantley Co. GA, 18411 129 F4
Brant Rock MA, 5100 151 E2
Braselton GA, 7511 121 D3
Brasher Falls NY, 669 80 B1
Bratenahl OH, 1197 204 F1
Brattleboro VT, 7414 94 C1
Brawley CA, 24953 53 E4
Braxton Co. WV, 14523 101 F3
Bray OK, 1209 51 E4
Braymer MO, 878 96 C1
Brazil IN, 7912 99 E1
Brazoria TX, 3019 132 A4
Brazoria Co. TX, 313166 132 A4
Brazos Co. TX, 194851 61 F1
Brea CA, 39282 229 F3
Breathitt Co. KY, 13878 111 D1
Breaux Bridge LA, 8139 133 F2
Breckenridge CO, 4540 41 D1
Breckenridge MI, 1328 76 A2
Breckenridge MN, 3386 27 F1
Breckenridge TX, 5780 59 D2
Breckenridge Hills MO, 4746 256 B2
Breckinridge Co. KY, 20059 99 F4
Brecksville OH, 13656 204 F3
Breese IL, 4442 98 B3
Breezy Pt. MD, 800 144 C4
Breezy Pt. MN, 2346 64 B4
Breinigsville PA, 4138 146 B1
Bremen GA, 6227 120 B4
Bremen IN, 4588 89 F2
Bremen KY, 197 109 E1
Bremen OH, 1425 101 D1
Bremer Co. IA, 24276 73 E3
Bremerton WA, 37729 12 C3
Bremond TX, 929 59 F4
Brenham TX, 15716 61 F2
Brent AL, 4947 127 F1
Brent FL, 21804 135 F2
Brentsville VA, 650 144 A4
Brentwood CA, 51481 36 B3
Brentwood MD, 3046 270 E2
Brentwood MO, 8055 256 B2
Brentwood NY, 60664 149 D4
Brentwood PA, 9643 250 B3
Brentwood TN, 37060 109 F4
Bressler PA, 1437 218 C2
Brevard NC, 7609 121 E1
Brevard Co. FL, 543376 141 E2
Brewer ME, 9482 83 D1
Brewerton NY, 4029 79 D3
Brewster MA, 2000 151 F3
Brewster MN, 473 72 A2
Brewster NE, 17 34 C2
Brewster NY, 2390 148 C2
Brewster OH, 2112 91 E3
Brewster WA, 2370 13 E2
Brewster Co. TX, 9232 62 C3
Brewster Hill NY, 2089 148 C1
Brewton AL, 5408 135 F1
Briar TX, 5665 59 E2
Briarcliff TX, 1438 61 D1
Briarcliffe Acres SC, 457 123 D4
Briarcliff Manor NY, 7867 148 B2
Briar Creek PA, 660 93 E3
Briarwood KY, 435 230 F1
Briceville TN, 650 110 C4
Brickerville PA, 1309 146 A2
Bridge City LA, 7706 239 B2
Bridge City TX, 7840 132 C3
Bridgehampton NY, 1756 149 F3
Bridgeport AL, 2418 120 A2
Bridgeport CA, 575 37 E3
Bridgeport CT, 144229 149 D2
Bridgeport IL, 1886 99 D3
Bridgeport MD, 2700 144 A1
Bridgeport MI, 6950 76 B3
Bridgeport NE, 1545 34 A3
Bridgeport NY, 1490 79 E3
Bridgeport PA, 4554 248 A1
Bridgeport TX, 5976 59 E2
Bridgeport WA, 2409 13 E2
Bridgeport WV, 8149 102 A2
Bridger MT, 708 24 B2
Bridgeton MO, 11550 256 B1
Bridgeton NJ, 25349 145 F1
Bridgetown OH, 14407 204 A2
Bridgeview IL, 16446 203 D5
Bridgeville DE, 2048 145 E4
Bridgeville PA, 5148 250 A3
Bridgewater MA, 7841 151 D2
Bridgewater NJ, 44464 147 D1
Bridgewater NY, 470 79 E3
Bridgewater PA, 9643 250 B3
Bridgewater SD, 492 27 E4
Bridgewater VA, 5644 102 C4
Bridgman MI, 2291 89 E1
Bridgton ME, 2071 82 B3
Brielle NJ, 4774 147 E2
Brier WA, 6087 262 B2
Brigantine NJ, 9450 147 F4
Brigham City UT, 17899 31 E3
Bright IN, 5693 100 B2
Brighton AL, 2945 195 D2
Brighton CO, 33352 41 E1
Brighton IL, 2254 98 A2
Brighton IA, 652 87 E2
Brighton MI, 7444 76 B4
Brighton NY, 36609 78 C3
Brighton TN, 2735 118 B1
Brightwaters NY, 3103 149 D4
Brightwood VA, 1001 102 C3
Brilliant AL, 900 119 E3
Brilliant OH, 1482 91 F4
Brillion WI, 3148 74 C1
Brimfield IL, 868 88 B3
Brinckerhoff NY, 2900 148 B1
Brinkley AR, 3188 117 F2
Brinnon WA, 797 12 C3
Brisbane CA, 4282 259 B3
Briscoe Co. TX, 1637 50 B4
Bristol CT, 60477 149 D1
Bristol FL, 996 137 D2
Bristol IN, 1602 89 F1
Bristol NH, 1688 81 F3
Bristol PA, 9726 147 D2
Bristol RI, 22954 151 D3
Bristol SD, 341 27 E2
Bristol TN, 26702 111 E3
Bristol VT, 2030 81 D2
Bristol VA, 17835 111 E3
Bristol WI, 2584 74 C4
Bristol Co. MA, 548285 151 D3
Bristol Co. RI, 49875 151 D3
Bristow OK, 4222 51 F2
Britt IA, 2069 72 C3
Brittany Farms PA, 3695 146 C2
Britton MI, 586 90 B1
Britton SD, 1241 27 E1
Broadalbin NY, 1327 80 C4
Broad Brook CT, 4069 150 A3
Broadmoor CA, 4176 259 B3
Broadus MT, 468 25 E2
Broadview IL, 7932 203 C4
Broadview Hts. OH, 19400 204 F3
Broadwater Co. MT, 5612 15 F4
Broadway NC, 1229 123 D1
Broadway VA, 3691 102 C3
Brock Hall MD, 9552 144 C3
Brockport NY, 8366 78 C3
Brockton MA, 93810 151 D2
Brockton MT, 255 17 E2
Brockway PA, 2072 92 B2
Brocton NY, 1486 78 A4
Brodhead KY, 1211 110 C1
Brodhead WI, 3293 74 B4
Brodheadsville PA, 1800 93 F3
Brogden NC, 2633 123 E1
Broken Arrow OK, 98850 106 A4
Broken Bow NE, 3559 35 D3
Broken Bow OK, 4120 116 B3
Bromley KY, 763 204 A3
Bronson FL, 1113 138 C4
Bronson MI, 2349 90 A1
Bronte TX, 999 58 C3
Bronwood GA, 225 128 C3
Bronx Co. NY, 1385108 148 B4
Brook IN, 997 89 D3
Brookdale SC, 4873 122 A4
Brooke VA, 650 103 D4
Brooke Co. WV, 24069 91 F4
Brookfield CT, 16354 148 C1
Brookfield IL, 18978 203 C5
Brookfield MA, 833 150 B2
Brookfield MO, 4542 97 D1
Brookfield OH, 1288 276 C1
Brookfield WI, 37920 234 B2
Brookfield Ctr. CT, 1800 148 C1
Brookhaven MS, 12513 126 B4
Brookhaven NY, 3451 149 D4
Brookhaven PA, 8006 248 A4
Brookings OR, 6336 28 A2
Brookings SD, 22056 27 F3
Brookings Co. SD, 31965 27 F3
Brookland AR, 1642 108 A4
Brooklandville MD, 2200 193 C1
Brooklawn NJ, 1955 248 C4
Brooklet GA, 1395 130 B2
Brookline MA, 58732 151 D1
Brookline NH, 4991 95 D1
Brooklyn CT, 981 150 B3
Brooklyn IL, 749 256 C2
Brooklyn IN, 1598 99 F1
Brooklyn IA, 1468 87 E1
Brooklyn MI, 1206 90 B1
Brooklyn OH, 11169 204 E2
Brooklyn WI, 1401 74 B3
Brooklyn Ctr. MN, 30104 235 B1
Brooklyn Hts. OH, 1543 204 F2
Brooklyn Park MD, 14373 193 C4
Brooklyn Park MN, 75781 235 B1
Brookneal VA, 1112 112 C2
Brook Park OH, 19212 204 E3
Brookport IL, 984 108 C2
Brooks GA, 524 128 C1
Brooks KY, 2401 100 A4
Brooks ME, 1022 82 C2
Brooks Co. GA, 16243 137 F1
Brooks Co. TX, 7223 63 E3
Brookshire TX, 4702 61 F2
Brookside AL, 1363 195 D1
Brookside DE, 14353 146 B4
Brookside OH, 632 91 F4
Brookside Vil. TX, 1523 220 C4
Brookston IN, 1554 89 E3
Brooksville FL, 7719 140 C1
Brooksville KY, 642 100 C3
Brooksville MS, 1223 127 D1
Brookville IN, 2596 100 A2
Brookville KY, 3465 148 C4
Brookville OH, 5884 100 B1
Brookville PA, 3924 92 B2
Brookwood AL, 1828 127 F1
Broomall PA, 10789 146 C3
Broome Co. NY, 200600 93 F1
Broomfield CO, 55889 41 E1
Broomfield Co. CO, 55889 41 E1
Brooten MN, 743 66 B3
Broussard LA, 8197 133 F2
Broward Co. FL, 1748066 143 E1
Browerville MN, 790 66 B2
Brown City MI, 1325 76 C3
Brown Co. IL, 6937 87 F4
Brown Co. IN, 15242 99 F2
Brown Co. KS, 9984 96 A1
Brown Co. MN, 25893 72 B1
Brown Co. NE, 3145 34 C1
Brown Co. OH, 44846 100 C3
Brown Co. SD, 36531 27 E1
Brown Co. TX, 38106 59 D3
Brown Co. WI, 248007 74 C1
Brown Deer WI, 11999 234 C1
Brownfield TX, 9657 58 A2
Browning MT, 1016 15 E2
Brownsboro TX, 1039 124 A3
Brownsburg IN, 21285 99 F1
Brownsdale MN, 676 73 D2
Browns Mills NJ, 11223 147 D3
Brownstown IL, 759 98 C2
Brownstown IN, 2947 99 F3
Browns Valley MN, 589 27 F1
Brownsville CA, 1069 36 C1
Brownsville KY, 836 109 F2
Brownsville MN, 466 73 F2
Brownsville OR, 1668 20 B3
Brownsville PA, 2331 102 B1
Brownsville TN, 10292 118 C1
Brownsville TX, 175023 63 F4
Brownsville WI, 581 74 C2
Brownton MN, 762 66 C4
Brownville NY, 1119 79 E1
Brownville Jct. ME, 750 84 C4
Brownwood TX, 19288 59 D4
Broxton GA, 1189 129 E4
Broyhill Park VA, 17000 270 B4
Bruce MS, 1939 118 C3
Bruce SD, 204 27 F3
Bruce WI, 779 67 E3
Bruceton TN, 1478 109 D4
Bruceville-Eddy TX, 1475 59 E4
Brule Co. SD, 5255 27 D4
Brundidge AL, 2076 128 B4
Brunson SC, 554 130 B1
Brunswick GA, 15383 139 D1
Brunswick ME, 15175 82 B3
Brunswick MD, 5870 144 A2
Brunswick MO, 858 97 D2
Brunswick OH, 34255 91 E2
Brunswick Co. NC, 107431 123 E3
Brunswick Co. VA, 17434 113 D3
Brush CO, 5463 33 F4
Brush Prairie WA, 2652 20 C1
Brushy OK, 900 116 B1
Brusly LA, 2589 134 A2
Bryan OH, 8545 90 B2
Bryan TX, 76201 61 F1
Bryan Co. GA, 30233 130 B3
Bryan Co. OK, 42416 59 F1
Bryans Road MD, 7244 144 B4
Bryant AR, 16688 117 E2
Bryant SD, 456 27 E3
Bryantville MA, 2600 151 E2
Bryn Athyn PA, 1375 248 D1
Bryn Mawr PA, 3779 146 C3
Bryson TX, 539 59 D2
Bryson City NC, 1424 121 D1
Buchanan GA, 1104 120 B4
Buchanan MI, 4456 89 E1
Buchanan NY, 2230 148 B2
Buchanan VA, 1178 112 B1
Buchanan Co. IA, 20958 73 E4
Buchanan Co. MO, 89201 96 B1
Buchanan Co. VA, 24098 111 F2
Buchanan Dam TX, 1519 61 D1
Buchtel OH, 558 101 E2
Buckeye AZ, 50876 54 B1
Buckeye Lake OH, 2746 101 D1
Buckfield ME, 1723 82 B2
Buckhannon WV, 5639 102 A2
Buckhead Ridge FL, 1450 141 E4
Buckingham PA, 1400 146 C2
Buckingham VA, 133 113 D1
Buckingham Co. VA, 17146 113 D1
Buckland AK, 416 154 B2
Buckley IL, 600 89 D4
Buckley MI, 697 69 F4
Buckley WA, 4354 12 C3
Bucklin KS, 794 42 C4
Bucklin MO, 467 97 D1
Buckner KY, 5837 100 A4
Buckner MO, 3076 96 C2
Bucks Co. PA, 625249 146 C1
Bucksport ME, 2885 83 D2
Bucksport SC, 876 123 D4
Bucoda WA, 562 12 C4
Bucyrus OH, 12362 90 C3
Buda IL, 538 88 B2
Buda TX, 7295 61 E2
Budd Lake NJ, 8968 94 A4
Bude MS, 1063 126 A4
Buellton CA, 4828 52 A2
Buena NJ, 4603 147 D4
Buena WA, 990 13 D4
Buena Park CA, 80530 228 E3
Buena Ventura Lakes FL, 26079 246 C5
Buena Vista CO, 2617 41 D2
Buena Vista GA, 2173 128 C2
Buena Vista MI, 6816 76 B2
Buena Vista VA, 6650 112 C1
Buena Vista Co. IA, 20260 72 B4
Buffalo IN, 692 89 E3
Buffalo IA, 1270 87 F2
Buffalo KY, 498 110 A1
Buffalo MN, 15453 66 C3
Buffalo MO, 3084 107 D1
Buffalo NY, 261310 78 B3
Buffalo ND, 188 19 E4
Buffalo OK, 1299 50 C1
Buffalo SC, 1266 121 F2
Buffalo SD, 330 25 F1
Buffalo TX, 1856 59 F4
Buffalo WV, 1236 101 E3
Buffalo WY, 4585 25 D3
Buffalo Ctr. IA, 905 72 C2
Buffalo City WI, 1023 73 E1
Buffalo Co. NE, 46102 35 D4
Buffalo Co. SD, 1912 27 D3
Buffalo Co. WI, 13587 67 E4
Buffalo Grove IL, 41496 203 C2
Buffalo Lake MN, 733 66 B4
Buford GA, 12225 120 C3
Buhl ID, 4122 30 C1
Buhl MN, 1000 64 C3
Buhler KS, 1327 43 E3
Buies Creek NC, 2942 123 D1
Bullard TX, 2463 124 A3
Bullhead SD, 348 26 C1
Bullhead City AZ, 39540 46 B3
Bullitt Co. KY, 74319 99 F4
Bulloch Co. GA, 70217 130 B2
Bullock Co. AL, 10914 128 B3
Bulls Gap TN, 738 111 D3
Bull Shoals AR, 1950 107 E3
Bull Valley IL, 1077 74 C4
Bulverde TX, 4630 61 D2
Buna TX, 2142 132 C2
Buncombe Co. NC, 238318 111 E4
Bunker Hill IL, 1774 98 B2
Bunker Hill IN, 888 89 F3
Bunker Hill OR, 1444 20 A4
Bunker Hill WV, 700 103 D2
Bunker Hill Vil. TX, 3633 220 B2
Bunkerville NV, 1303 46 B1
Bunkie LA, 4171 133 E1
Bunnell FL, 2676 139 E4
Buras LA, 945 134 C4
Burbank CA, 103340 52 C2
Burbank IL, 28925 203 D5
Burbank WA, 3291 21 E1
Burden KS, 535 43 F4
Bureau Co. IL, 34978 88 B2
Burgaw NC, 3872 123 E2
Burgettstown PA, 1388 91 F4

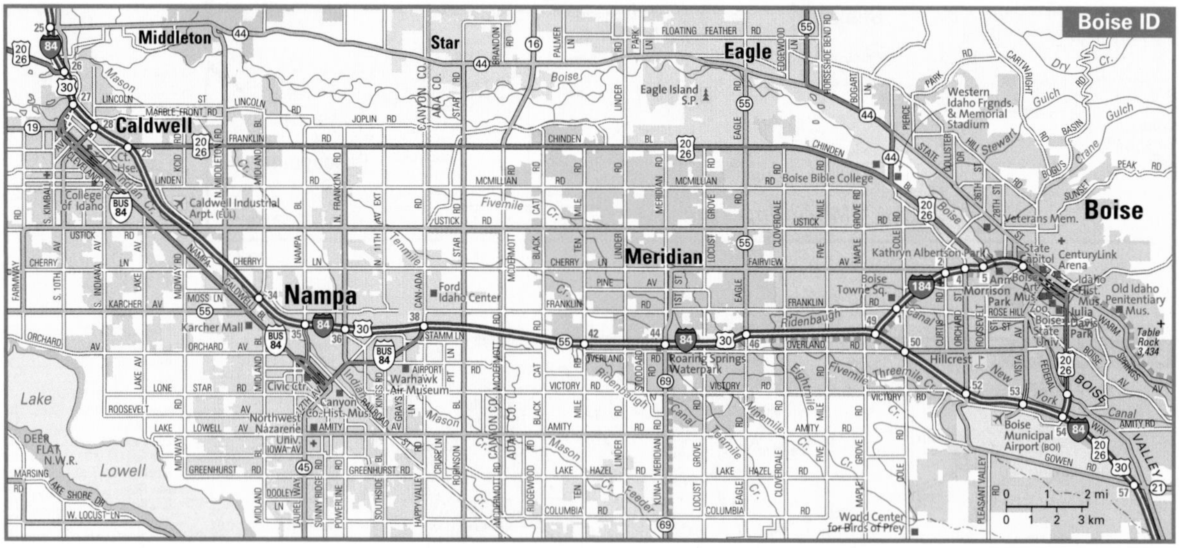

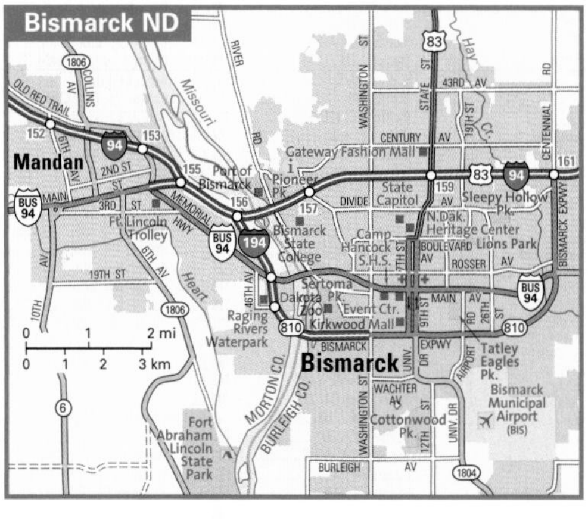

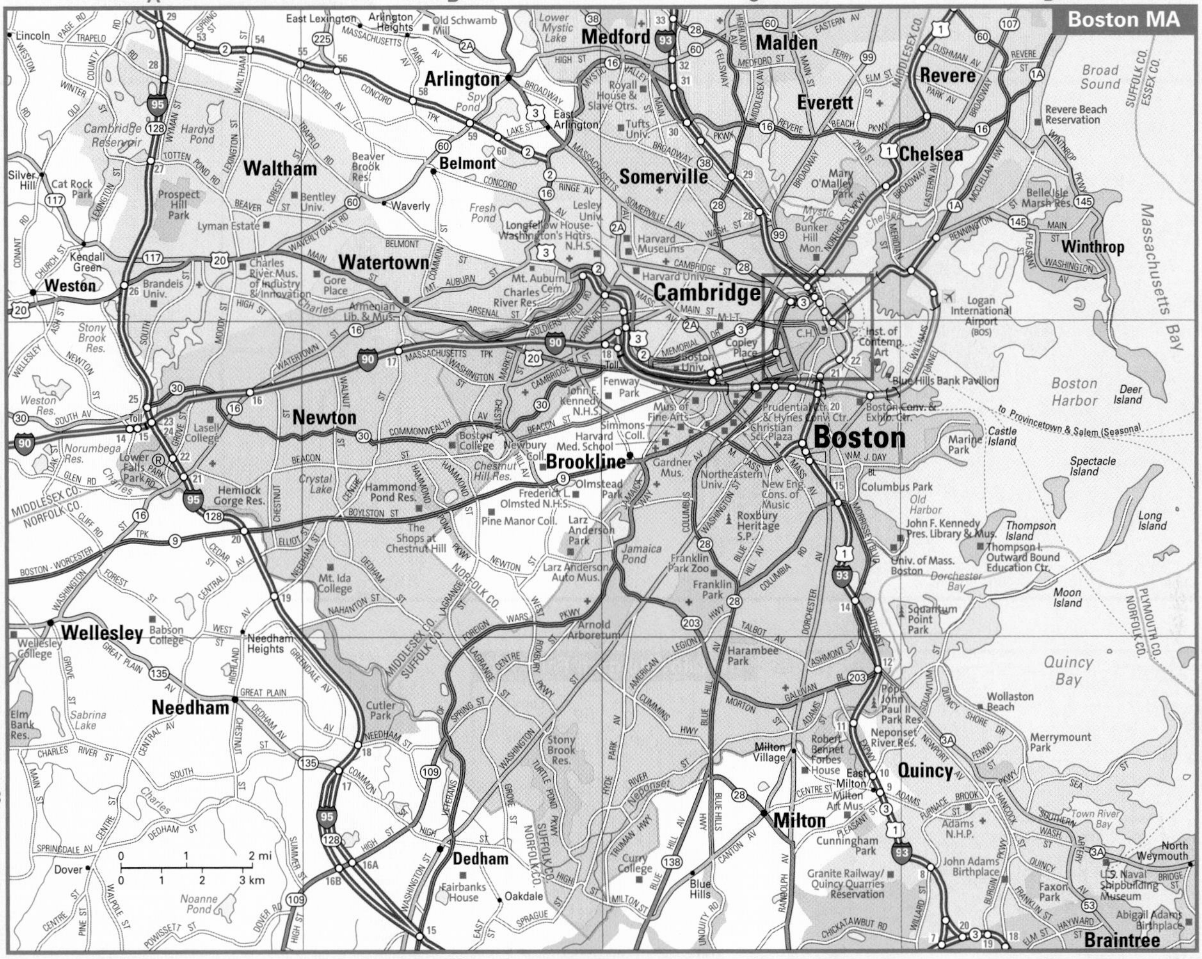

Arlington............B1
Arlington Hts.........B1
Belmont.............B1
Blue Hills...........C3
Boston..............C2
Brookline...........C2
Cambridge..........C1
Chelsea.............D1
Dedham.............B3
Dover..............A3
E. Arlington..........B1
E. Lexington.........B1
E. Milton............C3
Everett..............C1
Kendall Green.......A1
Lincoln..............A1
Malden..............C1
Medford.............C1
Milton..............C3
Milton Vil............C3
Needham...........A3
Needham Hts........A2
Newton.............B2
N. Weymouth........D3
Oakdale.............B3
Quincy..............D3
Revere..............D1
Silver Hill...........A1
Somerville...........C1
Waltham............A1
Watertown..........B1
Waverly.............B1
Wellesley...........A2
Weston.............A1
Winthrop............D1

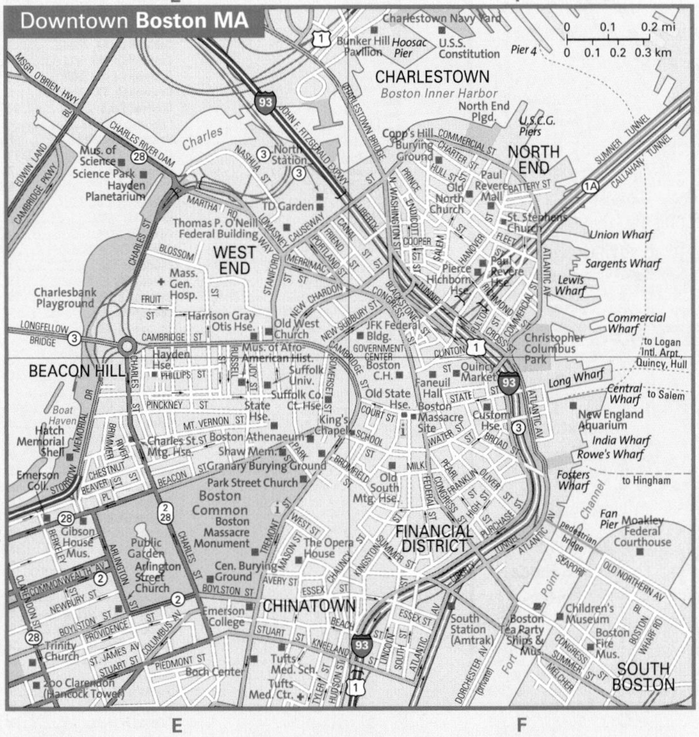

POINTS OF INTEREST
200 Clarendon (Hancock Tower)...........E2
Arlington Street Church...................E2
Boch Center.............................E2
Boston Athenaeum.......................E2
Boston City Hall..........................F2
Boston Fire Museum.....................F2
Boston Massacre Monument.............E2
Boston Massacre Site....................F2
Boston Tea Party Ships & Museum.......F2
Bunker Hill Pavilion.......................F1
Central Burying Ground..................E2
Charles Street Meeting House............E2
Children's Museum........................F2
Copp's Hill Burying Ground...............F1
Custom House.............................F2
Emerson College..........................E2
Faneuil Hall...............................F2
Gibson House Museum....................E2
Granary Burying Ground..................E2
Harrison Gray Otis House................E1
Hatch Memorial Shell.....................E2
Hayden House............................E2
Hayden Planetarium.......................E1
JFK Federal Building......................F1
King's Chapel.............................E2
Moakley Federal Courthouse..............F2
Museum of Afro-American Hist............E2
Museum of Science........................E1
New England Aquarium....................F2
North Station.............................E1
Old North Church..........................F1
Old South Meeting House.................F2
Old State House...........................F2
Old West Church...........................E1
The Opera House.........................E2
Park Street Church........................E2
Paul Revere House........................F1
Paul Revere Mall..........................F1
Pierce Hichborn House....................F1
Quincy Market.............................F2
St. Stephens Church.......................F1
Shaw Memorial.............................E2
South Station (Amtrak)....................F2
State House...............................E2
Suffolk County Court House...............E2
Suffolk Univ................................E2
TD Garden..................................E1
Thomas P. O'Neill Federal Building........E1
Trinity Church..............................E2
Suffolk County Court House...............E2
Tufts Medical School.......................E2
U.S.S. Constitution.........................F1

Burgin KY, *965*....................**110** B1
Burien WA, *33313*...................**12** C3
Burkburnett TX, *10811*.............**59** D1
Burke SD, *604*.......................**35** D1
Burke VA, *41055*....................**144** B3
Burke Co. GA, *23316*............**129** F1
Burke Co. NC, *90912*............**111** F4
Burke Co. ND, *1968*...............**18** A1
Burkesville KY, *1521*...............**110** A2
Burkeville VA, *432*..................**113** D2
Burleigh Co. ND, *81308*..........**18** C4
Burleson TX, *36690*..................**59** E3
Burleson Co. TX, *17187*...........**61** F1
Burley ID, *10345*.....................**31** D1
Burley WA, *2057*....................**262** A4
Burlingame CA, *28806*.............**259** B4
Burlingame KS, *934*..................**96** A3
Burlingham NY, *750*................**148** A1
Burlington CO, *4254*..................**42** A2
Burlington CT, *8190*..................**94** C3
Burlington IA, *25663*.................**87** F3
Burlington KS, *2674*..................**96** A4
Burlington KY, *15926*...............**100** B2
Burlington MA, *24498*..............**151** D1
Burlington NJ, *9920*................**147** D2
Burlington NC, *49963*..............**112** C4
Burlington ND, *1060*..................**18** B2
Burlington OH, *2676*................**101** D3
Burlington VT, *42417*..............**81** D2
Burlington WA, *8388*..................**12** C2
Burlington WI, *10464*.................**74** C4
Burlington WY, *288*...................**24** C3
Burlington Co. NJ, *448734*.......**147** D3
Burlington Jct. MO, *537*..............**86** B4
Burlison TN, *425*....................**118** B1
Burnet TX, *5987*.......................**61** D1
Burnet Co. TX, *42750*..............**61** D1
Burnett Co. WI, *15457*.............**67** D2
Burnettown SC, *2673*................**121** F4
Burney CA, *3154*.......................**28** C4
Burnham IL, *4206*....................**203** E6
Burnham PA, *2054*.....................**93** D3
Burning Sprs. KY, *600*..............**110** C2
Burns OR, *2806*.........................**21** E4
Burns TN, *1468*.......................**109** E4
Burns WY, *301*..........................**33** F3
Burns Flat OK, *2057*...................**51** D3
Burns Harbor IN, *1156*................**89** E2
Burnside KY, *611*.....................**110** B2
Burnsville MN, *60306*.................**67** D4
Burnsville MS, *936*..................**119** D2
Burnsville NC, *1693*.................**111** E4
Burnsville WV, *510*..................**102** A3
Burnt Hills NY, *2100*..................**94** B1
Burr Oak MI, *828*......................**90** A1
Burr Ridge IL, *10559*................**203** C5
Burrton KS, *901*........................**43** E3
Burt IA, *533*.............................**72** B3
Burt MI, *1228*...........................**76** B3
Burt Co. NE, *6858*....................**35** F2
Burton MI, *29999*......................**76** B3
Burton OH, *1455*........................**91** E2
Burton SC, *6976*......................**130** C2
Burtonsville MD, *8323*...............**144** B2
Burwell NE, *1210*.......................**35** D2
Busby MT, *745*..........................**25** D2
Bushnell FL, *2418*....................**140** C1
Bushnell IL, *3117*.......................**88** A4
Bushyhead OK, *1314*.................**106** A3
Butler AL, *1894*........................**127** D3
Butler GA, *1972*.......................**129** D2
Butler IN, *2684*..........................**90** A2
Butler KY, *612*.........................**100** B3
Butler MO, *4219*.........................**96** B4
Butler NJ, *7539*.......................**148** A3
Butler OH, *933*...........................**91** D4
Butler PA, *13757*........................**92** A3
Butler WI, *1841*........................**234** B1
Butler Beach FL, *4951*...............**139** E3
Butler Co. AL, *20947*...............**127** F3
Butler Co. IA, *14867*.................**73** D4
Butler Co. KS, *65880*.................**43** F4
Butler Co. KY, *12690*...............**109** F2
Butler Co. MO, *42794*...............**108** A2
Butler Co. NE, *8395*...................**35** E3
Butler Co. OH, *368130*.............**100** B2
Butler Co. PA, *183862*...............**92** A3
Butner NC, *7591*.......................**112** C4
Butte MT, *33525*.........................**23** E1
Butte NE, *326*............................**35** D1
Butte Co. CA, *220000*.................**36** C1
Butte Co. ID, *2891*.....................**23** D4
Butte Co. SD, *10110*...................**25** F2
Butte Falls OR, *423*......................**28** C1

Figures after entries indicate population, page number, and grid reference.

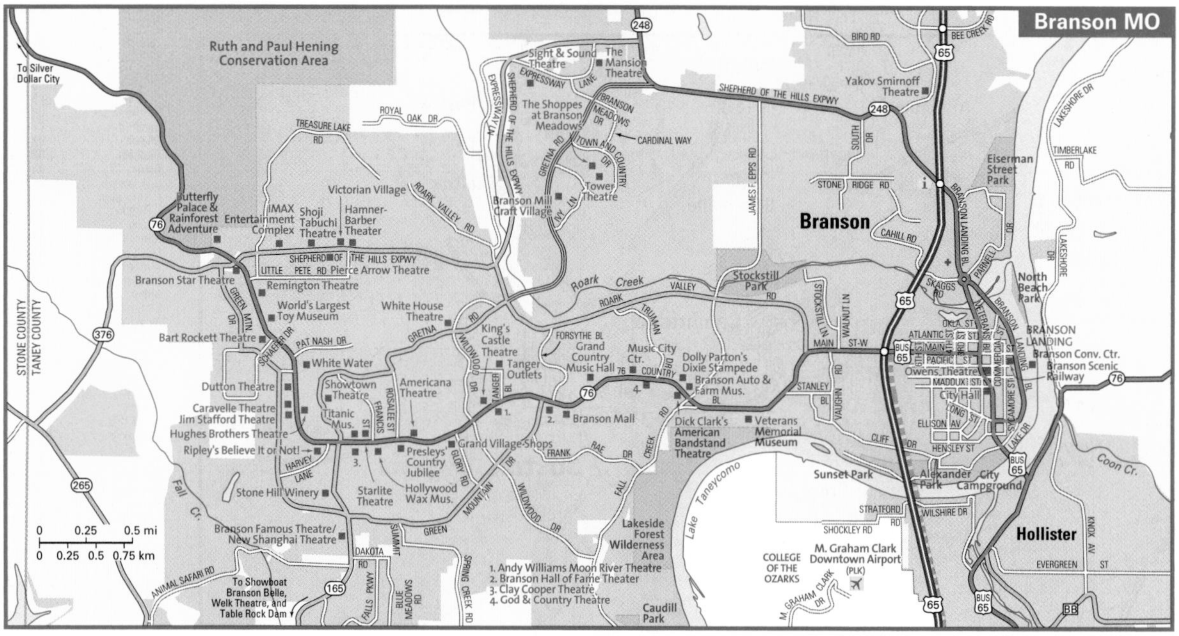

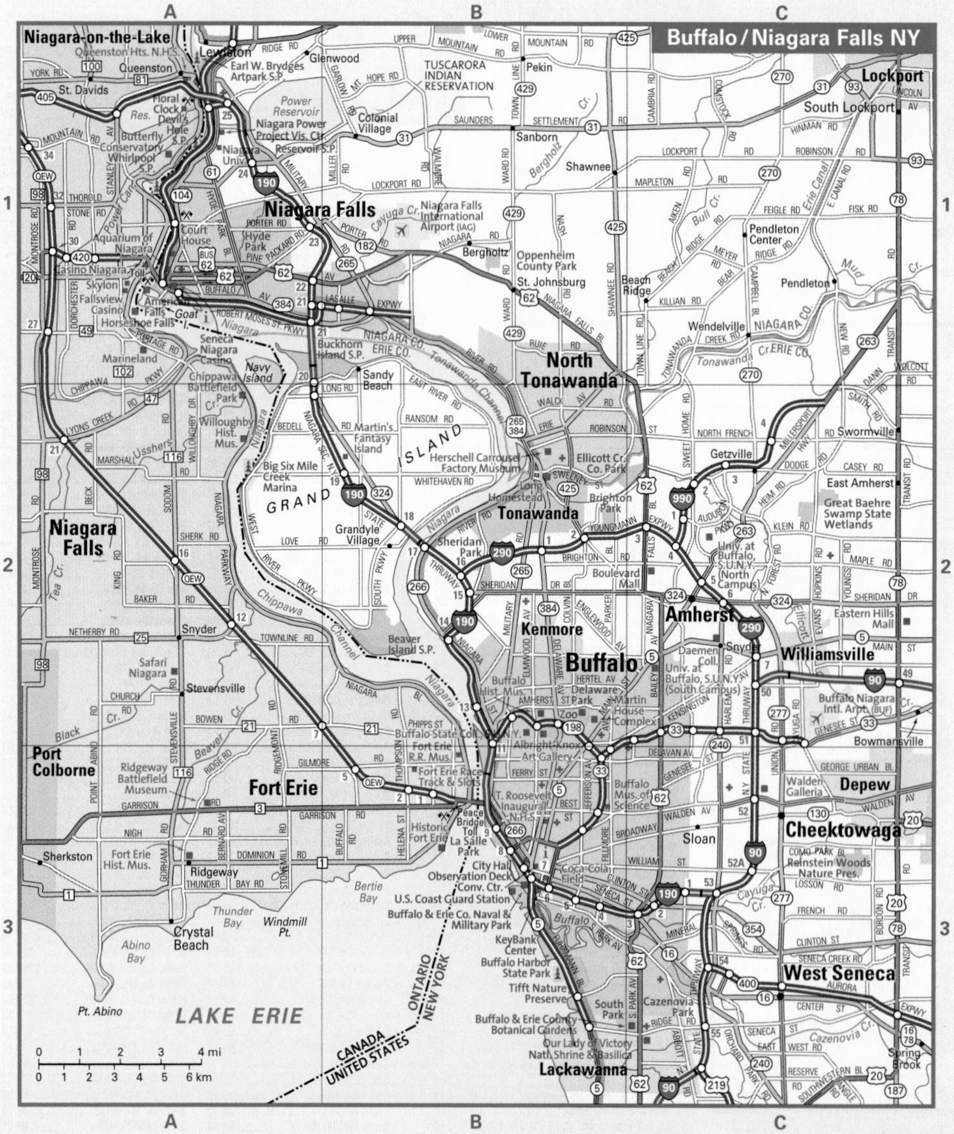

Amherst	C2
Beach Ridge	C1
Bergholtz	B1
Bowmansville	C2
Buffalo	B2
Cheektowaga	C3
Colonial Vil.	B1
Crystal Beach	A3
Depew	C3
E. Amherst	C2
Ft. Erie	A3
Getzville	C2
Glenwood	A1
Grandyle Vil.	B2
Kenmore	B2
Lackawanna	B3
Lewiston	A1
Lockport	C1
Niagara Falls, NY	A1
Niagara Falls, ON	A2
Niagara-on-the-Lake	A1
N. Tonawanda	B1
Pekin	B1
Pendleton	C1
Pendleton Ctr.	C1
Port Colborne	A3
Queenston	A1
Ridgeway	A3
St. Davids	A1
St. Johnsburg	B1
Sanborn	B1
Sandy Beach	B1
Shawnee	B1
Sherkston	A3
Sloan	C3
Snyder, NY	C2
Snyder, ON	A2
S. Lockport	C1
Spring Brook	C3
Stevensville	A2
Swormville	C2
Tonawanda	B2
Wendelville	C1
W. Seneca	C3
Williamsville	C2

Butterfield MN, *586* ... 72 B1
Buttonwillow CA, *1508* ... 45 D4
Butts Co. GA, *23655* ... 129 D1
Buttzville NJ, *146* ... 93 F3
Buxton NC, *1273* ... 115 F3
Buxton ND, *323* ... 19 E3
Buzzards Bay MA, *3859* ... 151 E3
Byers CO, *1160* ... 41 E1
Byers TX, *496* ... 59 D1
Byesville OH, *2438* ... 101 E1
Byfield MA, *850* ... 151 F1
Byhalia MS, *1302* ... 118 B2
Bylas AZ, *1962* ... 55 E2
Byng OK, *1175* ... 51 F3
Bynum AL, *1863* ... 120 A4
Byram MS, *11489* ... 126 B3
Byrdstown TN, *803* ... 110 B3
Byrnes Mill MO, *2781* ... 98 A3
Byron CA, *1277* ... 36 C4
Byron GA, *4512* ... 129 D2
Byron IL, *3753* ... 88 B1
Byron MI, *581* ... 76 B3
Byron MN, *4914* ... 73 D1
Byron WY, *593* ... 24 C3
Byron Ctr. MI, *5822* ... 75 F3

C

Cabarrus Co. NC, *178011* ... 122 B1
Cabazon CA, *2535* ... 53 D3
Cabell Co. WV, *96319* ... 101 E3
Cabin John MD, *2280* ... 270 B2
Cable WI, *206* ... 67 F1
Cabool MO, *2146* ... 107 E2
Cabot AR, *23776* ... 117 E2
Cabot VT, *233* ... 81 E2
Cache OK, *2796* ... 51 D4
Cache Co. UT, *112656* ... 31 F3
Cactus TX, *3179* ... 50 A2
Cactus Flats AZ, *1518* ... 55 E2
Caddo OK, *997* ... 51 F4
Caddo Co. OK, *29600* ... 51 D3
Caddo Mills TX, *1338* ... 59 F2
Caddo Par. LA, *254969* ... 124 C2
Caddo Valley AR, *635* ... 117 D3
Cade LA, *1723* ... 133 F2
Cadillac MI, *10355* ... 75 F1
Cadiz KY, *2558* ... 109 D2
Cadiz OH, *3353* ... 91 F4
Cadott WI, *1437* ... 67 F4
Cadyville NY, *700* ... 81 D1
Cahokia IL, *15241* ... 98 A3
Cairo GA, *9607* ... 137 E1
Cairo IL, *2831* ... 108 C2
Cairo NE, *785* ... 35 D3
Cairo NY, *1402* ... 94 B2
Cajah's Mtn. NC, *2823* ... 111 F4
Calabasas CA, *23058* ... 228 A2
Calabash NC, *1786* ... 123 D4
Calais ME, *3123* ... 83 E1
Calaveras Co. CA, *45578* ... 36 C3
Calcasieu Par. LA, *192768* ... 133 D2
Calcium NY, *3491* ... 79 E1
Calcutta OH, *3742* ... 91 F3
Caldwell AR, *555* ... 118 A1
Caldwell ID, *46237* ... 22 B4
Caldwell KS, *1068* ... 51 E1
Caldwell NJ, *7822* ... 240 A2
Caldwell OH, *1748* ... 101 F1
Caldwell TX, *4104* ... 61 F1
Caldwell Co. KY, *12984* ... 109 D2
Caldwell Co. MO, *9424* ... 96 C1
Caldwell Co. NC, *83029* ... 111 F4
Caldwell Co. TX, *38066* ... 61 E2
Caldwell Par. LA, *10132* ... 125 E3
Caledonia MI, *1511* ... 75 F4
Caledonia MN, *2868* ... 73 E2
Caledonia MS, *1041* ... 119 D4
Caledonia NY, *2201* ... 78 C3
Caledonia OH, *577* ... 90 C3
Caledonia Co. VT, *31227* ... 81 E2
Calera AL, *11620* ... 127 F1
Calera OK, *2164* ... 59 F1
Calexico CA, *38572* ... 53 E4
Calhan CO, *780* ... 41 E2
Calhoun GA, *15650* ... 120 B3
Calhoun KY, *763* ... 109 E1
Calhoun MO, *469* ... 96 C3
Calhoun TN, *490* ... 120 C1
Calhoun City MS, *1774* ... 118 C4
Calhoun Co. AL, *118572* ... 120 A4
Calhoun Co. AR, *5368* ... 117 E4
Calhoun Co. FL, *14625* ... 137 D2
Calhoun Co. GA, *6694* ... 128 C4
Calhoun Co. IL, *5089* ... 98 A2
Calhoun Co. IA, *9670* ... 72 B4
Calhoun Co. MI, *136146* ... 90 A1
Calhoun Co. MS, *14962* ... 118 C3
Calhoun Co. SC, *15175* ... 122 B4
Calhoun Co. TX, *21381* ... 61 F4
Calhoun Co. WV, *7627* ... 101 F3
Calhoun Falls SC, *2004* ... 121 E3
Calico Rock AR, *1545* ... 107 E4
Caliente NV, *1130* ... 38 C4
Califon NJ, *1076* ... 104 C1
California MD, *11857* ... 103 E4
California MO, *4278* ... 97 E3
California PA, *6795* ... 92 A4
California City CA, *14120* ... 52 C1
Calimesa CA, *7879* ... 229 K3
Calion AR, *494* ... 125 E1
Calipatria CA, *7705* ... 53 E4
Calistoga CA, *5155* ... 36 B3
Callahan FL, *1123* ... 139 D2

Entries in **bold black** indicate counties or parishes.
Entries in **bold color** indicate cities with detailed inset maps.

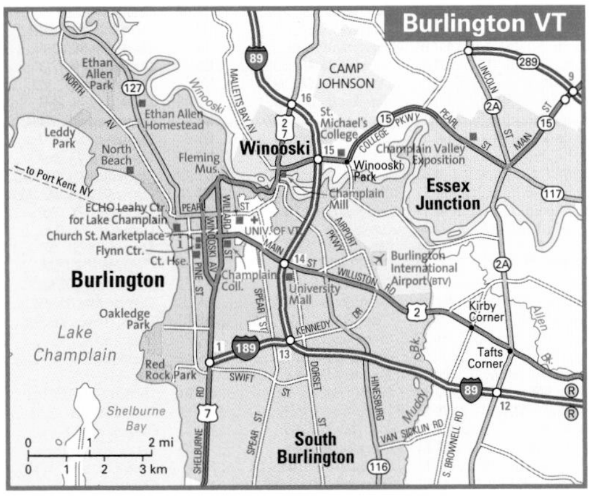

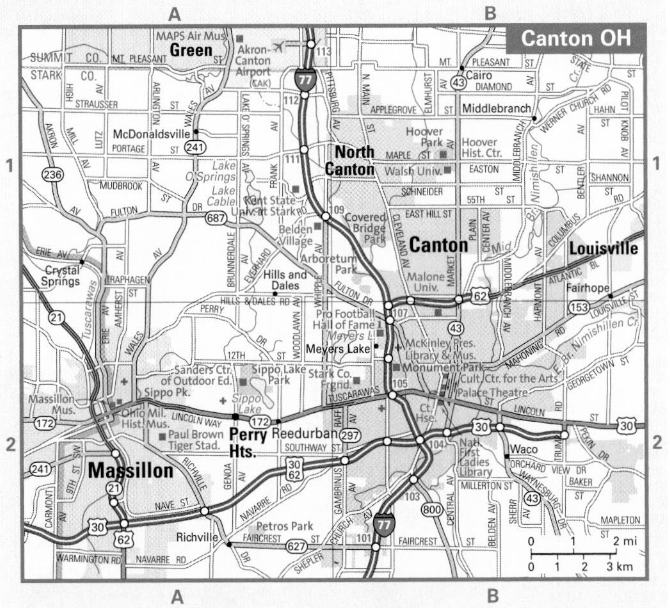

Cairo B1
Canton B1
Crystal Sprs. A1
Fairhope B1
Green A1
Hills and Dales A1
Louisville B1
Massillon A2
McDonaldsville A1
Meyers Lake B2
Middlebranch B1
N. Canton B1
Perry Hts. A2
Reedurban A2
Richville A2
Waco B2

Callahan Co. TX, *13544* 58 C3
Callaway FL, *14405* 136 C2
Callaway NE, *539* 34 C3
Callaway Co. MO, *44332* 97 E3
Calloway Co. KY, *37191* 109 D3
Calmar IA, *978* 73 E3
Cal-Nev-Ari NV, *244* 46 B3
Calpella CA, *679* 36 A2
Calumet MI, *726* 65 F3
Calumet OK, *507* 51 E3
Calumet City IL, *37042* 89 D2
Calumet Co. WI, *48971* 74 C1
Calumet Park IL, *7835* 203 E6
Calvert TX, *1192* 61 F1
Calvert Beach MD, *808* 103 E3
Calvert City KY, *2566* 109 D2
Calvert Co. MD, *88737* 144 C4
Calvert Manor MD, *650* 144 B4
Calverton MD, *17724* 144 B3
Calverton NY, *6510* 149 E3
Calverton Park MO, *1293* 256 B1
Camanche IA, *4448* 88 A1
Camargo KY, *1081* 100 C4
Camarillo CA, *65201* 52 B2
Camas WA, *19355* 20 C1
Camas Co. ID, *1117* 22 C4
Cambria CA, *6032* 44 B4
Cambria IL, *1228* 108 C1
Cambria WI, *767* 74 B2
Cambria Co. PA, *143679* 92 B4
Cambridge ID, *328* 22 B3
Cambridge IL, *2160* 88 A2
Cambridge IA, *827* 86 C1
Cambridge MD, *12326* 145 D4
Cambridge MA, *105162* 151 D1
Cambridge MN, *8111* 67 D3
Cambridge NE, *1063* 34 C4
Cambridge NY, *1870* 81 D4
Cambridge OH, *10635* 101 E1
Cambridge VT, *236* 81 D1
Cambridge WI, *1457* 74 B3
Cambridge City IN, *1870* 100 A1
Cambridge Sprs. PA, *2595* 92 A1
Camden AL, *2020* 127 F3
Camden AR, *12183* 117 D4
Camden DE, *3464* 145 E2
Camden IN, *611* 89 E3
Camden ME, *3570* 82 C2
Camden MI, *512* 90 A1
Camden NJ, *77344* 146 C3
Camden NY, *2231* 79 E3
Camden NC, *599* 115 E1
Camden OH, *2046* 100 B1
Camden SC, *6838* 122 B3
Camden TN, *3582* 109 D4
Camden Co. GA, *50513* 139 D1
Camden Co. MO, *44002* 97 D4
Camden Co. NJ, *513657* 147 D4
Camden Co. NC, *9980* 115 E1
Camden Pt. MO, *474* 96 B2
Camdenton MO, *3718* 97 D4
Cameron AZ, *885* 47 E2
Cameron LA, *406* 133 D3
Cameron MO, *9933* 96 C1
Cameron SC, *424* 122 B4
Cameron TX, *5552* 61 E1
Cameron WV, *946* 102 A1
Cameron WI, *1783* 67 E3
Cameron Co. PA, *5085* 92 C2
Cameron Co. TX, *406220* 63 F4
Cameron Par. LA, *6839* 133 D3
Camilla GA, *5360* 129 D4
Camillus NY, *1213* 79 D3
Camino CA, *1750* 36 C2
Campbell CA, *39349* 36 B4
Campbell FL, *2479* 141 D2
Campbell MO, *1992* 108 B3
Campbell OH, *8235* 91 F3
Campbell TX, *638* 59 F2
Campbell Co. KY, *90336* 100 B3
Campbell Co. SD, *1466* 26 C1
Campbell Co. TN, *40716* 110 C3
Campbell Co. VA, *54842* 112 C2
Campbell Co. WY, *46133* 25 E3
Campbell Hall NY, *750* 148 A1
Campbellsburg IN, *585* 99 F3
Campbellsburg KY, *813* 100 A3
Campbellsport WI, *2016* 74 C2
Campbellsville KY, *9108* 110 A1
Campbellton FL, *230* 136 C1
Camp Co. TX, *12401* 124 B1
Camp Douglas WI, *601* 74 A1
Camp Hill AL, *1014* 128 B2
Camp Hill PA, *7888* 93 D4
Campion CO, *1832* 33 E4
Campobello SC, *502* 121 F1
Camp Pt. IL, *1132* 87 F4
Camp Sprs. MD, *19096* 144 B3
Campti LA, *1056* 125 D3
Campton KY, *441* 111 D1
Campton NH, *3333* 81 F3
Camp Verde AZ, *10873* 47 D4
Camp Wood TX, *706* 60 C2
Cana VA, *1254* 112 A3
Canaan CT, *1212* 94 B2
Canaan ME, *300* 82 C1
Canaan NH, *524* 81 E3
Canaan VT, *392* 81 F1
Canadian TX, *2649* 50 C2
Canadian Co. OK, *115541* 51 E3
Canajoharie NY, *2229* 79 F3
Canal Fulton OH, *5479* 91 E3
Canal Pt. FL, *367* 141 E4
Canal Winchester OH, *7101* 101 D1
Canandaigua NY, *10545* 78 C3
Canaseraga NY, *550* 78 C4
Canastota NY, *4804* 79 E3
Canby MN, *1795* 27 F3
Canby OR, *15829* 20 C2
Candler Co. GA, *10998* 129 F2
Cando ND, *1115* 19 D2
Candor NY, *851* 93 E1
Candor NC, *840* 122 C1
Caney KS, *2203* 51 F1
Caneyville KY, *608* 109 F1
Canfield OH, *7515* 91 F3
Canisteo NY, *2270* 78 C4
Canistota SD, *656* 27 E4
Cannelton IN, *1563* 99 E4
Cannon Ball ND, *875* 18 C4
Cannon Beach OR, *1690* 20 B1
Cannon Co. TN, *13801* 110 A4
Cannondale CT, *141* 148 C2
Cannon Falls MN, *4083* 67 D4
Cannonsburg KY, *856* 101 D4
Canon GA, *804* 121 E3
Canon City CO, *16400* 41 E3
Canonsburg PA, *8992* 92 A4
Canterbury DE, *1200* 145 E3
Canton CT, *10292* 94 C3
Canton GA, *22958* 120 C3
Canton IL, *14704* 88 A4
Canton KS, *748* 43 E3
Canton MA, *21561* 151 D2
Canton MS, *13189* 126 B2
Canton MO, *2377* 87 F4
Canton NY, *6314* 80 B2
Canton NC, *4227* 121 E1
Canton OH, *73007* 91 E3
Canton OK, *625* 51 D2
Canton PA, *1976* 93 D2
Canton SD, *3057* 27 F4
Canton TX, *3581* 124 A2
Cantonment FL, *2300* 135 F2
Cantua Creek CA, *466* 44 C3
Canute OK, *541* 51 D3
Canutillo TX, *6321* 56 C3
Canyon TX, *13303* 50 A3
Canyon City OR, *703* 21 F3
Canyon Co. ID, *188923* 22 B4
Canyon Day AZ, *1209* 55 E1
Canyon Lake CA, *10561* 229 J5
Canyon Lake TX, *21262* 61 D2
Canyonville OR, *1884* 28 B1
Capac MI, *1890* 76 C3
Cape Canaveral FL, *9912* 141 E2
Cape Carteret NC, *1917* 115 D4
Cape Charles VA, *1009* 114 B3
Cape Coral FL, *154305* 142 C1
Cape Cottage ME, *2300* 251 B2
Cape Elizabeth ME, *9068* 82 B3
Cape Girardeau MO, *37941* 108 B1
Cape Girardeau Co. MO, *75674* 108 B1
Cape May NJ, *3607* 104 C4
Cape May Co. NJ, *97265* 104 C4
Cape May C.H. NJ, *5338* 104 C4
Cape Neddick ME, *2568* 82 B4
Cape Porpoise ME, *650* 82 B4
Cape St. Claire MD, *8747* 144 C3
Cape Vincent NY, *726* 79 D1
Capitan NM, *1489* 57 D1
Capitola CA, *9918* 44 B2
Capitol Hts. MD, *4337* 270 E3
Capitol Park DE, *700* 145 E2
Capron IL, *1376* 74 C4
Captain Cook HI, *3429* 153 E3
Caraway AR, *1279* 108 A4
Carbonado WA, *610* 12 C4
Carbon Cliff IL, *2134* 208 C2
Carbon Co. MT, *10078* 24 B2
Carbon Co. PA, *65249* 93 F3
Carbon Co. UT, *21403* 39 F1
Carbon Co. WY, *15885* 33 D2
Carbondale CO, *6427* 40 C2
Carbondale IL, *25902* 108 C1
Carbondale KS, *1437* 96 A3
Carbondale PA, *8891* 93 F2
Carbon Hill AL, *2021* 119 E4
Cardiff MD, *650* 146 A4
Cardiff NJ, *2100* 147 F4
Cardington OH, *2047* 90 C4
Cardwell MO, *713* 108 A4
Carefree AZ, *3363* 54 C1
Carencro LA, *7526* 133 F2
Carey ID, *604* 23 D4
Carey OH, *3674* 90 C3
Caribou ME, *8189* 85 D2
Caribou Co. ID, *6963* 31 E1
Carleton MI, *2345* 90 C1
Carlin NV, *2368* 30 B4
Carlinville IL, *5917* 98 B2
Carlisle AR, *2214* 117 F2
Carlisle IN, *692* 99 E3
Carlisle IA, *3876* 86 C2
Carlisle KY, *2010* 100 C4
Carlisle MA, *4852* 150 C1
Carlisle OH, *4915* 100 B1
Carlisle PA, *18682* 93 D4
Carlisle SC, *436* 122 A2
Carlisle Co. KY, *5104* 108 C2
Carl Jct. MO, *7445* 106 B2
Carlls Corner NJ, *1100* 145 F1
Carlsbad CA, *105328* 53 D4
Carlsbad NM, *26138* 57 E3
Carlsborg WA, *995* 12 B2
Carlstadt NJ, *6127* 240 C2
Carlton MN, *862* 64 C4
Carlton OR, *2007* 20 B2
Carlton Co. MN, *35386* 64 C4
Carlyle IL, *3281* 98 B3
Carlyss LA, *4670* 133 D2
Carmel IN, *79191* 99 F1
Carmel ME, *2416* 82 C1
Carmel NY, *6817* 148 C1
Carmel-by-the-Sea CA, *3722* 44 B3
Carmel Valley CA, *4407* 44 B3
Carmen AZ, *569* 55 D4
Carmi IL, *5240* 99 D4
Carmichael CA, *61762* 255 C2
Carnation WA, *1786* 12 C3
Carnegie OK, *1723* 51 D3
Carnegie PA, *7972* 250 A2
Carnesville GA, *577* 121 D3
Carney MD, *29941* 193 D1
Carney OK, *647* 51 F2
Carneys Pt. NJ, *7382* 146 B4
Caro MI, *4229* 76 B2
Caroleen NC, *652* 121 F1
Carolina RI, *970* 150 C4
Carolina Beach NC, *5706* 123 E3
Carolina Shores NC, *3048* 123 D4
Caroline Co. MD, *33066* 145 E4
Caroline Co. VA, *28545* 103 E4
Carol Stream IL, *39711* 203 B4
Carpendale WV, *977* 102 C1
Carpentersville IL, *37691* 88 C1
Carpinteria CA, *13040* 52 B2
Carrabelle FL, *2778* 137 D3
Carrboro NC, *19582* 112 C4
Carriere MS, *600* 134 C2
Carrier Mills IL, *1653* 108 C1
Carrington ND, *2065* 19 D3
Carrizo Sprs. TX, *5368* 60 C4
Carrizozo NM, *996* 56 C1
Carroll IA, *10103* 86 B1
Carroll Co. AR, *27446* 107 D4
Carroll Co. GA, *110527* 120 B4
Carroll Co. IL, *15387* 88 B1
Carroll Co. IN, *20155* 89 E4
Carroll Co. IA, *20816* 86 B1
Carroll Co. KY, *10811* 100 A3
Carroll Co. MD, *167134* 144 B1
Carroll Co. MS, *10597* 118 B4
Carroll Co. MO, *9295* 96 C2
Carroll Co. NH, *47818* 81 F3
Carroll Co. OH, *28836* 91 E3
Carroll Co. TN, *28522* 109 D4
Carroll Co. VA, *30042* 112 A3
Carrollton AL, *1019* 127 E1
Carrollton GA, *24388* 120 B4
Carrollton IL, *2484* 98 A2
Carrollton KY, *3938* 100 A3
Carrollton MI, *6602* 76 B2
Carrollton MS, *190* 118 B4
Carrollton MO, *3784* 96 C2
Carrollton OH, *3241* 91 F4
Carrollton TX, *119097* 59 F2
Carrolltown PA, *853* 92 B4
Carroll Valley PA, *3876* 103 D1
Carrollwood FL, *33365* 266 C1
Carson CA, *91714* 228 D4
Carson IA, *812* 86 A2
Carson ND, *293* 18 B4
Carson WA, *2279* 20 C1
Carson City MI, *1093* 76 A3
Carson City NV, *55274* 37 D2
Carson Co. TX, *6182* 50 B3
Carsonville MI, *527* 76 C2
Carter Co. KY, *27720* 101 D4
Carter Co. MO, *6265* 108 A2
Carter Co. MT, *1160* 25 F2
Carter Co. OK, *47557* 51 E4
Carter Co. TN, *57424* 111 E3
Carteret NJ, *22844* 147 E1
Carteret Co. NC, *66469* 115 E4
Carter Lake IA, *3785* 86 A2
Cartersville GA, *19731* 120 B3
Carterville IL, *5496* 108 C1
Carterville MO, *1891* 106 B2
Carthage AR, *343* 117 E3
Carthage IL, *2605* 87 F4
Carthage IN, *927* 100 A1
Carthage MS, *5075* 126 C2
Carthage MO, *14378* 106 C2
Carthage NY, *3747* 79 E1
Carthage NC, *2205* 122 C1
Carthage TN, *2306* 110 A3
Carthage TX, *6779* 124 C3
Caruthers CA, *2497* 44 C3
Caruthersville MO, *6168* 108 B4
Carver MA, *11574* 151 E3
Carver MN, *3724* 66 C4
Carver Co. MN, *91042* 66 C4
Cary IL, *18271* 88 C1
Cary MS, *313* 126 A2
Cary NC, *135234* 112 C4
Caryville TN, *2297* 110 C3
Casa Blanca AZ, *1388* 54 C2
Casa Blanca NM, *669* 48 B3
Casa Grande AZ, *48571* 54 C2
Cascade CO, *1655* 41 E2
Cascade ID, *939* 22 B3
Cascade IA, *2159* 73 F4
Cascade MD, *1112* 103 D1
Cascade MT, *685* 15 F3
Cascade WI, *709* 74 C2
Cascade Co. MT, *81327* 15 F3
Cascade Locks OR, *1144* 20 C1
Casco ME, *587* 82 B3
Casco WI, *583* 69 D4
Caseville MI, *777* 76 C1
Casey IL, *2769* 99 D2
Casey IA, *426* 86 B2
Casey Co. KY, *15955* 110 B1
Caseyville IL, *4245* 256 D2
Cashion OK, *802* 51 E2
Cashmere WA, *3063* 13 D3
Cashton WI, *1102* 73 F2
Casitas Sprs. CA, *1000* 52 B2
Casper WY, *55316* 33 D1
Caspian MI, *906* 68 C2
Cassadaga FL, *650* 141 D1
Cassadaga NY, *634* 78 A4
Cass City MI, *2428* 76 C2
Cass Co. IL, *13642* 98 A1
Cass Co. IN, *38966* 89 F3
Cass Co. IA, *13956* 86 B2
Cass Co. MI, *52293* 89 F1
Cass Co. MN, *28567* 64 B4
Cass Co. MO, *99478* 96 C3
Cass Co. NE, *25241* 35 F3
Cass Co. ND, *149778* 19 E3
Cass Co. TX, *30464* 124 C1
Casselberry FL, *26241* 141 D1
Casselton ND, *2329* 19 E4
Cassia Co. ID, *22952* 31 D2
Cass Lake MN, *770* 64 A3
Cassopolis MI, *1774* 89 F1
Cassville MO, *3266* 106 C3
Cassville NJ, *900* 147 E2
Cassville WV, *701* 102 A1
Cassville WI, *947* 73 F4
Castaic CA, *19015* 52 C2
Castalia OH, *852* 91 D2
Castanea PA, *1125* 93 D3
Castile NY, *1015* 78 B4
Castine ME, *1029* 83 D2
Castleberry AL, *583* 127 F4
Castle Dale UT, *1630* 39 F2
Castleford ID, *226* 30 C1
Castle Hayne NC, *1202* 123 E3
Castle Hills TX, *4116* 257 E2
Castle Rock CO, *48231* 41 E2
Castle Rock WA, *1982* 20 B1
Castle Shannon PA, *8316* 250 B3
Castleton VT, *1485* 81 D3
Castleton-on-Hudson NY, *1473* 94 B1
Castle Valley UT, *319* 40 A3
Castlewood SD, *627* 27 F3
Castlewood VA, *2045* 111 E2
Castro Co. TX, *8062* 50 A4
Castro Valley CA, *61388* 259 D3
Castroville CA, *6481* 44 B2
Castroville TX, *2680* 61 D3
Caswell Co. NC, *23719* 112 C3
Catahoula Par. LA, *10407* 125 F3
Catalina AZ, *7569* 55 D3
Catasauqua PA, *6436* 146 B1
Catawba NC, *603* 112 A4
Catawba SC, *1343* 122 A2
Catawba Co. NC, *154358* 122 A1
Catawba Island OH, *850* 91 D2
Catawissa PA, *1552* 93 E3
Catharpin VA, *600* 144 A3
Cathcart WA, *2458* 262 B2
Cathedral City CA, *51200* 53 E3
Cathlamet WA, *532* 20 B1
Catlettsburg KY, *1856* 101 D3
Catlin IL, *2040* 89 D4
Cato NY, *532* 79 D3
Catonsville MD, *41567* 144 C2
Catoosa OK, *7151* 106 A3
Catoosa Co. GA, *63942* 120 B2
Catron Co. NM, *3725* 48 A4
Catskill NY, *4081* 94 B2
Cattaraugus NY, *1002* 78 A4
Cattaraugus Co. NY, *80317* 78 A4
Cavalier ND, *1302* 19 E1
Cavalier Co. ND, *3993* 19 D1

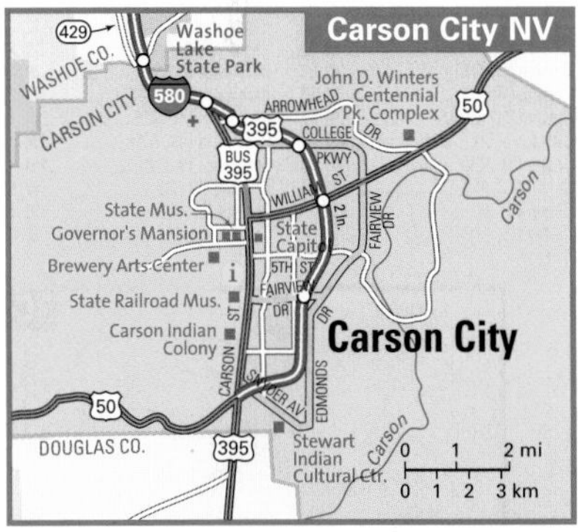

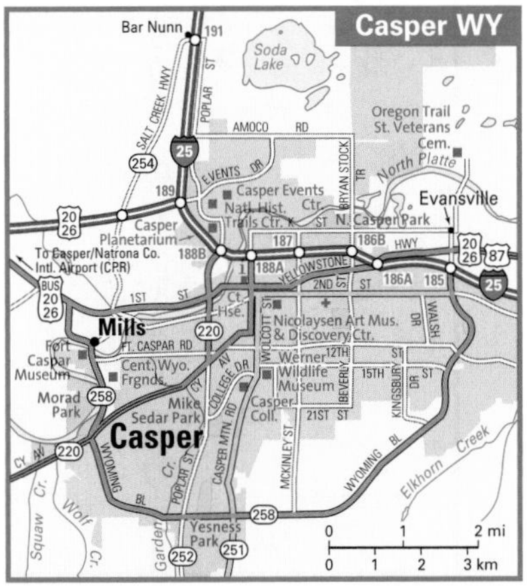

200
Cave City–Chisago County

Figures after entries indicate population, page number, and grid reference.

Cave City AR, *1904* 107 F4
Cave City KY, *2240* 110 A2
Cave Creek AZ, *5015* 54 C1
Cave Jct. OR, *1883* 28 B2
Cave Spr. GA, *1200* 120 B3
Cave Spr. VA, *24922* 112 B2
Cave Sprs. AR, *1729* 106 C3
Cavetown MD, *1473* 144 A1
Cawker City KS, *469* 43 D1
Cawood KY, *731* 111 D2
Cayce SC, *12528* 122 A3
Cayucos CA, *2592* 44 B4
Cayuga IN, *1162* 99 E1
Cayuga NY, *549* 79 D3
Cayuga Co. NY, *80026* 79 D4
Cayuga Hts. NY, *3729* 79 D4
Cazenovia NY, *2835* 79 E3
Cecil PA, *2476* 92 A4
Cecil Co. MD, *101108* 145 E1
Cecilia KY, *572* 110 A1
Cecilia LA, *1980* 133 F2
Cecilton MD, *663* 145 E1
Cedar Bluff AL, *1820* 120 A3
Cedar Bluff VA, *1137* 111 F2
Cedar Bluffs NE, *610* 35 F3
Cedar Brook NJ, *1100* 147 D4
Cedarburg WI, *11412* 74 C3
Cedar City UT, *28857* 39 D4
Cedar Co. IA, *18499* 87 F1
Cedar Co. MO, *13982* 106 C1
Cedar Co. NE, *8852* 35 E1
Cedar Creek NE, *390* 35 F3
Cedar Crest NM, *958* 48 C3
Cedaredge CO, *2253* 40 B2
Cedar Falls IA, *39260* 73 D4
Cedar Fort UT, *368* 31 E4
Cedar Grove FL, *3397* 136 C2
Cedar Grove MD, *950* 144 B2
Cedar Grove NJ, *12411* 148 A3
Cedar Grove NM, *747* 48 C3
Cedar Grove WV, *997* 101 F4
Cedar Grove WI, *2113* 75 D2
Cedar Hill MO, *1721* 98 A4
Cedar Hill TX, *45028* 207 C3
Cedar Hills OR, *8300* 251 C2
Cedarhurst NY, *6592* 241 G5
Cedar Key FL, *702* 138 B4
Cedar Lake IN, *11560* 89 D2
Cedar Park TX, *48937* 61 E1
Cedar Pt. NC, *1279* 115 D4
Cedar Rapids IA, *126326* 87 E1
Cedar Rapids NE, *382* 35 E3
Cedar Sprs. MI, *3509* 75 F3
Cedartown GA, *9750* 120 B3
Cedar Vale KS, *579* 51 F1
Cedarville AR, *1394* 116 C1
Cedarville IL, *741* 74 B4
Cedarville NJ, *776* 145 F2
Cedarville OH, *4019* 100 C1
Celebration FL, *7427* 141 D1
Celeste TX, *814* 59 F2
Celina OH, *10400* 90 B4
Celina TN, *1495* 110 A3
Celina TX, *6028* 59 F2
Celoron NY, *1112* 92 B1
Cement OK, *501* 51 E3
Cement City MI, *438* 90 B1
Centennial CO, *100377* 209 C4
Center CO, *2230* 41 D4
Center MO, *508* 97 F1
Center NE, *94* 35 E1
Center ND, *571* 18 B3
Center TX, *5193* 124 C3
Center Barnstead NH, *500* 81 F4
Centerbrook CT, *950* 149 E2
Center Brunswick NY, *900* 94 B1
Centerburg OH, *1773* 91 D4
Center City MN, *628* 67 D3
Centereach NY, *31578* 149 D3
Centerfield UT, *1367* 39 E2
Center Harbor NH, *1096* 81 F3
Center Hill FL, *988* 140 C1
Center Line MI, *8257* 210 C2
Center Moriches NY, *7580* 149 D4
Center Ossipee NH, *561* 81 F3
Center Pt. AL, *16921* 119 F4
Center Pt. IA, *2421* 87 E1
Center Pt. TX, *750* 61 D2
Centerport NY, *5508* 148 C3
Centerton AR, *9515* 106 C3
Centerton NJ, *2000* 147 D3
Centertown KY, *423* 109 E1
Center Valley PA, *1600* 146 C1
Centerville GA, *7148* 129 D2
Centerville IN, *2552* 100 B1
Centerville IA, *5528* 87 D3
Centerville LA, *800* 133 F3
Centerville MA, *9200* 151 F3
Centerville MO, *191* 108 A1
Centerville OH, *103* 100 B1
Centerville PA, *3263* 92 A4
Centerville SC, *6586* 121 E3
Centerville SD, *882* 35 F1
Centerville TN, *3644* 109 E4
Centerville TX, *892* 124 A4
Centerville UT, *15335* 31 E4
Central AZ, *645* 55 E2
Central SC, *5159* 121 E2
Central TN, *2279* 111 E3
Central Bridge NY, *593* 79 F4
Central City AR, *502* 116 C1
Central City CO, *663* 41 D1
Central City IL, *1172* 98 C3
Central City IA, *1257* 87 F1
Central City KY, *5978* 109 E1
Central City NE, *2934* 35 E3
Central City PA, *1124* 92 B4
Central Falls RI, *19376* 150 C3
Central High OK, *1199* 51 E4
Centralia IL, *13032* 98 C3
Centralia KS, *512* 43 F1
Centralia MO, *4027* 97 E2
Centralia WA, *16336* 12 B4
Central Islip NY, *34450* 149 D4
Central Lake MI, *952* 69 F3
Central Park WA, *2685* 12 B4
Central Pt. OR, *17169* 28 B2
Central Square NY, *1848* 79 D3
Central Valley (Woodbury)
NY, *1857* 148 B2
Central Vil. CT, *1400* 150 B3
Central Vil. MA, *600* 151 D4
Centre AL, *3489* 120 A3
Centre Co. PA, *153990* 92 C3
Centre Hall PA, *1265* 92 C3
Centreville AL, *2778* 127 F1
Centreville IL, *5309* 98 A3
Centreville MD, *4285* 145 D3
Centreville MI, *1425* 89 F1
Centreville MS, *1684* 134 A1
Centreville VA, *71135* 144 A3
Centuria WI, *948* 67 E3
Century FL, *1698* 135 F1
Ceres CA, *45417* 36 C4
Ceresco NE, *889* 35 F3
Cerritos CA, *49041* 228 E4
Cerro Gordo IL, *1403* 98 C1
Cerro Gordo Co. IA, *44151* 73 D3
Chackbay LA, *5177* 134 A3
Chadbourn NC, *1856* 123 D3
Chadron NE, *5851* 34 A1
Chaffee MO, *2955* 108 B2
Chaffee Co. CO, *17809* 41 D2
Chaffinville MA, *3100* 150 B1
Chagrin Falls OH, *4113* 91 E2
Chalco NE, *10994* 35 F3
Chalfant PA, *800* 250 D2
Chalfont PA, *4009* 146 C2
Chalkville AL, *3829* 195 F1
Challenge CA, *1069* 36 C1
Challis ID, *1081* 23 D3
Chalmers IN, *508* 89 E3
Chalmette LA, *16751* 134 B3
Chama NM, *1022* 48 C1
Chamberino NM, *919* 56 C3
Chamberlain SD, *2387* 27 D4
Chamberlayne Farms VA, *5456* 254 B1
Chambersburg PA, *20268* 103 D1
Chambers Co. AL, *34215* 128 B1
Chambers Co. TX, *35096* 132 B3
Chamblee GA, *9892* 120 C4
Chamisal NM, *310* 49 D2
Champaign IL, *81055* 88 C4
Champaign Co. IL, *201081* 89 D4
Champaign Co. OH, *40097* 90 C4
Champion Hts. OH, *6498* 91 F2
Champlain NY, *1101* 81 D1
Chancellor SD, *264* 27 F4
Chandler AZ, *236123* 54 C2
Chandler IN, *2887* 99 E4
Chandler OK, *3100* 51 F2
Chandler TX, *2734* 124 A2
Chandler Hts. AZ, *950* 54 C2
Chandlerville IL, *553* 88 A4
Chanhassen MN, *22952* 66 C4
Channahon IL, *12560* 88 C2
Channel Lake IL, *1664* 74 C4
Channelview TX, *38289* 132 B3
Channing TX, *363* 50 A2
Chantilly VA, *23039* 144 A3
Chanute KS, *9119* 106 A1
Chaparral NM, *14631* 56 C3
Chapel Hill NC, *57233* 112 C4
Chapel Hill TN, *1445* 119 F1
Chapin IL, *512* 98 A1
Chapin SC, *1445* 122 A3
Chaplin KY, *418* 100 A4
Chapman KS, *1393* 43 F2
Chapmanville WV, *1256* 101 E4
Chappaqua NY, *1436* 148 B2
Chappell NE, *929* 34 A3
Chardon OH, *5148* 91 E2
Charenton LA, *1903* 133 F3
Chariton IA, *4321* 87 D3
Chariton Co. MO, *7831* 97 D1
Charlack MO, *1363* 256 B2
Charleroi PA, *4120* 92 A4
Charles City IA, *7652* 73 D3
Charles City VA, *133* 113 E1
Charles City Co. VA, *7256* 113 E1
Charles Co. MD, *146551* 144 B4
Charles Mix Co. SD, *9129* 27 D4
Charleston AR, *2494* 116 C1
Charleston IL, *21838* 99 D2
Charleston ME, *300* 82 C1
Charleston MS, *2193* 118 B3
Charleston MO, *5947* 108 C2
Charleston SC, *120083* 131 D2
Charleston TN, *651* 120 C1
Charleston UT, *415* 31 F4
Charleston WV, *51400* 101 E4
Charleston Co. SC, *350209* 131 D2
Charlestown IN, *7585* 100 A3
Charlestown MD, *1183* 145 D1
Charlestown NH, *1152* 81 E4
Charlestown RI, *7827* 150 C4
Charles Town WV, *5259* 103 D2
Charlevoix MI, *2513* 69 F3
Charlevoix Co. MI, *25949* 70 B3
Charlo MT, *379* 15 D3
Charlotte MI, *9074* 76 A4
Charlotte NC, *731424* 122 A1
Charlotte TN, *1235* 109 E4
Charlotte TX, *1715* 61 D3
Charlotte Co. FL, *159978* 140 C4
Charlotte Co. VA, *12586* 113 D2
Charlotte C.H. VA, *543* 113 D2
Charlotte Hall MD, *1420* 144 C4
Charlotte Harbor FL, *3714* 140 C4
Charlottesville VA, *43475* 102 C4
Charlton MA, *12981* 150 B2
Charlton NY, *3954* 94 B1
Charlton City MA, *1400* 150 B2
Charlton Co. GA, *12171* 138 C1
Charlton Depot MA, *1200* 150 B2
Charter Oak CA, *9310* 229 F2
Charter Oak IA, *502* 86 A1
Chartley MA, *1600* 151 D2
Chase KS, *477* 43 D3
Chase City VA, *2351* 113 D2
Chase Co. KS, *2790* 43 F3
Chase Co. NE, *3966* 34 B4
Chaska MN, *23770* 66 C4
Chassahowitzka FL, *700* 140 B1
Chassell MI, *800* 65 F4
Chateaugay NY, *833* 80 C1
Chatfield MN, *2779* 73 E2
Chatham IL, *11500* 98 B1
Chatham LA, *557* 125 E2
Chatham MA, *1421* 151 F3
Chatham NJ, *8962* 148 A4
Chatham NY, *1770* 94 B2
Chatham VA, *1269* 112 C2
Chatham Co. GA, *265128* 130 B3
Chatham Co. NC, *63505* 112 C4
Chatom AL, *1288* 127 D4
Chatsworth GA, *4299* 120 C2
Chatsworth IL, *1205* 88 C3
Chattahoochee FL, *3652* 137 D1
Chattahoochee Co. GA, *11267* 128 C2
Chattanooga OK, *461* 51 D4
Chattanooga TN, *167674* 120 B2
Chattaroy WV, *756* 111 E1
Chattooga Co. GA, *26015* 120 B3
Chatwood PA, *3600* 146 B3
Chaumont NY, *624* 79 D1
Chauncey OH, *1049* 101 E2
Chautauqua Co. KS, *3669* 43 F4
Chautauqua Co. NY, *134905* 78 A4
Chauvin LA, *2912* 134 B4
Chaves Co. NM, *65645* 57 E2
Chazy NY, *565* 81 D1
Cheatham Co. TN, *39105* 109 E3
Cheat Lake WV, *7988* 102 B1
Chebanse IL, *1062* 89 D3
Cheboygan MI, *4867* 70 C2
Cheboygan Co. MI, *26152* 70 C3
Checotah OK, *3335* 116 A1
Cheektowaga NY, *75178* 78 B3
Chefornak AK, *418* 154 B3
Chehalis WA, *7259* 12 B4
Chelan WA, *3890* 13 E3
Chelan Co. WA, *72453* 13 D2
Chelmsford MA, *33802* 95 E1
Chelsea AL, *10183* 127 F1
Chelsea MA, *35177* 151 D1
Chelsea MI, *4944* 76 B4
Chelsea NY, *2300* 148 B1
Chelsea OK, *1964* 106 A3
Chelsea VT, *1250* 81 E3
Cheltenham MD, *650* 144 C4
Cheltenham PA, *5500* 248 C2
Chelyan WV, *776* 101 F4
Chemung Co. NY, *88830* 93 E1
Chenango Bridge NY, *2883* 93 E1
Chenango Co. NY, *50477* 79 E4
Chenequa WI, *590* 74 C3
Cheney KS, *2094* 43 E4
Cheney WA, *10590* 13 F3
Cheneyville LA, *625* 133 E1
Chenoa IL, *1785* 88 C3
Chenoweth OR, *1855* 21 D1
Chepachet RI, *1675* 150 C3
Cheraw SC, *5851* 122 C2
Cheriton VA, *487* 114 B3
Cherokee AL, *1048* 119 D2
Cherokee IA, *5253* 72 A4
Cherokee KS, *714* 106 B1
Cherokee OK, *1498* 51 D1
Cherokee Co. AL, *25989* 120 A3
Cherokee Co. GA, *214346* 120 C3
Cherokee Co. IA, *12072* 72 A3
Cherokee Co. KS, *21603* 106 B2
Cherokee Co. NC, *27444* 121 D1
Cherokee Co. OK, *46987* 106 B4
Cherokee Co. SC, *55342* 121 F2
Cherokee Co. TX, *50845* 124 A3
Cherokee Forest SC, *8000* 217 A1
Cherokee Vil. AR, *4671* 107 F3
Cherry Co. NE, *5713* 34 B1
Cherry Creek NY, *461* 78 A4
Cherryfield ME, *1157* 83 E2
Cherry Grove OH, *4378* 204 C3
Cherry Hill NJ, *71045* 146 C3
Cherry Hills Vil. CO, *5987* 209 C4
Cherryvale KS, *2367* 106 A2
Cherryvale SC, *2496* 122 B4
Cherry Valley AR, *651* 118 A1
Cherry Valley NY, *520* 79 F4
Cherryville NC, *5760* 122 A1
Chesaning MI, *2394* 76 B3
Chesapeake OH, *745* 101 D3
Chesapeake VA, *222209* 113 F3
Chesapeake WV, *1554* 101 F4
Chesapeake Beach MD, *5753* 144 C4
Chesapeake City MD, *673* 145 E1
Chesapeake Ranch Estates
MD, *10519* 103 F4
Cheshire CT, *29097* 149 D1
Cheshire MA, *514* 94 C1
Cheshire Co. NH, *77117* 81 E4
Chesilhurst NJ, *1634* 147 D4
Chesnee SC, *868* 121 F1
Chester CA, *2144* 29 D4
Chester CT, *3832* 149 E2
Chester IL, *8586* 98 B4
Chester MD, *4167* 145 D3
Chester MA, *627* 94 C2
Chester MT, *847* 15 F2
Chester NH, *4768* 81 F4
Chester NJ, *1649* 94 A4
Chester NY, *3969* 148 A2
Chester PA, *33972* 146 C3
Chester SC, *5607* 122 A2
Chester VT, *1005* 81 E4
Chester VA, *20987* 113 E1
Chester WV, *2585* 91 F3
Chester Co. PA, *498886* 146 B3
Chester Co. SC, *33140* 122 A2
Chester Co. TN, *17131* 119 D1
Chester Depot VT, *850* 81 E4
Chesterfield IN, *2547* 89 F4
Chesterfield MO, *47484* 98 A3
Chesterfield SC, *1472* 122 B2
Chesterfield VA, *3558* 113 E1
Chesterfield Co. SC, *46734* 122 B2
Chesterfield Co. VA, *316236* 113 E1
Chester Hts. PA, *2531* 146 B3
Chester Hill PA, *883* 92 C3
Chesterland OH, *2521* 91 E2
Chesterton IN, *13068* 89 E2
Chestertown MD, *5252* 145 D2
Chestnut Mtn. GA, *650* 121 D3
Chestnut Ridge NY, *7916* 148 B3
Cheswick PA, *1746* 250 D1
Cheswold DE, *1380* 145 E2
Chetek WI, *2221* 67 E3
Chetopa KS, *1125* 106 B2
Chevak AK, *938* 154 B3
Cheverly MD, *6173* 144 B3
Cheviot OH, *8375* 100 B2
Chevy Chase MD, *1953* 270 C2
Chevy Chase View MD, *920* 270 C1
Chewelah WA, *2607* 13 F2
Cheyenne OK, *801* 50 C3
Cheyenne WY, *59466* 33 E3
Cheyenne Co. CO, *1836* 42 A2
Cheyenne Co. KS, *2726* 42 B1
Cheyenne Co. NE, *9998* 34 A3
Cheyenne Wells CO, *846* 42 A2
Cheyney PA, *1600* 146 B3
Chicago IL, *2695598* 89 D1
Chicago Hts. IL, *30276* 89 D2
Chicago Ridge IL, *14305* 203 D5
Chichester NH, *2523* 81 F4
Chickamauga GA, *3101* 120 B2
Chickasaw AL, *6106* 135 E1
Chickasaw Co. IA, *12439* 73 E3
Chickasaw Co. MS, *17392* 118 C4
Chickasha OK, *16036* 51 E3
Chico CA, *86187* 36 B1
Chico TX, *1002* 59 E2
Chicopee MA, *55298* 150 A2
Chicora PA, *1043* 92 A3
Chicot Co. AR, *11800* 125 F1
Chiefland FL, *2245* 138 B4
Chilchinbito AZ, *506* 47 F1
Chilcoot CA, *387* 37 D1
Childersburg AL, *5175* 128 A1
Childress TX, *6105* 50 C4
Childress Co. TX, *7041* 50 C4
Chilhowie VA, *1781* 111 F2
Chillicothe IL, *6097* 88 B3
Chillicothe MO, *9515* 96 C1
Chillicothe OH, *21901* 101 D2
Chillicothe TX, *707* 50 C4
Chillum MD, *33513* 270 D2
Chiloquin OR, *734* 28 C1
Chilton WI, *3933* 74 C1
Chilton Co. AL, *43643* 127 F2
Chimayo NM, *3177* 49 D2
China TX, *1160* 132 C3
China Grove NC, *3563* 122 B1
China Grove TX, *1179* 61 D3
Chinchilla PA, *2098* 261 E1
Chincoteague VA, *2941* 114 C2
Chinle AZ, *4518* 47 F2
Chino CA, *77983* 229 G3
Chino Hills CA, *74799* 229 G3
Chinook MT, *1203* 16 B2
Chinook WA, *466* 20 B1
Chino Valley AZ, *10817* 47 D4
Chipita Park CO, *1709* 205 C1
Chipley FL, *3605* 136 C1
Chippewa Co. MI, *38520* 70 B1
Chippewa Co. MN, *12441* 66 A3
Chippewa Co. WI, *62415* 67 F3
Chippewa Falls WI, *13661* 67 F4
Chippewa Lake OH, *711* 91 E3
Chisago City MN, *4967* 67 D3
Chisago Co. MN, *53887* 67 D3

Cedar Rapids IA

Blackhawk B2	Dunbar A2	Malden B2	Rutledge B1	S. Charleston A2
Charleston A1	Knollwood B1	Port Amherst B2	Snow Hill B2	Tyler Mtn. A1

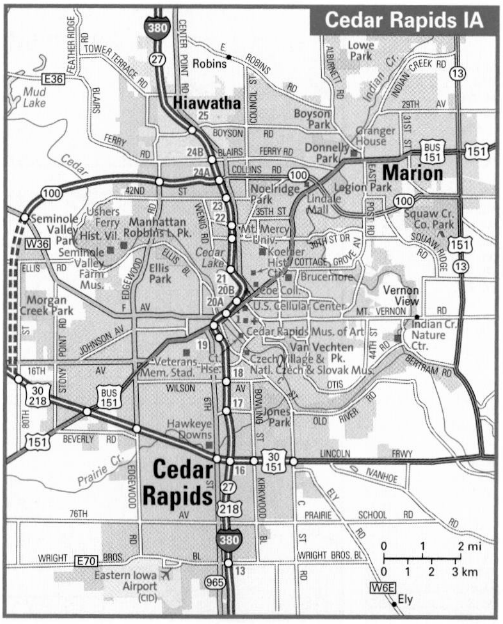

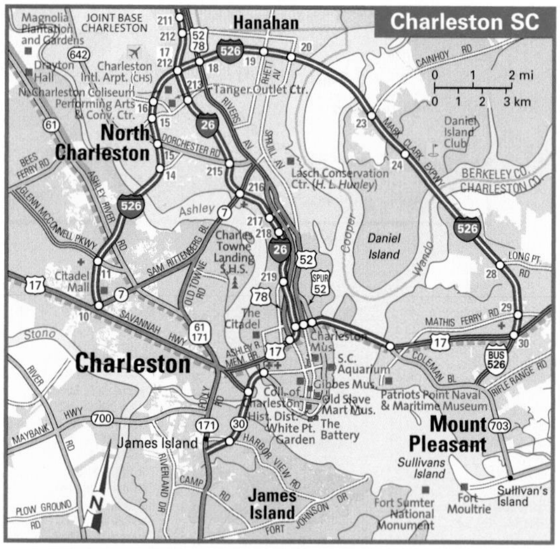

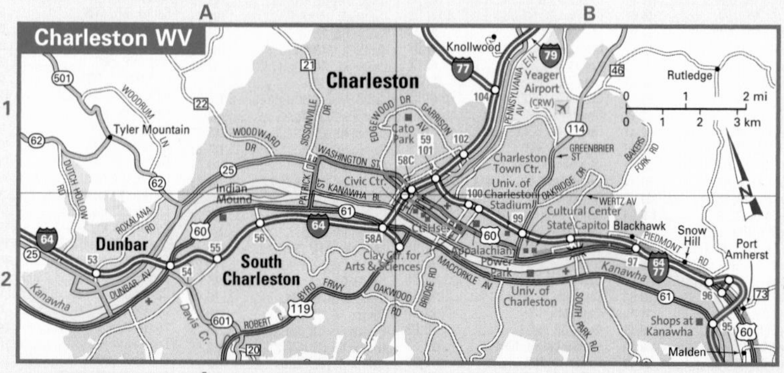

Entries in **bold black** indicate counties or parishes.
Entries in **bold color** indicate cities with detailed inset maps.

Chisholm ME, 1380 ... 82 B2
Chisholm MN, 4976 ... 64 C3
Chittenango NY, 5081 ... 79 E3
Chittenden VT, 1182 ... 81 D3
Chittenden Co. VT, 156545 ... 81 D2
Chocowinity NC, 820 ... 115 D3
Choctaw OK, 11146 ... 51 E3
Choctaw Co. AL, 13859 ... 127 E3
Choctaw Co. MS, 8547 ... 126 C1
Choctaw Co. OK, 15205 ... 116 A3
Choteau MT, 1684 ... 15 E3
Choudrant LA, 845 ... 125 E2
Chouteau OK, 2097 ... 106 A3
Chouteau Co. MT, 5813 ... 15 F2
Chowan Co. NC, 14793 ... 113 F4
Chowchilla CA, 18720 ... 44 C2
Chrisman IL, 1343 ... 99 D1
Chrisney IN, 481 ... 99 E4
Christiana PA, 1168 ... 146 A3
Christian Co. IL, 34800 ... 98 B1
Christian Co. KY, 73955 ... 109 E2
Christian Co. MO, 77422 ... 107 D2
Christiansburg OH, 526 ... 90 B4
Christiansburg VA, 21041 ... 112 A2
Christmas FL, 1146 ... 141 D1
Christopher IL, 2382 ... 98 C4
Chualar CA, 1190 ... 44 B3
Chubbuck ID, 13922 ... 31 E1
Chugwater WY, 212 ... 33 E2
Chuichu AZ, 269 ... 54 C2
Chula Vista CA, 243916 ... 53 D4
Chuluota FL, 2483 ... 141 D1
Church Hill MD, 745 ... 145 D2
Church Hill TN, 6737 ... 111 E3
Churchill OH, 2149 ... 276 C2
Churchill PA, 3011 ... 250 D2
Churchill Co. NV, 24877 ... 37 F1
Church Pt. LA, 4560 ... 133 E2
Church Rock NM, 1128 ... 48 A3
Churchton MD, 1800 ... 144 C3
Churchtown NJ, 3300 ... 146 B4
Churchville MD, 1200 ... 145 D1
Churchville NY, 1961 ... 78 C3
Churubusco IN, 1796 ... 90 A2
Cibecue AZ, 1713 ... 55 D1
Cibola Co. NM, 27213 ... 48 B4
Cibolo TX, 15349 ... 257 F1
Cicero IL, 83891 ... 89 D1
Cicero IN, 4812 ... 89 F4
Cimarron KS, 2184 ... 42 C4
Cimarron NM, 1021 ... 49 E1
Cimarron Co. OK, 2475 ... 50 A1
Cincinnati OH, 296943 ... 100 B2
Cinnaminson NJ, 15569 ... 146 C3
Circle MT, 615 ... 17 E3
Circle Pines MN, 4918 ... 235 C1
Circleville NY, 900 ... 148 A1
Circleville OH, 13314 ... 101 D1
Circleville UT, 547 ... 39 E3
Cisco TX, 3899 ... 59 D3
Cisne IL, 672 ... 98 C3
Cissna Park IL, 846 ... 89 D4
Citra FL, 800 ... 138 C4
Citronelle AL, 3905 ... 135 E1
Citrus Co. FL, 141236 ... 140 B1
Citrus Hts. CA, 83301 ... 36 C3
Citrus Park FL, 24252 ... 266 B1
Citrus Sprs. FL, 8622 ... 138 C4
City View SC, 1345 ... 217 A2
Clackamas OR, 5177 ... 251 D3
Clackamas Co. OR, 375992 ... 20 C2
Claflin KS, 645 ... 43 D3
Claiborne Co. MS, 9604 ... 126 A3
Claiborne Co. TN, 32213 ... 110 C3
Claiborne Par. LA, 17195 ... 125 D2
Clairton PA, 6796 ... 92 A4
Clallam Bay WA, 363 ... 12 B2
Clallam Co. WA, 71404 ... 12 B2
Clancy MT, 1661 ... 15 E4
Clanton AL, 8619 ... 127 F2
Clara City MN, 1360 ... 66 B4
Clare MI, 3118 ... 76 A2
Clare Co. MI, 30926 ... 76 A1
Claremont CA, 34926 ... 229 G2
Claremont MN, 548 ... 73 D1
Claremont NH, 13355 ... 81 E4
Claremont NC, 1352 ... 112 A4
Claremont VA, 378 ... 113 F2
Claremore OK, 18581 ... 106 A3
Clarence IA, 974 ... 87 F1
Clarence LA, 499 ... 125 D3
Clarence MO, 813 ... 97 E1
Clarence PA, 626 ... 92 C3
Clarence Ctr. NY, 2257 ... 78 B3
Clarendon AR, 1664 ... 117 F2
Clarendon TX, 2026 ... 50 B3
Clarendon Co. SC, 34971 ... 122 B4
Clarendon Hills IL, 8427 ... 203 C5
Clarinda IA, 5572 ... 86 B3
Clarion IA, 2850 ... 72 C4
Clarion PA, 5276 ... 92 B2
Clarion Co. PA, 39988 ... 92 A3
Clarissa MN, 681 ... 66 B2
Clark NJ, 14756 ... 147 E1
Clark SD, 1139 ... 27 E2
Clark Co. AR, 22995 ... 117 D4
Clark Co. ID, 982 ... 23 E3
Clark Co. IL, 16335 ... 99 D2
Clark Co. IN, 110232 ... 100 A3
Clark Co. KS, 2215 ... 42 C4
Clark Co. KY, 35613 ... 100 B4
Clark Co. MO, 7139 ... 87 E4
Clark Co. NV, 1951269 ... 46 A1
Clark Co. OH, 138333 ... 100 C1
Clark Co. SD, 3691 ... 27 E2
Clark Co. WA, 425363 ... 20 C1
Clark Co. WI, 34690 ... 67 F4
Clarkdale AZ, 4097 ... 47 D4
Clarke Co. AL, 25833 ... 127 E4
Clarke Co. GA, 116714 ... 121 D4
Clarke Co. IA, 9286 ... 86 C3
Clarke Co. MS, 16732 ... 127 D3
Clarke Co. VA, 14034 ... 103 D2
Clarkesville GA, 1733 ... 121 D2
Clarkfield MN, 863 ... 66 A4
Clark Fork ID, 536 ... 14 B2
Clarks LA, 1017 ... 125 E3
Clarksboro NJ, 2600 ... 146 C3
Clarksburg MD, 13766 ... 144 B2
Clarksburg WV, 16578 ... 102 A2
Clarksdale MS, 17962 ... 118 A3
Clarks Green PA, 1476 ... 261 E1
Clarks Grove MN, 706 ... 72 C2
Clarks Hill IN, 611 ... 89 E4
Clarkson KY, 875 ... 109 F1
Clarkson NE, 658 ... 35 F2
Clarks Summit PA, 5116 ... 93 F2
Clarkston GA, 7554 ... 190 E3

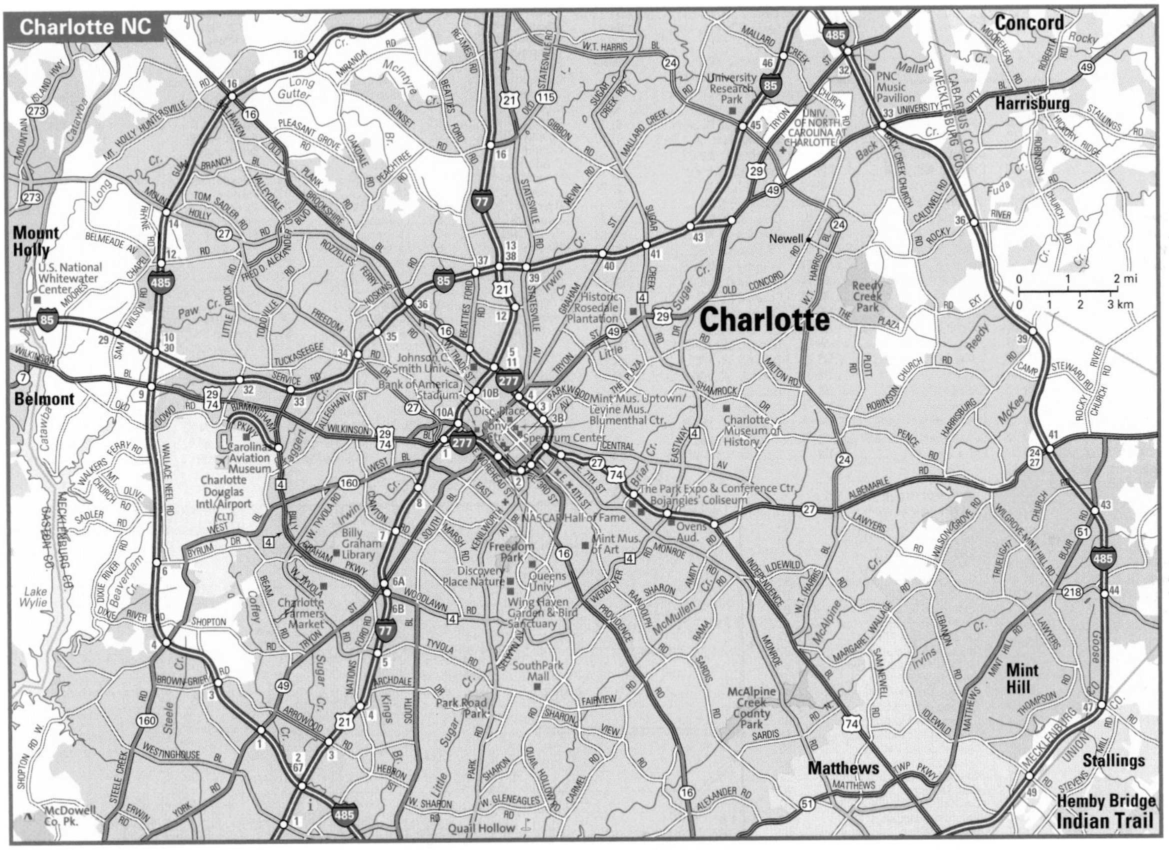

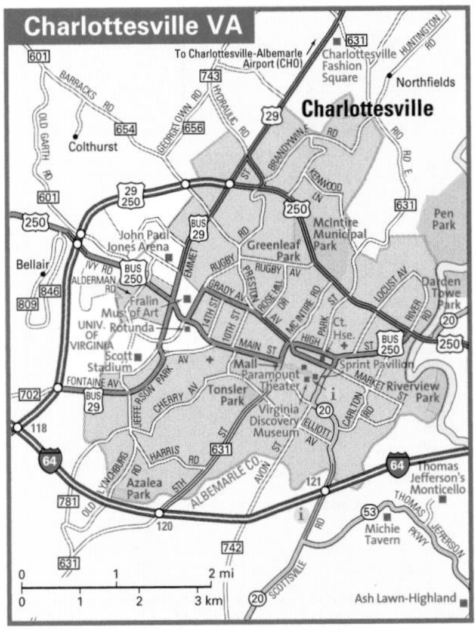

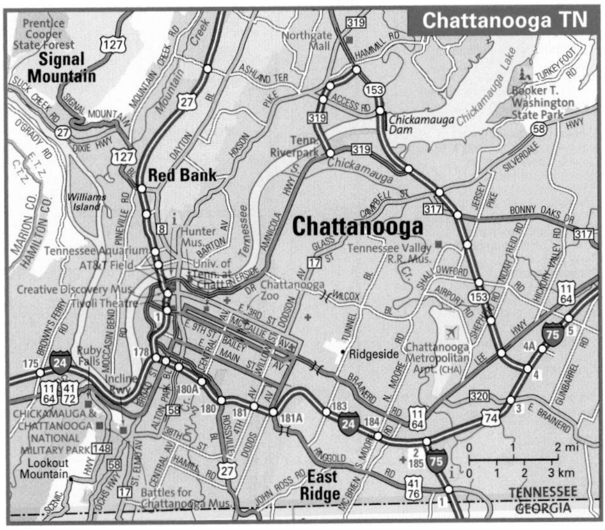

Clarkston UT, 666 ... 31 E2
Clarkston WA, 7229 ... 14 B4
Clarksville AR, 9178 ... 117 D1
Clarksville DE, 900 ... 145 F4
Clarksville IN, 21724 ... 100 A4
Clarksville IA, 1439 ... 73 D4
Clarksville MD, 900 ... 144 B2
Clarksville MO, 442 ... 97 F2
Clarksville TN, 132929 ... 109 E3
Clarksville TX, 3285 ... 116 B4
Clarksville VA, 1139 ... 113 D3
Clarksville City TX, 865 ... 124 B2
Clarkton MO, 1288 ... 108 B3
Clarkton NC, 837 ... 123 D3
Claryville KY, 2355 ... 100 B3
Clatskanie OR, 1737 ... 20 B1
Clatsop Co. OR, 37039 ... 20 B1
Claude TX, 1196 ... 50 B3
Claverack NY, 913 ... 94 B2
Clawson MI, 11825 ... 210 C2
Claxton GA, 2746 ... 130 A3
Clay AL, 9708 ... 119 F4
Clay KY, 1181 ... 109 D1
Clay WV, 491 ... 101 F3
Clay Ctr. KS, 4334 ... 43 E2
Clay Ctr. NE, 760 ... 35 E4
Clay City IL, 959 ... 99 D3
Clay City IN, 861 ... 99 E2
Clay City KY, 1077 ... 110 C1
Claycomo MO, 1430 ... 224 C2
Clay Co. AL, 13932 ... 128 B1
Clay Co. AR, 16083 ... 108 A3
Clay Co. FL, 190865 ... 139 D3
Clay Co. GA, 3183 ... 128 C4
Clay Co. IL, 13815 ... 98 C3
Clay Co. IN, 26890 ... 99 E2
Clay Co. IA, 16667 ... 72 B3
Clay Co. KS, 8535 ... 43 E2
Clay Co. KY, 21730 ... 110 C2
Clay Co. MN, 58999 ... 19 F4
Clay Co. MS, 20634 ... 118 C4
Clay Co. MO, 221939 ... 96 B2
Clay Co. NE, 6542 ... 35 E4
Clay Co. NC, 10587 ... 121 D1
Clay Co. SD, 13864 ... 35 F1
Clay Co. TN, 7861 ... 110 A3
Clay Co. TX, 10752 ... 59 D1
Clay Co. WV, 9386 ... 101 F3
Clayhatchee AL, 589 ... 128 B4
Claymont DE, 8253 ... 146 B3
Claypool AZ, 1538 ... 55 D1
Claypool Hill VA, 1776 ... 111 F2
Claysburg PA, 1625 ... 92 C4
Claysville PA, 829 ... 91 F4
Clayton AL, 3008 ... 128 B3
Clayton CA, 10897 ... 259 E2
Clayton DE, 2918 ... 145 E2
Clayton GA, 2047 ... 121 D2
Clayton IL, 709 ... 87 F4
Clayton IN, 972 ... 99 F1
Clayton LA, 711 ... 125 F4
Clayton MO, 15939 ... 98 A3
Clayton NJ, 8179 ... 146 C4
Clayton NM, 2980 ... 49 F1
Clayton NY, 1978 ... 79 E1
Clayton NC, 16116 ... 113 D4
Clayton OH, 13209 ... 100 B1
Clayton OK, 821 ... 116 A2
Clayton Co. GA, 259424 ... 120 C4
Clayton Co. IA, 18129 ... 73 F3
Clearbrook MN, 518 ... 64 A3
Clear Creek IN, 1800 ... 99 F2
Clear Creek Co. CO, 9088 ... 41 D1
Clearfield PA, 6215 ... 92 C3
Clearfield UT, 30112 ... 31 E3
Clearfield Co. PA, 81642 ... 92 C3
Clearlake CA, 15250 ... 36 B2
Clear Lake IA, 7777 ... 72 C3
Clear Lake SD, 1273 ... 27 F3
Clear Lake WA, 1002 ... 12 C2
Clear Lake WI, 1070 ... 67 E3
Clearlake Oaks CA, 2359 ... 36 B2
Clear Lake Shores TX, 1063 ... 132 B3
Clear Spr. MD, 358 ... 103 D1
Clearview WV, 565 ... 91 F4
Clearwater FL, 107685 ... 140 B2
Clearwater KS, 2481 ... 43 E4
Clearwater MN, 1735 ... 66 C3
Clearwater SC, 4370 ... 121 F4
Clearwater Co. ID, 8761 ... 14 C4
Clearwater Co. MN, 8695 ... 64 A3
Cleaton KY, 500 ... 109 E2
Cleburne TX, 29337 ... 59 E3
Cleburne Co. AL, 14972 ... 120 B4
Cleburne Co. AR, 25970 ... 107 E4
Cle Elum WA, 1872 ... 13 D3
Clementon NJ, 5000 ... 146 C3
Clemmons NC, 18627 ... 112 A4
Clemson SC, 13905 ... 121 E2
Clendenin WV, 1227 ... 101 F3
Cleona PA, 2080 ... 93 E4
Cleora OK, 1463 ... 106 B3
Clermont FL, 28742 ... 140 C1
Clermont IN, 1356 ... 99 F1
Clermont IA, 632 ... 73 E3
Clermont Co. OH, 197363 ... 100 C2
Cleveland AL, 1303 ... 119 F3
Cleveland FL, 2990 ... 140 C4
Cleveland GA, 3410 ... 121 D2
Cleveland MN, 719 ... 72 C1
Cleveland MS, 12334 ... 118 A4
Cleveland MO, 661 ... 96 B3
Cleveland NY, 750 ... 79 E3
Cleveland NC, 871 ... 112 A4
Cleveland OH, 396815 ... 91 E2
Cleveland OK, 3251 ... 51 F2
Cleveland TN, 41285 ... 120 B1
Cleveland TX, 7675 ... 132 B2
Cleveland UT, 464 ... 39 F2
Cleveland WI, 1485 ... 75 D2
Cleveland Co. AR, 8689 ... 117 E4
Cleveland Co. NC, 98078 ... 121 F1
Cleveland Co. OK, 255755 ... 51 E3
Cleveland Hts. OH, 46121 ... 91 E2
Clever MO, 2139 ... 107 D2
Cleves OH, 3234 ... 100 B2
Clewiston FL, 7155 ... 141 E4
Cliffside NC, 611 ... 121 F1
Cliffside Park NJ, 23594 ... 148 B3
Cliffwood Beach NJ, 3194 ... 147 E1
Clifton AZ, 3311 ... 55 E2
Clifton CO, 19889 ... 40 B2
Clifton ID, 259 ... 31 E2
Clifton IL, 1468 ... 89 D3
Clifton KS, 554 ... 43 E1
Clifton NJ, 84136 ... 148 B3
Clifton TN, 2694 ... 119 D1
Clifton TX, 3442 ... 59 E4
Clifton Forge VA, 3884 ... 112 B1
Clifton Hts. PA, 6652 ... 248 B3
Clifton Park NY, 4600 ... 94 B1
Clifton Sprs. NY, 2127 ... 78 C3
Climax MI, 767 ... 75 F4
Clinchco VA, 3372 ... 111 E2
Clinch Co. GA, 6798 ... 138 C1
Clint TX, 926 ... 56 C4

Figures after entries indicate population, page number, and grid reference.

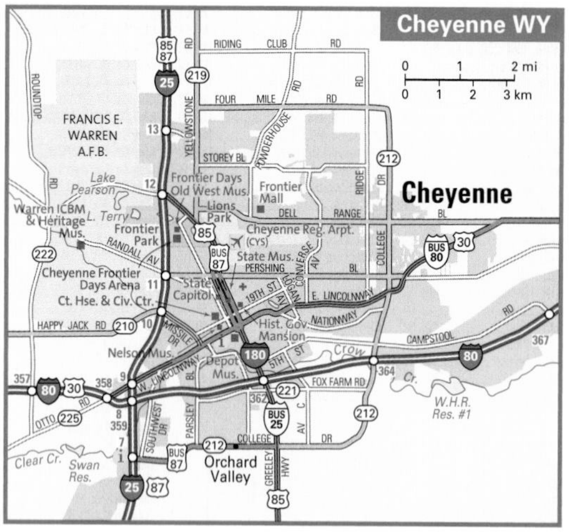

Clinton AR, 2602 .... 117 E1
Clinton CT, 3368 .... 149 E2
Clinton IL, 7225 .... 88 C4
Clinton IN, 4893 .... 99 E1
Clinton IA, 26885 .... 88 A1
Clinton KY, 1388 .... 108 C3
Clinton LA, 1653 .... 134 A1
Clinton ME, 1419 .... 82 C2
Clinton MD, 35970 .... 144 B4
Clinton MA, 7389 .... 150 C1
Clinton MI, 2336 .... 90 B1
Clinton MS, 25216 .... 126 B2
Clinton MO, 9008 .... 96 C4
Clinton MT, 1052 .... 15 D4
Clinton NJ, 2719 .... 147 D1
Clinton NY, 1942 .... 79 E3
Clinton NC, 8639 .... 123 E2
Clinton OH, 1214 .... 91 E3
Clinton OK, 9033 .... 51 D3
Clinton SC, 8490 .... 121 F3
Clinton TN, 9841 .... 110 C4
Clinton UT, 20426 .... 244 A2
Clinton WA, 928 .... 12 C2
Clinton WI, 2154 .... 74 B4
Clinton Co. IL, 37762 .... 98 B3
Clinton Co. IN, 33224 .... 89 E4
Clinton Co. IA, 49116 .... 88 A1
Clinton Co. KY, 10272 .... 110 B2
Clinton Co. MI, 75382 .... 76 A3
Clinton Co. MO, 20743 .... 96 B1
Clinton Co. NY, 82128 .... 80 C2
Clinton Co. OH, 42040 .... 100 C2
Clinton Co. PA, 39238 .... 92 C2
Clintondale NY, 1452 .... 148 B1
Clintonville WI, 4559 .... 68 C4
Clintwood VA, 1414 .... 111 E2
Clio AL, 1399 .... 128 B4
Clio MI, 2646 .... 76 B3
Clio SC, 726 .... 122 C2
Cloquet MN, 12124 .... 64 C4
Closter NJ, 8373 .... 148 B3
Cloud Co. KS, 9533 .... 43 E2
Cloudcroft NM, 674 .... 56 C2
Clover SC, 5094 .... 122 A1
Cloverdale CA, 8618 .... 36 A2
Cloverdale IN, 2172 .... 99 E1
Cloverdale VA, 3119 .... 112 B1
Cloverleaf TX, 22942 .... 220 D2
Cloverport KY, 1152 .... 109 F1
Clovis CA, 95631 .... 44 C2
Clovis NM, 37775 .... 49 F4
Clute TX, 11211 .... 132 A4
Clyde CA, 678 .... 259 D1
Clyde KS, 716 .... 43 E1
Clyde NY, 2093 .... 79 D3
Clyde NC, 1223 .... 121 E1
Clyde OH, 6325 .... 90 C2
Clyde TX, 3713 .... 58 C3
Clyde Hill WA, 2984 .... 262 B3
Clyde Park MT, 288 .... 23 F1
Clymer PA, 1357 .... 92 B3
Coachella CA, 40704 .... 53 E3
Coahoma TX, 817 .... 58 B3
Coahoma Co. MS, 26151 .... 118 A3
Coal City IL, 5587 .... 88 C2
Coal City WV, 1815 .... 111 F1
Coal Co. OK, 5925 .... 51 F4
Coal Creek CO, 2400 .... 41 E3
Coaldale PA, 2281 .... 93 E3
Coal Fork WV, 1233 .... 101 F4
Coalgate OK, 1967 .... 51 F4
Coal Grove OH, 2165 .... 101 D3
Coal Hill AR, 1012 .... 116 C1
Coaling AL, 1657 .... 127 F1
Coalinga CA, 13380 .... 44 C3
Coalmont TN, 841 .... 120 A1
Coal Mtn. GA, 700 .... 120 C3
Coal Run Vil. KY, 1706 .... 111 E1
Coal Valley IL, 3743 .... 88 A2
Coalville UT, 1363 .... 31 F4
Coatesville IN, 523 .... 99 E1

Coatesville PA, 13100 .... 146 B3
Coats NC, 2112 .... 123 D1
Cobb CA, 1778 .... 36 B2
Cobb Co. GA, 688078 .... 120 C4
Cobb Island MD, 1166 .... 103 E4
Cobden IL, 1157 .... 108 C1
Cobleskill NY, 4678 .... 79 F4
Coburg OR, 1035 .... 20 B3
Cochise Co. AZ, 131346 .... 55 E3
Cochiti NM, 528 .... 48 C3
Cochituate MA, 6569 .... 150 C1
Cochran GA, 5150 .... 129 E2
Cochran Co. TX, 3127 .... 57 F1
Cochranton PA, 1136 .... 92 A2
Cochranville PA, 668 .... 146 A3
Cocke Co. TN, 35662 .... 111 D4
Cockeysville MD, 20776 .... 144 C1
Cockrell Hill TX, 4193 .... 207 D2
Cocoa FL, 17140 .... 141 E2
Cocoa Beach FL, 11231 .... 141 E2
Cocoa West FL, 5925 .... 232 A2
Coconino Co. AZ, 134421 .... 47 D3
Coconut Creek FL, 52909 .... 233 B1
Codington Co. SD, 27227 .... 27 E2
Cody WY, 9520 .... 24 B3
Coeburn VA, 2139 .... 111 E2
Coeur d'Alene ID, 44137 .... 14 B3
Coffee Co. AL, 49948 .... 128 A4
Coffee Co. GA, 42356 .... 129 E4
Coffee Co. TN, 52796 .... 120 A1
Coffeen IL, 685 .... 98 B2
Coffeeville MS, 905 .... 118 B4
Coffey Co. KS, 8601 .... 96 A4
Coffeyville KS, 10295 .... 106 A2
Coggon IA, 658 .... 73 E4
Cohasset MA, 7542 .... 151 E1
Cohasset MN, 2698 .... 64 B3
Cohocton NY, 838 .... 78 C4
Cohoes NY, 16168 .... 94 B1
Cohutta GA, 661 .... 120 B2
Cokato MN, 2694 .... 66 C3
Cokeburg PA, 630 .... 92 A4
Coke Co. TX, 3320 .... 58 B4
Coker AL, 979 .... 127 E1
Cokeville WY, 535 .... 31 F2
Colbert GA, 592 .... 121 D3
Colbert OK, 1140 .... 59 F1
Colbert Co. AL, 54428 .... 119 E2
Colby KS, 5387 .... 42 B2
Colby WI, 1852 .... 68 A4
Colchester CT, 4781 .... 149 E1
Colchester IL, 1401 .... 87 F4
Colchester VT, 17067 .... 81 D2
Colcord OK, 815 .... 106 B3
Colden NY, 3323 .... 78 B4
Cold Spr. KY, 5912 .... 204 B3
Cold Spr. MN, 4025 .... 66 C3
Cold Spr. NY, 2013 .... 148 B1
Coldspring TX, 853 .... 132 B3
Coldwater KS, 828 .... 43 D4
Coldwater MI, 10945 .... 90 A1
Coldwater MS, 1677 .... 118 B2
Coldwater OH, 4427 .... 90 B4
Cole OK, 555 .... 51 E3
Colebrook NH, 1394 .... 81 F1
Cole Camp MO, 1121 .... 97 D3
Cole Co. MO, 75990 .... 97 E3
Coleman FL, 703 .... 140 C1
Coleman MI, 1243 .... 76 A2
Coleman TX, 4709 .... 58 C3
Coleman WI, 724 .... 68 C3
Coleman Co. TX, 8895 .... 58 C3
Coleraine MN, 1970 .... 64 B3
Coleridge NE, 473 .... 35 E1
Coles Co. IL, 53873 .... 99 D1
Colesville MD, 14647 .... 144 B2
Colfax CA, 1963 .... 36 C2
Colfax IL, 1061 .... 88 C4
Colfax IN, 691 .... 89 E4
Colfax IA, 2093 .... 87 D2
Colfax LA, 1558 .... 125 E4

Colfax WA, 2805 .... 14 A4
Colfax WI, 1158 .... 67 E4
Colfax Co. NE, 10515 .... 35 F3
Colfax Co. NM, 13750 .... 49 E1
Collbran CO, 708 .... 40 B2
College AK, 12964 .... 154 C2
Collegedale TN, 8282 .... 120 B2
College Park GA, 13942 .... 120 C4
College Park MD, 30413 .... 270 E1
College Place WA, 8765 .... 21 F1
College Sta. TX, 93857 .... 61 F1
Collegeville IN, 330 .... 89 E3
Collegeville PA, 5089 .... 146 B2
Colleton Co. SC, 38892 .... 130 C2
Colleyville TX, 22807 .... 59 E2
Collier Co. FL, 321520 .... 143 D1
Collierville TN, 43965 .... 118 B2
Collin Co. TX, 782341 .... 59 F2
Collingdale PA, 8786 .... 248 B4
Collingswood NJ, 13926 .... 146 C3
Collingsworth Co. TX, 3057 .... 50 C3
Collins GA, 584 .... 129 F3

Collins IA, 495 .... 87 D1
Collins MS, 2586 .... 126 C4
Collins Park DE, 8300 .... 274 D3
Collinsville AL, 1983 .... 120 A3
Collinsville IL, 25579 .... 98 B3
Collinsville MS, 1948 .... 127 D2
Collinsville OK, 5606 .... 106 A3
Collinsville TX, 1624 .... 59 F1
Collinsville VA, 7335 .... 112 B3
Collinwood TN, 982 .... 119 E1
Colma CA, 1792 .... 259 B3
Colman SD, 594 .... 27 F4
Colmar PA, 1800 .... 146 C2
Colmar Manor MD, 1404 .... 270 E3
Colmesneil TX, 596 .... 132 C1
Colo IA, 876 .... 87 D1
Cologne MN, 1519 .... 66 C4
Cologne NJ, 800 .... 147 D4
Coloma MI, 1483 .... 89 F1
Colome SD, 296 .... 34 C1
Colon MI, 1173 .... 90 A1
Colona IL, 5099 .... 88 A2
Colonia NJ, 17795 .... 147 E1
Colonial Beach VA, 3542 .... 103 E4
Colonial Hts. TN, 6934 .... 111 E3
Colonial Hts. VA, 17411 .... 113 E2
Colonial Park PA, 13229 .... 218 C1
Colonie NY, 7793 .... 94 B1
Colony KS, 408 .... 96 A4
Colorado City AZ, 4821 .... 46 C1
Colorado City CO, 2193 .... 41 E3
Colorado City TX, 4146 .... 58 B3
Colorado Co. TX, 20874 .... 61 F2
Colorado Sprs. CO, 416427 .... 41 E2
Colquitt GA, 1992 .... 137 D1
Colquitt Co. GA, 45498 .... 137 F1
Colstrip MT, 2214 .... 25 D1
Colton CA, 52154 .... 229 J2
Colton SD, 687 .... 27 F4
Columbia AL, 740 .... 128 B4
Columbia CA, 2297 .... 37 D3
Columbia CT, 4971 .... 149 F1
Columbia FL, 550 .... 138 C3
Columbia IL, 9707 .... 98 A3
Columbia KY, 4452 .... 110 B2
Columbia LA, 390 .... 125 F3
Columbia MD, 99615 .... 144 B2
Columbia MS, 6582 .... 126 B4
Columbia MO, 108500 .... 97 E3
Columbia NC, 891 .... 113 F4
Columbia PA, 10400 .... 103 E1
Columbia SC, 129272 .... 122 A3
Columbia TN, 34681 .... 119 F1
Columbia Beach MD, 700 .... 144 C3

CHICAGO MAP INDEX

Addison C4
Algonquin A2
Alsip D6
Arlington Hts. C2
Aurora A5
Bannockburn C2
Barrington B2
Barrington Hills A2
Bartlett A3
Batavia A4
Bedford Park D5
Bellwood C4
Bensenville C4
Berkeley C4
Berwyn D4
Bloomingdale B3
Blue Island D6
Bolingbrook B6
Bridgeview D5
Broadview C4
Brookfield C5
Buffalo Grove C2
Burbank D5
Burnham E6
Burr Ridge C5
Burtons Bridge A1
Calumet City E6
Calumet Park E6
Carol Stream B4
Carpentersville A2
Cary A2
Chicago E4
Chicago Ridge D5
Cicero D4
Clarendon Hills C5
Countryside C5
Crest Hill B6
Crestwood D6
Crystal Lake A1
Darien C5
Deerfield C2
Deer Park B2
Des Plaines C3
Diamond Lake B1
Dixmoor E6
Dolton E6
Downers Grove B5
E. Dundee A2
Elgin A3
Elk Grove Vil. C3
Elmhurst C4
Elmwood Park D4
Evanston D3
Evergreen Park D5
Forest Lake B1
Forest Park D4
Forest View D5
Fox River Grove A2
Franklin Park C4
Geneva A4
Glencoe D2
Glendale Hts. B4
Glen Ellyn B4
Glenview D2
Golf D3
Grayslake B1
Green Oaks C1
Hanover Park B3
Harvey E6
Harwood Hts. D3
Hawthorn Woods B1
Hazel Crest E6
Hickory Hills D5
Highland Park D2
Highwood D1
Hillside C4
Hinsdale C5
Hodgkins C5
Hoffman Estates B3
Holiday Hills A1
Homer Glen C6
Hometown D5
Indian Creek C1
Indian Head Park C5
Inverness B2
Island Lake A1
Itasca B3
Ivanhoe B1
Justice D5
Kenilworth D2
Kildeer B2
Knollwood C1
La Grange C5
La Grange Park C4
Lake Barrington B1
Lake Bluff C1
Lake Forest C1
Lake in the Hills A2
Lakemoor A1
Lake Zurich B2
Lemont B6
Libertyville C1
Lincolnshire C2
Lincolnwood D3
Lisle B5
Lockport B6
Lombard B4
Long Grove C2
Lyons D5
Markham D6
Maywood C4
McCook D5
McHenry A1
Medinah B3
Melrose Park C4
Merrionette Park D6
Mettawa C1
Midlothian D6
Montgomery A5
Morton Grove D3
Mount Prospect C3
Mundelein B1
Naperville B5
Niles D3
Norridge D3
N. Aurora A5
N. Barrington B2
Northbrook D2
N. Chicago C1
Northfield D2
Northlake C4
N. Riverside D4
Oak Brook C4
Oakbrook Terrace C4
Oak Forest D6
Oak Lawn D5
Oak Park D4
Oakwood Hills A1
Orland Hills C6
Orland Park C6
Oswego A5
Palatine B2
Palos Hts. D6
Palos Hills D5
Palos Park D6
Park Ridge C3
Phoenix E6
Plainfield A6
Port Barrington A1
Posen D6
Prairie Grove A1
Prospect Hts. C2
Riverdale E6
River Forest D4
River Grove D4
Riverside D4
Riverwoods C2
Robbins D6
Rolling Meadows B3
Romeoville B6
Rondout C1
Roselle B3
Rosemont C3
St. Charles A4
Schaumburg B3
Schiller Park C3
Skokie D3
Sleepy Hollow A2
S. Barrington B2
S. Elgin A3
S. Holland E6
Stickney D5
Stone Park C4
Streamwood B3
Summit D5
Tinley Park D6
Tower Lakes B1
Trout Valley A1
Valley View A3
Vernon Hills C1
Villa Park C4
Volo B1
Warrenville A4
Wauconda B1
Wayne A4
Westchester C4
W. Chicago A4
W. Dundee A2
Western Sprs. C5
Westmont C5
Wheaton B4
Wheeling C2
Willowbrook C5
Willow Sprs. C5
Wilmette D3
Winfield B4
Winnetka D2
Wood Dale C3
Woodridge B5
Worth D6

Columbia City IN, 8750 .... 89 F2
Columbia City OR, 1946 .... 20 C1
Columbia Co. AR, 24552 .... 125 D1
Columbia Co. FL, 67531 .... 138 C2
Columbia Co. GA, 124053 .... 121 F4
Columbia Co. NY, 63096 .... 94 B2
Columbia Co. OR, 49351 .... 20 B1
Columbia Co. PA, 67295 .... 93 E3
Columbia Co. WA, 4078 .... 13 F4
Columbia Co. WI, 56833 .... 74 B3
Columbia Falls MT, 4688 .... 15 D2
Columbia Hts. MN, 19496 .... 235 C2
Columbiana AL, 4197 .... 127 F1
Columbiana OH, 6384 .... 91 F3
Columbiana Co. OH, 107841 .... 91 F3
Columbiaville MI, 787 .... 76 B3
Columbiaville NY, 1200 .... 94 B2
Columbine Valley CO, 1256 .... 209 B4

POINTS OF INTEREST

875 N. Michigan Av. (John Hancock Ctr.) B1
900 North Michigan Shops B1
Adler Planetarium & Astronomy Museum C3
American Writers Museum B2
Art Institute of Chicago B2
Auditorium Building B2
Buckingham Fountain B2
Cadillac Palace Theatre B2
Centennial Fountain & Arc B2
Chicago Architecture Foundation B2
Chicago Board of Trade B2
Chicago Children's Museum C1
Chicago Cultural Center B2
Chicago Fire Marker A3
Chicago Mercantile Exchange A2
Chicago Stock Exchange B2
Chicago Theatre B2
Chicago Yacht Club C2
CIBC Theatre B2
City Hall B2
Civic Opera House A2
Cloud Gate B2
Crown Fountain B2
Daley Plaza B2
Dearborn Station B3
East-West University B3
The Field Museum C3
Ford Center for the Performing Arts B2
Goodman Theatre B2
Harris Theater B2
Harold Washington Library Center B2
Huntington Bank Pavilion at Northerly Island C3
James R. Thompson Center B2
Jane Addams' Hull House Mus. A3
John G. Shedd Aquarium C3
Merchandise Mart A2
Monadnock Building B2
Moody Bible Institute B1
Mus. of Broadcast Communications B2
Mus. of Contemporary Art B1
Mus. of Contemporary Photography B3
Navy Pier C1
Newberry Library B1
New Maxwell Street Market A3
Northwestern Univ. (Chi. Campus) C1
Petrillo Band Shell C2
Pritzker Pavilion B2
The Shops at North Bridge B1
Soldier Field C3
Spertus Institute B3
Symphony Center B2
Tribune Tower B1
Trump Intl. Hotel & Tower B2
UIC Forum A3
Union Station A2
Univ. of Illinois at Chicago A3
Water Tower B1
Water Tower Place B1
Willis Tower A2
Wrigley Building B1

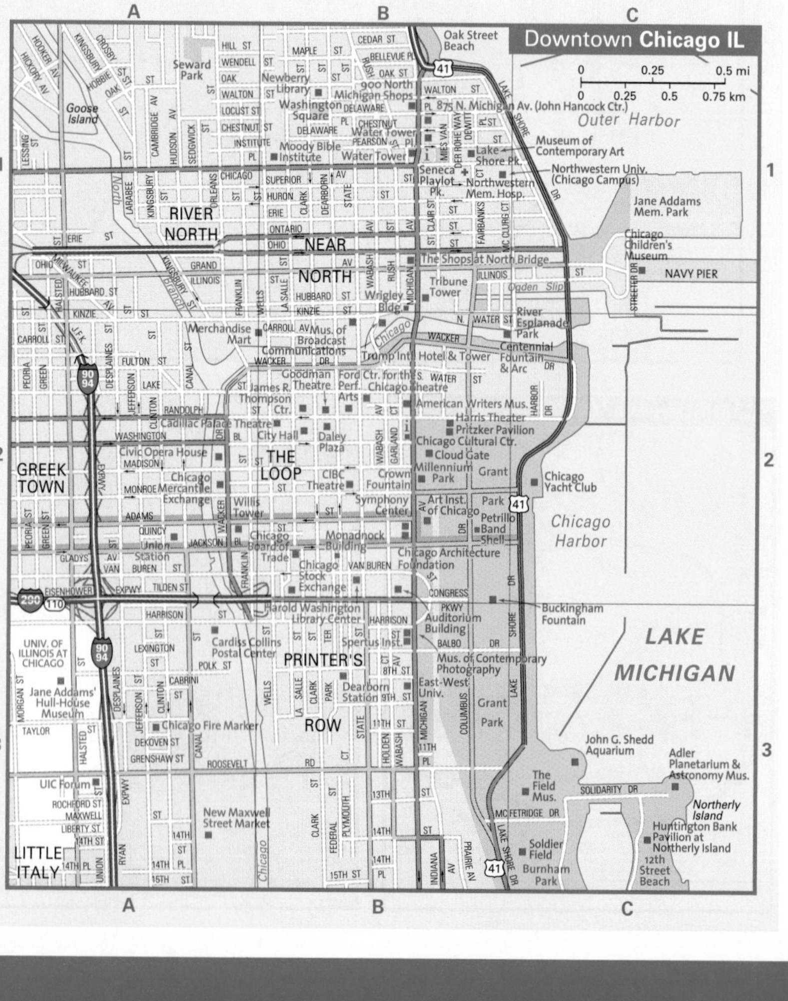

Entries in **bold black** indicate counties or parishes.
Entries in **bold color** indicate cities with detailed inset maps.

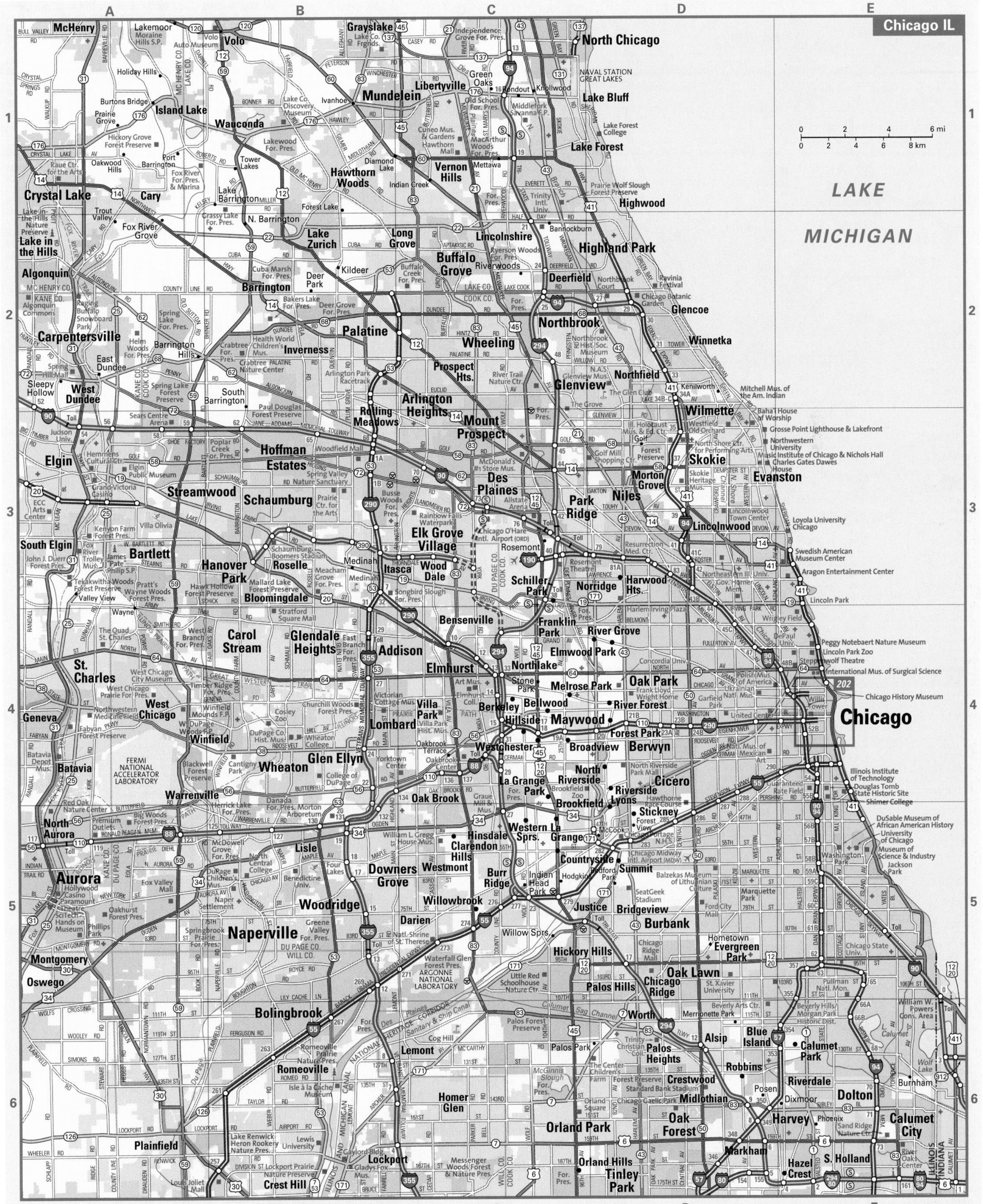

Figures after entries indicate population, page number, and grid reference.

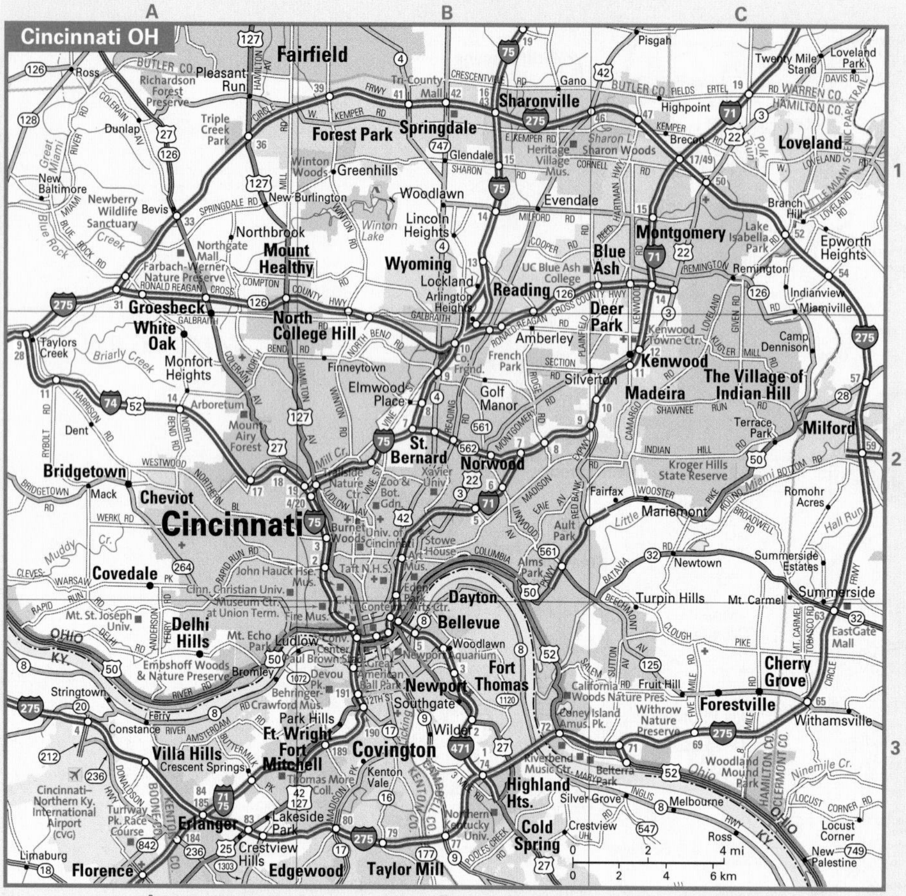

Columbus GA, *189885* **128** C2
Columbus IN, *44061* **99** F2
Columbus KS, *3312* **106** B2
Columbus MS, *23640* **119** D4
Columbus MT, *1893* **24** B1
Columbus NE, *22111* **35** E3
Columbus NJ, *750* **147** D2
Columbus NM, *1664* **56** B3
Columbus NC, *999* **121** F1
Columbus OH, *787033* **101** D1
Columbus TX, *3655* **61** F2
Columbus WI, *4991* **74** B3
Columbus Co. NC, *58098* **123** D3
Columbus Grove OH, *2137* **90** B3
Columbus Jct. IA, *1899* **87** F2
Colusa CA, *5971* **36** B2
Colusa Co. CA, *21419* **36** B2
Colver PA, *959* **92** B4
Colville WA, *4673* **13** F2
Colwich KS, *1327* **43** E4
Colwyn PA, *2546* **248** B4
Comal Co. TX, *108472* **61** D2
Comanche OK, *1663* **51** E4
Comanche TX, *4335* **59** D3
Comanche Co. KS, *1891* **43** D4
Comanche Co. OK, *124098* **51** D4
Comanche Co. TX, *13974* **59** D3
Combes TX, *2895* **63** F4
Comer GA, *1126* **121** E3
Comfort TX, *2363* **61** D2
Commack NY, *36124* **148** C3
Commerce CA, *12823* **228** D3
Commerce GA, *6544* **121** D3
Commerce OK, *2473* **106** B2
Commerce TX, *8078* **124** A1
Commerce City CO, *45913* **41** E1
Commercial Pt. OH, *1582* **101** D1
Como MS, *1279* **118** B3
Como TX, *702* **124** A1
Como WI, *2631* **74** C4
Compton CA, *96455* **52** C3
Comstock MI, *4472* **75** F4
Comstock NY, *1900* **81** D4
Comstock Park MI, *10088* **75** F3
Concho Co. TX, *4087* **58** C4
Concord AL, *1837* **195** D2

Amberley B2
Arlington Hts. B2
Bellevue B3
Bevis A1
Blue Ash C1
Branch Hill C1
Brecon C1
Bridgetown A2
Bromley A3
Camp Dennison C2
Cherry Grove C3
Cheviot A2
Cincinnati A2
Cold Spr. B3
Constance A3
Covedale A2
Covington B3
Crescent Sprs. A3
Crestview B3
Crestview Hills A3
Dayton B2
Deer Park C2
Delhi Hills A3
Dent A2
Dunlap A1
Edgewood B3
Elmwood Place B2
Epworth Hts. C1
Erlanger A3
Evendale B1
Fairfax C2
Fairfield B1
Finneytown B2
Florence A3
Forest Park B1
Forestville C3
Ft. Mitchell A3
Ft. Thomas B3
Ft. Wright B3
Fruit Hill C3
Gano B1
Glendale B1
Golf Manor B2
Greenhills B1
Groesbeck A2
Highland Hts. B3
Highpoint C1
Indianview C1
Kenton Vale B3
Kenwood C2
Lakeside Park A3
Limaburg A3
Lincoln Hts. B1
Lockland B1
Locust Corner C3
Loveland C1
Loveland Park C1
Ludlow A3
Mack A2
Madeira C2
Mariemont C2
Melbourne C3
Miamiville C1
Milford C2
Monfort Hts. A2
Montgomery C1
Mt. Carmel C2
Mt. Healthy A1
New Baltimore A1
New Burlington A1
New Palestine C3
Newport B3
Newtown C2
Northbrook A1
N. College Hill A2
Norwood B2
Park Hills B3
Pisgah C1
Pleasant Run A1
Reading B1
Remington C1
Romohr Acres C2
Ross, KY C3
Ross, OH A1
St. Bernard B2
Sharonville B1
Silver Grove C3
Silverton B2
Southgate B3
Springdale B1
Stringtown A3
Summerside C2
Summerside Estates C2
Taylor Mill B3
Taylors Creek A2
Terrace Park C2
The Vil. of Indian Hill C2
Turpin Hills C3
Twenty Mile Stand C1
Villa Hills A3
White Oak A2
Wilder B3
Withamsville C3
Woodlawn, KY B3
Woodlawn, OH B1
Wyoming B1

Cleveland E1
Cleveland Hts. F2
Cuyahoga Hts. F2
E. Cleveland F1
Euclid G1
Fairview Park D2
Garfield Hts. F3
Gates Mills G1
Glenwillow G3
Highland Hts. G1
Highland Hills G2
Hunting Valley G2
Independence F3
Lakewood E2
Linndale E2
Lyndhurst G2
Macedonia G3
Maple Hts. F3
Mayfield G1
Mayfield Hts. G2
Middleburg Hts. E3
Moreland Hills G2
Newburgh Hts. F2
Northfield G3
N. Olmsted D2
N. Randall G2
N. Ridgeville D3
N. Royalton E3
Oakwood G3
Olmsted Falls D3
Orange G2
Parma E3
Parma Hts. E3
Pepper Pike G2
Richmond Hts. G1
Rocky River E2
Sagamore Hills F3
Seven Hills F3
Shaker Hts. G2
Solon G3
S. Euclid G1
Strongsville E3
Twinsburg G3
University Hts. G2
Valley View F3
Walton Hills G3
Warrensville Hts. G2
Westlake D2
Wickliffe G1
Willoughby Hills G1
Woodmere G2

Avon D2
Avon Lake D2
Bay Vil. D2
Beachwood G2
Bedford G3
Bedford Hts. G3
Bentleyville G3
Berea D3
Bratenahl F1
Brecksville F3
Broadview Hts. F3
Brooklyn E2
Brooklyn Hts. F2
Brook Park E3

Entries in **bold black** indicate counties or parishes.
Entries in **bold color** indicate cities with detailed inset maps.

Concord CA, *122067* ... **36** B3
Concord MA, *17668* ... **150** C1
Concord MI, *1050* ... **90** B1
Concord MO, *16421* ... **256** B3
Concord NH, *42695* ... **81** F4
Concord NC, *79066* ... **122** B1
Concord TN, *1700* ... **110** C4
Concord VA, *1458* ... **112** C1
Concordia KS, *5395* ... **43** E1
Concordia MO, *2450* ... **96** C2
Concordia Par. LA, *20822* ... **125** F4
Concrete WA, *705* ... **12** C2
Condon OR, *682* ... **21** E2
Conecuh Co. AL, *13228* ... **127** F4
Conehatta MS, *1342* ... **126** C2
Conejos CO, *58* ... **49** D1
Conejos Co. CO, *8256* ... **41** D4
Conestoga PA, *1258* ... **146** A3
Confluence PA, *780* ... **102** B1
Congers NY, *8363* ... **148** B2
Congress AZ, *1975* ... **46** C4
Conklin NY, *5940* ... **93** F1
Conneaut OH, *12841* ... **91** F1
Conneaut Lake PA, *653* ... **91** F2
Conneaut Lake Park PA, *2502* ... **91** F2
Conneautville PA, *774* ... **91** F1
Connell WA, *4209* ... **13** F4
Connellsville PA, *7637* ... **102** B1
Connersville IN, *13481* ... **100** A1
Conover NC, *8165* ... **111** F4
Conovertown NJ, *1000* ... **147** F4
Conrad IA, *1108* ... **87** D1
Conrad MT, *2570* ... **15** E2
Conroe TX, *56207* ... **132** A2
Conshohocken PA, *7833* ... **146** C2
Constantia NY, *1182* ... **79** E3
Constantine MI, *2076* ... **89** F1
Continental OH, *1153* ... **90** B3
Contoocook NH, *1444* ... **81** F4
Contra Costa Co. CA, *1049025* ... **36** B3
Convent LA, *711* ... **134** A3
Converse IN, *1265* ... **89** F3
Converse LA, *440* ... **124** C3
Converse TX, *18198* ... **257** F2
Converse Co. WY, *13833* ... **33** E1
Convoy OH, *1085* ... **90** A3
Conway AR, *58908* ... **117** E1
Conway FL, *13467* ... **246** C3
Conway MO, *788* ... **107** D1
Conway NH, *1823* ... **81** F3
Conway NC, *836* ... **113** E3
Conway PA, *2176* ... **91** F3
Conway SC, *17103* ... **123** D4
Conway Co. AR, *21273* ... **117** E1
Conway Sprs. KS, *1272* ... **43** E4
Conyers GA, *15195* ... **120** C4
Conyngham PA, *1914* ... **93** E3
Cook MN, *574* ... **64** C3
Cook Co. GA, *17212* ... **129** E4
Cook Co. IL, *5194675* ... **89** D1
Cook Co. MN, *5176* ... **65** D2
Cooke Co. TX, *38437* ... **59** E1
Cookeville TN, *30435* ... **110** A4
Cooleemee NC, *960* ... **112** A4
Coolidge AZ, *11825* ... **54** C2
Coolidge GA, *525* ... **137** E1
Coolidge TX, *955* ... **59** F4
Cool Valley MO, *1196* ... **256** B1
Coon Rapids IA, *1305* ... **86** B1
Coon Rapids MN, *61476* ... **67** D3
Coon Valley WI, *765* ... **73** F2
Cooper TX, *1969* ... **124** A1
Cooper City FL, *28547* ... **233** A3
Cooper Co. MO, *17601* ... **97** D3
Coopersburg PA, *2386* ... **146** C1
Coopers Mills ME, *350* ... **82** C2
Cooperstown NY, *1852* ... **79** F4
Cooperstown ND, *984* ... **19** E3
Coopersville MI, *4275* ... **75** F3
Coopertown TN, *4278* ... **109** E3
Coosa Co. AL, *11539* ... **128** A1
Coosada AL, *1224* ... **128** A2
Coos Bay OR, *15967* ... **20** A4
Coos Co. NH, *33055* ... **81** F1
Coos Co. OR, *63043* ... **20** B4
Copalis Beach WA, *415* ... **12** B3
Copan OK, *733* ... **51** F1
Copenhagen NY, *801* ... **79** E2
Copiague NY, *22993* ... **148** C4
Copiah Co. MS, *29449* ... **126** A3
Coplay PA, *3192* ... **189** A1
Copley OH, *2000* ... **188** A1
Coppell TX, *38659* ... **207** C1
Copperas Cove TX, *32032* ... **59** E4
Copperhill TN, *354* ... **120** C2
Copperopolis CA, *3671* ... **36** C3
Coquille OR, *3866* ... **28** A1
Coral Gables FL, *46780* ... **143** E2
Coral Hills MD, *9895* ... **270** E4
Coral Sprs. FL, *121096* ... **143** E1
Coralville IA, *18907* ... **87** F2
Coram MT, *539* ... **15** D2
Coram NY, *39113* ... **149** D3
Coraopolis PA, *5677* ... **250** A1
Corbin KY, *7304* ... **110** C2
Corcoran CA, *24813* ... **45** D3
Corcoran MN, *5379* ... **66** C3
Cordaville MA, *2650* ... **150** C1
Cordele GA, *11147* ... **129** D3
Cordova AL, *2095* ... **119** E4
Cordova AK, *2239* ... **154** C3
Cordova IL, *672* ... **88** A2
Cordova MD, *562* ... **145** D3
Cordova NC, *1775* ... **122** C2
Cordova TN, *2800* ... **118** B1
Corea ME, *450* ... **83** E2
Corfu NY, *709* ... **78** B3
Corinna ME, *600* ... **82** C1
Corinne UT, *685* ... **31** E3
Corinth MS, *14573* ... **119** D2
Corinth NY, *2559* ... **80** C4
Corinth TX, *19935* ... **59** E2
Corn OK, *503* ... **51** D3
Cornelia GA, *4160* ... **121** D3
Cornelius NC, *24866* ... **122** A1
Cornelius OR, *11869* ... **20** B2
Cornell WI, *1467* ... **67** F3
Cornersville TN, *1194* ... **119** F1
Cornfields AZ, *255* ... **47** F2
Corning AR, *3377* ... **108** A3
Corning CA, *7663* ... **36** B1
Corning IA, *1635* ... **86** B3
Corning NY, *11183* ... **93** D1
Corning OH, *583* ... **101** E1
Cornish ME, *1269* ... **82** A3
Cornville AZ, *3280* ... **47** D4
Cornwall PA, *4112* ... **93** E4
Cornwall-on-Hudson NY, *3018* ... **148** B1
Corona CA, *152374* ... **53** D3
Coronado CA, *18912* ... **53** D4
Corpus Christi TX, *305215* ... **63** F2
Corrales NM, *8329* ... **48** C3
Corralitos CA, *2326* ... **44** B2
Correctionville IA, *821* ... **72** A4
Corrigan TX, *1595* ... **132** B1

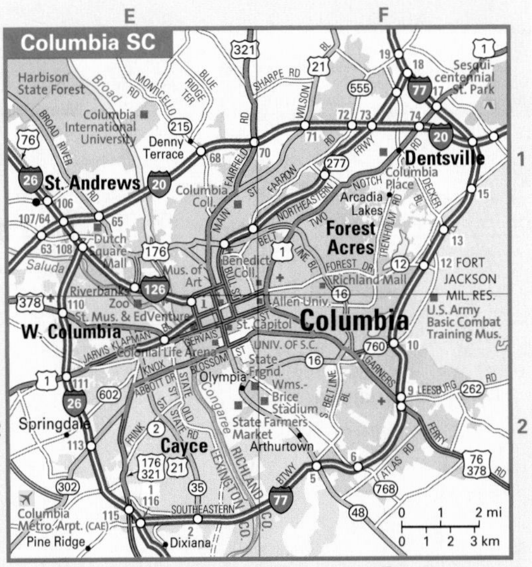

Arcadia Lakes ... F1
Arthurtown ... F2
Cayce ... E2
Columbia ... F2
Denny Terrace ... E1
Dentsville ... F1
Dixiana ... E2
Forest Acres ... F1
Olympia ... E2
Pineridge ... E2
St. Andrews ... E1
Springdale ... E2
W. Columbia ... E2

Black Forest ... D1
Cascade ... C1
Chipita Park ... C1
Colorado Sprs. ... D1
Crystola ... C1
Fountain ... D2
Green Mtn. Falls ... C1
Manitou Sprs. ... C2
Security-Widefield ... D2
Stratmoor Hills ... D2

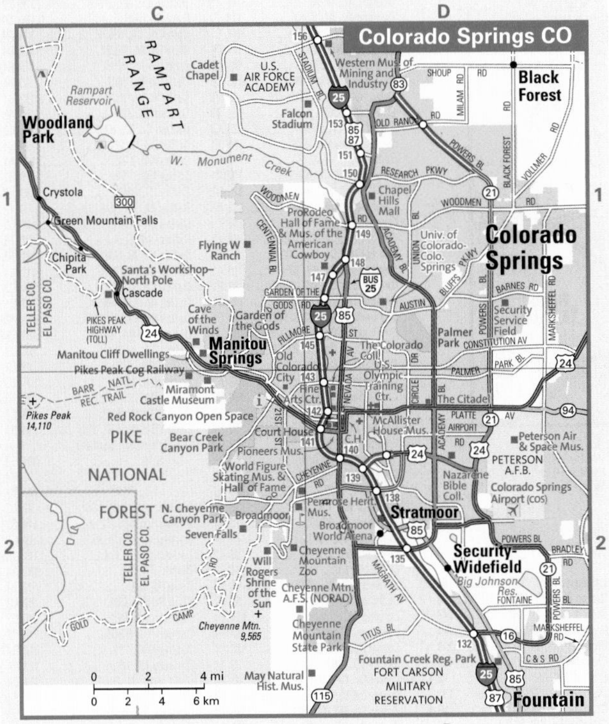

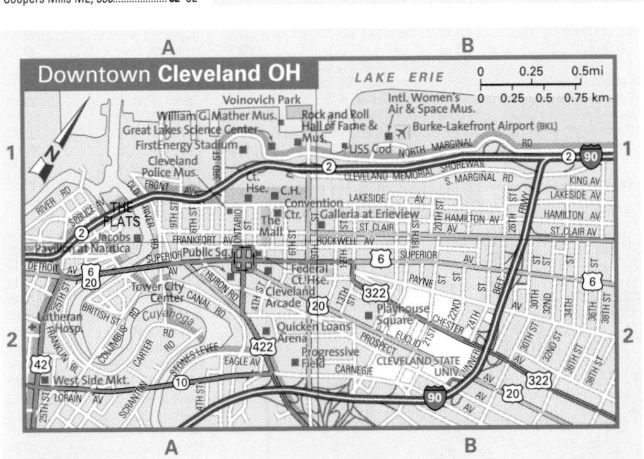

POINTS OF INTEREST

Burke-Lakefront Airport ... B1
Cleveland Arcade ... A2
Cleveland Police Museum ... A1
Cleveland State University ... B2
Convention Center ... A1
FirstEnergy Stadium ... A1
Galleria at Erieview ... B1
Great Lakes Science Center ... A1
International Women's Air & Space Museum ... B1
Jacobs Pavilion at Nautica ... A1
Playhouse Square ... B2
Progressive Field ... A2
Quicken Loans Arena ... A2
Rock and Roll Hall of Fame & Museum ... A1
Tower City Center ... A2
U.S.S. Cod ... B1
West Side Market ... A2
William G. Mather Museum ... A1

Corry PA, *6605* ... **92** A1
Corryton TN, *650* ... **110** C4
Corsica SD, *592* ... **27** E4
Corsicana TX, *23770* ... **59** F3
Corson Co. SD, *4050* ... **26** C1
Cortaro AZ, *1700* ... **55** D3
Corte Madera CA, *9253* ... **259** A2
Cortez CO, *8482* ... **40** B4
Cortez FL, *4241* ... **140** B3
Cortland IL, *4270* ... **88** C1
Cortland NE, *482* ... **35** F4
Cortland NY, *19204* ... **79** D4
Cortland OH, *7104* ... **91** F2
Cortland Co. NY, *49336* ... **79** E4
Corunna MI, *3497* ... **76** B3
Corvallis MT, *976* ... **15** D4
Corvallis OR, *54462* ... **20** B3
Corydon IN, *3122* ... **99** F4
Corydon IA, *1585* ... **87** D3
Corydon KY, *720* ... **109** E1
Coryell Co. TX, *75388* ... **59** E4
Coshocton OH, *11216* ... **91** E4
Coshocton Co. OH, *36901* ... **91** E4
Cosmopolis WA, *1649* ... **12** B4
Cosmos MN, *473* ... **66** B4
Costa Mesa CA, *109960* ... **228** E5
Costilla Co. CO, *3524* ... **41** E4
Cotati CA, *7265* ... **36** B3
Coto de Caza CA, *14866* ... **229** G5
Cottage City MD, *1305* ... **270** E3
Cottage Grove MN, *34589* ... **67** D4
Cottage Grove OR, *9686* ... **20** B4
Cottage Grove WI, *6192* ... **74** B3
Cottage Hill FL, *1300* ... **135** F1
Cottageville SC, *762* ... **130** C1
Cottageville WV, *750* ... **101** E3
Cotter AR, *970* ... **107** E3
Cottle Co. TX, *1505* ... **58** B1
Cotton Co. OK, *6193* ... **51** D4
Cottondale AL, *2000* ... **127** E1
Cottondale FL, *933* ... **136** C1
Cotton Plant AR, *649* ... **117** F2
Cottonport LA, *2006* ... **133** F1
Cotton Valley LA, *1009* ... **125** D2
Cottonwood AL, *1289* ... **137** D1
Cottonwood AZ, *226* ... **47** D4
Cottonwood CA, *3316* ... **28** C4
Cottonwood ID, *900* ... **22** B1
Cottonwood MN, *1212* ... **66** A4
Cottonwood Co. MN, *11687* ... **72** A1
Cottonwood Cove NV, *100* ... **46** B3
Cottonwood Falls KS, *903* ... **43** F3
Cottonwood Hts. UT, *33433* ... **257** B3
Cottonwood Shores TX, *1123* ... **61** D1
Cotuit MA, *2400* ... **151** E4
Cotulla TX, *3603* ... **60** C4
Coudersport PA, *2546* ... **92** C1
Coulee City WA, *562* ... **13** E3
Coulee Dam WA, *1098* ... **13** E2
Coulterville IL, *945* ... **98** B4
Council ID, *839* ... **22** B3
Council Bluffs IA, *62230* ... **86** A2
Council Grove KS, *2182* ... **43** F2
Country Club Hills MO, *1274* ... **256** B1
Country Club Vil. MO, *2449* ... **96** B1
Country Homes WA, *5841* ... **14** A3
Country Knolls NY, *2224* ... **94** B1
Countryside IL, *5895* ... **203** C5
Countryside VA, *10072* ... **144** A3
Coupeville WA, *1831* ... **12** C2
Courtdale PA, *732* ... **261** B1
Courtland AL, *609* ... **119** E2
Courtland MN, *611* ... **72** B1
Courtland MS, *511* ... **118** B3
Courtland VA, *1284* ... **113** E3
Courtney TX, *1500* ... **61** F1
Coushatta LA, *1964* ... **125** D3
Cove OR, *552* ... **21** F2
Covedale OH, *6447* ... **204** A2
Covelo CA, *1255* ... **36** A1
Coventry CT, *11504* ... **150** A3
Coventry Ctr. RI, *850* ... **150** C3
Covert MI, *650* ... **75** E4
Covina CA, *47796* ... **229** F2
Covington GA, *13118* ... **121** D4
Covington IN, *2645* ... **89** D4
Covington KY, *40640* ... **100** B2
Covington LA, *8765* ... **134** B2
Covington OH, *2584* ... **90** B4
Covington OK, *527* ... **51** E2
Covington TN, *9038* ... **118** B1
Covington VA, *5961* ... **112** B1
Covington WA, *17575* ... **262** B4
Covington Co. AL, *37765* ... **128** A4
Covington Co. MS, *19568* ... **126** C4
Cowan TN, *1737* ... **120** A1
Cowan Hts. CA, *4700* ... **229** F4
Coward SC, *752* ... **122** C4
Cowarts AL, *1871* ... **137** D1
Cowden IL, *629* ... **98** C2
Cowen WV, *541* ... **102** A3
Coweta OK, *9943* ... **106** A4
Coweta Co. GA, *127317* ... **128** C1
Cowley WY, *655* ... **24** C2
Cowley Co. KS, *36311* ... **43** F4
Cowlitz Co. WA, *102410* ... **20** C1
Cowpens SC, *2162* ... **121** F2
Coxsackie NY, *2813* ... **94** B2
Cozad NE, *3977* ... **34** C4
Crab Orchard KY, *841* ... **110** B1
Crab Orchard TN, *752* ... **110** B4
Crab Orchard WV, *2678* ... **111** F1
Crafton PA, *5951* ... **250** A2
Craig AK, *1201* ... **155** E4
Craig CO, *9464* ... **32** C4
Craig Beach OH, *1180* ... **91** F3
Craig Co. OK, *15029* ... **106** A2
Craig Co. VA, *5190* ... **112** B1
Craighead Co. AR, *96443* ... **108** A4
Craigmont ID, *501* ... **22** B1
Craigsville VA, *923* ... **102** B4
Craigsville WV, *2213* ... **102** A4
Crainville IL, *1254* ... **108** C1
Cramerton NC, *4165* ... **122** A1
Cranbury NJ, *2181* ... **147** D2
Crandall TX, *2858* ... **59** F2
Crandon WI, *1920* ... **68** B3
Crane MO, *1462* ... **106** C2
Crane TX, *3353* ... **58** A4
Crane Co. TX, *4375* ... **57** F4
Cranesville PA, *638* ... **91** F1
Cranford NJ, *22625* ... **147** E1
Cranston RI, *80387* ... **150** C3
Craven Co. NC, *103505* ... **115** D3
Crawford CO, *431* ... **40** C2
Crawford GA, *832* ... **121** E4
Crawford MS, *641* ... **127** D1
Crawford NE, *997* ... **33** F1
Crawford TX, *717* ... **59** E4
Crawford Co. AR, *61948* ... **116** C1
Crawford Co. GA, *12630* ... **129** D2
Crawford Co. IL, *19817* ... **99** D2
Crawford Co. IN, *10713* ... **99** F4
Crawford Co. IA, *17096* ... **86** A1
Crawford Co. KS, *39134* ... **106** B1
Crawford Co. MI, *14074* ... **70** C4
Crawford Co. MO, *24696* ... **97** F4
Crawford Co. OH, *43784* ... **90** C3
Crawford Co. PA, *88765* ... **91** F1
Crawford Co. WI, *16644* ... **73** F3
Crawfordsville AR, *479* ... **118** B1
Crawfordsville IN, *15915* ... **89** E4
Crawfordville FL, *3702* ... **137** E2
Crawfordville GA, *534* ... **121** E4
Creal Sprs. IL, *543* ... **108** C1
Creede CO, *290* ... **40** C4
Creedmoor NC, *4124* ... **112** C4
Creek Co. OK, *69967* ... **51** F2
Creekside KY, *305* ... **230** F1
Creighton NE, *1154* ... **35** E2
Crenshaw MS, *885* ... **118** B3
Crenshaw Co. AL, *13906* ... **128** A4
Creola AL, *1926* ... **135** E1
Cresaptown MD, *4592* ... **102** C1
Crescent IA, *617* ... **86** A2
Crescent OK, *1411* ... **51** E2
Crescent Beach FL, *931* ... **139** E3
Crescent City CA, *7643* ... **28** A2
Crescent City FL, *1577* ... **139** D4

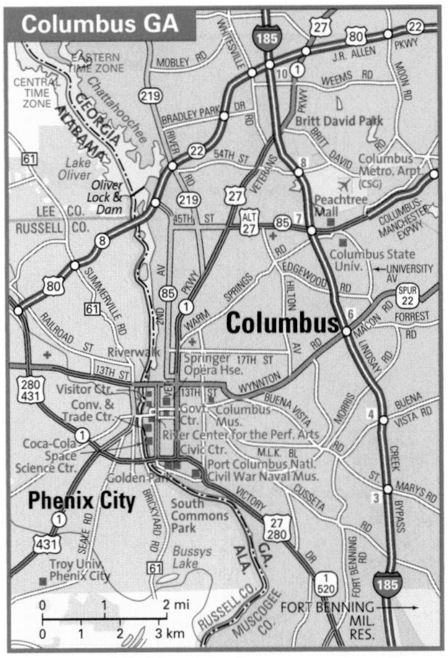

Figures after entries indicate population, page number, and grid reference.

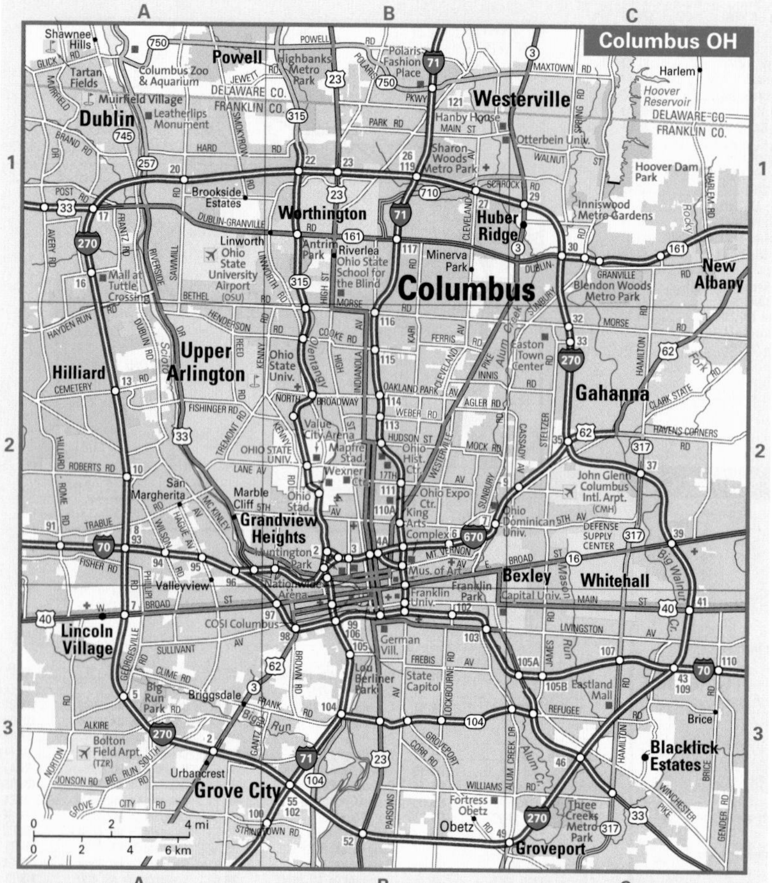

Bexley . . . C2	Gahanna . . . C2	Lincoln Vil. . . . A3	Powell . . . A1
Blacklick Estates . . . C3	Grandview Hts. . . . B2	Linworth . . . B1	Riverlea . . . B1
Brice . . . C3	Grove City . . . A3	Marble Cliff . . . A2	San Margherita . . . A2
Briggsdale . . . A3	Groveport . . . C3	Minerva Park . . . B1	Shawnee Hills . . . A1
Brookside Estates . . . A1	Harlem . . . C1	New Albany . . . C1	Upper Arlington . . . A2
Columbus . . . B1	Hilliard . . . A2	New Rome . . . A3	Urbancrest . . . A3
Dublin . . . A1	Huber Ridge . . . C1	Obetz . . . B3	Valleyview . . . A2
Westerville . . . C1	Whitehall . . . C2	Worthington . . . B1	

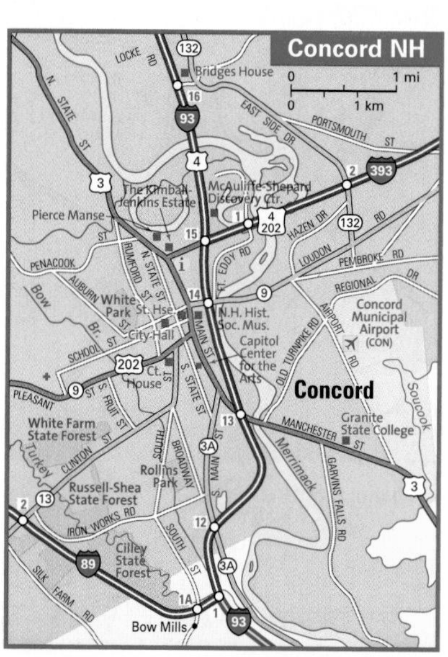

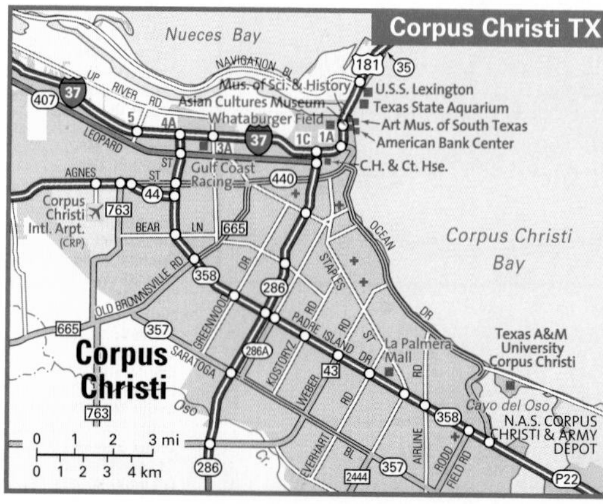

Crescent City IL, *615* **89** D3
Crescent Sprs. KY, *3801* **204** A3
Cresco IA, *3868* **73** E2
Cresson PA, *1711* **92** B4
Cressona PA, *1651* **146** A1
Crested Butte CO, *1487* **40** C2
Crest Hill IL, *20837* **89** D2
Crestline CA, *10770* **53** D2
Crestline OH, *4630* **91** D3
Creston IA, *7834* **86** B3
Creston OH, *2171* **91** E3
Crestview FL, *20978* **136** B1
Crestview KY, *475* **204** B3
Crestview Hills KY, *3148* **204** A3
Crestwood IL, *10950* **203** D6
Crestwood KY, *4531* **100** A4
Crestwood MO, *11912* **256** B3
Crestwood Vil. NJ, *7907* **147** E3
Creswell OR, *5031* **20** B4
Crete IL, *8259* **89** D2
Crete NE, *6960* **35** F4
Creve Coeur MO, *17833* **256** A2
Crewe VA, *2326* **113** D2
Cricket NC, *1855* **111** F4
Cridersville OH, *1852* **90** B3
Crimora VA, *2209* **102** C4
Cripple Creek CO, *1189* **41** E2
Crisfield MD, *2726* **103** F4
Crisp Co. GA, *23439* **129** D3
Crittenden KY, *3815* **100** B3
Crittenden Co. AR, *50902* **118** B1
Crittenden Co. KY, *9315* **109** D2
Crivitz WI, *984* **68** C3
Crocker MO, *1110* **97** E4
Crockett CA, *3094* **259** C1
Crockett TX, *6950* **124** A4
Crockett Co. TN, *14586* **108** C4
Crockett Co. TX, *3719* **60** A1
Crofton KY, *749* **109** E2
Crofton MD, *27348* **144** C3
Crofton NE, *726* **35** E1
Croghan NY, *618* **79** E2
Crompond NY, *2292* **148** B2
Cromwell CT, *13594* **149** E1
Crook Co. OR, *20978* **21** D3
Crook Co. WY, *7083* **25** F3
Crooked Lake Park FL, *1722* **141** D3
Crooks SD, *1269* **27** F4
Crookston MN, *7891* **19** F3
Crooksville OH, *2534* **101** E1
Crosby MN, *2386* **64** B4
Crosby ND, *1070* **18** A1
Crosby TX, *2299* **132** B3
Crosby Co. TX, *6059* **58** A1
Crosbyton TX, *1741* **58** B1
Cross City FL, *1728* **137** F3
Cross Co. AR, *17870* **118** A1
Crossett AR, *5507* **125** F1
Cross Hill SC, *507* **121** F3
Cross Keys NJ, *3600* **146** C4
Crosslake MN, *2141* **64** B4
Cross Plains TN, *1714* **109** F3
Cross Plains TX, *982* **59** D3
Cross Plains WI, *3538* **74** B3
Cross Roads TX, *1563* **59** F2
Crossville AL, *1862* **120** A3
Crossville IL, *745* **99** D4
Crossville TN, *10795* **110** B4
Crosswicks NJ, *900* **147** D2
Croswell MI, *2447* **76** C3
Crothersville IN, *1591* **99** F3
Croton Falls NY, *1200* **148** C2
Croton-on-Hudson NY, *8070* **148** B2
Crow Agency MT, *1616* **24** C1
Crowder MS, *712* **118** B3
Crowder OK, *430* **116** A1
Crowell TX, *948* **58** C1
Crowley LA, *13265* **133** E2
Crowley TX, *12838* **59** E2
Crowley Co. CO, *5823* **41** F3
Crown Hts. NY, *2840* **148** B1
Crown Pt. IN, *27317* **89** D2
Crown Pt. LA, *650* **134** B3
Crownpoint NM, *2278* **48** B2
Crown Pt. NY, *2119* **81** D3
Crownsville MD, *1757* **144** C3
Crow Wing Co. MN, *62500* **66** C1
Croydon PA, *9950* **248** E2
Crozet VA, *5565* **102** C4
Cruger MS, *386* **126** B1
Crump TN, *1428* **119** D1
Crystal MN, *22151* **235** B2
Crystal NM, *311* **48** A2
Crystal Beach FL, *4000* **266** A1
Crystal City MO, *4855* **98** A4
Crystal City TX, *7138* **60** C4
Crystal Falls MI, *1469* **68** C2
Crystal Lake CT, *1945* **150** A3
Crystal Lake IL, *40743* **88** C1
Crystal Lakes OH, *1483* **100** C1
Crystal River FL, *3108* **140** B1
Crystal Sprs. FL, *1327* **140** C2
Crystal Sprs. MS, *5044* **126** B3
Cuba IL, *1294* **88** A4
Cuba MO, *3356* **97** F4
Cuba NM, *731* **48** C2
Cuba NY, *1575* **92** C1
Cuba City WI, *2086* **74** A4
Cudahy CA, *23805* **228** D3
Cudahy WI, *18267* **75** D3
Cuddebackville NY, *750* **148** A1
Cudjoe Key FL, *1763* **143** D4
Cuero TX, *6841* **61** E3
Culberson Co. TX, *2398* **57** E4
Culbertson MT, *714* **17** F2
Culbertson NE, *595* **34** C4
Culdesac ID, *380* **14** B4
Cullen LA, *1163* **125** D1
Cullman AL, *14775* **119** F3
Cullman Co. AL, *80406* **119** F3
Culloden WV, *3061* **101** E3
Cullowhee NC, *6228* **121** D1
Culpeper VA, *16379* **103** D3
Culpeper Co. VA, *46689* **103** D3
Culver IN, *1353* **89** E2
Culver OR, *1357* **21** D3
Culver City CA, *38883* **228** C3
Cumberland IN, *5169* **99** F1
Cumberland KY, *2237* **111** D2
Cumberland MD, *20859* **102** C1
Cumberland NC, *4400* **123** D2
Cumberland VA, *393* **113** D1
Cumberland WI, *2170* **67** E3
Cumberland Ctr. ME, *2499* **82** B3
Cumberland Co. IL, *11048* **99** D2
Cumberland Co. KY, *6856* **110** A2
Cumberland Co. ME, *281674* **82** B3
Cumberland Co. NJ, *156898* **145** F2
Cumberland Co. NC, *319431* **123** D2
Cumberland Co. PA, *235406* **103** D1
Cumberland Co. TN, *56053* **110** B4
Cumberland Co. VA, *10052* **113** D1
Cumberland Foreside ME, *500* **82** B3
Cumberland Hill RI, *7934* **150** C2
Cumby TX, *777* **124** A1
Cuming Co. NE, *9139* **35** F2
Cumming GA, *5430* **120** C3
Cunningham KS, *454* **43** D4
Cupertino CA, *58302* **36** B4
Curlew FL, *5900* **266** A1
Currituck NC, *125* **115** E1
Currituck Co. NC, *23547* **115** E1
Curry Co. NM, *48376* **49** F4
Curry Co. OR, *22364* **28** A2
Curtis NE, *939* **34** C4
Curwensville PA, *2542* **92** B3
Cushing OK, *7826* **51** F2
Cushing TX, *612* **124** B3
Cushman AR, *452* **107** F4
Cusseta GA, *11267* **128** C3
Custer SD, *2067* **25** F4
Custer Co. CO, *4255* **41** E3
Custer Co. ID, *4368* **23** D3
Custer Co. MT, *11699* **25** E1
Custer Co. NE, *10939* **34** C3
Custer Co. OK, *27469* **51** D2
Custer Co. SD, *8216* **25** F4
Cut and Shoot TX, *1070* **132** A2
Cut Bank MT, *2869* **15** E1
Cutchogue NY, *3349* **149** E3
Cuthbert GA, *3873* **128** C3
Cutler CA, *5000* **45** D3
Cutler Bay FL, *24781* **143** E3
Cutlerville MI, *14370* **75** F3
Cut Off LA, *5976* **134** B3
Cutten CA, *3108* **28** A4
Cuyahoga Co. OH, *1280122* **91** E2
Cuyahoga Falls OH, *49652* **91** E3
Cuyahoga Hts. OH, *638* **204** F2
Cygnet OH, *597* **90** C2
Cynthiana IN, *545* **99** D4
Cynthiana KY, *6402* **100** B4
Cypress CA, *47802* **228** E4
Cypress Quarters FL, *1215* **141** E4
Cyril OK, *1059* **51** E3

D

Dacono CO, *4152* **41** E1
Dacula GA, *4442* **121** D3
Dade City FL, *6437* **140** C2
Dade Co. GA, *16633* **120** B2
Dade Co. MO, *7883* **106** C1
Dadeville AL, *3230* **128** B2
Daggett CA, *600* **53** D1
Daggett Co. UT, *1059* **32** A4
Dagsboro DE, *805* **145** F4
Dahlgren VA, *2653* **103** E4
Dahlonega GA, *5242* **120** C3
Daingerfield TX, *2560* **124** B1
Daisetta TX, *966* **132** B2
Dakota City IA, *843* **72** C4
Dakota City NE, *1919* **35** F2
Dakota Co. MN, *398552* **67** D4
Dakota Co. NE, *21006* **35** F2
Dale IN, *1593* **99** E4
Dale City VA, *65969* **144** A4
Dale Co. AL, *50251* **128** B4
Daleville AL, *5295* **128** B4
Daleville IN, *1647* **89** F4
Daleville VA, *2557* **112** B1
Dalhart TX, *7930* **50** A2
Dallam Co. TX, *6703* **50** A2
Dallas GA, *11544* **120** B4
Dallas NC, *4488* **122** A1
Dallas OR, *14583* **20** B2
Dallas PA, *2804* **93** E2
Dallas TX, *1197816* **59** F2
Dallas Ctr. IA, *1623* **86** C2
Dallas City IL, *945* **87** F3
Dallas Co. AL, *43820* **127** F3
Dallas Co. AR, *8116* **117** E4
Dallas Co. IA, *66135* **86** C2
Dallas Co. MO, *16777* **107** D1
Dallas Co. TX, *2368139* **59** F2
Dallastown PA, *4049* **103** E1
Dalton GA, *33128* **120** B2
Dalton MA, *6892* **94** C1
Dalton OH, *1830* **91** E3
Dalton PA, *1234* **93** F2
Dalton City IL, *544* **98** C1
Dalton Gardens ID, *2335* **14** B3
Dalworthington Gardens TX, *2259* **207** B3
Daly City CA, *101123* **36** B4
Dalzell SC, *3059* **122** B3
Damariscotta ME, *1142* **82** C3
Damascus MD, *15257* **144** B2
Damascus OR, *10539* **20** C2
Damascus VA, *814* **111** F3
Damon TX, *552* **132** A4
Dana IN, *608* **99** E1
Dana Pt. CA, *33351* **52** C3
Danboro PA, *1500* **146** C2
Danbury CT, *80893* **148** C2
Danbury NC, *189* **112** B3
Danbury TX, *1715* **132** A4
Dandridge TN, *2812* **111** D4
Dane WI, *995* **74** B3
Dane Co. WI, *488073* **74** B3
Danforth IL, *604* **89** D3
Dania Beach FL, *29639* **143** F2
Daniel MD, *650* **144** B1
Daniels Co. MT, *1751* **17** E1
Danielson CT, *4051* **150** B3
Danielsville GA, *560* **121** D3
Dannemora NY, *3936* **80** C1
Dansville NY, *4719* **78** C4
Dante VA, *649* **111** E2
Danube MN, *505* **66** B4
Danvers IL, *1154* **88** B4
Danvers MA, *26493* **151** F1
Danville AR, *2409* **117** D2
Danville CA, *42039* **36** B4
Danville IL, *33027* **89** D4
Danville IN, *9001* **99** F1
Danville IA, *934* **87** F3
Danville KY, *16218* **110** B1
Danville NH, *4387* **95** E1
Danville OH, *1044* **91** D4
Danville PA, *4699* **93** E3
Danville VT, *383* **81** E2
Danville VA, *43055* **112** C3
Danville WV, *691* **101** E4
Daphne AL, *21570* **135** E2
Darby MT, *720* **23** D1
Darby PA, *10687* **146** C3
Dardanelle AR, *4745* **117** D1
Dardenne Prairie MO, *11494* **98** A3
Dare Co. NC, *33920* **115** F2
Dares Beach MD, *1400* **144** C4
Darien CT, *20732* **148** C3
Darien GA, *1975* **130** B4
Darien IL, *22086* **203** C5
Darien WI, *1580* **74** C4
Darke Co. OH, *52959* **100** B1
Darlington IN, *843* **89** E4
Darlington SC, *6289* **122** C3
Darlington WI, *2451* **74** A4
Darlington Co. SC, *68681* **122** B3
Darmstadt IN, *1407* **99** D4
Darnestown MD, *6802* **144** B2
Darrington WA, *1347* **12** C2
Dasher GA, *912* **137** F1
Dassel MN, *1469* **66** C3
Dauphin PA, *791* **93** D4
Dauphin Co. PA, *268100* **93** D4
Dauphin Island AL, *1238* **135** E2
Davenport FL, *2888* **141** D2
Davenport IA, *99685* **88** A2
Davenport ND, *252* **19** E4
Davenport OK, *814* **51** F2
Davenport WA, *1734* **13** F3
David City NE, *2906* **35** F3
Davidson NC, *10944* **122** A1
Davidson Co. NC, *162878* **112** B4
Davidson Co. TN, *626681* **109** F4
Davidsville PA, *1130* **92** B4
Davie FL, *91992* **143** E2
Davie Co. NC, *41240* **112** A4
Daviess Co. IN, *31648* **99** E3
Daviess Co. KY, *96656* **109** E1
Daviess Co. MO, *8433* **96** C1
Davis CA, *65622* **36** B3
Davis IL, *677* **74** B4
Davis OK, *2683* **51** F4
Davis WV, *660* **102** B2
Davisboro GA, *2010* **129** F1
Davis Co. IA, *8753* **87** E3
Davis Co. UT, *306479* **31** E3
Davison MI, *5173* **76** B3
Davison Co. SD, *19504* **27** E4
Davy WV, *420* **111** F1
Dawes Co. NE, *9182* **34** A1
Dawson GA, *4540* **128** C3
Dawson MN, *1540* **27** F2
Dawson TX, *807* **59** F3
Dawson Co. GA, *22330* **120** C3
Dawson Co. MT, *8966* **17** F3
Dawson Co. NE, *24326* **35** D4
Dawson Co. TX, *13833* **58** A2
Dawson Sprs. KY, *2764* **109** E2
Dawsonville GA, *2536* **120** C3
Day Co. SD, *5710* **27** E2
Dayton ID, *463* **31** E2
Dayton IN, *1420* **89** E4
Dayton IA, *837* **72** C4
Dayton KY, *5338* **204** B2
Dayton MN, *4671* **66** C3
Dayton NV, *8964* **37** D2
Dayton NJ, *7063* **147** D1
Dayton OH, *141527* **100** B1
Dayton OR, *2534* **20** B2
Dayton TN, *7191* **120** B1
Dayton TX, *7242* **132** B3
Dayton VA, *1530* **102** C3
Dayton WA, *2526* **13** F4
Dayton WY, *757* **24** C2
Daytona Beach FL, *61005* **139** E4
Daytona Beach Shores FL, *4247* **139** E4
Dayville CT, *1600* **150** B3
Deadwood SD, *1270* **25** F3
Deaf Smith Co. TX, *19372* **49** F3
Deal NJ, *750* **147** F2
Deale MD, *4945* **144** C3
Deal Island MD, *471* **103** F4
Dearborn MI, *98153* **76** C4
Dearborn MO, *496* **96** B1
Dearborn Co. IN, *50047* **100** B2
Dearborn Hts. MI, *57774* **210** B3
Dearing KS, *431* **106** A2
DeArmanville AL, *700* **120** A4
Deary ID, *506* **14** B4
Deaver WY, *178* **24** B2
De Baca Co. NM, *2022* **49** E4
DeBary FL, *19320* **141** D1
De Beque CO, *504* **40** B2
Decatur AL, *55683* **119** F2
Decatur AR, *1699* **106** B3
Decatur GA, *19335* **120** C4
Decatur IL, *76122* **98** C1
Decatur IN, *9405* **90** A3
Decatur MI, *1819* **89** F1

Entries in **bold black** indicate counties or parishes.
Entries in **bold color** indicate cities with detailed inset maps.

Addison . . . D1
Arlington . . . C3
Avondale . . . A1
Balch Sprs. . . . E3
Bedford . . . B2
Benbrook . . . A3
Blue Mound . . . A2
Carrollton . . . D1
Cedar Hill . . . C3
Cockrell Hill . . . D2
Colleyville . . . B1
Coppell . . . C1
Crowley . . . A3
Dallas . . . D2
Dalworthington Gardens . . . B3
De Soto . . . D3
Duncanville . . . D3
Edgecliff . . . A3
Euless . . . C2
Everman . . . B3
Farmers Branch . . . D1
Flower Mound . . . C1
Forest Hill . . . B3
Ft. Worth . . . A2
Garland . . . E1
Grand Prairie . . . C3
Grapevine . . . C1
Haltom City . . . B2
Haslet . . . A1
Highland Park . . . D2
Hurst . . . B2
Hutchins . . . E3
Irving . . . C2
Keller . . . B1
Kennedale . . . B3
Lakeview . . . A1
Lake Worth . . . A2
Lancaster . . . D3
Lewisville . . . C1
Mansfield . . . B3
Mesquite . . . E2
Murphy . . . E1
Newark . . . A1
N. Richland Hills . . . B2
Pantego . . . B3
Plano . . . D1
Richardson . . . E1
Richland Hills . . . B2
River Oaks . . . A2
Roanoke . . . B1
Rowlett . . . E1
Sachse . . . E1
Saginaw . . . A2
Sansom Park . . . A2
Seagoville . . . E3
Southlake . . . B1
Sunnyvale . . . E1
Trophy Club . . . B1
University Park . . . D2
Watauga . . . B2
Westlake . . . B1
Westover Hills . . . A2
Westworth . . . A2
White Settlement . . . A2
Wilmer . . . E3
Wylie . . . E1

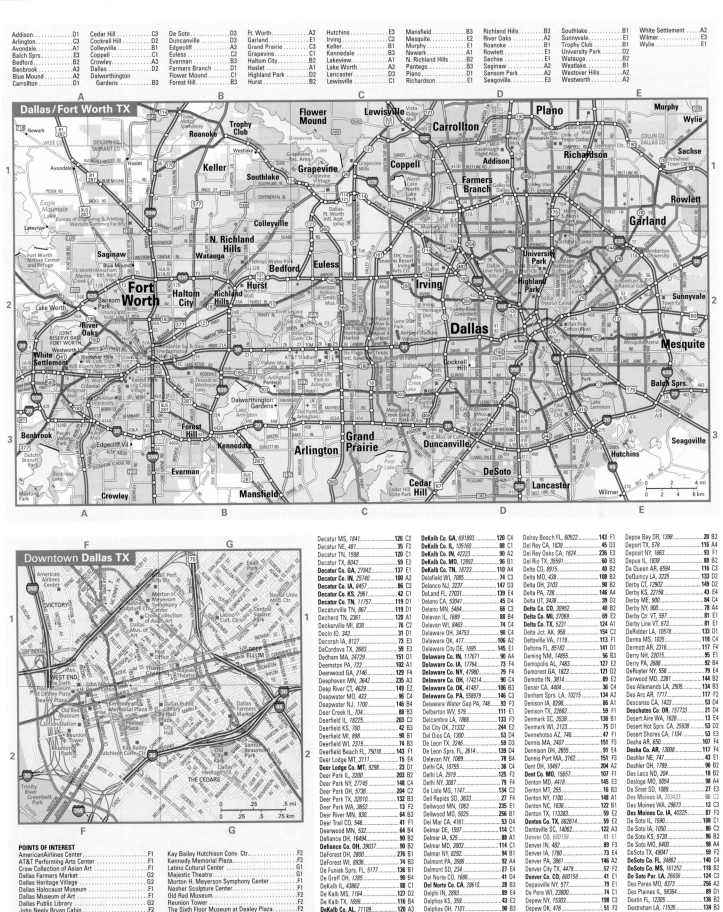

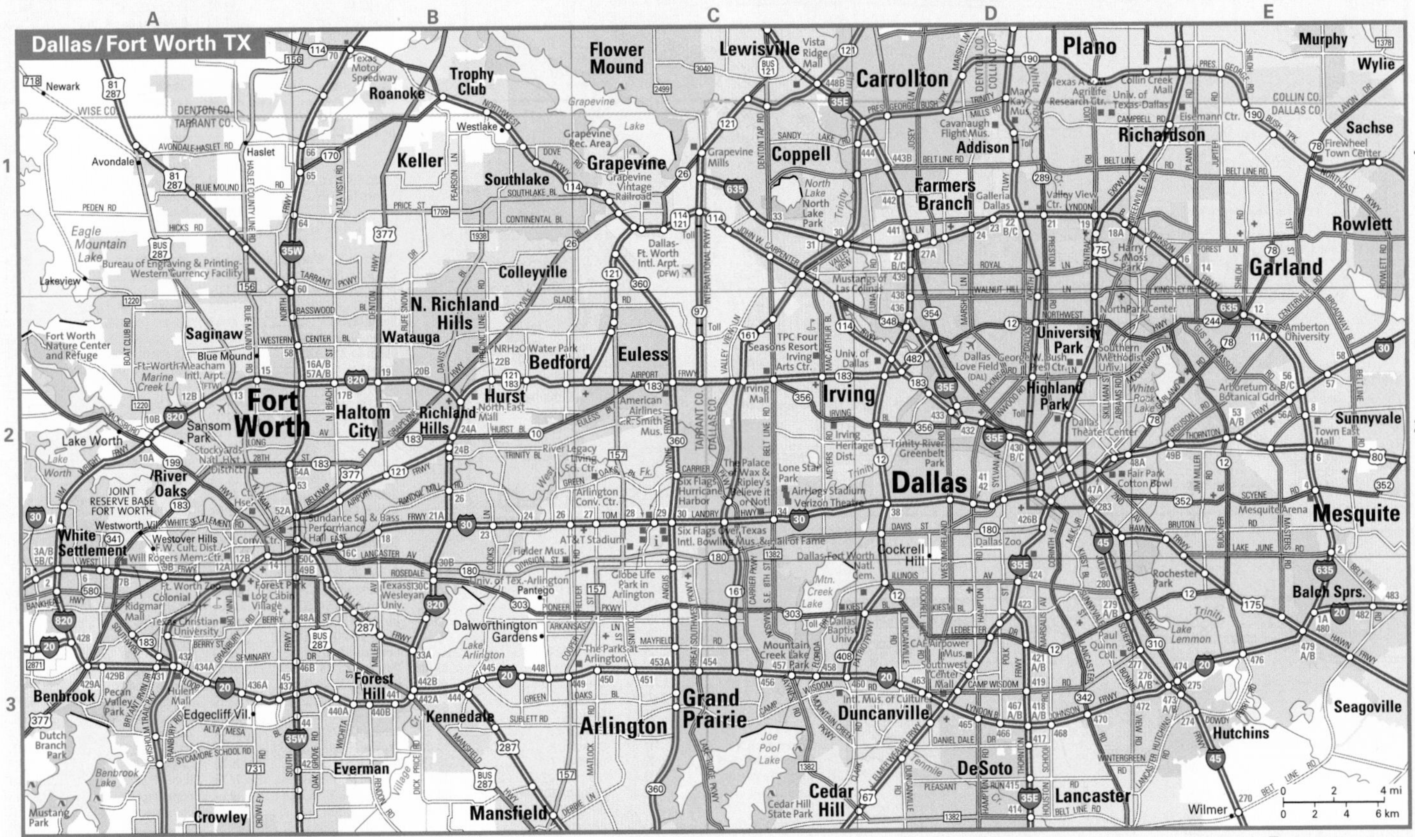

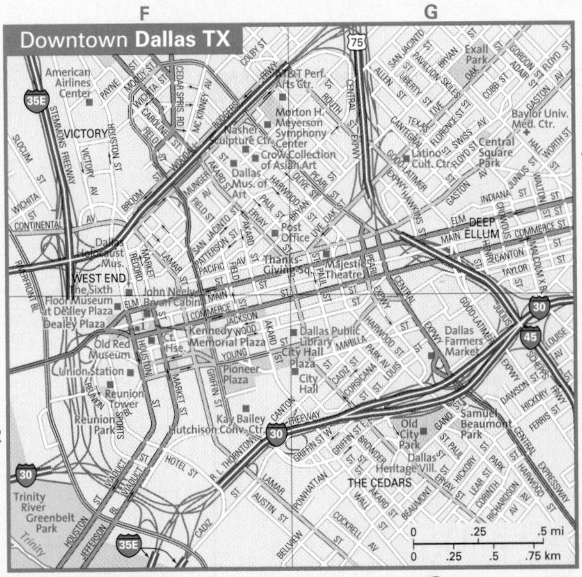

POINTS OF INTEREST

AmericanAirlines Center . . . F1
AT&T Performing Arts Center . . . F1
Crow Collection of Asian Art . . . F1
Dallas Farmers Market . . . G2
Dallas Heritage Village . . . G2
Dallas Holocaust Museum . . . F1
Dallas Museum of Art . . . F1
Dallas Public Library . . . G2
John Neely Bryan Cabin . . . F2
Kay Bailey Hutchison Conv. Ctr. . . . F2
Kennedy Memorial Plaza . . . F2
Latino Cultural Center . . . G1
Majestic Theatre . . . G1
Morton H. Meyerson Symphony Center . . . F1
Nasher Sculpture Center . . . F1
Old Red Museum . . . F2
Reunion Tower . . . F2
The Sixth Floor Museum at Dealey Plaza . . . F2

Decatur MS, *1841* . . . **126** C2
Decatur NE, *481* . . . **35** F2
Decatur TN, *1598* . . . **120** C1
Decatur TX, *6042* . . . **59** E2
Decatur Co. GA, *27842* . . . **137** E1
Decatur Co. IN, *25740* . . . **100** A2
Decatur Co. IA, *8457* . . . **86** C3
Decatur Co. KS, *2961* . . . **42** C1
Decatur Co. TN, *11757* . . . **119** D1
Decaturville TN, *867* . . . **119** D1
Decherd TN, *2361* . . . **120** A1
Deckerville MI, *830* . . . **76** C2
Declo ID, *343* . . . **31** D1
Decorah IA, *8127* . . . **73** E3
DeCordova TX, *2683* . . . **59** E3
Dedham MA, *24729* . . . **151** D1
Deemston PA, *722* . . . **102** A1
Deenwood GA, *2146* . . . **129** F4
Deephaven MN, *3642* . . . **235** A3
Deep River CT, *4629* . . . **149** E2
Deepwater MO, *433* . . . **96** C4
Deepwater NJ, *1700* . . . **146** B4
Deer Creek IL, *704* . . . **88** B3
Deerfield IL, *18225* . . . **203** C2
Deerfield KS, *700* . . . **42** B3
Deerfield MI, *898* . . . **90** B1
Deerfield WI, *2319* . . . **74** B3
Deerfield Beach FL, *75018* . . . **143** F1
Deer Lodge MT, *3111* . . . **15** E4
Deer Lodge Co. MT, *9298* . . . **23** D1
Deer Park IL, *3200* . . . **203** B2
Deer Park NY, *27745* . . . **148** C4
Deer Park OH, *5736* . . . **204** C2
Deer Park TX, *32010* . . . **132** B3
Deer Park WA, *3652* . . . **13** F2
Deer River MN, *930* . . . **64** B3
Deer Trail CO, *546* . . . **41** F1
Deerwood MN, *532* . . . **64** B4
Defiance OH, *16494* . . . **90** B2
Defiance Co. OH, *39037* . . . **90** B2
DeForest OH, *2800* . . . **276** B1
DeForest WI, *8936* . . . **74** B3
De Funiak Sprs. FL, *5177* . . . **136** B1
De Graff OH, *1285* . . . **90** B4
DeKalb IL, *43862* . . . **88** C1
De Kalb MS, *1164* . . . **127** D2
De Kalb TX, *1699* . . . **116** B4
DeKalb Co. AL, *71109* . . . **120** A3
DeKalb Co. GA, *691893* . . . **120** C4
DeKalb Co. IL, *105160* . . . **88** C1
DeKalb Co. IN, *42223* . . . **90** A2
DeKalb Co. MO, *12892* . . . **96** B1
DeKalb Co. TN, *18723* . . . **110** A4
Delafield WI, *7085* . . . **74** C3
Delanco NJ, *3237* . . . **147** D3
DeLand FL, *27031* . . . **139** E4
Delano CA, *53041* . . . **45** D4
Delano MN, *5464* . . . **66** C3
Delavan IL, *1689* . . . **88** B4
Delavan WI, *8463* . . . **74** C4
Delaware OH, *34753* . . . **90** C4
Delaware OK, *417* . . . **106** A2
Delaware City DE, *1695* . . . **145** E1
Delaware Co. IN, *117671* . . . **90** A4
Delaware Co. IA, *17764* . . . **73** F4
Delaware Co. NY, *47980* . . . **79** F4
Delaware Co. OH, *174214* . . . **90** C4
Delaware Co. OK, *41487* . . . **106** B3
Delaware Co. PA, *558979* . . . **146** C3
Delaware Water Gap PA, *746* . . . **93** F3
Delbarton WV, *579* . . . **111** E1
Delcambre LA, *1866* . . . **133** F3
Del City OK, *21332* . . . **244** E2
Del Dios CA, *1300* . . . **53** D4
De Leon TX, *2246* . . . **59** D3
De Leon Sprs. FL, *2614* . . . **139** D4
Delevan NY, *1089* . . . **78** B4
Delhi CA, *10755* . . . **36** C4
Delhi LA, *2919* . . . **125** F2
Delhi NY, *3087* . . . **79** F4
De Lisle MS, *1147* . . . **134** C2
Dell Rapids SD, *3633* . . . **27** F4
Dellwood MN, *1063* . . . **235** E1
Dellwood MO, *5025* . . . **256** B1
Del Mar CA, *4161* . . . **53** D4
Delmar DE, *1597* . . . **114** C1
Delmar IA, *525* . . . **88** A1
Delmar MD, *3003* . . . **114** C1
Delmar NY, *8292* . . . **94** B1
Delmont PA, *2686* . . . **92** A4
Delmont SD, *234* . . . **27** E4
Del Norte CO, *1686* . . . **41** D4
Del Norte Co. CA, *28610* . . . **28** B3
Delphi IN, *2893* . . . **89** E4
Delphos KS, *359* . . . **43** E2
Delphos OH, *7101* . . . **90** B3
Delray Beach FL, *60522* . . . **143** F1
Del Rey CA, *1639* . . . **45** D3
Del Rey Oaks CA, *1624* . . . **236** E3
Del Rio TX, *35591* . . . **60** B3
Delta CO, *8915* . . . **40** B2
Delta MO, *438* . . . **108** B2
Delta OH, *3103* . . . **90** B2
Delta PA, *728* . . . **146** A4
Delta UT, *3436* . . . **39** D2
Delta Co. CO, *30952* . . . **40** B2
Delta Co. MI, *37069* . . . **69** E2
Delta Co. TX, *5231* . . . **124** A1
Delta Jct. AK, *958* . . . **154** C2
Deltaville VA, *1119* . . . **113** F1
Deltona FL, *85182* . . . **141** D1
Deming NM, *14855* . . . **56** B3
Demopolis AL, *7483* . . . **127** E2
Demorest GA, *1823* . . . **121** D2
Demotte IN, *3814* . . . **89** E2
Denair CA, *4404* . . . **36** C4
Denham Sprs. LA, *10215* . . . **134** A2
Denison IA, *8298* . . . **86** A1
Denison TX, *22682* . . . **59** F1
Denmark SC, *3538* . . . **130** B1
Denmark WI, *2123* . . . **75** D1
Dennehotso AZ, *746* . . . **47** F1
Dennis MA, *2407* . . . **151** F3
Dennison OH, *2655* . . . **91** E4
Dennis Port MA, *3162* . . . **151** F3
Dent OH, *10497* . . . **204** A2
Dent Co. MO, *15657* . . . **107** F1
Denton MD, *4418* . . . **145** E3
Denton MT, *255* . . . **16** B3
Denton NY, *1100* . . . **148** A1
Denton NC, *1636* . . . **122** B1
Denton TX, *113383* . . . **59** E2
Denton Co. TX, *662614* . . . **59** E2
Dentsville SC, *14062* . . . **122** A3
Denver CO, *600158* . . . **41** E1
Denver IN, *482* . . . **89** F3
Denver IA, *1780* . . . **73** E4
Denver PA, *3861* . . . **146** A2
Denver City TX, *4479* . . . **57** F2
Denver Co. CO, *600158* . . . **41** E1
Depauville NY, *577* . . . **79** E1
De Pere WI, *23800* . . . **74** C1
Depew NY, *15303* . . . **198** C3
Depew OK, *476* . . . **51** F2
Depoe Bay OR, *1398* . . . **20** B2
Deport TX, *578* . . . **116** A4
Deposit NY, *1663* . . . **93** F1
Depue IL, *1838* . . . **88** B2
De Queen AR, *6594* . . . **116** C3
DeQuincy LA, *3235* . . . **133** D2
Derby CT, *12902* . . . **149** D2
Derby KS, *22158* . . . **43** E4
Derby ME, *900* . . . **84** C4
Derby NY, *900* . . . **78** A4
Derby Ctr. VT, *597* . . . **81** E1
Derby Line VT, *673* . . . **81** E1
DeRidder LA, *10578* . . . **133** D1
Derma MS, *1025* . . . **118** C4
Dermott AR, *2316* . . . **117** F4
Derry NH, *22015* . . . **95** E1
Derry PA, *2688* . . . **92** B4
DeRuyter NY, *558* . . . **79** E4
Derwood MD, *2381* . . . **144** B2
Des Allemands LA, *2505* . . . **134** B3
Des Arc AR, *1717* . . . **117** F2
Descanso CA, *1423* . . . **53** D4
Deschutes Co. OR, *157733* . . . **21** D4
Desert Aire WA, *1626* . . . **13** E4
Desert Hot Sprs. CA, *25938* . . . **53** D2
Desert Shores CA, *1104* . . . **53** E3
Desha AR, *650* . . . **107** F4
Desha Co. AR, *13008* . . . **117** F4
Deshler NE, *747* . . . **43** E1
Deshler OH, *1799* . . . **90** B2
Des Lacs ND, *204* . . . **18** B2
Desloge MO, *5054* . . . **98** A4
De Smet SD, *1089* . . . **27** E3
Des Moines IA, *203433* . . . **86** C2
Des Moines WA, *29673* . . . **12** C3
Des Moines Co. IA, *40325* . . . **87** F3
De Soto IL, *1590* . . . **108** C1
De Soto IA, *1050* . . . **86** C2
De Soto KS, *5720* . . . **96** B2
De Soto MO, *6400* . . . **98** A4
DeSoto TX, *49047* . . . **59** F2
DeSoto Co. FL, *34862* . . . **140** C4
DeSoto Co. MS, *161252* . . . **118** B2
De Soto Par. LA, *26656* . . . **124** C3
Des Peres MO, *8373* . . . **256** A2
Des Plaines IL, *58364* . . . **89** D1
Destin FL, *12305* . . . **136** B2
Destrehan LA, *11535* . . . **134** B3

Figures after entries indicate population, page number, and grid reference.

Barstow C2
Bettendorf B1
Buffalo. A2
Carbon Cliff C2
Cleveland C2
Coal Valley B2
Colona. C2
Davenport. A1
E. Moline. B1
Hampton C1
Le Claire C1
Milan. B2
Moline. B2
Panorama Park B1
Port Byron C1
Rapids City C1
Riverdale. B1
Rock Island A2
Silvis C2

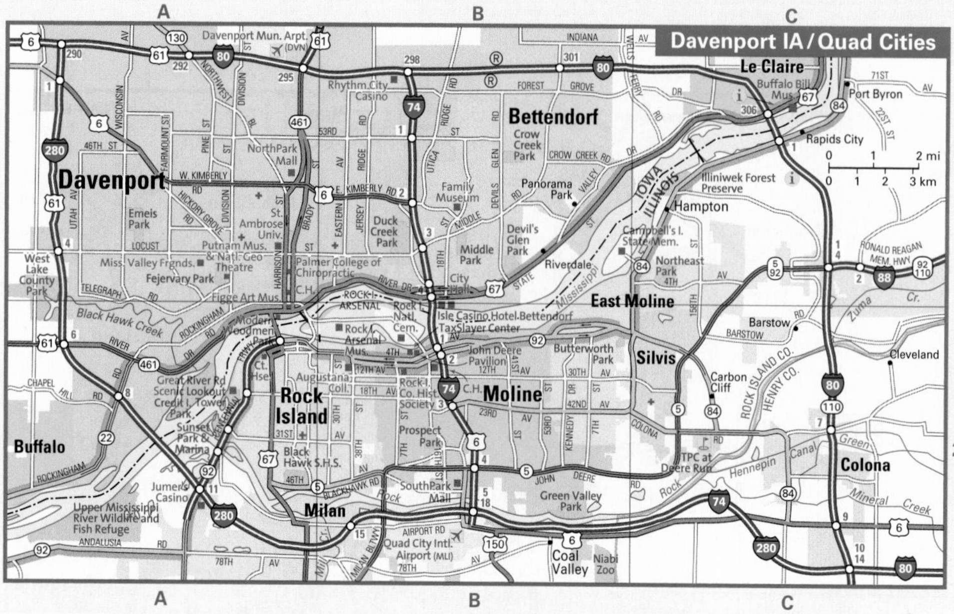

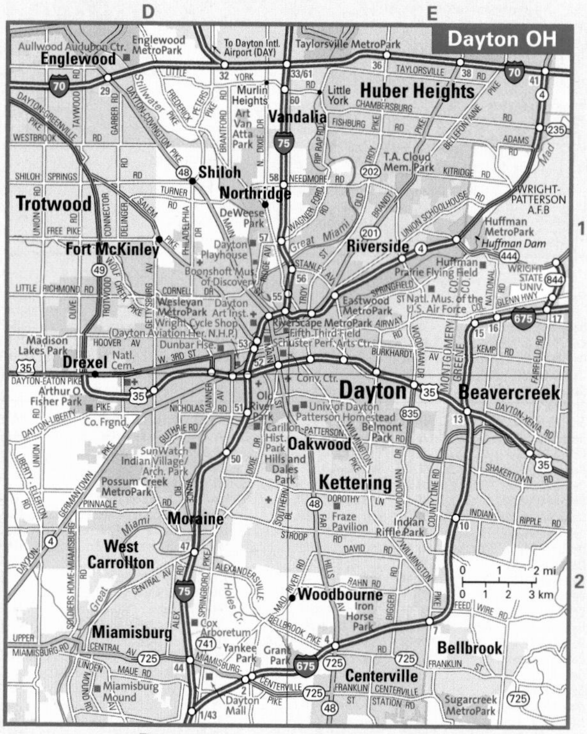

Beavercreek E2
Bellbrook E2
Centerville E2
Dayton. E2
Drexel D1
Englewood D1
Ft. McKinley. D1
Huber Hts. E1
Kettering. E2
Little York E1
Miamisburg D2
Moraine D2
Murlin Hts. D1
Northridge D1
Oakwood. E2
Riverside. E1
Shiloh D1
Trotwood D1
Vandalia E1
W. Carrollton D2
Woodbourne E2

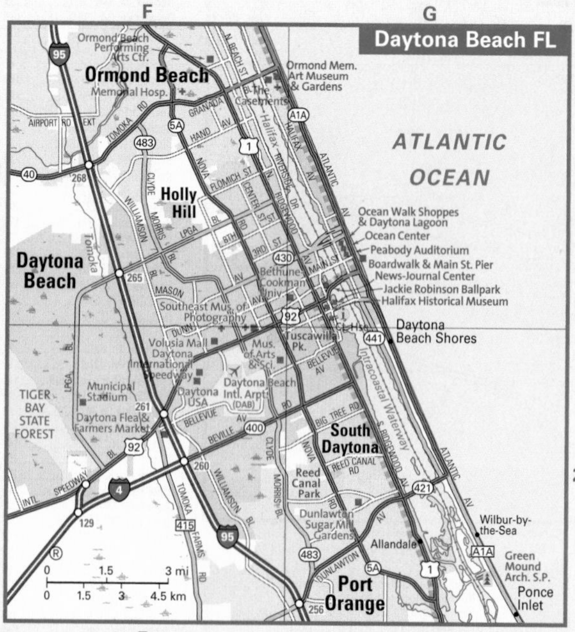

Allandale. G2
Daytona Beach F1
Daytona Beach Shores G2
Holly Hill F1
Ormond Beach F1
Ponce Inlet. G2
Port Orange G2
S. Daytona G2
Wilbur-by-the-Sea G2

Detroit MI, *713777* **76** C4
Detroit TX, *732* **116** A4
Detroit Beach MI, *2087* **90** C1
Detroit Lakes MN, *8569* **19** F4
Deuel Co. NE, *1941* **34** A3
Deuel Co. SD, *4364* **27** F2
De Valls Bluff AR, *619* **117** F2
Deville LA, *1764* **125** E4
Devils Lake ND, *7141* **19** D2
Devine TX, *4350* **61** D3
Devola OH, *2652* **101** F2
Devon PA, *1515* **248** A2
Dewar OK, *888* **116** A1
Dewey OK, *3432* **51** F1
Dewey Beach DE, *341* **145** F4
Dewey Co. OK, *4810* **51** D2
Dewey Co. SD, *5301* **26** C2
Dewey-Humboldt AZ, *3894* **47** D4
Deweyville TX, *1023* **132** C2
Deweyville UT, *332* **31** E3
DeWitt AR, *3292* **117** F3
De Witt IA, *5322* **88** A1
DeWitt MI, *4507* **76** A3
De Witt NE, *513* **35** F4
De Witt NY, *24071* **79** E3
De Witt Co. IL, *16561* **88** B4
DeWitt Co. TX, *20097* **61** E3
Dexter GA, *575* **129** E2
Dexter IA, *611* **86** C2
Dexter ME, *2158* **82** C1
Dexter MI, *4067* **76** B4
Dexter MO, *7864* **108** B2
Dexter NM, *1266* **57** E2
Dexter NY, *1052* **79** E1
Dexter OR, *750* **20** C4
Diablo CA, *1158* **259** D2
Diamond IL, *2527* **88** C2
Diamond MO, *902* **106** C2
Diamond Bar CA, *55544* **229** F3
Diamond City AR, *782* **107** D3
Diamondhead MS, *8425* **134** C2
Diamond Hill RI, *1100* **150** C2
Diamond Sprs. CA, *11037* **36** C2
Diamondville WY, *737* **31** F2
Diaz AR, *1318* **107** F4
D'Iberville MS, *9486* **135** D2
Diboll TX, *4776* **132** B1
Dickens TX, *286* **58** B1
Dickens Co. TX, *2444* **58** B1
Dickenson Co. VA, *15903* **111** E2
Dickey Co. ND, *5289* **27** D1
Dickeyville WI, *1061* **73** F4
Dickinson ND, *17787* **18** A4
Dickinson TX, *18680* **132** B4
Dickinson Co. IA, *16667* **72** B3
Dickinson Co. KS, *19754* **43** E2
Dickinson Co. MI, *26168* **69** D2
Dickson OK, *1207* **51** F4
Dickson TN, *14538* **109** E4
Dickson City PA, *6070* **93** F2
Dickson Co. TN, *49666* **109** E4
Dierks AR, *1133* **116** C3
Dieterich IL, *617* **98** C2
Dighton KS, *1038* **42** C3
Dighton MA, *6175* **151** D3
Dike IA, *1209* **73** D4
Dilkon AZ, *1184* **47** F3
Dill City OK, *562* **51** D3
Dilley TX, *3894* **60** C4
Dillingham AK, *2329* **154** B3
Dillon CO, *904* **41** D1
Dillon MT, *4134* **23** E2
Dillon SC, *6788* **122** C3
Dillon Co. SC, *32062* **122** C3
Dillonvale OH, *3474* **91** F4
Dillsboro IN, *1327* **100** A2
Dillsburg PA, *2563* **93** D4
Dillwyn VA, *447* **113** D1
Dilworth MN, *4024* **19** F4
Dimmit Co. TX, *9996* **60** C4
Dimmitt TX, *4393* **50** A4
Dimondale MI, *1234* **76** A4
Dinosaur CO, *339* **32** B4
Dinuba CA, *21453* **45** D3
Dinwiddie VA, *350* **113** E2
Dinwiddie Co. VA, *28001* **113** E2
District Hts. MD, *5837* **271** F4
Divernon IL, *1172* **98** B1
Divide Co. ND, *2071* **17** F1
Dixfield ME, *1076* **82** B2
Dixie Co. FL, *16422* **137** F3
Dixmoor IL, *3644* **203** E6
Dixon CA, *18351* **36** B3
Dixon IL, *15733* **88** B1
Dixon KY, *786* **109** E1
Dixon MO, *1549* **97** E4
Dixon MT, *203* **15** D3
Dixon Co. NE, *6000* **35** F1
D'Lo MS, *394* **126** B3
Dobbins Hts. NC, *866* **122** C2
Dobbs Ferry NY, *10875* **148** B3
Dobson NC, *1586* **112** A3
Dock Jct. GA, *7721* **139** D1
Doctor Phillips FL, *10981* **246** B3
Doctors Inlet FL, *1400* **139** D2
Doddridge Co. WV, *8202* **102** A2
Dodge NE, *612* **35** F2
Dodge Ctr. MN, *2670* **73** D1
Dodge City AL, *593* **119** F3
Dodge City KS, *27340* **42** C4
Dodge Co. GA, *21796* **129** E3
Dodge Co. MN, *20087* **73** D1
Dodge Co. NE, *36691* **35** F3
Dodge Co. WI, *88759* **74** C2
Dodgeville WI, *4693* **74** A3
Doerun GA, *774* **129** D4
Doland SD, *180* **27** E2
Dolan Sprs. AZ, *2033* **46** B3
Dolgeville NY, *2206* **79** F3
Dollar Bay MI, *1082* **65** F3
Dolores CO, *936* **40** B4
Dolores Co. CO, *2064* **40** B4
Dolton IL, *23153* **203** E6
Doña Ana NM, *1211* **56** B3
Dona Ana Co. NM, *209233* **56** B3
Donald OR, *979* **20** B2
Donaldsonville LA, *7436* **134** A2
Donalsonville GA, *2650* **137** D1
Dongola IL, *726* **108** C1
Doniphan MO, *1997* **108** A3
Doniphan NE, *829* **35** E4
Doniphan Co. KS, *7945* **96** B1
Donley Co. TX, *3677* **50** B3
Donna TX, *15798* **63** E4
Donnellson IA, *912* **87** F3
Donora PA, *4781* **92** A4
Doolittle MO, *630* **97** E4
Dooly Co. GA, *14918* **129** D3
Doon IA, *577* **27** F4
Door Co. WI, *27785* **69** D4
Dora AL, *2025* **119** F4
Doraville GA, *8330* **120** C4
Dorchester NE, *586* **35** F4
Dorchester WI, *876* **68** A4
Dorchester Co. MD, *32618* **103** F4
Dorchester Co. SC, *136555* **130** C1
Dormont PA, *8593* **250** B3
Dorr MI, *2800* **75** F4
Dorris CA, *939* **28** C2
Dorset VT, *249* **81** D4
Dorsey MD, *1000* **193** B4
Dortches NC, *935* **113** D4
Dos Palos CA, *4950* **44** C2
Dothan AL, *65496* **128** B4
Double Sprs. AL, *1083* **119** E3
Doubs MD, *750* **144** A2
Dougherty Co. GA, *94565* **128** C4
Douglas AL, *744* **120** A3
Douglas AZ, *17378* **55** E4
Douglas GA, *11589* **129** E4
Douglas MA, *8471* **150** C2
Douglas MI, *1232* **75** E4
Douglas WY, *6120* **33** E1
Douglas Co. CO, *285465* **41** E2
Douglas Co. GA, *132403* **120** C4
Douglas Co. IL, *19980* **99** D1
Douglas Co. KS, *110826* **96** A3
Douglas Co. MN, *36009* **66** B2
Douglas Co. MO, *13684* **107** E2
Douglas Co. NE, *517110* **35** F3
Douglas Co. NV, *46997* **37** D2
Douglas Co. OR, *107667* **20** B4
Douglas Co. SD, *3002* **27** E4
Douglas Co. WA, *38431* **13** E3
Douglas Co. WI, *44159* **64** C4
Douglass KS, *1700* **43** F4
Douglass Hills KY, *5484* **230** F2
Douglassville PA, *448* **146** B2
Douglasville GA, *30961* **120** C4
Dousman WI, *2302* **74** C3
Dove Creek CO, *735* **40** A4
Dover AR, *1378* **117** D1
Dover DE, *36047* **145** E2
Dover FL, *3702* **140** C2
Dover ID, *556* **14** B2
Dover MA, *2265* **151** D1
Dover NH, *29987* **82** A4
Dover NJ, *18157* **148** A3
Dover OH, *12826* **91** E4
Dover PA, *2007* **103** E1
Dover TN, *1417* **109** D3
Dover-Foxcroft ME, *2528* **82** C1
Dover Plains NY, *1323* **94** B3
Dowagiac MI, *5879* **89** F1
Dow City IA, *510* **86** A1
Dowling Park FL, *650* **137** F2
Downers Grove IL, *47833* **89** D1
Downey CA, *111772* **52** C2
Downey ID, *625* **31** E2
Downieville CA, *282* **36** C1
Downingtown PA, *7891* **146** B3
Downs IL, *1005* **88** C4
Downs KS, *900* **43** D1
Dows IA, *538* **72** C4
Doyle TN, *537* **110** A4
Doylestown OH, *3051* **91** E3
Doylestown PA, *8380* **146** C2
Doyline LA, *818* **125** D2
Drain OR, *1151* **20** B4
Drake ND, *275* **18** C2
Drakesboro KY, *515* **109** E2
Drakes Branch VA, *530* **113** D2
Draper UT, *42274* **31** E4
Dravosburg PA, *1792* **250** C3
Drayton ND, *824* **19** E2
Dresden OH, *1529* **91** D4
Dresden TN, *3005* **108** C3
Dresser WI, *895* **67** D3
Drew MS, *1927* **118** A4
Drew Co. AR, *18509* **117** F4
Drexel MO, *965* **96** B3
Drexel NC, *1858* **111** F4
Drexel OH, *2076* **208** D1
Drexel Hill PA, *28043* **146** C3
Driggs ID, *1660* **23** F4
Dripping Sprs. TX, *1788* **61** D2
Driscoll TX, *739* **63** F2
Druid Hills GA, *14568* **190** D3
Drummond MT, *309* **15** E4
Drumright OK, *2907* **51** F2
Dryden ME, *1100* **82** B2
Dryden MI, *951* **76** C3
Dryden NY, *1890* **79** D4
Dryden VA, *1208* **111** D2
Dry Mills ME, *700* **82** B3
Dry Prong LA, *436* **125** E4
Dry Ridge KY, *2191* **100** B3
Duarte CA, *21321* **228** E2
Dubach LA, *961* **125** E2
Dublin CA, *46036* **259** E3
Dublin GA, *16201* **129** E2
Dublin IN, *790* **100** A1
Dublin MD, *650* **145** D1
Dublin OH, *41751* **90** C4
Dublin PA, *2158* **146** C2
Dublin TX, *3654* **59** D3
Dublin VA, *2534* **112** A2
Dubois ID, *677* **23** E3
DuBois PA, *7794* **92** B3
Dubois WY, *971* **24** B4
Dubois Co. IN, *41889* **99** E3
Duboistown PA, *1205* **93** D2
Dubuque IA, *57637* **73** F4
Dubuque Co. IA, *93653* **73** F4
Duchesne UT, *1690* **32** A4
Duchesne Co. UT, *18607* **39** F1
Duck Hill MS, *732* **118** B4
Ducktown TN, *475* **120** C2
Ducor CA, *612* **45** D4
Dudley MA, *11390* **150** B2

Entries in **bold black** indicate counties or parishes.
Entries in **bold color** indicate cities with detailed inset maps.

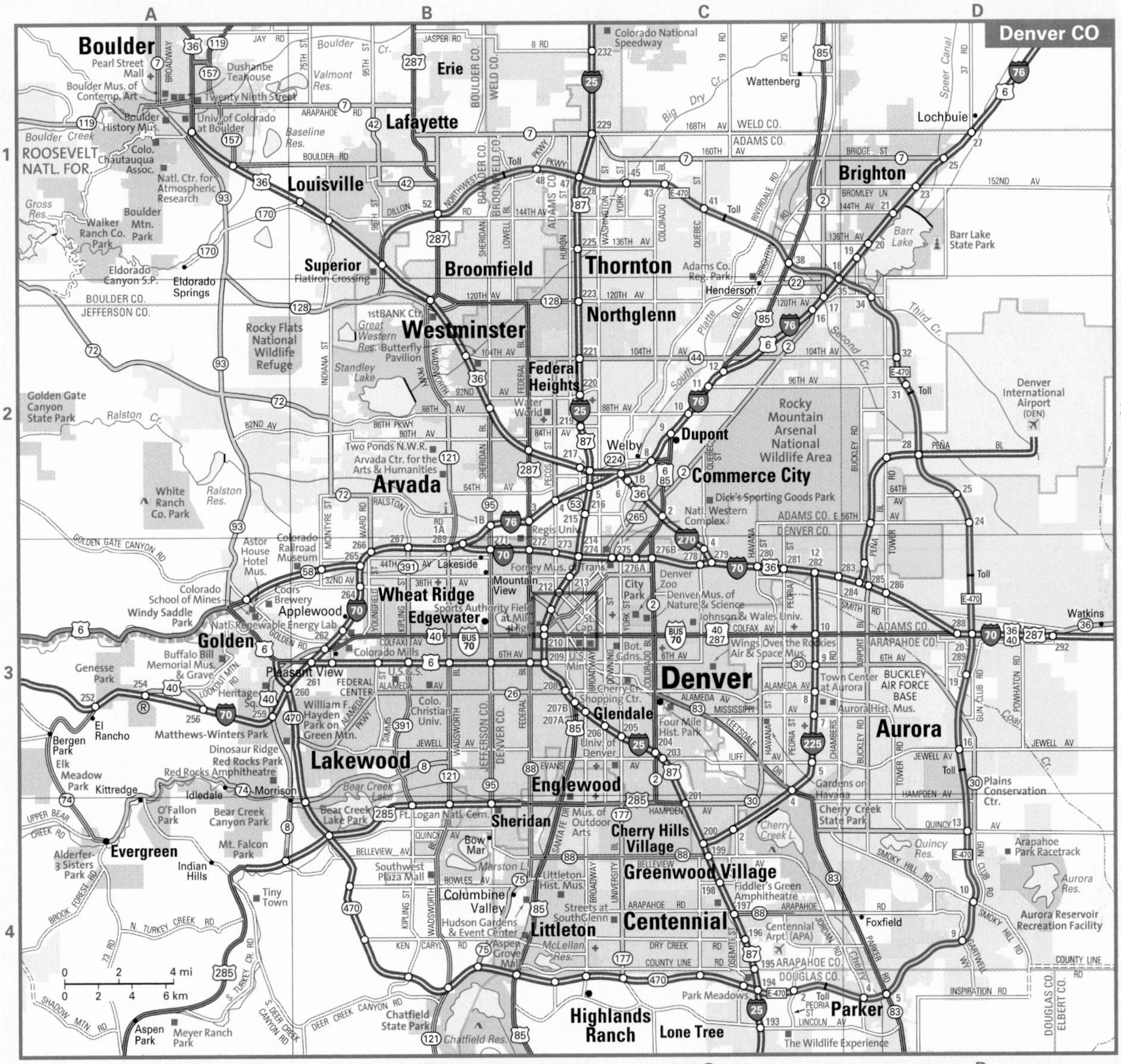

Applewood B3
Arvada. B2
Aspen Park. A4
Aurora. D3
Bergen Park A3
Boulder A1
Bow Mar. B4
Brighton D1
Broomfield B1
Centennial C4
Cherry Hills Vil. C4
Columbine Valley B4
Commerce City C2
Denver. C3
Dupont. C2
Edgewater B3
Eldorado Sprs. A1
El Rancho A3
Englewood C3
Erie. B1
Evergreen A4
Federal Hts. B2
Foxfield D4
Glendale C3
Golden. A3
Greenwood Vil. C4
Henderson C2
Highlands Ranch. C4
Idledale. A3
Indian Hills A4
Kittredge. A4
Lafayette. B1
Lakeside B3
Lakewood B3
Littleton. B4
Lochbuie. D1
Lone Tree C4
Louisville. B1
Morrison. A4
Mtn. View. B3
Northglenn C2
Parker. D4
Pleasant View B3
Sheridan. B4
Superior B1
Thornton C1
Watkins. D3
Wattenberg C1
Welby C2
Westminster. B2
Wheat Ridge B3

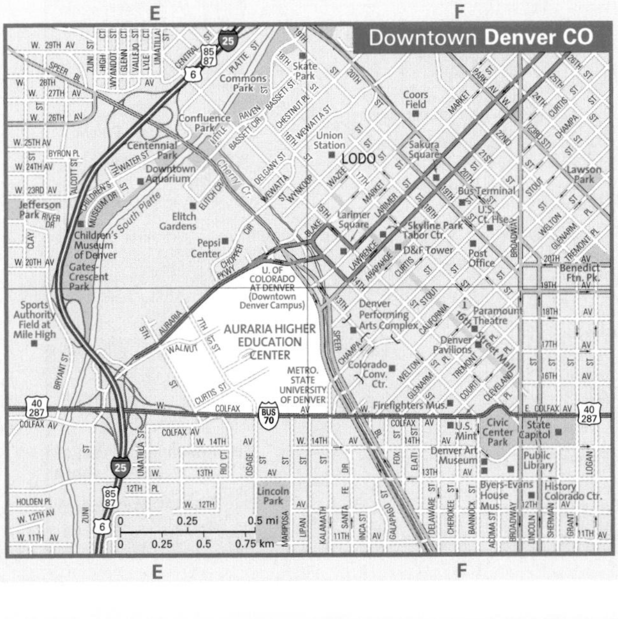

POINTS OF INTEREST

16th Street Mall. F2
Auraria Higher Education Center. E2
Bus Terminal F1
Byers-Evans House F2
Children's Museum of Denver E1
Colorado Convention Center. F2
Coors Field F1
D&F Tower F1
Denver Art Museum. F2
Denver Pavilions F2
Denver Performing Arts Complex F2
Downtown Aquarium E1
Elitch Gardens E1
Firefighters Museum F2
History Colorado Center F2
Larimer Square F1
LoDo F1
Metropolitan State Coll. of Denver E2
Paramount Theatre. F2
Pepsi Center E1
Post Office F1
Public Library. F2
Sakura Square. F1
Skate Park E1
Sports Authority Field at Mile High E2
State Capitol F2
Tabor Center F1
Union Station F1
U.S. Court House. F1
U.S. Mint. F2
Univ. of Colorado at Denver
(Downtown Denver Campus). E2

Dudleyville AZ, *959* **55** D2
Duenweg MO, *1121* **106** B2
Due West SC, *1247* **121** E3
Dufur OR, *604* **21** D2
Dugger IN, *920* **99** E2
Dukes Co. MA, *16535* **151** E4
Dulac LA, *1463* **134** B4
Dulce NM, *2743* **48** C1
Duluth GA, *26600* **120** C3
Duluth MN, *86265* **64** C4
Dumas AR, *4706* **117** F4
Dumas MS, *470* **118** C2
Dumas TX, *14691* **50** A2
Dumfries VA, *4961* **144** A4
Dumont CO, *364* **41** D1
Dumont IA, *637* **73** D4
Dunbar PA, *1042* **102** B1
Dunbar WV, *7907* **101** E4
Duncan AZ, *696* **55** F2
Duncan MS, *423* **118** A3
Duncan OK, *23431* **51** E4
Duncan SC, *3181* **121** F2
Duncannon PA, *1522* **93** D4
Duncansville PA, *1233* **92** C4
Duncanville TX, *38524* **59** F2
Dundalk MD, *63597* **144** C2
Dundas MN, *1367* **73** D1
Dundee FL, *3717* **141** D2
Dundee MI, *3957* **90** C1
Dundee NY, *1725* **79** D4
Dundee OR, *3162* **20** B2
Dundy Co. NE, *2008* **42** B1
Dunean SC, *3671* **217** A2
Dunedin FL, *35321* **140** B2
Dunellen NJ, *7227* **147** E1
Dunes City OR, *1303* **20** A4
Dunkerton IA, *852* **73** E4
Dunkirk IN, *2362* **90** A4
Dunkirk MD, *2520* **144** C4
Dunkirk NY, *12563* **78** A4
Dunkirk OH, *875* **90** C3
Dunklin Co. MO, *31953* **108** B4
Dunlap IL, *1386* **88** B3
Dunlap IN, *6235* **89** F2
Dunlap IA, *1042* **86** A1
Dunlap TN, *4815* **120** B1
Dunleith DE, *9100* **274** D2
Dunmore PA, *14057* **93** F2
Dunn NC, *9263* **123** D1
Dunn Co. ND, *3536* **18** A3
Dunn Co. WI, *43857* **67** E3
Dunnellon FL, *1733* **138** C4
Dunn Loring VA, *8803* **270** A3
Dunn's Corners RI, *500* **150** C4
Dunnstown PA, *1360* **93** D3
Dunseith ND, *773* **18** C1
Dunsmuir CA, *1650* **28** C3
Dunwoody GA, *46267* **190** E2
DuPage Co. IL, *916924* **89** D1
Duplin Co. NC, *58505* **115** C4
Dupo IL, *4138* **98** A3
Dupont CO, *4500* **209** C2
Dupont PA, *2711* **261** C2
DuPont WA, *8199* **12** C3
Dupree SD, *525* **26** B2
Duquesne MO, *1763* **106** B2
Duquesne PA, *5565* **250** D3
Du Quoin IL, *6109* **98** B4
Durand IL, *1443* **74** B4
Durand MI, *3446* **76** B3
Durand WI, *1931* **67** E4
Durango CO, *16887* **40** B4
Durant IA, *1832* **87** F2
Durant MS, *2673* **126** B1

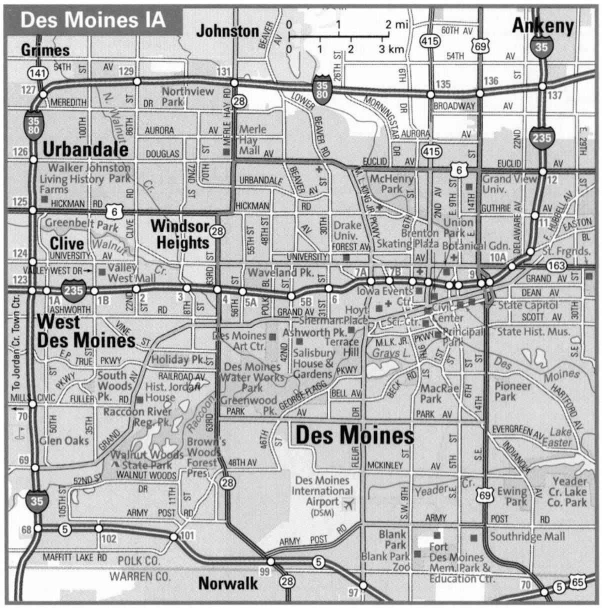

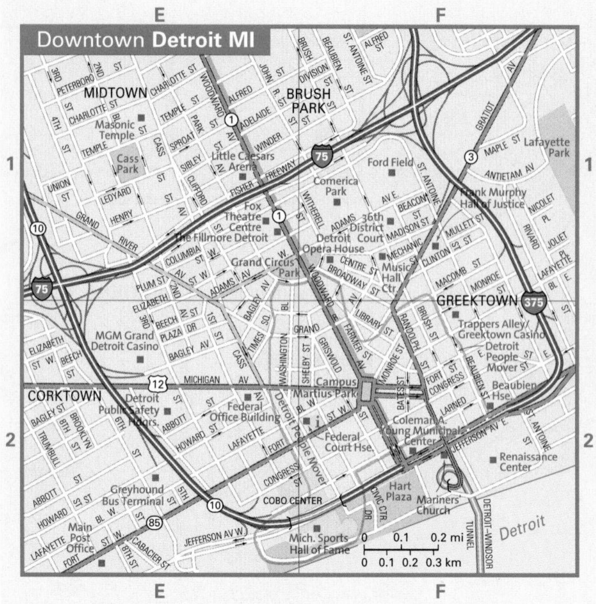

POINTS OF INTEREST
36th District Court . . . F1
Beaubien House . . . F2
Cobo Center . . . F2
Coleman A. Young Municipal Center . . . F2
Comerica Park . . . F1
Detroit Opera House . . . F1
Detroit People Mover . . . F2
Detroit Public Safety Headquarters . . . F1
Federal Court House . . . F2
Federal Office Building . . . E2
The Fillmore Detroit . . . E1
Ford Field . . . F1
Fox Theatre Centre . . . E1
Frank Murphy Hall of Justice . . . F1
Greyhound Bus Terminal . . . E2
Little Caesars Arena . . . E1
Main Post Office . . . E2
Mariners Church . . . F2
Masonic Temple . . . E1
MGM Grand Detroit Casino . . . E2
Michigan Sports Hall of Fame . . . F2
Music Hall Center . . . F1
Renaissance Center . . . F2
Trappers Alley/Greektown Casino . . . F2

Allen Park . . . B4
Auburn Hills . . . B1
Berkley . . . B2
Beverly Hills . . . B2
Bingham Farms . . . B2
Birmingham . . . B1
Bloomfield Hills . . . B1
Center Line . . . C2
Clawson . . . C2
Dearborn . . . B4
Dearborn Hts. . . . B3
Detroit . . . B3
Eastpointe . . . D2
Ecorse . . . C4
Elmstead . . . D4
Farmington . . . A2
Farmington Hills . . . A2
Ferndale . . . C2
Franklin . . . B2
Fraser . . . D2
Garden City . . . A3
Grosse Pointe . . . D3
Grosse Pointe Farms . . . D3
Grosse Pointe Park . . . D3
Grosse Pointe Shores . . . D3
Grosse Pointe Woods . . . D2
Hamtramck . . . C3
Harper Woods . . . D2
Hazel Park . . . C2
Highland Park . . . C3
Huntington Woods . . . B2
Huron Hts. . . . A1
Inkster . . . B4
Keego Harbor . . . A1
LaSalle . . . C4
Lathrup Vil. . . . B2
Lincoln Park . . . B4
Livonia . . . A3
Madison Hts. . . . C2
Melvindale . . . B4
Mt. Clemens . . . D1
Northville . . . A2
Novi . . . A2
Oak Park . . . B2
Oldcastle . . . D4
Oliver . . . C4
Orchard Lake . . . A1
Oxbow . . . A1
Pleasant Ridge . . . C2
Plymouth . . . A3
Pontiac . . . B1
Redford . . . B3
River Rouge . . . C4
Rochester Hills . . . B1
Romulus . . . A4
Roseville . . . D2
Royal Oak . . . B2
St. Clair Beach . . . D4
St. Clair Shores . . . D2
Southfield . . . B2
Sterling Hts. . . . C1
Sylvan Lake . . . B1
Taylor . . . B4
Tecumseh . . . D4
Troy . . . C1
Union Lake . . . A1
Utica . . . C1
Waldenburg . . . D1
Walled Lake . . . A2
Warren . . . C2
Wayne . . . A4
W. Acres . . . A1
Westland . . . A4
Windsor . . . C4
Wolverine Lake . . . A1

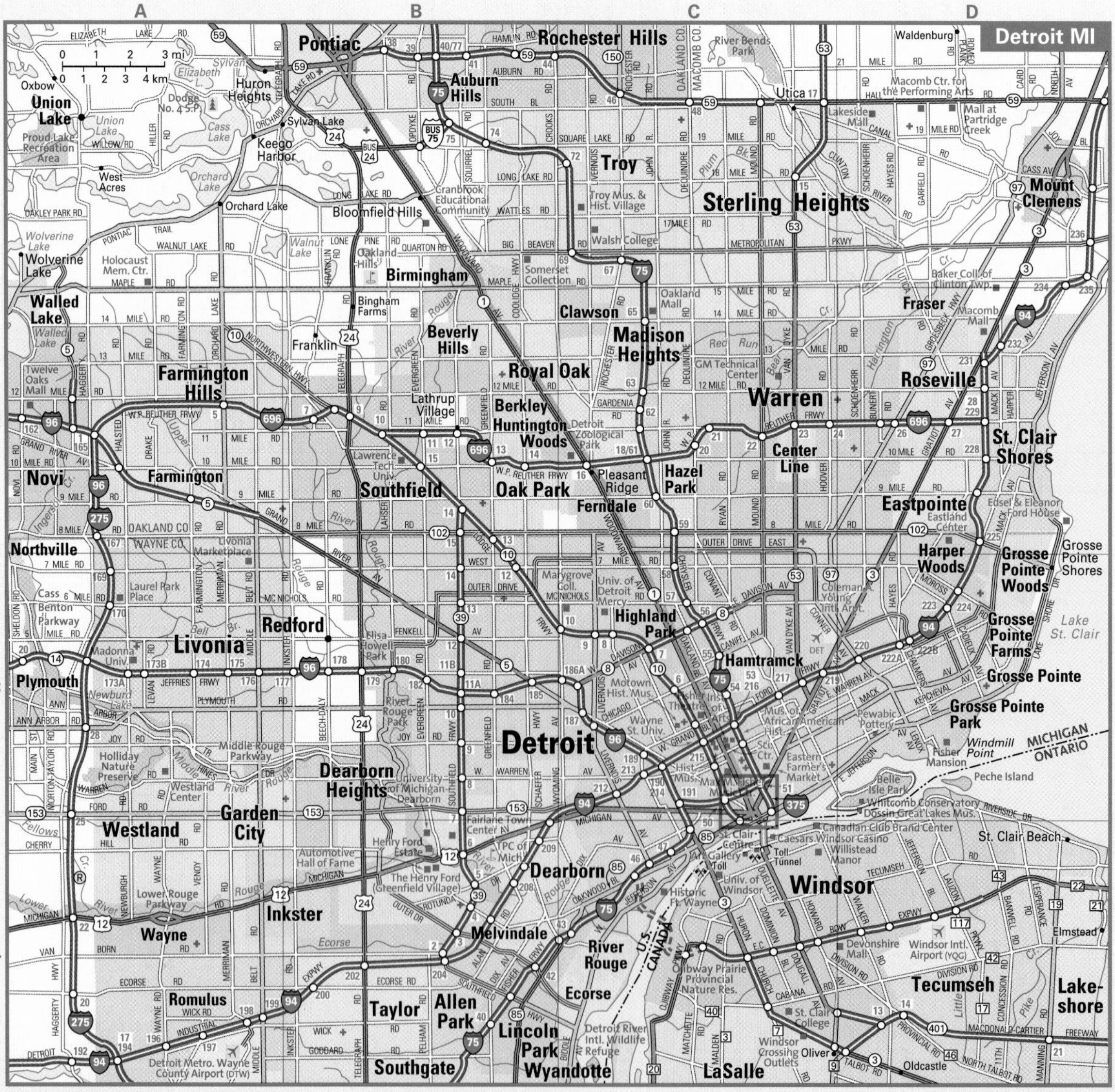

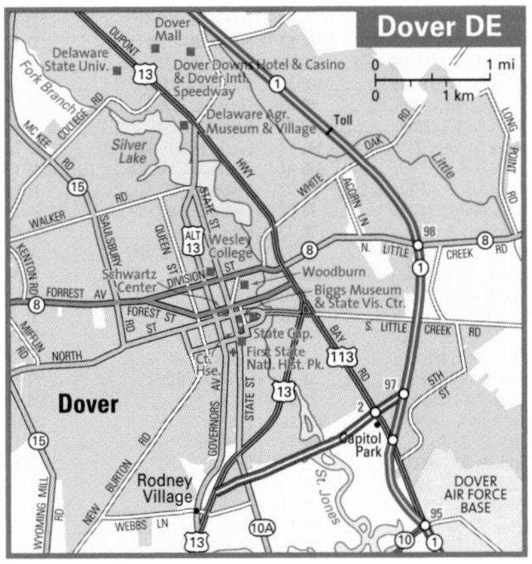

211
Durant–Elizabethtown

Entries in **bold black** indicate counties or parishes.
Entries in **bold color** indicate cities with detailed inset maps.

Durant OK, 15856 59 F1
Durham CA, 5518 36 B1
Durham CT, 2933 149 E1
Durham NH, 10345 82 A4
Durham NC, 228330 112 C4
Durham OR, 1351 251 C3
Durham Co. NC, 267587 112 C4
Duryea PA, 4917 93 F2
Dushore PA, 608 93 E2
Duson LA, 1716 133 E2
Dustin OK, 395 51 F3

Dover DE
Dover
Dover Mall
Delaware State Univ.
Dover Downs Hotel & Casino & Dover Int'l. Speedway
Delaware Agr. Museum & Village
Silver Lake
Wesley College
Schwartz Center
Woodburn
Biggs Museum & State Vis. Ctr.
State Cap.
First State Natl. Hist. Pk.
Capitol Park
Rodney Village
DOVER AIR FORCE BASE
1 mi
1 km

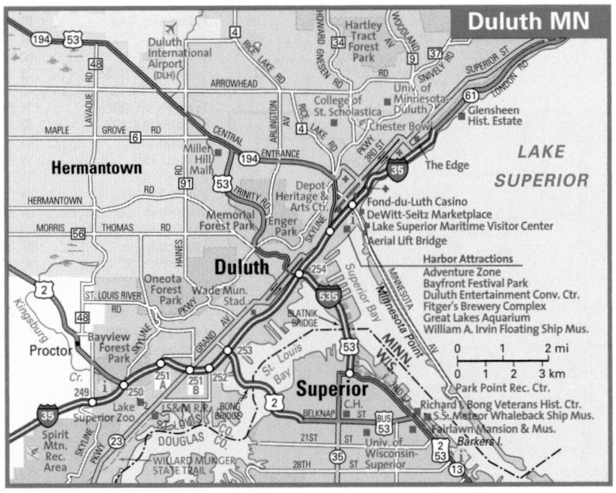

Duluth MN
Duluth International Airport (DLH)
Hartley Tract Forest Park
College of St. Scholastica
Univ. of Minnesota-Duluth
Glensheen Hist. Estate
Chester Bowl
Hermantown
LAKE SUPERIOR
The Edge
Fond-du-Luth Casino
DeWitt-Seitz Marketplace
Lake Superior Maritime Visitor Center
Aerial Lift Bridge
Harbor Attractions
Adventure Zone
Bayfront Festival Park
Duluth Entertainment Conv. Ctr.
Fitger's Brewery Complex
Great Lakes Aquarium
William A. Irvin Floating Ship Mus.
Duluth
Superior
Proctor
Bayview Forest Park
Oneota Forest Park
Wade Mun. Stad.
Enger Park
Memorial Forest Park
Lake Superior Zoo
Spirit Mtn. Rec. Area
Park Point Rec. Ctr.
Richard I. Bong Veterans Hist. Ctr.
S.S. Meteor Whaleback Ship Mus.
Fairlawn Mansion & Mus.
Barkers I.
Univ. of Wisconsin-Superior
Willard Munger State Trail

Dutchess Co. NY, 297488 148 C1
Dutch Neck NJ, 4400 147 D2
Dutton MT, 316 15 F2
Duval Co. FL, 864263 139 D2
Duval Co. TX, 11782 63 E2
Duvall WA, 6695 12 C3
Duxbury MA, 1802 151 E2
Duxbury VT, 1289 81 E2
Dwaar Kill NY, 1400 148 A1
Dwarf KY, 550 111 D1
Dwight IL, 4260 88 C3
Dyer AR, 876 116 C1
Dyer IN, 16390 89 D2
Dyer TN, 2341 108 C4
Dyer Co. TN, 38335 108 C4
Dyersburg TN, 17145 108 C4
Dyersville IA, 4058 73 F4
Dyess AR, 410 118 B1
Dysart IA, 1379 87 E1

E

Eads CO, 609 42 A3
Eagan MN, 64206 235 D4
Eagar AZ, 4885 48 A4
Eagle CO, 6508 40 C1
Eagle ID, 19908 22 B4
Eagle NE, 1024 35 F4
Eagle WI, 1950 74 C3
Eagle Bend MN, 535 66 B1
Eagle Butte SD, 1318 26 B2
Eagle Co. CO, 52197 40 C1
Eagle Grove IA, 3583 72 C4
Eagle Lake FL, 2255 140 C2
Eagle Lake ME, 625 85 D1
Eagle Lake MN, 2422 72 C1
Eagle Lake TX, 3639 61 F2
Eagle Mtn. UT, 21415 31 E4
Eagle Nest NM, 290 49 D1
Eagle Pass TX, 26248 60 B4
Eagle Pt. OR, 8469 28 C2
Eagle River MI, 71 65 F3
Eagle River WI, 1398 68 B2
Eagleton Vil. TN, 5052 110 C4
Eagleville PA, 4800 146 C2
Eagleville TN, 604 109 F4
Earle AR, 2414 118 A1
Earlham IA, 1450 86 C2
Earlimart CA, 8537 45 D4
Earlington KY, 1413 109 E2
Earlsboro OK, 628 51 F3
Earlville IL, 1701 88 C2
Earlville IA, 812 73 F4
Earlville NY, 872 79 E4
Earlville PA, 800 146 B2
Early IA, 557 72 A4
Early TX, 2762 59 D4
Early Co. GA, 11008 128 C4
Earlysville VA, 750 102 C4
Earth TX, 1065 50 A4
Easley SC, 19993 121 E2
E. Alton IL, 6301 98 A3
E. Arcadia NC, 487 123 E3
E. Arlington VT, 750 81 D4
E. Atlantic Beach NY, 2049 241 G5
E. Aurora NY, 6236 78 B4
E. Bank WV, 959 101 F4
E. Barre VT, 826 81 E2
E. Barrington NH, 400 81 F4
E. Baton Rouge Par. LA, 440171 134 A1
E. Bend NC, 612 112 A3
E. Berlin PA, 1521 103 E1
E. Bernard TX, 2272 61 F2
E. Bernstadt KY, 716 110 C2
E. Bethel MN, 11626 67 D3
E. Blackstone MA, 1600 150 C2
E. Brady PA, 942 92 A3
E. Brewster MA, 850 151 F3
E. Brewton AL, 2478 135 F1
E. Bridgewater MA, 12974 151 D2
E. Brookfield MA, 1323 150 B2
E. Brooklyn CT, 1638 150 B3
E. Brunswick NJ, 47512 147 E1
E. Butler PA, 732 92 A3
E. Camden AR, 931 117 E4
E. Canton OH, 1591 91 E3
E. Carbon UT, 1301 39 F1
E. Carroll Par. LA, 7759 126 A2
Eastchester NY, 19554 148 B3
E. Chicago IN, 29698 89 D2
E. Cleveland OH, 17843 91 E2
E. Dennis MA, 2753 151 F3
E. Douglas MA, 2557 150 C2
E. Dublin GA, 2441 129 E3
E. Dubuque IL, 1704 73 F4
E. Duke OK, 424 50 C4
E. Dundee IL, 2860 203 A2
E. Ellijay GA, 546 120 C2
E. End AR, 6998 117 E2
E. Falmouth MA, 6038 151 E4
E. Feliciana Par. LA, 20267 134 A1
E. Flat Rock NC, 4995 121 E1
E. Freehold NJ, 4894 147 E2
E. Freetown MA, 1200 151 D3
E. Gaffney SC, 3085 121 F1
E. Galesburg IL, 812 88 A3
Eastgate WA, 4958 262 B3
E. Glacier Park MT, 363 15 D2
E. Glastonbury CT, 1400 149 E1
E. Glenville NY, 6616 94 B1
E. Grand Forks MN, 8601 19 E2
E. Grand Rapids MI, 10694 215 B2
E. Greenbush NY, 4487 188 E3
E. Greenville PA, 2951 146 B1
E. Greenwich RI, 13146 150 C3
E. Gull Lake MN, 1004 64 A4
E. Haddam CT, 550 149 E1
Eastham MA, 5453 151 F3
E. Hampton CT, 2691 149 E1
Easthampton MA, 16053 150 A1
E. Hampton NY, 1083 149 F3
E. Hanover NJ, 11426 148 A3
E. Hardwick VT, 300 81 E2
E. Hartford CT, 51252 150 A3
E. Harwich MA, 4872 151 F3
E. Haven CT, 29257 149 D2
E. Helena MT, 1984 15 E4
E. Highland Park VA, 14796 254 B1
E. Holden ME, 475 83 D1
E. Hope ID, 210 14 B2
E. Ithaca NY, 2231 79 D4
E. Jordan MI, 2351 69 F3
Eastlake OH, 18577 91 E2
Eastland TX, 3960 59 D3
Eastland Co. TX, 18583 59 D3
E. Lansdowne PA, 2668 248 B3
E. Lansing MI, 48579 76 A4
E. Lebanon ME, 650 82 A4
E. Liverpool OH, 11195 91 F3
E. Longmeadow MA, 15720 150 A2
E. Los Angeles CA, 126496 228 D3
Eastman GA, 4962 129 E3
E. Marion MA, 550 151 E3
E. Marion NY, 926 149 E2
E. McKeesport PA, 2126 250 D3
E. Meadow NY, 38132 148 C4
E. Middlebury VT, 425 81 D3
E. Middletown NY, 5000 148 A1
E. Millcreek UT, 21385 257 B2
E. Millinocket ME, 1567 85 D4
E. Moline IL, 21302 88 A2
E. Montpelier VT, 80 81 E2
E. Moriches NY, 5249 149 E4
E. Mtn. TX, 580 124 B2
E. Naples FL, 23000 142 C2
E. Nassau NY, 587 94 B1
E. Newark NJ, 2406 240 B3
E. Newnan GA, 1321 128 C1
E. Northport ME, 350 82 C2
E. Northport NY, 20217 148 C3
E. Olympia WA, 900 12 C4
Easton CA, 2083 44 C3
Easton CT, 7488 148 C2
Easton ME, 1249 85 E2
Easton MD, 15945 145 D3
Easton PA, 26800 93 F3
Easton TX, 510 124 B2
E. Orange NJ, 64270 148 A4
E. Orleans MA, 6341 151 F3
Eastover NC, 3628 123 D1
Eastover SC, 813 122 B4
E. Palatka FL, 1654 139 D3
E. Palestine OH, 4721 91 F3
E. Palo Alto CA, 28155 259 D5
E. Patchogue NY, 22469 149 D4
E. Peoria IL, 23402 88 B3
E. Petersburg PA, 4506 146 A2
E. Pittsburgh PA, 1822 250 D2
Eastpoint FL, 2337 137 D3
E. Point GA, 33712 120 C4
Eastpointe MI, 32442 210 D2
Eastport ME, 1331 83 F1
Eastport NY, 1831 149 E3
E. Poultney VT, 400 81 D3
E. Prairie MO, 3176 108 C2
E. Prospect PA, 905 103 E1
E. Providence RI, 47037 150 C3
E. Quincy CA, 2489 36 C1
E. Quogue NY, 4757 149 E3
E. Randolph NY, 620 92 B1
E. Ridge TN, 20979 120 B2
E. Rochester NY, 6587 254 G2
E. Rockaway NY, 9818 147 F1
E. Rockingham NC, 3736 122 C2
E. Rutherford NJ, 8913 240 C2
E. St. Louis IL, 27006 98 A3
E. Sandwich MA, 3940 151 E3
E. Setauket NY, 15931 149 D3
E. Shoreham NY, 6666 149 D3
Eastsound WA, 750 12 C1
E. Spencer NC, 1534 112 A4
E. Stroudsburg PA, 9840 93 F3
E. Swanzey NH, 475 95 D1
E. Syracuse NY, 3084 265 B2
E. Tawakoni TX, 883 59 F2
E. Tawas MI, 2808 76 B1
E. Texas PA, 6000 146 B1
E. Thermopolis WY, 254 24 C4
E. Troy WI, 4281 74 C4
E. Vassalboro ME, 300 82 C2
Eastview MD, 650 144 B1
Eastview TN, 705 119 D2
E. Village CT, 1500 149 D2
Eastville VA, 305 114 B3
E. Wareham MA, 1700 151 E3
E. Washington PA, 2234 92 A4
E. Wenatchee WA, 13190 13 D3
E. Wilton ME, 550 82 B2
E. Winthrop ME, 650 82 B2
Eastwood LA, 4093 125 D2
E. York PA, 8777 275 F1
Eaton CO, 4365 33 E4
Eaton IN, 1805 90 A4
Eaton OH, 8407 100 B1
Eaton Co. MI, 107759 76 A4
Eaton Estates OH, 1222 91 D2
Eaton Park FL, 3000 266 E2
Eaton Rapids MI, 5214 76 A4
Eatons Neck NY, 1406 148 C3
Eatonton GA, 6480 129 E1
Eatontown NJ, 12709 147 E2
Eatonville FL, 2159 246 C1
Eatonville WA, 2758 12 C4
Eau Claire MI, 625 89 F1
Eau Claire WI, 65883 67 F4
Eau Claire Co. WI, 98736 67 F4
Ebensburg PA, 3351 92 B4
Eccles WV, 362 111 F1
Echo OR, 699 21 E1
Echols Co. GA, 4034 138 B1
Eclectic AL, 1001 128 A2
Economy PA, 8970 92 A3
Ecorse MI, 9512 210 C4
Ecru MS, 895 118 C3
Ector TX, 695 59 F1
Ector Co. TX, 137130 57 F3
Edcouch TX, 3161 63 E4
Eddington ME, 2052 83 D1
Eddy Co. NM, 53829 57 E2
Eddy Co. ND, 2385 19 D3
Eddystone PA, 2410 248 A4
Eddyville IA, 1024 87 D2
Eddyville KY, 2554 109 D2
Eden ID, 405 31 D1
Eden MD, 823 103 F4
Eden NY, 3516 78 A4
Eden NC, 15527 112 B3
Eden TX, 2766 58 C4
Eden WI, 875 74 C2
Eden WY, 281 32 A2
Eden Prairie MN, 60797 235 A4
Edenton NC, 5004 113 F4
Eden Valley MN, 1042 66 B3
Edenville NY, 650 148 A2
Edgar NE, 498 35 E4
Edgar WI, 1479 68 A4
Edgar Co. IL, 18576 99 D1
Edgard LA, 2441 134 B3
Edgartown MA, 3779 151 E4
Edgecliff Vil. TX, 2776 207 A3
Edgecombe Co. NC, 56552 113 E4
Edgefield SC, 4750 121 F4
Edgefield Co. SC, 26985 121 F4
Edgeley ND, 563 19 D4
Edgemere MD, 8669 144 C2
Edgemont SD, 774 25 F4
Edgemoor DE, 5677 146 B4
Edgerton KS, 1671 96 B3
Edgerton MN, 1189 27 F4
Edgerton MO, 546 96 B2
Edgerton OH, 2012 90 A2
Edgerton WI, 5461 74 B3
Edgerton WY, 195 25 D4
Edgewater AL, 883 195 D2
Edgewater CO, 5170 209 B3
Edgewater FL, 20750 139 E4
Edgewater NJ, 11513 240 D2
Edgewater Park NJ, 7968 147 D3
Edgewood FL, 2503 246 C3
Edgewood IN, 1913 89 F4
Edgewood IA, 864 73 F4
Edgewood KY, 8575 204 B3
Edgewood MD, 25562 145 D1
Edgewood NM, 3735 48 C3
Edgewood OH, 4432 91 F1
Edgewood PA, 3118 250 C2
Edgewood TX, 1441 124 A2
Edgewood WA, 9387 262 B5
Edina MN, 47941 67 D4
Edina MO, 1176 87 E4
Edinboro PA, 6438 92 A1
Edinburg IL, 1078 98 B1
Edinburg NJ, 900 147 D2
Edinburg ND, 196 19 E2
Edinburg TX, 77100 63 E4
Edinburg VA, 1041 102 C3
Edinburgh IN, 4480 99 F2
Edison GA, 1531 128 C4
Edison NJ, 99967 147 E1
Edisto Beach SC, 414 130 C2
Edmond OK, 81405 51 E2
Edmonds WA, 39709 12 C3
Edmondson AR, 427 118 B1
Edmonson Co. KY, 12161 109 F2
Edmonston MD, 1445 270 E2
Edmonton KY, 1595 110 A2
Edmore MI, 1201 75 F2
Edmore ND, 182 19 D2
Edmunds Co. SD, 4071 27 D2
Edmundson MO, 834 256 B1
Edna KS, 442 106 A2
Edna TX, 5499 61 F3
Edon OH, 834 90 A2
Edwards CO, 10266 40 C1
Edwards MS, 1034 126 A2
Edwardsburg MI, 1259 89 F1
Edwards Co. IL, 6721 99 D4
Edwards Co. KS, 3037 43 D4
Edwards Co. TX, 2002 60 B2
Edwardsville IL, 24293 98 B3
Edwardsville KS, 4340 96 B2
Edwardsville PA, 4816 261 A1
Effingham IL, 12328 98 C2
Effingham KS, 546 96 A1
Effingham Co. GA, 52250 130 B2
Effingham Co. IL, 34242 98 C2
Effort PA, 2269 93 F3
Egan SD, 278 27 F3
Egg Harbor City NJ, 4243 147 D4
Egypt PA, 2391 189 A1
Ehrenberg AZ, 1470 53 F3
Ehrhardt SC, 545 130 C1
Ekalaka MT, 332 25 F1
Elaine AR, 636 118 A3
Elam PA, 2000 146 B3
Elba AL, 3940 128 A4
Elba NY, 676 78 B3
Elberfeld IN, 625 99 E4
Elberta AL, 1498 135 F2
Elberta MI, 372 69 E4
Elberta UT, 256 39 E1
Elbert Co. CO, 23086 41 E2
Elbert Co. GA, 20166 121 E3
Elberton GA, 4653 121 E3
Elbow Lake MN, 1176 27 F1
Elbridge NY, 1058 79 D3
Elburn IL, 5602 88 C1
El Cajon CA, 99478 53 D4
El Campo TX, 11602 61 F3
El Cenizo TX, 249 63 D2
El Centro CA, 42598 53 E4
El Cerrito CA, 4590 229 H4
El Cerrito CA, 23549 259 B2
Eldersburg MD, 30531 144 B1
Eldon IA, 927 87 E3
Eldon MO, 4567 97 E4
Eldon OK, 368 106 B4
Eldora IA, 2732 73 D4
El Dorado AR, 18884 125 E1
Eldorado IL, 4122 109 D1
El Dorado KS, 13021 43 F4
Eldorado OK, 446 50 C4
Eldorado TX, 1951 60 B1
El Dorado Co. CA, 181058 36 C2
Eldorado Sprs. CO, 585 209 A1
El Dorado Sprs. MO, 3593 96 C4
Eldred PA, 825 92 C1
Eldridge IA, 5651 88 A2
Eleanor WV, 1518 101 E3
Electra TX, 2791 59 D1
Electric City WA, 968 13 E2
Eleele HI, 2390 152 B1
Elephant Butte NM, 1431 56 B2
Eleva WI, 670 67 F4
Elfers FL, 13986 140 B2
Elfrida AZ, 459 55 E4
Elgin AZ, 161 55 D4
Elgin IL, 108188 88 C1
Elgin IA, 683 73 E3
Elgin MN, 1089 73 E1
Elgin NE, 661 35 E2
Elgin ND, 642 18 B4
Elgin OK, 2156 51 D4
Elgin OR, 1711 21 F1
Elgin SC, 1311 122 A3
Elgin SC, 2426 122 B2
Elgin TX, 8135 61 E1
El Granada CA, 5467 259 B5
Elida OH, 1905 90 B3
Elihu KY, 650 110 B2
Elizabeth CO, 1358 41 E2
Elizabeth IL, 761 74 A4
Elizabeth LA, 532 133 E1
Elizabeth NJ, 124969 148 A4
Elizabeth PA, 1493 92 A4
Elizabeth WV, 823 101 F2
Elizabeth City NC, 18683 113 F3
Elizabeth Lake CA, 1756 52 C2
Elizabethton TN, 14176 111 E3
Elizabethtown IL, 299 109 D1
Elizabethtown KY, 28531 110 A1

El Paso TX
El Paso
Ciudad Juárez
Sunland Park
Canutillo
El Paso Mus. of Archaeology Wilderness Park
Border Patrol Mus.
Cohen Stadium
FORT BLISS CASTNER RANGE
FORT BLISS MILITARY RESERVATION
BIGGS ARMY AIRFIELD
FRANKLIN MOUNTAINS
Franklin Mountains State Park
McKelligon Canyon Amphitheater
Wyler Aerial Tramway
Fort Bliss Natl. Cem.
FORT BLISS
El Paso International Airport (ELP)
Sunland Park Racetrack & Casino
Western Playland Amusement Park
Sunland Park Mall
TEXAS
NEW MEXICO
UNITED STATES
MEXICO
Don Haskins Ctr.
Sun Bowl
Centennial Museum & Chihuahuan Desert Gardens
El Paso Mus. of Art
Conv. & Performing Arts Center
Magoffin Home S.H.S.
Chamizal Natl. Mem.
Chamizal Park
El Paso Holocaust Mus.
American Consulate
Bassett Place
Cielo Vista Mall
Ascarate Park
CHIHUAHUA
3 mi
4 km

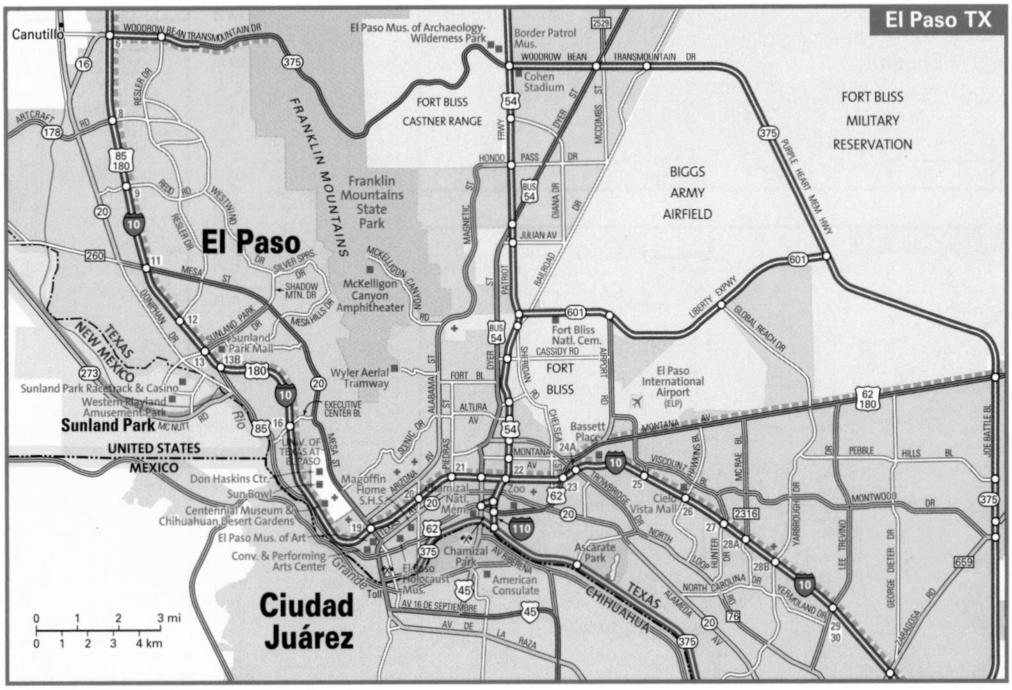

212
Elizabethtown – Ewing

Figures after entries indicate population, page number, and grid reference.

Elizabethtown NY, 754 ... 81 D2
Elizabethtown NC, 3583 ... 123 D2
Elizabethtown PA, 11545 ... 93 E4
Elizabethville PA, 1510 ... 93 D4
El Jebel CO, 3801 ... 40 C2
Elkader IA, 1273 ... 73 F3
Elk City OK, 11693 ... 50 C3
Elk Co. KS, 2882 ... 43 F4
Elk Co. PA, 31946 ... 92 B2
Elk Grove CA, 153015 ... 36 C3
Elk Grove Vil. IL, 33127 ... 203 C3
Elkhart IN, 50949 ... 89 F2
Elkhart KS, 2205 ... 50 A1
Elkhart TX, 1371 ... 124 A4
Elkhart Co. IN, 197559 ... 89 F2
Elkhart Lake WI, 967 ... 74 C2
Elkhorn CA, 1565 ... 236 E2
Elk Horn IA, 662 ... 86 B2
Elkhorn WI, 10084 ... 74 C4
Elkhorn City KY, 982 ... 111 E1
Elkin NC, 4001 ... 112 A3
Elkins AR, 2648 ... 106 C4
Elkins WV, 7094 ... 102 A3
Elkland PA, 1821 ... 93 D1
Elkmont AL, 434 ... 119 F2
Elk Mound WI, 878 ... 67 E4
Elko NV, 18297 ... 30 B4
Elko Co. NV, 48818 ... 30 C3
Elko New Market MN, 4110 ... 67 D4
Elk Pt. SD, 1963 ... 35 F1
Elk Rapids MI, 1642 ... 69 F4
Elkridge MD, 15593 ... 144 C2
Elk Ridge UT, 2436 ... 39 E1
Elk River MN, 22974 ... 66 C3
Elk Run Hts. IA, 1117 ... 73 E4
Elkton KY, 2062 ... 109 E2
Elkton MD, 15443 ... 145 E1
Elkton MI, 808 ... 76 C2
Elkton SD, 736 ... 27 F3
Elkton TN, 578 ... 119 F2
Elkton VA, 2726 ... 102 C3
Elkview WV, 1222 ... 101 F3
Elkville IL, 928 ... 98 B4
El Lago TX, 2706 ... 132 B3
Ellaville GA, 1812 ... 129 D3
Ellenboro NC, 873 ... 121 F1
Ellenboro WV, 363 ... 101 F2
Ellendale DE, 381 ... 145 F3
Ellendale MN, 691 ... 72 C2
Ellendale ND, 1394 ... 27 D1
Ellensburg WA, 18174 ... 13 D4
Ellenton FL, 4275 ... 266 B4
Ellenville NY, 4135 ... 94 A3
Ellerbe NC, 1054 ... 122 C2
Ellerslie MD, 572 ... 102 C1
Ellettsville IN, 6378 ... 99 F2
Ellicott NY, 2200 ... 78 B4
Ellicott City MD, 65834 ... 144 C2
Ellijay GA, 1619 ... 120 C2
Ellington CT, 12921 ... 150 A3
Ellington MO, 987 ... 108 A2
Ellinwood KS, 2131 ... 43 D3
Elliott Co. KY, 7852 ... 101 D4
Ellis KS, 2062 ... 42 C2
Ellis Co. KS, 28452 ... 43 D2
Ellis Co. OK, 4151 ... 50 C2
Ellis Co. TX, 149610 ... 59 F3
Ellisport WA, 1200 ... 262 A4
Elliston MT, 219 ... 15 E4
Elliston VA, 902 ... 112 B2
Ellisville MS, 4448 ... 126 C4
Ellisville MO, 9133 ... 256 A2
Elloree SC, 692 ... 122 B4
Ellsworth IA, 531 ... 72 C4
Ellsworth KS, 3120 ... 43 E2
Ellsworth ME, 7741 ... 83 D2
Ellsworth MI, 349 ... 69 F3
Ellsworth MN, 463 ... 27 F4
Ellsworth PA, 1027 ... 92 A4
Ellsworth WI, 3284 ... 67 E4
Ellsworth Co. KS, 6497 ... 43 E3
Ellwood City PA, 7921 ... 91 F3
Elma IA, 546 ... 73 D3
Elma NY, 2571 ... 78 B3
Elma WA, 3107 ... 12 B4
Elm City NC, 1298 ... 113 D4
Elm Creek NE, 901 ... 35 D4
Elmendorf TX, 1488 ... 61 D3
Elmer NJ, 1395 ... 145 F1
Elm Grove WI, 5934 ... 234 B2
Elmhurst IL, 44121 ... 89 D1
Elmira NY, 29200 ... 93 D1
El Mirage AZ, 31797 ... 249 A1
Elmira Hts. NY, 4097 ... 93 D1
Elm Mott TX, 1200 ... 59 E4
Elmo UT, 418 ... 39 F2
Elmont NY, 33198 ... 148 C4
Elmont VA, 500 ... 113 E1
El Monte CA, 113475 ... 228 E2
Elmore MN, 663 ... 72 C2
Elmore OH, 1410 ... 90 C2
Elmore City OK, 697 ... 51 E4
Elmore Co. AL, 79303 ... 128 A2
Elmore Co. ID, 27038 ... 22 B4
Elm Sprs. AR, 1535 ... 106 C3
Elmville CT, 1300 ... 150 B3
Elmwood IL, 2097 ... 88 A3
Elmwood NE, 634 ... 35 F4
Elmwood WI, 817 ... 67 E4
Elmwood Park IL, 24883 ... 203 D4
Elmwood Park NJ, 19403 ... 240 C1
Elmwood Place OH, 2188 ... 204 B2
Elnora IN, 640 ... 99 E3
Elnora NY, 2700 ... 94 B1
Elon NC, 9419 ... 112 C4
Eloy AZ, 16631 ... 54 C2
El Paso IL, 2810 ... 88 B3
El Paso TX, 649121 ... 56 C4
El Paso Co. CO, 622263 ... 41 E2
El Paso Co. TX, 800647 ... 56 C4
El Portal FL, 2325 ... 233 B4
El Prado NM, 400 ... 49 D1
El Reno OK, 16749 ... 51 E3
El Rio CA, 7198 ... 52 B2
El Rito NM, 808 ... 48 C2
Elroy WI, 1442 ... 74 A2
Elsa TX, 5660 ... 63 E4
Elsah IL, 673 ... 98 A2
Elsberry MO, 1934 ... 98 A2
El Segundo CA, 16654 ... 228 C3
Elsie MI, 966 ... 76 A3
Elsinore UT, 847 ... 39 E3
Elsmere DE, 6131 ... 146 B4
Elsmere KY, 8451 ... 100 B2
Elsmere NY, 3200 ... 188 D3
El Sobrante CA, 12669 ... 259 C1
Elton LA, 1128 ... 133 E2
Elvaton MD, 3500 ... 193 C5
Elverson PA, 1225 ... 146 B2
Elwood IL, 2279 ... 89 D2
Elwood IN, 8614 ... 89 F4
Elwood KS, 1224 ... 96 B1
Elwood NE, 707 ... 34 C4
Elwood NJ, 1437 ... 147 D4
Elwood UT, 1034 ... 31 E3
Ely IA, 1776 ... 87 E1
Ely MN, 3460 ... 64 C2
Ely NV, 4255 ... 38 B2
Elyria OH, 54533 ... 91 D2
Elysburg PA, 2194 ... 93 E3
Elysian MN, 652 ... 72 C1
Emanuel Co. GA, 22598 ... 129 F2
Emerado ND, 414 ... 19 E2
Emerald Isle NC, 3655 ... 115 D4
Emerson GA, 1470 ... 120 C3
Emerson NE, 840 ... 35 F2
Emerson NJ, 7401 ... 148 B3
Emery SD, 447 ... 27 E4
Emery UT, 288 ... 39 E2
Emery Co. UT, 10976 ... 39 F2
Emery Mills ME, 350 ... 82 A4
Emeryville CA, 10080 ... 259 C2
Emigsville PA, 2672 ... 103 E1
Emily MN, 813 ... 64 B4
Eminence KY, 2498 ... 100 A4
Eminence MO, 600 ... 107 F2
Emlenton PA, 625 ... 92 A2
Emmaus PA, 11211 ... 146 B1
Emmet AR, 518 ... 117 D4
Emmet Co. IA, 10302 ... 72 B3
Emmet Co. MI, 32694 ... 70 B3
Emmetsburg IA, 3904 ... 72 B3
Emmett ID, 6557 ... 22 B4
Emmitsburg MD, 2814 ... 103 D1
Emmonak AK, 762 ... 154 B2
Emmons Co. ND, 3550 ... 18 C4
Emmorton MD, 4000 ... 145 D1
Emory TX, 1239 ... 124 A1
Emory VA, 1251 ... 111 F2
Empire CO, 282 ... 41 D1
Empire LA, 993 ... 134 C4
Empire NV, 217 ... 29 E4
Empire City OK, 955 ... 51 E4
Emporia KS, 24916 ... 43 F3
Emporia VA, 5927 ... 113 E3
Emporium PA, 2073 ... 92 C2
Emsworth PA, 2449 ... 250 A1
Encampment WY, 450 ... 33 D3
Encinal TX, 559 ... 60 C4
Encinitas CA, 59518 ... 53 D4
Enderlin ND, 886 ... 19 E4
Endicott NY, 13392 ... 93 E1
Endicott WA, 289 ... 13 F4
Endwell NY, 11446 ... 93 E1
Energy IL, 1146 ... 108 C1
Enfield CT, 45441 ... 150 A2
Enfield IL, 596 ... 99 D4
Enfield NH, 1540 ... 81 E3
Enfield NC, 2532 ... 113 E4
Enfield Ctr. NH, 600 ... 81 E3
England AR, 2825 ... 117 E2
Englewood CO, 30255 ... 41 E1
Englewood FL, 14863 ... 140 C4
Englewood NJ, 27147 ... 148 B3
Englewood OH, 13465 ... 100 B1
Englewood TN, 1532 ... 120 C1
Englewood Beach FL, 1000 ... 140 C4
Englewood Cliffs NJ, 5281 ... 240 D1
English IN, 645 ... 99 F4
Englishtown NJ, 1847 ... 147 E2
Enhaut PA, 1007 ... 218 C2
Enid OK, 49379 ... 51 E1
Enigma GA, 1278 ... 129 E4
Enka NC, 1500 ... 121 E1
Ennis MT, 838 ... 23 E2
Ennis TX, 18513 ... 59 F3
Enoch UT, 5803 ... 39 D4
Enochville NC, 2925 ... 122 B1
Enola PA, 6111 ... 218 A1
Enon OH, 2415 ... 100 C1
Enoree SC, 665 ... 121 F2
Enosburg Falls VT, 1329 ... 81 D1
Ensley FL, 20602 ... 135 F2
Ensor KY, 500 ... 109 E1
Enterprise AL, 26562 ... 128 B4
Enterprise KS, 855 ... 43 F2
Enterprise MS, 526 ... 127 D3
Enterprise OR, 1940 ... 22 A2
Enterprise UT, 605 ... 38 C4
Enterprise WV, 961 ... 102 A2
Entiat WA, 1112 ... 13 D3
Enumclaw WA, 10669 ... 12 C3
Ephraim UT, 6135 ... 39 E2
Ephrata PA, 13394 ... 146 A2
Ephrata WA, 7664 ... 13 E3
Epping NH, 1681 ... 81 F4
Epps LA, 854 ... 125 F2
Epworth IA, 1860 ... 73 F4
Epworth Hts. OH, 3300 ... 204 C1
Equality IL, 595 ... 109 D1
Erath LA, 2114 ... 133 F3
Erath Co. TX, 37890 ... 59 D3
Erda UT, 4642 ... 31 E4
Erial NJ, 6200 ... 146 C4
Erick OK, 1052 ... 50 C3
Erie CO, 18135 ... 209 B1
Erie IL, 1602 ... 88 A2
Erie KS, 1150 ... 106 A1
Erie PA, 101786 ... 92 A1
Erie Co. NY, 919040 ... 78 B4
Erie Co. OH, 77079 ... 91 D2
Erie Co. PA, 280566 ... 92 A1
Erin TN, 1324 ... 109 E3
Erlanger KY, 18082 ... 100 B2
Erwin NC, 4405 ... 123 D1
Erwin TN, 6097 ... 111 E4
Erwinville LA, 2192 ... 134 A2
Escalante UT, 797 ... 39 E4
Escalon CA, 7132 ... 36 C4
Escambia Co. AL, 38319 ... 136 A1
Escambia Co. FL, 297619 ... 135 F1
Escanaba MI, 12616 ... 69 D2
Escatawpa MS, 3722 ... 195 C1
Escobares TX, 1188 ... 63 D4
Escondido CA, 143911 ... 53 D4
Esko MN, 1869 ... 64 C4
Eskridge KS, 534 ... 43 F2
Esmeralda Co. NV, 783 ... 37 F4
Espanola NM, 10224 ... 49 D2
Espanong NJ, 2700 ... 148 A3
Esparto CA, 3108 ... 36 B2
Espy PA, 1642 ... 93 E3
Essex CT, 6783 ... 149 E2
Essex IA, 798 ... 86 A3
Essex MD, 39262 ... 144 C2
Essex MA, 1471 ... 151 F1
Essex MO, 472 ... 108 B2
Essex Co. MA, 743159 ... 151 F1
Essex Co. NJ, 783969 ... 148 A3
Essex Co. NY, 39370 ... 80 C3
Essex Co. VT, 6306 ... 81 F1
Essex Co. VA, 11151 ... 103 E4
Essex Fells NJ, 2113 ... 240 A2
Essex Jct. VT, 9271 ... 81 D2
Essexville MI, 3478 ... 76 B2
Estacada OR, 2695 ... 20 C2
Estancia NM, 1655 ... 49 D4
Estelle LA, 16377 ... 239 C2
Estelline SD, 768 ... 27 F3
Estell Manor NJ, 1735 ... 104 C3
Ester AK, 2422 ... 154 C2
Estero FL, 22612 ... 142 C1
Estes Park CO, 5858 ... 33 E4
Estherville IA, 6360 ... 72 B2
Estherwood LA, 889 ... 133 E2
Estill SC, 2040 ... 130 B2
Estill Co. KY, 14672 ... 110 C1
Estill Sprs. TN, 2055 ... 120 A1
Estral Beach MI, 418 ... 90 C1
Ethan SD, 331 ... 27 E4
Ethel MS, 418 ... 126 C1
Ethete WY, 1553 ... 32 B1
Ethridge TN, 465 ... 119 E1
Etna CA, 737 ... 28 B3
Etna PA, 3451 ... 250 C1
Etna Green IN, 586 ... 89 F2
Etowah NC, 6944 ... 121 E1
Etowah TN, 3490 ... 120 C1
Etowah Co. AL, 104430 ... 120 A3
Ettrick VA, 6682 ... 113 E2
Ettrick WI, 524 ... 73 F1
Eubank KY, 319 ... 110 B2
Euclid OH, 48920 ... 91 E2
Eudora AR, 2269 ... 126 A1
Eudora KS, 6136 ... 96 B3
Eufaula AL, 13137 ... 128 B3
Eufaula OK, 2813 ... 116 A1
Eugene OR, 156185 ... 20 B4
Euharlee GA, 4136 ... 120 B3
Euless TX, 51277 ... 207 C2
Eunice LA, 10398 ... 133 E2
Eunice NM, 2922 ... 57 F3
Eupora MS, 2197 ... 118 C4
Eureka CA, 27191 ... 28 A4
Eureka IL, 5295 ... 88 B3
Eureka KS, 2633 ... 43 F4
Eureka MO, 10189 ... 98 A3
Eureka MT, 1037 ... 14 C1
Eureka NV, 610 ... 38 A1
Eureka SD, 868 ... 27 D1
Eureka UT, 669 ... 39 E1
Eureka Co. NV, 1987 ... 30 B4
Eureka Mill SC, 1476 ... 122 A2
Eureka Sprs. AR, 2073 ... 106 C3
Eustace TX, 991 ... 59 F3
Eustis FL, 18558 ... 140 C1
Eustis NE, 401 ... 34 C4
Eutaw AL, 2934 ... 127 E2
Eva AL, 519 ... 119 F3
Evadale TX, 1483 ... 132 C2
Evangeline Par. LA, 33984 ... 133 E1
Evans CO, 18537 ... 33 E4
Evans GA, 29011 ... 121 F4
Evans WV, 750 ... 101 E3
Evans City PA, 1833 ... 92 A3
Evans Co. GA, 11000 ... 130 B3
Evansdale IA, 4751 ... 73 E4
Evans Mills NY, 621 ... 79 E1
Evanston IL, 74486 ... 89 D1
Evanston WY, 12359 ... 31 F3
Evansville IL, 701 ... 98 B4
Evansville IN, 117429 ... 99 D4
Evansville MN, 612 ... 66 A2
Evansville WI, 5012 ... 74 B4
Evansville WY, 2544 ... 33 D1
Evaro MT, 322 ... 15 D4
Evart MI, 1903 ... 75 F1
Evarts KY, 962 ... 111 D2
Eveleth MN, 3718 ... 64 C3
Evendale OH, 2767 ... 204 B1
Evening Shade AR, 432 ... 107 F4
Everett MA, 41667 ... 197 C1
Everett PA, 1834 ... 102 C1
Everett WA, 103019 ... 12 C2
Everglades City FL, 479 ... 143 D2
Evergreen AL, 3944 ... 127 F4
Evergreen CO, 9038 ... 41 D1
Evergreen MT, 7616 ... 15 D2
Evergreen Park IL, 19852 ... 203 D5
Everly IA, 603 ... 72 A3
Everman TX, 6108 ... 207 B3
Everson PA, 793 ... 92 A4
Everson WA, 2481 ... 12 C1
Evesboro NJ, 2400 ... 147 D3
Ewa Beach HI, 14955 ... 152 A3
Ewa Villages HI, 6108 ... 152 A3
Ewing NE, 387 ... 35 E2
Ewing NJ, 35790 ... 147 D2

Erie PA

Fargo ND

Eugene OR
To Eugene Airport (EUG)
Santa Clara
Springfield
Eugene
Valley River Center
Owen Rose Garden
Gillespie Butte
5th St. Pub. Mkt.
Alton Science Factory
Springfield Museum
Glenwood
Hendricks Park
Maude Kerns Art Ctr.
Amazon Park
Rhododendron Garden
New Hope Christian College
Morse Ranch Park
Historical Museum
Westmoreland Park
McKenzie
Willamette

Evansville IN
Evansville
Evansville Regional Airport (EVV)
Igleheart Park
Moutoux Park
Kasson
Mesker Park
Mesker Amphitheatre
Mesker Park Zoo & Bot. Gdn.
Kleymeyer Park
Garvin Park
Bosse Field
Wesselman Woods Nat. Pres.
Eastland Mall
Univ. of Evansville
Victory Theatre
Tropicana Evansville
Evansville Hist. Dist.
Mus. of Arts, History & Science
Burdette Park Aquatic Center
Angel Mounds St. Hist. Site
Ohio
WARRICK CO.
VANDERBURGH CO.

Fayetteville AR
Springdale
Tontitown
Johnson
Fayetteville
Farmington
Shiloh Mus.
Arts Ctr. of the Ozarks
Arkansas & Missouri R.R.
Randal Tyson Park
Lake Fayetteville Park
Botanical Gdn. of the Ozarks
Northwest Arkansas Mall
County Fairgrounds
EXP. FARM
UNIV. OF ARKANSAS
Razorback Stad.
Bud Walton Arena
Old Main
Hist. Dist.
Ct. Hse.
Walton Arts Ctr.
Fayetteville Natl. Cem.
Combs Park
Lake Sequoyah
Kessler Mtn.
Clear Cr.

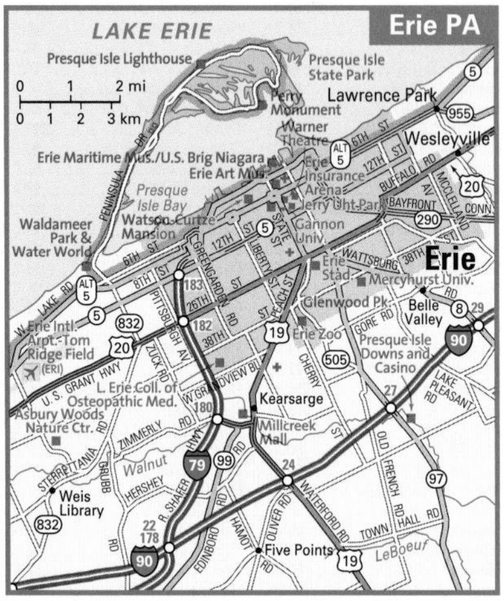

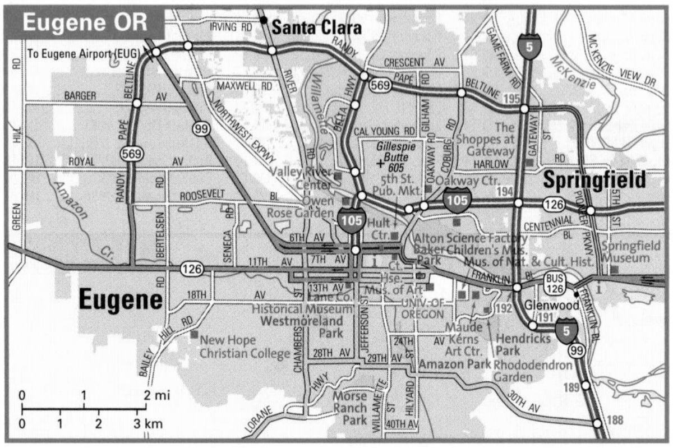

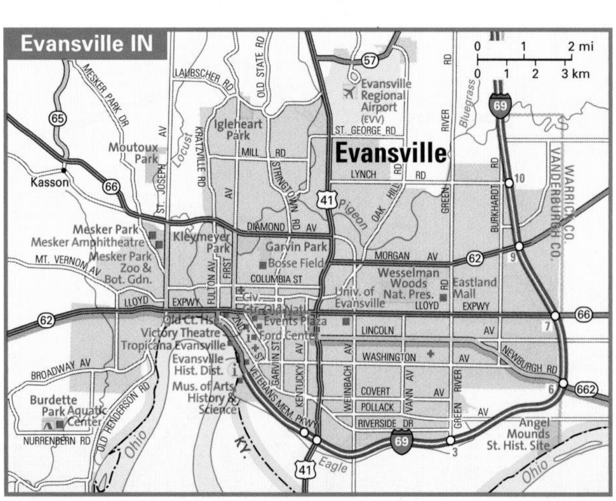

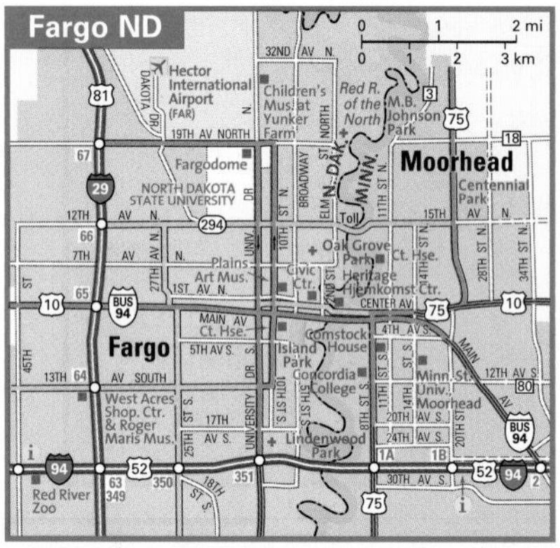

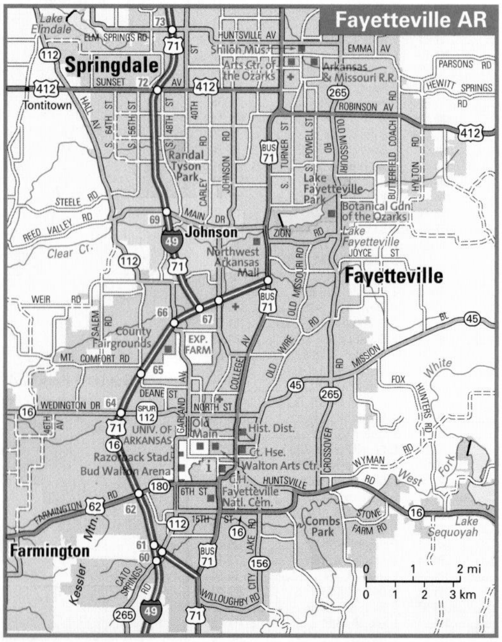

Entries in **bold black** indicate counties or parishes.
Entries in **bold color** indicate cities with detailed inset maps.

Ewing VA, 439 111 D3
Excel AL, 723 127 F4
Excelsior Sprs. MO, 11084 96 C2
Exeter CA, 10334 45 D3
Exeter MO, 772 106 C3
Exeter NE, 591 35 E4
Exeter NH, 9242 82 A4
Exeter PA, 5652 261 C1
Exeter RI, 6425 150 C4
Exira IA, 840 86 B2
Exmore VA, 1460 114 B3
Experiment GA, 2894 129 D1
Exton PA, 4842 146 B3
Eyota MN, 1977 73 E1

F

Fabens TX, 8257 56 C4
Factoryville PA, 1158 93 F2
Fairacres NM, 824 56 B3
Fairbank IA, 1113 73 E4
Fairbanks AK, 31535 154 C2
Fairbanks FL, 750 138 C3
Fairbanks ME, 700 82 B1
Fair Bluff NC, 951 123 D3
Fairborn OH, 32352 100 C1
Fairburn GA, 12950 120 C4
Fairbury IL, 3757 88 C3
Fairbury NE, 3942 43 E1
Fairchance PA, 1975 102 B1
Fairchild WI, 550 67 F4
Fairchilds TX, 763 132 A4
Fairfax CA, 7441 36 B3
Fairfax DE, 2300 274 E1
Fairfax IA, 2123 87 E1
Fairfax MN, 1235 66 B4
Fairfax MO, 638 86 A4
Fairfax OH, 1699 204 C2
Fairfax OK, 1380 51 F1
Fairfax SC, 2025 130 B1
Fairfax VT, 3765 81 D1
Fairfax VA, 22565 144 A3
Fairfax Co. VA, 1081726 144 A3
Fairfield AL, 11117 119 F4
Fairfield CA, 105321 36 B3
Fairfield CT, 59404 149 D2
Fairfield ID, 416 22 C4
Fairfield IL, 5154 99 D4
Fairfield IA, 9464 87 E3
Fairfield ME, 2638 82 C2
Fairfield MT, 708 15 E3
Fairfield NE, 387 35 E4
Fairfield NJ, 7466 240 A1
Fairfield OH, 42510 100 B2
Fairfield TX, 2951 59 F4
Fairfield WA, 612 14 B3
Fairfield Bay AR, 2338 117 E1
Fairfield Co. CT, 916829 149 D2
Fairfield Co. OH, 146156 101 D1
Fairfield Co. SC, 23956 122 A3
Fairfield Glade TN, 6989 110 B4
Fairgrove MI, 563 76 B2
Fair Grove MO, 1393 107 D1
Fairhaven MA, 16112 151 D3
Fair Haven MI, 1500 76 C4
Fair Haven NJ, 6121 147 E2
Fair Haven NY, 745 79 D3
Fair Haven VT, 2269 81 D3
Fairhope AL, 15326 135 E2
Fairland IN, 315 99 F1
Fairland MD, 23681 144 B2
Fairland OK, 1057 106 B2
Fair Lawn NJ, 32457 148 B3
Fairlawn OH, 7437 188 A1
Fairlawn VA, 2367 112 A2
Fairlea WV, 1747 112 A1
Fairless Hills PA, 8466 147 D2
Fairmead CA, 1447 44 C2
Fairmont MN, 10666 72 B2
Fairmont NE, 560 35 E4
Fairmont NC, 2663 123 D3
Fairmont WV, 18704 102 A2
Fairmont City IL, 2635 256 C2
Fairmount GA, 720 120 C3
Fairmount IL, 642 99 D1
Fairmount IN, 2954 89 F4
Fairmount MD, 457 103 F4
Fairmount NY, 10224 79 D3
Fairmount ND, 367 27 F1
Fairmount TN, 2825 120 B1
Fairmount Hts. MD, 1494 270 E3
Fair Oaks CA, 30912 255 C1
Fair Oaks GA, 8225 120 C4
Fair Oaks Ranch TX, 5986 61 D2
Fair Plain MI, 7631 89 E1
Fairplains NC, 2120 111 F3
Fairplay CO, 679 41 D2
Fairport NY, 5353 78 C3
Fairport Harbor OH, 3109 91 E1
Fairton NJ, 1264 145 F1
Fairview AL, 446 119 F3
Fairview GA, 6769 120 B2
Fairview MI, 600 70 C4
Fairview MT, 840 17 F2
Fairview NJ, 13835 148 B3
Fairview NC, 2678 121 E1
Fairview NC, 3300 122 B1
Fairview OK, 2579 51 D2
Fairview OR, 8920 20 C2
Fairview PA, 198 91 F1
Fairview TN, 7720 109 E4
Fairview TX, 7248 59 F2
Fairview UT, 1247 39 E1
Fairview WV, 408 102 A1
Fairview WY, 275 31 F1
Fairview Hts. IL, 17078 98 B3
Fairview Park IN, 1386 99 E1
Fairview Park OH, 16826 204 D2
Fairview Shores FL, 10239 246 C1
Fairway KS, 3882 224 B3
Faison NC, 961 123 E1
Faith NC, 807 122 B1
Faith SD, 421 26 B2
Falconer NY, 2420 92 B1
Falcon Hts. MN, 5321 235 C2
Falfurrias TX, 4981 63 E3
Falkville AL, 1279 119 F3
Fall Branch TN, 1291 111 E3
Fallbrook CA, 30534 53 D3
Fall City WA, 1993 12 C3
Fall Creek WI, 1315 67 F4
Falling Waters WV, 876 103 D1
Fallon NV, 8606 37 E1
Fallon Co. MT, 2890 17 F4
Fall River MA, 88857 151 D3
Fall River WI, 1712 74 B2
Fall River Co. SD, 7094 33 F1
Fall River Mills CA, 573 29 D3
Falls Church VA, 12332 144 B3
Falls City NE, 4325 86 A4
Falls City OR, 947 20 B2
Falls City TX, 611 61 E3
Falls Co. TX, 17866 59 F4
Falls Creek PA, 1037 92 B3
Fallston MD, 8958 144 C1
Fallston NC, 607 122 A1
Falmouth KY, 2169 100 B3
Falmouth MA, 3799 151 E4
Falmouth VA, 4274 103 D4
Falmouth Foreside ME, 1511 82 B3
Fancy Farm KY, 458 108 C2
Fannett TX, 2252 132 C3
Fannin Co. GA, 23682 120 C2
Fannin Co. TX, 33915 59 F1
Fanning Sprs. FL, 764 138 B3
Fanwood NJ, 7318 147 E1
Fargo ND, 105549 19 F4
Far Hills NJ, 919 148 A4
Faribault MN, 23352 73 D1
Faribault Co. MN, 14553 72 C2
Farley IA, 1537 73 F4
Farmer City IL, 2037 88 C4
Farmers Branch TX, 28616 207 D1
Farmersburg IN, 1118 99 E2
Farmers Mills NY, 800 148 C1
Farmersville CA, 10588 45 D3
Farmersville IL, 724 98 B2
Farmersville OH, 1009 100 B1
Farmersville PA, 991 189 B1
Farmersville TX, 3301 59 F2
Farmerville LA, 3860 125 E2
Farmingdale ME, 1970 82 C2
Farmingdale NJ, 1329 147 E2
Farmingdale NY, 8189 148 C4
Farmington AR, 5974 106 C4
Farmington CT, 24941 94 C3
Farmington IL, 2448 88 A3
Farmington IA, 664 87 E3
Farmington ME, 4288 82 B1
Farmington MI, 10372 210 A2
Farmington MN, 21086 67 D4
Farmington MS, 2186 119 D2
Farmington MO, 16240 108 A1
Farmington NH, 3885 81 F4
Farmington NM, 45877 48 B1
Farmington UT, 18275 31 E3
Farmington WV, 375 102 A1
Farmington Hills MI, 79740 210 A2
Farmingville NY, 15481 149 D3
Farmland IN, 1333 90 A4
Farmville NC, 4654 115 C2
Farmville VA, 8216 113 D2
Farragut IA, 485 86 A3
Farragut TN, 20676 110 C4
Farrell PA, 5111 91 F2
Farr West UT, 5928 244 A1
Farson WY, 313 32 A2
Farwell MI, 871 76 A2
Farwell TX, 1363 49 F4
Faulk Co. SD, 2364 27 D2
Faulkner Co. AR, 113237 117 E1
Faulkton SD, 736 27 D2
Fauquier Co. VA, 65203 144 A4
Favoretta FL, 650 139 E4
Fayette AL, 4619 119 E4
Fayette IA, 1338 73 E3
Fayette MS, 1614 126 A4
Fayette MO, 2688 97 D2
Fayette OH, 1283 90 B2
Fayette Co. AL, 17241 119 E4
Fayette Co. GA, 106567 120 C4
Fayette Co. IL, 22140 98 C2
Fayette Co. IN, 24277 100 A1
Fayette Co. IA, 20880 73 E4
Fayette Co. KY, 295803 100 B4
Fayette Co. OH, 29030 100 C1
Fayette Co. PA, 136606 102 B1
Fayette Co. TN, 38413 118 C1
Fayette Co. TX, 24554 61 E2
Fayette Co. WV, 46039 101 F4
Fayetteville AR, 73580 106 C4
Fayetteville GA, 15945 120 C4
Fayetteville NY, 4373 79 E3
Fayetteville NC, 200564 123 D2
Fayetteville PA, 3128 103 D1
Fayetteville TN, 6827 119 F1
Fayetteville WV, 2892 101 F4
Fearrington Vil. NC, 2339 112 C4
Feasterville PA, 3074 248 D1
Federal Hts. CO, 11467 209 B2
Federalsburg MD, 2739 145 E4
Federal Way WA, 89306 12 C3
Felicity OH, 818 100 C3
Felida WA, 7385 20 C1
Fellowship NJ, 4900 147 D3
Fellsmere FL, 5197 141 E3
Felton CA, 4057 236 D1
Felton DE, 1298 145 E3
Fennimore WI, 2497 73 F3
Fennville MI, 1398 75 E4
Fenton MI, 11756 76 B4
Fenton MO, 4022 256 A3
Fentress Co. TN, 17959 110 B3
Fenwick Island DE, 379 114 C1
Ferdinand IN, 2157 99 E4
Fergus Co. MT, 11586 16 B3
Fergus Falls MN, 13138 19 F4
Ferguson KY, 924 110 B2
Ferguson MO, 21203 256 B1
Fernandina Beach FL, 11487 139 D1
Fernan Lake Vil. ID, 186 14 B3
Ferndale CA, 1371 28 A4
Ferndale MD, 16746 193 C4
Ferndale MI, 19900 210 C2
Ferndale PA, 1636 146 C1
Ferndale WA, 11415 12 C1
Fernley NV, 19368 37 E1
Fern Park FL, 7704 246 C1
Ferrell NJ, 1100 146 C4
Ferrellsburg WV, 500 101 E4
Ferrelview MO, 451 96 B2
Ferriday LA, 3511 125 F4
Ferris TX, 2436 59 F3
Ferron UT, 1626 39 E2
Ferrum VA, 2043 112 B2
Ferry Co. WA, 7551 13 F2
Ferry Pass FL, 28921 135 F2
Ferrysburg MI, 2892 75 E3
Fertile MN, 842 19 F3
Fessenden ND, 479 18 C3
Festus MO, 11602 98 A4
Fieldale VA, 879 112 B3
Fielding UT, 455 31 E2
Fieldsboro NJ, 540 147 D2
Fife WA, 9173 262 B5
Fife Lake MI, 443 69 F4
Filer ID, 2508 30 C1
Fillmore CA, 15002 52 B2
Fillmore IN, 533 99 E1
Fillmore UT, 2435 39 D2
Fillmore Co. MN, 20866 73 E2
Fillmore Co. NE, 5890 35 E4
Fincastle KY, 817 230 F1
Fincastle VA, 353 112 B1
Findlay IL, 683 98 C1
Findlay OH, 41202 90 C3
Finley ND, 445 19 E3
Finley WA, 6012 21 E1
Finney Co. KS, 36776 42 B3
Finneytown OH, 12741 204 B2
Fircrest WA, 6497 262 A5
Firebaugh CA, 7549 44 C2
Firth ID, 477 23 E4
Firth NE, 590 35 F4
Firthcliffe NY, 4949 148 B1
Fisher IL, 1881 88 C4
Fisher Co. TX, 3974 58 B2
Fishers IN, 76794 99 F1
Fishersville VA, 7462 102 C4
Fishkill NY, 2171 148 B1
Fishkill Plains NY, 900 148 B1
Fiskdale MA, 2583 150 B2
Fitchburg MA, 40318 95 D1
Fitchburg WI, 25260 74 B3
Fitchville CT, 750 149 F1
Fitzgerald GA, 9053 129 E4
Fitzwilliam NH, 2396 95 D1
Five Corners MA, 2100 151 D2
Flagler CO, 561 41 F2
Flagler Beach FL, 4484 139 E4
Flagler Co. FL, 95696 139 D3
Flagstaff AZ, 65870 47 E3
Flagtown NJ, 3000 147 D1
Flanagan IL, 1110 88 C3
Flanders NY, 4472 149 E3
Flanders (E. Lyme) CT, 18459 149 F2
Flandreau SD, 2341 27 F3
Flasher ND, 232 18 B4
Flathead Co. MT, 90928 14 C2
Flat Lick KY, 960 110 C2
Flatonia TX, 1383 61 E2
Flat Rock MI, 9878 90 C1
Flat Rock NC, 1690 112 A3
Flat Rock NC, 3114 121 E1
Flatwoods KY, 7423 101 D3
Flatwoods WV, 277 102 A3
Fleetwood PA, 4085 146 B1
Fleming CO, 408 34 A4
Fleming Co. KY, 14348 100 C4
Fleming-Neon KY, 770 111 E2
Flemingsburg KY, 2658 100 C3
Flemington NJ, 4581 147 D1
Flemington PA, 1330 93 D3
Fletcher NC, 7187 121 E1
Fletcher OK, 1177 51 D4
Flint MI, 102434 76 B3
Flint TX, 1200 124 A3
Flippin AR, 1355 107 E3
Flohrville MD, 950 144 B1
Flomaton AL, 1440 135 F1
Floodwood MN, 528 64 C4
Flora IL, 5070 98 C3
Flora IN, 2036 89 E4
Flora MS, 1886 126 B2
Florala AL, 1980 136 B1
Floral City FL, 5217 140 C1
Floral Park NY, 15863 241 G3
Flora Vista NM, 2191 48 B1
Flordell Hills MO, 822 256 C1
Florence AL, 39319 119 E2
Florence AZ, 25536 54 C2
Florence CA, 60197 228 D3
Florence CO, 3881 41 E3
Florence KS, 465 43 F3
Florence KY, 29951 100 B2
Florence MS, 4141 126 B3
Florence MT, 765 15 D4
Florence NJ, 4426 147 D2
Florence OR, 8466 20 B4
Florence SC, 37056 122 C3
Florence SD, 374 27 E2
Florence TX, 1136 61 E1
Florence WI, 592 68 C2
Florence Co. SC, 136885 122 C3
Florence Co. WI, 4423 68 C2
Floresville TX, 6448 61 D3
Florham Park NJ, 11696 148 A4
Florida NY, 2833 148 A2
Florida City FL, 11245 143 E3
Florien LA, 633 125 D4
Florin CA, 47513 36 C3
Florissant MO, 52158 98 A3
Flourtown PA, 4538 248 B1
Flovilla GA, 653 129 D1
Flower Hill NY, 4665 241 G2
Flower Mound TX, 64669 207 C1
Flowery Branch GA, 5679 121 D3
Flowood MS, 7823 126 B3
Floyd VA, 425 112 B2
Floydada TX, 3038 58 B1
Floyd Co. GA, 96317 120 B3
Floyd Co. IN, 74578 99 F4
Floyd Co. IA, 16303 73 D3
Floyd Co. KY, 39451 111 E1
Floyd Co. TX, 6446 50 B4
Floyd Co. VA, 15279 112 A2
Flushing MI, 8389 76 B3
Flushing OH, 879 91 F4
Fluvanna Co. VA, 25691 113 D1
Flying Hills PA, 2568 146 A2
Foard Co. TX, 1336 58 C1
Fogelsville PA, 950 146 B1
Folcroft PA, 6606 248 B4
Foley AL, 14618 135 E2
Foley MN, 2603 66 C2

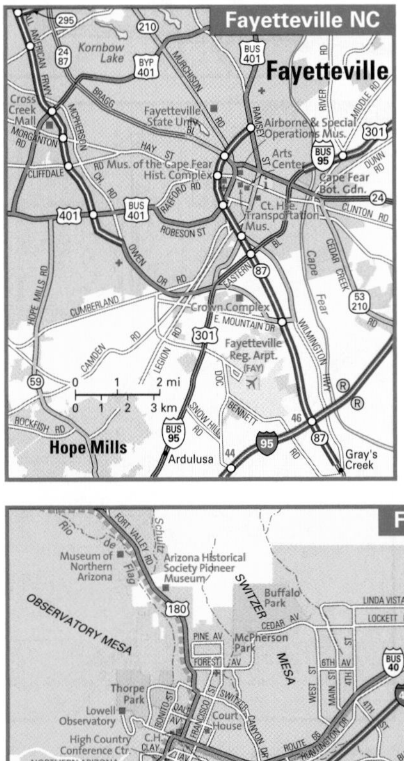

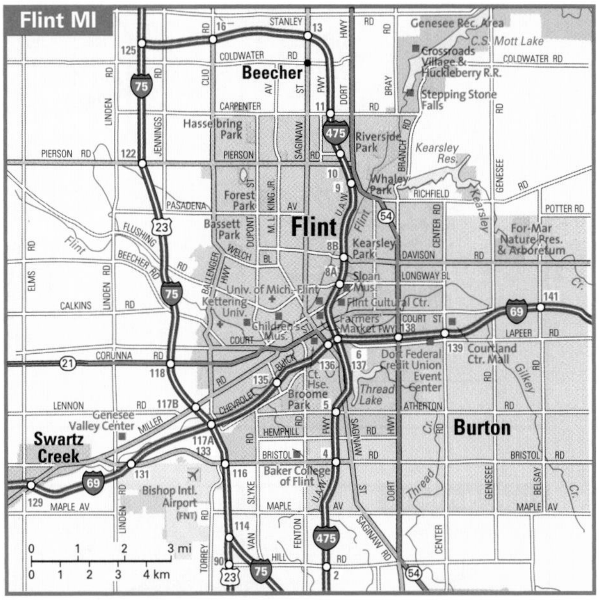

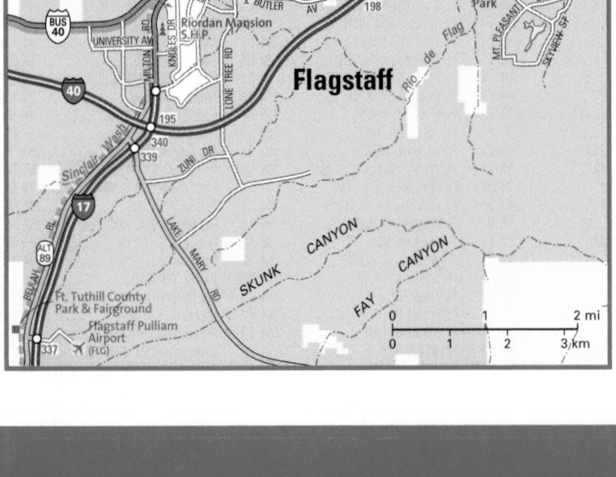

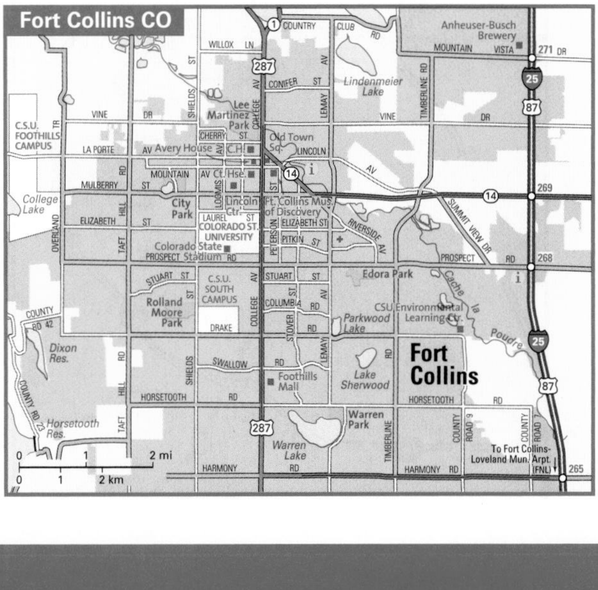

Figures after entries indicate population, page number, and grid reference.

Folkston GA, *2502* **139** D1
Follansbee WV, *2986* **91** F4
Folly Beach SC, *2617* **131** D2
Folsom CA, *72203* **36** C3
Folsom LA, *716* **134** B2
Folsom NJ, *1885* **147** D4
Folsom PA, *8323* **248** A4
Fonda IA, *631* **72** B4
Fonda NY, *795* **79** F3
Fond du Lac WI, *43021* **74** C2
Fond du Lac Co. WI, *101633* **74** C2
Fontana CA, *196069* **229** H2
Fontana WI, *1754* **74** C4
Fontanelle IA, *672* **86** B2
Foothill Farms CA, *33121* **255** C1
Footville WI, *808* **74** B4
Ford City CA, *4278* **52** B1
Ford City PA, *2991* **92** A3
Ford Co. IL, *14081* **88** C4
Ford Co. KS, *33848* **42** C4
Fordland MO, *800* **107** D2
Fordoche LA, *928* **133** F2
Fords NJ, *15187* **240** A6
Fords Prairie WA, *1959* **12** B4
Fordsville KY, *524* **109** F1
Fordville ND, *212* **19** E2
Fordyce AR, *4300* **117** E4
Foreman AR, *1011* **116** C4
Forest MS, *5684* **126** C2
Forest OH, *1461* **90** C3
Forest VA, *9106* **112** C1
Forest Acres SC, *10361* **205** F1
Forestbrook SC, *4612* **123** D4
Forest City FL, *13854* **246** B1
Forest City IA, *4151* **72** C3
Forest City NC, *7476* **121** F1
Forest City PA, *1911* **93** F2
Forest Co. PA, *7716* **92** B2
Forest Co. WI, *9304* **68** C2
Forestdale AL, *10162* **195** E1
Forestdale MA, *4099* **151** E3
Forest Dale VT, *800* **81** D3
Forest Grove OR, *21083* **20** B2
Forest Grove PA, *3800* **250** A1
Forest Hts. MD, *2447* **270** D5
Foresthill CA, *1483* **36** C2
Forest Hill LA, *818* **133** E1
Forest Hill TX, *12355* **59** E2
Forest Hills FL, *989* **139** D4
Forest Hills KY, *444* **230** F2
Forest Hills PA, *6518* **250** C2
Forest Lake IL, *1659* **203** B1
Forest Lake MN, *18375* **67** D3
Forest Park GA, *18468* **190** D5
Forest Park IL, *14167* **203** D4
Forest Park OH, *18720* **100** B2
Forest Park OK, *998* **244** E2
Forest View IL, *698* **203** D5
Forestville CA, *3293* **36** A3
Forestville MD, *12353* **271** F4
Forestville NY, *697* **78** A4
Forestville OH, *10532* **100** B2
Forgan OK, *547* **50** C1
Forked River NJ, *5244* **147** E3
Forkland AL, *649* **127** E2
Forks WA, *3532* **12** A2
Forman ND, *504* **27** E1
Forney TX, *14661* **59** F2
Forrest IL, *1220* **88** C3
Forrest City AR, *15371* **118** A2
Forrest Co. MS, *74934* **126** C4
Forreston IL, *1446* **88** B1
Forsyth GA, *3788* **129** D1
Forsyth IL, *3490* **98** C1
Forsyth MO, *2255* **107** D3
Forsyth MT, *1777* **25** D1
Forsyth Co. GA, *175511* **120** C3
Forsyth Co. NC, *350670* **112** A4
Ft. Ann NY, *484* **81** D4
Ft. Ashby WV, *1380* **102** C2
Ft. Meade FL, *5626* **140** C3
Ft. Mill SC, *10811* **122** A2
Ft. Mitchell KY, *8207* **204** A3
Ft. Montgomery NY, *1571* **148** B2
Ft. Morgan CO, *11315* **33** F4
Ft. Myers FL, *62298* **142** C1
Ft. Myers Beach FL, *6277* **142** C1
Ft. Myers Shores FL, *5487* **142** C1
Ft. Myers Villas FL, *11346* **142** C1
Ft. Oglethorpe GA, *9263* **120** B2
Ft. Payne AL, *14012* **120** A3
Ft. Peck MT, *233* **17** D2
Ft. Pierce FL, *41590* **141** E3
Ft. Pierre SD, *2078* **26** C3
Ft. Pillow TN, *650* **108** B4
Ft. Plain NY, *2322* **79** F3
Ft. Recovery OH, *1430* **90** A4
Ft. Salonga NY, *10008* **148** C3
Ft. Scott KS, *8087* **106** B1
Ft. Shaw MT, *280* **15** F3
Foster Ctr. RI, *355* **150** C3
Foster City CA, *30567* **259** C4
Foster Co. ND, *3343* **19** D3
Fostoria MI, *694* **76** C3
Fostoria OH, *13441* **90** C3
Fouke AR, *859* **124** C1
Fountain CO, *25846* **41** E2
Fountain NC, *427* **113** E4
Fountain City IN, *796* **100** B1
Fountain City WI, *859* **73** E1
Fountain Co. IN, *17240* **89** D4
Fountain Green UT, *1071* **39** E1
Fountain Hill PA, *4597* **146** C1
Fountain Hills AZ, *22489* **54** C1
Fountain Inn SC, *7799* **121** F2
Fountain Lake AR, *503* **117** D2
Fountain Valley CA, *55313* **228** E5
Four Corners OR, *15947* **20** B2
Four Corners TX, *12382* **220** A3
Four Mile NJ, *900* **147** D3
Francisco IN, *469* **99** E4
Francis Creek WI, *669* **75** D1
Franconia VA, *18245* **144** B3
Frankenmuth MI, *4944* **76** B3
Frankford DE, *847* **145** F4
Frankfort IL, *17782* **89** D2
Frankfort IN, *16422* **89** E4
Frankfort KS, *726* **43** F1
Frankfort KY, *25527* **100** B4
Frankfort MI, *1286* **69** E4
Frankfort NY, *2598* **79** F3
Frankfort OH, *1064* **101** D2
Franklin GA, *993* **128** C1
Franklin ID, *641* **31** E2
Franklin IL, *610* **98** B1
Franklin IN, *23712* **99** F2
Franklin KY, *8408* **109** F3
Franklin LA, *7660* **133** F3
Franklin ME, *300* **83** D2
Franklin MA, *31635* **150** C2

Bokeelia A1
Bonita Sprs. B2
Cape Coral A1
Captiva A2
Estero B2
Flamingo Bay A1
Ft. Myers. B1
Ft. Myers Beach B2
Ft. Myers Shores. B1
Ft. Myers Villas B1
Matlacha A1
N. Ft. Myers B1
Pine Island Ctr. A1
Pineland A1
Punta Rassa A2
St. James City A2
San Carlos Park. B2
Sanibel A2
Tice B1
Truckland B2

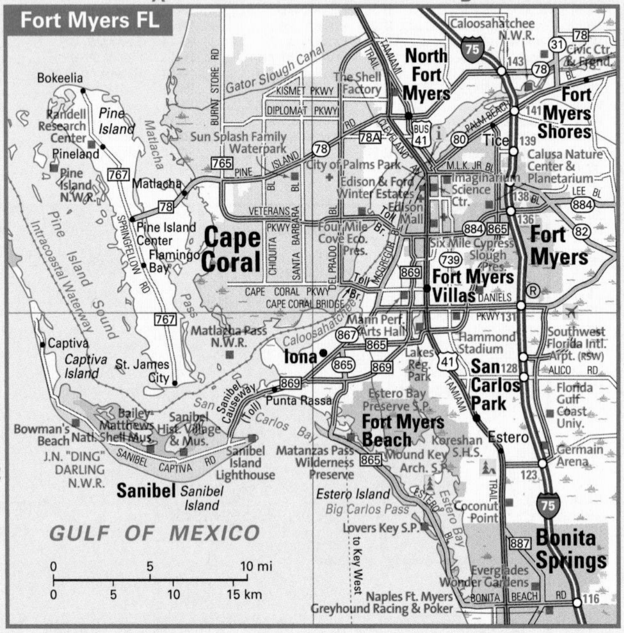

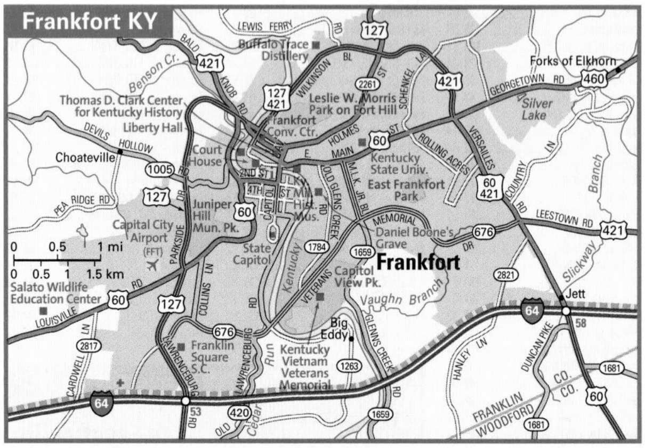

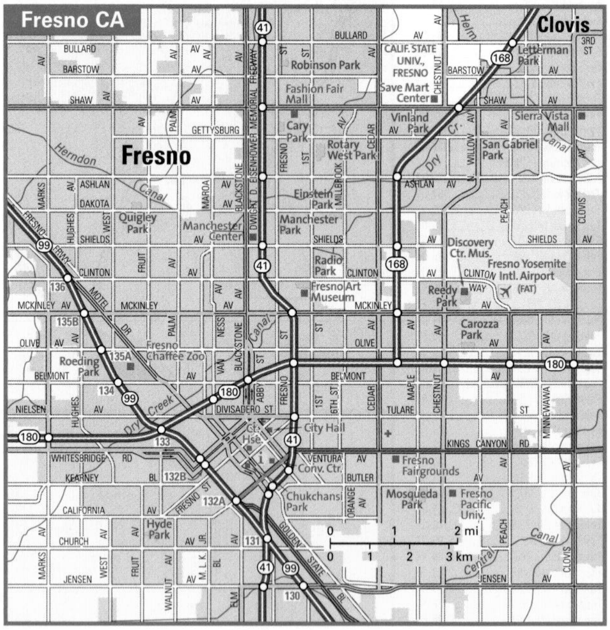

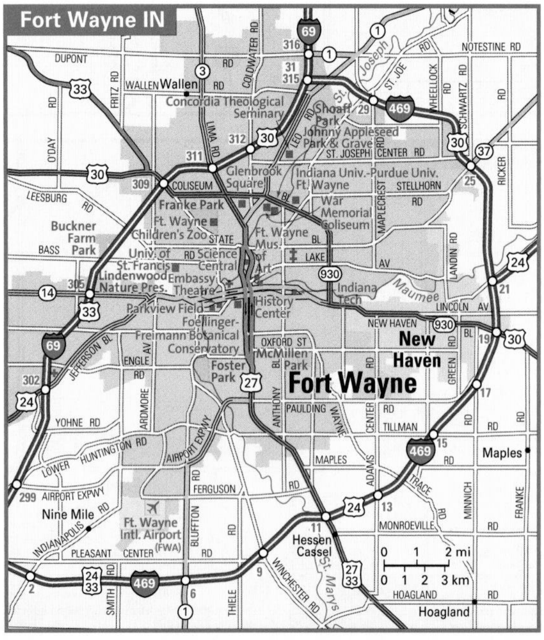

Ft. Atkinson WI, *12368* **74** B3
Ft. Belknap Agency MT, *1293* **16** C2
Ft. Bend Co. TX, *585375* **132** A4
Ft. Benton MT, *1464* **15** F2
Ft. Bragg CA, *7273* **36** A1
Ft. Branch IN, *2771* **99** D4
Ft. Bridger WY, *345* **32** A3
Ft. Calhoun NE, *908* **35** F3
Ft. Chiswell VA, *939* **112** A2
Ft. Cobb OK, *634* **51** D3
Ft. Collins CO, *143986* **33** E4
Ft. Covington NY, *1645* **80** C1
Ft. Davis TX, *1201* **62** B2
Ft. Defiance AZ, *3624* **48** A2
Ft. Deposit AL, *1344* **128** A3
Ft. Dodge IA, *25206* **72** C4
Ft. Dodge KS, *165* **42** C4
Ft. Duchesne UT, *714* **32** A4
Ft. Edward NY, *3375* **81** D4
Ft. Fairfield ME, *1825* **85** E2
Ft. Gaines GA, *1107* **128** C4
Ft. Garland CO, *433* **41** D4
Ft. Gates TX, *800* **59** E4
Ft. Gay WV, *705* **101** D4
Ft. Gibson OK, *4154* **106** A4
Ft. Grant AZ, *800* **55** E2
Ft. Hall ID, *3201* **31** E1
Ft. Hancock TX, *1750* **56** C4
Ft. Johnson NY, *490* **80** C4
Ft. Jones CA, *839* **28** B3
Ft. Kent ME, *2488* **85** D1
Ft. Kent Mills ME, *325* **85** D1
Ft. Laramie WY, *230* **33** E2
Ft. Lauderdale FL, *165521* **143** F2
Ft. Lawn SC, *895* **122** A2
Ft. Lee NJ, *35345* **148** B3
Ft. Loramie OH, *1478* **90** B4
Ft. Lupton CO, *7377* **41** E1
Ft. Madison IA, *11051* **87** F3
Ft. McKinley OH, *3989* **208** D1
Ft. Shawnee OH, *3726* **90** B3
Ft. Smith AR, *86209* **116** C1
Ft. Stockton TX, *8283* **62** C2
Ft. Sumner NM, *1031* **49** E4
Ft. Thomas KY, *16325* **204** B3
Ft. Thompson SD, *1282* **27** D3
Ft. Totten ND, *1243* **19** D2
Ft. Towson OK, *519* **116** A3
Fortuna CA, *11926* **28** A4
Ft. Valley GA, *9815* **129** D2
Fortville IN, *3929* **99** F1
Ft. Walton Beach FL, *19507* **136** B2
Ft. Washakie WY, *1759* **32** B1
Ft. Washington PA, *5446* **248** C1
Ft. Wayne IN, *253691* **90** A3
Ft. Wingate NM, *550* **48** A3
Ft. Worth TX, *741206* **59** E2
Ft. Wright KY, *5723* **204** B3
Ft. Yates ND, *184* **26** C1
Forty Fort PA, *4214* **261** B1
Ft. Yukon AK, *583* **154** C2
Fossil OR, *473* **21** E2
Fosston MN, *1527* **19** F3
Four Oaks NC, *1921* **123** D1
Four Seasons MO, *2217* **97** D4
Fowblesburg MD, *600* **144** C1
Fowler CA, *5570* **44** C3
Fowler CO, *1182* **41** F3
Fowler IN, *2317* **89** D3
Fowler KS, *590* **42** C4
Fowler MI, *1208* **76** A3
Fowlerville MI, *2886* **76** B4
Foxboro MA, *5625* **151** D2
Fox Chapel PA, *5388* **250** C1
Fox Chase KY, *447* **100** A4
Fox Crossing WI, *18892* **74** C1
Foxfield CO, *685* **209** D4
Fox Island WA, *3633* **262** A5
Fox Lake IL, *10579* **74** C4
Fox Lake WI, *1519* **74** B2
Fox Pt. WI, *6701* **234** D1
Fox River Grove IL, *4854* **88** C1
Frackville PA, *3805* **93** E3
Framingham MA, *68318* **150** C1
Francesville IN, *879* **89** E3
Francis UT, *1077* **31** F4
Franklin MI, *3150* **210** B2
Franklin MN, *510* **66** B4
Franklin NE, *1000* **43** D1
Franklin NH, *8477* **81** F4
Franklin NJ, *5045* **148** A2
Franklin NC, *3845* **121** D1
Franklin OH, *11771* **100** B1
Franklin PA, *323* **92** A2
Franklin TN, *62487* **109** F4
Franklin TX, *1564* **59** F4
Franklin VA, *8582* **113** F3
Franklin WV, *721* **102** B3
Franklin WI, *35451* **74** C3
Franklin Co. AL, *31704* **119** E3
Franklin Co. AR, *18125* **116** C1
Franklin Co. FL, *11549* **137** D3
Franklin Co. GA, *22084* **121** D3
Franklin Co. ID, *12786* **31** F2
Franklin Co. IL, *39561* **98** C4
Franklin Co. IN, *23087* **100** A2
Franklin Co. IA, *10680* **72** C4
Franklin Co. KS, *25992* **96** A3
Franklin Co. KY, *49285* **100** B4

Entries in **bold black** indicate counties or parishes.
Entries in **bold color** indicate cities with detailed inset maps.

Franklin Co. ME, 30768 82 B1
Franklin Co. MA, 71372 150 A1
Franklin Co. MS, 8118 126 A4
Franklin Co. MO, 101492 97 F3
Franklin Co. NE, 3225 43 D1
Franklin Co. NY, 51599 80 C2
Franklin Co. NC, 60619 113 D4
Franklin Co. OH, 1163414 101 D1
Franklin Co. PA, 149618 103 D1
Franklin Co. TN, 41052 120 A1
Franklin Co. TX, 10605 124 B1
Franklin Co. VT, 47746 81 D1
Franklin Co. VA, 56159 112 B2
Franklin Co. WA, 78163 13 F4
Franklin Furnace OH, 1660 101 D3
Franklin Grove IL, 1021 88 B1
Franklin Par. LA, 20767 125 F2
Franklin Park IL, 18333 203 C4
Franklin Park PA, 13470 92 A3
Franklin Sprs. GA, 952 121 E3
Franklin Square NY, 29320 241 G4
Franklinton LA, 3857 134 B1
Franklinton NC, 2023 113 D4
Franklinville NJ, 1500 145 F1
Franklinville NY, 1740 78 B4
Franklinville NC, 1164 112 B4
Frankston TX, 1229 124 A3
Frankton IN, 1862 89 F4
Frannie WY, 157 24 B2
Fraser CO, 1224 41 D1
Fraser MI, 14480 210 D2
Frazee MN, 1350 19 F4
Frazer MT, 362 17 E2
Frazeysburg OH, 1326 91 D4
Frazier Park CA, 2691 52 B1
Frederic WI, 1137 67 E2
Frederica DE, 774 145 E3
Frederick CO, 8679 41 E1
Frederick MD, 65239 144 A1
Frederick OK, 3940 51 D4
Frederick SD, 199 27 D1
Frederick Co. MD, 233385 144 A1
Frederick Co. VA, 78305 102 C2
Fredericksburg IA, 931 73 E3
Fredericksburg PA, 1357 92 A2
Fredericksburg PA, 987 93 E4
Fredericksburg TX, 10530 61 D2
Fredericksburg VA, 24286 103 D4
Fredericktown MO, 3985 108 A1
Fredericktown OH, 2493 91 D4
Fredonia AZ, 1314 47 D1
Fredonia KS, 2482 106 A1
Fredonia KY, 401 109 D2
Fredonia NY, 11230 78 A4
Fredonia PA, 502 91 F2
Fredonia WI, 2160 74 C2
Freeborn Co. MN, 31255 72 C2
Freeburg IL, 4354 98 B3
Freeburg PA, 575 93 D3
Freedom CA, 3070 44 B2
Freedom WI, 1500 74 C1
Freehold NJ, 12052 147 E2
Freeland MI, 6969 76 B2
Freeland PA, 3531 93 E3
Freeland WA, 2045 262 A1
Freeman MO, 482 96 B3
Freeman SD, 1306 27 E4
Freemansburg PA, 2636 146 C1
Freeport FL, 1787 136 B2
Freeport IL, 25638 74 B4
Freeport ME, 1485 82 B3
Freeport NY, 42860 147 F1
Freeport PA, 1813 92 A3
Freeport TX, 12049 133 E4
Freer TX, 2818 63 E2
Freestone Co. TX, 19816 59 F4
Freetown IN, 385 99 F2
Freetown NY, 2400 149 F3
Freeville NY, 520 79 D4
Freewood Acres NJ, 3100 147 E2
Fremont CA, 214089 36 B4
Fremont IN, 2138 90 A1
Fremont IA, 743 87 E2
Fremont MI, 4081 75 F2
Fremont NE, 26397 35 F3
Fremont NH, 4283 81 F4
Fremont NC, 1255 123 E1
Fremont OH, 16734 90 C2
Fremont WI, 679 74 B1
Fremont Co. CO, 46824 41 D3
Fremont Co. ID, 13242 23 F3
Fremont Co. IA, 7441 86 A3
Fremont Co. WY, 40123 32 C1
Fremont Hills MO, 826 107 D2
Frenchburg KY, 486 100 C4
French Camp CA, 3376 36 C4
French Lick IN, 1807 99 F3
French Settlement LA, 1116 134 A2
Frenchtown MT, 1825 15 D4
Frenchtown NJ, 1373 146 C1
Frenchville ME, 1225 85 D1
Fresno CA, 494665 44 C3
Fresno TX, 19069 220 B4
Fresno Co. CA, 930450 37 E4
Frewsburg NY, 1906 92 B1
Friant CA, 509 44 C2
Friars Pt. MS, 1200 118 A3
Friday Harbor WA, 2162 12 B2
Fridley MN, 27208 67 D3
Friedens PA, 1523 102 C1
Friedensburg PA, 858 146 A1
Friend NE, 1027 35 E4
Friendly MD, 9250 144 B4
Friendship ME, 1204 82 C3
Friendship NY, 1218 92 C1
Friendship TN, 668 108 C4
Friendship WI, 725 74 A1
Friendsville MD, 491 102 B1
Friendsville TN, 913 110 C4
Friendswood TX, 35805 132 B4
Fries VA, 484 112 A3
Frio Co. TX, 17217 60 C3
Friona TX, 4123 49 F4
Frisco CO, 2683 41 D1
Frisco TX, 116989 59 F2
Frisco City AL, 1309 127 F4
Fritch TX, 2117 50 B2
Froid MT, 185 17 F2
Fromberg MT, 438 24 B2
Frontenac FL, 1900 232 A1
Frontenac KS, 3437 106 B1
Frontenac MO, 3482 256 B2
Frontier ND, 214 19 F4
Frontier Co. NE, 2756 34 C4
Fronton TX, 180 63 D4
Front Royal VA, 14440 102 C3
Frost TX, 643 59 F3
Frostburg MD, 9002 102 C1
Frostproof FL, 2992 141 D3
Fruita CO, 12646 40 B2
Fruit Cove FL, 29362 139 D2
Fruit Hts. UT, 4701 31 E3
Fruit Hill OH, 3755 204 C3
Fruitland ID, 4684 22 A4
Fruitland IA, 977 87 F2
Fruitland MD, 4866 103 F4
Fruitland NM, 650 48 B1
Fruitland Park FL, 4078 140 C1
Fruitport MI, 1093 75 E3
Fruitville FL, 13224 266 C5
Fryeburg ME, 1631 81 F3
Fulda MN, 1318 72 A2
Fullerton CA, 135161 52 C3
Fullerton MD, 10100 193 D2
Fullerton NE, 1307 35 E3
Fulshear TX, 1134 132 A3
Fulton IL, 3481 88 A1
Fulton KY, 2445 108 C3
Fulton MD, 2049 144 B2
Fulton MS, 3961 119 D3
Fulton MO, 12790 97 E3
Fulton NY, 11896 79 D3
Fulton TX, 1358 61 E4
Fulton Co. AR, 12245 107 F3
Fulton Co. GA, 920581 120 C3
Fulton Co. IL, 37069 88 A4
Fulton Co. IN, 20836 89 F3
Fulton Co. KY, 6813 108 C3
Fulton Co. NY, 55531 79 F3
Fulton Co. OH, 42698 90 B2
Fulton Co. PA, 14845 103 D1
Fultondale AL, 8380 119 F4
Fultonville NY, 784 79 F3
Fuquay-Varina NC, 17937 123 D1
Furnas Co. NE, 4959 42 C1
Fyffe AL, 1018 120 A3

G

Gabbs NV, 269 37 F2
Gackle ND, 310 19 D4
Gadsden AL, 36856 120 A3
Gadsden AZ, 678 53 F4
Gadsden TN, 470 108 C4
Gadsden Co. FL, 46389 137 D2
Gaffney SC, 12414 121 F2
Gage Co. NE, 22311 35 F4
Gahanna OH, 33248 101 D1
Gail TX, 231 58 B2
Gainesboro TN, 962 110 A3
Gaines Co. TX, 17526 57 F2
Gainesville FL, 124354 138 C3
Gainesville GA, 33804 121 D3
Gainesville MO, 773 107 E3
Gainesville TX, 16002 59 E1
Gainesville VA, 11481 144 A3
Gaithersburg MD, 59933 144 B2
Galatia IL, 933 108 C1
Galax VA, 7042 112 A3
Galena AK, 470 154 C2
Galena IL, 3429 74 A4
Galena IN, 1818 99 F4
Galena KS, 3085 106 B2
Galena MO, 440 107 D2
Galena Park TX, 10887 220 C3
Galesburg IL, 32195 88 A3
Galesburg MI, 2009 75 F4
Gales Ferry CT, 1162 149 F1
Galesville WI, 1481 73 F1
Galeville NY, 4617 265 A1
Galien MI, 549 89 E1
Galilee RI, 700 150 C4
Galion OH, 10512 91 D3
Galisteo NM, 253 49 D3
Gallatin MO, 1786 96 C1
Gallatin TN, 30278 109 F3
Gallatin Co. IL, 5589 109 D1
Gallatin Co. KY, 8589 100 B3
Gallatin Co. MT, 89513 23 F2
Gallatin Gateway MT, 856 23 F1
Gallaway TN, 680 118 B1
Gallia Co. OH, 30934 101 E3
Galliano LA, 7676 134 B4
Gallipolis OH, 3641 101 E3
Gallitzin PA, 1668 92 B4
Gallup NM, 21678 48 A3
Galt CA, 23647 36 C3
Galva IL, 2589 88 A2
Galva KS, 870 43 E3
Galveston IN, 1311 89 F3
Galveston KY, 450 111 E1
Galveston TX, 47743 132 B4
Galveston Co. TX, 291309 132 B4
Gamaliel KY, 376 110 A3
Gambell AK, 681 154 A2
Gamber MD, 1000 144 B1
Gambier OH, 2391 91 D4
Gamewell NC, 4051 111 F4
Ganado AZ, 1210 47 F2
Ganado TX, 2003 61 F3
Gang Mills NY, 4185 93 D1
Gann Valley SD, 14 27 D3
Gansevoort NY, 800 81 D4
Gantt SC, 14229 217 A2
Gap PA, 1931 146 A3
Garber OK, 822 51 E1
Gardena CA, 58829 228 C4
Garden City AL, 492 119 F3
Garden City CO, 234 33 E4
Garden City GA, 8778 130 B3
Garden City ID, 10972 22 B4
Garden City KS, 26658 42 B3
Garden City MI, 27692 210 A3
Garden City MO, 1642 96 C3
Garden City NY, 22371 241 G3
Garden City SC, 9209 123 D4
Garden City TX, 334 58 A3
Garden City UT, 562 31 F2
Garden City South NY, 4024 241 G4
Garden Co. NE, 2057 34 A3
Gardendale AL, 13893 119 F4
Gardendale MI, 800 76 C3
Gardendale TX, 1574 58 A3
Garden Grove CA, 170883 228 E4
Garden Home OR, 6674 251 C2
Garden Plain KS, 849 43 E4
Garden Ridge TX, 3259 61 D2
Garden View PA, 2503 93 D2
Gardenville PA, 1000 146 C1
Gardiner ME, 5800 82 C2
Gardiner MT, 875 23 F2
Gardiner NY, 950 148 B1
Gardner IL, 1463 88 C2
Gardner KS, 19123 96 B3
Gardner MA, 20228 95 D1
Gardnertown NY, 4373 148 B1
Gardnerville NV, 5656 37 D2
Garfield AR, 502 106 C3
Garfield NJ, 30487 148 B3
Garfield TX, 1698 61 E2
Garfield WA, 597 14 B4
Garfield Co. CO, 56389 40 B1
Garfield Co. MT, 1206 17 D3
Garfield Co. NE, 2049 35 D2
Garfield Co. OK, 60580 51 E1
Garfield Co. UT, 5172 39 E3
Garfield Co. WA, 2266 14 A4
Garfield Hts. OH, 28849 91 E2
Garibaldi OR, 779 20 B2
Garland NC, 625 123 D2
Garland TX, 226876 59 F2
Garland UT, 2400 31 E2
Garland Co. AR, 96024 117 D2
Garnavillo IA, 745 73 F3
Garner IA, 3129 72 C3
Garner KY, 600 111 D1
Garner NC, 25745 113 D4
Garnett KS, 3415 96 A4
Garrard Co. KY, 16912 110 C1
Garretson SD, 1166 27 F4
Garrett IN, 6286 90 A2
Garrett Co. MD, 30097 102 B2
Garrett Park MD, 992 270 C1
Garrettsville OH, 2325 91 F2
Garrison KY, 866 101 D3
Garrison MD, 8823 193 A1
Garrison ND, 1453 18 B3
Garrison TX, 895 124 B3
Garrisonville VA, 2700 144 A4
Garvin Co. OK, 27576 51 E4
Garwin IA, 527 87 D1
Gary IN, 80294 89 D2
Gary SD, 227 27 F2
Gary WV, 968 111 F1
Garysburg NC, 1057 113 E3
Garyville LA, 2811 134 B3
Garza Co. TX, 6461 58 B2
Gas KS, 564 96 A4
Gas City IN, 5965 89 F4
Gasconade Co. MO, 15222 97 F3
Gasport NY, 1248 78 B3
Gassaway WV, 908 101 F3
Gassville AR, 2078 107 E3
Gaston IN, 871 89 F4
Gaston NC, 1152 113 E3
Gaston OR, 637 20 B2
Gaston SC, 1645 122 A4
Gaston Co. NC, 206086 122 A1
Gastonia NC, 71741 122 A1
Gate City VA, 2034 111 E3
Gates NY, 4910 78 C3
Gates OR, 471 20 C3
Gates TN, 647 108 B4
Gates Co. NC, 12197 113 F3
Gates Mills OH, 2270 204 G1
Gatesville NC, 321 113 F3
Gatesville TX, 15751 59 E4
Gatlinburg TN, 3944 111 D4
Gauley Bridge WV, 614 101 F4
Gautier MS, 18572 135 D2
Gayle Mill SC, 913 122 A2
Gaylord MI, 3645 70 C3
Gaylord MN, 2305 66 C4
Gaylordsville CT, 750 148 C1
Gays Mills WI, 491 73 F3
Gayville SD, 407 35 E1
Gearhart OR, 1462 20 B1
Geary OK, 1280 51 D3
Geary Co. KS, 34362 43 F2
Geauga Co. OH, 93389 91 E2
Geddes SD, 208 35 D1
Geistown PA, 2467 92 B4
Gem Co. ID, 16719 22 B3
Genesee ID, 955 14 B4
Genesee MI, 1800 76 B3
Genesee Co. MI, 425790 76 B3
Genesee Co. NY, 60079 78 B3
Geneseo IL, 6586 88 A2
Geneseo NY, 8031 78 C4
Geneva AL, 4452 136 C1
Geneva FL, 2940 141 D1
Geneva IL, 21495 88 C1
Geneva IN, 1293 90 A3
Geneva NE, 2217 35 E4
Geneva NY, 13261 79 D3
Geneva OH, 6215 91 F1
Geneva WA, 2321 12 C1
Geneva Co. AL, 26790 136 C1
Geneva-on-the-Lake OH, 1288 91 F1
Genoa IL, 5193 88 C1
Genoa NE, 1003 35 E3
Genoa OH, 2336 90 C2
Genoa City WI, 3042 74 C4
Genola UT, 1370 39 E1
Gentry AR, 3158 106 B3
Gentry Co. MO, 6738 86 B4
George IA, 1080 72 A2
George WA, 501 13 E4
George Co. MS, 22578 135 D1
Georgetown CA, 2367 36 C2
Georgetown CO, 1034 41 D1
Georgetown CT, 1805 148 C2
Georgetown DE, 6422 145 F4
Georgetown GA, 11823 128 C3
Georgetown ID, 476 31 F1
Georgetown IL, 4046 99 D1
Georgetown IN, 2876 99 F4
Georgetown KY, 29098 100 B4
Georgetown MA, 8183 151 F1
Georgetown OH, 4331 100 C3
Georgetown PA, 174 146 A3
Georgetown PA, 2200 261 A2
Georgetown SC, 9163 131 E1
Georgetown TX, 47400 61 E1
Georgetown Co. SC, 60158 122 C4
George West TX, 2445 61 D4
Georgia Ctr. VT, 375 81 D1
Georgiana AL, 1738 127 F4
Gerald MO, 1345 97 F3
Geraldine AL, 896 120 A3
Geraldine MT, 261 16 A3
Gerber CA, 1060 36 B1
Gering NE, 8500 33 F2
Gerlach NV, 206 29 E4
Germania NJ, 750 147 D4
Germantown IL, 1269 98 B3
Germantown MD, 86395 144 B2
Germantown NY, 845 94 B2
Germantown OH, 5547 100 B1
Germantown TN, 38844 118 B1
Germantown WI, 19749 74 C3
Germantown Hills IL, 3438 88 B3
Geronimo OK, 1268 51 D4
Geronimo TX, 1032 61 E2
Gerrardstown WV, 550 103 D2
Gervais OR, 2464 20 B2
Gettysburg OH, 513 90 B4
Gettysburg PA, 7620 103 E1
Gettysburg SD, 1162 26 C2
Geyserville CA, 862 36 A2
Ghent KY, 323 100 A3
Ghent NY, 564 94 B2
Ghent OH, 5261 188 A1
Gholson TX, 1061 59 E4
Giants Neck CT, 1000 149 F2
Gibbon MN, 772 66 B4
Gibbon NE, 1833 35 D4
Gibbsboro NJ, 2274 147 D3
Gibbstown NJ, 3739 146 C3
Gibraltar MI, 4656 90 C1
Gibsland LA, 979 125 D2
Gibson GA, 663 129 F1
Gibson MD, 650 145 D1
Gibson NC, 540 122 C2
Gibsonburg OH, 2581 90 C2
Gibson City IL, 3407 88 C4
Gibson Co. IN, 33503 99 E4
Gibson Co. TN, 49683 108 C4
Gibsonton FL, 14234 140 C3
Gibsonville NC, 6410 112 B4
Giddings TX, 4881 61 F2
Gideon MO, 1093 108 B3
Gifford FL, 9590 141 E3
Gifford IL, 975 89 D4
Gig Harbor WA, 7126 12 C3
Gila Bend AZ, 1922 54 B2
Gila Co. AZ, 53597 55 D1
Gilbert AZ, 208453 54 C2
Gilbert IA, 1082 86 C1
Gilbert LA, 521 125 F3
Gilbert MN, 1799 64 C3
Gilbert SC, 565 122 A4
Gilbert WV, 450 111 F1
Gilbertsville PA, 4832 146 B2
Gilbertville IA, 712 73 E4
Gilbertville MA, 1000 150 B1
Gilby ND, 237 19 E2
Gilchrist Co. FL, 16939 138 C3
Gilcrest CO, 1034 33 E4
Giles Co. TN, 29485 119 F1
Giles Co. VA, 17286 112 A1
Gilford NH, 7126 81 F3
Gilford Park NJ, 8700 147 E3
Gillespie IL, 3319 98 B2
Gillespie Co. TX, 24837 61 D1
Gillett AR, 691 117 F3
Gillett WI, 1386 68 C4
Gillette WY, 29087 25 E3
Gilliam Co. OR, 1871 21 D2
Gilman IL, 1814 89 D3
Gilman IA, 509 87 D1
Gilman VT, 375 81 F2
Gilmer TX, 4905 124 B2
Gilmer Co. GA, 28292 120 C2
Gilmer Co. WV, 8693 101 F2
Gilmore City IA, 504 72 B4
Gilpin Co. CO, 5441 41 D1
Gilroy CA, 48821 44 B2
Gilt Edge TN, 477 118 B1
Ginger Blue MO, 61 106 B3
Girard IL, 2103 98 B2
Girard KS, 2789 106 B1
Girard OH, 9958 91 F2
Girard PA, 3104 91 F1
Girardville PA, 1519 93 E3
Gisela AZ, 570 47 E4
Glacier Co. MT, 13399 15 E1
Gladbrook IA, 945 87 D1
Gladden AZ, 400 54 B1
Glades Co. FL, 12884 141 D4
Glade Spr. VA, 1456 111 F2
Gladewater TX, 6441 124 B2
Gladstone MI, 4973 69 D2
Gladstone MO, 25410 96 B2
Gladstone ND, 239 18 A4
Gladstone OR, 11497 251 D3
Gladwin MI, 2933 76 A1
Gladwin Co. MI, 25692 76 A1
Glandorf OH, 1001 90 B3
Glasco KS, 498 43 E2
Glasco NY, 2099 94 B2
Glascock Co. GA, 3082 129 F1
Glasford IL, 1022 88 B4
Glasgow DE, 14303 145 E1
Glasgow KY, 14028 110 A2
Glasgow MO, 1103 97 D2
Glasgow MT, 3250 17 D2
Glasgow VA, 1133 112 C1
Glasgow WV, 905 101 F4
Glasgow Vil. MO, 5429 256 C1
Glassboro NJ, 18579 146 C4
Glasscock Co. TX, 1226 58 A3
Glassmanor MD, 17295 270 D5
Glassport PA, 4483 250 C3
Glastonbury CT, 33089 150 A3
Gleason TN, 1445 108 C3
Glenaire MO, 545 224 C2
Glen Allen AL, 510 119 E4
Glen Allen VA, 14774 254 B1
Glen Alpine NC, 1517 111 F4
Glenarden MD, 6000 144 B3
Glenburn ND, 380 18 B2
Glenburn PA, 953 93 F2
Glen Burnie MD, 67639 144 C2
Glen Carbon IL, 12934 98 B3
Glencoe AL, 5160 120 A4
Glencoe IL, 8723 89 D1
Glencoe MN, 5631 66 C4
Glencoe OK, 601 51 F2
Glen Cove ME, 375 82 C2
Glen Cove NY, 26964 148 C3
Glendale AZ, 226721 54 C1
Glendale CA, 191719 52 C2
Glendale CO, 4184 209 C3
Glendale MO, 5925 256 B2
Glendale OH, 2155 204 B1
Glendale OR, 874 28 B1
Glendale RI, 800 150 C2
Glendale UT, 381 39 D4
Glen Dale WV, 1526 101 F1
Glendale WI, 12872 234 C1
Glendale Hts. IL, 34208 203 B4
Glendive MT, 4935 17 F3
Glendo WY, 205 33 E1
Glendora CA, 50073 229 F2
Glendora NJ, 4750 146 C3
Glen Elder KS, 445 43 D1
Glen Ellen CA, 784 36 B3
Glen Ellyn IL, 27450 203 B4
Glen Gardner NJ, 1704 104 C1
Glenham NY, 4300 148 B1
Glen Lyon PA, 1873 93 E2
Glen Mills MA, 750 151 F1

Ada B2
Cascade B2
Comstock Park A1
E. Grand Rapids B2
Grand Rapids B1
Grandville A2
Jenison A2
Kentwood B2
Marne A1
Tallmadge A1
Walker A2
Wyoming A2

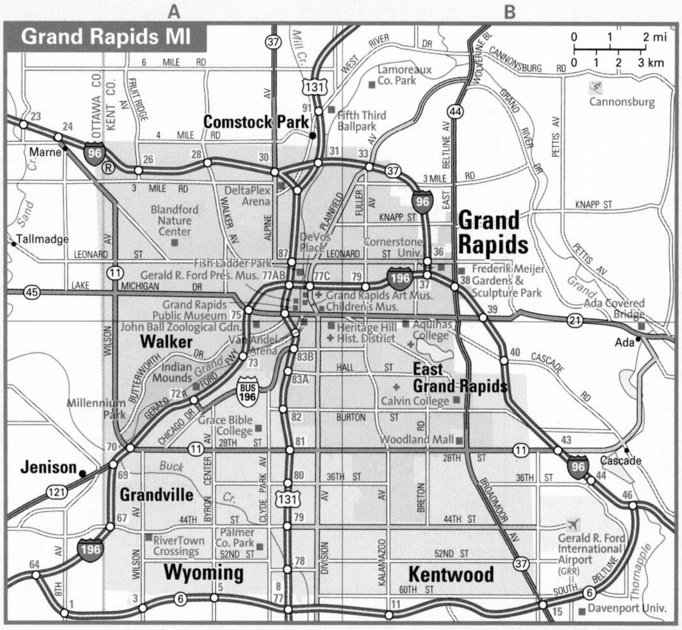

Glenmoor OH, *1987* **91** F3
Glenmora LA, *1342* **133** E1
Glennallen AK, *483* **154** C3
Glenn Co. CA, *28122* **36** B1
Glenn Dale MD, *13466* **144** C3
Glenn Hts. TX, *11278* **59** F3
Glenns Ferry ID, *1319* **30** C1
Glennville GA, *3569* **130** A3
Glenolden PA, *7153* **146** C3
Glenpool OK, *10808* **51** F2
Glen Raven NC, *2750* **112** C4
Glen Ridge NJ, *7527* **240** B2
Glen Rock NJ, *11601* **148** B3
Glen Rock PA, *2025* **103** E1
Glenrock WY, *2576* **33** D1
Glen Rose TX, *2444* **59** E3
Glen St. Mary FL, *437* **138** C2
Glens Falls NY, *14700* **81** D4
Glenside PA, *8384* **146** C2
Glen Ullin ND, *807* **18** B4
Glenview IL, *44692* **203** D2
Glenview KY, *531* **230** E1
Glenview Hills KY, *319* **230** E1
Glenville MN, *643* **73** D2
Glenville WV, *1537* **101** F3
Glenwood AR, *2228* **117** D3
Glenwood GA, *747* **129** F3
Glenwood IA, *5269* **86** A3
Glenwood MD, *650* **144** B2
Glenwood MN, *2564* **66** B2
Glenwood UT, *464* **39** E2
Glenwood City WI, *1242* **67** E3
Glenwood Sprs. CO, *9614* **40** C1
Glidden IA, *1146* **86** B1
Glide OR, *1795* **20** B4
Globe AZ, *7532* **55** D1
Glorieta NM, *430* **49** D3
Gloster MS, *960* **126** A4
Gloucester MA, *28789* **151** F1
Gloucester VA, *2269* **113** F1
Gloucester City NJ, *11456* **146** C3
Gloucester Co. NJ, *288288* **146** C4
Gloucester Co. VA, *36858* **113** F1
Gloucester Pt. VA, *9402* **113** F2
Glouster OH, *1791* **101** E2
Gloversville NY, *15665* **79** F3
Gloverville SC, *2831* **121** F4
Glyndon MD, *1200* **144** C1
Glyndon MN, *1394* **19** F4
Glynn Co. GA, *79626* **130** B4
Gnadenhutten OH, *1288* **91** E4
Gobles MI, *829* **75** F4
Goddard KS, *4344* **43** E4
Godeffroy NY, *650* **148** A1
Godfrey IL, *17982* **98** A2
Godley IL, *601* **88** C2
Godley TX, *1009* **59** E3
Goessel KS, *539* **43** E3
Goffstown NH, *3196* **81** F4
Gogebic Co. MI, *16427* **65** E4
Golconda IL, *668* **109** D1
Golconda NV, *214* **30** A3
Gold Bar WA, *2075* **12** C2
Gold Beach OR, *2253* **28** A2
Golden CO, *18867* **41** E1
Golden IL, *644* **87** F4
Golden Beach FL, *919* **233** C3
Golden Beach MD, *3796* **144** C4
Golden Bridge NY, *1578* **148** C2
Golden City MO, *765* **106** C1
Goldendale WA, *3407* **21** D1
Golden Gate FL, *23961* **142** C1
Golden Meadow LA, *2101* **134** B4
Goldenrod FL, *12039* **246** D1
Golden Valley MN, *20371* **235** B2
Golden Valley Co. MT, *884* **16** B4
Golden Valley Co. ND, *1680* **17** F3
Goldfield IA, *635* **72** C4
Goldfield NV, *268* **37** F4
Gold Hill OR, *1220* **28** B2
Goldonna LA, *430* **125** D3
Goldsboro NC, *36437* **123** E1
Goldsboro PA, *952* **93** D4
Goldsby OK, *1801* **51** E3
Goldthwaite TX, *1878* **59** D4
Goleta CA, *29888* **52** B2
Golf Manor OH, *3611* **204** B2
Goliad TX, *1908* **61** E4
Goliad Co. TX, *7210* **61** E3
Gonzales CA, *8187* **44** B3
Gonzales LA, *9781* **134** A2
Gonzales TX, *7237* **61** E2
Gonzales Co. TX, *19807* **61** E3
Gonzalez FL, *13273* **135** F2
Goochland VA, *861* **113** D1
Goochland Co. VA, *21717* **113** D1
Goodfield IL, *860* **88** B3
Good Hope AL, *2264* **119** F3
Goodhue MN, *1176* **73** D1
Goodhue Co. MN, *46183* **73** D1
Gooding ID, *3567* **30** C1
Gooding Co. ID, *15464* **30** C1
Goodland IN, *1043* **89** D3
Goodland KS, *4489* **42** B2
Goodlettsville TN, *15921* **109** F3
Goodman MS, *1386* **126** B1
Goodman MO, *1248* **106** B3
Goodrich MI, *1860* **76** B3
Goodsprings NV, *229* **46** A2
Good Thunder MN, *583* **72** C1
Goodview MN, *4036* **73** E1
Goodwater AL, *1475* **128** A1
Goodwell OK, *1293* **50** B1
Goodyear AZ, *65275* **54** C1
Goose Creek SC, *35938* **131** D1
Gordo AL, *1750* **127** E1
Gordon AL, *332* **137** D1
Gordon GA, *2017* **129** E1
Gordon NE, *1612* **34** A1
Gordon PA, *763* **93** E3
Gordon Co. GA, *55186* **120** B3
Gordonsville TN, *1213* **110** A4
Gordonsville VA, *1496* **102** C4
Gordonville PA, *508* **146** A3
Gore OK, *977* **116** B1
Goreville IL, *1049* **108** C1
Gorham ME, *6882* **82** B3
Gorham NH, *1600* **81** F2
Gorham NY, *617* **78** C4
Gorman NC, *1011* **112** C4
Gorman TX, *1083* **59** D3
Goshen AR, *1071* **106** C4
Goshen CA, *3006* **45** D3
Goshen IN, *31719* **89** F2
Goshen KY, *909* **100** A3
Goshen MD, *1300* **144** B2
Goshen NY, *5454* **148** A2
Goshen OR, *650* **20** B4
Goshen UT, *921* **39** E1
Goshen VA, *361* **102** B4
Goshen Co. WY, *13249* **33** F2
Gosnell AR, *3548* **108** B4
Gosper Co. NE, *2044* **34** C4
Gosport IN, *826* **99** E2
Gotha FL, *1915* **246** A2
Gothenburg NE, *3574* **34** C4
Gould AR, *837* **117** F3
Goulding FL, *4102* **247** B1
Goulds FL, *10103* **143** E3
Gouldtown NJ, *2300* **145** F1
Gouverneur NY, *3949* **79** E1
Gove KS, *80* **42** C2
Gove Co. KS, *2695* **42** C2
Gowanda NY, *2709* **78** A4
Gower MO, *1526* **96** B1
Gowrie IA, *1037* **72** B4
Grabill IN, *1053* **90** A2
Grace ID, *915* **31** F1
Graceville FL, *2278* **136** C1
Graceville MN, *577* **27** F1
Grady AR, *449* **117** F3
Grady Co. GA, *25011* **137** E1
Grady Co. OK, *52431* **51** E4
Graettinger IA, *844* **72** B3
Graford TX, *584* **59** D2
Grafton IL, *674* **98** A2
Grafton MA, *17765* **150** C2
Grafton ND, *4284* **19** E2
Grafton OH, *6636* **91** D2
Grafton WV, *5164* **102** A2
Grafton WI, *11459* **74** C3
Grafton Co. NH, *89118* **81** F2
Graham KY, *475* **109** E2
Graham NC, *14153* **112** C4
Graham TX, *8903* **59** D2
Graham WA, *23491* **12** C4
Graham Co. AZ, *37220* **55** E2
Graham Co. KS, *2597* **42** C2
Graham Co. NC, *8861* **121** D1
Grainger Co. TN, *22657* **111** D3
Grain Valley MO, *12854* **96** C2
Grambling LA, *4949* **125** E2
Gramercy LA, *3613* **134** B3
Granada CO, *517* **42** A3
Granbury TX, *7978* **59** E3
Granby CO, *1864* **41** D1
Granby CT, *11088* **94** C2
Granby MA, *1368* **150** A1
Granby MO, *2134* **106** C2
Grand Bay AL, *3672* **135** E2
Grand Blanc MI, *8276* **76** B3
Grand Canyon AZ, *2004* **47** D2
Grand Coteau LA, *947* **133** F2
Grand Coulee WA, *988* **13** E2
Grand Co. CO, *14843* **41** D1
Grand Co. UT, *9225* **40** A2
Grandfield OK, *1038* **51** D4
Grand Forks ND, *52838* **19** E2
Grand Forks Co. ND, *66861* **19** E3
Grand Haven MI, *10412* **75** E3
Grandin NJ, *1800* **147** D1
Grand Island NE, *48520* **35** E4
Grand Isle LA, *1296* **134** B4
Grand Isle VT, *1955* **81** D1
Grand Isle Co. VT, *6970* **81** D1
Grand Jct. CO, *58566* **40** B2
Grand Jct. IA, *824* **86** C1
Grand Lake CO, *471* **33** D4
Grand Ledge MI, *7786* **76** A4
Grand Marais MN, *1351* **65** D3
Grand Meadow MN, *1139* **73** D2
Grand Mound IA, *642* **88** A1
Grand Prairie TX, *175396* **207** C3
Grand Rapids MI, *188040* **75** F3
Grand Rapids MN, *10869* **64** B3
Grand Rapids OH, *965* **90** B2
Grand Ridge FL, *892* **137** D1
Grand Rivers KY, *382* **109** D2
Grand Saline TX, *3136* **124** A2
Grand Terrace CA, *12040* **229** J3
Grand Tower IL, *605* **108** B1
Grand Traverse Co. MI, *86986* **69** F4
Grandview CO, *600* **40** B4
Grand View ID, *452* **30** B1
Grandview IN, *749* **99** E4
Grandview IA, *556* **87** F2
Grandview MO, *24475* **96** B3
Grandview TX, *1561* **59** E3
Grandview WA, *10862* **21** E1
Grandview Hts. OH, *6536* **206** B2
Grandview Plaza KS, *1560* **43** F2
Grandville MI, *15378* **75** F3
Grandy NC, *1000* **115** F1
Granger IN, *30465* **89** F1
Granger IA, *1244* **86** C1
Granger TX, *1419* **61** E1
Granger WA, *3246* **13** E4
Grangeville ID, *3141* **22** B1
Granite OK, *2065* **50** C3
Granite UT, *1932* **257** B3
Granite City IL, *29849* **98** A3
Granite Co. MT, *3079* **15** D4
Granite Falls MN, *2897* **66** A4
Granite Falls NC, *4722* **111** F4
Granite Falls WA, *3364* **12** C2
Granite Quarry NC, *2930* **122** B1
Granite Shoals TX, *4910* **61** D1
Granite Sprs. NY, *2300* **148** B2
Graniteville SC, *2614* **121** F4
Graniteville VT, *784* **81** E2
Grannis AR, *554* **116** C3
Grant AL, *896* **120** A2
Grant MI, *894* **75** F3
Grant MN, *4096* **67** D3
Grant NE, *1165* **34** B4
Grant City MO, *859* **86** B4
Grant Co. AR, *17853* **117** E3
Grant Co. IN, *70061* **89** F3
Grant Co. KS, *7829* **42** B4
Grant Co. KY, *24662* **100** B3
Grant Co. MN, *6018* **27** F1
Grant Co. NE, *614* **34** B2
Grant Co. NM, *29514* **55** F2
Grant Co. ND, *2394* **18** B4
Grant Co. OK, *4527* **51** E1
Grant Co. OR, *7445* **21** F3
Grant Co. SD, *7356* **27** F2
Grant Co. WA, *89120* **13** E3
Grant Co. WV, *11937* **102** B2
Grant Co. WI, *51208* **73** F3
Grant Hollow NY, *700* **188** E1
Grant Par. LA, *22309* **125** E4
Grant Park IL, *1331* **89** D2
Grants NM, *9182* **48** B3
Grantsburg WI, *1341* **67** D2
Grantsdale MT, *750* **23** D1
Grants Pass OR, *34533* **28** B2
Grantsville MD, *766* **102** B1
Grantsville UT, *8893* **31** E4
Grantsville WV, *561* **101** F3
Grant Town WV, *613* **102** A1
Grantville GA, *3041* **128** C1
Grantville PA, *1000* **93** E4
Granville IL, *1427* **88** B2
Granville NY, *2543* **81** D4
Granville ND, *241* **18** C2
Granville OH, *5646* **91** D4
Granville Co. NC, *59916* **113** D3
Grapeland TX, *1489* **124** A4
Grapeview WA, *954* **12** C3
Grapevine TX, *46334* **59** E2
Grasonville MD, *3425* **145** D3
Grass Lake MI, *1173* **76** B4
Grass Valley CA, *12860* **36** C2
Graterford PA, *1400* **146** B2
Gratiot Co. MI, *42476* **76** A3
Gratis OH, *881* **100** B1
Graton CA, *1707* **36** A3
Gratz PA, *765* **93** E4
Gravel Ridge AR, *3232* **117** E2
Graves Co. KY, *37121* **108** C3
Gravette AR, *2325* **106** B3
Grawn MI, *772* **69** F4
Gray GA, *3276* **129** D1
Gray KY, *650* **110** C2
Gray LA, *5584* **134** A3
Gray ME, *884* **82** B3
Gray TN, *1222* **111** E3
Gray Co. KS, *6006* **42** C4
Gray Co. TX, *22535* **50** B3
Gray Court SC, *795* **121** F2
Grayland WA, *953* **12** B4
Grayling MI, *1884* **70** C4
Graymoor-Devondale KY, *2870* **230** E1
Grays Harbor Co. WA, *72797* **12** B3
Grayslake IL, *20957* **74** C4
Grayson GA, *2666* **121** D4
Grayson KY, *4217* **101** D4
Grayson LA, *532* **125** E3
Grayson Co. KY, *25746* **109** F1
Grayson Co. TX, *120877* **59** F1
Grayson Co. VA, *15533* **111** F3
Gray Summit MO, *2701* **98** A3

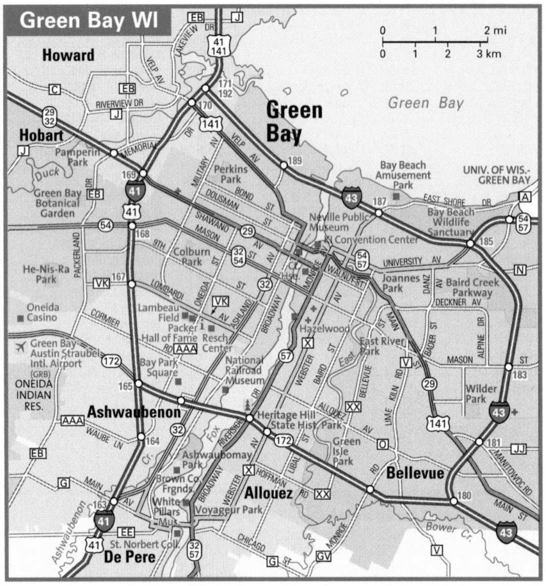

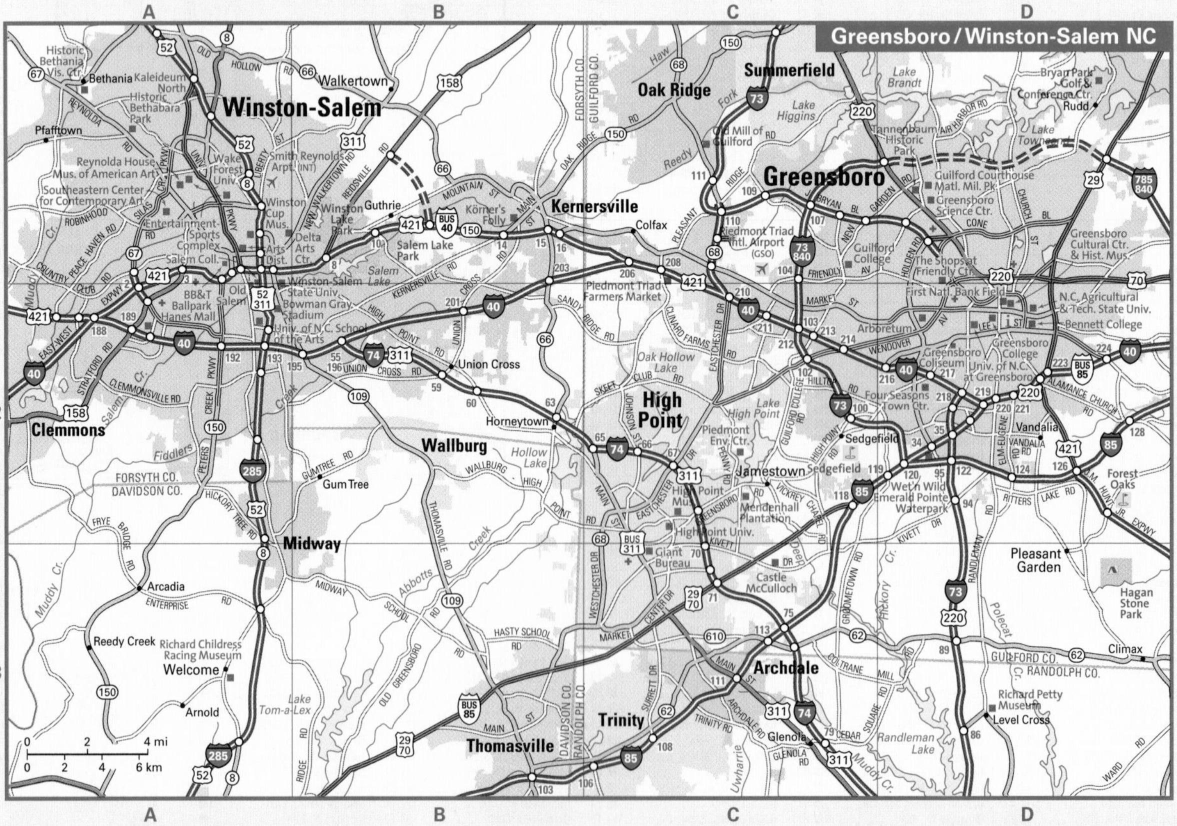

Arcadia A3	Climax D3	Guthrie B1	Level Cross D3	Reedy Creek A3	Trinity C3	Welcome A3
Archdale C3	Colfax C1	High Pt. C2	Midway A3	Rudd D1	Union Cross B2	Winston-Salem A1
Arnold A3	Glenola C3	Horneytown B2	Oak Ridge C1	Sedgefield C2	Vandalia D2	
Bethania A1	Greensboro C1	Jamestown C2	Pfafftown A1	Summerfield C1	Walkertown B1	
Clemmons A2	Gum Tree B2	Kernersville B1	Pleasant Garden D3	Thomasville B3	Wallburg B2	

217
Graysville–Harrisburg

Entries in **bold black** indicate counties or parishes.
Entries in **bold color** indicate cities with detailed inset maps.

Graysville AL, 2165 119 F4
Graysville TN, 1502 120 B1
Grayville IL, 1666 99 D4
Greasewood AZ, 547 47 F3
Great Barrington MA, 2231 94 B2
Great Bend KS, 15995 43 D3
Great Bend NY, 843 79 E1
Great Bend PA, 734 93 F1
Great Falls MT, 58505 15 F3
Great Falls SC, 1979 122 A2
Great Falls VA, 15427 144 B3
Great Meadows NJ, 303 94 A4
Great Mills MD, 2600 103 E4
Great Neck NY, 9989 148 B4
Great Neck Estates NY, 2761 241 G3
Great Neck Gardens NY, 1186 241 G2
Great Neck Plaza NY, 6707 241 G2
Great River NY, 1489 149 D4
Greece NY, 14519 78 C3
Greeley CO, 92889 33 E4
Greeley NE, 466 35 D3
Greeley Co. KS, 1247 42 B3
Greeley Co. NE, 2538 35 D3
Greeleyville SC, 438 122 B4
Green OH, 25699 91 E3
Green OR, 7515 28 B1
Greenacres CA, 5566 45 D4
Greenacres FL, 37573 143 F1
Greenback TN, 1064 110 C4
Green Bay WI, 104057 68 C4
Greenbelt MD, 23068 144 B3
Greenbrier AR, 4706 117 E1
Greenbrier TN, 6433 109 F3
Greenbrier Co. WV, 35480 102 A4
Greenbush MA, 550 151 E2
Greenbush MN, 719 19 F1
Greencastle IN, 10326 99 E1
Greencastle PA, 3996 103 D1
Green City MO, 657 87 D4
Green Co. KY, 11258 110 A1
Green Co. WI, 36842 74 B4
Green Cove Sprs. FL, 6908 139 D3
Green Creek NJ, 1300 104 C4
Greendale IN, 4520 100 B2
Greendale MO, 651 256 B2
Greendale WI, 14046 234 C3
Greene IA, 1130 73 D3
Greene ME, 4076 82 B2
Greene NY, 1580 79 E4
Greene Co. AL, 9045 127 E2
Greene Co. AR, 42090 108 A3
Greene Co. GA, 15994 121 E4
Greene Co. IL, 13886 98 A2
Greene Co. IN, 33165 99 E2
Greene Co. IA, 9336 86 B1
Greene Co. MS, 14400 127 D4
Greene Co. MO, 275174 107 D1
Greene Co. NY, 49221 94 A2
Greene Co. NC, 21362 115 C3
Greene Co. OH, 161573 100 C1
Greene Co. PA, 38686 102 A1
Greene Co. TN, 68831 111 D3
Greene Co. VA, 18403 102 C4
Greenevers NC, 634 123 E2
Greeneville TN, 15062 111 D4
Greenfield CA, 3991 44 B3
Greenfield IL, 1071 98 A2
Greenfield IN, 20602 99 F1
Greenfield IA, 1982 86 B2
Greenfield MA, 17456 94 C1
Greenfield MO, 1371 106 C1
Greenfield NH, 375 95 D1
Greenfield OH, 4639 100 C2
Greenfield TN, 2182 108 C4
Greenfield WI, 36720 234 C3
Green Forest AR, 2761 107 D3
Green Harbor MA, 2609 151 E2
Green Haven MD, 24287 144 C2
Green Haven NY, 3000 148 C1
Green Hill TN, 6618 109 F3
Greenhills OH, 3615 204 B1
Green Island NY, 2620 188 E2
Green Lake WI, 960 74 B2
Green Lake Co. WI, 19051 74 B2
Greenland AR, 1259 106 C4
Greenland NH, 3549 82 A4
Green Lane PA, 508 146 B2
Greenleaf ID, 846 22 A4
Greenlee Co. AZ, 8437 55 E2
Greenmount MD, 600 144 B1
Green Mtn. Falls CO, 640 205 C1
Green Oaks IL, 3866 203 C1
Green Park MO, 2622 256 B3
Green Pond NJ, 1400 148 A3
Greenport NY, 2197 149 E3
Green River UT, 952 39 F2
Green River WY, 12515 32 A3
Greensboro AL, 2497 127 E2
Greensboro FL, 602 137 D2
Greensboro GA, 3359 121 D4
Greensboro MD, 1931 145 E3
Greensboro NC, 269666 112 B4
Greensboro Bend VT, 232 81 E2
Greensburg IN, 11492 100 A2
Greensburg KS, 777 43 D4
Greensburg KY, 2163 110 A2
Greensburg LA, 718 134 B1
Greensburg PA, 14892 92 A4
Greens Fork IN, 361 100 A1
Green Sprs. OH, 1368 90 C2
Greensville Co. VA, 12243 113 E2
Greentown IN, 2415 89 F4
Greentown OH, 3804 91 E3
Green Tree PA, 4432 250 B2
Greenup IL, 1513 99 D2
Greenup KY, 1188 101 D3
Greenup Co. KY, 36910 101 D3
Green Valley AZ, 21391 55 D3
Green Valley CA, 600 52 C2
Green Valley IL, 709 88 B4
Green Valley MD, 12262 144 B2
Greenview IL, 778 88 B4
Green Vil. PA, 1100 103 D1
Greenville AL, 8135 128 A3
Greenville CA, 1129 36 C1
Greenville DE, 2326 146 B3
Greenville FL, 843 137 F2
Greenville GA, 876 128 C1
Greenville IL, 7000 98 B3
Greenville IN, 595 99 F4
Greenville KY, 4312 109 E2
Greenville ME, 1257 84 C4
Greenville MI, 8481 75 F3
Greenville MS, 34400 126 A1
Greenville MO, 511 108 A2
Greenville NH, 1108 95 D1
Greenville NY, 7116 94 B2
Greenville NC, 84554 115 D2
Greenville OH, 13227 90 A4
Greenville PA, 5919 91 F2
Greenville RI, 8658 150 C3
Greenville SC, 58409 121 E2
Greenville TX, 25557 59 F2
Greenville VA, 832 102 B4
Greenville WI, 950 74 C1
Greenville Co. SC, 451225 121 E2
Greenville Jct. ME, 850 84 C4
Greenwich CT, 12942 148 C3
Greenwich NY, 1777 81 D4
Greenwich OH, 1476 91 D3
Greenwood AR, 8952 116 C1
Greenwood DE, 973 145 E3
Greenwood FL, 686 137 D1
Greenwood IN, 49791 99 F1
Greenwood LA, 3219 124 C2
Greenwood MS, 15205 118 B4
Greenwood MO, 5221 96 B3
Greenwood NE, 568 35 F3
Greenwood SC, 23222 121 F3
Greenwood WI, 1026 68 A4
Greenwood Co. KS, 6689 43 F3
Greenwood Co. SC, 69661 121 F3
Greenwood Lake NY, 3154 148 A2
Greenwood Vil. CO, 13925 209 C4
Greer SC, 25515 121 F2
Greer Co. OK, 6239 50 C3
Greers Ferry AR, 891 117 E1
Gregg Co. TX, 121730 124 B2
Gregory SD, 1295 35 D1
Gregory TX, 1907 63 F2
Gregory Co. SD, 4271 35 D1
Greilickville MI, 1530 69 F4
Grenada MS, 13092 118 B4
Grenada Co. MS, 21906 118 B4
Gresham OR, 105594 20 C2
Gresham WI, 586 68 C4
Gresham Park GA, 7432 190 E4
Gretna FL, 1460 137 D2
Gretna LA, 17736 134 B3
Gretna NE, 4441 35 F3
Gretna VA, 1267 112 C2
Greybull WY, 1847 24 C3
Gridley CA, 6584 36 B2
Gridley IL, 1432 88 C3
Gridley KS, 341 96 A4
Griffin GA, 23643 129 D1
Griffith IN, 16893 89 D2
Grifton NC, 2617 115 D3
Griggs Co. ND, 2420 19 D3
Griggsville IL, 1226 98 A1
Grimes AL, 558 128 B4
Grimes IA, 8246 86 C2
Grimes Co. TX, 26604 132 A2
Grinnell IA, 9218 87 D1
Griswold IA, 1036 86 B2
Groesbeck OH, 6788 204 A2
Groesbeck TX, 4328 59 F4
Groom TX, 574 50 B3
Grosse Pointe MI, 5421 210 D3
Grosse Pointe Farms MI, 9479 210 D3
Grosse Pointe Park MI, 11555 210 D3
Grosse Pointe Shores MI, 3008 210 D3
Grosse Pointe Woods MI, 16135 76 C4
Grosse Tete LA, 647 133 F2
Grosvenor Dale CT, 700 150 B2
Groton CT, 10389 149 F2
Groton MA, 1124 95 D1
Groton NY, 2363 79 D4
Groton SD, 1458 27 E2
Groton VT, 437 81 E2
Groton Long Pt. CT, 518 149 F2
Grottoes VA, 2668 102 C4
Grove OK, 6623 106 B3
Grove City FL, 1804 140 C4
Grove City MN, 635 66 B3
Grove City OH, 35575 101 D1
Grove City PA, 8322 92 A2
Grove Hill AL, 1570 127 F4
Groveland CA, 601 37 D4
Groveland FL, 8729 140 C1
Groveland MA, 2800 95 E1
Groveport OH, 5363 101 D1
Grover NC, 708 122 A1
Grover Beach CA, 13156 52 A1
Groves TX, 16144 132 C3
Groveton NH, 1118 81 F2
Groveton TX, 1057 132 B1
Groveton VA, 14598 144 B4
Grovetown GA, 11216 121 F4
Grubbs AR, 386 107 F4
Gruetli-Laager TN, 1813 120 A1
Grundy VA, 1021 111 E2
Grundy Ctr. IA, 2706 73 D4
Grundy Co. IL, 50063 88 C2
Grundy Co. IA, 12453 73 D4
Grundy Co. MO, 10261 86 C4
Grundy Co. TN, 13703 120 A1
Gruver TX, 1194 50 B2
Guadalupe AZ, 5523 249 C3
Guadalupe CA, 7080 52 A1
Guadalupe Co. NM, 4687 49 E4
Guadalupe Co. TX, 131533 61 E3
Guerneville CA, 4534 36 A3
Guernsey WY, 1147 33 E2
Guernsey Co. OH, 40087 91 E4
Gueydan LA, 1398 133 E3
Guilderland NY, 35303 188 C2
Guildhall VT, 268 81 F2
Guilford CT, 22307 149 E2
Guilford ME, 903 82 C1
Guilford MD, 12918 193 A5
Guilford Co. NC, 488406 112 B4
Guin AL, 2376 119 E4
Gulf Breeze FL, 5763 135 F2
Gulf Co. FL, 15863 137 D3
Gulfport FL, 12029 140 B3
Gulfport MS, 67793 135 D2
Gulf Shores AL, 9741 135 E2
Gulf Stream FL, 786 143 F1
Gun Barrel City TX, 5672 59 F3
Gunnison CO, 5854 40 C3
Gunnison MS, 452 118 A4
Gunnison UT, 3285 39 E2
Gunnison Co. CO, 15324 40 C2
Gunter TX, 1498 59 F1
Guntersville AL, 8197 120 A3
Guntown MS, 2083 119 D3
Gurdon AR, 2212 117 D4
Gurley AL, 801 119 F2
Gurn Spr. NY, 600 80 C4
Gustavus AK, 442 155 D4
Gustine CA, 5520 36 C4
Guthrie KY, 1419 109 E3
Guthrie OK, 10191 51 E2
Guthrie TX, 160 58 C1
Guthrie Ctr. IA, 1569 86 B2
Guthrie Co. IA, 10954 86 B2
Guthriesville PA, 1800 146 B3
Guttenberg IA, 1919 73 F4
Guttenberg NJ, 11176 240 D2
Guymon OK, 11442 50 B1
Guys TN, 466 119 D2
Guyton GA, 1684 130 B2
Gwinn MI, 1917 69 D1
Gwinner ND, 753 27 E1
Gwinnett Co. GA, 805321 121 D4
Gwynn VA, 602 113 F1
Gypsum CO, 6477 40 C1
Gypsum KS, 405 43 E2

H

Haakon Co. SD, 1937 26 B3
Habersham Co. GA, 43041 121 D2
Hacienda Hts. CA, 54038 228 E3
Hackberry LA, 1261 133 D3
Hackensack NJ, 43010 148 B3
Hackett AR, 812 116 C1
Hackettstown NJ, 9724 94 A4
Hackleburg AL, 1516 119 E3
Haddam CT, 7635 149 E1
Haddonfield NJ, 11593 146 C3
Haddon Hts. NJ, 7473 248 D4
Hadley MA, 4793 150 A1
Hadley NY, 1009 80 C4
Hagaman NY, 1292 80 C4
Hagan GA, 996 129 F3
Hagerhill KY, 900 111 D1
Hagerman ID, 872 30 C1
Hagerman NM, 1257 57 E2
Hagerstown IN, 1787 100 A1
Hagerstown MD, 39662 144 A1
Hahira GA, 2737 137 F1
Hahnville LA, 3344 134 B3
Haiku HI, 8118 153 D1
Hailey ID, 7960 22 C4
Haileyville OK, 813 116 A2
Haines AK, 1713 155 D3
Haines OR, 416 21 F2
Haines City FL, 20535 141 D2
Halaula HI, 469 153 E2
Halawa HI, 14014 152 C3
Hale Ctr. TX, 2252 58 A1
Hale Co. AL, 15760 127 E2
Hale Co. TX, 36273 58 A1
Haledon NJ, 8318 148 B3
Haleiwa HI, 3970 152 A2
Hales Corners WI, 7692 74 C3
Haleyville AL, 4173 119 E3
Halfmoon NY, 18474 188 E1
Half Moon NC, 8352 115 D4
Half Moon Bay CA, 11324 36 B4
Halfway MD, 10701 144 A1
Halfway OR, 288 22 A2
Halifax MA, 7500 151 D2
Halifax NC, 234 113 E3
Halifax PA, 841 93 D4
Halifax VA, 1309 112 C2
Halifax Co. NC, 54691 113 E4
Halifax Co. VA, 36241 112 C2
Haliimaile HI, 964 153 D1
Hallam PA, 2673 103 E1
Hallandale Beach FL, 37113 143 F2
Hall Co. GA, 179684 121 D3
Hall Co. NE, 58607 35 D4
Hall Co. TX, 3353 50 B4
Hallettsville TX, 2550 61 F3
Halliday ND, 188 18 A3
Hallock MN, 981 19 E1
Hallowell ME, 2381 82 C2
Halls TN, 2255 108 C4
Hallsburg TX, 507 59 F4
Halls Crossroads TN, 2100 110 C4
Halls Gap KY, 450 110 B1
Hallstead PA, 1303 93 F1
Hallsville MO, 1491 97 E2
Hallsville TX, 3577 124 B2
Halsey OR, 904 20 B3
Halstad MN, 597 19 F3
Halstead KS, 2085 43 E3
Haltom City TX, 42409 207 B2
Hamblen Co. TN, 62544 111 D3
Hamburg AR, 2857 125 F1
Hamburg IA, 1187 86 A3
Hamburg MN, 513 66 C4
Hamburg NJ, 3277 148 A2
Hamburg NY, 9409 78 B4
Hamburg PA, 4289 146 A1
Hamden CT, 58180 149 D2
Hamden OH, 879 101 D2
Hamel IL, 816 98 B3
Hamilton AL, 6885 119 D3
Hamilton GA, 1016 128 C2
Hamilton IL, 2951 87 F4
Hamilton IN, 1532 90 A2
Hamilton MI, 1300 75 F4
Hamilton MO, 1809 96 C1
Hamilton MT, 4348 23 D1
Hamilton NY, 4239 79 E3
Hamilton NC, 408 113 E4
Hamilton OH, 62477 100 B2
Hamilton RI, 2500 150 C4
Hamilton TX, 3095 59 E4
Hamilton VA, 506 144 A2
Hamilton City CA, 1759 36 B1
Hamilton Co. FL, 14799 138 C2
Hamilton Co. IL, 8457 98 C4
Hamilton Co. IN, 274569 99 F1
Hamilton Co. IA, 15673 72 C4
Hamilton Co. KS, 2690 42 A3
Hamilton Co. NE, 9124 35 E4
Hamilton Co. NY, 4836 79 F2
Hamilton Co. OH, 802374 100 B2
Hamilton Co. TN, 336463 120 B1
Hamilton Co. TX, 8517 59 D4
Hamilton Square NJ, 12784 147 D2
Ham Lake MN, 15296 67 D3
Hamler OH, 576 90 B2
Hamlet IN, 800 89 E2
Hamlet NC, 6495 122 C2
Hamlin TX, 2124 58 C2
Hamlin WV, 1142 101 E4
Hamlin Co. SD, 5903 27 E3
Hammon OK, 568 50 C3
Hammond IL, 509 98 C1
Hammond IN, 80830 89 D2
Hammond LA, 20019 134 B2
Hammond WI, 1922 67 E4
Hammondsport NY, 661 78 C4
Hammondville AL, 488 120 A2
Hammonton NJ, 14791 147 D4
Hamorton PA, 1400 146 B3
Hampden ME, 4343 83 D1
Hampden Co. MA, 463490 150 A2
Hampden Sydney VA, 1450 113 D2
Hampshire IL, 5563 88 C1
Hampshire Co. MA, 158080 94 C2
Hampshire Co. WV, 23964 102 C2
Hampstead MD, 6323 144 B1
Hampstead NH, 8523 95 E1
Hampton AR, 1324 117 E4
Hampton FL, 500 138 C3
Hampton GA, 6987 129 D1
Hampton IL, 1863 208 C1
Hampton IA, 4461 73 D4
Hampton MD, 5052 193 C1
Hampton NE, 423 35 E4
Hampton NH, 9656 95 E1
Hampton NJ, 1401 104 C1
Hampton PA, 632 103 E1
Hampton SC, 2808 130 B2
Hampton TN, 1300 111 E3
Hampton VA, 137436 113 F2
Hampton Bays NY, 13603 149 E3
Hampton Beach NH, 2275 95 E1
Hampton Co. SC, 21090 130 B2
Hampton Park NY, 950 149 E3
Hamtramck MI, 22423 210 C3
Hana HI, 1235 153 E1
Hanahan SC, 17997 131 D1
Hanamaulu HI, 3835 152 B1
Hanapepe HI, 2638 152 B1
Hanceville AL, 2982 119 F3
Hancock MD, 1545 102 C1
Hancock MI, 4634 65 F3
Hancock MN, 765 66 A3
Hancock NH, 204 81 E4
Hancock NY, 1031 93 F1
Hancock Co. GA, 9429 129 E1
Hancock Co. IL, 19104 87 F4
Hancock Co. IN, 70002 100 A1
Hancock Co. IA, 11341 72 C3
Hancock Co. KY, 8565 109 F1
Hancock Co. ME, 54418 83 D1
Hancock Co. MS, 43929 134 C2
Hancock Co. OH, 74782 90 B3
Hancock Co. TN, 6819 111 D3
Hancock Co. WV, 30676 91 F4
Hand Co. SD, 3431 27 D3
Hanford CA, 53967 45 D3
Hankinson ND, 919 27 F1
Hanley Hills MO, 2101 256 B2
Hanna WY, 841 33 D2
Hanna City IL, 1225 88 B3
Hannibal MO, 17916 97 F1
Hannibal NY, 555 79 D3
Hanover CT, 700 149 F1
Hanover IL, 844 74 A4
Hanover IN, 3546 100 A3
Hanover KS, 682 43 F1
Hanover MA, 13164 151 E2
Hanover MN, 2938 66 C3
Hanover NH, 8636 81 E3
Hanover NJ, 13731 148 A3
Hanover OH, 921 91 D4
Hanover PA, 15289 103 E1
Hanover VA, 252 113 E1
Hanover Co. VA, 99863 103 D4
Hanover Park IL, 37973 203 B3
Hansen ID, 1144 30 C1
Hansford Co. TX, 5613 50 B2
Hanson KY, 742 109 E1
Hanson MA, 2118 151 D2
Hanson Co. SD, 3331 27 E4
Hapeville GA, 6373 190 D5
Happy TX, 678 50 A4
Happy Camp CA, 1190 28 B2
Happy Valley OR, 13903 251 D2
Harahan LA, 9277 239 B2
Haralson Co. GA, 28780 120 B4
Harbert MI, 1619 89 E1
Harbeson DE, 375 145 F4
Harbor OR, 2391 28 A2
Harbor Beach MI, 1703 76 C2
Harbor Bluffs FL, 2860 266 A2
Harbor Hills NY, 575 241 G2
Harbor Hills OH, 1509 101 D1
Harbor Sprs. MI, 1194 70 B3
Harbour Hts. FL, 2987 140 C4
Hardee Co. FL, 27731 140 C3
Hardeeville SC, 2952 130 B3
Hardeman Co. TN, 27253 118 C1
Hardeman Co. TX, 4139 50 C4
Hardin IL, 967 98 A2
Hardin KY, 615 109 D2
Hardin MO, 569 96 C2
Hardin MT, 3505 24 C1
Hardin TX, 819 132 B2
Hardin Co. IL, 4320 109 D1
Hardin Co. IA, 17534 73 D4
Hardin Co. KY, 105543 110 A1
Hardin Co. OH, 32058 90 C3
Hardin Co. TN, 26026 119 D1
Hardin Co. TX, 54635 132 C2
Harding Co. NM, 695 49 E2
Harding Co. SD, 1255 25 F1
Hardinsburg KY, 2343 109 F1
Hardwick GA, 3930 129 E1
Hardwick VT, 1345 81 E2
Hardy AR, 772 107 F3
Hardy Co. WV, 14025 102 C2
Harewood Park MD, 3400 145 D1
Harford Co. MD, 244826 144 C1
Hargill TX, 877 63 E4
Harker Hts. TX, 26700 59 E4
Harkers Island NC, 1207 115 E4
Harlan IA, 5106 86 A2
Harlan KY, 1745 111 D2
Harlan Co. KY, 29278 111 D2
Harlan Co. NE, 3423 35 D4
Harlem FL, 2658 141 D4
Harlem GA, 2666 129 F1
Harlem MT, 808 16 C2
Harleysville PA, 9286 146 C2
Harleyville SC, 677 130 C1
Harlingen TX, 64849 63 F4
Harlowton MT, 997 16 B4
Harmon Co. OK, 2922 50 C4
Harmony IN, 656 99 E1
Harmony MN, 1020 73 E2
Harmony NC, 531 112 A4
Harmony PA, 890 92 A3
Harmony RI, 985 150 C3
Harnett Co. NC, 114678 123 D1
Harney Co. OR, 7422 21 E4
Harold KY, 1400 111 E1
Harper KS, 1473 43 E4
Harper TX, 1192 60 C1
Harper Co. KS, 6034 43 E4
Harper Co. OK, 3685 50 C1
Harpersville AL, 1637 128 A1
Harper Woods MI, 14236 210 D2
Harrah OK, 5095 51 E3
Harrah WA, 625 13 D4
Harriman NY, 2424 148 B2
Harriman TN, 6350 110 B4
Harrington DE, 3562 145 E3
Harrington ME, 882 83 E2
Harrington WA, 424 13 F3
Harris MN, 1132 67 D3
Harrisburg AR, 2288 118 A1
Harrisburg IL, 9017 109 D1
Harrisburg NE, 100 33 F3

Greenville / Spartanburg SC

Apalache B1
Arcadia C1
Berea A2
Cherokee Forest A1
Clifton D1
Conestee A2
Converse D1
Cowpens D1
Crescent C2
Delmar D1
Drayton D1
Duncan C1
Dunean A2
E. Gantt A2
Fairforest C1
Fairview B1
Gantt A2
Glendale D1
Glenn Sprs. D2
Greenville A2
Greer B1
Lake Forest A2
Lyman C1
Marietta A1
Mauldin B2
Moore C2
Paris A1
Pauline D2
Pelham B2
Reidville C2
Renfrew A1
Roebuck D2
Sans Souci A2
Saxon C1
Simpsonville B2
Spartanburg D1
Startex C1
Switzer C2
Taylors B1
Travelers Rest A1
Welcome A2
Wellford C1
White Stone D1
Whitney D1

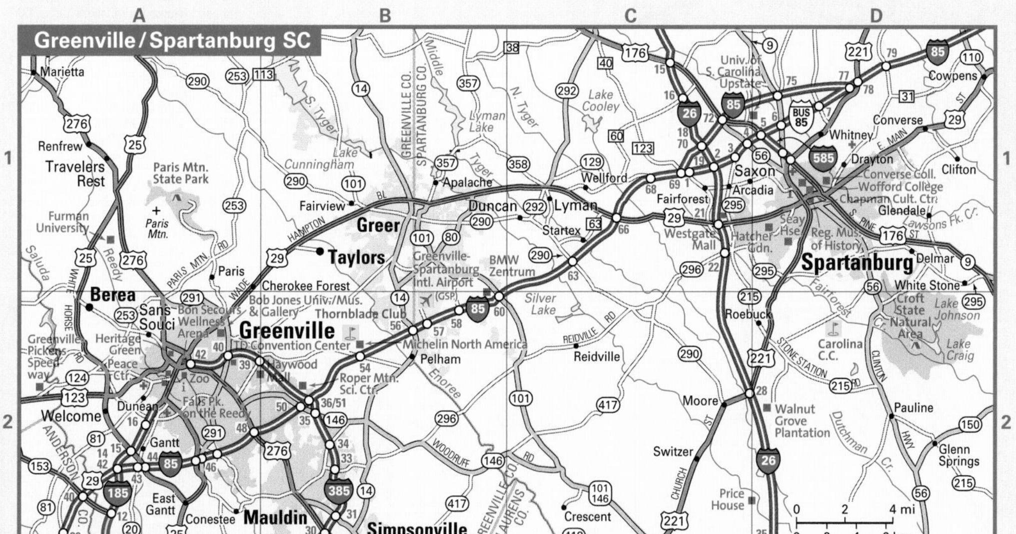

Figures after entries indicate population, page number, and grid reference.

Harrisburg NC, *11526* ... 122 B1
Harrisburg OR, *3567* ... 20 B3
Harrisburg PA, *49528* ... 93 D4
Harrisburg SD, *4089* ... 27 F4
Harris Co. GA, *32024* ... 128 C2
Harris Co. TX, *4092459* ... 132 A3
Harrison AR, *12943* ... 107 D3
Harrison GA, *489* ... 129 F2
Harrison ID, *203* ... 14 B3
Harrison ME, *2315* ... 82 B2
Harrison MI, *2114* ... 76 A1
Harrison NE, *251* ... 33 F1
Harrison NJ, *13620* ... 148 B4
Harrison NY, *27472* ... 148 C3
Harrison OH, *9897* ... 100 B2
Harrison TN, *7769* ... 120 B1
Harrisonburg LA, *348* ... 125 F3
Harrisonburg VA, *48914* ... 102 C3
Harrison Co. IN, *39364* ... 99 F4
Harrison Co. IA, *14928* ... 86 A1

Bressler ... C2
Camp Hill ... A2
Colonial Park ... C1
Eberlys Mill ... B2
Edgemont ... B1
Enhaut ... C2
Enola ... A1
Estherton ... B1
Fair Acres ... B2
Good Hope ... A1
Green Lane Farms ... B2
Harrisburg ... B1
Highland Park ... B2
Highspire ... C2
Lawnton ... C1
Lemoyne ... B2
Marsh Run ... C2
Mechanicsburg ... A2
New Cumberland ... B2
Oakleigh ... C2
Oberlin ... C2
Paxtang ... B1
Paxtang Manor ... C1
Paxtonia ... C1
Penbrook ... B1
Progress ... B1
Reesers Summit ... B2
Rossmoyne ... A2
Rossmoyne Manor ... A2
Rutherford Hts. ... C1
Shiremanstown ... A2
Steelton ... B2
Summerdale ... A1
W. Enola ... A1
W. Fairview ... A1
White Hill ... A2
Wormleysburg ... B2

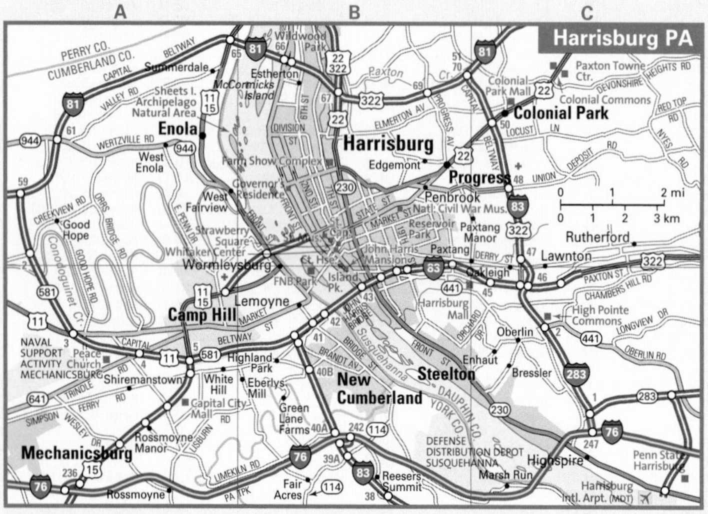

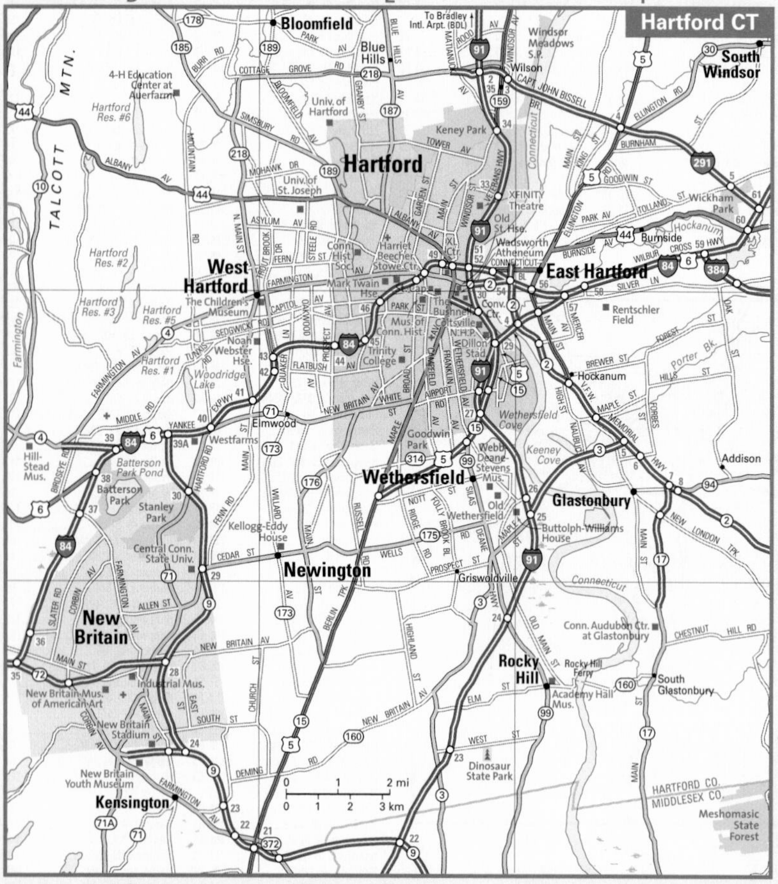

Addison ... F2
Bloomfield ... E1
Blue Hills ... E1
Burnside ... F1
E. Hartford ... F1
Elmwood ... E2
Glastonbury ... F2
Griswoldville ... E2
Hartford ... E1
Hockanum ... F2
Kensington ... D3
New Britain ... D3
Newington ... E2
Rocky Hill ... F3
S. Glastonbury ... F3
S. Windsor ... F1
W. Hartford ... D2
Wethersfield ... E2
Wilson ... E1

Harrison Co. KY, *18846* ... 100 B3
Harrison Co. MS, *187105* ... 134 C2
Harrison Co. MO, *8957* ... 86 C4
Harrison Co. OH, *15864* ... 91 E4
Harrison Co. TX, *65631* ... 124 B2
Harrison Co. WV, *69099* ... 102 A2
Harrisonville MO, *10019* ... 96 B3
Harristown IL, *1367* ... 98 C1
Harrisville MD, *600* ... 146 A4
Harrisville MI, *493* ... 71 D4
Harrisville NH, *961* ... 95 D1
Harrisville NY, *628* ... 79 E1
Harrisville PA, *897* ... 92 A3
Harrisville RI, *1605* ... 150 C2
Harrisville UT, *5567* ... 31 E3
Harrisville WV, *1876* ... 101 F2
Harrodsburg KY, *8340* ... 110 B1
Harrogate TN, *4389* ... 110 C3
Harrold SD, *124* ... 27 D3
Hart MI, *2126* ... 75 E2
Hart TX, *1114* ... 50 A4
Hart Co. GA, *25213* ... 121 E3
Hart Co. KY, *18199* ... 110 A2
Hartford AL, *2624* ... 136 C1
Hartford AR, *642* ... 116 C2
Hartford CT, *124775* ... 150 A3
Hartford IL, *1429* ... 98 A3
Hartford IA, *771* ... 86 C2
Hartford KS, *371* ... 43 F3
Hartford KY, *2672* ... 109 E1
Hartford MI, *2688* ... 89 F1
Hartford SD, *2534* ... 27 F4
Hartford WV, *614* ... 101 E2
Hartford WI, *14223* ... 74 C3
Hartford City IN, *6220* ... 90 A4
Hartford Co. CT, *894014* ... 150 A3
Hartington NE, *1554* ... 35 E1
Hartland ME, *813* ... 82 C1
Hartland VT, *380* ... 81 E3
Hartland WI, *9110* ... 74 C3
Hartley IA, *1672* ... 72 A3
Hartley Co. TX, *6062* ... 50 A2
Hartly DE, *74* ... 145 E2
Hartman AR, *519* ... 116 C1
Harts WV, *656* ... 101 E4
Hartselle AL, *14255* ... 119 F3
Hartshorne OK, *2125* ... 116 A2
Hartsville SC, *7764* ... 122 B3
Hartsville TN, *7870* ... 109 F3
Hartville MO, *613* ... 107 E2
Hartville OH, *2944* ... 91 E3
Hartwell GA, *4469* ... 121 E3
Harvard IL, *9447* ... 74 C4
Harvard MA, *6520* ... 150 C1
Harvard NE, *1013* ... 35 E4
Harvest AL, *5281* ... 119 F2
Harvey IL, *25282* ... 203 E6
Harvey LA, *20348* ... 239 C2
Harvey MI, *1393* ... 69 D1
Harvey ND, *1783* ... 18 C3
Harvey Co. KS, *34684* ... 43 E3
Harveysburg OH, *546* ... 100 C2
Harveys Lake PA, *2791* ... 93 E2
Harwich MA, *1798* ... 151 F3
Harwich Port MA, *1644* ... 151 F3
Harwinton CT, *5571* ... 94 C3
Harwood ND, *718* ... 19 F4
Harwood Hts. IL, *8612* ... 203 D3
Hasbrouck Hts. NJ, *11842* ... 240 C1
Haskell AR, *3990* ... 117 E3
Haskell OK, *2007* ... 106 A4
Haskell TX, *3322* ... 58 C2
Haskell Co. KS, *4256* ... 42 B4
Haskell Co. OK, *12769* ... 116 B1
Haskell Co. TX, *5899* ... 58 C2
Haskins OH, *1188* ... 90 C2
Haslet TX, *1517* ... 207 A1
Haslett MI, *19220* ... 76 A4
Hastings FL, *580* ... 139 D3
Hastings MI, *7350* ... 75 F4
Hastings MN, *22172* ... 67 D4
Hastings NE, *24907* ... 35 E4
Hastings PA, *1278* ... 92 B3
Hatboro PA, *7360* ... 146 C2
Hatch NM, *1648* ... 56 B2
Hatfield AR, *413* ... 116 C3
Hatfield IN, *813* ... 99 E4
Hatfield MA, *1318* ... 150 A1
Hatfield PA, *3290* ... 146 C2
Hatley MS, *482* ... 119 D4
Hatteras NC, *504* ... 115 F3
Hattiesburg MS, *45989* ... 126 C4
Hatton ND, *777* ... 19 E3
Haubstadt IN, *1577* ... 99 D4
Haughton LA, *3454* ... 125 D2
Hauppauge NY, *20882* ... 149 D3
Hauser ID, *678* ... 14 B3
Hauula HI, *4148* ... 152 A2
Havana FL, *1754* ... 137 E2
Havana IL, *3301* ... 88 A4
Havelock NC, *20735* ... 115 D4
Haven KS, *1237* ... 43 E4
Haverhill FL, *1873* ... 143 F1
Haverhill MA, *60879* ... 95 E1
Haverhill NH, *4697* ... 81 E3
Haverstraw NY, *11910* ... 148 B2
Havertown PA, *22300* ... 248 B3
Haviland KS, *701* ... 43 D4
Havre MT, *9310* ... 16 B2
Havre de Grace MD, *12952* ... 145 D1
Hawaiian Gardens CA, *14254* ... 228 E4
Hawaiian Ocean View HI, *4437* ... 153 E4
Hawaiian Paradise Park HI, *11404* ... 153 F3
Hawaii Co. HI, *185079* ... 153 E2
Hawarden IA, *2546* ... 35 F1
Hawesville KY, *945* ... 99 E4
Hawi HI, *1081* ... 153 E2
Hawkins TX, *1278* ... 124 B2
Hawkins Co. TN, *56833* ... 111 D3
Hawkinsville GA, *4589* ... 129 E3
Hawley MN, *2067* ... 19 F4
Hawley PA, *1211* ... 93 F2
Hawley TX, *634* ... 58 C2
Hawleyville CT, *800* ... 148 C1
Haw River NC, *2298* ... 112 C4
Hawthorn PA, *494* ... 92 B3
Hawthorne CA, *84293* ... 228 C3
Hawthorne FL, *1417* ... 138 C3
Hawthorne NV, *3269* ... 37 E3
Hawthorne NJ, *18791* ... 148 B3
Hawthorne NY, *4586* ... 148 B3
Hawthorn Woods IL, *7663* ... 203 B1
Haxtun CO, *946* ... 34 A4
Hayden AL, *444* ... 119 F4
Hayden AZ, *662* ... 55 D2
Hayden CO, *1810* ... 32 C4
Hayden ID, *13294* ... 14 B3
Hayden Lake ID, *574* ... 14 B3
Haydenville MA, *700* ... 150 A1
Hayes LA, *780* ... 133 E2
Hayes Ctr. NE, *214* ... 34 B4
Hayes Co. NE, *967* ... 34 B4
Hayesville NC, *311* ... 121 D2
Hayesville OR, *19936* ... 20 B2
Hayfield MN, *1340* ... 73 D2
Hayfork CA, *2368* ... 28 B4
Haymarket VA, *1782* ... 144 A3
Haynesville LA, *2327* ... 125 D1
Haynesville VA, *550* ... 103 E4
Hayneville AL, *932* ... 128 A3
Hays KS, *20510* ... 43 D2
Hays MT, *843* ... 16 C2
Hays NC, *1851* ... 112 A3
Hays Co. TX, *157107* ... 61 D2
Hay Sprs. NE, *570* ... 34 A1
Haysville KS, *10826* ... 43 E4
Hayti MO, *2939* ... 108 B3
Hayti SD, *381* ... 27 F3
Hayti Hts. MO, *626* ... 108 B3
Hayward CA, *144186* ... 36 B4
Hayward WI, *2318* ... 67 F2
Haywood Co. NC, *59036* ... 111 D4
Haywood Co. TN, *18787* ... 108 C4
Hazard KY, *4456* ... 111 D2
Hazardville CT, *4599* ... 150 A2
Hazel KY, *410* ... 109 D3
Hazel Crest IL, *14100* ... 203 E6
Hazel Green AL, *3630* ... 119 F2
Hazel Green WI, *1256* ... 74 A4
Hazel Park MI, *16422* ... 210 C2
Hazelton ID, *753* ... 31 D1
Hazelton ND, *235* ... 18 C4
Hazelwood MO, *25703* ... 256 B1
Hazen AR, *1468* ... 117 F2
Hazen ND, *2411* ... 18 B3
Hazlehurst GA, *4226* ... 129 F3
Hazlehurst MS, *4009* ... 126 B3
Hazleton IA, *823* ... 73 E4
Hazleton PA, *25340* ... 93 E3
Hazlettville DE, *450* ... 145 E2
Headland AL, *4510* ... 128 B4
Head of the Harbor NY, *1472* ... 149 D3
Healdsburg CA, *11254* ... 36 B3
Healdton OK, *2788* ... 51 E4
Healy AK, *1021* ... 154 C2
Heard Co. GA, *11834* ... 128 B1
Hearne TX, *4459* ... 61 F1
Heart Butte MT, *582* ... 15 E2
Heath OH, *10310* ... 101 D1
Heathcote NJ, *5821* ... 147 D1
Heath Sprs. SC, *790* ... 122 B2
Heathsville VA, *142* ... 103 E4
Heavener OK, *3414* ... 116 B2
Hebbronville TX, *4558* ... 63 E2
Hebbville MD, *10900* ... 193 A2
Heber AZ, *2722* ... 47 E4
Heber CA, *4275* ... 53 E4
Heber City UT, *11362* ... 31 F4
Heber Sprs. AR, *7165* ... 117 E1
Hebron CT, *9198* ... 149 E1
Hebron IL, *1216* ... 74 C4
Hebron IN, *3724* ... 89 E2
Hebron KY, *5929* ... 100 B2
Hebron MD, *1084* ... 103 F3
Hebron NE, *1579* ... 43 E1
Hebron ND, *747* ... 18 B4
Hebron OH, *2336* ... 101 D1
Hebron Estates KY, *1087* ... 100 A4
Hecla SD, *227* ... 27 E1
Hector AR, *450* ... 117 D1
Hector MN, *1151* ... 66 B4
Hedrick IA, *764* ... 87 E2
Hedwig Vil. TX, *2557* ... 220 B2
Heeia HI, *4963* ... 152 A3
Heflin AL, *3480* ... 120 A4
Heidelberg MS, *718* ... 127 D3
Heidelberg PA, *1244* ... 250 A3
Heilwood PA, *711* ... 92 B3
Helena AL, *16793* ... 127 F1
Helena AR, *6323* ... 118 A2
Helena GA, *2883* ... 129 E3
Helena MS, *1184* ... 195 C1
Helena MT, *28190* ... 15 E4
Helena OK, *1403* ... 51 D1
Helenwood TN, *865* ... 110 B3
Hellertown PA, *5898* ... 146 C1
Helmetta NJ, *2178* ... 147 E1
Helotes TX, *7341* ... 61 D2
Helper UT, *2201* ... 39 F1
Hemet CA, *78657* ... 53 D3
Hemingford NE, *803* ... 34 A2
Hemingway SC, *459* ... 122 C4
Hemlock MI, *1466* ... 76 B2
Hemphill TX, *1198* ... 124 C4
Hemphill Co. TX, *3807* ... 50 C2
Hempstead NY, *53891* ... 148 C4
Hempstead TX, *5770* ... 61 F2
Hempstead Co. AR, *22609* ... 116 C4
Henagar AL, *2344* ... 120 A2
Henderson KY, *28757* ... 109 E1
Henderson LA, *1674* ... 133 F2
Henderson MN, *886* ... 66 C4
Henderson NE, *991* ... 35 E4
Henderson NV, *257729* ... 46 B2
Henderson NC, *15368* ... 113 D3
Henderson TN, *6309* ... 119 D1
Henderson TX, *13712* ... 124 B3
Henderson Co. IL, *7331* ... 87 F3
Henderson Co. KY, *46250* ... 109 E1
Henderson Co. NC, *106740* ... 121 E1
Henderson Co. TN, *27769* ... 109 D4
Henderson Co. TX, *78532* ... 124 A2
Hendersonville NC, *13137* ... 121 E1
Hendersonville TN, *51372* ... 109 F3
Hendricks MN, *713* ... 27 F3
Hendricks Co. IN, *145448* ... 99 F1
Hendron KY, *4687* ... 108 C2
Hendry Co. FL, *39140* ... 143 D1
Henefer UT, *766* ... 31 F3
Henlopen Acres DE, *122* ... 145 F4
Hennepin IL, *757* ... 88 B2
Hennepin Co. MN, *1152425* ... 66 C4
Hennessey OK, *2131* ... 51 E2
Henniker NH, *1747* ... 81 F4
Henning MN, *802* ... 64 A4
Henning TN, *945* ... 108 B4
Henrico Co. VA, *306935* ... 113 E1
Henrietta NY, *42581* ... 78 C3
Henrietta TX, *3141* ... 59 D1
Henry IL, *2464* ... 88 B3
Henry SD, *267* ... 27 E2
Henry TN, *464* ... 109 D3
Henry Co. AL, *17302* ... 128 B4
Henry Co. GA, *203922* ... 129 D1
Henry Co. IL, *50486* ... 88 A2
Henry Co. IN, *49462* ... 100 A1
Henry Co. IA, *20145* ... 87 F3
Henry Co. KY, *15416* ... 100 A3
Henry Co. MO, *22272* ... 96 C4
Henry Co. OH, *28215* ... 90 B2
Henry Co. TN, *32330* ... 109 D3
Henry Co. VA, *54151* ... 112 B2
Henryetta OK, *5927* ... 51 F3

Entries in **bold black** indicate counties or parishes.
Entries in **bold color** indicate cities with detailed inset maps.

Henryville IN, *1905* 100 A3
Hephzibah GA, *4011* 129 F1
Heppner OR, *1291* 21 E2
Herculaneum MO, *3468* 98 A4
Hercules CA, *24060* 259 C1
Hereford PA, *930* 146 B1
Hereford TX, *15370* 50 A4
Herington KS, *2526* 43 F3
Herkimer NY, *7743* 79 F3
Herkimer Co. NY, *64519* 79 F2
Hermann MO, *2431* 97 F3
Hermantown MN, *9414* 64 C4
Herminie PA, *789* 92 A4
Hermiston OR, *16745* 21 E1
Hermitage AR, *830* 117 E4
Hermitage MO, *467* 97 D4
Hermitage PA, *16220* 91 F2
Hermon ME, *4437* 83 D1
Hermosa CO, *700* 40 B4
Hermosa SD, *398* 26 A4
Hermosa Beach CA, *19506* 228 C4
Hernandez NM, *946* 48 C2
Hernando FL, *9054* 140 C1
Hernando MS, *14090* 118 B2
Hernando Beach FL, *2299* 140 B1
Hernando Co. FL, *172778* 140 B1
Herndon VA, *23292* 144 A3
Heron Lake MN, *698* 72 A2
Herreid SD, *438* 26 C1
Herricks NY, *4295* 241 G3
Herriman UT, *21785* 31 E4
Herrin IL, *12501* 108 C1
Herscher IL, *1591* 89 D3
Hershey NE, *665* 34 B3
Hershey PA, *14257* 93 E4
Hertford NC, *2143* 113 F3
Hertford Co. NC, *24669* 113 F3
Hesperia CA, *90173* 53 D2
Hesperia MI, *954* 75 E2
Hessmer LA, *802* 133 F1
Hesston KS, *3709* 43 E3
Hettinger ND, *1226* 26 A1
Hettinger Co. ND, *2477* 18 A4
Heuvelton NY, *714* 80 B2
Hewitt TX, *13549* 59 E4
Hewitt WI, *828* 68 A4
Hewlett NY, *6819* 241 G4
Hewlett Harbor NY, *1263* 241 G5
Hewlett Neck NY, *445* 241 G5
Heyburn ID, *3089* 31 D1
Heyworth IL, *2841* 88 C4
Hialeah FL, *224669* 143 E2
Hialeah Gardens FL, *21744* 143 E2
Hiawassee GA, *880* 121 D2
Hiawatha IA, *7024* 87 E1
Hiawatha KS, *3172* 96 A1
Hibbing MN, *16361* 64 B3
Hickman KY, *2395* 108 C3
Hickman NE, *1657* 35 F4
Hickman Co. KY, *4902* 108 C3
Hickman Co. TN, *24690* 109 E4
Hickory MS, *530* 126 C2
Hickory NC, *40010* 111 F4
Hickory Co. MO, *9627* 97 D4
Hickory Flat MS, *601* 118 C2
Hickory Hills IL, *14049* 203 D5
Hickory Withe TN, *2574* 118 C1
Hicksville NY, *41547* 148 C4
Hicksville OH, *3581* 90 A2
Hico TX, *1379* 59 E3
Hidalgo TX, *11198* 63 E4
Hidalgo Co. NM, *4894* 55 F4
Hidalgo Co. TX, *774769* 63 E3
Hidden Hills CA, *1856* 228 A2
Hiddenite NC, *536* 112 A4
Hideaway TX, *3083* 124 A2
Higbee MO, *568* 97 E2
Higganum CT, *1698* 149 E1
Higginsville MO, *4797* 96 C2
High Bridge NJ, *3648* 104 C1
Highgate Ctr. VT, *600* 81 D1
Highgrove CA, *3988* 229 J3
Highland AR, *1045* 107 F3
Highland CA, *53104* 229 K2
Highland IL, *9919* 98 B3
Highland IN, *23727* 89 D2
Highland KS, *1012* 96 A1
Highland MD, *1034* 144 B2
Highland NY, *5647* 94 B3
Highland UT, *15523* 31 F4
Highland WI, *842* 74 A3
Highland Beach FL, *3539* 143 F1
Highland City FL, *10834* 140 C2
Highland Co. OH, *43589* 100 C2
Highland Co. VA, *2321* 102 B4
Highland Falls NY, *3900* 148 B2
Highland Hts. KY, *6923* 204 B3
Highland Hts. OH, *8345* 204 G1
Highland Hills OH, *1130* 204 G2
Highland Lakes NJ, *4933* 148 A2
Highland Mills NY, *3468* 148 B2
Highland Park IL, *29763* 89 D1
Highland Park MI, *11776* 210 C3
Highland Park NJ, *13982* 147 E1
Highland Park PA, *1380* 218 B2
Highland Park TX, *8564* 207 D2
Highlands NJ, *5005* 147 F1
Highlands NC, *924* 121 D2
Highlands TX, *7522* 132 B3
Highlands Co. FL, *98786* 141 D4
Highland Sprs. VA, *15711* 254 C2
Highlands Ranch CO, *96713* 209 C4
Highlandville MO, *911* 107 D2
Highmore SD, *795* 27 D3
High Pt. FL, *3686* 266 B2
High Pt. NC, *104371* 112 B4
High Ridge MO, *4305* 98 A3
High Rolls NM, *834* 56 C2
High Shoals NC, *696* 122 A1
Highspire PA, *2399* 218 C2
High Sprs. FL, *5350* 138 C3
Hightstown NJ, *5494* 147 D2
Hightsville NC, *739* 275 A1
Highwood IL, *5405* 203 D1
Hilbert WI, *1132* 74 C1
Hilda SC, *447* 130 B1
Hildale UT, *2726* 46 C1
Hiles WI, *404* 68 B2
Hillandale MD, *6043* 270 E1
Hillburn NY, *951* 148 B2
Hill City KS, *1474* 42 C2
Hill City MN, *633* 64 B4
Hill City SD, *948* 25 F4
Hill Country Vil. TX, *985* 257 E1
Hill Co. MT, *16096* 16 A1
Hill Co. TX, *35089* 59 E3
Hillcrest IL, *1326* 88 B1
Hillcrest NY, *7558* 148 B2
Hillcrest TX, *730* 132 B4
Hillcrest Hts. MD, *16469* 144 B3
Hilliard FL, *3086* 139 D1
Hilliard OH, *28435* 101 D1
Hillman MI, *701* 70 C3
Hills IA, *703* 87 F2
Hills MN, *686* 27 F4
Hillsboro AL, *552* 119 E2
Hillsboro IL, *6207* 98 B2
Hillsboro IN, *538* 89 E4
Hillsboro KS, *2993* 43 E3
Hillsboro MO, *2821* 98 A4
Hillsboro ND, *1603* 19 E3
Hillsboro OH, *6605* 100 C2
Hillsboro OR, *91611* 20 B2
Hillsboro TX, *8456* 59 E3
Hillsboro WI, *1417* 74 A2
Hillsboro Beach FL, *1875* 143 F1
Hillsborough CA, *10825* 259 B4
Hillsborough NH, *1976* 81 E4
Hillsborough NC, *6087* 112 C4
Hillsborough Co. FL, *1229226* 140 C3
Hillsborough Co. NH, *400721* 81 F4
Hillsdale IL, *523* 88 A2
Hillsdale MI, *8305* 90 B1
Hillsdale MO, *1478* 256 B2
Hillsdale NJ, *10219* 148 B3
Hillsdale Co. MI, *46688* 90 B1
Hillside IL, *8157* 203 C4
Hillside NJ, *21404* 148 A4
Hillside Lake NY, *1084* 148 B1
Hillsville VA, *2681* 112 A2
Hilltop MN, *744* 235 C1
Hillview KY, *8172* 100 A4
Hilmar CA, *4807* 36 C4
Hilo HI, *43263* 153 F3
Hilshire Vil. TX, *746* 220 B2
Hilton NY, *5886* 78 C3
Hilton Head Island SC, *37099* 130 C3
Hinckley IL, *2070* 88 C1
Hinckley MN, *1800* 67 D2
Hinckley UT, *696* 39 D2
Hindman KY, *777* 111 D1
Hinds Co. MS, *245285* 126 B3
Hines OR, *1563* 21 E4
Hinesburg VT, *658* 81 D2
Hinesville GA, *33437* 130 B3
Hingham MA, *5650* 151 D1
Hinsdale IL, *16816* 203 C5
Hinsdale MA, *1872* 94 C1
Hinsdale NH, *1548* 94 C1
Hinsdale Co. CO, *843* 40 C4
Hinson FL, *750* 137 E2
Hinton IA, *928* 35 F1
Hinton OK, *3196* 51 D3
Hinton WV, *2676* 112 A1
Hiram GA, *3546* 120 C4
Hiram OH, *1406* 91 E2
Hitchcock TX, *6961* 132 B4
Hitchcock Co. NE, *2908* 34 B4
Hitchins KY, *475* 101 D4
Hobart IN, *29059* 89 D2
Hobart OK, *3756* 51 D3
Hobart WA, *6221* 12 C3
Hobbs NM, *34122* 57 F2
Hobe Sound FL, *11521* 141 F4
Hoboken NJ, *50005* 148 B4
Hobson MT, *215* 16 B4
Hockessin DE, *13527* 146 B3
Hocking Co. OH, *29380* 101 D1
Hockley Co. TX, *22935* 58 A1
Hodge LA, *470* 125 E3
Hodgeman Co. KS, *1916* 42 C3
Hodgenville KY, *3206* 110 A1
Hodgkins IL, *1897* 203 C5
Hoffman MN, *681* 66 A2
Hoffman NC, *588* 122 C2
Hoffman Estates IL, *51895* 203 B3
Hogansville GA, *3060* 128 C1
Hohenwald TN, *3757* 119 E1
Hoisington KS, *2706* 43 D3
Hokah MN, *580* 73 F2
Hoke Co. NC, *46952* 123 D2
Hokendauqua PA, *3378* 189 A1
Hokes Bluff AL, *4286* 120 A3
Holbrook AZ, *5053* 47 F3
Holbrook MA, *10791* 151 D2
Holbrook NY, *27195* 149 D4
Holcomb KS, *2094* 42 B3
Holcomb MO, *635* 108 B3
Holden MA, *17346* 150 B1
Holden MO, *2252* 96 C3
Holden UT, *378* 39 E2
Holden WV, *876* 111 E1
Holden Beach NC, *575* 123 E4
Holdenville OK, *5771* 51 F3
Holdingford MN, *708* 66 B2
Holdrege NE, *5495* 35 D4
Holgate OH, *1109* 90 B2
Holiday FL, *22403* 140 B2
Holiday Hills IL, *610* 203 A1
Holiday Lakes TX, *1107* 132 A4
Holladay UT, *26472* 257 B2
Holland AR, *557* 117 E1
Holland IN, *626* 99 E4
Holland MA, *1464* 150 B2
Holland MI, *33051* 75 E4
Holland NY, *1206* 78 B4
Holland OH, *1764* 90 C2
Holland TX, *1121* 61 E1
Hollandale MS, *2702* 126 A1
Holley FL, *1630* 135 F2
Holley NY, *1811* 78 B3
Holliday TX, *1758* 59 D1
Hollidaysburg PA, *5791* 92 C4
Hollins VA, *14673* 112 B1
Hollis NH, *7684* 95 D1
Hollis OK, *2060* 50 C4
Hollis Ctr. ME, *450* 82 B3
Hollister CA, *34928* 44 B2
Hollister MO, *4426* 107 D3
Hollister NC, *674* 113 D3
Holliston MA, *13547* 150 C2
Hollow Creek KY, *783* 230 E3
Hollow Rock TN, *718* 109 D4
Holly CO, *802* 42 A3
Holly MI, *6086* 76 B4
Holly Grove AR, *602* 117 F2
Holly Hill FL, *11659* 139 E4
Holly Hill SC, *1277* 130 C1
Holly Park NJ, *2200* 147 E3
Holly Pond AL, *798* 119 F3
Holly Ridge NC, *1268* 115 C4
Holly Sprs. GA, *9189* 120 C3
Holly Sprs. MS, *7699* 118 C2
Holly Sprs. NC, *24661* 112 C4
Hollyvilla KY, *537* 100 A4
Hollywood AL, *1000* 120 A2
Hollywood FL, *140768* 143 F2
Hollywood MD, *650* 103 E4
Hollywood SC, *4714* 131 D2
Hollywood Park TX, *3062* 61 D2
Holmdel NJ, *16773* 147 E2
Holmen WI, *9005* 73 F1
Holmes Beach FL, *3836* 140 B3
Holmes Co. FL, *19927* 136 C1
Holmes Co. MS, *19198* 126 B1
Holmes Co. OH, *42366* 91 D4
Holstein IA, *1396* 72 A4
Holt AL, *3638* 127 E1
Holt MI, *23973* 76 A4
Holt Co. MO, *4912* 86 A4
Holt Co. NE, *10435* 35 D1
Holton KS, *3329* 96 A2
Holts Summit MO, *3247* 97 E3
Holtville CA, *5939* 53 E4
Holualoa HI, *8538* 153 E3
Holyoke CO, *2313* 34 A4
Holyoke MA, *39880* 150 A2
Holyrood KS, *447* 43 D3
Homecroft IN, *722* 99 F1
Homedale ID, *2633* 22 A4
Home Gardens CA, *11570* 229 H4
Homeland CA, *5969* 229 K4
Homeland GA, *910* 139 D1
Homeland Park SC, *6296* 121 E3
Homer AK, *5003* 154 C3
Homer GA, *1141* 121 D3
Homer IL, *1193* 99 D1
Homer LA, *3237* 125 D2
Homer MI, *1668* 90 A1
Homer NE, *549* 35 F2
Homer NY, *3291* 79 D4
Homer City PA, *1707* 92 B4
Homer Glen IL, *24220* 203 C6
Homerville GA, *2456* 138 C1
Homestead FL, *60512* 143 E3
Homestead PA, *3165* 250 C2
Homestead Valley CA, *3032* 259 A2
Hometown IL, *4349* 203 D5
Hometown PA, *1349* 93 E3
Hometown WV, *668* 101 E3
Homewood AL, *25167* 119 F4
Hominy OK, *3565* 51 F1
Homosassa FL, *2578* 140 B1
Homosassa Sprs. FL, *13791* 140 B1
Honaker VA, *1449* 111 E2
Honalo HI, *2423* 153 E3
Honaunau HI, *2567* 153 E3
Hondo TX, *8803* 60 C3
Honea Path SC, *3597* 121 E3
Honeoye NY, *579* 78 C4
Honeoye Falls NY, *2674* 78 C3
Honesdale PA, *4480* 93 F2
Honey Brook PA, *1713* 146 B2
Honey Grove TX, *1668* 59 F1
Honeyville UT, *1441* 31 E3
Honokaa HI, *2258* 153 E2
Honokowai HI, *7261* 153 D1
Honolulu HI, *337256* 152 A3
Honolulu Co. HI, *953207* 152 A3
Honomu HI, *509* 153 F3
Hood Co. TX, *51182* 59 E3
Hood River OR, *7167* 21 D1
Hood River Co. OR, *22346* 20 C2
Hooker OK, *1918* 50 B1
Hooker Co. NE, *736* 34 B2
Hooks TX, *2769* 116 C4
Hooksett NH, *4147* 81 F4
Hoonah AK, *760* 155 D4
Hooper NE, *830* 35 F3
Hooper UT, *7218* 244 A2
Hooper Bay AK, *1093* 154 B3
Hoopeston IL, *5351* 89 D4
Hoople ND, *242* 19 E2
Hoosick Falls NY, *3501* 94 B1
Hoover AL, *81619* 127 F1
Hooverson Hts. WV, *2590* 91 F4
Hooversville PA, *645* 92 B4
Hopatcong NJ, *15147* 148 A3
Hope AR, *10095* 117 D4
Hope IN, *2102* 99 F2
Hope ND, *258* 19 E3
Hope RI, *1900* 150 C3
Hopedale IL, *865* 88 B4
Hopedale MA, *3753* 150 C2
Hopedale OH, *950* 91 F4
Hope Mills NC, *15176* 123 D2
Hope Valley RI, *1612* 150 C4
Hopewell NJ, *1922* 147 D1
Hopewell TN, *1874* 120 B1
Hopewell VA, *22591* 113 E1
Hopewell Jct. NY, *376* 148 B1
Hopkins MI, *610* 75 F4
Hopkins MN, *17591* 235 A3
Hopkins MO, *532* 86 B4
Hopkins Co. KY, *46920* 109 E2
Hopkins Co. TX, *35161* 124 A1
Hopkins Park IL, *603* 89 D3
Hopkinsville KY, *31577* 109 E2

Honolulu HI

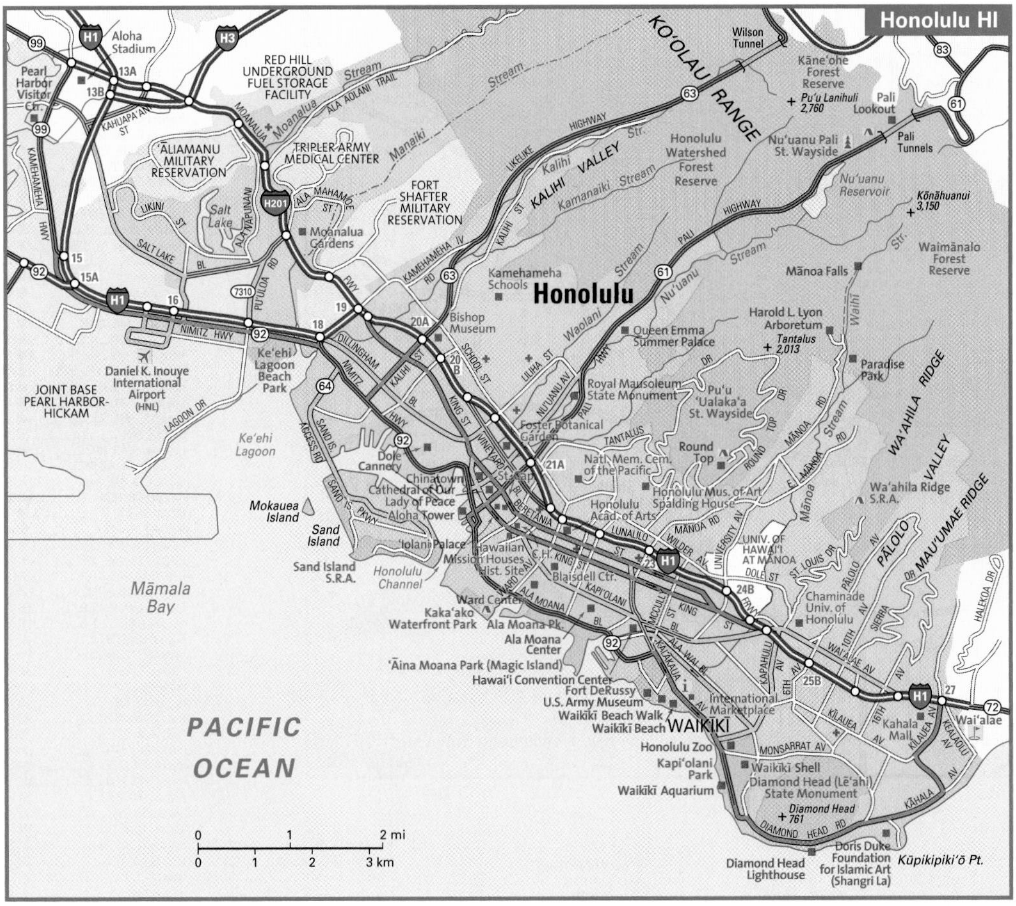

Hot Springs AR

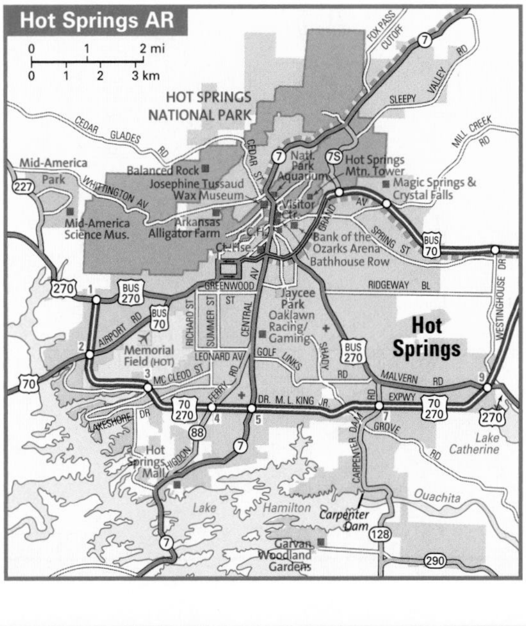

Figures after entries indicate population, page number, and grid reference.

Aldine C1
Barrett D1
Beaumont Place D2
Bellaire B3
Booth A4
Brookside Vil. C4
Bunker Hill Vil. B2
Channelview D2
Cloverleaf D2
Crabb A4
Crosby D1
Cypress A1
Deer Park D3
Four Corners A3
Fresno B4
Friendswood D4
Galena Park C3
Hedwig Vil. B2
Highlands D2
Hilshire Vil. B2
Houmont Park D2
Houston C2
Humble C1
Hunters Creek Vil. B2
Jacinto City C2
Jersey Vil. A1
La Porte D3
League City D4
Lynchburg D2
Magnolia Gardens D1
Meadows Place A3
Mission Bend A3
Missouri City B4
Nassau Bay D4
N. Houston B1
Pasadena D3
Pearland C4
Piney Pt. Vil. B2
Satsuma A1
Sheldon D2
S. Houston C3
Southside Place B3
Spring Valley Village B2
Stafford B4
Sugar Land A3
Webster D4
W. University Place B3

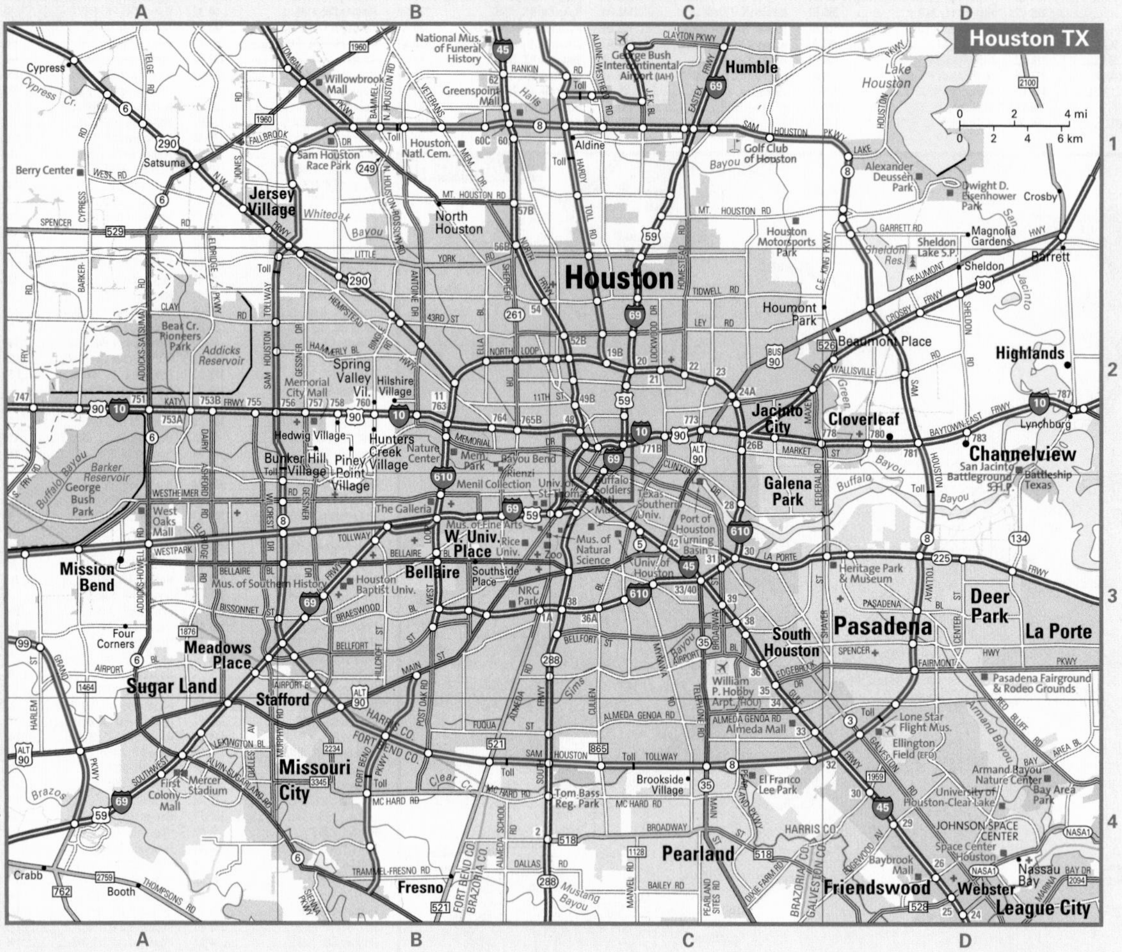

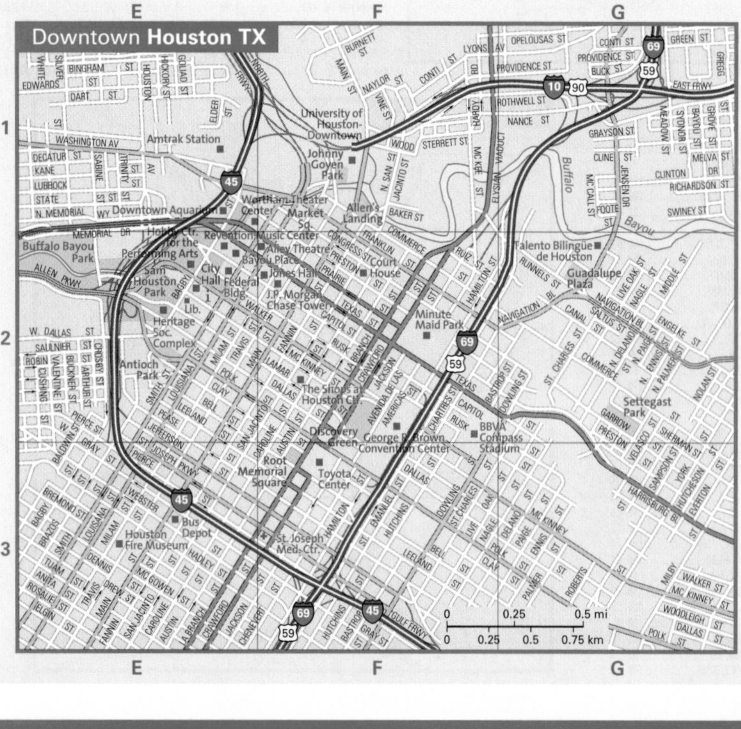

POINTS OF INTEREST
Allen's Landing F1
Alley Theatre F2
Amtrak Station E1
Bayou Music Center E2
Bayou Place E2
BBVA Compass Stadium F2
Bus Depot E3
City Hall E2
Court House F2
Downtown Aquarium E1
Federal Building E2
George R. Brown Convention Center F2
Heritage Society Complex E2
Hobby Center for the Performing Arts E2
Houston Fire Museum E3
Jones Hall F2
J.P. Morgan Chase Tower F2
Library E2
Minute Maid Park F2
The Shops at Houston Center F2
Talento Bilingüe de Houston G2
Toyota Center F3
Univ. of Houston-Downtown F1
Wortham Theater Center E1

Hopkinton IA, *628* 73 F4
Hopkinton MA, *2550* 150 C2
Hopkinton NH, *5589* 81 F4
Hopwood PA, *2090* 102 B1
Hoquiam WA, *8726* 12 B4
Horace ND, *2430* 19 E4
Horatio AR, *1044* 116 C4
Horicon WI, *3655* 74 C2
Horizon City TX, *16735* 56 C4
Hornbeak TN, *424* 108 C3
Hornbeck LA, *480* 125 D4
Hornell NY, *8563* 78 C4
Hornersville MO, *663* 108 B4
Horn Lake MS, *26066* 118 B2
Horry Co. SC, *269291* 123 D3
Horse Cave KY, *2311* 110 A2
Horseheads NY, *6461* 93 D1
Horse Pasture VA, *2227* 112 B3
Horseshoe Bay TX, *3418* 61 D1
Horseshoe Bend AR, *2184* 107 F3
Horseshoe Bend ID, *707* 22 B4
Horsham PA, *14842* 146 C2
Horton KS, *1776* 96 A1
Hortonville MA, *850* 151 D3
Hortonville WI, *2711* 74 C1
Hoschton GA, *1377* 121 D3
Hosmer SD, *208* 27 D1
Hospers IA, *698* 35 F1
Hotchkiss CO, *944* 40 B2
Hotchkissville CT, *1200* 149 D1
Hotevilla-Bacavi AZ, *957* 47 E2
Hot Spr. Co. AR, *32923* 117 D3
Hot Sprs. AR, *35193* 117 D3
Hot Sprs. MT, *544* 14 C3
Hot Sprs. NC, *560* 111 D4
Hot Sprs. SD, *3711* 25 F4
Hot Sprs. Co. WY, *4812* 24 B4
Hot Sprs. Vil. AR, *12807* 117 D2
Hot Sulphur Sprs. CO, *663* 41 D1
Houck AZ, *1024* 48 A3
Houghton MI, *7708* 65 F3
Houghton NY, *1693* 78 B4
Houghton Co. MI, *36628* 65 F4
Houghton Lake MI, *3427* 76 A1
Houlton ME, *4856* 85 E3
Houma LA, *33727* 134 A3
Housatonic MA, *1109* 94 B2
Houston AK, *1912* 154 C3
Houston DE, *374* 145 E3
Houston MN, *979* 73 E2
Houston MS, *3623* 118 C4
Houston MO, *2081* 107 E1
Houston PA, *1296* 92 A4
Houston TX, *2099451* 132 A3
Houston Acres KY, *507* 230 F2
Houston Co. AL, *101547* 137 D1
Houston Co. GA, *139900* 129 D2
Houston Co. MN, *19027* 73 F2
Houston Co. TN, *8426* 109 E3
Houston Co. TX, *23732* 124 A4
Houtzdale PA, *797* 92 C3
Hoven SD, *406* 27 D2
Howard KS, *687* 43 F4
Howard PA, *720* 92 C3
Howard SD, *858* 27 E4
Howard WI, *17399* 68 C4
Howard City MI, *1808* 75 F2
Howard Co. AR, *13789* 116 C3
Howard Co. IN, *82752* 89 F4
Howard Co. IA, *9566* 73 E3
Howard Co. MD, *287085* 144 B2
Howard Co. MO, *10144* 97 D2
Howard Co. NE, *6274* 35 D3
Howard Co. TX, *35012* 58 B3
Howard Lake MN, *1962* 66 C3
Howards Grove WI, *3188* 75 D2
Howe IN, *807* 90 A1
Howe OK, *802* 116 B2
Howe TX, *2600* 59 F1
Howell MI, *9489* 76 B4
Howell Co. MO, *40400* 107 E3
Howells NE, *561* 35 F2
Howells NY, *800* 148 A1
Howey-in-the-Hills FL, *1098* 140 C1
Howland ME, *1096* 85 D4
Hoxie AR, *2780* 108 A4
Hoxie KS, *1201* 42 C2
Hoyt KS, *669* 96 A2
Hoyt Lakes MN, *2017* 64 C3
Huachuca City AZ, *1853* 55 D4
Hubbard IA, *845* 72 C4
Hubbard OH, *7874* 276 C2
Hubbard OR, *3173* 20 C2
Hubbard TX, *1423* 59 F3
Hubbard Co. MN, *20428* 64 A3
Hubbard Lake MI, *1002* 71 D4
Hubbell MI, *946* 65 F3
Huber Hts. OH, *38101* 100 C1
Huber Ridge OH, *4604* 206 C1
Huddy KY, *900* 111 E1
Hudson CO, *2356* 41 E1
Hudson FL, *12158* 140 B2
Hudson IL, *1838* 88 C3
Hudson IN, *518* 90 A2
Hudson IA, *2282* 73 D4
Hudson MA, *14907* 150 C1
Hudson MI, *2307* 90 B1
Hudson NH, *7336* 95 E1
Hudson NY, *6713* 94 B2
Hudson NC, *3776* 111 F4
Hudson OH, *22262* 91 E2
Hudson SD, *296* 35 F1
Hudson TX, *4731* 124 B4
Hudson WI, *12719* 67 D4
Hudson WY, *458* 32 B1
Hudson Co. NJ, *634266* 148 B4
Hudson Falls NY, *7281* 81 D4
Hudsonville MI, *7116* 75 F3
Hudspeth Co. TX, *3476* 57 D4
Huerfano Co. CO, *6711* 41 E4
Hueytown AL, *16105* 119 F4
Huffs Church PA, *100* 146 B1
Hughes AR, *1441* 118 A2
Hughes Co. OK, *14003* 51 F3
Hughes Co. SD, *17022* 26 C3
Hughes Sprs. TX, *1760* 124 B1
Hughestown PA, *1392* 261 C2
Hughesville MD, *2197* 144 C4
Hughesville PA, *2128* 93 E2
Hughson CA, *6640* 36 C4
Hugo CO, *730* 41 F2
Hugo MN, *13332* 67 D3
Hugo OK, *5310* 116 A3
Hugoton KS, *3904* 42 B4
Huguenot NY, *900* 148 A1
Huguley AL, *2540* 128 B2
Hulbert OK, *590* 106 B4
Hulett WY, *383* 25 F3
Hull IA, *2175* 35 F1
Hull MA, *10293* 151 D1
Hulmeville PA, *1003* 147 D2
Humansville MO, *1048* 106 C1
Humarock MA, *2000* 151 E2
Humble TX, *15133* 132 B3
Humboldt IA, *4690* 72 B4
Humboldt KS, *1953* 106 A1
Humboldt NE, *877* 43 F1
Humboldt NV, *500* 29 F4
Humboldt SD, *589* 27 F4
Humboldt TN, *8452* 108 C4
Humboldt Co. CA, *134623* 28 A4
Humboldt Co. IA, *9815* 72 B3
Humboldt Co. NV, *16528* 29 F3
Humeston IA, *494* 86 C3
Hummelstown PA, *4538* 93 E4
Humphrey AR, *557* 117 F3

Entries in **bold black** indicate counties or parishes.
Entries in **bold color** indicate cities with detailed inset maps.

Humphrey NE, *760* ... 35 E3
Humphreys Co. MS, *9375* ... 126 B1
Humphreys Co. TN, *18538* ... 109 E4
Hungerford TX, *347* ... 61 F3
Hungry Horse MT, *826* ... 15 D2
Hunt Co. TX, *86129* ... 59 F2
Hunter ND, *261* ... 19 E3
Hunter TN, *1854* ... 111 E3
Hunterdon Co. NJ, *128349* ... 147 D1
Hunters Creek Vil. TX, *4367* ... 220 B2
Hunters Pt. AZ, *400* ... 48 A3
Huntersville NC, *46773* ... 122 A1
Huntertown IN, *4810* ... 90 A2
Huntingburg IN, *6057* ... 99 E4
Huntingdon PA, *7093* ... 92 C4
Huntingdon TN, *3985* ... 109 D4
Huntingdon Co. PA, *45913* ... 92 C3
Huntington AR, *635* ... 116 C1
Huntington IN, *17391* ... 89 F3
Huntington MA, *936* ... 94 C2
Huntington NY, *18046* ... 148 C3
Huntington OR, *440* ... 22 A3
Huntington TX, *2118* ... 124 B4
Huntington UT, *2129* ... 39 F2
Huntington VA, *11267* ... 270 C5
Huntington WV, *49138* ... 101 D3
Huntington Bay NY, *1425* ... 148 C3
Huntington Beach CA, *189992* ... 52 C3
Huntington Co. IN, *37124* ... 89 F3
Huntington Park CA, *58114* ... 228 D3
Huntington Sta. NY, *33029* ... 148 C3
Huntington Woods MI, *6238* ... 210 B2
Huntingtown MD, *3311* ... 144 C4
Hunting Valley OH, *705* ... 204 G2
Huntland TN, *872* ... 120 A2
Huntleigh MO, *334* ... 256 B2
Huntley IL, *24291* ... 88 C1
Huntley MT, *446* ... 24 C1
Hunts Pt. WA, *443* ... 262 B3
Huntsville AL, *180105* ... 119 F2
Huntsville AR, *2346* ... 106 C4
Huntsville MO, *1564* ... 97 E2
Huntsville TN, *1248* ... 110 B3
Huntsville TX, *38548* ... 132 A1
Huntsville UT, *608* ... 31 F3
Hurffville NJ, *4300* ... 146 C4
Hurley MS, *1551* ... 135 D1
Hurley NM, *1297* ... 55 F2
Hurley NY, *3458* ... 94 B2
Hurley SD, *415* ... 27 F4
Hurley WI, *1547* ... 65 E4
Hurlock MD, *2092* ... 145 E4
Huron CA, *6754* ... 44 C3
Huron OH, *7149* ... 91 D2
Huron SD, *12592* ... 27 E3
Huron Co. MI, *33118* ... 76 C2
Huron Co. OH, *59626* ... 91 D3
Hurricane UT, *13748* ... 39 D4
Hurricane WV, *6284* ... 101 E3
Hurst IL, *795* ... 108 C1
Hurst TX, *37337* ... 207 B2
Hurstbourne KY, *4216* ... 230 F2
Hurstbourne Acres KY, *1811* ... 230 F2
Hurt VA, *1304* ... 112 C2
Hurtsboro AL, *553* ... 128 B3
Hustisford WI, *1123* ... 74 C3
Hustonville KY, *405* ... 110 B1
Hutchins TX, *5338* ... 207 E3
Hutchinson KS, *42080* ... 43 E3
Hutchinson MN, *14178* ... 66 C4
Hutchinson Co. SD, *7343* ... 27 E4
Hutchinson Co. TX, *22150* ... 50 B2
Hutsonville IL, *554* ... 99 D2
Huttig AR, *597* ... 125 E1
Hutto TX, *14698* ... 61 E1
Huxley IA, *3317* ... 86 C1
Hyannis MA, *20097* ... 151 F3
Hyannis NE, *182* ... 34 B2
Hyannis Port MA, *3100* ... 151 F4
Hyattsville MD, *17557* ... 144 B3
Hyde PA, *1399* ... 92 C3
Hyde Co. NC, *5810* ... 113 F4
Hyde Co. SD, *1420* ... 27 D3
Hyden KY, *365* ... 111 D2
Hyde Park NY, *1908* ... 94 B3
Hyde Park UT, *3833* ... 31 E2
Hyde Park VT, *462* ... 81 E2
Hydesville CA, *1237* ... 28 A4
Hydetown PA, *526* ... 92 A2
Hydro OK, *969* ... 51 D3
Hymera IN, *801* ... 99 E2
Hyndman PA, *910* ... 102 C1
Hypoluxo FL, *2588* ... 143 F1
Hyrum UT, *7609* ... 31 E3
Hysham MT, *312* ... 25 D1

I

Iaeger WV, *302* ... 111 F1
Iberia MO, *736* ... 97 E4
Iberia Par. LA, *73240* ... 133 F3
Iberville Par. LA, *33387* ... 133 F2
Icard NC, *2664* ... 111 F4
Ida MI, *1100* ... 90 C1
Idabel OK, *7010* ... 116 B4
Ida Co. IA, *7089* ... 72 A4
Ida Grove IA, *2142* ... 72 A4
Idaho City ID, *485* ... 22 B4
Idaho Co. ID, *16267* ... 14 C4
Idaho Falls ID, *56813* ... 23 E4
Idalou TX, *2250* ... 58 A1
Ideal GA, *499* ... 129 D2
Ider AL, *723* ... 120 A2
Idyllwild CA, *3874* ... 53 D3
Idylwood VA, *17288* ... 270 B3
Ignacio CO, *697* ... 48 B1
Ilion NY, *8053* ... 79 F3
Illiopolis IL, *891* ... 98 B1
Ilwaco WA, *936* ... 12 B4
Imboden AR, *677* ... 107 F3
Imlay NV, *171* ... 29 F4
Imlay City MI, *3597* ... 76 C3
Immokalee FL, *24154* ... 143 D1
Imperial CA, *14758* ... 53 E4
Imperial MO, *4709* ... 98 A4
Imperial NE, *2071* ... 34 B4
Imperial PA, *2541* ... 91 F4
Imperial Beach CA, *26324* ... 53 D4
Imperial Co. CA, *174528* ... 53 F4
Ina IL, *2338* ... 98 C4
Incline Vil. NV, *8777* ... 37 D2
Independence CA, *669* ... 45 E2
Independence IA, *5966* ... 73 E4
Independence KS, *9483* ... 106 A2
Independence KY, *24757* ... 100 B3
Independence LA, *1665* ... 134 B1
Independence MN, *3504* ... 66 C4
Independence MO, *116830* ... 96 B2
Independence OH, *7133* ... 204 F3
Independence OR, *8590* ... 20 B2
Independence VA, *947* ... 111 F3
Independence WI, *1336* ... 73 E1
Independence Co. AR, *36647* ... 107 F4
Independent Hill VA, *7419* ... 144 A4
Indialantic FL, *2720* ... 141 E2
Indiana PA, *13975* ... 92 B3
Indiana Co. PA, *88880* ... 92 B3
Indianapolis IN, *820445* ... 99 F1
Indian Harbour Beach FL, *8225* ... 141 E2
Indian Head MD, *3844* ... 144 B4
Indian Head Park IL, *3809* ... 203 C5
Indian Hills CO, *1280* ... 209 A4
Indian Hills KY, *2868* ... 230 E1
Indian Neck CT, *3400* ... 149 D2
Indianola IA, *14782* ... 86 C2
Indianola MS, *10683* ... 118 A4
Indianola NE, *584* ... 34 C4
Indianola WA, *3500* ... 262 A2
Indian Pt. MO, *588* ... 107 D3
Indian River MI, *1959* ... 70 C3
Indian River Co. FL, *138028* ... 141 E3
Indian River Estates FL, *6220* ... 141 E3
Indian River Shores FL, *3901* ... 141 E3
Indian Rocks Beach FL, *4113* ... 140 B2
Indian Shores FL, *1420* ... 266 A2
Indian Sprs. NV, *991* ... 46 A1
Indian Sprs. Vil. AL, *2363* ... 127 F1

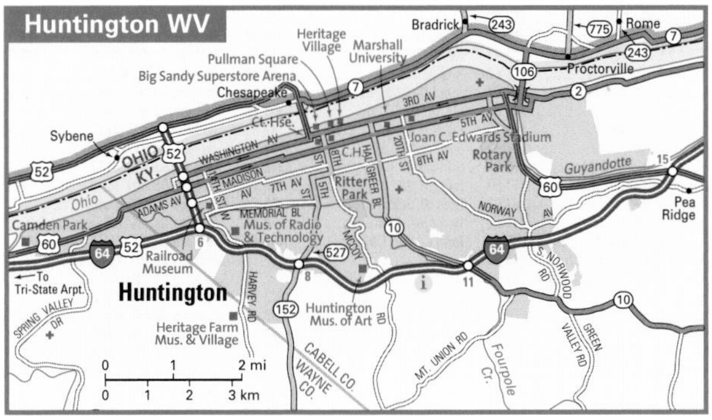

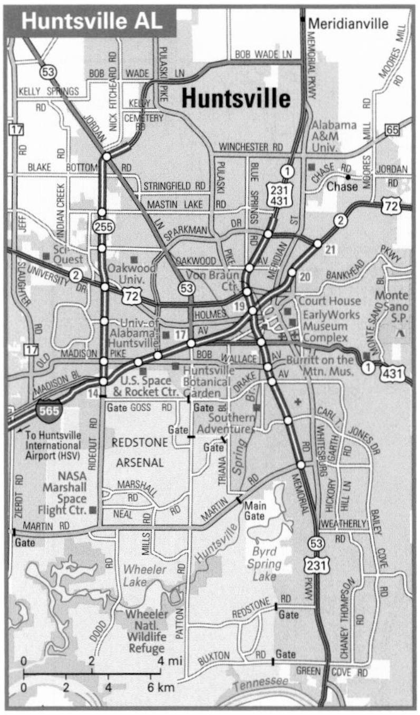

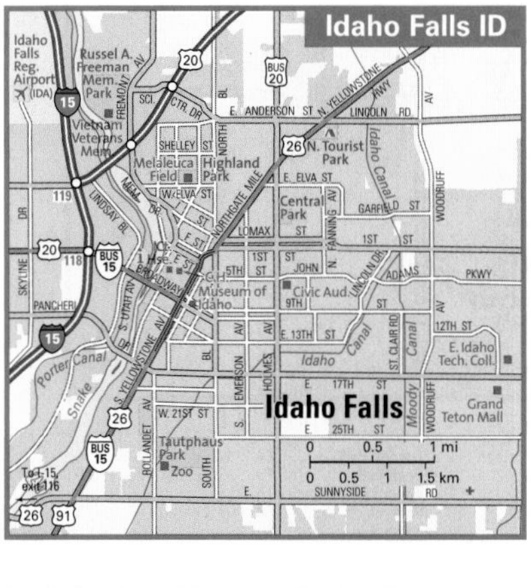

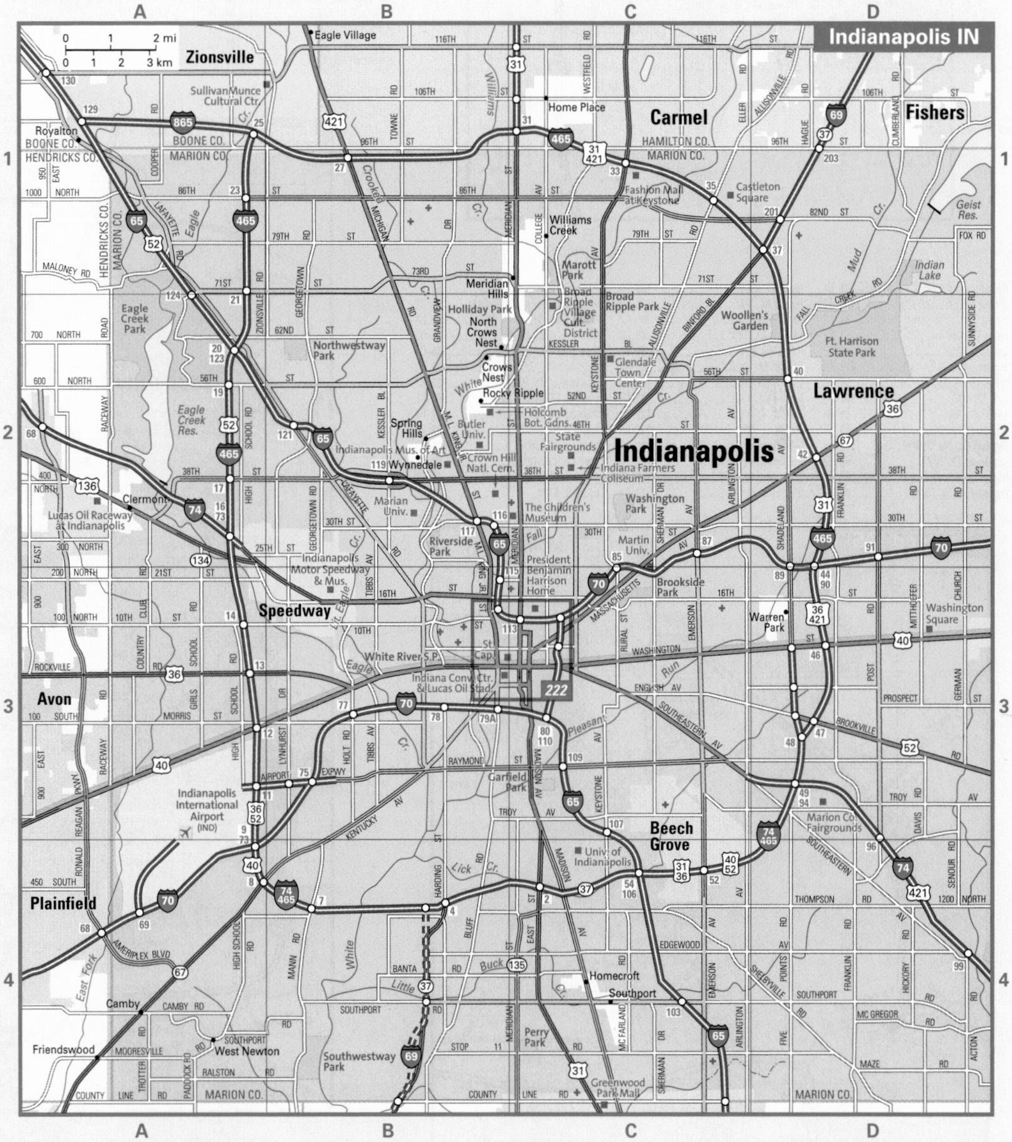

Avon ... A3	Crows Nest ... B2	Home Place ... C1	Plainfield ... A4	Spring Hills ... B2	Zionsville ... A1
Beech Grove ... C3	Eagle Vil. ... B1	Indianapolis ... C2	Rocky Ripple ... B2	Warren Park ... D3	
Camby ... A4	Fishers ... D1	Lawrence ... D2	Royalton ... A1	W. Newton ... A4	
Carmel ... C1	Friendswood ... A4	Meridian Hills ... C1	Southport ... C4	Williams Creek ... C1	
Clermont ... A2	Homecroft ... C4	N. Crows Nest ... B2	Speedway ... B3	Wynnedale ... B2	

POINTS OF INTEREST

- American Legion National Headquarters . . A1
- Artsgarden . . . A2
- Bankers Life Fieldhouse . . . B2
- Canal & State Park Cultural District . . . A2
- Circle Centre . . . A2
- City Market . . . B2
- Eiteljorg Museum . . . A2
- Herron School of Art . . . A2
- Indiana Avenue Cultural District . . . A1
- Indiana Convention Center . . . A2
- Indiana State Museum . . . A2
- Indiana Univ./Purdue Univ. Indianapolis . . A2
- Indiana War Memorial . . . A1
- James Whitcomb Riley Home . . . B1
- Lucas Oil Stadium . . . A2
- Madame Walker Theatre Center . . . A1
- Massachusetts Avenue Cultural District . . B1
- Morris-Butler House . . . B1
- NCAA Hall of Champions . . . A2
- Old National Centre . . . B1
- President Benjamin Harrison Home . . . B1
- Scottish Rite Cathedral . . . A1
- Soldiers & Sailors Monument . . . A2
- State Capitol . . . A2
- Victory Field . . . A2
- White River State Park . . . A2
- Zoo . . . A2

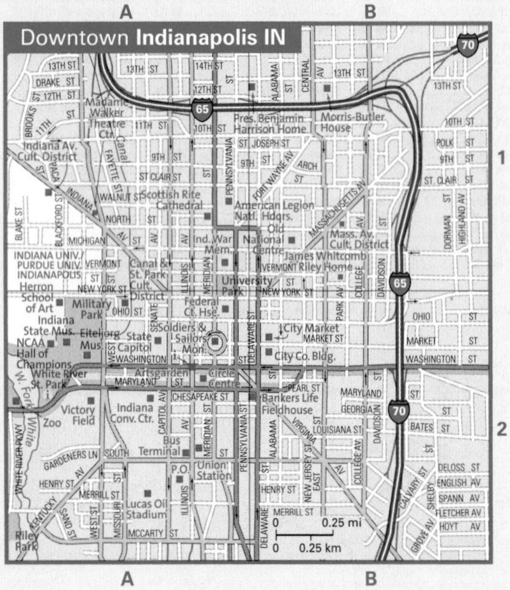

- Indiantown FL, *6083* . . . **141** E4
- Indian Trail NC, *33518* . . . **122** B2
- Indian Wells CA, *4958* . . . **53** E3
- Indio CA, *76036* . . . **53** E3
- Indrio FL, *550* . . . **141** E3
- Industry CA, *219* . . . **228** E3
- Industry PA, *1835* . . . **91** F3
- Inez KY, *717* . . . **101** D4
- Inez TX, *2098* . . . **61** F3
- Ingalls IN, *2394* . . . **99** F1
- **Ingham Co. MI,** *280895* . . . **76** A4
- Ingleside TX, *9387* . . . **63** F2
- Ingleside on the Bay TX, *615* . . . **63** F2
- Inglewood CA, *109673* . . . **52** C2
- Inglis FL, *1325* . . . **138** C4
- Ingold NC, *471* . . . **123** E2
- Ingram PA, *3330* . . . **250** A2
- Ingram TX, *1804* . . . **60** C2
- Inkom ID, *854* . . . **31** E1
- Inkster MI, *25369* . . . **210** B4
- Inman GA, *650* . . . **128** C1
- Inman KS, *1377* . . . **43** E3
- Inman SC, *2321* . . . **121** F2
- Inola OK, *1788* . . . **106** A4
- Intercession City FL, *900* . . . **141** D2
- Interlachen FL, *1403* . . . **139** D3
- Interlaken NJ, *820* . . . **147** F2
- Interlaken NY, *602* . . . **79** D4
- Interlochen MI, *583* . . . **69** F4
- International Falls MN, *6424* . . . **64** B2
- Inver Grove Hts. MN, *33880* . . . **235** D4
- Inverness CA, *1304* . . . **36** A3
- Inverness FL, *7210* . . . **140** C1
- Inverness IL, *7399* . . . **203** B2
- Inverness MS, *1019* . . . **126** B1
- Inwood FL, *6403* . . . **140** C2
- Inwood IA, *814* . . . **27** F4
- Inwood NY, *9792* . . . **147** F1
- Inwood WV, *2954* . . . **103** D2
- **Inyo Co. CA,** *18546* . . . **37** F4
- Inyokern CA, *1099* . . . **45** E4
- Iola KS, *5704* . . . **96** A4

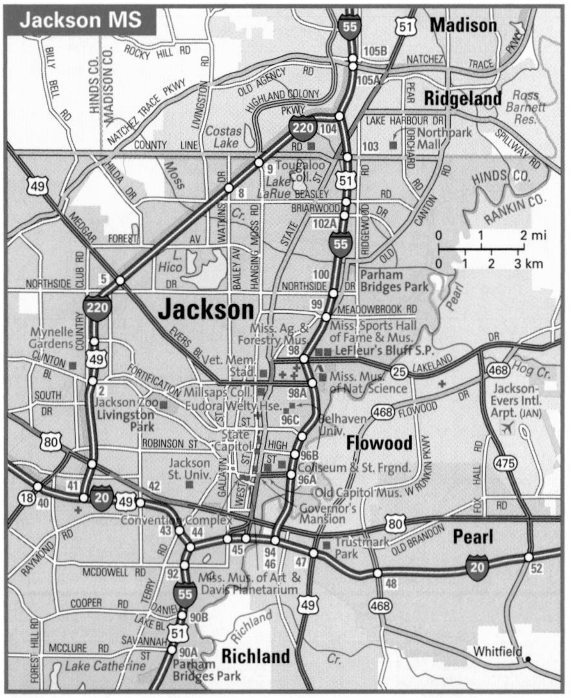

- Iola WI, *1301* . . . **68** B4
- Iona ID, *1803* . . . **23** E4
- Ione CA, *7918* . . . **36** C3
- Ione OR, *329* . . . **21** E2
- Ione WA, *447* . . . **13** F1
- Ionia MI, *11394* . . . **76** A3
- **Ionia Co. MI,** *63905* . . . **75** F3
- **Iosco Co. MI,** *25887* . . . **76** B1
- Iota LA, *1500* . . . **133** E2
- Iowa LA, *2996* . . . **133** D2
- Iowa City IA, *67862* . . . **87** F2
- Iowa Colony TX, *1170* . . . **132** A4
- **Iowa Co. IA,** *16355* . . . **87** E2
- **Iowa Co. WI,** *23687* . . . **74** A3
- Iowa Falls IA, *5238* . . . **73** D4
- Iowa Park TX, *6355* . . . **59** D1
- Ipswich MA, *4222* . . . **151** F1
- Ipswich SD, *954* . . . **27** D2
- Iraan TX, *1229* . . . **60** A1
- **Iredell Co. NC,** *159437* . . . **112** A4
- Irene SD, *420* . . . **35** E1
- Ireton IA, *609* . . . **35** F1
- **Irion Co. TX,** *1599* . . . **58** B4
- Irmo SC, *11097* . . . **122** A3
- Iron City TN, *328* . . . **119** E2
- **Iron Co. MI,** *11817* . . . **68** C1
- **Iron Co. MO,** *10630* . . . **108** A1
- **Iron Co. UT,** *46163* . . . **39** D4
- **Iron Co. WI,** *5916* . . . **68** A1
- Irondale AL, *12349* . . . **119** F4
- Irondequoit NY, *51692* . . . **78** C3
- Iron Gate VA, *388* . . . **112** B1
- Iron Mtn. MI, *7624* . . . **68** C2
- Iron Mtn. Lake MO, *737* . . . **108** A1
- Iron Ridge WI, *929* . . . **74** C2
- Iron River MI, *3029* . . . **68** C2
- Ironton MN, *572* . . . **64** B4
- Ironton MO, *1460* . . . **108** A1
- Ironton OH, *11129* . . . **101** D3
- Ironwood MI, *5387* . . . **65** E4
- Iroquois SD, *266* . . . **27** E3
- **Iroquois Co. IL,** *29718* . . . **89** D3
- Irrigon OR, *1826* . . . **21** E1
- Irvine CA, *212375* . . . **52** C3
- Irvine KY, *2715* . . . **110** C1
- Irving IL, *495* . . . **98** B2
- Irving TX, *216290* . . . **59** F2
- Irvington IL, *659* . . . **98** C3
- Irvington KY, *1181* . . . **99** F4
- Irvington NE, *950* . . . **245** A1
- Irvington NJ, *53926* . . . **148** A4
- Irvington NY, *6420* . . . **148** B3
- Irvington VA, *432* . . . **113** F1
- Irvona PA, *647* . . . **92** B3
- Irwin PA, *3973* . . . **92** A4
- Irwin SC, *1405* . . . **122** B2
- **Irwin Co. GA,** *9538* . . . **129** E4
- Irwindale CA, *1422* . . . **228** E2
- Irwinton GA, *589* . . . **129** E2
- Isabel SD, *135* . . . **26** B2
- **Isabella Co. MI,** *70311* . . . **76** A2
- Isanti MN, *5251* . . . **67** D3
- **Isanti Co. MN,** *37816* . . . **67** D2
- Iselin NJ, *18695* . . . **147** E1
- Ishpeming MI, *6470* . . . **65** F4
- Islamorada FL, *6119* . . . **143** E4
- Island KY, *458* . . . **109** E1
- Island City OR, *989* . . . **21** F2
- **Island Co. WA,** *78506* . . . **12** C2
- Island Falls ME, *793* . . . **85** D3
- Island Hts. NJ, *1673* . . . **147** E3
- Island Lake IL, *8080* . . . **74** C4
- Island Park ID, *286* . . . **23** F3
- Island Park NY, *4655* . . . **147** F1
- Island Pond VT, *821* . . . **81** E1
- Isla Vista CA, *23096* . . . **52** A2
- Isle MN, *751* . . . **67** D2
- Isle of Hope GA, *2402* . . . **130** C3
- Isle of Palms SC, *4133* . . . **131** D2
- Isle of Wight VA, *100* . . . **113** F2
- **Isle of Wight Co. VA,** *35270* . . . **113** F2
- Isleta NM, *491* . . . **48** C3
- Isleton CA, *804* . . . **36** C3
- Islip NY, *18689* . . . **149** D4
- Isola MS, *713* . . . **126** B1
- Issaquah WA, *30434* . . . **12** C3
- **Issaquena Co. MS,** *1406* . . . **126** A2
- Italy TX, *1863* . . . **59** F3
- Itasca IL, *8649* . . . **203** B3
- Itasca TX, *1644* . . . **59** E3
- **Itasca Co. MN,** *45058* . . . **64** B3
- **Itawamba Co. MS,** *23401* . . . **119** D3
- Ithaca MI, *2910* . . . **76** A3
- Ithaca NY, *30014* . . . **79** D4
- Itta Bena MS, *2049* . . . **118** B4
- Iuka IL, *489* . . . **98** C3
- Iuka MS, *3028* . . . **119** D2
- Iva SC, *1218* . . . **121** E3
- Ivanhoe CA, *4495* . . . **45** D3
- Ivanhoe MN, *559* . . . **27** F3
- Ivanhoe VA, *551* . . . **112** A2
- Ivey GA, *981* . . . **129** E1
- Ivins UT, *6753* . . . **38** C4
- Ixonia WI, *1624* . . . **74** C3
- **Izard Co. AR,** *13696* . . . **107** F4

J

- Jacinto City TX, *10553* . . . **220** C2
- **Jack Co. TX,** *9044* . . . **59** D2
- Jackman ME, *718* . . . **84** B4
- Jackman Sta. ME, *750* . . . **84** B4
- Jackpot NV, *1195* . . . **30** C2
- Jacksboro TN, *2020* . . . **110** C3
- Jacksboro TX, *4511* . . . **59** D2
- Jackson AL, *5228* . . . **127** E4
- Jackson CA, *4651* . . . **36** C3
- Jackson GA, *5045* . . . **129** D1
- Jackson KY, *2231* . . . **111** D1
- Jackson LA, *3842* . . . **134** A1
- Jackson MI, *33534* . . . **76** A4
- Jackson MN, *3299* . . . **72** B2
- Jackson MS, *173514* . . . 126 B2
- Jackson MO, *13758* . . . **108** B1
- Jackson NC, *513* . . . **113** E3
- Jackson OH, *6397* . . . **101** D2
- Jackson SC, *1700* . . . **130** B1
- Jackson TN, *65211* . . . **118** C1
- Jackson WI, *6753* . . . **74** C3
- Jackson WY, *9577* . . . **23** F4
- Jackson Ctr. OH, *1462* . . . **90** B4
- **Jackson Co. AL,** *53227* . . . **120** A2
- **Jackson Co. AR,** *17997* . . . **118** A1
- **Jackson Co. CO,** *1394* . . . **33** D4
- **Jackson Co. FL,** *49746* . . . **137** D1
- **Jackson Co. GA,** *60485* . . . **121** D3
- **Jackson Co. IL,** *60218* . . . **98** B4
- **Jackson Co. IN,** *42376* . . . **99** F3
- **Jackson Co. IA,** *19848* . . . **87** F1
- **Jackson Co. KS,** *13462* . . . **96** A2
- **Jackson Co. KY,** *13494* . . . **110** C1
- **Jackson Co. MI,** *160248* . . . **76** A4
- **Jackson Co. MN,** *10266* . . . **72** B2
- **Jackson Co. MS,** *139668* . . . **135** D2
- **Jackson Co. MO,** *674158* . . . **96** C3
- **Jackson Co. NC,** *40271* . . . **121** E1
- **Jackson Co. OH,** *33225* . . . **101** D3
- **Jackson Co. OK,** *26446* . . . **50** C4
- **Jackson Co. OR,** *203206* . . . **28** B1
- **Jackson Co. SD,** *3031* . . . **26** B4
- **Jackson Co. TN,** *11638* . . . **110** A3
- **Jackson Co. TX,** *14075* . . . **61** F3
- **Jackson Co. WV,** *29211* . . . **101** E3
- **Jackson Co. WI,** *20449* . . . **67** F4
- Jackson Par. LA, *16274* . . . **125** E2
- Jacksons Gap AL, *828* . . . **128** B1
- Jacksonville AL, *12548* . . . **120** A4
- Jacksonville AR, *28364* . . . **117** E2
- Jacksonville FL, *821784* . . . 139 D2
- Jacksonville IL, *19446* . . . **98** A1
- Jacksonville MD, *900* . . . **144** C1

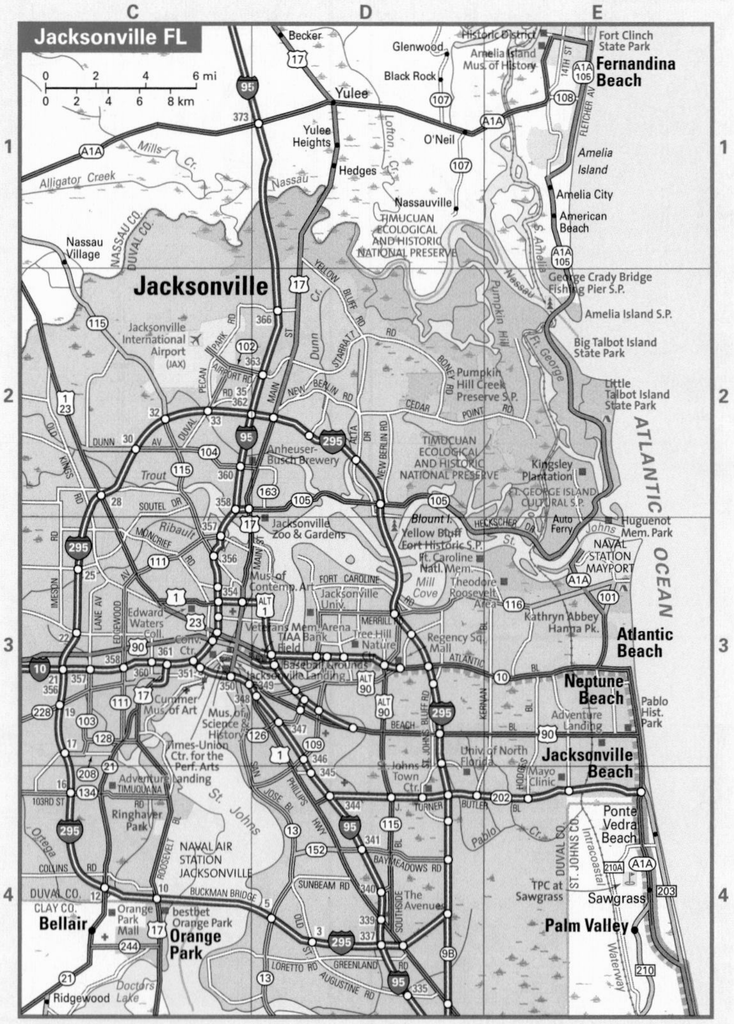

- Amelia City . . . E1
- American Beach . . . E1
- Atlantic Beach . . . E3
- Becker . . . D1
- Bellair . . . C4
- Black Rock . . . D1
- Fernandina Beach . . E1
- Glenwood . . . D1
- Hedges . . . D1
- Jacksonville . . . D2
- Jacksonville Beach . E3
- Nassau Vil. . . . C1
- Nassauville . . . D1
- Neptune Beach . . . E3
- O'Neil . . . D1
- Orange Park . . . C4
- Palm Valley . . . E4
- Ponte Vedra Beach . E4
- Ridgewood . . . C4
- Sawgrass . . . E4
- Yulee . . . D1
- Yulee Hts. . . . D1

Entries in **bold black** indicate counties or parishes.
Entries in **bold color** indicate cities with detailed inset maps.

Jacksonville NC, 70145 115 D4
Jacksonville OR, 2785 28 B2
Jacksonville PA, 637 92 B4
Jacksonville TX, 14544 124 A3
Jacksonville VT, 223 94 C1
Jacksonville Beach FL, 21362 139 D2
Jacobstown NJ, 950 147 D2
Jacobus PA, 1841 103 E1
Jaffrey NH, 2757 95 D1
Jal NM, 2047 57 F3
Jamaica Beach TX, 983 132 B4
Jamesburg NJ, 5915 147 E2
James City NC, 5899 115 D3
James City Co. VA, 67009 113 F1
Jamesport MO, 524 96 C1
Jamesport NY, 1710 149 E3
Jamestown CA, 3433 37 D3
Jamestown IN, 958 99 E1
Jamestown KS, 286 43 E1
Jamestown KY, 1794 110 B2
Jamestown MI, 750 75 F3
Jamestown NY, 31146 92 B1
Jamestown NC, 3382 112 B4
Jamestown ND, 15427 19 D4
Jamestown OH, 1993 100 C1
Jamestown PA, 617 91 F2
Jamestown RI, 5405 150 C4
Jamestown TN, 1959 110 B3
James Town WY, 536 32 A3
Jamesville NC, 491 113 F4
Jamul CA, 6163 53 D4
Jane Lew WV, 409 102 A2
Janesville CA, 1408 29 D4
Janesville IA, 930 73 D4
Janesville MN, 2256 72 C1
Janesville WI, 63575 74 B4
Jarales NM, 2475 48 C4
Jarratt VA, 638 113 E2
Jarrell TX, 984 61 E1
Jarrettsville MD, 2916 144 C1
Jasmine Estates FL, 18989 140 B2
Jasonville IN, 2222 99 E2
Jasper AL, 14352 119 E4
Jasper AR, 466 107 D4
Jasper FL, 4546 138 B2
Jasper GA, 3684 120 C3
Jasper IN, 15038 99 E4
Jasper MN, 633 27 F4
Jasper MO, 931 106 C1
Jasper OR, 700 20 B4
Jasper TN, 3279 120 A2
Jasper TX, 7590 132 C1
Jasper Co. GA, 13900 129 D1
Jasper Co. IL, 9698 99 D2
Jasper Co. IN, 33478 89 E3
Jasper Co. IA, 36842 87 D2
Jasper Co. MS, 17062 126 C3
Jasper Co. MO, 117404 106 C2
Jasper Co. SC, 24777 130 C3
Jasper Co. TX, 35710 132 C1
Jay FL, 533 135 F1
Jay ME, 4985 82 B2
Jay OK, 2448 106 B3
Jay Co. IN, 21253 90 A4
Jayton TX, 534 58 B2
Jeanerette LA, 5530 133 F3
Jean Lafitte LA, 1903 134 B3
Jeannette PA, 9654 92 A4
Jeddito AZ, 293 47 F2
Jeff Davis Co. GA, 15068 129 F3
Jeff Davis Co. TX, 2342 62 B2
Jefferson GA, 9432 121 D3
Jefferson IA, 4345 86 B1
Jefferson LA, 11193 239 B1
Jefferson MA, 1600 150 B1
Jefferson NC, 1611 111 F3
Jefferson OH, 3120 91 F1
Jefferson OR, 3098 20 B3
Jefferson PA, 631 103 E1
Jefferson SC, 753 122 B2
Jefferson SD, 547 35 F1
Jefferson TX, 2106 124 C2
Jefferson WI, 7973 74 B3
Jefferson City MO, 43079 97 E3
Jefferson City MT, 472 15 E4
Jefferson City TN, 8047 111 D4
Jefferson Co. AL, 658466 119 F4
Jefferson Co. AR, 77435 117 F3
Jefferson Co. CO, 534543 41 E1
Jefferson Co. FL, 14761 137 E2
Jefferson Co. GA, 16930 129 F1
Jefferson Co. ID, 26140 23 E4
Jefferson Co. IL, 38827 98 C4
Jefferson Co. IN, 32428 100 A3
Jefferson Co. IA, 16843 87 E3
Jefferson Co. KS, 19126 96 A2
Jefferson Co. KY, 741096 100 A4
Jefferson Co. MS, 7726 126 A3
Jefferson Co. MO, 218733 98 A4
Jefferson Co. MT, 11406 23 E1
Jefferson Co. NE, 7547 35 F4
Jefferson Co. NY, 116229 79 E2
Jefferson Co. OH, 69709 91 F4
Jefferson Co. OK, 6472 59 E1
Jefferson Co. OR, 21720 20 C3
Jefferson Co. PA, 45200 92 B2
Jefferson Co. TN, 51407 111 D4
Jefferson Co. TX, 252273 132 C3
Jefferson Co. WA, 29872 12 B3
Jefferson Co. WV, 53498 103 D2
Jefferson Co. WI, 83686 74 C3
Jefferson Davis Co. MS, 12487 126 B4
Jefferson Davis Par. LA, 31594 133 E2
Jefferson Hts. NY, 1094 94 B2
Jefferson Hills PA, 10619 92 A4
Jefferson Par. LA, 432552 134 B3
Jeffersontown KY, 26595 100 A4
Jefferson Valley NY, 14142 148 B2
Jeffersonville GA, 1035 129 E2
Jeffersonville IN, 44953 100 A4
Jeffersonville KY, 1506 100 C4
Jeffersonville OH, 1203 100 C1
Jeffersonville PA, 10200 248 A1
Jeffersonville VT, 729 81 D1
Jellico TN, 2355 110 C3
Jemez Pueblo NM, 1788 48 C3
Jemez Sprs. NM, 250 48 C2
Jemison AL, 2585 127 F1
Jena LA, 3398 125 E4
Jenison MI, 16538 75 F3
Jenkins KY, 2203 111 E2
Jenkins Co. GA, 8340 129 F2
Jenkintown PA, 4422 146 C2
Jenks OK, 16924 51 F2
Jennerstown PA, 695 92 B4
Jennings FL, 878 137 F2
Jennings LA, 10383 133 E2
Jennings MO, 14712 256 B1
Jennings Co. IN, 28525 100 A3
Jenny Lind AR, 650 116 C1
Jensen Beach FL, 11707 141 E4
Jerauld Co. SD, 2071 27 D3
Jericho NY, 13567 148 C4
Jericho VT, 1329 81 D2
Jermyn PA, 2169 93 F2
Jerome AZ, 444 47 D4
Jerome ID, 10890 30 C1
Jerome PA, 1017 92 B4
Jerome Co. ID, 22374 31 D1
Jersey Co. IL, 22985 98 A2
Jersey City NJ, 247597 148 B4
Jersey Shore PA, 4361 93 D2
Jersey Vil. TX, 7620 132 A3
Jerseyville IL, 8465 98 A2
Jerseyville NJ, 1000 147 E2
Jerusalem RI, 800 150 C4
Jessamine Co. KY, 48586 100 B4
Jessup MD, 7137 144 C2
Jessup PA, 4676 93 F2
Jesup GA, 10214 130 A4
Jesup IA, 2520 73 E4
Jetmore KS, 867 42 C3

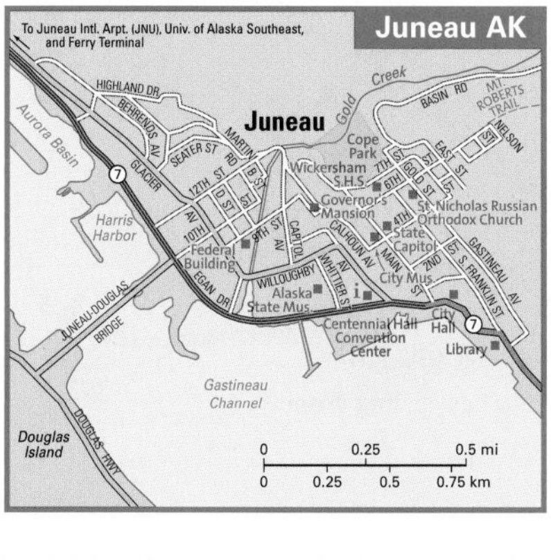

Jewell IA, 1215 72 C4
Jewell KS, 432 43 E1
Jewell Co. KS, 3077 43 E1
Jewett OH, 692 91 F4
Jewett TX, 1167 59 F4
Jewett City (Griswold) CT, 3487 149 F1
Jim Hogg Co. TX, 5300 63 E3
Jim Thorpe PA, 4781 93 F3
Jim Wells Co. TX, 40838 63 E2
Joanna SC, 1539 121 F3
Joaquin TX, 824 124 C3
Jo Daviess Co. IL, 22678 74 A4
John Day OR, 1744 21 F3
Johns Island SC, 650 131 D2
Johnson AR, 3354 106 C4
Johnson VT, 1443 81 E2
Johnsonburg PA, 2483 92 B2
Johnson City KS, 1495 42 B4
Johnson City NY, 15174 93 E1
Johnson City OR, 566 251 D3
Johnson City TN, 63152 111 E3
Johnson City TX, 1656 61 D1
Johnson Co. AR, 25540 117 D1
Johnson Co. GA, 9980 129 F2
Johnson Co. IL, 12582 108 C1
Johnson Co. IN, 139654 99 F2
Johnson Co. IA, 130882 87 F2
Johnson Co. KS, 544179 96 B3
Johnson Co. KY, 23356 111 D1
Johnson Co. MO, 52595 96 C3
Johnson Co. NE, 5217 35 F4
Johnson Co. TN, 18244 111 F3
Johnson Co. TX, 150934 59 E3
Johnson Co. WY, 8569 25 D4
Johnson Creek WI, 2738 74 C3
Johnsonville SC, 1480 122 C4
Johnston IA, 17278 86 C2
Johnston SC, 2362 121 F4
Johnston City IL, 3543 108 C1
Johnston Co. NC, 168878 113 D4
Johnston Co. OK, 10957 51 F4
Johnstown CO, 9887 33 E4
Johnstown NY, 8743 79 F3
Johnstown OH, 4632 91 D4
Johnstown PA, 20978 92 B4
Joiner AR, 576 118 B1
Joliet IL, 147433 89 D2
Joliet MT, 595 24 B2
Jollyville TX, 16151 61 E1
Jones OK, 2692 51 E3
Jonesboro AR, 67263 108 A4
Jonesboro GA, 4724 120 C4
Jonesboro IL, 1821 108 C1
Jonesboro IN, 1756 89 F4
Jonesboro LA, 4704 125 E3
Jonesborough TN, 5051 111 E3
Jonesburg MO, 768 97 F3
Jones Co. GA, 28669 129 D1
Jones Co. IA, 20638 87 F1
Jones Co. MS, 67761 126 C4
Jones Co. NC, 10153 115 D3
Jones Co. SD, 1006 26 C4
Jones Co. TX, 20202 58 C2
Jones Creek TX, 2020 132 A4
Jonesport ME, 1408 83 E2
Jonestown MS, 1298 118 A3
Jonestown PA, 64 93 E4
Jonestown TX, 1834 61 E1
Jonesville LA, 2265 125 F4
Jonesville MI, 2258 90 B1
Jonesville NC, 2285 112 A3
Jonesville SC, 911 121 F2
Jonesville VT, 375 81 D2
Jonesville VA, 1034 111 D3
Joplin MO, 50150 106 B2
Joplin MT, 157 15 F2
Joppatowne MD, 12616 145 D1
Jordan MN, 5470 66 C4
Jordan MT, 343 17 D3
Jordan NY, 1368 79 D3
Joseph OR, 1081 22 A2
Joseph City AZ, 1386 47 F3
Josephine TX, 812 59 F2
Josephine Co. OR, 82713 28 B2
Joshua TX, 5910 59 E3
Joshua Tree CA, 7414 53 E2
Jourdanton TX, 3871 61 D3
Juab Co. UT, 10246 39 D1
Judith Basin Co. MT, 2072 16 A3
Judsonia AR, 2019 117 F1
Julesburg CO, 1225 34 A3
Juliaetta ID, 579 14 B4
Julian CA, 1502 53 D4
Julian NC, 600 112 B4
Jumpertown MS, 480 119 D2
Junction TX, 2574 60 C1
Junction UT, 191 39 E3
Junction City AR, 581 125 E1
Junction City KS, 23353 43 F2
Junction City KY, 2241 110 B1
Junction City LA, 582 125 E1
Junction City OH, 819 101 E1
Junction City OR, 5392 20 B3
Juneau AK, 31275 155 E4
Juneau WI, 2814 74 C2
Juneau Co. WI, 26664 74 A1
Juniata NE, 755 35 D4
Juniata Co. PA, 24636 93 D3
Junior WV, 520 102 A2
Juno Beach FL, 3176 141 F4
Jupiter FL, 55156 141 F4
Jupiter Island FL, 817 141 F4
Jurupa Valley CA, 94235 229 H3
Justice IL, 12926 203 D5
Justin TX, 3246 59 E2
Justus PA, 950 261 E1

K

Kaaawa HI, 1379 152 A2
Kaanapali HI, 1045 153 D1
Kadoka SD, 654 26 B4
Kahaluu HI, 4738 152 A3
Kahoka MO, 2078 87 E4
Kahuku HI, 2614 152 A2
Kahului HI, 26337 153 D1
Kaibab AZ, 124 47 D1
Kaibito AZ, 1522 47 E1
Kailua HI, 38635 152 B3
Kailua-Kona HI, 11975 153 E3
Kake AK, 557 155 E4
Kalaheo HI, 4595 152 B1
Kalama WA, 2344 20 C1
Kalamazoo MI, 74262 75 F4
Kalamazoo Co. MI, 250331 75 F4
Kalaoa HI, 9644 153 E3
Kalaupapa HI, 152 C3
Kalawao Co. HI, 90 152 C3
Kaleva MI, 470 75 F1
Kalida OH, 1542 90 B3
Kalihiwai HI, 428 152 B1
Kalispell MT, 19927 15 D2
Kalkaska MI, 2020 69 F4
Kalkaska Co. MI, 17153 70 B4
Kalona IA, 2363 87 E2
Kamas UT, 1811 31 F4
Kamiah ID, 1295 22 B1
Kanab UT, 4312 47 D1
Kanabec Co. MN, 16239 67 D2
Kanarraville UT, 355 39 D4
Kanawha IA, 652 72 C3
Kanawha WV, 500 101 F2
Kanawha Co. WV, 193063 101 F4
Kandiyohi MN, 491 66 B3
Kandiyohi Co. MN, 42239 66 B3
Kane PA, 3730 92 B2
Kane Co. IL, 515269 88 C1
Kane Co. UT, 7125 39 E4
Kaneohe HI, 34597 152 A3
Kankakee IL, 27537 89 D3
Kankakee Co. IL, 113449 89 D2
Kannapolis NC, 42625 122 B1
Kanopolis KS, 492 43 E2
Kanosh UT, 474 39 D2
Kansas IL, 787 99 D1
Kansas OK, 802 106 B3
Kansas City KS, 145786 96 B2
Kansas City MO, 459787 96 B2
Kapaa HI, 10699 152 B1
Kapaau HI, 1734 153 E2
Kaplan LA, 4600 133 E3
Karlstad MN, 760 19 F2
Karnak IL, 499 108 C2
Karnes City TX, 3042 61 E3
Karnes Co. TX, 14824 61 E3
Karns TN, 1500 110 C4
Kasigluk AK, 569 154 B3
Kasota MN, 675 72 C1
Kasson IN, 1500 99 D4
Kasson MN, 5931 73 D1
Kathleen FL, 6332 140 C2
Kathleen GA, 650 129 D2
Katonah NY, 1679 148 C2
Katy TX, 14102 132 A3
Keavy KY, 450 110 C2
Kechi KS, 1909 43 E4
Keedysville MD, 1152 144 A1
Keegan ME, 550 85 E1
Keego Harbor MI, 2970 210 A1
Keene NH, 23409 95 D1
Keene TX, 6106 59 E3
Keener NC, 567 123 E2
Keenesburg CO, 1127 41 E1
Keeseville NY, 1815 81 D2
Keewatin MN, 1068 64 B3
Keiser AR, 759 108 B4
Keith Co. NE, 8368 34 B3
Keithsburg IL, 609 87 F3
Keizer OR, 36478 20 B2
Kekaha HI, 3537 152 B1
Keller TX, 39627 59 E2
Kellogg ID, 2120 14 B3
Kellogg IA, 599 87 D1
Kellyville OK, 1150 51 F2
Kelseyville CA, 3353 36 B2
Kelso MO, 586 108 B2
Kelso WA, 11925 20 B1
Kemah TX, 1773 132 B3
Kemblesville PA, 1000 146 B4
Kemmerer WY, 2656 31 F2
Kemp TX, 1154 59 F3
Kemper Co. MS, 10456 127 D2
Kempner TX, 1089 59 E4
Kenai AK, 7100 154 C3
Kenansville NC, 855 123 E2
Kenbridge VA, 1257 113 D2
Kendall FL, 75371 143 E2
Kendall NY, 750 78 B3
Kendall Co. IL, 114736 88 C2
Kendall Co. TX, 33410 61 D2
Kendall Park NJ, 9339 147 D1
Kendallville IN, 9862 90 A2
Kendrick FL, 600 138 C4
Kendrick ID, 303 14 B4
Kenedy TX, 3296 61 E3
Kenedy Co. TX, 416 63 F3
Kenefick TX, 563 132 B2
Kenesaw NE, 880 35 D4
Kenilworth IL, 2513 203 D2
Kenilworth NJ, 7914 240 A4
Kenilworth PA, 1907 146 B2
Kensington MD, 2213 270 C1
Kensington NY, 1161 241 G2
Kensington Park FL, 3901 266 C5
Kent CT, 2962 94 B3
Kent OH, 28904 91 E3
Kent WA, 92411 12 C3
Kent City MI, 1057 75 F3
Kent Co. DE, 162310 145 E3
Kent Co. MD, 20197 145 D2
Kent Co. MI, 602622 75 F3
Kent Co. RI, 166158 150 C3
Kent Co. TX, 808 58 B2
Kentfield CA, 6485 259 A1
Kentland IN, 1748 89 D3
Kenton DE, 261 145 E2
Kenton KY, 375 100 B3
Kenton OH, 8262 90 C3
Kenton TN, 1281 108 C3
Kenton Co. KY, 159720 100 B2
Kentwood LA, 2198 134 B1
Kentwood MI, 48707 75 F3
Kenvil NJ, 3009 148 A3
Kenwood MD, 9800 193 D2
Kenwood OH, 6981 204 C2
Kenwood Beach MD, 600 144 C4
Kenyon MN, 1815 73 D1
Keokuk IA, 10780 87 F4
Keokuk Co. IA, 10511 87 E2
Keosauqua IA, 1006 87 E3
Keota IA, 1009 87 E2
Keota OK, 564 116 B1
Kerens TX, 1573 59 F3
Kerhonkson NY, 1684 94 A3
Kerkhoven MN, 759 66 B3
Kerman CA, 13544 44 C3
Kermit TX, 5708 57 F3
Kern Co. CA, 839631 45 D4
Kernersville NC, 23123 112 B4
Kernville CA, 1395 45 E4
Kerr Co. TX, 49625 60 C2
Kerrville TX, 22347 60 C2
Kersey CO, 1454 33 E4
Kershaw SC, 1803 122 B2
Kershaw Co. SC, 61697 122 B3
Keshena WI, 1262 68 C4
Ketchikan AK, 8050 155 E4
Ketchum ID, 2689 22 C4

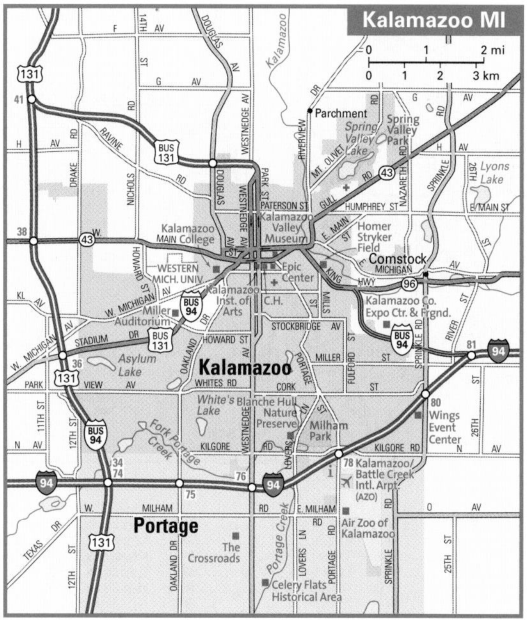

Kauai Co. HI, 67091 152 B1
Kaufman TX, 6703 59 F2
Kaufman Co. TX, 103350 59 F3
Kaukauna WI, 15462 74 C1
Kaumakani HI, 749 152 B1
Kaunakakai HI, 3425 152 C3
Kawkawlin MI, 1600 76 B2
Kaycee WY, 263 25 D4
Kay Co. OK, 46562 51 E1
Kayenta AZ, 5189 47 F1
Kaysville UT, 27300 31 E3
Keaau HI, 2253 153 F3
Kealakekua HI, 2019 153 E3
Keams Canyon AZ, 304 47 F2
Keansburg NJ, 10105 147 E1
Kearney MO, 8381 96 B2
Kearney NE, 30787 35 D4
Kearney Co. NE, 6489 35 D4
Kearneysville WV, 650 103 D2
Kearns UT, 35731 257 A2
Kearny AZ, 1950 55 D2
Kearny NJ, 40684 148 B4
Kearny Co. KS, 3977 42 B3
Keauhou HI, 3549 153 E3
Kenly NC, 1339 123 E1
Kenmare ND, 1096 18 B1
Kenmore NY, 15423 78 A3
Kenmore WA, 20460 262 B2
Kennebec SD, 240 26 C4
Kennebec Co. ME, 122151 82 B2
Kennebunk ME, 5214 82 B4
Kennebunkport ME, 1238 82 B4
Kennedale TX, 6763 207 B3
Kennedy AL, 447 119 D4
Kenner LA, 66702 134 B3
Kennesaw GA, 29783 120 C3
Kenneth City FL, 4980 266 A3
Kennett MO, 10932 108 B3
Kennett Square PA, 6072 146 B3
Kennewick WA, 73917 21 E1
Keno OR, 650 28 C2
Kenosha WI, 99218 75 D4
Kenosha Co. WI, 166426 74 C4
Kenova WV, 3216 101 D4
Kensett AR, 1648 117 F1
Kensington CA, 5077 259 C2
Kensington CT, 8459 149 E1
Kensington KS, 473 43 D1
Kettering OH, 56163 100 B1
Kettle Falls WA, 1595 13 F1
Kettleman City CA, 1439 44 C3
Kevil KY, 376 108 C2
Kewanee IL, 12916 88 A2
Kewanna IN, 613 89 E3
Kewaskum WI, 4004 74 C2
Kewaunee WI, 2952 75 D1
Kewaunee Co. WI, 20574 69 D4
Keweenaw Co. MI, 2156 65 F3
Keya Paha Co. NE, 824 35 D1
Key Biscayne FL, 12344 143 F2
Key Colony Beach FL, 797 143 D4
Keyes CA, 5601 36 C4
Key Largo FL, 10433 143 E3
Keyport NJ, 7240 147 E1
Keys OK, 565 106 B4
Keyser WV, 5439 102 C2
Keystone CO, 1079 41 D1
Keystone IA, 622 87 E1
Keystone SD, 337 25 F4
Keystone WV, 282 111 F1
Keystone Hts. FL, 1350 139 D3
Keysville VA, 832 113 D2

Figures after entries indicate population, page number, and grid reference.

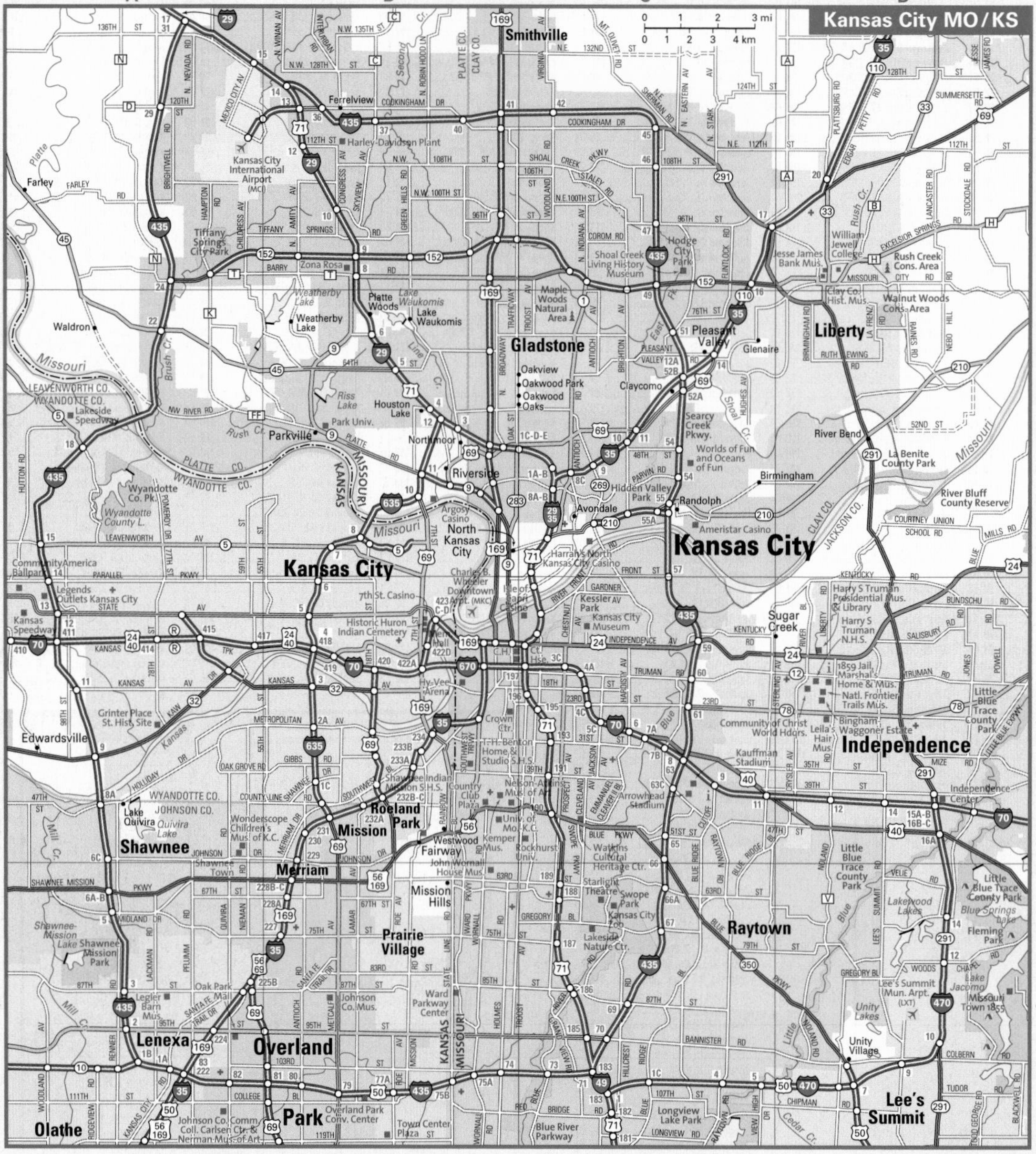

Avondale C2
Birmingham C2
Claycomo C2
Countryside B4
Edwardsville. A3
Fairway B3
Farley. A1
Ferrelview. B1
Gladstone C2
Glenaire C2
Houston Lake. B2
Independence D3
Kansas City, KS B2
Kansas City, MO C2
Lake Quivira A3
Lake Waukomis. B2
Lees Summit D4
Lenexa. A4
Liberty D2
Merriam B4
Mission B3
Mission Hills B4
N. Kansas City B2
Northmoor B2
Oaks. C2
Oakview C2
Oakwood. C2
Oakwood Park C2
Olathe A4
Overland Park B4
Parkville B2
Platte Woods B2
Pleasant Valley C2
Prairie Vil. B4
Randolph. C2
Raytown C4
River Bend D2
Riverside. B2
Roeland Park B3
Shawnee. A3
Smithville C1
Sugar Creek. D3
Unity Vil. D4
Waldron A2
Weatherby Lake B2
Westwood B3

Keytesville MO, *471* **97** D2
Key West FL, *24649* **142** C4
Kezar Falls ME, *750* **82** A3
Kiamesha Lake NY, *700* **148** A1
Kiawah Island SC, *1626* **131** D2
Kibler AR, *961* **116** C1
Kidder Co. ND, *2435* **18** C4
Kiefer OK, *1685* **51** F2
Kiel WI, *3738* **74** C2
Kiester MN, *501* **72** C2
Kihei HI, *20881* **153** D1
Kilauea HI, *2803* **152** B1
Kilbourne LA, *416* **125** F1
Kildeer IL, *3968* **203** B2
Kilgore TX, *12975* **124** B2
Killbuck OH, *817* **91** E4
Killdeer ND, *751* **18** A3
Kill Devil Hills NC, *6683* **115** F2
Killeen TX, *127921* **59** E4
Killen AL, *1108* **119** E2
Killian LA, *1206* **134** B2
Killona LA, *793* **239** A1
Kilmarnock VA, *1487* **113** F1
Kilmichael MS, *699* **118** C4
Kiln MS, *2238* **134** C2
Kimball MN, *762* **66** C3
Kimball NE, *2496* **33** F3
Kimball SD, *703* **27** D4
Kimball TN, *1395* **120** A2
Kimball WV, *194* **111** F1
Kimball Co. NE, *3821* **33** F3
Kimberling City MO, *2400* **107** D3
Kimberly AL, *2711* **119** F4
Kimberly ID, *3264* **30** C1
Kimberly WI, *6468* **74** C1
Kimberton PA, *2500* **146** B2
Kimble Co. TX, *4607* **60** C1
Kincaid IL, *1505* **98** B1
Kinde MI, *448* **76** C1
Kinder LA, *2477* **133** E2
Kinderhook NY, *1211* **94** B2
Kindred ND, *692* **19** E4
King NC, *6904* **112** A3
King WI, *1750* **74** B1
King and Queen Co. VA, *6945* **113** F1
King and Queen C.H. VA, *85* **113** F1
King City CA, *12874* **44** B3
King City MO, *1013* **86** B4
King City OR, *3111* **251** C3
King Co. TX, *286* **58** C1
King Co. WA, *1931249* **12** C3
King Cove AK, *938* **154** B4
Kingfield ME, *997* **82** B1
Kingfisher OK, *4633* **51** E2
Kingfisher Co. OK, *15034* **51** E2
King George VA, *4457* **103** E4
King George Co. VA, *23584* **103** E4
Kingman AZ, *28068* **46** B3
Kingman IN, *511* **99** E1
Kingman KS, *3177* **43** E4
Kingman Co. KS, *7858* **43** E4
King of Prussia PA, *19936* **146** C2
King Salmon AK, *374* **154** B3
Kings Beach CA, *3796* **37** D2
Kingsburg CA, *11382* **45** D3
Kingsbury TX, *782* **61** E2
Kingsbury Co. SD, *5148* **27** E3
Kings Co. CA, *152982* **44** C3
Kings Co. NY, *2504700* **147** F1
Kingsford MI, *5133* **68** C2
Kingsford Hts. IN, *1435* **89** E2
Kingsland AR, *447* **117** E4
Kingsland GA, *15946* **139** D1
Kingsland TX, *6030* **61** D1
Kingsley IA, *1411* **35** F1
Kingsley MI, *1480* **69** F4
Kings Mtn. NC, *10296* **122** A1
Kings Park NY, *17282* **149** D3
Kings Pt. NY, *5005* **148** B4
Kingsport TN, *48205* **111** E3
Kingston GA, *637* **120** B3
Kingston ID, *650* **14** B3
Kingston IL, *1164* **88** C1
Kingston KY, *600* **110** C1
Kingston MA, *5591* **151** E2
Kingston MI, *440* **76** C2
Kingston MO, *348* **96** C1
Kingston NH, *6025* **95** E1
Kingston NJ, *1493* **147** D1
Kingston NY, *23893* **94** B2
Kingston OH, *1032* **101** D2
Kingston OK, *1601* **59** F1
Kingston PA, *13182* **93** E2
Kingston RI, *6974* **150** C4
Kingston TN, *5934* **110** B4
Kingston WA, *2099* **12** C3

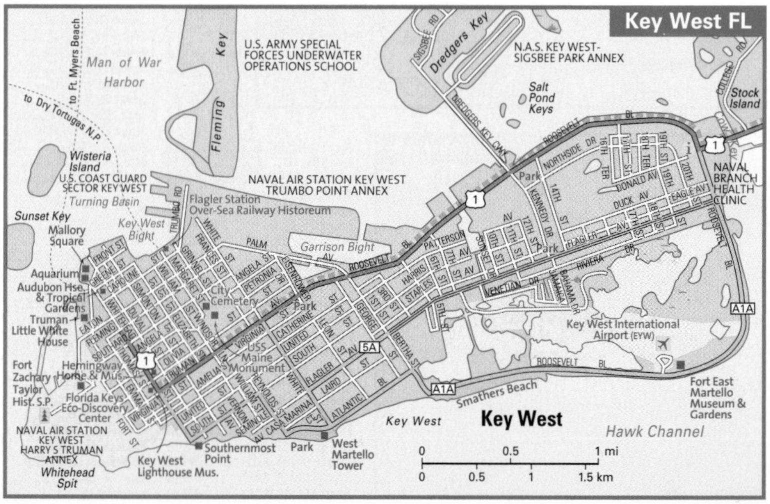

Entries in **bold black** indicate counties or parishes.
Entries in **bold color** indicate cities with detailed inset maps.

Kingston Sprs. TN, *2756* ... **109** E4
Kingstown MD, *1733* ... **145** D2
Kingstown NC, *681* ... **121** F1
Kingstree SC, *3328* ... **122** C4
Kingsville MD, *4318* ... **193** E1
Kingsville TX, *26213* ... **63** F2
King William VA, *252* ... **113** E1
King William Co. VA, *15935* ... **113** E1
Kingwood TX, *37400* ... **132** B3
Kingwood WV, *2939* ... **102** B2
Kinmundy IL, *796* ... **98** C3
Kinnelon NJ, *10248* ... **148** A3
Kinney Co. TX, *3598* ... **60** B3
Kinsey AL, *2198* ... **128** B4
Kinsley KS, *1457* ... **43** D4
Kinsman OH, *616* ... **91** F2
Kinston AL, *540* ... **128** A4
Kinston NC, *21677* ... **115** C3
Kinzers PA, *800* ... **146** A3
Kiowa CO, *723* ... **41** E2
Kiowa KS, *1026* ... **51** D1
Kiowa OK, *731* ... **116** A2
Kiowa Co. CO, *1398* ... **42** A3
Kiowa Co. KS, *2553* ... **43** D4
Kiowa Co. OK, *9446* ... **51** D3
Kipnuk AK, *639* ... **154** B3
Kirby TX, *8000* ... **61** D3
Kirbyville TX, *2142* ... **132** C1
Kirkland IL, *1744* ... **88** C1
Kirkland WA, *48787* ... **12** C3
Kirklin IN, *788* ... **89** F4
Kirksville MO, *17505* ... **87** D4
Kirkwood DE, *1800* ... **145** E1
Kirkwood IL, *714* ... **87** F3
Kirkwood MO, *27540* ... **98** A3
Kirtland NM, *7875* ... **48** B1
Kirtland OH, *6866* ... **91** E2
Kiryas Joel NY, *20175* ... **148** B2
Kismet KS, *459* ... **42** B4
Kissimmee FL, *59682* ... **141** D2
Kit Carson Co. CO, *8270* ... **41** F1
Kitsap Co. WA, *251133* ... **12** C3
Kittanning PA, *4044* ... **92** A3
Kittery ME, *4562* ... **82** B4
Kittery Pt. ME, *1012* ... **82** B4
Kittitas WA, *1381* ... **13** D4
Kittitas Co. WA, *40915* ... **13** D3
Kittredge CO, *1304* ... **209** A4
Kittson Co. MN, *4552* ... **19** F1
Kitty Hawk NC, *3272* ... **115** F2
Klamath CA, *779* ... **28** A3
Klamath Co. OR, *66380* ... **28** C2
Klamath Falls OR, *20840* ... **28** C2
Klawock AK, *755* ... **155** E4
Kleberg Co. TX, *32061* ... **63** F2
Klemme IA, *507* ... **72** C3
Klickitat WA, *362* ... **21** D1
Klickitat Co. WA, *20318* ... **21** D1
Knightdale NC, *11401* ... **113** D4
Knights FL, *1000* ... **266** D1
Knightsen CA, *1568* ... **36** C3
Knights Landing CA, *995* ... **36** B2
Knightstown IN, *2182* ... **100** A1
Knightsville IN, *872* ... **99** E1
Knippa TX, *689* ... **60** C3
Knob Noster MO, *2709* ... **96** C3
Knollcrest CT, *1300* ... **148** C1
Knollwood CT, *2500* ... **149** E2
Knott Co. KY, *16346* ... **111** D1
Knox IN, *3704* ... **89** E2
Knox PA, *1146* ... **92** A2
Knox City TX, *1130* ... **58** C1
Knox Co. IL, *52919* ... **88** A3
Knox Co. IN, *38440* ... **99** E3
Knox Co. KY, *31883* ... **110** C2
Knox Co. ME, *39736* ... **82** C2
Knox Co. MO, *4131* ... **87** E4
Knox Co. NE, *8701* ... **35** E1
Knox Co. OH, *60921* ... **91** D4
Knox Co. TN, *432226* ... **110** C4
Knox Co. TX, *3719* ... **58** C1
Knoxville AR, *731* ... **117** D1
Knoxville GA, *69* ... **129** D2
Knoxville IL, *2911* ... **88** A3
Knoxville IA, *7313* ... **87** D2
Knoxville PA, *629* ... **93** D1
Knoxville TN, *178874* ... **110** C4
Kodiak AK, *6130* ... **154** C4
Kohler WI, *2120* ... **75** D2
Kokomo IN, *45468* ... **89** F4
Kolin LA, *600* ... **125** E4
Koloa HI, *2144* ... **152** B1
Komatke AZ, *821* ... **54** C2
Konawa OK, *1298* ... **51** F3
Koochiching Co. MN, *13311* ... **64** B2
Koontz Lake IN, *1557* ... **89** E2
Kooskia ID, *607* ... **22** B1
Kootenai ID, *678* ... **14** B2
Kootenai Co. ID, *138494* ... **14** B3
Koppel PA, *762* ... **91** F3
Kopperston WV, *616* ... **111** F1
Kosciusko MS, *7402* ... **126** C1
Kosciusko Co. IN, *77358* ... **89** F2
Kossuth Co. IA, *15543* ... **72** C3
Kotlik AK, *577* ... **154** B2
Kotzebue AK, *3201* ... **154** B1
Kountze TX, *2123* ... **132** C2
Kouts IN, *1879* ... **89** E2
Kreamer PA, *822* ... **93** D3
Krebs OK, *2053* ... **116** A2
Kremmling CO, *1444* ... **41** D1
Kress TX, *715* ... **50** A4
Krotz Sprs. LA, *1198* ... **133** F2
Krum TX, *4157* ... **59** E2
Kualapuu HI, *2027* ... **152** C3
Kulm ND, *354* ... **27** D1
Kulpmont PA, *2924* ... **93** E3
Kulpsville PA, *8194* ... **146** C2
Kuna ID, *15210* ... **22** B4
Kure Beach NC, *2012* ... **123** E3
Kurtistown HI, *1298* ... **153** F3
Kuttawa KY, *649* ... **109** D2
Kutztown PA, *5012* ... **146** B1
Kwethluk AK, *721* ... **154** B3
Kykotsmovi Vil. AZ, *746* ... **47** E2
Kyle SD, *846* ... **26** B4
Kyle TX, *28016* ... **61** E2

L

Labadieville LA, *1854* ... **134** A3
La Barge WY, *551* ... **32** A2
LaBelle FL, *4640* ... **141** D4
La Belle MO, *660* ... **87** E4
Labette Co. KS, *21607* ... **106** A2
La Blanca TX, *2488* ... **63** E4
La Cañada Flintridge CA, *20246* ... **228** D1
Lac du Flambeau WI, *1969* ... **68** A2
La Center KY, *1009* ... **108** C2
La Center WA, *2800* ... **20** C1
Lacey WA, *42393* ... **12** C4
Laceys Spr. AL, *750* ... **119** F2
La Cienega NM, *3819* ... **48** C3
Lackawanna NY, *18141* ... **78** B3
Lackawanna Co. PA, *214437* ... **93** F2
Laclede Co. MO, *35571* ... **107** D1
Lacombe LA, *8679* ... **134** C2
Lacon IL, *1937* ... **88** B3
Lacona NY, *582* ... **79** E2
Laconia NH, *15951* ... **81** F3
La Conner WA, *891* ... **12** C2
Lacoochee FL, *1714* ... **140** C1
LaCoste TX, *1119* ... **61** D3
Lac qui Parle Co. MN, *7259* ... **27** F2
La Crescent MN, *4830* ... **73** F2
La Crescenta CA, *18532* ... **228** D1
La Croft OH, *1144* ... **91** F3
La Crosse IN, *551* ... **89** E2
La Crosse KS, *1342* ... **43** D3
La Crosse VA, *604* ... **113** D3
La Crosse WI, *51320* ... **73** F2
La Crosse Co. WI, *114638* ... **73** F2
La Cygne KS, *1149* ... **96** B4
Ladd IL, *1295* ... **88** B2
Laddonia MO, *513* ... **97** F2
Ladera Hts. CA, *6498* ... **228** C3
Ladoga IN, *985* ... **99** E1
Ladonia AL, *3142* ... **128** C2
Ladonia TX, *612* ... **59** F1
Ladson SC, *13790* ... **131** D1
Ladue MO, *8521* ... **256** B2
Lady Lake FL, *13926* ... **140** C1
Ladysmith VA, *750* ... **103** D4
Ladysmith WI, *3414* ... **67** F3
La Farge WI, *746* ... **73** F2
La Fargeville NY, *608* ... **79** E1
Lafayette AL, *3003* ... **128** B1
Lafayette CA, *23893* ... **259** D2
Lafayette CO, *24453* ... **41** E1
LaFayette GA, *7121* ... **120** B2
Lafayette IN, *67140* ... **89** E4
Lafayette LA, *120623* ... **133** F2
Lafayette MN, *504* ... **72** B1
Lafayette NJ, *700* ... **148** A3
Lafayette OR, *3742* ... **20** B2
Lafayette TN, *4474* ... **110** A3
Lafayette Co. AR, *7645* ... **125** D1
Lafayette Co. FL, *8870* ... **137** F3
Lafayette Co. MS, *47351* ... **118** C3
Lafayette Co. MO, *33381* ... **96** C2
Lafayette Co. WI, *16836* ... **74** A4
Lafayette Par. LA, *221578* ... **133** F2
La Feria TX, *7302* ... **63** F4
Lafitte LA, *972* ... **134** B3
Laflin PA, *1487* ... **261** B2
LaFollette TN, *7456* ... **110** C3
La Fontaine IN, *875* ... **89** F3
Lafourche Par. LA, *96318* ... **134** B4
Lago Vista TX, *6041* ... **61** E1
La Grande OR, *13082* ... **21** F2
LaGrange GA, *29588* ... **128** C1
La Grange IL, *15550* ... **203** C5
Lagrange IN, *2625* ... **90** A2
La Grange KY, *8082* ... **100** A3
La Grange MO, *931* ... **97** F1
La Grange NC, *2873* ... **123** E1
LaGrange OH, *2103* ... **91** D2
La Grange TX, *4641* ... **61** F2
La Grange WY, *448* ... **33** F3
LaGrange Co. IN, *37128* ... **90** A2
La Grange Park IL, *13579* ... **203** C4
Lagrangeville NY, *1100* ... **148** B1
La Grulla TX, *1622* ... **63** E4
Laguna NM, *1241* ... **48** B3
Laguna Beach CA, *22723* ... **52** C3
Laguna Beach FL, *3932* ... **136** C2
Laguna Hts. TX, *3488* ... **63** F4
Laguna Hills CA, *30344* ... **229** G5
Laguna Niguel CA, *62979* ... **229** G6
Laguna Vista TX, *3117* ... **63** F4
Laguna Woods CA, *16192* ... **229** G5
Lagunitas CA, *1835* ... **36** B3
La Habra CA, *60239* ... **228** E3
La Habra Hts. CA, *5325* ... **228** E3
Lahaina HI, *11704* ... **153** D1
La Harpe IL, *1235* ... **87** F3
La Harpe KS, *578* ... **96** A4
Lahoma OK, *611* ... **51** E2
Laie HI, *6138* ... **152** A2
Laingsburg MI, *1283* ... **76** A3
La Jara CO, *818* ... **41** D4
La Joya TX, *3985* ... **63** E4
La Junta CO, *7077* ... **41** F3
Lake MS, *324* ... **126** C2
Lake Alfred FL, *5015* ... **140** C2
Lake Aluma OK, *88* ... **224** E2
Lake Andes SD, *879* ... **35** D1
Lake Ariel PA, *1000* ... **93** F2
Lake Arrowhead CA, *12424* ... **53** D2
Lake Arthur LA, *2738* ... **133** E2
Lake Arthur NM, *436* ... **57** E2
Lake Barcroft VA, *9558* ... **270** B4
Lake Barrington IL, *4973* ... **203** B1
Lake Benton MN, *683* ... **27** F3
Lake Bluff IL, *5722* ... **75** D4
Lake Butler FL, *15400* ... **138** C3

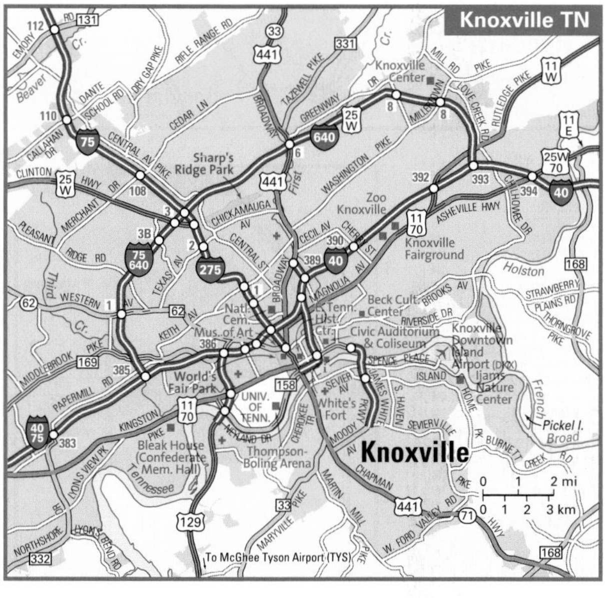

Bird in Hand ... C2
E. Petersburg ... A1
Lancaster ... B2
Landisville ... A1
Leacock ... C1
Leola ... C1
Millersville ... A2
Mountville ... A2
Neffsville ... B1
Rohrerstown ... A2
Salunga ... A1
Smoketown ... C2

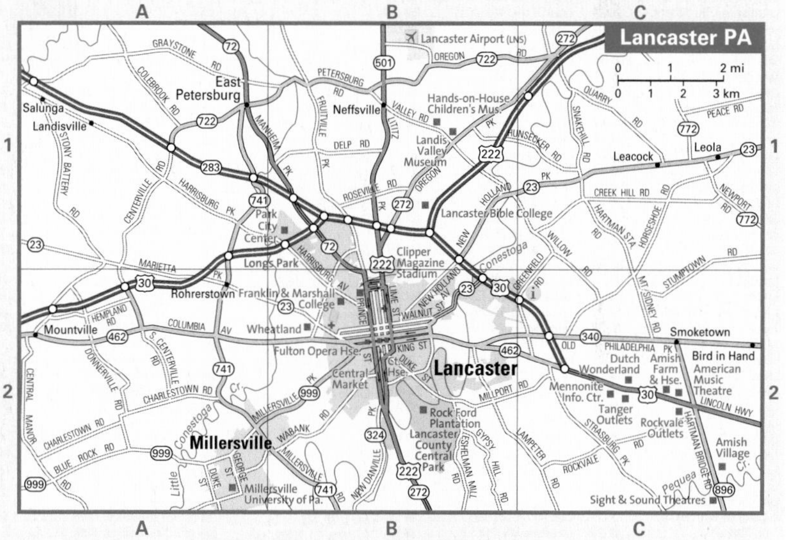

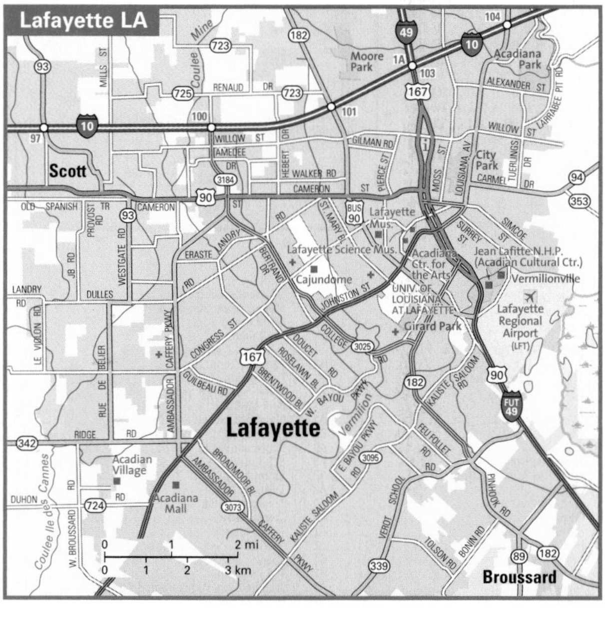

Lake Carmel NY, *8282* ... **148** C1
Lake Charles LA, *71993* ... **133** D2
Lake City AR, *2082* ... **108** A4
Lake City CO, *408* ... **40** C3
Lake City FL, *12046* ... **138** C2
Lake City GA, *2612* ... **190** D5
Lake City IA, *1727* ... **72** B4
Lake City MI, *836* ... **75** F1
Lake City MN, *5063* ... **73** E1
Lake City PA, *3031* ... **91** F1
Lake City SC, *6675* ... **122** C4
Lake City TX, *509* ... **61** E4
Lake Clarke Shores FL, *3376* ... **143** F1
Lake Co. CA, *64665* ... **36** B2
Lake Co. CO, *7310* ... **41** D2
Lake Co. FL, *297052* ... **141** D1
Lake Co. IL, *703462* ... **74** C4
Lake Co. IN, *496005* ... **89** D2
Lake Co. MI, *11539* ... **75** F1
Lake Co. MN, *10866* ... **65** D3
Lake Co. MT, *28746* ... **15** D3
Lake Co. OH, *230041* ... **91** E1
Lake Co. OR, *7895* ... **21** D4
Lake Co. SD, *11200* ... **27** F3
Lake Co. TN, *7832* ... **108** B3
Lake Crystal MN, *2549* ... **72** C1
Lake Dallas TX, *7105* ... **59** F2
Lake Delton WI, *2914* ... **74** A2
Lake Elmo MN, *8069* ... **235** E2
Lake Elsinore CA, *51821* ... **53** D3
Lake Erie Beach NY, *3872* ... **78** A4
Lakefield MN, *1694* ... **72** A2
Lake Forest CA, *77264* ... **229** G5
Lake Forest IL, *19375* ... **75** D4
Lake Forest Park WA, *12598* ... **262** B2
Lake Geneva WI, *7651* ... **74** C4

Figures after entries indicate population, page number, and grid reference.

Lake George NY, *906* **80** C4
Lake Grove NY, *11163* **149** D3
Lake Hamilton AR, *2135* **117** D3
Lake Hamilton FL, *1231* **141** D2
Lake Havasu City AZ, *52527* **46** B4
Lakehead CA, *461* **28** C4
Lake Helen FL, *2624* **139** E4
Lakehills TX, *5150* **61** D2
Lakehurst NJ, *2654* **147** E3
Lake in the Hills IL, *28965* **203** A2
Lake Isabella CA, *3466* **45** E4
Lake Isabella MI, *1681* **76** A2
Lake Jackson TX, *26849* **132** A4
Lake Junaluska NC, *2734* **121** E1
Lakeland FL, *97422* **140** C2
Lakeland GA, *3366* **137** F1
Lakeland MN, *1796* **67** D4
Lakeland NY, *2786* **265** A1
Lakeland TN, *12430* **118** B1
Lakeland Vil. CA, *11541* **229** J5
Lake Linden MI, *1007* **65** F3
Lake Lotawana MO, *1939* **96** C3
Lake Lure NC, *1192* **121** F1
Lake Luzerne NY, *1227* **80** C4
Lake Mary FL, *13822* **141** D1
Lake Michigan Beach MI, *1216* **89** E1
Lake Mills IA, *2100* **72** C2
Lake Mills WI, *5708* **74** B3
Lake Mohawk NJ, *9916* **148** A3
Lake Mohegan NY, *6010* **148** B2
Lakemont PA, *1868* **92** C4
Lake Montezuma AZ, *4706* **47** D4
Lakemoor IL, *6017* **203** A1
Lakemore OH, *3068* **188** B2
Lake Nebagamon WI, *1069* **64** C4
Lake Norden SD, *467* **27** F3
Lake Odessa MI, *2018* **75** F3
Lake of the Woods IL, *2912* **88** C4
Lake of the Woods Co. MN, *4045* **64** A1
Lake Orion MI, *2973* **76** C4
Lake Oswego OR, *36619* **20** C2
Lake Ozark MO, *1586* **97** D4
Lake Panasoffkee FL, *3551* **140** C1
Lake Park FL, *8155* **141** F4
Lake Park GA, *733* **137** F1
Lake Park IA, *1105* **72** A2
Lake Park MN, *783* **19** F4
Lake Peekskill NY, *3800* **148** B2
Lake Placid FL, *2223* **141** D3
Lake Placid NY, *2521* **80** C2
Lake Pleasant NY, *100* **79** F2
Lake Pocotopaug CT, *3436* **149** E1
Lakeport CA, *4753* **36** A2
Lakeport MI, *700* **76** C3
Lakeport TX, *974* **124** B2
Lake Preston SD, *599* **27** E3
Lake Providence LA, *3991* **126** A2
Lake Quivira KS, *906* **224** A3
Lake Ridge VA, *41058* **144** A4
Lake St. Croix Beach MN, *1051* **67** D4
Lake St. Louis MO, *14545* **98** A3
Lakeshire MO, *1432* **256** B3
Lake Shore MD, *19477* **144** C2
Lake Shore MN, *1004* **64** A4
Lakeside CA, *20648* **53** D4
Lakeside CT, *1300* **149** D1
Lakeside MT, *2669* **15** D2
Lakeside OR, *1699* **20** A4
Lakeside VA, *11849* **113** E1
Lakeside City TX, *997* **59** D1
Lakeside Park KY, *2668* **204** A3
Lakesite TN, *1826* **120** B1
Lakes of the Four Seasons IN, *7033* **89** D2
Lake Sta. IN, *12572* **89** D2
Lake Stevens WA, *28069* **12** C2
Lake Success NY, *2934* **241** G3
Lake Summerset IL, *2048* **74** B4
Lake Tanglewood TX, *796* **50** A3
Lake Tapawingo MO, *730* **96** C2
Laketon IN, *623* **89** F3
Lake View AL, *1943* **127** F1
Lakeview AR, *741* **107** E3
Lake View AR, *443* **118** A3
Lakeview CA, *2104* **229** K4
Lake View IA, *1142* **72** B4
Lakeview MI, *1007* **75** F2
Lake View NY, *2100* **78** A4
Lakeview NY, *5615* **241** G4
Lakeview OH, *1072* **90** B4
Lakeview OR, *2294* **29** D2
Lake View SC, *807* **122** C3
Lake Villa IL, *8741* **74** C4
Lake Vil. AR, *2575* **125** F1
Lake Vil. IN, *765* **89** D3
Lakeville CT, *928* **94** B2
Lakeville IN, *786* **89** F2
Lakeville MA, *9821* **151** D3
Lakeville MN, *55954* **67** D4
Lake Waccamaw NC, *1480* **123** D3
Lake Wales FL, *14225* **141** D2
Lake Waukomis MO, *870* **224** B2
Lakeway TX, *11391* **61** E1
Lake Winnebago MO, *1131* **96** B3
Lakewood CA, *80048* **228** D4
Lakewood CO, *142980* **41** E1
Lakewood IL, *3811* **88** C1
Lakewood NJ, *53805* **147** E2
Lakewood NY, *3002* **92** B1
Lakewood OH, *52131* **91** E2
Lakewood TN, *2302* **109** F3
Lakewood WA, *58163* **12** C3
Lakewood Club MI, *1291* **75** E2
Lakewood Park FL, *11323* **141** E3
Lakewood Park ND, *425* **19** D2
Lake Worth FL, *34910* **143** F1
Lake Worth TX, *4584* **207** A2
Lake Wylie SC, *8841* **122** A1
Lake Zurich IL, *19631* **89** D1
Lakin KS, *2216* **42** B3
Lakota ND, *672* **19** D2
La Luz NM, *1697* **56** C2
Lamar AR, *1605* **117** D1
Lamar CO, *7804* **42** A3
Lamar MO, *4532* **106** C1
Lamar SC, *989* **122** B3
Lamar Co. AL, *14564* **119** D4
Lamar Co. GA, *18317* **129** D1
Lamar Co. MS, *55658* **126** C4
Lamar Co. TX, *49793* **116** A4
La Marque TX, *14509* **132** B4
Lamb Co. TX, *13977* **50** A4
Lambert MS, *1638* **118** B3
Lamberton MN, *824* **72** A1
Lambertville MI, *9953* **90** C1
Lambertville NJ, *3906* **147** D2
Lame Deer MT, *2052* **25** D1
La Mesa CA, *57065* **53** D4
La Mesa NM, *728* **56** C3
Lamesa TX, *9422* **58** A2
La Mirada CA, *48527* **228** E3
La Moille IL, *726* **88** B2
Lamoille Co. VT, *24475* **81** E1
Lamoni IA, *2324* **86** C3
Lamont CA, *15120* **45** D4
Lamont IA, *461* **73** E4
Lamont OK, *417* **51** E1
La Monte MO, *1140* **97** D3
LaMoure ND, *889* **19** D4
LaMoure Co. ND, *4139* **19** D4
Lampasas TX, *6681* **59** D4
Lampasas Co. TX, *19677* **59** D4
Lampeter PA, *1669* **146** A3
Lanai City HI, *3102* **152** C4
Lanare CA, *589* **44** C3
Lanark IL, *1457* **88** B1
Lanark PA, *1500* **146** C1
Lanark Vil. FL, *550* **137** D3
Lancaster CA, *156633* **52** C2
Lancaster KY, *3442* **110** B1
Lancaster MA, *8055* **150** C1
Lancaster MO, *728* **87** D4
Lancaster NH, *1725* **81** F2
Lancaster NY, *10352* **78** B3
Lancaster OH, *38780* **101** D1
Lancaster PA, *59322* **146** A3
Lancaster SC, *8526* **122** B2
Lancaster TX, *36361* **59** F2
Lancaster VA, *100* **113** F1
Lancaster WI, *3868* **73** F3
Lancaster Co. NE, *285407* **35** F3
Lancaster Co. PA, *519445* **146** A3
Lancaster Co. SC, *76652* **122** B2
Lancaster Co. VA, *11391* **113** F1
Lander WY, *7487* **32** B1
Lander Co. NV, *5775* **30** A4
Landfall MN, *686* **235** E3
Landis NC, *3109* **122** B1
Landisville PA, *1893* **225** A1
Land O' Lakes FL, *31996* **140** B2
Landover MD, *23078* **270** E3
Landover Hills MD, *1687* **271** F2
Landrum SC, *2376* **121** F1
Lane SC, *508* **122** C4
Lane Co. KS, *1750* **42** C3
Lane Co. OR, *351715* **20** C4
Lanesboro MN, *754* **73** E2
Lanesboro PA, *506* **93** F1
Lanesborough MA, *2990* **94** C1
Lanesville CT, *3100* **148** C1
Lanesville IN, *564* **99** F4
Lanett AL, *6468* **128** B2
Langdon ND, *1878* **19** D1
Langdon Place KY, *936* **230** F1
Langford SD, *313* **27** E1
Langhorne PA, *1622* **147** D2
Langlade Co. WI, *19977* **68** B3
Langley OK, *819* **106** B3
Langley VA, *3500* **270** B2
Langley WA, *1035* **12** C2
Langley Park MD, *18755* **270** D2
Langston OK, *1724* **51** E2
Lanham MD, *10157* **271** F2
Lanier Co. GA, *10078* **137** F1
Lannon WI, *1107* **234** A1
Lanoka Harbor NJ, *3800* **147** E3
Lansdale PA, *16269* **146** C2
Lansdowne MD, *8409* **193** C3
Lansdowne PA, *10620* **146** C3
L'Anse MI, *2011* **65** F4
Lansford ND, *245* **18** B2
Lansford PA, *3941* **93** E3
Lansing IA, *999* **73** F2
Lansing KS, *11265* **96** B2
Lansing MI, *114297* **76** A4
Lansing NY, *3529* **79** D4
Lantana FL, *10423* **143** F1
Laona WI, *583* **68** C3
La Palma CA, *15568* **228** E4
La Paz IN, *561* **89** F2
La Paz Co. AZ, *20489* **54** A1
Lapeer MI, *8841* **76** C3
Lapeer Co. MI, *88319* **76** C3
Lapel IN, *2068* **89** F4
La Pine OR, *1653* **21** D4
Laplace LA, *29872* **134** B3
La Plata MD, *8753* **144** B4
La Plata MO, *1366* **97** E1
La Plata Co. CO, *51334* **40** B4
Laporte CO, *2450* **33** E4
La Porte IN, *22053* **89** E2
Laporte PA, *316* **93** E2
La Porte TX, *33800* **132** B3
La Porte City IA, *2285* **73** E4
LaPorte Co. IN, *111467* **89** E2
La Prairie MN, *665* **64** B3
La Pryor TX, *1643* **60** C3
La Puente CA, *39816* **228** E3
Lapwai ID, *1137* **14** B4
La Quinta CA, *37467* **53** E3
Laramie WY, *30816* **33** E3
Laramie Co. WY, *91738* **33** E3
Larchmont NY, *5864* **241** F1
Larchwood IA, *866* **27** F4
Laredo TX, *236091* **63** D2
Largo FL, *77648* **140** B2
Largo MD, *10709* **271** F3
Larimer Co. CO, *299630* **33** E4
Larimore ND, *1346* **19** E2
Larkspur CA, *11926* **259** A1
Larksville PA, *4480* **261** A1
Larned KS, *4054* **43** D3
Larose LA, *7400* **134** B3
La Rue OH, *747* **90** C4
Larue Co. KY, *14193* **110** A1
La Sal UT, *395* **40** A3
La Salle CO, *1955* **33** E4
LaSalle IL, *9609* **88** B2
La Salle Co. IL, *113924* **88** C2
La Salle Co. TX, *6886* **60** C4
La Salle Par. LA, *14890* **125** E3
Las Animas CO, *2410* **41** F3
Las Animas Co. CO, *15507* **41** F4
Lasara TX, *1039* **63** E4
Las Cruces NM, *97618* **56** C3
Las Lomas CA, *3024* **236** E2
Lassen Co. CA, *34895* **29** D4
Las Vegas NV, *583756* **46** A2
Las Vegas NM, *13753* **49** D3
Latah Co. ID, *37244* **14** B4
Latham NY, *10100* **188** E2
Lathrop CA, *18023* **36** C4
Lathrop MO, *2086* **96** B1
Lathrup Vil. MI, *4075* **210** B2
Latimer IA, *507* **72** C4
Latimer MS, *6079* **135** D2
Latimer Co. OK, *11154* **116** B2
Laton CA, *1824* **44** C3
Latrobe PA, *8338* **92** A4
Latta OK, *800* **51** F4
Latta SC, *1379* **122** C3
Lattingtown NY, *1739* **148** C3
Lauderdale MN, *2379* **235** C2
Lauderdale-by-the-Sea FL, *6056* **233** C2
Lauderdale Co. AL, *92709* **119** E2
Lauderdale Co. MS, *80261* **127** D3
Lauderdale Co. TN, *27815* **108** B4
Lauderdale Lakes FL, *32593* **233** B2
Lauderhill FL, *66887* **233** B2
Laughlin NV, *7323* **46** B3
La Union NM, *1106* **56** C3
Laura KY, *600* **111** E1
Laurel DE, *3708* **145** E4
Laurel FL, *8171* **140** B4
Laurel IN, *512* **100** A1
Laurel MD, *25115* **144** B2
Laurel MS, *18540* **126** C4
Laurel MT, *6718* **24** B1
Laurel NE, *964* **35** F2
Laurel NY, *1394* **149** E3
Laurel VA, *16713* **113** E1
Laurel Bay SC, *5891* **130** C2
Laurel Co. KY, *58849* **110** C2
Laureldale NJ, *800* **147** D4
Laureldale PA, *3911* **146** B1
Laurel Hill FL, *537* **136** B1
Laurel Hill NC, *1254* **122** C2
Laurel Park NC, *2180* **121** E1
Laurel Run PA, *500* **261** B2
Laurence Harbor NJ, *6536* **147** E1
Laurens IA, *1258* **72** B3
Laurens NY, *263* **79** F4
Laurens SC, *9139* **121** F3
Laurens Co. GA, *48434* **129** E3
Laurens Co. SC, *66537* **121** F3
Laurie MO, *945* **97** D4
Laurinburg NC, *15962* **122** C2
Laurium MI, *1977* **65** F3
Lavaca AR, *2289* **116** C1
Lavaca Co. TX, *19263* **61** E3
Lava Hot Sprs. ID, *407* **31** E1
La Vale MD, *3551* **102** C1
Lavalette WV, *1073* **101** D4
Lavallette NJ, *1875* **147** E3
La Vergne TN, *32588* **109** F4
La Verkin UT, *4060* **39** D4
La Verne CA, *31063* **229** F2
Laverne OK, *1344* **50** C1
La Vernia TX, *1034* **61** D3
La Veta CO, *800* **41** E4
La Villa TX, *1957* **63** E4
Lavina MT, *187* **24** B1
La Vista NE, *15758* **35** F3
Lavonia GA, *2156* **121** E3
Lawai HI, *2363* **152** B1
Lawndale CA, *32769* **228** C3
Lawndale NC, *606* **121** F1
Lawnside NJ, *2945* **146** C3

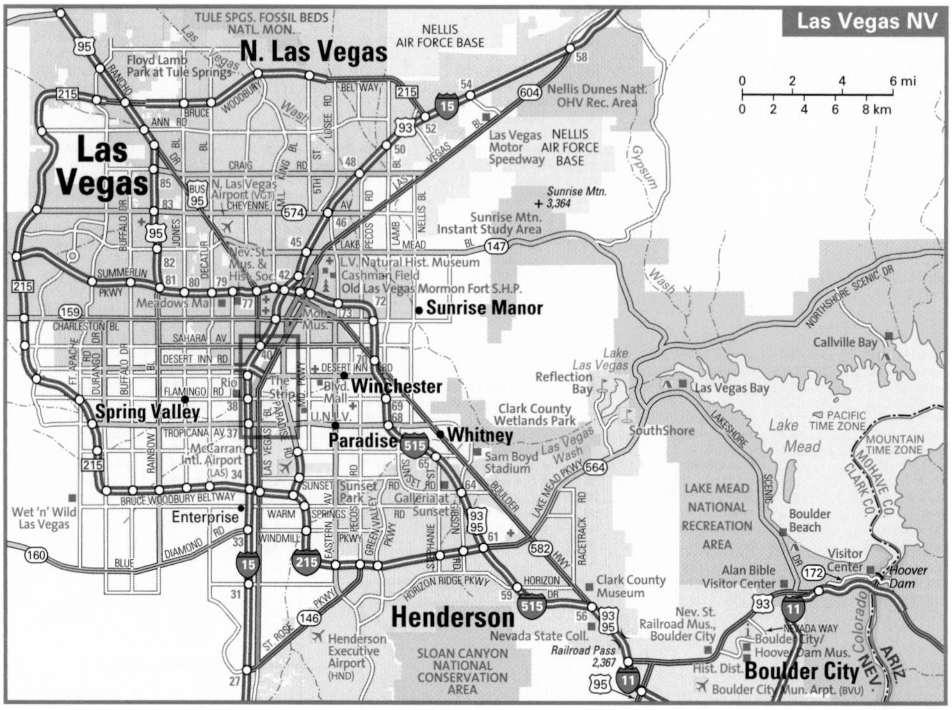

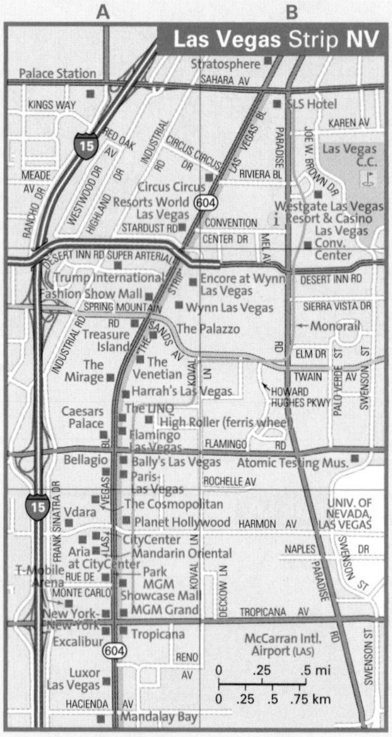

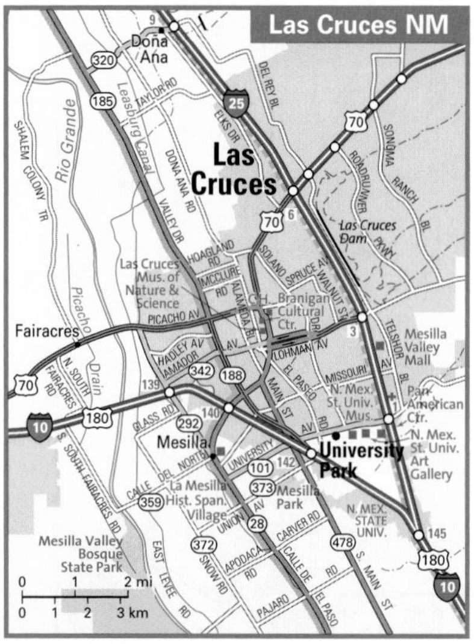

POINTS OF INTEREST
Aria at CityCenter A3
Atomic Testing Museum B2
Bally's Las Vegas A2
Bellagio A2
Caesars Palace A2
Circus Circus B1
CityCenter A3
The Cosmopolitan A3
Encore at Wynn Las Vegas A2
Excalibur A3
Fashion Show Mall A2
Flamingo Las Vegas A2
Harrah's Las Vegas A2
High Roller (ferris wheel) A2
Las Vegas Convention Center B1
The LINQ A2
Luxor Las Vegas A3
Mandalay Bay A3
Mandarin Oriental A3
McCarran Intl. Airport B3
MGM Grand A3
The Mirage A2
New York-New York A3
Palace Station A1
The Palazzo A2
Paris-Las Vegas A2
Park MGM A3
Planet Hollywood A3
Resorts World Las Vegas A1
Showcase Mall A3
SLS Hotel B1
Stratosphere B1
T-Mobile Arena A3
Treasure Island A2
Tropicana A3
Trump International A2
Univ. of Nevada, Las Vegas B3
Vdara A3
The Venetian A2
Westgate Las Vegas Hotel & Casino B1
Wynn Las Vegas A2

Entries in **bold black** indicate counties or parishes.
Entries in **bold color** indicate cities with detailed inset maps.

Becknerville C3
Boonesboro C3
Clays Ferry C3
Clintonville C1
Colby C2
E. Hickman B3
Faywood A1
Ford C3
Ft. Garrett A2
Georgetown A1
Hootentown C3
Hutchison C1
Keene A3
Lexington B1
Lisletown C3
Locust Grove C3
Midway A1
New Zion B1
Nicholasville A3
Nugent Crossroads . . . A1
Old Pine Grove C2
Paris C1
Pinckard A3
Pine Grove C2
Pisgah A2
Troy A3
Wallace A1
Wyandotte C2

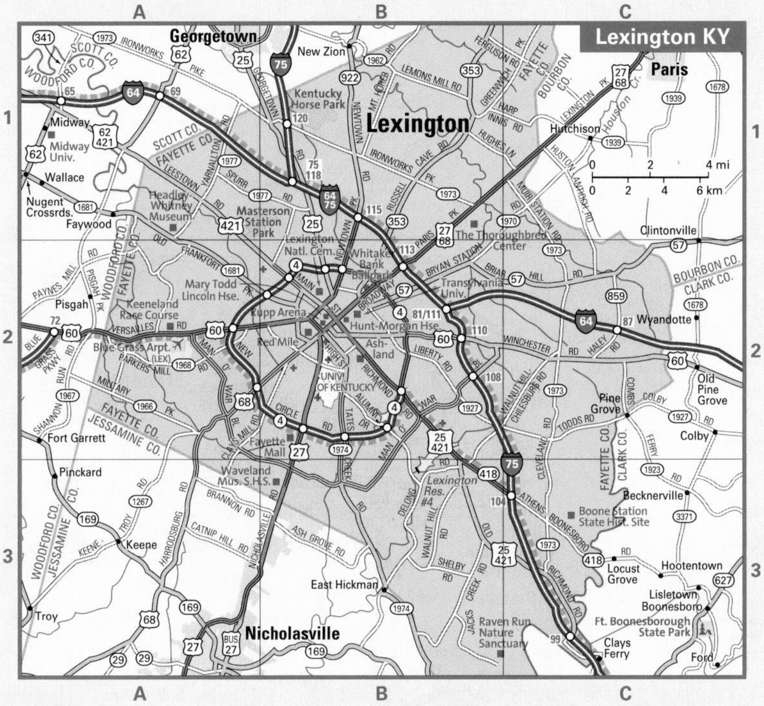

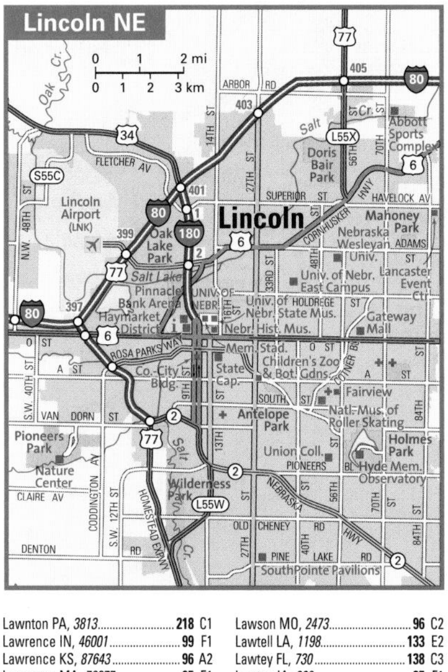

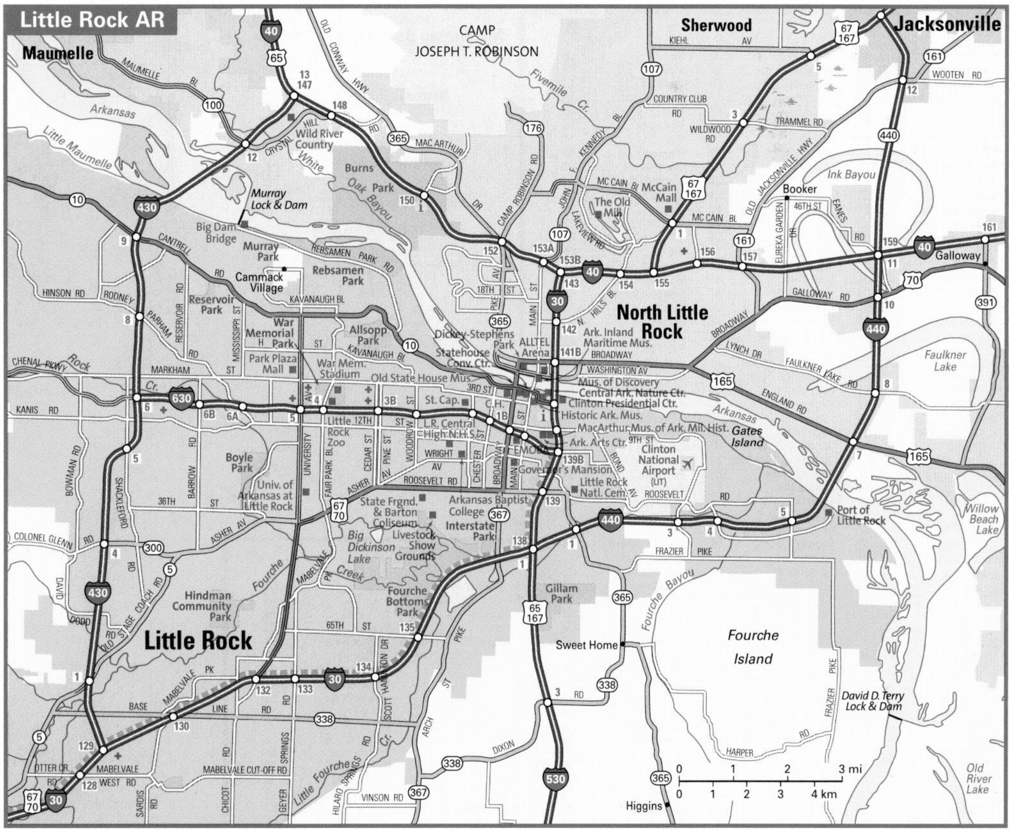

Lawnton PA, *3813* **218** C1
Lawrence IN, *46001* **99** F1
Lawrence KS, *87643* **96** A2
Lawrence MA, *76377* **95** E1
Lawrence MI, *996* **89** F1
Lawrence NY, *6483* **147** F1
Lawrenceburg IN, *5042* **100** B2
Lawrenceburg KY, *10505* **100** B4
Lawrenceburg TN, *10428* **119** E1
Lawrence Co. AL, *34339* **119** E3
Lawrence Co. AR, *17415* **107** F4
Lawrence Co. IL, *16833* **99** D3
Lawrence Co. IN, *46134* **99** F3
Lawrence Co. KY, *15860* **101** D4
Lawrence Co. MS, *12929* **126** B4
Lawrence Co. MO, *38634* **106** C2
Lawrence Co. OH, *62450* **101** D3
Lawrence Co. PA, *91108* **91** F3
Lawrence Co. SD, *24097* **25** F3
Lawrence Co. TN, *41869* **119** E1
Lawrenceville GA, *28546* **120** C4
Lawrenceville IL, *4348* **99** D3
Lawrenceville NJ, *3887* **147** D2
Lawrenceville PA, *581* **93** D1
Lawrenceville VA, *1438* **113** D2
Lawson MO, *2473* **96** C2
Lawtell LA, *1198* **133** E2
Lawtey FL, *730* **138** C3
Lawton IA, *908* **35** F1
Lawton MI, *1900* **89** F1
Lawton OK, *96867* **51** D4
Laysville CT, *1100* **149** F2
Layton UT, *67311* **31** E3
Laytonville CA, *1227* **36** A1
Leachville AR, *1993* **108** A4
Leacock PA, *6625* **146** A2
Lea Co. NM, *64727* **57** F2
Lead SD, *3124* **25** F3
Leadville CO, *2602* **41** D2
Leadwood MO, *1282* **98** A4
League City TX, *83560* **132** B4
Leake Co. MS, *23805* **126** C2
Leakesville MS, *898* **135** D1
Leakey TX, *425* **60** C2
Lealman FL, *19879* **266** B3
Leander TX, *26521* **61** E1
Leary GA, *618* **128** C4
Leary TX, *495* **116** C4
Leavenworth KS, *35251* **96** B2
Leavenworth WA, *1965* **13** D3
Leavenworth Co. KS, *76227* **96** B2
Leavittsburg OH, *1973* **276** A1
Leawood MO, *682* **106** B2
Lebanon DE, *2458* **145** E2
Lebanon IL, *4418* **98** B3
Lebanon IN, *15792* **89** E4
Lebanon KY, *5539* **110** B1
Lebanon MO, *14474* **107** E1
Lebanon NH, *13151* **81** E3
Lebanon NJ, *1358* **147** D1
Lebanon OH, *20033* **100** B2
Lebanon OR, *15518* **20** B3
Lebanon PA, *25477* **93** E4
Lebanon TN, *26190* **109** F3
Lebanon VA, *3424* **111** E2
Lebanon Co. PA, *133568* **93** E4
Lebanon Jct. KY, *1813* **100** A4
Lebec CA, *1468* **52** B1
Lebo KS, *940* **96** A3
Lecanto FL, *5882* **140** B1
Le Center MN, *2499* **72** C1
Le Claire IA, *3765* **88** A2
Lecompte LA, *1227* **133** E1
Lecompton KS, *625* **96** A2
Ledbetter KY, *1683* **109** D2
Ledgewood NJ, *1100* **148** A3
Ledyard Ctr. CT, *15172* **149** F1
Lee MA, *2051* **94** C2
Leechburg PA, *2156* **92** A3
Lee Co. AL, *140247* **128** B2
Lee Co. AR, *10424* **118** A2
Lee Co. FL, *618754* **142** C1
Lee Co. GA, *28298* **129** D4
Lee Co. IL, *36031* **88** B2
Lee Co. IA, *35862* **87** F3
Lee Co. KY, *7887* **110** C1
Lee Co. MS, *82910* **119** D3
Lee Co. NC, *57866* **123** D1
Lee Co. SC, *19220* **122** B3
Lee Co. TX, *16612* **61** F1
Lee Co. VA, *25587* **111** D3
Leeds AL, *11773* **119** F4
Leeds ND, *427* **19** D2
Leeds UT, *820* **39** D4
Leelanau Co. MI, *21708* **69** F4
Leesburg AL, *1027* **120** A3
Leesburg FL, *20117* **140** C1
Leesburg GA, *2896* **129** D4
Leesburg IN, *555* **89** F2
Leesburg NJ, *850* **145** F2
Leesburg OH, *1314* **100** C2
Leesburg VA, *42616* **144** A2
Leesport PA, *1918* **146** A1
Lee's Summit MO, *91364* **96** B3
Leesville LA, *6612* **133** D1
Leeton MO, *566* **96** C3
Leetonia OH, *1959* **91** F3
Leflore Co. MS, *32317* **118** B4
Le Flore Co. OK, *50384* **116** B2
Lefors TX, *497* **50** B3
Le Grand CA, *1659* **37** D4
Le Grand IA, *938* **87** D1
Lehi UT, *47407* **31** E4
Lehigh IA, *416* **72** C4
Lehigh Acres FL, *86784* **143** D1
Lehigh Co. PA, *349497* **93** F3
Lehighton PA, *5500* **93** F3
Leicester MA, *10970* **150** B1
Leigh NE, *405* **35** E3
Leighton AL, *729* **119** E2
Leipsic DE, *183* **145** E2
Leipsic OH, *2093* **90** B3
Leisure City FL, *22655* **143** E3
Leisuretowne NJ, *3582* **147** D3
Leitchfield KY, *6699* **109** F1
Leitersburg MD, *573* **103** D1
Leithsville PA, *1200* **146** C1
Leland IL, *977* **88** C2
Leland MI, *377* **69** F3
Leland MS, *4481* **126** A1
Leland NC, *13527* **123** E3
Le Mars IA, *9826* **35** F1
Lemay MO, *16645* **256** B3
Lemhi Co. ID, *7936* **23** D2
Lemitar NM, *330* **48** C4
Lemmon SD, *1227* **26** B1
Lemmon Valley NV, *5040* **37** D1
Lemon Grove CA, *25320* **53** D4
Lemont IL, *16000* **89** D2
Lemont PA, *2270* **92** C3
Lemoore CA, *24531* **44** C3
Lemoyne PA, *4553* **218** B2
Lena IL, *2912* **74** A4
Lenawee Co. MI, *99892* **90** B1
Lenexa KS, *48190* **96** B2
Lennon MI, *511* **76** B3
Lennox CA, *22753* **228** C3
Lennox SD, *2111* **27** F4
Lenoir NC, *18228* **111** F4
Lenoir City TN, *8642* **110** C4
Lenoir Co. NC, *59495* **115** D3
Lenox GA, *873* **129** E4
Lenox IA, *1407* **86** B3
Lenox MA, *5077* **94** B2
Lenwood CA, *3543* **53** D1
Lenzburg IL, *521* **98** B4
Leo-Cedarville IN, *3603* **90** A2
Leola AR, *501* **117** E3
Leola PA, *7214* **146** A2
Leola SD, *457* **27** D1
Leominster MA, *40759* **150** C1
Leon IA, *1977* **86** C3
Leon KS, *704* **43** F4
Leonard ND, *223* **19** E4
Leonard TX, *1990* **59** F1
Leonardo NJ, *2757* **147** E1
Leonardtown MD, *2930* **103** E4
Leonardville KS, *449* **43** F2
Leon Co. FL, *275487* **137** E2
Leon Co. TX, *16801* **124** A4
Leonia NJ, *8937* **240** D1
Leon Valley TX, *10151* **61** D2
Leonville LA, *1084* **133** F2
Leoti KS, *1534* **42** B3
Lepanto AR, *1893* **118** B1
Le Roy IL, *3560* **88** C4
LeRoy KS, *561* **96** A4
Le Roy MN, *929* **73** D2
Le Roy NY, *4391* **78** B3
Leslie AR, *441* **107** E4
Leslie MI, *1851* **76** A4
Leslie Co. KY, *11310* **111** D2
Lesslie SC, *3112* **122** A2
Lester Prairie MN, *1730* **66** C4
Le Sueur MN, *4058* **72** C1
Le Sueur Co. MN, *27703* **72** C1
Letcher Co. KY, *24519* **111** D2
Leupp AZ, *951* **47** E3
Levan UT, *841* **39** E1
Levant ME, *2171* **83** D1
Levelland TX, *13542* **57** F1
Level Plains AL, *2085* **128** B4
Levittown NY, *51881* **148** C4
Levittown PA, *52983* **147** D2
Levy Co. FL, *40801* **138** C4
Lewes DE, *2747* **145** F3
Lewis KS, *451* **43** D3
Lewis and Clark Co. MT, *63395* **15** E3
Lewisburg KY, *810* **109** E2
Lewisburg OH, *1820* **100** B1
Lewisburg PA, *5792* **93** D3
Lewisburg TN, *11100* **119** F1
Lewisburg WV, *3830* **112** A1
Lewis Co. ID, *3821* **22** B1
Lewis Co. KY, *13870* **100** C3
Lewis Co. MO, *10211* **87** F4
Lewis Co. NY, *27087* **79** E2
Lewis Co. TN, *12161* **119** E1
Lewis Co. WA, *75455* **12** C4
Lewis Co. WV, *16372* **102** A2
Lewisport KY, *1670* **99** E4
Lewis Run PA, *617* **92** B1
Lewiston CA, *1193* **28** B4
Lewiston ID, *31894* **14** B4
Lewiston ME, *36592* **82** B2
Lewiston MI, *1392* **70** C4
Lewiston MN, *1620* **73** E1
Lewiston NY, *2701* **78** A3
Lewiston UT, *1766* **31** E2
Lewiston Woodville NC, *549* **113** E4
Lewistown IL, *2384* **88** A4
Lewistown MD, *600* **144** A1
Lewistown MO, *534* **87** E4
Lewistown MT, *5901* **16** B4
Lewistown PA, *8338* **93** D4
Lewisville AR, *1280* **125** D1
Lewisville ID, *458* **23** E4
Lewisville NC, *12639* **112** A4
Lewisville TX, *95290* **59** F2
Lexington AL, *735* **119** E2
Lexington GA, *228* **121** E4

Figures after entries indicate population, page number, and grid reference.

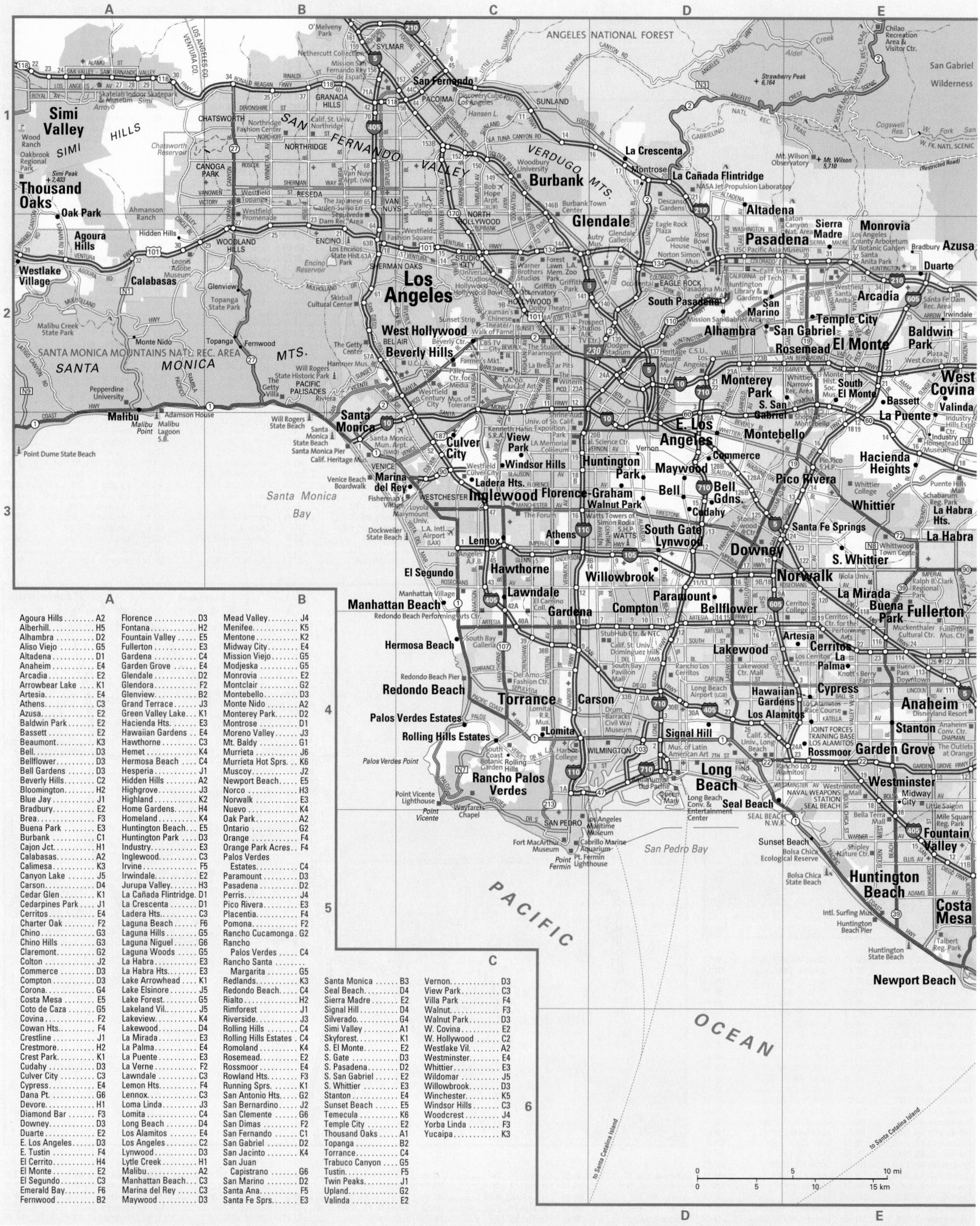

Agoura Hills A2
Alberhill H5
Alhambra D2
Aliso Viejo G5
Altadena D1
Anaheim E4
Arcadia E2
Arrowbear Lake K1
Artesia E4
Athens C3
Azusa E2
Baldwin Park E2
Bassett E2
Beaumont K3
Bell D3
Bellflower D3
Bell Gardens D3
Beverly Hills C2
Bloomington H2
Blue Jay J1
Bradbury E2
Brea F3
Buena Park E3
Burbank C1
Cajon Jct. H1
Calabasas A2
Calimesa K3
Canyon Lake J5
Carson D4
Cedar Glen K1
Cedarpines Park J1
Cerritos E4
Charter Oak F2
Chino G3
Chino Hills G3
Claremont G2
Colton J2
Commerce D3
Compton D3
Corona G4
Costa Mesa E5
Coto de Caza G5
Covina F2
Cowan Hts. F4
Crestline J1
Crestmore H2
Crest Park K1
Cudahy D3
Culver City C3
Cypress E4
Dana Pt. G6
Devore H1
Diamond Bar F3
Downey D3
Duarte E2
E. Los Angeles D3
E. Tustin F4
El Cerrito H4
El Monte E2
El Segundo C3
Emerald Bay F6
Fernwood B2
Florence D3
Fontana H2
Fountain Valley E5
Fullerton E3
Gardena C4
Garden Grove E4
Glendale D2
Glendora F2
Glenview B2
Grand Terrace J3
Green Valley Lake K1
Hacienda Hts. E3
Hawaiian Gardens E4
Hawthorne C3
Hemet K4
Hermosa Beach C4
Hesperia J1
Hidden Hills A2
Highgrove J3
Highland K2
Home Gardens H4
Homeland K4
Huntington Beach E5
Huntington Park D3
Industry E3
Inglewood C3
Irvine F5
Irwindale E2
Jurupa Valley H3
La Cañada Flintridge D1
La Crescenta D1
Ladera Hts. C3
Laguna Beach F6
Laguna Hills G5
Laguna Niguel G6
Laguna Woods G5
La Habra E3
La Habra Hts. E3
Lake Arrowhead K1
Lake Elsinore J5
Lake Forest G5
Lakeland Vil. J5
Lakeview K4
Lakewood D4
La Mirada E3
La Palma E4
La Puente E3
La Verne F2
Lawndale C3
Lemon Hts. F4
Lennox C3
Loma Linda J3
Lomita C4
Long Beach D4
Los Alamitos E4
Los Angeles C2
Lynwood D3
Lytle Creek H1
Malibu A2
Manhattan Beach C3
Marina del Rey C3
Maywood D3
Mead Valley J4
Menifee K5
Mentone K2
Midway City E4
Mission Viejo G5
Modjeska G5
Monrovia E2
Montclair G2
Montebello D3
Monte Nido A2
Monterey Park D2
Montrose D1
Moreno Valley J3
Mt. Baldy G1
Murrieta J6
Murrieta Hot Sprs. K6
Muscoy J2
Newport Beach E5
Norco H3
Norwalk E3
Nuevo K4
Oak Park A2
Ontario G2
Orange F4
Orange Park Acres F4
Palos Verdes Estates C4
Paramount D3
Pasadena D2
Perris J4
Pico Rivera E3
Placentia F4
Pomona F2
Rancho Cucamonga G2
Rancho Palos Verdes C4
Rancho Santa Margarita G5
Redlands K3
Redondo Beach C4
Rialto H2
Rimforest J1
Riverside J3
Rolling Hills C4
Rolling Hills Estates C4
Romoland K4
Rosemead E2
Rossmoor E4
Rowland Hts. F3
Running Sprs. K1
San Antonio Hts. G2
San Bernardino J2
San Clemente G6
San Dimas F2
San Fernando C1
San Gabriel D2
San Jacinto K4
San Juan Capistrano G6
San Marino D2
Santa Ana F5
Santa Fe Sprs. E3
Santa Monica B3
Seal Beach D4
Sierra Madre E2
Signal Hill D4
Silverado G4
Simi Valley A1
Skyforest K1
S. El Monte E2
S. Gate D3
S. Pasadena D2
S. San Gabriel E2
S. Whittier E3
Stanton E4
Sunset Beach E5
Temecula K6
Temple City E2
Thousand Oaks A1
Topanga B2
Torrance C4
Trabuco Canyon G5
Tustin F5
Twin Peaks J1
Upland G2
Valinda E2
Vernon D3
View Park C3
Villa Park F4
Walnut F3
Walnut Park D3
W. Covina E2
W. Hollywood C2
Westlake Vil. A2
Westminster E4
Whittier E3
Wildomar J5
Willowbrook D3
Winchester K5
Windsor Hills C3
Woodcrest J4
Yorba Linda F3
Yucaipa K3

Entries in **bold black** indicate counties or parishes.
Entries in **bold color** indicate cities with detailed inset maps.

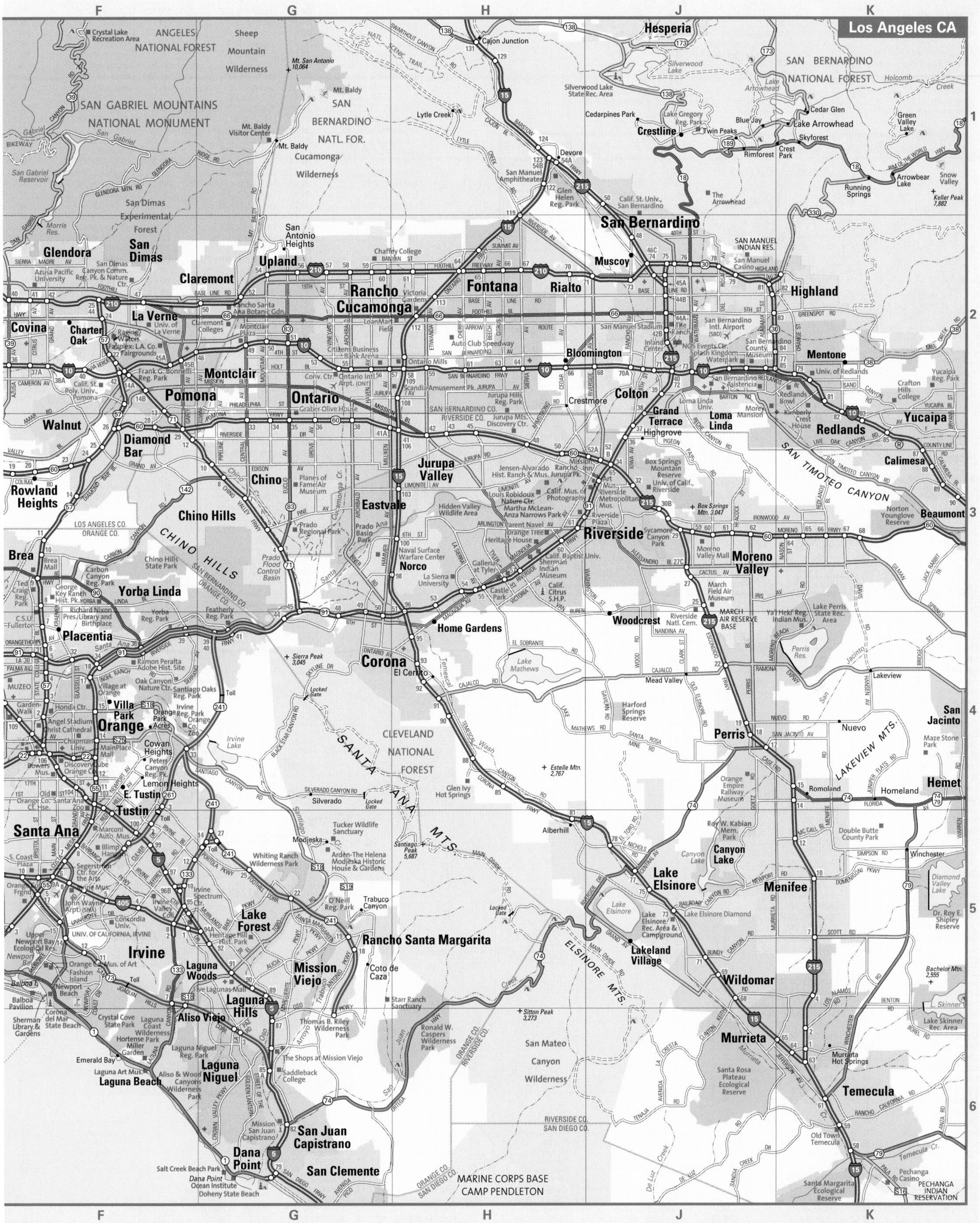

POINTS OF INTEREST

Angels Flight A1
Bradbury Building. A1
California Plaza A1
Cathedral of Our Lady of the Angels. .A1
Chinese American Museum B1
City Hall. B1
City Market. A2
Convention Center A2
Court House A1
Dodger Stadium B1
El Pueblo de Los Angeles Hist. Mon . .B1
Flower District. A2
GRAMMY Museum. A2
Institute of Contemporary Art. B2
Japanese American Natl. Museum. . .B1
Jewelry District. A2
L.A. Center Studios. A1
L.A. Live A2
Library. A1
Los Angeles State Historical Park. . . .B1
Microsoft Theatre. A2
Mt. St. Mary's University. A2
Museum of Contemporary Art (MOCA) A1
Museum of Neon Art A2
Music Center. .A1
Post Office B1
STAPLES Center A2
The Geffen Contemporary at MOCA . .B1
Union Station. B1
Walt Disney Concert Hall A1

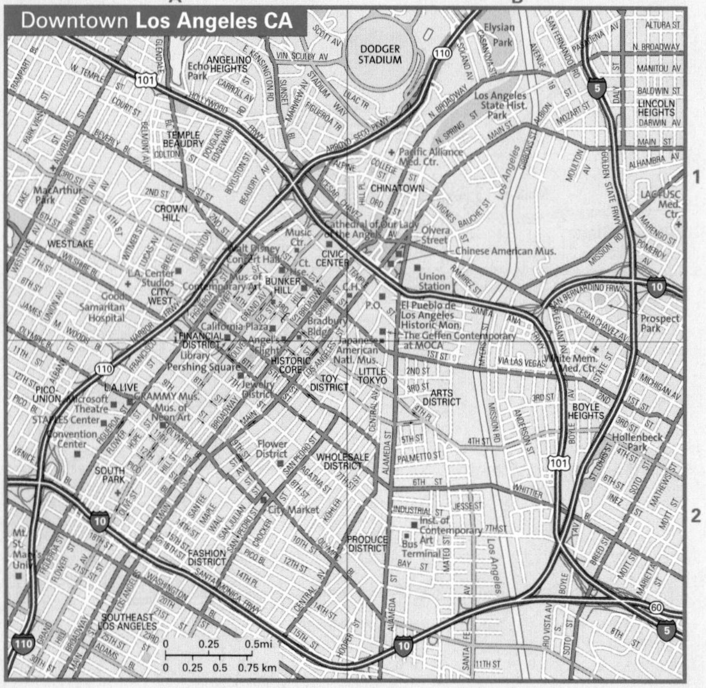

Lincoln Hts. OH, 3286 .... 204 B1
Lincolnia VA, 22855 .... 270 B4
Lincoln Par. LA, 46735 .... 125 E2
Lincoln Park CO, 3546 .... 41 E3
Lincoln Park MI, 38144 .... 90 C1
Lincoln Park NJ, 10521 .... 148 A3
Lincolnshire IL, 7275 .... 203 C2
Lincolnton GA, 1566 .... 121 E4
Lincolnton NC, 10486 .... 122 A1
Lincoln Vil. OH, 9032 .... 206 A3
Lincolnville SC, 1139 .... 131 D1
Lincolnville Ctr. ME, 325 .... 82 C2
Lincolnwood IL, 12590 .... 203 D3
Lincroft NJ, 6135 .... 147 E2
Lind WA, 564 .... 13 F4
Linda CA, 17773 .... 36 C2
Lindale GA, 4191 .... 120 B3
Lindale TX, 4818 .... 124 A2
Lindcove CA, 406 .... 45 D3
Linden AL, 2123 .... 127 E2
Linden CA, 1784 .... 36 C3
Linden IN, 759 .... 89 E4
Linden MI, 3991 .... 76 B3
Linden NJ, 40499 .... 147 E1
Linden TN, 908 .... 119 E1
Linden TX, 1988 .... 124 C1
Linden WI, 549 .... 74 A3
Lindenhurst IL, 14462 .... 74 C4
Lindenhurst NY, 27253 .... 148 C4
Lindenwold NJ, 17613 .... 146 C3
Lindon UT, 10070 .... 31 F4
Lindsay CA, 11768 .... 45 D3
Lindsay OK, 2840 .... 51 E4
Lindsay TX, 1018 .... 59 E1
Lindsborg KS, 3458 .... 43 E3
Lindstrom MN, 4442 .... 67 D3
Linesville PA, 1040 .... 91 F2
Lineville AL, 2395 .... 128 B1
Lingle WY, 468 .... 33 F2
Linglestown PA, 6334 .... 93 D4
Linn KS, 410 .... 43 F1
Linn MO, 1459 .... 97 E3
Linn TX, 801 .... 63 E3
Linn Co. IA, 211226 .... 87 E1
Linn Co. KS, 9656 .... 96 B4
Linn Co. MO, 12761 .... 97 D1
Linn Co. OR, 116672 .... 20 C3
Linneus MO, 278 .... 97 D1
Linn Valley KS, 804 .... 96 B4
Lino Lakes MN, 20216 .... 235 D7
Linthicum MD, 10324 .... 193 C4
Linton IN, 5413 .... 99 E2
Linton ND, 1097 .... 26 C1
Linwood IN, 700 .... 89 F4
Linwood KS, 375 .... 96 B2
Linwood MI, 1200 .... 76 B2
Linwood NJ, 7092 .... 147 F4
Lionville PA, 6189 .... 146 B3
Lipscomb AL, 2210 .... 195 D2
Lipscomb TX, 37 .... 50 C2
Lipscomb Co. TX, 3302 .... 50 C2
Lisbon IA, 2152 .... 87 F1
Lisbon ME, 9077 .... 82 B3
Lisbon NH, 980 .... 81 E2
Lisbon ND, 2154 .... 19 E4
Lisbon OH, 2821 .... 91 F3
Lisbon Falls ME, 4100 .... 82 B3
Lisle IL, 22390 .... 203 B5
Lisman AL, 539 .... 127 D3
Litchfield CT, 1258 .... 94 C3
Litchfield IL, 6939 .... 98 B2
Litchfield ME, 3110 .... 82 B2
Litchfield MI, 1369 .... 90 A1
Litchfield MN, 6726 .... 66 B3
Litchfield Co. CT, 189927 .... 94 B3
Litchfield Park AZ, 5476 .... 249 A2
Lithia Sprs. GA, 15491 .... 120 C4
Lithonia GA, 1924 .... 120 C4
Lithopolis OH, 1106 .... 101 D1
Lititz PA, 9369 .... 146 A2
Little Canada MN, 9773 .... 235 D2
Little Chute WI, 10449 .... 74 C1
Little Compton RI, 3492 .... 151 D4
Little Creek DE, 224 .... 145 E2
Little Cypress TX, 1800 .... 132 C2
Little Eagle SD, 319 .... 26 C1
Little Elm TX, 25898 .... 59 F2
Little Falls MN, 8343 .... 66 C2
Little Falls NJ, 11694 .... 148 A3
Little Falls NY, 4946 .... 79 F3
Little Ferry NJ, 10626 .... 240 C2
Littlefield TX, 6372 .... 58 A1
Little Flock AR, 2585 .... 106 C3
Littlefork MN, 647 .... 64 B2
Little Heaven DE, 1400 .... 145 E3
Little River KS, 557 .... 43 E3
Little River SC, 8960 .... 123 D4
Little River-Academy TX, 1961 .... 61 E1
Little River Co. AR, 13171 .... 116 C4
Little Rock AR, 193524 .... 117 E2
Littlerock CA, 1377 .... 52 C2
Little Silver NJ, 5950 .... 147 E2
Littlestown PA, 4434 .... 103 E1
Littleton CO, 41737 .... 41 E1
Littleton NH, 4412 .... 81 F2
Littleton NC, 674 .... 113 D3
Little Valley NY, 1143 .... 92 B1
Littleville AL, 1011 .... 119 E2
Live Oak CA, 17158 .... 36 C2
Live Oak CA, 17158 .... 236 D1
Live Oak FL, 6850 .... 138 B2
Live Oak TX, 13131 .... 61 D2
Live Oak Co. TX, 11531 .... 61 D4
Livermore CA, 80968 .... 36 B4
Livermore KY, 1365 .... 109 E1
Livermore Falls ME, 1594 .... 82 B2
Liverpool NY, 2347 .... 265 A1
Liverpool PA, 955 .... 93 D4
Livingston AL, 3485 .... 127 D2
Livingston CA, 13058 .... 36 C4
Livingston IL, 858 .... 98 B2
Livingston LA, 1769 .... 134 A2
Livingston MT, 7044 .... 23 F1
Livingston NJ, 29366 .... 148 A4
Livingston TN, 4058 .... 110 A3
Livingston TX, 5335 .... 132 B1
Livingston WI, 664 .... 74 A3
Livingston Co. IL, 38950 .... 88 C3
Livingston Co. KY, 9519 .... 109 D2
Livingston Co. MI, 180967 .... 76 B4
Livingston Co. MO, 15195 .... 96 C1
Livingston Co. NY, 65393 .... 78 C4
Livingston Manor NY, 1221 .... 94 A2
Livingston Par. LA, 128026 .... 134 B2
Livonia LA, 1442 .... 133 F2
Livonia MI, 96942 .... 76 B4
Livonia NY, 1409 .... 78 C3
Llangollen Estates DE, 5600 .... 145 E1
Llano TX, 3232 .... 61 D1
Llano Co. TX, 19301 .... 61 D1
Lloyd Harbor NY, 3660 .... 148 C3
Loa UT, 572 .... 39 E3
Loami IL, 745 .... 98 B1
Lobelville TN, 897 .... 109 D4
Lochbuie CO, 4726 .... 209 D1
Lochearn MD, 25333 .... 144 C2
Loch Lynn Hts. MD, 552 .... 102 B2
Loch Sheldrake NY, 800 .... 94 A3
Lockeford CA, 3233 .... 36 C3
Lockesburg AR, 739 .... 116 C4
Lockhart AL, 516 .... 136 B1
Lockhart FL, 13060 .... 246 B1
Lockhart TX, 12698 .... 61 E2
Lock Haven PA, 9772 .... 93 D3
Lockland OH, 3449 .... 204 B1
Lockney TX, 1842 .... 50 B4
Lockport IL, 24839 .... 89 D2
Lockport LA, 2578 .... 134 B3
Lockport NY, 21165 .... 78 B3
Lockwood MO, 936 .... 106 C1
Locust NC, 2930 .... 122 B1
Locust Fork AL, 1186 .... 119 F4
Locust Grove GA, 5402 .... 129 D1
Locust Grove OK, 1423 .... 106 B3
Locust Valley NY, 3406 .... 148 C3
Lodge Grass MT, 428 .... 24 C2
Lodge Pole MT, 265 .... 16 C2
Lodi CA, 62134 .... 36 C3
Lodi NJ, 24136 .... 240 C1
Lodi OH, 2746 .... 91 D3
Lodi WI, 3050 .... 74 B3

Lexington IL, 2060 .... 88 C3
Lexington KY, 295803 .... 100 B4
Lexington MA, 31394 .... 151 D1
Lexington MI, 1178 .... 76 C3
Lexington MN, 2049 .... 235 C1
Lexington MS, 1731 .... 126 B1
Lexington MO, 4726 .... 96 C2
Lexington NE, 10230 .... 34 C4
Lexington NC, 18931 .... 112 B4
Lexington OH, 4822 .... 91 D3
Lexington OK, 2152 .... 51 E3
Lexington SC, 17870 .... 122 A3
Lexington TN, 7652 .... 109 D4
Lexington TX, 1177 .... 61 E1
Lexington VA, 7042 .... 112 C1
Lexington Co. SC, 262391 .... 122 A4
Lexington Park MD, 11626 .... 103 F4
Libby MT, 2628 .... 14 C2
Liberal KS, 20525 .... 50 B1
Liberal MO, 759 .... 106 B1
Liberty IL, 516 .... 97 F1
Liberty IN, 2133 .... 100 B1
Liberty KY, 2168 .... 110 B1
Liberty ME, 300 .... 82 C2
Liberty MS, 728 .... 134 A1
Liberty MO, 29149 .... 96 B2
Liberty NY, 4392 .... 94 A3
Liberty NC, 2656 .... 112 B4
Liberty PA, 2551 .... 250 C3
Liberty SC, 3269 .... 121 E2
Liberty TN, 310 .... 110 A4
Liberty TX, 8397 .... 132 B3
Liberty Ctr. OH, 1180 .... 90 B2
Liberty City TX, 2351 .... 124 B2
Liberty Corner NJ, 1700 .... 147 D1
Liberty Co. FL, 8365 .... 137 D2
Liberty Co. GA, 63453 .... 130 B3
Liberty Co. MT, 2339 .... 15 F1
Liberty Co. TX, 75643 .... 132 B2
Liberty Hill TX, 967 .... 61 E1
Liberty Lake WA, 7591 .... 14 B3
Libertyville IL, 20315 .... 74 C4
Licking MO, 3124 .... 107 E1
Licking Co. OH, 166492 .... 91 D4
Lidgerwood ND, 652 .... 27 E1
Lido Beach NY, 2897 .... 147 F1
Lighthouse Pt. FL, 10344 .... 143 F1
Ligonier IN, 4405 .... 89 F2
Ligonier PA, 1573 .... 92 B4
Lihue HI, 6455 .... 152 B1
Lilbourn MO, 1190 .... 108 B3
Lilburn GA, 11596 .... 120 C4
Lillington NC, 3194 .... 123 D1
Lilly PA, 968 .... 92 B4
Lily KY, 1200 .... 110 C2
Lilydale MN, 623 .... 235 D3
Lily Lake IL, 993 .... 88 C1
Lima MT, 221 .... 23 E3
Lima NY, 2139 .... 78 C3
Lima OH, 38771 .... 90 B3
Lima PA, 2735 .... 248 A4
Lime Lake NY, 867 .... 78 B4
Limeport PA, 1100 .... 146 C1
Limerick ME, 2240 .... 82 A3
Limerick PA, 850 .... 146 B2
Lime Sprs. IA, 496 .... 73 E2
Limestone ME, 1075 .... 85 E1
Limestone Co. AL, 82782 .... 119 F2
Limestone Co. TX, 23384 .... 59 F4
Limon CO, 1880 .... 41 F2
Lincoln AL, 6266 .... 120 A4
Lincoln AR, 2249 .... 106 B4
Lincoln CA, 42819 .... 36 C2
Lincoln DE, 950 .... 145 F3
Lincoln ID, 3647 .... 23 E4
Lincoln IL, 14504 .... 88 B4
Lincoln KS, 1297 .... 43 E2
Lincoln ME, 2884 .... 85 D4
Lincoln MA, 6362 .... 197 A1
Lincoln MO, 1190 .... 97 D4
Lincoln MT, 1013 .... 15 E4
Lincoln NE, 258379 .... 35 F4
Lincoln NH, 993 .... 81 F3
Lincoln ND, 2406 .... 18 C4
Lincoln Beach OR, 2045 .... 20 B2
Lincoln City OR, 7930 .... 20 B2
Lincoln Co. AR, 14134 .... 117 F3
Lincoln Co. CO, 5467 .... 41 F2
Lincoln Co. GA, 7996 .... 121 E4
Lincoln Co. ID, 5208 .... 31 D1
Lincoln Co. KS, 3241 .... 43 E2
Lincoln Co. KY, 24742 .... 110 B1
Lincoln Co. ME, 34457 .... 82 C2
Lincoln Co. MN, 5896 .... 27 F3
Lincoln Co. MS, 34869 .... 126 B4
Lincoln Co. MO, 52566 .... 97 F2
Lincoln Co. MT, 19687 .... 14 C2
Lincoln Co. NE, 36288 .... 34 C3
Lincoln Co. NV, 5345 .... 38 B4
Lincoln Co. NM, 20497 .... 49 D4
Lincoln Co. NC, 78265 .... 122 A1
Lincoln Co. OK, 34273 .... 51 F2
Lincoln Co. OR, 46034 .... 20 B3
Lincoln Co. SD, 44828 .... 35 F1
Lincoln Co. TN, 33361 .... 119 F1
Lincoln Co. WA, 10570 .... 13 F3
Lincoln Co. WV, 21720 .... 101 E4
Lincoln Co. WI, 28743 .... 68 A3
Lincoln Co. WY, 18106 .... 32 A2
Lincolndale NY, 1521 .... 148 C2

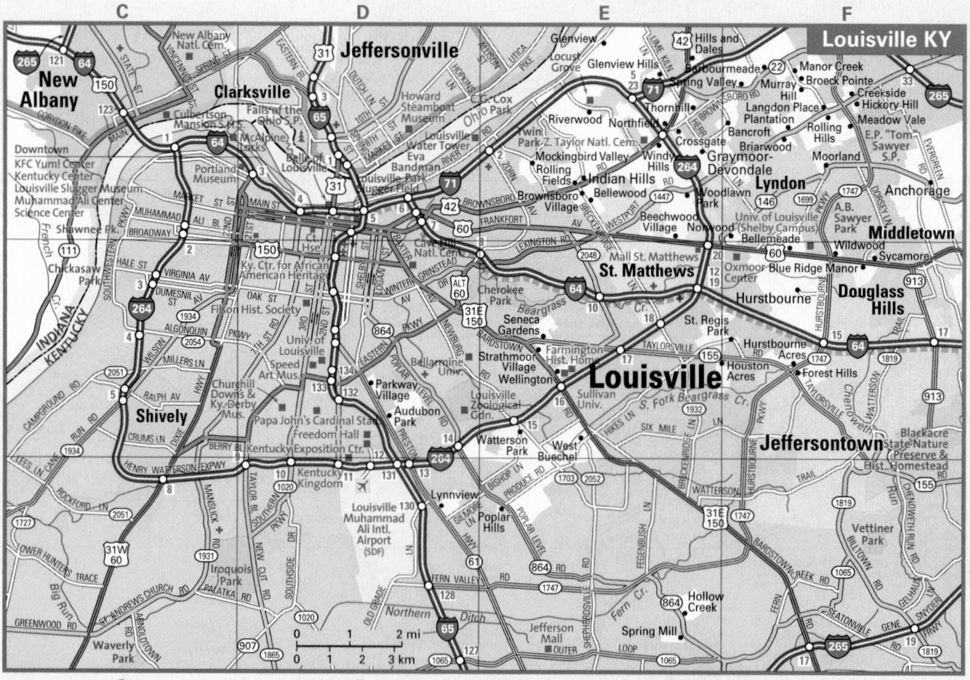

Bancroft F1
Barbourmeade. F1
Beechwood Vil. E1
Bellemeade F2
Bellewood E1
Blue Ridge Manor. F2
Briarwood. F1
Broeck Pointe F1
Brownsboro Vil.. . . . . .E1
Clarksville D1
Creekside F1
Crossgate E1
Douglass Hills F2
Fincastle F1
Forest Hills F2
Glenview. E1
Glenview Hills E1
Graymoor-Devondale E1
Hickory Hill. F1
Hills and Dales. E1
Hollow Creek E3
Houston Acres. F2
Hurstbourne F2
Hurstbourne Acres F2
Indian Hills E1
Jeffersontown F2
Jeffersonville D1
Langdon Place. F1
Louisville. E2
Lyndon. F1
Lynnview. D3
Manor Creek F1
Meadow Vale F1
Middletown F1
Mockingbird Valley. E1
Moorland F1
Murray Hill F1
New Albany C1
Northfield E1
Norwood. F1
Parkway Vil. D2
Plantation F1
Poplar Hills. E3
Riverwood E1
Rolling Fields E1
Rolling Hills F1
St. Matthews E1
St. Regis Park F2
Seneca Gardens E2
Shively. C2
Spring Mill E3
Spring Valley F1
Strathmoor Vil.. . . . . .E2
Sycamore F2
Thornhill E1
Watterson Park. E2
Wellington E2
W. Buechel E2
Wildwood F2
Windy Hills. E1
Woodlawn Park. E1

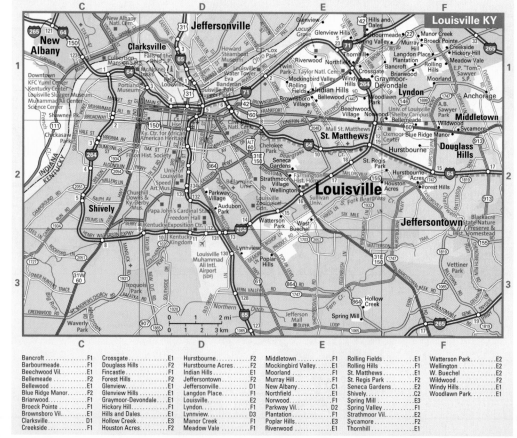

Entries in **bold black** indicate counties or parishes.
Entries in **bold color** indicate cities with detailed inset maps.

Logan IA, 1534 86 A2
Logan KS, 589 42 C1
Logan NM, 1042 49 F3
Logan OH, 7152 101 D1
Logan UT, 48174 31 E2
Logan WV, 1779 101 E4
Logan Co. AR, 22353 116 C1
Logan Co. CO, 22709 34 A4
Logan Co. IL, 30305 98 B1
Logan Co. KS, 2756 42 B2
Logan Co. KY, 26835 109 F2
Logan Co. NE, 763 34 C3
Logan Co. ND, 1990 18 C4
Logan Co. OH, 45858 90 B4
Logan Co. OK, 41848 51 E2
Logan Co. WV, 36743 101 E4
Lone Oak KY, 454 108 C2
Lone Oak TX, 598 59 F2
Lone Pine CA, 2035 45 E3
Lone Rock WI, 888 74 A3
Lone Star LA, 1400 239 A2
Lone Star TX, 1581 124 B1
Lone Tree CO, 10218 209 C4
Lone Tree IA, 1300 87 F2
Lone Wolf OK, 438 51 D3
Long Beach CA, 462257 52 C3
Long Beach IN, 1179 89 E1
Long Beach MD, 1821 103 E3
Long Beach MS, 14792 135 D2
Long Beach NY, 33275 147 F1
Long Beach WA, 1392 12 B4
Longboat Key FL, 6888 140 B3
Lorain Co. OH, 301356 91 D2
Loraine TX, 602 58 B3
Lorane PA, 4236 146 B2
Lordsburg NM, 2797 55 F3
Lordstown OH, 3417 91 F2
Loreauville LA, 887 133 F3
Lorena TX, 1691 59 E4
Lorenzo TX, 1147 58 A1
Loretto KY, 713 110 A1
Loretto MN, 650 66 C3
Loretto PA, 1302 92 B4
Loretto TN, 1714 119 E2
Loris SC, 2396 123 D3
Lorton VA, 18610 144 B4
Los Alamitos CA, 11449 228 E4
Los Alamos CA, 1890 52 A1

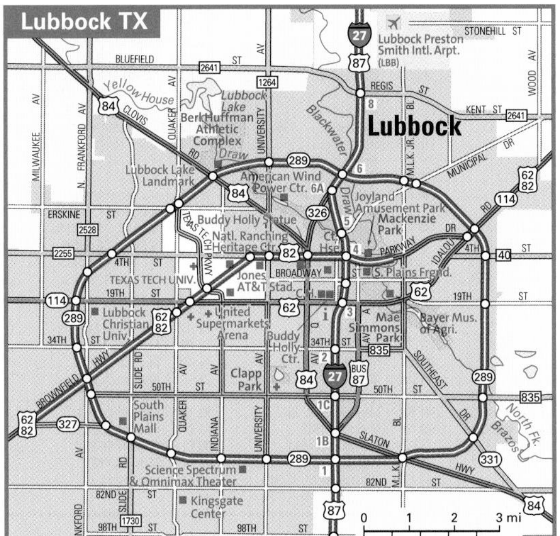

Logandale NV, 800 46 B1
Logansport IN, 18396 89 E3
Logansport LA, 1555 124 C3
Loganville GA, 10458 121 D4
Loganville PA, 1240 103 E1
Log Cabin TX, 714 59 F3
Log Lane Vil. CO, 873 33 F4
Loleta CA, 783 28 A4
Lolita TX, 555 61 F3
Lolo MT, 3892 15 D4
Loma Linda CA, 23261 229 J3
Loma Linda MO, 725 106 B2
Loma Rica CA, 2368 36 C2
Lombard IL, 43165 203 B4
Lometa TX, 856 59 D4
Lomira WI, 2430 74 C2
Lomita CA, 20256 228 C4
Lompoc CA, 42434 52 A2
Lonaconing MD, 1214 102 C1
London AR, 1039 117 D1
London KY, 7993 110 C2
London OH, 9904 100 C1
Londonderry NH, 11037 95 E1
Londonderry VT, 1709 81 D4
Londontowne MD, 7595 144 C3
Lone Grove OK, 5054 51 E4
Lone Jack MO, 1050 96 C3
Long Branch NJ, 30719 147 F2
Long Co. GA, 14464 130 B3
Long Creek IL, 1328 98 C1
Long Green MD, 1000 144 C1
Long Grove IL, 8043 203 C2
Long Grove IA, 808 88 A1
Long Lake MN, 1768 66 C4
Longmeadow MA, 15784 150 A2
Longmont CO, 86270 41 E1
Long Pond MA, 1500 151 E3
Longport NJ, 895 147 F4
Long Prairie MN, 3458 66 B2
Longton KS, 348 43 F4
Long Valley NJ, 1879 94 A4
Long View NC, 4871 111 F4
Longview TX, 80455 124 B2
Longview WA, 36648 20 B1
Longwood FL, 13657 141 D1
Lonoke AR, 4245 117 F2
Lonoke Co. AR, 68356 117 F2
Lonsdale MN, 3674 67 D4
Loogootee IN, 2751 99 E3
Lookout Mtn. GA, 1602 120 B2
Lookout Mtn. TN, 1832 120 B2
Loomis CA, 6430 36 C2
Loomis NE, 382 35 D4
Lorain OH, 64097 91 D2
Los Alamos NM, 12019 48 C2
Los Alamos Co. NM, 17950 48 C2
Los Altos CA, 28976 36 B4
Los Altos Hills CA, 7922 259 C6
Los Angeles CA, 3792621 52 C2
Los Angeles Co. CA, 9818605 52 C2
Los Banos CA, 35972 44 B2
Los Chavez NM, 5446 48 C4
Los Fresnos TX, 5542 63 F4
Los Gatos CA, 29413 36 B4
Los Indios TX, 1083 63 F4
Los Lunas NM, 14835 48 C4
Los Molinos CA, 2037 36 B1
Los Olivos CA, 1132 52 A2
Los Osos CA, 14276 44 B4
Los Padillas NM, 1800 48 C3
Los Ranchos de Albuquerque NM, 6024 48 C3
Lost Creek WV, 496 102 A2
Lost Hills CA, 2412 44 C4
Lost Nation IA, 446 87 F1
Lott TX, 759 59 F4
Loudon TN, 5381 110 C4
Loudon Co. TN, 48556 110 C4
Loudonville NY, 10800 94 B1
Loudonville OH, 2641 91 D3
Loudoun Co. VA, 312311 144 A2

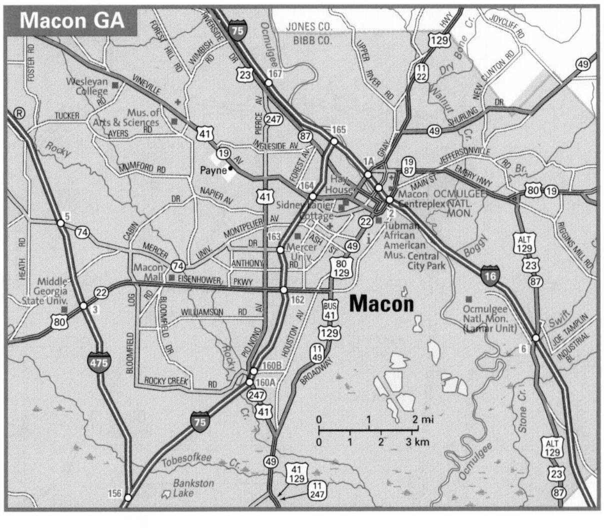

Loughman FL, 2680 141 D2
Louisa KY, 2467 101 D4
Louisa VA, 1555 103 D4
Louisa Co. IA, 11387 87 F2
Louisa Co. VA, 33153 103 D4
Louisburg KS, 4315 96 B3
Louisburg NC, 3359 113 D4
Louise TX, 995 61 F3
Louisiana MO, 3364 97 F2
Louisville AL, 519 128 B3
Louisville CO, 18376 41 E1
Louisville GA, 2493 129 F1
Louisville IL, 1139 98 C3
Louisville KY, 597337 100 A4
Louisville MS, 6631 126 C1
Louisville NE, 1106 35 F3
Louisville OH, 9186 91 E3
Louisville TN, 2439 110 C4
Loup City NE, 1029 35 D3
Loup Co. NE, 632 35 D2
Love Co. OK, 9423 59 E1
Lovelady TX, 649 132 A1
Loveland CO, 66859 33 E4
Loveland OH, 12081 100 B2
Loveland Park OH, 1523 204 C1
Lovell WY, 2360 24 C2
Lovelock NV, 1894 29 F4
Loves Park IL, 23996 74 B4
Lovettsville VA, 1613 144 A2
Loveville MD, 650 103 E4
Lovilia IA, 538 87 D3
Loving NM, 1413 57 E3
Loving Co. TX, 82 57 E3
Lovingston VA, 520 112 C1
Lovington IL, 1130 98 C1
Lovington NM, 11009 57 F2
Lowden IA, 789 87 F1
Lowell AR, 7327 106 C3
Lowell IN, 9276 89 D2
Lowell MA, 106519 95 E1
Lowell MI, 3783 75 F3
Lowell NC, 3526 122 A1
Lowell OH, 549 101 F1
Lowell OR, 1045 20 C4
Lowellville OH, 1155 91 F3
Lower Brule SD, 613 27 D3
Lower Lake CA, 1294 36 B2
Lowesville NC, 2945 122 A1
Low Moor VA, 258 112 B1
Lowndes Co. AL, 11299 127 F3
Lowndes Co. GA, 109233 137 F1
Lowndes Co. MS, 59779 127 D1
Lowry City MO, 640 96 C4
Lowville NY, 3470 79 E2
Loxley AL, 1632 135 E2
Loyal WI, 1261 68 A4
Loyalhanna PA, 3428 92 B4
Loyall KY, 1461 111 D2
Loyalton CA, 769 37 D1
Lubbock TX, 229573 58 A1
Lubbock Co. TX, 278831 58 A1
Lubec ME, 349 83 F1
Lubeck WV, 1311 101 E2
Lucama NC, 1108 113 D4
Lucas KS, 393 43 D2
Lucas OH, 615 91 D3
Lucas TX, 5166 59 F2
Lucas Co. IA, 8898 87 D3
Lucas Co. OH, 441815 90 C2
Lucasville OH, 2757 101 D3
Luce Co. MI, 6631 69 F1
Lucedale MS, 2923 135 D1
Lucerne CA, 3067 36 B2
Lucerne WY, 535 24 C4
Lucernemines PA, 937 92 B4
Luck WI, 1119 67 E3
Luckey OH, 1012 90 C2
Ludington MI, 8076 75 E1
Ludingtonville NY, 1000 148 C1
Ludlow KY, 4407 204 A3
Ludlow MA, 21103 150 A2
Ludlow VT, 811 81 E4
Ludowici GA, 1703 130 B4
Lufkin TX, 35067 124 B4
Lugoff SC, 7434 122 B3
Lukachukai AZ, 1701 48 A1
Lula GA, 2758 121 D3
Luling LA, 12119 239 A2
Luling TX, 5411 61 E2
Lumber City GA, 1328 129 F3
Lumberport WV, 876 102 A2
Lumberton MS, 2086 134 C1
Lumberton NJ, 12331 147 D3
Lumberton NC, 21542 123 D2
Lumberton TX, 11943 132 C2
Lumpkin GA, 2741 128 C3
Lumpkin Co. GA, 29966 120 C2
Luna Co. NM, 25095 56 A3
Luna Pier MI, 1436 90 C1
Lunenburg MA, 1760 95 D1
Lunenburg VT, 1328 81 F2
Lunenburg VA, 165 113 D2
Lunenburg Co. VA, 12914 113 D2
Lupton AZ, 25 48 A3
Luray VA, 4895 102 C3
Lusby MD, 1835 103 F3
Lusk WY, 1567 33 E1
Lutcher LA, 3559 134 B3
Luther OK, 1221 51 E2
Luthersville GA, 874 128 C1
Luttrell TN, 1074 110 C3
Lutz FL, 19344 140 B2
Luverne AL, 2800 128 A4
Luverne MN, 4745 27 F4
Luxemburg WI, 2515 69 D4
Luxora AR, 1178 108 B4
Luzerne PA, 2845 261 B1
Luzerne Co. PA, 320918 93 E3
Lycoming Co. PA, 116111 93 D2
Lydia LA, 952 133 F3
Lydick IN, 1300 89 E2
Lyerly GA, 540 120 B3
Lyford TX, 2611 63 F4
Lykens PA, 1779 93 E4
Lyle MN, 551 73 D2
Lyle WA, 499 21 D1
Lyman NE, 341 33 F2
Lyman SC, 3243 121 F2
Lyman WA, 438 12 C2
Lyman WY, 2115 32 A3
Lyman Co. SD, 3755 26 C4
Lynbrook NY, 19427 147 F1
Lynch KY, 747 111 D2
Lynchburg MS, 2437 118 B2
Lynchburg OH, 1499 100 C2
Lynchburg SC, 373 122 B3
Lynchburg TN, 6362 119 F1
Lynchburg VA, 75568 112 C1
Lynch Hts. DE, 550 145 F3
Lynch Sta. VA, 500 112 C2
Lyndell PA, 1000 146 B3
Lynden WA, 11951 12 C1
Lyndhurst NJ, 19290 240 C2
Lyndhurst OH, 14001 204 G2
Lyndhurst VA, 1490 102 C4
Lyndon KS, 1052 96 A3
Lyndon KY, 11002 230 F1
Lyndon NY, 4600 265 B2
Lyndon VT, 5448 81 E2
Lyndon Ctr. VT, 1200 81 E2
Lyndonville NY, 838 78 B3
Lyndonville VT, 1207 81 E2
Lyndora PA, 6685 92 A3
Lynn AL, 659 119 E3
Lynn IN, 1097 90 A4
Lynn MA, 90329 151 D1
Lynn Co. TX, 5915 58 A2
Lynn Haven FL, 18493 136 C2
Lynnview KY, 914 230 D3
Lynnville IN, 888 99 E4
Lynnwood WA, 35836 12 C3
Lynwood CA, 69772 228 D3
Lynx MS, 350 118 A3
Lyon Co. IA, 11581 27 F4
Lyon Co. KS, 33690 43 F3
Lyon Co. KY, 8314 109 D2
Lyon Co. MN, 25857 72 A1
Lyon Co. NV, 51980 37 E2
Lyons CO, 2033 33 E4
Lyons GA, 4367 129 F3
Lyons IL, 10729 203 D5
Lyons IN, 742 99 E2
Lyons KS, 3739 43 E3
Lyons MI, 789 76 A3
Lyons NE, 851 35 F2
Lyons NY, 3619 79 D3
Lyons OH, 562 90 B2
Lyons OR, 1161 20 C3
Lyons Falls NY, 566 79 E2
Lyons Plain CT, 2100 148 C2
Lytle TX, 2492 61 D3

M

Mabank TX, 3035 59 F3
Mabel MN, 780 73 E2
Maben MS, 871 118 C4
Mableton GA, 37115 120 C4
Mabscott WV, 1408 111 F1
Mabton WA, 2286 21 E1
Macclenny FL, 6374 138 C2
Macedon NY, 1523 78 C3
Macedonia OH, 11188 91 E2
Machesney Park IL, 23499 74 B4
Machias ME, 1274 83 E1
Machias NY, 471 78 B4
Mack OH, 11585 204 A2
Mackay ID, 517 23 D4
Mackinac Co. MI, 11113 70 B2
Mackinac Island MI, 492 70 C2
Mackinaw IL, 1950 88 B4
Mackinaw City MI, 806 70 C2
Macksville KS, 549 43 D3
Macomb IL, 19288 88 A4
Macomb Co. MI, 840978 76 C4
Macon AR, 1100 117 E2
Macon GA, 91351 129 D2
Macon IL, 1138 98 C1
Macon MS, 2768 127 D1
Macon MO, 5471 97 E1

Fitchburg A2	McFarland B2	Shorewood Hills A2
Madison A1	Middleton A1	Sun Prairie B1
Maple Bluff B1	Monona B2	Waunakee A1

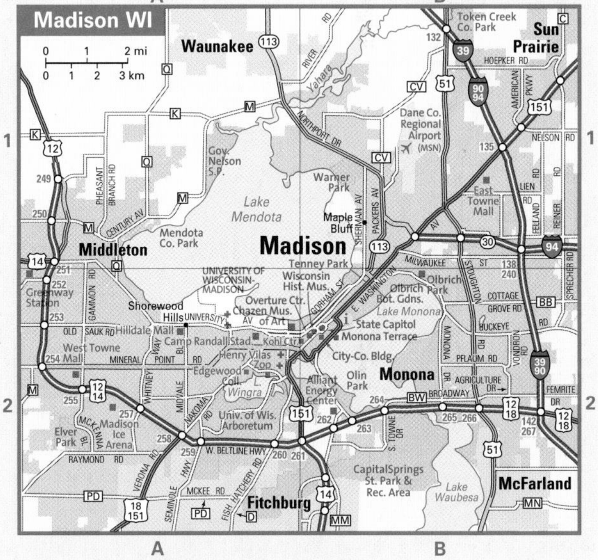

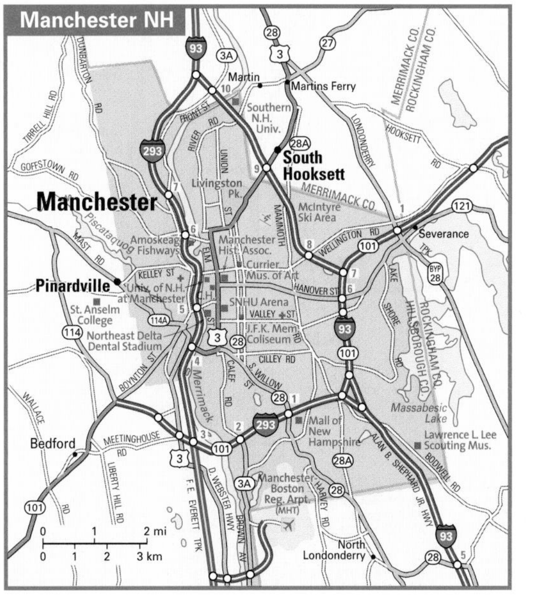

Figures after entries indicate population, page number, and grid reference.

Macon Co. AL, *21452* 128 B3
Macon Co. GA, *14740* 129 D2
Macon Co. IL, *110768* 98 C1
Macon Co. MO, *15566* 97 D1
Macon Co. NC, *33922* 121 D1
Macon Co. TN, *22248* 110 A3
Macoupin Co. IL, *47765* 98 B2
Macungie PA, *3074* 146 B1
Macy NE, *1023* 35 F2
Madawaska ME, *2967* 85 D1
Maddock ND, *382* 19 D2
Madeira OH, *8726* 204 C2
Madeira Beach FL, *4263* 140 B3
Madelia MN, *2308* 72 B1
Madera CA, *61416* 44 C2
Madera Co. CA, *150865* 44 C2
Madill OK, *3770* 51 F4
Madison AL, *42938* 119 F2
Madison AR, *769* 118 A2
Madison CT, *18812* 149 E2
Madison FL, *2843* 137 F2
Madison GA, *3979* 121 D4
Madison IL, *3891* 98 A3
Madison IN, *11967* 100 A3
Madison KS, *701* 43 F3
Madison ME, *2630* 82 B1
Madison MN, *1551* 27 F2
Madison MS, *24149* 126 B2
Madison MO, *554* 97 E2
Madison NE, *2438* 35 E2
Madison NJ, *15845* 148 A4
Madison NC, *2246* 112 B3
Madison OH, *3184* 91 F1
Madison SD, *6474* 27 F3
Madison VA, *229* 102 C4
Madison WV, *3076* 101 E4
Madison WI, *233209* 74 B3
Madison Co. AL, *334811* 119 F2
Madison Co. AR, *15717* 106 C4
Madison Co. FL, *19224* 137 F2
Madison Co. GA, *28120* 121 E3
Madison Co. ID, *37536* 23 F4
Madison Co. IL, *269282* 98 B3
Madison Co. IN, *131636* 89 F4
Madison Co. IA, *15679* 86 C2
Madison Co. KY, *82916* 110 C1
Madison Co. MS, *95203* 126 B2
Madison Co. MO, *12226* 108 A1
Madison Co. MT, *7691* 23 E2
Madison Co. NE, *34876* 35 E2
Madison Co. NY, *73442* 79 E4
Madison Co. NC, *20764* 111 E4
Madison Co. OH, *43435* 100 C1
Madison Co. TN, *98294* 108 C4
Madison Co. TX, *13664* 61 F1
Madison Co. VA, *13308* 102 C3
Madison Hts. MI, *29694* 210 C2
Madison Hts. VA, *11285* 112 C1
Madison Lake MN, *1017* 72 C1
Madison Par. LA, *12093* 126 A3
Madisonville KY, *19591* 109 E1
Madisonville LA, *748* 134 B2
Madisonville TN, *4577* 120 C1
Madisonville TX, *4396* 61 F1
Madras OR, *6046* 21 D3
Madrid IA, *2543* 86 C1
Madrid NY, *757* 80 B1
Maeser UT, *3601* 32 A4
Magalia CA, *11310* 36 C1
Magazine AR, *847* 116 C1
Magdalena NM, *938* 48 B4
Magee MS, *4408* 126 C3
Maggie Valley NC, *1150* 121 E1
Magna UT, *26505* 257 A2
Magnolia AR, *11577* 125 D1
Magnolia DE, *225* 145 E2
Magnolia MS, *2420* 134 B1
Magnolia NJ, *4341* 248 D4
Magnolia NC, *939* 123 E2
Magnolia OH, *978* 91 E3
Magnolia TX, *1393* 132 A2
Magoffin Co. KY, *13333* 111 D1
Mahanoy City PA, *4162* 93 E3
Mahaska Co. IA, *22381* 87 D2
Mahnomen MN, *1214* 19 F3
Mahnomen Co. MN, *5413* 19 F3
Mahomet IL, *7258* 88 C4
Mahoning Co. OH, *238823* 91 F3
Mahopac NY, *8369* 148 C2
Mahtomedi MN, *7676* 235 E1
Mahwah NJ, *25890* 148 B3
Maiden NC, *3310* 122 A1
Maili HI, *9488* 152 A3
Maine NY, *1000* 93 E1
Maineville OH, *975* 100 B2
Maitland FL, *15751* 141 D1
Maize KS, *3420* 43 E4
Majestic KY, *600* 111 E1
Major Co. OK, *7527* 51 D2
Makaha HI, *8278* 152 A3
Makakilo City HI, *18248* 152 A3
Makawao HI, *7184* 153 D1
Makena HI, *99* 153 D1
Malabar FL, *2757* 141 E2
Malad City ID, *2095* 31 E2
Malaga CA, *947* 44 C3
Malaga NJ, *1700* 145 F1
Malakoff TX, *2324* 59 F3
Malcolm NE, *382* 35 F4
Malden MA, *59450* 151 D1
Malden MO, *4275* 108 B3
Malden WV, *750* 200 B2
Malheur Co. OR, *31313* 22 A4
Malibu CA, *12645* 52 B2
Malin OR, *805* 29 D2
Mallory WV, *1654* 111 F1
Malone FL, *2088* 137 D1
Malone NY, *5911* 80 C1
Malone WA, *475* 12 B4
Malta ID, *193* 31 D2
Malta IL, *1164* 88 C1
Malta MT, *1997* 16 C2
Malta NY, *2100* 94 B1
Malta OH, *671* 101 E1
Maltby WA, *10830* 262 B2
Malvern AL, *1448* 136 C1
Malvern AR, *10318* 117 D3
Malvern IA, *1142* 86 A3
Malvern OH, *1189* 91 E3
Malvern PA, *2998* 146 B3
Malverne NY, *8514* 241 G4
Mamaroneck NY, *18929* 148 C3
Mammoth AZ, *1426* 55 D2
Mammoth Hot Sprs. WY, *263* 23 F2
Mammoth Lakes CA, *8234* 37 E4
Mammoth Spr. AR, *977* 107 F3
Mamou LA, *3242* 133 E2
Man WV, *759* 111 F1
Manahawkin NJ, *2303* 147 E4
Manasquan NJ, *5897* 147 E2
Manassa CO, *991* 41 D4
Manassas VA, *37821* 144 A4
Manassas Park VA, *14273* 144 A3
Manatee Co. FL, *322833* 140 C3
Manawa WI, *1371* 74 B1
Mancelona MI, *1390* 70 B4
Manchaca TX, *1133* 61 E2
Manchaug MA, *850* 150 C2
Manchester CT, *30577* 150 A3
Manchester GA, *4230* 128 C2
Manchester IA, *5179* 73 F4
Manchester KY, *1255* 110 C2
Manchester ME, *2465* 82 B2
Manchester MD, *4808* 103 E1
Manchester MI, *2091* 90 B1
Manchester MO, *18094* 256 A3
Manchester NH, *109565* 81 F4
Manchester NY, *1709* 78 C3
Manchester OH, *2023* 100 C3
Manchester PA, *2763* 93 E4
Manchester TN, *10102* 120 A1
Manchester VT, *749* 81 D4
Manchester WA, *5413* 262 A3
Manchester-by-the-Sea MA, *5228* 151 F1
Manchester Ctr. VT, *2120* 81 D4
Mancos CO, *1336* 40 B4
Mandan ND, *18331* 18 C4
Mandaree ND, *596* 18 A3
Manderson SD, *626* 26 A4
Mandeville AR, *700* 116 C4
Mandeville LA, *11560* 134 B2
Mangham LA, *672* 125 F2
Mango FL, *11313* 266 C2
Mangonia Park FL, *1888* 141 F4
Mangum OK, *3010* 50 C3
Manhasset NY, *8080* 148 C4
Manhasset Hills NY, *3592* 241 G3
Manhattan IL, *7051* 89 D2
Manhattan KS, *52281* 43 F2
Manhattan MT, *1520* 23 F1
Manhattan Beach CA, *35135* 228 C3
Manheim PA, *4858* 93 E4
Manila AR, *3342* 108 B4
Manila UT, *310* 32 A3
Manilla IA, *776* 86 A1
Manistee MI, *6226* 75 E1
Manistee Co. MI, *24733* 70 A4
Manistique MI, *3097* 69 E2
Manito IL, *1642* 88 B4
Manitou Beach MI, *2019* 90 B1
Manitou Sprs. CO, *4992* 41 E2
Manitowoc WI, *33736* 75 D1
Manitowoc Co. WI, *81442* 75 D1
Mankato KS, *869* 43 E1
Mankato MN, *39309* 72 C1
Manlius NY, *4704* 79 E3
Manly IA, *1323* 73 D3
Mannford OK, *3076* 51 F2
Manning IA, *1500* 86 B1
Manning ND, *74* 18 A3
Manning SC, *4108* 122 B4
Mannington WV, *2063* 102 A1
Mannsville OK, *863* 51 F4
Manokotak AK, *442* 154 B3
Manomet MA, *2900* 151 E3
Manor PA, *3239* 92 A4
Manor TX, *5037* 61 E1
Manorhaven NY, *6556* 241 G2
Manorville NY, *14314* 149 D3
Mansfield AR, *1139* 116 C2
Mansfield IL, *906* 88 C4
Mansfield LA, *5001* 124 C3
Mansfield MA, *7360* 151 D2
Mansfield MO, *1296* 107 E2
Mansfield OH, *47821* 91 D3
Mansfield PA, *3625* 93 D1
Mansfield TX, *56368* 59 E3
Mansfield Ctr. CT, *947* 150 B3
Mansfield Four Corners CT, *700* 150 B3
Manson IA, *1690* 72 B4
Manson WA, *1468* 13 E2
Mansura LA, *1419* 133 F1
Mantachie MS, *1144* 119 D3
Manteca CA, *67096* 36 C4
Manteno IL, *9204* 89 D2
Manteo NC, *1434* 115 F2
Manti UT, *3276* 39 E2
Manton MI, *1287* 75 F1
Mantorville MN, *1197* 73 D1
Mantua OH, *1043* 91 E2
Mantua UT, *687* 31 E3
Mantua VA, *7135* 270 A4
Manvel ND, *360* 19 E2
Manvel TX, *5179* 132 A4
Manville NJ, *10344* 147 D1
Manville RI, *3800* 150 C2
Many LA, *2853* 125 D4
Many Farms AZ, *1348* 47 F2

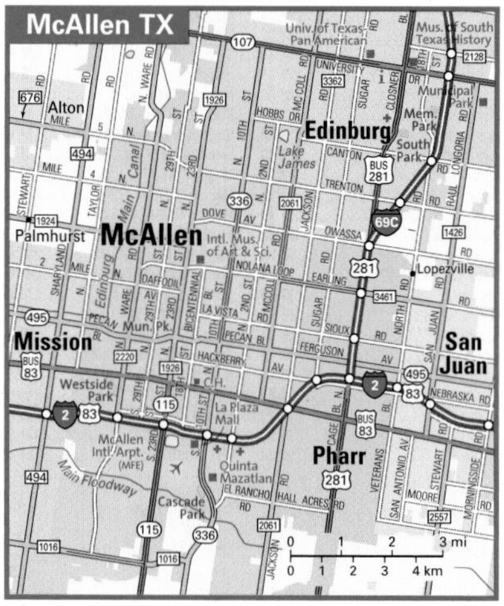

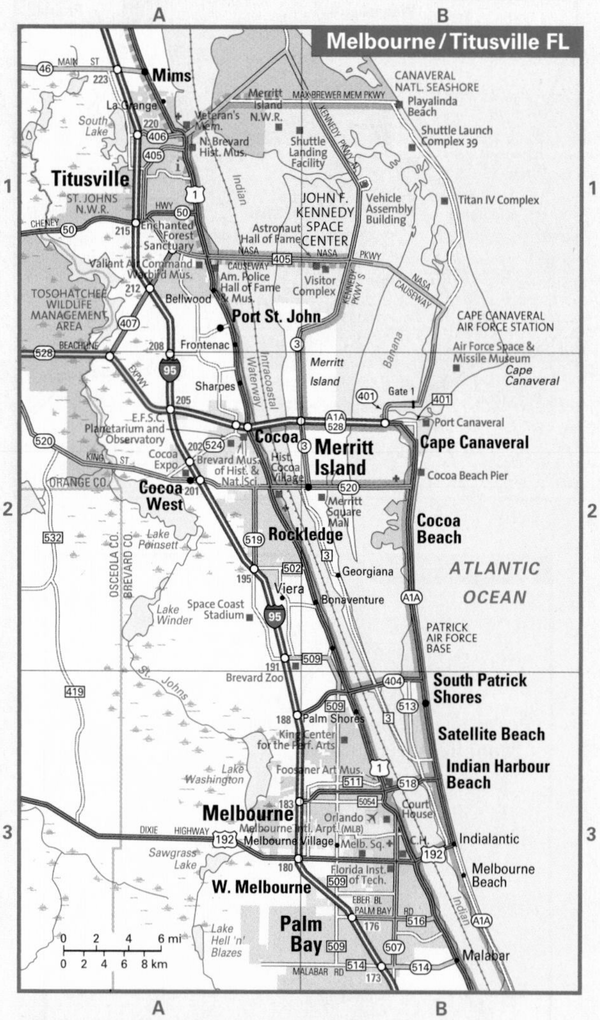

Bellwood A1
Bonaventure B2
Cape Canaveral B2
Cocoa A2
Cocoa Beach B2
Cocoa West A2
Frontenac A1
Georgiana B2
Indialantic B3
Indian Harbour Beach B3
La Grange A1
Malabar B3
Melbourne A3
Melbourne Beach B3
Melbourne Vil. B3
Merritt Island B2
Mims A1
Palm Bay B3
Palm Shores B3
Pineda B2
Port St. John A1
Rockledge A2
Satellite Beach B3
Sharpes A2
S. Patrick Shores B3
Titusville A1
Viera A2
W. Melbourne B3

Entries in **bold black** indicate counties or parishes.
Entries in **bold color** indicate cities with detailed inset maps.

Manzanita OR, 598 .... 20 B1
Manzanola CO, 434 .... 41 F3
Maple Bluff WI, 1313 .... 74 B3
Maple Grove MN, 61567 .... 67 D3
Maple Hts. OH, 23138 .... 91 E2
Maple Hill KS, 620 .... 43 F2
Maple Lake MN, 2059 .... 66 C3
Maple Park IL, 1310 .... 88 C1
Maple Plain MN, 1768 .... 66 C4
Maple Rapids MI, 672 .... 76 A3
Maple Shade NJ, 19195 .... 146 C3
Maplesville AL, 708 .... 127 F2
Mapleton IA, 1224 .... 86 A1
Mapleton ME, 683 .... 85 D2
Mapleton MN, 1756 .... 72 C1
Mapleton ND, 762 .... 19 E4
Mapleton UT, 7979 .... 39 E1
Maple Valley WA, 22684 .... 12 C3
Maplewood MN, 38018 .... 235 D2
Maplewood MO, 8046 .... 256 B2
Maplewood NJ, 23867 .... 240 A3
Mappsville VA, 440 .... 114 C2
Maquoketa IA, 6141 .... 88 A1
Marana AZ, 34961 .... 55 D3
Marathon FL, 8297 .... 143 D4
Marathon NY, 919 .... 79 E4
Marathon City WI, 1524 .... 68 A4
Marathon Co. WI, 134063 .... 68 A4
Marble MN, 701 .... 64 B3
Marble Cliff OH, 573 .... 206 A2
Marble Falls TX, 6077 .... 61 D1
Marblehead MA, 19808 .... 151 D1
Marblehead OH, 903 .... 91 D2
Marble Hill MO, 1477 .... 108 B1
Marbleton WY, 1094 .... 32 A1
Marbury MD, 1200 .... 144 B4
Marceline MO, 2233 .... 97 D1
Marcellus MI, 1198 .... 89 F1
Marcellus NY, 1813 .... 79 D3
Marco Island FL, 16413 .... 142 C2
Marcus IA, 1117 .... 72 A3
Marcus Hook PA, 2397 .... 146 C3
Marengo IL, 7648 .... 88 C1
Marengo IN, 828 .... 99 F4
Marengo IA, 2528 .... 87 E1
Marengo Co. AL, 21027 .... 127 E3
Marfa TX, 1981 .... 62 B3
Margaret AL, 4428 .... 119 F4
Margaretville NY, 596 .... 94 A2
Margate FL, 53284 .... 143 E1
Margate City NJ, 6354 .... 147 F4
Marianna AR, 4115 .... 118 A2
Marianna FL, 6102 .... 137 D1
Marianna PA, 494 .... 102 A1
Maricopa AZ, 43482 .... 54 C2
Maricopa CA, 1154 .... 52 B1
Maricopa Co. AZ, 3817117 .... 54 B1
Mariemont OH, 3403 .... 204 C2
Maries Co. MO, 9176 .... 97 E4
Marietta GA, 56579 .... 120 C4
Marietta OH, 14085 .... 101 F2
Marietta OK, 106 .... 59 E1
Marietta PA, 2588 .... 93 E4
Marietta SC, 2228 .... 121 E2
Marietta WA, 3906 .... 12 C1
Marina CA, 19718 .... 44 B3
Marina del Rey CA, 8866 .... 228 C3
Marin Co. CA, 252409 .... 36 B3
Marine IL, 960 .... 98 B3
Marine City MI, 4248 .... 76 C4
Marine on St. Croix MN, 689 .... 67 D3
Marinette WI, 10968 .... 69 D3
Marinette Co. WI, 41749 .... 68 C3
Maringouin LA, 1098 .... 133 F2
Marinwood CA, 6357 .... 259 A1
Marion AL, 3686 .... 127 F2
Marion AR, 12345 .... 118 B1
Marion CT, 1900 .... 149 D1
Marion IL, 17193 .... 108 C1
Marion IN, 29948 .... 89 F4
Marion IA, 34768 .... 87 E1
Marion KS, 1927 .... 43 F3
Marion KY, 3039 .... 109 D1
Marion LA, 765 .... 125 E1
Marion MD, 600 .... 103 F4
Marion MA, 5123 .... 151 E3
Marion MI, 872 .... 75 F1
Marion MS, 1479 .... 127 D2
Marion NY, 1511 .... 78 C3
Marion NC, 7838 .... 111 E4
Marion OH, 36837 .... 90 C4
Marion PA, 953 .... 103 D1
Marion SC, 6939 .... 122 C3
Marion SD, 784 .... 27 F4
Marion VA, 5968 .... 111 F2
Marion WI, 1260 .... 68 B4
Marion Co. AL, 30776 .... 119 E3
Marion Co. AR, 16653 .... 107 E3
Marion Co. FL, 331298 .... 139 D4
Marion Co. GA, 8742 .... 128 C3
Marion Co. IL, 39437 .... 98 C3
Marion Co. IN, 903393 .... 99 F1
Marion Co. IA, 33309 .... 87 D2
Marion Co. KS, 12660 .... 43 F3
Marion Co. KY, 19820 .... 110 B1
Marion Co. MS, 27088 .... 126 C4
Marion Co. MO, 28781 .... 97 F1
Marion Co. OH, 66501 .... 90 C3
Marion Co. OR, 315335 .... 20 C2
Marion Co. SC, 33062 .... 122 C3
Marion Co. TN, 28237 .... 120 A1
Marion Co. TX, 10546 .... 124 C2
Marion Co. WV, 56418 .... 102 A1
Marion Hts. PA, 611 .... 93 E3
Marionville MO, 2225 .... 106 C2
Mariposa CA, 2173 .... 37 D4
Mariposa Co. CA, 18251 .... 37 D4
Marissa IL, 1979 .... 98 B4
Marked Tree AR, 2566 .... 118 B1
Markesan WI, 1476 .... 74 B2
Markham IL, 12508 .... 203 D6
Markham TX, 1082 .... 61 F3
Markle IN, 1095 .... 90 A3
Markleeville CA, 210 .... 37 D2
Marks MS, 1735 .... 118 B3
Marksville LA, 5702 .... 133 F1
Marlboro NJ, 40191 .... 147 E2
Marlboro NY, 3669 .... 148 B1
Marlboro Co. SC, 28933 .... 122 C3
Marlborough CT, 6267 .... 149 E1
Marlborough MA, 38499 .... 150 C1
Marlborough MO, 2179 .... 256 B3
Marlborough NH, 1094 .... 95 D1
Marlette MI, 1875 .... 76 C3
Marley MD, 11200 .... 144 C2
Marlin TX, 5967 .... 59 F4
Marlinton WV, 1054 .... 102 A4
Marlow OK, 4662 .... 51 E4
Marlowe WV, 1300 .... 103 D1
Marlow Hts. MD, 5618 .... 270 E4
Marlton MD, 9031 .... 144 C3
Marlton NJ, 10133 .... 147 D3
Mar-Mac NC, 3615 .... 123 E1
Marmaduke AR, 1111 .... 108 A3
Marmet WV, 1503 .... 101 F4
Marmora NJ, 1600 .... 147 F4
Maroa IL, 1801 .... 98 C1
Marquette KS, 641 .... 43 E3
Marquette MI, 21355 .... 69 D1
Marquette Co. MI, 67077 .... 65 F4
Marquette Co. WI, 15404 .... 74 B2
Marrero LA, 33141 .... 134 B3
Mars PA, 1699 .... 92 A3
Marseilles IL, 5094 .... 88 C2
Marshall AR, 1355 .... 107 E4
Marshall IL, 3933 .... 99 D2
Marshall MI, 7088 .... 76 A4
Marshall MN, 13680 .... 72 A1
Marshall MO, 13065 .... 97 D2
Marshall NC, 872 .... 111 E4
Marshall TX, 23523 .... 124 C2
Marshall VA, 1480 .... 103 D3
Marshall WI, 3862 .... 74 B3
Marshallberg NC, 403 .... 115 E4
Marshall Co. AL, 93019 .... 119 F3
Marshall Co. IL, 12640 .... 88 B3
Marshall Co. IN, 47051 .... 89 F2
Marshall Co. IA, 40648 .... 87 D1
Marshall Co. KS, 10117 .... 43 F1
Marshall Co. KY, 31448 .... 109 D2
Marshall Co. MN, 9439 .... 19 F2
Marshall Co. MS, 37144 .... 118 C2
Marshall Co. OK, 15840 .... 51 F4
Marshall Co. SD, 4656 .... 27 E1
Marshall Co. TN, 30617 .... 119 F1
Marshall Co. WV, 33107 .... 102 A1
Marshallton DE, 1700 .... 146 B4
Marshallton PA, 1441 .... 146 B3
Marshalltown IA, 27552 .... 87 D1
Marshallville GA, 1448 .... 129 D2
Marshallville OH, 756 .... 91 E3
Marshfield MA, 4335 .... 151 E2
Marshfield MO, 6633 .... 107 D1
Marshfield VT, 273 .... 81 E2
Marshfield WI, 19118 .... 68 A4
Marshfield Hills MA, 2356 .... 151 E2
Mars Hill ME, 980 .... 85 E2
Mars Hill NC, 1869 .... 111 E4
Marshville NC, 2402 .... 122 B2
Marsing ID, 1031 .... 22 A4
Marston MO, 503 .... 108 B3
Marstons Mills MA, 8000 .... 151 E3
Mart TX, 2209 .... 59 F4
Martha Lake WA, 15473 .... 262 B2
Marthasville MO, 1136 .... 97 F3
Martin KY, 634 .... 111 E1
Martin LA, 594 .... 125 D3
Martin SD, 1071 .... 34 B1
Martin TN, 11473 .... 108 C3
Martin City MT, 500 .... 15 D2
Martin Co. FL, 146318 .... 141 E4
Martin Co. IN, 10334 .... 99 E3
Martin Co. KY, 12929 .... 111 E1
Martin Co. MN, 20840 .... 72 B2
Martin Co. NC, 24505 .... 113 F4
Martin Co. TX, 4799 .... 58 A3
Martindale TX, 1116 .... 61 E2
Martinez CA, 35824 .... 36 B3
Martins Additions MD, 933 .... 270 C2
Martinsburg PA, 1958 .... 92 C4
Martinsburg WV, 17227 .... 103 D2
Martins Creek PA, 631 .... 93 F3
Martins Ferry OH, 6915 .... 91 F4
Martinsville IL, 1167 .... 99 D2
Martinsville IN, 11828 .... 99 F2
Martinsville NJ, 11980 .... 147 D1
Martinsville VA, 13821 .... 112 B3
Marty SD, 402 .... 35 D1
Marvell AR, 1186 .... 118 A2
Marvin NC, 5579 .... 122 A2
Mary Esther FL, 3851 .... 136 B2
Maryland City MD, 16093 .... 193 A5
Maryland Hts. MO, 27472 .... 256 A1

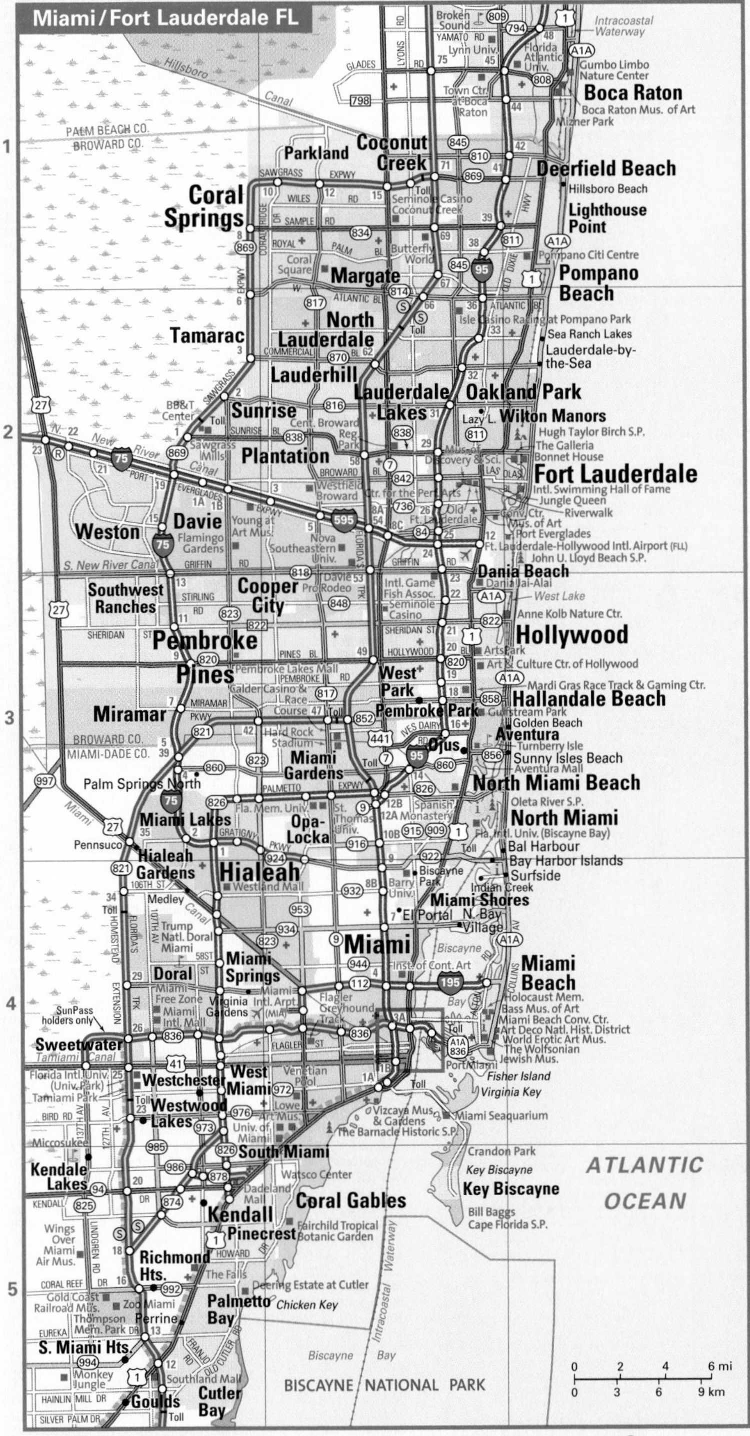

Aventura B3
Bal Harbour B3
Bay Harbor Islands C4
Biscayne Park B4
Boca Raton C1
Coconut Creek B1
Cooper City A3
Coral Gables B5
Coral Sprs. A1
Cutler Bay A5
Dania Beach B3
Davie A2
Deerfield Beach C1
El Portal B4
Ft. Lauderdale C2
Golden Beach C3
Goulds A5
Hallandale Beach C3
Hialeah A4
Hialeah Gardens A4
Hillsboro Beach C1
Hollywood B3
Indian Creek B4
Kendale Lakes A5
Kendall A5
Key Biscayne B5
Lauderdale-by-the-Sea C2
Lauderdale Lakes B2
Lauderhill B2
Lazy Lake B2
Lighthouse Pt. C1
Margate B1
Medley A4
Miami B4
Miami Beach C4
Miami Gardens B3
Miami Lakes A3
Miami Shores B4
Miami Sprs. A4
Miramar A3
N. Bay Vil. B4
N. Lauderdale B2
N. Miami C3
N. Miami Beach B3
Oakland Park B2
Opa-Locka B3
Ojus B3
Palmetto Bay A5
Palm Springs North A3
Parkland B1
Pembroke Park B3
Pembroke Pines A3
Perrine A5
Pinecrest A5
Plantation B2
Pompano Beach C1
Richmond Hts. A5
Rockdale A5
S. Miami A5
S. Miami Hts. A5
Southwest Ranches A3
Sunny Isles Beach C3
Sunrise B2
Surfside C4
Sweetwater A4
Tamarac A2
Virginia Gardens A4
W. Miami A4
Westchester A4
Weston A2
West Park B3
Westwood Lakes A4
Wilton Manors C2

POINTS OF INTEREST

AmericanAirlines Arena E1
Bayside Marketplace E2
Flagler Palm Cottage D2
Freedom Tower D1
Frost Museum of Science E1
HistoryMiami D2
James L. Knight Center D2
Jungle Island E1
Klipsch Amphitheater at Bayfront Park E2
Knight Concert Hall E1
Miami Children's Museum E1
Miami Herald Building E1
Miami Seaplane Base E1
Olympia Theater D2
PortMiami E2
Sanford & Dolores Ziff Ballet Opera House D1

Figures after entries indicate population, page number, and grid reference.

Marysvale UT, 408 ..... 39 E3
Marysville CA, 12072 ..... 36 C2
Marysville KS, 3294 ..... 43 F1
Marysville MI, 9959 ..... 76 C3
Marysville OH, 22094 ..... 90 C4
Marysville PA, 2534 ..... 93 D4
Marysville WA, 60020 ..... 12 C2
Maryville IL, 7487 ..... 256 D1
Maryville MO, 11972 ..... 86 B4
Maryville TN, 27465 ..... 110 C4
Marywood MD, 6000 ..... 145 D1
Masaryktown FL, 1040 ..... 140 B1
Mascot TN, 2411 ..... 110 C4
Mascotte FL, 5101 ..... 140 C1
Mascoutah IL, 7483 ..... 98 B3
Mashpee MA, 1000 ..... 151 E3
Mason MI, 8252 ..... 76 A4
Mason NV, 500 ..... 37 E2
Mason NH, 1382 ..... 95 D1
Mason OH, 30712 ..... 100 B2
Mason TN, 1609 ..... 118 C1
Mason TX, 2114 ..... 60 C1
Mason WV, 968 ..... 101 E2
Masonboro NC, 11812 ..... 123 E3
Mason City IL, 2343 ..... 88 B4
Mason City IA, 28079 ..... 73 D3
Mason Co. IL, 14666 ..... 88 A4
Mason Co. KY, 17490 ..... 100 C3
Mason Co. MI, 28705 ..... 75 E1
Mason Co. TX, 4012 ..... 60 C1
Mason Co. WA, 60699 ..... 12 B3
Mason Co. WV, 27324 ..... 101 E3
Masontown PA, 3450 ..... 102 B1
Masontown WV, 546 ..... 102 B1
Masonville KY, 1014 ..... 109 E1
Masonville NJ, 7300 ..... 147 D3
Massac Co. IL, 15429 ..... 108 C2
Massapequa NY, 21685 ..... 148 C4
Massapequa Park NY, 17008 ..... 148 C4
Massena NY, 10936 ..... 80 B1
Massillon OH, 32149 ..... 91 E3
Mastic NY, 15481 ..... 149 D4
Mastic Beach NY, 12930 ..... 149 D4
Masury OH, 2064 ..... 91 F2
Matador TX, 607 ..... 58 B1
Matagorda Co. TX, 36702 ..... 132 A4
Matamoras PA, 2469 ..... 94 A3
Matawan NJ, 8810 ..... 147 E1
Matewan WV, 499 ..... 111 E1
Matherville IL, 723 ..... 88 A2
Mathews LA, 2209 ..... 134 B3
Mathews VA, 555 ..... 113 F1
Mathews Co. VA, 8978 ..... 113 F1
Mathis TX, 4942 ..... 61 E4
Mathiston MS, 698 ..... 118 C4
Matlacha FL, 677 ..... 142 C1
Mattapoisett MA, 2915 ..... 151 E3
Mattawa WA, 4437 ..... 13 E4
Mattawamkeag ME, 825 ..... 85 D4
Mattawan MI, 1997 ..... 89 F1
Mattawoman MD, 3100 ..... 144 B4
Matteson IL, 19009 ..... 89 D2
Matthews IN, 596 ..... 89 F4
Matthews MO, 628 ..... 108 B2
Matthews NC, 27198 ..... 122 B1
Mattituck NY, 4219 ..... 149 E3
Mattoon IL, 18555 ..... 98 C2
Mattydale NY, 6446 ..... 79 D3
Matunuck RI, 750 ..... 150 C4
Maud OH, 4800 ..... 100 B2
Maud OK, 1048 ..... 51 F3
Maud TX, 1056 ..... 124 C1
Maugansville MD, 3071 ..... 103 D1
Maui Co. HI, 154834 ..... 153 D1
Mauldin SC, 22889 ..... 121 F2
Maumee OH, 14286 ..... 90 C2
Maumelle AR, 17163 ..... 117 E2
Maunawili HI, 2040 ..... 152 B3
Maupin OR, 418 ..... 21 D2
Maurertown VA, 770 ..... 102 C3
Maurice LA, 964 ..... 133 F2
Mauriceville TX, 3252 ..... 132 C2
Maury City TN, 674 ..... 108 C4
Maury Co. TN, 80956 ..... 109 E4
Mauston WI, 4423 ..... 74 A2
Maverick Co. TX, 54258 ..... 60 B3
Mavisdale VA, 550 ..... 111 E2
Max ND, 334 ..... 18 B3
Max Meadows VA, 562 ..... 112 A2
Maxton NC, 2426 ..... 122 C2
Maxwell CA, 1103 ..... 36 B2
Maxwell IA, 920 ..... 86 C1
Maxwell NM, 254 ..... 49 E1
Maybee MI, 562 ..... 90 C1
Maybeury WV, 234 ..... 111 F1
Maybrook NY, 2958 ..... 148 B1
Mayer AZ, 1497 ..... 47 D4
Mayer MN, 1749 ..... 66 C4
Mayersville MS, 547 ..... 126 A1
Mayes Co. OK, 41259 ..... 106 A3
Mayesville SC, 731 ..... 122 B3
Mayfield KY, 10024 ..... 108 C3
Mayfield NY, 832 ..... 80 C4
Mayfield OH, 3460 ..... 204 G1
Mayfield PA, 1807 ..... 93 F2
Mayfield UT, 496 ..... 39 E2
Mayfield Hts. OH, 19155 ..... 91 E2
Mayflower AR, 2234 ..... 117 E2
Maynard IA, 518 ..... 73 E4
Maynard MA, 10106 ..... 150 C1
Maynardville TN, 2413 ..... 110 C3
Mayo FL, 1237 ..... 137 F3
Mayo MD, 8298 ..... 144 C3
Mayo SC, 1592 ..... 121 F1
Mayodan NC, 2478 ..... 112 B3
Maypearl TX, 934 ..... 59 F3
Mays Chapel MD, 11420 ..... 193 C1
Mays Landing NJ, 2135 ..... 105 D3
Maysville GA, 1798 ..... 121 D3
Maysville KY, 9011 ..... 100 C3
Maysville MO, 1114 ..... 96 B1
Maysville NC, 1019 ..... 115 D4
Maysville OK, 1232 ..... 51 E4
Maytown AL, 385 ..... 195 D1
Mayville MI, 950 ..... 76 C3
Mayville NY, 1711 ..... 78 A4
Mayville ND, 1858 ..... 19 E3
Mayville WI, 5154 ..... 74 C2
Maywood CA, 27395 ..... 228 D3
Maywood IL, 24090 ..... 203 C4
Maywood NJ, 9555 ..... 240 C1
Maywood NY, 4200 ..... 188 D2
Maywood Park OR, 752 ..... 251 D2
Mazeppa MN, 842 ..... 73 D1
Mazomanie WI, 1652 ..... 74 A3
Mazon IL, 1015 ..... 88 C2
McAdoo PA, 2300 ..... 93 E3
McAfee NJ, 2600 ..... 148 A2
McAlester OK, 18383 ..... 116 A2
McAlisterville PA, 971 ..... 93 D3
McAllen TX, 129877 ..... 63 E4
McArthur OH, 1701 ..... 101 D2
McBain MI, 656 ..... 75 F1
McBee SC, 867 ..... 122 B3
McCall ID, 2991 ..... 22 B2
McCamey TX, 1887 ..... 58 A4
McCammon ID, 809 ..... 31 E1
McCandless PA, 28457 ..... 92 A4
McCaysville GA, 1056 ..... 120 C2
McClain Co. OK, 34506 ..... 51 E3
McCleary WA, 1653 ..... 12 B4
McClellandville DE, 2400 ..... 146 B4
McClellanville SC, 499 ..... 131 E1
McCloud CA, 1101 ..... 28 C3
McClure OH, 725 ..... 90 B2
McClure PA, 941 ..... 93 D3
McClusky ND, 380 ..... 18 C3
McColl SC, 2174 ..... 122 C2
McComb MS, 12790 ..... 126 B4
McComb OH, 1648 ..... 90 B3
McCone Co. MT, 1734 ..... 17 E3
McConnellsburg PA, 1220 ..... 103 D1
McConnelsville OH, 1784 ..... 101 E1
McCook NE, 7698 ..... 42 C1
McCook Co. SD, 5618 ..... 27 E4
McCordsville IN, 4797 ..... 99 F1
McCormack Corners NY, 2300 ..... 188 C2
McCormick SC, 2783 ..... 121 F4
McCormick Co. SC, 10233 ..... 121 F4
McCracken Co. KY, 65565 ..... 108 C2
McCreary Co. KY, 18306 ..... 110 C2
McCrory AR, 1729 ..... 117 F1
McCulloch Co. TX, 8283 ..... 58 C4
McCune KS, 405 ..... 106 B1
McCurtain OK, 516 ..... 116 B1
McCurtain Co. OK, 33151 ..... 116 B3
McDermitt NV, 172 ..... 30 A2
McDonald OH, 3263 ..... 276 B2
McDonald PA, 2149 ..... 92 A4
McDonald Co. MO, 23083 ..... 106 C3
McDonough GA, 22084 ..... 120 C4
McDonough Co. IL, 32612 ..... 87 F3
McDowell Co. NC, 44996 ..... 111 E4
McDowell Co. WV, 22113 ..... 111 F1
McDuffie Co. GA, 21875 ..... 129 F1
McEwen TN, 1750 ..... 109 E4
McFarland CA, 12707 ..... 45 D4
McFarland WI, 7808 ..... 74 B3
McGaheysville VA, 500 ..... 102 C4
McGehee AR, 4219 ..... 117 F4
McGill NV, 1148 ..... 38 B2
McGrath AK, 346 ..... 154 C2
McGraw NY, 1053 ..... 79 E4
McGregor IA, 871 ..... 73 F3
McGregor TX, 4987 ..... 59 E4
McHenry IL, 26992 ..... 74 C4
McHenry KY, 388 ..... 109 E1
McHenry Co. IL, 308760 ..... 74 C4
McHenry Co. ND, 5395 ..... 18 C2
McIntosh FL, 452 ..... 138 C4
McIntosh MN, 625 ..... 19 F3
McIntosh SD, 173 ..... 26 B1
McIntosh Co. GA, 14333 ..... 130 B4
McIntosh Co. ND, 2809 ..... 27 D1
McIntosh Co. OK, 20252 ..... 116 A1
McIntyre GA, 650 ..... 129 E2
McKean Co. PA, 43450 ..... 92 B1
McKee KY, 800 ..... 110 C1
McKee City NJ, 2800 ..... 147 F4
McKeesport PA, 19731 ..... 92 A4
McKees Rocks PA, 6104 ..... 250 B1
McKenna WA, 716 ..... 12 C4
McKenney VA, 483 ..... 113 E2
McKenzie AL, 530 ..... 127 F4
McKenzie TN, 5310 ..... 109 D4
McKenzie Co. ND, 6360 ..... 17 F2
McKinley Co. NM, 71492 ..... 48 A2
McKinleyville CA, 15177 ..... 28 A4
McKinney TX, 131117 ..... 59 F2
McKownville NY, 2600 ..... 188 D3
McLain MS, 441 ..... 135 D1
McLaughlin SD, 663 ..... 26 C1
McLean IL, 830 ..... 88 B4
McLean TX, 778 ..... 50 B3
McLean VA, 48115 ..... 144 B3
McLean Co. IL, 169572 ..... 88 C4
McLean Co. KY, 9531 ..... 109 E1
McLean Co. ND, 8962 ..... 18 B3
McLeansboro IL, 2883 ..... 98 C4
McLennan Co. TX, 234906 ..... 59 F4
McLeod Co. MN, 36651 ..... 66 C4
McLoud OK, 4044 ..... 51 E3
McLouth KS, 880 ..... 96 A2
McMechen WV, 1926 ..... 101 F1
McMinn Co. TN, 52266 ..... 120 C1
McMinnville OR, 32187 ..... 20 B2
McMinnville TN, 13605 ..... 110 A4
McMullen Co. TX, 707 ..... 61 D4
McMurray PA, 4647 ..... 92 A4
McNairy Co. TN, 26075 ..... 119 D1
McNary AZ, 528 ..... 47 F4
McNeil AR, 516 ..... 125 D1
McPherson KS, 13155 ..... 43 E3
McPherson Co. KS, 29180 ..... 43 E3
McPherson Co. NE, 539 ..... 34 B3
McPherson Co. SD, 2459 ..... 27 D1
McQueeney TX, 2545 ..... 61 D2
McRae AR, 682 ..... 117 F1
McRae GA, 5740 ..... 129 E3
McRoberts KY, 784 ..... 111 E2
McSherrystown PA, 3038 ..... 103 E1
McVeigh KY, 550 ..... 111 E1
McVille ND, 349 ..... 19 E3
Mead CO, 3405 ..... 33 E4
Mead NE, 569 ..... 35 F3
Mead WA, 7275 ..... 14 A3
Meade KS, 1721 ..... 42 C4
Meade Co. KS, 4575 ..... 42 C4
Meade Co. KY, 28602 ..... 99 F4
Meade Co. SD, 25434 ..... 26 A3
Meadow TX, 593 ..... 58 A1
Meadowlakes TX, 1777 ..... 61 D1
Meadows Place TX, 4660 ..... 132 A3
Meadow Vale KY, 736 ..... 230 F1
Meadow Valley CA, 464 ..... 36 C1
Meadowview VA, 967 ..... 111 F2
Meadville MS, 449 ..... 126 A4
Meadville PA, 13388 ..... 92 A2
Meagher Co. MT, 1891 ..... 15 F4
Mebane NC, 11393 ..... 112 C4
Mecca CA, 8577 ..... 53 E3
Mechanic Falls ME, 2237 ..... 82 B2
Mechanicsburg OH, 1644 ..... 90 C4
Mechanicsburg PA, 8981 ..... 93 D4
Mechanicsville IA, 1146 ..... 87 F1
Mechanicsville MD, 1508 ..... 103 E3
Mechanicsville VA, 36348 ..... 113 E1
Mechanicville NY, 5196 ..... 94 B1
Mecklenburg Co. NC, 919628 ..... 122 B1
Mecklenburg Co. VA, 32727 ..... 113 D2
Mecosta Co. MI, 42798 ..... 75 F2
Medanales NM, 450 ..... 48 C2
Medaryville IN, 614 ..... 89 E3
Medfield MA, 6483 ..... 151 D2
Medford MA, 56173 ..... 151 D1
Medford MN, 1239 ..... 73 D1
Medford NJ, 22858 ..... 147 D3
Medford NY, 24142 ..... 149 D4
Medford OK, 996 ..... 51 E1
Medford OR, 74907 ..... 28 B2
Medford WI, 4326 ..... 68 A3
Medford Lakes NJ, 4146 ..... 147 D3
Media PA, 5327 ..... 146 C3
Mediapolis IA, 1560 ..... 87 F3
Medical Lake WA, 5060 ..... 13 F3
Medicine Bow WY, 284 ..... 33 D2
Medicine Lake MT, 225 ..... 17 F2
Medicine Lodge KS, 2009 ..... 43 D4
Medina MN, 4892 ..... 66 C3
Medina NY, 6065 ..... 78 B3
Medina ND, 308 ..... 19 D4
Medina OH, 26678 ..... 91 E3
Medina TN, 3479 ..... 108 C4
Medina WA, 2969 ..... 262 B3
Medina Co. OH, 172332 ..... 91 E3
Medina Co. TX, 46006 ..... 60 C3

Bayside D1
Brookfield B2
Brown Deer C1
Butler B1
Cudahy D3
Elm Grove B2
Fox Pt. D1
Glendale C1
Greendale C3
Greenfield C3
Hales Corners B3
Lannon A1
Menomonee Falls B1
Milwaukee C2
New Berlin B3
Pewaukee (city) A2
Pewaukee (village) A2
River Hills D1
St. Francis D3
Shorewood D2
Sussex A1
Waukesha A2
Wauwatosa C2
W. Allis C3
W. Milwaukee C3
Whitefish Bay D1

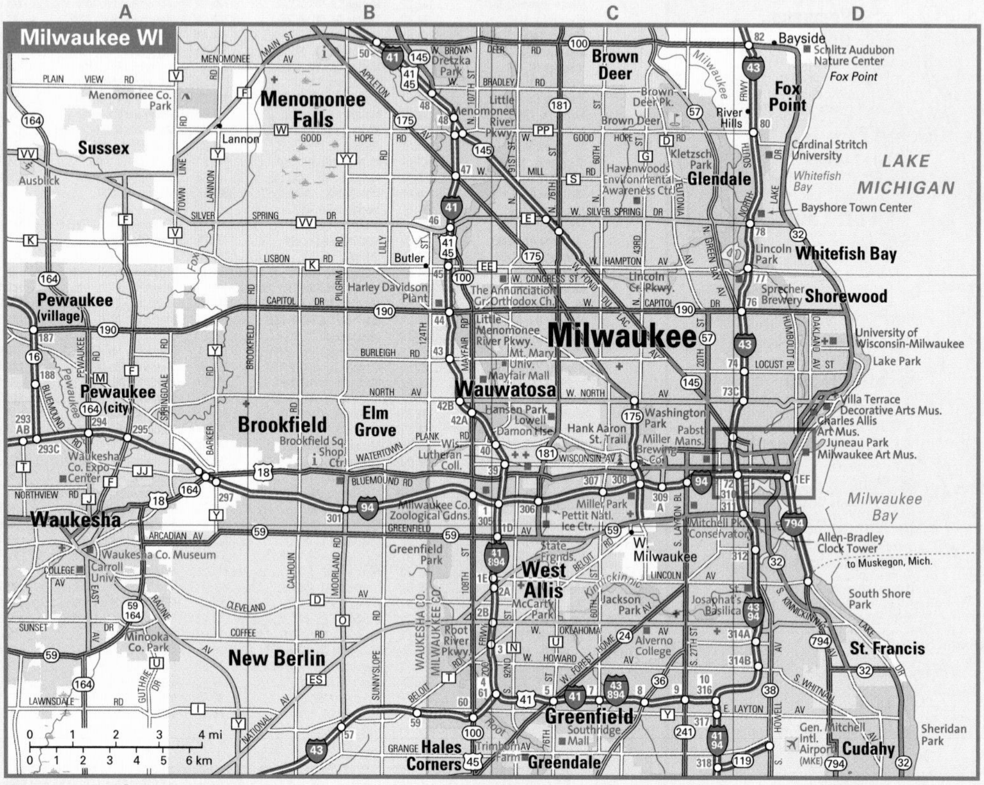

POINTS OF INTEREST

Amtrak/Intermodal Station F2
Betty Brinn Children's Museum G2
Broadway Theatre Center F2
Court House E1
Cudahy Gardens G2
Discovery World at Pier Wisconsin G2
Federal Plaza F2
Fiserv Forum F1
Grain Exchange F2
Haggerty Museum of Art E2
Harley-Davidson Museum F2
Helfaer Theatre E2
Historic Third Ward F2
Lakeshore State Park G2
Maier Festival Park G2
Marcus Ctr. for the Performing Arts F1
Marquette University E2
Miller High Life Theatre F1
Milwaukee Art Museum & War Memorial Center G1
Milwaukee County Hist. Society F1
Milwaukee Institute of Art & Design F2
Milwaukee Public Market F2
Milwaukee Public Museum E1
Milwaukee School of Engineering F1
Pabst Theater F1
Post Office F2
Potawatomi Hotel & Casino E2
St. Joan of Arc Chapel E2
The Shops of Grand Avenue F2
State Office Building F1
UW-Milwaukee Panther Arena F1
Wisconsin Center F2
Wisconsin Conservatory of Music G1

Entries in **bold black** indicate counties or parishes.
Entries in **bold color** indicate cities with detailed inset maps.

Medinah IL, *2500* **203** B3
Medley FL, *838* **233** A4
Medora IN, *693* **99** F3
Medora ND, *112* **18** A4
Medulla FL, *8892* **140** C2
Medway ME, *1489* **85** D4
Medway MA, *12752* **150** C2
Meeker CO, *2475* **40** B1
Meeker OK, *1144* **51** F3
Meeker Co. MN, *23300* **66** B3
Meenon WI, *250* **67** E2
Meeteetse WY, *327* **24** B3
Meggett SC, *1226* **131** D2
Mehlville MO, *28380* **98** A3
Meigs GA, *1035* **137** E1
Meigs Co. OH, *23770* **101** E2
Meigs Co. TN, *11753* **110** B4
Meiners Oaks CA, *3571* **52** B2
Melba ID, *513* **22** B4
Melbourne AR, *1848* **107** E4
Melbourne FL, *76068* **141** E2
Melbourne IA, *830* **87** D1
Melbourne KY, *401* **204** C3
Melbourne Beach FL, *3101* **141** E2
Melbourne Vil. FL, *662* **141** E2
Melcher-Dallas IA, *1288* **87** D2
Melfa VA, *408* **114** C3
Melissa TX, *4695* **59** F2
Mellen WI, *731* **65** D4
Mellette SD, *210* **27** E2
Mellette Co. SD, *2048* **26** C4
Melrose MN, *3598* **66** B2
Melrose NM, *651* **49** F4
Melrose NY, *800* **94** B1
Melrose WI, *503* **73** F1
Melrose Park IL, *25411* **203** C4
Melrose Park NY, *2294* **79** D3
Melvern KS, *385* **96** A3
Melville LA, *1041* **133** F1
Melvindale MI, *10715* **210** B4
Memphis FL, *7848* **140** B3
Memphis MI, *1183* **76** C3
Memphis MO, *1822* **87** E4
Memphis TN, *646889* **118** B1
Memphis TX, *2290* **50** B4
Memphis Jct. KY, *550* **109** F2
Mena AR, *5737* **116** C2
Menahga MN, *1306* **64** A4
Menan ID, *741* **23** E4
Menands NY, *3990* **188** E3
Menard TX, *1471* **60** C1
Menard Co. IL, *12705* **88** B4
Menard Co. TX, *2242* **60** C1
Menasha WI, *17353* **74** C1
Mendenhall MS, *2504* **126** B3
Mendenhall PA, *1600* **146** B3
Mendham NJ, *4981* **148** A4
Mendocino CA, *894* **36** A2
Mendocino Co. CA, *87841* **36** A1
Mendon IL, *953* **87** F4
Mendon MA, *5839* **150** C2
Mendon MI, *870* **89** F1
Mendon OH, *662* **90** B3
Mendon UT, *1282* **31** E3
Mendota CA, *11014* **44** C3
Mendota IL, *7372* **88** B2
Mendota Hts. MN, *11071* **235** D3
Menifee CA, *77519* **53** D3
Menifee Co. KY, *6306* **100** C4
Menlo GA, *474* **120** B3
Menlo Park CA, *32026* **259** C5
Menno SD, *608* **27** E4
Menominee MI, *8599* **69** D3
Menominee Co. MI, *24029* **69** D3
Menominee Co. WI, *4232* **68** C3
Menomonee Falls WI, *35626* **74** C3
Menomonie WI, *16264* **67** E4
Mentone AL, *360* **120** B2
Mentone CA, *8720* **53** D2
Mentone IN, *1001* **89** F2
Mentone TX, *19* **57** E4
Mentor OH, *47159* **91** E2
Mentor TN, *1500* **110** C4
Mentor-on-the-Lake OH, *7443* **91** E1
Mequon WI, *23132* **74** C3
Meraux LA, *5816* **134** C3
Merced CA, *78958* **37** D4
Merced Co. CA, *255793* **44** C2
Mercedes TX, *15570* **63** E4
Mercer PA, *2002* **91** F2
Mercer Co. IL, *16434* **87** F2
Mercer Co. KY, *21331* **110** B1
Mercer Co. MO, *3785* **86** C4
Mercer Co. NJ, *366513* **147** D2
Mercer Co. ND, *8424* **18** B3
Mercer Co. OH, *40814* **90** A4
Mercer Co. PA, *116638* **91** F2
Mercer Co. WV, *62264* **112** A1
Mercer Island WA, *22699* **262** B3
Mercersburg PA, *1561* **103** D1
Mercerville NJ, *13230* **147** D2
Merchantville NJ, *3821* **248** D3
Meredith NH, *1718* **81** F3
Meredosia IL, *1044* **98** A1
Meriden CT, *60868* **149** D1
Meriden KS, *813* **96** A2
Meridian ID, *75092* **22** B4
Meridian MS, *41148* **127** D2
Meridian PA, *3881* **92** A3
Meridian TX, *1493* **59** E3
Meridian Hills IN, *1616* **99** F1
Meridianville AL, *6021* **119** F2
Merigold MS, *439* **118** A4
Meriwether Co. GA, *21992* **128** C1
Merkel TX, *2590* **58** C3
Merlin OR, *1615* **28** B1
Mermentau LA, *661* **133** E2
Merriam KS, *11003* **224** B4
Merriam Woods MO, *1761* **107** D3
Merrick NY, *22097* **148** C4
Merrick Co. NE, *7845* **35** E3
Merrifield VA, *15212* **270** A3
Merrill IA, *755* **35** F1
Merrill MI, *778* **76** A2
Merrill OR, *844* **28** C2
Merrill WI, *9661* **68** B3
Merrillan WI, *542* **73** F1
Merrillville IN, *35246* **89** D2
Merrimac MA, *6338* **151** F1
Merrimack NH, *25494* **95** D1
Merrimack Co. NH, *146445* **81** F4
Merrionette Park IL, *1900* **203** D6
Merritt Island FL, *34743* **141** E2
Mer Rouge LA, *628* **125** F2
Merrow CT, *1000* **150** A3
Merryville LA, *1103* **133** D1
Merton WI, *3346* **74** C3
Mertzon TX, *781* **58** B4
Mertztown PA, *664* **146** B1
Mesa AZ, *439041* **54** C1
Mesa WA, *489* **13** E4
Mesa Co. CO, *146723* **40** B2
Mescalero NM, *1338* **56** C2
Mesilla NM, *2196* **56** C3
Mesita NM, *804* **48** B3
Mesquite NV, *15276* **46** B1
Mesquite NM, *1112* **56** C3
Mesquite TX, *139824* **59** F2
Metairie LA, *138481* **134** B3
Metamora IL, *3636* **88** B3
Metamora MI, *565* **76** C3
Metamora OH, *627* **90** B2
Metcalfe MS, *1067* **118** A4
Metcalfe Co. KY, *10099* **110** A2
Methuen MA, *47255* **95** E1
Metlakatla AK, *1405* **155** E4
Metolius OR, *710* **21** D3
Metropolis IL, *6537* **108** C2
Metter GA, *4130* **129** F2
Metuchen NJ, *13574* **147** E1
Metzger OR, *3765* **251** C2

Apple Valley C4
Arden Hills C1
Bald Eagle E1
Birchwood Vil. E1
Blaine C1
Bloomington B4
Brooklyn Ctr. B1
Brooklyn Park B1
Burnsville B4
Circle Pines C1
Columbia Hts. C2
Coon Rapids B1
Cottage Grove E4
Crystal B2
Deephaven A3
Dellwood E1
Eagan D4
Eden Prairie A4
Edina B3
Falcon Hts. C2
Fridley C1
Gem Lake D1
Golden Valley B2
Grant E1
Hilltop C1
Hopkins A3
Hugo E1
Inver Grove Hts. D4
Lake Elmo E2
Landfall E3
Lauderdale C2
Lexington C1
Lilydale D3
Lino Lakes D1
Little Canada D2
Mahtomedi E1
Maple Grove A1
Maplewood D2
Medicine Lake A2
Mendota C3
Mendota Hts. D3
Minneapolis B3
Minnetonka A3
Mounds View C1
New Brighton C1
New Hope B2
Newport D3
Nininger E4
N. Oaks D1
N. St. Paul D2
Oakdale E2
Osseo A1
Pine Sprs. E2
Plymouth A2
Richfield B3
Robbinsdale B2
Rosemount D4
Roseville C2
St. Anthony C2
St. Louis Park B2
St. Paul D2
St. Paul Park E4
Savage B4
Shakopee A4
Shoreview C1
S. St. Paul D3
Spring Lake Park C1
Sunfish Lake D3
Vadnais Hts. D1
Wayzata A2
W. St. Paul D3
White Bear Lake D1
Willernie E1
Withrow E1
Woodbury E3
Woodland A3

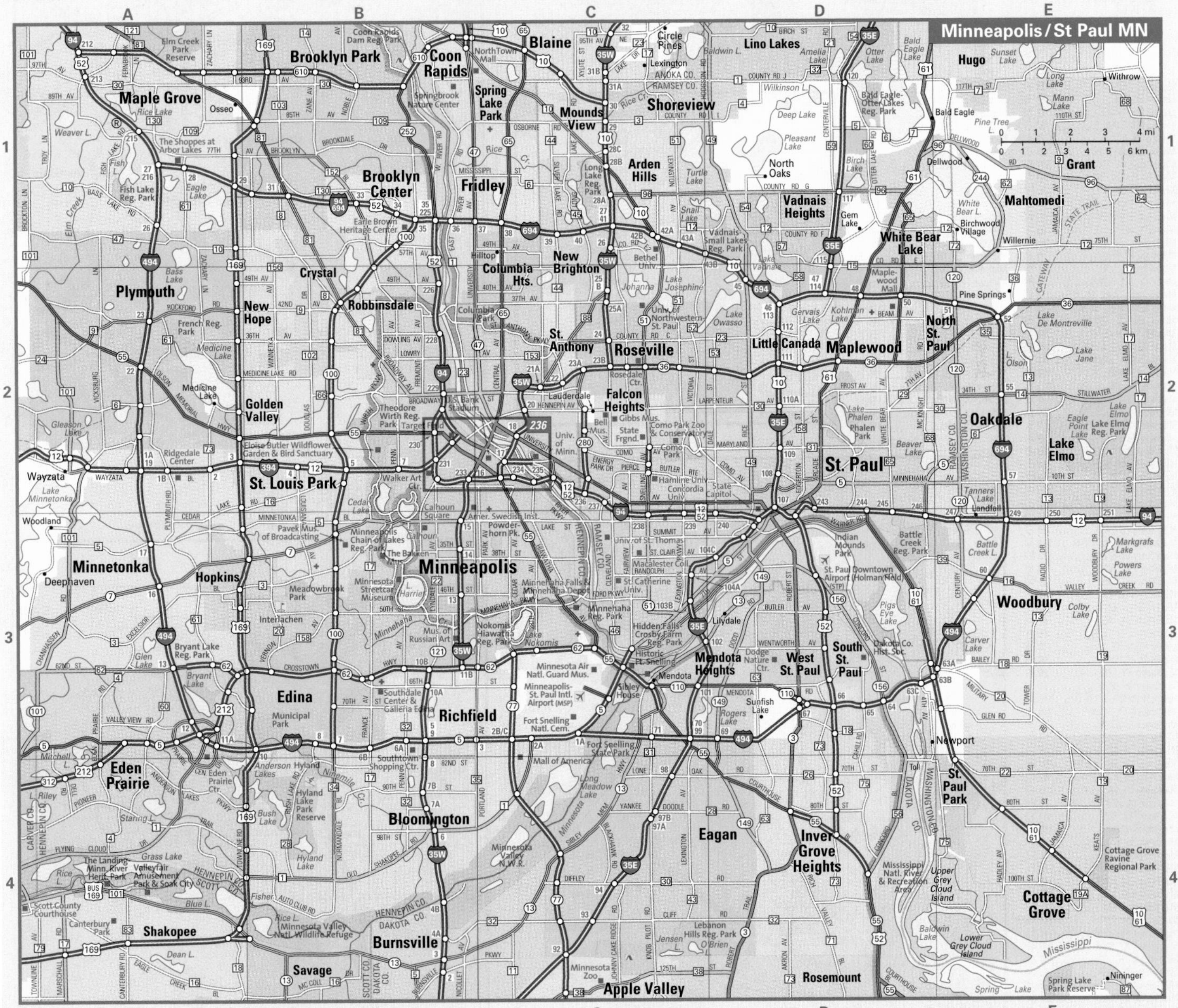

Figures after entries indicate population, page number, and grid reference.

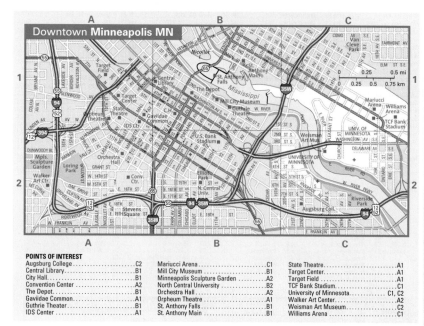

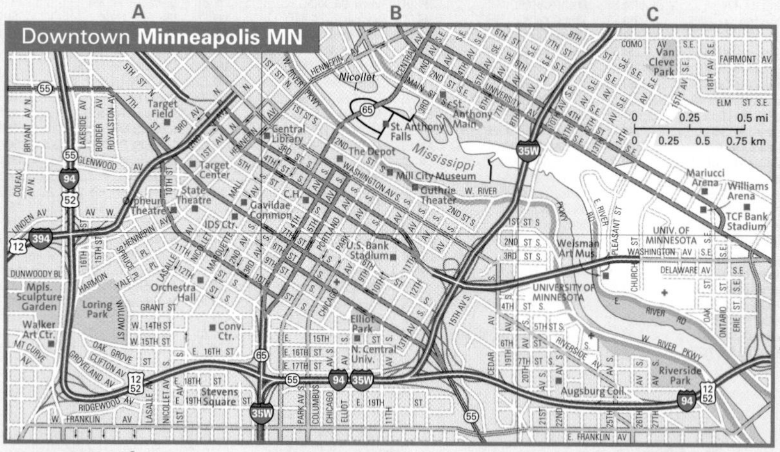

POINTS OF INTEREST

Augsburg College.....C2
Central Library.....B1
City Hall.....B1
Convention Center.....A2
The Depot.....B1
Gaviidae Common.....A1
Guthrie Theater.....B1
IDS Center.....A1
Mariucci Arena.....C1
Mill City Museum.....B1
Minneapolis Sculpture Garden.....A2
North Central University.....B2
Orchestra Hall.....A2
Orpheum Theatre.....A1
St. Anthony Falls.....B1
St. Anthony Main.....B1
State Theatre.....A1
Target Center.....A1
Target Field.....A1
TCF Bank Stadium.....C1
University of Minnesota.....C1, C2
Walker Art Center.....A2
Weisman Art Museum.....C2
Williams Arena.....C1

Mexia TX, *7459*.....**59** F4
Mexico IN, *836*.....**89** F3
Mexico ME, *1743*.....**82** B2
Mexico MO, *11543*.....**97** E2
Mexico NY, *1624*.....**79** D2
Mexico Beach FL, *1072*.....**136** C3
Meyersdale PA, *2184*.....**102** C1
Meyers Lake OH, *569*.....**199** B2
Miami AZ, *1837*.....**55** D1
Miami FL, *399457*.....143 F2
Miami OK, *13570*.....**106** B2
Miami TX, *597*.....**50** B2
Miami Beach FL, *87779*.....**143** F2
Miami Co. IN, *36903*.....**89** F3
Miami Co. KS, *32787*.....**96** B3
Miami Co. OH, *102506*.....**90** B4
Miami-Dade Co. FL, *2496435*.....**143** E2
Miami Gardens FL, *107167*.....**143** E2
Miami Lakes FL, *29361*.....**233** A3
Miamisburg OH, *20181*.....**100** B1
Miami Shores FL, *10493*.....**143** F2
Miami Sprs. FL, *13809*.....**143** E2
Micanopy FL, *600*.....**138** C4
Micaville NC, *750*.....**111** E4
Micco FL, *9052*.....**141** E2
Michie TN, *591*.....**119** D2
Michigan ND, *294*.....**19** E2
Michigan Ctr. MI, *4672*.....**90** B1
Michigan City IN, *31479*.....**89** E1
Middleboro MA, *7319*.....**151** D3
Middlebourne WV, *815*.....**101** F2
Middleburg FL, *13008*.....**139** D3
Middleburg PA, *1309*.....**93** D3
Middleburg VA, *673*.....**144** A3
Middleburgh NY, *1500*.....**79** F4
Middleburg Hts. OH, *15946*.....**204** E3
Middlebury CT, *6974*.....**149** D1
Middlebury IN, *3420*.....**89** F2
Middlebury VT, *6588*.....**81** D3
Middle Falls NY, *750*.....**81** D4
Middlefield CT, *4281*.....**149** E1
Middlefield OH, *2694*.....**91** F2
Middle Haddam CT, *900*.....**149** E1
Middle Island NY, *10483*.....**149** D3
Middle Pt. OH, *593*.....**90** B3
Middleport NY, *1840*.....**78** B3
Middleport OH, *2530*.....**101** E2
Middle River MD, *25191*.....**144** C2
Middlesboro KY, *10334*.....**110** C3
Middlesex NJ, *13635*.....**147** D1
Middlesex NC, *822*.....**113** D4
Middlesex Co. CT, *165676*.....**149** E1
Middlesex Co. MA, *1503085*.....**151** D1
Middlesex Co. NJ, *809858*.....**147** E2
Middlesex Co. VA, *10959*.....**113** F1
Middleton ID, *5524*.....**22** B4
Middleton MA, *7744*.....**151** F1
Middleton TN, *706*.....**118** C2
Middleton WI, *17442*.....**74** B3
Middletown CA, *1323*.....**36** B2
Middletown CT, *47648*.....**149** E1
Middletown DE, *18871*.....**145** E1
Middletown IN, *2322*.....**89** F4
Middletown IA, *318*.....**87** F3
Middletown KY, *7218*.....**100** A4
Middletown MD, *4136*.....**144** A1
Middletown NY, *28086*.....**148** A1
Middletown OH, *48694*.....**100** B1
Middletown PA, *8901*.....**93** E4
Middletown PA, *7378*.....**189** B1
Middletown RI, *16150*.....**151** D4
Middletown VA, *1265*.....**102** C2
Middle Valley TN, *12684*.....**120** B1
Middleville MI, *3319*.....**75** F4
Middleville NY, *512*.....**79** F3
Midfield AL, *5365*.....**119** F4
Midland MI, *41863*.....**76** B2
Midland NC, *3073*.....**122** B1
Midland PA, *2635*.....**91** F3
Midland TX, *111147*.....**58** A3
Midland WA, *8962*.....**262** A5
Midland City AL, *2344*.....**128** B4
Midland Co. MI, *83629*.....**76** A2
Midland Co. TX, *136872*.....**58** A3
Midlothian IL, *14819*.....**203** D6
Midlothian TX, *18037*.....**59** F3
Midlothian VA, *3300*.....**113** E1
Midtown TN, *1360*.....**110** B4
Midvale UT, *27964*.....**257** B3
Midway AL, *499*.....**128** B3
Midway DE, *1500*.....**145** F4
Midway FL, *3004*.....**137** E2
Midway GA, *2121*.....**130** B3
Midway KY, *1641*.....**100** B4
Midway LA, *1291*.....**125** E4
Midway NM, *971*.....**57** E2
Midway NC, *4679*.....**112** B4
Midway PA, *2125*.....**91** F4
Midway TN, *2491*.....**111** D4
Midway UT, *3845*.....**31** F4
Midwest WY, *404*.....**25** D4
Midwest City OK, *54371*.....**51** E3
Mifflin PA, *642*.....**93** D4
Mifflinburg PA, *3540*.....**93** D3
Mifflin Co. PA, *46682*.....**93** D3
Mifflintown PA, *936*.....**93** D4
Mifflinville PA, *1253*.....**93** E3
Milaca MN, *2946*.....**66** C2
Milam TX, *1480*.....**124** C4
Milam Co. TX, *24757*.....**61** F1
Milan GA, *700*.....**129** E3
Milan IL, *5099*.....**88** A2
Milan IN, *1899*.....**100** A2
Milan MI, *5836*.....**90** C1
Milan MO, *1960*.....**87** D4
Milan NM, *3245*.....**48** B3
Milan OH, *1367*.....**91** D2
Milan TN, *7851*.....**108** C4
Milbank SD, *3353*.....**27** F2
Milbridge ME, *1279*.....**83** E2

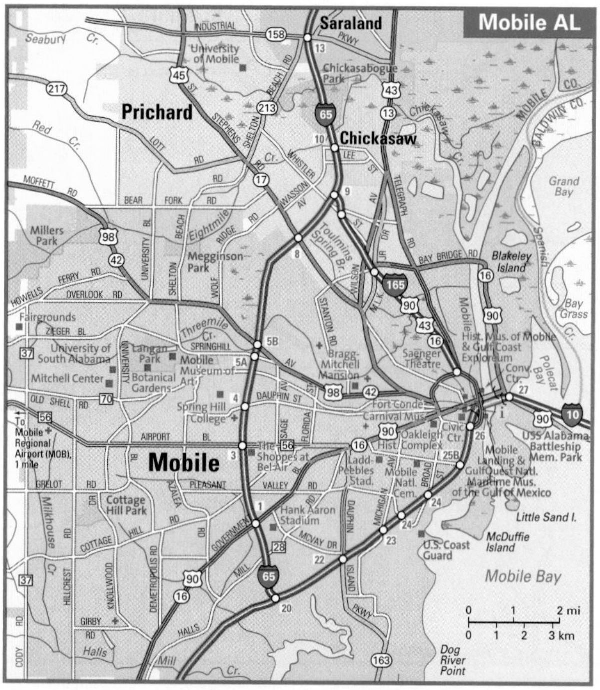

Aptos.....D1
Aromas.....E2
Ben Lomond.....D1
Bolsa Knolls.....E2
Capitola.....D1
Carmel-by-the-Sea.....D3
Carmel Highlands.....D3
Carmel Valley.....E3
Castroville.....E2
Corralitos.....E1
Del Rey Oaks.....E3
Elkhorn.....E2
Felton.....D1
Freedom.....E1
Gabilan Acres.....E2
Gilroy.....E1
La Selva Beach.....D1
Las Lomas.....E2
Live Oak.....D1
Marina.....E2
Monterey.....D3
Moss Landing.....E2
Mt. Hermon.....D1
Opal Cliffs.....D1
Pacific Grove.....D3
Pajaro.....E1
Paradise Park.....D1
Pebble Beach.....D3
Prunedale.....E2
Rio del Mar.....D1
Salinas.....E3
Sand City.....E3
Santa Cruz.....D1
Scotts Valley.....D1
Seaside.....E3
Soquel.....D1
Spreckels.....E3
Twin Lakes.....D1
Watsonville.....E1
Zayante.....D1

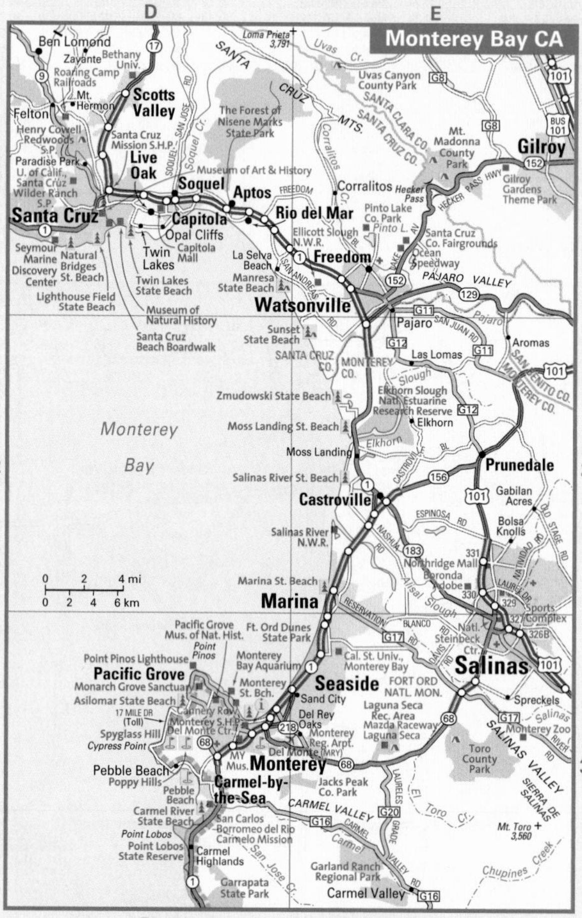

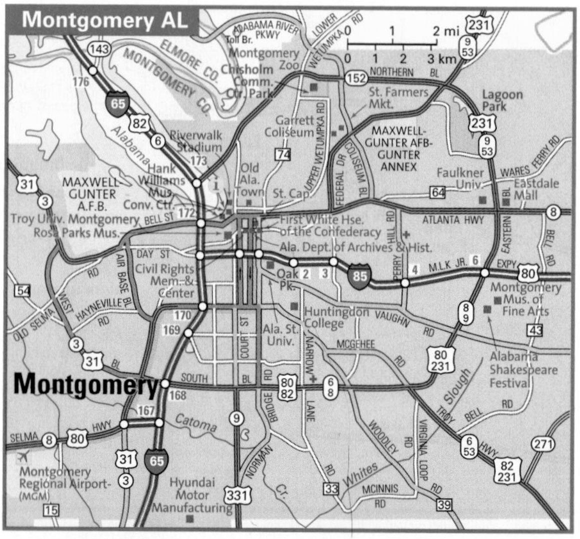

Entries in **bold black** indicate counties or parishes.
Entries in **bold color** indicate cities with detailed inset maps.

Miles TX, *829* **58** C4
Milesburg PA, *1123* **92** C3
Miles City MT, *8410* **17** E4
Milford CT, *51271* **149** D2
Milford DE, *9559* **145** F3
Milford IL, *1306* **89** D3
Milford IN, *1562* **89** F2
Milford IA, *2898* **72** A3
Milford KS, *530* **43** F2
Milford ME, *2233* **83** D1
Milford MD, *29042* **193** B2
Milford MA, *25055* **150** C2
Milford MI, *6175* **76** B4
Milford NE, *2090* **35** F4
Milford NH, *8835* **95** D1
Milford NJ, *1233* **146** C1
Milford NY, *415* **79** F4
Milford OH, *6709* **100** B2
Milford PA, *1021* **94** A3
Milford TX, *728* **59** F3
Milford UT, *1409* **39** D3
Milford Ctr. OH, *792* **90** C4
Milford Square PA, *897* **146** C1
Mililani Town HI, *27629* **152** A3
Millard Co. UT, *12503* **39** D2
Millbourne PA, *1159* **248** B3
Millbrae CA, *21532* **259** B4
Millbrook AL, *14640* **128** A2
Millbrook NY, *1452* **94** B3
Millburn NJ, *19765* **240** A3
Millbury MA, *13261* **150** C2
Millbury OH, *1200* **90** C2
Mill City NV, *300* **29** F4
Mill City OR, *1855* **20** C3
Mill Creek WA, *18244* **12** C3
Mill Creek WV, *724* **102** A3
Milledgeville GA, *17715* **129** E1
Milledgeville IL, *1032* **88** B1
Mille Lacs Co. MN, *26097* **66** C2
Millen GA, *3120* **129** F2
Miller MO, *699* **106** C2
Miller SD, *1489* **27** D3
Miller Co. AR, *43462* **124** C1
Miller Co. GA, *6125* **128** C4
Miller Co. MO, *24748* 97 E4
Miller Place NY, *12339* **149** D3
Millersburg IN, *903* **89** F2
Millersburg KY, *792* **100** B4
Millersburg OH, *3025* **91** E4
Millersburg OR, *1329* **20** B3
Millersburg PA, *2557* **93** D4
Millers Creek NC, *2112* **111** F3
Millers Falls MA, *1139* **94** C1
Millersport OH, *1044* **101** D1
Millerstown PA, *673* **93** D4
Millersville PA, *8168* **146** A3
Millersville TN, *6440* **109** F3
Millerton NY, *958* **94** B2
Mill Hall PA, *1613* **93** D3
Milliken CO, *5610* **33** E4
Millington MI, *1072* **76** B3
Millington NJ, *3500* **148** A4
Millington TN, *10176* **118** B1
Millinocket ME, *4466* **85** D4
Millis MA, *4403* **150** C2
Mill Neck NY, *997* **148** C3
Millport AL, *1049* **119** D4
Millry AL, *546* **127** D4
Mills WY, *3461* **33** D1
Millsboro DE, *3877* **145** F4
Mills Co. IA, *15059* **86** A3
Mills Co. TX, *4936* **59** D4
Millstadt IL, *4011* **98** A3
Millstone KY, *117* **111** E2
Milltown IN, *818* **99** F4
Milltown NJ, *6893* **147** E1
Milltown WI, *917* **67** E3
Millvale PA, *3744* **250** B1
Mill Valley CA, *13903* **36** B4
Millville CA, *727* **28** C4
Millville DE, *544* **145** F4
Millville NJ, *28400* **145** F1
Millville OH, *708* **100** B2
Millville PA, *948* **93** E3
Millville UT, *1829* **31** E3
Millwood NY, *2300* **148** B2
Millwood WA, *1786* **14** A3
Milner GA, *610* **129** D1
Milnor ND, *653* **27** E1
Milo IA, *775* **86** C2
Milo ME, *1847* **84** C4
Milpitas CA, *66790* **36** B4
Milroy IN, *604* **100** A2
Milroy PA, *1498* **93** D3
Milton DE, *2576* **145** F3
Milton FL, *8826* **135** F1
Milton IN, *490* **100** A1
Milton IA, *443* **87** E3
Milton KY, *574* **100** A3
Milton MA, *27003* **151** D1
Milton NH, *575* **81** F4
Milton NY, *1251* **148** B1
Milton PA, *7042* **93** D3
Milton VT, *1861* **81** D1
Milton WA, *6968* **262** B5
Milton WV, *2423* **101** E3
Milton WI, *5546* **74** B4
Milton-Freewater OR, *7050* **21** F1
Miltonvale KS, *539* **43** E2
Milwaukee WI, *594833* 74 C3
Milwaukee Co. WI, *947735* **75** D3
Milwaukie OR, *20291* **251** D2
Mimosa Park LA, *4500* **239** A2
Mims FL, *7058* **141** E1
Mina NV, *155* **37** F3
Minatare NE, *816* **33** F2
Minco OK, *1632* **51** E3
Minden IA, *599* **86** A2
Minden LA, *13082* **125** D2
Minden NE, *2923* **35** D4
Minden NV, *3001* **37** D2
Mineola NY, *18799* **148** C4
Mineola TX, *4515* **124** A2
Miner MO, *984* **108** B2
Mineral VA, *467* **103** D4
Mineral City OH, *727* **91** E4
Mineral Co. CO, *712* **40** C4
Mineral Co. MT, *4223* **14** C3
Mineral Co. NV, *4772* **37** E3
Mineral Co. WV, *28212* **102** C2
Mineral Pt. WI, *2487* **74** A3
Mineral Ridge OH, *3892* **276** B2
Mineral Sprs. AR, *1208* **116** C4
Mineral Sprs. NC, *2639* **122** B2
Mineral Wells TX, *16788* **59** E2
Mineral Wells WV, *1950* **101** E2
Miner Co. SD, *2389* **27** E3
Minersville PA, *4397* **93** E3
Minersville UT, *907* **39** D3
Minerva OH, *3720* **91** F3
Minerva Park OH, *1272* **206** B1
Minetto NY, *1069* **79** D2
Mineville NY, *1269* **81** D2
Mingo Co. WV, *26839* **101** E4
Mingo Jct. OH, *3454* **91** F4
Minidoka Co. ID, *20069* **31** D1
Minier IL, *1252* **88** B4
Minneapolis KS, *2032* **43** E2
Minneapolis MN, *382578* 67 D4
Minnehaha Co. SD, *169468* **27** F4
Minneola FL, *9403* **140** C1
Minneola KS, *745* **42** C4
Minneota MN, *1392* **27** F3
Minnesota Lake MN, *687* **72** C2
Minnetonka MN, *49734* **235** A3
Minnewaukan ND, *224* **19** D2
Minoa NY, *3449* **79** E3
Minocqua WI, *451* **68** B2
Minong WI, *527* **67** E2
Minonk IL, *2078* **88** B3
Minooka IL, *10924* **88** C2
Minor Hill TN, *537* **119** E2
Minot ME, *2248* **82** B3
Minot MA, *1100* **151** E2
Minot ND, *40888* **18** B2
Minster OH, *2805* **90** B4
Mint Hill NC, *22722* **122** B1
Minto ND, *604* **19** E2
Minturn CO, *1027* **41** D1
Mio MI, *1826* **70** C4
Miramar FL, *122041* **143** E2
Miramar Beach FL, *6146* **136** B2
Misenheimer NC, *728* **122** B1
Mishawaka IN, *48252* **89** F2
Mishicot WI, *1442* **75** D1
Missaukee Co. MI, *14849* **75** F1
Mission KS, *9323* **224** B3
Mission OR, *1037* **21** F1
Mission SD, *1182* **26** C4
Mission TX, *77058* **63** E4
Mission Bend TX, *36501* **220** A3
Mission Hills KS, *3498* **224** B4
Mission Viejo CA, *93305* **52** C3
Mississippi Co. AR, *46480* **108** B4
Mississippi Co. MO, *14358* **108** C2
Mississippi State MS, *4005* **119** D4
Missoula MT, *66788* 15 D4
Missoula Co. MT, *109299* **15** D4
Missouri City TX, *67358* **132** A3
Missouri Valley IA, *2838* **86** A2
Mitchell IN, *4350* **99** F3
Mitchell NE, *1702* **33** F2
Mitchell SD, *15254* **27** E4
Mitchell Co. GA, *23498* **137** E1
Mitchell Co. IA, *10776* **73** D2
Mitchell Co. KS, *6373* **43** E2
Mitchell Co. NC, *15579* **111** E4
Mitchell Co. TX, *9403* **58** B3
Mitchellville AR, *360* **117** F4
Mitchellville IA, *2254* **87** D2
Mi-Wuk Vil. CA, *941* **37** D3
Moab UT, *5046* **40** A3
Moapa NV, *1025* **46** B1
Moberly MO, *13974* **97** E2
Mobile AL, *195111* 135 E1
Mobile Co. AL, *412992* **135** E1
Mobridge SD, *3465* **26** C2
Mocksville NC, *5051* **112** A4
Moclips WA, *207* **12** B3
Modena NY, *1100* **148** B1
Modena PA, *535* **146** B3
Modesto CA, *201165* **36** C4
Modoc Co. CA, *9686* **29** D3
Moenkopi AZ, *964* **47** E2
Moffat Co. CO, *13795* **32** B4
Mogadore OH, *3853* **188** B2
Mohall ND, *783* **18** B1
Mohave Co. AZ, *200186* **46** B3
Mohave Valley AZ, *16715* **46** B3
Mohawk MI, *750* **65** F3
Mohawk NY, *2731* **79** F3
Mohegan CT, *3500* **149** F1
Mohnton PA, *3043* **146** A2
Mohrsville PA, *383* **146** A1
Mojave CA, *4238* **52** C1
Mokelumne Hill CA, *646* **36** C3
Mokuleia HI, *1811* **152** A2
Molalla OR, *8108* **20** C2
Molena GA, *368* **128** C1
Moline IL, *43483* **88** A2
Moline KS, *371* **43** F4
Moline Acres MO, *2442* **256** C1
Molino FL, *1277* **135** F1
Momence IL, *3310* **89** D2
Mona UT, *1547* **39** E1
Monaca PA, *5737* **91** F3
Monahans TX, *6953* **57** F4
Monarch Mill SC, *1811* **121** F2
Moncks Corner SC, *7885* **131** D1
Mondovi WI, *2777* **67** E4
Monee IL, *5148* **89** D2
Monessen PA, *7720* **92** A4
Monett MO, *8873* **106** C2
Monette AR, *1501* **108** A4
Monfort Hts. OH, *11948* **204** A2
Moniteau Co. MO, *15607* **97** D3
Monmouth IL, *9444* **88** A3
Monmouth ME, *3785* **82** B2
Monmouth OR, *9534* **20** B2
Monmouth Beach NJ, *3279* **147** F2
Monmouth Co. NJ, *630380* **147** E2
Monmouth Jct. NJ, *2887* **147** D1
Mono Co. CA, *14202* **37** E4
Monon IN, *1777* **89** E3
Monona IA, *1549* **73** F3
Monona WI, *7533* **74** B3
Monona Co. IA, *9243* **86** A1
Monongah WV, *1044* **102** A2
Monongahela PA, *4300* **92** A4
Monongalia Co. WV, *96189* **102** A1
Monponsett MA, *1700* **151** E2
Monroe CT, *19650* **149** D2
Monroe GA, *13234* **121** D4
Monroe IN, *842* **90** A3
Monroe IA, *1830* **87** D2
Monroe LA, *48815* **125** E2
Monroe MI, *20733* **90** C1
Monroe NY, *8364* **148** B2
Monroe NC, *32797* **122** B2
Monroe OH, *12442* **100** B2
Monroe OR, *617* **20** B3
Monroe UT, *2256* **39** E3
Monroe VA, *1200* **112** C1
Monroe WA, *17304* **12** C3
Monroe WI, *10827* **74** B4
Monroe City IN, *545* **99** E3
Monroe City MO, *2531* **97** E1
Monroe Co. AL, *23068* **127** F4
Monroe Co. AR, *8149* **118** A2
Monroe Co. FL, *73090* **143** D3
Monroe Co. GA, *26424* **129** D1
Monroe Co. IL, *32957* **98** A4
Monroe Co. IN, *137974* **99** F2
Monroe Co. IA, *7970* **87** D3
Monroe Co. KY, *10963* **110** A2
Monroe Co. MI, *152021* **90** C1
Monroe Co. MS, *36989* **119** D4
Monroe Co. MO, *8840* **97** E2
Monroe Co. NY, *744344* **78** C3
Monroe Co. OH, *14642* **101** F1
Monroe Co. PA, *169842* **93** F3
Monroe Co. TN, *44519* **120** C1
Monroe Co. WV, *13502* **112** A1
Monroe Co. WI, *44673* **73** F1
Monroeville AL, *6519* **127** F4
Monroeville IN, *1235* **90** A3
Monroeville OH, *1400* **91** D2
Monroeville PA, *28386* **92** A4
Monrovia CA, *36590* **228** E2
Monrovia IN, *1063* **99** F1
Monsey NY, *18412* **148** B2
Monson MA, *2107* **150** A2
Montague CA, *1443* **28** C3
Montague MA, *8489* **94** C1
Montague MI, *2361* **75** E2
Montague TX, *304* **59** E1
Montague Co. TX, *19719* **59** E1
Mont Alto PA, *1705* **103** D1
Montana City MT, *2715* **15** E4
Montara CA, *2909* **259** A4
Montauk NY, *3326* **149** F3
Mont Belvieu TX, *3835* **132** B3
Montcalm WV, *726* **111** F1
Montcalm Co. MI, *63342* **75** F2
Montclair CA, *36664* **229** G2
Montclair NJ, *37669* **148** A3
Mont Clare PA, *1900* **146** B2
Monteagle TN, *1192* **120** A1
Monte Alto TX, *1924* **63** E4
Montebello CA, *62500* **228** D3
Montecito CA, *8965* **52** B2
Montegut LA, *1540* **134** B4

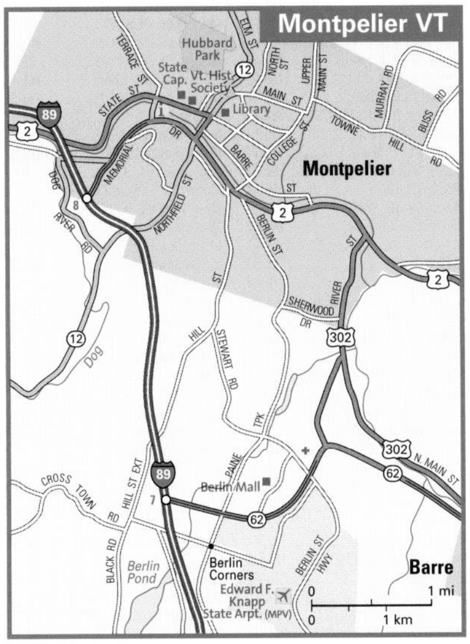

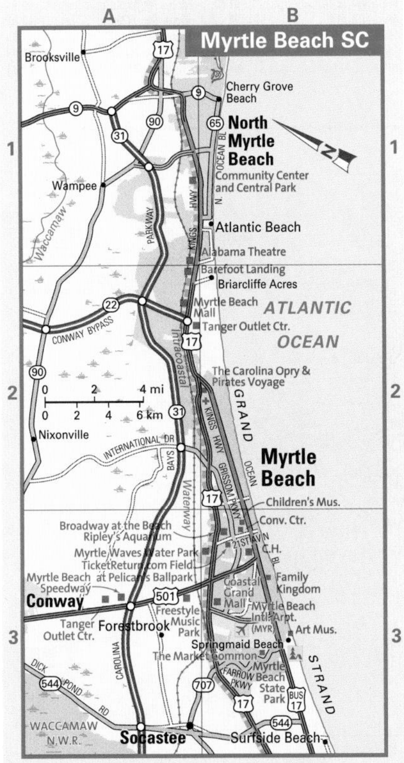

Atlantic Beach . . . B1
Briarcliffe Acres . B2
Brooksville A1
Cherry Grove Beach B1
Conway A3
Forestbrook A3
Myrtle Beach B2
Nixonville A2
N. Myrtle Beach . B1
Socastee A3
Springmaid Beach B3
Surfside Beach . . B3
Wampee A1

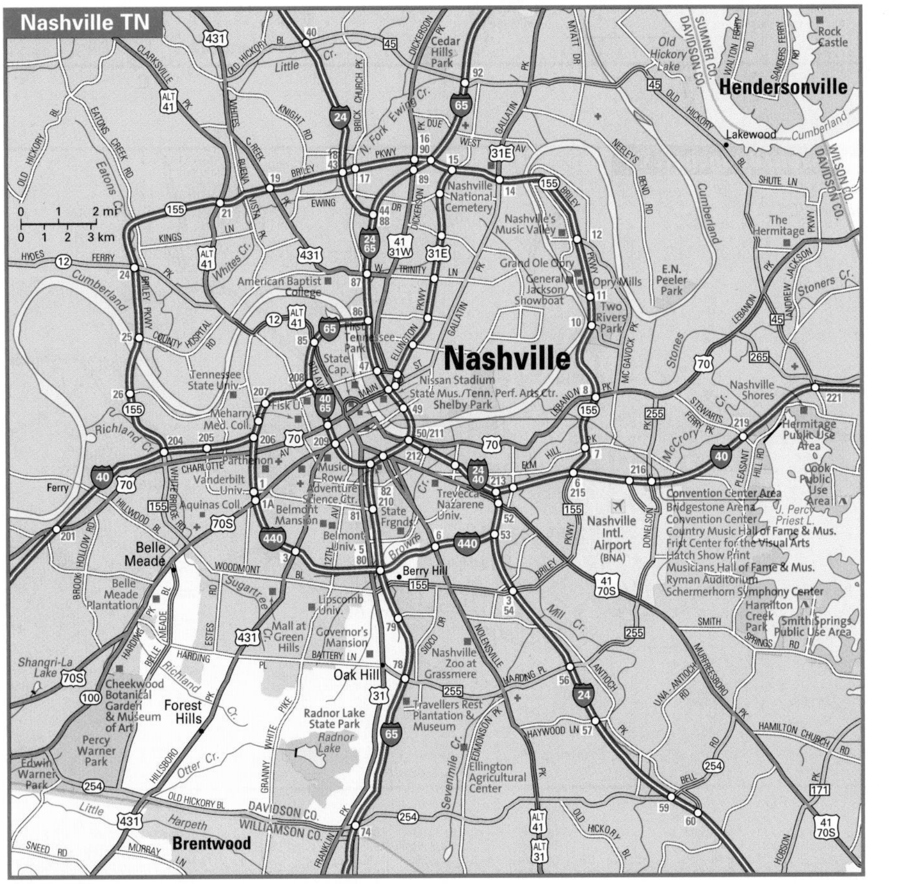

Figures after entries indicate population, page number, and grid reference.

Montello WI, *1495* **74** B2
Monterey CA, *27810* **44** B3
Monterey TN, *2850* **110** B4
Monterey VA, *147* **102** B3
Monterey Co. CA, *415057* **44** B3
Monterey Park CA, *60269* **228** D2
Monte Rio CA, *1152* **36** A3
Montesano WA, *3976* **12** B4
Montevallo AL, *6323* **127** F1
Montevideo MN, *5383* **66** A4
Monte Vista CO, *4444* **41** D4
Montezuma GA, *3460* **129** D3
Montezuma IN, *1022* **99** E1
Montezuma IA, *1462* **87** D2
Montezuma KS, *966* **42** C4
Montezuma Co. CO, *25535* **48** A1
Montezuma Creek UT, *335* **40** A4
Montfort WI, *718* **74** A3
Montgomery AL, *205764* **128** A2
Montgomery IL, *18438* **203** A5
Montgomery LA, *730* **125** D4
Montgomery MN, *2956* **72** C1
Montgomery NY, *3814* **148** A1
Montgomery OH, *10251* **204** C1
Montgomery PA, *1579* **93** D2
Montgomery WV, *1638* **101** F4
Montgomery City MO, *2834* **97** F2
Montgomery Co. AL, *229363* **128** A3
Montgomery Co. AR, *9487* **116** C3
Montgomery Co. GA, *9123* **129** F3
Montgomery Co. IL, *30104* **98** B2
Montgomery Co. IN, *38124* **89** E4
Montgomery Co. IA, *10740* **86** B3
Montgomery Co. KS, *35471* **106** A1
Montgomery Co. KY, *26499* **100** C4
Montgomery Co. MD, *971777* **144** B2
Montgomery Co. MS, *10925* **118** B4
Montgomery Co. MO, *12236* **97** F2
Montgomery Co. NY, *50219* **94** A1
Montgomery Co. NC, *27798* **122** C1
Montgomery Co. OH, *535153* **100** B1
Montgomery Co. PA, *799874* **146** B2
Montgomery Co. TN, *172331* **109** E3
Montgomery Co. TX, *455746* **132** A2
Montgomery Co. VA, *94392* **112** A2
Montgomery Vil. MD, *32032* **144** B2
Montgomeryville PA, *12624* **146** C2
Monticello AR, *9467* **117** F4
Monticello FL, *2506* **137** E2
Monticello GA, *2657* **129** D1
Monticello IL, *5548* **98** C1
Monticello IN, *5378* **89** E3
Monticello IA, *3796* **87** F1
Monticello KY, *6188* **110** B2
Monticello MN, *12759* **66** C3
Monticello MS, *1571* **126** B4
Monticello MO, *98* **87** E4
Monticello NY, *6726* **148** A1
Monticello UT, *1972* **40** A4
Monticello WI, *1217* **74** B4
Montmorency Co. MI, *9765* **70** C4
Montour Co. PA, *18267* **93** E3
Montour Falls NY, *1711* **79** D4
Montoursville PA, *4615* **93** D2
Montpelier ID, *2597* **31** F2
Montpelier IN, *1805* **90** A4
Montpelier OH, *4072* **90** B2
Montpelier VT, *7855* **81** E2
Montreal WI, *807* **65** E4
Montreat NC, *723* **111** E4
Montrose AR, *354* **125** F1
Montrose CA, *18532* **228** D1
Montrose CO, *19132* **40** B3
Montrose IA, *898* **87** F4
Montrose MI, *1657* **76** B3
Montrose MN, *2847* **66** C3
Montrose NY, *2731* **148** B2
Montrose OH, *5177* **188** A1
Montrose PA, *1617* **93** E1
Montrose SD, *472* **27** F4
Montrose Co. CO, *41276* **40** B3
Montross VA, *384* **103** E4
Montvale NJ, *7844* **148** B3
Montverde FL, *1463* **140** C1
Mont Vernon NH, *2409* **95** D1
Montville NJ, *21150* **148** A3
Montz LA, *1918* **239** A1
Monument CO, *5530* **41** E2
Monument Beach MA, *2790* **151** E3
Moodus CT, *1413* **149** E1
Moody AL, *11726* **119** F4
Moody ME, *1000* **82** B4
Moody TX, *1371* **59** E4
Moody Co. SD, *6486* **27** F3
Moonachie NJ, *2708* **240** C2
Moorcroft WY, *1009* **25** E3
Moore ID, *189* **23** D4
Moore MT, *193* **16** B4
Moore OK, *55081* **51** E3
Moore TX, *475* **61** D3
Moore Co. NC, *88247* **122** C1
Moore Co. TN, *6362* **120** A1
Moore Co. TX, *21904* **50** A2
Moorefield WV, *2544* **102** C2
Moore Haven FL, *1680* **141** D4
Mooreland OK, *1190* **51** D1
Moores Hill IN, *597* **100** A2
Moorestown NJ, *19487* **147** D3
Mooresville IN, *9326* **99** F1
Mooresville NC, *32711* **122** B1
Moorhead MN, *38065* **19** F4
Moorhead MS, *2405* **118** A4
Mooringsport LA, *793* **124** C2
Moorland KY, *431* **230** F1
Moorpark CA, *34421* **52** B2
Moose Lake MN, *2751* **64** C4
Moosic PA, *5719* **261** D2
Moosup CT, *3231* **150** B3
Mora MN, *3571* **67** D2
Mora NM, *656* **49** D2
Mora Co. NM, *4881* **49** D2
Morada CA, *3828* **36** C3
Moraga CA, *16016* **259** D2
Moraine OH, *6307* **100** B1
Moran KS, *558* **96** A4
Moravia IA, *665* **87** D3
Moravia NY, *1282* **79** D4
Moravian Falls NC, *1901* **111** F4
Moreauville LA, *929* **133** F1
Morehead KY, *6845* **100** C4
Morehead City NC, *8661* **115** E4
Morehouse MO, *973* **108** B2
Morehouse Par. LA, *27979* **125** F1
Moreland KY, *550* **110** B1
Moreland Hills OH, *3320* **204** G2
Morenci AZ, *1489* **55** E2
Morenci MI, *2220* **90** B1
Moreno Valley CA, *193365* **53** D3
Morgan GA, *240* **128** C4
Morgan MN, *896* **72** B1
Morgan UT, *3687* **31** F3
Morgan City LA, *12404* **134** A3
Morgan Co. AL, *119490* **119** F3
Morgan Co. CO, *28159* **33** F4
Morgan Co. GA, *17868* **121** D4
Morgan Co. IL, *35547* **98** A1
Morgan Co. IN, *68894* **99** F2
Morgan Co. KY, *13923* **100** C4
Morgan Co. MO, *20565* **97** D3
Morgan Co. OH, *15054* **101** E1
Morgan Co. TN, *21987* **110** B3
Morgan Co. UT, *9469* **31** F3
Morgan Co. WV, *17541* **102** C1
Morganfield KY, *3285* **109** D1
Morgan Hill CA, *37882* **44** B2
Morgan's Pt. Resort TX, *4170* **59** E4
Morganton NC, *16918* **111** F4
Morgantown IN, *986* **99** F2
Morgantown KY, *2394* **109** F2
Morgantown PA, *826* **146** B2
Morgantown WV, *29660* **102** A1
Morganville NJ, *5040* **147** E1
Morganza LA, *610* **133** F1
Moriarty NM, *1910* **49** D3
Moriches NY, *2838* **149** D4
Morley MI, *493* **75** F2
Morley MO, *697* **108** B2
Morningdale MA, *2500* **275** D1
Morningside MD, *2015* **271** F4
Morning Sun IA, *836* **87** F3
Moro OR, *324* **21** D2
Morocco IN, *1129* **89** D3
Morongo Valley CA, *3552* **53** D2
Moroni UT, *1423* **39** E1
Morrice MI, *927* **76** B3
Morrill NE, *921* **33** F2
Morrill Co. NE, *5042* **34** A2
Morrilton AR, *6767* **117** E1
Morris AL, *1859* **119** F4
Morris IL, *13636* **88** C2
Morris MN, *5286* **27** F1
Morris NY, *583* **79** E4
Morris OK, *1479* **116** A1
Morris Co. KS, *5923* **43** F3
Morris Co. NJ, *492276* **94** A4
Morris Co. TX, *12934* **124** B1

Acushnet C1
Bliss Corner C2
Braleys C1
Coury Hts. C1
Eagleville A2
Fairhaven C2
Fall River B1
Faunce Corner C1
Head of Westport B2
Hixville B1
Idlewood C2
Island Park A2
Lakeside B2
Long Plain C1
New Bedford C2
N. Dartmouth C2
N. Fairhaven C2
N. Tiverton A2
Ocean Grove A1
Sherwood Forest C1
Somerset A1
S. Dartmouth C2
S. Swansea A1
Summit Grove B2
Swansea A1
The Hummocks A2
Tiverton A2
Westport Factory B2

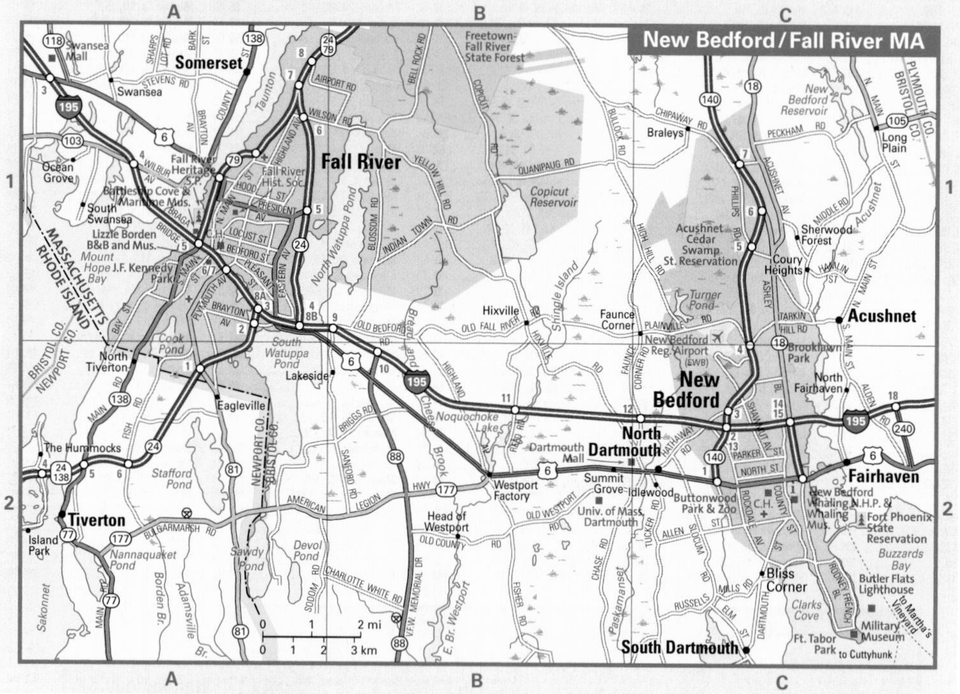

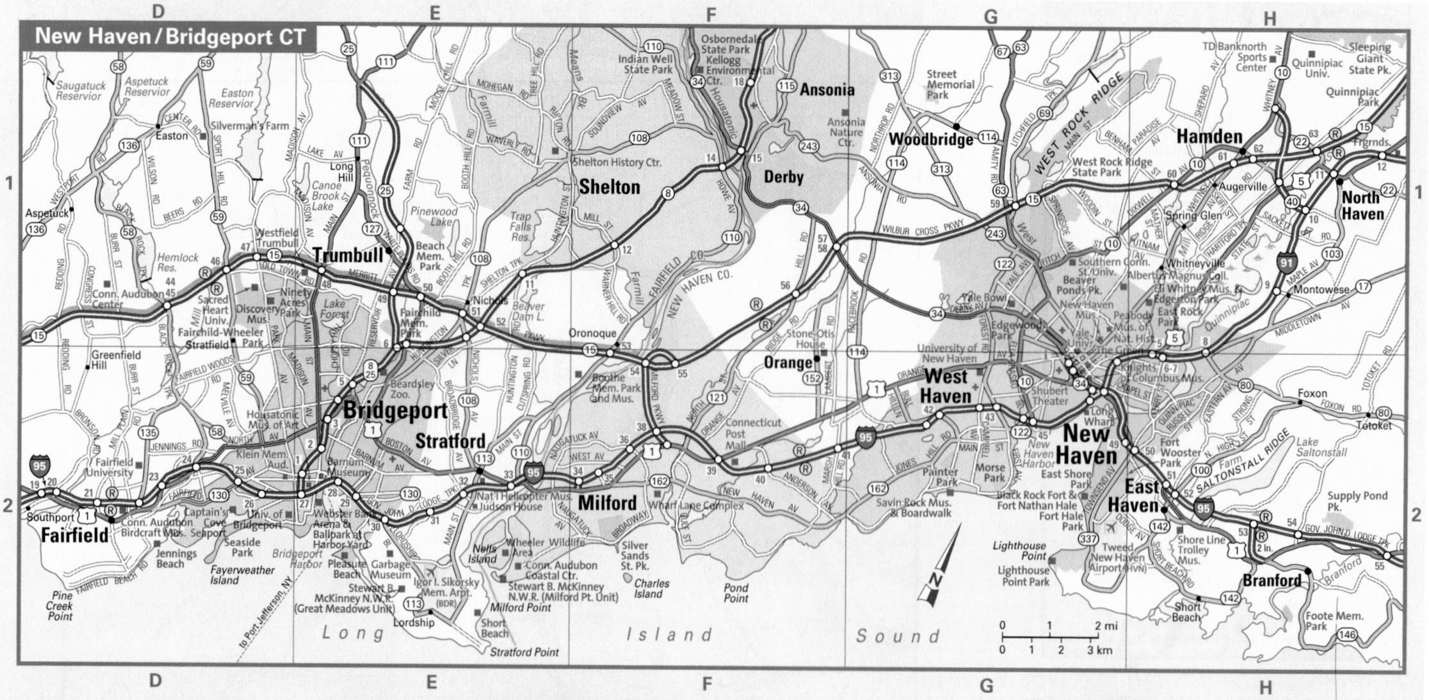

Ansonia F1
Aspetuck D1
Augerville H1
Branford H2
Bridgeport E2
Derby F1
E. Haven H2
Easton D1
Fairfield D2
Foxon H2
Greenfield Hill D2
Hamden H1
Long Hill E1
Lordship E2
Milford F2
Montowese H1
New Haven G2
Nichols E1
N. Haven H1
Orange F2
Oronoque F1
Shelton F1
Short Beach H2
Southport D2
Spring Glen H1
Stratfield D1
Stratford E2
Totoket H2
Trumbull E1
W. Haven G2
Whitneyville H1
Woodbridge G1

Entries in **bold black** indicate counties or parishes.
Entries in **bold color** indicate cities with detailed inset maps.

Ama.....B2
Arabi.....C1
Avondale.....B2
Belle Chasse.....C2
Boutte.....A2
Braithwaite.....D2
Bridge City.....B2
Caernarvon.....D2
Chalmette.....C2
Dalcour.....C2
Des Allemands.....A2
Destrehan.....A2
English Turn.....C2
Estelle.....C2
Frenier.....A1
Gretna.....C2
Hahnville.....A1
Harahan.....B2
Harvey.....C2
Jefferson.....B1
Kenilworth.....D2
Kenner.....B1
Killona.....A1
Laplace.....A1
Lone Star.....A2
Lucy.....A1
Luling.....A2
Marrero.....C2
Meraux.....D2
Metairie.....C1
Mimosa Park.....A2
Montz.....A1
New Orleans.....D1
New Sarpy.....A1
Norco.....A1
Oakville.....C2
Paradis.....A2
Poydras.....D2
River Ridge.....B1
St. Bernard.....D2
St. Rose.....B1
Scarsdale.....C2
Taft.....A1
Terrytown.....C2
Toca.....D2
Verret.....D2
Violet.....D2
Waggaman.....B2
Westwego.....B2

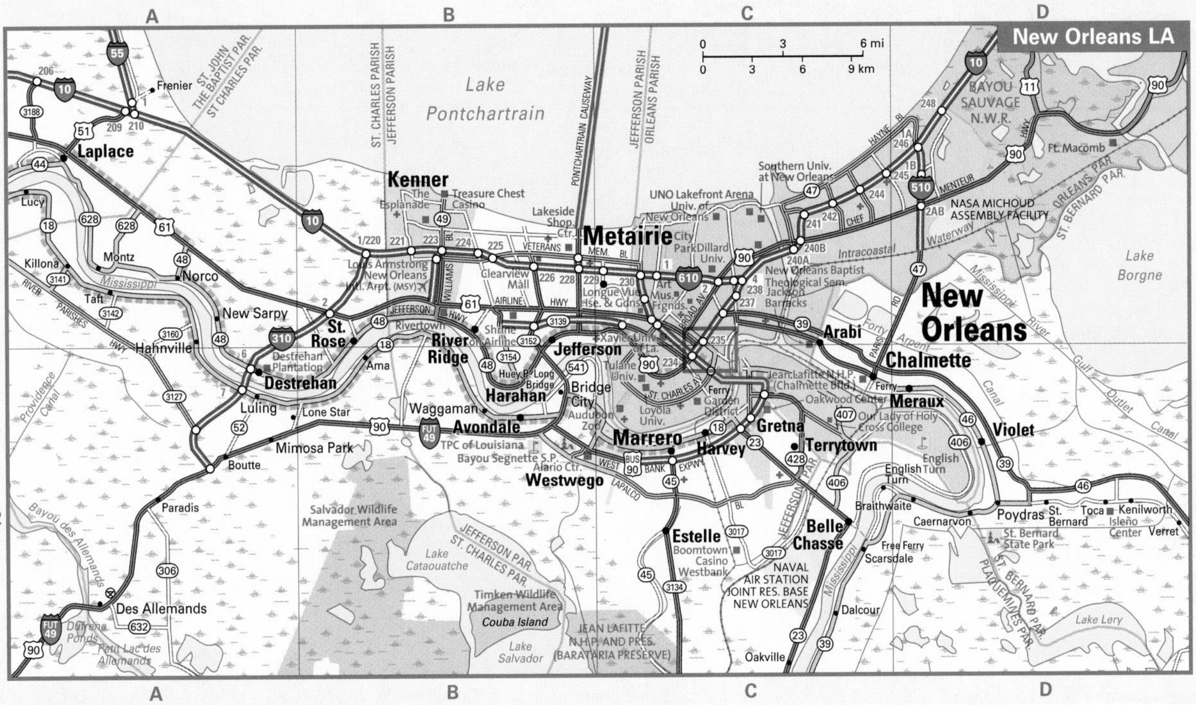

POINTS OF INTEREST

Audubon Aquarium of the Americas.....F2
Audubon Insectarium.....F2
The Cabildo.....F1
Contemporary Arts Center.....F2
Creole Queen.....F2
Ernest N. Morial Convention Center.....F2
French Quarter (Vieux Carré).....F1
Harrah's.....F2
Jackson Square.....F1
Jean Lafitte Natl. Hist. Park (Visitor Center).....F1
Louisiana's Civil War Museum at Confederate Memorial Hall.....F2
Mercedes-Benz Superdome.....E2
M. Jackson Theatre for the Performing Arts.....F1
National World War II Museum.....F2
New Orleans Jazz N.H.P. Visitor Center.....F1
Ogden Museum.....F2
Old U.S. Mint.....F1
One Canal Place.....F2
Orpheum Theatre.....F1
Pontalba Buildings.....F1
The Presbytère.....F1
Public Library.....E2
Saenger Theatre.....F1
St. Charles Avenue Streetcar.....F2
St. Louis Cathedral.....F1
Smoothie King Center.....E2
Woldenberg Riverfront Park.....F2

Morrison CO, *428*.....**209** A4
Morrison IL, *4188*.....**88** A1
Morrison OK, *733*.....**51** F2
Morrison TN, *694*.....**120** A1
Morrison Co. MN, *33198*.....**66** C2
Morrisonville IL, *1056*.....**98** B2
Morrisonville NY, *1545*.....**81** D1
Morris Plains NJ, *5532*.....**148** A3
Morristown IN, *1218*.....**100** A1
Morristown MN, *987*.....**72** C1
Morristown NJ, *18411*.....**148** A4
Morristown TN, *29137*.....**111** D3
Morrisville NY, *2199*.....**79** E3
Morrisville NC, *18576*.....**112** C4
Morrisville PA, *1443*.....**102** A1
Morrisville PA, *8728*.....**147** D2
Morrisville VT, *1958*.....**81** E2
Morrisville VA, *550*.....**144** A4
Morro Bay CA, *10234*.....**44** B4
Morrow GA, *6445*.....**120** C4
Morrow OH, *1188*.....**100** C2
Morrow Co. OH, *34827*.....**91** D4
Morrow Co. OR, *11173*.....**21** E2
Morse LA, *812*.....**133** E2
Morton IL, *16267*.....**88** B3
Morton MS, *3462*.....**126** C2
Morton PA, *2669*.....**248** B4
Morton TX, *2006*.....**57** F1
Morton WA, *1126*.....**12** C4
Morton Co. KS, *3233*.....**42** A4
Morton Co. ND, *27471*.....**18** B4
Morton Grove IL, *23270*.....**203** D3
Mortons Gap KY, *863*.....**109** E2
Morven GA, *565*.....**137** F1
Morven NC, *511*.....**122** B2
Moscow ID, *23800*.....**14** B4
Moscow ME, *577*.....**82** B1
Moscow PA, *2026*.....**93** F2
Moscow TN, *556*.....**118** C2
Moscow Mills MO, *2509*.....**97** F2
Moses Lake WA, *20366*.....**13** E3
Mosheim TN, *2362*.....**111** D3
Mosier OR, *433*.....**21** D1
Mosinee WI, *3988*.....**68** B4
Mosquero NM, *93*.....**49** E2
Moss Beach CA, *3103*.....**259** A5
Moss Bluff LA, *11557*.....**133** D2
Mosses AL, *1029*.....**127** F3
Moss Pt. MS, *13704*.....**135** D2
Mossville IL, *1000*.....**88** B3
Mossyrock WA, *759*.....**12** C4
Motley MN, *671*.....**64** A4
Motley Co. TX, *1210*.....**50** B4
Mott ND, *721*.....**18** A4
Moulton AL, *3471*.....**119** E3
Moulton IA, *605*.....**87** D3
Moulton TX, *886*.....**61** E2
Moultrie GA, *14268*.....**137** E1
Moultrie Co. IL, *14846*.....**98** C1
Mound MN, *9052*.....**66** C4
Mound Bayou MS, *1533*.....**118** A4
Mound City IL, *588*.....**108** C2
Mound City KS, *694*.....**96** B4
Mound City MO, *1159*.....**86** A4
Mound City SD, *71*.....**26** C1
Moundridge KS, *1737*.....**43** E3
Mounds IL, *810*.....**108** C2
Mounds OK, *1168*.....**51** F2
Mounds View MN, *12155*.....**235** C1
Moundsville WV, *9318*.....**101** F1
Mound Valley KS, *407*.....**106** A2
Moundville AL, *2427*.....**127** E1
Mt. Aetna MD, *561*.....**144** A1
Mountainair NM, *928*.....**48** C4
Mountainaire AZ, *1119*.....**47** E3
Mtn. Brook AL, *20413*.....**119** F4
Mountainburg AR, *631*.....**116** C1
Mtn. City GA, *1088*.....**121** D2
Mtn. City TN, *2531*.....**111** F3
Mtn. City TX, *648*.....**61** E2
Mtn. Grove MO, *4789*.....**107** E2
Mtn. Home AR, *12448*.....**107** E3
Mtn. Home ID, *14206*.....**30** B1
Mtn. Home NC, *3622*.....**121** E1
Mountainhome PA, *1182*.....**93** F2
Mtn. Iron MN, *2869*.....**64** C3
Mtn. Lake MN, *2104*.....**72** B1
Mtn. Lake Park MD, *2092*.....**102** B2
Mtn. Lakes NJ, *4160*.....**148** A3
Mtn. Pine AR, *770*.....**117** D2
Mtn. Ranch CA, *1628*.....**36** C3
Mountainside NJ, *6685*.....**148** A4
Mtn. Top PA, *10982*.....**93** E2
Mtn. View AR, *2748*.....**107** E4
Mtn. View CA, *74066*.....**259** D5
Mtn. View CO, *507*.....**209** B3
Mtn. View HI, *3924*.....**153** F3
Mtn. View MO, *2719*.....**107** F2
Mtn. View OK, *795*.....**51** D3
Mtn. View WY, *1286*.....**32** A3
Mtn. Vil. AK, *813*.....**154** B2
Mtn. Vil. CO, *1320*.....**40** B3
Mt. Airy GA, *1284*.....**121** D3
Mt. Airy MD, *9288*.....**144** B1
Mt. Airy NC, *10388*.....**112** A3
Mt. Angel OR, *3286*.....**20** C2
Mt. Arlington NJ, *5050*.....**148** A3
Mt. Ayr IA, *1691*.....**86** C3
Mt. Bethel NJ, *1000*.....**147** D1
Mt. Calvary WI, *762*.....**74** C2
Mt. Carmel IL, *7284*.....**99** D3
Mt. Carmel OH, *4741*.....**204** C2
Mt. Carmel PA, *5893*.....**93** E3
Mt. Carmel TN, *5429*.....**111** E3
Mt. Carroll IL, *1717*.....**88** A1
Mt. Clemens MI, *16314*.....**76** C4
Mt. Cobb PA, *1799*.....**93** F2
Mt. Crested Butte CO, *801*.....**40** C2
Mt. Dora FL, *12370*.....**141** D1
Mt. Enterprise TX, *447*.....**124** B3
Mt. Ephraim NJ, *4676*.....**248** C4
Mt. Freedom NJ, *2000*.....**148** A3
Mt. Gay WV, *1779*.....**101** E4
Mt. Gilead NC, *1181*.....**122** B1
Mt. Gilead OH, *3660*.....**91** D4
Mt. Healthy OH, *6098*.....**204** A1
Mt. Holly NJ, *10602*.....**147** D3
Mt. Holly NC, *13656*.....**122** A1
Mt. Holly Sprs. PA, *2030*.....**93** D4
Mt. Hope KS, *813*.....**43** E4
Mt. Hope WV, *1414*.....**101** F4
Mt. Horeb WI, *7009*.....**74** A3
Mt. Ida AR, *1076*.....**116** C2
Mt. Ivy NY, *6878*.....**148** B2
Mt. Jackson VA, *1994*.....**102** C3
Mt. Jewett PA, *919*.....**92** B1
Mt. Joy PA, *7410*.....**93** E4
Mt. Juliet TN, *23671*.....**109** F3
Mt. Kisco NY, *10877*.....**148** C2
Mountlake Terrace WA, *19909*.....**262** B2
Mt. Lebanon PA, *33137*.....**92** A4
Mt. Morris IL, *2998*.....**88** B1
Mt. Morris MI, *3086*.....**76** B3
Mt. Morris NY, *2986*.....**78** C4
Mt. Nebo PA, *1000*.....**146** A3
Mt. Olive AL, *4079*.....**119** F4
Mt. Olive IL, *2099*.....**98** B2
Mt. Olive MS, *982*.....**126** C3
Mt. Olive NC, *4589*.....**123** E1
Mt. Oliver PA, *3403*.....**250** B2
Mt. Olivet KY, *299*.....**100** C3
Mt. Orab OH, *3664*.....**100** C2
Mt. Pleasant AR, 401.....**107** F4
Mt. Pleasant IA, *8668*.....**87** F3
Mt. Pleasant MI, *26016*.....**76** A2
Mt. Pleasant NC, *1652*.....**122** B1
Mt. Pleasant PA, *4454*.....**92** A4
Mt. Pleasant SC, *67843*.....**131** D2
Mt. Pleasant TN, *4561*.....**119** E1
Mt. Pleasant TX, *15564*.....**124** B1
Mt. Pleasant UT, *3260*.....**39** E1
Mt. Pleasant WI, *26197*.....**75** D4
Mt. Plymouth FL, *4011*.....**141** D1
Mt. Pocono PA, *3170*.....**93** F3
Mt. Prospect IL, *54167*.....**203** C3
Mt. Pulaski IL, *1566*.....**98** B1
Mountrail Co. ND, *7673*.....**18** A2
Mt. Rainier MD, *8080*.....**270** E2
Mt. Royal NJ, *1800*.....**146** C3
Mt. Savage MD, *873*.....**102** C1
Mt. Shasta CA, *3394*.....**28** C3
Mt. Sidney VA, *663*.....**102** C4
Mt. Sinai NY, *12118*.....**149** D3
Mt. Sterling IL, *2025*.....**98** A1
Mt. Sterling KY, *6895*.....**100** C4
Mt. Sterling OH, *1782*.....**101** D1
Mt. Union PA, *2447*.....**92** C4
Mt. Vernon AL, *1574*.....**135** E1
Mt. Vernon GA, *2451*.....**129** F3
Mt. Vernon IL, *15277*.....**98** C4
Mt. Vernon IN, *6687*.....**99** D4
Mt. Vernon IA, *4506*.....**87** F1
Mt. Vernon KY, *2477*.....**110** C1
Mt. Vernon MD, *779*.....**103** F4
Mt. Vernon MO, *4575*.....**106** C2
Mt. Vernon NY, *4400*.....**78** A4
Mt. Vernon NY, *67292*.....**148** B3
Mt. Vernon OH, *16990*.....**91** D4
Mt. Vernon OR, *527*.....**21** E3
Mt. Vernon SD, *462*.....**27** E4
Mt. Vernon TX, *2662*.....**124** B1
Mt. Vernon VA, *12416*.....**144** B4
Mt. Vernon WA, *31743*.....**12** C2
Mt. Victory OH, *627*.....**90** C4
Mt. View RI, *750*.....**150** C4
Mountville PA, *2802*.....**103** E1
Mt. Washington KY, *9117*.....**100** A4
Mt. Wolf PA, *1393*.....**93** E4
Mt. Zion GA, *1696*.....**120** B4
Mt. Zion IL, *5833*.....**98** C1
Moville IA, *1618*.....**35** F1
Moweaqua IL, *1831*.....**98** C1
Mower Co. MN, *39163*.....**73** D2
Moxee WA, *3308*.....**13** D4
Moyie Sprs. ID, *718*.....**14** B1
Mud Lake ID, *358*.....**23** E4
Muenster TX, *1544*.....**59** E1
Muhlenberg Co. KY, *31499*.....**109** E2
Muir MI, *604*.....**76** A3

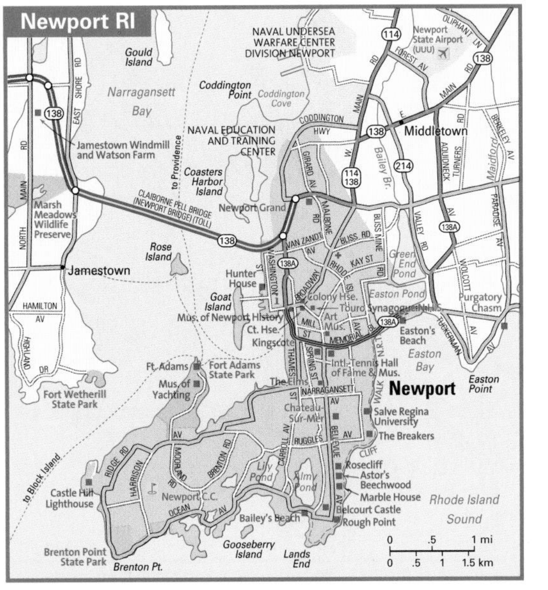

Figures after entries indicate population, page number, and grid reference.

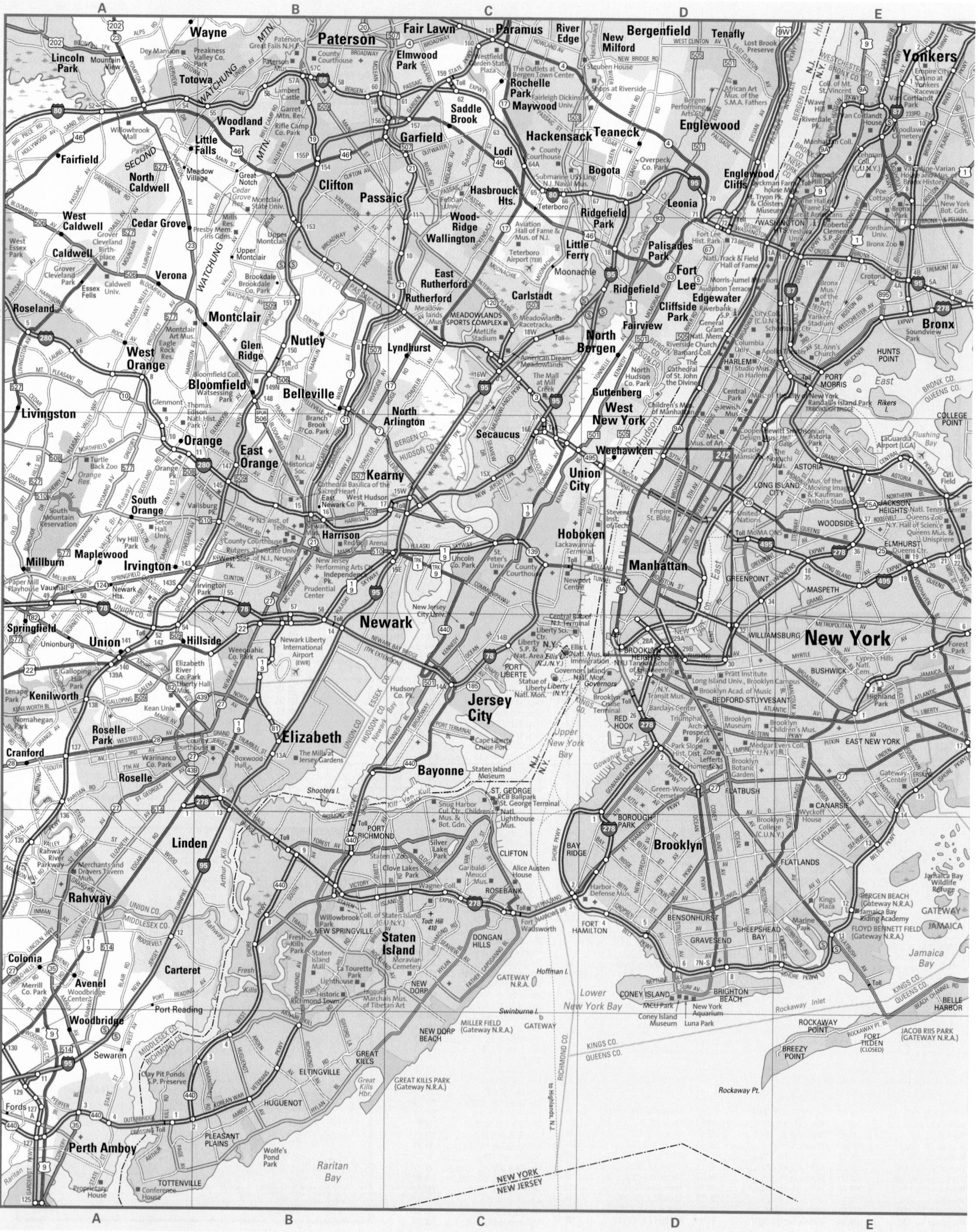

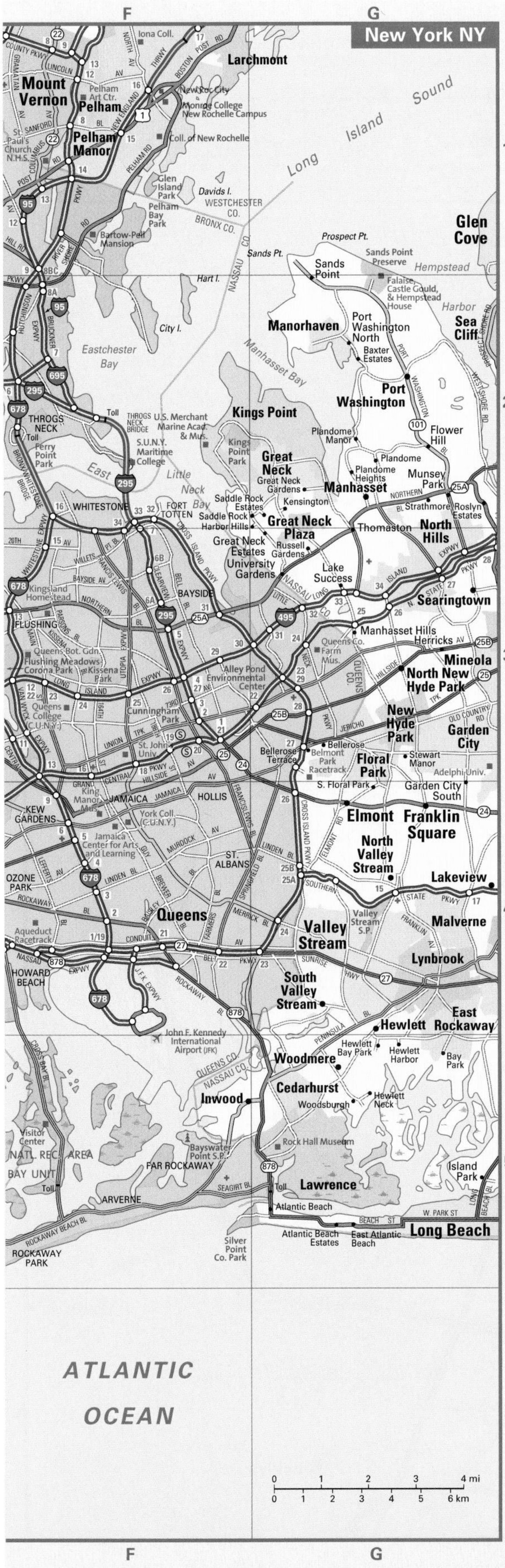

Atlantic Beach G5
Atlantic Beach Estates G5
Avenel A5
Baxter Estates G2
Bayonne C4
Bay Park G5
Bellerose G3
Bellerose Terrace G3
Belleville B2
Bergenfield D1
Bloomfield B2
Bogota D1
Brookdale B2
Caldwell A2
Carlstadt C2
Carteret A5
Cedar Grove A2
Cedarhurst G5
Cliffside Park D2
Clifton B1
Colonia A5
Cranford A4
E. Atlantic Beach G5
E. Newark B3
E. Orange B3
E. Rockaway G4
E. Rutherford C2
Edgewater D2
Elizabeth B4
Elmont G4
Elmwood Park C1
Englewood D1
Englewood Cliffs D1
Essex Fells A2
Fairfield A1
Fair Lawn C1
Fairview D2
Floral Park G3
Flower Hill G2
Fords A6
Ft. Lee D2
Franklin Square G4
Garden City G3
Garden City South G4
Garfield C1
Glen Cove G1
Glen Ridge B2
Great Neck G2
Great Neck Estates G3
Great Neck Gardens G2
Great Neck Plaza G2
Great Notch B1
Guttenberg D2
Hackensack C1
Harbor Hills G2
Harrison B3
Hasbrouck Hts. C1
Herricks G3
Hewlett G4
Hewlett Bay Park G5
Hewlett Harbor G5
Hewlett Neck G5
Hillside A4
Hoboken C3
Inwood F5
Irvington A3
Island Park G5
Jersey City C4
Kearny B3
Kenilworth A4
Kensington G2
Kings Pt. G2
Lake Success G3
Lakeview G4
Larchmont F1
Lawrence G5
Leonia D1
Lincoln Park A1
Linden A5
Little Falls A1
Little Ferry C2
Livingston A2
Lodi C1
Long Beach G5
Lynbrook G4
Lyndhurst C2
Malverne G4
Manhasset G2
Manhasset Hills G3
Manorhaven G2
Maplewood A3
Maywood C1
Meadow Vil. A1
Millburn A3
Mineola G3
Montclair B2
Moonachie C2
Mtn. View A1
Mt. Vernon F1
Munsey Park G2
Newark B4
Newark Hts. A3
New Hyde Park G3
New Milford D1
New York E4
N. Arlington C2
N. Bergen D2
N. Caldwell A1
N. Hills G3
N. New Hyde Park G3
N. Valley Stream G4
Nutley B2
Orange A3
Palisades Park D2
Paramus C1
Passaic B1
Paterson B1
Pelham F1
Pelham Manor F1
Perth Amboy A6
Plandome G2
Plandome Hts. G2
Plandome Manor G2
Port Reading A5
Port Washington G2
Port Washington North G2
Rahway A5
Ridgefield D2
Ridgefield Park D1
River Edge C1
Rochelle Park C1
Roseland A2
Roselle A4
Roselle Park A4
Roslyn Estates G2
Russell Gardens G3
Rutherford C2
Saddle Brook C1
Saddle Rock G2
Saddle Rock Estates G2
Sands Pt. G2
Sea Cliff G2
Searingtown G3
Secaucus C3
Sewaren A6
S. Floral Park G4
S. Orange A3
S. Valley Stream G4
Springfield A4
Stewart Manor G3
Strathmore G2
Teaneck D1
Tenafly D1
Teterboro C1
Thomaston G3
Totowa A1
Union A4
Unionburg A4
Union City C3
University Gardens G3
Upper Montclair B2
Valley Stream G4
Vauxhall A3
Verona A2
Wallington C2
Wayne A1
Weehawken D3
W. Caldwell A2
W. New York D2
W. Orange A2
Woodbridge A6
Woodland Park B1
Woodmere G5
Wood-Ridge C2
Woodsburgh G5
Yonkers E1

Muir PA, 451 .... 93 E4
Mukilteo WA, 20254 .... 12 C2
Mukwonago WI, 7355 .... 74 C3
Mulberry AR, 1655 .... 116 C1
Mulberry FL, 3817 .... 140 C2
Mulberry IN, 1254 .... 89 E4
Mulberry KS, 520 .... 106 B1
Mulberry NC, 2332 .... 111 F3
Mulberry OH, 3323 .... 100 B2
Mulberry Grove IL, 634 .... 98 B3
Muldraugh KY, 947 .... 99 F4
Muldrow OK, 3466 .... 116 B1
Muleshoe TX, 5158 .... 49 F4
Mulga AL, 836 .... 195 D1
Mullan ID, 692 .... 14 C3
Mullen NE, 509 .... 34 B2
Mullens WV, 1559 .... 111 F1
Mullica Hill NJ, 3982 .... 146 C4
Mulliken MI, 553 .... 76 A4
Mullins SC, 4663 .... 122 C3
Multnomah Co. OR, 735334 .... 20 C2
Mulvane KS, 6111 .... 43 E4
Muncie IN, 70085 .... 90 A4
Muncy PA, 2477 .... 93 D2
Munday TX, 1300 .... 58 C1
Mundelein IL, 31064 .... 74 C4
Munds Park AZ, 631 .... 47 E3
Munford AL, 1292 .... 120 A4
Munford TN, 5927 .... 118 B1
Munfordville KY, 1615 .... 110 A2
Munhall PA, 11406 .... 250 C3
Munich ND, 210 .... 19 D1
Munising MI, 2355 .... 69 E1
Munroe Falls OH, 5012 .... 188 B1
Munsey Park NY, 2693 .... 241 G2
Munsons Corners NY, 2728 .... 79 D4
Munster IN, 23603 .... 89 D2
Murchison TX, 594 .... 124 A3
Murdo SD, 488 .... 26 C4
Murfreesboro AR, 1641 .... 116 C3
Murfreesboro NC, 2835 .... 113 E3
Murfreesboro TN, 108755 .... 109 F4
Murphy ID, 97 .... 30 B1
Murphy MO, 8690 .... 98 A3
Murphy NC, 1627 .... 120 C2
Murphy TX, 17708 .... 207 E1
Murphys CA, 2213 .... 37 D3
Murphysboro IL, 7970 .... 108 C1
Murray IA, 756 .... 86 C3
Murray KY, 17741 .... 109 D3
Murray NE, 463 .... 86 A3
Murray UT, 46746 .... 31 E4
Murray Co. GA, 39628 .... 120 C2
Murray Co. MN, 8725 .... 72 A1
Murray Co. OK, 13488 .... 51 F4
Murray Hill KY, 582 .... 230 F1
Murrayville IL, 587 .... 98 A1
Murrells Inlet SC, 7547 .... 123 D4
Murrieta CA, 103466 .... 53 D3
Murrieta Hot Sprs. CA, 2948 .... 229 K6
Murrysville PA, 20079 .... 92 A4
Muscatine IA, 22886 .... 87 F2
Muscatine Co. IA, 42745 .... 87 F2
Muscle Shoals AL, 13146 .... 119 E2
Muscoda WI, 1299 .... 74 A3
Muscogee Co. GA, 189885 .... 128 C2
Muscoy CA, 10644 .... 229 J2
Muskego WI, 24135 .... 74 C3
Muskegon MI, 38401 .... 75 E3
Muskegon Co. MI, 172188 .... 75 F3
Muskegon Hts. MI, 10856 .... 75 E3
Muskingum Co. OH, 86074 .... 91 E4
Muskogee OK, 39223 .... 106 A4
Muskogee Co. OK, 70990 .... 106 A4
Musselshell Co. MT, 4538 .... 16 C4
Mustang OK, 17395 .... 51 E3
Mustang Ridge TX, 861 .... 61 E2
Muttontown NY, 3497 .... 148 C3
Myers Corner NY, 6790 .... 148 B1
Myerstown PA, 3062 .... 146 A1
Myersville MD, 1626 .... 144 A1
Myricks MA, 600 .... 151 D3
Myrtle MS, 490 .... 118 C2
Myrtle Beach SC, 27109 .... 123 D4
Myrtle Creek OR, 3439 .... 28 B1
Myrtle Grove FL, 15870 .... 135 F2
Myrtle Grove NC, 8875 .... 123 E3
Myrtle Pt. OR, 2514 .... 28 A1
Mystic CT, 4205 .... 149 F2
Mystic IA, 425 .... 87 D3
Mystic Island NJ, 8493 .... 147 E4
Myton UT, 569 .... 32 A4

N

Naalehu HI, 866 .... 153 E4
Naches WA, 795 .... 13 D4
Naco AZ, 1046 .... 55 E4
Nacogdoches TX, 32996 .... 124 B4
Nacogdoches Co. TX, 64524 .... 124 B4
Nageezi NM, 286 .... 48 B2
Nags Head NC, 2757 .... 115 F2
Nahant MA, 3410 .... 151 D1
Nahunta GA, 1053 .... 129 F4
Nain VA, 700 .... 102 C2
Naknek AK, 544 .... 154 B3
Nambe NM, 1818 .... 49 D2
Nameloc Hts. MA, 1500 .... 151 E3
Nampa ID, 81557 .... 22 B4
Nanakuli HI, 12666 .... 152 A3
Nance Co. NE, 3735 .... 35 E3
Nanticoke PA, 10465 .... 93 E2
Nantucket MA, 7446 .... 151 F4
Nantucket Co. MA, 10172 .... 151 F4
Nanty Glo PA, 2734 .... 92 B4
Nanuet NY, 17882 .... 148 B3
Napa CA, 76915 .... 36 B3
Napa Co. CA, 136484 .... 36 B2
Napanoch NY, 1174 .... 94 A3
Napaskiak AK, 405 .... 154 B3
Napavine WA, 1766 .... 12 B4
Naperville IL, 141853 .... 88 C1
Naples FL, 19537 .... 142 C2
Naples NY, 1041 .... 78 C4
Naples TX, 1378 .... 124 B1
Naples UT, 1755 .... 32 A4
Naples Manor FL, 5562 .... 142 C2
Naples Park FL, 5967 .... 142 C1
Napoleon MI, 1258 .... 90 B1
Napoleon ND, 792 .... 18 C4
Napoleon OH, 8749 .... 90 B2
Napoleonville LA, 660 .... 134 A3
Nappanee IN, 6648 .... 89 F2
Naranja FL, 8303 .... 143 E3
Narberth PA, 4282 .... 248 B3
Narragansett Pier RI, 3409 .... 150 C4
Narrows VA, 2029 .... 112 A1
Naschitti NM, 301 .... 48 A2
Nash TX, 2960 .... 116 C4
Nash Co. NC, 95840 .... 113 D4
Nashotah WI, 1395 .... 74 C3
Nashua IA, 1663 .... 73 D3
Nashua MT, 290 .... 17 D2
Nashua NH, 86494 .... 95 D1
Nashville AR, 4627 .... 116 C4
Nashville GA, 4939 .... 129 E4
Nashville IL, 3258 .... 98 B4
Nashville IN, 803 .... 99 F2
Nashville MI, 1628 .... 76 A4
Nashville NC, 5352 .... 113 D4
Nashville TN, 601222 .... 109 F4
Nashwauk MN, 983 .... 64 B3
Nassau DE, 1600 .... 145 F4
Nassau NY, 1133 .... 94 B1
Nassau Bay TX, 4002 .... 132 B3
Nassau Co. FL, 73314 .... 139 D2
Nassau Co. NY, 1339532 .... 148 C4
Nassau Vil. FL, 1900 .... 222 C1
Nassawadox VA, 499 .... 114 B3
Natalbany LA, 2984 .... 134 B2
Natalia TX, 1431 .... 61 D3
Natchez LA, 597 .... 125 D4
Natchez MS, 15792 .... 125 F4
Natchitoches LA, 18323 .... 125 D3
Natchitoches Par. LA, 39566 .... 125 D4
Natick MA, 33006 .... 150 C1
National City CA, 58582 .... 258 B2
National Park NJ, 3036 .... 146 C3
Natrona Co. WY, 75450 .... 33 D1
Natrona Hts. PA, 10934 .... 92 A3
Naturita CO, 546 .... 40 B3
Naugatuck CT, 31862 .... 149 D1
Nauvoo IL, 1149 .... 87 F4
Navajo NM, 1645 .... 48 A2
Navajo Co. AZ, 107449 .... 47 F3
Navarre OH, 1957 .... 91 E3
Navarro Co. TX, 47735 .... 59 F3
Navasota TX, 7049 .... 61 F1
Navesink NJ, 2020 .... 147 F1
Naylor MO, 632 .... 108 A3
Naytahwaush MN, 578 .... 19 F3
Nazareth KY, 1000 .... 100 A4
Nazareth PA, 5746 .... 93 F3
Nazlini AZ, 489 .... 47 F2
Neah Bay WA, 865 .... 12 A2
Neapolis OH, 423 .... 90 B2
Nebraska City NE, 7289 .... 86 A3
Necedah WI, 916 .... 74 A1
Neche ND, 371 .... 19 E1
Nederland CO, 1445 .... 41 D1
Nederland TX, 17547 .... 132 C3
Nedrow NY, 2244 .... 79 D3
Needham MA, 28886 .... 151 D1
Needles CA, 4844 .... 46 B4
Needville TX, 2823 .... 132 A4
Neelyville MO, 483 .... 108 A3
Neenah WI, 25501 .... 74 C1
Neffs OH, 993 .... 101 F1
Negaunee MI, 4568 .... 65 F4
Neillsville WI, 2463 .... 68 A4
Nekoosa WI, 2580 .... 74 A1
Neligh NE, 1599 .... 35 E2
Nelliston NY, 596 .... 79 F3
Nelson GA, 1314 .... 120 C3
Nelson NE, 488 .... 35 E4
Nelson Co. KY, 43437 .... 100 A4
Nelson Co. ND, 3126 .... 19 E2
Nelson Co. VA, 15020 .... 112 C1
Nelsonville NY, 628 .... 148 B1
Nelsonville OH, 5392 .... 101 E2
Nemacolin PA, 937 .... 102 A1
Nemaha Co. KS, 10178 .... 96 A1
Nemaha Co. NE, 7248 .... 86 A4
Nenana AK, 378 .... 154 C2
Neodesha KS, 2486 .... 106 A1
Neoga IL, 1636 .... 98 C2
Neola IA, 842 .... 86 A2
Neola UT, 461 .... 32 A4
Neopit WI, 690 .... 68 C4
Neosho MO, 11835 .... 106 B2
Neosho WI, 574 .... 74 C3
Neosho Co. KS, 16512 .... 106 A1
Neotsu OR, 650 .... 20 B2
Nephi UT, 5389 .... 39 E1
Neptune NJ, 28394 .... 147 F2
Neptune Beach FL, 7037 .... 139 D2
Neptune City NJ, 4869 .... 147 F2
Nesbit MS, 700 .... 118 B2
Nesconset NY, 13387 .... 149 D3
Nescopeck PA, 1583 .... 93 E3
Neshoba Co. MS, 29676 .... 126 C2
Nesquehoning PA, 3349 .... 93 F3
Ness City KS, 1449 .... 42 C3
Ness Co. KS, 3107 .... 42 C3
Netarts OR, 748 .... 20 B2
Netcong NJ, 3232 .... 94 A4
Nettleton MS, 1992 .... 119 D3
Nevada IA, 6798 .... 86 C1
Nevada MO, 8386 .... 106 C1
Nevada OH, 760 .... 90 C3
Nevada City CA, 3068 .... 36 C2
Nevada Co. AR, 8997 .... 117 D4
Nevada Co. CA, 98764 .... 36 C2
New Albany IN, 36372 .... 99 F4
New Albany MS, 8034 .... 118 C3
New Albin IA, 522 .... 73 F2
New Alexandria PA, 560 .... 92 A4
Newark AR, 1176 .... 107 F4
Newark CA, 42573 .... 259 D5
Newark DE, 31454 .... 146 B4
Newark IL, 992 .... 88 C2
Newark NJ, 277140 .... 148 B4
Newark NY, 9145 .... 78 C3
Newark OH, 47573 .... 91 D4
Newark TX, 1005 .... 59 E2
Newark Valley NY, 997 .... 93 E1
New Athens IL, 2054 .... 98 B4
New Auburn MN, 456 .... 66 C4
New Auburn WI, 548 .... 67 F3
New Augusta MS, 644 .... 126 C4
Newaygo MI, 1976 .... 75 F2
Newaygo Co. MI, 48460 .... 75 F2
New Baden IL, 3349 .... 98 B3
New Baltimore MI, 12084 .... 76 C4
New Baltimore NY, 800 .... 94 B1
New Baltimore VA, 8119 .... 144 A3
New Beaver PA, 1502 .... 91 F3
New Bedford MA, 95072 .... 151 D4
Newberg OR, 22068 .... 20 B2
New Berlin IL, 1346 .... 98 B1
New Berlin NY, 1028 .... 79 E4
New Berlin PA, 873 .... 93 D3
New Berlin WI, 39584 .... 74 C3
New Bern NC, 29524 .... 115 D3
Newbern TN, 3313 .... 108 C4
Newberry FL, 4950 .... 138 C3
Newberry MI, 1519 .... 69 F1
Newberry SC, 10277 .... 121 F3
Newberry Co. SC, 37508 .... 121 F3
New Bethlehem PA, 989 .... 92 B3
New Bloomfield MO, 669 .... 97 E3
New Bloomfield PA, 1077 .... 93 D4
Newborn GA, 696 .... 121 D4
New Boston IL, 683 .... 87 F2
New Boston NH, 5321 .... 81 F4
New Boston OH, 2272 .... 101 D3
New Boston TX, 4550 .... 116 B4
New Braunfels TX, 57740 .... 61 D2
New Bremen OH, 2978 .... 90 B4
New Brighton MN, 21456 .... 235 C1
New Brighton PA, 6025 .... 91 F3
New Britain CT, 73206 .... 149 E1
New Britain PA, 3152 .... 146 C2
New Brockton AL, 1146 .... 128 A4
New Brunswick NJ, 55181 .... 147 E1
New Buffalo MI, 1883 .... 89 E1
Newburg WV, 329 .... 102 B2
Newburg WI, 1254 .... 74 C2
Newburgh IN, 3325 .... 99 E4
Newburgh NY, 28866 .... 148 B1
Newburgh Hts. OH, 2167 .... 204 F2
Newbury VT, 365 .... 81 E2
Newburyport MA, 17416 .... 151 F1
New Canaan CT, 19984 .... 148 C2
New Carlisle IN, 1861 .... 89 E1
New Carlisle OH, 5785 .... 100 C1
New Carrollton MD, 12135 .... 144 B3
New Castle CO, 4518 .... 40 C1
New Castle DE, 5285 .... 146 B4

Figures after entries indicate population, page number, and grid reference.

New Castle IN, *18114* **100** A1
New Castle KY, *912* **100** A3
Newcastle ME, *667* **82** C3
Newcastle OK, *7685* **51** E3
New Castle PA, *23273* **91** F3
Newcastle TX, *585* **59** D2
New Castle VA, *153* **112** B1
Newcastle WA, *10380* **262** B3
Newcastle WY, *3532* **25** F4
New Castle Co. DE, *538479* **145** E1
New Chapel Hill TX, *594* **124** B3
New City NY, *33559* **148** B2
Newcomb MD, *600* **145** D4
Newcomb NM, *339* **48** A2
Newcomerstown OH, *3822* **91** E4
New Concord OH, *2491* **101** E1
New Cordell OK, *2915* **51** D3
New Cumberland PA, *7277* **218** B2
New Cumberland WV, *1103* **91** F4
Newdale ID, *323* **23** F4
New Deal TX, *794* **58** A1
New Durham NH, *2638* **81** F4
New Eagle PA, *2184* **92** A4
New Effington SD, *256* **27** F1
New Egypt NJ, *2512* **147** D3
Newell IA, *876* **72** B4
Newell SD, *603* **25** F3
Newell WV, *1376* **91** F3
New Ellenton SC, *2052* **121** F4
Newellton LA, *1187* **126** A3
New England ND, *600* **18** A4
New Era MI, *451* **75** E2
New Fairfield CT, *14261* **148** C1
New Fairview TX, *1258* **59** E2
Newfane NY, *3822* **78** B3
Newfane VT, *118* **81** E4
Newfield NJ, *1553* **145** F1
Newfield NY, *647* **79** D4
Newfields NH, *301* **82** A4
New Florence MO, *769* **97** F3
New Florence PA, *689* **92** B4
New Franklin MO, *1089* **97** D2
New Franklin OH, *14227* **91** E3
New Freedom PA, *4464* **103** E1
New Glarus WI, *2172* **74** B3
New Gloucester ME, *5461* **82** B3
New Gretna NJ, *600* **147** E4
Newhall IA, *875* **87** E1
New Hamburg NY, *1200* **148** B1
New Hampton IA, *3571* **73** E3
New Hampton NY, *1200* **148** A1
New Hanover PA, *1800* **146** B2
New Hanover Co. NC, *202667* **123** E3
New Harmony IN, *789* **99** D4
New Hartford CT, *6746* **94** C2
New Hartford IA, *516* **73** D4
New Haven CT, *129779* **149** D2
New Haven IN, *14794* **90** A3
New Haven KY, *855* **110** A1
New Haven MI, *4642* **76** C4
New Haven MO, *2089* **97** F3
New Haven WV, *1560* **101** E2
New Haven Co. CT, *862477* **149** D1
New Hebron MS, *447* **126** B4
New Hempstead NY, *5132* **148** B2
New Holland OH, *801* **101** D1
New Holland PA, *5378* **146** A2
New Holstein WI, *3236* **74** C1
New Hope AL, *2810* **119** F2
New Hope GA, *750* **120** B4
New Hope MN, *20339* **235** B2
New Hope MS, *3193* **119** D4
New Hope NC, *4500* **123** E1
New Hope PA, *2528* **147** D2
New Hope TN, *1082* **120** A2
New Hope VA, *797* **102** C4
New Houlka MS, *626* **118** C3
New Hyde Park NY, *9712* **241** G3
New Iberia LA, *30617* **133** F3
Newington CT, *30562* **149** E1
New Ipswich NH, *5099* **95** D1
New Jerusalem PA, *649* **146** B1
New Johnsonville TN, *1951* **109** D4
New Kensington PA, *13116* **92** A4
New Kent VA, *239* **113** F1
New Kent Co. VA, *18429* **113** F1
Newkirk OK, *2317* **51** E1
New Knoxville OH, *879* **90** B4
Newland NC, *698* **111** F4
New Lebanon OH, *3995* **100** B1
New Leipzig ND, *221* **18** B4
New Lenox IL, *24394* **89** D2

POINTS OF INTEREST

601 Lexington Avenue D2
African Burial Ground Natl. Mon. B5
Algonquin Hotel C2
Alvin Alley American Dance Th. .C1
American Folk Art Museum C1
American Standard Building C2
Americas Society D1
Appellate Division of the Supreme Court of New York C3
Battery Park A6
Bernard M. Baruch College of the City University of N.Y. C3
Brookfield Place A5
Carnegie Hall C1
Castle Clinton Natl. Monument A6
Central Park D1
Central Park Zoo D1
Chanin Building D2
Chrysler Building D2
City Hall B5
Comcast Building C2
ConEdison Building C4
The Cooper Union C4
Criminal Courts Building B5
Cunard Building A6
Daily News Building D2
David Geffen Hall C1
David H. Koch Theatre C1
Empire State Building C3
Fashion Institute of Technology & Museum B3
Federal Hall National Memorial A6
Federal Reserve Bank A6
Flatiron Building C3
Fordham University C1
Foundation Building C4
Fraunces Tavern A6
French Building C2
The Frick Collection D1
Fuller Building D1
General Assembly Building D2
General Electric Building D2
Grace Church C4
Grand Central Terminal D2
High Line Park B2
Home Savings of America Building C2
Hotel Chelsea B3
Hunter College (C.U.N.Y.) D1
Intrepid Sea, Air & Space Mus. B1
Irish Hunger Memorial A5
Italian American Museum B5
Jacob Javits Convention Center .B2
Japan Society D2
Jazz at Lincoln Center Frederick P. Rose Hall C1
Jefferson Market Library B4
John Jay College (C.U.N.Y.) C1
Lever House D2
Lincoln Center C1
Lower East Side Tenement Mus. Natl. Hist. Site C5
Lyceum Theatre C2
Macdougal Alley B4
Macy's C2
Madame Tussauds-New York C2
Madison Square Garden B2
Manhattan Cruise Terminal B1
Manhattan Mall C2
Meatpacking District A3
Merchant's House Museum B4
Met Breuer D1
Met Life Building D2
Metropolitan Opera House C1
Morgan Library & Museum C2
Municipal Building B5
Museum at Eldridge Street B5
Museum of American Finance A6
Museum of Arts & Design C1
Museum of Chinese in America B5
Museum of Jewish Heritage A6
Museum of Modern Art D2
Museum of Sex C3
National Geographic Encounter C2
National Museum of the American Indian A6
Natl. Sept. 11 Mem. & Mus. A6
New Mus. of Contemporary Art B5
New York City Fire Museum A4
New York Edition Hotel C3
New York Supreme & Co. Court B5
New York Life Insurance Company Building C3
New York Mercantile Exchange .A5
The New York Public Library C2
New York Stock Exchange A6
New York Univ. B4
Old New York Co. Court House B5
One World Trade Ctr. (Freedom Tower) A5
Pace University New York City Campus B5
Paley Center for Media D2
Paramount Building C2
Pennsylvania Station B2
Pier 17 Pavilion B6
Plaza Hotel D1
Port Authority Bus Terminal B2
Public Theater B4
Radio City Music Hall C2
Rockefeller Center C2
Roosevelt Island Aerial Tram D2
Rubin Museum of Art B3
St. Patrick's Cathedral D2
St. Paul's Chapel A6
Salmagundi Club B4
Seagram Building D2
Seaport Museum B6
Secretariat Building D2
Sheridan Square B4
Skyscraper Museum A6
Society of Illustrators D1
South Street Seaport B6
Stonewall National Monument B4
The Oculus A6
Theodore Roosevelt Birthplace Natl. Hist. Site C3
Times Square C2
Tisch Childrens Zoo D1
Trinity Church A6
Trump Tower D1
Ukrainian Museum C4
United Nations D2
U.S. Court House B5
Villard Houses D2
Waldorf-Astoria D2
Washington Arch B4
Washington Square B4
Whitney Mus. of American Art A3
Wollman Rink D1
Woolworth Building A5
World Trade Center A5

Entries in **bold black** indicate counties or parishes.
Entries in **bold color** indicate cities with detailed inset maps.

New Lexington OH, 4731 ... 101 E1
New Lisbon WI, 2554 ... 74 A2
New Llano LA, 2504 ... 133 D1
New London CT, 27620 ... 149 F2
New London IA, 1897 ... 87 F3
New London MN, 1251 ... 66 B3
New London MO, 974 ... 97 F1
New London NH, 1415 ... 81 E4
New London OH, 2461 ... 91 D3
New London PA, 1100 ... 146 B3
New London TX, 998 ... 124 B3
New London WI, 7295 ... 74 C1
New London Co. CT, 274055 ... 150 B4
New Lothrop MI, 581 ... 76 B3
New Madison OH, 892 ... 100 B1
New Madrid MO, 3116 ... 108 B3
New Madrid Co. MO, 18956 ... 108 B3
Newman CA, 10224 ... 36 C4
Newman IL, 865 ... 99 D1
Newman Grove NE, 721 ... 35 E2
Newmanstown PA, 2478 ... 146 A2
New Market AL, 1597 ... 119 F2
New Market IN, 636 ... 99 E1
Newmarket NH, 5297 ... 82 A4
New Market TN, 1334 ... 111 D4
New Market VA, 2146 ... 102 C3
New Martinsville WV, 5366 ... 101 F1
New Matamoras OH, 896 ... 101 F1
New Meadows ID, 496 ... 22 B2
New Miami OH, 2249 ... 100 B2
New Middletown OH, 1621 ... 91 F3
New Milford CT, 6523 ... 148 C1
New Milford NJ, 16341 ... 240 D1
New Milford NY, 850 ... 148 A2
New Milford PA, 868 ... 93 F1
New Millford IL, 541 ... 88 B1
Newnan GA, 33039 ... 128 C1
New Orleans LA, 343829 ... 134 B3
New Oxford PA, 1783 ... 103 E1
New Palestine IN, 2055 ... 99 F1
New Paltz NY, 6818 ... 94 B3
New Paris IN, 1494 ... 89 F2
New Paris OH, 1629 ... 100 B1
New Pekin IN, 1401 ... 99 F3
New Philadelphia OH, 17288 ... 91 E4
New Philadelphia PA, 1085 ... 93 E3
New Plymouth ID, 1538 ... 22 A4
Newport AR, 7879 ... 117 F1
Newport DE, 1055 ... 146 B4
Newport IN, 515 ... 99 E1
Newport KY, 15273 ... 100 B2
Newport ME, 1776 ... 82 C1
Newport MN, 3435 ... 235 D3
Newport NH, 4769 ... 81 E4
Newport NY, 640 ... 79 F3
Newport NC, 4150 ... 115 D4
Newport OH, 1003 ... 101 F2
Newport OR, 9989 ... 20 B3
Newport PA, 1574 ... 93 D4
Newport RI, 24672 ... 151 D4
Newport TN, 6945 ... 111 D4
Newport VT, 4589 ... 81 E1
Newport WA, 2126 ... 14 B2
Newport Beach CA, 85186 ... 52 C3
Newport Ctr. VT, 274 ... 81 E1
Newport Co. RI, 82888 ... 151 D4
Newport News VA, 180719 ... 113 F2
New Port Richey FL, 14911 ... 140 B2
New Prague MN, 7321 ... 66 C4
New Preston CT, 1182 ... 148 C1
New Providence NJ, 12171 ... 148 A4
New Richland MN, 1203 ... 72 C2
New Richmond OH, 2582 ... 100 B3
New Richmond WI, 8375 ... 67 E3
New River AZ, 14952 ... 54 C1
New Roads LA, 4831 ... 133 F1
New Rochelle NY, 77062 ... 148 B3
New Rockford ND, 1391 ... 19 D3
New Salem ND, 946 ... 18 B4
New Salem PA, 808 ... 102 B1
New Salem PA, 579 ... 275 E2
New Sarpy LA, 1464 ... 239 A1
New Sharon IA, 1293 ... 87 D2
New Site AL, 773 ... 128 B1
New Smyrna Beach FL, 22464 ... 139 E4
New Stanton PA, 2173 ... 92 A4
New Straitsville OH, 722 ... 101 E1
New Strawn KS, 394 ... 96 A4
New Stuyahok AK, 510 ... 154 B3
New Summerfield TX, 1111 ... 124 B3
New Tazewell TN, 3037 ... 111 D3
Newton AL, 1511 ... 128 B4
Newton GA, 654 ... 128 C4
Newton IL, 2849 ... 99 D2
Newton IA, 15254 ... 87 D2
Newton KS, 19132 ... 43 E3
Newton MA, 85146 ... 151 D1
Newton MS, 3373 ... 126 C2
Newton NH, 4603 ... 95 E1
Newton NJ, 7997 ... 94 A4
Newton NC, 12968 ... 111 F4
Newton TX, 2478 ... 132 C1
Newton UT, 789 ... 31 E2
Newton Co. AR, 8330 ... 107 D4
Newton Co. GA, 99958 ... 121 D4
Newton Co. IN, 14244 ... 89 D3
Newton Co. MS, 21720 ... 126 C2
Newton Co. MO, 58114 ... 106 C2
Newton Co. TX, 14445 ... 133 D1
Newton Falls OH, 4795 ... 91 F2
Newton Grove NC, 569 ... 123 D1
Newtonville NJ, 800 ... 147 D4
Newtonville NY, 2100 ... 188 E2
Newtown CT, 1941 ... 148 C1
New Town ND, 1925 ... 18 A2
Newtown OH, 2672 ... 204 C2
Newtown PA, 2248 ... 147 D2
New Ulm MN, 13522 ... 72 B1
New Underwood SD, 660 ... 26 A3
New Vernon NJ, 1200 ... 148 A4
New Vienna OH, 1224 ... 100 C2
Newville AL, 539 ... 128 B4
Newville PA, 1326 ... 93 D4
New Washington IN, 566 ... 100 A3
New Washington OH, 967 ... 91 D3
New Washoe City NV, 2900 ... 37 D2
New Waterford OH, 1238 ... 91 F3
New Waverly TX, 1032 ... 132 A2
New Whiteland IN, 5472 ... 99 F1
New Wilmington PA, 2466 ... 91 F3
New Windsor IL, 748 ... 88 A2
New Windsor MD, 1396 ... 144 B1
New Windsor NY, 8922 ... 148 B1
New York NY, 8175133 ... 148 B4
New York Co. NY, 1585873 ... 148 B4
New York Mills MN, 1199 ... 64 A4
Nezperce ID, 466 ... 22 B1
Nez Perce Co. ID, 39265 ... 22 B1
Niagara WI, 1624 ... 68 C2
Niagara Co. NY, 216469 ... 78 B3
Niagara Falls NY, 50193 ... 78 A3
Niantic CT, 3114 ... 149 F2
Niantic IL, 707 ... 98 C1
Nibley UT, 5438 ... 31 E3
Nice CA, 2731 ... 36 B2
Niceville FL, 12749 ... 136 B2
Nicholas Co. KY, 7135 ... 100 C4
Nicholas Co. WV, 26233 ... 101 F4
Nicholasville KY, 28015 ... 100 B4
Nicholls GA, 2798 ... 129 F4
Nichols NY, 512 ... 93 E1
Nichols Hills OK, 3710 ... 244 D2
Nicholson GA, 1696 ... 121 D3
Nicholson MS, 3092 ... 134 C2
Nicholson PA, 767 ... 93 F2
Nickelsville VA, 383 ... 111 E2
Nickerson KS, 1070 ... 43 E3
Nickerson NE, 369 ... 35 F3
Nicksville AZ, 425 ... 55 E4
Nicollet MN, 1093 ... 72 C1
Nicollet Co. MN, 32727 ... 72 B1
Nicoma Park OK, 2393 ... 244 F2
Niederwald TX, 565 ... 61 E2
Nikiski AK, 4493 ... 154 C3
Niland CA, 1006 ... 53 E3
Niles IL, 29803 ... 203 D3
Niles MI, 11600 ... 89 F1
Niles OH, 19266 ... 91 F2
Ninety Six SC, 1998 ... 121 F3
Ninnekah OK, 1002 ... 51 E3
Niobrara Co. WY, 2484 ... 33 E1
Niota TN, 719 ... 120 C1
Nipomo CA, 16714 ... 52 A1
Niskayuna NY, 4859 ... 188 D2
Nisland SD, 232 ... 25 F3
Nissequogue NY, 1749 ... 149 D3
Nisswa MN, 1971 ... 64 A4
Nitro WV, 7178 ... 101 E3
Niwot CO, 4006 ... 41 E1
Nixa MO, 19022 ... 107 D2
Nixon NV, 374 ... 37 D1
Nixon TX, 2385 ... 61 E3
Noank CT, 1796 ... 149 F2
Noatak AK, 514 ... 154 B1
Noble IL, 677 ... 99 D3
Noble OK, 6481 ... 51 E3
Nobleboro ME, 1626 ... 82 C3
Noble Co. IN, 47536 ... 89 F2
Noble Co. OH, 14645 ... 101 F1
Noble Co. OK, 11561 ... 51 E2
Nobles Co. MN, 21378 ... 72 A2
Noblesville IN, 51969 ... 89 F4
Nocatee FL, 4524 ... 140 C4
Nocona TX, 3033 ... 59 E1
Nodaway Co. MO, 23370 ... 86 B4
Noel MO, 1832 ... 106 B3
Nogales AZ, 20837 ... 55 D4
Nokesville VA, 1354 ... 144 A4
Nokomis FL, 3167 ... 140 B4
Nokomis IL, 2256 ... 98 B2
Nolan Co. TX, 15216 ... 58 B3
Nolanville TX, 4259 ... 59 E4
Nolensville TN, 5861 ... 109 F4
Nome AK, 3598 ... 154 B2
Nome TX, 588 ... 132 C3
Nooksack WA, 1338 ... 12 C1
Noonday TX, 777 ... 124 A3
Noorvik AK, 668 ... 154 B2
Nora Sprs. IA, 1431 ... 73 D3
Norborne MO, 708 ... 96 C2
Norco CA, 27063 ... 53 D2
Norco LA, 3074 ... 134 B3
Norcross GA, 9116 ... 120 C4
Norfolk CT, 553 ... 94 C2
Norfolk MA, 10460 ... 151 D2
Norfolk NE, 24210 ... 35 E2
Norfolk NY, 1327 ... 80 B1
Norfolk VA, 242803 ... 113 F2
Norfolk Co. MA, 670850 ... 151 D2
Norfork AR, 511 ... 107 E3
Norlina NC, 1118 ... 113 D3
Normal IL, 52497 ... 88 C4
Norman AR, 378 ... 116 C3
Norman OK, 110925 ... 51 E3
Norman Co. MN, 6852 ... 19 F3
Normandy MO, 5008 ... 256 B2
Normandy Park WA, 6335 ... 262 B4
Normangee TX, 685 ... 59 F4
Norman Park GA, 972 ... 129 D4
Normans MD, 650 ... 145 D3
Norphlet AR, 844 ... 125 E1
Norridge IL, 14572 ... 203 D3
Norridgewock ME, 1438 ... 82 C1
Norris SC, 813 ... 121 E2
Norris TN, 1491 ... 110 C4
Norris City IL, 1275 ... 99 D4
Norristown PA, 34324 ... 146 C2
North SC, 754 ... 122 A4

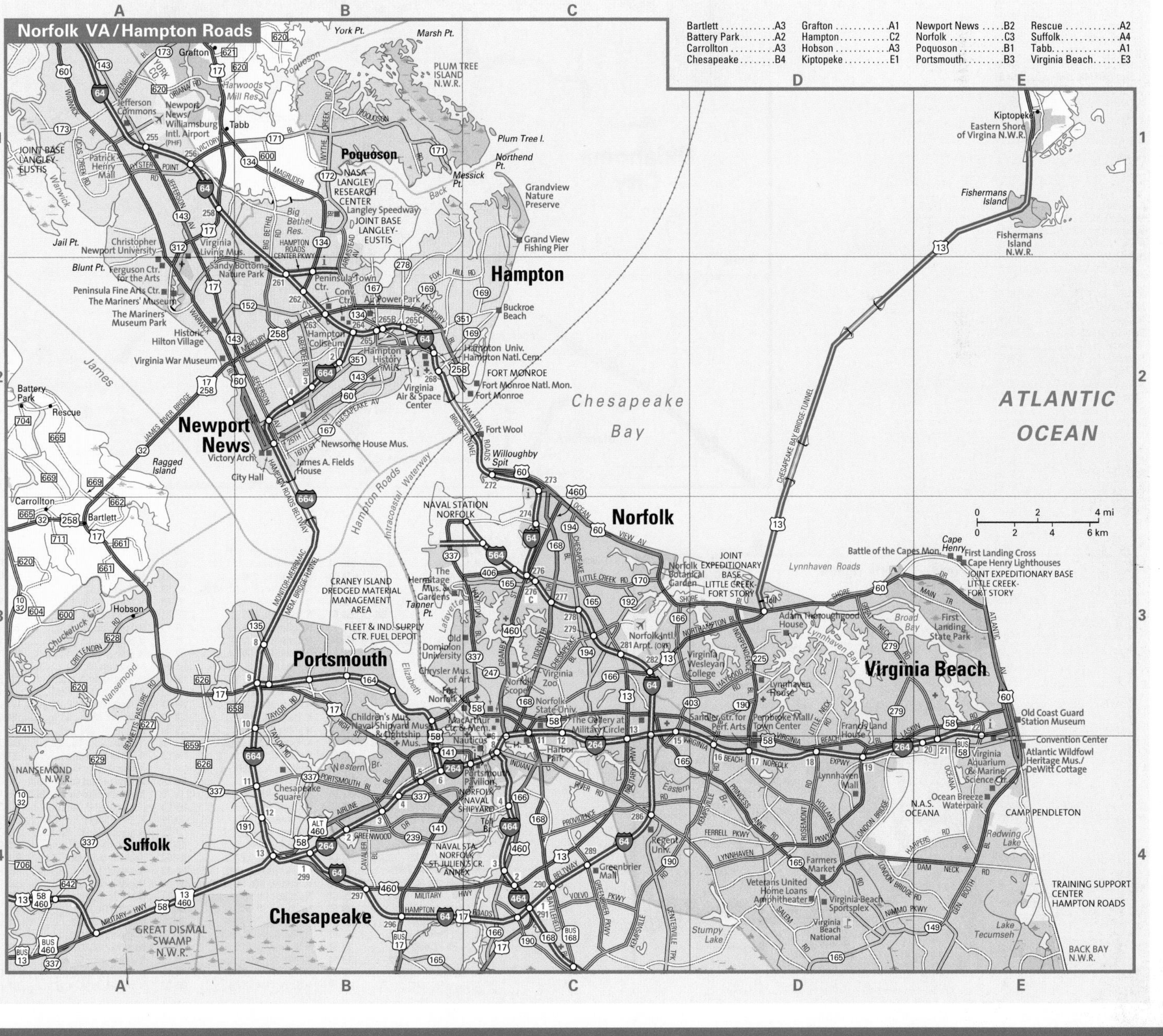

Figures after entries indicate population, page number, and grid reference.

N. Acton MA, *3000*........ **150** C1
N. Adams MA, *13708*........ **94** C1
N. Adams MI, *477*........ **90** B1
N. Albany OR, *4300*........ **20** B3
N. Amherst MA, *6819*........ **150** A1
Northampton MA, *28549*........ **150** A1
Northampton PA, *9926*........ **93** F3
Northampton Co. NC, *22099*........ **113** E3
Northampton Co. PA, *297735*........ **93** F3
Northampton Co. VA, *12389*........ **114** B3
N. Anson ME, *400*........ **82** B1
N. Apollo PA, *1297*........ **92** A4
N. Arlington NJ, *15392*........ **240** C2
N. Atlanta GA, *40456*........ **190** E2
N. Attleboro MA, *28712*........ **150** C2
N. Augusta SC, *21348*........ **121** F4
N. Aurora IL, *16760*........ **88** C1
N. Baltimore OH, *3432*........ **90** C2
N. Barrington IL, *3047*........ **203** B2
N. Bay Vil. FL, *7137*........ **233** B4
N. Beach MD, *1978*........ **144** C4
N. Beach Haven NJ, *2235*........ **147** E4
N. Bellport NY, *11545*........ **149** D4
N. Bend NE, *1177*........ **35** F3
N. Bend OR, *9695*........ **20** A4
N. Bend WA, *5731*........ **12** C3
N. Bennington VT, *1643*........ **94** C1
N. Bergen NJ, *58092*........ **240** D2
N. Berwick ME, *1615*........ **82** B4
N. Bonneville WA, *956*........ **20** C1
Northborough MA, *6167*........ **150** C1
N. Boston NY, *2521*........ **78** B4
N. Braddock PA, *4857*........ **250** C2
N. Branch MI, *1033*........ **76** C3
N. Branch MN, *10125*........ **67** D3
N. Branch NJ, *1500*........ **147** D1
N. Branford CT, *14398*........ **149** E2
N. Brentwood MD, *517*........ **270** E2
Northbridge MA, *15707*........ **150** C2
Northbrook IL, *33170*........ **89** D1
Northbrook OH, *10668*........ **204** A1
N. Brookfield MA, *2265*........ **150** B1
N. Brunswick NJ, *40742*........ **147** E1
N. Caldwell NJ, *6183*........ **240** A1
N. Canton OH, *17488*........ **91** E3
N. Cape May NJ, *3226*........ **104** C4
N. Carrollton MS, *473*........ **118** B4
N. Carver MA, *700*........ **151** E3
N. Catasauqua PA, *2849*........ **189** A1
N. Charleston SC, *97471*........ **131** D2
N. Chevy Chase MD, *465*........ **270** C1
N. Chicago IL, *32574*........ **75** D4
N. Chili NY, *4300*........ **78** C3
N. Clarendon VT, *700*........ **81** D3
N. Cohasset MA, *1600*........ **151** E1
N. College Hill OH, *9397*........ **204** A2
N. Collins NY, *1232*........ **78** A4
N. Conway NH, *2349*........ **81** F3
N. Corbin KY, *1773*........ **110** C2
N. Courtland AL, *632*........ **119** E2
N. Crossett AR, *3119*........ **125** F1
Northdale FL, *22079*........ **266** C1
N. Dartmouth MA, *2200*........ **238** C2
N. Decatur GA, *16698*........ **190** E3
N. Dighton MA, *1400*........ **151** D3
N. Druid Hills GA, *18947*........ **190** E3
North East MD, *3572*........ **145** D1
N. East PA, *4294*........ **92** A1
N. Eastham MA, *1806*........ **151** F3
Northeast Harbor ME, *500*........ **83** D2
N. Easton MA, *3700*........ **151** D2
N. Edwards CA, *1058*........ **52** C1
N. English IA, *1041*........ **87** E2
N. Enid OK, *860*........ **51** E1
Northern Cambria PA, *3835*........ **92** B3
N. Fairfield OH, *560*........ **91** D3
N. Fair Oaks CA, *14687*........ **259** C5
N. Falmouth MA, *3084*........ **151** E4
N. Ferrisburg VT, *500*........ **81** D2
Northfield CT, *800*........ **149** D1
Northfield IL, *5420*........ **203** D2
Northfield KY, *1020*........ **230** E1
Northfield MA, *1089*........ **94** C1
Northfield MN, *20007*........ **73** D1
Northfield NH, *2200*........ **81** F4
Northfield NJ, *8624*........ **147** F4
Northfield OH, *3677*........ **204** G3
Northfield VT, *2101*........ **81** E2
Northfield Falls VT, *650*........ **81** E2
N. Fond du Lac WI, *5014*........ **74** C2
Northford CT, *1600*........ **149** D2
Northfork WV, *429*........ **111** F1
N. Miami OK, *433*........ **106** B2
N. Miami Beach FL, *41523*........ **143** F2
N. Middleboro MA, *850*........ **151** D3
N. Middletown KY, *643*........ **100** C4
N. Salem IN, *518*........ **99** E1
N. Salem NY, *650*........ **148** C2
N. Salt Lake UT, *16322*........ **31** E4
N. Scituate MA, *5077*........ **151** E2

Arcadia........F1
Bethany........D2
Choctaw........F2
Del City........E2
Edmond........E1
Forest Park........E2
Jones........F1
Lake Aluma........E2
Midwest City........F2
Moore........E3
Mustang........C3
Newcastle........D4
Nichols Hills........D2
Nicoma Park........F2
Norman........E4
Oklahoma City........C3
Piedmont........C1
Richland........C1
Smith Vil........E2
Spencer........E2
The Village........D1
Valley Brook........E3
Warr Acres........D2
Woodlawn Park........D2
Yukon........C2

Clinton........A2
Eden........B1
Farr West........A1
Harrisville........A1
Hooper........A2
Marriott-Slaterville........A1
N. Ogden........B1
Ogden........B2
Plain City........A1
Pleasant View........A1
Riverdale........A2
Roy........A2
S. Ogden........A2
S. Weber........B2
Sunset........A2
Uintah........B2
Warren........A1
Washington Terrace........A2
W. Haven........A1
W. Point........A2
W. Weber........A1

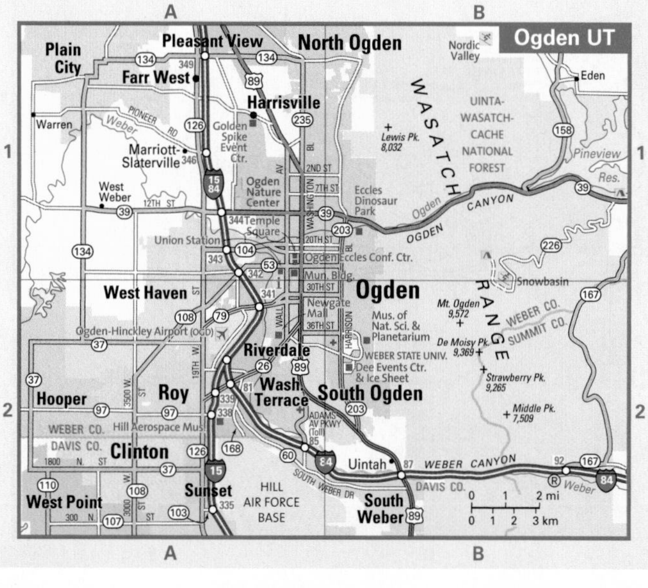

N. Fork Vil. OH, *1726*........ **101** D2
N. Ft. Myers FL, *39407*........ **142** C1
N. Freedom WI, *701*........ **74** A2
Northglenn CO, *35789*........ **209** C2
N. Grafton MA, *3600*........ **150** C2
N. Grosvenor Dale CT, *1530*........ **150** B2
N. Hartland VT, *302*........ **81** E3
N. Hartsville SC, 3251........ **122** B3
N. Hatfield MA, *550*........ **150** A1
N. Haven CT, *24093*........ **149** D2
N. Haven NY, *833*........ **149** E3
N. Haverhill NH, *450*........ **81** E2
N. Hero VT, *810*........ **81** D1
N. Hickory NC, *4300*........ **111** F4
N. Highlands CA, *42694*........ **36** C3
N. Hills NY, *5075*........ **241** G3
N. Hodge LA, *436*........ **125** E3
N. Hornell NY, *778*........ **78** C4
N. Houston TX, *4900*........ **132** A3
N. Hudson WI, *3768*........ **67** D4
N. Industry OH, *1800*........ **91** E3
N. Judson IN, *1772*........ **89** E2
N. Kansas City MO, *4208*........ **224** B2
N. Kingsville OH, *2923*........ **91** F1
Northlake IL, *12323*........ **203** C4
N. Las Vegas NV, *216961*........ **46** B2
N. Lauderdale FL, *41023*........ **233** B2
N. Lewisburg OH, *1490*........ **90** C4
N. Liberty IN, *1896*........ **89** E2
N. Liberty IA, *13374*........ **87** E1
N. Little Rock AR, *62304*........ **117** E2
N. Logan UT, *6163*........ **31** E2
N. Manchester IN, *6112*........ **89** F3
N. Mankato MN, *13394*........ **72** C1
N. Miami FL, *58786*........ **143** F2
N. Muskegon MI, *3786*........ **75** E3
N. Myrtle Beach SC, *13752*........ **123** D4
N. Naples FL, *13400*........ **142** C1
N. New Hyde Park NY, *14899*........ **241** G3
N. Newton KS, *1759*........ **43** E3
N. Oaks MN, *4469*........ **235** D1
N. Ogden UT, *17357*........ **31** E3
N. Olmsted OH, *32718*........ **91** E2
N. Oxford MA, *1200*........ **150** B2
N. Palm Beach FL, *12015*........ **141** F4
N. Pembroke MA, *3292*........ **151** E2
N. Perry OH, *893*........ **91** E1
N. Plainfield NJ, *21936*........ **147** E1
N. Plains OR, *1947*........ **20** B1
N. Platte NE, *24733*........ **34** C3
N. Plymouth MA, *3600*........ **151** E2
N. Pole AK, *2117*........ **154** C2
Northport AL, *23330*........ **127** E1
N. Port FL, *57357*........ **140** C4
Northport MI, *526*........ **69** F3
Northport NY, *7401*........ **148** C3
N. Powder OR, *439*........ **21** F2
N. Prairie WI, *2141*........ **74** C3
N. Providence RI, *32078*........ **150** C3
N. Randall OH, *1027*........ **204** G2
N. Redington Beach FL, *1417*........ **266** A3
N. Richland Hills TX, *63343*........ **207** B2
Northridge OH, *7572*........ **208** D1
Northridge OH, *6853*........ **100** C1
N. Ridgeville OH, *29465*........ **91** D2
N. River Shores FL, *3079*........ **141** E4
N. Riverside IL, *6672*........ **203** D4
N. Rose NY, *636*........ **79** D3
N. Royalton OH, *30444*........ **91** E2
N. St. Paul MN, *11460*........ **235** D2
N. Scituate RI, *950*........ **150** C3
N. Sea NY, *4458*........ **149** E3
N. Shore LA, *1800*........ **134** C2
N. Sioux City SD, *2530*........ **35** F1
N. Somers CT, *1626*........ **150** A2
N. Springfield VT, *573*........ **81** E4
N. Springfield VA, *7274*........ **270** A5
N. Stonington CT, *5233*........ **149** F1
N. Swansea MA, *1100*........ **151** D3
N. Syracuse NY, *6800*........ **79** D3
N. Terre Haute IN, *4305*........ **99** E1
N. Tonawanda NY, *31568*........ **78** A3
N. Topsail Beach NC, *743*........ **115** D4
N. Troy VT, *620*........ **81** E1
N. Truro MA, *550*........ **151** F2
N. Tunica MS, *1035*........ **118** B2
N. Turner ME, *400*........ **82** B2
Northumberland PA, *3804*........ **93** D3
Northumberland Co. PA, *94528*........ **93** E3
Northumberland Co. VA, *12330*........ **103** F4
N. Uxbridge MA, *4200*........ **150** C2
N. Valley Stream NY, *16628*........ **241** G4
N. Vassalboro ME, *750*........ **82** C2
N. Vernon IN, *6728*........ **100** A2
Northville MA, *2400*........ **151** D2
Northville MI, *5970*........ **210** A2
Northville NY, *1099*........ **80** C4
Northville NY, *801*........ **149** E3
N. Wales PA, *3229*........ **146** C2
N. Walpole NH, *828*........ **81** E4
N. Webster IN, *1146*........ **89** F2
Northwest NC, *735*........ **123** E3
N. Westchester CT, *800*........ **149** E1
N. Wildwood NJ, *4041*........ **104** C4
N. Wilkesboro NC, *4245*........ **111** F4

Entries in **bold black** indicate counties or parishes.
Entries in **bold color** indicate cities with detailed inset maps.

N. Windham ME, 4904 ... 82 B3
Northwood IA, 1989 ... 73 D2
Northwood NH, 4241 ... 81 F4
Northwood ND, 945 ... 19 E3
Northwood OH, 5265 ... 90 C2
Northwoods MO, 4227 ... 256 B2
N. Woodstock NH, 528 ... 81 F3
Northwye MO, 550 ... 97 E4
N. York PA, 1914 ... 275 E1
Norton KS, 2928 ... 42 C1
Norton MA, 19031 ... 151 D2
Norton OH, 12085 ... 91 E3
Norton VA, 3958 ... 111 E2
Norton Co. KS, 5671 ... 42 C1
Norton Shores MI, 23994 ... 75 E3
Nortonville KS, 637 ... 96 A2
Nortonville KY, 1204 ... 109 E2
Norwalk CA, 105549 ... 52 C3
Norwalk CT, 85603 ... 148 C2
Norwalk IA, 8945 ... 86 C2
Norwalk OH, 17012 ... 91 D2
Norwalk WI, 638 ... 73 F2
Norway IA, 545 ... 87 E1
Norway ME, 2748 ... 82 B2
Norway MI, 2845 ... 69 D2
Norwell MA, 10506 ... 151 E2
Norwich CT, 40493 ... 149 F1
Norwich KS, 491 ... 43 E4
Norwich NY, 7190 ... 79 E4
Norwich VT, 878 ... 81 E3
Norwood CO, 518 ... 40 B3
Norwood KY, 370 ... 230 F1
Norwood MA, 28602 ... 151 D2
Norwood MO, 665 ... 107 E2
Norwood NY, 1657 ... 80 B1
Norwood NC, 2379 ... 122 B1
Norwood OH, 19207 ... 100 B2
Norwood PA, 5890 ... 248 B4
Norwood Young America MN, 3549 ... 66 C4
Notasulga AL, 965 ... 128 B2
Nottingham NH, 4785 ... 81 F4
Nottoway VA, 84 ... 113 D2
Nottoway Co. VA, 15853 ... 113 D2
Notus ID, 531 ... 22 B4
Novato CA, 51904 ... 36 B3
Novi MI, 55224 ... 76 B4
Novinger MO, 456 ... 87 D4
Nowata OK, 3731 ... 106 A3
Nowata Co. OK, 10536 ... 106 A2
Noxapater MS, 472 ... 126 C1
Noxon MT, 218 ... 14 C2
Noxubee Co. MS, 11545 ... 127 D1
Noyack NY, 3568 ... 149 E3
Nuangola PA, 679 ... 93 E3
Nuckolls Co. NE, 4500 ... 35 E4
Nucla CO, 711 ... 40 B3
Nueces Co. TX, 340223 ... 63 F2
Nuevo CA, 6447 ... 53 D3
Nuiqsut AK, 402 ... 154 C1
Nunda NY, 1377 ... 78 B4
Nunn CO, 416 ... 33 E4
Nutley NJ, 28370 ... 148 B3
Nutter Fort WV, 1593 ... 102 A2
Nyack NY, 6765 ... 148 B3
Nye Co. NV, 43946 ... 37 F3
Nyssa OR, 3267 ... 22 A4

O

Oacoma SD, 451 ... 27 D4
Oak Bluffs MA, 3735 ... 151 E4
Oakboro NC, 1859 ... 122 B1
Oak Brook IL, 7883 ... 203 C4
Oakbrook Terrace IL, 2134 ... 203 C4
Oak City UT, 578 ... 39 D2
Oak Creek CO, 884 ... 32 C4
Oak Creek WI, 34451 ... 74 C3
Oakdale CA, 20675 ... 36 C4
Oakdale CT, 1100 ... 149 F1
Oakdale KY, 4937 ... 109 D2
Oakdale LA, 7780 ... 133 E1
Oakdale MA, 1100 ... 150 C1
Oakdale MN, 27378 ... 235 E2
Oakdale NY, 7974 ... 149 D4
Oakdale PA, 1459 ... 92 A4
Oakes ND, 1856 ... 27 E1
Oakesdale WA, 422 ... 14 A3
Oakfield ME, 732 ... 85 D3
Oakfield NY, 1813 ... 78 B3
Oakfield WI, 1075 ... 74 C2
Oak Forest IL, 27962 ... 89 D2
Oak Grove AL, 528 ... 128 A1
Oak Grove IL, 396 ... 88 A2
Oak Grove KY, 7489 ... 109 E3
Oak Grove LA, 1727 ... 125 F1
Oak Grove MI, 700 ... 70 C4
Oak Grove MN, 8031 ... 67 D3
Oak Grove MS, 1400 ... 126 C4
Oak Grove OR, 16629 ... 251 D3
Oak Grove SC, 10291 ... 122 A3
Oak Grove TN, 4425 ... 111 E3
Oak Grove Hts. AR, 889 ... 108 A4
Oak Grove Village MO, 509 ... 96 C2
Oak Harbor OH, 2759 ... 90 C2
Oak Harbor WA, 22075 ... 12 C2
Oak Hill FL, 1792 ... 141 E1
Oak Hill OH, 1551 ... 101 D3
Oak Hill WV, 7730 ... 101 F4
Oak Hills IL, 2400 ... 256 D2
Oakhurst CA, 2829 ... 37 D4
Oakhurst NJ, 3995 ... 147 F2
Oakhurst OK, 2185 ... 51 F2
Oak Island NC, 6783 ... 123 E4
Oakland CA, 390724 ... 36 B4
Oakland FL, 2538 ... 141 D1
Oakland IL, 880 ... 99 D1
Oakland IA, 1527 ... 86 A2
Oakland ME, 2602 ... 82 C2
Oakland MD, 1925 ... 102 B2
Oakland MD, 2100 ... 144 B1
Oakland MS, 527 ... 118 B3
Oakland MO, 1381 ... 256 B3
Oakland NE, 1244 ... 35 F2
Oakland NJ, 12754 ... 148 A3
Oakland OK, 1057 ... 51 F4
Oakland OR, 927 ... 20 B4
Oakland PA, 616 ... 93 F1
Oakland TN, 6623 ... 118 C1
Oakland City IN, 2429 ... 99 E4
Oakland Co. MI, 1202362 ... 76 B4
Oakland Park FL, 41363 ... 143 F1
Oak Lawn IL, 56690 ... 89 D1
Oakley ID, 763 ... 31 D2
Oakley KS, 2045 ... 42 B2
Oakley UT, 1470 ... 31 F4
Oaklyn NJ, 4038 ... 248 D4
Oakman AL, 789 ... 119 E4
Oakmont PA, 6303 ... 92 A4
Oak Orchard DE, 750 ... 145 F4
Oak Park CA, 13811 ... 228 A2
Oak Park IL, 51878 ... 89 D1
Oak Park MI, 29319 ... 76 C4
Oak Park Hts. MN, 4339 ... 67 D3
Oak Ridge NJ, 750 ... 148 A3
Oak Ridge NC, 6185 ... 112 B4
Oakridge OR, 3205 ... 20 C4
Oak Ridge TN, 29330 ... 110 C4
Oak Ridge North TX, 3049 ... 132 A2
Oak Shade NJ, 1500 ... 147 D3
Oakton VA, 34166 ... 144 A3
Oaktown IN, 608 ... 99 E3
Oak Trail Shores TX, 2755 ... 59 E3
Oak View CA, 4066 ... 52 B2
Oakville CT, 9047 ... 149 D1
Oakville MO, 36143 ... 98 A3
Oakville WA, 684 ... 12 B4
Oakwood GA, 3970 ... 121 D3
Oakwood IL, 1595 ... 89 D4
Oakwood OH, 607 ... 90 B3
Oakwood OH, 3667 ... 204 G3
Oakwood OH, 9202 ... 208 E2
Oakwood Beach NJ, 700 ... 145 E1
Oakwood Hills IL, 2083 ... 203 A1
Oasis NV, 29 ... 30 C3
Oberlin KS, 1788 ... 42 C1
Oberlin LA, 1770 ... 133 E2
Oberlin OH, 8286 ... 91 D2
Oberlin PA, 588 ... 218 C2
Obetz OH, 4532 ... 206 B3
Obion TN, 1119 ... 108 C3
Obion Co. TN, 31807 ... 108 C3
Oblong IL, 1466 ... 99 D2
O'Brien Co. IA, 14398 ... 72 A3
Ocala FL, 56315 ... 138 C4
Occidental CA, 1115 ... 36 A3
Occoquan VA, 934 ... 144 B4
Oceana WV, 1394 ... 111 F1
Oceana Co. MI, 26570 ... 75 E2
Ocean Bluff MA, 4970 ... 151 E2
Ocean Breeze Park FL, 355 ... 141 E4
Ocean City FL, 5550 ... 136 B2
Ocean City MD, 7102 ... 114 C1
Ocean City NJ, 11701 ... 147 F4
Ocean Co. NJ, 576567 ... 147 E3
Ocean Gate NJ, 2011 ... 147 E3
Ocean Grove MA, 2811 ... 151 D3
Ocean Grove NJ, 3342 ... 147 F2
Oceano CA, 7286 ... 52 A1
Ocean Park WA, 1573 ... 12 B4
Ocean Pines MD, 11710 ... 114 C1
Oceanport NJ, 5832 ... 147 F2
Ocean Reef Club FL, 1000 ... 143 E3
Ocean Ridge FL, 1786 ... 143 F1
Ocean Shores WA, 5569 ... 12 B4
Oceanside CA, 167086 ... 53 D3
Oceanside NY, 32109 ... 147 F1
Oceanside OR, 361 ... 20 B2
Ocean Sprs. MS, 17442 ... 135 D2
Ocean View DE, 1882 ... 145 F4
Ochelata OK, 424 ... 51 F1
Ocheyedan IA, 490 ... 72 A2
Ochiltree Co. TX, 10223 ... 50 B2
Ochlocknee GA, 676 ... 137 E1
Ocilla GA, 3414 ... 129 E4
Ocoee FL, 35579 ... 141 D1
Oconee Co. GA, 32808 ... 121 D4
Oconee Co. SC, 74273 ... 121 E2
Oconomowoc WI, 15759 ... 74 C3
Oconto WI, 4513 ... 69 D4
Oconto Co. WI, 37660 ... 68 C4
Oconto Falls WI, 2891 ... 68 C4
Ocracoke NC, 948 ... 115 E3
Odebolt IA, 1013 ... 72 A4
Odell IL, 1046 ... 88 C3
Odell OR, 2255 ... 20 C1
Odem TX, 2389 ... 61 E4
Odenton MD, 37132 ... 144 C2
Odenville AL, 3585 ... 119 F4
Odessa DE, 364 ... 145 E1
Odessa FL, 7267 ... 140 B2
Odessa MO, 5300 ... 96 C2
Odessa NY, 591 ... 79 D4
Odessa TX, 99940 ... 58 A3
Odessa WA, 910 ... 13 F3
Odin IL, 1076 ... 98 C3
Odon IN, 1354 ... 99 E3
O'Donnell TX, 831 ... 58 A2
Oelwein IA, 6415 ... 73 E4
O'Fallon IL, 28281 ... 98 B3
O'Fallon MO, 79329 ... 98 A3
Ogallala NE, 4737 ... 34 B3
Ogden IL, 810 ... 89 D4
Ogden IA, 2044 ... 86 C1
Ogden KS, 2087 ... 43 F2
Ogden NC, 6766 ... 123 E3
Ogden UT, 82825 ... 31 E3
Ogden Dunes IN, 1110 ... 89 E2
Ogdensburg NJ, 2410 ... 148 A3
Ogdensburg NY, 11128 ... 80 B1
Ogemaw Co. MI, 21699 ... 76 B1
Oglala SD, 1290 ... 34 A1
Oglala Lakota Co. SD, 13586 ... 26 A4
Ogle Co. IL, 53497 ... 88 B1
Oglesby IL, 3791 ... 88 B2
Oglethorpe GA, 1328 ... 129 D3
Oglethorpe Co. GA, 14899 ... 121 E4
Ogunquit ME, 1226 ... 82 B4
Ohatchee AL, 1170 ... 120 A4
Ohio City OH, 705 ... 90 B3
Ohio Co. IN, 6128 ... 100 A2
Ohio Co. KY, 23842 ... 109 F1
Ohio Co. WV, 44443 ... 91 F4
Ohioville PA, 3533 ... 91 F3
Oil City LA, 1008 ... 124 C2
Oil City PA, 10557 ... 92 A2
Oildale CA, 32684 ... 45 D4
Oilton OK, 1013 ... 51 F2
Ojai CA, 7461 ... 52 B2
Okaloosa Co. FL, 180822 ... 136 B2
Okanogan WA, 2552 ... 13 E2
Okanogan Co. WA, 41120 ... 13 E1
Okarche OK, 1215 ... 51 E2
Okauchee WI, 4422 ... 74 C3
Okawville IL, 1434 ... 98 B3
Okay OK, 620 ... 106 A4
Okeechobee FL, 5621 ... 141 E4
Okeechobee Co. FL, 39996 ... 141 E3
Okeene OK, 1204 ... 51 D2
Okemah OK, 3223 ... 51 F3
Okemos MI, 21369 ... 76 A4
Okfuskee Co. OK, 12191 ... 51 F3
Oklahoma City OK, 579999 ... 51 E3
Oklahoma Co. OK, 718633 ... 51 E2
Okmulgee OK, 12321 ... 51 F2
Okmulgee Co. OK, 40069 ... 51 F2
Okoboji IA, 807 ... 72 A2
Okolona MS, 2692 ... 119 D3
Oktibbeha Co. MS, 47671 ... 118 C4
Ola AR, 1281 ... 117 D2
Olanta SC, 563 ... 122 C4
Olathe CO, 1849 ... 40 B3
Olathe KS, 125872 ... 96 B3
Olcott NY, 1241 ... 78 B3
Old Bennington VT, 139 ... 94 C1
Old Bridge NJ, 23753 ... 147 E1
Oldenburg IN, 674 ... 100 A2
Old Field NY, 918 ... 149 D3
Old Forge NY, 756 ... 79 F2
Old Forge PA, 8313 ... 93 F2
Old Fort NC, 908 ... 111 E4
Oldham SD, 133 ... 27 E3
Oldham Co. KY, 60316 ... 100 A4
Oldham Co. TX, 2052 ... 49 F3
Old Lyme CT, 7486 ... 149 E2
Old Mystic CT, 3554 ... 149 F2
Old Orchard Beach ME, 8624 ... 82 B4
Old River-Winfree TX, 1245 ... 132 B3
Old Saybrook CT, 10512 ... 149 E2
Oldsmar FL, 13591 ... 140 B2
Oldtown ID, 184 ... 14 B2
Old Town ME, 7840 ... 83 D1
Old Zionsville PA, 950 ... 146 B1
Olean NY, 14452 ... 92 C1
Oley PA, 1282 ... 146 B1
Olin IA, 698 ... 87 F1
Olive Branch MS, 33484 ... 118 B2
Olive Hill KY, 1599 ... 101 D4
Olivehurst CA, 13656 ... 36 C2
Oliver PA, 2535 ... 102 B1
Oliver Co. ND, 1846 ... 18 B4
Oliver Sprs. TN, 3231 ... 110 C4
Olivet MI, 1605 ... 76 A4
Olivet NJ, 1408 ... 145 F1
Olivet SD, 74 ... 35 E1
Olivette MO, 7737 ... 256 B2
Olivia MN, 2484 ... 66 B4
Olla LA, 1385 ... 125 E3
Olmos Park TX, 2237 ... 257 E2
Olmsted Co. MN, 144248 ... 73 E1
Olmsted Falls OH, 9024 ... 204 D3
Olney IL, 9115 ... 99 D3
Olney MD, 33844 ... 144 B2
Olney TX, 3285 ... 59 D1
Olney Sprs. CO, 345 ... 41 F3
Olpe KS, 546 ... 43 F3
Olton TX, 2215 ... 50 A4
Olustee OK, 607 ... 50 C4
Olympia WA, 46478 ... 12 B4
Olympian Vil. MO, 774 ... 98 A4
Olyphant PA, 5151 ... 261 E2
Omaha NE, 408958 ... 86 A2
Omaha TX, 1021 ... 124 B1
Omak WA, 4845 ... 13 E2
Omao HI, 1301 ... 152 B1
Omega GA, 1221 ... 129 D4
Omro WI, 3517 ... 74 C1
Onaga KS, 702 ... 43 F1
Onalaska TX, 1764 ... 132 B1
Onalaska WI, 17736 ... 73 F2
Onamia MN, 878 ... 66 C2
Onancock VA, 1263 ... 114 C3
Onarga IL, 1368 ... 89 D3
Onawa IA, 2998 ... 35 F2
Onaway ID, 187 ... 14 B4
Onaway MI, 880 ... 70 C3
Oneco FL, 7500 ... 140 B3
Oneida IL, 700 ... 88 A3
Oneida NY, 11393 ... 79 E3
Oneida TN, 3752 ... 110 B3
Oneida WI, 1070 ... 68 C4
Oneida Co. ID, 4286 ... 31 E2
Oneida Co. NY, 234878 ... 79 E2
Oneida Co. WI, 35998 ... 68 B2
O'Neill NE, 3705 ... 35 D2
Onekama MI, 411 ... 75 E1
Oneonta AL, 6567 ... 119 F4
Oneonta NY, 13901 ... 79 F4
Onida SD, 658 ... 26 C3
Onley VA, 516 ... 114 C3
Onondaga Co. NY, 467026 ... 79 E3
Onset MA, 1573 ... 151 E3
Onslow Co. NC, 177772 ... 115 D4
Onsted MI, 917 ... 90 B1
Ontario CA, 163924 ... 52 C2
Ontario OH, 6225 ... 91 D3
Ontario OR, 11366 ... 22 A4
Ontario Co. NY, 107931 ... 78 C4
Ontonagon MI, 1494 ... 65 E4
Ontonagon Co. MI, 6780 ... 65 E4
Onyx CA, 475 ... 45 E4
Oolitic IN, 1184 ... 99 F3
Oologah OK, 1146 ... 106 A3
Ooltewah TN, 687 ... 120 B2
Oostburg WI, 2887 ... 75 D2
Opal Cliffs CA, 6458 ... 236 D1
Opa-Locka FL, 15219 ... 143 E2
Opelika AL, 26477 ... 128 B2
Opelousas LA, 16634 ... 133 F2
Opp AL, 6659 ... 128 A4
Oppelo AR, 781 ... 117 E1
Oquawka IL, 1371 ... 87 F3
Oracle AZ, 3686 ... 55 D2
Oracle Jct. AZ, 550 ... 55 D3
Oradell NJ, 7978 ... 148 B3
Oran MO, 1294 ... 108 B2
Orange CA, 136416 ... 52 C3
Orange CT, 13956 ... 149 D2
Orange MA, 4018 ... 95 D1
Orange NJ, 32868 ... 240 A3
Orange OH, 3323 ... 204 G2
Orange TX, 18595 ... 132 C2
Orange VA, 4721 ... 103 D4
Orange Beach AL, 5441 ... 135 F2
Orangeburg NY, 4568 ... 148 B3
Orangeburg SC, 13964 ... 122 A4
Orangeburg Co. SC, 92501 ... 122 A4
Orange City FL, 10599 ... 141 D1
Orange City IA, 6004 ... 35 F1
Orange Co. CA, 3010232 ... 52 C3
Orange Co. FL, 1145956 ... 141 D1
Orange Co. IN, 19840 ... 99 F3
Orange Co. NY, 372813 ... 148 A2
Orange Co. NC, 133801 ... 112 C4
Orange Co. TX, 81837 ... 132 C2
Orange Co. VT, 28936 ... 81 E3
Orange Co. VA, 33481 ... 103 D4
Orange Cove CA, 9078 ... 45 D3
Orange Grove TX, 1318 ... 61 E4
Orange Lake FL, 650 ... 138 C4
Orange Lake NY, 6982 ... 148 B1
Orange Park FL, 8412 ... 139 D2
Orangeville IL, 793 ... 74 B4
Orangeville UT, 1470 ... 39 F2
Orbisonia PA, 424 ... 92 C4
Orchard Beach MD, 4400 ... 193 D5
Orchard City CO, 3119 ... 40 B2
Orchard Lake MI, 2375 ... 210 A1
Orchard Mesa CO, 6836 ... 40 B2
Orchard Park NY, 3246 ... 78 B4
Orchards WA, 19556 ... 20 C1
Orcutt CA, 28905 ... 52 A1
Ord NE, 2112 ... 35 D3
Orderville UT, 577 ... 39 D4
Ordway CO, 1080 ... 41 F3
Oreana IL, 875 ... 98 C1
Ore City TX, 1144 ... 124 B2
Orefield PA, 1600 ... 146 B1
Oregon IL, 3721 ... 88 B1
Oregon MO, 857 ... 96 B1
Oregon OH, 20291 ... 90 C2
Oregon WI, 9231 ... 74 B3
Oregon City OR, 31859 ... 20 C2
Oregon Co. MO, 10881 ... 107 F3
Oreland PA, 5678 ... 248 C1
Orem UT, 88328 ... 31 F4
Orfordville WI, 1442 ... 74 B4
Orient NY, 743 ... 149 F2
Oriental NC, 900 ... 115 E3
Orient Park FL, 5703 ... 266 C2
Orinda CA, 17643 ... 259 C2
Orion IL, 1861 ... 88 A2
Oriskany NY, 1400 ... 79 E3
Oriskany Falls NY, 732 ... 79 E3
Orland CA, 7291 ... 36 B1
Orland ME, 2134 ... 83 D2
Orland Hills IL, 7149 ... 203 C6
Orlando FL, 238300 ... 141 D1
Orland Park IL, 56767 ... 89 D2
Orleans IN, 2142 ... 99 F3
Orleans IA, 608 ... 72 B2
Orleans MA, 1621 ... 151 F3
Orleans NE, 386 ... 43 D1
Orleans VT, 818 ... 81 E1
Orleans Co. NY, 42883 ... 78 B3
Orleans Co. VT, 27231 ... 81 E1
Orleans Par. LA, 343829 ... 134 B2
Orlinda TN, 859 ... 109 F3
Orlovista FL, 6123 ... 246 B2
Ormond Beach FL, 38137 ... 139 E4
Ormond-by-the-Sea FL, 7406 ... 139 E4
Orofino ID, 3142 ... 14 B4
Orono ME, 9474 ... 83 D1
Orono MN, 7437 ... 66 C4
Oronoco MN, 1300 ... 73 D1
Oronogo MO, 2381 ... 106 B2
Orosi CA, 8770 ... 45 D3
Oro Valley AZ, 41011 ... 55 D3
Oroville CA, 15546 ... 36 C1
Oroville WA, 1686 ... 13 E1
Orrick MO, 837 ... 96 C2
Orrington ME, 3526 ... 83 D1
Orrs Island ME, 550 ... 82 B3
Orrville OH, 8380 ... 91 E3
Orting WA, 6746 ... 12 C3
Ortonville MI, 1442 ... 76 B3
Ortonville MN, 1916 ... 27 F2
Orwell OH, 1660 ... 91 F2
Orwigsburg PA, 3099 ... 146 A1
Osage IA, 3619 ... 73 D3
Osage WY, 208 ... 25 F4
Osage Beach MO, 4351 ... 97 D4
Osage City KS, 2943 ... 96 A3
Osage Co. KS, 16295 ... 96 A3
Osage Co. MO, 13878 ... 97 F4
Osage Co. OK, 47472 ... 51 F1
Osakis MN, 1740 ... 66 B2
Osawatomie KS, 4447 ... 96 B3
Osborne KS, 1431 ... 43 D2
Osborne Co. KS, 3858 ... 43 D2
Osburn ID, 1555 ... 14 B3
Oscawana Corners NY, 1500 ... 148 B2
Osceola AR, 7757 ... 108 B4
Osceola IN, 2463 ... 89 F2
Osceola IA, 4929 ... 86 C3
Osceola MO, 947 ... 96 C4
Osceola NE, 880 ... 35 E3
Osceola WI, 2568 ... 67 D3
Osceola Co. FL, 268685 ... 141 D2
Osceola Co. IA, 6462 ... 72 A2
Osceola Co. MI, 23528 ... 75 F1
Osceola Mills PA, 1141 ... 92 C3
Oscoda MI, 903 ... 76 C1
Oscoda Co. MI, 8640 ... 70 C4
Osgood IN, 1624 ... 100 A2
Oshkosh NE, 884 ... 34 A3
Oshkosh WI, 66083 ... 74 C1
Oskaloosa IA, 11463 ... 87 D2
Oskaloosa KS, 1113 ... 96 A2
Oslo FL, 1900 ... 141 E3
Osmond NE, 783 ... 35 E2
Osprey FL, 6100 ... 140 B4
Osseo MN, 2430 ... 235 A1
Osseo WI, 1701 ... 67 F4
Ossian IN, 3289 ... 90 A3

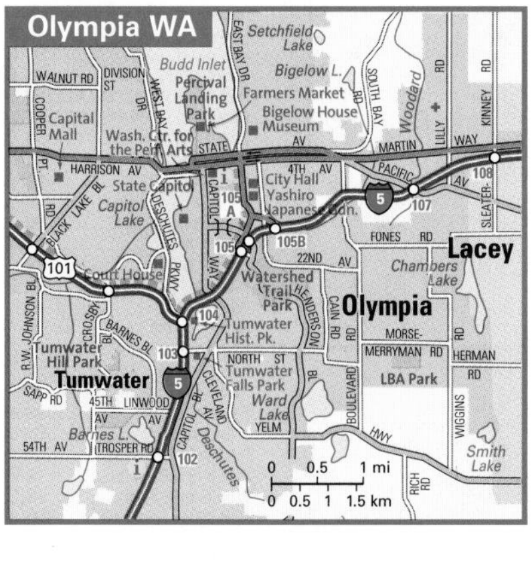

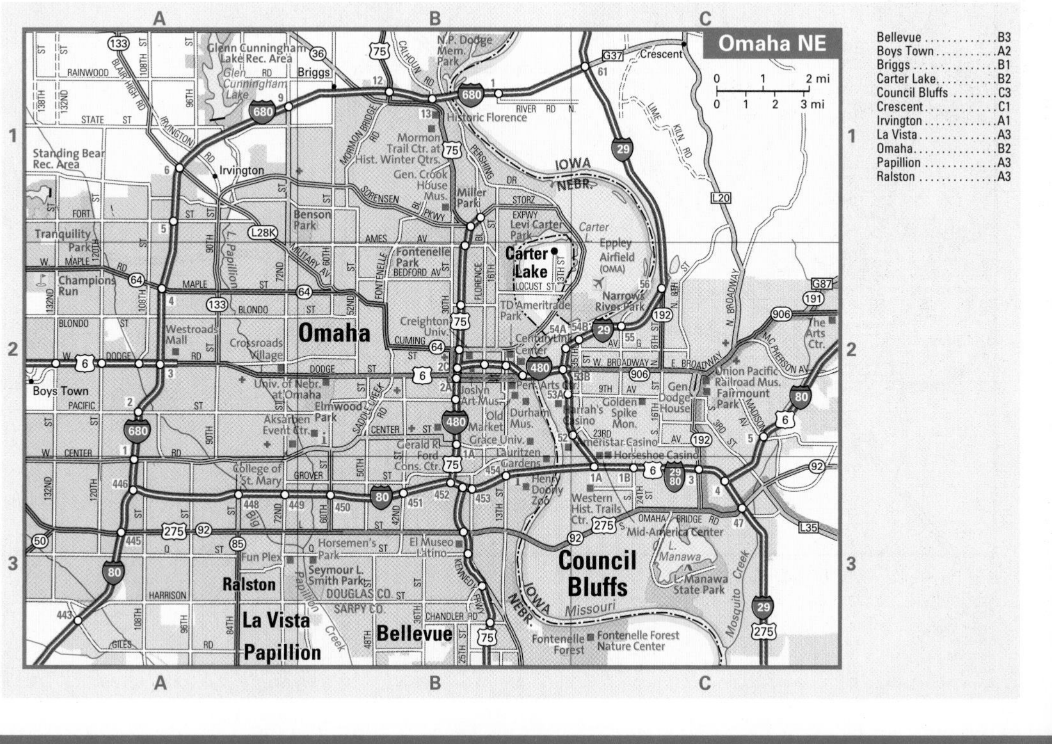

Figures after entries indicate population, page number, and grid reference.

Ossian IA, *845* **73** E3
Ossineke MI, *938* **71** D4
Ossining NY, *25060* **148** B2
Ossipee NH, *4345* **81** F3
Ossipee NC, *543* **112** B4
Osterville MA, *2900* **151** E4
Oswego IL, *30355* **88** C2
Oswego KS, *1829* **106** B2
Oswego NY, *18142* **79** D2
Oswego Co. NY, *122109* **79** E2
Osyka MS, *440* **134** B1
Otego NY, *1010* **79** F4
Otero Co. CO, *18831* **41** F4
Otero Co. NM, *63797* **57** D3
Othello WA, *7364* **13** E4
Otho IA, *542* **72** C4
Otis CO, *475* **41** F1
Otisville MI, *864* **76** B3
Otisville NY, *1068* **148** A1
Otoe Co. NE, *15740* **35** F4
Otsego MI, *3956* **75** F4
Otsego MN, *13571* **66** C3
Otsego Co. MI, *24164* **70** C3
Otsego Co. NY, *62259* **79** F4
Ottawa IL, *18768* **88** C2
Ottawa KS, *12649* **96** A3
Ottawa OH, *4460* **90** B3
Ottawa Co. KS, *6091* **43** E2
Ottawa Co. MI, *263801* **75** E3
Ottawa Co. OH, *41428* **90** C2
Ottawa Co. OK, *31848* **106** B2
Ottawa Hills OH, *4517* **267** A1
Otterbein IN, *1262* **89** E4
Otter Tail Co. MN, *57303* **19** F4
Ottoville OH, *976* **90** B3
Ottumwa IA, *25023* **87** E3
Otway NC, *700* **115** E4
Ouachita Co. AR, *26120* **117** D4
Ouachita Par. LA, *153720* **125** E2
Ouray CO, *1000* **40** C3
Ouray Co. CO, *4436* **40** B3
Outagamie Co. WI, *176695* **74** C1
Overall TN, *800* **109** F4
Overbrook KS, *1058* **96** A3
Overgaard AZ, *2722* **47** F4
Overland MO, *16062* **256** B2
Overland Park KS, *173372* **96** B3
Overlea MD, *12275* **144** C2
Overton NE, *594* **35** D4
Overton NV, *1700* **46** B1
Overton TX, *2554* **124** B3
Overton Co. TN, *22083* **110** B3
Ovid CO, *318* **34** A3
Ovid MI, *1603* **76** A3
Ovid NY, *602* **79** D4
Oviedo FL, *33342* **141** D1
Ovilla TX, *3492* **59** F3
Owasso OK, *28915* **106** A3
Owatonna MN, *25599* **73** D1
Owego NY, *3896* **93** E1
Owen WI, *940* **68** A4
Owen Co. IN, *21575* **99** E2
Owen Co. KY, *10841* **100** B3
Owens VA, *600* **103** E4
Owensboro KY, *57265* **109** E1
Owens Cross Roads AL, *1521* **119** F2
Owensville IN, *1284* **99** D4
Owensville MO, *2676* **97** F4
Owensville OH, *794* **100** B2
Owenton KY, *1327* **100** B3
Owings MD, *2149* **144** C4
Owings Mills MD, *30622* **144** C1
Owingsville KY, *1530* **100** C4
Owosso MI, *15194* **76** B3
Owsley Co. KY, *4755* **110** C1
Owyhee NV, *953* **30** B2
Owyhee Co. ID, *11526* **22** A4
Oxbow ND, *305* **19** F4
Oxford AL, *21348* **120** A4
Oxford AR, *670* **107** E3
Oxford CT, *12272* **149** D1
Oxford GA, *2134* **121** D4
Oxford IN, *1162* **89** D4
Oxford IA, *807* **87** E1
Oxford KS, *1049* **43** E4
Oxford ME, *1263* **82** B2
Oxford MD, *651* **145** D4
Oxford MA, *6103* **150** B2
Oxford MI, *3436* **76** C3
Oxford MS, *18916* **118** C3
Oxford NE, *779* **35** D4
Oxford NJ, *1090* **93** F3
Oxford NY, *1450* **79** E4
Oxford NC, *8461* **113** D3
Oxford OH, *21371* **100** B1
Oxford PA, *5077* **146** A3
Oxford WI, *607* **74** B2
Oxford Co. ME, *57833* **82** A2
Oxford Jct. IA, *496* **87** F1
Oxnard CA, *197899* **52** B2
Oxon Hill MD, *17722* **144** B3
Oyster Bay NY, *6707* **148** C3
Oyster Bay Cove NY, *2197* **148** C3
Oyster Creek TX, *1111* **132** A4
Ozark AL, *14907* **128** B4
Ozark AR, *3684* **116** C1
Ozark MO, *17820* **107** D2
Ozark Co. MO, *9723* **107** E3
Ozaukee Co. WI, *86395* **75** D2
Ozawkie KS, *645* **96** A2
Ozona TX, *3225* **60** B1

P

Paauilo HI, *595* **153** F2
Pablo MT, *2254* **15** D3
Pace FL, *20039* **135** F2
Pacheco CA, *3685* **259** D1
Pacific MO, *7002* **98** A3
Pacific WA, *6606* **262** B5
Pacifica CA, *37234* **36** B4
Pacific City OR, *1035* **20** B2
Pacific Co. WA, *20920* **12** B4
Pacific Grove CA, *15041* **44** B3
Pacific Jct. IA, *507* **86** A3
Pacolet SC, *2235* **121** F2
Paddock Lake WI, *2992* **74** C4
Paden OK, *461* **51** F3
Paden City WV, *2633* **101** F1
Paducah KY, *25024* **108** C2
Paducah TX, *1186* **58** C1
Page AZ, *7247* **47** E1
Page Co. IA, *15932* **86** B3
Page Co. VA, *24042* **102** C3
Pagedale MO, *3304* **256** B2
Pageland SC, *2760* **122** B2
Pagosa Sprs. CO, *1727* **40** C4
Paguate NM, *421* **48** B3
Pahala HI, *1356* **153** E4
Pahoa HI, *945* **153** F3
Pahokee FL, *5649* **141** E4
Pahrump NV, *36441* **46** A2
Paia HI, *2668* **153** D1
Paincourtville LA, *911* **134** A3
Painesville OH, *19563* **91** E1
Painted Post NY, *1809* **93** D1
Paint Rock TX, *273* **58** C4
Paintsville KY, *3459* **111** D1
Paisley FL, *818* **139** D4
Pajaro CA, *3070* **236** E1
Pala CA, *700* **53** D3
Palacios TX, *4718* **61** F3
Palatine IL, *68557* **89** D1
Palatine Bridge NY, *737* **79** F3
Palatka FL, *10558* **139** D3
Palenville NY, *1037* **94** B2
Palermo CA, *5382* **36** C2
Palermo NJ, *2300* **147** F4
Palestine AR, *681* **118** A2
Palestine IL, *1369* **99** D2
Palestine TX, *18712* **124** A3
Palisade CO, *2692* **40** B2
Palisades Park NJ, *19622* **148** B3
Palm Bay FL, *103190* **141** E2
Palm Beach FL, *8348* **143** F1
Palm Beach Co. FL, *1320134* **141** E4
Palm Beach Gardens FL, *48452* **141** F4
Palm Beach Shores FL, *1142* **141** F4
Palm City FL, *23120* **141** E4
Palm Coast FL, *75180* **139** E3
Palmdale CA, *152750* **52** C2
Palm Desert CA, *48445* **53** E3
Palmer AK, *5937* **154** C3
Palmer MA, *12140* **150** A2
Palmer NE, *472* **35** E3
Palmer TN, *672* **120** B1
Palmer TX, *2000* **59** F3
Palmer Lake CO, *2420* **41** E2
Palmer Park MD, *7000* **271** F3
Palmerton PA, *5414* **93** F3
Palmetto FL, *12606* **140** B3
Palmetto GA, *4488* **120** C4
Palmetto Bay FL, *23410* **143** E3
Palm Harbor FL, *57439* **140** B2
Palm River FL, *17589* **266** C2
Palm Shores FL, *900* **141** E2

Altamonte Sprs. C1
Apopka A1
Azalea Park D2
Bay Hill B3
Belle Isle C3
Bertha D1
Buena Ventura Lakes C5
Casselberry C1
Celebration A5
Clarcona B1
Conway C3
Doctor Phillips B3
Eatonville C1
Edgewood C3
Fairview Shores C1
Fairvilla C2
Fern Park C1
Flamingo C4
Forest City B1
Goldenrod D1
Gotha A2
Jamestown D1
Kissimmee B5
Lake Buena Vista B4
Lake Cain Hills B3
Lockhart B1
Maitland C1
Morningside Park C3
Narcoossee D5
Ocoee A2
Orlando C2
Orlovista B2
Piedmont B1
Pine Castle C3
Pine Hills B2
Sky Lake C3
Slavia D1
S. Apopka B1
Taft C4
Tangelo Park B3
Union Park D2
Vineland B4
Williamsburg B4
Windermere A3
Winter Garden A2
Winter Park C1
Winter Sprs. D1

Entries in **bold black** indicate counties or parishes.
Entries in **bold color** indicate cities with detailed inset maps.

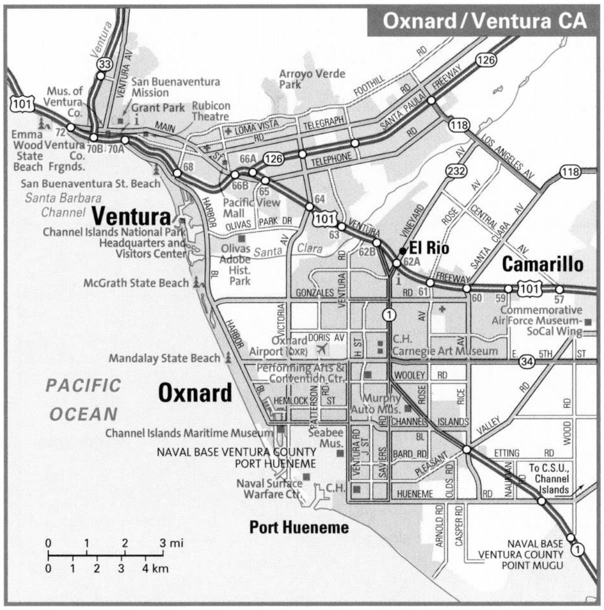

Palm Sprs. CA, *44552* 53 D3
Palm Sprs. FL, *18928* **143** F1
Palm Valley FL, *20019* **139** D2
Palmview TX, *5460* **63** E4
Palmyra IL, *698* **98** B2
Palmyra IN, *930* **99** F3
Palmyra MO, *3595* **97** F1
Palmyra NE, *545* **35** F4
Palmyra NJ, *7398* **146** C3
Palmyra NY, *3536* **78** C3
Palmyra PA, *7320* **93** E4
Palmyra VA, *104* **102** C4
Palmyra WI, *1781* **74** C3
Palo IA, *1026* **87** E1
Palo Alto CA, *64403* **36** B4
Palo Alto Co. IA, *9421* **72** B3
Palo Cedro CA, *1269* **28** C4
Palo Pinto TX, *333* **59** D2
Palo Pinto Co. TX, *28111* **59** D2
Palos Hts. IL, *12515* **203** D6
Palos Hills IL, *17484* **203** D5
Palos Park IL, *4847* **203** D6
Palos Verdes Estates CA, *13438* . **228** C4
Palouse WA, *998* **14** B4
Pamlico Co. NC, *13144* **115** E3
Pampa TX, *17994* **50** B3
Pamplico SC, *1226* **122** C3
Pana IL, *5847* **98** C2
Panaca NV, *963* **38** C4
Panacea FL, *816* **137** E3
Panama OK, *1413* **116** B1
Panama City FL, *36484* 136 C2
Panama City Beach FL, *12018* **136** C2
Pandora OH, *1153* **90** B3
Pangburn AR, *601* **117** F1
Panguitch UT, *1520* **39** D4
Panhandle TX, *2452* **50** B3
Panola Co. MS, *34707* **118** B3
Panola Co. TX, *23796* **124** C3

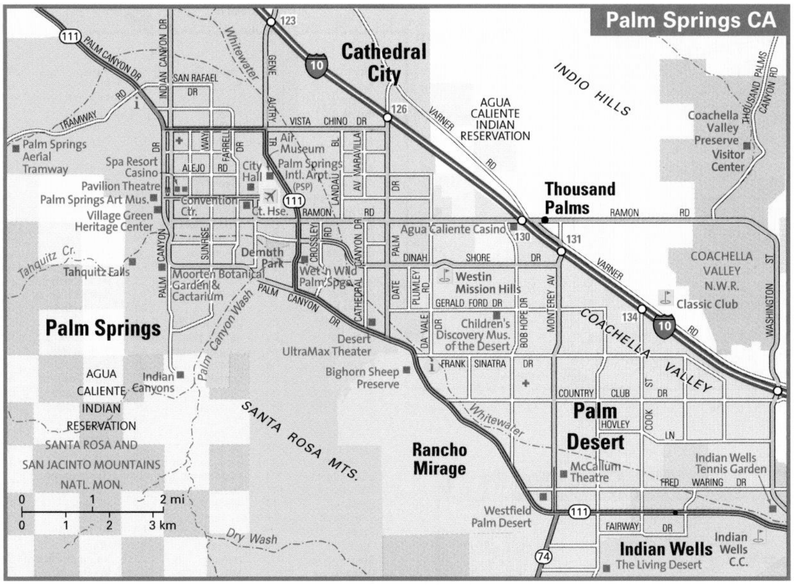

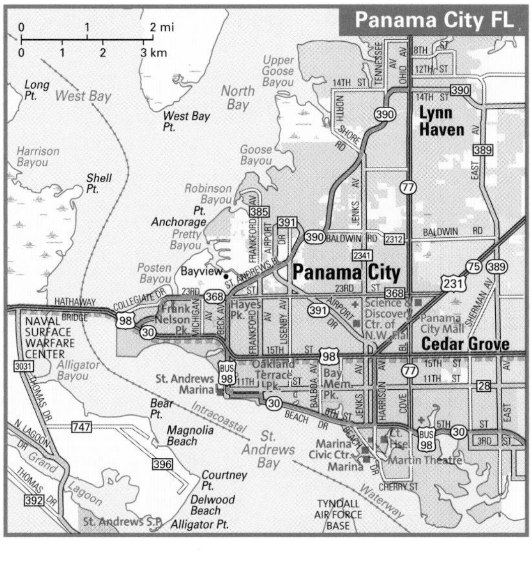

Panora IA, *1124* **86** B2
Panorama Vil. TX, *1965* **132** A2
Pantano AZ, *350* **55** D3
Pantego TX, *2394* **207** B3
Panthersville GA, *9749* **190** E4
Paola KS, *5602* **96** B3
Paoli IN, *3677* **99** F3
Paoli OK, *610* **51** E4
Paoli PA, *5575* **146** B3
Paonia CO, *1451* **40** C2
Papaikou HI, *1314* **153** F3
Papillion NE, *18894* **35** F3
Parachute CO, *1085* **40** B1
Paradis LA, *1298* **239** A2
Paradise CA, *26218* **36** C1
Paradise PA, *1129* **146** A3
Paradise UT, *904* **31** E3
Paradise Hills NM, *4256* **48** C3
Paradise Valley AZ, *12820* **249** C2
Paragon IN, *659* **99** F2
Paragonah UT, *488* **39** D4
Paragould AR, *26113* **108** A4
Paramount CA, *54098* **228** D3
Paramus NJ, *26342* **148** B3
Pardeeville WI, *2115* **74** B2
Paris AR, *3532* **116** C1
Paris ID, *513* **31** F2
Paris IL, *8837* **99** D1
Paris KY, *8553* **100** B4
Paris ME, *4793* **82** B2
Paris MO, *1220* **97** E2
Paris TN, *10156* **109** D3
Paris TX, *25171* **116** A4
Parish NY, *450* **79** D2

Parishville NY, *647* **80** B1
Park City KS, *7297* **43** E4
Park City KY, *537* **110** A2
Park City MT, *983* **24** B1
Park City UT, *7558* **31** F4
Park Co. CO, *16206* **41** D2
Park Co. MT, *15636* **23** F2
Park Co. WY, *28205* **24** B3
Parke Co. IN, *17339* **99** E1
Parker AZ, *3083* **46** B4
Parker CO, *45297* **41** E1
Parker FL, *4317* **136** C2
Parker ID, *305* **23** E4
Parker PA, *840* **92** A3
Parker SD, *1022* **27** F4
Parker City IN, *1419* **90** A4
Parker Co. TX, *116927* **59** E2
Parkersburg IA, *1870* **73** D4
Parkersburg WV, *31492* **101** E2
Parkers Prairie MN, *1011* **66** B1
Parkertown NJ, *1700* **147** E4
Parkesburg PA, *3593* **146** A3
Park Falls WI, *2462* **68** A2
Park Hill OK, *3909* **106** B4
Park Hills KY, *2970* **204** B3
Park Hills MO, *8759* **98** A4
Parkin AR, *1105* **118** A1
Parkland FL, *23962* **143** E1

Parkland WA, *35803* **12** C3
Park Lane CT, *650* **148** C1
Park Rapids MN, *3709* **64** A4
Park Ridge IL, *37480* **203** C3
Park Ridge NJ, *8645* **148** B3
Park River ND, *1403* **19** E2
Parks AZ, *1188* **47** D3
Parks LA, *653* **133** F2
Parkside PA, *2328* **248** A4
Parksley VA, *842* **114** C2
Parkston SD, *1508* **27** E4
Park View IA, *2389* **88** A1
Parkville MD, *30734* **144** C1
Parkville MO, *5554* **224** B2
Parkway Vil. KY, *650* **230** D2
Parlier CA, *14494* **45** D3
Parma ID, *1983* **22** A4
Parma MI, *769* **76** A4
Parma MO, *713* **108** B3
Parma OH, *81601* **91** E2
Parma Hts. OH, *20718* **204** E3
Parmelee SD, *562* **26** C4
Parmer Co. TX, *10269* **49** F4
Parowan UT, *2790* **39** D4
Parrish AL, *982* **119** E4
Parshall ND, *903* **18** B2
Parsons KS, *10500* **106** A1
Parsons TN, *2373* **109** D4

Parsons WV, *1485* **102** B2
Pasadena CA, *137122* **52** C2
Pasadena MD, *12093* **193** D5
Pasadena TX, *149043* **132** B3
Pascagoula MS, *22392* **135** D2
Pasco WA, *59781* **21** E1
Pascoag RI, *4577* **150** C2
Pasco Co. FL, *464697* **140** B2
Paso Robles CA, *29793* **44** C4
Pasquotank Co. NC, *40661* **115** E1
Passaic NJ, *69781* **148** B3
Passaic Co. NJ, *501226* **148** A3
Pass Christian MS, *4613* **134** C2
Patagonia AZ, *913* **55** D4
Pataskala OH, *14962* **101** D1
Patchogue NY, *11798* **149** D4
Pateros WA, *667* **13** E2
Paterson NJ, *146199* **148** B3
Patoka IL, *584* **98** C3
Patoka IN, *735* **99** D3
Patrick Co. VA, *18490* **112** B3
Patrick Sprs. VA, *1845* **112** B3
Patten ME, *1200* **85** D3
Pattenburg NJ, *800* **146** C1
Patterson AR, *452* **117** F1
Patterson CA, *20413* **36** C4
Patterson GA, *730* **129** F4
Patterson LA, *6112* **134** A3

Bellview A1
Brent B1
Brownsville B2
Ensley A1
Ferry Pass B1
Goulding B1
Gulf Breeze B2
Myrtle Grove A2
Pensacola B1
Pleasant Grove A2
Warrington A2
W. Pensacola A1

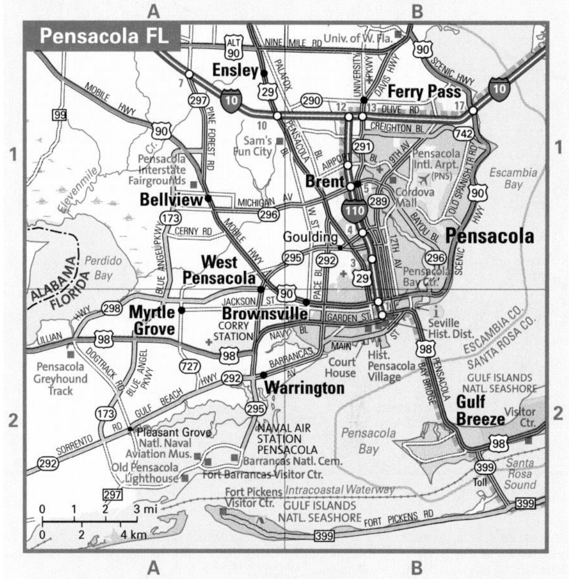

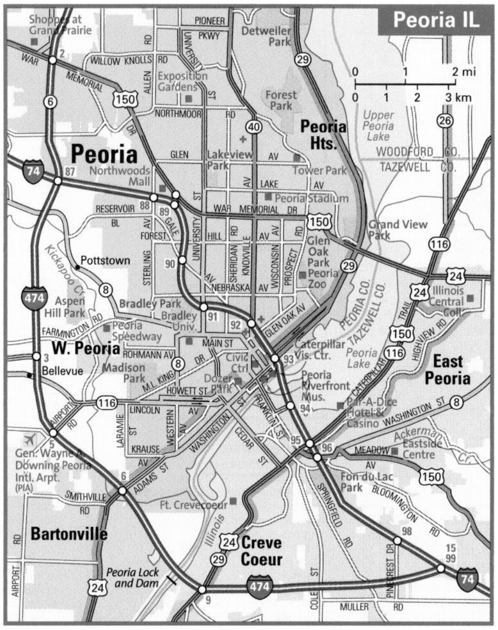

Figures after entries indicate population, page number, and grid reference.

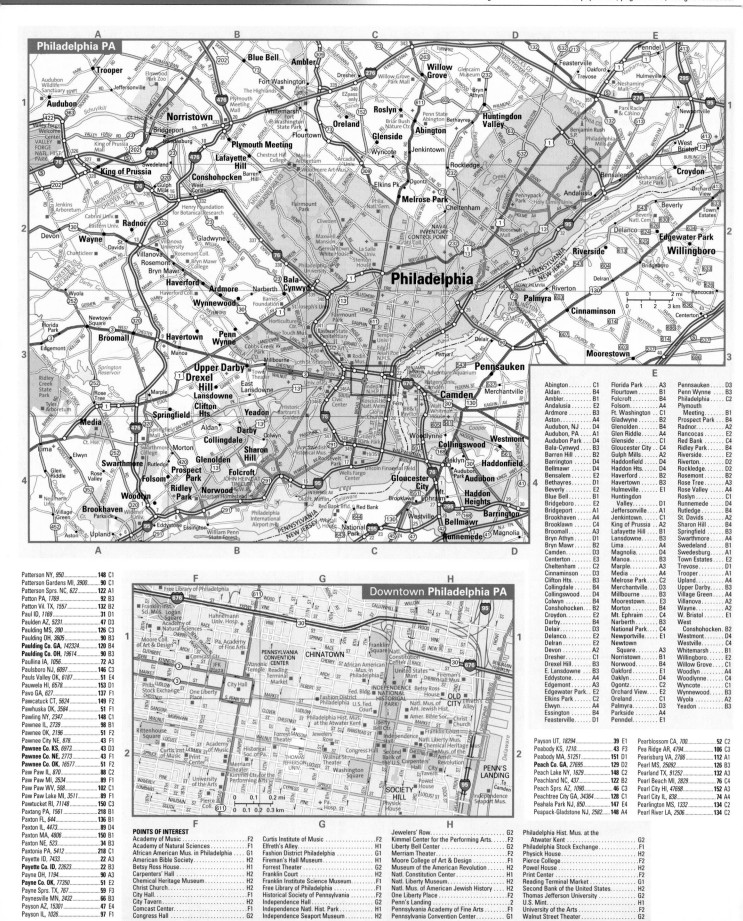

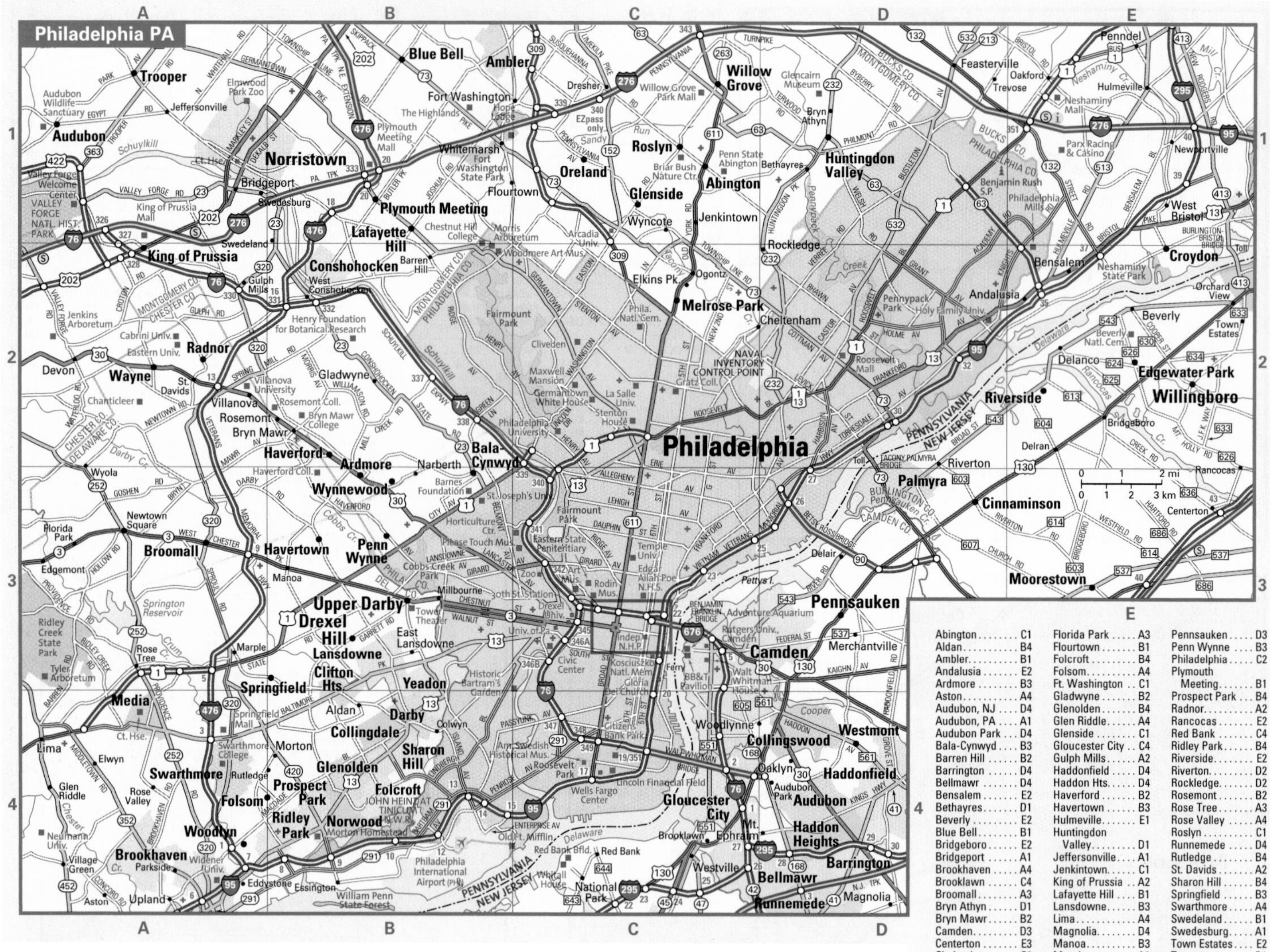

Abington C1
Aldan. B4
Ambler. B1
Andalusia E2
Ardmore B3
Aston. A4
Audubon, NJ D4
Audubon, PA A1
Audubon Park . . . D4
Bala-Cynwyd B3
Barren Hill B2
Barrington D4
Bellmawr D4
Bensalem E2
Bethayres. D1
Beverly E2
Blue Bell. B1
Bridgeboro E2
Bridgeport A1
Brookhaven A4
Brooklawn C4
Broomall. A3
Bryn Athyn D1
Bryn Mawr B2
Camden. D3
Centerton E3
Cheltenham C2
Cinnaminson D3
Clifton Hts. B3
Collingdale B4
Collingswood D4
Colwyn B4
Conshohocken. . . B2
Croydon. E2
Darby. B4
Delair. D3
Delanco. E2
Delran E2
Devon A2
Dresher. C1
Drexel Hill. B3
E. Lansdowne . . . B3
Eddystone. A4
Edgemont A3
Edgewater Park. . E2
Elkins Park C2
Elwyn. A4
Essington B4
Feasterville. D1
Florida Park A3
Flourtown B1
Folcroft B4
Folsom. A4
Ft. Washington . . C1
Gladwyne B2
Glenolden B4
Glen Riddle. A4
Glenside C1
Gloucester City . . C4
Gulph Mills. A2
Haddonfield D4
Haddon Hts. D4
Haverford B2
Havertown B3
Hulmeville. E1
Huntingdon Valley. D1
Jeffersonville. . . . A1
Jenkintown. C1
King of Prussia . . A2
Lafayette Hill B1
Lansdowne. B3
Lima A4
Magnolia. D4
Manoa. B3
Marple. A3
Media A4
Melrose Park C2
Merchantville. . . . D3
Millbourne B3
Moorestown. E3
Morton B4
Mt. Ephraim C4
Narberth B3
National Park. . . . C4
Newportville. E1
Newtown Square. A3
Norristown B1
Norwood. B4
Oakford E1
Oaklyn D4
Ogontz. C2
Orchard View. . . . E2
Oreland C1
Palmyra. D3
Parkside A4
Penndel. E1
Pennsauken D3
Penn Wynne B3
Philadelphia C2
Plymouth Meeting. B1
Prospect Park . . . B4
Radnor. A2
Rancocas E2
Red Bank C4
Ridley Park. B4
Riverside. E2
Riverton. D2
Rockledge. D2
Rosemont B2
Rose Tree A3
Rose Valley A4
Roslyn C1
Runnemede D4
Rutledge B4
St. Davids A2
Sharon Hill B4
Springfield B3
Swarthmore A4
Swedeland B1
Swedesburg. A1
Town Estates E2
Trevose D1
Trooper A1
Upland. A4
Upper Darby. B3
Village Green A4
Villanova A2
Wayne. A2
W. Bristol E1
West Conshohocken. B2
Westmont. D4
Westville. C4
Whitemarsh B1
Willingboro. E2
Willow Grove C1
Woodlyn A4
Woodlynne. C4
Wyncote C1
Wynnewood. B3
Wyola A2
Yeadon B3

Patterson NY, *950* **148** C1
Patterson Gardens MI, *3900* **90** C1
Patterson Sprs. NC, *622* **122** A1
Patton PA, *1769* **92** B3
Patton Vil. TX, *1557* **132** B2
Paul ID, *1169* **31** D1
Paulden AZ, *5231* **47** D3
Paulding MS, *200* **126** C3
Paulding OH, *3605* **90** B3
Paulding Co. GA, *142324* **120** B4
Paulding Co. OH, *19614* **90** B3
Paullina IA, *1056* **72** A3
Paulsboro NJ, *6097* **146** C3
Pauls Valley OK, *6187* **51** E4
Pauwela HI, *6578* **153** D1
Pavo GA, *627* **137** F1
Pawcatuck CT, *5624* **149** F2
Pawhuska OK, *3584* **51** F1
Pawling NY, *2347* **148** C1
Pawnee IL, *2739* **98** B1
Pawnee OK, *2196* **51** F2
Pawnee City NE, *878* **43** F1
Pawnee Co. KS, *6973* **43** D3
Pawnee Co. NE, *2773* **43** F1
Pawnee Co. OK, *16577* **51** F2
Paw Paw IL, *870* **88** C2
Paw Paw MI, *3534* **89** F1
Paw Paw WV, *508* **102** C1
Paw Paw Lake MI, *3511* **89** F1
Pawtucket RI, *71148* **150** C3
Paxtang PA, *1561* **218** B1
Paxton FL, *644* **136** B1
Paxton IL, *4473* **89** D4
Paxton MA, *4806* **150** B1
Paxton NE, *523* **34** B3
Paxtonia PA, *5412* **218** C1
Payette ID, *7433* **22** A3
Payette Co. ID, *22623* **22** B3
Payne OH, *1194* **90** A3
Payne Co. OK, *77350* **51** E2
Payne Sprs. TX, *767* **59** F3
Paynesville MN, *2432* **66** B3
Payson AZ, *15301* **47** E4
Payson IL, *1026* **97** F1

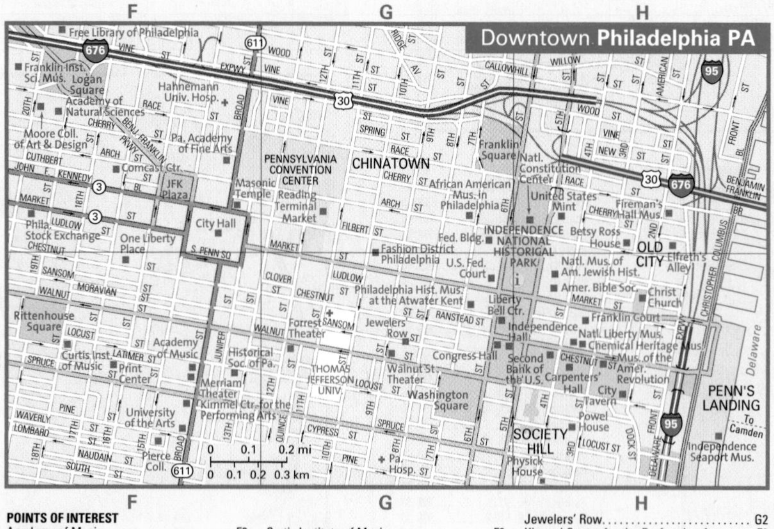

POINTS OF INTEREST

Academy of Music F2
Academy of Natural Sciences F1
African American Mus. in Philadelphia G1
American Bible Society H2
Betsy Ross House H1
Carpenters' Hall H2
Chemical Heritage Museum H2
Christ Church H2
City Hall F1
City Tavern H2
Comcast Center F1
Congress Hall G2
Curtis Institute of Music F2
Elfreth's Alley H1
Fashion District Philadelphia G1
Fireman's Hall Museum H1
Forrest Theater G2
Franklin Court H2
Franklin Institute Science Museum F1
Free Library of Philadelphia F1
Historical Society of Pennsylvania F2
Independence Hall G2
Independence Natl. Hist. Park H1
Independence Seaport Museum H2
Jewelers' Row G2
Kimmel Center for the Performing Arts F2
Liberty Bell Center G2
Merriam Theater F2
Moore College of Art & Design F1
Museum of the American Revolution H2
Natl. Constitution Center H1
Natl. Liberty Museum H2
Natl. Mus. of American Jewish History H2
One Liberty Place F2
Penn's Landing 2
Pennsylvania Academy of Fine Arts F1
Pennsylvania Convention Center G1
Philadelphia Hist. Mus. at the Atwater Kent G2
Philadelphia Stock Exchange F1
Physick House H2
Pierce College F2
Powel House H2
Print Center F2
Reading Terminal Market G1
Second Bank of the United States H2
Thomas Jefferson University G2
U.S. Mint H1
University of the Arts F2
Walnut Street Theater G2

Payson UT, *18294* **39** E1
Peabody KS, *1210* **43** F3
Peabody MA, *51251* **151** D1
Peach Co. GA, *27695* **129** D2
Peach Lake NY, *1629* **148** C2
Peachland NC, *437* **122** B2
Peach Sprs. AZ, *1090* **46** C3
Peachtree City GA, *34364* **128** C1
Peahala Park NJ, *850* **147** E4
Peapack-Gladstone NJ, *2582* **148** A4
Pearblossom CA, *700* **52** C2
Pea Ridge AR, *4794* **106** C3
Pearisburg VA, *2786* **112** A1
Pearl MS, *25092* **126** B3
Pearland TX, *91252* **132** A3
Pearl Beach MI, *2829* **76** C4
Pearl City HI, *47698* **152** A3
Pearl City IL, *838* **74** A4
Pearlington MS, *1332* **134** C2
Pearl River LA, *2506* **134** C2

Entries in **bold black** indicate counties or parishes.
Entries in **bold color** indicate cities with detailed inset maps.

Pearl River NY, *15876* **148** B3
Pearl River Co. MS, *55834* **134** C1
Pearsall TX, *9146* **61** D3
Pearson GA, *2117* **129** E4
Pecatonica IL, *2195* **74** B4
Peck ID, *197* **14** B4
Peck MI, *632* **76** C3
Pecksville NY, *1300* **148** C1
Peconic NY, *683* **149** E3
Pecos NM, *1392* **49** D3
Pecos TX, *8780* **57** F4
Pecos Co. TX, *15507* **57** F4
Peculiar MO, *4608* **96** B3
Peebles OH, *1782* **100** C3
Peekskill NY, *23583* **148** B2
Pe Ell WA, *632* **12** B4
Peeples Valley AZ, *428* **47** D4
Peever SD, *168* **27** F2
Pegram TN, *2093* **109** E4
Pekin IL, *34094* **88** B4
Pelahatchie MS, *1334* **126** B2
Peletier NC, *644* **115** D4
Pelham AL, *21352* **127** F1
Pelham GA, *3898* **137** E1
Pelham NH, *12897* **95** E1
Pelham NY, *6910* **148** B3
Pelham Manor NY, *5486* **148** B3
Pelican Rapids MN, *2464* **19** F4
Pelion SC, *674* **122** A4
Pella IA, *10352* **87** D2
Pell City AL, *12695* **120** A4
Pellston MI, *822* **70** C3
Pemberton NJ, *1409* **147** D3
Pemberville OH, *1371* **90** C2
Pembina ND, *592* **19** E1
Pembina Co. ND, *7413* **19** E1
Pembroke GA, *2196* **130** B3
Pembroke KY, *869* **109** E2
Pembroke ME, *879* **83** E1
Pembroke MA, *16927* **151** E2
Pembroke NC, *2973* **122** C2
Pembroke VA, *1128* **112** A1
Pembroke Park FL, *6102* **233** B3
Pembroke Pines FL, *154750* **143** E2
Pemiscot Co. MO, *18296* **108** B4
Pena Blanca NM, *709* **48** C3
Pen Argyl PA, *3595* **93** F3
Peñasco NM, *589* **49** D2
Penbrook PA, *3008* **218** B1
Pender NE, *1002* **35** F2
Pender Co. NC, *52217* **115** C4
Pendleton IN, *4253* **99** F1
Pendleton MO, *43* **97** F3
Pendleton OR, *16612* **21** F1
Pendleton SC, *2964* **121** E2
Pendleton Co. KY, *14877* **100** B3
Pendleton Co. WV, *7695* **102** B3
Pend Oreille Co. WA, *13001* **14** B2
Penhook VA, *801* **112** B2
Peninsula OH, *565* **91** E2
Penitas TX, *4403* **63** E4
Penndel PA, *2328* **147** D2
Penney Farms FL, *749* **139** D3
Penn Hills PA, *42329* **92** A4
Pennington NJ, *2585* **147** D2
Pennington Co. MN, *13930* **19** F2
Pennington Co. SD, *100948* **26** A4
Pennington Gap VA, *1781* **111** D2
Pennock MN, *508* **66** B3
Pennsauken NJ, *35885* **146** C3
Pennsboro WV, *1171* **101** F2
Pennsburg PA, *3843* **146** B1
Pennsbury Vil. PA, *661* **250** A2
Penns Creek PA, *715* **93** D3
Penns Grove NJ, *5147* **146** B4
Pennsville NJ, *11888* **145** E1
Pennville IN, *701* **90** A4
Penn Wynne PA, *5697* **248** B3
Penn Yan NY, *5159* **78** C4
Penobscot Co. ME, *153923* **83** D1
Penrose CO, *3582* **41** E3
Pensacola FL, *51923* **135** F2
Pensacola Beach FL, *750* **135** F2
Pentwater MI, *857* **75** E2
Peoria AZ, *154065* **54** C1
Peoria IL, *115007* **88** B3
Peoria Co. IL, *186494* **88** B3
Peoria Hts. IL, *6156* **88** B3
Peosta IA, *1377* **73** F4
Peotone IL, *4142* **89** D2
Pepeekeo HI, *1789* **153** F3
Pepin WI, *837* **73** E1
Pepin Co. WI, *7469* **67** E4
Pepperell MA, *2504* **95** D1
Pepper Pike OH, *5979* **204** G2
Pequannock NJ, *16658* **148** A3
Pequot Lakes MN, *2162* **64** A4
Peralta NM, *3660* **48** C4
Percy IL, *970* **98** B4
Perham MN, *2985* **19** F4
Peridot AZ, *1350* **55** D2
Perkasie PA, *8511* **146** C1
Perkins OK, *2831* **51** F2
Perkins Corner CT, *1000* **150** B3
Perkins Co. NE, *2970* **34** B4
Perkins Co. SD, *2982* **26** B2
Perkinston MS, *700* **135** D1
Perkiomenville PA, *1000* **146** B2
Perquimans Co. NC, *13453* **113** F4
Perris CA, *68386* **53** D3
Perry FL, *7017* **137** F2
Perry GA, *13839* **129** D2
Perry IA, *7702* **86** C1

Avondale A2
Chandler C3
El Mirage A1
Ft. McDowell D1
Fountain Hills D1
Gilbert D3
Glendale A2
Goodyear A2
Guadalupe C3
Komatke B3
Litchfield Park A2
Maricopa Vil. A3
Mesa D2
Paradise Valley C2
Peoria A1
Phoenix B1
Queen Creek D3
Rio Verde D1
Santa Cruz B3
Scottsdale C1
Sun City A1
Sun City West A1
Surprise A1
Tempe C3
Tolleson A2
Youngtown A1

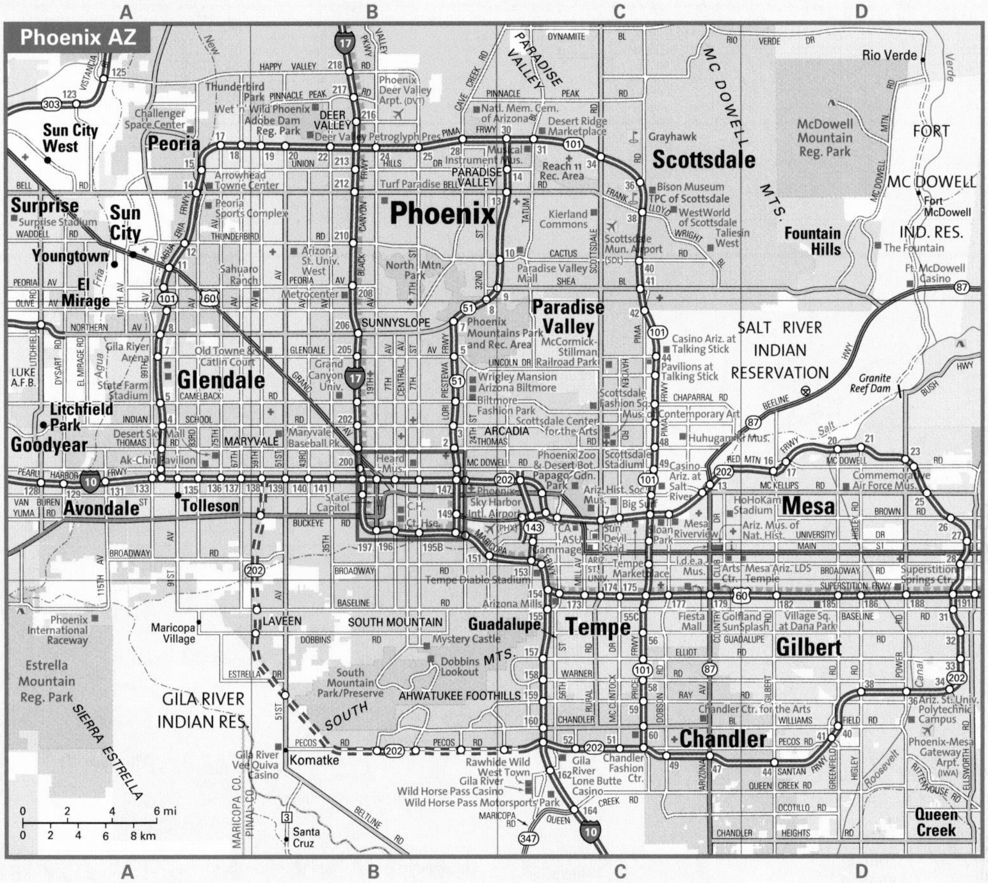

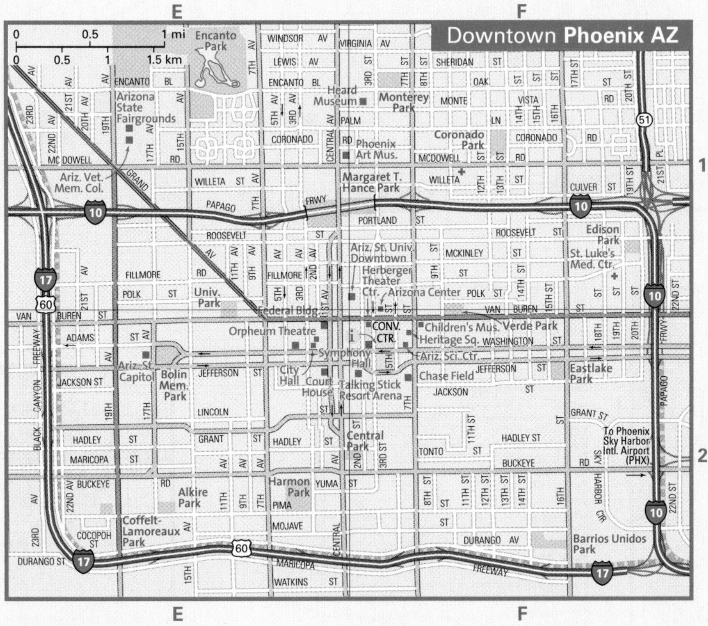

POINTS OF INTEREST

Arizona Center F1
Arizona Science Center F2
Arizona State Capitol E2
Arizona State Fairgrounds E1
Arizona Veterans Memorial Coliseum E1
Chase Field F2
Children's Museum F2
City Hall E2
Convention Center F2
Heard Museum F1
Herberger Theater Center F2
Heritage Square F2
Orpheum Theatre E2
Phoenix Art Museum E1
Symphony Hall F2
Talking Stick Resort Arena F2

Perry KS, *929* **96** A2
Perry LA, *1300* **133** F3
Perry MI, *2188* **76** B3
Perry MO, *693* **97** F2
Perry NY, *3673* **78** B4
Perry OH, *1663* **91** E1
Perry OK, *5126* **51** E2
Perry UT, *4512* **31** E3
Perry Co. AL, *10591* **127** F2
Perry Co. AR, *10445* **117** D2
Perry Co. IL, *22350* **98** B4
Perry Co. IN, *19338* **99** E4
Perry Co. KY, *28712* **111** D2
Perry Co. MS, *12250* **135** D1
Perry Co. MO, *18971* **108** B1
Perry Co. OH, *36058* **101** E1
Perry Co. PA, *45969* **93** D4
Perry Co. TN, *7915* **119** E1
Perry Hall MD, *28474* **144** C1
Perry Hts. OH, *8441* **91** E3
Perryman MD, *2342* **145** D1
Perryopolis PA, *1784* **92** A4
Perrysburg OH, *20623* **90** C2
Perrysville IN, *456* **89** D4
Perrysville OH, *735* **91** D3
Perryton TX, *8802* **50** B2

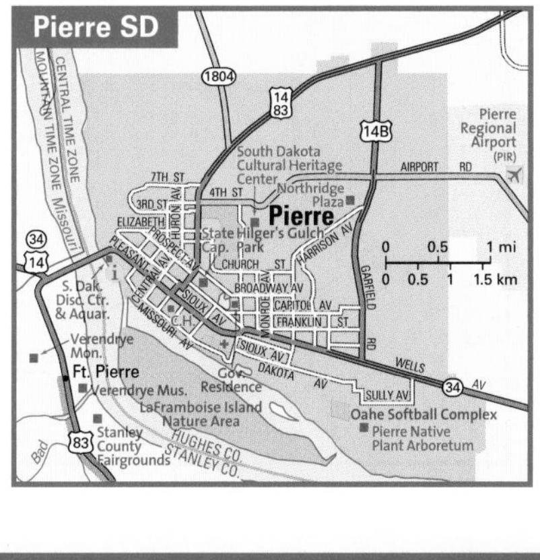

Perryville AR, *1460* **117** D2
Perryville KY, *751* **110** B1
Perryville MD, *4361* **145** D1
Perryville MO, *8225* **108** B1
Pershing Co. NV, *6753* **29** F4
Person Co. NC, *39464* **112** C3
Perth Amboy NJ, *50814* **147** E1
Peru IL, *10295* **88** B2
Peru IN, *11417* **89** F3
Peru NE, *865* **86** A4
Peru NY, *1591* **81** D2
Peshastin WA, *650* **13** D3
Peshtigo WI, *3502* **69** D3
Petal MS, *10454* **126** C4
Petaluma CA, *57941* **36** B3
Peterborough NH, *3103* **95** D1
Petersburg AK, *2948* **155** E4
Petersburg IL, *2260* **98** B1
Petersburg IN, *2383* **99** E3
Petersburg KY, *620* **100** B2
Petersburg MI, *1146* **90** C1
Petersburg NJ, *2900* **148** A3
Petersburg PA, *455* **93** C4
Petersburg TN, *544* **119** F1
Petersburg TX, *1202* **58** A1
Petersburg VA, *32420* **113** E2
Petersburg WV, *2467* **102** B2
Peterstown WV, *653* **112** A1
Petersville AL, *3137* **119** E2
Petoskey MI, *5670* **70** B3
Petroleum Co. MT, *494* **16** C3
Petrolia TX, *686* **59** D1
Petros TN, *583* **110** C4
Pettis Co. MO, *42201* **97** D3
Pettit OK, *954* **106** B4
Pettus TX, *558* **61** E4
Pevely MO, *5484* **98** A4
Pewamo MI, *469* **76** A3
Pewaukee (city) WI, *13195* **234** A2
Pewaukee (village) WI, *8166* **234** A2
Pewee Valley KY, *1456* **100** A4
Pflugerville TX, *46936* **61** E1
Pharr TX, *70400* **63** E4
Phelan CA, *14304* **53** D2
Phelps KY, *893* **111** E1
Phelps NY, *1989* **78** C3
Phelps Co. MO, *45156* **97** F4
Phelps Co. NE, *9188* **35** D4
Phenix City AL, *32822* **128** C2
Philadelphia MS, *7477* **126** C2
Philadelphia NY, *1252* **79** E1
Philadelphia PA, *1517550* **146** C3
Philadelphia TN, *656* **110** C4
Philadelphia Co. PA, *1526006* **146** C3
Phil Campbell AL, *1148* **119** E3
Philip SD, *779* **26** B3
Philippi WV, *2966* **102** A2
Philipsburg MT, *820* **15** D4
Philipsburg PA, *2770* **92** C3
Phillips ME, *990* **82** B1
Phillips WI, *1478* **68** A2
Phillipsburg KS, *2581* **43** D1
Phillipsburg NJ, *14950* **93** F3
Phillipsburg OH, *557* **100** B1
Phillips Co. AR, *21757* **118** A3
Phillips Co. CO, *4442* **34** A4
Phillips Co. KS, *5642* **43** D1
Phillips Co. MT, *4253* **16** C2
Philmont NY, *1379* **94** B2
Philo IL, *1466* **99** D1
Philo OH, *733* **101** E1
Philomath OR, *4584* **20** B3
Philpot KY, *850* **109** E1
Phoenix AZ, *1445632* **54** C1
Phoenix IL, *1964* **203** E6
Phoenix NY, *2382* **79** D3
Phoenix OR, *4538* **28** B2
Phoenixville PA, *16440* **146** B2
Pia Oik AZ, *450* **54** B3
Piatt Co. IL, *16729* **98** C1
Picacho AZ, *471* **54** C2
Picayune MS, *10878* **134** C2
Picher OK, *20* **106** B2
Pickaway Co. OH, *55698* **101** D1
Pickens MS, *1157* **126** B1
Pickens SC, *3126* **121** E2
Pickens Co. AL, *19746* **119** D4
Pickens Co. GA, *29431* **120** C3
Pickens Co. SC, *119224* **121** E2

Figures after entries indicate population, page number, and grid reference.

Pickensville AL, *608* **127** D1
Pickerington OH, *18291* **101** D1
Pickett Co. TN, *5077* **110** B3
Pico Rivera CA, *62942* **228** E3
Picture Rocks PA, *678* **93** E2
Piedmont AL, *4878* **120** A4
Piedmont CA, *10667* **259** C2
Piedmont MO, *1977* **108** A2
Piedmont OK, *5720* **51** E2
Piedmont SC, *5103* **121** E2
Piedmont SD, *222* **25** F3
Piedmont WV, *876* **102** B2
Pierce CO, *834* **33** E4
Pierce ID, *508* **14** C4
Pierce NE, *1767* **35** E2
Pierce City MO, *1292* **106** C2
Pierce Co. GA, *18758* **129** F4
Pierce Co. NE, *7266* **35** E2
Pierce Co. ND, *4357* **18** C2
Pierce Co. WA, *795225* **12** C4
Pierce Co. WI, *41019* **67** E4
Pierceton IN, *1015* **89** F2
Pierre SD, *13646* 26 C3
Pierre Part LA, *3169* **134** A3
Pierron IL, *600* **98** B3
Pierson FL, *1736* **139** D4
Pierz MN, *1393* **66** C2
Pigeon LA, *600* **134** A2
Pigeon MI, *1208* **76** C2
Pigeon Cove MA, *1700* **151** F1
Pigeon Forge TN, *5875* **111** D4
Piggott AR, *3849* **108** B3
Pike Co. AL, *32899* **128** A4
Pike Co. AR, *11291* **117** D3
Pike Co. GA, *17869* **128** C1
Pike Co. IL, *16430* **98** A1
Pike Co. IN, *12845* **99** E3
Pike Co. KY, *65024* **111** E1
Pike Co. MS, *40404* **126** B4
Pike Co. MO, *18516* **97** F2
Pike Co. OH, *28709* **101** D2
Pike Co. PA, *57369* **93** F2
Pikesville MD, *30764* **144** C1
Piketon OH, *2181* **101** D2
Pikeville KY, *6903* **111** E1
Pikeville NC, *678* **123** E1
Pikeville TN, *1608* **120** B1
Pilot Grove MO, *768* **97** D3
Pilot Knob MO, *746* **108** A1
Pilot Mtn. NC, *1477* **112** A3
Pilot Pt. TX, *3856* **59** F1
Pilot Rock OR, *1502* **21** F2
Pilot Sta. AK, *568* **154** B3
Pima AZ, *2387* **55** E2
Pima Co. AZ, *980263* **54** C3
Pimmit Hills VA, *6094* **270** B3
Pinal Co. AZ, *375770* **55** D2
Pinardville NH, *4780* **81** F4
Pinch WV, *3262* **101** F3
Pinckard AL, *647* **128** B4
Pinckney MI, *2427* **76** B4
Pinckneyville IL, *5648* **98** B4
Pinconning MI, *1307* **76** B2
Pine AZ, *1963* **47** E4
Pine Beach NJ, *2127* **147** E3
Pine Bluff AR, *49083* **117** E3
Pinebluff NC, *1337* **122** C1
Pine Bluffs WY, *1129* **33** F3
Pine Bush NY, *1780* **148** A1
Pine Castle FL, *10805* **141** D1
Pine City MN, *3123* **67** D2
Pine Co. MN, *29750* **64** C4
Pinecrest FL, *600* **140** C3
Pinecrest FL, *18223* **233** A5
Pineda FL, *1100* **141** E2
Pinedale WY, *2030* **32** A1
Pine Forest TX, *487* **132** C2
Pine Grove CA, *2219* **36** C3
Pine Grove PA, *2186* **146** A1
Pine Grove WV, *552* **101** F1
Pine Grove Mills PA, *1502* **92** C3
Pine Haven WY, *490* **25** E3
Pine Hill AL, *975* **127** E3
Pine Hill NJ, *10233* **146** C3
Pine Hills FL, *60076* **246** B2
Pinehurst ID, *1619* **14** B3
Pinehurst MA, *7152* **151** D1
Pinehurst NC, *13124* **122** C1
Pinehurst TX, *4624* **132** A2
Pinehurst TX, *2274* **132** C2
Pine Island MN, *3263* **73** D1
Pine Island NY, *700* **148** A2
Pine Island TX, *988* **61** F2
Pine Island Ctr. FL, *1854* **214** A1
Pine Knoll Shores NC, *1339* **115** D4
Pine Knot KY, *1621* **110** C3
Pineland FL, *407* **142** C1
Pineland TX, *850* **124** C4
Pine Lawn MO, *3275* **256** B2
Pine Level NC, *1700* **123** E1
Pinellas Co. FL, *916542* **140** B2
Pinellas Park FL, *49079* **140** B3
Pine Mtn. GA, *1304* **128** C2
Pine Plains NY, *1353* **94** B2
Pine Pt. ME, *600* **82** B3
Pine Prairie LA, *1610* **133** E1
Pine Ridge SC, *2064* **122** A4
Pine Ridge SD, *3308* **34** A1
Pine River MN, *944* **64** A4
Pinesdale MT, *917* **15** D4
Pinetop-Lakeside AZ, *4282* **47** F4
Pinetops NC, *1374* **113** E4
Pinetown DE, *1100* **145** F4
Pine Valley CA, *1510* **53** D4
Pine Valley NY, *813* **93** D1

Acmetonia D1
Aspinwall C1
Avalon A1
Baldwin C3
Bellevue B1
Ben Avon A1
Ben Avon Hts. A1
Bethel Park B3
Blawnox C1
Braddock C2
Braddock Hills C2
Brentwood B3
Bridgeville A3
Broughton B3
Carnegie A2
Castle Shannon B3
Chalfant D2
Cheswick D1
Churchill D2
Coraopolis A1
Crafton A2
Cuddy A3
Dormont B3
Dravosburg C3
Duquesne D3
E. McKeesport D3
E. Pittsburgh D2
Edgewood C2
Emsworth A1
Etna C1
Evergreen B1
Ewingsville A2
Forest Grove A1
Forest Hills C2
Fox Chapel C1
Glassport C3
Glenfield A1
Glen Osborne A1
Glenshaw C1
Green Tree B2
Groveton A1
Haysville A1
Heidelberg A3
Homestead C2
Ingram A2
Kenmawr A2
Kirwan Hts. A3
Liberty C3
McKeesport D3
McKees Rocks B1
Millvale B1
Monroeville D2
Moon Run A2
Morgan A3
Mt. Lebanon B3
Mt. Oliver B2
Munhall C3
N. Braddock C2
Oakmont D1
Penn Hills D2
Pennsbury Vil. A2
Perrysville B1
Pitcairn D2
Pittock A1
Pittsburgh B2
Pleasant Hills C3
Plum D1
Port Vue C3
Presto A3
Rankin C2
Rennerdale A2
Rosslyn Farms A2
Sandy Creek D1
Sharpsburg C1
Springdale D1
Stewartsville D3
Swissvale C2
Sygan A3
Thornburg A2
Trafford D3
Turtle Creek D2
Upper St. Clair A3
Verona D1
Wall D3
W. Homestead C2
W. Mifflin C3
W. Park A1
W. View B1
Whitaker C2
Whitehall B3
White Oak D3
Wilkinsburg C2
Wilmerding D3

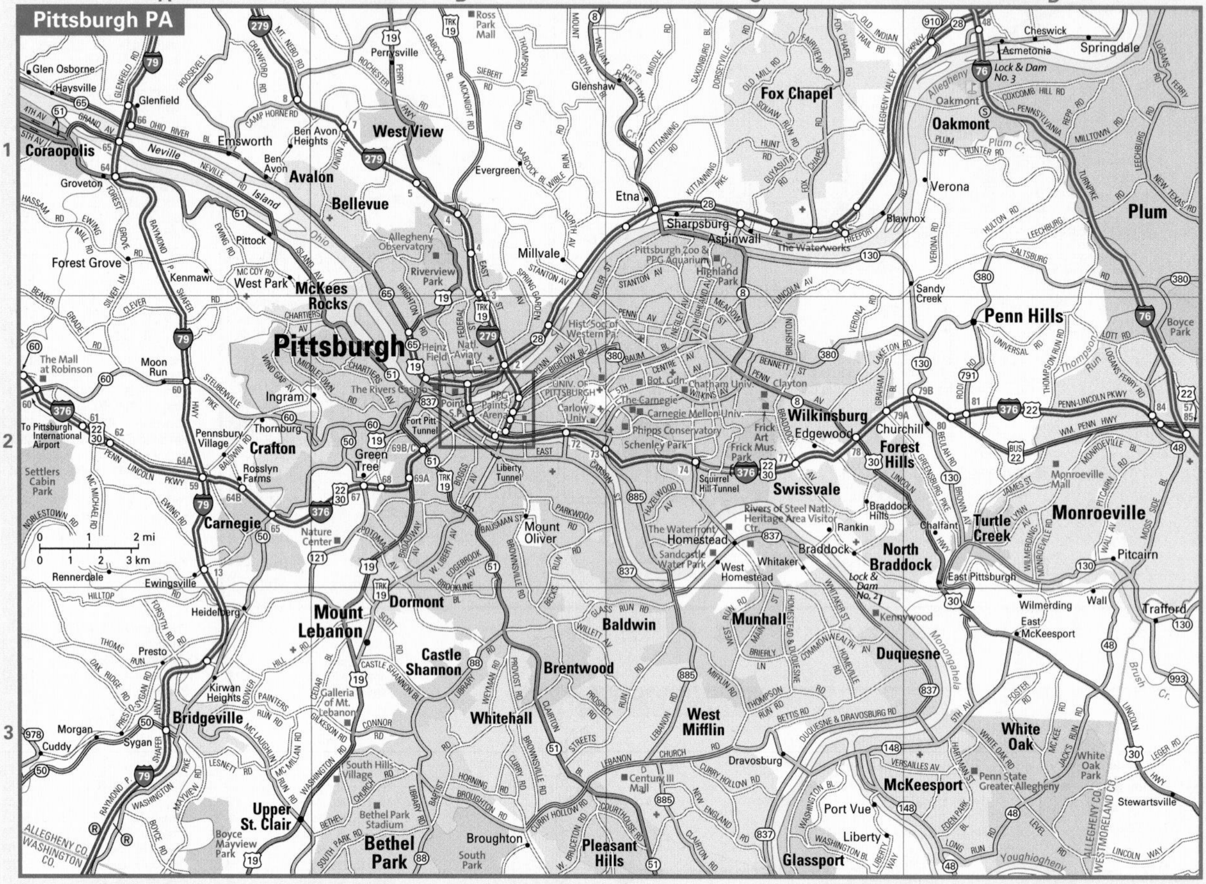

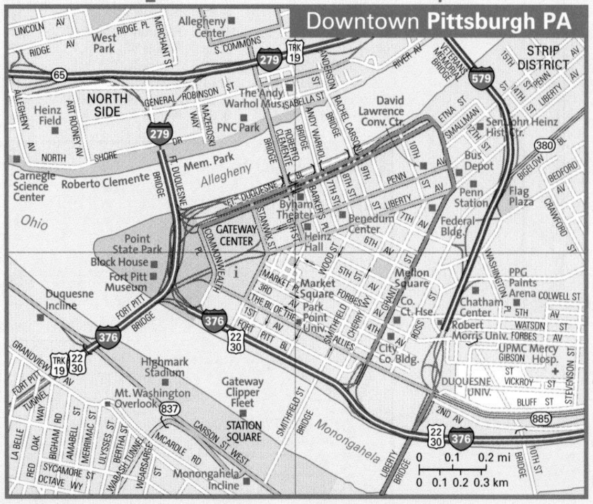

POINTS OF INTEREST
Allegheny Center E1
The Andy Warhol Museum E1
Benedum Center F1
Block House E2
Bus Depot F1
Byham Theater F1
Carnegie Science Center E1
Chatham Center F2
City County Building F2
County Court House F2
David Lawrence Convention Center F1
Duquesne Incline E2
Duquesne University F2
Federal Building F1
Fort Pitt Museum E2
Gateway Center E1
Gateway Clipper Fleet E2
Heinz Field E1
Heinz Hall F1
Highmark Stadium E2
Monongahela Incline E2
Mt. Washington Overlook E2
Penn Station F1
PNC Park E1
Point Park University F2
Point State Park E1
PPG Paints Arena F2
Robert Morris University F2
Senator John Heinz Hist. Center F1
Station Square E2

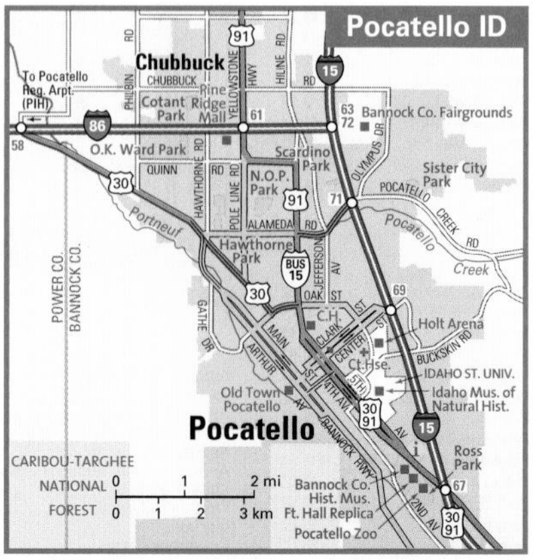

Entries in **bold black** indicate counties or parishes.
Entries in **bold color** indicate cities with detailed inset maps.

Pineview GA, *523* **129** E3
Pineville KY, *1732* **110** C2
Pineville LA, *14555* **125** E4
Pineville MO, *791* **106** B3
Pineville NC, *7479* **122** A2
Pineville WV, *668* **111** F1
Pinewald NJ, *2500* **147** E3
Pinewood SC, *538* **122** B4
Piney Green NC, *13293* **115** D4
Piney Pt. MD, *864* **103** E4
Piney Pt. Vil. TX, *3125* **220** B2
Pink OK, *2058* **51** E3
Pink Hill NC, *552* **123** E2
Pinnacle NC, *894* **112** A3
Pinole CA, *18390* **259** C1
Pinon AZ, *904* **47** F2
Pinson AL, *7163* **119** F4
Pioche NV, *1002* **38** C3
Pioneer OH, *1380* **90** B2
Pioneer Vil. KY, *2030* **100** A4
Piper City IL, *826* **88** C3
Piperton TN, *1445* **118** B2
Pipestone MN, *4317* **27** F3
Pipestone Co. MN, *9596* **27** F3
Piqua OH, *20522* **90** B4
Pirtleville AZ, *1744* **55** E4
Piru CA, *2063* **52** B2
Piscataquis Co. ME, *17535* **84** C3
Pisgah AL, *722* **120** A2
Pisgah Forest NC, *1100* **121** E1
Pisinemo AZ, *321* **54** C3
Pismo Beach CA, *7655* **52** A1
Pitcairn PA, *3294* **250** D2
Pitkin Co. CO, *17148* **40** C2
Pitman NJ, *9011* **146** C4
Pitt Co. NC, *168148* **113** E4
Pittman Ctr. TN, *502* **111** D4
Pittsboro IN, *2928* **99** F1
Pittsboro MS, *202* **118** C4
Pittsboro NC, *3743* **112** C4
Pittsburg CA, *63264* **36** B3
Pittsburg IL, *572* **108** C1
Pittsburg KS, *20233* **106** B1
Pittsburg TX, *4497* **124** B1
Pittsburg Co. OK, *45837* **116** A2
Pittsburgh PA, *305704* 92 A4
Pittsfield IL, *4576* **98** A1
Pittsfield ME, *3150* **82** C1
Pittsfield MA, *44737* **94** C1
Pittsfield NH, *1576* **81** F4
Pittsford NY, *1355* **78** C3
Pittsford VT, *740* **81** D3
Pittston ME, *2548* **82** C2
Pittston PA, *7739* **93** F2
Pittstown NY, *700* **94** B1
Pittsville MD, *1417* **114** C1
Pittsville WI, *874* **74** A1
Pittsylvania Co. VA, *63506* **112** C2
Piute Co. UT, *1556* **39** E3
Pixley CA, *3310* **45** D4
Placentia CA, *50533* **229** F4
Placer Co. CA, *348432* **36** C2
Placerville CA, *10389* **36** C2
Placid Lakes FL, *3054* **141** D4
Placitas NM, *4977* **48** C3
Plain WI, *773* **74** A3
Plain City OH, *4225* **90** C4
Plain City UT, *5476* **31** E3
Plain Dealing LA, *1015* **124** C1
Plainfield CT, *15443* **149** F1
Plainfield IL, *39581* **88** C2
Plainfield IN, *27631* **99** F1
Plainfield NH, *205* **81** E3
Plainfield NJ, *49808* **147** E1
Plainfield VT, *401* **81** E2
Plainfield WI, *862* **74** B1
Plains GA, *776* **128** C3
Plains KS, *1146* **42** C4
Plains MT, *1048* **14** C3
Plains PA, *4335* **261** B2
Plains TX, *1481* **57** F2
Plainsboro NJ, *21213* **147** D2
Plainview AR, *608* **117** D2
Plainview MN, *3340* **73** E1
Plainview NE, *1246* **35** E2
Plainview NY, *26217* **148** C4
Plainview TN, *2125* **110** C4
Plainview TX, *22194* **50** A4
Plainville CT, *17382* **149** D1
Plainville IN, *476* **99** E3
Plainville KS, *1903* **43** D2
Plainville MA, *8264* **150** C2
Plainwell MI, *3804* **75** F4
Plaistow NH, *7609* **95** E1
Planada CA, *4584* **37** D4
Plandome NY, *1349* **148** C4
Plandome Hts. NY, *1005* **241** G2
Plandome Manor NY, *872* **241** G2
Plankinton SD, *707* **27** E4
Plano IL, *10856* **88** C2
Plano TX, *259841* **59** F2
Plantation FL, *84955* **143** E2
Plantation KY, *832* **230** F1
Plant City FL, *34721* **140** C2
Plantersville MS, *1155* **119** D3
Plantsville CT, *10387* **149** D1
Plaquemine LA, *7119* **134** A2
Plaquemines Par. LA, *23042* **134** C4
Platte SD, *1230* **27** D4
Platte City MO, *4691* **96** B2
Platte Co. MO, *89322* **96** B2
Platte Co. NE, *32237* **35** E3
Platte Co. WY, *8667* **33** E2
Plattekill NY, *1260* **148** B1
Platteville CO, *2485* **33** E4
Platteville WI, *11224* **74** A4
Plattsburg MO, *2319* **96** B1
Plattsburgh NY, *19989* **81** D1
Plattsmouth NE, *6502* **86** A3
Pleak TX, *1044* **132** A4
Pleasantdale NY, *1600* **94** B1
Pleasant Gap PA, *2879* **92** C3
Pleasant Garden NC, *4489* **112** B4
Pleasant Grove AL, *10110* **119** F4
Pleasant Grove OH, *1742* **101** E1
Pleasant Grove UT, *33509* **31** F4
Pleasant Groves AL, *420* **120** A2
Pleasant Hill CA, *33152* **259** D2
Pleasant Hill IL, *966* **97** F2
Pleasant Hill IA, *8785* **86** C2
Pleasant Hill LA, *723* **125** D3
Pleasant Hill MO, *8113* **96** C3
Pleasant Hill OH, *1200* **90** B4
Pleasant Hill TN, *563* **110** B4
Pleasant Hills MD, *3379* **144** C1
Pleasant Hills PA, *8268* **250** C3
Pleasant Hope MO, *614* **107** D1
Pleasant Lake IN, *750* **90** A2
Pleasant Lake MA, *800* **151** F3
Pleasant Lake MI, *850* **76** A4
Pleasant Mills NJ, *100* **147** D4
Pleasanton CA, *70285* **36** B4
Pleasanton KS, *1216* **96** B4
Pleasanton TX, *8934* **61** D3
Pleasant Plains IL, *802* **98** B1
Pleasant Plains NJ, *922* **147** E3
Pleasant Pt. ME, *600* **83** F1
Pleasant Prairie WI, *19719* **74** C4
Pleasant Ridge MI, *2526* **210** C2
Pleasant Run OH, *4953* **204** A1
Pleasants Co. WV, *7605* **101** F2
Pleasant Valley MO, *2961* **96** B2
Pleasant Valley NY, *1145* **94** B3
Pleasant Valley PA, *800* **146** C1
Pleasant Valley WV, *3149* **102** A2
Pleasant View IN, *850* **99** F1
Pleasant View TN, *4149* **109** E3
Pleasant View UT, *7979* **31** E3
Pleasantville IA, *1694* **87** D2
Pleasantville NJ, *20249* **147** F4
Pleasantville NY, *7019* **148** B2
Pleasantville OH, *960* **101** D1
Pleasantville PA, *892* **92** A2
Pleasure Beach CT, *1600* **149** F2
Pleasureville KY, *834* **100** A4
Pleasureville PA, *3200* **275** F1
Plentywood MT, *1734* **17** F1
Plover WI, *12123* **74** B1
Pluckemin NJ, *6000* **147** D1
Plum PA, *27126* **92** A4
Plumas Co. CA, *20007* **36** C1
Plum City WI, *599* **67** E4
Plumerville AR, *826* **117** E1
Plum Grove TX, *600* **132** B2
Plummer ID, *1044* **14** B3
Plum Pt. RI, *850* **150** C4
Plum Sprs. KY, *453* **109** F2
Plymouth CA, *1005* **36** C3
Plymouth DE, *350* **145** E3
Plymouth IN, *10033* **89** F2
Plymouth MA, *7494* **151** E2
Plymouth MI, *9132* **76** B4
Plymouth MN, *70576* **67** D4
Plymouth NE, *409* **35** F4
Plymouth NH, *4456* **81** F3
Plymouth NC, *3878* **113** F4
Plymouth OH, *1857* **91** D3
Plymouth PA, *5951* **261** A1
Plymouth UT, *414* **31** E2
Plymouth WI, *8445* **74** C2
Plymouth Co. IA, *24986* **35** F1
Plymouth Co. MA, *494919* **151** E3
Plymouth Meeting PA, *6177* **248** B1
Plympton MA, *550* **151** E2
Poca WV, *974* **101** E3
Pocahontas AR, *6608* **108** A3
Pocahontas IL, *784* **98** B3
Pocahontas IA, *1789* **72** B4
Pocahontas VA, *389* **111** F1
Pocahontas Co. IA, *7310* **72** B4
Pocahontas Co. WV, *8719* **102** A4
Pocasset MA, *2851* **151** E3
Pocatello ID, *54255* 31 E1
Pocola OK, *4056* **116** B1
Pocomoke City MD, *4184* **114** C2
Pocono Pines PA, *1409* **93** F3
Poestenkill NY, *1061* **94** B1
Poinciana FL, *53193* **141** D2
Poinsett Co. AR, *24583* **118** A1
Point TX, *820* **124** A1
Pt. Arena CA, *474* **36** A2
Pt. Blank TX, *559* **132** B1
Pt. Clear AL, *2125* **135** E2
Pt. Comfort TX, *737* **61** F4
Pointe a la Hache LA, *187* **134** C3
Pointe Coupee Par. LA, *22802* **133** F2
Pt. Hope AK, *674* **154** B1

Cape Cottage B2
Cape Elizabeth B2
Cumberland Foreside B1
Eight Corners A2
Falmouth B1
Falmouth Foreside B1
Portland B2
S. Portland A2
Westbrook A1
W. Falmouth A1

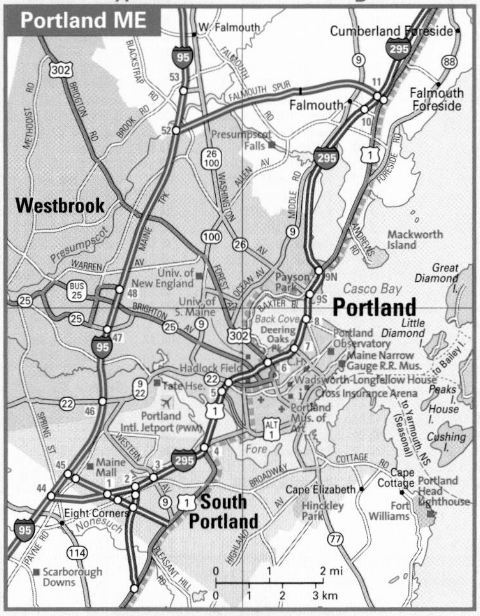

Beaverton C2
Carver D3
Cedar Hills C2
Clackamas D3
Durham C3
Garden Home C2
Gladstone D3
Gresham D2
Happy Valley D2
Johnson City D3
King City C3
Lake Oswego C3
Maywood Park D2
Metzger C2
Milwaukie D2
Oak Grove D3
Oregon City D3
Portland D2
Raleigh Hills C2
Rivergrove C3
Tigard C3
Tualatin C3
Vancouver D1
W. Linn D3
W. Slope C2

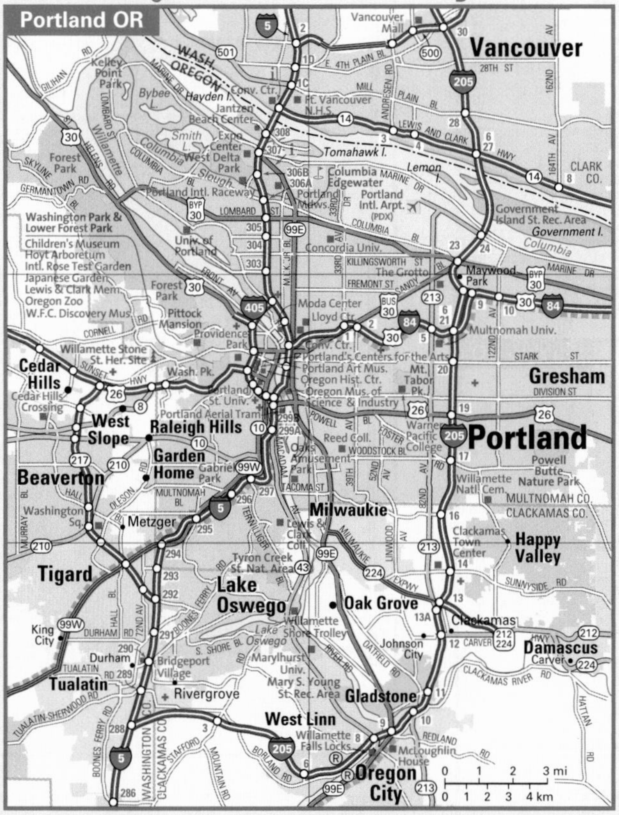

Abbott Run F1
Albion E1
Arctic E3
Ashton E1
Attleboro F1
Barrington F3
Berkeley E1
Central Falls F1
Centredale E2
Cranston E3
E. Providence F2
Esmond E1
Georgiaville E1
Hughesdale E2
Johnston E2
Lime Rock E1
Lonsdale F1
N. Providence E2
Pawtucket F2
Phenix E3
Providence E2
Quidnick E3
Quinnville E1
Riverside F3
Rumford F2
Saylesville F1
Seekonk F2
Stillwater E1
Thornton E2
Valley Falls F1
Warwick F3
W. Barrington F3
W. Warwick E3

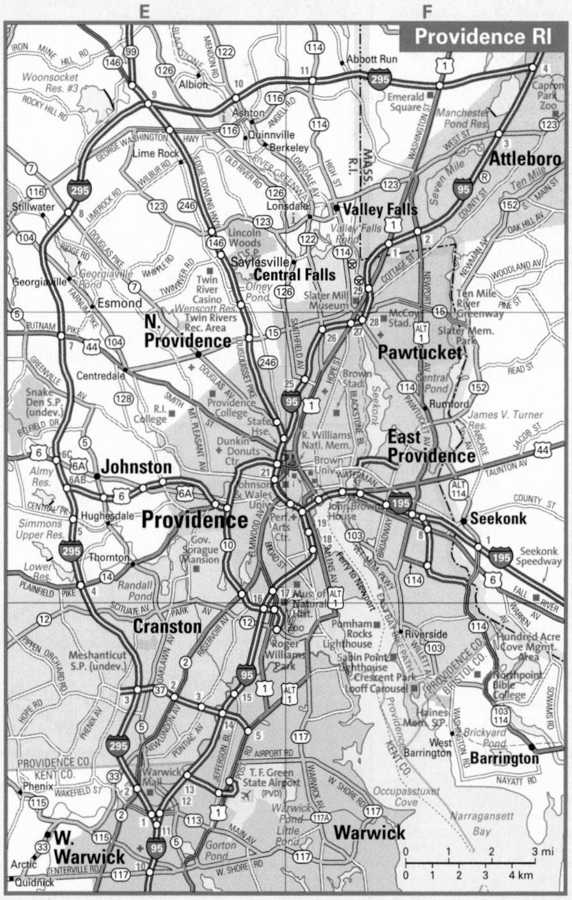

Figures after entries indicate population, page number, and grid reference.

Pt. Judith RI, 900 ... 150 C4
Pt. Marion PA, 1159 ... 102 B1
Pt. of Rocks MD, 1466 ... 144 A2
Pt. Pleasant NJ, 18392 ... 147 E2
Pt. Pleasant WV, 4350 ... 101 E3
Pt. Pleasant Beach NJ, 4665 ... 147 E2
Pt. Reyes Sta. CA, 848 ... 36 B3
Poipu HI, 979 ... 152 B1
Pojoaque NM, 1907 ... 49 D2
Polacca AZ, 1100 ... 47 F2
Poland OH, 2555 ... 276 C3
Polk PA, 816 ... 92 A2
Polk City FL, 1562 ... 140 C2
Polk City IA, 3418 ... 86 C1
Polk Co. AR, 20662 ... 116 C3
Polk Co. FL, 602095 ... 140 C3
Polk Co. GA, 41475 ... 120 B4
Polk Co. IA, 430640 ... 86 C1
Polk Co. MN, 31600 ... 19 F2
Polk Co. MO, 31137 ... 107 D1
Polk Co. NE, 5406 ... 35 E3
Polk Co. NC, 20510 ... 121 F1
Polk Co. OR, 75403 ... 20 B2
Polk Co. TN, 16825 ... 120 C1
Polk Co. TX, 45413 ... 132 B1
Polk Co. WI, 44205 ... 67 E3
Polkton NC, 3375 ... 122 B2
Polkville NC, 545 ... 121 F1
Pollock SD, 241 ... 26 C1
Pollock Pines CA, 6871 ... 36 C2
Polo IL, 2355 ... 88 B1
Polo MO, 575 ... 96 C1
Polson MT, 4488 ... 15 D3
Pomeroy IA, 662 ... 72 B4
Pomeroy OH, 1852 ... 101 E2
Pomeroy WA, 1425 ... 13 F4
Pomona CA, 149058 ... 52 C2
Pomona KS, 832 ... 96 A3
Pomona NJ, 7124 ... 105 D3
Pomona NY, 3103 ... 148 B2
Pomona Park FL, 912 ... 139 D4
Pomonkey MD, 750 ... 144 B4
Pompano Beach FL, 99845 ... 143 F1
Pompton Lakes NJ, 11097 ... 148 A3
Pompton Plains NJ, 6500 ... 148 A3
Ponca NE, 961 ... 35 F1
Ponca City OK, 25387 ... 51 E1
Ponce de Leon FL, 598 ... 136 C1
Ponce Inlet FL, 3032 ... 139 E4
Poncha Sprs. CO, 737 ... 41 D3
Ponchatoula LA, 6559 ... 134 B2
Pond Creek OK, 856 ... 51 E1
Pondera Co. MT, 6153 ... 15 E2
Ponderay ID, 1137 ... 14 B2
Ponderosa NM, 387 ... 48 C2
Ponemah MN, 724 ... 64 A2
Ponte Vedra Beach FL, 1100 ... 139 D2
Pontiac IL, 11931 ... 88 C3
Pontiac MI, 59515 ... 76 C4
Pontoon Beach IL, 5836 ... 256 D1
Pontotoc MS, 5625 ... 118 C3
Pontotoc Co. MS, 29957 ... 118 C3
Pontotoc Co. OK, 37492 ... 51 F4
Pooler GA, 19140 ... 130 B3
Poolesville MD, 4883 ... 144 A2
Pope Co. AR, 61754 ... 117 D1
Pope Co. IL, 4470 ... 109 D1
Pope Co. MN, 10995 ... 66 A3
Poplar CA, 1496 ... 45 D3
Poplar MT, 810 ... 17 E2
Poplar WI, 603 ... 64 C4
Poplar Bluff MO, 17023 ... 108 A2
Poplar Grove IL, 5023 ... 74 B4
Poplar Hills KY, 362 ... 230 E3
Poplarville MS, 2894 ... 134 C1
Poquetanuck CT, 1100 ... 149 F1
Poquonock CT, 2200 ... 150 A3
Poquonock Bridge CT, 1727 ... 149 F2
Poquoson VA, 12150 ... 113 F2
Poquott NY, 953 ... 149 D3
Porcupine SD, 1062 ... 26 B4
Portage IN, 36828 ... 89 E2
Portage MI, 46292 ... 89 F1
Portage PA, 2638 ... 92 B4
Portage WI, 10324 ... 74 B2
Portage Co. OH, 161419 ... 91 E3
Portage Co. WI, 70019 ... 74 B1
Portage Lakes OH, 6968 ... 188 A2
Portageville MO, 3228 ... 108 B3
Portal GA, 638 ... 129 F2
Portales NM, 12280 ... 49 F4
Port Allegany PA, 2157 ... 92 C1
Port Allen LA, 5180 ... 134 A2
Port Angeles WA, 19038 ... 12 B2
Port Aransas TX, 3480 ... 63 F2
Port Arthur TX, 53818 ... 132 C3
Port Austin MI, 664 ... 76 C1
Port Barre LA, 2055 ... 133 F2
Port Barrington IL, 1517 ... 203 A1
Port Byron IL, 1647 ... 88 A2
Port Byron NY, 1290 ... 79 D3
Port Carbon PA, 1889 ... 93 E3
Port Charlotte FL, 54392 ... 140 C4
Port Chester NY, 28967 ... 148 C3
Port Clinton OH, 6056 ... 90 C2
Port Deposit MD, 653 ... 145 D1
Port Edwards WI, 1818 ... 74 A1
Porter IN, 4858 ... 89 E2
Porter OK, 566 ... 106 A4
Porter WA, 207 ... 12 B4
Porter Corners NY, 800 ... 80 C4
Porter Co. IN, 164343 ... 89 E2
Porterdale GA, 1429 ... 121 D4
Porter Hts. TX, 1653 ... 132 A2
Porterville CA, 54165 ... 45 D3
Port Ewen NY, 3546 ... 94 B2
Port Gibson MS, 1567 ... 126 A3
Port Hadlock WA, 3580 ... 12 C2
Port Henry NY, 1194 ... 81 D3
Port Hueneme CA, 21723 ... 52 B2
Port Huron MI, 30184 ... 77 D3
Portia AR, 437 ... 107 F4
Port Isabel TX, 5006 ... 63 F4
Port Jefferson NY, 7750 ... 149 D3
Port Jefferson Sta. NY, 7838 ... 149 D3
Port Jervis NY, 8828 ... 148 A2
Port La Belle FL, 3530 ... 141 D4
Portland AR, 430 ... 125 F1
Portland CT, 5862 ... 149 E1
Portland IN, 6223 ... 90 A4
Portland ME, 66194 ... 82 B3
Portland MI, 3883 ... 76 A3
Portland ND, 606 ... 19 E3
Portland OR, 583776 ... 20 C2
Portland PA, 519 ... 93 F3
Portland TN, 11480 ... 109 F3
Portland TX, 15099 ... 63 F2
Port Lavaca TX, 12248 ... 61 F4
Port Leyden NY, 672 ... 79 E2
Port Ludlow WA, 2603 ... 12 C2
Port Matilda PA, 606 ... 92 C3
Port Monmouth NJ, 3818 ... 147 E1
Port Neches TX, 13040 ... 132 C3
Port Norris NJ, 1377 ... 145 F2
Portola CA, 2104 ... 37 D1
Portola Valley CA, 4353 ... 259 C6
Port Orange FL, 56048 ... 139 E4
Port Orchard WA, 11144 ... 12 C3
Port Orford OR, 1133 ... 28 A1
Port Reading NJ, 3728 ... 240 A5
Port Republic NJ, 1115 ... 147 E4
Port Richey FL, 2671 ... 140 B2
Port Royal PA, 925 ... 93 D4
Port Royal SC, 10678 ... 130 C2
Port St. Joe FL, 3445 ... 137 D3
Port St. John FL, 12267 ... 141 E1
Port St. Lucie FL, 164603 ... 141 E4
Port Salerno FL, 10091 ... 141 E4
Port Sanilac MI, 623 ... 76 C2
Portsmouth NH, 20779 ... 82 A4
Portsmouth OH, 20226 ... 101 D3
Portsmouth RI, 17389 ... 151 D4
Portsmouth VA, 95535 ... 113 F2
Port Sulphur LA, 1760 ... 134 C4
Port Townsend WA, 9113 ... 12 C2
Portville NY, 1014 ... 92 C1
Port Vincent LA, 741 ... 134 A2
Port Vue PA, 3798 ... 250 C3
Port Washington NY, 15846 ... 148 C3
Port Washington WI, 11250 ... 75 D2
Port Washington North NY, 3154 ... 241 G2
Port Wentworth GA, 5359 ... 130 B3
Porum OK, 727 ... 116 A1
Posen IL, 5987 ... 203 D6
Posey Co. IN, 25910 ... 99 D4
Poseyville IN, 1045 ... 99 D4
Post TX, 5376 ... 58 B2
Post Falls ID, 27574 ... 14 B3
Poston AZ, 285 ... 53 F2
Postville IA, 2227 ... 73 E3
Poteau OK, 8520 ... 116 B2
Poteet TX, 3260 ... 61 D3
Poth TX, 1908 ... 61 D3
Potlatch ID, 804 ... 14 B4
Potomac IL, 750 ... 89 D4
Potomac MD, 44965 ... 144 B3
Potomac Hts. MD, 1117 ... 144 B4
Potosi MO, 2660 ... 98 A4
Potosi TX, 2991 ... 58 C3
Potosi WI, 688 ... 73 F4
Potsdam NY, 9428 ... 80 B1
Pottawatomie Co. KS, 21604 ... 43 F2
Pottawatomie Co. OK, 69442 ... 51 F3
Pottawattamie Co. IA, 93158 ... 86 A2
Potter Co. PA, 17457 ... 92 C2
Potter Co. SD, 2329 ... 27 D2
Potter Co. TX, 121073 ... 50 A3
Pottersville NY, 424 ... 80 C3
Potter Valley CA, 646 ... 36 A2
Potterville MI, 2617 ... 76 A4
Pottsboro TX, 2160 ... 59 F1
Potts Camp MS, 523 ... 118 C2
Pottstown PA, 22377 ... 146 B2
Pottsville AR, 2838 ... 117 D1
Pottsville PA, 14324 ... 93 E3
Potwin KS, 449 ... 43 F3
Poughkeepsie NY, 32736 ... 148 B1
Poughquag NY, 900 ... 148 C1
Poulan GA, 851 ... 129 D4
Poulsbo WA, 9200 ... 12 C3
Poultney VT, 1612 ... 81 D4
Pound VA, 1037 ... 111 E2
Pound Ridge NY, 800 ... 148 C2
Poway CA, 47811 ... 53 D4
Powderly KY, 745 ... 109 E2
Powder River Co. MT, 1743 ... 25 E2
Powder Sprs. GA, 13940 ... 120 C4
Powell AL, 955 ... 120 A2
Powell OH, 11500 ... 90 C4
Powell TN, 7500 ... 110 C4
Powell WY, 6314 ... 24 B3
Powell Co. KY, 12613 ... 100 C4
Powell Co. MT, 7027 ... 15 D3
Powells Crossroads TN, 1322 ... 120 B1
Powellton WV, 619 ... 101 F4
Power Co. ID, 7817 ... 31 E1
Powers OR, 689 ... 28 A1
Powers Lake ND, 280 ... 18 A2
Powers Lake WI, 1615 ... 74 C4
Poweshiek Co. IA, 18914 ... 87 D1
Powhatan VA, 550 ... 113 D1
Powhatan Co. VA, 28046 ... 113 E1
Powhatan Pt. OH, 1592 ... 101 F1
Pownal VT, 3560 ... 94 C1
Poydras LA, 2351 ... 134 C3
Poynette WI, 2528 ... 74 B2
Prague OK, 2386 ... 51 F3
Prairie City IA, 1680 ... 87 D2
Prairie City OR, 909 ... 21 F3
Prairie Co. AR, 8715 ... 117 F2
Prairie Co. MT, 1179 ... 17 E4
Prairie Creek AR, 2066 ... 106 C3
Prairie du Chien WI, 5911 ... 73 F3
Prairie du Rocher IL, 604 ... 98 A4
Prairie du Sac WI, 3972 ... 74 A3
Prairie Grove AR, 4380 ... 106 C4
Prairie Grove IL, 1904 ... 203 A1
Prairie View TX, 5576 ... 61 F2
Prairie Vil. KS, 21447 ... 224 B4
Prairieville LA, 26895 ... 134 A2
Pratt KS, 6835 ... 43 D4
Pratt WV, 602 ... 101 F4
Pratt Co. KS, 9656 ... 43 D4
Prattsburgh NY, 656 ... 78 C4
Prattville AL, 33960 ... 128 A2
Preble Co. OH, 42270 ... 100 B1
Premont TX, 2653 ... 63 E2
Prentice WI, 660 ... 68 A3
Prentiss MS, 1081 ... 126 B4
Prentiss Co. MS, 25276 ... 119 D2
Prescott AZ, 39843 ... 47 D4
Prescott AR, 3296 ... 117 D4
Prescott WI, 4258 ... 67 D4
Prescott Valley AZ, 38822 ... 47 D4
Presho SD, 497 ... 26 C4
Presidential Lakes Estates NJ, 2365 ... 147 D3
Presidio TX, 4426 ... 62 B4
Presidio Co. TX, 7818 ... 62 B3
Presque Isle ME, 9692 ... 85 D2
Presque Isle Co. MI, 13376 ... 70 C3
Preston GA, 453 ... 128 C3
Preston ID, 5204 ... 31 E2
Preston IA, 1012 ... 88 A1
Preston MD, 719 ... 145 E4
Preston MN, 1325 ... 73 E2
Preston Co. WV, 33520 ... 102 B2
Prestonsburg KY, 3255 ... 111 E1
Pretty Prairie KS, 680 ... 43 E4
Price UT, 8715 ... 39 F1
Price Co. WI, 14159 ... 68 A2
Priceville AL, 2658 ... 119 F3
Prichard AL, 22659 ... 135 E1
Priest River ID, 1751 ... 14 B2
Primghar IA, 909 ... 72 A3
Prince Edward Co. VA, 23368 ... 113 D2
Prince Frederick MD, 2538 ... 144 C4
Prince George VA, 750 ... 113 E2
Prince George Co. VA, 35725 ... 113 E2
Prince George's Co. MD, 863420 ... 144 C3
Princes Lakes IN, 1312 ... 99 F2
Princess Anne MD, 3290 ... 103 F4
Princeton FL, 22038 ... 143 E3
Princeton IL, 7660 ... 88 B2
Princeton IN, 8644 ... 99 D4
Princeton IA, 886 ... 88 A2
Princeton KY, 6329 ... 109 D2
Princeton MN, 4698 ... 66 C3
Princeton MO, 1166 ... 86 C4
Princeton NJ, 12307 ... 147 D2
Princeton NC, 1194 ... 123 E1
Princeton TX, 6807 ... 59 F2
Princeton WV, 6432 ... 111 F1
Princeton WI, 1214 ... 74 B2
Princeton Jct. NJ, 2465 ... 147 D2
Princeville HI, 2158 ... 152 B1
Princeville IL, 1738 ... 88 B3
Princeville NC, 2082 ... 113 E4
Prince William Co. VA, 402002 ... 144 A4
Prineville OR, 9253 ... 21 D3
Pringle PA, 979 ... 261 B1
Prior Lake MN, 22796 ... 67 D4
Proctor MN, 3057 ... 64 C4
Proctor VT, 1877 ... 81 D3
Proctorville OH, 574 ... 101 E3
Progreso TX, 5507 ... 63 E4
Progress PA, 9765 ... 218 B1
Progress Vil. FL, 5392 ... 266 C2
Prophetstown IL, 2080 ... 88 A2
Prospect CT, 9234 ... 149 D1
Prospect KY, 4698 ... 100 A4
Prospect OH, 1112 ... 90 C4
Prospect PA, 1169 ... 92 A3
Prospect Hts. IL, 16256 ... 203 C2
Prospect Park PA, 327 ... 248 B4
Prosper TX, 9423 ... 59 F2
Prosperity SC, 1180 ... 122 A3
Prosser WA, 5714 ... 21 E1
Protection KS, 514 ... 43 D4
Provencal LA, 611 ... 125 D4
Providence FL, 1100 ... 140 C2
Providence KY, 3193 ... 109 D1
Providence RI, 178042 ... 150 C3
Providence UT, 7075 ... 31 E3
Providence Co. RI, 626667 ... 150 C3
Provincetown MA, 2642 ... 151 F2
Provo UT, 112488 ... 31 F4
Prowers Co. CO, 12551 ... 42 A3
Prudenville MI, 1682 ... 76 A1
Prue OK, 465 ... 51 F2
Prunedale CA, 17560 ... 44 B2
Pruntytown WV, 600 ... 102 A2
Pryor MT, 618 ... 24 C2
Pryor OK, 9539 ... 106 A3
Pueblo CO, 106595 ... 41 E3
Pueblo Co. CO, 159063 ... 41 E3
Pueblo Pintado NM, 192 ... 48 B2
Pueblo West CO, 29637 ... 41 E3
Puhi HI, 2906 ... 152 B1
Pukalani HI, 7574 ... 153 D1
Pukwana SD, 285 ... 27 D4
Pulaski NY, 2365 ... 79 D2
Pulaski TN, 7870 ... 119 F1
Pulaski VA, 9086 ... 112 A2
Pulaski WI, 3539 ... 68 C4
Pulaski Co. AR, 382748 ... 117 E2
Pulaski Co. GA, 12010 ... 129 E3
Pulaski Co. IL, 6161 ... 108 C2
Pulaski Co. IN, 13402 ... 89 E3
Pulaski Co. KY, 63063 ... 110 B2
Pulaski Co. MO, 52274 ... 97 E4
Pulaski Co. VA, 34872 ... 112 A2
Pullman MI, 700 ... 75 E4
Pullman WA, 29799 ... 14 B4
Pumphrey MD, 5317 ... 193 C4
Pumpkin Ctr. CA, 700 ... 45 D4
Pumpkin Ctr. NC, 2222 ... 115 D4
Punaluu HI, 1164 ... 152 A2
Punta Gorda FL, 16641 ... 140 C4
Punta Rassa FL, 1750 ... 142 C1
Punxsutawney PA, 5962 ... 92 B3
Pupukea HI, 4551 ... 152 A2
Purcell OK, 5884 ... 51 E3
Purcellville VA, 7727 ... 144 A2
Purdy MO, 1098 ... 106 C2
Purdys NY, 1200 ... 148 C2
Purvis MS, 2175 ... 134 C1
Puryear TN, 671 ... 109 D3
Pushmataha Co. OK, 11572 ... 116 A3
Putnam CT, 7214 ... 150 B3
Putnam Co. FL, 74364 ... 139 D3
Putnam Co. GA, 21218 ... 129 E1
Putnam Co. IL, 6006 ... 88 B2
Putnam Co. IN, 37963 ... 99 E1
Putnam Co. MO, 4979 ... 87 D4
Putnam Co. NY, 99710 ... 148 B2
Putnam Co. OH, 34499 ... 90 B3
Putnam Co. TN, 72321 ... 110 A3
Putnam Co. WV, 55486 ... 101 E3
Putnam Lake NY, 3844 ... 148 C1
Putney GA, 2898 ... 129 D4
Putney KY, 600 ... 111 D2
Putney VT, 523 ... 81 E4
Puxico MO, 881 ... 108 B2
Puyallup WA, 37022 ... 12 C3
Pyatt AR, 221 ... 107 D3

Q

Quaker City OH, 502 ... 101 F1
Quaker Hill CT, 4200 ... 149 F2
Quakertown PA, 8979 ... 146 C1
Quanah TX, 2641 ... 50 C4
Quantico VA, 480 ... 144 A4
Quapaw OK, 906 ... 106 B2
Quarryville CT, 2500 ... 150 A3
Quarryville PA, 2576 ... 146 A3
Quartz Hill CA, 10912 ... 52 C2
Quartzsite AZ, 3677 ... 54 A1
Quasqueton IA, 554 ... 73 E4
Quay Co. NM, 9041 ... 49 F3
Quechee VT, 656 ... 81 E3
Queen Anne's Co. MD, 47798 ... 145 D3
Queen City MO, 598 ... 87 D4
Queen City TX, 1476 ... 124 C1
Queen Creek AZ, 26361 ... 54 C2
Queens Co. NY, 2230722 ... 148 B4
Queenstown MD, 664 ... 145 D3
Quenemo KS, 388 ... 96 A3
Questa NM, 1770 ... 49 D1
Quidnessett RI, 3600 ... 150 C4
Quidnick RI, 6300 ... 150 C3
Quilcene WA, 596 ... 12 C3
Quimby IA, 319 ... 72 A4
Quinby SC, 932 ... 122 C3
Quince Orchard MD, 23044 ... 144 B2
Quincy CA, 1728 ... 36 C1
Quincy FL, 7972 ... 137 D2
Quincy IL, 40633 ... 97 F1
Quincy MA, 92271 ... 151 D1

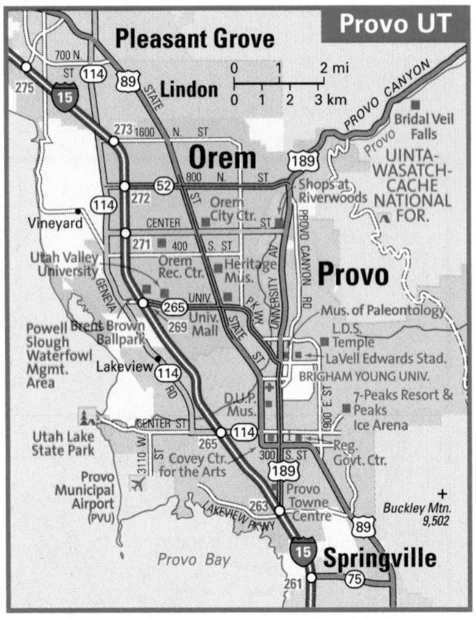

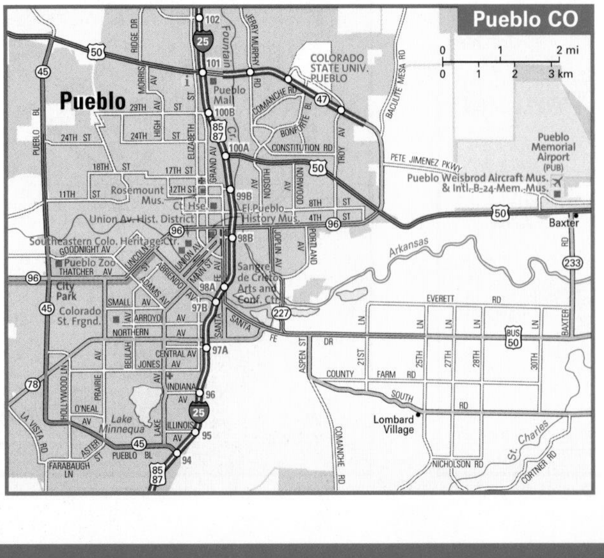

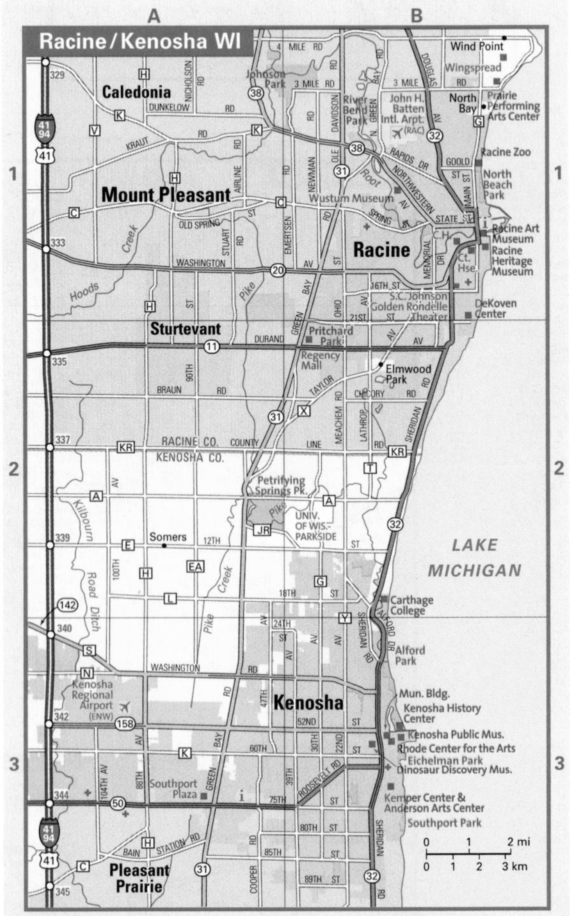

Elmwood Park	B2	Mount Pleasant	A1	Racine	B1
Franksville	A1	N. Bay	B1	Sturtevant	A2
Kenosha	A3	Pleasant Prairie	A3	Wind Pt.	B1

Entries in **bold black** indicate counties or parishes.
Entries in **bold color** indicate cities with detailed inset maps.

Quincy MI, *1652* **90** A1
Quincy OH, *706* **90** B4
Quincy PA, *1200* **103** D1
Quincy WA, *6750* **13** E3
Quinebaug CT, *1133* **150** B2
Quinhagak AK, *669* **154** B3
Quinlan TX, *1394* **59** F2
Quinnesec MI, *1191* **68** C2
Quinter KS, *918* **42** C2
Quinton OK, *1051* **116** A1
Quinwood WV, *290* **102** A4
Quitman AR, *762* **117** E1
Quitman GA, *3850* **137** F1
Quitman MS, *2323* **127** D3
Quitman TX, *1809* **124** A2
Quitman Co. GA, *2513* **128** C3
Quitman Co. MS, *8223* **118** B3
Quogue NY, *967* **149** E3

R

Rabun Co. GA, *16276* **121** D2
Raceland KY, *2424* **101** D3
Raceland LA, *10193* **134** B3
Racine MN, 442 .... **73** D2
Racine OH, *675* **101** E2
Racine WV, *256* **101** E4
Racine WI, *78860* **75** D4
Racine Co. WI, *195408* **74** C4
Radcliff KY, *21688* **99** F4
Radcliffe IA, *545* **72** C4
Radford VA, *16408* **112** A2
Radium Sprs. NM, *1699* **56** B3
Radnor PA, *30878* **248** A2
Raeford NC, *4611* **122** C2
Ragland AL, *1639* **120** A4
Rahway NJ, *27346* **147** E1
Rainbow City AL, *9602* **120** A4
Rainelle WV, *1505* **101** F4
Rainier OR, *1895* **20** B1
Rainier WA, *1794* **12** C4
Rains SC, *650* **122** C3
Rains Co. TX, *10914* **124** A1
Rainsville AL, *4948* **120** A3
Raleigh MS, *1462* **126** C3
Raleigh NC, *403892* **113** D4
Raleigh Co. WV, *78859* **101** F4
Raleigh Hills OR, *5896* **251** C2
Ralls TX, *1944* **58** B1
Ralls Co. MO, *10167* **97** F2
Ralston NE, *5943* **245** A3
Ralston WY, *280* **24** B3
Ramah NM, *370* **48** A3
Ramona CA, *20292* **53** D4
Ramona OK, *535* **51** F1
Ramsay MI, *750* **65** E4
Ramseur NC, *1692* **112** B4
Ramsey IL, *1037* **98** C2
Ramsey MN, *23668* **67** D3
Ramsey NJ, *14473* **148** B3
Ramsey Co. MN, *508640* **67** D3
Ramsey Co. ND, *11451* **19** D2
Ranburne AL, *409* **120** B4
Ranchester WY, *855* **25** D2
Rancho Cordova CA, *64776* **36** C3
Rancho Cucamonga CA, *165269* **229** G2
Rancho Mirage CA, *17218* **53** E3
Rancho Palos Verdes CA, *41643* **228** C4
Rancho Santa Fe CA, *3117* **53** D4
Rancho Santa Margarita CA, *47853* **229** G5
Ranchos de Taos NM, *2518* **49** D2
Rancocas NJ, *8400* **147** D3
Rand WV, *1631* **101** F4
Randall MN, *650* **66** B2
Randall Co. TX, *120725* **50** A3
Randallstown MD, *32430* **144** C1
Randle Cliff Beach MD, *800* **144** C4
Randleman NC, *4113* **112** B4
Randlett OK, *438* **51** D4
Randolph ME, *1772* **82** C2
Randolph MA, *32112* **151** D2
Randolph NE, *944* **35** E2
Randolph NY, *1286* **92** B1
Randolph UT, *464* **31** F3
Randolph VT, *1974* **81** E3
Randolph WI, *1811* **74** B2
Randolph Ctr. VT, *850* **81** E3
Randolph Co. AL, *22913* **128** B1
Randolph Co. AR, *17969* **107** F3
Randolph Co. GA, *7719* **128** C4
Randolph Co. IL, *33476* **98** B4
Randolph Co. IN, *26171* **90** A4
Randolph Co. MO, *25414* **97** E2
Randolph Co. NC, *141752* **112** B4
Randolph Co. WV, *29405* **102** B3
Randolph Hills MD, *14300* **270** C1
Random Lake WI, *1594* **74** C2
Rangeley ME, *1052* **82** B1
Rangely CO, *2365* **40** B1
Ranger TX, *2468* **59** D3
Rankin IL, *561* **89** D4
Rankin PA, *2122* **250** C2
Rankin TX, *778* **58** A4
Rankin Co. MS, *141617* **126** B2
Ranlo NC, *3434* **122** A1
Ransom Canyon TX, *1096* **58** A1
Ransom Co. ND, *5457* **19** E4
Ransomville NY, *1419* **78** A3
Ranson WV, *4440* **103** D2
Rantoul IL, *12941* **88** C4
Rapid City SD, *67956* **26** A3
Rapides Par. LA, *131613* **125** E4
Rapids NY, *1636* **78** B3
Rapids City IL, *959* **208** C1
Rappahannock Co. VA, *7373* **103** D3
Raritan NJ, *6881* **147** D1
Rathdrum ID, *6826* **14** B3
Ratliff FL, *4667* **139** D2
Raton NM, *6885* **49** E1
Raubsville PA, *1088* **146** C1
Ravalli Co. MT, *40212* **23** D1
Raven VA, *2270* **111** F2
Ravena NY, *3268* **94** B1
Ravenden AR, *470* **107** F3
Ravenel SC, *2465* **131** D2
Ravenna KY, *605* **110** C1
Ravenna MI, *1219* **75** F3
Ravenna NE, *1360* **35** D3
Ravenna OH, *11724* **91** E3
Ravensdale WA, *1101* **12** C3
Ravenswood WV, *3876* **101** E3
Ravia OK, *528* **51** F4
Ravine PA, *662* **93** E4
Rawlings MD, *693* **102** C1
Rawlins WY, *9259* **32** C2
Rawlins Co. KS, *2519* **42** B1
Rawson OH, *570* **90** B3
Ray ND, *592* **18** A2
Ray City GA, *1090* **137** F1
Ray Co. MO, *23494* **96** C2
Raymond IL, *1006* **98** B2
Raymond ME, *4299* **82** B3
Raymond MN, *764* **66** B4
Raymond MS, *1933* **126** B3
Raymond NH, *2855* **81** F4
Raymond WA, *2882* **12** B4
Raymondville TX, *11284* **63** F4
Raymore MO, *19206* **96** B3
Rayne LA, *7953* **133** E2
Raynham MA, *11739* **151** D2
Raynham Ctr. MA, *4100* **151** D3
Raytown MO, *29526* **96** B2
Rayville LA, *3695* **125** F2
Readfield ME, *2360* **82** B2
Reading MA, *24747* **151** D1
Reading MI, *1078* **90** A1
Reading OH, *10385* **204** B1
Reading PA, *88082* **146** A2
Readington NJ, *16126* **147** D1
Readlyn IA, *808* **73** E4
Readsboro VT, *321* **94** C1
Reagan Co. TX, *3367* **58** A4
Real Co. TX, *3309* **60** C2
Reamstown PA, *3361* **146** A2
Reardan WA, *571* **13** F3
Reaville NJ, *1200* **147** D1
Rector AR, *1977* **108** A3
Red Bank NJ, *12206* **147** E2
Red Bank SC, *9617* **122** A4
Red Bank TN, *11651* **120** B1
Red Bay AL, *3158* **119** D3
Red Bluff CA, *14076* **36** B1
Red Boiling Sprs. TN, *1112* **110** A3
Red Bud IL, *3698* **98** B4
Redby MN, *1334* **64** A2
Red Cloud NE, *1020* **43** D1
Red Creek NY, *532* **79** D3
Reddick FL, *506* **138** C4
Redding CA, *89861* **28** C4
Redding CT, *8270* **148** C2
Redding Ridge CT, *900* **148** C2
Red Feather Lakes CO, *343* **33** E4
Redfield AR, *1297* **117** E3
Redfield IA, *835* **86** C2
Redfield SD, *2333* **27** D2
Redford MI, *51622* **210** B3
Redford NY, *477* **80** C2
Redgranite WI, *2149* **74** B1
Red Hill PA, *2383* **146** B1
Red Hill SC, *13223* **123** D4
Red Hook NY, *1961* **94** B2
Redington Beach FL, *1427* **140** B3
Redington Shores FL, *2121* **266** A2
Red Jacket WV, *581* **111** E1
Redkey IN, *1353* **90** A4
Red Lake MN, *1731* **64** A2
Red Lake Co. MN, *4089* **19** F2
Red Lake Falls MN, *1427* **19** F2
Redland MD, *17242* **144** B2
Redlands CA, *68747* **53** D2
Red Level AL, *487* **128** A4
Red Lick TX, *1008* **116** C4
Red Lion PA, *6373* **103** E1
Red Lodge MT, *2125* **24** B2
Red Mesa AZ, *480* **47** F1
Redmond OR, *26215* **21** D3
Redmond UT, *730* **39** E2
Redmond WA, *54144* **12** C3
Red Oak IA, *5742* **86** A3
Red Oak NC, *3430* **113** D4
Red Oak OK, *549* **116** B2
Red Oak TX, *10769* **59** F3
Red Oaks Mill NY, *3613* **148** B1
Redondo Beach CA, *66748* **228** C4
Red River NM, *477* **49** D1
Red River Co. TX, *12860* **116** B4
Red River Par. LA, *9091* **125** D3
Red Sprs. NC, *3428* **122** C2
Redwater MS, *633* **126** C2
Redwater TX, *1057* **124** C1
Redway CA, *1225* **36** A1
Red Willow Co. NE, *11055* **42** C1
Red Wing MN, *16459* **67** E4
Redwood NY, *605* **79** E1
Redwood City CA, *76815* **36** B4
Redwood Co. MN, *16059* **66** B4
Redwood Estates CA, *1600* **36** B4
Redwood Falls MN, *5254* **66** B4
Redwood Valley CA, *1729* **36** A2
Reece City AL, *653* **120** A3
Reed City MI, *2425* **75** F2
Reed Creek GA, *2604* **121** E3
Reedley CA, *24194* **45** D3
Reedsburg WI, *9200* **74** A2
Reedsport OR, *4154* **20** A4
Reedsville PA, *641* **93** D3
Reedsville WV, *593* **102** B1
Reedsville WI, *1206* **74** C1
Reedville VA, *600* **103** F4
Reelsboro NC, *800* **115** D3
Reese MI, *1454* **76** B2
Reeseville WI, *708* **74** B3
Reeves Co. TX, *13783* **57** E4
Reeves Crossing DE, *450* **145** E3
Reform AL, *1702* **127** E1
Refton PA, *298* **146** A3
Refugio TX, *2890* **61** E4
Refugio Co. TX, *7383* **61** E4
Regent ND, *160* **18** A4
Rehobeth AL, *1297* **136** C1
Rehoboth MA, *10172* **151** D3
Rehoboth NM, *375* **48** A3
Rehoboth Beach DE, *1327* **145** F4
Reidland KY, *4491* **109** D2
Reidsville GA, *4944* **129** F3
Reidsville NC, *14520* **112** B3
Reidville SC, *601* **121** F2
Reinbeck IA, *1664* **73** D4
Reisterstown MD, *25968* **144** C1
Reliance SD, *191* **27** D4
Reliance WY, *714* **32** B3
Remerton GA, *1123* **137** F1
Remington IN, *1185* **89** E3
Remington VA, *598* **103** D3
Remsen IA, *1663* **35** F1
Remsen NY, *508* **79** F3
Remsenburg NY, *2642* **149** E4
Reno NV, *225221* **37** D1
Reno TX, *2494* **59** E2

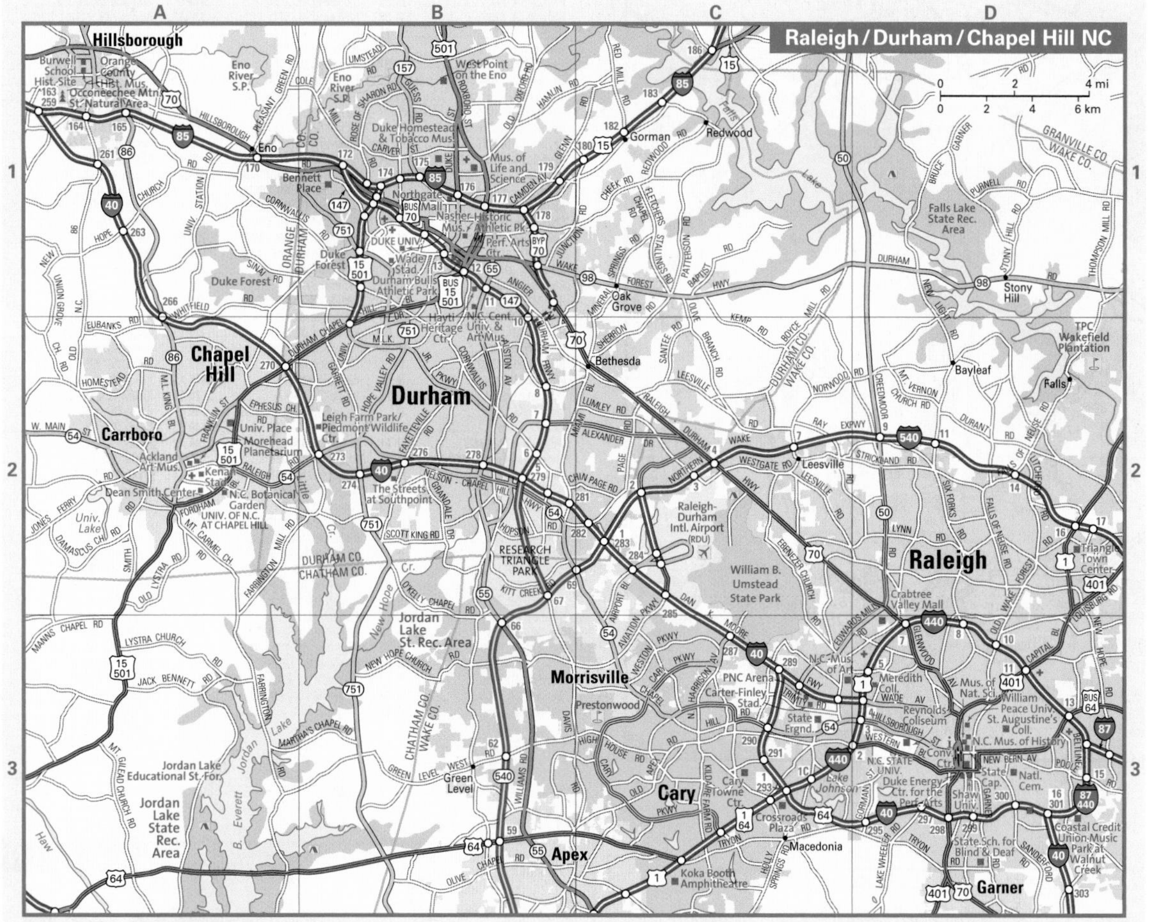

Apex B3	Carrboro A2	Durham B2	Garner D3	Hillsborough A1	Morrisville C3	Redwood C1
Bayleaf D2	Cary C3	Eno A1	Gorman C1	Leesville C2	Oak Grove C1	Stony Hill D1
Bethesda C2	Chapel Hill A2	Falls D2	Green Level B3	Macedonia C3	Raleigh D2	

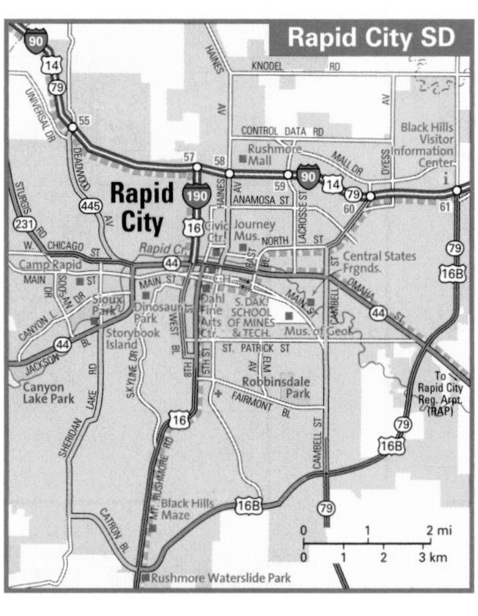

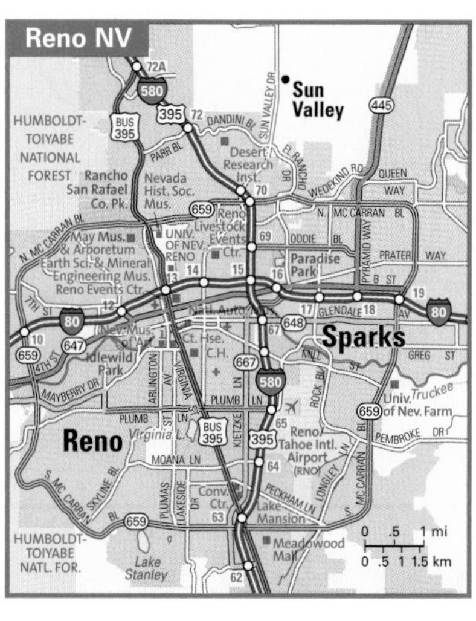

Figures after entries indicate population, page number, and grid reference.

Atlee B1
Bellwood B3
Bensley B3
Bon Air A2
Borkeys Store C1
Centralia B3
Chamberlayne Farms B1
Chester B3
Chesterfield B3
E. Highland Park B1
Fair Oaks C2
Glen Allen B1
Greendale B1
Highland Sprs. C2
Hunton B1
Lakeside B1
Laurel B1
Mechanicsville C1
Midlothian A2
Newmans C1
Old Cold Harbor C1
Pearsons Corner C1
Richmond B2
Rivermont C3
Sandston C2
Seven Pines C2
Short Pump A1
Studley C1
Varina C2

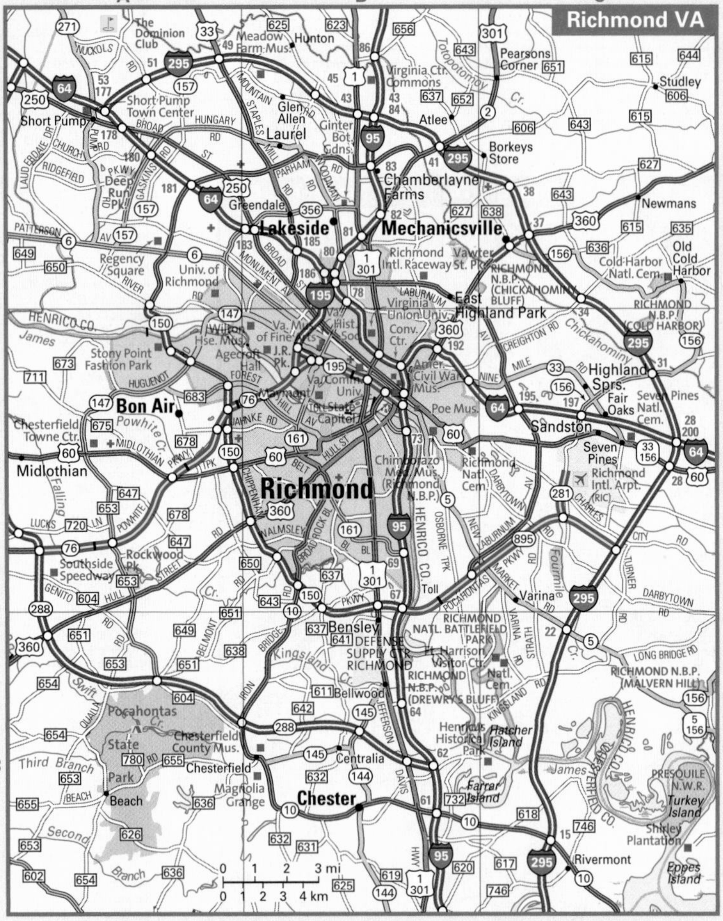

Reno TX, *2767* **116** A4
Reno Co. KS, *64511* **43** E4
Renova MS, *668* **118** A4
Renovo PA, *1228* **92** C2
Rensselaer IN, *5859* **89** E3
Rensselaer NY, *9392* **94** B1
Rensselaer Co. NY, *159429* **94** B1
Renton WA, *90927* **12** C3
Renville MN, *1287* **66** B4
Renville Co. MN, *15730* **66** B4
Renville Co. ND, *2470* **18** B1
Republic MI, *570* **65** F4
Republic MO, *14751* **107** D2
Republic OH, *549* **90** C3
Republic PA, *1096* **102** B1
Republic WA, *1073* **13** F1
Republic Co. KS, *4980* **43** E1
Resaca GA, *544* **120** B2
Reserve LA, *9766* **134** B3
Reserve NM, *289* **55** F1
Reston VA, *58404* **144** A3
Revere MA, *51755* **151** D1
Rexburg ID, *25484* **23** E4
Reyno AR, *456* **108** A3
Reynolds GA, *1086* **129** D2
Reynolds IN, *533* **89** E3
Reynolds ND, *301* **19** E3
Reynoldsburg OH, *35893* **101** D1
Reynolds Co. MO, *6696* **107** F1
Reynoldsville PA, *2759* **92** B3
Rhea Co. TN, *31809* **110** B4
Rhinebeck NY, *2657* **94** B2
Rhinelander WI, *7798* **68** B2
Rhome TX, *1522* **59** E2
Rialto CA, *99171* **53** D2
Rib Lake WI, *910* **68** A3
Rice MN, *1275* **66** C2
Rice TX, *923* **59** F3
Riceboro GA, *809* **130** B4
Rice City RI, *425* **150** C3
Rice Co. KS, *10083* **43** E3
Rice Co. MN, *64142* **72** C1
Rice Lake WI, *8438* **67** E3
Riceville IA, *785* **73** D3
Riceville TN, *670* **120** C1
Richardson TX, *99223* **207** E1
Richardson Co. NE, *8363* **86** A4
Richardton ND, *529* **18** A4
Richboro PA, *6563* **146** C2
Rich Co. UT, *2264* **31** F3
Rich Creek VA, *774* **112** A1
Richey MT, *177* **17** E3
Richfield ID, *482* **31** D1
Richfield MN, *35228* **235** B3
Richfield NC, *613* **122** B1
Richfield OH, *3648* **91** E2
Richfield UT, *7551* **39** E2
Richfield Sprs. NY, *1264* **79** F3
Richford VT, *1361* **81** E1
Richgrove CA, *2882* **45** D4
Rich Hill MO, *1396* **96** B4
Richland GA, *1473* **128** C3
Richland IA, *584* **87** E2
Richland MI, *751* **75** F4
Richland MS, *6912* **126** B3
Richland MO, *1863* **97** E4
Richland NJ, *750* **147** D4
Richland PA, *1519* **146** A2
Richland WA, *48058* **13** E4
Richland Ctr. WI, *5184* **74** A3
Richland Co. IL, *16233* **99** D3
Richland Co. MT, *9746* **17** F2
Richland Co. ND, *16321* **19** E4
Richland Co. OH, *124475* **91** D3
Richland Co. SC, *384504* **122** B3
Richland Co. WI, *18021* **74** A2
Richland Hills TX, *7801* **207** B2
Richland Par. LA, *20725* **125** F3
Richlands NC, *1520* **115** D4
Richlands VA, *5823* **111** F2
Richlandtown PA, *1327* **146** C1
Richmond CA, *103701* **36** B3
Richmond IL, *1874* **74** C4
Richmond IN, *36812* **100** B1
Richmond KS, *464* **96** A3
Richmond KY, *31364* **110** C1
Richmond LA, *577* **126** A2
Richmond ME, *1760* **82** C3
Richmond MI, *5735* **76** C4
Richmond MN, *1422* **66** B3
Richmond MO, *5797* **96** C2
Richmond TX, *11679* **132** A3
Richmond UT, *2470* **31** E2
Richmond VT, *723* **81** D2
Richmond VA, *204214* **113** E1
Richmond Co. GA, *200549* **130** A1
Richmond Co. NY, *468730* **147** E1
Richmond Co. NC, *46639* **122** C2
Richmond Co. VA, *9254* **103** E4
Richmond Hts. FL, *8541* **143** E2
Richmond Hts. MO, *8603* **256** B2
Richmond Hts. OH, *10546* **204** G1
Richmond Hill GA, *9281* **130** B3
Richmondville NY, *918* **79** F4
Rich Square NC, *958* **113** E3
Richton MS, *1068* **127** D4
Richwood LA, *3392* **125** E2
Richwood OH, *2229* **90** C4
Richwood TX, *3510* **132** A4
Richwood WV, *2051* **102** A4
Riddle OR, *1185* **28** B1
Ridge NY, *13336* **149** D3
Ridgebury CT, *1200* **148** C2
Ridgebury NY, *850* **148** A2
Ridgecrest CA, *27616* **45** E4
Ridgecrest LA, *694* **125** F4
Ridge Farm IL, *882* **99** D1
Ridgefield CT, *7645* **148** C2
Ridgefield NJ, *11032* **240** D2
Ridgefield WA, *4763* **20** C1
Ridgefield Park NJ, *12729* **240** D1
Ridgeland MS, *24047* **126** B2
Ridgeland SC, *4036* **130** C2
Ridgely MD, *1639* **145** E3
Ridgely TN, *1795* **108** B3
Ridge Manor FL, *4513* **140** C1
Ridge Spr. SC, *737* **121** F4
Ridgetop TN, *1874* **109** F3
Ridgeville IN, *803* **90** A4
Ridgeville SC, *1979* **130** C1
Ridgeway MO, *464* **86** C4
Ridgeway VA, *742* **112** B3
Ridgeway WV, *750* **103** D2
Ridgeway WI, *653* **74** A3
Ridgewood NJ, *24958* **148** B3
Ridgway CO, *924* **40** B3
Ridgway IL, *869* **109** D1
Ridgway PA, *4078* **92** B2
Ridley Park PA, *7002* **248** B4
Riegelsville PA, *868* **146** C1
Riesel TX, *1007* **59** F4
Rifle CO, *9172* **40** B1
Rigby ID, *3945* **23** E4
Riggins ID, *419* **22** B2
Riley KS, *939* **43** F2
Riley Co. KS, *71115* **43** F2
Rillito AZ, *97* **55** D3
Rimersburg PA, *951* **92** A3
Rincon GA, *8836* **130** B3
Rindge NH, *6014* **95** D1
Rineyville KY, *550* **110** A1
Ringgold GA, *3580* **120** B2
Ringgold LA, *1495* **125** D2
Ringgold Co. IA, *5131* **86** B3
Ringling OK, *1037* **51** E4
Ringoes NJ, *1100* **147** D1
Ringtown PA, *818* **93** E3
Ringwood NJ, *12228* **148** A2
Rio FL, *965* **141** E4
Rio WI, *1059* **74** B2
Rio Arriba Co. NM, *40246* **48** C1
Rio Blanco Co. CO, *6666* **40** B1
Rio Bravo TX, *4794* **63** D2
Rio Dell CA, *3368* **28** A4
Rio del Mar CA, *9216* **236** D1
Rio Grande NJ, *2670* **104** C4
Rio Grande OH, *830* **101** E3
Rio Grande City TX, *13834* **63** E4
Rio Grande Co. CO, *11982* **41** D4
Rio Hondo TX, *2356* **63** F4
Rio Linda CA, *15106* **255** B1
Rio Rancho NM, *87521* **48** C3
Rio Rico AZ, *18962* **55** D4
Rio Verde AZ, *1811* **54** C1
Rio Vista CA, *7360* **36** B3
Rio Vista TX, *873* **59** E3
Ripley CA, *692* **53** F3
Ripley MS, *5395* **118** C2
Ripley NY, *872* **78** A4
Ripley OH, *1750* **100** C3
Ripley OK, *403* **51** F2
Ripley TN, *8445* **108** B4
Ripley WV, *3252* **101** E3
Ripley Co. IN, *28818* **100** A2
Ripley Co. MO, *14100* **108** A3
Ripon CA, *14297* **36** C4
Ripon WI, *7733* **74** B2
Ririe ID, *656* **23** E4
Rising Star TX, *835* **59** D3
Rising Sun DE, *2458* **145** E2
Rising Sun IN, *2304* **100** B2
Rising Sun MD, *2781* **146** A4
Risingsun OH, *606* **90** C2
Rison AR, *1344* **117** E4
Ritchie Co. WV, *10449* **101** F2
Rittman OH, *6491* **91** E3
Ritzville WA, *1673* **13** F3
Riverbank CA, *22678* **36** C4
River Bend NC, *3119* **115** D3
River Bluff KY, *403* **100** A4
Riverdale CA, *3153* **44** C3
Riverdale GA, *15134* **120** C4
Riverdale IL, *13549* **203** E6
Riverdale IA, *405* **208** B1

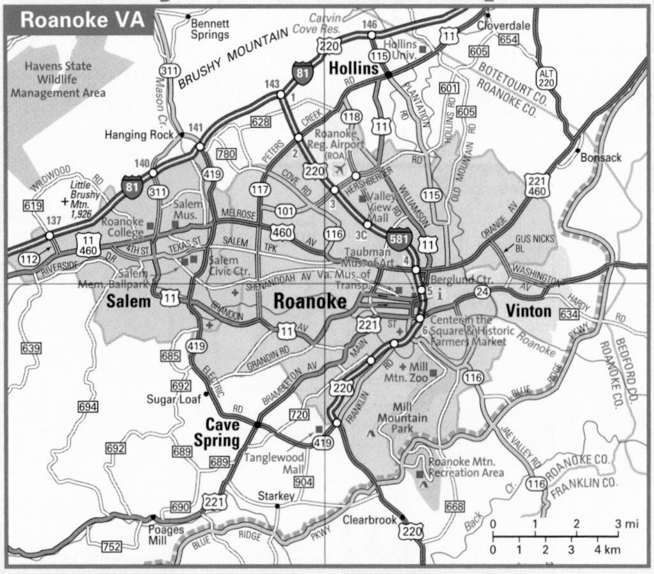

Bennett Sprs. D1
Bonsack E1
Cave Spr. D2
Clearbrook E2
Cloverdale E1
Hanging Rock D1
Hollins E1
Poages Mill D2
Roanoke D2
Salem D2
Starkey D2
Sugar Loaf D2
Vinton E2

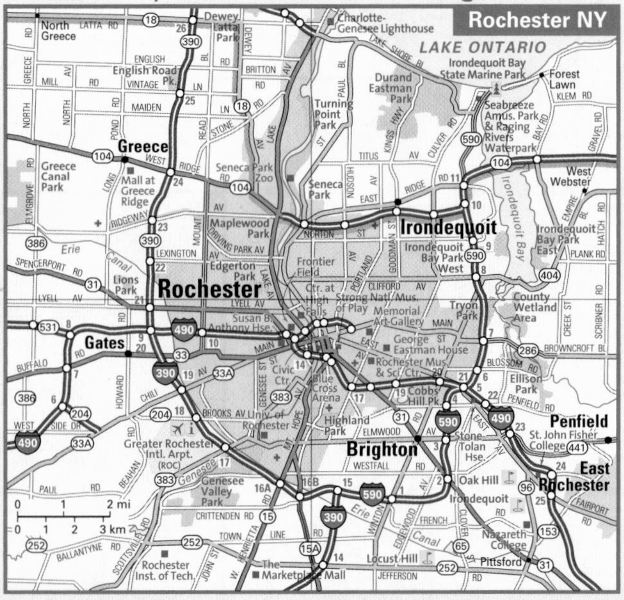

Brighton G2
E. Rochester G2
Forest Lawn G1
Gates F2
Greece F1
Irondequoit G1
N. Greece F1
Penfield G2
Pittsford G2
Rochester F1

Entries in **bold black** indicate counties or parishes.
Entries in **bold color** indicate cities with detailed inset maps.

Riverdale ND, *205* 18 B3
Riverdale UT, *8426* 244 A2
Riverdale Park MD, *6956* 270 E2
River Edge NJ, *11340* 240 C1
River Falls AL, *526* 128 A4
River Falls WI, *15000* 67 D4
River Forest IL, *11172* 203 D4
River Grove IL, *10227* 203 D4
Rivergrove OR, *289* 251 C3
Riverhead NY, *13299* 149 E3
River Hills WI, *1597* 234 D1
River Oaks TX, *7427* 207 A2
River Ridge LA, *13494* 239 B1
River Rouge MI, *7903* 210 C4
Riverside AL, *2208* 120 A4
Riverside CA, *303871* 53 D2
Riverside IL, *8875* 203 D4
Riverside IA, *993* 87 F2
Riverside MO, *2937* 224 B2
Riverside NJ, *7765* 147 D3
Riverside NY, *497* 149 E3
Riverside OH, *25201* 100 C1
Riverside PA, *381* 93 E3
Riverside Co. CA, *2189641* 53 E3
Riverton IL, *3455* 98 B1
Riverton KS, *929* 106 B2
Riverton NJ, *2779* 146 C3
Riverton UT, *38753* 31 E4
Riverton WY, *10615* 32 B1
Riverview FL, *71050* 140 C2
Riverview MO, *2856* 256 C1
Riverwood KY, *446* 230 E1
Riverwoods IL, *3660* 203 C2
Rives Jct. MI, *650* 76 A4
Rivesville WV, *934* 102 A1
Riviera Beach FL, *32488* 141 F4
Riviera Beach MD, *12677* 144 C2
Roachdale IN, *926* 99 E1
Roaming Shores OH, *1508* 91 F2
Roane Co. TN, *54181* 110 B4
Roane Co. WV, *14926* 101 F3
Roan Mtn. TN, *1360* 111 E3
Roanoke AL, *6074* 128 B1
Roanoke IL, *2065* 88 B3
Roanoke IN, *1722* 90 A3
Roanoke TX, *5962* 207 B1
Roanoke VA, *97032* 112 B2
Roanoke Co. VA, *92376* 112 B1
Roanoke Rapids NC, *15754* 113 E3
Roaring Spr. PA, *2585* 92 C4
Robards KY, *515* 109 E1
Robbins IL, *5337* 203 D6
Robbins NC, *1097* 122 C1
Robbinsdale MN, *13953* 235 B2
Robbinsville NJ, *3041* 147 D2
Robbinsville NC, *620* 121 D1
Robersonville NC, *1488* 113 E4
Roberta GA, *1007* 129 D2
Robert Lee TX, *1049* 58 B3
Roberts ID, *580* 23 E4
Roberts WI, *1651* 67 E4
Roberts Co. SD, *10149* 27 F1
Roberts Co. TX, *929* 50 B2
Robertsdale AL, *5276* 135 E2
Robertson Co. KY, *2282* 100 C3
Robertson Co. TN, *66283* 109 F3
Robertson Co. TX, *16622* 61 F1
Robertsville NJ, *11297* 147 E2
Robeson Co. NC, *134168* 123 D2
Robesonia PA, *2061* 146 A2
Robins IA, *3142* 87 E1
Robinson IL, *7713* 99 D2
Robinson TX, *10509* 59 E4
Robstown TX, *11487* 63 F2
Roby TX, *643* 58 B2
Rochdale MA, *1400* 150 B2
Rochelle GA, *1174* 129 E3
Rochelle IL, *9574* 88 B1
Rochelle Park NJ, *6079* 240 C1
Rochester IL, *3689* 98 B1
Rochester IN, *6218* 89 F3
Rochester MN, *106769* 73 D1
Rochester NH, *29752* 81 F4
Rochester NY, *210565* 78 C3
Rochester PA, *3657* 91 F3
Rochester VT, *299* 81 D3
Rochester WA, *2388* 12 B4
Rochester WI, *3682* 74 C4
Rochester Hills MI, *70995* 76 C4
Rock MA, *850* 151 D3
Rockaway NJ, *6438* 148 A3
Rockaway Beach MO, *841* 107 D3
Rockaway Beach OR, *1312* 20 B1
Rockbridge Co. VA, *22307* 102 B4
Rockcastle Co. KY, *17056* 110 C2
Rock Co. MN, *9687* 27 F4
Rock Co. NE, *1526* 35 D2
Rock Co. WI, *160331* 74 B4
Rock Creek MN, *1628* 67 D2
Rock Creek OH, *529* 91 F2
Rockdale MD, *16100* 144 C2
Rockdale TX, *5595* 61 E1
Rockdale Co. GA, *85215* 120 C4
Rockfall CT, *1500* 149 E1
Rock Falls IL, *9266* 88 B1
Rockford AL, *477* 128 A1
Rockford IL, *152871* 74 B4
Rockford IA, *860* 73 D3
Rockford MI, *5719* 75 F3
Rockford MN, *4316* 66 C3
Rockford OH, *1120* 90 A3
Rockford TN, *856* 110 C4
Rockford WA, *470* 14 B3
Rock Hall MD, *1310* 145 D2
Rock Hill MO, *4635* 256 B2
Rock Hill NY, *1742* 148 A1
Rock Hill SC, *66154* 122 A2
Rockingham NC, *9558* 122 C2
Rockingham Co. NH, *295223* 81 F4
Rockingham Co. NC, *93643* 112 B3
Rockingham Co. VA, *76314* 102 C3
Rock Island IL, *39018* 88 A2
Rock Island OK, *646* 116 B1
Rock Island WA, *788* 13 E3
Rock Island Co. IL, *147546* 88 A2
Rockland ID, *295* 31 E1
Rockland ME, *7297* 82 C2
Rockland MA, *17489* 151 D2
Rockland WI, *594* 73 F1
Rockland Co. NY, *311687* 148 B2
Rockledge AL, *600* 120 A3
Rockledge FL, *24926* 141 E2
Rockledge PA, *2543* 248 D2
Rocklin CA, *56974* 36 C2
Rockmart GA, *4199* 120 B3
Rock Mills AL, *600* 128 B1
Rock Pt. AZ, *642* 47 F1
Rockport AR, *755* 117 D3
Rockport IN, *2270* 99 E4
Rockport KY, *266* 109 E1
Rockport ME, *3209* 82 C2
Rockport MA, *4966* 151 F1
Rock Port MO, *1318* 86 A4
Rockport TX, *8766* 61 E4
Rock Rapids IA, *2549* 27 F4
Rock River WY, *245* 33 D2
Rocksprings TX, *1182* 60 B2
Rock Sprs. WY, *23036* 32 B3
Rockton IL, *7685* 74 B4
Rockvale CO, *487* 41 E3
Rock Valley IA, *3354* 35 F1
Rockville CT, *7474* 150 A3
Rockville IN, *2607* 99 E1
Rockville MD, *61209* 144 B2
Rockville MN, *2448* 66 C3
Rockville RI, *425* 150 C4
Rockwall TX, *37490* 59 F2
Rockwall Co. TX, *78337* 59 F2
Rockwell AR, *3780* 117 D3
Rockwell IA, *1039* 73 D3
Rockwell NC, *2108* 122 B1
Rockwell City IA, *1709* 72 B4
Rockwood MI, *3289* 90 C1
Rockwood PA, *890* 102 B1
Rockwood TN, *5562* 110 B4
Rocky Ford CO, *3957* 41 F3
Rocky Hill CT, *18760* 149 E1
Rocky Hill NJ, *682* 147 D1
Rocky Mount NC, *57477* 113 E4
Rocky Mount VA, *4799* 112 B2
Rocky Pt. NY, *14014* 149 D3
Rocky Ridge UT, *733* 39 E1
Rocky Ripple IN, *606* 221 B2
Rocky River OH, *20213* 204 E2
Rocky Top TN, *1781* 110 C3
Rodeo CA, *8679* 259 C1
Roebuck SC, *2200* 121 F2
Roeland Park KS, *6731* 224 B3
Roessleville NY, *10800* 188 D2
Roff OK, *725* 51 F4
Roger Mills Co. OK, *3647* 50 C2
Rogers AR, *55964* 106 C3
Rogers MN, *8597* 66 C3
Rogers TX, *1218* 61 E1
Rogers City MI, *2827* 71 D3
Rogers Co. OK, *86905* 106 A3
Rogersville AL, *1257* 119 E2
Rogersville MO, *3073* 107 D2
Rogersville TN, *4420* 111 D3
Rogue River OR, *2131* 28 B2
Rohnert Park CA, *40971* 36 B3
Roland IA, *1284* 86 C1
Roland OK, *3169* 116 B1
Rolesville NC, *3786* 113 D4
Rolette ND, *594* 18 C1
Rolette Co. ND, *13937* 18 C1
Rolfe IA, *584* 72 B3
Rolla KS, *442* 50 B1
Rolla MO, *19559* 97 F4
Rolla ND, *1280* 18 C1
Rolling Fields KY, *646* 230 E1
Rolling Fork MS, *2143* 126 A1
Rolling Hills CA, *1860* 228 C4
Rolling Hills KY, *959* 230 F1
Rolling Hills WY, *440* 33 D1
Rolling Hills Estates CA, *8067* 228 C4
Rolling Meadows IL, *24099* 203 B3
Rolling Prairie IN, *582* 89 E2
Rollingstone MN, *664* 73 E1
Rollinsford NH, *2527* 82 A4
Roma TX, *9765* 63 D4
Romancoke MD, *800* 145 D3
Roman Forest TX, *1538* 132 B2
Rome GA, *36303* 120 B3
Rome IL, *1738* 88 B3
Rome NY, *33725* 79 E3
Rome City IN, *1361* 90 A2
Romeo CO, *404* 41 D4
Romeo MI, *3596* 76 C4
Romeoville IL, *39680* 89 D2
Romney WV, *1848* 102 C2
Romoland CA, *1684* 229 K4
Romulus MI, *23989* 90 C1
Ronan MT, *1871* 15 D3
Ronceverte WV, *1765* 112 A1
Ronkonkoma NY, *19082* 149 D3
Roodhouse IL, *1814* 98 A2
Rooks Co. KS, *5181* 43 D2
Roosevelt NJ, *882* 147 E2
Roosevelt UT, *6046* 32 A4
Roosevelt Co. MT, *10425* 17 E2
Roosevelt Co. NM, *19846* 49 F4
Roosevelt Park MI, *3831* 75 E3
Roper NC, *611* 113 F4
Ropesville TX, *434* 58 A1
Rosalia WA, *550* 14 A3
Rosamond CA, *18150* 52 C1
Rosaryville MD, *18150* 144 C4
Rosburg WA, *317* 12 B4
Roscoe IL, *10785* 74 B4
Roscoe NY, *541* 94 A2
Roscoe SD, *329* 27 D2
Roscoe TX, *1322* 58 B3
Roscommon MI, *1075* 70 C4
Roscommon Co. MI, *24449* 76 A1
Roseau MN, *2633* 19 F1
Roseau Co. MN, *15629* 19 F1
Roseboro NC, *1191* 123 D2
Rose Bud AR, *482* 117 E1
Rosebud SD, *1587* 34 C1
Rosebud TX, *1412* 59 F4
Rosebud Co. MT, *9233* 17 D4
Roseburg OR, *21181* 28 B1
Rose City MI, *653* 76 B1
Rose City TX, *502* 132 C2
Rosedale IN, *725* 99 E1
Rosedale LA, *793* 133 F2
Rosedale MD, *19257* 144 C2
Rosedale MS, *1873* 118 A4
Rosedale Beach DE, *750* 145 F4
Rose Haven MD, *1400* 144 C4
Rose Hill KS, *3931* 43 F4
Rose Hill NC, *1626* 123 E2
Rose Hill VA, *714* 111 D3
Rose Hill VA, *20226* 270 C5
Roseland FL, *1472* 141 E3
Roseland LA, *1123* 134 B1
Roseland NJ, *5819* 240 A2
Roselawn IN, *4131* 89 D3
Roselle IL, *22763* 203 B3
Roselle NJ, *21085* 147 E1
Roselle Park NJ, *13297* 147 E1
Rose Lodge OR, *1894* 20 B2
Rosemead CA, *53764* 228 E2
Rosemont CA, *22681* 255 C3
Rosemont IL, *4202* 203 C3
Rosemount MN, *21874* 235 D4
Rosemount OH, *2112* 101 D3
Rosenberg TX, *30618* 132 A3
Rosendale NY, *1349* 94 B3
Rosendale WI, *1063* 74 C2
Rosenhayn NJ, *1098* 145 F1
Rosepine LA, *1692* 133 D1
Roseto PA, *1567* 93 F3
Rose Valley PA, *913* 248 A4
Roseville CA, *118788* 36 C2
Roseville IL, *989* 88 A3
Roseville MI, *47299* 210 D2
Roseville MN, *33660* 235 C2
Roseville OH, *1852* 101 E1
Roseville Park DE, *6200* 146 B4
Rosholt SD, *423* 27 F1
Rosiclare IL, *1160* 109 D1
Roslyn PA, *16900* 248 C1
Roslyn SD, *183* 27 E2
Roslyn WA, *893* 13 D3
Roslyn Estates NY, *1251* 241 G2
Rosman NC, *576* 121 E1
Ross CA, *2415* 259 A1
Ross OH, *3417* 100 B2
Ross Co. OH, *78064* 101 D2
Rossford OH, *6293* 267 B2
Rossiter PA, *646* 92 B3
Rossmoor CA, *10244* 228 E4
Rossmoor NJ, *2666* 147 E2
Rossville GA, *4105* 120 B2
Rossville IL, *1331* 89 D4
Rossville IN, *1653* 89 E4
Rossville KS, *1151* 43 F2
Rossville MD, *15147* 193 E2
Roswell GA, *88346* 120 C3
Roswell NM, *48366* 57 E1
Rotan TX, *1508* 58 B2
Rothsay MN, *493* 19 F4
Rothschild WI, *5269* 68 B4
Rothsville PA, *3044* 146 A2
Rotonda FL, *8759* 140 C4
Rotterdam NY, *20652* 94 B1
Rotterdam Jct. NY, *918* 94 B1
Rougemont NC, *978* 112 C3
Rough Rock AZ, *414* 47 F1
Round Hill VA, *539* 103 D2
Round Lake NY, *623* 94 B1
Round Mtn. NV, *550* 37 F2
Round Pond ME, *325* 82 C3
Round Rock AZ, *789* 47 F1
Round Rock TX, *99887* 61 E1
Roundup MT, *1788* 16 C4
Rouses Pt. NY, *2209* 81 D1
Routt Co. CO, *23509* 32 C4
Rouzerville PA, *917* 103 D1
Rowan Co. KY, *23333* 100 C4
Rowan Co. NC, *138428* 112 A4
Rowland NC, *1037* 122 C3
Rowland Hts. CA, *48993* 229 F3
Rowlesburg WV, *584* 102 B2
Rowlett TX, *56199* 207 E1
Rowley MA, *1416* 151 F1
Roxana DE, *375* 145 F4
Roxboro NC, *8362* 112 C3
Roxie MS, *497* 126 A4
Roxton TX, *650* 116 A4
Roy NM, *234* 49 E2
Roy UT, *36884* 31 E3
Royal Ctr. IN, *861* 89 E3
Royal City WA, *2140* 13 E4
Royal Oak MD, *750* 145 D4
Royal Oak MI, *57236* 76 C4
Royal Palm Beach FL, *34140* 143 E1
Royal Pines NC, *4272* 121 E1
Royalton IL, *1151* 98 C4
Royalton MN, *1242* 66 C2
Royersford PA, *4752* 146 B2
Royse City TX, *9349* 59 F2
Royston GA, *2582* 121 E3
Rubonia FL, *1700* 266 B4
Ruch OR, *840* 28 B2
Rudyard MT, *258* 15 F2
Rugby ND, *2876* 18 C2
Ruidoso NM, *8029* 57 D2
Ruidoso Downs NM, *2815* 57 D2
Rule TX, *636* 58 C2
Ruleville MS, *3007* 118 A4
Rumford ME, *4218* 82 B2
Rumson NJ, *7122* 147 F2
Runaway Bay TX, *1286* 59 E2
Runge TX, *1031* 61 E3
Runnels Co. TX, *10501* 58 C3
Runnemede NJ, *8468* 146 C3
Running Sprs. CA, *4862* 229 K1
Rupert ID, *5554* 31 D1
Rupert WV, *942* 102 A4
Rural Hall NC, *2937* 112 B3
Rural Retreat VA, *1483* 111 F2
Rural Valley PA, *876* 92 B3
Rush City MN, *3079* 67 D2
Rush Co. IN, *17392* 100 A1
Rush Co. KS, *3307* 43 D3
Rushford MN, *1731* 73 E2
Rushford Vil. MN, *807* 73 E2
Rushmere VA, *1018* 113 F2
Rush Sprs. OK, *1231* 51 E4
Rush Valley UT, *447* 31 E4
Rushville IL, *3192* 88 A4
Rushville IN, *6341* 100 A1
Rushville NE, *890* 34 A1

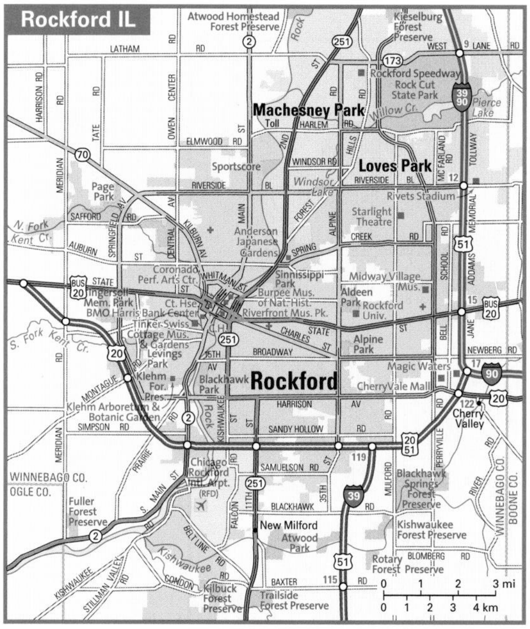

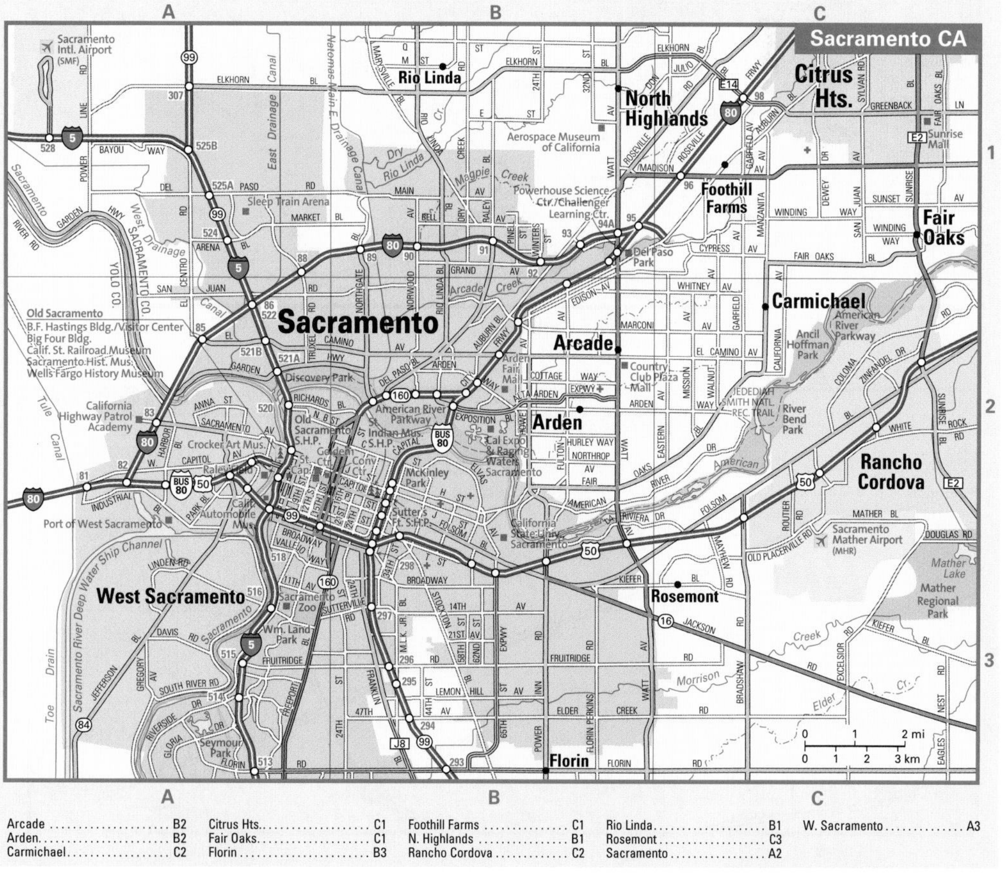

Arcade B2
Arden B2
Carmichael C2
Citrus Hts. C1
Fair Oaks C1
Florin B3
Foothill Farms C1
N. Highlands B1
Rancho Cordova C2
Rio Linda B1
Rosemont C3
Sacramento A2
W. Sacramento A3

Figures after entries indicate population, page number, and grid reference.

Affton B3
Alorton C3
Ballwin A2
Bella Villa B3
Bellefontaine Neighbors C1
Bellerive B2
Belleville D3
Bel-Nor B2
Bel-Ridge B2
Benevolent Hts. D3
Berkeley B1
Beverly Hills B2
Black Jack B1
Breckenridge Hills B2
Brentwood B2
Bridgeton B1
Brooklyn C2
Cahokia C3
Calverton Park B1
Caseyville D2
Cedar Park D1
Centreville C3
Champ A1
Charlack B2
Chesterfield A2
Clayton B2
Collinsville D2
Columbia C3
Concord B3
Cool Valley B1
Country Club Hills B1
Country Life Acres A2
Crestwood B3
Creve Coeur A2
Crystal Lake Park B2
Dellwood B1
Des Peres A2
Dupo C3
E. Carondelet C3
E. St. Louis C2
Edmundson B1
Edwardsville D1
Ellisville A2
Fairmont City C2
Fairview Hts. D2
Fenton A3
Ferguson B1
Flordell Hills C1
Florissant B1
Forest Acres D2
Frontenac B2
Glasgow Vil. C1
Glen Carbon D1
Glendale B2
Granite City C1
Greendale B2
Green Park B3
Hanley Hills B2
Hartford D1
Hazelwood B1
Hillsdale B2
Hollywood Hts. D2
Huntleigh B2
Imbs C3
Jennings B1
Kinloch B1
Kirkwood B3
Ladue B2
Lakeshire B3
Lemay B3
Mackenzie B3
Madison C2
Manchester A3
Maplewood B2
Marlborough B3
Maryland Hts. A1
Maryville D1
Mattese B3
Mehlville B3
Mitchell D1
Moline Acres C1
Murphy A3
Normandy B2
N. Dupo C3
Northwoods B2
Oak Hills D2
Oakland B3
Oakville B3
O'Fallon D2
Olivette B2
Overland B2
Pagedale B2
Parkdale A3
Peerless Park A3
Pine Lawn B2
Poag D1
Pontoon Beach D1
Richmond Hts. B2
Riverview C1
Robertson B1
Rock Hill B2
St. Ann B1
St. Charles A1
St. George B3
St. John B1
St. Louis C2
St. Peters A1
Sappington B3
Sauget C2
Shoveltown B1
Shrewsbury B3
Signal Hill D3
S. Roxana D1
Spanish Lake C1
Sunset Hills B3
Swansea D3
Town and Country A2
Twin Oaks A3
University City B2
Valley Park A3
Venice C2
Vinita Park B2
Warson Woods B2
Washington Park D2
Webster Groves B3
Wellston B2
Westwood A2
Wilbur Park B3
Wildwood A3
Winchester A2
Woodson Terrace B1

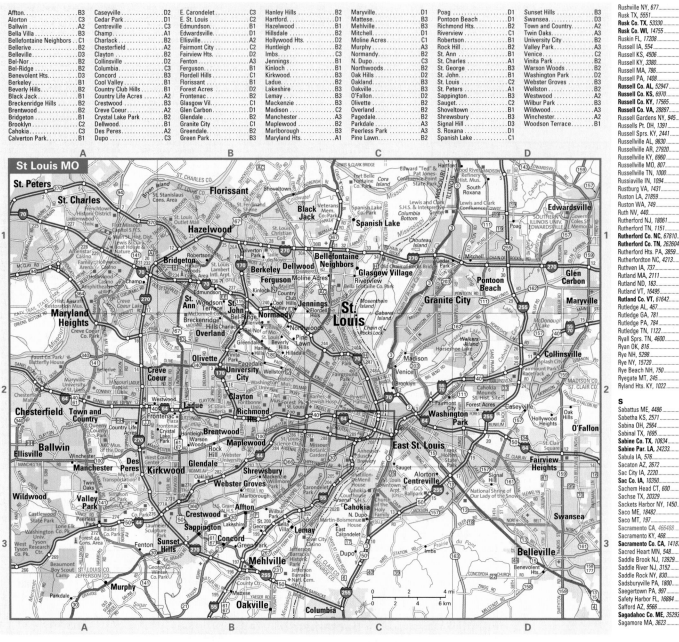

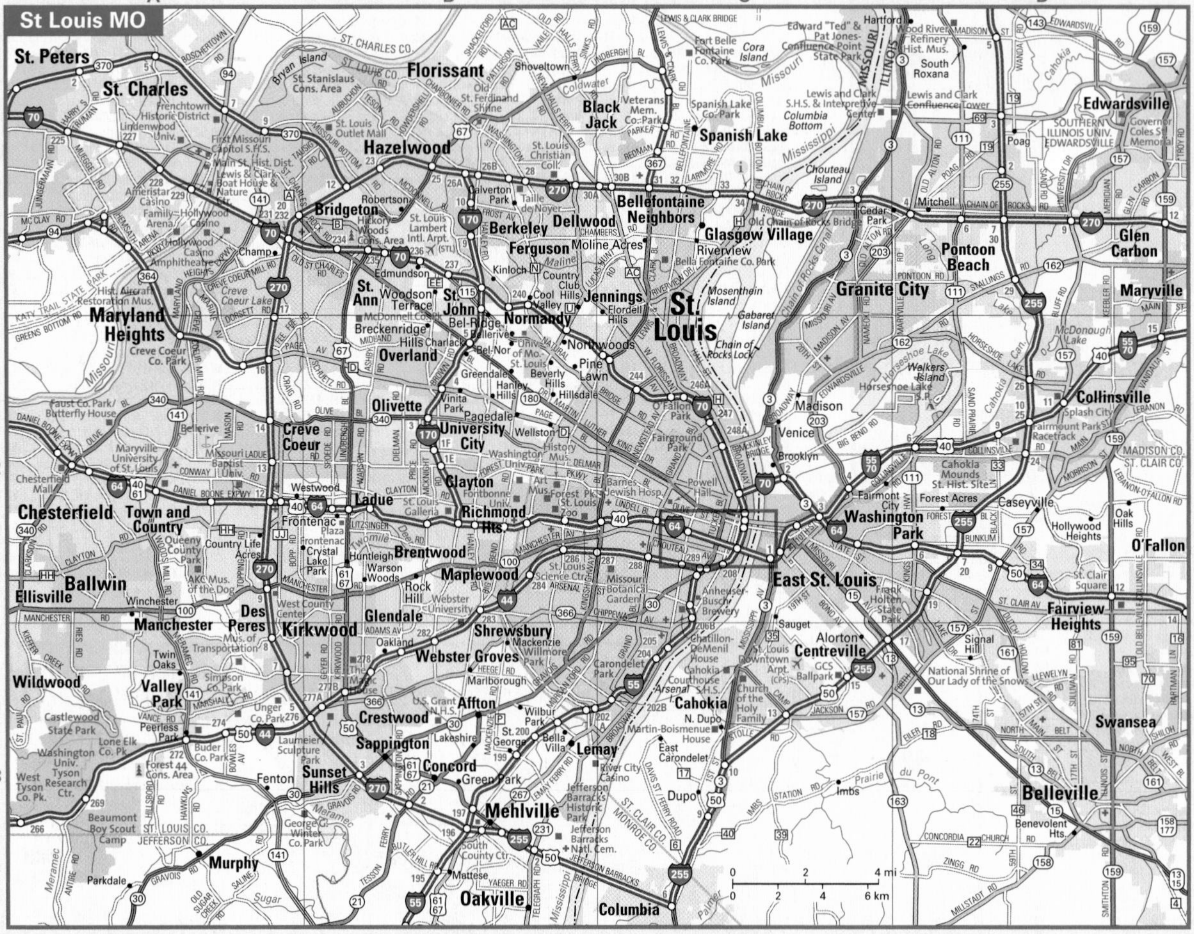

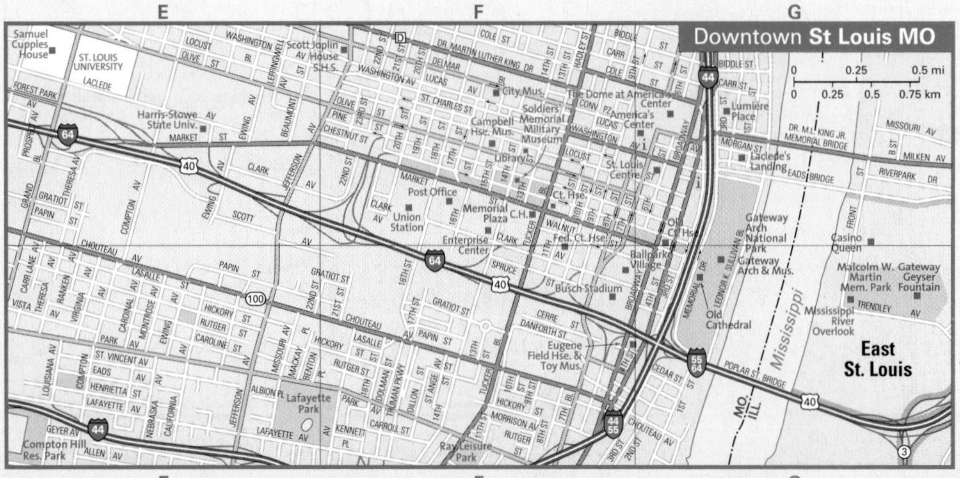

POINTS OF INTEREST

America's Center G1
Ballpark Village F2
Busch Stadium F2
Campbell House Museum F1
Casino Queen G1
City Hall F1
City Museum F1
Court House F1
Enterprise Center F1
Eugene Field House & Toy Museum F2
Federal Court House F1
Gateway Arch & Museum G2
Gateway Arch National Park G1
Gateway Geyser Fountain G2
Harris-Stowe State University E1
Jefferson Natl. Expansion Memorial G1
Laclede's Landing G1
Library F1
Lumière Place G1
Mississippi River Overlook G2
Old Cathedral G2
Old Court House G1
Post Office F1
St. Louis Centre G1
St. Louis University E1
Samuel Cupples House E1
Scott Joplin House State Hist. Site F1
Soldiers' Memorial Military Museum F1
The Dome at America's Center G1
Union Station F1

Rushville NY, *677* **78** C4
Rusk TX, *5551* **124** B3
Rusk Co. TX, *53330* **124** B3
Rusk Co. WI, *14755* **67** F3
Ruskin FL, *17208* **140** B3
Russell IA, *554* **87** D3
Russell KS, *4506* **43** D2
Russell KY, *3380* **101** D3
Russell MA, *786* **94** C2
Russell PA, *1408* **92** B1
Russell Co. AL, *52947* **128** C3
Russell Co. KS, *6970* **43** D2
Russell Co. KY, *17565* **110** B2
Russell Co. VA, *28897* **111** F2
Russell Gardens NY, *945* **241** G3
Russells Pt. OH, *1391* **90** B4
Russell Sprs. KY, *2441* **110** B2
Russellville AL, *9830* **119** E3
Russellville AR, *27920* **117** D1
Russellville KY, *6960* **109** E2
Russellville MO, *807* **97** E3
Russellville TN, *1000* **111** D3
Russiaville IN, *1094* **89** F4
Rustburg VA, *1431* **112** C2
Ruston LA, *21859* **125** E2
Ruston WA, *749* **262** A5
Ruth NV, *440* **38** B2
Rutherford NJ, *18061* **148** B3
Rutherford TN, *1151* **108** C4
Rutherford Co. NC, *67810* **121** F1
Rutherford Co. TN, *262604* **109** F4
Rutherford Hts. PA, *3859* **218** C1
Rutherfordton NC, *4213* **121** F1
Ruthven IA, *737* **72** B3
Rutland MA, *2111* **150** B1
Rutland ND, *163* **27** E1
Rutland VT, *16495* **81** D3
Rutland Co. VT, *61642* **81** D3
Rutledge AL, *467* **128** A4
Rutledge GA, *781* **121** D4
Rutledge PA, *784* **248** B4
Rutledge TN, *1122* **111** D3
Ryall Sprs. TN, *4600* **120** B2
Ryan OK, *816* **59** E1
Rye NH, *5298* **82** A4
Rye NY, *15720* **148** C3
Rye Beach NH, *750* **82** A4
Ryegate MT, *245* **16** B4
Ryland Hts. KY, *1022* **100** B2

S

Sabattus ME, *4486* **82** B2
Sabetha KS, *2571* **96** A1
Sabina OH, *2564* **100** C2
Sabinal TX, *1695* **60** C3
Sabine Co. TX, *10834* **124** C4
Sabine Par. LA, *24233* **125** D4
Sabula IA, *576* **88** A1
Sacaton AZ, *2672* **54** C2
Sac City IA, *2220* **72** B4
Sac Co. IA, *10350* **72** A4
Sachem Head CT, *600* **149** E2
Sachse TX, *20329* **207** E1
Sackets Harbor NY, *1450* **79** D1
Saco ME, *18482* **82** B4
Saco MT, *197* **17** D2
Sacramento CA, *466488* **36** C3
Sacramento KY, *468* **109** E1
Sacramento Co. CA, *1418788* **36** C3
Sacred Heart MN, *548* **66** B4
Saddle Brook NJ, *13929* **240** C1
Saddle River NJ, *3152* **148** B3
Saddle Rock NY, *830* **241** G2
Sadsburyville PA, *1800* **146** B3
Saegertown PA, *997* **92** A1
Safety Harbor FL, *16884* **140** B2
Safford AZ, *9566* **55** E2
Sagadahoc Co. ME, *35293* **82** B3
Sagamore MA, *3623* **151** E3

Entries in **bold black** indicate counties or parishes.
Entries in **bold color** indicate cities with detailed inset maps.

Sagamore Beach MA, *1200*	151	E3
Sagaponack NY, *313*	149	F3
Sag Harbor NY, *2169*	149	F3
Saginaw MI, *51508*	76	B2
Saginaw TX, *19806*	207	A2
Saginaw Co. MI, *200169*	76	B3
Sagle ID, *425*	14	B2
Saguache CO, *485*	41	D3
Saguache Co. CO, *6108*	41	D3
Sahuarita AZ, *25259*	55	D3
St. Albans VT, *6918*	81	D1
St. Albans WV, *11044*	101	E4
St. Albans Bay VT, *425*	81	D1
St. Andrew NY, *800*	148	B1
St. Andrews SC, *20493*	205	E1
St. Ann MO, *13020*	256	B1
St. Anne IL, *1257*	89	D3
St. Ansgar IA, *1107*	73	D2
St. Anthony ID, *3542*	23	E4
St. Anthony MN, *8226*	235	C2
St. Augusta MN, *3317*	66	C3
St. Augustine FL, *12975*	139	D3
St. Augustine Beach FL, *6176*	139	E3
St. Augustine Shores FL, *7359*	139	D3
St. Bernard LA, *1500*	134	C3
St. Bernard OH, *4368*	204	B2
St. Bernard Par. LA, *35897*	134	C3
St. Bonifacius MN, *2283*	66	C4
St. Charles IL, *32974*	88	C1
St. Charles IA, *653*	86	C2
St. Charles MD, *33379*	144	B4
St. Charles MI, *2054*	76	B3
St. Charles MN, *3735*	73	E1
St. Charles MO, *65794*	98	A3

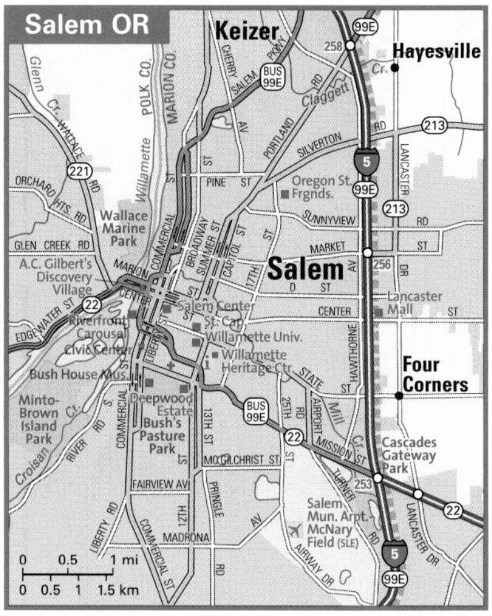

Alamo Hts.	E2
Balcones Hts.	E2
Bracken	F1
Buena Vista	E3
Castle Hills	E2
China Grove	F3
Cibolo	F1
Converse	F2
Garden Ridge	F1
Grey Forest	D1
Helotes	D1
Hill Country Vil.	E1
Hollywood Park	E1
Kirby	F2
Leon Valley	D2
Live Oak	F2
Macdona	D3
Olmos Park	E2
San Antonio	F3
Sayers	F3
Schertz	F1
Selma	F1
Shavano Park	E1
Southton	E3
Terrell Hills	E2
Universal City	F1
Von Ormy	D3
Windcrest	F2

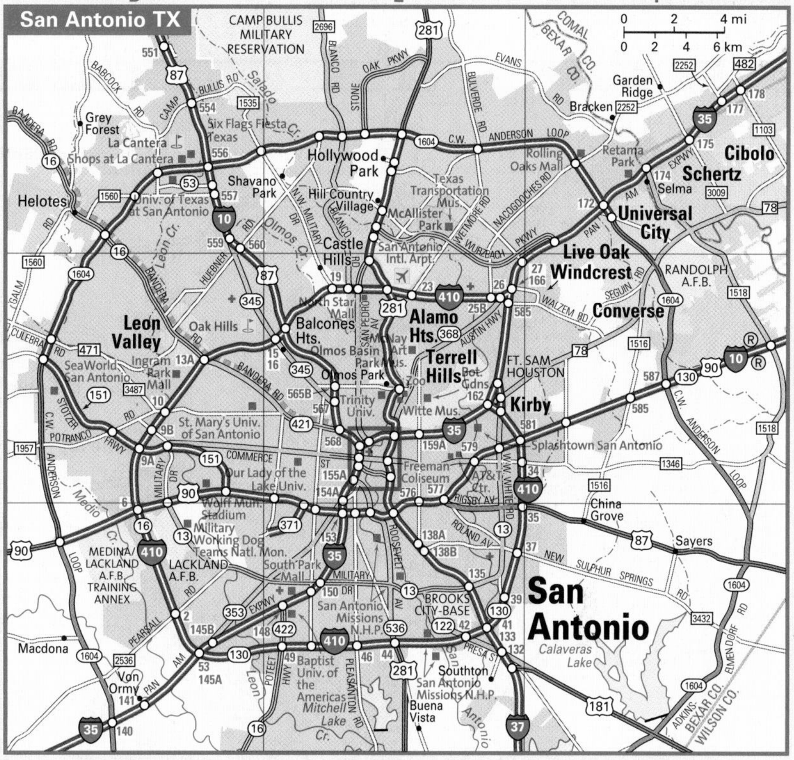

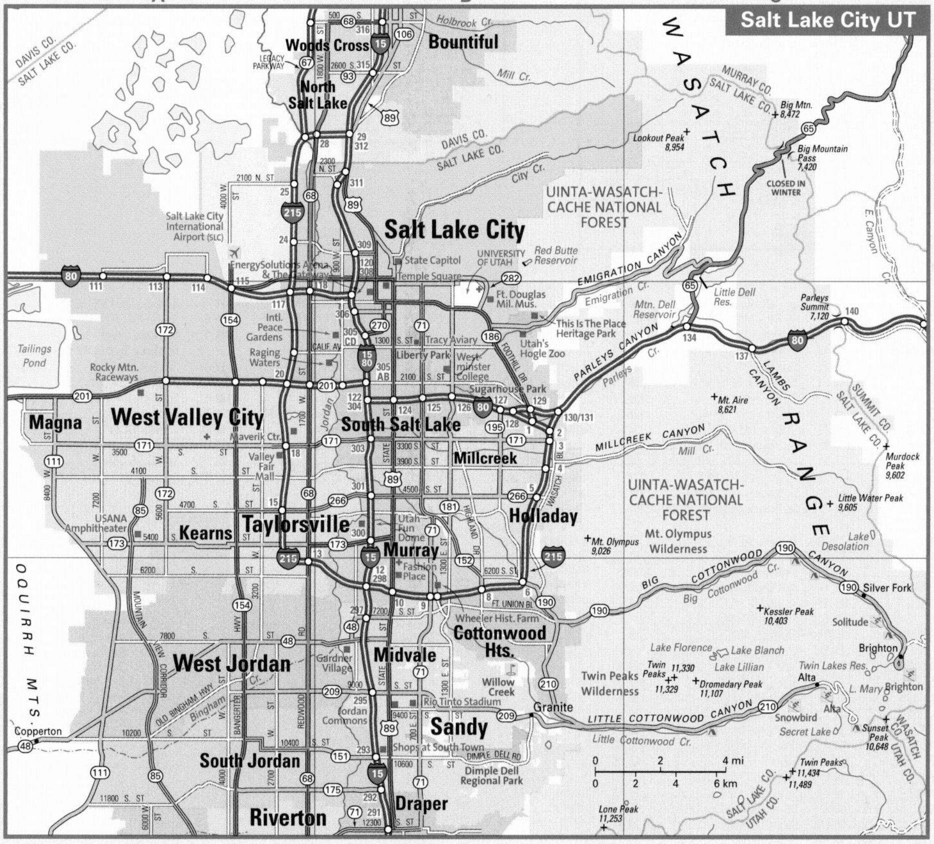

Alta	C3	Draper	B3	Magna	A2	Riverton	A3	S. Salt Lake	B2
Bountiful	B1	E. Millcreek	B2	Midvale	B3	Salt Lake City	B1	Taylorsville	A2
Brighton	C3	Granite	B3	Mill Creek	B2	Sandy	B3	W. Jordan	A3
Copperton	A3	Holladay	B2	Murray	B2	Silver Fork	C3	W. Valley City	A2
Cottonwood Hts.	B3	Kearns	A2	N. Salt Lake	B1	S. Jordan	A3	Woods Cross	B1

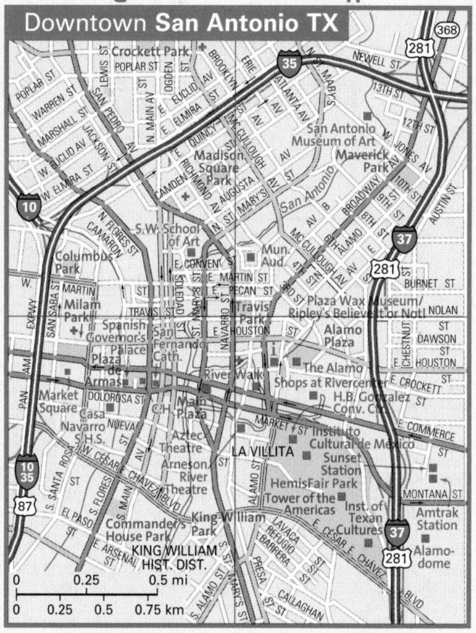

POINTS OF INTEREST

The Alamo	H2
Alamodome	H2
Amtrak Station	H2
Arneson River Theater	H2
Aztec Theatre	G2
Casa Navarro State Historic Site	G2
H.B. Gonzalez Convention Center	H2
HemisFair Park	H2
Institute of Texan Cultures	H2
Instituto Cultural de México	H2
Market Square	G2
Municipal Auditorium	H1
Plaza Wax Museum/Ripley's Believe It or Not!	H2
River Walk	H2
San Antonio Museum of Art	H1
San Fernando Cathedral	G2
Shops at Rivercenter	H2
Spanish Governor's Palace	G2
Sunset Station	H2
Southwest School of Art	G1
Tower of the Americas	H2

Figures after entries indicate population, page number, and grid reference.

Bonita C2
Chula Vista B3
Coronado A2
El Cajon C1
Imperial Beach B3
Lakeside C1
La Mesa C2
Lemon Grove C2
National City B2
San Diego C2
Santee C1
Spring Valley C2
Sunnyside C2
Tijuana, MX C3

POINTS OF INTEREST

Automotive Museum E1
Balboa Park E1
Balboa Stadium E1
Casa del Prado E1
Civic Center D2
Comic-Con Center for Popular Culture E1
Copley Symphony Hall E2
County Court House D2
Cruise Ship Terminal D2
Fleet & Industrial Supply Center D2
Fleet Science Center E1
Gaslamp Quarter & W. H. Davis House E2
House of Hospitality E1
Maritime Museum D2
Museum of Contemporary Art, San Diego D2
The New Children's Museum D2
The Old Globe Theatre E1
Petco Park E2
San Diego Air & Space Museum E1
San Diego Convention Center D2
San Diego International Airport D1
San Diego Museum of Art E1
San Diego Museum of Man E1
San Diego Natural History Museum E1
San Diego Zoo E1
Santa Fe Depot D2
Seaport Village D2
Spanish Village Art Center E1
Spreckels Organ Pavilion E1
Spreckels Theatre D2
Starlight Bowl E1
Timken Museum of Art E1
USS Midway Aircraft Carrier Museum D2
Veterans Museum & Memorial Center E1
Waterfront Park D1
Westfield Horton Plaza D2

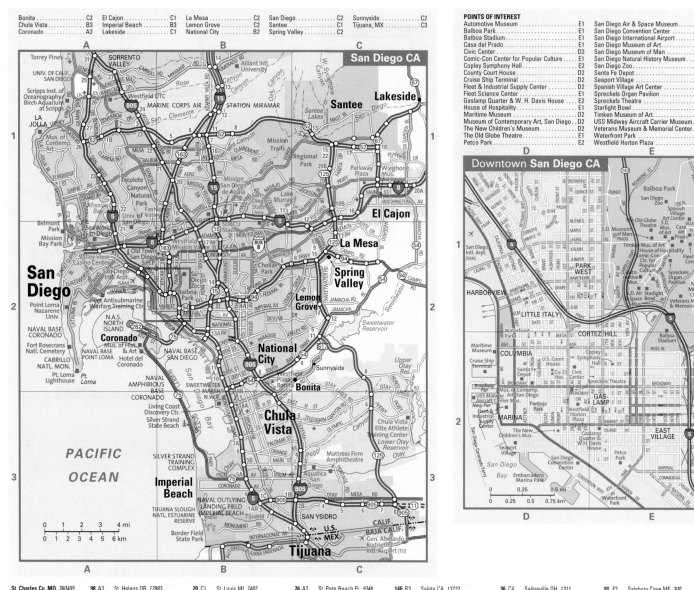

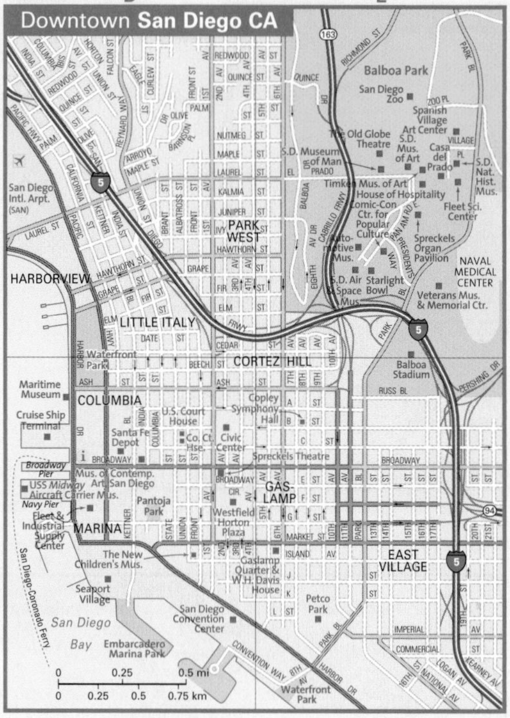

St. Charles Co. MO, *360485* **98** A3
St. Charles Par. LA, *52780* **134** B3
St. Clair MI, *5485* **76** C3
St. Clair MN, *868* **72** C1
St. Clair MO, *4724* **97** F4
St. Clair PA, *3004* **93** E3
St. Clair Co. AL, *83593* **120** A4
St. Clair Co. IL, *270056* **98** B4
St. Clair Co. MI, *163040* **76** C3
St. Clair Co. MO, *9805* **96** C4
St. Clair Shores MI, *59715* **76** C4
St. Clairsville OH, *5184* **91** F4
St. Cloud FL, *35183* **141** D2
St. Cloud MN, *65842* **66** C3
St. Croix Co. WI, *84345* **67** E3
St. Croix Falls WI, *2133* **67** D3
St. David AZ, *1699* **55** E3
St. David IL, *589* **88** A4
St. Edward NE, *705* **35** E3
Ste. Genevieve MO, *4410* **98** B4
Ste. Genevieve Co. MO, *18145* **98** A4
St. Elmo IL, *1426* **98** C2
St. Francis KS, *1329* **42** B1
St. Francis MN, *7218* **67** D3
St. Francis SD, *709* **34** C1
St. Francis WI, *9365* **234** D3
St. Francis Co. AR, *28258* **118** A2
St. Francisville IL, *697* **99** D3
St. Francisville LA, *1765* **134** A1
St. Francois Co. MO, *65359* **98** A4
St. Gabriel LA, *6677* **134** A2
St. George KS, *639* **43** F2
St. George ME, *2580* **82** C3
St. George MO, *1337* **256** B3
St. George SC, *2084* **130** C1
St. George UT, *72897* **46** C1
St. Hedwig TX, *2094* **61** D3
St. Helen MI, *2668* **76** A1
St. Helena CA, *5814* **36** B3
St. Helena Par. LA, *11203* **134** A1
St. Helens OR, *12883* **20** C1
St. Henry OH, *2427* **90** A4
St. Ignace MI, *2452* **70** C2
St. Ignatius MT, *842* **15** D3
St. Jacob IL, *1098* **98** B3
St. James MD, *2953* **144** A1
St. James MN, *4605* **72** B1
St. James MO, *4216* **97** F4
St. James NY, *13338* **149** D3
St. James NC, *3165* **123** E4
St. James City FL, *3784* **142** C1
St. James Par. LA, *22102* **134** A3
St. Jo TX, *1043* **59** E1
St. John IN, *14850* **89** D2
St. John KS, *1295* **43** D3
St. John MO, *6517* **256** B1
St. John ND, *341* **18** C1
St. John WA, *537* **13** F3
St. Johns AZ, *3480* **48** A4
St. Johns MI, *7865* **76** A3
St. Johnsbury VT, *6193* **81** E2
St. Johnsbury Ctr. VT, *1000* **81** E2
St. Johns Co. FL, *190039* **139** D3
St. Johnsville NY, *1732* **79** F3
St. John the Baptist Par. LA, *45924* **134** B2
St. Joseph IL, *3967* **89** D4
St. Joseph LA, *1176* **126** A3
St. Joseph MI, *8365* **89** E1
St. Joseph MN, *6534* **66** C3
St. Joseph MO, *76780* **96** B1
St. Joseph TN, *782* **119** E2
St. Joseph Co. IN, *266931* **89** F2
St. Joseph Co. MI, *61295* **89** F1
St. Landry Par. LA, *83384* **133** F1
St. Lawrence PA, *1809* **146** B2
St. Lawrence SD, *198* **27** D3
St. Lawrence Co. NY, *111944* **79** F1
St. Leo FL, *1340* **140** C2
St. Libory IL, *615* **98** B4
St. Louis MI, *7482* **76** A2
St. Louis MO, *319294* **98** A3
St. Louis Co. MN, *200226* **64** C3
St. Louis Co. MO, *998954* **98** A3
St. Louis Park MN, *45250* **235** B2
St. Lucie FL, *590* **141** E3
St. Lucie Co. FL, *277789* **141** E3
St. Maries ID, *2402* **14** B3
St. Martin Par. LA, *52160* **133** F2
St. Martins MO, *1140* **97** E3
St. Martinville LA, *6114* **133** F2
St. Mary Par. LA, *54650* **134** A3
St. Mary's AK, *507* **154** B2
St. Marys GA, *17121* **139** D1
St. Marys KS, *2627* **43** F2
St. Marys OH, *8332* **90** B4
St. Marys PA, *13070* **92** B2
St. Marys WV, *1860* **101** F2
St. Mary's City MD, *900* **103** F4
St. Mary's Co. MD, *105151* **103** E3
St. Matthews KY, *17472* **230** E1
St. Matthews SC, *2021* **122** B4
St. Meinrad IN, *706* **99** E4
St. Michael MN, *16399* **66** C3
St. Michaels AZ, *1443* **48** A2
St. Michaels MD, *1029* **145** D3
St. Nazianz WI, *783* **74** C1
St. Paris OH, *2089* **90** B4
St. Paul AK, *479* **154** A3
St. Paul IN, *1031* **100** A2
St. Paul KS, *629* **106** B1
St. Paul MN, *285068* **67** D4
St. Paul MO, *1829* **98** A3
St. Paul NE, *2290* **35** D3
St. Paul OR, *421* **20** B2
St. Paul TX, *1066* **59** F2
St. Paul TX, *542* **61** E4
St. Paul VA, *970* **111** E2
St. Paul Park MN, *5279* **235** E4
St. Pauls NC, *2035* **123** D2
St. Pete Beach FL, *9346* **140** B3
St. Peter MN, *11196* **72** C1
St. Peters MO, *52575* **98** A3
St. Petersburg FL, *244769* **140** B3
St. Regis MT, *319* **14** C3
St. Regis Falls NY, *464* **80** C1
St. Regis Park KY, *1454* **230** F2
St. Robert MO, *4340* **107** E1
St. Rose LA, *8122* **134** B3
St. Simons Island GA, *12743* **139** D1
St. Stephen MN, *851* **66** C2
St. Stephen SC, *1697* **131** D1
St. Stephens NC, *8759* **111** F4
St. Tammany Par. LA, *233740* **134** B2
St. Thomas ND, *331* **19** E2
Saks AL, *10744* **120** A4
Salado TX, *2126* **61** E1
Salamanca NY, *5815* **92** B1
Sale Creek TN, *2845* **120** B1
Salem AR, *1635* **107** F3
Salem AR, *2789* **117** E2
Salem IL, *7485* **98** C3
Salem IN, *6319* **99** F3
Salem KY, *752* **109** D2
Salem MA, *41340* **151** D1
Salem MO, *4950* **107** F1
Salem NH, *28776* **95** E1
Salem NJ, *5146* **145** E1
Salem NM, *942* **56** B2
Salem NY, *946* **81** D4
Salem NC, *2218* **111** F4
Salem OH, *12303* **91** F3
Salem OR, *154637* **20** B2
Salem SD, *1347* **27** E4
Salem UT, *6423* **39** E1
Salem VA, *24802* **112** B2
Salem WV, *1586* **102** A2
Salem Co. NJ, *66083* **145** F1
Salem Lakes WI, *14558* **74** C4
Salesville AR, *450* **107** E3
Salida CA, *13722* **36** C4
Salida CO, *5236* **41** D3
Salina KS, *47707* **43** E2
Salina OK, *1396* **106** B3
Salina UT, *2489* **39** E2
Salinas CA, *150441* **44** B3
Saline MI, *8810* **90** B1
Saline Co. AR, *107118* **117** D2
Saline Co. IL, *24913* **98** C4
Saline Co. KS, *55606* **43** E2
Saline Co. MO, *23370* **97** D2
Saline Co. NE, *14200* **35** E4
Salineville OH, *1311* **91** F3
Salisbury CT, *3977* **94** B2
Salisbury MD, *30343* **114** C1
Salisbury MA, *4869* **151** F1
Salisbury MO, *1618* **97** D2
Salisbury NC, *33662* **112** A4
Salisbury PA, *727* **102** B1
Salisbury Beach MA, *1300* **151** F1
Salix PA, *1149* **92** B4
Sallisaw OK, *8880* **116** B1
Salmon ID, *3112* **23** D2
Salome AZ, *1530* **54** A1
Salsbury Cove ME, *300* **83** D2
Saltillo MS, *4752* **119** D3
Salt Lake City UT, *186440* **31** E4
Salt Lake Co. UT, *1029655* **31** E4
Salt Lick KY, *303* **100** C4
Salton City CA, *3763* **53** E3
Saltsburg PA, *873* **92** A4
Salt Sprs. FL, *600* **139** D4
Saltville VA, *2077* **111** F2
Saluda NC, *713* **121** E1
Saluda SC, *3565* **121** F3
Saluda VA, *769* **113** F1

SAN FRANCISCO BAY MAP INDEX

Alameda C3
Alamo D2
Albany C2
Antioch E1
Ashland D3
Atherton C5
Bay Pt. D1
Belmont C5
Belvedere B2
Benicia C1
Berkeley C2
Brisbane B3
Broadmoor B3
Burlingame B4
Campbell E6
Canyon C2
Castro Valley D3
Clayton E2
Clyde D1
Colma B3
Concord D1
Corte Madera A2
Crockett C1
Cupertino D6
Daly City B3
Danville D2
Diablo D2
Dublin E3
E. Palo Alto C5
El Cerrito B2
El Granada B5
El Sobrante C1
Emeryville C2
Fairfax A1
Foster City C4
Fremont D5
Greenbrae A2
Half Moon Bay B5
Hayward D4
Hercules C1
Hillsborough B4
Homestead Valley A2
Ignacio A1
Kensington C2
Kentfield A2
Ladera C5
Lafayette D2
La Honda C6
Larkspur A2
Livermore E3
Los Altos D6
Los Altos Hills C6
Marinwood A1
Martinez D1
Menlo Park C5
Millbrae B4
Mill Valley A2
Milpitas E5
Montara A4
Moraga D2
Moss Beach A5
Mtn. View D5
Muir Beach A2
Newark D5
N. Fair Oaks C5
N. Richmond B2
Novato A1
Oakland C3
Orinda C2
Pacheco D1
Pacifica A4
Palo Alto D5
Pescadero B6
Piedmont C2
Pinole C1
Pittsburg E1
Pleasant Hill D2
Pleasanton E4
Port Costa C1
Portola Valley C6
Redwood City C5
Richmond B2
Rodeo C1
Ross A1
San Anselmo A1
San Bruno B4
San Carlos C5
San Francisco A3
San Gregorio B6
San Jose E6
San Leandro C3
San Lorenzo D4
San Mateo B4
San Pablo B1
San Quentin A2
San Rafael B1
San Ramon D3
Santa Clara D6
Santa Venetia A1
Saratoga D6
Sausalito B2
S. San Francisco B4
Stinson Beach A2
Sunnyvale D6
Sunol E4
Tamalpais Valley A2
Tara Hills B1
Tiburon B2
Union City D4
Vallejo C1
Vine Hill D1
Walnut Creek D2
Woodacre A1
Woodside C5

Entries in **bold black** indicate counties or parishes.
Entries in **bold color** indicate cities with detailed inset maps.

Figures after entries indicate population, page number, and grid reference.

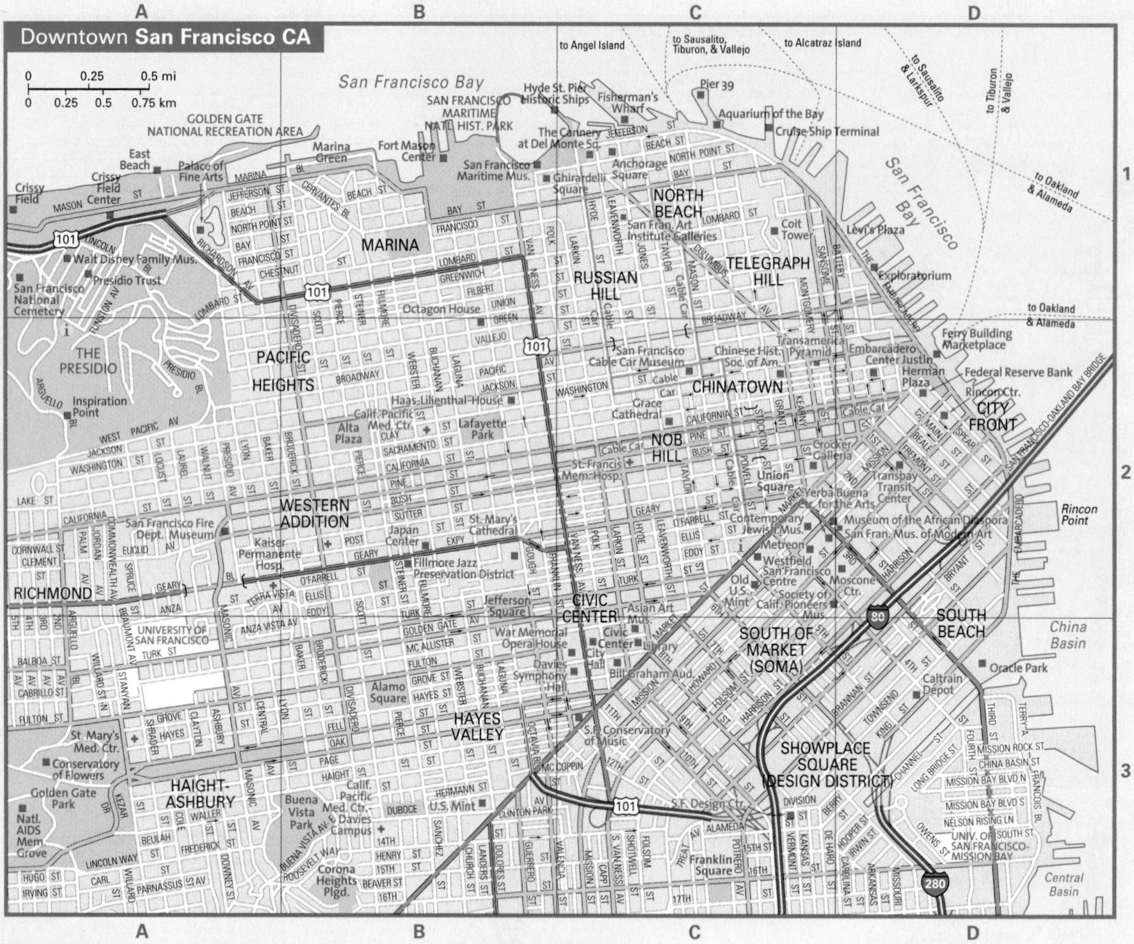

POINTS OF INTEREST

Anchorage Square C1
Aquarium of the Bay. C1
Asian Art Museum C3
AT&T Park D3
Bill Graham Auditorium C3
Caltrain Depot D3
The Cannery at Del Monte Square C1
Chinese Historical Society of America. C2
City Hall. C3
Coit Tower C1
Conservatory of Flowers A3
Contemporary Jewish Mus. C2
Crissy Field. A1
Crissy Field Center A1
Crocker Galleria C2
Cruise Ship Terminal C1
Davies Symphony Hall. C3
East Beach. A1
Embarcadero Center D2
Exploratorium. D1
Federal Reserve Bank D2
Fillmore Jazz Preservation District B2
Ferry Building Marketplace D2
Fisherman's Wharf C1
Fort Mason Center B1
Ghirardelli Square. B1
Golden Gate Natl. Rec. Area. . . . A1
Golden Gate Park A3
Grace Cathedral C2
Haas-Lilienthal House B2
Hyde Street Pier Historic Ships . C1
Inspiration Point A2
Japan Center. B2
Levi's Plaza D1
Library. C3
Metreon C2
Moscone Center D2
Museum of the African Diaspora. D2
National AIDS Memorial Grove . A3
Octagon House B2
Old U.S. Mint C2
Palace of Fine Arts. A1
Pier 39. . . . . C1
The Presidio. A2
Presidio Trust A1
Rincon Center D2
St. Mary's Cathedral. B2
San Francisco Art Institute Galleries. C1
San Francisco Cable Car Mus. . . C2
San Francisco Cons. of Music . . C3
San Francisco Design Center. . . C3
San Francisco Fire Dept. Mus. . . A2
San Francisco Maritime Mus. . . B1
San Francisco Maritime Natl. Hist. Park B1
San Francisco Museum of Modern Art D2
San Francisco Natl. Cemetery . . A1
Soc. of Calif. Pioneers Mus. C2
Transamerica Pyramid. C2
Transbay Transit Center D2
U.S. Mint. B3
Univ. of San Francisco. A3
Univ. of San Francisco-Mission Bay. D3
Walt Disney Family Mus.. . . . . A1
War Memorial Opera House. C3
Westfield San Francisco Centre. C2
Yerba Buena Center for the Arts C2

Saluda Co. SC, *19875* **121** F3
Salunga PA, *2695* **225** A1
Salyersville KY, *1883* **111** D1
Sammamish WA, *45780* **12** C3
Samoset FL, *3854* **266** B4
Sampit SC, *700* **131** E1
Sampson Co. NC, *63431* **123** D1
Samson AL, *1940* **136** C1
Samsula FL, *5047* **139** E4
San Andreas CA, *2783* **36** C3
San Angelo TX, *93200* **58** B4
San Anselmo CA, *12336* **259** A1
San Antonio FL, *1138* **140** C2
San Antonio TX, *1327407* **61** D3
San Antonio Hts. CA, *3371* **229** G2
San Ardo CA, *517* **44** B3
Sanatoga PA, *8378* **146** B2
Sanatorium MS, *900* **126** B3
San Augustine TX, *2108* **124** C4
San Augustine Co. TX, *8865* **124** C4
San Benito TX, *24250* **63** F4
San Benito Co. CA, *55269* **44** B3
San Bernardino CA, *209924* **53** D2
San Bernardino Co. CA, *2035210* .. **45** F4
Sanborn IA, *1404* **72** A3
Sanborn Co. SD, *2355* **27** E3
Sanbornville NH, *1056* **81** F3
San Bruno CA, *41114* **36** B4
San Carlos AZ, *4038* **55** D2
San Carlos CA, *28406* **259** C5
San Carlos Park FL, *16824* **142** C1
San Clemente CA, *63522* **52** C3
Sanders Co. MT, *11413* **14** C3
Sanderson TX, *837* **62** C3
Sandersville GA, *5912* **129** E1
Sandersville MS, *731* **126** C3
Sand Hills MA, *2400* **151** E2
Sandia Park NM, *237* **48** C3
San Diego CA, *1307402* **53** D4
San Diego TX, *4488* **63** E2
San Diego Co. CA, *3095313* **53** E4
San Dimas CA, *33371* **229** F2
Sand Lake MI, *1412* **75** F3
Sandoval IL, *1274* **98** C3
Sandoval Co. NM, *131561* **48** C2
Sandown NH, *5986* **95** E1
Sand Pt. AK, *976* **154** B4
Sandpoint ID, *7365* **14** B2
Sand Ridge NY, *849* **79** D3
Sand Rock AL, *560* **120** A3
Sands Pt. NY, *2675* **241** G2
Sand Sprs. OK, *18906* **51** F2
Sand Sprs. TX, *835* **58** B3
Sandston VA, *7571* **113** E1
Sandstone MN, *2849* **67** D2
Sandusky MI, *2679* **76** C2
Sandusky OH, *25793* **91** D2
Sandusky Co. OH, *60944* **90** C2
Sandwich IL, *7421* **88** C2
Sandwich MA, *2962* **151** E3
Sandy OR, *9570* **20** C2
Sandy PA, *1429* **92** B3
Sandy UT, *87461* **31** E4
Sandy Creek NY, *771* **79** E2
Sandy Hook KY, *675* **101** D4
Sandy Lake PA, *659* **92** A2
Sandy Sprs. GA, *93853* **120** C4

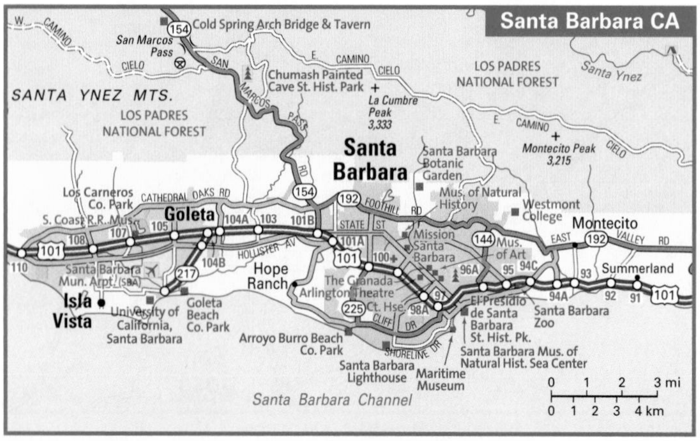

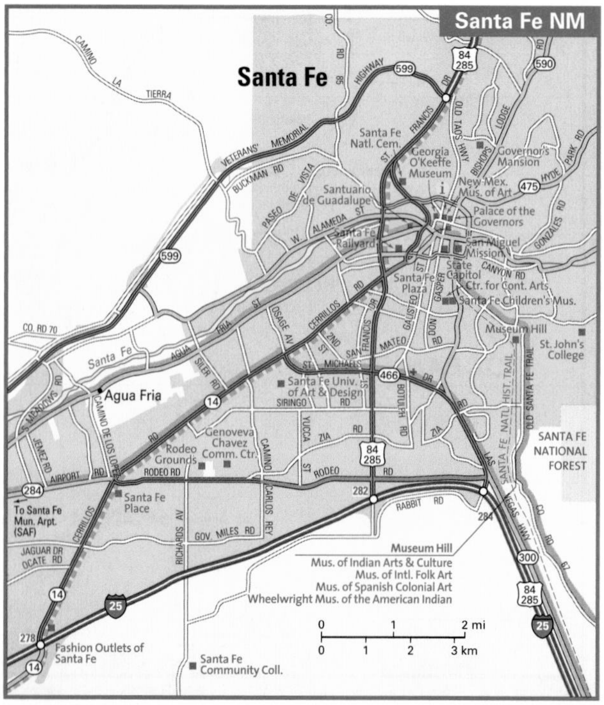

Entries in **bold black** indicate counties or parishes.
Entries in **bold color** indicate cities with detailed inset maps.

Sandy Sprs. SC, *750* ... 121 E2
Sandy Valley NV, *2051* ... 46 A2
Sandyville MD, *1000* ... 144 B1
San Elizario TX, *13603* ... 56 C4
San Felipe TX, *747* ... 61 F2
San Felipe Pueblo NM, *2404* ... 48 C3
San Fernando CA, *23645* ... 52 C2
Sanford CO, *879* ... 41 D4
Sanford FL, *53570* ... 141 D1
Sanford ME, *9761* ... 82 A4
Sanford MI, *859* ... 76 A2
Sanford NC, *28094* ... 122 C1
San Francisco CA, *805235* ... 36 B4
San Francisco Co. CA, *805235* ... 36 B4
San Gabriel CA, *39718* ... 228 D2
Sangamon Co. IL, *197465* ... 98 B1
Sanger CA, *24270* ... 45 D3
Sanger TX, *6916* ... 59 E1
Sangerville ME, *1270* ... 82 C1
Sanibel FL, *6469* ... 142 C1
Sanilac Co. MI, *43114* ... 76 C2
San Jacinto CA, *44199* ... 53 D3
San Jacinto Co. TX, *26384* ... 132 B1
San Joaquin CA, *4001* ... 44 C3
San Joaquin Co. CA, *685306* ... 36 C3
San Jon NM, *216* ... 49 F3
San Jose CA, *945942* ... 36 B4
San Jose IL, *642* ... 88 B4
San Juan Bautista CA, *1862* ... 44 B2
San Juan Capistrano CA, *34593* ... 52 C3
San Juan Co. CO, *699* ... 40 C4
San Juan Co. NM, *130044* ... 48 B1
San Juan Co. UT, *14746* ... 39 F4
San Juan Co. WA, *15769* ... 12 C2
Sankertown PA, *675* ... 92 B4
San Leandro CA, *84950* ... 36 B4
San Lorenzo CA, *23452* ... 259 D4
San Lucas CA, *269* ... 44 B3
San Luis AZ, *25505* ... 53 F4
San Luis CO, *629* ... 41 D4
San Luis Obispo CA, *45119* ... 44 C4
San Luis Obispo Co. CA, *269637* ... 44 C4
San Manuel AZ, *3551* ... 55 D2
San Marcos CA, *83781* ... 53 D4
San Marcos TX, *44894* ... 61 E2
San Marino CA, *13147* ... 228 D2
San Martin CA, *7027* ... 44 B2
San Mateo CA, *97207* ... 36 B4
San Mateo FL, *1000* ... 139 D3
San Mateo Co. CA, *718451* ... 36 B4
San Miguel CA, *2336* ... 44 C4
San Miguel NM, *1153* ... 56 C3
San Miguel Co. CO, *7359* ... 40 B3
San Miguel Co. NM, *29393* ... 49 E3
Sanostee NM, *371* ... 48 A1
San Pablo CA, *29139* ... 259 B1
San Patricio Co. TX, *64804* ... 61 E4
San Perlita TX, *573* ... 63 F3
Sanpete Co. UT, *27822* ... 39 E2
San Rafael CA, *57713* ... 36 B3
San Ramon CA, *72148* ... 36 B4
San Remo NY, *12200* ... 149 D3
San Saba TX, *3099* ... 59 D4
San Saba Co. TX, *6131* ... 59 D4
Sansom Park TX, *4686* ... 207 A2
Sans Souci SC, *7869* ... 217 A2
Santa Ana CA, *324528* ... 52 C3
Santa Ana Pueblo NM, *610* ... 48 C3
Santa Anna TX, *1099* ... 58 C4
Santa Barbara CA, *88410* ... 52 B2
Santa Barbara Co. CA, *423895* ... 52 B1
Santa Clara CA, *116468* ... 259 D6
Santa Clara NM, *1686* ... 55 F2
Santa Clara OR, *12800* ... 20 B3
Santa Clara UT, *6003* ... 46 C1
Santa Clara Co. CA, *1781642* ... 36 C4
Santa Clarita CA, *176320* ... 52 C2
Santa Claus IN, *2481* ... 99 E4
Santa Cruz CA, *59946* ... 44 A2
Santa Cruz NM, *368* ... 49 D2
Santa Cruz Co. AZ, *47420* ... 55 D4
Santa Cruz Co. CA, *262382* ... 44 A2
Santa Fe NM, *67947* ... 49 D2
Santa Fe TX, *12222* ... 132 B4
Santa Fe Co. NM, *144170* ... 49 D3
Santa Fe Sprs. CA, *16223* ... 228 E3
Santa Margarita CA, *1259* ... 44 C4
Santa Maria CA, *99553* ... 52 A1
Santa Maria TX, *733* ... 63 F4
Santa Monica CA, *89736* ... 52 C2
Santa Nella CA, *1380* ... 44 B2
Santa Paula CA, *29321* ... 52 B2
Santaquin UT, *9128* ... 39 E1
Santa Rosa AZ, *628* ... 54 C3
Santa Rosa CA, *167815* ... 36 B3
Santa Rosa NM, *2848* ... 49 E3
Santa Rosa TX, *2873* ... 63 F4
Santa Rosa Co. FL, *151372* ... 135 F1
Santa Teresa NM, *4258* ... 56 C3
Santa Venetia CA, *4292* ... 259 A1
Santa Ynez CA, *4418* ... 52 A2
Santee CA, *53413* ... 53 D4
Santee SC, *961* ... 122 B4
Santo Domingo Pueblo NM, *2456* ... 48 C3
San Ysidro NM, *2090* ... 48 C3
Sappington MO, *7580* ... 256 B3
Sapulpa OK, *20544* ... 51 F2
Saraland AL, *13405* ... 135 E1
Saranac MI, *1325* ... 75 F3
Saranac Lake NY, *5406* ... 80 C2
Sarasota FL, *51917* ... 140 B3
Sarasota Co. FL, *379448* ... 140 C4
Saratoga CA, *29926* ... 36 B4
Saratoga WY, *1690* ... 33 D3
Saratoga Co. NY, *219607* ... 80 C4
Saratoga Sprs. NY, *26586* ... 80 C4
Sarcoxie MO, *1330* ... 106 C2
Sardinia OH, *980* ... 100 C2
Sardis GA, *999* ... 130 B1
Sardis MS, *1703* ... 118 B3
Sardis TN, *381* ... 119 D1
Sardis City AL, *1704* ... 120 A3
Sarepta LA, *891* ... 125 D1
Sargent GA, *700* ... 120 B4
Sargent NE, *525* ... 35 D3
Sargent Co. ND, *3829* ... 27 E1
Sarita TX, *238* ... 63 F3
Sarpy Co. NE, *158840* ... 35 F3
Sartell MN, *15876* ... 66 C2
Satanta KS, *1133* ... 42 B4
Satellite Beach FL, *10109* ... 141 E2
Satsop WA, *675* ... 12 B4
Satsuma AL, *6168* ... 135 E1
Satsuma FL, *700* ... 139 D3
Satus WA, *746* ... 21 E1
Saucier MS, *1342* ... 135 D2
Saugatuck MI, *925* ... 75 E4
Saugerties NY, *3971* ... 94 B2
Saugus MA, *26628* ... 151 D1
Sauk Centre MN, *4317* ... 66 B2
Sauk City WI, *3410* ... 74 A3
Sauk Co. WI, *61976* ... 74 A3
Sauk Rapids MN, *12773* ... 66 C2
Saukville WI, *4451* ... 74 C2
Sault Ste. Marie MI, *14144* ... 70 C1
Saunders Co. NE, *20780* ... 35 F3
Saunderstown RI, *1600* ... 150 C4
Sauquoit NY, *1000* ... 79 E3
Sausalito CA, *7061* ... 259 B2
Savage MD, *7054* ... 144 C2
Savage MN, *26911* ... 67 D4
Savanna IL, *3062* ... 88 A1
Savanna OK, *686* ... 116 A2
Savannah GA, *136286* ... 130 B3
Savannah MO, *5057* ... 96 B1
Savannah TN, *6982* ... 119 D1
Savona NY, *827* ... 78 C4
Savoonga AK, *671* ... 154 A2
Savoy IL, *7280* ... 88 C4
Savoy TX, *831* ... 59 F1
Sawgrass FL, *4880* ... 222 E4
Sawmill AZ, *748* ... 48 A2
Sawmills NC, *5240* ... 111 F4
Sawyer ND, *357* ... 18 B2
Sawyer Co. WI, *16557* ... 67 F2
Saxapahaw NC, *1648* ... 112 C4
Saxis VA, *241* ... 103 F4
Saxon SC, *3424* ... 217 C1
Saxonburg PA, *1525* ... 92 A3
Saxton PA, *736* ... 92 C4
Saxtons River VT, *565* ... 81 E4
Saybrook IL, *693* ... 88 C4
Saybrook OH, *850* ... 91 F1
Saybrook Manor CT, *1052* ... 149 E2
Saylorsburg PA, *1126* ... 93 F3
Saylorville IA, *3301* ... 86 C2
Sayre OK, *4375* ... 50 C3
Sayre PA, *5587* ... 93 E1
Sayreville NJ, *42704* ... 147 E1
Sayville NY, *16853* ... 149 D4
Scammon KS, *482* ... 106 B2
Scammon Bay AK, *474* ... 154 B2
Scandia KS, *372* ... 43 E1
Scanlon MN, *991* ... 64 C4
Scappoose OR, *6592* ... 20 B1
Scarborough ME, *4403* ... 82 B3
Scarbro WV, *486* ... 101 F4
Scarsdale NY, *17166* ... 148 B3
Schaefferstown PA, *941* ... 146 A2
Schaghticoke NY, *592* ... 94 B1
Schaller IA, *772* ... 72 A4
Schaumburg IL, *74227* ... 203 B3
Schenectady NY, *66135* ... 94 B1
Schenectady Co. NY, *154727* ... 94 B1
Schererville IN, *29243* ... 89 D2
Schertz TX, *31465* ... 257 F1
Schiller Park IL, *11793* ... 203 C3
Schleicher Co. TX, *3461* ... 60 B1
Schleswig IA, *882* ... 86 A1
Schley Co. GA, *5010* ... 128 C3
Schnecksville PA, *2935* ... 146 B1
Schofield WI, *2169* ... 68 B4
Schoharie NY, *922* ... 94 A1
Schoharie Co. NY, *32749* ... 79 F4
Schoolcraft MI, *1525* ... 89 F1
Schoolcraft Co. MI, *8485* ... 69 E1
Schram City IL, *586* ... 98 B2
Schriever LA, *6853* ... 134 A3
Schroon Lake NY, *833* ... 80 C3
Schulenburg TX, *2852* ... 61 F2
Schulter OK, *509* ... 51 F3
Schurz NV, *658* ... 37 E2
Schuyler NE, *6211* ... 35 F3
Schuyler Co. IL, *7544* ... 88 A4
Schuyler Co. MO, *4431* ... 87 E4
Schuyler Co. NY, *18343* ... 79 D4
Schuyler Falls NY, *650* ... 81 D1
Schuylerville NY, *1386* ... 81 D4
Schuylkill Co. PA, *148289* ... 146 A1
Schuylkill Haven PA, *5437* ... 146 A1
Schwenksville PA, *1385* ... 146 B2
Science Hill KY, *693* ... 110 B2
Scio OH, *763* ... 91 F4
Scio OR, *838* ... 20 B3
Scioto Co. OH, *79499* ... 101 D3
Scipio UT, *327* ... 39 E2
Scituate MA, *5245* ... 151 E2
Scobey MT, *1017* ... 17 E1
Scooba MS, *732* ... 127 D2
Scotch Plains NJ, *23510* ... 148 A4
Scotchtown NY, *9212* ... 148 A1
Scotia CA, *850* ... 28 A4
Scotia NY, *7729* ... 94 B1
Scotland MA, *1900* ... 151 D2
Scotland PA, *1395* ... 103 D1
Scotland SD, *841* ... 35 E1
Scotland Co. MO, *4843* ... 87 E4
Scotland Co. NC, *36157* ... 122 C2
Scotland Neck NC, *2059* ... 113 E4
Scott LA, *8614* ... 133 F2
Scott City KS, *3816* ... 42 B3
Scott City MO, *4565* ... 108 B2
Scott Co. AR, *11233* ... 116 C2
Scott Co. IL, *5355* ... 98 A1
Scott Co. IN, *24181* ... 100 A3
Scott Co. IA, *165224* ... 88 A2
Scott Co. KS, *4936* ... 42 B3
Scott Co. KY, *47173* ... 100 B4
Scott Co. MN, *129928* ... 66 C4
Scott Co. MS, *28264* ... 126 C2
Scott Co. MO, *39191* ... 108 B2
Scott Co. TN, *22228* ... 110 C3
Scott Co. VA, *23177* ... 111 E2
Scottdale GA, *10631* ... 190 E3
Scottdale PA, *4384* ... 92 A4
Scott Depot WV, *2600* ... 101 E3
Scottsbluff NE, *15039* ... 33 F2
Scotts Bluff Co. NE, *36970* ... 33 F2
Scottsboro AL, *14770* ... 120 A2
Scottsburg IN, *6747* ... 100 A3
Scottsdale AZ, *217385* ... 54 C1
Scotts Hill TN, *984* ... 119 D1
Scotts Mills OR, *357* ... 20 C2
Scottsmoor FL, *600* ... 141 E1
Scotts Valley CA, *11580* ... 44 A2
Scottsville KY, *4226* ... 109 F2
Scottsville NY, *2001* ... 78 C3
Scottsville VA, *566* ... 113 D1
Scottville MI, *1214* ... 75 E1
Scranton IA, *557* ... 86 B1

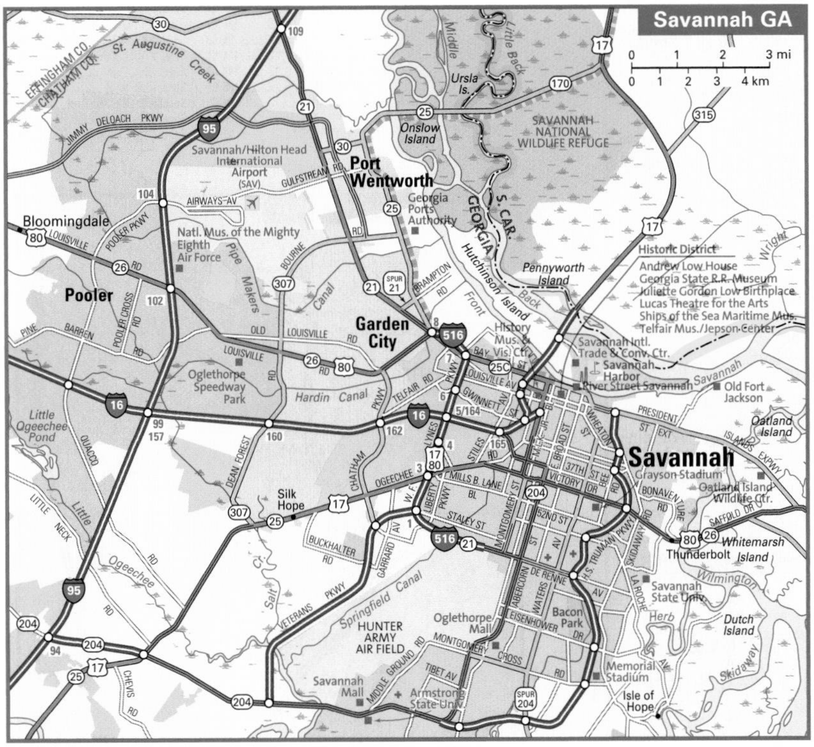

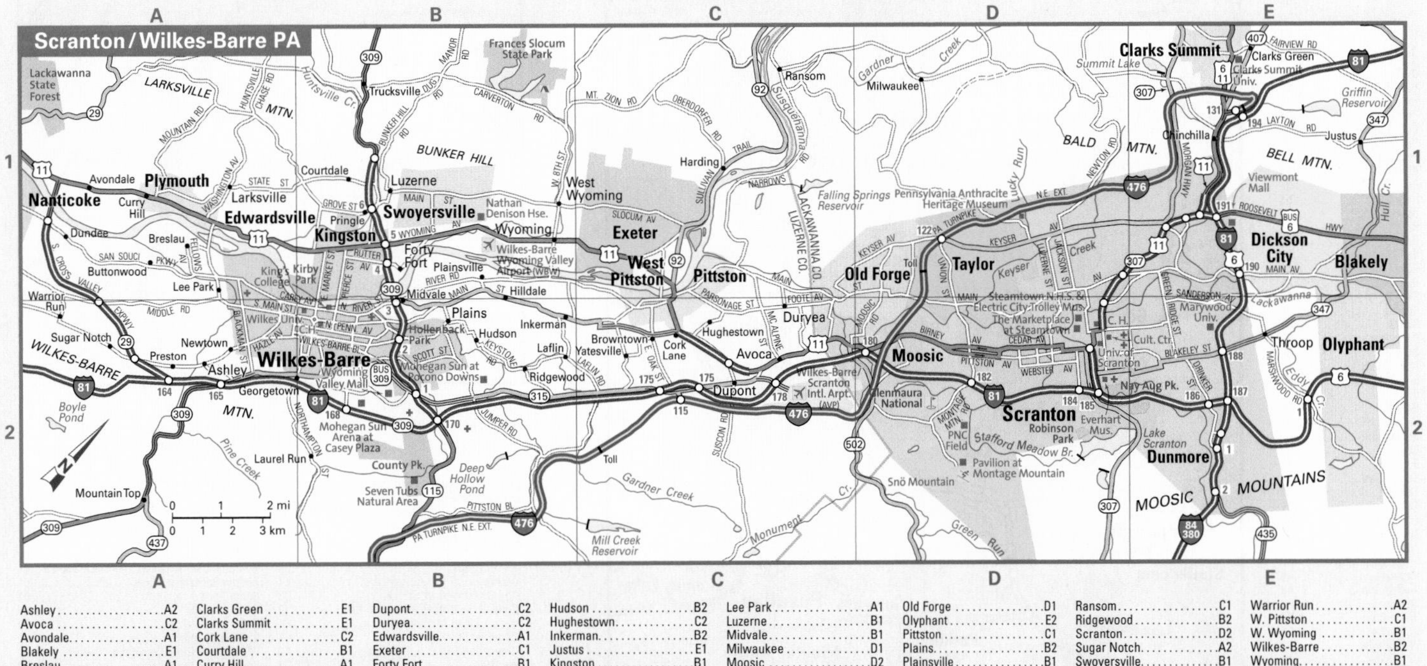

A
Ashley ... A2
Avoca ... C2
Avondale ... A1
Blakely ... E1
Breslau ... A1
Browntown ... C2
Buttonwood ... A1
Chinchilla ... E1
Clarks Green ... E1
Clarks Summit ... E1
Cork Lane ... C2
Courtdale ... B1
Curry Hill ... A1
Dickson City ... E1
Dundee ... A1
Dunmore ... E2
B
Dupont ... C2
Duryea ... C2
Edwardsville ... A1
Exeter ... C1
Forty Fort ... B1
Georgetown ... A2
Harding ... C1
Hilldale ... B1
Hudson ... B2
Hughestown ... C2
Inkerman ... B2
Justus ... E1
Kingston ... B1
Laflin ... B2
Larksville ... A1
Laurel Run ... B2
C
Lee Park ... A1
Luzerne ... B1
Midvale ... B1
Milwaukee ... D1
Moosic ... D2
Mtn. Top ... A2
Nanticoke ... A1
Newtown ... A2
D
Old Forge ... D1
Olyphant ... E2
Pittston ... C1
Plains ... B2
Plainsville ... B1
Plymouth ... A1
Preston ... A2
Pringle ... B1
Ransom ... C1
Ridgewood ... B2
Scranton ... D2
Sugar Notch ... A2
Swoyersville ... B1
Taylor ... D1
Throop ... E2
Trucksville ... B1
E
Warrior Run ... A2
W. Pittston ... C1
W. Wyoming ... B1
Wilkes-Barre ... B2
Wyoming ... B1
Yatesville ... C2

Figures after entries indicate population, page number, and grid reference.

Scranton KS, *710* **96** A3
Scranton ND, *281* **26** A1
Scranton PA, *76089* 93 F2
Scranton SC, *932* **122** C4
Scraper OK, *191* **106** B4
Screven GA, *766* **129** F4
Screven Co. GA, *14593* **130** B2
Scribner NE, *857* **35** F3
Scurry Co. TX, *16921* **58** B2
Seaboard NC, *632* **113** E3
Sea Breeze NC, *1969* **123** E3
Sea Bright NJ, *1412* **147** F2
Seabrook MD, *17287* **271** F2
Seabrook NH, *8693* **95** E1
Seabrook NJ, *1719* **145** F1
Seabrook TX, *11952* **132** B3
Seabrook Island SC, *1714* **131** D2
Sea Cliff NY, *4995* **148** C3
Seadrift TX, *1364* **61** F4
Seaford DE, *6928* **145** E4
Seaford VA, *2000* **113** F2
Seagate NC, *4590* **123** E3
Sea Girt NJ, *1828* **147** F2
Seagoville TX, *14835* **59** F2
Seagraves TX, *2417* **57** F2
Sea Isle City NJ, *2114* **105** D4
Seal Beach CA, *24168* **228** D4
Sealy TX, *6019* **61** F2
Seaman OH, *944* **100** C3
Sea Ranch Lakes FL, *670* **233** C2
Searchlight NV, *539* **46** B3
Searcy AR, *22858* **117** F1
Searcy Co. AR, *8195* **107** E4
Searingtown NY, *4915* **241** G3
Searsport ME, *992* **83** D2
Seaside CA, *33025* **44** B3
Seaside OR, *6457* **20** B1
Seaside Hts. NJ, *2887* **147** E3
Seaside Park NJ, *1579* **147** E3
SeaTac WA, *26909* **12** C3
Seat Pleasant MD, *4542* **271** F3
Seattle WA, *608660* 12 C3
Sebago Lake ME, *550* **82** B3
Sebastian FL, *21929* **141** E3
Sebastian TX, *1917* **63** F4
Sebastian Co. AR, *125744* **116** C1
Sebastopol CA, *7379* **36** B3
Sebeka MN, *711* **64** A4
Sebewaing MI, *1759* **76** B2
Sebree KY, *1603* **109** E1
Sebring FL, *10491* **141** D3
Sebring OH, *4420* **91** F3
Secaucus NJ, *16264* **240** C3
Second Mesa AZ, *962* **47** F2
Secretary MD, *535* **145** D4
Section AL, *770* **120** A2
Security CO, *29845* **41** E2
Sedalia MO, *21387* **97** D3
Sedalia NC, *623* **112** B4
Sedan KS, *1124* **43** F4
Sedgefield NC, *1100* **112** B4
Sedgwick KS, *1695* **43** E3
Sedgwick Co. CO, *2379* **34** A4
Sedgwick Co. KS, *498365* **43** E4
Sedley VA, *470* **113** F2
Sedona AZ, *10031* **47** D3
Sedro-Woolley WA, *10540* **12** C2
Seeley CA, *1739* **53** E4
Seeley Lake MT, *1659* **15** D3
Seelyville IN, *1029* **99** E2
Seffner FL, *7579* **266** D2
Seguin TX, *25175* **61** E2
Seiling OK, *860* **51** D2
Seisholtzville PA, *1400* **146** B1
Selah WA, *7147* **13** D4
Selawik AK, *829* **154** B2
Selby SD, *642* **26** C2
Selbyville DE, *2167* **114** C1
Selden NY, *19851* **149** D3
Selfridge ND, *160* **26** C1
Seligman AZ, *445* **46** C3
Seligman MO, *851* **106** C3
Selinsgrove PA, *5654* **93** D3
Selkirk NY, *1400* **94** B1
Sellersburg IN, *6128* **100** A3
Sellersville PA, *4249* **146** C2
Sells AZ, *2495* **54** C3
Selma AL, *20756* **127** F2
Selma CA, *23219* **45** D3
Selma IN, *866* **90** A4
Selma NC, *6073* **123** E1
Selma TX, *5540* **257** F1
Selma VA, *529* **112** B1
Selmer TN, *4396* **119** D1
Selmont AL, *3502* **127** F2
Seminole FL, *17233* **140** B2
Seminole OK, *7488* **51** F3
Seminole TX, *6430* **57** F2
Seminole Co. FL, *422718* **141** D1
Seminole Co. GA, *8729* **137** D1
Seminole Co. OK, *25482* **51** F3
Senath MO, *1767* **108** B4
Senatobia MS, *8165* **118** B2
Seneca IL, *2371* **88** C2
Seneca KS, *1991* **43** F1
Seneca MO, *2336* **106** B2
Seneca PA, *1065* **92** A2
Seneca SC, *8102* **121** E2
Seneca Co. NY, *35251* **79** D4
Seneca Co. OH, *56745* **90** C3
Seneca Falls NY, *6681* **79** D3

Alderwood Manor B2
Algona B5
Arletta A5
Auburn B4
Bainbridge Island A3
Bay View A1
Beaux Arts B3
Bellevue B3
Bethel A4
Bonney Lake B5
Bothell B2
Bremerton A3
Brier B2
Brownsville A3
Burien B4
Burley A4
Burton A4
Cathcart B2
Clinton B1
Clyde Hill B3
Colby A3
Covington B4
Des Moines B4
Dockton A4
Eastgate B3
Edgewood B5
Edmonds B2
Ellisport A4
Everett B1
Federal Way B4
Fife B5
Fircrest A5
Fox Island A5
Freeland A1
Gig Harbor A4
Glendale B1
Hansville A1
Hunts Pt. B3
Indianola A2
Kenmore B2
Kent B4
Keyport A2
Kingston A2
Kirkland B2
Lake Forest Park B2
Lake Stevens B1
Lakewood A5
Langley A1
Lofall A2
Lynnwood B2
Maltby B2
Manchester A3
Martha Lake B2
Marysville B1
Maxwelton A1
McMillan B5
Medina B3
Mercer Island B3
Midland A5
Mill Creek B2
Milton B5
Mountlake Terrace B2
Mukilteo B1
Newcastle B3
Normandy Park B4
Olalla A4
Pacific B5
Parkland A5
Portage A4
Port Gamble A2
Port Orchard A3
Poulsbo A2
Purdy A4
Puyallup B5
Redmond B3
Redondo B4
Renton B4
Retsil A3
Rollingbay A3
Rosedale A4
Ruston A5
SeaTac B4
Seattle B2
Shine A2
Shoreline B2
Skyway B4
Snohomish B1
S. Colby A3
S. Hill B5
S. Prairie B5
Southworth A3
Steilacoom A5
Summit B5
Sumner B5
Suquamish A2
Tacoma A5
Tahlequah A4
Tracyton A3
Tukwila B4
Tulalip B1
University Place A5
Vashon A4
Vashon Hts. A3
Wauna A4
White Ctr. B4
Wollochet A5
Woodinville B2
Woodway A2
Yarrow Pt. B3

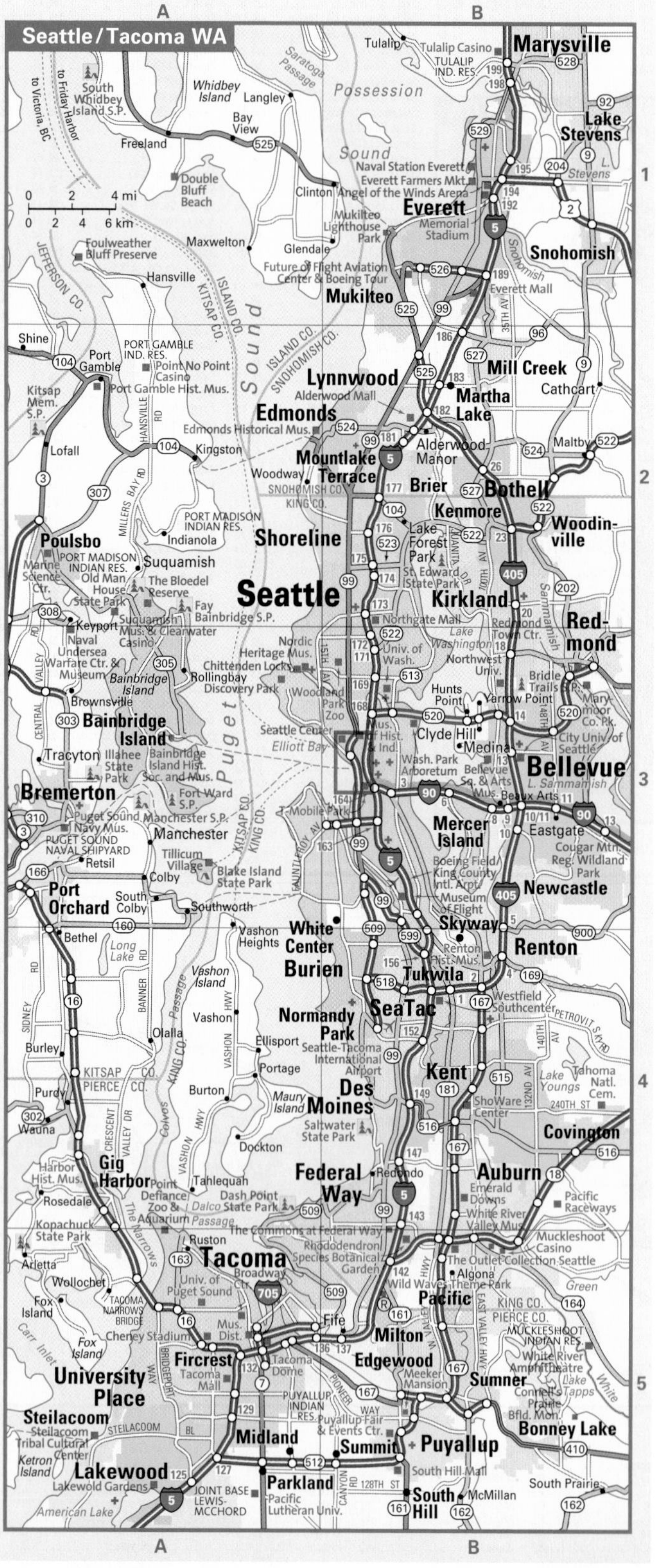

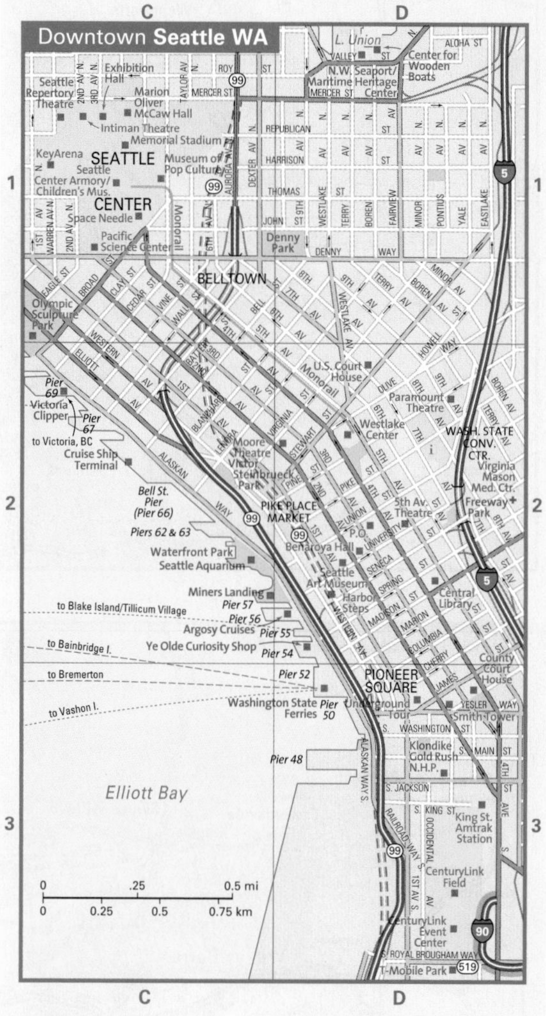

POINTS OF INTEREST

5th Avenue Theatre D2
Argosy Cruises D2
Benaroya Hall D2
Center for Wooden Boats D1
Central Library D2
CenturyLink Event Center D3
CenturyLink Field D3
Cruise Ship Terminal C2
Exhibition Hall C1
Harbor Steps D2
KeyArena C1
King Street Amtrak Station D3
Klondike Gold Rush Natl. Hist. Park D3
Marion Oliver McCaw Hall C1
Memorial Stadium C1
Miners Landing C2
Monorail C1, D2
Moore Theatre D2
Museum of Pop Culture C1
Northwest Seaport/ Maritime Heritage Center D1
Pacific Science Center C1
Paramount Theatre D2
Pike Place Market D2
Post Office D2
Safeco Field D3
The Seattle Aquarium C2
Seattle Art Museum D2
Seattle Center C1
Seattle Center Armory/Childrens Museum C1
Seattle Repertory Theatre C1
Smith Tower D3
Space Needle C1
Underground Tour D3
Victoria Clipper C2
Washington State Convention Center D2
Washington State Ferries D3
Westlake Center D2
Ye Old Curiosity Shop D2

Entries in **bold black** indicate counties or parishes.
Entries in **bold color** indicate cities with detailed inset maps.

Seneca Gardens KY, 696 ... 230 E2
Senoia GA, 3307 ... 128 C1
Sentinel OK, 901 ... 51 D3
Sequatchie Co. TN, 14112 ... 120 B1
Sequim WA, 6606 ... 12 B2
Sequoyah Co. OK, 42391 ... 116 B1
Sergeant Bluff IA, 4227 ... 35 F2
Sergeantsville NJ, 650 ... 147 D1
Sesser IL, 1931 ... 98 C4
Setauket NY, 15477 ... 149 D3
Seth Ward TX, 2025 ... 50 A4
Seven Corners VA, 9255 ... 270 B4
Seven Fields PA, 2887 ... 92 A3
Seven Hills OH, 11804 ... 204 F3
Seven Lakes NC, 4888 ... 122 C1
Seven Mile OH, 751 ... 100 B2
Seven Pts. TX, 1455 ... 59 F3
Severance CO, 3165 ... 33 E4
Severn MD, 44231 ... 144 C2
Severna Park MD, 37634 ... 144 C2
Sevier Co. AR, 17058 ... 116 C3
Sevier Co. TN, 89889 ... 111 D4
Sevier Co. UT, 20802 ... 39 E2
Sevierville TN, 14807 ... 111 D4

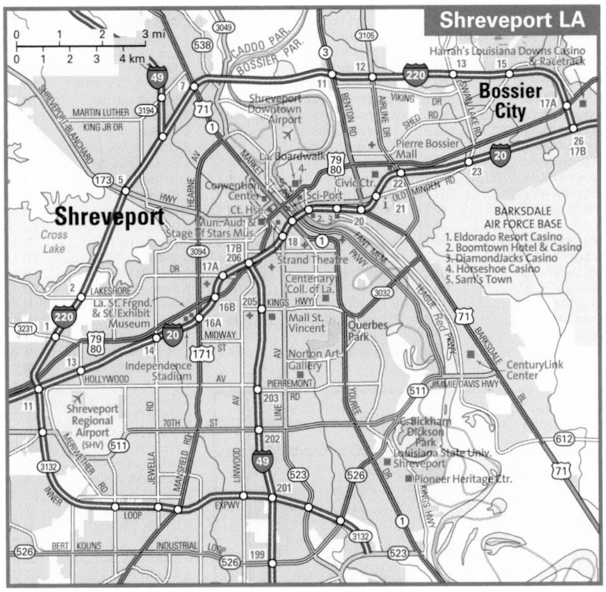

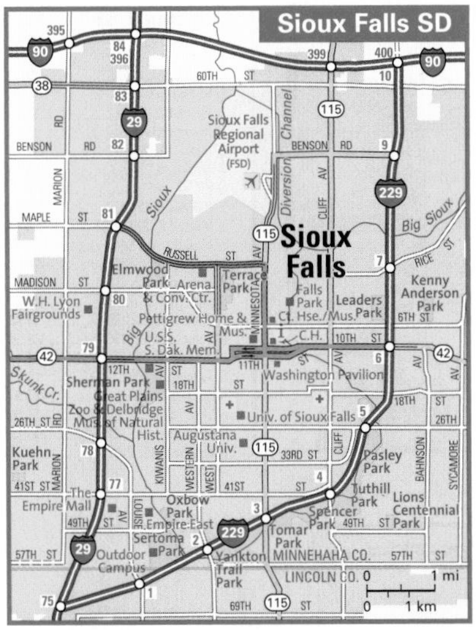

Seville OH, 2296 ... 91 E3
Sewanee TN, 2311 ... 120 A1
Seward AK, 2693 ... 154 C3
Seward NE, 6964 ... 35 F4
Seward Co. KS, 22952 ... 42 B4
Seward Co. NE, 16750 ... 35 E4
Sewaren NJ, 2756 ... 240 A6
Sewell NJ, 3400 ... 146 C4
Sewickley PA, 3827 ... 92 A4
Seymour CT, 16144 ... 149 D2
Seymour IN, 17503 ... 99 F2
Seymour IA, 701 ... 87 D3
Seymour MO, 1921 ... 107 D2
Seymour TN, 10919 ... 110 C4
Seymour TX, 2740 ... 58 C1
Seymour WI, 1418 ... 68 C4
Seymourville LA, 2200 ... 134 A2
Shabbona IL, 925 ... 88 C1
Shackelford Co. TX, 3378 ... 58 C2
Shadeland IN, 1610 ... 89 E4
Shady Cove OR, 2904 ... 28 B1
Shady Pt. OK, 1026 ... 116 B1
Shady Rest CT, 550 ... 148 C1
Shady Side MD, 5803 ... 144 C3
Shadyside OH, 3785 ... 101 F1
Shady Spr. WV, 2998 ... 111 F1
Shafter CA, 16988 ... 45 D4
Shaker Hts. OH, 28448 ... 91 E2
Shakopee MN, 37076 ... 66 C4
Shalimar FL, 717 ... 136 B2
Shallotte NC, 3675 ... 123 D4
Shallowater TX, 2484 ... 58 A1
Shamokin PA, 7374 ... 93 E3
Shamokin Dam PA, 1686 ... 93 D3
Shamrock TX, 1910 ... 50 C3
Shandon CA, 1295 ... 44 C4
Shannock RI, 900 ... 150 C4
Shannon GA, 1862 ... 120 B3
Shannon IL, 757 ... 88 B1
Shannon MS, 1753 ... 119 D3
Shannon Co. MO, 8441 ... 107 F2
Shannon Hills AR, 3143 ... 117 E2
Shannontown SC, 4100 ... 122 B4
Sharkey Co. MS, 4916 ... 126 A2
Sharon CT, 729 ... 94 B2
Sharon MA, 5658 ... 151 D2
Sharon PA, 14038 ... 91 F2
Sharon SC, 494 ... 122 A2
Sharon TN, 944 ... 108 C3
Sharon WI, 1605 ... 74 C4
Sharon Hill PA, 5697 ... 248 B4
Sharon Sprs. KS, 748 ... 42 B2
Sharon Sprs. NY, 547 ... 79 F4
Sharonville OH, 13560 ... 100 B2
Sharp Co. AR, 17264 ... 107 F4
Sharpes FL, 3411 ... 141 E1
Sharpsburg MD, 705 ... 144 A1
Sharpsburg NC, 2024 ... 113 E4
Sharpsburg PA, 3446 ... 250 C1
Sharpsville IN, 607 ... 89 F4
Sharpsville PA, 4415 ... 91 F2
Sharptown MD, 651 ... 145 E4
Shasta Co. CA, 177223 ... 28 C3
Shasta Lake CA, 10164 ... 28 C4
Shattuck OK, 1356 ... 50 C2
Shavano Park TX, 3035 ... 257 E1
Shaver Lake CA, 634 ... 45 D2
Shaw MS, 1952 ... 118 A4
Shawanee TN, 2865 ... 111 D3
Shawano WI, 9305 ... 68 C4
Shawano Co. WI, 41949 ... 68 C4
Shawnee KS, 62209 ... 96 B2
Shawnee OH, 724 ... 101 E1
Shawnee OK, 29857 ... 51 F3
Shawnee Co. KS, 177934 ... 96 A2
Shawneetown IL, 1239 ... 109 D1
Shawsville VA, 1310 ... 112 B2
Sheboygan WI, 49288 ... 75 D2
Sheboygan Co. WI, 115507 ... 74 C2
Sheboygan Falls WI, 7775 ... 75 D2
Sheep Sprs. NM, 237 ... 48 A2
Sheffield AL, 9039 ... 119 E2
Sheffield IL, 926 ... 88 B2
Sheffield IA, 1172 ... 73 D3
Sheffield MA, 3335 ... 94 B2
Sheffield PA, 1132 ... 92 B2
Sheffield Lake OH, 9137 ... 91 D2
Shelbiana KY, 600 ... 111 E1
Shelbina MO, 1704 ... 97 E1
Shelburn IN, 1252 ... 99 E2
Shelburne VT, 592 ... 81 D2
Shelburne Falls MA, 1731 ... 94 C1
Shelby IA, 641 ... 86 A2
Shelby MI, 2065 ... 75 E2
Shelby MS, 2229 ... 118 A4
Shelby MT, 3376 ... 15 E2
Shelby NE, 714 ... 35 E3
Shelby NC, 20323 ... 121 F1
Shelby OH, 9317 ... 91 D3
Shelby Co. AL, 195085 ... 127 F1
Shelby Co. IL, 22363 ... 98 C2
Shelby Co. IN, 44436 ... 99 F1
Shelby Co. IA, 12167 ... 86 A1
Shelby Co. KY, 42074 ... 100 A4
Shelby Co. MO, 6373 ... 97 E1
Shelby Co. OH, 49423 ... 90 B4
Shelby Co. TN, 927644 ... 118 B1
Shelby Co. TX, 25448 ... 124 C3
Shelbyville IL, 4700 ... 98 C2
Shelbyville IN, 19191 ... 99 F1
Shelbyville KY, 14045 ... 100 A4
Shelbyville MO, 552 ... 97 E1
Shelbyville TN, 20335 ... 119 F1
Sheldon IL, 1070 ... 89 D3
Sheldon IA, 5188 ... 35 F1
Sheldon MO, 543 ... 106 C1
Sheldon TX, 1990 ... 220 D2
Shelley ID, 4409 ... 23 E4
Shell Knob MO, 1379 ... 106 C3
Shell Lake WI, 1347 ... 67 E2
Shellman GA, 1083 ... 128 C4
Shell Pt. SC, 2336 ... 130 C2
Shell Rock IA, 1296 ... 73 D4
Shellsburg IA, 983 ... 87 E1
Shelly PA, 1200 ... 146 C1
Shelter Island NY, 1333 ... 149 E3
Shelter Island Hts. NY, 1048 ... 149 E3
Shelton CT, 39559 ... 149 D2
Shelton NE, 1059 ... 35 D4
Shelton WA, 9834 ... 12 B3
Shenandoah IA, 5150 ... 86 A3
Shenandoah PA, 5071 ... 93 E3
Shenandoah TX, 2134 ... 132 A2
Shenandoah VA, 2373 ... 102 C3
Shenandoah Co. VA, 41993 ... 102 C3
Shepherd MI, 1515 ... 76 A2
Shepherd TX, 2319 ... 132 B2
Shepherdstown WV, 1734 ... 103 D2
Shepherdsville KY, 11222 ... 100 A4
Sherando VA, 688 ... 102 C4
Sherborn MA, 4119 ... 150 C1
Sherburn MN, 1137 ... 72 B2
Sherburne NY, 1367 ... 79 E4
Sherburne Co. MN, 88499 ... 66 C3
Sheridan AR, 4603 ... 117 E3
Sheridan CA, 1238 ... 36 C2
Sheridan CO, 5664 ... 209 B4
Sheridan IL, 2137 ... 88 C2
Sheridan IN, 2665 ... 89 F4
Sheridan MI, 649 ... 76 A3
Sheridan MT, 642 ... 23 E2
Sheridan OR, 6127 ... 20 B2
Sheridan WY, 17444 ... 25 D3
Sheridan Co. KS, 2556 ... 42 C1
Sheridan Co. MT, 3384 ... 17 E1
Sheridan Co. NE, 5469 ... 34 A2
Sheridan Co. ND, 1321 ... 18 C3
Sheridan Co. WY, 29116 ... 25 D2
Sherman IL, 4148 ... 98 B1
Sherman MS, 650 ... 118 C3
Sherman NY, 730 ... 92 A1
Sherman TX, 38521 ... 59 F1
Sherman Co. KS, 6010 ... 42 B2
Sherman Co. NE, 3152 ... 35 D3
Sherman Co. OR, 1765 ... 21 D2
Sherman Co. TX, 3034 ... 50 A2
Sherrard IL, 640 ... 88 A2
Sherrill NY, 3071 ... 79 E3
Sherrills Ford NC, 941 ... 112 A4
Sherwood ND, 242 ... 18 B1
Sherwood OH, 827 ... 90 B2
Sherwood OR, 18194 ... 20 B2
Sherwood WI, 2713 ... 74 C1
Sherwood Manor CT, 5410 ... 150 A2
Sheyenne ND, 204 ... 19 D3
Shiawassee Co. MI, 70648 ... 76 B4
Shickshinny PA, 838 ... 93 E3
Shidler OK, 441 ... 51 F1
Shields MI, 6587 ... 76 B2
Shillington PA, 5273 ... 146 A2
Shiloh NJ, 516 ... 145 F1
Shiloh OH, 721 ... 91 D3
Shiloh OH, 11272 ... 208 D1
Shiloh PA, 11218 ... 275 E1
Shiner TX, 2069 ... 61 E3
Shinglehouse PA, 1127 ... 92 C1
Shingle Sprs. CA, 4432 ... 36 C3
Shingletown CA, 2283 ... 28 C4
Shinnecock Hills NY, 2188 ... 149 E3
Shinnston WV, 2201 ... 102 A2
Shiocton WI, 921 ... 74 C1
Ship Bottom NJ, 1156 ... 147 E4
Shipman IL, 624 ... 98 B2
Shippensburg PA, 5492 ... 103 D1
Shiprock NM, 8295 ... 48 A1
Shipshewana IN, 658 ... 89 F2
Shiremanstown PA, 1569 ... 218 A2
Shirley IN, 830 ... 100 A1
Shirley MA, 1441 ... 95 D1
Shirley NY, 27854 ... 149 D4
Shishmaref AK, 563 ... 154 B2
Shively KY, 15264 ... 99 F4
Shoals IN, 756 ... 99 E3
Shoemakersville PA, 1378 ... 146 A1
Shokan NY, 1183 ... 94 A2
Shongopovi AZ, 831 ... 47 E2
Shonto AZ, 591 ... 47 E1
Shore Acres NJ, 4500 ... 147 E3
Shoreacres TX, 1493 ... 132 B3
Shoreham MI, 862 ... 89 E1
Shoreham Beach MD, 1300 ... 144 C3
Shoreline WA, 53007 ... 12 C3
Shoreview MN, 25043 ... 235 C1
Shorewood IL, 15615 ... 88 C2
Shorewood MN, 7307 ... 66 C4
Shorewood WI, 13162 ... 234 D2
Shorewood Hills WI, 1565 ... 231 A2
Short Beach CT, 5100 ... 149 D2
Shortsville NY, 1439 ... 78 C3
Shoshone ID, 1461 ... 30 C1
Shoshone Co. ID, 12765 ... 14 B3
Shoshoni WY, 649 ... 32 C1
Show Low AZ, 10660 ... 47 F4
Shreve OH, 1514 ... 91 D3
Shreveport LA, 199311 ... 124 C2
Shrewsbury MA, 35608 ... 150 C1
Shrewsbury MO, 6254 ... 256 B3
Shrewsbury NJ, 3809 ... 147 E2
Shrewsbury PA, 3823 ... 103 E1
Shrub Oak NY, 2011 ... 148 B2
Shubuta MS, 441 ... 127 D3
Shullsburg WI, 1226 ... 74 A4
Shuqualak MS, 501 ... 127 D1
Sibley IA, 2798 ... 72 A2
Sibley LA, 1218 ... 125 D2
Sibley Co. MN, 15226 ... 66 C4
Sicily Island LA, 526 ... 125 F3
Sicklerville NJ, 6000 ... 147 D4
Sidell IL, 617 ... 99 D1
Sidman PA, 431 ... 92 B4
Sidney IL, 1233 ... 99 D1
Sidney IA, 1138 ... 86 A3
Sidney MT, 5191 ... 17 F3
Sidney NE, 6757 ... 34 A3
Sidney NY, 3900 ... 79 E4
Sidney OH, 21229 ... 90 B4
Sidon MS, 509 ... 126 B1
Sierra Blanca TX, 553 ... 57 D4
Sierra Co. CA, 3240 ... 37 D1
Sierra Co. NM, 11988 ... 56 B2
Sierra Madre CA, 10917 ... 228 E2
Sierra Vista AZ, 43888 ... 55 E4
Siesta Key FL, 6565 ... 140 B4
Signal Hill CA, 11016 ... 228 D4
Signal Mtn. TN, 7554 ... 120 B1
Sigourney IA, 2059 ... 87 E2
Sigurd UT, 429 ... 39 E2
Sikeston MO, 16318 ... 108 B2
Silas AL, 452 ... 127 D3
Siler City NC, 7887 ... 112 C4
Siletz OR, 1212 ... 20 B3
Silica OH, 1100 ... 90 C2
Siloam Sprs. AR, 15039 ... 106 B3
Silsbee TX, 6611 ... 132 C2
Silt CO, 2930 ... 40 C1
Silters NY, 600 ... 94 B1
Silver Bay MN, 1887 ... 65 D3
Silver Bow Co. MT, 34200 ... 23 E1
Silver City NM, 10315 ... 55 F2
Silver City NC, 882 ... 122 C2
Silver Cliff CO, 587 ... 41 D3
Silver Creek MO, 623 ... 106 B2
Silver Creek NE, 362 ... 35 E3
Silver Creek NY, 2656 ... 78 A4
Silverdale PA, 871 ... 146 C2
Silverdale WA, 19204 ... 12 C3
Silver Grove KY, 1102 ... 100 B2
Silverhill AL, 706 ... 135 E2
Silver Hill MD, 5950 ... 270 E4
Silver Lake IN, 915 ... 89 F3
Silver Lake KS, 1439 ... 96 A2
Silver Lake MA, 1000 ... 151 E2
Silver Lake MN, 837 ... 66 C4
Silver Lake NC, 5598 ... 123 E3
Silver Lake OH, 2519 ... 188 B1
Silver Ridge NJ, 1133 ... 147 E3
Silver Spr. MD, 71452 ... 144 B3
Silver Sprs. FL, 6400 ... 139 D4
Silver Sprs. NV, 5296 ... 37 E2
Silver Sprs. NY, 782 ... 78 B4
Silver Sprs. Shores FL, 6539 ... 139 D4
Silverthorne CO, 3887 ... 41 D1
Silverton CO, 637 ... 40 C4
Silverton NJ, 9200 ... 147 E3
Silverton OH, 4788 ... 204 B2
Silverton OR, 9222 ... 20 C2
Silverton TX, 731 ... 50 B4
Silvis IL, 7479 ... 208 C2
Simi Valley CA, 124237 ... 52 B2
Simla CO, 618 ... 41 F2
Simmesport LA, 2161 ... 133 F1
Simms MT, 354 ... 15 E3
Simonton TX, 814 ... 61 F2
Simpson LA, 638 ... 125 D4
Simpson Co. KY, 17327 ... 109 F2
Simpson Co. MS, 27503 ... 126 B3
Simpsonville KY, 2484 ... 100 A4
Simpsonville MD, 4400 ... 144 B2
Simpsonville SC, 18238 ... 121 F2
Simsboro LA, 841 ... 125 E2
Simsbury CT, 23656 ... 94 C3
Sinclair WY, 433 ... 32 C2
Sinclairville NY, 588 ... 78 A4
Sinking Spr. PA, 4008 ... 146 A2
Sinton TX, 5665 ... 61 E4
Sioux Ctr. IA, 7048 ... 35 F1
Sioux City IA, 82684 ... 35 F1
Sioux Co. IA, 33704 ... 35 F1
Sioux Co. NE, 1311 ... 33 F1
Sioux Co. ND, 4153 ... 26 B1
Sioux Falls SD, 153888 ... 27 F4
Sioux Rapids IA, 775 ... 72 A3
Sippewisset MA, 950 ... 151 E4
Sipsey AL, 437 ... 119 F4
Siren WI, 806 ... 67 E2
Siskiyou Co. CA, 44900 ... 28 C3
Sisseton SD, 2470 ... 27 F1
Sissonville WV, 4028 ... 101 E3
Sister Bay WI, 876 ... 69 D3
Sister Lakes MI, 1000 ... 89 F1
Sisters OR, 2038 ... 21 D3
Sistersville WV, 1396 ... 101 F1
Sitka AK, 8881 ... 155 D4
Six Mile SC, 675 ... 121 E2
Skagit Co. WA, 116901 ... 12 C2
Skagway AK, 920 ... 155 D3
Skamania Co. WA, 11066 ... 12 C4
Skaneateles NY, 2450 ... 79 D3
Skellytown TX, 473 ... 50 B3
Skiatook OK, 7397 ... 51 F1
Skidaway Island GA, 8341 ... 130 C3
Skidmore TX, 925 ... 61 E4
Skidway Lake MI, 3392 ... 76 B1
Skippack PA, 3758 ... 146 C2
Skokie IL, 64784 ... 89 D1
Skowhegan ME, 6297 ... 82 C1
Sky Lake FL, 6153 ... 246 C3
Skyline AL, 851 ... 120 A2
Skyway WA, 15645 ... 262 B4
Slater IA, 1489 ... 86 C1
Slater MO, 1856 ... 97 D2

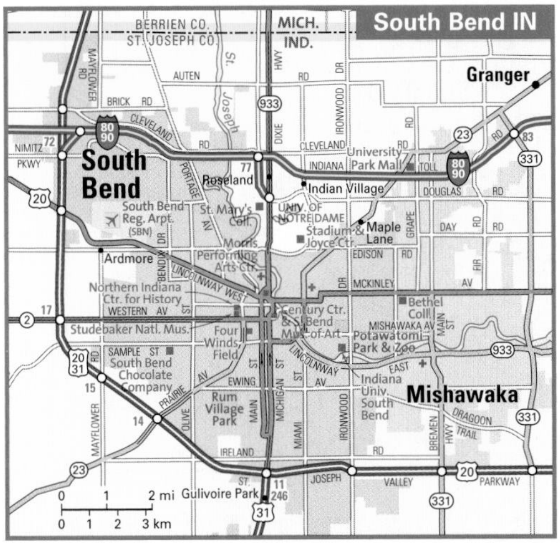

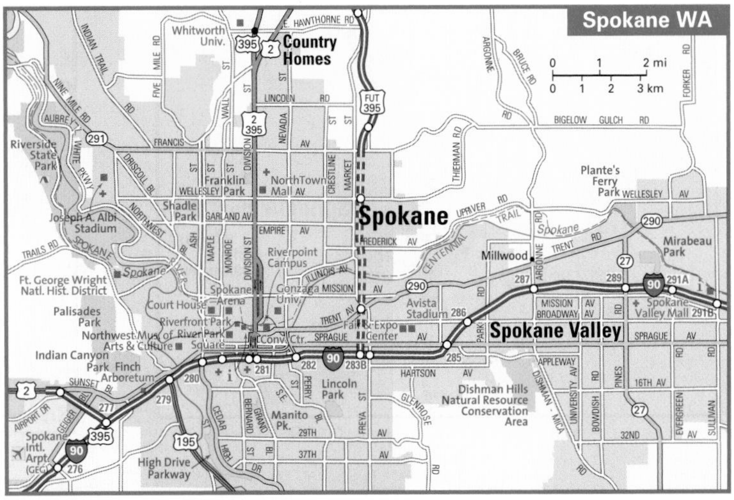

Figures after entries indicate population, page number, and grid reference.

Slater SC, *2176* **121** E2
Slatersville RI, *2600* **150** C2
Slatington PA, *4232* **93** F3
Slaton TX, *6121* **58** A1
Slaughter LA, *997* **134** A1
Slaughter Beach DE, *207* **145** F3
Slaughterville OK, *4137* **51** E3
Slayton MN, *2153* **72** A1
Sledge MS, *545* **118** B3
Sleepy Eye MN, *3599* **72** B1
Sleepy Hollow IL, *3304* **203** A2
Sleepy Hollow NY, *9870* **148** B3
Slidell LA, *27068* **134** C2
Sligo PA, *720* **92** A3
Slinger WI, *5068* **74** C3
Slingerlands NY, *2900* **188** D3
Slippery Rock PA, *3625* **92** A3
Sloan IA, *973* **35** F2
Sloan NY, *3661* **198** C3
Sloatsburg NY, *3039* **148** B2
Slocomb AL, *1980* **136** C1
Slocum RI, *350* **150** C4
Slope Co. ND, *727* **18** A4
Smackover AR, *1865* **125** E1
Smallwood MD, *950* **144** B1
Smallwood NY, *580* **94** A3
Smelterville ID, *627* **14** B3
Smethport PA, *1655* **92** C1
Smith Ctr. KS, *1665* **43** D1
Smith Co. KS, *3853* **43** D1
Smith Co. MS, *16491* **126** C3
Smith Co. TN, *19166* **110** A3
Smith Co. TX, *209714* **124** B2
Smithers WV, *813* **101** F4
Smithfield NC, *10966* **123** E1
Smithfield OH, *869* **91** F4
Smithfield PA, *875* **102** B1
Smithfield UT, *9495* **31** E2
Smithfield VA, *8089* **113** F2
Smithland KY, *301* **109** D2
Smith River CA, *866* **28** A2
Smithsburg MD, *2975* **144** A1
Smiths Grove KY, *714* **109** F2
Smiths Sta. AL, *4926* **128** C2
Smithton IL, *3693* **98** B3
Smithton MO, *570* **97** D3
Smithtown NY, *26470* **149** D3
Smith Valley NV, *1603* **37** D2
Smithville GA, *575* **129** D3
Smithville IN, *3184* **99** F2
Smithville MS, *942* **119** D3
Smithville MO, *8425* **96** B2
Smithville NJ, *7242* **147** E4
Smithville OH, *1252* **91** E3
Smithville PA, *1000* **146** A3
Smithville TN, *4530* **110** A4
Smithville TX, *3817* **61** E2
Smyrna DE, *10023* **145** E2
Smyrna GA, *51271* **120** C4
Smyrna TN, *39974* **109** F4
Smyth Co. VA, *32208* **111** F2
Snead AL, *835* **119** F3
Sneads FL, *1849* **137** D1
Sneads Ferry NC, *2646* **115** D4
Sneedville TN, *1387* **111** D3
Snellville GA, *18242* **120** C4
Snohomish WA, *9098* **12** C2
Snohomish Co. WA, *713335* **12** C2
Snook TX, *511* **61** F1
Snoqualmie WA, *10670* **12** C3
Snowflake AZ, *5590* **47** F4
Snow Hill MD, *2103* **114** C2
Snow Hill NC, *1595* **115** C3
Snowmass Vil. CO, *2826* **40** C2
Snow Shoe PA, *765* **92** C3
Snyder OK, *1394* **51** D4
Snyder TX, *11202* **58** B2
Snyder Co. PA, *39702* **93** D3
Soap Lake WA, *1514* **13** E3
Socastee SC, *19952* **123** D4
Social Circle GA, *4262* **121** D4
Society Hill SC, *563* **122** C3
Socorro NM, *9051* **56** B1
Socorro TX, *32013* **56** C4
Socorro Co. NM, *17866* **48** C4
Soda Sprs. ID, *3058* **31** F1
Sodaville OR, *308* **20** B3
Soddy-Daisy TN, *12714* **120** B1
Sodus NY, *1819* **78** C3
Sodus Pt. NY, *900* **79** D3
Solana FL, *742* **140** C4
Solana Beach CA, *12867* **53** D4
Solano Co. CA, *413344* **36** B3
Soldiers Grove WI, *592* **73** F2
Soldotna AK, *4163* **154** C3
Soledad CA, *25738* **44** B3
Solomon AZ, *426* **55** E2
Solomon KS, *1095* **43** E2
Solomons MD, *2368* **103** F4
Solon IA, *2037* **87** F1
Solon OH, *23348* **91** E2
Solon Sprs. WI, *600* **64** C4
Solvang CA, *5245* **52** A2
Solvay NY, *6584* **265** A2
Solway TN, *1200* **110** C4
Somerdale NJ, *5151* **146** C3
Somers CT, *1789* **150** A2
Somers MT, *1109* **15** D2
Somers NY, *2000* **148** C2
Somers WI, *1100* **74** C4
Somerset KY, *11196* **110** B2
Somerset MD, *1216* **270** C2
Somerset MA, *18165* **151** D3
Somerset NJ, *22083* **147** E1
Somerset OH, *1481* **101** E1
Somerset PA, *6277* **102** B1
Somerset TX, *1631* **61** D3
Somerset WI, *2635* **67** D3
Somerset Co. ME, *52228* **82** B1
Somerset Co. MD, *26470* **103** F4
Somerset Co. NJ, *323444* **147** D1
Somerset Co. PA, *77742* **92** B4
Somers Pt. NJ, *10795* **147** F4
Somersworth NH, *11766* **82** A4
Somerton AZ, *14287* **53** F4
Somervell Co. TX, *8490* **59** E3
Somerville MA, *75754* **151** D1
Somerville NJ, *12098* **147** D1
Somerville TN, *3094* **118** C1
Somerville TX, *1376* **61** F1
Somis CA, *900* **52** B2
Somonauk IL, *1893* **88** C2
Sonoita AZ, *818* **55** D4
Sonoma CA, *10648* **36** B3
Sonoma Co. CA, *483878* **36** A2
Sonora CA, *4903* **37** D3
Sonora KY, *513* **110** A1
Sonora TX, *3027* **60** B1
Sopchoppy FL, *457* **137** E3
Soperton GA, *3115* **129** F2
Sophia WV, *1344* **111** F1
Soquel CA, *9644* **236** D1
Sorento IL, *498* **98** B2
Sorrento LA, *1401* **134** A2
Souderton PA, *6618* **146** C2
Soulsbyville CA, *2215* **37** D3
Sound Beach NY, *7612* **149** D3
Sound View CT, *1200* **149** F2
Sour Lake TX, *1813* **132** C2
S. Acton MA, *2700* **150** C1
S. Amboy NJ, *8631* **147** E1
S. Amherst MA, *4994* **150** A1
S. Amherst OH, *1688* **91** D2
Southampton NY, *3109* **149** E3
Southampton PA, *8000* **146** C2
Southampton Co. VA, *18570* **113** E3
S. Apopka FL, *5728* **246** B1
Southaven MS, *48982* **118** B2
S. Barrington IL, *4565* **203** B2
S. Bay FL, *4876* **143** E1
S. Belmar NJ, *1806* **147** F2
S. Beloit IL, *7892* **74** B4
S. Bend IN, *101168* **89** F2
S. Bend WA, *1637* **12** B4
S. Berlin MA, *800* **150** C1
S. Berwick ME, *2300* **82** A4
S. Bethany DE, *449* **145** F4
S. Bloomfield OH, *1744* **101** D1
Southborough MA, *9767* **150** C1
S. Boston VA, *8142* **112** C3
S. Bound Brook NJ, *4563* **147** D1
Southbridge MA, *16719* **150** B2
S. Bridgewater MA, *2600* **151** D2
S. Burlington VT, *17904* **81** D2
Southbury CT, *550* **149** D1
S. Cairo NY, *700* **94** B2
S. Carthage TN, *1322* **110** A3
S. Casco ME, *650* **82** B3
S. Charleston OH, *1693* **100** C1
S. Charleston WV, *13450* **101** E4
S. Chatham MA, *800* **151** F3
S. China ME, *325* **82** C2
S. Cle Elum WA, *532* **13** D3
S. Coatesville PA, *1303* **146** B3
S. Coffeyville OK, *785* **106** A2
S. Congaree SC, *2306* **122** A4
S. Connellsville PA, *1970* **102** B1
S. Corning NY, *1145* **93** D1
S. Dartmouth MA, *1900* **151** D4
S. Dayton NY, *620* **78** A4
S. Daytona FL, *12252* **139** E4
S. Deerfield MA, *1880* **150** A1
S. Dennis MA, *3643* **151** F3
S. Dos Palos CA, *1620* **44** C2
S. Dover NY, *750* **148** C1
S. Duxbury MA, *3360* **151** E2
S. Easton MA, *3600* **151** D2
S. Elgin IL, *21985* **88** C1
S. Eliot ME, *3550* **82** A4
S. El Monte CA, *20116* **228** E2
Southern Pines NC, *12334* **122** C1
Southern Shores NC, *2714* **115** F2
S. Euclid OH, *22295* **204** G1
S. Fallsburg NY, *2870* **94** A3
Southfield MI, *71739* **76** C4
S. Floral Park NY, *1764* **241** G4
S. Fork CO, *386* **40** C4
S. Fork PA, *928* **92** B4
S. Fulton TN, *2354* **108** C3
S. Gastonia NC, *5433* **122** A1
S. Gate CA, *94396* **228** D3
Southgate KY, *3803* **204** B3
S. Gate MD, *28672* **193** C5
S. Glastonbury CT, *1900* **149** E1
S. Glens Falls NY, *3518* **81** D4
S. Greensburg PA, *2117* **92** A4
S. Hadley MA, *17514* **150** A1
S. Hadley Falls MA, *4300* **150** A2
S. Haven KS, *390* **51** E1
S. Haven MI, *4403* **75** E4
S. Heart ND, *301* **18** A4
S. Hill NY, *6673* **79** D4
S. Hill VA, *4650* **113** D3
S. Hill WA, *52431* **262** B5
S. Holland IL, *22030* **203** E6
S. Hooksett NH, *5418* **81** F4
S. Houston TX, *16983* **220** C3
S. Hutchinson KS, *2457* **43** E3
Southington CT, *42077* **149** D1
S. Jacksonville IL, *3331* **98** A1
S. Jamesport NY, *1100* **149** E3
S. Jordan UT, *50418* **31** E4
S. Killingly CT, *750* **150** B3
Southlake TX, *26575* **207** B1
S. Lake Tahoe CA, *21403* **37** D2
S. Lancaster MA, *1894* **150** C1
S. Lebanon ME, *350* **81** F4

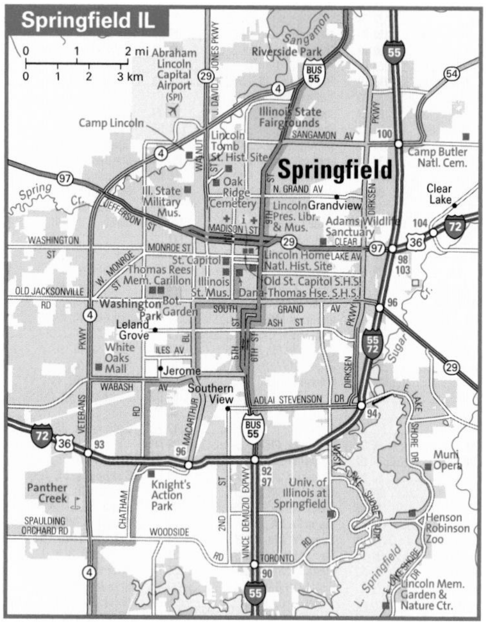

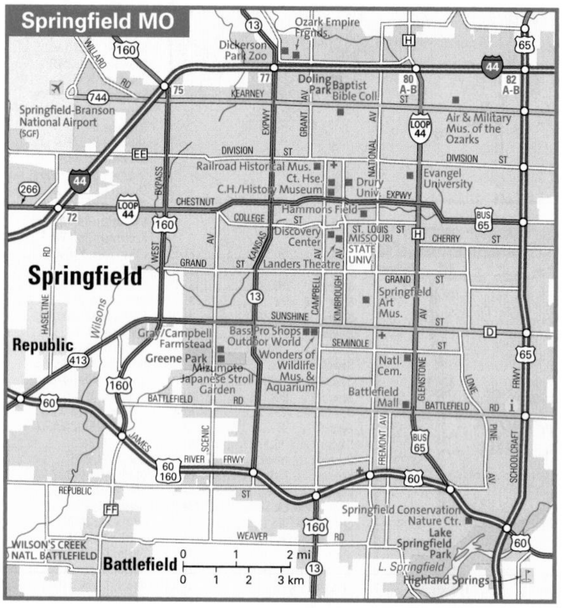

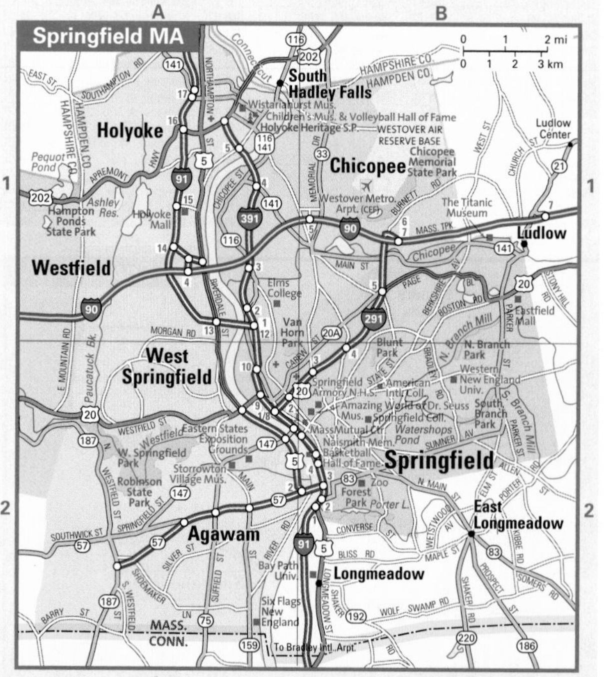

Agawam A2	Holyoke A1	Ludlow Ctr. B1	Westfield A1
Chicopee B1	Longmeadow B2	S. Hadley Falls A1	W. Springfield A2
E. Longmeadow B2	Ludlow B1	Springfield B2	

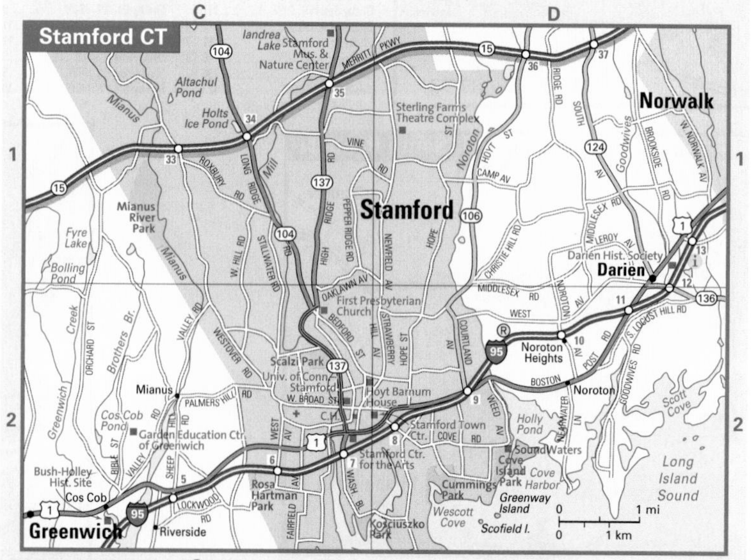

Cos Cob C2	Greenwich C2	Noroton D2	Norwalk D1	Stamford D1
Darien D1	Mianus C2	Noroton Hts. D2	Riverside C2	

Entries in **bold black** indicate counties or parishes.
Entries in **bold color** indicate cities with detailed inset maps.

S. Lebanon OH, 4115 100 B2
S. Lockport NY, 8324 78 B3
S. Lyon MI, 11327 76 B4
Southmayd TX, 992 59 F1
S. Miami FL, 11657 143 E2
S. Miami Hts. FL, 35696 233 A5
S. Middleboro MA, 750 151 E3
S. Mills NC, 454 113 F3
S. Milwaukee WI, 21156 75 D3
S. Monroe MI, 6433 90 C1
Southmont NC, 1470 112 B4
S. Naknek AK, 137 154 B3
S. Ogden UT, 16532 244 A2
Southold NY, 5748 149 E3
S. Orange NJ, 16198 240 A3
S. Orleans MA, 1100 151 F3
S. Padre Island TX, 2816 63 F4
S. Palm Beach FL, 1171 143 F1
S. Paris ME, 2267 82 B2
S. Pasadena CA, 25619 228 D2
S. Pasadena FL, 4964 140 B3
S. Patrick Shores FL, 5875 141 E2
S. Pekin IL, 1146 88 B4
S. Pittsburg TN, 2992 120 A2
S. Plainfield NJ, 23385 147 E1
S. Point OH, 3958 101 D3
Southport FL, 1500 136 C2
Southport IN, 1712 99 F1
Southport NY, 7238 93 D1
Southport NC, 2833 123 E4
S. Portland ME, 25002 82 B3
S. Pottstown PA, 2081 146 B2
S. Range MI, 758 65 F3
S. River NJ, 16008 147 E1
S. Rockwood MI, 1675 90 C1
S. Roxana IL, 2053 256 D1
S. Royalton VT, 694 81 E3
S. Russell OH, 3810 91 E2
S. St. Paul MN, 20160 235 D3
S. Salt Lake UT, 23617 257 B2
S. Sanford ME, 4536 82 B2
S. San Francisco CA, 63632 259 B4
S. San Gabriel CA, 8070 228 E2
S. Shaftsbury VT, 683 94 C1
S. Shore KY, 1122 101 D3
S. Shore SD, 225 27 F2
Southside AL, 8412 120 A4
Southside Place TX, 1715 220 B3
S. Sioux City NE, 13353 35 F2
S. Toms River NJ, 3684 147 E3
S. Torrington WY, 550 33 F2
S. Tucson AZ, 5652 55 D3
S. Valley Stream NY, 5962 241 G4
S. Venice FL, 13949 140 B4
S. Wallins KY, 859 111 D2
S. Walpole MA, 1900 151 D2
S. Waverly PA, 1027 93 E1
S. Weber UT, 6051 244 B2
S. Webster OH, 866 101 D3
S. Weldon NC, 705 113 E3
Southwest City MO, 970 106 B3
Southwest Harbor ME, 720 83 D2
S. Westport MA, 600 151 D4
S. Weymouth MA, 11100 151 D2
S. Whitley IN, 1751 89 F3
S. Whittier CA, 57156 228 E3
Southwick MA, 9706 150 A2
S. Williamson KY, 602 111 E1
S. Williamsport PA, 6379 93 D2
S. Willington CT, 1700 150 A3
S. Wilmington IL, 681 88 C2
S. Windham CT, 1421 149 F1
S. Windham ME, 1374 82 B3
S. Windsor CT, 25709 150 A3
Southwood Acres CT, 7657 150 A2
S. Woodstock CT, 1291 150 B3
S. Yarmouth MA, 11092 151 F3
S. Zanesville OH, 1989 101 E1
Spalding NE, 487 35 E3
Spalding Co. GA, 64073 128 C1
Spanaway WA, 27227 12 C3
Spanish Fork UT, 34691 39 E1
Spanish Fort AL, 6798 135 E1
Spanish Lake MO, 19650 256 C1
Sparkman AR, 427 117 D4
Sparks GA, 2052 137 F1
Sparks MD, 1800 144 C1
Sparks NV, 90264 37 D1
Sparrow Bush NY, 1100 94 A3
Sparta GA, 1400 129 E1
Sparta IL, 4302 98 B4
Sparta MI, 4140 75 F3
Sparta MO, 1756 107 D2
Sparta NJ, 19722 148 A3
Sparta NC, 1770 112 A3
Sparta TN, 4925 110 A4
Sparta WI, 9522 73 F1
Spartanburg SC, 37013 121 F2
Spartanburg Co. SC, 284307 121 F2
Spavinaw OK, 437 106 B3
Spearfish SD, 10494 25 F3
Spearman TX, 3368 50 B2
Spearville KS, 773 42 C4
Speedway IN, 11812 99 F1
Speigner AL, 1700 128 A2
Spencer IN, 2217 99 E2
Spencer IA, 11233 72 A3
Spencer MA, 5700 150 B1
Spencer NE, 455 35 D1
Spencer NY, 759 93 E1
Spencer NC, 3267 112 A4
Spencer OH, 753 91 D3
Spencer OK, 3912 51 E3
Spencer TN, 1601 110 A4
Spencer WV, 2322 101 F3
Spencer WI, 1925 68 A4
Spencer Co. IN, 20952 99 E4
Spencer Co. KY, 17061 100 A4
Spencerport NY, 3601 78 C3
Spencerville OH, 2223 90 B3
Speonk NY, 2675 149 E3
Sperry OK, 1206 51 F2
Spiceland IN, 890 100 A1
Spicer MN, 1167 66 B3
Spindale NC, 4321 121 F1
Spink Co. SD, 6415 27 E2
Spinnerstown PA, 1826 146 C1
Spirit Lake ID, 1945 14 B2
Spirit Lake IA, 4840 72 B2
Spiro OK, 2164 116 B1
Splendora TX, 1615 132 B2
Spofford NH, 500 94 C1
Spokane WA, 208916 14 A3
Spokane Co. WA, 471221 14 B2
Spokane Valley WA, 89755 14 B3
Spooner WI, 2682 67 E2
Spotswood NJ, 8257 147 E1
Spotsylvania VA, 3833 103 D4
Spotsylvania Co. VA, 122397 103 D4
Spottsville KY, 325 99 E4
Spout Sprs. NC, 550 123 D1
Sprague WA, 446 13 F3
Spreckels CA, 673 236 E3
Spring TX, 54298 132 A2
Spring Arbor MI, 2881 90 B1
Springboro OH, 17409 100 B1
Spring City PA, 3323 146 B2
Spring City TN, 1981 110 B4
Spring City UT, 988 39 E1
Spring Creek NV, 12361 30 B4
Springdale AR, 69797 106 C4
Springdale OH, 11223 204 B1
Springdale PA, 3405 250 D1
Springdale SC, 2574 205 E2
Springdale UT, 529 39 D4
Springer NM, 1047 49 E2
Springer OK, 700 51 E4
Springerville AZ, 1961 48 A4
Springfield CO, 1451 42 A4
Springfield FL, 8903 136 C2
Springfield GA, 2852 130 B2
Springfield IL, 116250 98 B1
Springfield KY, 2519 110 B1
Springfield LA, 487 134 B2
Springfield MA, 153060 150 A2
Springfield MI, 5260 75 F4
Springfield MN, 2152 72 B1
Springfield MO, 159498 107 D2
Springfield NE, 1529 35 F3
Springfield NJ, 15817 148 A4
Springfield OH, 60608 100 C1
Springfield OR, 59403 20 B4
Springfield PA, 23677 146 C3
Springfield SC, 524 122 A4
Springfield SD, 1989 35 E1
Springfield TN, 16440 109 F3
Springfield VT, 3979 81 E4
Springfield VA, 30484 144 B3
Spring Garden Estates MD, 2400 144 A1
Spring Glen UT, 1126 39 F1
Spring Green WI, 1628 74 A3
Spring Grove IL, 5778 74 C4
Spring Grove MN, 1330 73 E2
Spring Grove PA, 2167 103 E1
Spring Hill FL, 98621 140 B1
Spring Hill KS, 5437 96 B3
Springhill LA, 5269 125 D1
Spring Hill TN, 29036 109 E4
Spring Hope NC, 1320 113 D4
Spring Lake MI, 2323 75 E3
Spring Lake NJ, 2993 147 F2
Spring Lake NC, 11964 123 D1
Spring Lake Hts. NJ, 4713 147 E2
Spring Lake Park MN, 6412 235 C1
Spring Mill KY, 287 230 E3
Springport MI, 800 76 A4
Springs NY, 6592 149 F3
Springtown TX, 2658 59 E2
Springvale ME, 3292 82 A4
Spring Valley CA, 28205 53 D4
Spring Valley IL, 5558 88 B2
Spring Valley KY, 654 230 F1
Spring Valley MN, 2479 73 D2
Spring Valley NY, 31347 148 B2
Spring Valley WI, 1352 67 E4
Spring Valley Vil. TX, 3715 220 B2
Springview NE, 242 34 C1
Springville AL, 4080 119 F4
Springville CA, 934 45 D3
Springville IA, 1074 87 F1
Springville NJ, 2400 147 D3
Springville NY, 4296 78 B4
Springville UT, 29466 39 E1
Springwater NY, 549 78 C4
Spruce Pine NC, 2175 111 E4
Spry PA, 4891 275 F2
Spur TX, 1318 58 B1
Squaw Valley CA, 3162 45 D3
Staatsburg NY, 377 94 B3
Stacy MN, 1456 67 D3
Stafford CT, 11307 150 B2
Stafford KS, 1042 43 D3
Stafford TX, 17693 132 A3
Stafford VA, 4320 103 D3
Stafford Co. KS, 4437 43 D3
Stafford Co. VA, 128961 144 A4
Stafford Sprs. CT, 4988 150 A2
Stallings NC, 13831 122 B1
Stamford CT, 122643 148 C3
Stamford NY, 1119 79 F4
Stamford TX, 3124 58 C2
Stamping Ground KY, 643 100 B4
Stamps AR, 1693 125 D1
Stanardsville VA, 367 102 C4
Stanberry MO, 1185 86 B4
Standing Pine MS, 504 126 C2
Standish ME, 469 82 B3
Standish MI, 1509 76 B1
Stanfield AZ, 740 54 C2
Stanfield NC, 1486 122 B1
Stanfield OR, 2043 21 E1
Stanford IL, 596 88 B4
Stanford KY, 3487 110 B1
Stanford MT, 401 16 B3
Stanhope NJ, 3610 94 A4
Stanislaus Co. CA, 514453 36 C4
Stanley KY, 400 109 E1
Stanley NC, 3556 122 A1
Stanley ND, 1458 18 A2
Stanley VA, 1689 102 C3
Stanley WI, 3608 67 F4
Stanley Co. SD, 2966 26 C3
Stanleytown VA, 1422 112 B2
Stanly Co. NC, 60585 122 B1
Stannards NY, 798 92 C1
Stanton CA, 38186 228 E4
Stanton DE, 5000 146 B4
Stanton IA, 689 86 B3
Stanton KY, 2733 110 C1
Stanton MI, 1417 76 A3
Stanton NE, 1577 35 E2
Stanton ND, 366 18 B3
Stanton TN, 452 118 C1
Stanton TX, 2492 58 A3
Stanton Co. KS, 2235 42 B4
Stanton Co. NE, 6129 35 E2
Stantonsburg NC, 784 123 E1
Stanwood IA, 684 87 F1
Stanwood WA, 6231 12 C2
Staples MN, 2981 64 A4
Stapleton NE, 305 34 C3
Star ID, 5793 22 B4
Star NC, 876 122 C1
Starbuck MN, 1302 66 A2
Star City AR, 2274 117 F4
Star City WV, 1825 102 A1
Star Cross NJ, 1400 145 F1
Stark Co. IL, 5994 88 B3
Stark Co. ND, 24199 18 A4
Stark Co. OH, 375586 91 E3
Starke FL, 5449 138 C3
Starke Co. IN, 23363 89 E2
Starkey VA, 600 254 D2
Starks LA, 664 133 D2
Starkville MS, 23888 118 C4
Star Lake NY, 809 79 F1
Star Prairie WI, 561 67 E3
Starr Co. TX, 60968 63 E3
Startex SC, 859 217 C1
Startup WA, 676 12 C2
Star Valley AZ, 2310 47 E4
Stateburg SC, 1380 122 B4
State Ctr. IA, 1468 87 D1
State College PA, 42034 92 C3
State Line MS, 565 127 D4
Stateline NV, 842 37 D2
State Line PA, 2709 103 D1
Statenville GA, 1040 137 F1
State Road NC, 900 112 A3
Statesboro GA, 28422 130 B2
Statesville NC, 24532 112 A4
Statham GA, 2408 121 D4
Staunton IL, 5139 98 B2
Staunton IN, 534 99 E2
Staunton VA, 23746 102 B4
Stayton OR, 7644 20 C3
Steamboat AZ, 284 47 F2
Steamboat Sprs. CO, 12088 33 D4
Stearns KY, 1416 110 B3
Stearns Co. MN, 150642 66 B3
Stebbins AK, 556 154 B2
Stedman NC, 1028 123 D2
Steele AL, 1043 120 A4
Steele MO, 2172 108 B4
Steele ND, 715 18 C4
Steele Co. MN, 36576 73 D1
Steele Co. ND, 1975 19 E3
Steeleville IL, 2083 98 B4
Steelton PA, 5990 218 B2
Steelville MO, 1642 97 F4
Steilacoom WA, 5985 12 C3
Steinhatchee FL, 1047 137 F3
Stephen MN, 658 19 E2
Stephens AR, 891 125 D1
Stephens City VA, 1829 102 C2
Stephens Co. GA, 26175 121 D2
Stephens Co. OK, 45048 51 E4
Stephens Co. TX, 9630 59 D2
Stephenson MI, 862 69 D3
Stephenson VA, 1100 103 D2
Stephenson Co. IL, 47711 74 B4
Stephenville TX, 17123 59 D3
Sterling CO, 14777 34 A4
Sterling CT, 3519 150 B3
Sterling IL, 15370 88 B1
Sterling KS, 2328 43 E3
Sterling MA, 7808 150 C1
Sterling MI, 530 76 B1
Sterling NE, 476 35 F4
Sterling OK, 793 51 E4
Sterling VA, 27822 144 A3
Sterling City TX, 888 58 B3
Sterling Co. TX, 1143 58 B4
Sterling Forest NY, 700 148 A2
Sterling Hts. MI, 129699 76 C4
Sterlington LA, 1594 125 E2
Stetsonville WI, 541 68 A3
Steuben Co. IN, 34185 90 A2
Steuben Co. NY, 98990 78 C4
Steubenville KY, 550 110 B2
Steubenville OH, 18659 91 F4
Stevens Co. KS, 5724 42 B4
Stevens Co. MN, 9726 27 F2
Stevens Co. WA, 43531 13 F2
Stevens Creek VA, 550 112 A2
Stevenson AL, 2046 120 A2
Stevenson CT, 800 149 D2
Stevenson WA, 1465 20 C1
Stevens Pt. WI, 26717 68 B4
Stevensville MD, 6803 145 D3
Stevensville MI, 1142 89 E1
Stevensville MT, 1809 15 D4
Stewardson IL, 734 98 C2
Stewart MN, 571 66 B4
Stewart Co. GA, 6058 128 C3
Stewart Co. TN, 13324 109 D3
Stewart Manor NY, 1896 241 G3
Stewartstown PA, 2089 103 E1
Stewartsville MO, 750 96 B1
Stewartville MN, 5916 73 D2
Stickney IL, 6786 203 D5
Stickney SD, 284 27 E4
Stigler OK, 2685 116 B1
Stillman Valley IL, 1120 88 B1
Stillmore GA, 532 129 F2

Bayberry A1	Galeville A1	Nedrow A2	Taunton A2
Collamer B1	Jamesville B2	N. Syracuse B1	Westvale A2
DeWitt B2	Lakeland A1	Onondaga Hill A2	
E. Syracuse B2	Liverpool A1	Solvay A2	
Fairmount A2	Lyndon B2	Split Rock A2	
Franklin Park B1	Mattydale B1	Syracuse A2	

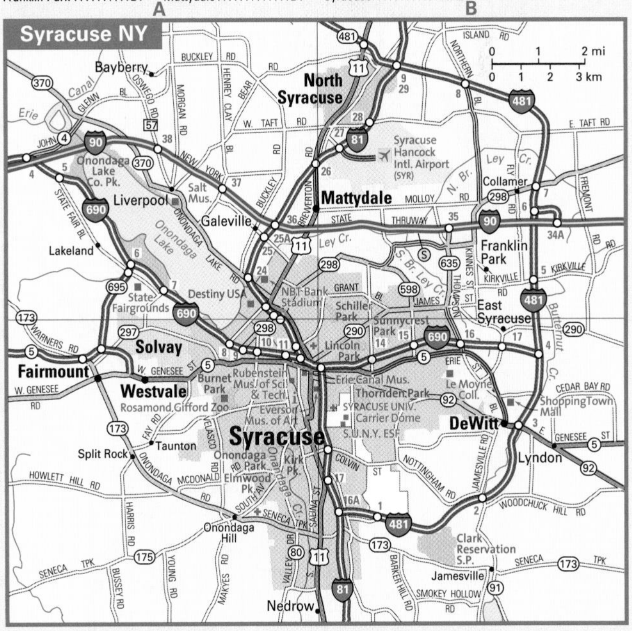

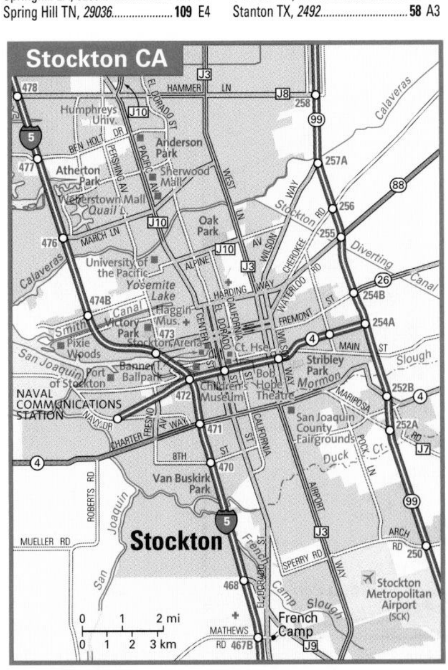

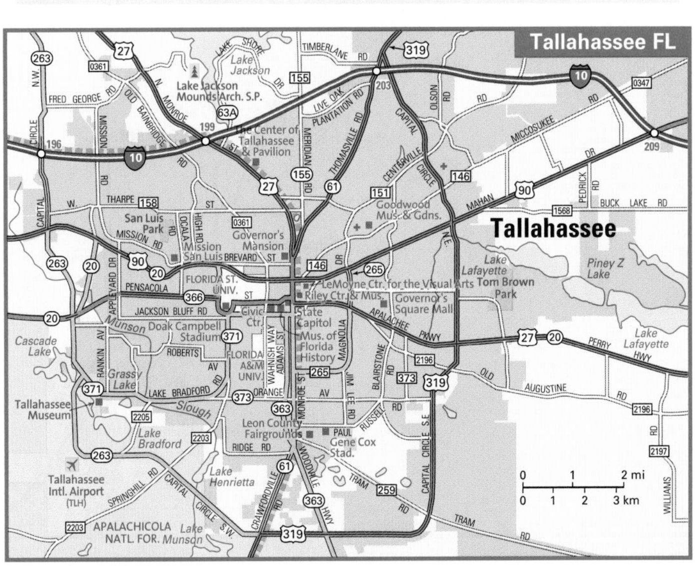

Figures after entries indicate population, page number, and grid reference.

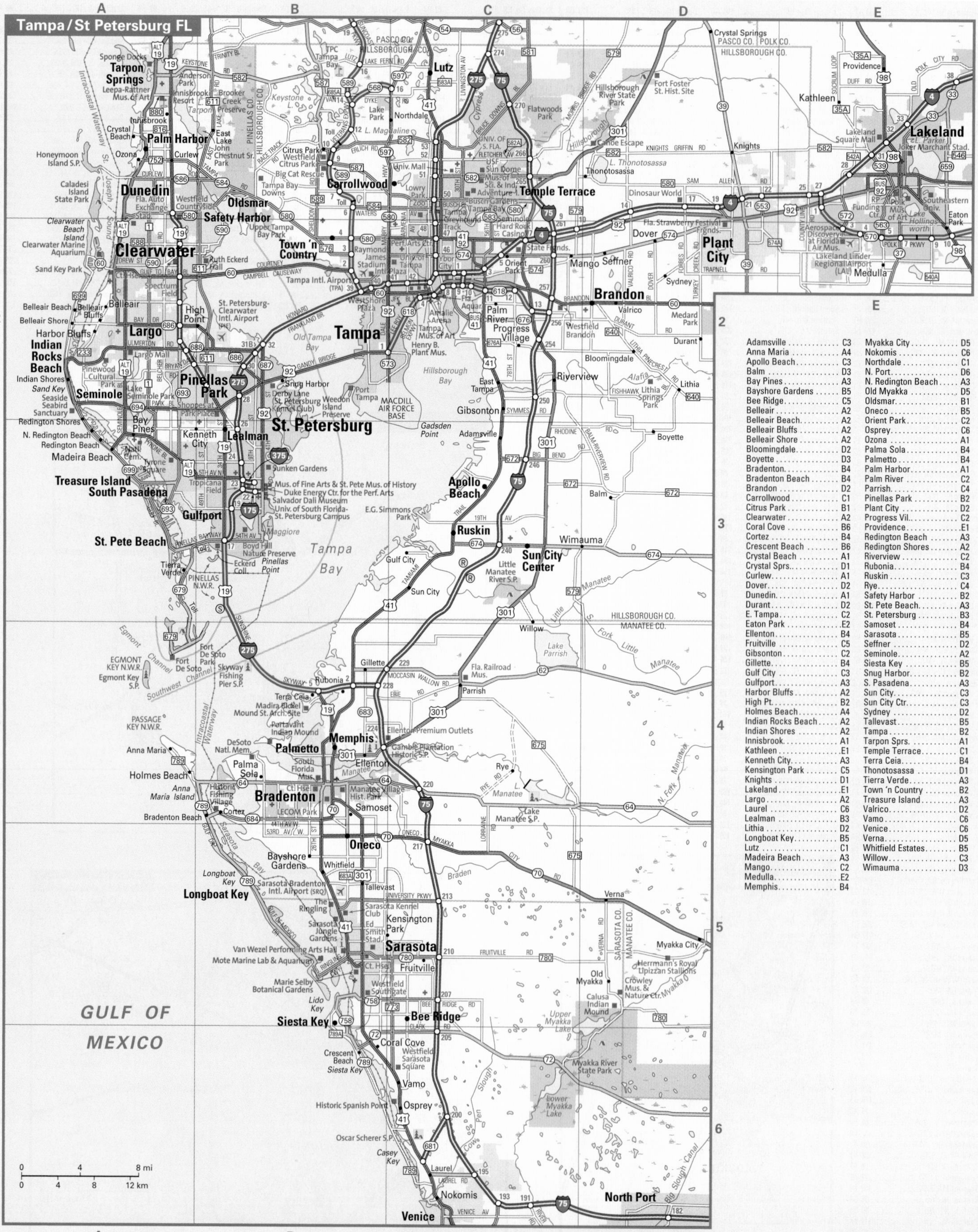

E

Adamsville C3
Anna Maria A4
Apollo Beach C3
Balm D3
Bay Pines A3
Bayshore Gardens B5
Bee Ridge C5
Belleair A2
Belleair Beach A2
Belleair Bluffs A2
Belleair Shore A2
Bloomingdale D2
Boyette D3
Bradenton B4
Bradenton Beach B4
Brandon D2
Carrollwood C1
Citrus Park B1
Clearwater A2
Coral Cove B6
Cortez B4
Crescent Beach B6
Crystal Beach A1
Crystal Sprs. D1
Curlew A1
Dover D2
Dunedin A1
Durant D2
E. Tampa C2
Eaton Park E2
Ellenton B4
Fruitville C5
Gibsonton C2
Gillette B4
Gulf City C3
Gulfport A3
Harbor Bluffs A2
High Pt. B2
Holmes Beach A4
Indian Rocks Beach A2
Indian Shores A2
Innisbrook A1
Kathleen E1
Kenneth City A3
Kensington Park C5
Knights D1
Lakeland E1
Largo A2
Laurel C6
Lealman B3
Lithia D2
Longboat Key B5
Lutz C1
Madeira Beach A3
Mango C2
Medulla E2
Memphis B4
Myakka City D5
Nokomis C6
Northdale C1
N. Port D6
N. Redington Beach A3
Old Myakka D5
Oldsmar B1
Oneco B5
Orient Park C2
Osprey C6
Ozona A1
Palma Sola B4
Palmetto B4
Palm Harbor A1
Palm River C2
Parrish C4
Pinellas Park B2
Plant City D2
Progress Vil. C2
Providence E1
Redington Beach A3
Redington Shores A2
Riverview C2
Rubonia B4
Ruskin C3
Rye C4
Safety Harbor B2
St. Pete Beach A3
St. Petersburg B3
Samoset B4
Sarasota B5
Seffner D2
Seminole A2
Siesta Key B5
Snug Harbor B2
S. Pasadena A3
Sun City C3
Sun City Ctr. C3
Sydney D2
Tallevast B5
Tampa B2
Tarpon Sprs. A1
Temple Terrace C1
Terra Ceia B4
Thonotosassa D1
Tierra Verde A3
Town 'n Country B2
Treasure Island A3
Valrico D2
Vamo C6
Venice C6
Verna D5
Whitfield Estates B5
Willow C3
Wimauma D3

267
Stillwater–Terre Haute

Entries in **bold black** indicate counties or parishes.
Entries in **bold color** indicate cities with detailed inset maps.

Stillwater ME, *1600* **83** D1
Stillwater MN, *18225* **67** D3
Stillwater NY, *1738* **94** B1
Stillwater OK, *45688* **51** F2
Stillwater Co. MT, *9117* **24** B1
Stilwell KS, *1200* **96** B3
Stilwell OK, *3949* **106** B4
Stimson Crossing WA, *773* **12** C2
Stinnett TX, *1881* **50** B2
Stinson Beach CA, *632* **259** A2
Stites ID, *221* **22** B1
Stockbridge GA, *25636* **120** C4
Stockbridge MA, *1947* **94** B2
Stockbridge MI, *1218* **76** B4
Stockbridge WI, *636* **74** C1
Stockdale TX, *1442* **61** E3
Stock Island FL, *3919* **142** C4
Stockton CA, *291707* **36** C3
Stockton IL, *1862* **74** A4
Stockton KS, *1329* **43** D2
Stockton MN, *697* **73** E1
Stockton MO, *1819* **106** C1
Stockton NJ, *538* **146** C1
Stockton UT, *616* **31** E4
Stockton Sprs. ME, *1481* **83** D2
Stockville NE, *25* **34** C4
Stoddard WI, *774* **73** F2
Stoddard Co. MO, *29968* **108** B2
Stokes Co. NC, *47401* **112** B3
Stokesdale NC, *5047* **112** B3
Stoneboro PA, *1051* **92** A2
Stone Co. AR, *12394* **107** E4
Stone Co. MS, *17786* **135** D1
Stone Co. MO, *32202* **107** D3
Stonega VA, *475* **111** D2
Stoneham MA, *21437* **151** D1
Stone Harbor NJ, *866* **104** C4
Stone Mtn. GA, *5802* **120** C4
Stone Park IL, *4946* **203** C4
Stone Ridge NY, *1173* **94** B3
Stoneville NC, *1056* **112** B3
Stonewall LA, *1814* **124** C3
Stonewall MS, *1088* **127** D3
Stonewall OK, *470* **51** F4
Stonewall Co. TX, *1490* **58** B2
Stonewood WV, *1806* **102** A2
Stoney Creek Mills PA, *5900* **146** B2
Stonington CT, *929* **149** F2
Stonington IL, *932* **98** C1
Stonington ME, *1152* **83** D2
Stony Brook NY, *13740* **149** D3
Stony Creek CT, *900* **149** E2
Stony Pt. NY, *12147* **148** B2
Stony Pt. NC, *1317* **112** A4
Storey Co. NV, *4010* **37** D2
Storm Lake IA, *10600* **72** A4
Stormstown PA, *2366* **92** C3
Storrs CT, *15344* **150** B3
Story WY, *828* **25** D3
Story City IA, *3431* **86** C1
Story Co. IA, *89542* **86** C1
Stottville NY, *1375* **94** B2
Stoughton MA, *26962* **151** D2
Stoughton WI, *12611* **74** B3
Stoutsville OH, *560* **101** D1
Stover MO, *1094* **97** D3
Stow OH, *34837* **91** E2
Stowe PA, *3695* **146** B2
Stowe VT, *495* **81** E2
Stowell TX, *1756* **132** C3
Strafford MO, *2358* **107** D2
Strafford Co. NH, *123143* **81** F4
Straitsville CT, *1000* **149** D1
Strasburg CO, *2447* **41** E1
Strasburg IL, *467* **98** C2
Strasburg ND, *409* **26** C1
Strasburg OH, *2608* **91** E4
Strasburg PA, *2809* **146** A3
Strasburg VA, *6398* **102** C2
Stratford CA, *1277* **44** C3
Stratford CT, *51384* **149** D2
Stratford IA, *743* **72** C4
Stratford NJ, *7040* **146** C3
Stratford OK, *1525* **51** F4
Stratford TX, *2017* **50** A2
Stratford WI, *1578* **68** A4
Stratham NH, *7255* **82** A4
Strathmoor Vil. KY, *648* **230** E2
Strathmore CA, *2819* **45** D3
Strathmore NJ, *7258* **147** E1
Stratmoor Hills CO, *6650* **205** D2
Stratton CO, *658* **42** A2
Stratton ME, *425* **82** B1
Stratton NE, *343* **42** B1
Strawberry AZ, *961* **47** E4
Strawberry Pt. IA, *1279* **73** E4
Strawn TX, *653* **59** D3
Streamwood IL, *39858* **203** B3
Streator IL, *14190* **88** C3
Streetsboro OH, *16028* **91** E2
Stroh IN, *700* **90** A2
Stromsburg NE, *1171* **35** E3
Strong AR, *558* **125** E1
Strong ME, *1259* **82** B1
Strong City KS, *485* **43** F3
Stronghurst IL, *883* **87** F3
Strongsville OH, *44750* **91** E2
Stroud OK, *2690* **51** F2
Stroudsburg PA, *5567* **93** F3
Strum WI, *1114* **67** F4
Struthers OH, *10713* **91** F3
Stryker OH, *1335* **90** B2
Stuart FL, *15593* **141** E4
Stuart IA, *1648* **86** B2
Stuart NE, *590* **35** D1
Stuart VA, *1408* **112** B3
Stuarts Draft VA, *9235* **102** C4
Sturbridge MA, *2253* **150** B2
Sturgeon MO, *872* **97** E2
Sturgeon Bay WI, *9144* **69** D4
Sturgis KY, *1898* **109** D1
Sturgis MI, *10994* **90** A1
Sturgis SD, *6627* **25** F3
Sturtevant WI, *6970* **74** C4
Stutsman Co. ND, *21100* **19** D3
Stuttgart AR, *9326* **117** F3
Suamico WI, *11346* **68** C4
Subiaco AR, *572* **116** C1
Sublette KS, *1453* **42** B4
Sublette Co. WY, *10247* **32** A1
Sublimity OR, *2681* **20** C2
Succasunna NJ, *9152* **148** A3
Sudan TX, *958* **57** F1
Sudbury MA, *17659* **150** C1
Suffern NY, *10723* **148** B2
Suffield CT, *14704* **150** A2
Suffolk VA, *84585* **113** F3
Suffolk Co. MA, *722023* **151** D1
Suffolk Co. NY, *1493350* **149** D3
Sugar City ID, *1514* **23** E4
Sugar Creek MO, *3345* **224** D3
Sugarcreek OH, *2220* **91** E4
Sugarcreek PA, *5294* **92** A2
Sugar Grove IL, *8997* **88** C1
Sugar Grove PA, *614* **92** B1
Sugar Grove VA, *758* **111** F2
Sugar Hill GA, *18522* **120** C3
Sugar Land TX, *78817* **132** A3
Sugarland Run VA, *11799* **144** A3
Sugar Loaf NY, *700* **148** A2
Sugar Notch PA, *989* **261** A2
Suisun City CA, *28111* **36** B3
Suitland MD, *25825* **144** B3
Sulligent AL, *1927* **119** D4
Sullivan IL, *4440* **98** C1
Sullivan IN, *4249* **99** E2
Sullivan MO, *7081* **97** F4
Sullivan WI, *669* **74** C3
Sullivan City TX, *4002* **63** E4
Sullivan Co. IN, *21475* **99** E2
Sullivan Co. MO, *6714* **87** D4
Sullivan Co. NH, *43742* **81** E4
Sullivan Co. NY, *77547* **94** A2
Sullivan Co. PA, *6428* **93** E2
Sullivan Co. TN, *156823* **111** E3
Sullivan's Island SC, *1791* **131** D2
Sully IA, *821* **87** D2
Sully Co. SD, *1373* **26** C3
Sulphur LA, *20410* **133** D2
Sulphur OK, *4929* **51** F4
Sulphur Rock AR, *456* **107** F4
Sulphur Sprs. AR, *1101* **106** B3
Sulphur Sprs. TX, *15449* **124** A1
Sultan WA, *4651* **12** C3
Sumas WA, *1307* **12** C1
Sumiton AL, *2520* **119** F4
Summerdale AL, *862* **135** E2
Summerfield NC, *10232* **112** B3
Summerland Key FL, *600* **143** D4
Summers Co. WV, *13927* **112** A1
Summerside OH, *5083* **204** C2
Summersville MO, *502* **107** F2
Summersville WV, *3572* **101** F4
Summerton SC, *1000* **122** B4
Summertown TN, *866* **119** E1
Summerville GA, *4534* **120** B3
Summerville SC, *43392* **131** D1
Summit AR, *604* **107** E3
Summit IL, *11054* **203** D5
Summit KY, *3400* **101** D3
Summit MS, *1705* **126** B4
Summit NJ, *21457* **148** A4
Summit SD, *288* **27** F2
Summit WA, *7985* **262** B5
Summit Co. CO, *27994* **41** D1
Summit Co. OH, *541781* **91** E3
Summit Co. UT, *36324* **31** F4
Summitville IN, *967* **89** F4
Sumner IL, *3174* **99** D3
Sumner IA, *2028* **73** E3
Sumner MS, *316* **118** B3
Sumner WA, *9451* **12** C3
Sumner Co. KS, *24132* **51** E1
Sumner Co. TN, *160645* **109** F3
Sumrall MS, *1421* **126** C4
Sumter SC, *40524* **122** B4
Sumter Co. AL, *13763* **127** E2
Sumter Co. FL, *93420* **140** C1
Sumter Co. GA, *32819* **129** D3
Sumter Co. SC, *107456* **122** B4
Sun LA, *470* **134** C1
Sunapee NH, *3365* **81** E4
Sunbright TN, *552* **110** B3
Sunburst MT, *375* **15** E1
Sunbury OH, *4389* **91** D4
Sunbury PA, *9905* **93** D3
Sun City AZ, *37499* **54** C1
Sun City Ctr. FL, *19258* **140** C3
Sun City West AZ, *24535* **249** A1
Suncook NH, *5379* **81** F4
Sundance WY, *1182* **25** F3
Sunderland MD, *1400* **144** C4
Sunderland MA, *3777* **150** A1
Sundown TX, *1397* **57** F1
Sunfield MI, *578* **76** A4
Sunfish Lake MN, *521* **235** D3
Sunflower MS, *1159* **118** A4
Sunflower Co. MS, *29450* **118** A4
Sun Lakes AZ, *13975* **54** C2
Sunland Park NM, *14106* **56** C4
Sunman IN, *1049* **100** A2
Sunnybrook MD, *2300* **144** C1
Sunny Isles Beach FL, *20832* **233** C3
Sunnyside UT, *377* **39** F1
Sunnyside WA, *15858* **13** E4
Sunnyvale CA, *140081* **36** B4
Sunol CA, *913* **259** E4
Sun Prairie WI, *29364* **74** B3
Sunray TX, *1926* **50** A2
Sunrise FL, *84439* **143** E1
Sunrise Beach Vil. TX, *713* **61** D1
Sunset LA, *2897* **133** F2
Sunset UT, *5122* **244** A2
Sunset Beach NC, *3572* **123** D4
Sunset Hills MO, *8496* **256** B3
Sun Valley ID, *1406* **22** C4
Superior AZ, *2837* **55** D2
Superior CO, *12483* **209** B1
Superior MT, *812* **14** C3
Superior NE, *1957* **43** E1
Superior WI, *27244* **64** C4
Superior WY, *336* **32** B2
Supreme LA, *1052* **134** A3
Suquamish WA, *4140* **262** A2
Surf City NJ, *1205* **147** E4
Surf City NC, *1853* **123** E3
Surfside FL, *5744* **233** C4
Surfside Beach SC, *3837* **123** D4
Surfside Beach TX, *482* **133** E4
Surgoinsville TN, *1801* **111** D3
Suring WI, *544* **68** C4
Surprise AZ, *117517* **54** C1
Surrey ND, *934* **18** B2
Surry VA, *262* **113** F2
Surry Co. NC, *73673* **112** A3
Surry Co. VA, *7058* **113** F2
Susan VA, *244* **113** F1
Susan Moore AL, *763* **119** F3
Susanville CA, *17947* **29** D4
Susquehanna PA, *1643* **93** F1
Susquehanna Co. PA, *43356* **93** E2
Sussex NJ, *2130* **148** A2
Sussex VA, *256* **113** E2
Sussex WI, *10518* **74** C3
Sussex Co. DE, *197145* **145** F4
Sussex Co. NJ, *149265* **148** A2
Sussex Co. VA, *12087* **113** E2
Sutcliffe NV, *253* **37** D1
Sutherland IA, *649* **72** A3
Sutherland NE, *1286* **34** B3
Sutherlin OR, *7810* **20** B4
Sutter CA, *2904* **36** B2
Sutter Co. CA, *94737* **36** B2
Sutter Creek CA, *2501* **36** C3
Sutton AK, *1447* **154** C3
Sutton MA, *8963* **150** C2
Sutton NE, *1502* **35** E4
Sutton WV, *994* **101** F3
Sutton Co. TX, *4128* **60** B1
Suttons Bay MI, *618* **69** F4
Suwanee GA, *15355* **120** C3
Suwannee Co. FL, *41551* **138** B2
Swain Co. NC, *13981* **121** D1
Swainsboro GA, *7277* **129** F2
Swampscott MA, *13787* **151** D1
Swannanoa NC, *4576* **121** E1
Swann Keys DE, *700* **145** F4
Swanquarter NC, *324* **115** E3
Swansboro NC, *2663* **115** D4
Swansea IL, *13430* **98** B3
Swansea SC, *827* **122** A4
Swanton OH, *3690* **90** B2
Swanton VT, *2386* **81** D1
Swan Valley ID, *204* **23** F4
Swarthmore PA, *6194* **146** C3
Swartz LA, *4536* **125** F2
Swartz Creek MI, *5758* **76** B3
Swayzee IN, *981* **89** F4
Swea City IA, *536* **72** B2
Swedesboro NJ, *2584* **146** C4
Sweeny TX, *3684* **132** A4
Sweet Briar VA, *750* **112** C1
Sweet Grass Co. MT, *3651* **24** A1
Sweet Home OR, *8925* **20** C3
Sweetser IN, *1229* **89** F3
Sweet Sprs. MO, *1484* **97** D3
Sweetwater FL, *13499* **143** E2
Sweetwater TN, *5764* **120** C1
Sweetwater TX, *10906* **58** B3
Sweetwater Co. WY, *43806* **32** B2
Swepsonville NC, *1154* **112** C4
Swift Co. MN, *9783* **66** A3
Swifton AR, *798* **107** F4
Swifts Beach MA, *2700* **151** E3
Swift Trail Jct. AZ, *2935* **55** E2
Swiftwater PA, *800* **93** F3
Swink CO, *617* **41** F3
Swisher IA, *879* **87** E1
Swisher Co. TX, *7854* **50** A4
Swissvale PA, *8983* **250** C2
Switzer WV, *595* **111** E1
Switzerland Co. IN, *10613* **100** B3
Swoyersville PA, *5062* **93** E2
Sycamore GA, *711* **129** D4
Sycamore IL, *17519* **88** C1
Sycamore OH, *861* **90** C3
Sycaway NY, *3000* **188** E2
Sykesville MD, *4436* **144** B1
Sykesville PA, *1157* **92** B3
Sylacauga AL, *12749* **128** A1
Sylva NC, *2588* **121** D1
Sylvan Beach NY, *897* **79** E3
Sylvania AL, *1837* **120** A2
Sylvania GA, *2956* **130** B2
Sylvania OH, *18965* **90** C2
Sylvan Lake MI, *1720* **210** B1
Sylvan Lake NY, *1200* **148** C1
Sylvan Shores FL, *2424* **141** D3
Sylvan Sprs. AL, *1542* **195** D2
Sylvester GA, *6188* **129** D4
Symsonia KY, *615* **109** D2
Syosset NY, *18829* **148** C3
Syracuse IN, *2810* **89** F2
Syracuse KS, *1812* **42** B3
Syracuse NE, *1942* **35** F4
Syracuse NY, *145170* **79** D3
Syracuse OH, *826* **101** E2
Syracuse UT, *24331* **31** E3

T

Tabor IA, *1040* **86** A3
Tabor SD, *423* **35** E1
Tabor City NC, *2511* **123** D3
Tacna AZ, *602* **54** A2
Tacoma WA, *198397* **12** C3
Taft CA, *9327* **52** B1
Taft FL, *2205* **246** C4
Taft TX, *3048* **61** E4
Tahlequah OK, *15753* **106** B4
Tahoe City CA, *1761* **37** D2
Tahoka TX, *2673* **58** A2
Taholah WA, *840* **12** A3
Takoma Park MD, *16715* **270** D2
Talbot Co. GA, *6865* **128** C2
Talbot Co. MD, *37782* **145** D3
Talbott TN, *1400* **111** D4
Talbotton GA, *970* **128** C2
Talco TX, *516* **124** B1
Talcottville CT, *4500* **150** A3
Talent OR, *6066* **28** B2
Taliaferro Co. GA, *1717* **121** E4
Talihina OK, *1114* **116** B2
Talkeetna AK, *876* **154** C3
Talladega AL, *15676* **120** A4
Talladega Co. AL, *82291* **128** A1
Tallahassee FL, *181376* **137** E2
Tallahatchie Co. MS, *15378* **118** B4
Tallapoosa GA, *3170* **120** B4
Tallapoosa Co. AL, *41616* **128** B1
Tallassee AL, *4819* **128** A2
Tallevast FL, *1100* **266** B5
Talleyville DE, *6300* **146** B3
Tallmadge OH, *17537* **91** E3
Tallula IL, *488* **98** B1
Tallulah LA, *7335* **126** A2
Talmage CA, *1130* **36** A2
Talmo GA, *180* **121** D3
Taloga OK, *299* **51** D2
Talty TX, *1535* **59** F2
Tama IA, *2877* **87** D1
Tama Co. IA, *17767* **87** D1
Tamalpais Valley CA, *10691* **259** A2
Tamaqua PA, *7107* **93** E3
Tamarac FL, *60427* **143** E1
Tamaroa IL, *638* **98** B4
Tamms IL, *632* **108** C2
Tampa FL, *335709* **140** B2
Tampico IL, *790* **88** B2
Taney Co. MO, *51675* **107** D3
Taneytown MD, *6728* **103** E1
Tangelo Park FL, *2231* **246** B3
Tangent OR, *1164* **20** B3
Tangier VA, *727* **114** B2
Tangipahoa LA, *748* **134** B1
Tangipahoa Par. LA, *121097* **134** B1
Tanner AL, *900* **119** F2
Tannersville PA, *1000* **93** F3
Tanque Verde AZ, *16901* **55** D3
Tantallon MD, *7900* **144** B4
Taos MO, *878* **97** E3
Taos NM, *5716* **49** D1
Taos Co. NM, *32937* **49** D1
Tappahannock VA, *2375* **103** E4
Tappan NY, *6613* **148** B3
Tappen ND, *197* **18** C4
Tara Hills CA, *5126* **259** B1
Tarboro NC, *11415* **113** E4
Tarentum PA, *4530* **92** A3
Tariffville CT, *1324* **150** A3
Tarkiln RI, *950* **150** C2
Tarkio MO, *1583* **86** A4
Tarpon Sprs. FL, *23484* **140** B2
Tarrant AL, *6397* **119** F4
Tarrant Co. TX, *1809034* **59** E2
Tarrytown NY, *11277* **148** B3
Tasso TN, *1300* **120** B1
Tatamy PA, *1203* **93** F3
Tate Co. MS, *28886* **118** B2
Tattnall Co. GA, *25520* **129** F3
Tatum NM, *798* **57** F2
Tatum TX, *1385* **124** B2
Taunton MA, *55874* **151** D3
Tavares FL, *13951* **140** C1
Tavernier FL, *2136* **143** E4
Tawas City MI, *1827* **76** B1
Taylor AL, *2375* **136** C1
Taylor AZ, *4112* **47** F4
Taylor AR, *566* **125** D1
Taylor MI, *63131* **90** C1
Taylor NE, *190* **35** D2
Taylor PA, *6263* **261** D1
Taylor TX, *15191* **61** E1
Taylor Co. FL, *22570* **137** F3
Taylor Co. GA, *8906* **129** D2
Taylor Co. IA, *6317* **86** B3
Taylor Co. KY, *24512* **110** B1
Taylor Co. TX, *131506* **58** C3
Taylor Co. WV, *16895* **102** A2
Taylor Co. WI, *20689* **67** F3
Taylor Creek FL, *4348* **141** E4
Taylor Lake Vil. TX, *3544* **132** B3
Taylor Mill KY, *6604* **204** B3
Taylors SC, *21617* **121** F2
Taylors Falls MN, *976* **67** D3
Taylor Sprs. IL, *583* **98** B2
Taylorsville IN, *919* **99** F2
Taylorsville KY, *763* **100** A4
Taylorsville MD, *900* **144** B1
Taylorsville MS, *1353* **126** C3
Taylorsville NC, *2098* **111** F4
Taylorsville UT, *58652* **257** A2
Taylortown NJ, *1200* **148** A3
Taylortown NC, *722* **122** C1
Taylorville IL, *11246* **98** B1
Tazewell TN, *2218* **111** D3
Tazewell VA, *4627* **111** F2
Tazewell Co. IL, *135394* **88** B4
Tazewell Co. VA, *45078* **111** F2
Tchula MS, *2096* **126** B1
Tea SD, *3806* **27** F4
Teague TX, *3560* **59** F4
Teaneck NJ, *38633* **148** B3
Teaticket MA, *1692* **151** E4
Teays Val. WV, *13175* **101** E3
Tecumseh MI, *8521* **90** B1
Tecumseh NE, *1677* **35** F4
Tecumseh OK, *6457* **51** F3
Teec Nos Pos AZ, *730* **48** A1
Tega Cay SC, *7620* **122** A2
Tehachapi CA, *14414* **52** C1
Tehama CA, *418* **36** B1
Tehama Co. CA, *63463* **36** B1
Tekamah NE, *1736* **35** F2
Tekoa WA, *778* **14** B3
Tekonsha MI, *717* **90** A1
Telfair Co. GA, *16500* **129** E3
Telford PA, *4872* **146** C2
Tell City IN, *7272* **99** E4
Teller Co. CO, *23350* **41** E2
Tellico Plains TN, *880* **120** C1
Telluride CO, *2325* **40** B3
Temecula CA, *100097* **53** D3
Tempe AZ, *161719* **54** C1
Temperance MI, *8517* **90** C1
Temple GA, *4228* **120** B4
Temple OK, *1002* **51** E4
Temple PA, *1877* **146** B1
Temple TX, *66102* **59** E4
Temple City CA, *35558* **228** E2
Temple Hills MD, *7852* **270** E5
Temple Terrace FL, *24541* **140** C2
Templeton CA, *7674* **44** C4
Templeton MA, *8013* **95** D1
Tenafly NJ, *14488* **148** B3
Tenaha TX, *1160* **124** C3
Tenants Harbor ME, *500* **82** C3
Tenino WA, *1695* **12** C4
Tennent NJ, *1100* **147** E2
Tennessee Ridge TN, *1368* **109** D3
Tennille GA, *1539* **129** E1
Tensas Par. LA, *5252* **125** F3
Ten Sleep WY, *260* **24** C3
Tequesta FL, *5629* **141** F4
Terra Alta WV, *1477* **102** B2
Terra Bella CA, *3310* **45** D4
Terrace Hts. WA, *6937* **13** D4
Terrace Park OH, *2251* **204** C2
Terrebonne OR, *1257* **21** D3
Terrebonne Par. LA, *111860* **134** A4
Terre Haute IN, *60785* **99** E2

Harbor View B1
Holland A2
Lime City B2
Maumee A2
Moline B2
Northwood B2
Oregon B1
Ottawa Hills A1
Perrysburg A2
Rossford B2
Stony Ridge B2
Sylvania A1
Toledo A1
Walbridge B2

Toledo OH
A
B
1
2
MICHIGAN
OHIO
Sylvania
Ottawa Hills
Toledo
Oregon
Harbor View
Holland
Rossford
Northwood
Maumee
Walbridge
Perrysburg
Moline
Lime City
Stony Ridge
Maumee Bay
Univ. of Toledo
Toledo Zoo
0 1 2 3 mi
0 1 2 3 4 km

Topeka KS
Topeka
Kansas
Lake Shawnee
Lake Sherwood
Pauline
Topeka Reg. Airport (FOE)
Combat Air Mus.
0 1 2 mi
0 1 2 3 km

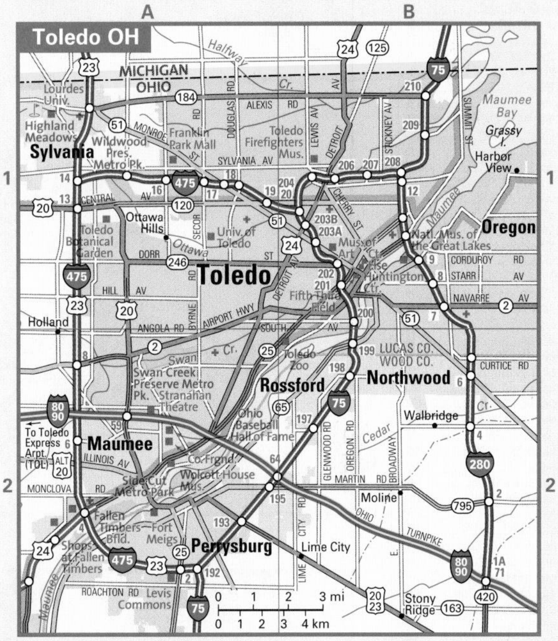

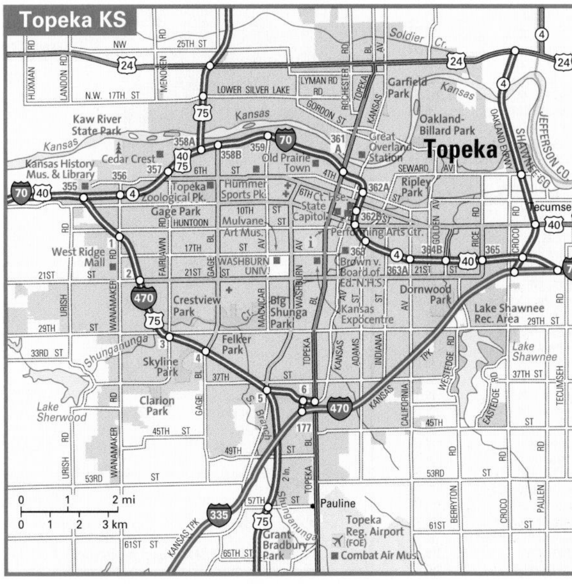

268
Terre Hill–Troy

Figures after entries indicate population, page number, and grid reference.

Terre Hill PA, 1295 146 A2
Terrell TX, 15816 59 F2
Terrell Co. GA, 9315 128 C4
Terrell Co. TX, 984 60 A2
Terrell Hills TX, 4878 257 E2
Terry MS, 1063 126 B3
Terry MT, 605 17 E4
Terry Co. TX, 12651 57 F2
Terrytown LA, 23319 134 B3
Terrytown NE, 1198 33 F2
Terryville CT, 5387 149 D1
Terryville NY, 11849 149 D3
Tesuque NM, 925 49 D2
Teton ID, 735 23 F4
Teton Co. ID, 10170 23 F4
Teton Co. MT, 6073 15 E3
Teton Co. WY, 21294 24 A3
Tetonia ID, 269 23 F4
Teutopolis IL, 1530 98 C2
Tewksbury MA, 28961 95 E1
Texarkana AR, 29919 116 C4
Texarkana TX, 36411 116 C4
Texas MA, 1300 150 B2
Texas City TX, 45099 132 B4
Texas Co. MO, 26008 107 E1
Texas Co. OK, 20640 50 A1
Texhoma OK, 926 50 A1
Texico NM, 1130 49 F4
Thatcher AZ, 4865 55 E2
Thaxton MS, 643 118 C3
Thayer IL, 693 98 B1
Thayer KS, 497 106 A1
Thayer MO, 2243 107 F3
Thayer Co. NE, 5228 35 E4
Thayne WY, 366 31 F1
The Colony TX, 36328 59 F2
The Dalles OR, 13620 21 D2
Thedford NE, 188 34 C2
The Hills TX, 2472 61 E1
Theodore AL, 6130 135 E2
The Pinery CO, 10517 41 E1
The Plains OH, 3080 101 E2
Theresa NY, 863 79 E1
Theresa WI, 1262 74 C2
Thermal CA, 2865 53 E3
Thermalito CA, 6646 36 C1
Thermopolis WY, 3009 24 C4
The Village OK, 8929 51 E3
The Vil. of Indian Hill OH, 5785 204 C2
The Woodlands TX, 93847 132 A2
Thibodaux LA, 14566 134 A3
Thief River Falls MN, 8573 19 F2
Thiells NY, 5032 148 B2
Thiensville WI, 3235 74 C3
Thomas OK, 1181 51 D2
Thomas WV, 586 102 B2
Thomasboro IL, 1126 88 C4
Thomas Co. GA, 44720 137 E1
Thomas Co. KS, 7900 42 B2
Thomas Co. NE, 647 34 C2
Thomaston CT, 1910 149 D1
Thomaston GA, 9170 128 C1
Thomaston ME, 1875 82 C3
Thomaston NY, 2617 241 G3
Thomasville AL, 4209 127 E3
Thomasville GA, 18413 137 E1
Thomasville NC, 26757 112 B4
Thompson IA, 502 72 C2
Thompson ND, 986 19 E3
Thompson Falls MT, 1313 14 C3
Thompson's Sta. TN, 2194 109 F4
Thompsontown PA, 697 93 D4
Thompsonville CT, 8577 150 A2
Thompsonville IL, 543 98 C4
Thompsonville MI, 441 69 F4
Thomson GA, 6778 121 E4
Thomson IL, 590 88 A1
Thonotosassa FL, 13014 140 C2
Thoreau NM, 1865 48 B3
Thorndale PA, 3407 146 B3
Thorndale TX, 1336 61 E1
Thorne Bay AK, 471 155 E4
Thornton AR, 407 117 E4
Thornton CA, 1131 36 C3
Thornton CO, 118772 41 E1
Thornton TX, 526 59 F4
Thorntown IN, 1520 89 E4
Thornville OH, 991 101 D1
Thornwood NY, 3759 148 B2
Thorofare NJ, 1500 146 C3
Thorp WI, 1621 67 F4
Thorsby AL, 1980 127 F1
Thousand Oaks CA, 126683 52 B2
Thousand Palms CA, 7715 53 E3
Thrall TX, 839 61 E1
Three Bridges NJ, 850 147 D1
Three Forks MT, 1869 23 F1
Three Oaks MI, 1622 89 E1
Three Pts. AZ, 5581 55 D3
Three Rivers CA, 2182 45 D3
Three Rivers MA, 2939 150 A2
Three Rivers MI, 7811 89 F1
Three Rivers TX, 1848 61 D4
Three Way TN, 1709 108 C4
Throckmorton TX, 828 59 D2
Throckmorton Co. TX, 1641 59 D2
Throop PA, 4088 261 E2
Thurmont MD, 6170 144 A1
Thurston OH, 604 101 D1
Thurston Co. NE, 6940 35 F2
Thurston Co. WA, 252264 12 C4
Tiana NY, 2200 149 E3
Tiburon CA, 8962 259 B2
Tice FL, 4470 142 C1
Tickfaw LA, 694 134 B2
Ticonderoga NY, 3382 81 D3
Tidioute PA, 688 92 B2
Tierra Amarilla NM, 382 48 C1
Tierra Verde FL, 3721 266 A3
Tieton WA, 1191 13 D4
Tiffin IA, 1947 87 E1
Tiffin OH, 17963 90 C3
Tift Co. GA, 40118 129 E4
Tifton GA, 16350 129 E4
Tigard OR, 48035 20 C2
Tigerton WI, 741 68 B4
Tignall GA, 546 121 E4
Tijeras NM, 541 48 C3
Tiki Island TX, 968 132 B4
Tilden IL, 934 98 B4
Tilden NE, 953 35 E2
Tilden TX, 261 61 D4
Tilghman MD, 784 145 D4
Tillamook OR, 4935 20 B2
Tillamook Co. OR, 25250 20 B1
Tillman Co. OK, 7992 51 D4
Tillmans Corner AL, 17398 135 E2
Tillson NY, 1586 94 B3
Tilton IL, 2724 89 D4
Tilton NH, 3567 81 F4
Tiltonsville OH, 1372 91 F4
Timber Lake SD, 443 26 C2
Timberlake VA, 12183 112 C1
Timberon NM, 348 57 D2
Timberville VA, 2522 102 C3
Timmonsville SC, 2320 122 C3
Timpson TX, 1155 124 C3
Tinley Park IL, 56703 89 D2
Tinton Falls NJ, 17892 147 E2
Tioga LA, 1500 125 E4
Tioga ND, 1230 18 A2
Tioga PA, 666 93 D1
Tioga TX, 803 59 F1
Tioga Co. NY, 51125 93 E1
Tioga Co. PA, 41981 93 D1
Tionesta PA, 483 92 A2
Tippah Co. MS, 22232 118 C2
Tipp City OH, 9689 100 B1
Tippecanoe Co. IN, 172780 89 E4
Tipton CA, 2543 45 D3
Tipton IN, 5106 89 F4
Tipton IA, 3221 87 F1
Tipton MO, 3262 97 D3
Tipton OK, 847 51 D4
Tipton PA, 1083 92 C3
Tipton Co. IN, 15936 89 F4
Tipton Co. TN, 61081 118 B1
Tiptonville TN, 4464 108 B3
Tishomingo OK, 3034 51 F4
Tishomingo Co. MS, 19593 119 D2
Tiskilwa IL, 829 88 B2
Titonka IA, 476 72 C3
Titus Co. TX, 32334 124 B1
Titusville FL, 43761 141 E1
Titusville NJ, 800 147 D2
Titusville PA, 5601 92 A2
Tiverton RI, 7557 151 D4
Tivoli NY, 1118 94 B2
Toano VA, 1400 113 F1
Toast NC, 1450 112 A3
Tobaccoville NC, 2441 112 A3
Toccoa GA, 8491 121 D2
Todd Co. KY, 12460 109 E2
Todd Co. MN, 24895 66 B1
Todd Co. SD, 9612 34 C1
Togiak AK, 817 154 B3
Tohatchi NM, 808 48 A2
Tok AK, 1258 155 D2
Toksook Bay AK, 590 154 B3
Toledo IL, 1238 99 D2
Toledo IA, 2341 87 D1
Toledo OH, 287208 90 C2
Toledo OR, 3465 20 B3
Toledo WA, 725 12 C4
Tolland CT, 13146 150 A3
Tolland Co. CT, 152691 149 E1
Tolles CT, 650 149 D1
Tolleson AZ, 6545 249 A2
Tolono IL, 3447 99 D1
Toluca IL, 1414 88 B3
Tomah WI, 9093 74 A1
Tomahawk WI, 3397 68 B3
Tomball TX, 10753 132 A2
Tom Bean TX, 1045 59 F1
Tombstone AZ, 1380 55 E4
Tome NM, 1867 48 C4
Tom Green Co. TX, 110224 58 C4
Tomkins Cove NY, 1400 148 B2
Tompkins Co. NY, 101564 79 D4
Tompkinsville KY, 2402 110 A3
Toms River NJ, 88791 147 E3
Tonalea AZ, 549 47 E2
Tonasket WA, 1032 13 E1
Tonawanda NY, 15130 78 A3
Tonganoxie KS, 4996 96 B2
Tonica IL, 768 88 B2
Tonkawa OK, 3216 51 E1
Tonopah NV, 2478 37 F3
Tontitown AR, 2460 106 C4
Tooele UT, 31605 31 E4
Tooele Co. UT, 58218 31 D4
Tool TX, 2240 59 F3
Toole Co. MT, 5324 15 F1
Toombs Co. GA, 27223 129 F3
Toomsboro GA, 472 129 E2
Topeka IN, 1153 89 F2
Topeka KS, 127473 96 A2
Toppenish WA, 8949 13 D4
Topsfield MA, 2717 151 F1
Topsham ME, 5931 82 B3
Topton PA, 2069 146 B1
Toquerville UT, 1370 39 D4
Tornillo TX, 1568 56 C4
Toronto OH, 5091 91 F4
Toronto SD, 212 27 F3
Torrance CA, 145438 52 C3
Torrance Co. NM, 16383 49 D4
Torreon NM, 326 48 B2
Torreon NM, 244 48 C4
Torrington CT, 36383 94 C3
Torrington WY, 6501 33 F2
Totowa NJ, 10804 240 A1
Toughkenamon PA, 1492 146 B3
Toulon IL, 1292 88 B3
Towaco NJ, 2700 148 A3
Towanda KS, 1450 43 F4
Towanda PA, 2919 93 E1
Towaoc CO, 1087 40 B4
Tower MN, 500 64 C3
Tower City ND, 253 19 E4
Tower City PA, 1346 93 E4
Tower Hill IL, 611 98 C2
Tower Lakes IL, 1283 203 B1
Town and Country MO, 10815 256 A2
Town Creek AL, 1100 119 E2
Towner ND, 533 18 C2
Towner Co. ND, 2246 19 D1
Town Line NY, 2367 78 B3
Town 'n Country FL, 78442 266 B2
Town of Pines IN, 708 89 E2
Towns Co. GA, 10471 121 D2
Townsend DE, 2049 145 E1
Townsend MA, 1128 95 D1
Townsend MT, 1878 15 F4
Towson MD, 55197 144 C1
Tracy CA, 82922 36 C4
Tracy MN, 2163 72 A1
Tracy City TN, 1481 120 A1
Tracyton WA, 5233 262 A3
Traer IA, 1703 87 E1
Trafalgar IN, 1101 99 F2
Trafford AL, 646 119 F4
Trafford PA, 3174 250 D3
Trail Creek IN, 2052 89 E2
Traill Co. ND, 8121 19 E3
Trainer PA, 1828 146 C3
Tramway NC, 750 122 C1
Tranquillity CA, 799 44 C3
Transylvania Co. NC, 33090 121 E1
Trappe MD, 1077 145 D4
Trappe PA, 3509 146 B2
Trapper Creek AK, 481 154 C3
Traskwood AR, 518 117 E3
Travelers Rest SC, 4576 121 E2
Traver CA, 713 45 D3
Traverse City MI, 14674 69 F4
Traverse Co. MN, 3558 27 F1
Travis Co. TX, 1024266 61 E1
Treasure Co. MT, 718 17 D4
Treasure Island FL, 6705 140 B3
Trego Co. KS, 3001 42 C2
Tremont IL, 2236 88 B4
Tremont PA, 1752 146 A1
Tremonton UT, 7647 31 E3
Trempealeau WI, 1529 73 F1
Trempealeau Co. WI, 28816 67 F4
Trent SD, 232 27 F4
Trenton FL, 1999 138 C3
Trenton GA, 2301 120 B2
Trenton IL, 2715 98 B3
Trenton KY, 384 109 E3
Trenton MI, 18853 90 C1
Trenton MO, 6001 86 C4
Trenton NE, 560 42 B1
Trenton NJ, 84913 147 D2
Trenton NC, 287 115 D3
Trenton OH, 11869 100 B2
Trenton TN, 4264 108 C4
Trenton TX, 635 59 F1
Trenton UT, 464 31 E2
Trent Woods NC, 4155 115 D3
Treutlen Co. GA, 6885 129 F2
Trevorton PA, 1834 93 E3
Trevose PA, 3550 146 C2
Trexlertown PA, 1988 146 B1
Treynor IA, 919 86 A2
Trezevant TN, 859 108 C4
Triadelphia WV, 811 91 F4
Triana AL, 496 119 F2
Triangle VA, 8188 144 A4
Tribes Hill NY, 1003 94 A1
Tribune KS, 741 42 B3
Tri-City OR, 3931 28 B1
Trigg Co. KY, 14339 109 D3
Tri-Lakes IN, 1421 90 A2
Trilby FL, 419 140 C1
Trimble CO, 650 40 B4
Trimble TN, 637 108 C3
Trimble Co. KY, 8809 100 A3
Trimont MN, 747 72 B2
Trinidad CO, 9096 41 E4
Trinidad TX, 886 59 F3
Trinity AL, 2095 119 F2
Trinity NC, 6614 112 B4
Trinity TX, 2697 132 A1
Trinity Co. CA, 13786 28 B4
Trinity Co. TX, 14585 132 B1
Trion GA, 1827 120 B2
Tripoli IA, 1313 73 E4
Tripp SD, 647 35 E1
Tripp Co. SD, 5644 26 C4
Triumph LA, 216 134 C4
Trona CA, 18 45 E4
Trooper PA, 5744 146 C2
Trophy Club TX, 8024 207 B1
Tropic UT, 530 39 E4
Trotwood OH, 24431 100 B1
Troup TX, 1869 124 B3
Troup Co. GA, 67044 128 C1
Trousdale Co. TN, 7870 109 F3
Trout Creek MT, 242 14 C3
Troutdale OR, 15962 20 C2
Troutdale VA, 178 111 F3
Trout Lake WA, 557 21 D1
Troutman NC, 2383 112 A4
Trout Valley IL, 537 203 A1
Troutville VA, 431 112 B1
Trowbridge Park MI, 2176 69 D1
Troy AL, 18033 128 A3
Troy ID, 862 14 B4
Troy IL, 9888 98 B3
Troy KS, 1010 96 B1

Trenton NJ

Bakersville	B1	Fallsington	A2	Mercerville	B1	Trenton	B2
Ewing	A1	Lawrenceville	B1	Morrisville	A2	W. Trenton	A1
Ewingville	A1	Lewisville	B1	Slackwood	B1	White Horse	B2

Tucson AZ
CORONADO NATIONAL FOREST
PUSCH RIDGE WILDERNESS
Marana
Casas Adobes
Catalina Foothills
Flowing Wells
SAGUARO NATIONAL PARK (WEST)
Tucson
TUCSON MOUNTAIN PARK
South Tucson
Drexel Hts.
Tanque Verde
DAVIS-MONTHAN A.F.B.
SAGUARO NATL. PARK (EAST)
PASCUA YAQUI INDIAN RESERVATION
TOHONO O'ODHAM (SAN XAVIER) INDIAN RESERVATION

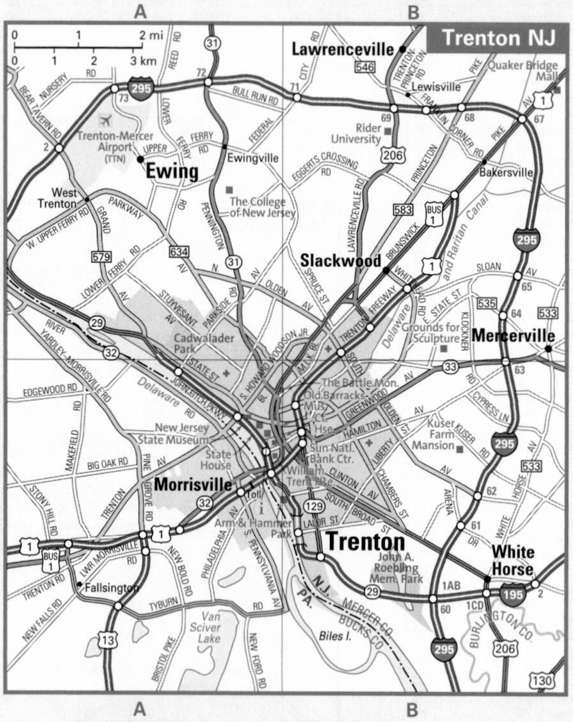

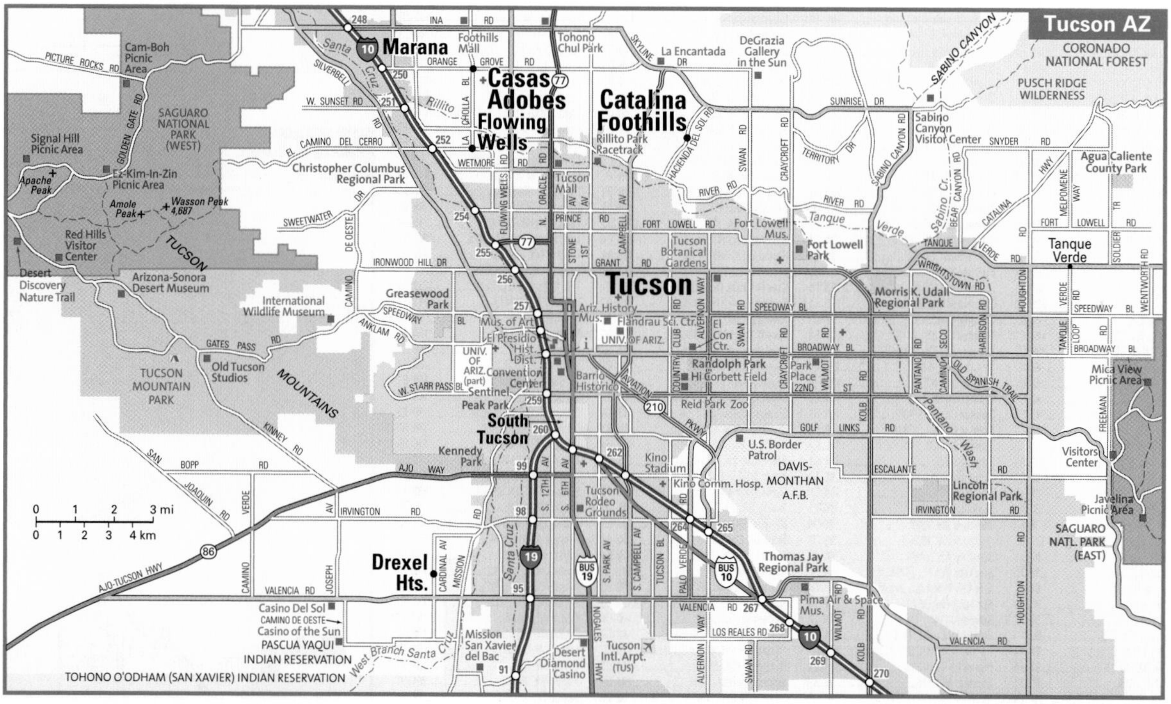

Entries in **bold black** indicate counties or parishes.
Entries in **bold color** indicate cities with detailed inset maps.

Troy MI, 80980 ... 76 C4
Troy MO, 10540 ... 97 F2
Troy MT, 938 ... 14 C2
Troy NH, 1221 ... 95 D1
Troy NY, 50129 ... 94 B1
Troy NC, 3189 ... 122 C1
Troy OH, 25058 ... 100 B1
Troy PA, 1354 ... 93 D1
Troy TN, 1371 ... 108 C3
Troy TX, 1645 ... 59 E4
Troy VT, 243 ... 81 E1
Truckee CA, 16180 ... 37 D2
Truman MN, 1115 ... 72 B2
Trumann AR, 7243 ... 108 A4
Trumansburg NY, 1797 ... 79 D4
Trumbauersville PA, 974 ... 146 C1
Trumbull CT, 36018 ... 149 D2
Trumbull Co. OH, 210312 ... 91 F2
Trussville AL, 19933 ... 119 F4
Truth or Consequences NM, 6475 ... 56 B2
Tryon NE, 157 ... 34 B3
Tryon NC, 1646 ... 121 F1
Tryon OK, 491 ... 51 F2
Tsaile AZ, 1205 ... 48 A2
Tupper Lake NY, 3667 ... 79 F1
Turbeville SC, 766 ... 122 B4
Turbotville PA, 705 ... 93 D3
Turley NM, 425 ... 48 B1
Turley OK, 2756 ... 51 F2
Turlock CA, 68549 ... 36 C4
Turner ME, 4972 ... 82 B2
Turner OR, 1854 ... 20 B2
Turner Co. GA, 8930 ... 129 D4
Turner Co. SD, 8347 ... 27 F4
Turners Falls MA, 4470 ... 94 C1
Turnersville NJ, 3742 ... 146 C4
Turon KS, 387 ... 43 D4
Turpin Hills OH, 5099 ... 204 C3
Turrell AR, 615 ... 118 B1
Turtle Creek PA, 5349 ... 250 D2
Turtle Lake ND, 581 ... 18 C3
Turtle Lake WI, 1050 ... 67 E3
Tusayan AZ, 558 ... 47 D2
Tuscaloosa AL, 90468 ... 127 E1
Tuscaloosa Co. AL, 194656 ... 119 E4
Tuscarawas OH, 1056 ... 91 E4
Tuscarawas Co. OH, 92582 ... 91 E4
Tuscarora PA, 980 ... 93 E3
Tuscola IL, 4480 ... 99 D1
Tyler Co. WV, 9208 ... 101 F2
Tylersport PA, 950 ... 146 C2
Tylertown MS, 1609 ... 134 B1
Tyndall SD, 1067 ... 35 E1
Tyrone GA, 6879 ... 120 C4
Tyrone NM, 637 ... 55 F2
Tyrone OK, 762 ... 50 B1
Tyrone PA, 5477 ... 92 C3
Tyronza AR, 762 ... 118 B1
Tyrrell Co. NC, 4407 ... 113 F4
Tysons VA, 19627 ... 270 A3
Ty Ty GA, 725 ... 129 D4

U
Ubly MI, 858 ... 76 C2
Ucon ID, 1108 ... 23 E4
Udall KS, 746 ... 43 F4
Uhrichsville OH, 5413 ... 91 E4
Uinta Co. WY, 21118 ... 31 F3
Uintah UT, 1322 ... 244 B2
Uintah Co. UT, 32588 ... 32 A4
Ukiah CA, 16075 ... 36 A2
Ulah NC, 800 ... 122 C1
Uledi PA, 1100 ... 102 B1
Ulen MN, 547 ... 19 F3
Union City IN, 3584 ... 90 A4
Union City MI, 1599 ... 90 A1
Union City NJ, 66455 ... 148 B4
Union City OH, 1666 ... 90 A4
Union City OK, 1645 ... 51 E3
Union City PA, 3320 ... 92 A1
Union City TN, 10895 ... 108 C3
Union Co. AR, 41639 ... 125 E1
Union Co. FL, 15535 ... 138 C3
Union Co. GA, 21356 ... 120 C2
Union Co. IL, 17808 ... 108 C1
Union Co. IN, 7516 ... 100 B1
Union Co. IA, 12534 ... 86 B3
Union Co. KY, 15007 ... 109 D1
Union Co. MS, 27134 ... 118 C3
Union Co. NJ, 536499 ... 147 E1
Union Co. NM, 4549 ... 49 F1
Union Co. NC, 201292 ... 122 B2
Union Co. OH, 52300 ... 90 C4
Union Co. OR, 25748 ... 21 F2
Union Co. PA, 44947 ... 93 D3
Union Co. SC, 28961 ... 121 F2
Union Co. SD, 14399 ... 35 F1
Union Co. TN, 19109 ... 110 C3
Union Gap WA, 6047 ... 13 D4
Upper Arlington OH, 33771 ... 101 D1
Upper Darby PA, 82795 ... 248 B3
Upper Lake CA, 1052 ... 36 A2
Upper Marlboro MD, 631 ... 144 C3
Upper Saddle River NJ, 8208 ... 148 B3
Upper Sandusky OH, 6596 ... 90 C3
Upshur Co. TX, 39309 ... 124 B2
Upshur Co. WV, 24254 ... 102 A3
Upson Co. GA, 27153 ... 129 D2
Upton KY, 683 ... 110 A1
Upton MA, 3013 ... 150 C2
Upton WY, 1100 ... 25 F3
Upton Co. TX, 3355 ... 58 A4
Urania LA, 1313 ... 125 E3
Urbana IL, 41250 ... 88 C4
Urbana IA, 1458 ... 87 E1
Urbana OH, 11793 ... 90 B4
Urbancrest OH, 960 ... 206 A3
Urbandale IA, 39463 ... 86 C2
Urbanna VA, 476 ... 113 F1
Urich MO, 476 ... 96 C3
Ursa IL, 626 ... 87 F4
Usquepaug RI, 350 ... 150 C4
Utah Co. UT, 516564 ... 39 E1
Utica IN, 776 ... 100 A4
Utica MI, 4757 ... 210 C1
Utica MS, 820 ... 126 A3
Utica NE, 861 ... 35 E4
Utica NY, 62235 ... 79 E3
Utica OH, 2132 ... 91 D4
Utica SC, 1489 ... 121 E2
Uvalda GA, 598 ... 129 F3
Uvalde TX, 15751 ... 60 C3
Uvalde Co. TX, 26405 ... 60 C3
Uxbridge MA, 13457 ... 150 C2

V
Vacaville CA, 92428 ... 36 B3
Vader WA, 621 ... 12 B4
Vadito NM, 270 ... 49 D2
Vadnais Hts. MN, 12302 ... 235 D1
Vado NM, 3194 ... 56 C3
Vaiden MS, 734 ... 126 C1
Vail AZ, 10208 ... 55 D3
Vail CO, 5305 ... 41 D1
Vails Gate NY, 3369 ... 148 B1
Valatie NY, 1819 ... 94 B2
Valders WI, 962 ... 74 C1
Valdese NC, 4490 ... 111 F4
Valdez AK, 3976 ... 154 C3
Valdosta GA, 54518 ... 137 F1
Vale OR, 1874 ... 22 A4
Valencia NM, 2192 ... 48 C4
Valencia Co. NM, 76569 ... 48 C4
Valentine NE, 2737 ... 34 C1
Valhalla NY, 3162 ... 148 B3
Valier IL, 669 ... 98 C4
Valier MT, 509 ... 15 E2
Valinda CA, 22822 ... 228 E2
Vallejo CA, 115942 ... 36 B3
Vallersville MA, 2000 ... 151 E3
Valley AL, 9524 ... 128 B2
Valley NE, 1875 ... 35 F3
Valley Brook OK, 765 ... 244 E3
Valley Ctr. CA, 9277 ... 53 D3
Valley Ctr. KS, 6822 ... 43 E4
Valley City ND, 6585 ... 19 E4
Valley Cottage NY, 9107 ... 148 B2
Valley Co. ID, 9862 ... 22 C2
Valley Co. MT, 7369 ... 17 D2
Valley Co. NE, 4260 ... 35 D3
Valley Falls KS, 1192 ... 96 A2
Valley Falls RI, 11547 ... 150 C3
Valley Farms AZ, 300 ... 54 C2
Valley Forge PA, 1200 ... 146 B2
Valley Grove WV, 378 ... 91 F4
Valley Head AL, 558 ... 120 A2
Valley Mills TX, 1203 ... 59 E4
Valley Park MO, 6942 ... 256 A3
Valley Sprs. CA, 3553 ... 36 C3
Valley Sprs. SD, 759 ... 27 F4
Valley Stream NY, 37511 ... 148 C4
Valley View OH, 2034 ... 204 F3
Valleyview OH, 620 ... 206 A2
Valley View PA, 1683 ... 93 E3
Valley View TX, 757 ... 59 E1
Valliant OK, 754 ... 116 B3
Valmeyer IL, 1263 ... 98 A4
Valparaiso FL, 5036 ... 136 B2
Valparaiso IN, 31730 ... 89 E2
Valparaiso NE, 570 ... 35 F3
Valrico FL, 35545 ... 266 D2
Val Verde CA, 2468 ... 52 C2
Val Verde Co. TX, 48879 ... 60 B2
Vamo FL, 4727 ... 140 B4
Van TX, 2632 ... 124 A2
Van Alstyne TX, 3046 ... 59 F1
Van Buren AR, 22791 ... 116 C1
Van Buren IN, 864 ... 89 F3
Van Buren ME, 1937 ... 85 E1
Van Buren MO, 819 ... 107 F2
Van Buren Co. AR, 17295 ... 117 E1
Van Buren Co. IA, 7570 ... 87 E3
Van Buren Co. MI, 76258 ... 75 F4
Van Buren Co. TN, 5548 ... 110 A4
Vance AL, 1529 ... 127 F1
Vanceboro NC, 1005 ... 115 D3
Vanceburg KY, 1518 ... 100 C3
Vance Co. NC, 45422 ... 113 D3
Vancleave MS, 5886 ... 135 D2
Vancouver WA, 161791 ... 20 C1
Vandalia IL, 7042 ... 98 C3
Vandalia MO, 3899 ... 97 F2
Vandalia OH, 15246 ... 100 B1
Vandenberg Vil. CA, 6497 ... 52 A1
Vander NC, 1146 ... 123 D2
Vanderbilt MI, 562 ... 70 C3
Vanderburgh Co. IN, 179703 ... 99 D4
Vandercook Lake MI, 4721 ... 90 B1
Vandergrift PA, 5205 ... 92 A4
Vandling PA, 751 ... 93 F2
Van Etten NY, 537 ... 93 E1
Vanhiseville NJ, 700 ... 147 E2
Van Horn TX, 2063 ... 57 D4
Van Horne IA, 682 ... 87 E1
Van Lear KY, 1100 ... 111 E1
Vanlue OH, 359 ... 90 C3
Van Meter IA, 1016 ... 86 C2
Vansant VA, 470 ... 111 E2
Van Vleck TX, 1844 ... 132 A4
Van Wert OH, 10846 ... 90 B3
Van Wert Co. OH, 28744 ... 90 B3
Van Zandt Co. TX, 52579 ... 124 A2
Vardaman MS, 1316 ... 118 C4
Varnamtown NC, 541 ... 123 E4
Varnell GA, 1744 ... 120 B2
Varnville SC, 2162 ... 130 B2
Vashon WA, 10624 ... 262 A4
Vashon Hts. WA, 1100 ... 262 A3
Vass NC, 720 ... 122 C1
Vassalboro ME, 4047 ... 82 C2
Vassar MI, 2697 ... 76 B3
Vaughn MT, 658 ... 15 F3
Vaughn NM, 446 ... 49 D4
Veazie ME, 1744 ... 83 D1
Veblen SD, 531 ... 27 E1
Veedersburg IN, 2180 ... 89 D4
Vega TX, 884 ... 50 A3
Velma OK, 620 ... 51 E4
Velva ND, 1084 ... 18 B2
Venango Co. PA, 54984 ... 92 A2
Veneta OR, 4561 ... 20 B3
Venice FL, 20748 ... 140 B4
Venice IL, 1890 ... 256 C2
Venice LA, 202 ... 134 C4
Venice Gardens FL, 7104 ... 140 C4
Ventnor City NJ, 10650 ... 147 F4
Ventura CA, 106433 ... 52 B2
Ventura IA, 717 ... 72 C3
Ventura Co. CA, 823318 ... 52 B2
Venus TX, 2960 ... 59 E3
Verden OK, 530 ... 51 E3
Verdi NV, 1415 ... 37 D1
Verdigre NE, 575 ... 35 E1
Vergennes VT, 2588 ... 81 D2
Vermilion OH, 10594 ... 91 D2
Vermilion Co. IL, 81625 ... 89 D4
Vermilion Par. LA, 57999 ... 133 E3
Vermillion SD, 10571 ... 35 F1
Vermillion Co. IN, 16212 ... 99 E1

Bixby	C3	Broken Arrow	C3	Jenks	B3	Sand Sprs.	A2	Tiger	C1
Bowden	A3	Catoosa	C1	Oakhurst	A3	Sapulpa	A3	Tulsa	B2

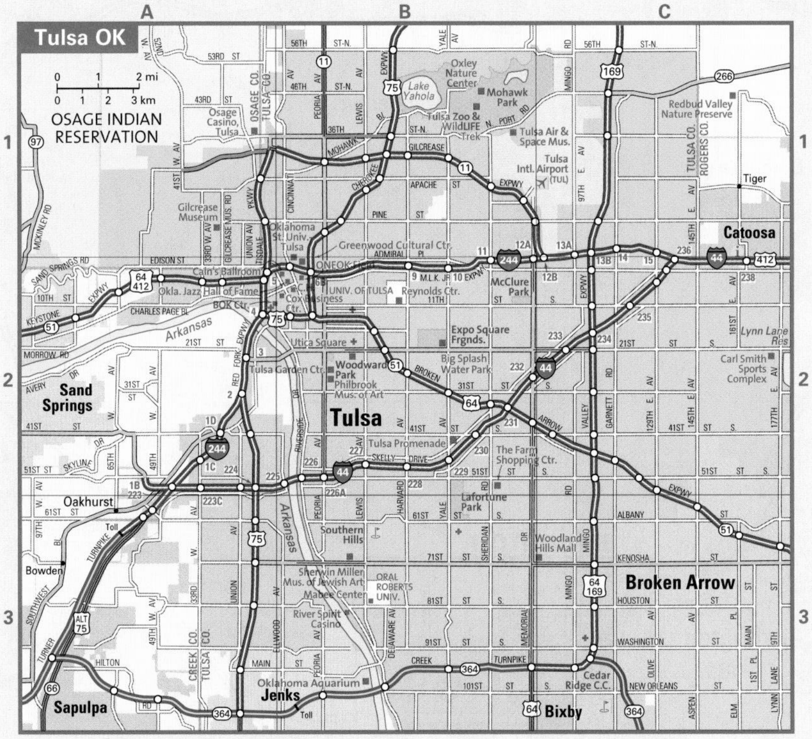

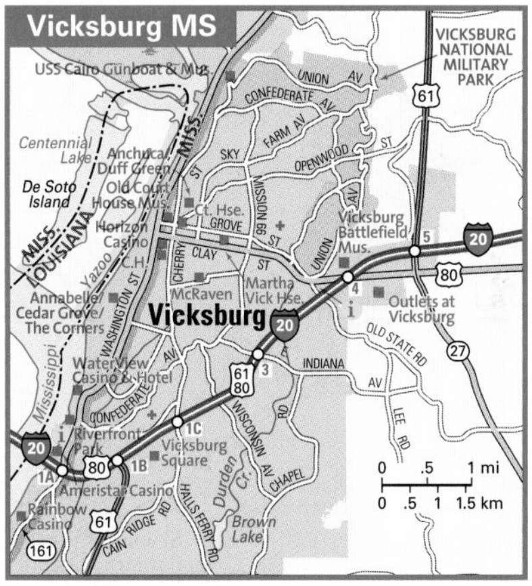

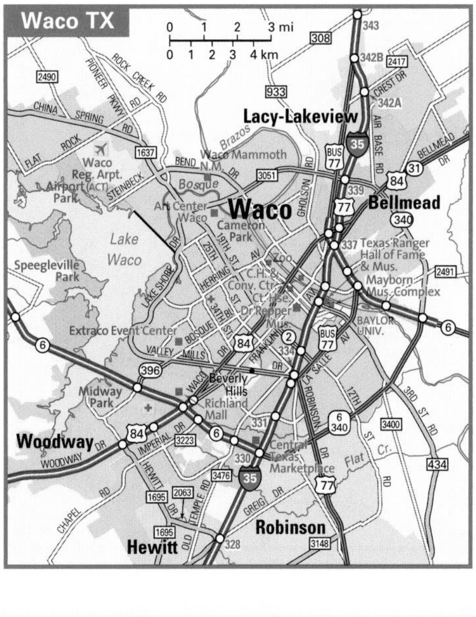

Figures after entries indicate population, page number, and grid reference.

Adelphi .E1
Alexandria C5
Annandale B4
Arlington C3
Bailey's Crossroads B4
Ballston C3
Barcroft C4
Belle Haven C5
Belle View C5
Beltsville .E1
Berwyn Hts. .E2
Bethesda C2
Bladensburg .E3
Bren Mar Park B5
Brentwood .E2
Broyhill Park B4
Cabin John B2
Calverton .E1
Camp Sprs. .E5
Canterbury Woods A4
Capitol Hts. .E3
Cherrydale C3
Chesterbrook B3
Cheverly .E3
Chevy Chase C2
Chevy Chase View C1
Chillum D2
Clarendon C3
College Park .E1
Colmar Manor .E3
Coral Hills .E4
Cottage City .E3
Crystal City C4
District Hts. .F4
Dodge Park .F3
Dunn Loring A3
E. Falls Church B3
Edmonston .E2
Fairfax A4
Fairmount Hts. .E3
Falls Church B3
Forest Hts. D5
Forestville .F4
Ft. Foote Vil. D5
Franconia B5
Garrett Park C1
Glassmanor D5
Glenarden .F3
Glendale A2
Glen Echo B2
Glen Echo Hts. C2
Greenbelt .F1
Groveton C5
Hillandale .E1
Hillcrest Hts. .E4
Huntington C5
Hyattsville .E2
Idylwood B3
Kensington C1
Kentland .F3
Kings Park A5
Knollwood .E1
Lake Barcroft B4
Landover .E3
Landover Hills .F2
Langley B2
Langley Park D2
Lanham .F2
Largo .F3
Lewisdale .E2
Lincolnia B4
Luxmanor C1
Mantua A4
Marlow Hts. .E4
Martins Additions C2
McLean B2
Merrifield A3
Morningside .F4
Mt. Rainier .E2
New Carrollton .F2
N. Brentwood .E2
N. Chevy Chase C1
N. Springfield A5
Oaklawn .E5
Oakview .E1
Oxon Hill D5
Palmer Park .F3
Pimmit Hills B3
Potomac A1
Randolph Hills C1
Ravensworth A5
Ritchie .F4
Riverdale Hts. .E2
Riverdale Park .E2
Rosedale Estates .E5
Rose Hill C5
Rosslyn C3
Seabrook .F2
Seat Pleasant .F3
Seven Corners B4
Shirlington C4
Silver Hill .E4
Silver Spr. D2
Somerset C2
Springfield B5
Spring Hill A2
Suitland .E4
Takoma Park D2
Temple Hills .E5
Tysons A3
University Park .E2
Vienna A3
Virginia Hills C5
Walker Mill .F4
Washington D3
Westover B3
W. Springfield A5
Wheaton D1
White Oak D1
Woodyard .F5

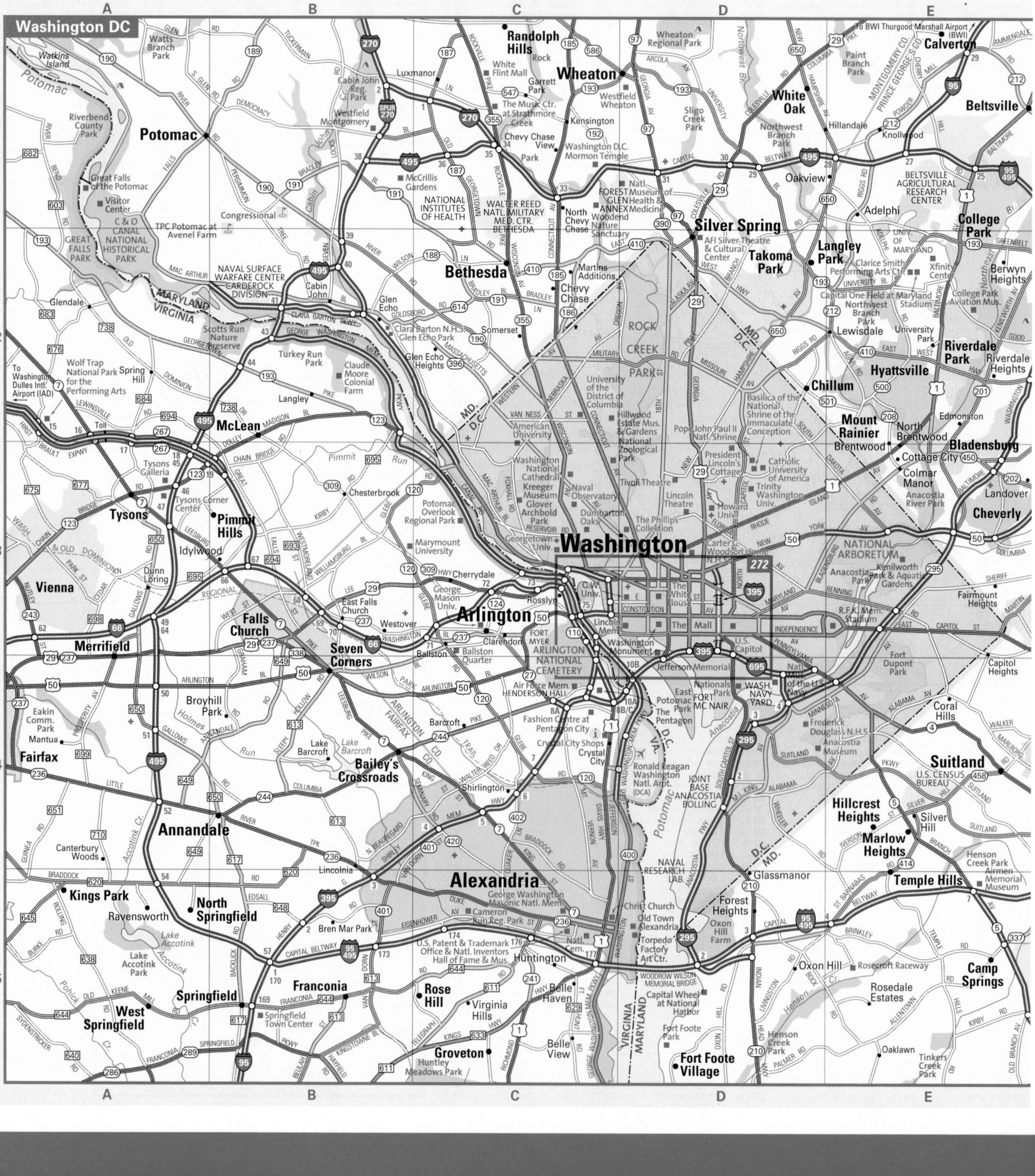

271
Vermont–Waynesboro

Entries in **bold black** indicate counties or parishes.
Entries in **bold color** indicate cities with detailed inset maps.

Vermont IL, *667* 88 A4
Vermontville MI, *759* 76 A4
Vernal UT, *9089* 32 A4
Verndale MN, *602* 64 A4
Vernon AL, *2000* 119 D4
Vernon CT, *29179* 150 A3
Vernon FL, *687* 136 C2
Vernon IN, *318* 100 A2
Vernon MI, *783* 76 B3
Vernon NY, *1172* 79 E3
Vernon TX, *11002* 51 D4
Vernon VT, *2141* 94 C1
Vernon Co. MO, *21159* 96 C4
Vernon Co. WI, *29773* 73 F2
Vernon Hills IL, *25113* 203 C1
Vernonia OR, *2151* 20 B1
Vernon Par. LA, *52334* 125 D4
Vernon Valley NJ, *1626* 148 A2
Vero Beach FL, *15220* 141 E3
Verona MS, *3006* 119 D3
Verona MO, *619* 106 C2
Verona NJ, *13332* 148 A3
Verona NC, *700* 115 D4
Verona PA, *2474* 250 D1
Verona VA, *4239* 102 C4
Verona WI, *10619* 74 B3
Verplanck NY, *1729* 148 B2
Versailles CT, *750* 149 F1
Versailles IN, *2113* 100 A2
Versailles KY, *8568* 100 B4
Versailles MO, *2482* 97 D3
Versailles OH, *2687* 90 B4
Vesper WI, *584* 68 A4
Vestal NY, *3900* 93 E1
Vestal Ctr. NY, *850* 93 E1
Vestavia Hills AL, *34033* 119 F4
Vevay IN, *1683* 100 A3
Vian OK, *1466* 116 B1
Viborg SD, *782* 35 F1
Viburnum MO, *693* 107 F1
Vici OK, *699* 51 D2
Vicksburg MI, *2906* 89 F1
Vicksburg MS, *23856* 126 A2
Victor CO, *397* 41 E2
Victor ID, *1928* 23 F4
Victor IA, *893* 87 E1
Victor MT, *745* 15 D4
Victor NY, *2696* 78 C3
Victoria KS, *1214* 43 D2
Victoria MN, *7345* 66 C4
Victoria TX, *62592* 61 F3
Victoria VA, *1725* 113 D2
Victoria Co. TX, *86793* 61 F3
Victorville CA, *115903* 53 D2
Victory Gardens NJ, *1520* 148 A3
Vidalia GA, *10473* 129 F3
Vidalia LA, *4299* 125 F4
Vidor TX, *10579* 132 C2
Vienna GA, *4011* 129 D3
Vienna IL, *1434* 108 C1
Vienna LA, *386* 125 E2
Vienna MO, *610* 97 E4
Vienna VA, *15687* 144 B3
Vienna WV, *10749* 101 E2
View Park CA, *10958* 228 C3
Vigo Co. IN, *107848* 99 E2
Vilano Beach FL, *2678* 139 E3
Vilas Co. WI, *21430* 68 B2
Village Green NY, *3891* 79 D3
Village Green PA, *7822* 248 A4
Villages of Oriole FL, *4758* 143 F1
Villa Grove IL, *2537* 99 D1
Villa Hills KY, *7489* 204 A3
Villa Park CA, *5812* 229 F4
Villa Park IL, *21904* 203 C4
Villa Rica GA, *13956* 120 B4
Villa Ridge MO, *2636* 98 A3
Villas NJ, *9483* 104 C4
Ville Platte LA, *7430* 133 E1
Villisca IA, *1252* 86 B3
Vilonia AR, *3815* 117 E1
Vimy Ridge AR, *600* 117 E2
Vinalhaven ME, *1235* 83 D3
Vincennes IN, *18423* 99 D3
Vincent AL, *1988* 128 A1
Vincent CA, *15922* 52 C2
Vincentown NJ, *750* 147 D3
Vinco PA, *1305* 92 B4
Vine Grove KY, *4520* 110 A1
Vine Hill CA, *3761* 259 D1
Vineland MN, *1001* 66 C1
Vineland NJ, *60724* 145 F1
Vinemont AL, *425* 119 F3
Vineyard Haven MA, *2114* 151 E4
Vinings GA, *9734* 190 C2
Vinita OK, *5743* 106 B3
Vinita Park MO, *1880* 256 B2
Vinton CA, *387* 37 D1
Vinton IA, *5257* 87 E1
Vinton LA, *3212* 133 D2
Vinton TX, *1971* 56 C3
Vinton VA, *8098* 112 B2
Vinton Co. OH, *13435* 101 E2
Viola DE, *157* 145 E3
Viola IL, *955* 88 A2
Viola WI, *699* 73 F2
Violet LA, *4973* 134 C3
Virden IL, *3425* 98 B2
Virgin UT, *596* 39 D4
Virginia IL, *1611* 98 A1
Virginia MN, *8712* 64 C3
Virginia Beach VA, *437994* 114 B4
Virginia City MT, *190* 23 E2
Virginia City NV, *855* 37 D2
Virginia Gardens FL, *2375* 233 A4
Viroqua WI, *4362* 73 F2
Visalia CA, *124442* 45 D3
Vista CA, *93834* 53 D3
Vivian LA, *3671* 124 C1
Volcano HI, *2575* 153 F4
Volga SD, *1768* 27 F3
Volin SD, *161* 35 E1
Voluntown CT, *2631* 149 F1
Volusia Co. FL, *494593* 139 E4
Vonore TN, *1474* 120 C1
Voorheesville NY, *2789* 94 B1

W

Wabash IN, *10666* 89 F3
Wabasha MN, *2521* 73 E1
Wabasha Co. MN, *21676* 73 E1
Wabash Co. IL, *11947* 99 D3
Wabash Co. IN, *32888* 89 F3
Wabasso FL, *609* 141 E3
Wabasso MN, *696* 72 A1
Wabaunsee Co. KS, *7053* 43 F2
Waco TX, *124805* 59 E4
Waconia MN, *10697* 66 C4
Waddington NY, *972* 80 B1
Wade MS, *1074* 135 D2
Wade NC, *556* 123 D1
Wadena MN, *4088* 64 A4
Wadena Co. MN, *13843* 64 A4
Wadesboro NC, *5813* 122 B2
Wading River NY, *7719* 149 D3
Wadley AL, *751* 128 B1
Wadley GA, *2061* 129 F1
Wadsworth NV, *834* 37 D1
Wadsworth OH, *21567* 91 E3
Waelder TX, *1065* 61 E2
Wagener SC, *797* 122 A4
Waggaman LA, *10015* 239 B2
Wagner SD, *1566* 35 E1
Wagoner OK, *8323* 106 A4
Wagoner Co. OK, *73085* 106 A4
Wagon Mound NM, *314* 49 E2
Wagontown PA, *1100* 146 B3
Wagram NC, *840* 122 C2
Wahiawa HI, *17821* 152 A2
Wahkiakum Co. WA, *3978* 12 B4
Wahoo NE, *4508* 35 F3
Wahpeton ND, *7766* 27 F1
Waialua HI, *3860* 152 A2
Waianae HI, *13177* 152 A3
Waiehu HI, *8841* 153 D1
Waihee HI, *7310* 153 D1
Waikane HI, *778* 152 A2
Waikapu HI, *2965* 153 D1
Waikoloa Vil. HI, *6362* 153 E3
Wailua HI, *2254* 152 B1
Wailuku HI, *15313* 153 D1
Waimalu HI, *13730* 152 A3
Waimanalo HI, *5451* 152 B3
Waimanalo Beach HI, *4481* 152 B3
Waimea HI, *1855* 152 B1
Waimea (Kamuela) HI, *9212* 153 E2
Wainscott NY, *650* 149 F3
Wainwright AK, *556* 154 C1
Waipahu HI, *38216* 152 A3
Waipio Acres HI, *5236* 152 A3
Waite Park MN, *6715* 66 C3
Waitsburg WA, *1217* 13 F4
Waitsfield VT, *164* 81 D2
Wakarusa IN, *1758* 89 F2
Wakeby MA, *1600* 151 E3
Wake Co. NC, *900993* 113 D4
WaKeeney KS, *1862* 42 C2
Wakefield KS, *980* 43 F2
Wakefield MA, *24932* 151 D1
Wakefield MI, *1851* 65 E4
Wakefield NE, *1451* 35 F2
Wakefield RI, *8487* 150 C4
Wakefield VA, *11275* 113 F2
Wake Forest NC, *30117* 113 D4
Wakeman OH, *1047* 91 D2
Wake Vil. TX, *5492* 124 C1
Wakonda SD, *321* 35 F1
Wakulla Co. FL, *30776* 137 E2
Walbridge OH, *3019* 267 B2
Walcott IA, *1629* 87 F2
Walden CO, *608* 33 D4
Walden NY, *6978* 148 B1
Walden TN, *1898* 120 B1
Waldo AR, *1372* 125 D1
Waldo FL, *1015* 138 C3
Waldoboro ME, *1233* 82 C2
Waldo Co. ME, *38786* 82 C2
Waldorf MD, *67752* 144 B4
Waldport OR, *2033* 20 B3
Waldron AR, *3618* 116 C2
Waldron IN, *804* 100 A2
Waldron MI, *538* 90 B1
Wales MA, *1737* 150 B2
Wales WI, *2549* 74 C3
Waleska GA, *644* 120 C3
Walford IA, *1463* 87 E1
Walhalla ND, *996* 19 E1
Walhalla SC, *4263* 121 E2
Walker IA, *791* 73 E4
Walker LA, *6138* 134 A2
Walker MI, *23537* 75 F3
Walker MN, *941* 64 A3
Walker Co. AL, *67023* 119 E4
Walker Co. GA, *68756* 120 B2
Walker Co. TX, *67861* 132 A1
Walker Mill MD, *11302* 271 F4
Walkersville MD, *5800* 144 A1
Walkerton IN, *2144* 89 E2
Walkertown NC, *4675* 112 B4
Walker Valley NY, *853* 148 A1
Walkerville MT, *675* 23 E1
Wall PA, *580* 250 D3
Wall SD, *766* 26 B3
Wallace ID, *784* 14 B3
Wallace NC, *3880* 123 E2
Wallace VA, *550* 111 E3
Wallace Co. KS, *1485* 42 B2
Walla Walla WA, *31731* 21 F1
Walla Walla Co. WA, *58781* 21 F1
Wallburg MI, *3047* 112 B4
Walled Lake MI, *6999* 210 A2
Waller TX, *2326* 61 F2
Waller Co. TX, *43205* 132 A3
Wallingford CT, *44736* 149 D1
Wallingford VT, *830* 81 D4
Wallington NJ, *11335* 148 B3
Wallis TX, *1252* 61 F2
Wallkill NY, *2288* 148 B1
Wall Lake IA, *819* 72 B4
Wallowa OR, *808* 22 A1
Wallowa Co. OR, *7008* 22 A1
Walnut CA, *29172* 229 F3
Walnut IL, *1416* 88 B2
Walnut IA, *785* 86 A2
Walnut MS, *771* 118 C2
Walnut Cove NC, *1425* 112 B3
Walnut Creek CA, *64173* 36 B4
Walnut Creek NC, *835* 123 E1
Walnut Grove AL, *698* 120 A3
Walnut Grove CA, *1542* 36 C3
Walnut Grove GA, *1330* 121 D4
Walnut Grove MN, *871* 72 A1
Walnut Grove MS, *1911* 126 C2
Walnut Grove MO, *665* 106 C1
Walnut Grove TN, *864* 109 F3
Walnut Hill TN, *2394* 111 E3
Walnut Park CA, *15966* 228 D3
Walnutport PA, *2070* 93 F3
Walnut Ridge AR, *4890* 108 A4
Walnut Sprs. TX, *827* 59 E3
Walpole MA, *5918* 151 D2
Walpole NH, *605* 81 E4
Walsenburg CO, *3068* 41 E4
Walsh CO, *546* 42 A4
Walsh Co. ND, *11119* 19 E2
Walterboro SC, *5398* 130 C1
Walterhill TN, *401* 109 F4
Walters OK, *2551* 51 D4
Walthall MS, *144* 118 C4
Walthall Co. MS, *15443* 134 B1
Waltham MA, *60632* 151 D1
Walthill NE, *780* 35 F2
Walthourville GA, *4111* 130 B3
Walton IN, *1049* 89 F3
Walton KY, *3635* 100 B3
Walton NY, *3088* 93 F1
Walton Co. FL, *55043* 136 B2
Walton Co. GA, *83768* 121 D4
Walton Hills OH, *2281* 204 G3
Walworth WI, *2816* 74 C4
Walworth Co. SD, *5438* 26 C2
Walworth Co. WI, *102228* 74 C4
Wamac IL, *1185* 98 C3
Wamego KS, *4372* 43 F2
Wampsville NY, *543* 79 E3
Wamsutter WY, *451* 32 C3
Wanakah NY, *3199* 78 A4
Wanamassa NJ, *4532* 147 E2
Wanamingo MN, *1086* 73 D1
Wanaque NJ, *11116* 148 A3
Wanatah IN, *1048* 89 E2
Wanblee SD, *725* 26 B4
Wanchese NC, *1642* 115 F2
Wapakoneta OH, *9867* 90 B4
Wapanucka OK, *438* 51 F4
Wapato WA, *4997* 13 D4
Wapella IL, *558* 88 C4
Wapello IA, *2067* 87 F2
Wapello Co. IA, *35625* 87 D3
Waples TX, *800* 59 E3
Wappingers Falls NY, *5522* 148 B1
War WV, *862* 111 F1
Ward AR, *4067* 117 F2
Ward Co. ND, *61675* 18 B2
Ward Co. TX, *10658* 57 F4
Warden WA, *2692* 13 E4
Wardner ID, *188* 14 B3
Wardsville MO, *1506* 97 E3
Ware MA, *6170* 150 B1
Ware Co. GA, *36312* 129 F4
Wareham MA, *21221* 151 E3
Ware Shoals SC, *2170* 121 F3
Waretown NJ, *1569* 147 E3
Warm Beach WA, *2437* 12 C2
Warm Sprs. GA, *485* 128 C1
Warm Sprs. OR, *2945* 21 D3
Warm Sprs. VA, *123* 102 B4
Warner NH, *444* 81 F4
Warner OK, *1641* 116 A1
Warner SD, *457* 27 D2
Warner Robins GA, *66588* 129 D2
Warr Acres OK, *10043* 244 D2
Warren AR, *6003* 117 E4
Warren IL, *1428* 74 A4
Warren IN, *1239* 90 A3
Warren ME, *3794* 82 C2
Warren MA, *1405* 150 B2
Warren MI, *134056* 76 C4
Warren MN, *1563* 19 F2
Warren OH, *41557* 91 F2
Warren PA, *9710* 92 B1
Warren RI, *10611* 151 D3
Warren Co. GA, *5834* 129 F1
Warren Co. IL, *17707* 88 A3
Warren Co. IN, *8508* 89 D4
Warren Co. IA, *46225* 86 C2
Warren Co. KY, *113792* 109 F2
Warren Co. MS, *48773* 126 A2
Warren Co. MO, *32513* 97 F3
Warren Co. NJ, *108692* 93 F3
Warren Co. NY, *65707* 80 C3
Warren Co. NC, *20972* 113 D3
Warren Co. OH, *212693* 100 C2
Warren Co. PA, *41815* 92 B1
Warren Co. TN, *39839* 110 A4
Warren Co. VA, *37575* 103 D2
Warren Glen NJ, *650* 146 C1
Warren Park IN, *1480* 99 F1
Warrensburg IL, *1210* 98 C1
Warrensburg MO, *18838* 96 C3
Warrensburg NY, *3103* 80 C4
Warrensville PA, *1100* 93 D2
Warrensville Hts. OH, *13542* 204 G2
Warrenton GA, *1937* 129 F1
Warrenton MO, *7880* 97 F3
Warrenton NC, *862* 113 D3
Warrenton OR, *4989* 20 B1
Warrenton VA, *9611* 103 D3
Warrenville IL, *13140* 203 A4
Warrick Co. IN, *59689* 99 E4
Warrington FL, *14531* 135 F2
Warrington PA, *5400* 146 C2
Warrior AL, *3176* 119 F4
Warrior Run PA, *584* 261 A2
Warroad MN, *1781* 64 A1
Warsaw IL, *1607* 87 F4
Warsaw IN, *13559* 89 F2
Warsaw KY, *1615* 100 B3
Warsaw MN, *627* 72 C1
Warsaw MO, *2127* 97 D4
Warsaw NY, *3473* 78 B4
Warsaw NC, *3054* 123 E2
Warsaw OH, *682* 91 D4
Warsaw VA, *1512* 103 E4
Warson Woods MO, *1962* 256 B2
Wartburg TN, *918* 110 B4
Wartrace TN, *651* 120 A1
Warwick NY, *6731* 148 A2
Warwick RI, *82672* 150 C3
Wasatch Co. UT, *23530* 31 F4
Wasco CA, *25545* 45 D4
Wasco OR, *410* 21 D1
Wasco Co. OR, *25213* 21 D2
Waseca MN, *9410* 72 C1
Waseca Co. MN, *19136* 72 C1
Washakie Co. WY, *8533* 24 C4
Washburn IL, *1155* 88 B3
Washburn IA, *876* 73 E4
Washburn ME, *997* 85 D2
Washburn ND, *1246* 18 B3
Washburn WI, *2117* 65 D4
Washburn Co. WI, *15911* 67 E2
Washington CT, *600* 148 C1
Washington DC, *601723* 144 B3
Washington GA, *4134* 121 E4
Washington IL, *15134* 88 B3
Washington IN, *11509* 99 E3
Washington IA, *7266* 87 E2
Washington KS, *1131* 43 F1
Washington LA, *964* 133 F2
Washington MO, *13982* 97 F3
Washington NJ, *6461* 93 F3
Washington NC, *9744* 115 D3
Washington OK, *618* 51 E3
Washington PA, *13663* 91 F4
Washington UT, *18761* 46 C1
Washington VT, *1047* 81 E2
Washington VA, *135* 103 D3
Washington WV, *1175* 101 E2
Washington Co. AL, *17581* 127 E4
Washington Co. AR, *203065* 106 B4
Washington Co. CO, *4814* 34 A4
Washington Co. FL, *24896* 136 C2
Washington Co. GA, *21187* 129 E1
Washington Co. ID, *10198* 22 A3
Washington Co. IL, *14716* 98 B4
Washington Co. IN, *28262* 99 F3
Washington Co. IA, *21704* 87 E2
Washington Co. KS, *5799* 43 E1
Washington Co. KY, *11717* 110 B1
Washington Co. ME, *32856* 83 E1
Washington Co. MD, *147430* 103 D1
Washington Co. MN, *238136* 67 D3
Washington Co. MS, *51137* 126 A1
Washington Co. MO, *25195* 97 F4
Washington Co. NE, *20234* 35 F3
Washington Co. NY, *63216* 81 D4
Washington Co. NC, *13228* 113 F4
Washington Co. OH, *61778* 101 E2
Washington Co. OK, *50976* 106 A2
Washington Co. OR, *529710* 20 B2
Washington Co. PA, *207820* 92 A4
Washington Co. RI, *126979* 150 C4
Washington Co. TN, *122979* 111 E3
Washington Co. TX, *33718* 61 F2
Washington Co. UT, *138115* 38 C4
Washington Co. VT, *59534* 81 E2
Washington Co. VA, *54876* 111 F3
Washington Co. WI, *131887* 74 C2
Washington C.H. OH, *14192* 100 C1
Washington Crossing NJ, *950* 147 D2
Washington Crossing PA, *1300* 147 D2
Washington Hts. NY, *1689* 148 A1
Washington Par. LA, *47168* 134 B1
Washington Park IL, *4196* 256 D2
Washington Terrace UT, *9067* 244 A2
Washingtonville NY, *5899* 148 B1
Washingtonville OH, *801* 91 F3
Washita Co. OK, *11629* 51 D3
Washoe Co. NV, *421407* 29 E4
Washougal WA, *14095* 20 C2
Washtenaw Co. MI, *344791* 90 B1
Wasilla AK, *7831* 154 C3
Waskom TX, *2160* 124 C2
Wataga IL, *843* 88 A3
Watauga TN, *458* 111 E3
Watauga TX, *23497* 207 B2
Watauga Co. NC, *51079* 111 F3
Watchung NJ, *5801* 147 E1
Waterboro ME, *6214* 82 B3
Waterbury CT, *110366* 149 D1
Waterbury VT, *1763* 81 D2
Waterbury Ctr. VT, *850* 81 E2
Waterford CA, *8456* 36 C4
Waterford CT, *2887* 149 F2
Waterford MI, *73150* 76 B4
Waterford NY, *1990* 188 E1
Waterford PA, *1517* 92 A1
Waterford WI, *5368* 74 C4
Waterford Works NJ, *1000* 147 D4
Waterloo IL, *9811* 98 A4
Waterloo IN, *2242* 90 A2
Waterloo IA, *68406* 73 E4
Waterloo MD, *900* 144 C2
Waterloo NE, *848* 35 F3
Waterloo NY, *5171* 79 D3
Waterloo WI, *3333* 74 B3
Waterman IL, *1506* 88 C1
Water Mill NY, *1559* 149 E3
Waterproof LA, *688* 125 F3
Watertown CT, *3574* 149 D1
Watertown FL, *2829* 138 C2
Watertown MA, *31915* 151 D1
Watertown MN, *4205* 66 C4
Watertown NY, *27023* 79 E1
Watertown SD, *21482* 27 F2
Watertown TN, *1477* 109 F4
Watertown WI, *23861* 74 C3
Water Valley MS, *3392* 118 B3
Waterville KS, *680* 43 F1
Waterville ME, *15722* 82 C2
Waterville MN, *1868* 72 C1
Waterville NY, *1583* 79 E3
Waterville OH, *5523* 90 C2
Waterville WA, *1138* 13 E3
Watervliet MI, *1735* 89 F1
Watervliet NY, *10254* 188 E2
Watford City ND, *1744* 18 A3
Wathena KS, *1364* 96 B1
Watkins MN, *962* 66 C3
Watkins Glen NY, *1859* 79 D4
Watkinsville GA, *2832* 121 D4
Watonga OK, *5111* 51 D2
Watonwan Co. MN, *11211* 72 B1
Watseka IL, *5255* 89 D3
Watson IL, *754* 98 C2
Watson LA, *1047* 134 A2
Watsontown PA, *2351* 93 D3
Watsonville CA, *51199* 44 B2
Watterson Park KY, *976* 230 E2
Waubay SD, *576* 27 E2
Wauchula FL, *5001* 140 C3
Wauconda IL, *13603* 203 B1
Waukee IA, *13790* 86 C2
Waukegan IL, *89078* 75 D4
Waukesha WI, *70718* 74 C3
Waukesha Co. WI, *389891* 74 C3
Waukomis OK, *1286* 51 E2
Waukon IA, *3897* 73 E3
Waunakee WI, *12097* 74 B3
Wauneta NE, *577* 34 B4
Waupaca WI, *6069* 74 B1
Waupaca Co. WI, *52410* 68 B4
Waupun WI, *11340* 74 C2
Wauregan CT, *1205* 150 B3
Waurika OK, *2064* 51 E4
Wausa NE, *634* 35 E1
Wausau WI, *39106* 68 B4
Wausaukee WI, *575* 68 C3
Wauseon OH, *7332* 90 B2
Waushara Co. WI, *24496* 74 B1
Wautoma WI, *2218* 74 B1
Wauwatosa WI, *46396* 234 C2
Wauzeka WI, *711* 73 F3
Waveland MS, *6435* 134 C2
Waverly FL, *767* 141 D2
Waverly IL, *1307* 98 B1
Waverly IA, *9874* 73 D4
Waverly KS, *592* 96 A3
Waverly MN, *1357* 66 C3
Waverly MO, *849* 96 C2
Waverly NE, *3277* 35 F4
Waverly NY, *4444* 93 E1
Waverly OH, *4408* 101 D2
Waverly TN, *4105* 109 D4
Waverly VA, *2149* 113 E2
Waverly Hall GA, *735* 128 C2
Waxahachie TX, *29621* 59 F3
Waxhaw NC, *9859* 122 B2
Waycross GA, *14649* 129 F4
Wayland IA, *966* 87 E2
Wayland MA, *12994* 150 C1
Wayland MI, *4079* 75 F4
Wayland NY, *1865* 78 C4
Waymart PA, *1341* 93 F2
Wayne IL, *2431* 203 A4
Wayne MI, *17593* 210 A4
Wayne NE, *5660* 35 F2
Wayne NJ, *53918* 148 A3
Wayne OH, *887* 90 C2
Wayne OK, *688* 51 E3
Wayne PA, *1000* 146 C3
Wayne WV, *1413* 101 D4
Wayne City IL, *1032* 98 C4
Wayne Co. GA, *30099* 130 A4
Wayne Co. IL, *16760* 98 C3
Wayne Co. IN, *68917* 100 A1
Wayne Co. IA, *6403* 87 D3
Wayne Co. KY, *20813* 110 B3
Wayne Co. MI, *1820584* 76 B4
Wayne Co. MS, *20747* 127 D4
Wayne Co. MO, *13521* 108 A2
Wayne Co. NE, *9595* 35 F2
Wayne Co. NY, *93772* 79 D3
Wayne Co. NC, *122623* 123 E1
Wayne Co. OH, *114520* 91 E3
Wayne Co. PA, *52822* 93 F1
Wayne Co. TN, *17021* 119 E1
Wayne Co. UT, *2778* 39 F3
Wayne Co. WV, *42481* 101 E4
Wayne Lakes OH, *718* 100 B1
Waynesboro GA, *5766* 129 F1
Waynesboro MS, *5043* 127 D4
Waynesboro PA, *10568* 103 D1
Waynesboro TN, *2449* 119 E1

F
Howard University
Beltsville Campus
Technology Univ.
BELTSVILLE
AGRICULTURAL
RESEARCH
CENTER
Beaverdam
Greenbelt
Greenbelt Museum
NASA Goddard Space Flight Center
GREEN-BELT PARK
New Carrollton
Seabrook
Lanham
Landover Hills
Dodge Park
Glenarden
Kentland
Palmer Park
FedExField
The Boulevard at the Capital Centre
Largo
Seat Pleasant
Walker Mill
Walker Mill Reg. Park
Ritchie
District Heights
Forestville
Morningside
JOINT BASE
ANDREWS NAVAL
AIR FACILITY
Woodyard
1
2
3
4
5
0 1 2 mi
0 1 2 3 km
F

Figures after entries indicate population, page number, and grid reference.

Waynesboro VA, *21006* **102** C4
Waynesburg OH, *923* **91** E3
Waynesburg PA, *4176* **102** A1
Waynesfield OH, *847* **90** B4
Waynesville MO, *4830* **107** E1
Waynesville NC, *9869* **121** E1
Waynesville OH, *2834* **100** C1
Waynetown IN, *958* **89** E4
Waynoka OK, *927* **51** D1
Wayzata MN, *3688* **235** A2
Weakley Co. TN, *35021* **108** C3
Weare NH, *8785* **81** F4
Weatherby Lake MO, *1723* **224** B2
Weatherford OK, *10833* **51** D3
Weatherford TX, *25250* **59** E2
Weatherly PA, *2525* **93** F3
Weaubleau MO, *418* **96** C4
Weaver AL, *3038* **120** A4
Weaverville CA, *3600* **28** B4
Weaverville NC, *3120* **111** E4
Webb AL, *1430* **128** B4
Webb MS, *565* **118** B4
Webb City MO, *10996* **106** B2
Webb Co. TX, *250304* **60** C4
Webbers Falls OK, *616* **116** B1
Webberville MI, *1272* **76** B4
Weber City VA, *1327* **111** E3
Weber Co. UT, *231236* **31** F3
Webster FL, *785* **140** C1
Webster MD, *1200* **145** D1
Webster MA, *11412* **150** B2
Webster NY, *5399* **78** C3
Webster NC, *363* **121** D1
Webster SD, *1886* **27** E2
Webster TX, *10400* **132** B3
Webster WI, *653* **67** E2
Webster City IA, *8070* **72** C4
Webster Co. GA, *2799* **128** C3
Webster Co. IA, *38013* **72** B4
Webster Co. KY, *13621* **109** E1
Webster Co. MS, *10253* **118** C4
Webster Co. MO, *36202* **107** D2
Webster Co. NE, *3812* **35** E4
Webster Co. WV, *9154* **102** A3
Webster Groves MO, *22995* **256** B3
Webster Par. LA, *41207* **125** D2
Webster Sprs. WV, *776* **102** A3
Weddington NC, *9459* **122** B2
Wedowee AL, *823* **128** B1
Weed CA, *2967* **28** C3
Weedsport NY, *1815* **79** D3
Weehawken NJ, *12554* **148** B4
Weeki Wachee Gardens FL, *1146* **140** B1
Weeping Water NE, *1050* **35** F4
Weidman MI, *959* **76** A2
Weigelstown PA, *12875* **103** E1
Weimar CA, *1100* **36** C2
Weimar TX, *2151* **61** F2
Weiner AR, *716* **108** A4
Weippe ID, *441* **14** B4
Weir KS, *686* **106** B2
Weir MS, *459* **126** C1
Weir TX, *450* **61** E1
Weirsdale FL, *750* **139** D4
Weirton WV, *19746* **91** F4
Weiser ID, *5507* **22** A3
Welaka FL, *701* **139** D4
Welby CO, *14846* **209** C2
Welch OK, *619* **106** B2
Welch WV, *2406* **111** F1
Welcome LA, *800* **134** A3
Welcome MN, *686* **72** B2
Welcome NC, *4162* **112** B4
Welcome SC, *6668* **217** A2
Weld Co. CO, *252825* **33** F4
Weldon CA, *2642* **45** E4
Weldon NC, *1655* **113** E3
Weldon Spr. MO, *5443* **98** A3
Weleetka OK, *998* **51** F3
Wellesley MA, *27982* **151** D1
Wellfleet MA, *2749* **151** F2
Wellford SC, *2378* **217** C1
Welling OK, *771* **106** B4
Wellington CO, *6289* **33** E4
Wellington FL, *56508* **143** E1
Wellington KS, *8172* **43** E4
Wellington KY, *565* **230** E2
Wellington MO, *812* **96** C2
Wellington OH, *4802* **91** D2
Wellington TX, *2189* **50** C4
Wellington UT, *1676* **39** F1
Wellman IA, *1408* **87** E2
Wells ME, *9400* **82** B4
Wells MN, *2343* **72** C2
Wells NV, *1292* **30** C3
Wells TX, *790* **124** B4
Wells VT, *397* **81** D4
Wellsboro IN, *600* **89** E2
Wellsboro PA, *3263* **93** D1
Wellsburg IA, *707* **73** D4
Wellsburg NY, *580* **93** D1
Wellsburg WV, *2805* **91** F4
Wells Co. IN, *27636* **90** A3
Wells Co. ND, *4207* **18** C3
Wells River VT, *399* **81** E2
Wellston MO, *2313* **256** B2
Wellston OH, *5663* **101** D2
Wellston OK, *788* **51** F2
Wellsville KS, *1857* **96** B3
Wellsville MO, *1217* **97** F2
Wellsville NY, *4679* **92** C1
Wellsville OH, *3541* **91** F3
Wellsville UT, *3432* **31** E3
Wellton AZ, *2882* **54** A2
Welsh LA, *3226* **133** E2
Wenatchee WA, *31925* **13** D3
Wendell ID, *2782* **30** C1
Wendell NC, *5845* **113** D4
Wenden AZ, *728* **54** B1
Wendover UT, *1400* **31** D4
Wenham MA, *4440* **151** F1
Wenona IL, *1056* **88** B3
Wenonah NJ, *2278* **146** C3
Wentworth NC, *2807* **112** B3
Wentzville MO, *29070* **98** A3

POINTS OF INTEREST

Arena Stage . . . E4
Arlington Natl. Cemetery . . . A4
Arthur M. Sackler Gallery . . . E3
Art Museum of the Americas . . . C2
Arts & Industries Building . . . E3
Sewall-Belmont House . . . G2
Belmont-Paul Women's Equality National Monument . . . C2
Bureau of Engraving & Printing . . . D3
Cathedral of St. Matthew the Apostle . . . C1
Daughters of the American Revolution Constitution Hall . . . C2
Decatur House . . . C1
Dept. of Agriculture . . . D3
Dept. of Commerce . . . D2
Dept. of Education . . . E3
Dept. of Energy . . . E3
Dept. of Housing and Urban Development . . . E3
Dept. of Justice . . . E2
Dept. of Labor . . . F2
Dept. of State . . . C2
Dept. of the Interior . . . C2
Dept. of the Treasury . . . D2
Dept. of Transportation . . . G4
Dept. of Veterans Affairs . . . D1
District of Columbia Court House . . . E2
District of Columbia War Memorial . . . C3
Donald W. Reynolds Center for American Art & Portraiture . . . E2
The Ellipse . . . D2
Environmental Protection Agency . . . D2
Fish Wharf . . . D4
Folger Shakespeare Library . . . G3
Ford's Theatre Natl. Hist. Site . . . E2
Franklin Delano Roosevelt Memorial . . . C3
Freer Gallery of Art . . . D3
Friendship Archway . . . E1
Gallaudet Univ. . . . G1
George Mason Memorial . . . C4
Georgetown Univ. Law Center . . . F2
George Washington Univ. . . . C2
Government Publishing Office . . . F1
Hirshhorn Mus. & Sculpture Garden . . . E3
Ice Skating Rink . . . E2
Internal Revenue Service . . . E2
International Spy Museum . . . E3
James Madison Building . . . G3
J. Edgar Hoover FBI Building . . . E2
John Adams Building . . . G3
John Ericsson Memorial . . . B3
John F. Kennedy Center for the Performing Arts . . . B2
John F. Kennedy Gravesite . . . A4
Judiciary Square . . . E2
Korean War Veterans Memorial . . . C3
Koshland Science Museum . . . E2
Lafayette Square . . . D1
Lansburgh Theatre . . . E2
L'Enfant Plaza . . . E3
Library of Congress . . . G3
Lincoln Memorial . . . B3
Lyndon B. Johnson Memorial Grove . . . B4
The Mall . . . E3
Marine Corps War Memorial (Iwo Jima Memorial) . . . A3
Martin Luther King, Jr. Mem. Library . . . E2
Martin Luther King, Jr. Natl. Memorial . . . C3
Museum of the Bible . . . E3
NASA . . . E4
Natl. Air & Space Museum . . . E3
The Natl. Archives . . . E2
Natl. Building Museum . . . E2
Natl. Gallery of Art East Building . . . E3
Natl. Gallery of Art West Building . . . E2
Natl. Geographic Society & Explorers Hall . . . D1
Natl. Mus. of African Art . . . E3
Natl. Mus. of African Amerian Hist. & Culture . . . D3
Natl. Mus. of American Hist. . . . E2
Natl. Mus. of Natural Hist. . . . E2
Natl. Mus. of the American Indian . . . E3
Natl. Mus. of Women in the Arts . . . D1
Natl. Postal Museum . . . F2
Natl. Theatre . . . D2
Natl. WWI Memorial . . . D2
Natl. WWII Memorial . . . C3
Navy-Merchant Marine Memorial . . . C4
The Netherlands Carillon . . . A3
Newseum . . . E2
Octagon House . . . C2
Old Stone House . . . B1
Organization of American States . . . C2
Reflecting Pool . . . C3
Renwick Gallery . . . C2
Ronald Reagan Building and Intl. Trade Center . . . D2
Seabees of the U.S. Navy Memorial . . . A3
The Shops at Georgetown Park . . . A1
Sidney Harman Hall . . . E2
Signers of the Declaration of Independence Memorial . . . C3
Smithsonian Institution Building (The Castle) . . . E3
The Supreme Court . . . G3
Taft Memorial Carillon . . . F2
Theodore Roosevelt Memorial . . . A2
Thomas Jefferson Building . . . G3
Thomas Jefferson Memorial . . . D4
Union Station . . . F2
United Spanish War Veterans Memorial . . . A3
U.S. Botanic Garden . . . F3
U.S. Capitol . . . F3
U.S. Capitol Visitor Center . . . F3
U.S. Claims Court . . . D1
U.S. District Court House . . . E2
U.S. Grant Memorial . . . F3
U.S. Holocaust Memorial Museum . . . D3
U.S. Navy Memorial & Naval Heritage Center . . . E2
U.S. Postal Service Headquarters . . . E3
Verizon Center . . . E2
Vietnam Veterans Memorial . . . C2
Vietnam Women's Memorial . . . C3
Warner Theatre . . . D2
Washington Convention Center . . . E1
The Washington Design Center . . . D1
Washington Harbour . . . A1
Washington Monument . . . D3
Washington Post . . . D1
The White House . . . D2
White House Visitor Center . . . D2
Women in Military Service for America Memorial . . . A4
Zero Milestone . . . D2

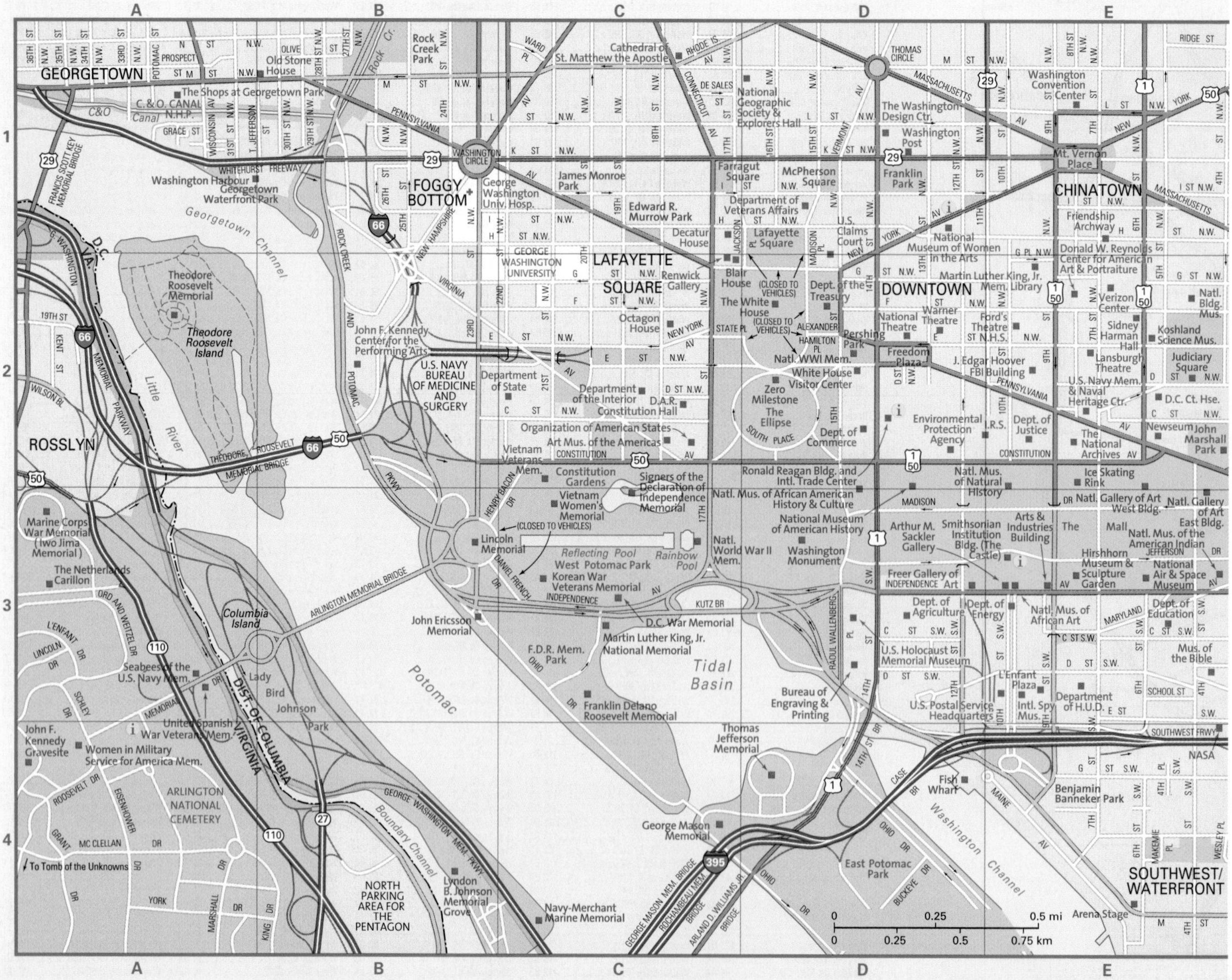

Entries in **bold black** indicate counties or parishes.
Entries in **bold color** indicate cities with detailed inset maps.

Wernersville PA, *2494* …… **146** A2
Weslaco TX, *35670* …… **63** E4
Wesley Chapel FL, *44092* …… **140** C2
Wesley Chapel NC, *7463* …… **122** B2
Wesley Hills NY, *5628* …… **148** B2
Wesleyville PA, *3341* …… **92** A1
Wessington SD, *170* …… **27** D3
Wessington Sprs. SD, *956* …… **27** D3
Wesson MS, *1925* …… **126** B4
West TX, *2807* …… **59** E3
W. Alexandria OH, *1340* …… **100** B1
W. Allis WI, *60411* …… **74** C3
W. Alton MO, *522* …… **98** A3
W. Babylon NY, *43213* …… **148** C4
W. Baden Sprs. IN, *574* …… **99** F3
W. Baraboo WI, *1248* …… **74** A2
W. Barnstable MA, *1500* …… **151** E3
W. Barrington RI, *4500* …… **150** C3
W. Baton Rouge Par. LA, *23788* …… **134** A2
W. Bend IA, *785* …… **72** B3
W. Bend WI, *31078* …… **74** C2
W. Berlin NJ, *4000* …… **147** D3
W. Blocton AL, *1240* …… **127** F1
Westborough MA, *4045* …… **150** C1
W. Bountiful UT, *5265* …… **31** E4
W. Bowdoin ME, *325* …… **82** B3
W. Boylston MA, *7669* …… **150** C1
W. Branch IA, *2322* …… **87** F2
W. Branch MI, *2139* …… **76** B1
W. Bridgewater MA, *6634* …… **151** D2
Westbrook CT, *6599* …… **149** E2
Westbrook ME, *17494* …… **82** B3
Westbrook MN, *739* …… **72** A1
W. Brookfield MA, *1413* …… **150** B1
W. Buechel KY, *1230* …… **230** E2
W. Burke VT, *343* …… **81** E1
W. Burlington IA, *2968* …… **87** F3
Westbury NY, *15146* …… **148** C4
W. Buxton ME, *425* …… **82** B3
Westby WI, *2200* …… **73** F2
W. Caldwell NJ, *10759* …… **240** A2
W. Carroll Par. LA, *11604* …… **125** F2
W. Carrollton OH, *13143* …… **100** B1
W. Carthage NY, *2012* …… **79** E1
Westchester IL, *16718* …… **203** C4
W. Chester PA, *18461* …… **146** B3
Westchester Co. NY, *949113* …… **148** B2
W. Chicago IL, *27086* …… **203** A4
West City IL, *661* …… **98** C4
Westcliffe CO, *568* …… **41** D3
W. College Corner IN, *676* …… **100** B1
W. Columbia SC, *14988* …… **205** E2
W. Columbia TX, *3905* …… **132** A4
W. Concord MA, *6028* …… **150** C1
W. Concord MN, *782* …… **73** D1
W. Conshohocken PA, *1320* …… **248** B2
W. Covina CA, *106098* …… **228** E2
W. Creek NJ, *1500* …… **147** E4
W. Crossett AR, *1256* …… **125** F1
W. Dennis MA, *2242* …… **151** F3
W. Des Moines IA, *56609* …… **86** C2
W. Dummerston VT, *325* …… **94** C1
W. Dundee IL, *7331* …… **88** C1
W. Elmira NY, *4967* …… **93** D1
W. End AL, *3924* …… **120** A4
W. Enfield ME, *350* …… **85** D4
Westerly RI, *17936* …… **150** B4
Western Grove AR, *384* …… **107** D4
Westernport MD, *1888* …… **102** B2
Western Sprs. IL, *12975* …… **203** C5
Westerville OH, *36120* …… **90** C4
W. Fairlee VT, *726* …… **81** E3
W. Fairview PA, *1282* …… **218** A1
W. Falmouth ME, *950* …… **251** A1
W. Falmouth MA, *1738* …… **151** E4
W. Fargo ND, *25830* …… **19** E4
W. Feliciana Par. LA, *15625* …… **133** F1
Westfield IL, *601* …… **99** D2
Westfield IN, *30068* …… **89** F4
Westfield MA, *41094* …… **150** A2
Westfield NJ, *30316* …… **147** E1
Westfield NY, *3224* …… **78** A4
Westfield PA, *1064* …… **93** D1
Westfield TX, *1700* …… **132** A3
Westfield WI, *1254* …… **74** B2
Westfield Ctr. OH, *1115* …… **91** E3
W. Fork AR, *2317* …… **106** C4
W. Frankfort IL, *8182* …… **98** C4
W. Freehold NJ, *13613* …… **147** E2
W. Friendship MD, *700* …… **144** B2
W. Gate of Lomond VA, *7493* …… **144** A3
W. Glacier MT, *125* …… **15** D2
W. Glens Falls NY, *7071* …… **80** C4
W. Grove PA, *2854* …… **146** B3
W. Hamlin WV, *774* …… **101** E4
Westhampton NY, *3079* …… **149** E3
Westhampton Beach NY, *1721* …… **149** E4
W. Hartford CT, *63268* …… **150** A3
W. Hartford VT, *375* …… **81** E3
W. Haven CT, *55564* …… **149** D2
W. Haven UT, *10272* …… **244** A1
W. Hazleton PA, *4594* …… **93** E3
W. Helena AR, *8689* …… **118** A2
W. Hollywood CA, *34399* …… **228** C2
W. Homestead PA, *1929* …… **250** C2
Westhope ND, *429* …… **18** B1
W. Hurley NY, *1939* …… **94** B2
W. Islip NY, *28335* …… **148** C4
W. Jefferson NC, *1299* …… **111** F3
W. Jefferson OH, *4222* …… **101** D1
W. Jordan UT, *103712* …… **31** E4
W. Kennebunk ME, *1176* …… **82** B4
W. Kingston RI, *500* …… **150** C4
W. Kittanning PA, *1175* …… **92** A3
W. Lafayette IN, *29596* …… **89** E4
W. Lafayette OH, *2321* …… **91** E4
Westlake LA, *4568* …… **133** D2
Westlake OH, *32729* …… **91** E2
W. Lake Hills TX, *3063* …… **61** E1
Westlake Vil. CA, *8270* …… **52** B2
Westland MI, *84094* …… **76** B4
W. Lebanon IN, *723* …… **89** D4
W. Leechburg PA, *1294* …… **92** A3
Westley CA, *603* …… **36** C4
W. Liberty IA, *3736* …… **87** F2
W. Liberty KY, *3435* …… **101** D4
W. Liberty OH, *1805* …… **90** B4
W. Liberty WV, *1542* …… **91** F4
W. Linn OR, *25109* …… **20** C2
W. Logan WV, *424* …… **101** E4
W. Long Branch NJ, *8097* …… **147** F2
W. Mahopac NY, *2700* …… **148** B2
W. Mansfield OH, *682* …… **90** C4
W. Mayfield PA, *1239* …… **91** F3
W. Medway MA, *3500* …… **150** C2
W. Melbourne FL, *18355* …… **141** E2
W. Memphis AR, *26245* …… **118** B1
Westmere NY, *7284* …… **94** B1
W. Miami FL, *5965* …… **143** E2
W. Middlesex PA, *863* …… **91** F2
W. Mifflin PA, *20313* …… **250** C3
W. Milford NJ, *27839* …… **148** A2
W. Milford WV, *630* …… **102** A2
W. Milton OH, *4630* …… **100** B1
W. Milwaukee WI, *4206* …… **234** C3
Westminster CA, *89701* …… **228** E4
Westminster CO, *106114* …… **41** E1
Westminster MD, *18590* …… **144** B1
Westminster MA, *7277* …… **95** D1
Westminster SC, *2418* …… **121** E2
Westminster VT, *291* …… **81** E4
W. Monroe LA, *13065* …… **125** E2
Westmont IL, *24685* …… **203** C5
Westmont PA, *5181* …… **92** B4
Westmoreland KS, *778* …… **43** F2
Westmoreland TN, *2206* …… **109** F3
Westmoreland Co. PA, *365169* …… **92** B4
Westmoreland Co. VA, *17454* …… **103** E4
Westmorland CA, *2225* …… **53** E4
W. Mystic CT, *3600* …… **149** F2
W. Newton PA, *2633* …… **92** A4
W. New York NJ, *49708* …… **148** B4
W. Odessa TX, *22707* …… **57** F3
W. Okoboji IA, *289* …… **72** A3
Weston CT, *10276* …… **148** C2
Weston FL, *65333* …… **143** E2
Weston ID, *437* …… **31** E2
Weston MO, *1641* …… **96** B2
Weston NE, *324* …… **35** F3
Weston OH, *1590* …… **90** B2
Weston OR, *667* …… **21** F1
Weston TX, *563* …… **59** F1
Weston WV, *4110* …… **102** A2
Weston WI, *14868* …… **68** B4
Weston Co. WY, *7208* …… **25** F4
Weston Lakes TX, *2482* …… **132** A3
Weston Mills NY, *1472* …… **92** C1
W. Orange NJ, *46207* …… **148** A4
W. Orange TX, *3443* …… **132** C3
W. Ossipee NH, *325* …… **81** F3
Westover TN, *900* …… **118** C1
Westover Hills TX, *682* …… **207** A2
W. Palm Beach FL, *99919* …… **143** F1
W. Paris ME, *1722* …… **82** B2
W. Pelham MA, *1300* …… **150** A1
W. Pelzer SC, *880* …… **121** E2
W. Pensacola FL, *21339* …… **135** F2
W. Peoria IL, *4458* …… **88** B3
Westphalia MI, *923* …… **76** A3
W. Pittston PA, *4868* …… **261** C1
W. Plains MO, *11986* …… **107** E3
W. Point CA, *674* …… **36** C3
W. Point GA, *3474* …… **128** B1
Westpoint IN, *425* …… **89** E4
W. Point IA, *966* …… **87** F3
W. Point KY, *797* …… **99** F4
W. Point MS, *11307* …… **119** D4
W. Point NE, *3364* …… **35** F2
W. Point UT, *9511* …… **31** E3
W. Point VA, *3306* …… **113** F1
Westport CT, *26391* …… **148** C2
Westport IN, *1379* …… **100** A2
Westport KY, *268* …… **100** A3
Westport NY, *518* …… **81** D2
Westport OR, *321* …… **20** B1
Westport WA, *2099* …… **12** B4
W. Portsmouth OH, *3149* …… **101** D3
W. Redding CT, *500* …… **148** C2
W. Richland WA, *11811* …… **13** E4
W. Rockport ME, *425* …… **82** C2
W. Rutland VT, *2024* …… **81** D3
W. Sacramento CA, *48744* …… **36** C3
W. St. Paul MN, *19540* …… **235** D3
W. Salem IL, *897* …… **99** D3
W. Salem OH, *1464* …… **91** D3
W. Salem WI, *4799* …… **73** F2
W. Sand Lake NY, *2660* …… **94** B1
W. Sayville NY, *5011* …… **149** D4
W. Selmont AL, *3502* …… **127** F2
W. Seneca NY, *44711* …… **78** B3
W. Siloam Sprs. OK, *846* …… **106** B4
W. Slope OR, *6554* …… **251** C2
W. Springfield MA, *28391* …… **150** A2
W. Springfield VA, *22460* …… **270** A5
W. Sterling MA, *450* …… **150** B1
W. Stockbridge MA, *1416* …… **94** B2
W. Suffield CT, *600* …… **150** A2
W. Swanzey NH, *1308* …… **95** D1
W. Tawakoni TX, *1576* …… **59** F2
W. Terre Haute IN, *2236* …… **99** E2
W. Topsham VT, *175* …… **81** E2
Westtown NY, *700* …… **148** A2
W. Townshend VT, *150* …… **81** E4
W. Union IA, *2486* …… **73** E3
W. Union OH, *3241* …… **100** C3
W. Union WV, *825* …… **101** F2
W. Unity OH, *1671* …… **90** B2
W. University Place TX, *14787* …… **132** A3
W. Upton MA, *2326* …… **150** C2
Westvale NY, *4963* …… **265** A2
W. Valley City UT, *129480* …… **31** E4
W. View PA, *6771* …… **250** B1
Westville IL, *3202* …… **99** D1
Westville IN, *5853* …… **89** E2
Westville NJ, *4288* …… **248** C4
Westville OK, *1639* …… **106** B4
W. Wareham MA, *2064* …… **151** E3
W. Warren MA, *1100* …… **150** B2
W. Warwick RI, *29191* …… **150** C3
Westway TX, *4188* …… **56** C3
Westwego LA, *8534* …… **134** B3
W. Wendover NV, *4410* …… **31** D4
W. Willington CT, *450* …… **150** A3
W. Winfield NY, *826* …… **79** F3
Westwood CA, *1647* …… **29** D4
Westwood KS, *1506* …… **224** B3
Westwood KY, *4746* …… **101** D3
Westwood MA, *14618* …… **151** D2
Westwood NJ, *10908* …… **148** B3
Westwood Lakes FL, *11838* …… **143** E2
Westworth Vil. TX, *2472* …… **207** A2
W. Wyoming PA, *2725* …… **261** B1
W. Yarmouth MA, *6012* …… **151** F3
W. Yellowstone MT, *1271* …… **23** F3
W. York PA, *4617* …… **275** C1
Wethersfield CT, *26668* …… **150** A3
Wetmore KS, *368* …… **96** A1
Wetumka OK, *1282* …… **51** F3
Wetumpka AL, *6528* …… **128** A2
Wetzel Co. WV, *16583* …… **102** A1
Wewahitchka FL, *1981* …… **137** D2
Wewoka OK, *3430* …… **51** F3

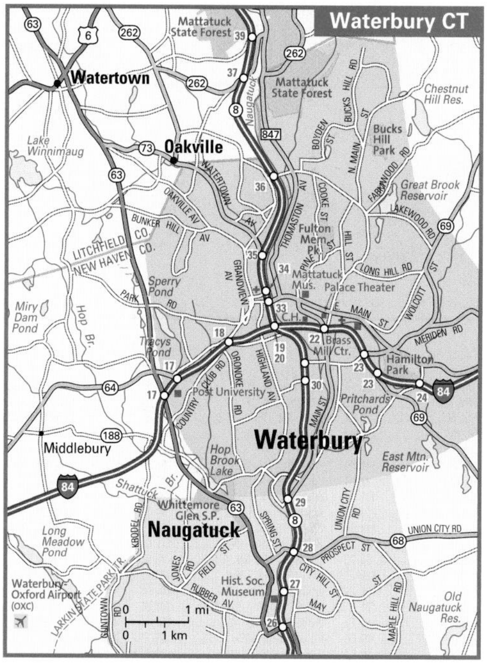

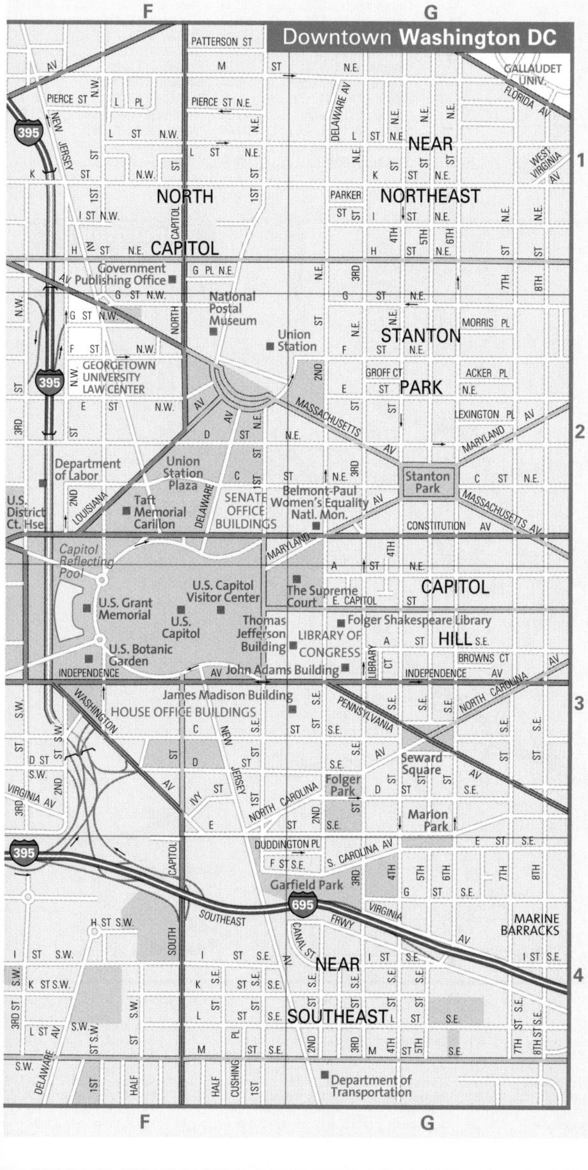

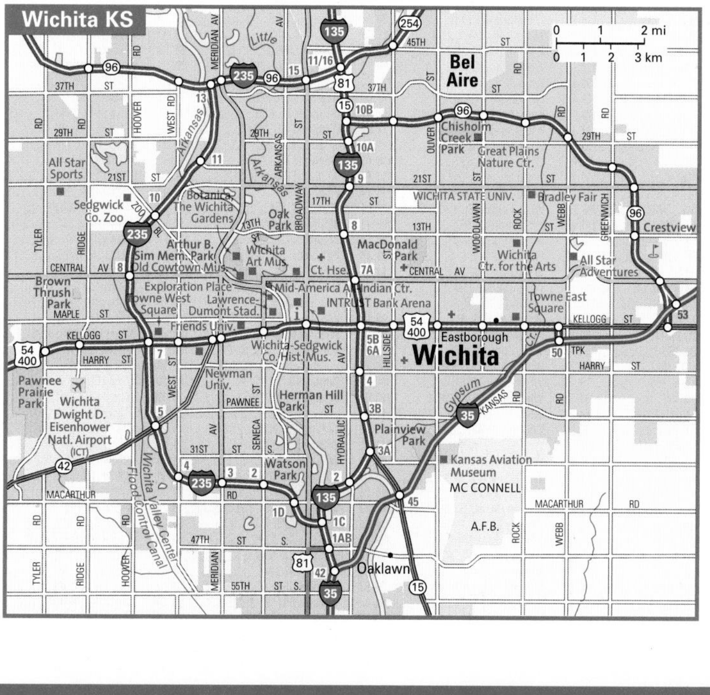

Figures after entries indicate population, page number, and grid reference.

Wexford Co. MI, 32735 ... 69 F4
Weyauwega WI, 1900 ... 74 B1
Weyers Cave VA, 2473 ... 102 C4
Weymouth MA, 53743 ... 151 D2
Wharton NJ, 6522 ... 148 A3
Wharton OH, 358 ... 90 C3
Wharton TX, 8832 ... 61 F3
Wharton Co. TX, 41280 ... 61 F3
What Cheer IA, 646 ... 87 E2
Whatcom Co. WA, 201140 ... 12 C1
Whately MA, 425 ... 150 A1
Wheatfield IN, 853 ... 89 E2
Wheatland CA, 3456 ... 36 C2
Wheatland IN, 480 ... 99 E3
Wheatland IA, 764 ... 87 F1
Wheatland WY, 3627 ... 33 E2
Wheatland Co. MT, 2168 ... 16 B4
Wheatley AR, 355 ... 118 A2
Wheaton IL, 52894 ... 89 D1
Wheaton MD, 48284 ... 144 B3
Wheaton MN, 1424 ... 27 F1
Wheaton MO, 696 ... 106 C2
Wheat Ridge CO, 30166 ... 209 B3
Wheeler MS, 300 ... 119 D2
Wheeler OR, 414 ... 20 B1
Wheeler TX, 1592 ... 50 C3
Wheeler Co. GA, 7421 ... 129 E3
Wheeler Co. NE, 818 ... 35 D2
Wheeler Co. OR, 1441 ... 21 E3
Wheeler Co. TX, 5410 ... 50 C3
Wheelersburg OH, 6437 ... 101 D3
Wheeling IL, 37648 ... 89 D1
Wheeling WV, 28486 ... 91 F4
Wheelwright KY, 780 ... 111 E1
Wheelwright MA, 425 ... 150 B1
Whigham GA, 471 ... 137 E1
Whippany NJ, 3800 ... 148 A3
Whispering Pines NC, 2928 ... 122 C1
Whitaker PA, 1271 ... 250 C2
Whitakers NC, 744 ... 113 E4
White GA, 670 ... 120 C3
White SD, 485 ... 27 F3
White Bear Lake MN, 23797 ... 235 D1
White Bird ID, 91 ... 22 B1
White Bluff TN, 3206 ... 109 E4
White Castle LA, 1883 ... 134 A2
White Ctr. WA, 13495 ... 262 B4
White City FL, 3719 ... 141 E3
White City KS, 618 ... 43 F2
White City OR, 7975 ... 28 B2
White Cloud MI, 1408 ... 75 F2
White Co. AR, 77076 ... 117 F1
White Co. GA, 27144 ... 121 D2
White Co. IL, 14665 ... 99 D4
White Co. IN, 24643 ... 89 E3
White Co. TN, 25841 ... 110 A4
White Deer TX, 1000 ... 50 B3
White Earth MN, 580 ... 19 F3
Whiteface TX, 449 ... 57 F1
Whitefield NH, 1142 ... 81 F2
Whitefish MT, 6357 ... 15 D2
Whitefish Bay WI, 14110 ... 234 D1
Whiteford MD, 700 ... 146 A4
White Hall AL, 858 ... 127 F2
White Hall AR, 5526 ... 117 E3
White Hall IL, 2520 ... 98 A2
Whitehall MI, 2706 ... 75 E2
Whitehall MT, 1038 ... 23 E1
Whitehall NY, 2614 ... 81 D3
Whitehall OH, 18062 ... 206 C2
Whitehall PA, 14268 ... 146 B1
Whitehall PA, 13944 ... 250 B3
Whitehall VA, 250 ... 102 C4
White Hall VA, 300 ... 103 D2
White Hall WV, 648 ... 102 A2
Whitehall WI, 1558 ... 73 F1
White Haven PA, 1097 ... 93 F3
White Horse NJ, 9494 ... 147 D2
White Horse PA, 475 ... 146 A3
White Horse Beach MA, 2300 ... 151 E3
Whitehouse OH, 4149 ... 90 B2
White House TN, 10255 ... 109 F3
Whitehouse TX, 7660 ... 124 B3
White House Sta. NJ, 2089 ... 147 D1
White Island Shores MA, 2106 ... 151 E3
White Lake NY, 475 ... 94 A3
White Lake NC, 802 ... 123 D2
White Lake SD, 372 ... 27 D4
Whiteland IN, 4169 ... 99 F1
Whitelaw WI, 757 ... 75 D1
White Marsh MD, 9513 ... 193 E2
White Marsh VA, 600 ... 113 F1
White Oak MD, 17403 ... 270 D1
White Oak OH, 19167 ... 204 A2
White Oak PA, 7862 ... 92 A4
White Oak TX, 6469 ... 124 B2
White Pigeon MI, 1522 ... 89 F1
White Pine MI, 474 ... 65 E4
White Pine TN, 2196 ... 111 D4
White Pine Co. NV, 10030 ... 38 B1
White Plains KY, 884 ... 109 E2
White Plains MD, 3600 ... 144 B4
White Plains NY, 56853 ... 148 B3
White Plains NC, 1074 ... 112 A3
Whiteriver AZ, 4104 ... 55 E1
White River SD, 581 ... 26 C4
White River Jct. VT, 2286 ... 81 E3
White Rock NM, 5725 ... 48 C2
Whiterocks UT, 289 ... 32 A4
White Salmon WA, 2224 ... 21 D1
Whitesboro NY, 3772 ... 79 E3
Whitesboro TX, 3793 ... 59 F1
Whitesburg GA, 588 ... 120 B4
Whitesburg KY, 2139 ... 111 D2
White Settlement TX, 16116 ... 207 A2
White Shield ND, 336 ... 18 B3
Whiteside Co. IL, 58498 ... 88 A1
White Sprs. FL, 777 ... 138 C2
White Stone VA, 352 ... 113 F1
White Sulphur Sprs. MT, 939 ... 15 F4
White Sulphur Sprs. WV, 2444 ... 112 B1
Whitesville KY, 552 ... 109 F1
Whitesville NY, 400 ... 92 C1
Whitesville WV, 514 ... 101 F4
White Swan WA, 793 ... 13 D4
Whiteville NC, 5394 ... 123 D3
Whiteville TN, 4638 ... 118 C1
Whitewater KS, 718 ... 43 E3
Whitewater WI, 14390 ... 74 C3
Whitewood SD, 927 ... 25 F3
Whitewright TX, 1604 ... 59 F1
Whitfield FL, 2882 ... 140 B3
Whitfield Co. GA, 102599 ... 120 B2
Whiting IN, 4997 ... 89 D2
Whiting IA, 762 ... 35 F2
Whiting NJ, 1800 ... 147 E3
Whiting WI, 1724 ... 68 B4
Whitinsville MA, 6704 ... 150 C2
Whitley City KY, 1170 ... 110 C3
Whitley Co. IN, 33292 ... 89 F3
Whitley Co. KY, 35637 ... 110 C2
Whitman MA, 14489 ... 151 D2
Whitman Co. WA, 44776 ... 14 A4
Whitmire SC, 1441 ... 121 F3
Whitmore Lake MI, 6423 ... 76 B4
Whitmore Vil. HI, 4499 ... 152 A2
Whitney TX, 2087 ... 59 E3
Whitney Pt. NY, 964 ... 79 E4
Whitsett NC, 590 ... 112 B4
Whittemore IA, 504 ... 72 B3
Whittemore MI, 384 ... 76 B1
Whittier CA, 85331 ... 52 C2
Whitwell TN, 1699 ... 120 B1
Why AZ, 167 ... 54 B3
Wibaux MT, 589 ... 17 F4
Wibaux Co. MT, 1017 ... 17 F4
Wichita KS, 382368 ... 43 E4
Wichita Co. KS, 2234 ... 42 B3
Wichita Co. TX, 131500 ... 59 D1
Wichita Falls TX, 104553 ... 59 D1
Wickenburg AZ, 6363 ... 54 B1
Wickes AR, 754 ... 116 C3
Wickett TX, 498 ... 57 F4
Wickford RI, 1900 ... 150 C4
Wickliffe KY, 688 ... 108 C2
Wickliffe OH, 12750 ... 91 E2
Wicomico Church VA, 250 ... 113 F1
Wicomico Co. MD, 98733 ... 114 C1
Widefield CO, 29845 ... 205 D2
Wiggins CO, 893 ... 33 F4
Wiggins MS, 4390 ... 135 D1
Wilbarger Co. TX, 13535 ... 58 C1
Wilber NE, 1855 ... 35 F4
Wilberforce OH, 2271 ... 100 C1
Wilbraham MA, 3915 ... 150 A2
Wilbur WA, 884 ... 13 F3
Wilbur Park MO, 471 ... 256 B3
Wilburton OK, 2843 ... 116 A2
Wilcox NE, 358 ... 35 D4
Wilcox PA, 383 ... 92 B2
Wilcox Co. AL, 11670 ... 127 F3
Wilcox Co. GA, 9255 ... 129 E3
Wilder ID, 1533 ... 22 A4
Wilder KY, 3035 ... 204 B3
Wilder VT, 1690 ... 81 E3
Wilderness VA, 300 ... 103 D4
Wildomar CA, 32176 ... 53 D3
Wild Rose WI, 725 ... 74 B1
Wildwood FL, 6709 ... 140 C1
Wildwood MO, 35517 ... 98 A3
Wildwood NJ, 5325 ... 104 C4
Wildwood TX, 1235 ... 132 C2
Wildwood Crest NJ, 3270 ... 104 C4
Wiley CO, 405 ... 42 A3
Wilhoit AZ, 868 ... 47 D4
Wilkes-Barre PA, 41498 ... 93 E2
Wilkesboro NC, 3413 ... 111 F4
Wilkes Co. GA, 10593 ... 121 E4
Wilkes Co. NC, 69340 ... 112 A3
Wilkeson WA, 477 ... 12 C3
Wilkin Co. MN, 6576 ... 19 F4
Wilkinsburg PA, 15930 ... 250 C2
Wilkinson Co. GA, 9563 ... 129 E2
Wilkinson Co. MS, 9878 ... 125 F4
Willacoochee GA, 1391 ... 129 E4
Willacy Co. TX, 22134 ... 63 F3
Willamina OR, 2025 ... 20 B2
Willard MO, 5288 ... 107 D2
Willard NM, 253 ... 49 D4
Willard OH, 6236 ... 91 D3
Willard UT, 1772 ... 31 E3
Willards MD, 958 ... 114 C1
Will Co. IL, 677560 ... 89 D2
Willcox AZ, 3757 ... 55 E3
Willernie MN, 507 ... 235 E1
Williams AZ, 3023 ... 47 D3
Williams CA, 5123 ... 36 B2
Williams IA, 344 ... 72 C4
Williams OR, 1072 ... 28 B2
Williams Bay WI, 2564 ... 74 C4
Williamsburg CO, 662 ... 41 E3
Williamsburg FL, 7646 ... 246 B4
Williamsburg IA, 3068 ... 87 E2
Williamsburg KS, 397 ... 96 A3
Williamsburg KY, 5245 ... 110 C3
Williamsburg MA, 550 ... 150 A1
Williamsburg NM, 449 ... 56 B2
Williamsburg OH, 2490 ... 100 C2
Williamsburg PA, 1254 ... 92 C4
Williamsburg VA, 14068 ... 113 F2
Williamsburg Co. SC, 34423 ... 122 C4
Williams Co. ND, 22398 ... 17 F2
Williams Co. OH, 37642 ... 90 A2
Williams Creek IN, 407 ... 221 C1
Williamsfield IL, 578 ... 88 A3
Williamson NY, 2495 ... 78 C3
Williamson WV, 3191 ... 111 E1
Williamson Co. IL, 66357 ... 108 C1
Williamson Co. TN, 183182 ... 109 F4
Williamson Co. TX, 422679 ... 61 E1
Williamsport IN, 1898 ... 89 D4
Williamsport MD, 2137 ... 103 D1
Williamsport OH, 1023 ... 101 D1
Williamsport PA, 29381 ... 93 D2
Williamston MI, 3854 ... 76 A4
Williamston NC, 5511 ... 113 E4
Williamston SC, 3934 ... 121 E2
Williamstown KY, 3925 ... 100 B3
Williamstown MA, 4325 ... 94 C1
Williamstown NJ, 15567 ... 146 C4
Williamstown NY, 475 ... 79 E2
Williamstown PA, 1387 ... 93 E4
Williamstown VT, 1162 ... 81 E2
Williamstown WV, 2908 ... 101 F2
Williamsville DE, 350 ... 114 C1
Williamsville IL, 1476 ... 98 B1
Williamsville MS, 400 ... 126 C1
Williamsville NY, 5300 ... 198 C2
Willimantic CT, 17737 ... 150 B3
Willingboro NJ, 36530 ... 147 D3
Willis TX, 5662 ... 132 A2
Willisburg KY, 282 ... 110 B1
Williston FL, 2768 ... 138 C4
Williston MD, 155 ... 145 E3
Williston ND, 14716 ... 17 F2
Williston OH, 487 ... 90 C2
Williston SC, 3139 ... 130 B1
Williston TN, 395 ... 118 C1
Williston VT, 8698 ... 81 D2
Willisville IL, 633 ... 98 B4
Willis Wharf VA, 475 ... 114 B3
Willits CA, 4888 ... 36 A2
Willmar MN, 19610 ... 66 B3
Willoughby OH, 22268 ... 91 E2
Willoughby Hills OH, 9485 ... 204 G1
Willow AK, 2102 ... 154 C3
Willowbrook CA, 35983 ... 228 D3
Willowbrook IL, 8540 ... 203 C5
Willow City ND, 163 ... 18 C2
Willow Creek CA, 1710 ... 28 B4
Willow Creek MT, 210 ... 23 E1
Willow Grove PA, 15726 ... 146 C2
Willowick OH, 14171 ... 91 E2
Willow Lake SD, 263 ... 27 E3
Willow Park TX, 3982 ... 59 E2
Willows CA, 6166 ... 36 B1
Willows MD, 900 ... 144 C4
Willow Sprs. IL, 5524 ... 203 C5
Willow Sprs. MO, 2184 ... 107 E2
Willow Street PA, 7578 ... 146 A3
Willsboro NY, 753 ... 81 D2
Willshire OH, 397 ... 90 A3
Wills Pt. TX, 3524 ... 59 F2
Willwood WY, 100 ... 24 B3
Wilmar AR, 511 ... 117 F4
Wilmer AL, 500 ... 135 E1
Wilmer TX, 3682 ... 207 E3
Wilmerding PA, 2190 ... 250 D3
Wilmette IL, 27087 ... 89 D1
Wilmington DE, 70851 ... 146 B4
Wilmington IL, 142 ... 88 C2
Wilmington NC, 106476 ... 123 E3
Wilmington OH, 12520 ... 100 C2
Wilmington VT, 463 ... 94 C1
Wilmington Island GA, 15138 ... 130 C3
Wilmington Manor DE, 7889 ... 274 D3
Wilmore KY, 3686 ... 100 B4
Wilmot AR, 550 ... 125 F1
Wilmot SD, 492 ... 27 F2
Wilsall MT, 178 ... 23 F1
Wilson AR, 903 ... 118 B1
Wilson KS, 781 ... 43 D2
Wilson LA, 595 ... 134 A1
Wilson NY, 1264 ... 78 B3
Wilson NC, 49167 ... 113 D4
Wilson OK, 1724 ... 51 E4
Wilson PA, 7896 ... 93 F3
Wilson TX, 489 ... 58 A2
Wilson WY, 1482 ... 23 F4
Wilson Co. KS, 9409 ... 106 A1
Wilson Co. NC, 81234 ... 113 E4
Wilson Co. TN, 113993 ... 109 F3
Wilson Co. TX, 42918 ... 61 E3
Wilson's Mills NC, 2277 ... 123 D1
Wilsonville AL, 1827 ... 128 A1
Wilsonville IL, 586 ... 98 B2
Wilsonville OR, 19509 ... 20 C2
Wilton AL, 687 ... 127 F1
Wilton AR, 374 ... 116 C4
Wilton CA, 5363 ... 36 C3
Wilton CT, 17960 ... 148 C2
Wilton IA, 2802 ... 87 F2
Wilton ME, 2198 ... 82 B2
Wilton NH, 1163 ... 95 D1
Wilton NY, 600 ... 80 C4
Wilton ND, 711 ... 18 C3
Wilton WI, 504 ... 73 F2
Wilton Manors FL, 11632 ... 233 C2
Wimauma FL, 6373 ... 140 C3
Wimberley TX, 2626 ... 61 D2
Wimbledon ND, 216 ... 19 D3
Winamac IN, 2490 ... 89 E3
Winchendon MA, 4213 ... 95 D1
Winchester CA, 2534 ... 53 D3
Winchester ID, 340 ... 22 B1
Winchester IL, 1593 ... 98 A1
Winchester IN, 4935 ... 90 A4
Winchester KS, 551 ... 96 A2
Winchester KY, 18368 ... 100 B4
Winchester MA, 21374 ... 151 D1
Winchester MO, 1547 ... 256 A2
Winchester NH, 1733 ... 94 C1
Winchester OH, 1051 ... 100 C3
Winchester OK, 516 ... 51 F2
Winchester TN, 8530 ... 120 A1
Winchester VA, 26203 ... 103 D2
Winchester Bay OR, 382 ... 20 A4
Windber PA, 4138 ... 92 B4
Windcrest TX, 5364 ... 61 D2
Winder GA, 14099 ... 121 D3
Windermere FL, 2462 ... 141 D1
Windfall IN, 708 ... 89 F4
Wind Gap PA, 2720 ... 93 F3
Windham CT, 23733 ... 149 F1
Windham NH, 13592 ... 95 E1
Windham OH, 2209 ... 91 F2
Windham Co. CT, 118428 ... 150 B3
Windham Co. VT, 44513 ... 81 E4
Wind Lake WI, 5342 ... 74 C3
Windom MN, 4646 ... 72 B2
Window Rock AZ, 2712 ... 48 A2
Wind Pt. WI, 1723 ... 75 D4
Windsor CA, 26801 ... 36 B3
Windsor CO, 18644 ... 33 E4
Windsor CT, 28778 ... 150 A3
Windsor IL, 1187 ... 98 C2
Windsor MO, 2901 ... 96 C3
Windsor NY, 916 ... 93 F1
Windsor NC, 3630 ... 113 F4
Windsor PA, 1319 ... 103 E1
Windsor VT, 2066 ... 81 E4
Windsor VA, 2626 ... 113 F2
Windsor WI, 6345 ... 74 B3
Windsor Co. VT, 56670 ... 81 E3
Windsor Hts. WV, 423 ... 91 F4
Windsor Hills CA, 10958 ... 228 C3
Windsor Locks CT, 12498 ... 150 A2
Windthorst TX, 409 ... 59 D1
Windy Hills KY, 2385 ... 230 E1
Winfall NC, 594 ... 113 F3
Winfield AL, 4717 ... 119 E4
Winfield IL, 9080 ... 203 B4
Winfield IN, 4383 ... 89 D2
Winfield IA, 1134 ... 87 F3
Winfield KS, 12301 ... 43 F4
Winfield MO, 1404 ... 98 A2
Winfield TN, 967 ... 110 C3
Winfield TX, 524 ... 124 B1
Winfield WV, 2301 ... 101 E3
Wingate NC, 3491 ... 122 B2
Wingdale NY, 1500 ... 148 C1
Wingo KY, 632 ... 108 C3
Winifred MT, 208 ... 16 B3
Wink TX, 940 ... 57 F4
Winkelman AZ, 353 ... 55 D2
Winkler Co. TX, 7110 ... 57 F3
Winlock WA, 1339 ... 12 B4
Winnebago IL, 3101 ... 74 B4
Winnebago MN, 1437 ... 72 C2
Winnebago NE, 774 ... 35 F2
Winnebago Co. IL, 295266 ... 74 B4
Winnebago Co. IA, 10866 ... 72 C2
Winnebago Co. WI, 166994 ... 74 C1
Winneconne WI, 2383 ... 74 C1

Five Forks ... A1
Gloucester Pt. ... C2
Hayes ... C1
Lackey ... C2
Newport News ... C2
Scotland ... A2
Wicomico ... C1
Williamsburg ... A1
Yorktown ... C2

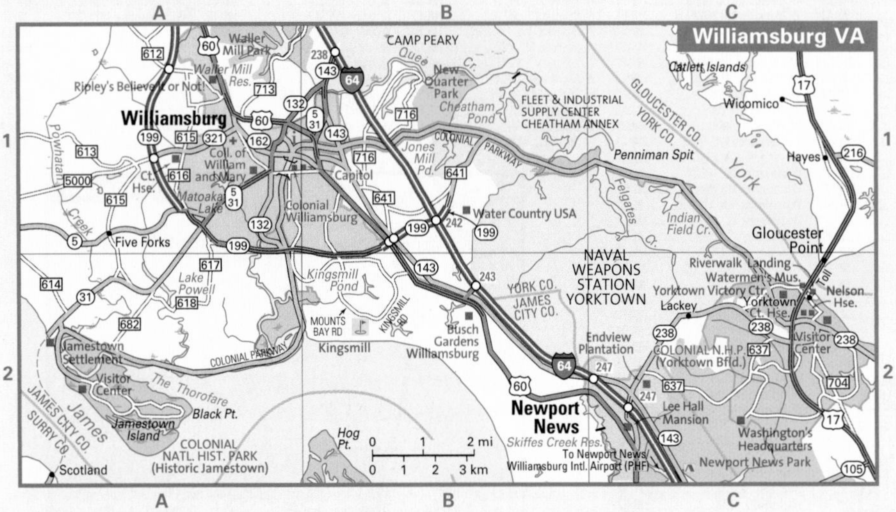

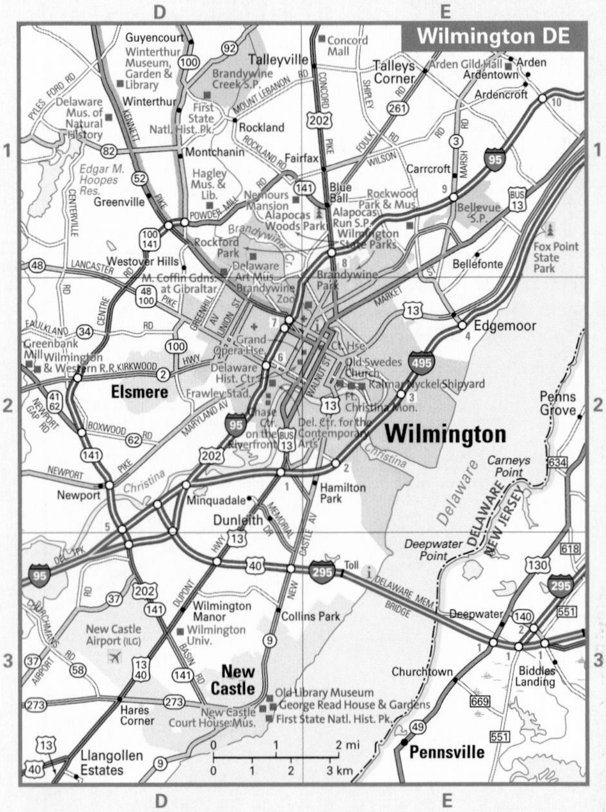

Arden ... E1
Ardencroft ... E1
Ardentown ... E1
Bellefonte ... E1
Biddles Landing ... E3
Blue Ball ... E1
Carrcroft ... E1
Churchtown ... E3
Collins Park ... D3
Deepwater ... E3
Dunleith ... D2
Edgemoor ... E2
Elsmere ... D2
Fairfax ... E1
Greenville ... D1
Guyencourt ... D1
Hamilton Park ... E2
Hares Corner ... D3
Llangollen Estates ... D3
Minquadale ... D2
Montchanin ... D1
New Castle ... D3
Newport ... D2
Penns Grove ... E2
Pennsville ... E3
Rockland ... D1
Talleys Corner ... E1
Talleyville ... E1
Westover Hills ... D1
Wilmington ... E2
Wilmington Manor ... D3
Winterthur ... D1

Entries in **bold black** indicate counties or parishes.
Entries in **bold color** indicate cities with detailed inset maps.

Winnecunnet MA, *750*..... **151** D2
Winnemucca NV, *7396*..... **30** A3
Winner SD, *2897*..... **26** C4
Winneshiek Co. IA, *21056*..... **73** E3
Winnetka IL, *12187*..... **203** D2
Winnett MT, *182*..... **16** C4
Winnfield LA, *4840*..... **125** E3
Winnie TX, *3254*..... **132** C3
Winnisquam NH, *850*..... **81** F4
Winn Par. LA, *15313*..... **125** E3
Winnsboro LA, *4910*..... **125** F3
Winnsboro SC, *3550*..... **122** A3
Winnsboro TX, *3434*..... **124** A1
Winnsboro Mills SC, *1898*..... **122** A3
Winona MN, *27592*..... **73** E1
Winona MS, *5043*..... **118** B4
Winona MO, *1335*..... **107** F2
Winona OH, *475*..... **91** F3
Winona TX, *576*..... **124** B2
Winona Co. MN, *51461*..... **73** E1
Winona Lake IN, *4908*..... **89** F2
Winooski VT, *7267*..... **81** D2
Winside NE, *427*..... **35** E2
Winslow AZ, *9655*..... **47** E3
Winslow AR, 391..... **106** C4
Winslow IN, *864*..... **99** E4
Winslow ME, *7794*..... **82** C2
Winslow NJ, *700*..... **147** D4
Winsted CT, *7712*..... **94** C2
Winsted MN, *2355*..... **66** C4
Winston OR, *5379*..... **28** B1
Winston Co. AL, *24484*..... **119** E3
Winston Co. MS, *19198*..... **127** D1
Winston-Salem NC, *229617*..... **112** B4
Winstonville MS, *191*..... **118** A4
Winter Beach FL, *2067*..... **141** E3
Winter Garden FL, *34568*..... **141** D1
Winter Harbor ME, *426*..... **83** D2
Winterhaven CA, *394*..... **53** F4
Winter Haven FL, *33874*..... **140** C2
Winter Park CO, *999*..... **41** D1
Winter Park FL, *27852*..... **141** D1
Winterport ME, *1340*..... **83** D2
Winters CA, *6624*..... **36** B3
Winters TX, *2562*..... **58** C3
Winterset IA, *5190*..... **86** C2
Winter Sprs. FL, *33282*..... **141** D1
Winterstown PA, *632*..... **103** E1
Wintersville OH, *3924*..... **91** F4
Winterville GA, *1122*..... **121** D4
Winterville NC, *9269*..... **115** D3
Winthrop CT, *400*..... **149** E2
Winthrop IA, *850*..... **73** E4
Winthrop ME, *2650*..... **82** B2
Winthrop MA, *17497*..... **151** D1
Winthrop MN, *1399*..... **66** C4
Winthrop NY, *510*..... **80** B1
Winthrop Harbor IL, *6742*..... **75** D4
Winton CA, *10613*..... **36** C4
Winton NC, *769*..... **113** F3
Wirt Co. WV, *5717*..... **101** F2
Wiscasset ME, *1097*..... **82** C3
Wisconsin Dells WI, *2678*..... **74** A2
Wisconsin Rapids WI, *18367*..... **74** A1
Wisdom MT, *98*..... **23** D1
Wise VA, *3286*..... **111** E2
Wise Co. TX, *59127*..... **59** E2
Wise Co. VA, *41452*..... **111** E2
Wishek ND, *1002*..... **27** D1
Wisner LA, *964*..... **125** F3
Wisner NE, *1170*..... **35** F2
Wister OK, *1102*..... **116** B2
Withamsville OH, *7021*..... **204** C3
Withee WI, *487*..... **68** A4
Witherbee NY, *347*..... **81** D2
Witt IL, *903*..... **98** B2
Witt TN, *500*..... **111** D4
Wittenberg WI, *1081*..... **68** B4
Wittmann AZ, *763*..... **54** B1
Wixom MI, *13498*..... **76** B4
Woburn MA, *38120*..... **151** D1
Wofford KY, *375*..... **110** C2
Wofford Hts. CA, *2200*..... **45** E4
Wolcott CT, *16228*..... **149** D1
Wolcott IN, *1001*..... **89** E3
Wolcott NY, *1701*..... **79** D3
Wolcottville IN, *998*..... **90** A2
Wolfdale PA, *2888*..... **91** F4
Wolfeboro NH, *2838*..... **81** F3
Wolfeboro Falls NH, *1000*..... **81** F3
Wolfe City TX, *1412*..... **59** F1
Wolfe Co. KY, *7355*..... **111** D1
Wolfforth TX, *3670*..... **58** A1
Wolf Lake MI, *4104*..... **75** E3
Wolf Pt. MT, *2621*..... **17** E2
Wolsey SD, *376*..... **27** E3
Wolverine Lake MI, *4312*..... **210** A1
Womelsdorf PA, *2810*..... **146** A2
Wonewoc WI, *816*..... **74** A2
Wonnie KY, *250*..... **111** D1
Woodacre CA, *1348*..... **259** A1
Woodbine GA, *1412*..... **139** D1
Woodbine IA, *1459*..... **86** A1
Woodbine KY, *550*..... **110** C2
Woodbine MD, *425*..... **144** B2
Woodbine NJ, *2472*..... **104** C4
Woodbourne NY, *1600*..... **94** A3
Woodbourne OH, *7910*..... **208** E2
Woodbranch TX, *1282*..... **132** B2
Woodbridge CT, *9264*..... **149** D2
Woodbridge NJ, *19265*..... **147** E1
Woodbridge VA, *4055*..... **144** B4
Woodburn IN, *1520*..... **90** A3
Woodburn KY, *355*..... **109** F2
Woodburn OR, *24080*..... **20** B2
Woodbury CT, *9734*..... **149** D1
Woodbury GA, *961*..... **128** C1
Woodbury MN, *61961*..... **67** D4
Woodbury NJ, *10174*..... **146** C3
Woodbury TN, *2680*..... **110** A4
Woodbury VT, *200*..... **81** E2
Woodbury Co. IA, *102172*..... **35** F2
Woodbury Hts. NJ, *3055*..... **146** C3
Wood Co. OH, *125488*..... **90** C2
Wood Co. TX, *41964*..... **124** A2
Wood Co. WV, *86956*..... **101** E2
Wood Co. WI, *74749*..... **68** A4
Woodcreek TX, *1457*..... **61** D2
Woodcrest CA, *14347*..... **229** J4
Wood Dale IL, *13770*..... **203** C3
Woodfield MD, *2500*..... **144** B2
Woodfin NC, *6123*..... **111** E4
Woodford Co. IL, *38664*..... **88** B3
Woodford Co. KY, *24939*..... **100** B4
Woodhaven MI, *12875*..... **90** C1
Wood Heights MO, *742*..... **96** C2
Woodhull IL, *811*..... **88** A2
Woodhull NY, *400*..... **93** D1
Woodinville NY, *600*..... **148** C1
Woodinville WA, *10938*..... **12** C3
Woodlake CA, *7279*..... **45** D3
Wood Lake MN, *439*..... **66** A4
Woodland CA, *55468*..... **36** B3
Woodland GA, *408*..... **128** C2
Woodland MI, *425*..... **76** A4
Woodland MN, *437*..... **235** A3
Woodland NC, *809*..... **113** E3
Woodland WA, *5509*..... **20** C1
Woodland (Baileyville) ME, *952*..... **83** E1
Woodland Beach MI, *2049*..... **90** C1
Woodland Hills UT, *1344*..... **39** E1
Woodland Park CO, *7200*..... **41** E2
Woodland Park NJ, *11819*..... **240** B1
Woodlawn IL, *698*..... **98** C4
Woodlawn KY, *229*..... **204** B3
Woodlawn MD, *1600*..... **145** D1
Woodlawn MD, *37879*..... **193** B2
Woodlawn OH, *3294*..... **204** B1
Woodlawn VA, *2343*..... **112** A3
Woodlawn Park KY, *942*..... **230** E1
Woodlyn PA, *9485*..... **248** A4
Woodlynne NJ, *2978*..... **248** C4
Woodmere NY, *17121*..... **241** G5
Woodmere OH, *884*..... **204** G2
Woodmont CT, *1488*..... **149** D2
Woodmore MD, *3936*..... **144** C3
Woodport NJ, *2000*..... **148** A3
Woodridge IL, *32971*..... **203** B5
Wood-Ridge NJ, *7626*..... **240** C2
Woodridge NY, *847*..... **94** A3
Wood River IL, *10657*..... **98** A3
Wood River NE, *1325*..... **35** D4
Woodruff SC, *4090*..... **121** F2
Woodruff WI, *966*..... **68** B2
Woodruff Co. AR, *7260*..... **117** F1
Woodsboro MD, *1141*..... **144** A1
Woodsboro TX, *1512*..... **61** E4
Woodsburgh NY, *778*..... **241** G5
Woods Co. OK, *8878*..... **51** D1
Woods Cross UT, *9761*..... **257** B1
Woodsfield OH, *2384*..... **101** F1
Woods Hole MA, *781*..... **151** E4
Woodside CA, *5287*..... **259** C5
Woodside DE, *181*..... **145** E2
Woodside MT, *175*..... **15** D4
Woods Landing WY, *100*..... **33** D3
Woodson AR, *403*..... **117** E3
Woodson IL, *512*..... **98** A1
Woodson Co. KS, *3309*..... **96** A4
Woodson Terrace MO, *4063*..... **256** B1
Woodstock AL, *1428*..... **127** F1
Woodstock GA, *23896*..... **120** C3
Woodstock IL, *24770*..... **74** C4
Woodstock NY, *2088*..... **94** B2
Woodstock VT, *900*..... **81** E3
Woodstock VA, *5097*..... **102** C3
Woodstock Valley CT, *750*..... **150** B2
Woodstown NJ, *3505*..... **145** F1
Woodsville NH, *1126*..... **81** E2
Woodville AL, *746*..... **120** A2
Woodville CA, *1740*..... **45** D3
Woodville FL, *2978*..... **137** E2
Woodville GA, *321*..... **121** E4
Woodville MA, *500*..... **150** C2
Woodville MS, *1096*..... **134** A1
Woodville OH, *2135*..... **90** C2
Woodville TX, *2586*..... **132** C1
Woodville WI, *1344*..... **67** E4
Woodward IA, *1024*..... **86** C1
Woodward OK, *12051*..... **50** C1
Woodward Co. OK, *20081*..... **51** D2
Woodway TX, *8452*..... **59** E4
Woodway WA, *1307*..... **262** A2
Woodworth LA, *1096*..... **133** E1
Woody Creek CO, *263*..... **40** C2
Woonsocket RI, *41186*..... **150** C2
Woonsocket SD, *655*..... **27** E3
Wooster AR, *860*..... **117** E1
Wooster OH, *26119*..... **91** E3
Worcester MA, *181045*..... **150** C1
Worcester NY, *1113*..... **79** F4
Worcester VT, *112*..... **81** E2
Worcester Co. MD, *51454*..... **114** C2
Worcester Co. MA, *798552*..... **150** B1
Worden IL, *1044*..... **98** B3
Worden MT, *577*..... **24** C1
Workmans Corners DE, *400*..... **145** F4
Worland WY, *5487*..... **24** C4
Worley ID, *257*..... **14** B3
Wormleysburg PA, *3070*..... **218** B2
Worth IL, *10789*..... **203** D6
Wortham TX, *1073*..... **59** F3
Worth Co. GA, *21679*..... **129** D4
Worth Co. IA, *7598*..... **73** D2
Worth Co. MO, *2171*..... **86** B4
Worthing SD, *877*..... **27** F4
Worthington IN, *1463*..... **99** E2
Worthington IA, *401*..... **73** F4
Worthington KY, *1609*..... **101** D3
Worthington MN, *12764*..... **72** A2
Worthington OH, *13575*..... **90** C4
Worthington PA, *639*..... **92** A3
Wounded Knee SD, *382*..... **34** A1
Wrangell AK, *2369*..... **155** E4
Wray CO, *2342*..... **42** A1
Wrens GA, *2187*..... **129** F1
Wrentham MA, *10955*..... **151** D2
Wright FL, *23127*..... **136** B2
Wright WY, *1807*..... **25** E4
Wright City MO, *3119*..... **97** F3
Wright City OK, *762*..... **116** B3
Wright Co. IA, *13229*..... **72** C4
Wright Co. MN, *124700*..... **66** C3
Wright Co. MO, *18815*..... **107** E2
Wrightsboro NC, *4896*..... **123** E3
Wrightstown NJ, *802*..... **147** D3
Wrightstown PA, *650*..... **147** D2
Wrightstown WI, *2827*..... **74** C1
Wrightsville AR, *2114*..... **117** E2
Wrightsville GA, *2195*..... **129** E2
Wrightsville PA, *2310*..... **103** E1
Wrightsville Beach NC, *2477*..... **123** E3
Wrightwood CA, *4525*..... **52** C2
Wrigley TN, *281*..... **109** E4
Wurtland KY, *995*..... **101** D3
Wurtsboro NY, *1246*..... **148** A1
Wyalusing PA, *596*..... **93** E2
Wyandot Co. OH, *22615*..... **90** C3
Wyandotte MI, *25883*..... **90** C1
Wyandotte OK, *333*..... **106** B2
Wyandotte Co. KS, *157505*..... **96** B2
Wyanet IL, *991*..... **88** B2
Wyckoff NJ, *16836*..... **148** B3
Wycombe PA, *650*..... **146** C2
Wykoff MN, *444*..... **73** E2
Wylie TX, *41427*..... **59** F2

Auburn..... C2
Bramanville..... D2
Chaffinville..... C1
Cherry Valley..... C2
Dorothy Pond..... D2
E. Millbury..... D2
Edgemere..... D2
Leicester..... C2
Millbury..... D2
Morningdale..... D1
Pondville..... C2
Rochdale..... C2
Stoneville..... C2
Worcester..... C1

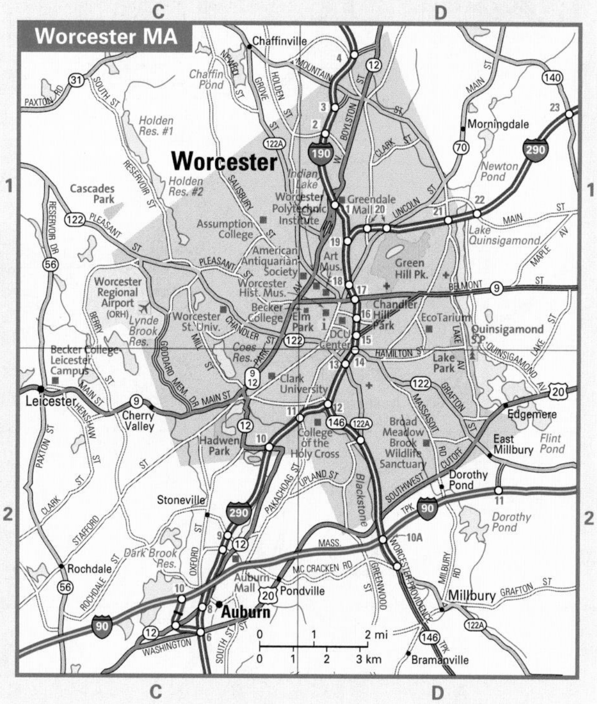

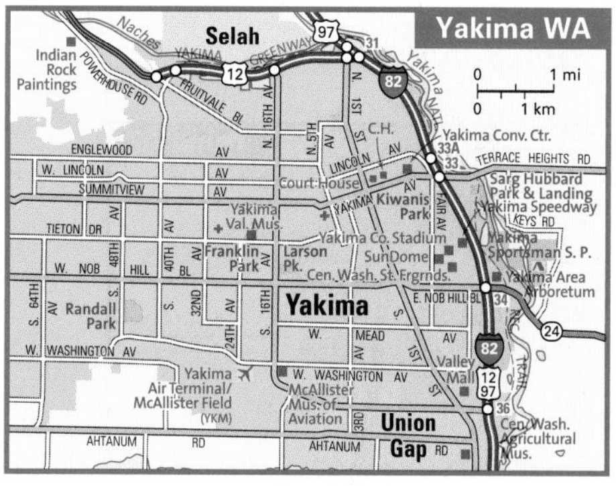

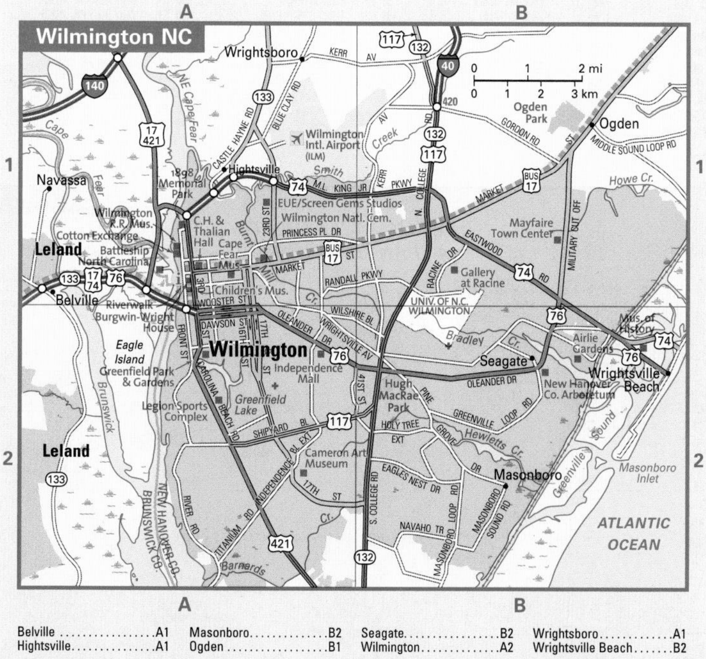

Belville..... A1
Hightsville..... A1
Masonboro..... B2
Ogden..... B1
Seagate..... B2
Wilmington..... A2
Wrightsboro..... A1
Wrightsville Beach..... B2

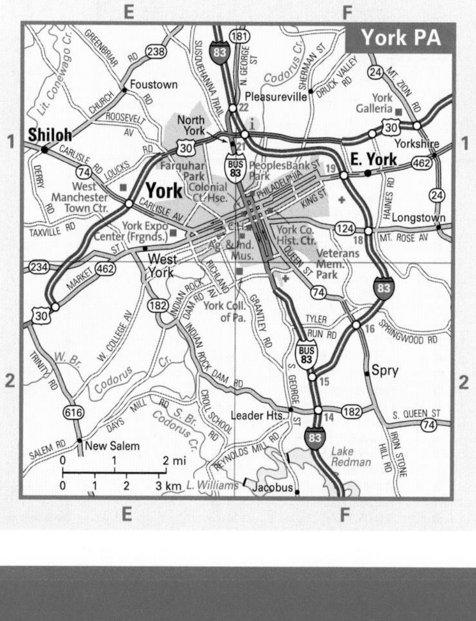

E. York..... F1
Foustown..... E1
Jacobus..... F2
Leader Hts..... F2
Longstown..... F1
New Salem..... E2
N. York..... E1
Pleasureville..... F1
Shiloh..... E1
Spry..... F2
W. York..... E1
York..... E1
Yorkshire..... F1

Figures after entries indicate population, page number, and grid reference.

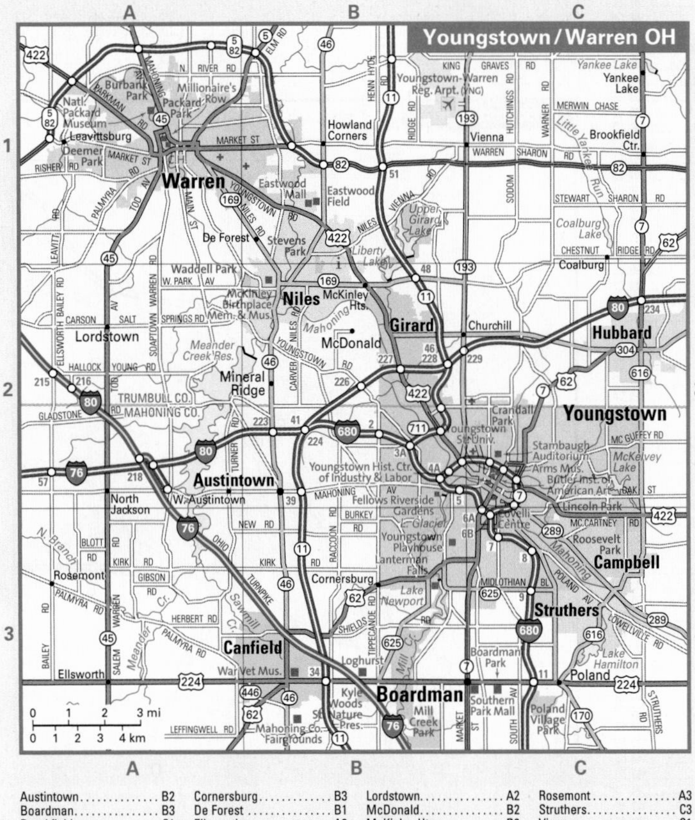

A		B		C	

Austintown	B2	Cornersburg	B3	Lordstown	A2	Rosemont	A3
Boardman	B3	De Forest	B1	McDonald	B2	Struthers	C3
Brookfield	C1	Ellsworth	A3	McKinley Hts.	B2	Vienna	C1
Campbell	C3	Girard	B2	Mineral Ridge	B2	Warren	A1
Canfield	B3	Howland Corners	B1	Niles	B2	W. Austintown	A2
Churchill	C2	Hubbard	C2	N. Jackson	A2	Yankee Lake	C1
Coalburg	C1	Leavittsburg	A1	Poland	C3	Youngstown	C2

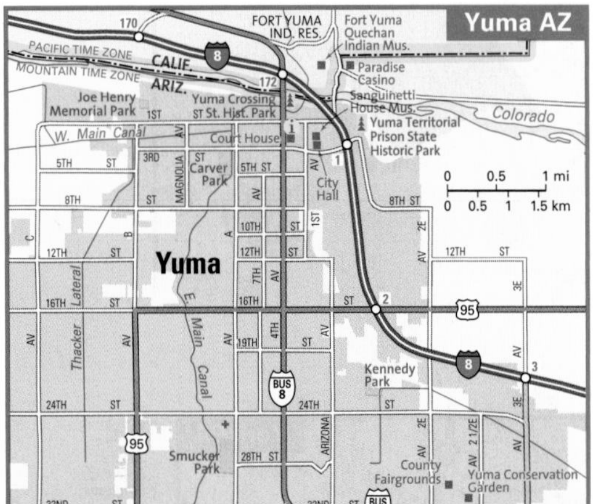

Wymore NE, *1457* **43** F1
Wynantskill NY, *3276* **188** E2
Wyncote PA, *3044* **248** C1
Wyndmere ND, *429* **27** F1
Wynne AR, *8367* **118** A1
Wynnewood OK, *2212* **51** E4
Wynona OK, *437* **51** F1
Wyocena WI, *768* **74** B2
Wyodak WY, *125* **25** E3
Wyola MT, *215* **24** C2
Wyoming DE, *1313* **145** E2
Wyoming IL, *1429* **88** B3
Wyoming IA, *515* **87** F1
Wyoming MI, *72125* **75** F3
Wyoming MN, *7791* **67** D3
Wyoming NY, *434* **78** B3
Wyoming OH, *8428* **204** B1
Wyoming PA, *3073* **261** B1
Wyoming RI, *270* **150** C4
Wyoming Co. NY, *42155* **78** B4
Wyoming Co. PA, *28276* **93** E2
Wyoming Co. WV, *23796* **111** F1
Wyomissing PA, *10461* **146** A2
Wythe Co. VA, *29235* **112** A2
Wytheville VA, *8211* **112** A2

X

Xenia IL, *391* **98** C3
Xenia OH, *25719* **100** C1

Y

Yachats OR, *690* **20** B3
Yacolt WA, *1566* **20** C1
Yadkin Co. NC, *38406* **112** A3
Yadkinville NC, *2959* **112** A4
Yah-ta-hey NM, *590* **48** A2
Yakima WA, *91067* **13** D4
Yakima Co. WA, *243231* **13** D4
Yakutat AK, *662* **155** D3
Yalaha FL, *1364* **140** C1
Yale MI, *1955* **76** C3
Yale OK, *1227* **51** F2
Yalesville CT, *3600* **149** D1
Yalobusha Co. MS, *12678* **118** B3
Yamhill OR, *1024* **20** B2
Yamhill Co. OR, *99193* **20** B2
Yampa CO, *429* **40** C1
Yancey Co. NC, *17818* **111** E4
Yanceyville NC, *2039* **112** C3
Yankeetown FL, *502* **138** C4
Yankton SD, *14454* **35** E1
Yankton Co. SD, *22438* **35** E1
Yaphank NY, *5945* **149** D3
Yardley PA, *2434* **147** D2
Yardville NJ, *7186* **147** D2
Yarmouth ME, *5869* **82** B3
Yarmouth MA, *24807* **151** F3
Yarmouth Port MA, *5320* **151** F3
Yarnell AZ, *649* **47** D4
Yarrow Pt. WA, *1001* **262** B3
Yates Ctr. KS, *1417* **96** A4
Yates City IL, *693* **88** A3
Yates Co. NY, *25348* **78** C4
Yatesville GA, *357* **129** D1
Yatesville PA, *607* **261** C2
Yavapai Co. AZ, *211033* **47** D4
Yazoo City MS, *11403* **126** B2
Yazoo Co. MS, *28065* **126** B2
Yeadon PA, *11443* **146** C3
Yeagertown PA, *1050* **93** D3
Yell Co. AR, *22185* **117** D2
Yellow House PA, 475 ..... **146** B2
Yellow Medicine Co. MN, *10438* . **66** A4
Yellow Sprs. MD, *1100* **144** A1
Yellow Sprs. OH, *3487* **100** C1
Yellowstone Co. MT, *147972* **24** C1
Yellville AR, *1204* **107** E3
Yelm WA, *6848* **12** C4
Yemassee SC, *1027* **130** C2
Yerington NV, *3048* **37** E2
Yerkes KY, *500* **111** D2
Yermo CA, *900* **53** D1
Yoakum TX, *5815* **61** E3
Yoakum Co. TX, *7879* **57** F2
Yoder WY, *151* **33** F2
Yoe PA, *1018* **103** E1
Yolo CA, *450* **36** B2
Yolo Co. CA, *200849* **36** B2
Yoncalla OR, *1047* **20** B4
Yonkers NY, *195976* **148** B3
Yorba Linda CA, *64234* **229** F3
York AL, *2538* **127** D2
York NE, *7766* **35** E4
York NY, *450* **78** C3
York PA, *43718* **103** E1
York SC, *7736* **122** A2
York Beach ME, *1400* **82** B4
York Co. ME, *197131* **82** B4
York Co. NE, *13665* **35** E4
York Co. PA, *434972* **103** E1
York Co. SC, *226073* **122** A2
York Co. VA, *65464* **113** F2
York Harbor ME, *3033* **82** B4
York Haven PA, *709* **93** E4
Yorkshire NY, *1180* **78** B4
Yorkshire VA, *7541* **144** A3
York Sprs. PA, *574* **103** E1
Yorktown IN, *9405* **89** F4
Yorktown NY, *36318* **148** B2
Yorktown TX, *2092* **61** E3
Yorktown VA, *195* **113** F2
Yorktown Hts. NY, *1781* **148** B2
York Vil. ME, *2000* **82** B4
Yorkville IL, *16921* **88** C2
Yorkville OH, *1079* **91** F4
Young AZ, *666* **47** E4
Young Co. TX, *18550* **59** D2
Young Harris GA, *899* **121** D2
Youngstown NY, *1935* **78** A3
Youngstown OH, *66982* **91** F3
Youngstown PA, *326* **92** B4
Youngsville LA, *8105* **133** F2
Youngsville NC, *1157* **113** D4
Youngsville PA, *1729* **92** B1
Youngtown AZ, *6156* **249** A1
Youngwood PA, *3050* **92** A4
Yountville CA, *2933* **36** B3
Ypsilanti MI, *19435* **90** C1
Yreka CA, *7765* **28** C2
Yuba City CA, *64925* **36** C2
Yuba Co. CA, *72155* **36** C2
Yucaipa CA, *51367* **53** D2
Yucca Valley CA, *20700* **53** E2
Yukon OK, *22709* **51** E3
Yulee FL, *11491* **139** D2
Yuma AZ, *93064* **53** F4
Yuma CO, *3524* **42** A1
Yuma Co. AZ, *195751* **54** A2
Yuma Co. CO, *10043* **34** A4
Yutan NE, *1174* **35** F3

Z

Zacata VA, *450* **103** E4
Zachary LA, *14960* **134** A1
Zanesville IN, *600* **90** A3
Zanesville OH, *25487* **101** E1
Zap ND, *237* **18** B3
Zapata TX, *5089* **63** D3
Zapata Co. TX, *14018* **63** D3
Zavala Co. TX, *11677* **60** C3
Zavalla TX, *713* **132** C1
Zearing IA, *554* **87** D1
Zeb OK, *497* **106** B4
Zebulon GA, *1174* **128** C1
Zebulon KY, *700* **111** E1
Zebulon NC, *4433* **113** D4
Zeeland MI, *5504* **75** F3
Zeigler IL, *1801* **98** C4
Zelienople PA, *3812* **92** A3
Zephyr Cove NV, *565* **37** D2
Zephyrhills FL, *13288* **140** C2
Zia Pueblo NM, *737* **48** C3
Ziebach Co. SD, *2801* **26** B2
Zillah WA, *2964* **13** E4
Zimmerman MN, *5228* **66** C3
Zion IL, *24413* **75** D4
Zion KY, *550* **109** E1
Zion PA, *2030* **92** C3
Zion Crossroads VA, 375 ..... **102** C4
Zionsville IN, *14160* **99** F1
Zolfo Sprs. FL, *1827* **140** C3
Zumbrota MN, *3252* **73** D1
Zuni Pueblo NM, *6302* **48** A3
Zwolle LA, *1759* **125** D4

PUERTO RICO

Aceitunas PR, *1436* **187** D1
Adjuntas PR, *4406* **187** D1
Aguada PR, *3212* **187** D1
Aguadilla PR, *13310* **187** D1
Aguas Buenas PR, *4204* **187** E1
Aguilita PR, *4747* **187** E1
Aibonito PR, *8249* **187** E1
Añasco PR, *5075* **187** D1
Arecibo PR, *44191* **187** E1
Arroyo PR, *6396* **187** E1
Bajadero PR, *3710* **187** E1
Barceloneta PR, *3785* **187** E1
Barranquitas PR, *2695* **187** E1
Bayamón PR, *185996* **187** E1
Betances PR, *876* **187** D1
Boquerón PR, *1218* **187** D1
Cabo Rojo PR, *9803* **187** D1
Caguas PR, *82243* **187** E1
Camuy PR, *3704* **187** D1
Canóvanas PR, *7297* **187** F1
Carolina PR, *157832* **187** F1
Cataño PR, *28140* **187** E1
Cayey PR, *16680* **187** E1
Cayuco PR, *1120* **187** D1
Ceiba PR, *5633* **187** F1
Ceiba PR, *3698* **187** E1
Ciales PR, *2591* **187** E1
Cidra PR, *5109* **187** E1
Coamo PR, *11522* **187** E1
Coco PR, *5758* **187** E1
Comerío PR, *4020* **187** E1
Comunas PR, *1900* **187** F1
Coquí PR, *3293* **187** E1
Corazón PR, *2131* **187** E1
Corozal PR, *10160* **187** E1
Coto Norte PR, *1604* **187** E1
Daguao PR, *1604* **187** F1
Dorado PR, *13258* **187** E1
Duque PR, *1320* **187** F1
El Mangó PR, *1482* **187** F1
Esperanza PR, *1219* **187** F1
Fajardo PR, *28930* **187** F1
Florida PR, *4711* **187** E1
Guánica PR, *7254* **187** D1
Guayabal PR, *2036* **187** E1
Guayama PR, *22691* **187** E1
Guayanilla PR, *3949* **187** D1
Guaynabo PR, *75443* **187** E1
Gurabo PR, *7609* **187** F1
Hatillo PR, *4439* **187** D1
Hormigueros PR, *12443* **187** D1
Humacao PR, *18629* **187** F1
Isabela PR, *11255* **187** D1
Jagual PR, *1062* **187** E1
Jayuya PR, *2759* **187** E1
Jobos PR, *2479* **187** E1
Juana Diaz PR, *7916* **187** E1
Juncos PR, *7564* **187** F1
La Parguera PR, *1044* **187** D1
La Plena PR, *865* **187** E1
Lajas PR, *4586* **187** D1
Lares PR, *4917* **187** D1
Las Marías PR, *2049* **187** D1
Las Marías PR, *998* **187** D1
Las Piedras PR, *5883* **187** F1
Levittown PR, *26960* **187** E1
Loíza PR, *3875* **187** F1
Los Llanos PR, *2118* **187** E1
Luquillo PR, *7761* **187** F1
Manatí PR, *14011* **187** E1
Maricao PR, *868* **187** D1
Maunabo PR, *1668* **187** F1
Mayagüez PR, *70463* **187** D1
Moca PR, *3861* **187** D1
Mora PR, *1583* **187** D1
Morovis PR, *2032* **187** E1
Naguabo PR, *4443* **187** F1
Naranjito PR, *1655* **187** E1
Orocovis PR, *722* **187** E1
Palmarejo PR, *1087* **187** D1
Palomas PR, *1742* **187** D1
Patillas PR, *4333* **187** E1
Peñuelas PR, *5859* **187** D1
Playita PR, *2192* **187** F1
Pole Ojea PR, *1695* **187** D1
Ponce PR, *132502* **187** E1
Potala Pastillo PR, *3092* **187** E1
Puerto Real PR, *5983* **187** D1
Punta Santiago PR, *4964* **187** F1
Quebrada PR, *995* **187** D1
Quebradillas PR, *5282* **187** D1
Rafael Capó PR, *1700* **187** D1
Rincón PR, *1456* **187** D1
Río Grande PR, *12677* **187** F1
Sabana Eneas PR, *1576* **187** D1
Sabana Grande PR, *8179* **187** D1
Sabana Hoyos PR, *1783* **187** E1
Salinas PR, *4771* **187** E1
San Antonio PR, *7574* **187** E1
San Antonio PR, *2300* **187** D1
San Germán PR, *10989* **187** D1
San Isidro PR, *6828* **187** F1
San Juan PR, *381931* **187** E1
San Lorenzo PR, *8037* **187** F1
San Sebastián PR, *9622* **187** D1
Santa Isabel PR, *5976* **187** E1
Santo Domingo PR, *3156* **187** D1
Tallaboa PR, *925* **187** D1
Toa Alta PR, *3713* **187** E1
Trujillo Alto PR, *48437* **187** E1
Utuado PR, *8397* **187** E1
Vázquez PR, *1890* **187** E1
Vega Alta PR, *10266* **187** E1
Vega Baja PR, *25905* **187** E1
Vieques PR, *3316* **187** F1
Villalba PR, *3384* **187** E1
Yabucoa PR, *6047* **187** F1
Yauco PR, *17186* **187** D1
Yaurel PR, *1050* **187** E1

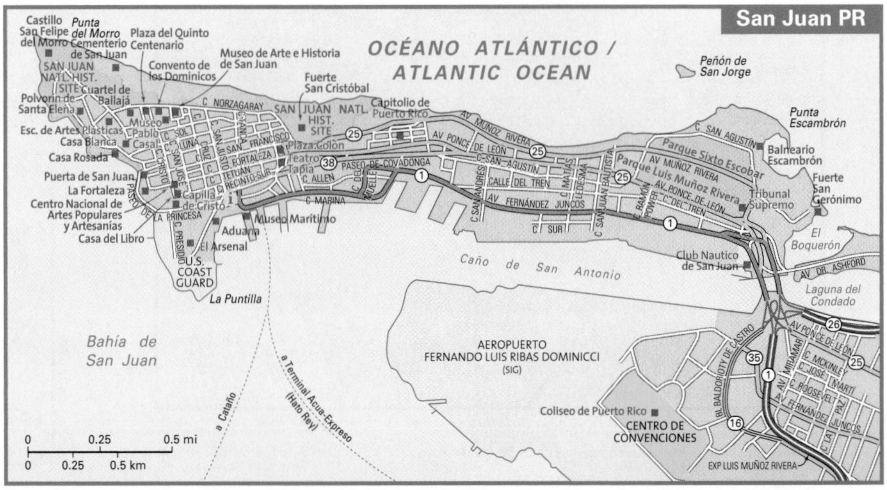

Entries in **bold color** indicate cities with detailed inset maps.

CANADA

Abbotsford BC, 115463 163 D3
Aberdeen SK, 534 165 F1
Acton ON, 7767 172 C2
Acton Vale QC, 7299 175 D3
Adstock QC, 1629 175 E2
Airdrie AB, 20382 164 C2
Air Ronge SK, 955 160 B3
Ajax ON, 73753 173 D2
Aklavik NT, 632 155 D1
Alban ON, 1084 170 C3
Albanel QC, 2455 176 B3
Alberta Beach AB, 762 158 C4
Alberton PE, 1115 179 E3
Aldergrove BC, 11910 163 D3
Alexandria ON, 3369 174 B3
Alfred ON, 1348 174 B3
Alix AB, 825 164 C2
Allan SK, 679 165 F2
Alliston ON, 9679 172 C1
Alma QC, 25918 176 C3
Almonte ON, 4659 174 A3
Altona MB, 3434 167 E4
Amherst NS, 9470 180 C1
Amherstburg ON, 20339 172 A4
Amos QC, 13044 171 E1
Amqui QC, 6473 178 B1
Ange-Gardien QC, 1994 175 D3
Angus ON, 9722 172 C1
Annapolis Royal NS, 550 180 B3
Antigonish NS, 4754 181 E1
Arborg MB, 959 167 E3
Arcola SK, 532 166 C4
Armagh QC, 1603 175 F1
Armstrong BC, 4256 164 A3
Arnold's Cove NL, 1024 183 E4
Arnprior ON, 7192 174 A3
Arthur ON, 2284 172 C2
Asbestos QC, 6580 175 E3
Ascot Corner QC, 2342 175 E3
Ashcroft BC, 1788 163 E1
Asquith SK, 574 165 F2
Assiniboia SK, 2483 166 A4
Athabasca AB, 2415 159 D3
Athens ON, 1026 174 A4
Atholville NB, 1381 178 C2
Atikokan ON, 3560 168 C4
Aurora ON, 40167 173 D2
Austin QC, 1201 175 D3
Avondale NL, 701 183 E4
Ayer's Cliff QC, 1102 175 D3
Aylesford NS, 807 180 C2
Aylmer ON, 7126 172 C3
Aylmer QC, 36085 174 B3
Ayr ON, 3636 172 C3
Baddeck NS, 907 181 F1
Badger NL, 906 183 D3
Baie-Comeau QC, 23079 177 D2
Baie-du-Febvre QC, 1135 175 D2
Baie-Ste-Anne NB, 1600 179 D3
Baie-St-Paul QC, 7290 176 C4
Baie Verte NL, 1492 183 D2
Balcarres SK, 622 166 B3
Balgonie SK, 1239 166 B3
Balmoral NB, 1836 178 C2
Bancroft ON, 4089 171 E4
Banff AB, 7135 164 B3
Barraute QC, 2010 171 E2
Barrhead AB, 4213 158 C3
Barrie ON, 103710 173 D1
Barry's Bay ON, 1259 171 E4
Bas-Caraquet NB, 1689 179 D2
Bashaw AB, 825 164 C1
Bassano AB, 1320 165 D3
Bathurst NB, 12924 179 D2
Battleford SK, 3820 159 F4
Bay Bulls NL, 1014 183 F4
Bayfield ON, 909 172 B2
Bay Roberts NL, 5237 183 E4
Beachburg ON, 870 174 A3
Beamsville ON, 9047 173 D3
Beauceville QC, 6261 175 E2
Beauharnois QC, 6387 174 C3
Beaumont AB, 7006 159 D4
Beaumont QC, 2153 175 E1
Beaupré QC, 2761 175 E1
Beauséjour MB, 2772 167 F3
Beauval SK, 843 159 F2
Beaverlodge AB, 2110 157 F1
Beaverton ON, 3065 173 D1
Bécancour QC, 11051 175 D2
Bedford NS 181 D3
Bedford QC, 2667 175 D4
Beechville NS, 2312 181 D3
Beeton ON, 3822 173 D2
Behchokö NT, 1894 155 F2
Beiseker AB, 838 164 C2
Bella Bella BC, 1253 156 C4
Belledune NB, 1923 178 C2
Bellefeuille QC, 14066 174 C3
Belleville ON, 45986 173 E1
Belmont ON, 1819 172 B3
Beloeil QC, 19053 175 D3
Benito MB, 415 166 C2
Bentley AB, 1035 164 C2
Beresford NB, 4414 179 D2
Berthierville QC, 3939 175 D2
Bertrand NB, 1269 179 D2
Berwick NS, 2282 180 C2
Betsiamites QC, 1625 178 A1
Bible Hill NS, 5741 181 D2
Bienfait SK, 786 166 C4
Biggar SK, 2243 165 F2
Big River SK, 741 159 F3
Binscarth MB, 445 166 C3
Birch Hills SK, 957 160 B4
Birchy Bay NL, 612 183 E2
Birtle MB, 715 167 D3
Bishop's Falls NL, 3688 183 D3
Black Diamond AB, 1866 164 C3
Blackfalds AB, 3042 164 C2
Black Lake QC, 4109 175 E2
Blacks Hbr. NB, 1082 180 A2
Blackville NB, 1015 178 C4
Blaine Lake SK, 508 160 B4
Blainville QC, 36029 174 C3
Blairmore AB, 1993 164 C4
Blanc-Sablon QC, 1201 183 D1
Blenheim ON, 4795 172 B4
Blind Bay BC, 2464 163 F1
Blind River ON, 3969 170 B3
Blue Mts. ON, 6116 172 C1
Bluewater ON, 6919 172 B2
Blyth ON, 987 172 B2
Bobcaygeon ON, 2854 173 E1
Bois-Blanc NB, 857 179 D2
Boischatel QC, 4303 175 E1
Boissevain MB, 1495 167 D4
Bolton ON, 20553 173 D2
Bon Accord AB, 1532 159 D4
Bonaventure QC, 2756 179 D2
Bonavista NL, 4021 183 E3
Bonnyville AB, 5709 159 E3
Borden-Carleton PE, 798 179 E4
Bothwell ON, 1002 172 B3
Botwood NL, 3221 183 D2
Bouctouche NB, 2426 179 D4
Bourget ON, 1005 174 B3
Bowden AB, 1174 164 C2
Bowen Island BC, 2957 163 D3
Bow Island AB, 1704 165 D4
Bowmanville ON, 32556 173 D2
Bowser BC, 1307 162 C3
Bowsman MB, 320 166 C2
Boyle AB, 836 159 D3
Bracebridge ON, 13751 171 D4
Bradford ON, 16978 173 D2
Bradford-W. Gwillimbury ON, 22228 173 D1
Bragg Creek AB, 678 164 C3
Brampton ON, 325428 173 D2
Brandon MB, 39716 167 D4
Brant ON, 31669 172 C3
Brantford ON, 86417 172 C3
Brantville NB, 1153 179 D3
Bridgenorth ON, 2279 173 E1
Bridgetown NS, 1035 180 B3
Bridgewater NS, 7621 180 C3
Brigham QC, 2250 175 D3
Brighton ON, 9449 173 E2
Brigus NL, 784 183 E4
Bristol NB, 719 178 B4
Broadview SK, 669 166 C3
Brochet MB, 226 161 D1
Brockville ON, 21375 174 B4
Bromont QC, 4808 175 D3
Bromptonville QC, 5571 175 E3
Brooklin ON, 5789 173 D2
Brooklyn NS, 1078 180 C4
Brooks AB, 11604 165 D3
Brookside NS, 1286 181 D3
Brownsburg-Chatham QC, 6770 174 C3
Bruderheim AB, 1202 159 D4
Bruno SK, 571 166 B2
Brussels ON, 1143 172 B2
Buchans NL, 877 183 D3
Buckingham QC, 11668 174 B3
Buffalo Creek BC, 701 157 F4
Buffalo Lake AB, 722 157 F1
Buffalo Narrows SK, 1137 159 F2
Burford ON, 1841 172 C3
Burgeo NL, 1782 182 C4
Burin NL, 2470 183 E4
Burk's Falls ON, 940 171 D4
Burlington ON, 150836 173 D3
Burnaby BC, 193954 163 D3
Burns Lake BC, 1942 157 D2
Burnt Islands NL, 801 182 C4
Bury QC, 1171 175 E3
Cabano QC, 3213 178 A2
Cache Creek BC, 1056 163 E1
Caledon ON, 50595 172 C2
Caledon East ON, 1974 172 C2
Caledonia ON, 8582 172 C3
Caledon Vil. ON, 1651 172 C2
Calgary AB, 878866 164 C3
Calmar AB, 1902 159 D4
Cambridge NS, 723 180 C2
Cambridge ON, 110372 172 C3
Cambridge-Narrows NB, 654 180 B1
Campbellford ON, 3675 173 E1
Campbell River BC, 28456 162 B2
Campbellton NB, 7798 178 C2
Camperville MB, 524 167 D2
Camrose AB, 14854 159 D4
Canal Flats BC, 709 164 B3
Candle Lake SK, 503 160 B4
Canmore AB, 10792 164 B3
Canning NS, 811 180 C2
Cannington ON, 2007 173 D1
Canora SK, 2200 166 C2
Canso NS, 992 181 F2
Cantley QC, 5898 174 B3
Cap-aux-Meules QC, 1659 179 F3
Cap-Chat QC, 2913 178 C1
Cap-de-la-Madeleine QC, 32534 175 D2
Cape Breton Reg. Mun. NS, 105968 181 F1
Cape St. George NL, 926 182 C3
Caplan QC, 2010 179 D2
Cap-Pele NB, 2266 179 E4
Capreol ON, 3471 170 C3
Cap-St-Ignace QC, 3204 175 F1
Cap-Santé QC, 2571 175 E1
Caraquet NB, 4442 179 D2
Carberry MB, 1513 167 D4
Carbonear NL, 4759 183 E4
Cardigan PE, 382 179 F4
Cardinal ON, 1739 174 B4
Cardston AB, 3475 164 C4
Carleton Place ON, 9083 174 A3
Carleton-St-Omer QC, 4010 178 C2
Carlisle ON, 2180 172 C2
Carlyle SK, 1260 166 C4
Carmacks YT, 431 155 D3
Carman MB, 2831 167 E4
Carmanville NL, 798 183 E2
Carnduff SK, 1017 166 C4
Caronport SK, 1040 166 A3
Carrot River SK, 1017 160 C4
Carseland AB, 662 164 C3
Carstairs AB, 2254 164 C2
Cartwright MB, 304 167 D4
Cartwright NL, 629 183 F1
Casselman ON, 2910 174 B3
Cassidy BC, 978 162 C3
Castlegar BC, 7002 164 A4
Castor AB, 935 165 D2
Catalina NL, 995 183 E3
Causapscal QC, 2634 178 B1
Cavendish PE, 267 179 E4
Cawston BC, 1013 163 F3
Cayuga ON, 1643 172 C3
Cedar BC, 4440 162 C3
Central Saanich BC, 15348 163 D4
Centreville NS, 1047 180 C2
Centreville-Wareham-Trinity NL, 1146 183 E3
Chalk River ON, 975 171 E3
Chambly QC, 20342 175 D3
Chambord QC, 1693 176 B3
Champlain QC, 1623 175 D2
Chandler QC, 2817 179 D1
Channel-Port aux-Basques NL, 4637 182 C4
Chapais QC, 1795 176 A2
Chapleau ON, 2832 170 B2
Charlesbourg QC, 70310 175 E1
Charlie Lake BC, 1727 158 A2
Charlo NB, 1449 178 C2
Charlottetown PE, 32245 179 E4
Charny QC, 10507 175 E1
Chase BC, 2460 163 F1
Châteauguay QC, 41003 174 C3
Château-Richer QC, 3442 175 E1
Chatham ON, 44156 172 B4
Chatham-Kent ON, 107341 172 A4
Chemainus BC, 2706 162 C3
Chertsey QC, 4112 174 C2
Chesley ON, 1880 172 B1
Chester NS, 1590 180 C3
Chestermere AB, 3414 164 C3
Chesterville ON, 1498 174 B4
Chéticamp NS 181 E3
Chetwynd BC, 2591 157 E1
Chibougamau QC, 7922 176 A2
Chicoutimi QC, 60008 176 C3
Chilliwack BC, 62927 163 E3
Chipman NB, 1432 178 C4
Christina Lake BC, 1035 164 A4
Churchbridge SK, 796 166 C3
Chute-aux-Outardes QC, 1968 177 D2
Clair NB, 863 178 A3
Clairmont AB, 1481 157 F1
Clarence-Rockland ON, 19612 174 B3
Clarenville NL, 5104 183 E3
Claresholm AB, 3622 164 C4
Clarington ON, 69834 173 D2
Clarke's Beach NL, 1257 183 E4
Clark's Hbr. NS, 944 180 B4
Clermont QC, 3078 176 C4
Clinton ON, 3117 172 B2

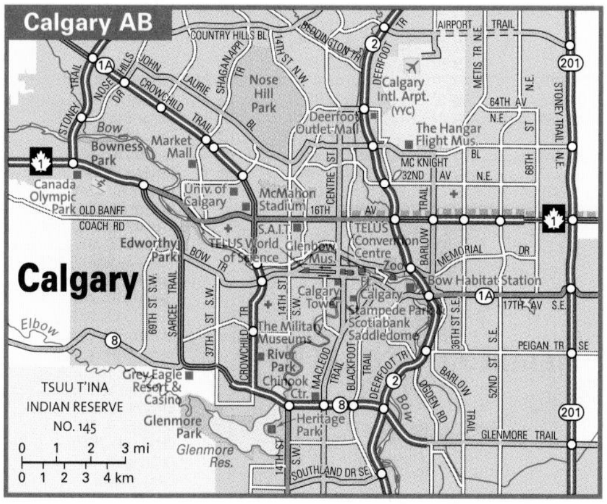

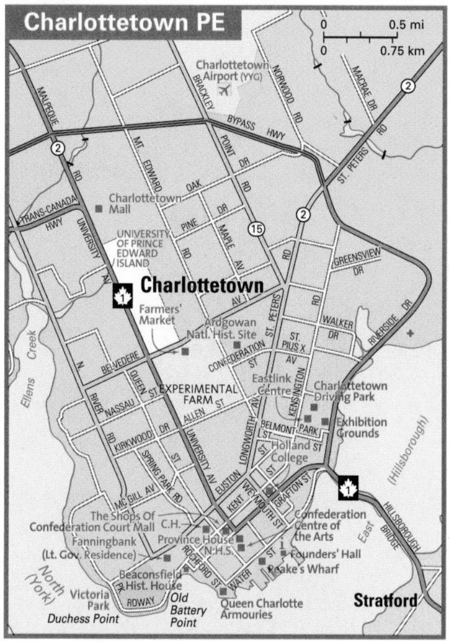

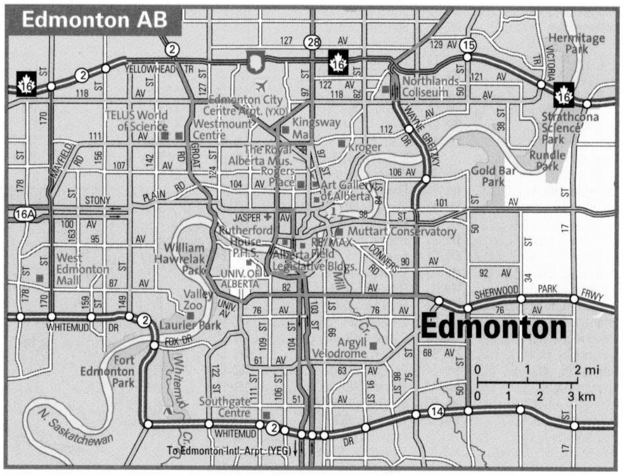

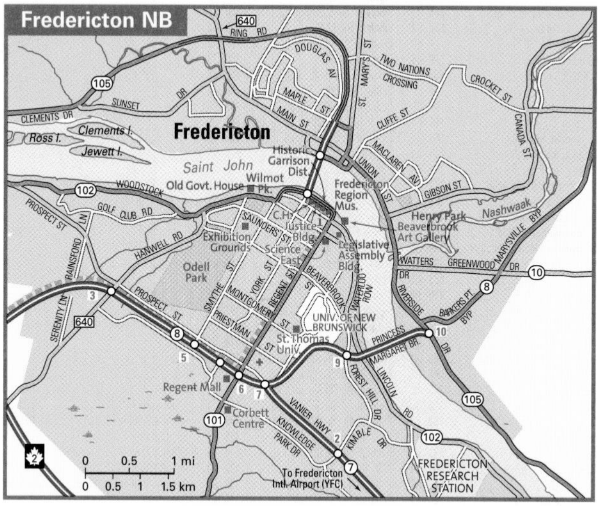

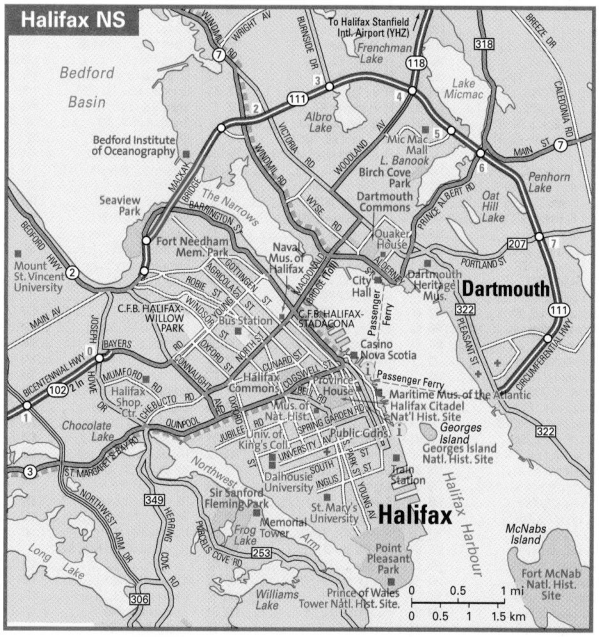

278
Clyde River–L'Islet

Figures after entries indicate population, page number, and grid reference.

Clyde River PE, 581 ... 179 E4
Coaldale AB, 6008 ... 165 D4
Coalhurst AB, 1476 ... 165 D4
Coaticook QC, 8988 ... 175 E4
Cobalt ON, 1229 ... 171 D2
Cobble Hill BC, 1753 ... 163 D4
Cobourg ON, 17172 ... 173 E2
Cocagne NB, 2659 ... 179 D4
Cochrane AB, 11798 ... 164 C3
Cochrane ON, 5690 ... 170 C1
Colborne ON, 2040 ... 173 E2
Colchester ON, 2184 ... 172 A4
Coldbrook NS, 2189 ... 180 C2
Cold Lake AB, 11520 ... 159 E3
Coldstream BC, 9106 ... 164 A3
Coleraine QC, 1642 ... 175 E2
Collingwood ON, 16039 ... 172 C1
Comox BC, 11172 ... 162 C2
Compton QC, 3047 ... 175 E3
Conception Bay South NL, 19772 ... 183 F4
Conception Hbr. NL, 801 ... 183 E4
Constance Bay ON, 2327 ... 174 A3
Contrecoeur QC, 5222 ... 175 D3
Cookshire QC, 1543 ... 175 E3
Cookstown ON, 1449 ... 173 D1
Coombs BC, 1372 ... 162 C3
Coquitlam BC, 112890 ... 163 D3
Cormack NL, 675 ... 182 C2
Cormorant MB, 400 ... 161 D3
Corner Brook NL, 20103 ... 182 C3
Cornwall ON, 45640 ... 174 B4
Cornwall PE, 4412 ... 179 E4
Coronach SK, 822 ... 166 A4
Coronation AB, 902 ... 165 D2
Coteau-du-Lac QC, 5573 ... 174 C3
Côte-Nord-du-Golfe-du-St-Laurent QC, 1183 ... 182 B1
Courtenay BC, 18304 ... 162 C2
Cowansville QC, 12032 ... 175 D3
Cowichan Bay BC, 1288 ... 163 D4
Cox's Cove NL, 719 ... 182 C2
Crabtree QC, 3330 ... 174 C2
Cranbrook BC, 18476 ... 164 B4
Crane River MB, 161 ... 167 D2
Creemore ON, 1317 ... 172 C1
Creighton SK, 1556 ... 161 D3
Creston BC, 4795 ... 164 B4
Crossfield AB, 2389 ... 164 C2
Cross Lake MB, 294 ... 161 E3
Crowsnest Pass AB, 6262 ... 164 C4
Crystal Beach ON, 6686 ... 173 D3
Crystal City MB, 414 ... 167 D4
Cudworth SK, 766 ... 165 F1
Cumberland BC, 2618 ... 162 C3
Cumberland House SK, 632 ... 160 C4
Cupar SK, 602 ... 166 B3
Cupids NL, 775 ... 183 E4
Cut Knife SK, 556 ... 159 F4
Dalhousie NB, 3975 ... 178 C2
Dalmeny SK, 1610 ... 165 F2
Danville QC, 4301 ... 175 D3
Dartmouth NS ... 181 D3
Dauphin MB, 8085 ... 167 D3
Davidson SK, 1035 ... 165 F2
Dawson YT, 1251 ... 155 D2
Dawson Creek BC, 10754 ... 157 F1
Daysland AB, 779 ... 159 D4
Deep River ON, 4135 ... 171 E3
Deer Lake NL, 4769 ... 182 C2
Dégelis QC, 3317 ... 178 A2
Delburne AB, 719 ... 164 C2
Déléage QC, 1999 ... 174 B2
Delhi ON, 4002 ... 172 C3
Déline NT, 536 ... 155 E2
Delisle QC, 4208 ... 176 C3
Delisle SK, 884 ... 165 F2
Deloraine MB, 1026 ... 167 D4
Delson QC, 7024 ... 174 C3
Delta BC, 96950 ... 163 D3
Denare Beach SK, 784 ... 161 D3
Denman Island BC, 1016 ... 162 C3
Deschaillons-sur-St-Laurent QC, 1061 ... 175 D2
Deschambault Lake SK, 896 ... 160 C3
Deseronto ON, 1796 ... 173 F1
Des Ruisseaux QC, 5401 ... 174 B2
Devon AB, 4969 ... 159 D4
Didsbury AB, 3932 ... 164 C2
Dieppe NB, 14951 ... 179 D4
Digby NS, 2111 ... 180 B3
Disraeli QC, 2635 ... 175 E2
Doaktown NB, 955 ... 178 C4
Dolbeau-Mistassini QC, 14879 ... 176 B3
Dominion NS ... 181 F1
Donnacona QC, 5479 ... 175 E2
Dorchester NB, 954 ... 180 C1
Dover NL, 730 ... 183 E3
Drayton ON, 1520 ... 172 C2
Drayton Valley AB, 5801 ... 158 C4
Dresden ON, 2582 ... 172 B4
Drumheller AB, 7785 ... 165 D2
Drummond NB, 932 ... 178 B3
Drummondville QC, 46599 ... 175 D3
Dryden ON, 8198 ... 168 C3
Duchess AB, 836 ... 165 D3
Duck Bay MB, 454 ... 167 D2
Duck Lake SK, 624 ... 160 B4
Dudswell QC, 1644 ... 175 E3
Duncan BC, 4699 ... 162 C4
Dundalk ON, 1972 ... 172 C1
Dundee NB, 883 ... 178 C2
Dundurn SK, 596 ... 165 F2
Dunham QC, 3215 ... 175 D4
Dunnottar MB, 487 ... 167 E3
Dunnville ON, 5686 ... 173 D3
Durham ON, 2709 ... 172 C1
Dutton ON, 1374 ... 172 B3
E. Angus QC, 3570 ... 175 E3
E. Broughton QC, 2367 ... 175 E2
Eastend SK, 576 ... 165 E4
E. Gwillimbury ON, 20555 ... 173 D1
Eckville AB, 1019 ... 164 C2
Edmonton AB, 666104 ... 159 D4
Edmundston NB, 17373 ... 178 B3
Edson AB, 7585 ... 158 C4
Eel River Crossing NB, 1335 ... 178 C2
Eganville ON, 1230 ... 174 A3
Elkford BC, 2589 ... 164 C4
Elkhorn MB, 470 ... 166 C4
Elk Pt. AB, 1440 ... 159 E4
Elliot Lake ON, 11956 ... 170 C3
Elmira ON, 8155 ... 172 C2
Elmsdale NS, 1580 ... 181 D2
Elmvale ON, 2176 ... 172 C1
Elrose SK, 517 ... 165 F2
Embree NL, 745 ... 183 E2
Embrun ON, 4468 ... 174 B3
Emerson MB, 655 ... 167 E4
Enderby BC, 2818 ... 164 A3
Enfield NS, 2006 ... 181 D2
Englee NL, 694 ... 183 D1
Englehart ON, 1595 ... 171 D2
Erickson MB, 448 ... 167 D3
Erin ON, 11052 ... 172 C2
Errington BC, 2122 ... 162 C3
Eskasoni NS ... 181 F1
Espanola ON, 5449 ... 170 C3
Essex ON, 20085 ... 172 A4
Esterhazy SK, 2348 ... 166 C3
Estevan SK, 10242 ... 166 C4
Eston SK, 1048 ... 165 E3
Ethelbert MB, 335 ... 167 D2
Evansburg AB, 765 ... 158 C4
Everett ON, 1146 ... 172 C1
Exeter ON, 4452 ... 172 B3
Fairisle NB, 989 ... 179 D3
Fairview AB, 3150 ... 158 B2
Falher AB, 1109 ... 158 B2
Falkland BC, 747 ... 163 F1
Fall River NS, 4393 ... 181 D3
Fanny Bay BC, 744 ... 162 C3
Farnham QC, 7747 ... 175 D3
Faro YT, 313 ... 155 E3
Fatima QC, 2686 ... 179 F3
Fenelon Falls ON, 1874 ... 173 D1
Fergus ON, 16732 ... 172 C2
Ferme-Neuve QC, 2947 ... 174 B1
Fermont QC, 2918 ... 183 E1
Fernie BC, 4611 ... 164 C4
Ferryland NL, 607 ... 183 F4
Flatrock NL, 1138 ... 183 F4
Flin Flon MB, 6000 ... 161 D3
Florence NS, 2650 ... 180 C2
Florenceville NB, 762 ... 178 B4
Foam Lake SK, 1218 ... 166 B2
Fogo NL, 803 ... 183 E2
Forest ON, 2857 ... 172 B3
Forestburg AB, 870 ... 165 D1
Forestville QC, 3748 ... 178 A1
Ft. Chipewyan AB, 902 ... 155 F2
Fort-Coulonge QC, 1661 ... 174 A3
Ft. Erie ON, 28143 ... 173 D3
Ft. Frances ON, 8315 ... 168 B4
Ft. Good Hope NT, 549 ... 155 E2
Ft. Liard NT, 530 ... 155 E3
Ft. Macleod AB, 2990 ... 164 C4
Ft. McMurray AB, 38667 ... 159 E1
Ft. McPherson NT, 761 ... 155 D1
Ft. Nelson BC, 4188 ... 155 F3
Ft. Providence NT, 753 ... 155 F2
Ft. Qu'Appelle SK, 1940 ... 166 B3
Ft. Resolution NT, 525 ... 155 F2
Ft. St. James BC, 1927 ... 157 D2
Ft. St. John BC, 16034 ... 158 A2
Ft. Saskatchewan AB, 13121 ... 159 D4
Ft. Simpson NT, 1163 ... 155 F2
Ft. Smith NT, 2185 ... 155 F2
Fortune NL, 1615 ... 183 D4
Ft. Vermilion AB, 818 ... 155 F3
Fox Creek AB, 2337 ... 158 B3
Frampton QC, 1293 ... 175 E2
Frankford ON, 2487 ... 173 E1
Franklin QC, 1603 ... 174 C4
Fraser Lake BC, 1268 ... 157 D2
Fredericton NB, 47560 ... 180 A1
Fredericton Jct. NB, 692 ... 180 A1
Frelighsburg QC, 1081 ... 175 D4
French Creek BC, 4790 ... 162 C3
French River ON, 2810 ... 171 D3
Frontenac QC, 1498 ... 175 E3
Fruitvale BC, 2025 ... 164 A4
Gabriola Island BC, 3522 ... 162 C3
Gagetown NB, 682 ... 180 B1
Gambo NL, 2084 ... 183 E3
Gananoque ON, 5167 ... 173 F1
Gander NL, 9651 ... 183 E3
Garnish NL, 665 ... 183 D4
Gaspé QC, 14932 ... 179 D1
Gatineau QC, 102898 ... 174 B3
Genelle BC, 823 ... 164 A4
Gentilly QC, 2079 ... 175 D2
Georgetown ON, 31510 ... 172 C2
Georgetown PE, 721 ... 179 F4
Georgina ON, 39263 ... 173 D1
Geraldton ON, 2224 ... 169 E3
Gibbons AB, 2654 ... 159 D4
Gibsons BC, 3906 ... 163 D3
Gift Lake AB, 809 ... 158 C2
Gilbert Plains MB, 757 ... 167 D3
Gillam MB, 1178 ... 161 F1
Gimli MB, 1657 ... 167 E3
Girardville QC, 1285 ... 176 B3
Glace Bay NS, 21187 ... 181 F4
Gladstone MB, 848 ... 167 D3
Glenboro MB, 656 ... 167 D4
Glencoe ON, 2152 ... 172 B3
Glenwood NL, 845 ... 183 E3
Glovertown NL, 2163 ... 183 E3
Goderich ON, 7604 ... 172 B2
Golden BC, 4020 ... 164 B2
Gold River BC, 1359 ... 162 B2
Gold River NS, 1015 ... 180 C3
Gore Bay ON, 898 ... 170 C4
Granby QC, 44121 ... 175 D3
Grand Bank NL, 2841 ... 183 D4
Grand Bay-Westfield NB, 4949 ... 180 B2
Grand Bend ON, 1949 ... 172 B3
Grand Ctr. AB, 11780 ... 159 E3
Grande-Anse NB, 853 ... 179 D2
Grande Cache AB, 3828 ... 157 F2
Grande-Digue NB, 2109 ... 179 D4
Grande Prairie AB, 36983 ... 157 F1
Grande-Rivière QC, 3556 ... 179 D1
Grande-Vallée QC, 1309 ... 179 D1
Grand Falls (Grand-Sault) NB, 5858 ... 178 B3
Grand Falls-Windsor NL, 13340 ... 183 D3
Grand Forks BC, 4054 ... 164 A4
Grand Manan NB, 2610 ... 180 A3
Grand-Mère QC, 13179 ... 175 D2
Grand Rapids MB, 355 ... 161 E4
Grand-Remous QC, 1216 ... 174 B2
Grand Valley ON, 1757 ... 172 C2
Grandview MB, 814 ... 167 D3
Gravelbourg SK, 1187 ... 165 F3
Gravenhurst ON, 10899 ... 171 D4
Greater Napanee ON, 15132 ... 173 F1
Greater Sudbury ON, 155219 ... 170 C3
Greenstone ON, 5662 ... 169 E3
Greenwood BC, 666 ... 164 A4
Greenwood NS, 2184 ... 180 C2
Grenfell SK, 1067 ... 166 C3
Grenville-sur-la-Rouge QC, 1315 ... 174 C3
Gretna MB, 563 ... 167 E4
Grimsby ON, 21297 ... 173 D3
Grimshaw AB, 2435 ... 158 B2
Grindrod BC, 1419 ... 164 A3
Guelph ON, 106170 ... 172 C2
Gull Lake SK, 1016 ... 165 E3
Guysborough NS, 462 ... 181 E2
Hagersville ON, 2484 ... 172 C3
Hague SK, 711 ... 165 F1
Haileybury ON, 4543 ... 171 D2
Haines Jct. YT, 531 ... 155 D3
Haldimand ON, 43728 ... 173 D3
Halifax NS, 359111 ... 181 D3
Halton Hills ON, 48184 ... 172 C2
Hamilton ON, 490268 ... 172 C3
Hamiota MB, 858 ... 167 D3
Hammonds Plains Road NS, 1162 ... 181 D3
Hampton NB, 3997 ... 180 B2
Hanna AB, 2986 ... 165 D2
Hanover ON, 6869 ... 172 C1
Hantsport NS, 1202 ... 180 C2
Happy Valley-Goose Bay NL, 7969 ... 183 F1
Harbour Breton NL, 2079 ... 183 D4
Harbour Grace NL, 3380 ... 183 E4
Hardisty AB, 743 ... 165 D1
Hardwicke NB, 1083 ... 179 D3
Hare Bay NL, 1065 ... 183 E3
Harrison Hot Sprs. BC, 1343 ... 163 E3
Harriston ON, 2034 ... 172 C2
Harrow ON, 2935 ... 172 A4
Hartland NB, 902 ... 178 B4
Hartney MB, 446 ... 167 D4
Hastings ON, 1208 ... 173 E1
Haute-Aboujagane NB, 947 ... 179 E4
Havelock ON, 1328 ... 173 E1
Havre-aux-Maisons QC, 2057 ... 179 F3
Havre Boucher NS, 401 ... 181 E1
Havre-St-Pierre QC, 3291 ... 177 F1
Hawkesbury ON, 10314 ... 174 B3
Hay River NT, 3510 ... 155 F2
Hearst ON, 5825 ... 170 B1
Heart's Delight-Islington NL, 736 ... 183 E4
Hebbville NS, 877 ... 180 C3
Hébertville QC, 2425 ... 176 C3
Henryville QC, 1482 ... 175 D4
Hensall ON, 1194 ... 172 B2
Herbert SK, 812 ... 165 F3
Hermitage NL, 602 ... 183 D4
Hérouxville QC, 1275 ... 175 D1
Herring Cove NS, 1530 ... 181 D3
Highlands BC, 1674 ... 163 D4
High Level AB, 3444 ... 155 F3
High Prairie AB, 2737 ... 158 C2
High River AB, 9345 ... 164 C3
Hillsborough NB, 1288 ... 180 C1
Hillsburgh ON, 1198 ... 172 C2
Hinton AB, 9405 ... 158 B4
Holyrood NL, 1906 ... 183 E4
Hope BC, 6184 ... 163 E3
Hornby Island BC, 966 ... 162 C3
Hornepayne ON, 1312 ... 169 F3
Houston BC, 3577 ... 156 C2
Hudson QC, 4796 ... 174 C3
Hudson Bay SK, 1783 ... 160 C4
Hudson's Hope BC, 1039 ... 158 A2
Hull QC, 66246 ... 174 B3
Humber Arm South NL, 1800 ... 182 C3
Humboldt SK, 5161 ... 166 B2
Hunter River PE, 354 ... 179 E4
Huntingdon QC, 2666 ... 174 C4
Huntsville ON, 17338 ... 171 D4
Huron East ON, 9680 ... 172 B2
Iberville QC, 9424 ... 175 D3
Île-à-la-Crosse SK, 1268 ... 159 F2
Indian Head SK, 1758 ... 166 B3
Ingersoll ON, 10977 ... 172 C3
Inkerman NB, 936 ... 179 D2
Innisfail AB, 6928 ... 164 C2
Innisfil ON, 28666 ... 173 D1
Inuvik NT, 2894 ... 155 D1
Invermere BC, 2858 ... 164 B3
Inverness NS, 1702 ... 181 E1
Iqaluit NU, 5236 ... 7
Irishtown-Summerside NL, 1304 ... 182 C3
Iroquois ON, 1228 ... 174 B4
Iroquois Falls ON, 5217 ... 170 C1
Irricana AB, 1038 ... 164 C2
Isle-aux Morts NL, 813 ... 182 C4
Ituna SK, 709 ... 166 B3
Jarvis ON, 2180 ... 172 C3
Jasper AB, 3716 ... 158 B4
Joe Batt's Arm-Barr'd Islands-Shoal Bay NL, 889 ... 183 E2
Joliette QC, 17837 ... 174 C2
Jonquière QC, 54842 ... 176 C3
Kaleden BC, 1269 ... 163 F3
Kamloops BC, 77281 ... 163 F1
Kamsack SK, 2009 ... 166 C2
Kanata ON, 70320 ... 174 A3
Kapuskasing ON, 9238 ... 170 C1
Kars ON, 1539 ... 174 B3
Kaslo BC, 1032 ... 164 B4
Kawartha Lakes ON, 69179 ... 173 D1
Kedgwick NB, 1184 ... 178 B2
Kelowna BC, 96288 ... 163 F2
Kelvington SK, 1007 ... 166 B2
Kemptville ON, 4004 ... 174 B3
Kenora ON, 15838 ... 167 F4
Kensington PE, 1385 ... 179 E4
Kent BC, 4926 ... 163 E3
Kentville NS, 5610 ... 180 C2
Keremeos BC, 1197 ... 163 F3
Kerrobert SK, 1111 ... 165 E2
Keswick ON ... 173 D1
Keswick Ridge NB, 1331 ... 180 A1
Kikino AB, 927 ... 159 D3
Killam AB, 1004 ... 165 D1
Killarney MB, 2221 ... 167 D4
Kimberley BC, 6484 ... 164 B4
Kincardine ON, 6410 ... 172 B1
Kindersley SK, 4548 ... 165 E2
Kingsey Falls QC, 2023 ... 175 D3
King's Pt. NL, 771 ... 183 D2
Kingston NS, 3009 ... 180 C2
Kingston ON, 114195 ... 173 F1
Kingsville ON, 19619 ... 172 A4
Kinistino SK, 702 ... 160 B4
Kipling SK, 1037 ... 166 C3
Kippens NL, 1802 ... 182 C3
Kirkland Lake ON, 8616 ... 171 D2
Kitchener ON, 190399 ... 172 C2
Kitimat BC, 10285 ... 156 B2
Kitscoty AB, 671 ... 159 E4
Kugluktuk NU, 1212 ... 155 F1
La Baie QC, 19940 ... 176 C3
Labelle QC, 2272 ... 174 B2
Labrador City NL, 7744 ... 183 E1
Labrecque QC, 1288 ... 176 C3
Lac-au-Saumon QC, 1539 ... 178 B1
Lac-aux-Sables QC, 1313 ... 175 D1
Lac-Beauport QC, 5519 ... 175 E1
Lac-Bouchette QC, 1370 ... 176 B3
Lac-Brome QC, 5444 ... 175 D3
Lac-Drolet QC, 1165 ... 175 E3
Lac du Bonnet MB, 1089 ... 167 F3
Lac-Etchemin QC, 2276 ... 175 F2
Lachine QC, 40222 ... 174 C3
Lachute QC, 11628 ... 174 C3
Lac La Biche AB, 2776 ... 159 D3
Lac-Mégantic QC, 5897 ... 175 E3
Lacolle QC, 1503 ... 174 C4
Lacombe AB, 9384 ... 164 C2
La Conception QC, 1050 ... 174 B2
La Crête AB, 1783 ... 155 F3
Lac-Supérieur QC, 1439 ... 174 C2
Ladysmith BC, 6587 ... 162 C3
La Guadeloupe QC, 1716 ... 175 E2
Lake Country BC, 9267 ... 163 F2
Lake Cowichan BC, 2827 ... 162 C4
Lake Echo NS, 3169 ... 181 D3
Lakefield ON, 2734 ... 173 E1
Lake Louise AB, 1041 ... 164 B2
Lakeshore ON, 28746 ... 172 A4
La Loche SK, 2136 ... 159 E1
La Malbaie QC, 9143 ... 176 C4
Lambton QC, 1525 ... 175 E3
Lambton Shores ON, 10571 ... 172 B3
Lamèque NB, 1580 ... 179 D2
La Minerve QC, 1080 ... 174 B2
Lamont AB, 1692 ... 159 D4
Lampman SK, 650 ... 166 C4
Lanark ON, 869 ... 174 A4
Landrienne QC, 1072 ... 171 E1
Langdon AB, 1685 ... 164 C3
L'Ange-Gardien QC, 2815 ... 175 E1
Langenburg SK, 1107 ... 166 C3
Langford BC, 18840 ... 163 D4
Langham SK, 1145 ... 165 F1
Langley BC, 23643 ... 163 D3
Lanigan SK, 1289 ... 166 B2
L'Annonciation QC, 1984 ... 174 B2
Lanoraie QC, 3869 ... 175 D2
L'Anse-St-Jean QC, 1155 ... 176 C3
Lantz NS, 1459 ... 181 D2
Lantzville BC, 3643 ... 162 C3
La Pêche QC, 6453 ... 174 A3
La Plaine QC, 15673 ... 174 C3
La Pocatière QC, 4518 ... 175 F1
Lappe ON, 1406 ... 169 D4
La Prairie QC, 18896 ... 174 C3
Lark Hbr. NL, 613 ... 182 C2
La Ronge SK, 2727 ... 160 B3
LaSalle ON, 25285 ... 172 A4
La Sarre QC, 7728 ... 171 D1
L'Ascension-de-Notre-Seigneur QC, 1731 ... 176 C3
La Scie NL, 1063 ... 183 D2
Lashburn SK, 783 ... 159 E4
L'Assomption QC, 15615 ... 174 C3
Laterrière QC, 4969 ... 176 C3
La Tuque QC, 11298 ... 175 D1
Laurentian Hills ON, 2750 ... 171 E4
Laurier-Station QC, 2376 ... 175 E2
Laurierville QC, 1528 ... 175 E2
Laval QC, 343005 ... 174 C3
Lavaltrie QC, 5967 ... 175 D3
L'Avenir QC, 1277 ... 175 D3
Lawn NL, 779 ... 183 D4
Lawrencetown NS, 650 ... 180 C2
Leader SK, 914 ... 165 E3
Leaf Rapids MB, 1309 ... 161 D2
Leamington ON, 27138 ... 172 A4
Lebel-sur-Quévillon QC, 3236 ... 171 E1
Le Bic QC, 2872 ... 178 A1
Leduc AB, 15032 ... 159 D4
Legal AB, 1058 ... 159 D4
Le Goulet NB, 969 ... 179 D2
Lennoxville QC, 4963 ... 175 E3
L'Épiphanie QC, 4208 ... 174 C3
Léry QC, 2378 ... 174 C3
Les Coteaux QC, 3010 ... 174 C3
Les Éboulements QC, 1027 ... 176 C4
Les Escoumins QC, 2106 ... 178 A1
Les Méchins QC, 1220 ... 178 C1
L'Étang-du-Nord QC, 2944 ... 179 F3
Lethbridge AB, 67374 ... 165 D4
Lévis QC, 40926 ... 175 E1
Lewisporte NL, 3312 ... 183 E2
Lillooet BC, 2741 ... 163 E1
Lincoln NB, 1990 ... 180 A1
Lincoln ON, 20612 ... 173 D3
Lindsay ON, 17757 ... 173 D1
Lions Bay BC, 1379 ... 163 D3
L'Islet QC, 3866 ... 175 F1

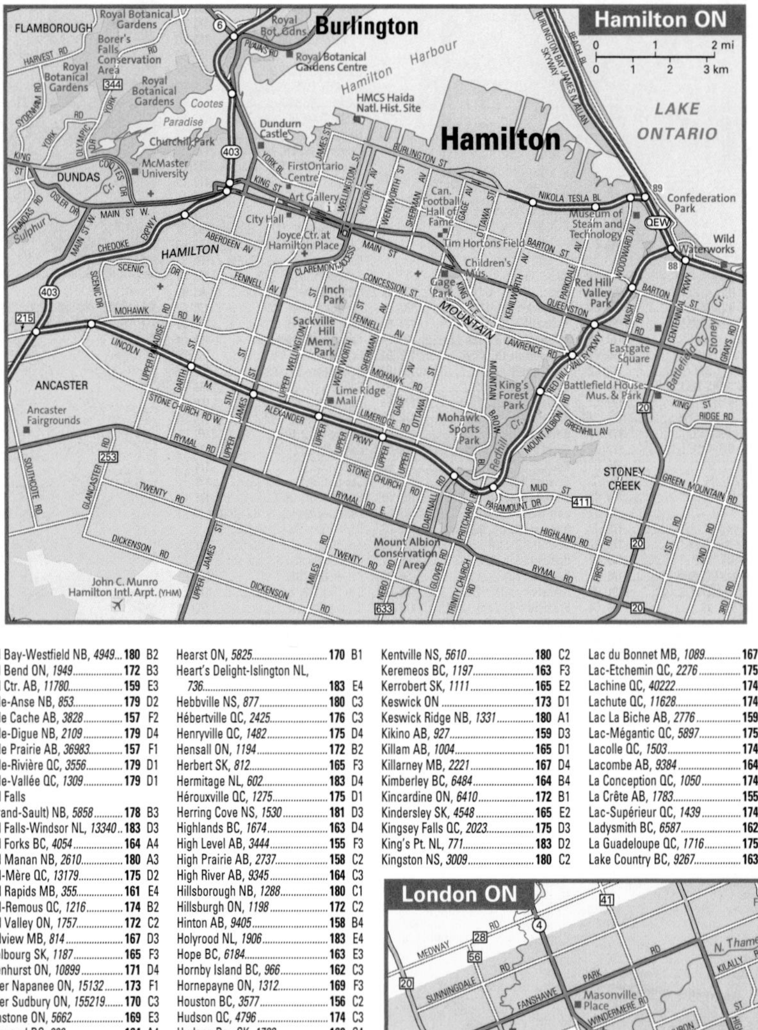

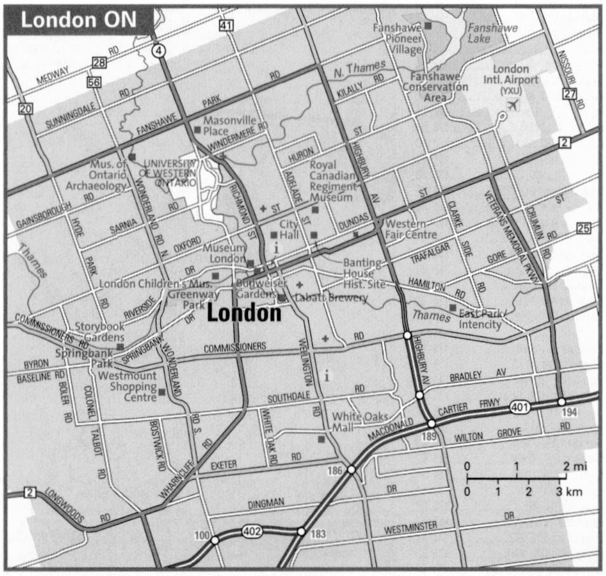

Entries in **bold color** indicate cities with detailed inset maps.

Montréal QC

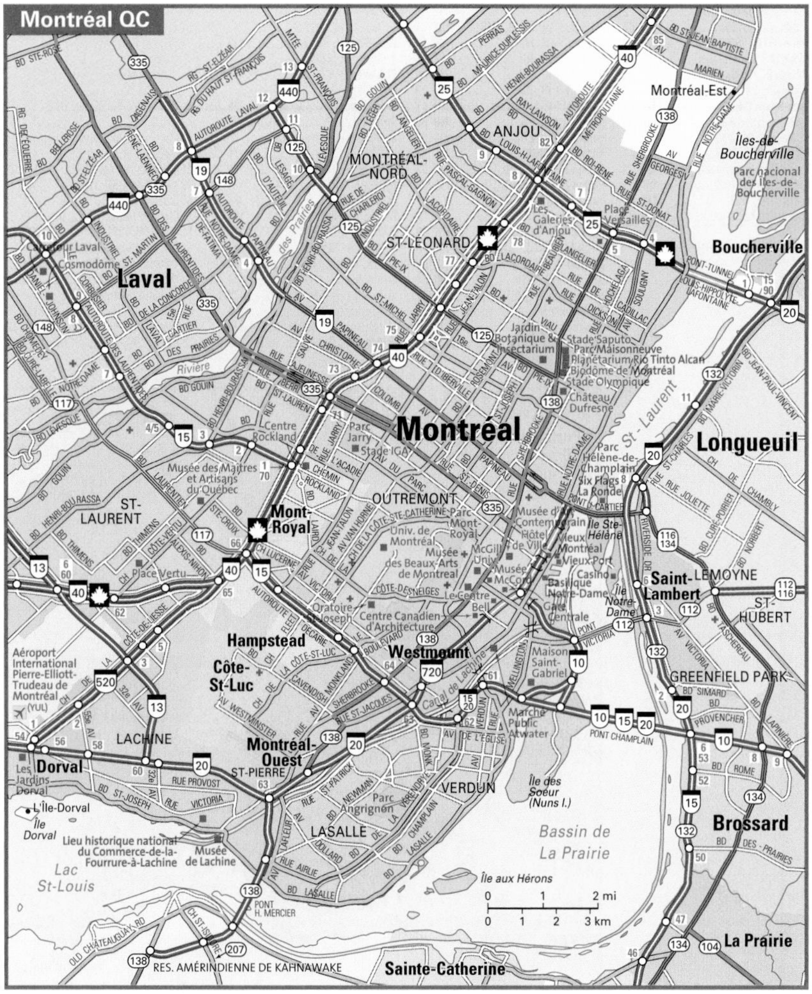

L'Isle-Verte QC, 1519 178 A2
Listowel ON, 5905 172 C2
Little Current ON, 1564 170 C4
Lively ON, 6704 170 C3
Liverpool NS, 2888 180 C4
Lloydminster AB, 13148 159 E4
Lloydminster SK, 7840 159 E4
Lockeport NS, 701 180 C4
Logan Lake BC, 2185 163 E1
London ON, 336539 172 B3
Longlac ON, 1748 169 E3
Longue-Rive QC, 1352 178 A1
Longueuil QC, 128016 174 C3
Loretteville QC, 13737 175 E1
L'Orignal ON, 2033 174 B3
Lorrainville QC, 1411 171 D2
Louisbourg NS, 1071 181 F4
Louiseville QC, 7622 175 D2
Lourdes NL, 650 182 C3
Lucan ON, 2010 172 B3
Lucknow ON, 1207 172 B2
Lumby BC, 1618 164 A3
Lumsden NL, 622 183 E2
Lumsden SK, 1581 166 B3
Lunenburg NS, 2568 180 C3
Luseland SK, 602 165 E2
Lynn Lake MB, 699 161 D1
Lyster QC, 1685 175 E2
Macamic QC, 1519 171 D1
MacGregor MB, 882 167 E4
Mackenzie BC, 5206 157 E1
Macklin SK, 1330 165 E2
Madoc ON, 1730 173 E1
Magog QC, 14283 175 D3
Magrath AB, 1993 165 D4
Mahone Bay NS, 991 180 C3
Maidstone SK, 995 159 F4
Maisonnette NB, 605 179 D2
Malartic QC, 3704 171 E2
Manawan QC, 1646 174 C1
Manigotagan MB, 192 167 F3
Manitou MB, 775 167 E4
Manitouwadge ON, 2949 169 F3
Maniwaki QC, 3571 174 A2
Manning AB, 1293 158 B1
Mannville AB, 722 159 E4
Maple Creek SK, 2270 165 E4
Maple Ridge BC, 63169 163 D3
Marathon ON, 4416 169 E4
Maria QC, 2458 178 C2
Marieville QC, 7240 175 D3
Markdale ON, 1433 172 C1
Markham ON, 208615 173 D2
Markstay-Warren ON, 2627 171 D3
Marmora ON, 1589 173 E1
Marshall SK, 633 159 E4
Martensville SK, 4365 165 F2
Marystown NL, 5908 183 E4
Mascouche QC, 29556 174 C3
Mashteuiatsh QC, 1861 176 B3
Maskinongé QC, 1087 175 D2
Masset BC, 926 156 A2
Masson-Angers QC, 9799 174 B3
Matagami QC, 1939 171 E1
Matane QC, 11635 178 B1
Mattawa ON, 2270 171 D3
Maxville ON, 864 174 B3
Mayerthorpe AB, 1570 158 C4
Mayo YT, 366 155 D2
McAdam NB, 1513 180 A1
McBride BC, 711 157 F3
McCreary MB, 522 167 D3
McLennan AB, 804 158 B2
McWatters QC, 1815 171 D2
Meadow Lake SK, 4582 159 F3
Meadows NL, 676 182 C3
Meaford ON, 10381 172 C1
Medicine Hat AB, 51249 165 D4
Melfort SK, 5559 160 B4
Melita MB, 1111 167 D4
Melocheville QC, 2449 174 C3
Melville SK, 4453 166 C3
Memramcook NB, 4719 180 C1
Mercier QC, 9442 174 C3
Merrickville-Wolford ON, 2812 174 B4
Merritt BC, 7088 163 E2
Merville BC, 2069 162 C2
Messines QC, 1322 174 A2
Métabetchouan-
Lac-à-la-Croix QC, 4198 176 C3
Metcalfe ON, 1610 174 B3
Metchosin BC, 4857 163 D4
Middleton NS, 1744 180 C2
Midland ON, 16214 172 C1
Mildmay ON, 1191 172 B2
Milestone SK, 542 166 B4
Milk River AB, 879 165 D4
Mill Bay BC, 1974 163 D4
Millbrook ON, 1467 173 E1
Mille-Isles QC, 1209 174 C3
Millet AB, 2037 159 D4
Milltown-Head of Bay
d'Espoir NL, 884 183 D3
Milton NS, 1004 180 C4
Milton ON, 31471 172 C2
Milverton ON, 1707 172 C2
Minitonas MB, 538 167 D2
Minnedosa MB, 2426 167 D3
Minto NB, 2776 178 C4
Minto ON, 8164 172 C2
Mirabel QC, 27330 174 C3
Miracle Beach BC, 1627 162 B2
Miramichi NB, 18508 179 D3
Mira Road NS, 1268 181 F1
Miscou Ctr. NB, 643 179 D2
Miscouche PE, 766 179 E4
Mission BC, 31272 163 D3
Mississauga ON, 612925 173 D2
Mississippi Mills ON, 11647 174 A3
Mistissini QC, 1814 176 B1
Mitchell ON, 4181 172 B2
Moncton NB, 61046 179 D4
Mono ON, 6922 172 C2
Montague PE, 1945 179 F4
Mont-Carmel QC, 1244 176 C4
Mont-Joli QC, 5886 178 B1
Mont-Laurier QC, 7365 174 B2
Montmagny QC, 11654 175 F1
Montréal QC, 1039534 174 C3
Montrose BC, 1067 164 A4
Moose Jaw SK, 32131 166 B3
Moose Lake MB, 740 161 D4
Moosomin SK, 2361 166 C3
Morden MB, 6142 167 E4
Morin-Heights QC, 2575 174 C3
Morinville AB, 6540 159 D4
Morris MB, 1673 167 E4
Morrisburg ON, 2583 174 B4
Mt. Albert ON, 2615 173 D1
Mt. Brydges ON, 2221 172 B3
Mt. Forest ON, 4584 172 C2
Mt. Moriah NL, 700 182 C3
Mt. Pearl NL, 24964 183 F4
Mt. Uniacke NS 181 D2
Mulgrave NS, 904 181 E1
Mundare AB, 653 159 D4
Munster ON, 1390 174 A3
Murdochville QC, 1171 179 D1
Murray Hbr. PE, 357 179 F4
Murray River PE, 435 179 F4
Musgrave Hbr. NL, 1294 183 E2
Musgravetown NL, 640 183 E3
Nackawic NB, 1042 180 A1
Naicam SK, 761 166 B2
Nakusp BC, 1698 164 A3
Nanaimo BC, 73000 162 C3
Nanoose Bay BC, 4723 162 C3
Nantes QC, 1424 175 E3
Nanton AB, 1841 164 C3
Napanee ON, 7760 173 F1
Napierville QC, 3073 174 C3
Naramata BC, 1791 163 F2
Nauwigewauk NB, 1508 180 B2
Neepawa MB, 3325 167 D3
Neguac NB, 1697 179 D3
Nelson BC, 9298 164 B4
Neuville QC, 3346 175 E1
New Aiyansh BC, 716 156 B1
New Carlisle QC, 1431 179 D2
New Glasgow NS, 9432 181 D2
New Hamburg ON, 7003 172 C3
New Hazelton BC, 750 156 C1
New Liskeard ON, 4906 171 D2
Newmarket ON, 65788 173 D2
New Maryland NB, 4284 180 A1
Newport QC, 1808 179 D2
New Richmond QC, 3760 178 C2
New Tecumseth ON, 26141 173 D2
New Victoria NS, 1049 181 F1
New Waterford NS, 10185 181 F1
New-Wes-Valley NL, 2832 183 E2
Niagara Falls ON, 78815 173 D3
Niagara-on-the-Lake ON, 13839 173 D3
Nicholas Denys NB, 1034 178 C2
Nicolet QC, 7928 175 D2
Nigadoo NB, 983 179 D2
Nipawin SK, 4275 160 C4
Nipigon ON, 1964 169 E3
Niverville MB, 1921 167 E4
Nobleton ON, 3472 173 D2
Nominingue QC, 2064 174 B2
Norfolk ON, 60847 172 C3
Normandin QC, 3524 176 B3
Norman's Cove-
Long Cove NL, 852 183 E4
Norman Wells NT, 666 155 E2
Norris Arm NL, 843 183 D3
Norris Pt. NL, 786 182 C2
N. Battleford SK, 13692 159 F4
N. Bay ON, 52771 171 D3
N. Cowichan BC, 26148 162 C4
Northeastern Manitoulin
and the Islands ON, 2531 170 C4
N. Perth ON, 12055 172 C2
N. Rustico PE, 637 179 E4
N. Saanich BC, 10436 163 D4
N. Sydney NS 181 F1
N. Tetagouche NB, 973 178 C2
N. Vancouver BC, 44303 163 D3
Norton NB, 1370 180 B1
Norway House MB, 456 161 E4
Norwich ON, 2510 172 C3
Norwood ON, 1653 173 E1
Notre Dame
de Lourdes MB, 619 167 E4
Notre-Dame-
des-Érables NB, 958 179 D2
Notre-Dame-des-Pins QC, 1030 175 E2
Notre-Dame-
du-Bon-Conseil QC, 1453 175 D2
Notre-Dame-du-Lac QC, 2152 178 A2
Notre-Dame-du-Laus QC, 1382 174 B2
Notre-Dame-
du-Mont-Carmel QC, 5055 175 D2
Notre-Dame-du-Nord QC, 1109 171 D2
Notre-Dame-
du-Portage QC, 1172 178 A2
Nouvelle QC, 1960 178 C2
Noyan QC, 1093 175 D4
Oak Bay BC, 17798 163 D4
Oak Lake MB, 359 167 D4
Oakville ON, 144738 173 D2
Oka QC, 3194 174 C3
Okanagan Falls BC, 1971 163 F3
Okotoks AB, 11664 164 C3
Old Perlican NL, 714 183 E3
Olds AB, 6607 164 C2
O'Leary PE, 860 179 E4
Oliver BC, 4224 163 F3
Omemee ON, 1319 173 E1
Onaping ON, 4104 170 C3
108 Mile Ranch BC, 2441 157 F4
150 Mile House BC, 1142 157 E4
100 Mile House BC, 1739 157 F4
Onoway AB, 847 159 D4
Orangeville ON, 25248 172 C2
Orillia ON, 29121 173 D1
Ormstown QC, 3647 174 C4
Oromocto NB, 8843 180 B1
Orono ON, 1666 173 D2
Osgoode ON, 2571 174 B3
Oshawa ON, 139051 173 D2
Osler SK, 823 165 F1
Osoyoos BC, 4295 163 F3
Ottawa ON, 774072 174 B3
Outlook SK, 2129 165 F2
Owen Sound ON, 21431 172 C1
Oxbow SK, 1132 166 C4
Oxford NS, 1332 181 D1
Oyen AB, 1020 165 E2
Pabos QC, 1427 179 D1
Pabos Mills QC, 1452 179 D2
Paisley ON, 1033 172 B1
Palmarolle QC, 1527 171 D1
Palmerston ON, 2518 172 C2
Papineauville QC, 2247 174 B3
Paquetville NB, 667 179 D2
Paradise NL, 9598 183 F4
Paris ON, 9881 172 C3
Parkhill ON, 1752 172 B3
Parksville BC, 10323 162 C3
Parrsboro NS, 1529 180 C2
Parry Sound ON, 6124 171 D4
Pasadena NL, 3133 182 C3
Paspébiac QC, 3326 179 D2
Peace River AB, 6240 158 B2
Peachland BC, 4654 163 F2
Pelham ON, 15272 173 D3
Pelican Narrows SK, 690 160 C3
Pelly Crossing YT, 328 155 D3
Pemberton BC, 1637 163 D2
Pembroke ON, 13490 174 A3
Penetanguishene ON, 8316 172 C1
Penhold AB, 1729 164 C2
Pense SK, 533 166 B3
Penticton BC, 30985 163 F3
Percé QC, 3614 179 E1
Perth ON, 6003 174 A4
Perth-Andover NB, 1908 178 B4
Petawawa ON, 14398 171 E4
Peterborough ON, 71446 173 E1
Peterview NL, 811 183 D2
Petitcodiac NB, 1444 180 C1
Petit-Matane QC, 1365 178 B1
Petit-Rocher NB, 1966 179 D2
Petrolia ON, 4849 172 B3
Pickering ON, 87139 173 D2
Picton ON, 4563 173 F2
Pictou NS, 3875 181 D1
Picture Butte AB, 1701 165 D4
Pilot Butte SK, 1850 166 B3
Pilot Mound MB, 676 167 D4
Pinawa MB, 1500 167 F3
Pincher Creek AB, 3666 164 C4
Pinehouse SK, 1038 159 F2
Pintendre QC, 6209 175 E1
Pitt Meadows BC, 14670 163 D3
Placentia NL, 4426 183 E4
Plantagenet ON, 1103 174 B3
Plaster Rock NB, 1219 178 B3
Plessisville QC, 6756 175 E2
Plum Coulee MB, 725 167 E4
Plympton-Wyoming ON, 7359 172 B3
Pohénégamook QC, 3097 178 A3
Pointe-à-la-Croix QC, 1513 178 C2
Pointe-au-Père QC, 4171 178 B1
Pointe-aux-Outardes QC, 1413 178 B1
Pointe-Calumet QC, 5604 174 C3
Pointe-du-Lac QC, 6902 175 D2
Pt. Edward ON, 2101 172 A3
Pointe-Lebel QC, 1931 177 D2
Pointe-Sapin NB, 627 179 D3
Pointe-Verte NB, 1041 178 C2
Pt. Leamington NL, 685 183 D2
Ponoka AB, 6330 164 C1
Ponteix SK, 550 165 F4
Pontiac QC, 4643 174 A3
Pont-Lafrance NB, 754 179 D3
Pont-Landry NB, 1342 179 D2
Pont-Rouge QC, 7146 175 E1
Porcupine ON, 7196 170 C1
Porcupine Plain SK, 820 166 C1
Portage la Prairie MB, 12976 167 E4
Port Alberni BC, 17743 162 C3
Port Alice BC, 1126 162 A1
Port au Choix NL, 1010 182 C1
Port au Port East NL, 642 182 C3
Port-Cartier QC, 6412 177 E2
Port Colborne ON, 18450 173 D3
Port Coquitlam BC, 51257 163 D3
Port-Daniel-Gascons QC, 1559 179 D2
Port Dover ON, 5527 172 C3

Ottawa ON

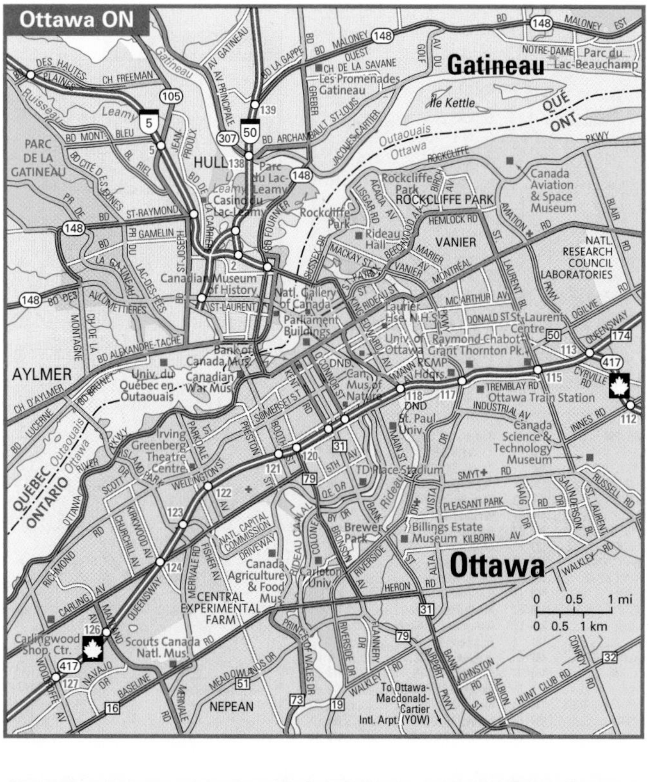

Figures after entries indicate population, page number, and grid reference.

Port Edward BC, *659* ... **156** B2
Port Elgin ON, *6766* ... **172** B1
Port Hardy BC, *4574* ... **162** A1
Port Hawkesbury NS, *3701* ... **181** E1
Port Hope ON, *15605* ... **173** E2
Port McNeill BC, *2821* ... **162** A1
Portneuf QC, *1436* ... **175** E1
Port Perry ON, *7244* ... **173** D2
Port Saunders NL, *812* ... **183** D1
Port Stanley ON, *2521* ... **172** B3
Pouce Coupe BC, *833* ... **157** F1
Pouch Cove NL, *1669* ... **183** F4
Powassan ON, *3252* ... **171** D3
Powell River BC, *12983* ... **162** C2
Quispamsis NB, *13757* ... **180** B2
Racine QC, *1153* ... **175** D3
Radium Hot Springs BC, *735* ... **164** B3
Radville SK, *735* ... **166** B4
Rainbow Lake AB, *976* ... **155** F3
Rainy River ON, *981* ... **167** F4
Ramea NL, *754* ... **182** C4
Rapid City MB, *424* ... **167** D3
Rawdon QC, *8648* ... **174** C2
Raymond AB, *3200* ... **165** D4
Raymore SK, *625* ... **166** B2
Redcliff AB, *4372* ... **165** D3
Red Deer AB, *67707* ... **164** C2
Red Lake ON, *4233* ... **168** B2
Rimouski-Est QC, *2058* ... **178** A1
Ripon QC, *1265* ... **174** B3
River Hebert NS, *676* ... **180** C1
Rivers MB, *1119* ... **167** D4
Riverton MB, *594* ... **167** E3
Riverview NB, *17010* ... **179** D4
Rivière-au-Renard QC, *2524* ... **179** D1
Rivière-Beaudette QC, *1464* ... **174** C3
Rivière-Bleue QC, *1477* ... **178** A3
Rivière-du-Loup QC, *17772* ... **178** A2
Rivière-Ouelle QC, *1177* ... **176** C4
Rivière-Verte NB, *856* ... **178** B3
Robert's Arm NL, *886* ... **183** D2
Roberts Creek BC, *3080* ... **163** D3
Robertsonville QC, *1705* ... **175** E2
Robertville NB, *954* ... **178** C2
Roberval QC, *10906* ... **176** B3
Roblin MB, *1818* ... **166** C3
Robson BC, *1599* ... **164** A4
Rocanville SK, *887* ... **166** C3
Rock Forest QC, *18667* ... **175** E3
Rockland ON, *8542* ... **174** B3
Rockwood ON, *2789* ... **172** C2
Rocky Hbr. NL, *1002* ... **182** C2
Rocky Mtn. House AB, *6208* ... **164** C2
Roddickton NL, *1003* ... **183** D1
Rodney ON, *1102* ... **172** B4
Rogersville NB, *1248* ... **179** D4
Rose Blanche-
  Harbour Le Cou NL, *668* ... **182** C4
Rosetown SK, *2471* ... **165** F2
Rossburn MB, *568* ... **167** D3
Rossland BC, *3646* ... **164** A4
Ross River YT, *337* ... **155** E3
Rosthern SK, *1504* ... **165** F1
Rothesay NB, *11505* ... **180** B2
Rouyn-Noranda QC, *28270* ... **171** D2
Roxboro QC, *5642* ... **174** C3
Roxton Falls QC, *1300* ... **175** D3
Roxton Pond QC, *3527* ... **175** D3
Royston BC, *1699* ... **162** C2
Rusagonis NB, *2698* ... **180** A1
Russell MB, *1587* ... **166** C3
Russell ON, *4059* ... **174** B3
Saanich BC, *103654* ... **163** D4
Sackville NB, *5361* ... **180** C1
Sacré-Coeur QC, *2053* ... **178** A2
St. Adolphe MB, *1140* ... **167** E4
St-Agapit QC, *2906* ... **175** E2
St-Aimé-des-Lacs QC, *1073* ... **176** C4
St-Alban QC, *1170* ... **175** D1
St. Alban's NL, *1372* ... **183** D4
St. Albert AB, *53081* ... **159** D4
St-Albert QC, *1475* ... **175** D2
St-Alexandre QC, *2388* ... **175** D3
St-Alexandre-
  de-Kamouraska QC, *1849* ... **178** A2
St-Alexis-des-Monts QC, *2909* ... **175** D2
St-Alphonse-Rodriguez QC,
  2691 ... **174** C2
St-Ambroise QC, *3463* ... **176** C3
St-André-Avellin QC, *3434* ... **174** B3
St-André-d'Argenteuil QC, *2867* ... **174** C3
St. Andrews NB, *1869* ... **180** A2
St-Anselme QC, *3224* ... **175** E2
St. Anthony NL, *2730* ... **183** D1
St-Antoine NB, *1472* ... **179** D4
St-Antoine QC, *11488* ... **174** C3
St-Antoine-de-Tilly QC, *1417* ... **175** E2
St-Antonin QC, *3395* ... **178** A2
St-Apollinaire QC, *3930* ... **175** E2
St-Armand QC, *1263* ... **175** D4
St-Charles NB, *806* ... **179** D4
St. Charles ON, *1245* ... **171** D3
St-Charles-Borromée QC,
  10668 ... **174** C2
St-Charles-de-Bellechasse QC,
  2237 ... **175** E1
St-Charles-de-Mandeville QC,
  1878 ... **174** C2
St-Charles-sur-Richelieu QC,
  1736 ... **175** D3
St-Chrysostome QC, *2590* ... **174** C4
St. Claude MB, *558* ... **167** E4
St-Claude QC, *1080* ... **175** E3
St-Clet QC, *1586* ... **174** C3
St-Côme QC, *1923* ... **174** C2
St-Côme-Linière QC, *3239* ... **175** F2
St-Constant QC, *22577* ... **174** C3
St-Cyprien QC, *1231* ... **178** A2
St-Cyrille-de-Wendover QC,
  3863 ... **175** D2
St-Damase QC, *1327* ... **175** D3
St-Damien QC, *1983* ... **174** C2

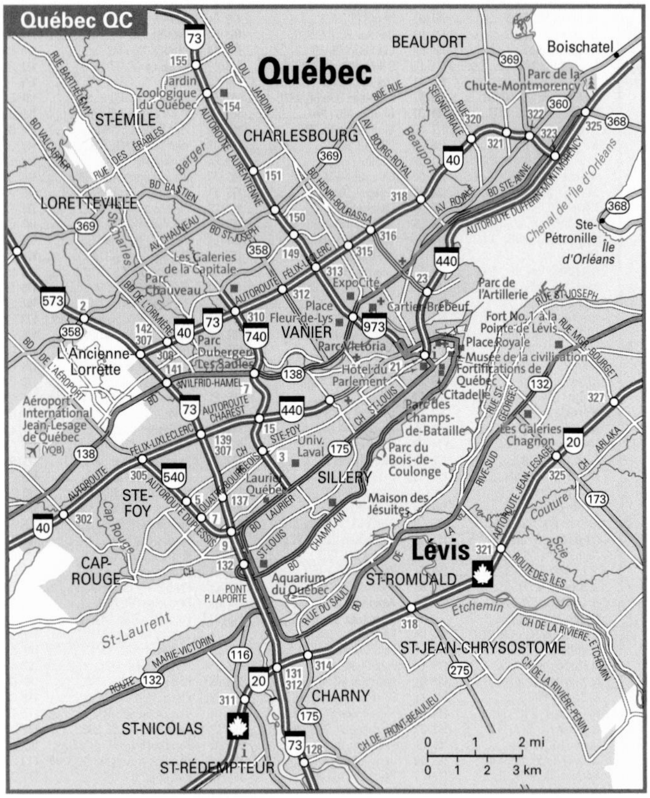

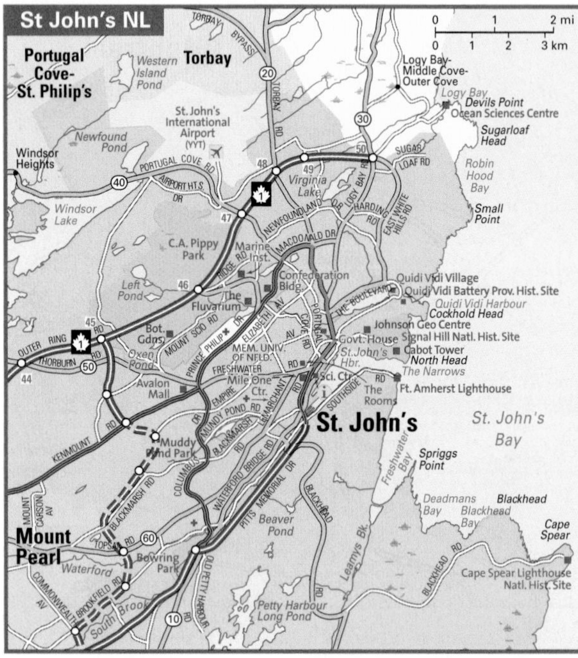

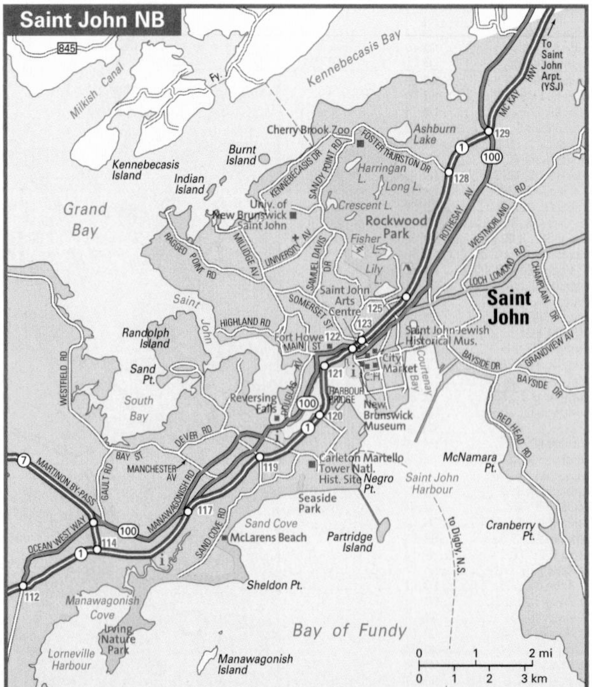

Powerview MB, *750* ... **167** F3
Pré-d'en-Haut NB, *964* ... **180** C1
Preeceville SK, *1074* ... **166** C2
Prescott ON, *4228* ... **174** B4
Prévost QC, *8280* ... **174** C3
Price QC, *1800* ... **178** B1
Prince Albert SK, *34291* ... **160** B4
Prince Edward ON, *24901* ... **173** F2
Prince George BC, *72406* ... **157** E2
Prince Rupert BC, *14643* ... **156** B2
Princeton BC, *2610* ... **163** F3
Princeville QC, *5703* ... **175** E2
Provost AB, *1980* ... **165** E2
Pugwash NS, *810* ... **181** D1
Qualicum Beach BC, *6921* ... **162** C3
Qu'Appelle SK, *648* ... **166** B3
Québec QC, *169076* ... 175 E1
Queens Reg. Mun. NS, *11694* ... **180** C4
Quesnel BC, *10044* ... **157** E3
Quinte West ON, *41409* ... **173** E1
Redvers SK, *917* ... **166** C4
Redwater AB, *2172* ... **159** D4
Regina SK, *178225* ... 166 B3
Regina Beach SK, *1039* ... **166** B3
Renfrew ON, *7942* ... **174** A3
Renous NB, *1183* ... **178** C3
Repentigny QC, *54550* ... **174** C3
Reserve Mines NS, *1732* ... **181** F1
Revelstoke BC, *7500* ... **164** A3
Rexton NB, *810* ... **179** D4
Richelieu QC, *4851* ... **175** D3
Richibucto NB, *1341* ... **179** D4
Richmond BC, *164345* ... **163** D3
Richmond ON, *3287* ... **174** B3
Richmond QC, *3424* ... **175** D3
Richmond Hill ON, *132030* ... **173** D2
Ridgetown ON, *3358* ... **172** B4
Rigaud QC, *6095* ... **174** C3
Rimbey AB, *2118* ... **164** C1
Rimouski QC, *31305* ... **178** A1
St-Arsène QC, *1156* ... **178** A2
St-Arthur NB, *832* ... **178** C2
St-Aubert QC, *1365* ... **175** F1
St-Augustin-de-Desmaures QC,
  15727 ... **175** E1
St-Basile QC, *2575* ... **175** E1
St-Benoît-Labre QC, *1543* ... **175** E2
St-Bernard QC, *2028* ... **175** E2
St. Bernard's-
  Jacques Fontaine NL, *657* ... **183** E4
St-Boniface QC, *3998* ... **175** D2
St. Brieux SK, *505* ... **166** B1
St-Bruno QC, *2384* ... **176** C3
St-Bruno-de-Guigues QC, *1129* ... **171** D2
St-Calixte QC, *4912* ... **174** C2
St-Canut QC, *3430* ... **174** C3
St-Casimir QC, *1582* ... **175** D2
St. Catharines ON, *129170* ... **173** D3
St-Césaire QC, *4850* ... **175** D3
St-Damien-de-Buckland QC,
  1880 ... **175** E2
St-David-de-Falardeau QC,
  2347 ... **176** C3
St-Denis-sur-Richelieu QC,
  2183 ... **175** D3
St-Dominique QC, *2231* ... **175** D3
St-Donat QC, *3444* ... **174** C2
Ste-Adèle QC, *9215* ... **174** C2
Ste-Agathe-de-Lotbinière QC,
  1191 ... **175** E2
Ste-Agathe-des-Monts QC,
  7116 ... **174** C2
Ste-Angèle-de-Mérici QC, *1066* ... **178** B1
Ste. Anne MB, *1513* ... **167** E4
Ste-Anne-de-Beaupré QC, *2752* ... **175** E1
Ste-Anne de Kent NB, *1150* ... **179** D4
Ste-Anne-de-la-Pérade QC,
  2151 ... **175** D2

Entries in **bold color** indicate cities with detailed inset maps.

Ste-Anne-de-Madawaska NB, *1168* **178** B3
Ste-Anne-des-Monts QC, *6835* **178** C1
Ste-Anne-des-Plaines QC, *12908* **174** C3
Ste-Barbe QC, *1338* **174** C3
Ste-Béatrix QC, *1608* **174** C2
Ste-Blandine QC, *2218* **178** B1
Ste-Brigide-d'Iberville QC, *1279* **175** D3
Ste-Catherine-de-Hatley QC, *1970* **175** D3
Ste-Catherine-de-la-Jacques-Cartier QC, *4681* **175** E1
Ste-Cécile NB, *883* **179** D2
Ste-Claire QC, *3135* **175** E2
Ste-Clotilde-de-Châteauguay QC, *1558* **174** C3
Ste-Clotilde-de-Horton QC, *1527* **175** D2
Ste-Croix QC, *1533* **175** E2
St-Édouard QC, *1195* **174** C3
Ste-Élisabeth QC, *1474* **174** C2
Ste-Émélie-de-l'Énergie QC, *1500* **174** C2
Ste-Félicité QC, *1256* **178** B1
Ste-Foy QC, *72547* **175** E1
Ste-Hélène-de-Bagot QC, *1521* **175** D3
Ste-Hénédine QC, *1168* **175** E2
Ste-Jeanne-d'Arc QC, *1128* **176** B3
Ste-Julie QC, *26580* **174** C3
Ste-Justine QC, *1884* **175** F2
Ste-Luce QC, *1478* **178** B1
St-Elzéar QC, *1769* **175** E2
Ste-Madeleine QC, *2011* **175** D3
Ste-Marcelline de-Kildare QC, *1279* **174** C2
Ste-Marguerite-Estérel QC, *2274* **174** C2
Ste-Marie QC, *11320* **175** E2
Ste-Marie-St-Raphaël NB, *1135* **179** D2
Ste-Marthe-du-Cap QC, *6162* **175** D2
Ste-Martine QC, *3740* **174** C3
Ste-Mélanie QC, *2633* **174** C2
Ste-Perpétue QC, *1990* **175** F1
St-Éphrem-de-Beauce QC, *2585* **175** E2
Ste-Rosalie QC, *4170* **175** D3
Ste. Rose du Lac MB, *1047* **167** D3
Ste-Sophie QC, *8966* **174** C3
St-Esprit QC, *1850* **174** C3
Ste-Thècle QC, *2513* **175** D1
Ste-Thérèse QC, *24269* **174** C3
Ste-Thérèse-de-Gaspé QC, *1165* **179** D1

St-Étienne-de-Lauzon QC, *8897* **175** E2
St-Eugène QC, *1084* **175** D3
St-Eustache QC, *40378* **174** C3
Ste-Véronique QC, *1050* **174** B2
St-Fabien QC, *1848* **178** A1

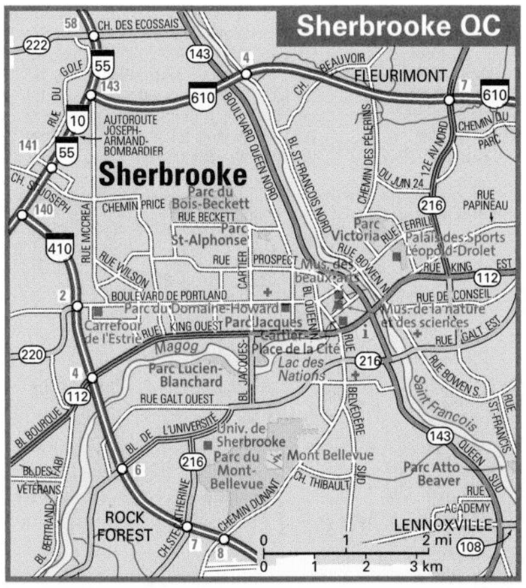

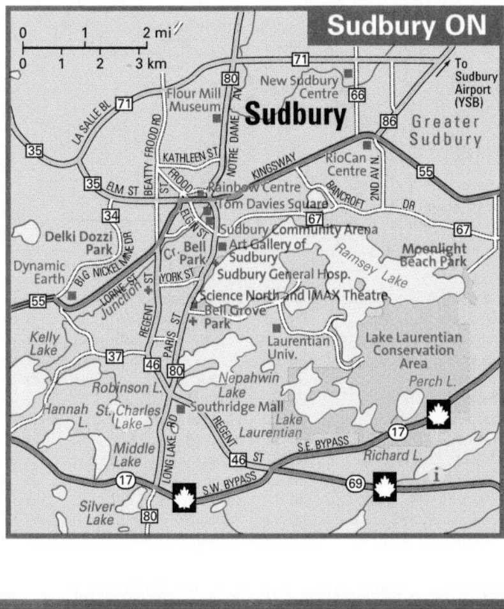

St-Faustin-Lac-Carré QC, *2790* **174** C2
St-Félicien QC, *10622* **176** B3
St-Félix-de-Kingsey QC, *1521* **175** D3
St-Félix-de-Valois QC, *5465* **174** C2
St-Ferdinand QC, *2477* **175** E2
St-Ferréol-les-Neiges QC, *2014* **175** E1
St-Flavien QC, *1492* **175** E2
St-François-de-la-Rivière-du-Sud QC, *1604* **175** E1
St-François-du-Lac QC, *1976* **175** D2
St-Frédéric QC, *1087* **175** E2
St-Fulgence QC, *2003* **176** C3
St-Gabriel QC, *2775* **174** C2
St-Gabriel-de-Rimouski QC, *1208* **178** B1
St-Gédéon QC, *1923* **176** C3
St-Gédéon-de-Beauce QC, *1829* **175** F3
St. George NB, *1509* **180** A2
St. George ON, *2510* **172** C3
St. George's NL, *1354* **182** C3
St-Georges QC, *20787* **175** F2
St-Georges QC, *3854* **175** D2
St-Georges-de-Cacouna QC, *1098* **178** A2
St-Germain-de-Grantham QC, *3661* **175** D3
St-Gervais QC, *1910* **175** E1
St-Gilles QC, *1803* **175** E2
St-Grégoire QC, *1217* **175** D2
St-Guillaume QC, *1575* **175** D3
St-Henri QC, *3807* **175** E1
St-Hilarion QC, *1148* **176** C4
St-Honoré QC, *3835* **176** C3
St-Honoré-de-Shenley QC, *1664* **175** E2
St-Hubert QC, *75912* **174** C3
St-Hubert-de-Rivière-du-Loup QC, *1322* **178** A2
St-Hugues QC, *1277* **175** D3
St-Hyacinthe QC, *38739* **175** D3
St-Ignace NB, *651* **179** D4
St-Ignace-de-Loyola QC, *1880* **175** D2
St-Irénée NB, *862* **179** D3
St-Isidore NB, *877* **179** D3
St-Isidore QC, *2667* **175** E2
St. Jacobs ON, *1227* **172** C2
St-Jacques QC, *3692* **174** C2
St. Jacques-Coomb's Cove NL, *707* **183** D4
St-Jean-de-Dieu QC, *1768* **178** A2
St-Jean-de-Matha QC, *3602* **174** C2
St-Jean-Port-Joli QC, *3372* **175** F1
St-Jean-sur-Richelieu QC, *37386* **175** D3
St-Jérôme QC, *24583* **174** C3
Saint John NB, *69661* **180** B2
St. John's NL, *99182* **183** F4
St-Joseph-de-Beauce QC, *4487* **175** E2
St-Jovite QC, *3955* **174** C2
St-Jude QC, *1126* **175** D3
St-Laurent QC, *77391* **175** E1
St. Lawrence NL, *1558* **183** D4

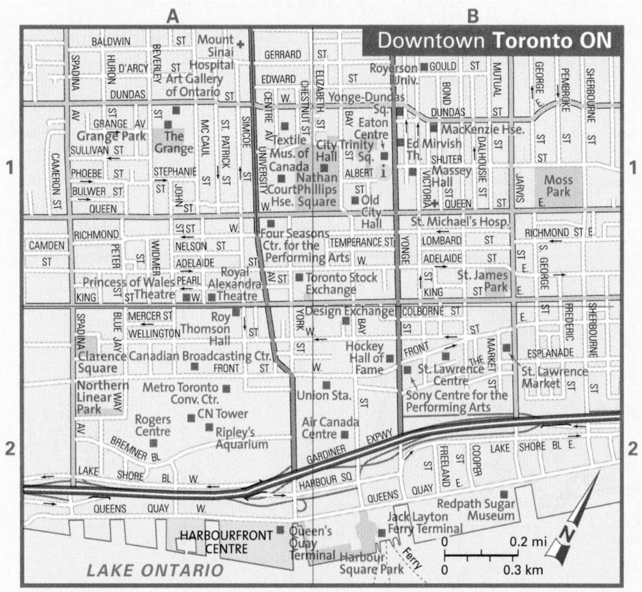

POINTS OF INTEREST

Air Canada Centre B2
Art Gallery of Ontario A1
Canadian Broadcasting Center . .A2
CN Tower .A2
Design Exchange B2
Eaton Centre B1
Ed Mirvish Theatre B1
Four Seasons Centre for the Performing Arts A1
The Grange A1
Harbourfront Centre A2
Hockey Hall of Fame. B2
Jack Layton Ferry Terminal. B2
MacKenzie House. B1
Massey Hall B1
Metro Toronto Convention Ctr.. . .A2
Old City Hall B1
Princess of Wales Theatre A1
Queen's Quay Terminal A2
Redpath Sugar Museum B2
Ripley's Aquarium. A2
Rogers Centre A2
Royal Alexandra Theatre. A1
Royerson University B1
Roy Thomson Hall. A2
Saint Lawrence Centre B2
Saint Lawrence Market. B2
Sony Centre for the Perf. Arts . . .B2
Textile Museum of Canada A1
Toronto Stock Exchange A1
Union Station. B2
Yonge-Dundas Square. B1

St-Lazare MB, *265* **166** C3
St-Lazare-de-Bellechasse QC, *1183* **175** E1
St-Léolin NB, *802* **179** D2
St. Leonard NB, *1385* **178** B3
St-Léonard-d'Aston QC, *2231* **175** D2
St-Léon-de-Standon QC, *1268* **175** F2
St-Léon-le-Grand QC, *1144* **178** B1
St-Liboire QC, *2829* **175** D3
St-Lin-Laurentides QC, *12384* **174** C3
St-Louis-de-France QC, *7246* **175** D2
St-Louis-de-Kent NB, *991* **179** D4
St-Ludger QC, *1203* **175** E3
St. Lunaire-Griquet NL, *822* **183** D1
St-Malachie QC, *1348* **175** E2
St-Marc-des-Carrières QC, *2855* **175** D1
St-Marc-sur-Richelieu QC, *1957* **175** D3
St-Martin QC, *2598* **175** F2
St. Marys ON, *6293* **172** B3
St-Mathieu-du-Parc QC, *1266* **175** D2
St-Maxime-du-Mont-Louis QC, *1288* **179** D1
St-Michel-de-Bellechasse QC, *1633* **175** E1
St-Michel-des-Saints QC, *2414* **174** C1
St-Narcisse QC, *1858* **175** D2
St-Nazaire QC, *2028* **176** C3
St-Nicéphore QC, *9966* **175** D3
St-Nicolas QC, *16645* **175** E1
St-Ours QC, *1624* **175** D3
St-Pacôme QC, *1706* **175** F1
St-Pamphile QC, *2847* **175** F1
St-Pascal QC, *3643* **178** A2
St-Patrice-de-Beaurivage QC, *1105* **175** E2
St. Paul AB, *5061* **159** E4
St-Paulin QC, *1576* **175** D2
St-Pie QC, *2396* **175** D3
St-Pierre-Jolys MB, *893* **167** E4
St-Pierre-les-Becquets QC, *1273* **175** D2
St-Placide QC, *1537* **174** C3
St-Polycarpe QC, *1657* **174** C3
St-Prime QC, *2702* **176** B3
St-Prosper QC, *3802* **175** F2
St-Quentin NB, *2280* **178** B3
St-Raphaël QC, *2231* **175** E1
St-Raymond QC, *8836* **175** E1
St-Rémi QC, *5736* **174** C3
St-Roch-de-Richelieu QC, *1760* **175** D3
St-Sauveur NB, *817* **179** D3
St-Sauveur-des-Monts QC, *3316* **174** C3
St-Siméon QC, *1211* **179** D2
St-Simon NB, *816* **179** D2

Figures after entries indicate population, page number, and grid reference.

St-Stanislas QC, *1076* **175** D2
St. Stephen NB, *4667* **180** A2
St-Théodore-d'Acton QC, *1544* **175** D3
St. Thomas ON, *33236* **172** B3
St-Timothée QC, *8299* **174** C3
St-Tite QC, *3845* **175** D1
St-Tite-des-Caps QC, *1426* **175** E1
St-Ubalde QC, *1460* **175** D1
St-Ulric QC, *1649* **178** B1
St-Urbain QC, *1430* **176** C4
St-Valère QC, *1308* **175** D2
St-Victor QC, *2460* **175** E2
St. Walburg SK, *672* **159** F4
St-Wenceslas QC, *1132* **175** D2
St-Zacharie QC, *2100* **175** F2
St-Zénon QC, *1180* **174** C2
St-Zotique QC, *4158* **174** C3
Salaberry-de-Valleyfield QC, *26170* **174** C3
Salisbury NB, *1954* **180** C1
Salmo BC, *1120* **164** B4
Salmon Arm BC, *15210* **163** F1
Salmon Cove NL, *746* **183** E4
Salmon River NS, *2259* **180** B4
Sandy Bay SK, *1092* **160** C2
Saratoga Beach BC, *1627* **162** B2
Sarnia ON, *70876* **172** A3
Saskatoon SK, *196811* 165 F2
Saugeen Shores ON, *11388* **172** B1
Sault Ste. Marie ON, *74566* **170** B3
Sayabec QC, *1999* **178** B1
Schomberg ON, *1216* **173** D2
Scott QC, *1705* **175** E2
Scoudouc NB, *1047* **179** D4
Seaforth ON, *2692* **172** B2
Sechelt BC, *7775* **162** C3
Sedgewick AB, *865* **165** D1
Selkirk MB, *9752* **167** E3
Senneterre QC, *3275* **171** E2
Sept-Îles QC, *23791* **177** E2
Sexsmith AB, *1653* **157** F1
Shannon QC, *3668* **175** E1
Shaunavon SK, *1775* **165** F4
Shawinigan QC, *17535* **175** D2
Shawinigan-Sud QC, *11544* **175** D2
Shawville QC, *1582* **174** A3
Shediac NB, *4892* **179** D4
Shediac Bridge NB, *950* **179** D4
Shediac Cape NB, *787* **179** D4
Shelburne NS, *2013* **180** B4
Shelburne ON, *4122* **172** C2
Shellbrook SK, *1276* **160** B4
Sherbrooke QC, *75916* 175 E3
Sherwood Park AB, *47645* **164** C1
Shippagan NB, *2872* **179** D2
Shoal Lake MB, *801* **167** D3
Shubenacadie NS, *906* **181** D2
Sicamous BC, *2720* **164** A3
Sidney BC, *10929* **163** D4
Silver Creek BC, *1062* **163** F1
Simcoe ON, *14175* **172** C3
Sioux Lookout ON, *5336* **168** C2
Slave Lake AB, *6600* **158** C3
Smithers BC, *5414* **156** C2
Smiths Falls ON, *9140* **174** A4
Smithville ON, *3317* **173** D3
Smoky Lake AB, *1011* **159** D3
Smooth Rock Falls ON, *1830* **170** C1
Snow Lake MB, *1207* **161** D3
Somerset MB, *459* **167** E4
Sooke BC, *8735* **162** C4
Sorel-Tracy QC, *34194* **175** D2
Sorrento BC, *1197* **163** F1
Souris MB, *1683* **167** D4
Souris PE, *1248* **179** F4
Southampton ON, *3360* **172** B1
S. Bruce Peninsula ON, *8090* **172** B1
Southey SK, *693* **166** B3
S. Huron ON, *10019* **172** B3
S. Indian Lake MB, *808* **161** E1
S. River ON, *1040* **171** D4
Spallumcheen BC, *5134* **164** A3
Spaniard's Bay NL, *2694* **183** E4
Sparwood BC, *3812* **164** C4
Spirit River AB, *1100* **157** F1
Spiritwood SK, *907* **159** F4
Springdale NL, *3045* **183** D2
Springhill NS, *4091* **180** C1
Springside SK, *525* **166** C2
Sproat Lake BC, *1888* **162** C3
Spruce Grove AB, *15983* **159** D4
Squamish BC, *14247* **163** D2
Stanstead QC, *2995* **175** D4
Stayner ON, *3885* **172** C1
Steinbach MB, *9227* **167** E4
Stellarton NS, *4809* **181** D2
Stephenville NL, *7109* **182** C3
Stephenville Crossing NL, *1993* **182** C3
Stettler AB, *5215* **165** D2
Stewiacke NS, *1388* **181** D2
Stirling AB, *877* **165** D4
Stirling ON, *2149* **173** E1
Stoke QC, *2475* **175** E3
Stonewall MB, *4012* **167** E3
Stoney Pt. ON, *1316* **172** A4
Stony Mtn. MB, *1700* **167** E3
Stony Plain AB, *9589* **159** D4
Stouffville ON, *11073* **173** D2
Stoughton SK, *720* **166** C4
Strasbourg SK, *760* **166** B3
Stratford ON, *29676* **172** C2
Strathmore AB, *7621* **164** C3
Strathroy ON, *12805* **172** B3
Sturgeon Falls ON, *5978* **171** D3
Sturgis SK, *627* **166** C2
Sudbury ON, *103879* 170 C3
Summerford NL, *1010* **183** E2
Summerland BC, *10713* **163** F2
Summerside PE, *14654* **179** E4
Sundre AB, *2267* **164** C2
Sundridge ON, *983* **171** D4
Sunny Corner NB, *910* **178** C3
Surrey BC, *347825* **163** D3
Sussex NB, *4182* **180** B1
Sussex Corner NB, *1321* **180** B1
Sutton ON, *6324* **173** D1
Sutton QC, *1631* **175** D4
Swan Hills AB, *1807* **158** C3
Swan River MB, *4032* **166** C2
Swift Current SK, *14821* **165** F3
Sydney NS, *33913* **181** F1
Sydney Mines NS, *16068* **181** F1
Sydney River NS, *4496* **181** F1
Sylvan Lake AB, *7493* **164** C2
Taber AB, *7671* **165** D4
Tabusintac NB, *893* **179** D3
Tappen BC, *788* **163** F1
Tara ON, *905* **172** B1
Tatamagouche NS, *738* **181** D1
Tavistock ON, *2513* **172** C3
Taylor BC, *1143* **158** A2
Tecumseh ON, *25105* **172** A4
Teeswater ON, *1109* **172** B2
Telkwa BC, *1371* **156** C2
Temagami ON, *893* **171** D3
Témiscaming QC, *2903* **171** D3
Terrace BC, *12109* **156** C2
Terrace Bay ON, *1950* **169** E4
Terrebonne QC, *43149* **174** C3
Teulon MB, *1058* **167** E3
Thamesford ON, *1748* **172** C3
Thamesville ON, *928* **172** B4
The Pas MB, *5795* **161** D4
Thessalon ON, *1386* **170** B3
Thetford Mines QC, *16628* **175** E2
Thompson MB, *13256* **161** E2
Thornbury ON, *1865* **172** C1
Thorold ON, *18048* **173** D3
Thorsby AB, *799* **159** D4
Three Hills AB, *2902* **164** C2
Thunder Bay ON, *109016* **169** D4
Thurso QC, *2436* **174** B3
Tide Head NB, *1149* **178** C2
Tignish PE, *831* **179** E3
Tilbury ON, *4599* **172** A4
Tillsonburg ON, *14052* **172** C3
Timberlea NS, *4781* **181** D3
Timmins ON, *43686* **170** C1
Tisdale SK, *3063* **160** C4
Tofield AB, *1818* **159** D4
Tofino BC, *1466* **162** B3
Torbay NL, *5474* **183** F4
Toronto ON, *2481494* 173 D2
Tottenham ON, *4829* **173** D2
Tracadie-Sheila NB, *4724* **179** D3
Trail BC, *7575* **164** A4
Treherne MB, *644* **167** E4
Trent Hills ON, *12569* **173** E1
Trenton NS, *2798* **181** D2
Trenton ON **173** E2
Trepassey NL, *889* **183** E4
Tring-Jonction QC, *1333* **175** E2
Triton NL, *1102* **183** D2
Trochu AB, *1033* **164** C2
Trois-Pistoles QC, *3635* **178** A2
Trois-Rivières QC, *46264* **175** D2
Truro NS, *11457* **181** D2
Tuktoyaktuk NT, *930* **155** D1
Tumbler Ridge BC, *1851* **157** F1
Turner Valley AB, *1608* **164** C3
Tweed ON, *1539* **173** E1
Twillingate NL, *2611* **183** E2
Two Hills AB, *1091* **159** E4
Ucluelet BC, *1559* **162** B3
Union Bay BC, *1167* **162** C3
Unity SK, *2243* **165** E2
Upton QC, *1986* **175** D3
Uxbridge ON, *8540* **173** D2
Val-Comeau NB, *823* **179** D3
Valcourt QC, *2411* **175** D3
Val-David QC, *3819* **174** C2
Val-des-Monts QC, *7842* **174** B3
Val-d'Or QC, *22748* **171** E2
Valemount BC, *1195* **157** F3
Val-Joli QC, *1532* **175** E3
Vallée-Jonction QC, *1882* **175** E2
Valleyview AB, *1856* **158** B3
Val-Morin QC, *2216* **174** C2
Val-Senneville QC, *2479* **171** E2
Vancouver BC, *545671* 163 D3
Vanderhoof BC, *4390* **157** D2
Vankleek Hill ON, *2022* **174** B3
Varennes QC, *19653* **174** C3
Vaudreuil-Dorion QC, *19920* **174** C3
Vauxhall AB, *1112* **165** D4
Vegreville AB, *5376* **159** D4
Venise-en-Québec QC, *1243* **175** D4
Verchères QC, *4782* **174** C3
Verdun QC, *60564* **174** C3
Vermilion AB, *3948* **159** E4
Vernon BC, *33494* **164** A3
Victoria BC, *74125* 163 D4
Victoria NL, *1798* **183** E4
Victoriaville QC, *38841* **175** E2
Viking AB, *1052* **159** E4
Ville-Marie QC, *2770* **171** D2
Virden MB, *3109* **167** D4
Vulcan AB, *1762* **164** C3
Wabana NL, *2679* **183** F4
Wabasca AB, *1114* **159** D2
Wabowden MB, *497* **161** E3
Wabush NL, *1894* **183** E1
Wadena SK, *1412* **166** B2
Wainwright AB, *5117* **159** E4
Wakaw SK, *884* **165** F1
Waldheim SK, *889* **165** F1
Walkerton ON, *4970* **172** B1
Wallaceburg ON, *11114* **172** A3
Warfield BC, *1739* **164** A4
Warman SK, *3481* **165** F2
Warwick QC, *4874* **175** E2
Wasaga Beach ON, *12419* **172** C1
Waterford ON, *2871* **172** C3
Waterloo ON, *86543* **172** C2
Waterloo QC, *3993* **175** D3
Waterville NS, *808* **180** C2
Waterville QC, *1824* **175** E3
Watford ON, *1625* **172** B3
Watrous SK, *1808* **166** B2
Watson SK, *794* **166** B2
Watson Lake YT, *912* **155** E3
Waverley NS, *934* **181** D3
Wawa ON, *3279* **169** F4
Wawanesa MB, *516* **167** D4
Wawota SK, *538* **166** C4
Wedgeport NS, *1217* **180** B4
Weedon QC, *2646* **175** E3
Welland ON, *48402* **173** D3
Wellesley ON, *1666* **172** C2
Wellington ON, *1943* **173** E2
Wellington PE, *382* **179** E4
Wembley AB, *1497* **157** F1
Wentworth-Nord QC, *1121* **174** C3
Westbank BC, *15700* **163** F2
Western Shore NS, *1015* **180** C3
Westlock AB, *4819* **159** D3
W. Lorne ON, *1458* **172** B4
W. Nipissing ON, *13114* **171** D3
W. Vancouver BC, *41421* **163** D3
Westville NS, *3879* **181** D2
Wetaskiwin AB, *11154* **159** D4
Weyburn SK, *9534* **166** B4
Wheatley ON, *1920* **172** A4
Whistler BC, *8896* **163** D2
Whitbourne NL, *930* **183** E4
Whitby ON, *87413* **173** D2
Whitchurch-Stouffville ON, *22008* **173** D2
White City SK, *1013* **166** B3
Whitecourt AB, *8334* **158** C3
Whitehorse YT, *19058* **155** D3
White Rock BC, *18250* **163** D3
Whitewood SK, *947* **166** C3
Wiarton ON, *2349* **172** B1
Wickham QC, *2516* **175** D3
Wikwemikong ON, *1352* **170** C4
Wilkie SK, *1282* **165** E2
Williams Lake BC, *11153* **157** E4
Winchester ON, *2427* **174** B4
Windermere BC, *1060* **164** B3
Windsor NS, *3778* **180** C2
Windsor ON, *208402* **172** A4
Windsor QC, *5321* **175** E3
Wingham ON, *2885* **172** B2
Winkler MB, *7943* **167** E4
Winnipeg MB, *619544* 167 E4
Winnipeg Beach MB, *801* **167** E3
Winnipegosis MB, *621* **167** D2
Witless Bay NL, *1056* **183** F4
Wolfville NS, *3658* **180** C2
Wolseley SK, *766* **166** C3
Wood Buffalo AB, *41466* **159** E1
Woodstock NB, *5198* **178** B4
Woodstock ON, *33061* **172** C3
Woodville ON, *871* **173** D1
Wotton QC, *1568* **175** E3
Wright QC, *1137* **174** A2
Wynyard SK, *1919* **166** B2
Wyoming ON, *2200* **172** B3
Yamachiche QC, *2631* **175** D2
Yarmouth NS, *7561* **180** B4
Yellowknife NT, *16541* **155** F2
Yorkton SK, *15107* **166** C3
Youbou BC, *727* **162** C3

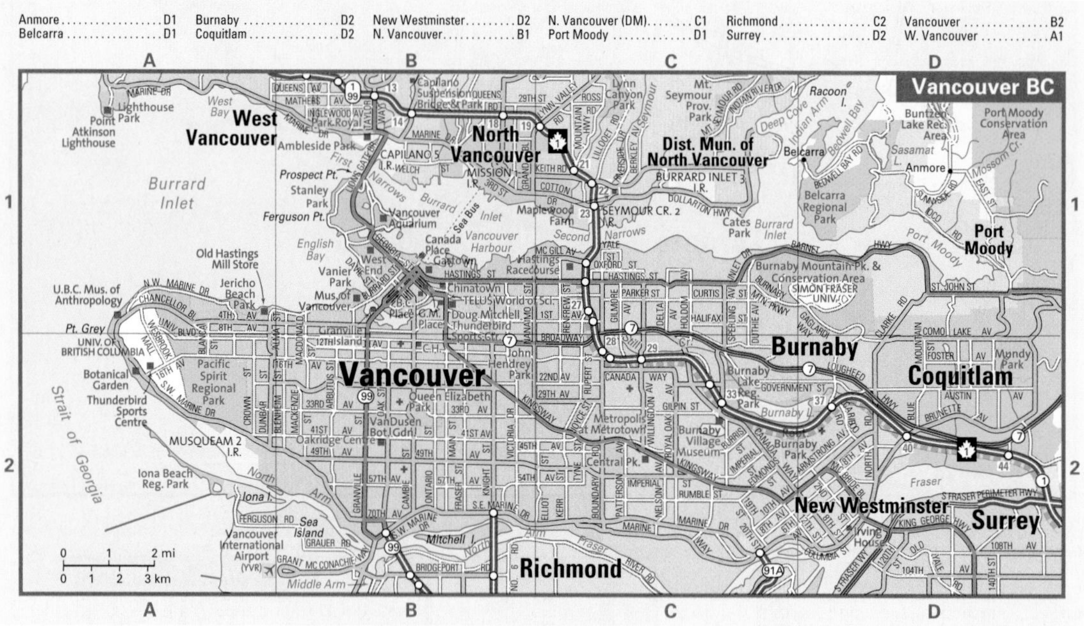

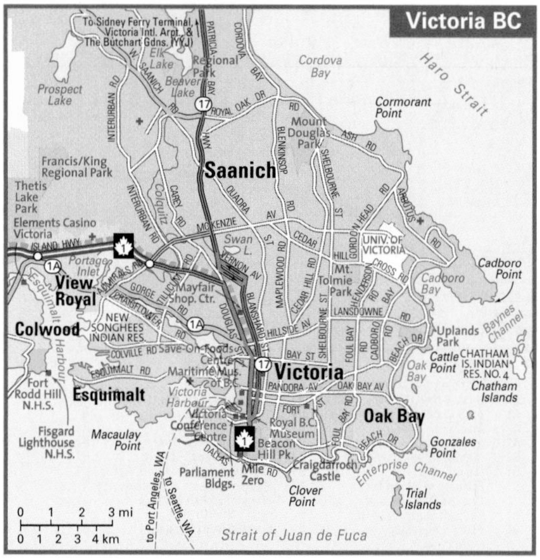

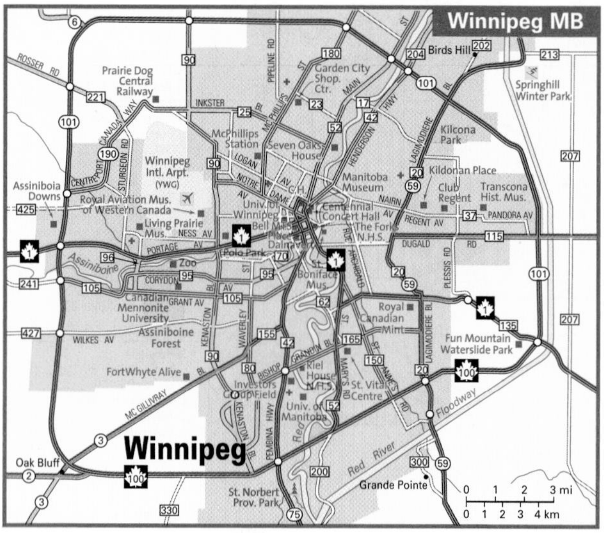

283
Acámbaro–Zumpango del Río

Entries in **bold color** indicate cities with detailed inset maps.

MEXICO

Acámbaro, 57972 ... 186 B3
Acaponeta, 17906 ... 186 A2
Acapulco, 673479 ... 186 B4
Acayucan, 50934 ... 187 D3
Actopan, 24097 ... 186 C2
Agua Dulce, 36079 ... 187 D3
Agua Prieta, 77254 ... 184 C1
Aguascalientes, 722250 ... 186 B2
Ajalpan, 28031 ... 186 C3
Álamo, 23281 ... 186 C2
Allende, 17753 ... 185 E2
Altamira, 59536 ... 186 C2
Alvarado, 23776 ... 187 D3
Apan, 26642 ... 186 C3
Apatzingán, 99010 ... 186 B3
Apizaco, 49506 ... 186 C3
Apodaca, 212118 ... 185 E3
Arcelia, 16609 ... 186 B3
Arriaga, 24447 ... 187 D4
Atlixco, 86690 ... 186 C3
Atoyac de Álvarez, 21407 ... 186 B4
Autlán de Navarro, 45382 ... 186 A2
Berriozábal, 16897 ... 187 D4
Caborca, 59922 ... 184 B1
Cabo San Lucas, 68463 ... 184 C4
Calvillo, 17966 ... 186 B2
Campeche, 220389 ... 187 E2
Cananea, 31560 ... 184 C1
Cancún, 628306 ... 187 F2
Cárdenas, 91558 ... 187 D3
Castaños, 19035 ... 185 E3
Catemaco, 27615 ... 187 D3
Celaya, 340387 ... 186 B2
Cerro Azul, 22268 ... 186 C2
Champotón, 30881 ... 187 E3
Chapala, 17998 ... 186 A2
Chetumal, 151243 ... 187 F3
Chiapa, 27654 ... 187 E4
Chihuahua, 809232 ... 185 D2
Chilpancingo, 187251 ... 186 C4
Cholula, 87897 ... 186 C3
Cintalapa, 42467 ... 187 D4
Cd. Acuña, 134233 ... 185 E2
Cd. Altamirano, 25168 ... 186 B3
Cd. Camargo, 37400 ... 185 D3
Cd. Constitución, 40935 ... 184 B4
Cd. del Carmen, 169466 ... 187 E3
Cd. Guzmán, 97750 ... 186 A3
Cd. Hidalgo, 60542 ... 186 B3
Cd. Ixtepec, 25381 ... 187 D4
Cd. Juárez, 1321004 ... 185 D1
Cd. Lerdo, 79669 ... 185 D4
Cd. Madero, 197216 ... 186 C2
Cd. Mante, 84787 ... 186 C1
Cd. Mendoza, 35641 ... 186 C3
Cd. Miguel Alemán, 16946 ... 185 F3
Cd. Obregón, 298625 ... 184 C3
Cd. Valles, 124644 ... 186 C2
Cd. Victoria, 305155 ... 185 F4
Coatepec, 53621 ... 186 C3
Coatzacoalcos, 235983 ... 187 D3
Colima, 137383 ... 186 A3
Comalcalco, 41458 ... 187 D3
Comitán de Domínguez, 97537 ... 187 E4
Comonfort, 23683 ... 186 B2
Córdoba, 140896 ... 186 C3
Cosamaloapan, 30577 ... 187 D3
Cosoleacaque, 22454 ... 187 D3
Costa Rica, 24874 ... 184 C4
Cozumel, 77236 ... 187 F2
Cuauhtémoc, 114007 ... 184 C2
Cuautla, 154358 ... 186 C3
Cuernavaca, 338650 ... 186 C3
Culiacán, 675773 ... 184 C4
Delicias, 118071 ... 185 D2
Dolores Hidalgo, 59240 ... 186 B2
Durango, 518709 ... 185 D4
Ébano, 24296 ... 186 C2
Emiliano Zapata, 16340 ... 187 E3
Empalme, 42516 ... 184 B2
Ensenada, 279765 ... 184 A1
Escárcega, 29477 ... 187 E3
Escuinapa de Hidalgo, 30790 ... 186 A1
Felipe Carrillo Puerto, 16427 ... 187 F3
Francisco I. Madero, 26201 ... 185 E3
Fresnillo, 120944 ... 185 E4
Frontera, 69462 ... 185 E3
Frontera, 69462 ... 187 E3
Garza García, 120868 ... 185 E3
Gómez Palacio, 257352 ... 185 D3
Guadalajara, 1495182 ... 186 A2
Guadalupe, 673616 ... 185 E3
Guadalupe, 673616 ... 186 B1
Guamúchil, 63743 ... 184 C4
Guanajuato, 72237 ... 186 B2
Guasave, 71196 ... 184 C3
Guaymas, 113082 ... 184 B2
Hermosillo, 715061 ... 184 B2
Hidalgo del Parral, 104836 ... 185 D3
Huajuapan de León, 53043 ... 186 C3
Huatabampo, 30475 ... 184 C3
Huatusco, 31305 ... 186 C3
Huauchinango, 56206 ... 186 C2
Huejutla de Reyes, 40015 ... 186 C2
Huetamo de Núñez, 21507 ... 186 B3
Huimanguillo, 27344 ... 187 D3
Huixtla, 32033 ... 187 E4
Hunucmá, 24910 ... 187 E2
Iguala, 118468 ... 186 C3
Irapuato, 380941 ... 186 B2
Ixmiquilpan, 34814 ... 186 C2
Ixtlán del Río, 21474 ... 186 A2
Izucar de Matamoros, 36531 ... 186 C3
Jacona, 56934 ... 186 B3
Jalostotitlán, 24423 ... 186 B2
Jáltipan de Morelos, 32778 ... 187 D3
Jérez de García Salinas, 43064 ... 186 A1
Jiménez, 34281 ... 185 D3
Jiutepec, 162427 ... 186 C3
Juchitán de Zaragoza, 74825 ... 187 D4
Kanasín, 77240 ... 187 F2
La Barca, 35219 ... 186 B2
Lagos de Moreno, 98206 ... 186 B2
La Paz, 215178 ... 184 B4
La Piedad de Cabadas, 83323 ... 186 B2
Las Choapas, 42693 ... 187 D3
Lázaro Cárdenas, 79200 ... 186 B3
León, 1238962 ... 186 B2
Linares, 63104 ... 185 F4
Loma Bonita, 31485 ... 187 D3
Loreto, 17714 ... 186 B2
Los Mochis, 256613 ... 184 C3
Los Reyes de Salgado, 39209 ... 186 B3
Macuspana, 32225 ... 187 E3
Magdalena de Kino, 19609 ... 184 B1
Manzanillo, 130035 ... 186 A3
Martínez de la Torre, 60074 ... 186 C2
Matamoros, 449815 ... 185 E4
Matamoros, 449815 ... 185 F3
Matehuala, 77328 ... 185 E4
Matías Romero, 20127 ... 187 D4
Mazatlán, 381583 ... 185 D4
Melchor Múzquiz, 35060 ... 185 E3
Meoqui, 22574 ... 185 D2
Mérida, 777615 ... 187 F2

Cancún MX
Isla Mujeres
Laguna Chakmochuk
Ruinas El Cerrito
El Meco
Aeropista
Punta Sam
Ruinas El Meco
Bahía Mujeres
Playa Garrafón
Punta Sur
Puerto Juárez
Cancún
Palacio de Gobierno
Plaza de Toros
Centro de Convenciones
Punta Cancún
Laguna Nichupté
ZONA HOTELERA
Alfredo V. Bonfil
Ruinas San Miguelito
Ruinas El Rey
Playa El Rey
Canal Nizuc
Aeropuerto Internacional de Cancún (CUN)
MAR CARIBE / CARIBBEAN SEA
Punta Nizuc
Ventura Park

México MX
Cuautitlán Izcalli
Tultitlán
Villa Nicolás Romero
San Francisco Coacalco
Sto. Tomás Chiconautla
Santa Catarina
Acolman
Xometla
San Pedro Tepetitlán
Buenavista
Ecatepec de Morelos
Tepexpan
Ciudad López Mateos
Tequisistlán
Nexquipayac
Tezoyuca
Chiconcuac
Santa Clara
Tlalnepantla
San Salvador Atenco
Chiautla
Texcoco Lake Bed
Texcoco
Naucalpan
México
Santiago Tepatlaxco
San Francisco Chimalpa
San Bernardino
Montecillo
Coatlinchan
Santiago Cuautlalpan
Magdalena Chichicaspa
Chimalhuacán
San Vicente Chicoloapan
Netzahualcóyotl
Dos Ríos
Cuajimalpa
Los Reyes
San Lorenzo Acopilco
Valle de Chalco
Ixtapaluca
PARQUE NACIONAL DESIERTO DE LOS LEONES
Six Flags México
Museo Arqueológico de Cuicuilco
Parque Ecológico de Xochimilco
Xico
Tláhuac
Xochimilco
Chalco

Buenavista ... D1
Chalco ... E3
Chiautla ... E1
Chiconcuac ... E1
Chimalhuacán ... E2
Ciudad López Mateos ... C1
Coatlinchan ... E2
Cuajimalpa ... C3
Cuautitlán Izcalli ... C1
Dos Rìos ... C3
Ecatepec de Morelos ... D1
Fuentes del Valle ... D1
Ixtapaluca ... E3
Los Reyes ... E3
México ... D2
Magdalena Chichicaspa ... C2
Montecillo ... E2
Naucalpan ... C2
Netzahualcóyotl ... E2
Nexquipayac ... E1
Nicolás Romero ... C1
San Bernardino ... E2
San Francisco Chimalpa ... C2
San Francisco Coacalco ... D1
San Lorenzo Acopilco ... C3
San Pedro Tepetitlán ... E1
San Salvador Atenco ... E1
San Vicente Chicoloapan ... E2
Santa Catarina ... E1
Santa Clara ... D1
Santo Tomás Chipiltepec ... E1
Santiago Cuautlalpan ... E2
Santiago Tepatlaxco ... C2
Tepexpan ... E1
Tequisistlán ... E1
Texcoco ... E2
Tezoyuca ... E1
Tláhuac ... E3
Tlalnepantla ... C1
Tultitlán ... D1
Valle de Chalco ... E3
Xico ... E3
Xochimilco ... D3
Xometla ... E1

Mexicali, 689775 ... 184 A1
México, 8555272 ... 186 C3
Minatitlán, 112046 ... 187 D3
Misantla, 26827 ... 186 C3
Monclova, 215271 ... 185 E3
Montemorelos, 45108 ... 185 F4
Monterrey, 1135512 ... 185 E3
Morelia, 597511 ... 186 B3
Moroleón, 43200 ... 186 B2
Naranjos, 20073 ... 186 C2
Navojoa, 113836 ... 184 C3
Navolato, 29153 ... 184 C4
Netzahualcóyotl, 1104585 ... 186 C3
Nogales, 212533 ... 184 B1
Nueva Italia de Ruiz, 29598 ... 186 B3
Nueva Rosita, 38158 ... 185 E3
Nuevo Casas Grandes, 55553 ... 184 C2
Nuevo Laredo, 373725 ... 185 F3
Oaxaca, 255029 ... 186 C4
Ocotlán, 83769 ... 186 A2
Ocozocoautla, 39180 ... 187 D4
Orizaba, 120844 ... 186 C3
Pachuca, 256584 ... 186 C2
Pánuco, 40754 ... 186 C2
Papantla, 53546 ... 186 C2
Paraíso, 25186 ... 187 D3
Parras de la Fuente, 33817 ... 185 E4
Pátzcuaro, 55298 ... 186 B3
Perote, 37516 ... 186 C3
Petatlán, 21659 ... 186 B4
Piedras Negras, 150178 ... 185 E2
Playa del Carmen, 149923 ... 187 F2
Poza Rica, 185242 ... 186 C2
Progreso, 40005 ... 187 E2
Puebla, 1434062 ... 186 C3
Puerto Peñasco, 56756 ... 184 B1
Puerto Vallarta, 203342 ... 186 A2
Puruándiro, 30571 ... 186 B2
Querétaro, 626495 ... 186 B2
Reynosa, 589466 ... 185 F3
Rincón de Romos, 27988 ... 186 B2
Río Bravo, 95647 ... 185 F3
Río Grande, 32944 ... 185 E4
Río Verde, 53128 ... 186 B2
Sabinas Hidalgo, 29988 ... 185 E3
Sahuayo, 64431 ... 186 B2
Salamanca, 160169 ... 186 B2
Salina Cruz, 71464 ... 187 D4
Saltillo, 709671 ... 185 E4
Salvatierra, 37203 ... 186 B2
San Andrés Tuxtla, 61769 ... 187 D3
San Buenaventura, 17743 ... 185 E3
San Cristóbal de las Casas, 158027 ... 187 E4
San Felipe, 28452 ... 186 B2
San Fernando, 29665 ... 185 F4
San Francisco del Rincón, 71139 ... 186 B2
San José del Cabo, 69788 ... 184 C4
San Juan de los Lagos, 48684 ... 186 B2
San Juan del Río, 138878 ... 186 B2
San Luis de la Paz, 49914 ... 186 B2
San Luis Potosí, 722772 ... 186 B2
San Luis Río Colorado, 158089 ... 184 A1
San Miguel de Allende, 69811 ... 186 B2
San Nicolás de los Garza, 443273 ... 185 E3
San Pedro de las Colonias, 48746 ... 185 E3
Santa Catarina, 201233 ... 185 E3
Santiago, 36840 ... 185 E4
Santiago Papasquiaro, 26121 ... 185 D4
Sayula, 26789 ... 186 A3
Silao, 74242 ... 186 B2
Sombrerete, 17535 ... 185 D4
Tacámbaro de Codallos, 18742 ... 186 B3
Tala, 35396 ... 186 A2
Tamazunchale, 24562 ... 186 C2
Tampico, 297284 ... 186 C2
Tantoyuca, 30587 ... 186 C2
Tapachula, 202672 ... 187 E4
Taxco, 52217 ... 186 B3
Teapa, 26548 ... 187 E3
Tecamachalco, 28679 ... 186 C3
Tecate, 64764 ... 184 A1
Tecomán, 85689 ... 186 A3
Tehuacán, 248716 ... 186 C3
Tehuantepec, 36888 ... 187 D4
Tejupilco de Hidalgo, 17994 ... 186 B3
Teloloapan, 23549 ... 186 B3
Tenancingo, 25195 ... 186 B3
Tenosique, 32579 ... 187 E3
Teocaltiche, 23726 ... 186 B2
Tepatitlán, 91959 ... 186 B2
Tepeji de Ocampo, 29486 ... 186 C3
Tepic, 332863 ... 186 A2
Tequila, 29203 ... 186 A2
Tequisquiapan, 29799 ... 186 B2
Tequixquiac, 16789 ... 186 C3
Teziutlán, 58699 ... 186 C3
Ticul, 32796 ... 187 F2
Tierra Blanca, 47824 ... 186 C3
Tijuana, 1300983 ... 184 A1
Tizayuca, 43250 ... 186 C3
Tizimín, 46971 ... 187 F2
Tlapa de Comonfort, 46975 ... 186 C3
Tlapacoyan, 35338 ... 186 C3
Tlaxcala, 14692 ... 186 C3
Toluca, 489333 ... 186 B3
Tonalá, 408759 ... 186 A2
Tonalá, 29557 ... 187 D4
Torreón, 608836 ... 185 D3
Tres Valles, 18078 ... 187 D3
Tulancingo, 102406 ... 186 C2
Tuxpam, 84750 ... 186 C2
Tuxpan, 22481 ... 186 A2
Tuxpan, 27523 ... 186 A3
Tuxtepec, 101810 ... 187 D3
Tuxtla Gutiérrez, 537102 ... 187 E4
Umán, 39611 ... 187 E2
Uruapan, 264439 ... 186 B3
Valladolid, 48973 ... 187 F2
Valle de Santiago, 68058 ... 186 B2
Valle Hermoso, 48918 ... 185 F3
Veracruz, 428323 ... 187 D3
Víctor Rosales, 32721 ... 186 B1
Villa Flores, 28257 ... 187 D4
Villahermosa, 353577 ... 187 E3
Xalapa, 424755 ... 186 C3
Xicotepec de Juárez, 39803 ... 186 C2
Zacapu, 52806 ... 186 B3
Zacatecas, 129011 ... 186 B1
Zacatlán, 33736 ... 186 C2
Zamora de Hidalgo, 141627 ... 186 B3
Zapopan, 1142483 ... 186 A2
Zapotiltic, 22833 ... 186 A3
Zihuatanejo, 67408 ... 186 B3
Zitácuaro, 84307 ... 186 B3
Zumpango, 50742 ... 186 C3
Zumpango del Río, 18158 ... 186 B3

Guadalajara MX
Nuevo México
Mascuala
Base Aérea Militar Emilio Carranza
Zapopan
Parque Bosque El Centinela
Barranca de Oblatos
Estadio Jalisco
Parque Huentitán y Zoológico
Museo Trompo Mágico
Matatlán
Bosque Los Colomos
El Aguacate
Colimilla
Univ. Autónoma de Guadalajara
Guadalajara
Instituto Cultural Cabañas
Parque Solidaridad
Coyula
Bosque La Primavera
Parque del Sol
Cerro de la Reina
Tonalá
El Vado
SANTA ANA TEPETITLÁN
Tlaquepaque
La Tijera
Los Gavilanes
La Calerilla
La Punta
Las Pintitas
San Agustín
Santa Anita
Santa Cruz del Valle
San Francisco de la Soledad
Puente Grande
El Verde
San Sebastián El Grande
Aeropuerto Internacional de Guadalajara Miguel Hidalgo y Costilla (GDL)
El Quince
San Antonio Juanacaxtle

Colimilla ... B1
Coyula ... B1
El Aguacate ... B1
El Quince ... B2
El Vado ... B2
El Verde ... B2
Guadalajara ... A1
La Calerilla ... A2
La Punta ... B2
La Tijera ... A2
Las Pintitas ... B2
Los Gavilanes ... A2
Mascuala ... B1
Matatlán ... B1
Nuevo México ... A1
Puente Grande ... B2
San Antoni Juanacaxtle ... B2
San Francisco de la Soledad ... B2
San Agustín ... A2
San Sebastián El Grande ... A2
Santa Anita ... A2
Santa Cruz del Valle ... A2
Tlaquepaque ... A2
Tonalá ... B2
Zapopan ... A1

Monterrey MX
General Escobedo
Apodaca
MEZQUITAL
Aeropuerto Internacional General Mariano Escobedo (MTY)
San Nicolás de los Garza
Universidad Autónoma de Nuevo León
Monterrey
CERRO DE LAS MITRAS
Parque Niños Héroes
Santa Catarina
Guadalupe
San Pedro Garza García
PARQUE NACIONAL CUMBRES DE MONTERREY
Instituto Tecnológico de Monterrey
Parque Ecológico Chipinque
CERRO DE LA SILLA
Ciudad Benito Juárez
Jardines de la Silla

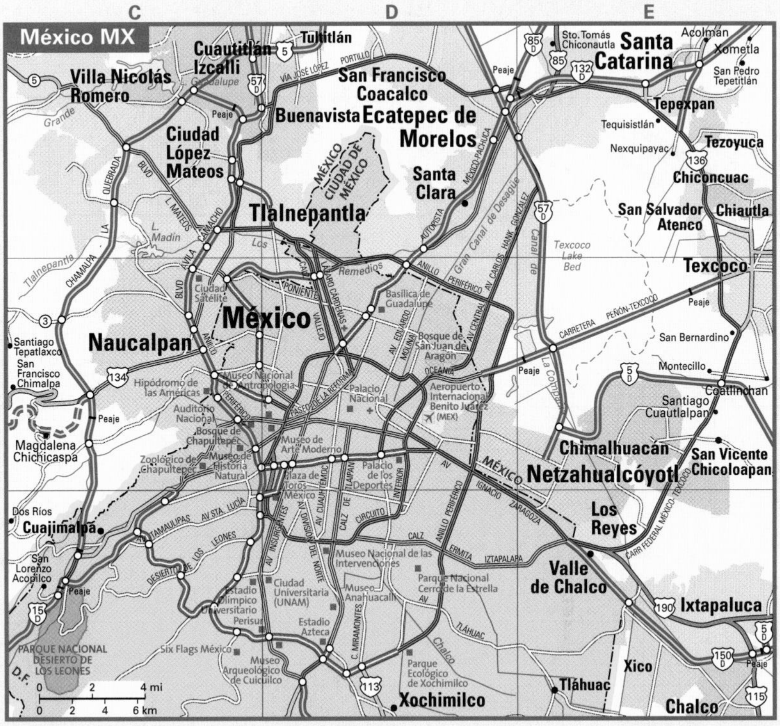

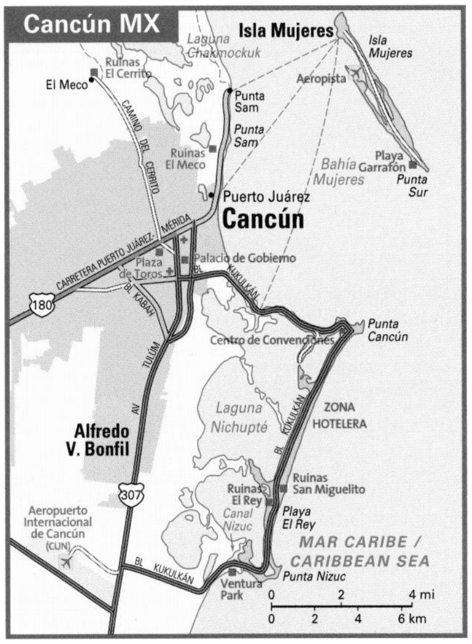

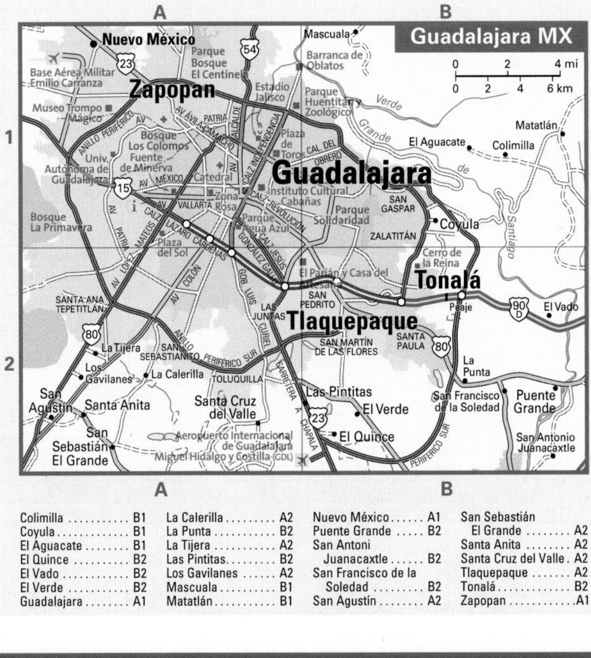

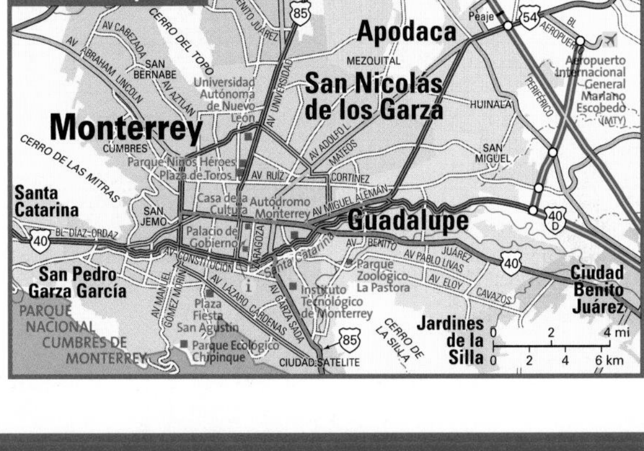

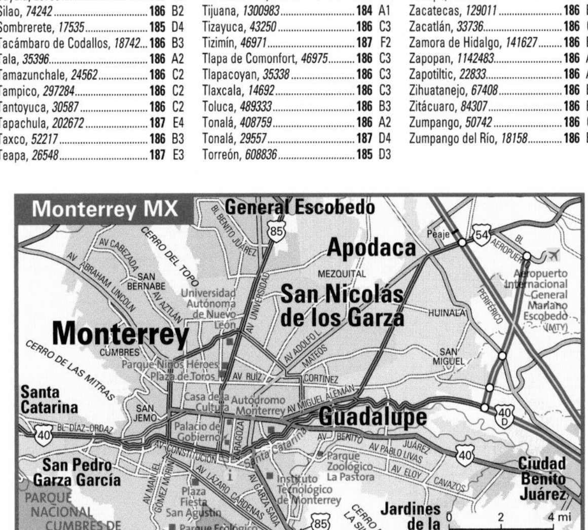

Miles

	Albuquerque, NM	Amarillo, TX	Anchorage, AK	Atlanta, GA	Baltimore, MD	Billings, MT	Birmingham, AL	Bismarck, ND	Boise, ID	Boston, MA	Buffalo, NY	Calgary, AB	Charleston, SC	Charleston, WV	Charlotte, NC	Cheyenne, WY	Chicago, IL	Cincinnati, OH	Cleveland, OH	Columbus, OH	Dallas, TX	Denver, CO	Des Moines, IA	Detroit, MI	El Paso, TX	Halifax, NS	Houston, TX	Indianapolis, IN	Jackson, MS	Jacksonville, FL	Kansas City, MO	Las Vegas, NV	Little Rock, AR	Los Angeles, CA	Louisville, KY
Albany, NY	2095	1811	4421	1010	333	2083	1093	1675	2526	172	292	2512	913	634	771	1789	832	730	484	621	1680	1833	1155	571	2326	877	1768	795	1331	1094	1282	2586	1354	2859	832
Albuquerque, NM		286	3563	1490	1902	991	1274	1333	966	2240	1808	1498	1793	1568	1649	538	1352	1409	1619	1476	754	438	1091	1608	263	2945	994	1298	1157	1837	894	578	900	806	1320
Amarillo, TX			3734	1206	1618	988	991	1398	1266	1957	1524	1669	1510	1285	1365	534	1069	1126	1335	1192	470	434	808	1324	438	2662	711	1014	874	1517	610	864	617	1092	1036
Anchorage, AK				4304	4297	2601	4253	2724	2745	4592	4133	2065	4495	4093	4348	3056	3584	3890	3935	3946	4087	3300	3421	3872	4002	4821	4328	3771	4294	4652	3547	3356	3929	3403	3886
Atlanta, GA					679	1889	150	1559	2218	1100	910	2395	317	503	238	1482	717	476	726	577	792	1403	967	735	1437	1805	800	531	386	344	801	2067	528	2237	419
Baltimore, MD						1959	795	1551	2401	422	370	2388	583	352	441	1665	708	521	377	420	1399	1690	1031	532	2045	1128	1470	600	1032	763	1087	2445	1072	2705	602
Billings, MT							1839	413	626	2254	1796	536	2157	1755	2012	455	1246	1552	1597	1608	1433	554	1007	1534	1255	2806	1673	1432	1836	2237	1088	965	1530	1239	1547
Birmingham, AL								1509	2170	1215	909	2346	466	578	389	1434	667	475	725	576	647	1356	919	734	1292	1921	678	481	241	494	753	1852	381	2092	369
Bismarck, ND									1039	1846	1388	794	1749	1347	1604	594	838	1144	1189	1200	1342	693	675	1126	1597	2398	1582	1024	1548	1906	801	1378	1183	1702	1139
Boise, ID										2697	2239	735	2520	2182	2375	737	1708	1969	2040	2036	1711	833	1369	1977	1206	3249	1952	1852	2115	2566	1376	760	1808	1033	1933
Boston, MA											462	2683	1003	741	861	1961	1003	862	654	760	1819	2004	1326	741	2465	714	1890	940	1453	1184	1427	2757	1493	3046	964
Buffalo, NY												2224	899	431	695	1502	545	442	197	333	1393	1546	868	277	2039	1167	1513	508	1134	1080	995	2299	1066	2572	545
Calgary, AB													2586	2184	2441	991	1675	1981	2026	2037	2114	1234	1512	1963	1936	2912	2355	1862	2385	2743	1638	1291	2020	1565	1977
Charleston, SC														468	204	1783	907	622	724	637	1109	1705	1204	879	1754	1708	1110	721	703	238	1102	2371	900	2554	610
Charleston, WV															265	1445	506	209	255	168	1072	1367	802	410	1718	1446	1192	320	816	649	764	2122	745	2374	251
Charlotte, NC																1637	761	476	520	433	1031	1559	1057	675	1677	1566	1041	575	625	385	956	2225	754	2453	464
Cheyenne, WY																	972	1233	1304	1300	979	100	633	1241	801	2513	1220	1115	1382	1829	640	843	1076	1116	1197
Chicago, IL																		302	346	359	936	1015	337	283	1543	1555	1108	184	750	1065	532	1768	662	2042	299
Cincinnati, OH																			253	105	958	1200	599	261	1605	1567	1079	116	700	803	597	1955	632	2215	106
Cleveland, OH																				144	1208	1347	669	171	1854	1359	1328	319	950	904	806	2100	882	2374	356
Columbus, OH																					1059	1266	665	192	1706	1465	1179	176	801	818	663	2021	733	2281	207
Dallas, TX																						887	752	1218	647	2524	241	913	406	1049	554	1331	327	1446	852
Denver, CO																							676	1284	701	2556	1127	1088	1290	1751	603	756	984	1029	1118
Des Moines, IA																								606	1283	1878	992	481	931	1315	194	1429	567	1703	595
Detroit, MI																									1799	1278	1338	318	960	1060	795	2037	891	2310	366
El Paso, TX																										3171	758	1489	1051	1642	1085	717	974	801	1499
Halifax, NS																											2595	1646	2158	1889	2133	3309	2198	3583	1669
Houston, TX																												839	445	884	795	1474	447	1558	972
Indianapolis, IN																													675	879	485	1843	587	2104	112
Jackson, MS																														598	747	1735	269	1851	594
Jacksonville, FL																															1148	2415	873	2441	766
Kansas City, MO																																1358	382	1632	516
Las Vegas, NV																																	1478	274	1874
Little Rock, AR																																		1706	526
Los Angeles, CA																																			2126

Kilometers

	Albany, NY	Albuquerque, NM	Amarillo, TX	Anchorage, AK	Atlanta, GA	Baltimore, MD	Billings, MT	Birmingham, AL	Bismarck, ND	Boise, ID	Boston, MA	Buffalo, NY	Calgary, AB	Charleston, SC	Charleston, WV	Charlotte, NC	Cheyenne, WY	Chicago, IL	Cincinnati, OH	Cleveland, OH	Columbus, OH	Dallas, TX	Denver, CO	Des Moines, IA	Detroit, MI	El Paso, TX	Halifax, NS	Houston, TX	Indianapolis, IN	Jackson, MS	Jacksonville, FL	Kansas City, MO	Las Vegas, NV	Little Rock, AR	Los Angeles, CA	Louisville, KY
Albuquerque, NM	3371																																			
Amarillo, TX	2914	460																																		
Anchorage, AK	7113	5733	6008																																	
Atlanta, GA	1625	2397	1940	6925																																
Baltimore, MD	536	3060	2603	6914	1093																															
Billings, MT	3352	1595	1590	4185	3039	3152																														
Birmingham, AL	1759	2050	1595	6843	241	1279	2959																													
Bismarck, ND	2695	2145	2249	4383	2508	2496	665	2428																												
Boise, ID	4064	1554	2037	4417	3569	3863	1007	3492	1672																											
Boston, MA	277	3604	3149	7389	1770	679	3627	1955	2970	4339																										
Buffalo, NY	470	2909	2452	6650	1464	595	2890	1463	2233	3603	743																									
Calgary, AB	4042	2410	2685	3323	3854	3842	862	3775	1278	1183	4317	3578																								
Charleston, SC	1469	2885	2430	7232	510	938	3471	750	2814	4055	1614	1446	4161																							
Charleston, WV	1020	2523	2068	6586	809	566	2824	930	2167	3511	1192	693	3514	753																						
Charlotte, NC	1241	2653	2196	6996	383	710	3237	626	2581	3821	1385	1118	3928	328	426																					
Cheyenne, WY	2879	866	859	4917	2385	2679	732	2307	956	1186	3155	2417	1595	2869	2325	2634																				
Chicago, IL	1339	2175	1720	5767	1154	1139	2005	1073	1348	2748	1614	877	2695	1459	814	1224	1564																			
Cincinnati, OH	1175	2267	1812	6259	766	838	2497	764	1841	3168	1387	711	3187	1001	336	766	1984	486																		
Cleveland, OH	779	2605	2148	6331	1168	607	2570	1167	1913	3282	1052	317	3260	1165	410	837	2098	557	407																	
Columbus, OH	999	2375	1918	6349	928	676	2587	927	1931	3276	1223	536	3278	1025	270	697	2092	578	169	232																
Dallas, TX	2703	1213	756	6576	1274	2251	2306	1041	2159	2753	2927	2241	3401	1784	1725	1659	1575	1506	1541	1944	1704															
Denver, CO	2949	705	698	5310	2257	2719	891	2182	1115	1340	3224	2488	1986	2743	2200	2508	161	1633	1931	2167	2037	1427														
Des Moines, IA	1858	1755	1300	5504	1556	1659	1620	1479	1086	2203	2134	1397	2433	1937	1290	1701	1018	542	964	1076	1070	1210	1088													
Detroit, MI	919	2587	2130	6230	1183	856	2468	1181	1812	3181	1192	446	3158	1414	660	1086	1997	455	420	275	309	1960	2066	975												
El Paso, TX	3743	423	705	6439	2312	3290	2019	2079	2570	1940	3966	3281	3115	2822	2764	2698	1289	2483	2582	2983	2745	1041	1128	2064	2895											
Halifax, NS	1411	4739	4283	7757	2904	1815	4515	3091	3858	5228	1149	1878	4685	2748	2327	2520	4043	2502	2521	2187	2357	4061	4113	3022	2056	5102										
Houston, TX	2845	1599	1144	6964	1287	2365	2692	1091	2545	3141	3041	2434	3789	1786	1918	1675	1963	1783	1736	2137	1897	388	1813	1596	2153	1220	4175									
Indianapolis, IN	1279	2088	1632	6068	854	965	2304	774	1648	2980	1512	817	2996	1160	515	925	1794	296	187	513	283	1469	1751	774	512	2396	2648	1350								
Jackson, MS	2142	1862	1406	6909	621	1660	2954	388	2491	3403	2338	1825	3837	1131	1313	1006	2224	1207	1126	1529	1289	653	2076	1498	1545	1691	3472	716	1086							
Jacksonville, FL	1760	2956	2441	7485	553	1228	3599	795	3067	4129	1905	1738	4413	383	1044	619	2943	1714	1292	1455	1316	1688	2817	2116	1706	2642	3039	1422	1414	962						
Kansas City, MO	2063	1438	981	5707	1289	1749	1751	1212	1289	2214	2296	1601	2636	1773	1229	1538	1030	856	961	1297	1067	891	970	312	1279	1746	3432	1279	780	1202	1847					
Las Vegas, NV	4161	930	1390	5400	3326	3934	1553	2980	2217	1223	4436	3699	2077	3815	3414	3580	1356	2845	3146	3379	3252	2142	1216	2299	3278	1154	5324	2372	2965	2792	3886	2185				
Little Rock, AR	2179	1448	993	6322	850	1725	2462	613	1903	2909	2402	1715	3250	1448	1199	1213	1731	1065	1017	1419	1179	526	1583	912	1434	1567	3537	719	944	433	1405	615	2378			
Los Angeles, CA	4600	1297	1757	5475	3599	4352	1994	3366	2739	1662	4901	4138	2518	4109	3820	3947	1796	3286	3564	3820	3670	2327	1656	2740	3717	1289	5765	2507	3385	2978	3928	2626	441	2745		
Louisville, KY	1339	2124	1667	6253	674	969	2489	594	1833	3110	1551	877	3181	981	404	747	1926	481	171	573	333	1371	1799	957	589	2412	2685	1564	180	956	1232	830	3015	846	3421	
Memphis, TN	1953	1662	1207	6570	626	1501	2615	388	2151	3144	2177	1492	3498	1223	975	988	1958	867	793	1194	956	750	1796	1158	1210	1789	3311	943	747	339	1179	862	2592	225	2959	621
México, MX	4520	2352	2051	8061	2821	3899	3641	2624	3952	3985	4574	4058	4737	3319	3541	3208	2911	3421	3360	3760	3522	1815	2750	3002	3776	1926	5709	1535	3287	2249	2956	2684	2846	2344	2981	3187
Miami, FL	2315	3467	2951	7997	1064	1784	4109	1307	3578	4639	2460	2293	4925	938	1599	1175	3455	2224	1836	2011	1871	2200	3329	2626	2254	3152	3595	1932	1924	1472	555	2359	4397	1915	4439	1744
Milwaukee, WI	1495	2294	1837	5651	1308	1295	1891	1228	1234	2813	1770	1033	2579	1614	967	1379	1628	143	640	713	730	1625	1697	608	611	2602	2658	1920	449	1344	1866	922	2909	1202	3350	634
Minneapolis, MN	2003	2154	1697	5110	1817	1804	1350	1736	693	2357	2280	1541	2039	2122	1477	1887	1418	658	1149	1223	1241	1607	1487	396	1121	2462	3168	1995	959	1852	2376	710	2698	1310	3139	1144
Mobile, AL	2162	2162	1780	7258	534	1630	3249	415	2840	3704	2306	1874	4187	1033	1347	920	2526	1485	1176	1578	1339	1028	2378	1794	1595	1981	1981	761	1186	301	660	1496	3092	735	3268	1006
Montréal, QC	370	3495	3038	6607	1997	907	3368	2074	2711	4079	504	639	3535	1842	1323	1614	2895	1353	1311	946	1167	2851	2965	1874	907	3802	1150	3044	1403	2436	2132	2187	4177	2327	4616	1480
Nashville, TN	1614	2008	1553	6534	389	1152	2652	312	2116	3179	1828	1152	3463	874	636	639	1995	763	452	854	615	1096	1870	1167	870	2137	2962	1289	462	681	948	899	2938	571	3305	282
New Orleans, LA	2317	2053	1598	7207	761	1837	3146	565	2790	3595	2515	2018	4135	1260	1490	1147	2417	1504	1319	1722	1482	845	2267	1797	1736	1799	3649	579	1329	298	895	1500	2983	732	3084	1149
New York, NY	243	3242	2785	7062	1398	309	3297	1585	2640	4008	346	644	3990	1244	829	1015	2824	1282	1023	750	861	2557	2895	1804	1001	3596	1480	2671	1150	1968	1533	1934	4106	2031	4537	1189
Oklahoma City, OK	2492	879	422	6245	1519	2179	1974	1173	1828	2423	2726	2031	3070	2008	1644	1773	1244	1298	1389	1726	1496	336	1096	879	1709	1186	3862	722	1210	985	2077	560	1809	571	2175	1245
Omaha, NE	2079	1566	1168	5409	1591	1879	1455	1514	991	1986	2354	1617	2338	2076	1532	1841	800	763	1184	1297	1290	1076	870	219	1195	1989	3242	1464	994	1504	2150	302	2082	917	2521	1133
Orlando, FL	1987	3112	2595	7641	708	1455	3754	951	3223	4283	2130	1965	4570	610	1271	845	3099	1868	1480	1681	1541	1844	2972	2270	1899	2796	3266	1577	1569	1117	227	2003	4042	1559	4084	1389
Ottawa, ON	486	3392	2936	6455	1866	842	3265	1971	2608	3977	665	536	3384	1780	1221	1483	2793	1252	1208	845	1064	2748	2862	1772	805	3701	1324	2941	1302	2333	2069	2085	4074	2224	4515	1377
Philadelphia, PA	359	3144	2689	7010	1258	167	3249	1443	2592	3961	516	666	3939	1102	730	874	2776	1236	927	703	763	2415	2806	1755	953	3455	1651	2529	1054	1826	1393	1836	4023	1891	4441	1091
Phoenix, AZ	4121	750	1212	5776	3006	3807	1929	2772	2674	1598	4354	3659	2454	3514	3274	3390	1615	2927	3018	3355	3125	1733	1455	2507	3337	695	5490	1911	2838	2385	3334	2188	459	2200	594	2874
Pittsburgh, PA	780	2687	2230	6526	1088	396	2766	1228	2109	3477	953	349	3455	1033	349	705	2293	751	470	219	306	2005	2349	1273	470	3046	2087	2198	595	1590	1323	1379	3564	1480	3984	634
Portland, ME	434	3762	3305	7546	1926	837	3784	2113	3128	4497	172	901	4475	1772	1350	1543	3313	1772	1545	1208	1381	3084	3382	2291	1348	4124	872	3199	1670	2494	2061	2454	4594	2558	5059	1709
Portland, OR	4753	2245	2727	3902	4259	4553	1430	4182	2093	695	5030	4291	1371	4743	4199	4508	1876	3438	3858	3973	3965	3443	2029	2893	3870	2843	5918	3831	3669	4093	4817	2904	1911	3599	1562	3800
Québec, QC	582	3734	3279	6846	2209	1120	3607	2314	2951	4320	624	879	3775	2055	1564	1826	3136	1595	1564	1187	1406	3091	3205	2114	1147	4043	940	3284	1644	2676	2344	2428	4417	2566	4858	1720
Raleigh, NC	1028	2867	2412	7157	637	497	3395	880	2739	4014	1173	1033	4085	449	504	254	2829	1385	840	914	776	1913	2703	1862	1165	2951	2307	1928	1028	1260	740	1733	3797	1430	4164	907
Rapid City, SD	2816	1353	1347	4795	2431	2616	610	2354	515	1496	3091	2354	1472	2935	2288	2700	491	1469	1961	2034	2051	1733	650	1012	1932	1778	3979	2121	1772	2346	2991	1142	1665	1759	2106	1955
Reno, NV	4420	1641	2101	4843	3926	4220	1545	3849	2208	692	4697	3958	2069	4410	3866	4175	1543	3105	3525	3640	3632	3110	1696	2560	3537	2116	5585	3334	3335	3760	4484	2571	711	3266	835	3467
Richmond, VA	776	3018	2563	7065	848	245	3303	1091	2647	4016	920	780	3994	689	518	465	2832	1290	853	758	832	2106	2716	1812	1009	3146	2055	2140	1031	1471	980	1746	3932	1582	4315	920
St. Louis, MO	1667	1691	1234	6113	883	1353	2158	806	1694	2619	1900	1205	3041	1368	824	1133	1435	473	563	901	671	1022	1376	702	883	1998	3036	1389	385	813	1442	405	2590	669	2986	425
Salt Lake City, UT	3578	1004	1551	4729	3083	3379	882	3006	1545	550	3854	3115	1406	3569	3025	3334	702	2262	2682	2796	2790	2269	854	1717	2695	1390	4742	2655	2492	2917	3643	1728	671	2425	1112	2624
San Antonio, TX	3142	1316	825	6833	1609	2689	2414	1413	2573	2833	3366	2679	3511	2108	2162	1997	1683	2043	1981	2383	2143	436	1522	1623	2397	895	4500	322	1908	1036	1744	1307	2047	965	2182	1810
San Diego, CA	4697	1327	1788	5673	3485	4383	2095	3252	2840	1763	4932	4235	2619	3995	3850	3870	1897	3387	3595	3921	3701	2212	1757	2841	3818	1175	5866	2393	3414	2864	3813	2727	542	2740	200	3450
San Francisco, CA	4769	1788	2248	4940	4212	4570	1892	3977	2814	1039	5044	4307	2409	4721	4216	4439	1892	3453	3873	3987	3981	2940	2045	2907	3886	1900	5932	3118	3685	3591	4541	2919	925	3237	619	3817
Seattle, WA	4664	2354	2837	3623	4352	4465	1313	4275	1977	805	4940	4203	1093	4784	4137	4549	1986	3318	3810	3883	3900	3553	2138	2932	3781	3128	5828	3940	3619	4203	4911	3012	2021	3709	1847	3804
Tampa, FL	2076	3136	2619	7664	732	1545	3778	975	3247	4307	2220	2053	4592	698	1360	935	3123	1892	1504	1772	1667	1868	2996	2294	1921	2821	3355	1601	1593	1141	315	2026	4064	1583	4108	1413
Toronto, ON	644	2962	2505	6595	1541	909	2835	1541	2179	3546	917	171	3524	1619	864	1290	2362	821	779	488	708	2319	2433	1342	375	3269	1681	2512	870	1903	1910	1654	3644	1794	4084	948
Vancouver, BC	4878	2570	3052	3430	4566	4679	1527	4491	2191	1018	5155	4417	899	4998	4352	4763	2201	3533	4024	4098	4116	3768	2354	3147	3995	3358	6043	4156	3834	4418	5126	3229	2237	3924	2077	4018
Washington, DC	594	3051	2594	6903	1023	61	3142	1220	2486	3854	737	618	3831	867	557	639	2669	1128	832	595	669	2191	2713	1649	846	3231	1873	2306	959	1603	1158	1743	3928	1667	4348	959
Wichita, KS	2367	1138	681	5921	1591	2053	1717	1348	1503	2166	2600	1905	2814	2077	1533	1842	986	1171	1263	1601	1371	591	838	628	1583	1445	3736	978	1084	1241	2151	309	2053	747	2434	1134
Winnipeg, MB	2730	2587	2285	4385	2542	2531	1324	2463	668	2336	3006	2269	1313	2850	2203	2615	1821	1384	1876	1948	1966	2193	1892	1121	1847	3010	3361	2581	1685	2526	3102	1324	3012	1939	3453	1870

Milles

	Memphis, TN	México, MX	Miami, FL	Milwaukee, WI	Minneapolis, MN	Mobile, AL	Montréal, QC	Nashville, TN	New Orleans, LA	New York, NY	Oklahoma City, OK	Omaha, NE	Orlando, FL	Ottawa, ON	Philadelphia, PA	Phoenix, AZ	Pittsburgh, PA	Portland, ME	Portland, OR	Québec, QC	Raleigh, NC	Rapid City, SD	Reno, NV	Richmond, VA	St. Louis, MO	Salt Lake City, UT	San Antonio, TX	San Diego, CA	San Francisco, CA	Seattle, WA	Tampa, FL	Toronto, ON	Vancouver, BC	Washington, DC	Wichita, KS	Winnipeg, MB
Albany, NY	1214	2809	1439	929	1245	1344	230	1003	1440	151	1549	1292	1235	302	223	2561	485	270	2954	362	639	1750	2747	482	1036	2224	1953	2919	2964	2899	1290	400	3032	369	1471	1697
Albuquerque, NM	1033	1462	2155	1426	1339	1344	2172	1248	1276	2015	546	973	1934	2108	1954	466	1670	2338	1395	2321	1782	841	1020	1876	1051	624	818	825	1111	1463	1949	1841	1597	1896	707	1608
Amarillo, TX	750	1275	1834	1142	1055	1106	1888	965	993	1731	262	726	1613	1825	1671	753	1386	2054	1695	2038	1499	837	1306	1593	767	964	513	1111	1397	1763	1628	1557	1897	1612	423	1420
Anchorage, AK	4083	5010	4970	3512	3176	4511	4106	4061	4479	4389	3881	3362	4749	4012	4357	3590	4056	4690	2425	4255	4448	2980	3010	4391	3799	2939	4247	3526	3070	2252	4763	4099	2132	4290	3680	2725
Atlanta, GA	389	1753	661	813	1129	332	1241	242	473	869	944	989	440	1160	782	1868	676	1197	2647	1373	396	1511	2440	527	549	1916	1000	2166	2618	2705	455	958	2838	636	989	1580
Baltimore, MD	933	2423	1109	805	1121	1013	564	716	1142	192	1354	1168	904	523	104	2366	246	520	2830	696	309	1626	2623	152	841	2100	1671	2724	2840	2775	960	565	2908	38	1276	1573
Billings, MT	1625	2263	2554	1175	839	2019	2093	1648	1955	2049	1227	904	2333	2029	2019	1199	1719	2352	889	2242	2110	379	960	2053	1341	548	1500	1302	1176	816	2348	1762	949	1953	1067	823
Birmingham, AL	241	1631	812	763	1079	258	1289	194	351	985	729	941	591	1225	897	1723	763	1313	2599	1438	547	1463	2392	678	501	1868	878	2021	2472	2657	606	958	2791	758	838	1531
Bismarck, ND	1337	2456	2224	767	431	1765	1685	1315	1734	1641	1136	616	2003	1621	1611	1662	1311	1944	1301	1834	1702	320	1372	1645	1053	960	1599	1765	1749	1229	2018	1354	1362	1545	934	415
Boise, ID	1954	2477	2883	1748	1465	2302	2535	1976	2234	2491	1506	1234	2662	2472	2462	993	2161	2795	432	2685	2495	930	430	2496	1628	342	1761	1096	646	500	2677	2204	633	2395	1346	1452
Boston, MA	1353	2843	1529	1100	1417	1433	313	1136	1563	215	1694	1463	1324	413	321	2706	592	107	3126	388	729	1921	2919	572	1181	2395	2092	3065	3135	3070	1380	570	3204	458	1616	1868
Buffalo, NY	927	2522	1425	642	958	1165	397	716	1254	400	1262	1005	1221	333	414	2274	217	560	2667	546	642	1463	2460	485	749	1936	1665	2632	2677	2612	1276	106	2745	384	1184	1410
Calgary, AB	2174	2944	3061	1603	1267	2602	2197	2152	2570	2480	1908	1453	2840	2103	2448	1525	2147	2781	852	2346	2539	915	1286	2482	1890	874	2182	1628	1497	679	2854	2190	559	2381	1749	816
Charleston, SC	760	2063	583	1003	1319	642	1145	543	783	773	1248	1290	379	1106	685	2184	642	1101	2948	1277	279	1824	2741	428	850	2218	1310	2483	2934	2973	434	1006	3106	539	1291	1771
Charleston, WV	606	2201	994	601	918	837	822	395	926	515	1022	952	790	759	454	2035	217	839	2610	972	313	1422	2403	322	512	1880	1344	2393	2620	2571	845	537	2705	346	953	1369
Charlotte, NC	614	1994	730	857	1173	572	1003	397	713	631	1102	1144	525	922	543	2107	438	959	2802	1135	158	1678	2595	289	704	2072	1241	2405	2759	2827	581	802	2960	397	1145	1625
Cheyenne, WY	1217	1809	2147	1012	881	1570	1799	1240	1502	1755	773	497	1926	1736	1725	1004	1425	2059	1166	1949	1758	305	959	1760	892	436	1046	1179	1176	1234	1941	1468	1368	1659	613	1132
Chicago, IL	539	2126	1382	89	409	923	841	474	935	797	807	474	1161	778	768	1819	467	1101	2137	991	861	913	1930	802	294	1406	1270	2105	2146	2062	1176	510	2196	701	728	860
Cincinnati, OH	493	2088	1141	398	714	731	815	281	820	636	863	736	920	751	576	1876	292	960	2398	972	522	1219	2191	530	350	1667	1231	2234	2407	2368	935	484	2501	517	785	1166
Cleveland, OH	742	2337	1250	443	760	981	588	531	1070	466	1073	806	1045	525	437	2085	136	751	2469	738	568	1264	2262	471	560	1738	1481	2437	2478	2413	1101	303	2547	370	995	1211
Columbus, OH	594	2189	1163	454	771	832	725	382	921	535	930	802	958	661	474	1942	190	858	2464	874	482	1275	2257	517	417	1734	1332	2300	2474	2424	1036	440	2558	416	852	1222
Dallas, TX	466	1128	1367	1010	999	639	1772	681	525	1589	209	669	1146	1708	1501	1077	1246	1917	2140	1921	1189	1077	1933	1309	635	1410	271	1375	1827	2208	1161	1441	2342	1362	367	1363
Denver, CO	1116	1709	2069	1055	924	1478	1843	1162	1409	1799	681	541	1847	1779	1744	904	1460	2102	1261	1992	1680	404	1054	1688	855	531	946	1092	1271	1329	1862	1512	1463	1686	521	1176
Des Moines, IA	720	1866	1632	378	246	1115	1165	725	1117	1121	546	136	1411	1101	1091	1558	791	1424	1798	1314	1157	629	1591	1126	436	1067	1009	1766	1807	1822	1426	834	1956	1025	390	697
Detroit, MI	752	2347	1401	380	697	991	564	541	1079	622	1062	743	1180	500	592	2074	292	838	2405	713	724	1201	2198	627	549	1675	1490	2373	2415	2350	1194	233	2483	526	984	1148
El Paso, TX	1112	1197	1959	1617	1530	1231	2363	1328	1118	2235	737	1236	1738	2300	2147	432	1893	2563	1767	2513	1834	1105	1315	1955	1242	864	556	730	1181	1944	1753	2032	2087	2008	898	1871
Halifax, NS	2058	3548	2234	1652	1969	1231	715	1841	2268	920	2400	2015	2030	823	1026	3412	1297	542	3678	584	1434	2473	3471	1277	1887	2947	2797	3646	3687	3622	2085	1045	3756	1164	2322	2089
Houston, TX	586	954	1201	1193	1240	473	1892	801	360	1660	449	910	980	1828	1572	1188	1366	1988	2381	2041	1198	1318	2072	1330	863	1650	200	1487	1938	2449	995	1561	2583	1433	608	1604
Indianapolis, IN	464	2043	1196	279	596	737	872	287	826	715	752	618	975	809	655	1764	370	1038	2280	1022	639	1101	2073	641	239	1549	1186	2122	2290	2249	990	541	2383	596	674	1047
Jackson, MS	211	1398	915	835	1151	187	1514	423	185	1223	612	935	694	1450	1135	1482	988	1550	2544	1663	783	1458	2337	914	505	1813	644	1780	2232	2612	709	1183	2746	996	771	1570
Jacksonville, FL	733	1837	345	1160	1477	410	1325	589	556	953	1291	1336	141	1286	866	2072	822	1281	2994	1457	460	1859	2787	609	896	2264	1084	2370	2822	3052	196	1187	3186	720	1337	1928
Kansas City, MO	536	1668	1466	573	441	930	1359	559	932	1202	348	188	1245	1296	1141	1360	857	1525	1805	1509	1077	710	1598	1085	252	1074	812	1695	1814	1872	1259	1028	2007	1083	192	823
Las Vegas, NV	1611	1769	2733	1808	1677	1922	2596	1826	1854	2552	1124	1294	2512	2532	2500	285	2215	2855	1188	2745	2360	1035	442	2444	1610	417	1272	337	575	1256	2526	2265	1390	2441	1276	1872
Little Rock, AR	140	1457	1190	747	814	457	1446	355	455	1262	355	570	969	1382	1175	1367	920	1590	2237	1595	889	1093	2030	983	416	1507	600	1703	2012	2305	984	1115	2439	1036	464	1205
Los Angeles, CA	1839	1853	2759	2082	1951	2031	2869	2054	1917	2820	1352	1567	2538	2806	2760	369	2476	3144	971	3019	2588	1309	519	2682	1856	691	1356	124	385	1148	2553	2538	1291	2702	1513	2146
Louisville, KY	386	1981	1084	394	711	625	920	175	714	739	774	704	863	856	678	1786	394	1062	2362	1069	564	1215	2155	572	264	1631	1125	2144	2372	2364	878	589	2497	596	705	1162
Memphis, TN		1595	1051	624	940	395	1306	215	396	1123	487	724	830	1243	1035	1500	780	1451	2382	1456	749	1247	2175	843	294	1652	739	1841	2144	2440	845	975	2574	896	597	1359
México, MX			2154	2200	2113	1426	2900	1810	1313	2619	1323	1783	1933	2838	2525	1484	2375	2941	2819	3051	2151	2365	2367	2283	1825	2135	853	1683	2233	2996	1948	2570	3139	2386	1481	2477
Miami, FL				1478	1794	727	1671	907	874	1299	1609	1654	232	1631	1211	2390	1167	1627	3312	1803	805	2176	3105	954	1214	2581	1401	2688	3140	3370	274	1532	3504	1065	1655	2246
Milwaukee, WI					337	1019	939	569	1020	894	880	514	1257	875	865	1892	564	1198	2063	1088	956	842	1970	899	367	1446	1343	2145	2186	1991	1272	607	2124	799	769	789
Minneapolis, MN						1335	1255	886	1337	1211	793	383	1573	1192	1181	1805	881	1515	1727	1405	1273	606	1839	1216	621	1315	1257	2014	2055	1654	1588	924	1788	1115	637	452
Mobile, AL							1575	450	146	1203	799	1119	506	1481	1115	1662	1019	1531	2731	1707	730	1641	2545	861	688	2000	673	1960	2411	2799	521	1214	2933	970	958	1787
Montréal, QC								1094	1632	383	1625	1300	1466	121	454	2637	607	282	2963	155	871	1758	2756	714	1112	2232	2043	2931	2972	2907	1522	330	3041	600	1547	1374
Nashville, TN									539	906	703	747	686	1031	818	1715	569	1234	2405	1244	532	1269	2198	626	307	1675	954	2056	2360	2463	701	764	2597	679	748	1337
New Orleans, LA										1332	731	1121	653	1570	1245	1548	1108	1660	2663	1783	871	1643	2431	1002	690	1932	560	1846	2298	2731	668	1302	2865	1106	890	1755
New York, NY											1469	1258	1094	439	91	2481	367	313	2920	515	499	1716	2713	342	956	2189	1861	2839	2929	2864	1150	507	2998	228	1391	1665
Oklahoma City, OK												463	1388	1563	1408	1012	1124	1792	1934	1776	1237	871	1727	1331	505	1204	466	1370	1657	2002	1403	1295	2136	1350	161	1158
Omaha, NE													1433	1238	1228	1440	928	1561	1662	1451	1265	525	1455	1263	440	932	927	1630	1672	1719	1448	971	1853	1162	307	638
Orlando, FL														1427	1006	2169	963	1422	3091	1598	601	1955	2884	750	993	2360	1180	2467	2918	3149	82	1327	3283	860	1434	2025
Ottawa, ON															451	2575	545	382	2901	257	831	1696	2694	675	1050	2170	1981	2869	2910	2845	1483	268	2978	562	1485	1280
Philadelphia, PA																2420	306	419	2890	586	411	1686	2683	254	895	2160	1774	2779	2900	2835	1062	522	2968	140	1330	1633
Phoenix, AZ																	2136	2804	1335	2788	2249	1308	883	2343	1517	651	987	358	750	1513	2184	2307	1655	2362	1173	2075
Pittsburgh, PA																		690	2590	758	497	1386	2383	341	611	1859	1519	2494	2599	2534	1019	321	2668	240	1046	1332
Portland, ME																			3223	264	827	2019	3016	670	1279	2493	2189	3162	3233	3168	1478	668	3301	556	1714	1966
Portland, OR																				3114	2923	1268	578	2925	2057	771	2322	1093	638	170	3106	2633	313	2824	1775	1463
Québec, QC																					1003	1908	2905	846	1261	2381	2193	3080	3122	3057	1654	479	3190	732	1696	1523
Raleigh, NC																						1777	2716	157	825	2193	1398	2563	2894	2926	656	820	3060	265	1266	1724
Rapid City, SD																							1151	1720	963	628	1335	1372	1368	1195	1970	1429	1328	1620	712	792
Reno, NV																								2718	1850	524	1870	642	217	755	2899	2426	898	2617	1568	1867
Richmond, VA																									834	2194	1530	2684	2934	2869	805	660	3003	108	1274	1667
St. Louis, MO																										1326	968	1875	2066	2125	1008	782	2259	837	441	1075
Salt Lake City, UT																											1419	754	740	839	2375	1902	973	2094	1044	1455
San Antonio, TX																												1285	1737	2275	1195	1714	2410	1635	624	1621
San Diego, CA																													508	1271	2481	2601	1414	2720	1531	2209
San Francisco, CA																														816	2933	2643	958	2834	1784	2193
Seattle, WA																															3164	2577	140	2769	1843	1390
Tampa, FL																																1383	3297	916	1448	2039
Toronto, ON																																	2711	563	1217	1375
Vancouver, BC																																		2902	1977	1375
Washington, DC																																			1272	1566
Wichita, KS																																				956

Kilomètres

	Memphis, TN	México, MX	Miami, FL	Milwaukee, WI	Minneapolis, MN	Mobile, AL	Montréal, QC	Nashville, TN	New Orleans, LA	New York, NY	Oklahoma City, OK	Omaha, NE	Orlando, FL	Ottawa, ON	Philadelphia, PA	Phoenix, AZ	Pittsburgh, PA	Portland, ME	Portland, OR	Québec, QC	Raleigh, NC	Rapid City, SD	Reno, NV	Richmond, VA	St. Louis, MO	Salt Lake City, UT	San Antonio, TX	San Diego, CA	San Francisco, CA	Seattle, WA	Tampa, FL	Toronto, ON	Vancouver, BC	Washington, DC	Wichita, KS
México, MX	2566																																		
Miami, FL	1691	3466																																	
Milwaukee, WI	1004	3540	2378																																
Minneapolis, MN	1512	3400	2887	542																															
Mobile, AL	636	2294	1170	1640	2148																														
Montréal, QC	2101	4666	2689	1511	2019	2534																													
Nashville, TN	346	2912	1459	916	1426	724	1760																												
New Orleans, LA	637	2113	1406	1641	2151	235	2626	867																											
New York, NY	1807	4214	2090	1438	1948	1936	616	1458	2143																										
Oklahoma City, OK	784	2129	2589	1416	1276	1286	2615	1131	1176	2364																									
Omaha, NE	1165	2869	2661	827	616	1800	2092	1202	1804	2024	745																								
Orlando, FL	1335	3110	373	2023	2531	814	2359	1104	1051	1760	2233	2306																							
Ottawa, ON	2000	4566	2624	1408	1918	2383	194	1659	2526	706	2515	1992	2296																						
Philadelphia, PA	1665	4063	1948	1392	1900	1794	730	1316	2003	146	2265	1976	1619	726																					
Phoenix, AZ	2414	2388	3846	3044	2904	2674	4243	2759	2491	3992	1628	2317	3490	4143	3894																				
Pittsburgh, PA	1255	3821	1878	907	1418	1640	977	916	1783	591	1809	1493	1549	877	492	3437																			
Portland, ME	2335	4732	2618	1928	2438	2463	454	1986	2671	504	2883	2512	2288	615	674	4512	1110																		
Portland, OR	3833	4536	5329	3319	2779	4394	4767	3870	4285	4698	3112	2674	4973	4668	4650	2148	4167	5186																	
Québec, QC	2343	4909	2901	1751	2261	2747	249	2002	2869	829	2858	2335	2571	414	943	4486	1220	425	5010																
Raleigh, NC	1205	3461	1295	1538	2048	1175	1401	856	1401	803	1990	2035	967	1337	661	3619	800	1331	4703	1614															
Rapid City, SD	2006	3805	3501	1355	975	2640	2829	2042	2644	2761	1401	845	3146	2729	2713	2105	2230	3249	2040	3070	2859														
Reno, NV	3500	3809	4996	3170	2959	4095	4434	3537	3911	4365	2779	2341	4640	4335	4317	1421	3834	4853	930	4674	4370	1852													
Richmond, VA	1356	3673	1535	1446	1957	1385	1149	1007	1612	550	2142	2032	1207	1086	409	3770	549	1078	4706	1361	253	2767	4373												
St. Louis, MO	473	2936	1953	591	999	1107	1789	494	1110	1538	813	708	1598	1689	1440	2441	983	2058	3310	2029	1327	1549	2977	1342											
Salt Lake City, UT	2658	3435	4153	2327	2116	3218	3591	2695	3109	3522	1937	1500	3797	3492	3475	1047	2991	4011	1241	3831	3529	1010	843	3530	2134										
San Antonio, TX	1189	1372	2254	2161	2023	1083	3287	1535	901	2994	750	1492	1899	3187	2854	1588	2444	3522	3736	3529	2249	2148	3009	2462	1558	2283									
San Diego, CA	2962	2708	4325	3451	3241	3154	4716	3308	2970	4568	2204	2623	3969	4616	4471	576	4013	5088	1759	4956	4124	2208	1033	4319	3017	1213	2068								
San Francisco, CA	3450	3593	5052	3517	3306	3879	4782	3797	3697	4713	2666	2690	4695	4682	4666	1207	4182	5202	1027	5023	4656	2201	349	4721	3324	1191	2795	817							
Seattle, WA	3926	4821	5422	3204	2661	4504	4677	3963	4394	4608	3221	2766	5067	4578	4562	2434	4077	5097	274	4919	4708	1923	1215	4616	3419	1350	3660	2045	1313						
Tampa, FL	1360	3134	441	2047	2555	838	2449	1128	1075	1850	2257	2330	132	2386	1709	3514	1640	2378	4998	2661	1056	3170	4664	1295	1622	3821	1923	3992	4719	5091					
Toronto, ON	1569	4135	2465	977	1487	1953	531	1229	2095	816	2084	1562	2135	431	840	3712	516	1075	4236	771	1319	2299	3903	1062	1258	3060	2758	4185	4253	4146	2225				
Vancouver, BC	4142	5051	5638	3418	2877	4719	4893	4179	4610	4824	3437	2981	5282	4792	4776	2663	4293	5311	504	5133	4924	2137	1445	4832	3635	1566	3878	2275	1541	225	5305	4362			
Washington, DC	1442	3839	1714	1286	1794	1561	965	1093	1780	367	2172	1870	1384	904	225	3800	386	895	4544	1178	426	2607	4211	174	1347	3369	2631	4376	4560	4455	1474	906	4669		
Wichita, KS	961	2383	2663	1237	1025	1541	2489	1204	1432	2238	259	494	2307	2389	2140	1887	1683	2758	2856	2729	2037	1146	2523	2050	710	1680	1004	2463	2870	2965	2330	1958	3181	2047	
Winnipeg, MB	2187	3985	3614	1270	727	2875	2211	2151	2824	2679	1863	1027	3258	2060	2627	3339	2143	3163	2354	2451	2774	1274	3004	2682	1730	2341	2608	3554	3529	2237	3281	2212	2212	2520	1538

TEMPERATURE CONVERSIONS

°F	°C	°C	°F
110	43.3	40	104
100	37.8	35	95
90	32.2	30	86
80	26.7	25	77
70	21.1	20	68
60	15.6	15	59
50	10.0	10	50
40	4.4	5	41
32	0	0	32
30	-1.1	-5	23
20	-6.7	-10	14
10	-12.2	-15	5
0	-17.8	-20	-4
-10	-23.3	-25	-13
-20	-28.9	-30	-22
-30	-34.4	-35	-31
-40	-40.0	-40	-40
-50	-45.6	-45	-49

DISTANCE CONVERSIONS

MILES	KM	KM	MILES
1	1.6	1	0.6
5	8.0	2	1.2
10	16.1	5	3.1
15	24.1	10	6.2
20	32.2	15	9.3
25	40.2	20	12.4
30	48.3	25	15.5
35	56.3	30	18.6
40	64.4	40	24.9
45	72.4	50	31.1
50	80.5	60	37.3
55	88.5	70	43.5
60	96.6	80	49.7
65	104.6	90	55.9
70	112.7	100	62.1
75	120.7	110	68.4
80	128.7	120	74.6
85	136.8	130	80.8
90	144.8	140	87.0
95	152.9	150	93.2
100	160.9	160	99.4

VOLUME CONVERSIONS

GALLONS	LITERS	LITERS	GALLONS
1	3.8	1	0.26
2	7.6	2	0.5
3	11.4	3	0.8
4	15.1	4	1.1
5	18.9	5	1.3
10	37.9	10	2.6
15	56.8	20	5.3
20	75.7	30	7.9
25	94.6	40	10.6
30	113.6	50	13.2
40	151.4	75	19.8
50	189.3	100	26.4

Legend:
- Interstate Route
- Other Route
- 206 Distance in Miles
- 332 Distance in Kilometers
- 4:15 Approximate Travel Time
- ● **Miami** City on Distance Chart, pp. 284–285
- • Fort Pierce Other City

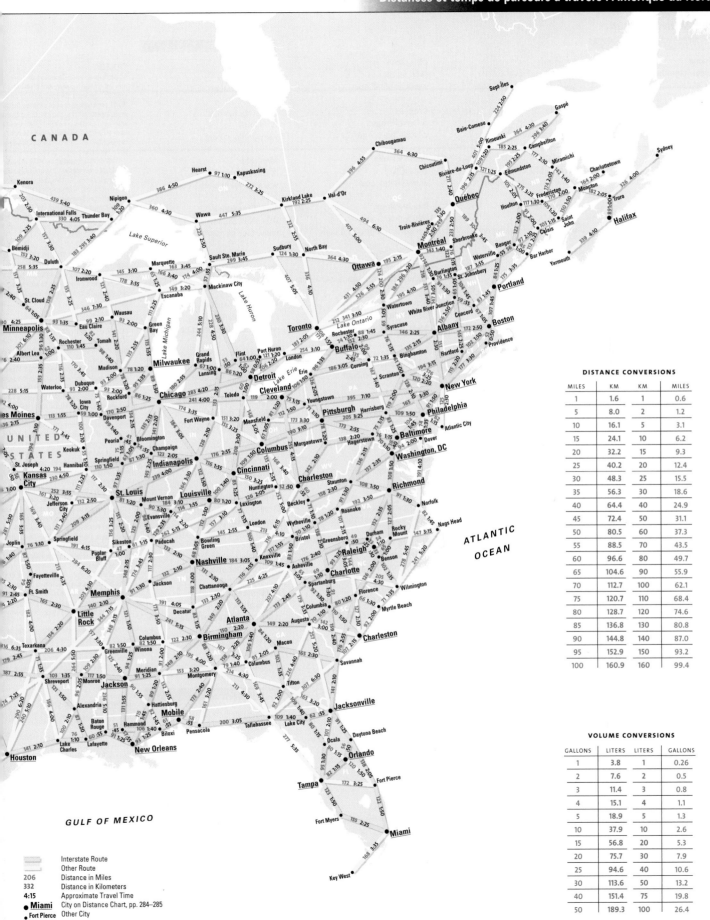

Distances and driving times may vary depending on actual route traveled and driving conditions.

TOURISM INFORMATION

UNITED STATES

Alabama
@TweetHomeAla
www.alabama.travel

Alaska
@alaskatravlnews
www.travelalaska.com

Arizona
@ArizonaTourism
www.visitarizona.com

Arkansas
@artourism
www.arkansas.com

California
@VisitCA
www.visitcalifornia.com

Colorado
@Colorado
www.colorado.com

Connecticut
@CTvisit
www.ctvisit.com

Delaware
@DelawareTourism
www.visitdelaware.com

District of Columbia
@washingtondc
www.washington.org

Florida
@VisitFlorida
www.visitflorida.com

Georgia
@ExploreGeorgia
www.exploregeorgia.org

Hawai'i
@gohawaii
www.gohawaii.com

Idaho
@visitidaho
www.visitidaho.org

Illinois
@enjoyillinois
www.enjoyillinois.com

Indiana
@visitindiana
www.visitindiana.com

Iowa
@Travel_Iowa
www.traveliowa.com

Kansas
@TravelKS
www.travelks.com

Kentucky
@KentuckyTourism
www.kentuckytourism.com

Louisiana
@LouisianaTravel
www.louisianatravel.com

Maine
@visitmaine
www.visitmaine.com

Maryland
@TravelMD
www.visitmaryland.org

Massachusetts
@VisitMA
www.massvacation.com

Michigan
@PureMichigan
www.michigan.org

Minnesota
@ExploreMinn
www.exploreminnesota.com

Mississippi
@visitms
www.visitmississippi.org

Missouri
@VisitMO
www.visitmo.com

Montana
@visitmontana
www.visitmt.com

Nebraska
@NebraskaTourism
www.visitnebraska.com

Nevada
@TravelNevada
www.travelnevada.com

New Hampshire
@VisitNH
www.visitnh.gov

New Jersey
@Visit_NJ
www.visitnj.org

New Mexico
@NewMexico
www.newmexico.org

New York
@I_LOVE_NY
www.iloveny.com

North Carolina
@VisitNC
www.visitnc.com

North Dakota
@NorthDakota
www.ndtourism.com

Ohio
@OhioFindItHere
www.ohio.org

Oklahoma
@TravelOK
www.travelok.com

Oregon
@TravelOregon
www.traveloregon.com

Pennsylvania
@visitPA
www.visitpa.com

Rhode Island
@RITourism
www.visitrhodeisland.com

South Carolina
@Discover_SC
www.discoversouthcarolina.com

South Dakota
@southdakota
www.travelsouthdakota.com

Tennessee
@TNVacation
www.tnvacation.com

Texas
@TexasTourism
www.traveltex.com

Utah
@VisitUtah
www.visitutah.com

Vermont
@VermontTourism
www.vermontvacation.com

Virginia
@VisitVirginia
www.virginia.org

Washington
@ExperienceWA
www.experiencewa.com

West Virginia
@GoToWV
www.gotowv.com

Wisconsin
@TravelWI
www.travelwisconsin.com

Wyoming
@TravelWI
www.wyomingtourism.org

Puerto Rico
@discover_PR
www.discoverpuertorico.com

CANADA

Alberta
@TravelAlberta
www.travelalberta.us

British Columbia
@HelloBC
www.hellobc.com

Manitoba
@TravelManitoba
www.travelmanitoba.com

New Brunswick
@SeeNewBrunswick
www.tourismnewbrunswick.ca

Newfoundland & Labrador
@NLtweets
www.newfoundlandlabrador.com

Northwest Territories
@spectacularNWT
www.spectacularnwt.com

Nova Scotia
@VisitNovaScotia
www.novascotia.com

Nunavut
@NunavutTourism
www.nunavuttourism.com

Ontario
@OntarioTravel
www.ontariotravel.net

Prince Edward Island
@tourismpei
www.tourismpei.com

Québec
@TourismQuebec
www.quebecoriginal.com

Saskatchewan
@Saskatchewan
www.tourismsaskatchewan.com

Yukon
@TravelYukon
www.travelyukon.com

MEXICO

@WeVisitMexico
www.visitmexico.com

BORDER CROSSING INFORMATION

TRAVEL ADVISORY

All U.S. citizens are now required to present a passport, passport card, or WHTI (Western Hemisphere Travel Initiative)-compliant document when entering the United States by air, sea or land. U.S. citizens traveling directly to or from Puerto Rico and the U.S. Virgin Islands are not required to have a passport. For more detailed information and updated schedules, please see http://travel.state.gov.

CANADA

All persons entering Canada must carry bo proof of citizenship and proof of identity. A valid U.S. passport, passport card or other WHTI-compliant document satisfies these requirements for U.S. citizens. U.S. citizens entering Canada from a third country must have a valid U.S. passport. A visa is not required for U.S. citizens to visit Canada fo up to 180 days.

U.S. driver's licenses are valid in Canad individual provinces and territories specify the length of time. Drivers should be prepa to present proof of their vehicle's registrati ownership, and insurance. International vis tors to Canada who are not U.S. citizens mu present a valid passport and visa (if require Citizens of Mexico require a visa to enter Canada.

UNITED STATES (FROM CANADA)

Canadian driver's licenses are valid in the U.S.; lengths of time vary depending on sta Drivers should be prepared to present proo of their vehicle's registration, ownership, a insurance.

MEXICO

All persons entering Mexico must carry pro of citizenship, either a valid passport or the original birth certificate (U.S. citizens shoul bear in mind the requirements set by the U. government for re-entry to the U.S.). Visas are not required for stays of up to 180 days. Naturalized citizens and alien permanent residents should carry the appropriate offic documentation. Individuals under the age o 18 traveling alone, with one parent, or with other adults must carry notarized parental/ legal guardian authorization. All U.S. citizen visiting for up to 180 days must also procure a tourist permit, obtainable from Mexican consulates, tourism offices, border crossing points, and airlines serving Mexico. Howeve tourist cards are not needed for visits short than 72 hours to areas within the Border Zo (extending approximately 25 km into Mexico

U.S. driver's licenses are valid in Mexico Visitors who wish to drive beyond the Baja California Peninsula or the Border Zone must obtain a temporary import permit for their vehicles. To acquire a permit, one mus submit evidence of citizenship and of the vehicle's title and registration, as well as a valid driver's license. A processing fee must be paid. Permits are available at border crossings or selected Mexican consulates. Mexican law also requires the posting of a refundable bond to guarantee the departure of the vehicle.

All visitors driving in Mexico should be aware that U.S. auto insurance policies are not valid and that full-coverage insurance from a Mexican insurance company is mandatory. Many U.S. insurance companies sell short-term tourist auto insurance for travel i Mexico.

IMPORTANT WEB SITES

U.S. State Department, www.travel.state.gov
U.S. Customs and Border Protection, www.cbp.gov
Canada Border Services Agency, www.cbsa-asfc.gc.ca
Citizenship and Immigration Canada, www.cic.gc.ca
Mexican Ministry of Foreign Affairs, www.gob.mx/sre
Mexican National Institute of Migration, www.gob.mx/inm

OMMON ABBREVIATIONS	
rch.	Archaeological
ld.	Battlefield
ons.	Conservation
nt.	Entrance
st.	Historic(al)
em.	Memorial
on.	Monument
tn.	Mountain
ts.	Mountains
us.	Museum
atl.	National
at.	Natural
N.H.S.	National Historic Site
N.H.P.	National Historical Park
N.M.P.	National Military Park
N.R.A.	National Recreation Area
Pk. Hqtrs.	Park Headquarters
Pres.	Preserve
Prov.	Provincial
Rec.	Recreation(al)
Res.	Reservation–Reserve
S.H.S.	State Historic Site
S.P.	State Park
Sta.	Station
Vis. Ctr.	Visitor Center

ALABAMA	PAGE	GRID	LATITUDE LONGITUDE
ational Park & Rec. Areas			
reedom Riders Natl. Mon.	120	A4	33.635108 -85.908448
orseshoe Bend N.M.P.-Vis. Ctr.	128	B1	32.977130 -85.739600
ussell Cave Natl. Mon.-Main Road	120	A2	34.980220 -85.809650
ussell Cave Natl. Mon.-Vis. Ctr.	120	A2	34.980400 -85.809800
uskegee Airmen N.H.S.	128	B2	32.424942 -85.691052
uskegee Airmen N.H.S.-Pk. Hqtrs.	128	B2	32.428600 -85.708500
uskegee Institute N.H.S.	128	B2	32.428751 -85.704120
uskegee Institute N.H.S.-Pk. Hqtrs.	128	B2	32.428600 -85.708500
tate Park & Rec. Areas			
ladon Springs S.P.	127	E4	31.730920 -88.195580
lue Springs S.P.	128	B4	31.661990 -85.508150
ucks Pocket S.P.	120	A3	34.469560 -86.049080
athedral Caverns S.P.	120	A2	34.572299 -86.221499
heaha S.P.	120	A4	33.474490 -85.807260
hewacla S.P.	128	B2	32.554520 -85.481920
esoto S.P.	120	A3	34.495460 -85.618860
lorala S.P.	136	B1	30.998590 -86.329980
rank Jackson S.P.	128	A4	31.291400 -86.255900
ulf S.P.	135	F2	30.270490 -87.582130
oe Wheeler S.P.	119	E2	34.793020 -87.379950
ake Guntersville S.P.	120	A3	34.367530 -86.222850
ake Lurleen S.P.	127	E1	33.295880 -87.676870
akepoint Resort S.P.	128	C3	31.990320 -85.114970
leaher S.P.	135	E1	30.669720 -87.936030
Monte Sano S.P.	119	F2	34.745220 -86.511650
Oak Mtn. S.P.	127	F1	33.324710 -86.758740
Paul M. Grist S.P.	127	F2	32.595380 -86.996080
Rickwood Caverns S.P.	119	F4	33.876870 -86.867230
Roland Cooper S.P.	127	F3	32.055350 -87.245330
Wind Creek S.P.	128	A1	32.856820 -85.946540

ALASKA	PAGE	GRID	LATITUDE LONGITUDE
National Park & Rec. Areas			
Admiralty Island Natl. Mon.	155	E4	57.618060 -134.161110
Aleutian WWII Natl. Hist. Area	154	A4	53.888889 -166.527222
Aniakchak Natl. Mon. & Pres.	154	B4	56.833333 -158.250556
Bering Land Bridge Natl. Pres.	154	B2	65.595320 -164.301800
Cape Krusenstern Natl. Mon.	154	B1	67.471630 -163.312300
Denali Natl. Park & Pres.-Denali Vis. Ctr.	154	C2	63.737000 -148.895000
Denali Natl. Park & Pres.-Eielson Vis. Ctr.	154	C2	63.440900 -150.239000
Gates of the Arctic Natl. Park & Pres.-Anaktuvuk Pass Ranger Sta.	154	C1	68.139900 -151.735400
Gates of the Arctic Natl. Park & Pres.-Arctic Interagency Vis. Ctr.	154	C1	67.253700 -150.187000
Gates of the Arctic Natl. Park & Pres.-Bettles Ranger Sta.	154	C1	66.912500 -151.667100
Gates of the Arctic Natl. Park & Pres.-Coldfoot Ranger Sta.	154	C1	67.253700 -150.187000
Glacier Bay Natl. Park & Pres.-Glacier Bay Lodge & Vis. Ctr.	155	D3	58.454900 -135.882600
Katmai Natl. Park & Pres.	154	C3	58.667030 -156.524600
Kenai Fjords Natl. Park-Vis. Ctr.	154	C3	60.105300 -149.435000
Klondike Gold Rush N.H.P.	155	D3	60.113550 -149.441342
Kobuk Valley Natl. Park	154	B1	67.073230 -159.839500
Lake Clark Natl. Park & Pres.	154	C3	60.471450 -154.576390
Misty Fiords Natl. Mon.	155	E4	55.472600 -130.429700
Noatak Natl. Pres.	154	C1	67.320740 -162.646370
White Mts. N.R.A.	154	C2	65.524300 -147.156400
Wrangell-Saint Elias Natl. Park & Pres.-Kennecott Vis. Ctr.	155	D3	61.485600 -142.881100
Wrangell-Saint Elias Natl. Park & Pres.-Wrangell-Saint Elias Vis. Ctr.	155	D3	61.964300 -145.317900
Yukon-Charley Rivers Natl. Pres.	155	D2	65.341680 -143.120650
State Park & Rec. Areas			
Afognak Island S.P.	154	C4	58.227100 -152.067300
Chilkat S.P.	155	D3	59.211111 -135.398056
Chugach S.P.	154	C3	61.037440 -149.780830
Denali S.P.	154	C3	62.734600 -150.199600
Point Bridget S.P.	155	E3	58.671225 -134.958801
Shuyak Island S.P.	154	C4	58.533100 -152.486100
Wood-Tikchik S.P.	154	B3	59.909600 -158.672000

ARIZONA	PAGE	GRID	LATITUDE LONGITUDE
National Park & Rec. Areas			
Agua Fria Natl. Mon.	47	D4	34.276490 -112.114350
Canyon de Chelly Natl. Mon.-Vis. Ctr.	48	A2	36.153200 -109.539000
Casa Grande Ruins Natl. Mon.-Ent. Sta.	54	C2	32.994700 -111.537000
Chiricahua Natl. Mon.-Main Road	55	E3	32.009250 -109.382230
Chiricahua Natl. Mon.-Ent. Sta.	55	E3	32.007500 -109.388900
Coronado Natl. Mem.-Vis. Ctr.	55	E4	31.346300 -110.254000
Fort Bowie N.H.S.-Vis. Ctr.	55	E3	32.146600 -109.435000
Glen Canyon N.R.A.-Ent. Sta.	47	E1	36.943300 -111.493600
Grand Canyon Natl. Park-East Ent.	47	D2	36.038800 -111.828000
Grand Canyon Natl. Park-North Ent.	47	D2	36.334900 -112.116000
Grand Canyon Natl. Park-South Ent.	47	D2	36.000100 -112.121600
Grand Canyon-Parashant Natl. Mon.	46	C2	36.452170 -113.724367
Ironwood Forest Natl. Mon.	54	C3	32.478380 -111.530220
Lake Mead N.R.A.-Boulder City Ent.	46	C2	36.020800 -114.796000
Lake Mead N.R.A.-Henderson Ent.	46	C2	36.105400 -114.901200
Lake Mead N.R.A.-Las Vegas-Rt 147 Ent.	46	C2	36.161000 -114.905100
Lake Mead N.R.A.-South Ent.	46	C2	35.225600 -114.551000
Montezuma Castle Natl. Mon.-Vis. Ctr.	47	D4	34.611600 -111.839000
Navajo Natl. Mon.-Betatakin Ruin	47	E1	36.683500 -110.541470
Navajo Natl. Mon.-Inscription House Ruin-Closed To Public	47	E1	36.661250 -110.775940
Navajo Natl. Mon.-Keet Seel Ruin	47	E1	36.683500 -110.541470
Navajo Natl. Mon.-Vis. Ctr.	47	E1	36.678200 -110.541000
Organ Pipe Cactus Natl. Mon.-Vis. Ctr.	54	B3	31.954800 -112.801000
Petrified Forest Natl. Park-North Ent.	47	F3	35.069600 -109.778000
Petrified Forest Natl. Park-South Ent.	47	F3	34.799600 -109.885000
Pipe Spring Natl. Mon.-Vis. Ctr.	47	D1	36.862500 -112.737000
Saguaro Natl. Park-East	55	D3	32.178430 -110.737990
Saguaro Natl. Park-Vis. Ctr.	55	D3	32.180200 -110.736000
Saguaro Natl. Park-West	55	D3	32.251660 -111.191660
Sonoran Desert Natl. Mon.	54	C2	33.001730 -112.421220
Sunset Crater Volcano Natl. Mon.-Vis. Ctr.	47	E3	35.368800 -111.543000
Tonto Natl. Mon.-Vis. Ctr.	55	D1	33.645200 -111.113000
Tumacácori N.H.P.-Vis. Ctr.	55	D4	31.567800 -111.051000
Tuzigoot Natl. Mon.-Pk. Hqtrs.	47	D4	34.561000 -111.853000
Vermilion Cliffs Natl. Mon.	47	D1	36.806389 -111.741111
Walnut Canyon Natl. Mon.-Walnut Canyon Vis. Ctr.	47	E3	35.171700 -111.509000
Wupatki Natl. Mon.-Vis. Ctr.	47	E3	35.520300 -111.372000
State Park & Rec. Areas			
Alamo Lake S.P.	46	C4	34.234270 -113.553220
Boyce Thmpson Arbrtum S.P.	55	D2	33.311150 -111.055790
Buckskin Mtn. S.P.	46	B4	34.255000 -114.134070
Catalina S.P.	55	D3	32.416760 -110.937500
Cattail Cove S.P.	46	B4	34.355075 -114.165877
Dead Horse Ranch S.P.	47	D4	34.748490 -112.022930
Homolovi Ruins S.P.	47	E3	35.023940 -110.630120
Kartchner Caverns S.P.	55	D3	31.840770 -110.342710
Lake Havasu S.P.	46	B4	34.473970 -114.345850
Lost Dutchman S.P.	54	C1	33.464920 -111.481350
Lyman Lake S.P.	48	A4	34.362870 -109.375370
Oracle S.P.	55	D2	32.610239 -110.740619
Patagonia Lake S.P.	55	D4	31.488970 -110.853790
Picacho Peak S.P.	54	C2	32.646340 -111.398090
Red Rock S.P.	47	D4	34.818920 -111.836700
Roper Lake S.P.	55	E2	32.758710 -109.709520
Slide Rock S.P.	47	D3	34.944340 -111.752810
Tonto Nat. Bridge S.P.	47	E4	34.323400 -111.449460

ARKANSAS	PAGE	GRID	LATITUDE LONGITUDE
National Park & Rec. Areas			
Fort Smith N.H.S.-Main Road	116	B1	35.387480 -94.429660
Fort Smith N.H.S.-Vis. Ctr.	116	B1	35.385800 -94.429800
Hot Springs Natl. Park-Main Road	117	D2	34.511660 -93.053980
Hot Springs Natl. Park-Vis. Ctr.	117	D2	34.513800 -93.053400
Pea Ridge N.M.P.-Main Road	106	C3	36.442600 -94.025980
Pea Ridge N.M.P.-Vis. Ctr.	106	C3	36.443800 -94.025900
State Park & Rec. Areas			
Bull Shoals-White River S.P.	107	E3	36.365590 -92.557490
Conway Cemetery S.P.	124	C1	33.101909 -93.683161
Crater of Diamonds S.P.	116	C3	34.038610 -93.667630
Crowley's Ridge S.P.	108	A4	36.044840 -90.666770
Degray Lake Resort S.P.-North Ent.	117	D3	34.248870 -93.116880
Degray Lake Resort S.P.-South Ent.	117	D3	34.217390 -93.085820
Hampson Arch. Mus. S.P.	118	B1	35.568990 -90.041060
Historic Washington S.P.	116	C4	33.774005 -93.683235
Hobbs S.P.-Cons. Area	106	C3	36.244880 -93.972640
Jacksonport S.P.	107	F4	35.641440 -91.305350
Jenkins' Ferry Bfld. S.P.	117	E3	34.212070 -92.547490
Lake Charles S.P.	107	F4	36.066870 -91.132700
Lake Chicot S.P.	126	A1	33.373070 -91.194940
Lake Dardanelle S.P.	117	D1	35.251690 -93.213380
Lake Fort Smith S.P.	106	C4	35.654040 -94.150140
Lake Frierson S.P.	108	A4	35.988570 -90.717540
Lake Ouachita S.P.	117	D2	34.610990 -93.165520
Lake Poinsett S.P.	118	A1	35.535510 -90.688700
Louisiana Purchase S.P.	118	A2	35.150340 -90.734990
Lower White River Mus. S.P.	117	F2	34.977035 -91.495131
Mammoth Spring S.P.	107	F3	36.496010 -91.535960
Marks' Mills Battleground S.P.	117	E4	33.781085 -92.256427
Moro Bay S.P.	125	E1	33.298890 -92.348940
Mount Magazine S.P.	116	C1	35.149900 -93.563600
Mount Nebo S.P.	117	D1	35.224870 -93.229930
Ozark Folk Center S.P.	107	E4	35.883480 -92.116340
Parkin Arch. S.P.	118	A1	35.268607 -90.554809
Petit Jean S.P.	117	D1	35.128320 -92.898530
Poison Springs Bfld. S.P.	117	D4	33.638340 -93.005250
Powhatan Hist. S.P.	107	F4	36.083234 -91.117858
Prairie Grove Bfld. S.P.	106	C4	35.983120 -94.305590
Toltec Mounds Arch. S.P.	117	E2	34.647370 -92.058510
Village Creek S.P.	118	A1	35.199650 -90.724540
White Oak Lake S.P.	117	D4	33.687490 -93.117240
Withrow Springs S.P.	106	C4	36.203800 -93.578200
Woolly Hollow S.P.	117	E1	35.286402 -92.285646

CALIFORNIA	PAGE	GRID	LATITUDE LONGITUDE
National Park & Rec. Areas			
Amboy Crater Natl. Nat. Landmark	53	E2	34.542196 -115.790920
Berryessa Snow Mountain Natl. Mon.	36	B2	38.902521 -123.411455
Carrizo Plain Natl. Mon.	52	B1	35.191000 -119.792000
Castle Mountains Natl. Mon.	53	F1	35.250563 -115.116773
Channel Islands Natl. Park	52	B2	34.248500 -119.267000
Death Valley Natl. Park-Furnace Creek Vis. Ctr.	45	F3	36.461800 -116.867000
Devils Postpile Natl. Mon.	37	E4	37.630330 -119.084300
Giant Sequoia Natl. Mon.-North Unit	45	D2	36.705501 -118.824821
Giant Sequoia Natl. Mon.-South Unit	45	E3	36.062389 -118.317784
Golden Gate N.R.A.-Marin Headlands	36	B4	37.830900 -122.525000
Golden Gate N.R.A.-Mott Vis. Ctr.	36	B4	37.799800 -122.460000
Joshua Tree Natl. Park-Indian Cove	53	E3	34.120000 -116.156000
Joshua Tree Natl. Park-North Ent.	53	E3	34.078300 -116.037000
Joshua Tree Natl. Park-West Ent.	53	E3	34.093600 -116.266000
Kings Canyon Natl. Park-East Ent.	45	D2	36.715870 -118.940420
Kings Canyon Natl. Park-West Ent.	45	D2	36.723720 -118.956490
Lassen Volcanic Natl. Park-Ent.	29	D4	40.537900 -121.571000
Lava Beds Natl. Mon.-Vis. Ctr.	29	D2	41.713900 -121.509000
Manzanar N.H.S.	45	E3	36.732260 -118.148500
Mojave Trails Natl. Mon.	53	E2	34.169528 -115.788162
Pinnacles Natl. Park-East Ent.	44	B3	36.483200 -121.162000
Pinnacles Natl. Park-West Ent.	44	B3	36.473300 -121.224400
Point Reyes Natl. Seashore-Bear Valley Vis. Ctr.	36	A3	38.043100 -122.799000
Point Reyes Natl. Seashore-Kenneth C. Patrick Vis. Ctr.	36	A3	38.027800 -122.961000
Point Reyes Natl. Seashore-Vis. Ctr.	36	A3	37.996500 -123.021000
Redwood Natl. Park-Kuchel Vis. Ctr.	28	A3	41.286800 -124.090900
Redwood Natl. Park-Prairie Creek Vis. Ctr.	28	A3	41.365300 -124.022000
Sand to Snow Natl. Mon.	53	D2	34.045197 -117.054096
San Gabriel Mountains Natl. Mon.	52	C2	34.286213 -117.884488
Santa Monica Mts. N.R.A.-Vis. Ctr.	52	B2	34.188600 -118.887000
Santa Rosa & San Jacinto Mts. Natl. Mon.	53	E3	33.755173 -116.729736
Sequoia Natl. Park-North Ent.	45	D3	36.647900 -118.826370
Sequoia Natl. Park-South Ent.	45	D3	36.487130 -118.836810
Shasta-Trinity N.R.A.	28	C4	40.633204 -122.601127
Trona Pinnacles Natl. Nature Landmark	45	F4	35.611944 -117.369444
Whiskeytown-N.R.A.	28	C4	40.751500 -122.320580
Yosemite Natl. Park-Arch Rock Ent.	37	D3	37.687500 -119.730000
Yosemite Natl. Park-Big Oak Flat Ent.	37	D3	37.800800 -119.874000
Yosemite Natl. Park-Hetch Hetchy Ent.	37	D3	37.893500 -119.842000
Yosemite Natl. Park-South Ent.	37	D3	37.507000 -119.632000
Yosemite Natl. Park-Tioga Pass Ent.	37	D3	37.910700 -119.258000
State Park & Rec. Areas			
Ahjumawi Lava Springs S.P.	29	D3	41.107140 -121.468600
Anza-Borrego Desert S.P.	53	E4	33.256550 -116.399340
Big Basin Redwoods S.P.	44	A2	37.168380 -122.221530
Bothe-Napa Valley S.P.	36	B3	38.553410 -122.525640
Butano S.P.	44	A2	37.200660 -122.344140
Carlsbad State Beach	53	D3	33.147530 -117.345280
Castle Crags S.P.	28	C3	41.149280 -122.317480
China Camp S.P.	36	B3	38.003990 -122.466480
Clear Lake S.P.	36	B2	39.009780 -122.805400
Cuyamaca Rancho S.P.	53	D4	32.933790 -116.562560
Del Norte Coast Redwoods S.P.	28	A3	41.603280 -124.100130
Doheny State Beach	52	C3	33.463820 -117.688830
Donner Mem. S.P.	37	D2	39.323880 -120.228370
Ed Z'Berg-Sugar Pine Point S.P.	37	D2	39.056290 -120.119200
Emerald Bay S.P.	37	D2	38.956710 -120.108850
Fremont Peak S.P.	44	B3	36.760340 -121.502670
Garrapata S.P.	44	B3	36.475310 -121.936280
Gaviota S.P.	52	A2	34.475250 -120.228590
Grizzly Creek Redwoods S.P.	28	B4	40.486630 -123.903520
Grover Hot Springs S.P.	37	D3	38.695230 -119.836760
Henry Cowell Redwoods S.P.	44	A2	37.044020 -122.070990
Henry W. Coe S.P.	44	B2	37.085600 -121.467340
Humboldt Lagoons S.P.	28	A3	41.284330 -124.089720
Humboldt Redwoods S.P.	28	A4	40.284740 -124.056950
Jedediah Smith Redwoods S.P.	28	A2	41.798190 -124.084030
Julia Pfeiffer Burns S.P.	44	B3	36.160700 -121.668210
Manchester S.P.	36	A2	38.980450 -123.703020
Marina State Beach	44	B3	36.683030 -121.809440
McGrath State Beach	52	B2	34.227270 -119.256460
Mendocino Headlands S.P.	36	A2	39.307570 -123.798910
Morro Bay S.P.	44	B4	35.354020 -120.843800
Morro Strand State Beach	44	B4	35.435390 -120.888060
Mount Diablo S.P.	36	B4	37.844210 -121.950200
Mount Tamalpais S.P.	36	B3	37.904290 -122.604040
Navarro River Redwoods S.P.	36	A2	39.175000 -123.676390

Pacheco S.P.	44	B2	37.055650 -121.016250
Palomar Mtn. S.P.	53	D3	33.325340 -116.893330
Patrick's Point S.P.	28	A3	41.135690 -124.150500
Pfeiffer Big Sur S.P.	44	B3	36.250930 -121.786550
Placerita Canyon S.P.	52	C2	34.377530 -118.470290
Plumas-Eureka S.P.	36	C1	39.758360 -120.695360
Point Dume State Beach	52	B2	34.003110 -118.807250
Point Sal State Beach	52	A1	34.897760 -120.642760
Prairie Creek Redwoods S.P.	28	A3	41.355490 -124.073670
Red Rock Canyon S.P.	52	C1	35.359734 -117.978351
Russian Gulch S.P.	36	A2	39.330990 -123.805050
Saddleback Butte S.P.	52	C2	34.689820 -117.824340
Samuel P. Taylor S.P.	36	B3	38.004660 -122.708400
San Gregorio State Beach	36	B4	37.321490 -122.401640
San Onofre State Beach	53	D3	33.383380 -117.580790
Sonoma Coast State Beach	36	A3	38.441060 -123.122970
Sunset State Beach	44	B2	36.897780 -121.835450
The Forest of Nisene Marks S.P.	44	B2	37.042024 -121.856231
Tolowa Dunes S.P.	28	A2	41.825800 -124.187500
Trinidad State Beach	28	A3	41.061090 -124.142290
Van Damme S.P.	36	A2	39.273990 -123.790490
Westport-Union Landing State Beach	36	A1	39.658350 -123.784930
Wilder Ranch S.P.	44	A2	36.962160 -122.080850
Zmudowski State Beach	44	B2	36.845580 -121.804300

COLORADO	PAGE	GRID	LATITUDE LONGITUDE
National Park & Rec. Areas			
Arapaho N.R.A.	41	D1	40.197870 -105.869440
Bent's Old Fort N.H.S.	41	F3	38.045980 -103.431440
Black Canyon-Gunnison Natl. Park-North Ent.	40	C3	38.586890 -107.695940
Black Canyon-Gunnison Natl. Park-South Ent.	40	C3	38.553980 -107.686390
Browns Canyon Natl. Mon.	41	D2	38.753093 -105.973528
Canyons of the Ancients Natl. Mon.	40	A4	37.587880 -108.916890
Colorado Natl. Mon.-Northwest Ent.	40	B2	39.117620 -108.730910
Colorado Natl. Mon.-Southeast Ent.	40	B2	39.032860 -108.631460
Colorado Natl. Mon.-South Ent.	40	B2	39.021100 -108.659540
Colorado Natl. Mon.-Southwest Ent.	40	B2	39.055070 -108.742500
Curecanti N.R.A.-East Ent.	40	C3	38.515010 -107.020560
Curecanti N.R.A.-North Ent.	40	C3	38.463380 -107.419580
Curecanti N.R.A.-South Ent.	40	C3	38.473160 -107.076450
Curecanti N.R.A.-West Ent.	40	C3	38.444680 -107.341980
Dinosaur Natl. Mon.-East Ent.	32	B4	40.443120 -108.517790
Dinosaur Natl. Mon.-South Ent.	32	B4	40.243920 -108.973750
Florissant Fossil Beds Natl. Mon.	41	E2	38.937440 -105.283400
Great Sand Dunes Natl. Park-Ent. Sta.	41	D4	37.725000 -105.519000
Hovenweep Natl. Mon.-Cutthroat	40	A4	37.413000 -108.974280
Hovenweep Natl. Mon.-Hackberry	40	A4	37.398890 -109.036680
Hovenweep Natl. Mon.-Holly	40	A4	37.398890 -109.036680
Hovenweep Natl. Mon.-Horseshoe	40	A4	37.464610 -108.974680
Mesa Verde Natl. Park-Ent. Sta.	40	B4	37.331100 -108.416000
Rocky Mtn. Natl. Park-Beaver Meadows Ent.	33	E4	40.367300 -105.578000
Rocky Mtn. Natl. Park-Fall River Ent.	33	E4	40.404000 -105.590000
Rocky Mtn. Natl. Park-Grand Lake Ent.	33	E4	40.267300 -105.833000
Rocky Mtn. Natl. Park-Wild Basin Ent.	33	E4	40.219000 -105.534000
Sand Creek Massacre N.H.S.	42	A3	38.541250 -102.505910
Yucca House Natl. Mon.	40	B4	37.251678 -108.684911
State Park & Rec. Areas			
Barr Lake S.P.	41	E1	39.938160 -104.733470
Boyd Lake S.P.	33	E4	40.428990 -105.045400
Castlewood Canyon S.P.	41	E2	39.325860 -104.737640
Crawford S.P.	40	C3	38.708000 -107.617550
Eleven Mile S.P.	41	D2	38.948570 -105.526450
Golden Gate Canyon S.P.	41	D1	39.875560 -105.453650
Harvey Gap S.P.	40	C1	39.606210 -107.659010
Highline Lake S.P.	40	B2	39.270910 -108.835930
Jackson Lake S.P.	33	F4	40.409110 -104.070130
James M. Robb-Colorado River S.P.-Corn Lake	40	B2	39.062709 -108.455110
James M. Robb-Colorado River S.P.-Island Acres	40	B2	39.165709 -108.300610
John Martin Reservoir S.P.	42	A3	38.065390 -102.927110
Lake Pueblo S.P.	41	E3	38.258130 -104.719160
Lathrop S.P.	41	E4	37.602830 -104.833740
Lory S.P.	33	E4	40.593143 -105.185413
Mancos S.P.	40	B4	37.399890 -108.266750
Mueller S.P.	41	E2	38.884940 -105.157710
Navajo S.P.	48	B1	37.067800 -107.407599
North Sterling S.P.	34	A4	40.787740 -103.264990
Paonia S.P.	40	C2	38.980440 -107.342900
Pearl Lake S.P.	33	D4	40.790160 -106.894610
Ridgway S.P.	40	B3	38.229710 -107.729410
Rifle Falls S.P.	40	B1	39.695290 -107.701090
Rifle Gap S.P.	40	B1	39.627460 -107.762520
Roxborough S.P.	41	E2	39.451300 -105.070200
San Luis Lakes S.W.A.	41	D4	37.663130 -105.734480
Spinney Mtn. S.P.	41	D2	39.014760 -105.625880
Stagecoach S.P.	33	D4	40.286100 -106.866920
Staunton S.P.	41	D1	39.509959 -105.394411
Steamboat Lake S.P.	32	C4	40.805240 -106.943600
Sweitzer Lake S.P.	40	B2	38.712050 -108.042640
Sylvan Lake S.P.	40	C1	39.516710 -106.753170
Trinidad Lake S.P.	49	E1	37.149700 -104.563650
Vega S.P.	40	B2	39.226890 -107.810250
Yampa River S.P.	32	C4	40.533190 -107.444483

CONNECTICUT	PAGE	GRID	LATITUDE LONGITUDE
National Park & Rec. Areas			
Weir Farm N.H.S.	148	C2	41.255890 -73.455980
State Park & Rec. Areas			
Bigelow Hollow S.P.	150	B2	41.991600 -72.134840
Bluff Point S.P.	149	F2	41.335800 -72.033520
Chatfield Hollow S.P.	150	A4	41.361400 -72.580190
Day Pond S.P.	150	A4	41.553432 -72.418419
Devil's Hopyard S.P.	150	A4	41.486529 -72.342462
Gay City S.P.	150	A3	41.716100 -72.434470
Gillette Castle S.P.	150	A4	41.430670 -72.427990
Hammonasset Beach S.P.	149	E2	41.273640 -72.562350
Haystack Mtn. S.P.	94	C2	42.002010 -73.209960
Hurd S.P.	150	A4	41.530650 -72.537650
John A. Minetto S.P.	94	C2	41.884020 -73.170280
Lake Waramaug S.P.	148	C1	41.706290 -73.382460
Mashamoquet Brook S.P.	150	B3	41.860320 -71.987230
Mount Riga S.P.	94	B2	42.028830 -73.428620
Putnam Mem. S.P.	148	C2	41.344200 -73.381500
Rocky Neck S.P.	149	F2	41.316920 -72.242690
Selden Neck S.P.	150	A4	41.287500 -72.331100
Silver Sands S.P.	149	D2	41.198410 -73.076180
Southford Falls S.P.	149	D1	41.455700 -73.166150
Squantz Pond S.P.	148	C1	41.508580 -73.471040
Stoddard Hill S.P.	150	B4	41.461900 -72.065500
Sunrise Resort S.P.	149	E1	41.502642 -72.477201
Wadsworth Falls S.P.	150	A4	41.536080 -72.687380
West Rock Ridge S.P.	149	D2	41.347810 -72.968260

DELAWARE	PAGE	GRID	LATITUDE LONGITUDE
State Park & Rec. Areas			
Cape Henlopen S.P.	145	F3	38.782360 -75.103010
Delaware Seashore S.P.	145	F4	38.614420 -75.071540
Fenwick Island S.P.	145	F4	38.469740 -75.051550
Fort Delaware S.P.	145	E1	39.578700 -75.588320
Fort Dupont S.P.	145	E1	39.568930 -75.588590
Holts Landing S.P.	145	F4	38.584080 -75.128380
Killens Pond S.P.	145	E3	38.990320 -75.544920
Lums Pond S.P.	145	E1	39.570520 -75.733490
Trap Pond S.P.	145	E4	38.525860 -75.483170
White Clay Creek S.P.	146	B4	39.709810 -75.776560

FLORIDA	PAGE	GRID	LATITUDE LONGITUDE
National Park & Rec. Areas			
Biscayne Natl. Park-Dante Fascell Vis. Ctr.	143	F3	25.464400 -80.334900
Canaveral Natl. Seashore	141	E1	28.611410 -80.808390
Castillo de San Marcos Natl. Mon.	139	D3	29.897747 -81.311461
Dry Tortugas Natl. Park-Vis. Ctr.	142	B4	24.628500 -82.873400
Everglades Natl. Park-Ent.	143	E3	25.394400 -80.589300
Fort Matanzas Natl. Mon.	139	E3	29.715660 -81.234190
Gulf Islands Natl. Seashore	135	F2	30.362880 -87.139630
State Park & Rec. Areas			
Alafia River S.P.	140	C3	27.789920 -82.120830
Amelia Island S.P.	139	D2	30.543900 -81.449700
Anastasia S.P.	139	E3	29.874740 -81.285030
Anclote Key Pres. S.P.	140	B2	28.193070 -82.850660
Avalon S.P.	141	E3	27.542840 -80.318060
Bahia Honda S.P.	143	D4	24.659540 -81.277810
Bald Point S.P.	138	A3	29.902700 -84.408600
Big Lagoon S.P.	135	F2	30.322290 -87.401170
Big Shoals S.P.	138	C2	30.339115 -82.683182
Big Talbot Island S.P.	139	D2	30.460500 -81.421950
Blue Spring S.P.	141	D1	28.952270 -81.331300
Bulow Creek S.P.	139	E4	29.388000 -81.132399
Bulow Plantation Ruins Hist. S.P.	139	E4	29.433590 -81.144590
Caladesi Island S.P.	140	B2	28.059890 -82.813780
Cedar Key Mus. S.P.	138	B4	29.151172 -83.048299
Charlotte Harbor Pres. S.P.	140	C4	26.850691 -82.022026
Collier-Seminole S.P.	143	D2	25.991630 -81.591700
Crystal River Pres. S.P. & Arch. S.P.	140	B1	28.909530 -82.628680
Curry Hammock S.P.	143	E4	24.742640 -80.984793
Dade Bfld. Hist. S.P.	140	C1	28.654430 -82.124970
Deleon Springs S.P.	139	D4	29.131920 -81.360400
Delnor-Wiggins Pass S.P.	142	C1	26.272500 -81.826900
Dudley Farm Hist. S.P.	138	C3	29.649617 -82.630738
Eden Gardens S.P.	136	B2	30.361530 -86.125010
Egmont Key S.P.	140	B3	27.723490 -82.679390
Fakahatchee Strand Pres. S.P.	143	D2	25.961900 -81.364600
Faver-Dykes S.P.	139	E3	29.668050 -81.268030
Florida Caverns S.P.	137	D1	30.809160 -85.212270
Fort Clinch S.P.	139	D1	30.698010 -81.434300
Fort Cooper S.P.	140	C1	28.801300 -82.309200
Fort Pierce Inlet S.P.-East Ent.	141	E3	27.485160 -80.299430
Fort Pierce Inlet S.P.-West Ent.	141	E3	27.475930 -80.316980
Gasparilla Island S.P.	140	C4	26.718200 -82.261400
Grayton Beach S.P.	136	B2	30.328930 -86.155790
Henderson Beach S.P.	136	B2	30.387000 -86.447499
Highlands Hammock S.P.	141	D3	27.476554 -81.557148
Hontoon Island S.P.	141	D1	28.976680 -81.35769
Hugh Taylor Birch S.P.	143	F1	26.138220 -80.10445
Indian Key Hist. S.P.	143	E4	24.888056 -80.67805
John Gorrie Mus. S.P.	137	D3	29.725768 -84.98324
John Pennekamp Coral Reef S.P.	143	E3	25.127620 -80.40965
Jonathan Dickinson S.P.	141	F4	27.002920 -80.09998
Kissimmee Prairie Pres. S.P.	141	D3	27.538826 -81.02294
Lafayette Blue Springs S.P.	138	B2	30.115136 -83.22941
Lake Griffin S.P.	140	C1	28.857450 -81.90224
Lake Kissimmee S.P.	141	D2	27.971930 -81.38022
Lake Louisa S.P.	140	C1	28.460070 -81.75162
Lake Manatee S.P.	140	C3	27.475140 -82.33680
Little Talbot Island S.P.	139	D2	30.460500 -81.42195
Long Key S.P.	143	E4	24.821580 -80.81951
Lovers Key S.P.	142	C1	26.391000 -81.87780
Manatee Springs S.P.	138	B4	29.496230 -82.95863
Myakka River S.P.	140	C4	27.242670 -82.33224
Natural Bridge Bfld. Hist. S.P.	138	A2	30.284730 -84.15226
O'Leno S.P.	138	C3	29.809100 -82.55070
Olustee Bfld. Hist. S.P.	138	C2	30.214650 -82.42896
Oscar Scherer S.P.	140	B4	27.168840 -82.47736
Paynes Prairie Pres. S.P.	138	C3	29.520720 -82.30040
Perdido Key S.P.	135	F2	30.291480 -87.46536
Ponce De Leon Springs S.P.	136	C1	30.713260 -85.92249
Rainbow Springs S.P.	138	C4	29.103818 -82.43878
Ravine Gardens S.P.	139	D3	29.637490 -81.64683
River Rise Pres. S.P.	138	C3	29.859961 -82.60539
Saint Sebastian River Pres. S.P.	141	E3	27.815241 -80.51382
San Marcos de Apalache Hist. S.P.	138	A2	30.152890 -84.21003
Savannas Pres. S.P.	141	E3	27.245960 -80.25027
Sebastian Inlet S.P.	141	E2	27.870200 -80.45359
Silver River S.P.	139	D4	29.202550 -82.05361
Suwannee River S.P.	138	B2	30.389610 -83.15785
Three Rivers S.P.	137	D1	30.736800 -84.93650
Tomoka S.P.	139	E4	29.342210 -81.08620
Torreya S.P.	137	D2	30.553530 -84.94674
Troy Spring S.P.	138	B3	29.918000 -82.89330
Waccasassa Bay Pres. S.P.	138	B4	29.188100 -82.92550
Washington Oaks Gardens S.P.	139	E3	29.634670 -81.20550
Wekiwa Springs S.P.	141	D1	28.710490 -81.46281
Windley Key Fossil Reef Geological S.P.	143	E4	24.914100 -80.64280
Yulee Sugar Mill Ruins Hist. S.P.	140	B1	28.784730 -82.60737

GEORGIA	PAGE	GRID	LATITUDE LONGITUDE
National Park & Rec. Areas			
Chattahoochee River N.R.A.	120	C3	34.002910 -84.34918
Chickamauga & Chattanooga N.M.P.	120	B2	34.941430 -85.25879
Cumberland Island Natl. Seashore	139	D1	30.720300 -81.54876
Ed Jenkins N.R.A.	120	C2	34.682900 -84.19820
Fort Frederica Natl. Mon.	130	B4	31.219790 -81.38657
Fort Pulaski Natl. Mon.	130	C3	32.016520 -80.89168
Jimmy Carter N.H.S.	128	C3	32.034090 -84.40160
Kennesaw Mtn. Natl. Battlefied Park-Vis. Ctr.	120	C3	33.983000 -84.57790
Ocmulgee Natl. Mon.	129	D2	32.848560 -83.60214
State Park & Rec. Areas			
Amicalola Falls S.P.	120	C2	34.558940 -84.24889
Black Rock Mtn. S.P.	121	D2	34.918150 -83.40031
Bobby Brown State Outdoor Rec. Area	121	E3	33.979030 -82.58896
Cloudland Canyon S.P.	120	B2	34.830430 -85.48204
Crooked River S.P.	139	D1	30.844840 -81.55935
Elijah Clark S.P.	121	E4	33.854210 -82.391913
Florence Marina S.P.	128	C3	32.090988 -85.043263
Fort Mtn. S.P.	120	C2	34.763090 -84.68933
Fort Yargo S.P.	121	D4	33.984940 -83.73358
Franklin D. Roosevelt S.P.	128	C2	32.848670 -84.79323
General Coffee S.P.	129	E4	31.511490 -82.74536
George L. Smith S.P.	130	A2	32.570310 -82.10376
George T. Bagby S.P.	128	C4	31.739940 -85.07482
Georgia Veterans S.P.	129	D3	31.957951 -83.903787
Gordonia-Alatamaha S.P.	130	A3	32.081900 -82.123550
Hamburg S.P.	129	E1	33.208800 -82.774870
Hard Labor Creek S.P.	121	D4	33.677820 -83.593840
Hart State Outdoor Rec. Area	121	E3	34.376040 -82.910260
High Falls S.P.	129	D1	33.176590 -84.020280
Indian Springs S.P.	129	D1	33.247480 -83.921190
James H. "Sloppy" Floyd S.P.	120	B3	34.440260 -85.347580
John Tanner S.P.	120	B4	33.602750 -85.167070
Laura S. Walker S.P.	138	C1	31.143130 -82.212920
Little Ocmulgee S.P.	129	E3	32.100590 -82.886360
Magnolia Springs S.P.	130	A1	32.875760 -81.962560
Mistletoe S.P.	121	E4	33.638770 -82.390540
Moccasin Creek S.P.	121	D2	34.845160 -83.589140
Panola Mtn. S.P.	120	C4	33.622042 -84.173078
Providence Canyon State Outdoor Rec. Area	128	C3	32.068270 -84.929150
Red Top Mtn. S.P.	120	C3	34.145950 -84.720190
Reed Bingham S.P.	137	F1	31.161310 -83.538880
Richard B. Russell S.P.	121	E3	34.166778 -82.745691
Seminole S.P.	137	D1	30.811420 -84.873570
Skidaway Island S.P.	130	C3	31.947720 -81.052550
Sprewell Bluff State Outdoor Rec. Area	128	C2	32.857269 -84.482657
Stephen C. Foster S.P.	138	C1	30.827020 -82.361310

	PAGE	GRID	LATITUDE LONGITUDE
ılah Gorge S.P.	121	D2	34.736350 -83.391950
aloo S.P.	121	E3	34.501940 -83.082320
coi S.P.	121	D2	34.724620 -83.728170
oria Bryant S.P.	121	E3	34.299380 -83.158770
el S.P.	121	D2	34.766190 -83.922000
son Mill Bridge S.P.	121	E3	34.041140 -83.126990

HAWAII

HAWAII	PAGE	GRID	LATITUDE LONGITUDE
tional Park & Rec. Areas			
eakala Natl. Park-Main Road	153	D1	20.769130 -156.242850
eakala Natl. Park-Kipahulu Ent.	153	D1	20.662000 -156.045600
eakala Natl. Park-North Ent.	153	D1	20.769000 -156.243000
vaii Volcanoes Natl. Park-Ent.	153	F4	19.428700 -155.254500
nouliuli Natl. Mon.	152	A3	21.354145 -158.090528
aupapa N.H.P.	152	C3	21.174110 -157.002830
ite Park & Rec. Areas			
ıpuaa O Kahana S.P.	152	A2	21.555210 -157.873260
ena S.P.	152	B1	22.220930 -159.579600
ena Point S.P.	152	A2	21.551270 -158.244180
ımahina State Wayside Park	153	D1	20.871610 -156.170310
kee S.P.	152	B1	22.112580 -159.671050
kena S.P.	153	D1	20.634030 -156.444180
aau S.P.	152	C3	21.174110 -157.002830
ihale S.P.	152	B1	22.084480 -159.756700
ia Kaa State Wayside	153	D1	20.817560 -156.125800
ianapanapa S.P.	153	E1	20.786230 -156.003010
ilua River S.P.	152	B1	22.044180 -159.337250
ilua Valley State Wayside	153	D1	20.840110 -156.139980
iluku River S.P.	153	F3	19.713340 -155.130490
imea Canyon S.P.	152	B1	22.031990 -159.671100

IDAHO

IDAHO	PAGE	GRID	LATITUDE LONGITUDE
tional Park & Rec. Areas			
y of Rocks Natl. Res.	31	D2	42.078950 -113.677650
aters of the Moon Natl. Mon. & Pres.	23	D4	43.462030 -113.559930
german Fossil Beds Natl. Mon.	30	C1	42.760980 -114.928220
nidoka Natl. Hist. Site	31	D1	42.636944 -114.232222
z Perce N.H.P.-Clearwater Bfld.	22	B1	46.072600 -115.975400
z Perce N.H.P.-East Kamiah Site	22	B1	46.216600 -115.992400
z Perce N.H.P.-Vis. Ctr.	22	B1	46.446500 -116.817000
z Perce N.H.P.-White Bird Bfld.	22	B1	45.794400 -116.282000
wtooth N.R.A.	22	C3	44.211000 -114.946000
ate Park & Rec. Areas			
ar Lake S.P.	31	F2	42.026180 -111.257690
uneau Dunes S.P.	30	B1	42.910940 -115.713890
stle Rocks S.P.	31	D2	42.135400 -113.670000
vorshak S.P.	14	B4	46.577610 -116.327310
gle Island S.P.	22	B4	43.684510 -116.400300
ragut S.P.	14	B2	47.952790 -116.602170
rriman S.P.	23	F3	44.321000 -111.471200
lls Gate S.P.	14	B4	46.380500 -117.044780
nrys Lake S.P.	23	F3	44.620000 -111.373060
eyburn S.P.	14	B3	47.353840 -116.748770
ke Cascade S.P.	22	B3	44.520686 -116.046685
ke Walcott S.P.	31	D1	42.674850 -113.482570
nd of the Yankee Fork S.P.	22	C3	44.475190 -114.208860
cky Peak S.P.	22	B4	43.530880 -116.055160
assacre Rocks S.P.	31	D1	42.672200 -112.990800
cCroskey S.P.	14	B4	47.721080 -116.826310
d Mission S.P.	14	B3	47.549420 -116.356940
onderosa S.P.	22	B2	44.926810 -116.083860
iest Lake S.P.	14	B1	48.622082 -116.827798
ound Lake S.P.	14	B2	48.166110 -116.634230
ousand Springs S.P.-Box Canyon	30	C1	42.709800 -114.791900
ousand Springs S.P.-Malad Gorge	30	C1	42.864400 -114.854600
ousand Springs S.P.-Niagara Springs	30	C1	42.662800 -114.672400
ree Island Crossing S.P.	30	C1	42.945280 -115.314850
inchester Lake S.P.	22	B1	46.232280 -116.635570

ILLINOIS

ILLINOIS	PAGE	GRID	LATITUDE LONGITUDE
ational Park & Rec. Areas			
ncoln Home N.H.S.	98	B1	39.798120 -89.645150
onald Reagan Boyhood Home N.H.S.	88	B1	41.836700 -89.481100
ate Park & Rec. Areas			
ople River Canyon S.P.	74	A4	42.443990 -90.053280
gyle Lake S.P.	87	F4	40.450680 -90.805080
anner Marsh State Fish & Wildlife Area	88	B4	40.539600 -89.864500
eall Woods S.P.	99	D4	38.351540 -87.836380
eaver Dam S.P.	98	B2	39.214390 -89.959390
g Bend State Fish & Wildlife Area	88	A2	41.634900 -90.044600
uffalo Rock S.P.	88	C2	41.329720 -88.913090
arlyle Lake State Fish & Wildlife Area	98	C3	38.768500 -89.193900
astle Rock S.P.	88	B1	41.978230 -89.357040
ave-In-Rock S.P.	109	D1	37.468010 -88.159950
hain O'Lakes S.P.	74	C4	42.458390 -88.211950
hannahon S.P.	88	C2	41.415826 -88.223133
offeen Lake State Fish & Wildlife Area	98	B2	39.057000 -89.412400
rawford County State Fish & Wildlife Area	99	D2	39.099800 -87.713100
elabar S.P.	87	F3	40.957830 -90.939460
es Plaines State Fish & Wildlife Area	88	C2	41.376600 -88.207400
ixon Springs S.P.	108	C1	37.383600 -88.672830
onnelley–Depue State Fish & Wildlife Area	88	B2	41.324000 -89.314100
Edward R. Madigan State Fish & Wildlife Area	88	B4	40.115280 -89.402240
Eldon Hazlet State Rec. Area	98	B3	38.667610 -89.327200
Ferne Clyffe S.P.	108	C1	37.532550 -88.966430
Fort Massac S.P.	108	C2	37.161720 -88.693850
Fox Ridge S.P.	99	D2	39.406020 -88.134810
Gebhard Woods S.P.	88	C2	41.357350 -88.440210
Giant City S.P.	108	C1	37.612250 -89.181790
Green River State Wildlife Area	88	B2	41.631600 -89.516500
Hamilton County State Fish & Wildlife Area	98	C4	38.065100 -88.404700
Hazel & Bill Rutherford Wildlife Prairie S.P.	88	B3	40.734180 -89.747270
Henderson County Cons. Area	87	F3	40.857505 -90.975005
Horseshoe Lake State Fish & Wildlife Area	108	C2	37.130465 -89.338505
Illini S.P.	88	C2	41.318770 -88.711070
Illinois Beach S.P.	75	D4	42.429920 -87.820150
Iroquois County State Wildlife Area	89	D3	40.994300 -87.598700
Jim Edgar Panther Creek State Fish & Wildlife Area	98	B1	40.011700 -90.177005
Johnson-Sauk Trail S.P.	88	A2	41.327510 -89.904850
Jubilee College S.P.	88	B3	40.844580 -89.827260
Kankakee River S.P.	89	D2	41.203400 -88.001880
Kaskaskia River State Fish & Wildlife Area	98	B4	38.229700 -89.879500
Kickapoo State Rec. Area	89	D4	40.138290 -87.737770
Lake Le Aqua-Na State Rec. Area	74	A4	42.422800 -89.823900
Lake Murphysboro S.P.	108	C1	37.771800 -89.382670
Lasalle Lake State Fish & Wildlife Area	88	C2	41.238400 -88.655500
Lincoln Trail S.P.	99	D2	39.346480 -87.696460
Lowden S.P.	88	B1	42.034860 -89.324950
Mackinaw River State Fish & Wildlife Area	88	B4	40.545801 -89.294301
Marshall State Fish & Wildlife Area	88	B3	41.007900 -89.410100
Matthiessen S.P.	88	C2	41.285010 -89.010050
Mautino State Fish & Wildlife Area	88	B2	41.323100 -89.718900
Middle Fork State Fish & Wildlife Area	89	D4	40.258300 -87.795900
Mississippi Palisades S.P.	88	A1	42.135820 -90.163300
Mississippi River State Fish & Wildlife Area	98	A2	38.991900 -90.542100
Morrison-Rockwood S.P.	88	A1	41.856350 -89.950120
Nauvoo S.P.	87	F4	40.543590 -91.386650
Newton Lake State Fish & Wildlife Area	99	D2	38.922400 -88.306700
Pere Marquette S.P.	98	A2	38.968110 -90.497430
Prophetstown S.P.	88	B2	41.672090 -89.920310
Pyramid S.P.	98	B4	38.004110 -89.425680
Ray Norbut State Fish & Wildlife Area	98	A1	39.685000 -90.648500
Red Hills S.P.	99	D3	38.728850 -87.838660
Rend Lake State Fish & Wildlife Area	98	C4	38.043800 -88.988900
Rice Lake State Fish & Wildlife Area	88	A4	40.476785 -89.949205
Saline County State Fish & Wildlife Area	109	D1	37.691300 -88.379100
Sam Dale Lake State Fish & Wildlife Area	98	C3	38.536005 -88.565605
Sam Parr State Fish & Wildlife Area	99	D2	39.011022 -88.126955
Sanganois State Fish & Wildlife Area	88	A4	40.091605 -90.283205
Sangchris Lake State Rec. Area	98	B1	39.656830 -89.487940
Shabbona Lake S.P.	88	C1	41.732250 -88.864930
Shelbyville State Fish & Wildlife Area	98	C2	39.566300 -88.566200
Siloam Springs S.P.	97	F1	39.899340 -90.955050
Silver Springs State Fish & Wildlife Area.	88	C2	41.627500 -88.518550
Snakeden Hollow State Fish & Wildlife Area	88	A3	41.030200 -90.080100
South Shore S.P.	98	B3	38.610250 -89.314570
Starved Rock S.P.	88	C2	41.321750 -89.010850
Stephen A. Forbes State Rec. Area	98	C3	38.718140 -88.743250
Ten Mile Creek State Fish & Wildlife Area	98	C4	38.081200 -88.594200
Turkey Bluffs State Fish & Wildlife Area	98	B4	37.877200 -89.771100
Walnut Point S.P.	99	D1	39.705150 -88.030390
Wayne Fitzgerrell S.P.	98	C4	38.089250 -88.937010
Weinberg-King S.P.	87	F4	40.226830 -90.899700
Weldon Springs S.P.	88	C4	40.125080 -88.921400
White Pines Forest S.P.	88	B1	41.988730 -89.461590
Wolf Creek S.P.	98	C2	39.488310 -88.680370
Woodford State Fish & Wildlife Area	88	B3	40.878900 -89.444800

INDIANA

INDIANA	PAGE	GRID	LATITUDE LONGITUDE
National Park & Rec. Areas			
George Rodgers Clark N.H.P.	99	D3	38.677880 -87.535350
Indiana Dunes Natl. Lakeshore	89	D1	41.653160 -87.062630
Lincoln Boyhood Natl. Mem.	99	E4	38.116800 -86.997860
State Park & Rec. Areas			
Bass Lake State Beach	89	E2	41.220100 -86.580200
Brown County S.P.	99	F2	39.197170 -86.215830
Chain O' Lakes S.P.	90	A2	41.336000 -85.422950
Charlestown S.P.	100	A3	38.448300 -85.644700
Clifty Falls S.P.	100	A3	38.761220 -85.420720
Fort Harrison S.P.	99	F1	39.871921 -86.018859
Harmonie S.P.	99	D4	38.089210 -87.934080
Indiana Dunes S.P.	89	E2	41.651470 -87.062620
Lincoln S.P.	99	E4	38.118370 -86.980080
McCormick's Creek S.P.	99	E2	39.283340 -86.726680
O'Bannon Woods S.P.	99	F4	38.200600 -86.254678
Ouabache S.P.	90	A3	40.728090 -85.111060
Pokagon S.P.	90	A1	41.707960 -85.029320
Potato Creek S.P.	89	E2	41.534950 -86.360290
Prophetstown S.P.	89	E4	40.500211 -86.829548
Shades S.P.	99	E1	39.941630 -87.057670
Shakamak S.P.	99	E2	39.181800 -87.232200
Spring Mill S.P.	99	F3	38.723330 -86.418460
Summit Lake S.P.	100	A1	40.018680 -85.302720
Tippecanoe River S.P.	89	E3	41.117330 -86.602750
Turkey Run S.P.	99	E1	39.882010 -87.200550
Versailles S.P.	100	A2	39.063900 -85.205330
Whitewater Mem. S.P.	100	B1	39.611300 -84.942300

IOWA

IOWA	PAGE	GRID	LATITUDE LONGITUDE
National Park & Rec. Areas			
Effigy Mounds Natl. Mon.	73	F3	43.089310 -91.192350
Herbert Hoover N.H.S.	87	F1	41.671390 -91.346640
State Park & Rec. Areas			
Ambrose A. Call S.P.	72	B3	43.049650 -94.243430
Backbone S.P.	73	E4	42.600730 -91.532700
Beed's Lake S.P.	73	D4	42.767209 -93.241705
Bellevue S.P.	88	A1	42.247870 -90.416920
Black Hawk S.P.	72	B4	42.302700 -95.048680
Bobwhite S.P.	86	C3	40.710200 -93.393850
Cold Springs S.P.	86	B2	41.289540 -95.083810
Crystal Lake S.P.	72	C3	43.224895 -93.792925
Echo Valley S.P.	73	E3	42.944040 -91.776880
Elk Rock S.P.	87	D2	41.400470 -93.063050
Fort Defiance S.P.	72	B2	43.393260 -94.851290
George Wyth Mem. S.P.	73	E4	42.536980 -92.394210
Green Valley S.P.	86	B3	41.114490 -94.377270
Heery Woods S.P.	73	D4	42.766450 -92.675250
Honey Creek S.P.	87	D3	40.863940 -92.939050
Lake Ahquabi S.P.	86	C2	41.286710 -93.572690
Lake Anita S.P.	86	B2	41.434150 -94.762470
Lake Icaria S.P.	86	B3	41.053380 -94.756990
Lake Keomah S.P.	87	D2	41.286570 -92.541660
Lake Macbride S.P.	87	F1	41.803090 -91.570950
Lake Wapello S.P.	87	D3	40.824890 -92.570530
Ledges S.P.	86	C1	41.998970 -93.896110
Maquoketa Caves S.P.	87	F1	42.119890 -90.770950
McIntosh Woods S.P.	72	C3	43.132580 -93.457580
Mini-Wakan S.P.	72	B2	43.498460 -95.102320
Nine Eagles S.P.	86	C3	40.591250 -93.765130
Oakland Mills S.P.	87	E3	40.935400 -91.619370
Palisades-Kepler S.P.	87	F1	41.916880 -91.497050
Pammel S.P.	86	C2	41.295590 -94.073150
Pikes Point S.P.	72	A2	43.405300 -95.162860
Pilot Knob S.P.	72	C3	43.255470 -93.574840
Prairie Rose S.P.	86	A2	41.601590 -95.210660
Preparation Canyon S.P.	86	A1	41.901570 -95.911670
Rice Lake S.P.	72	C2	43.401350 -93.502490
Rock Creek S.P.	87	D1	41.760580 -92.835410
Spring Lake S.P.	86	B1	42.070600 -94.291500
Stone S.P.	35	F1	42.555460 -96.476050
Trappers Bay S.P.	72	A2	43.453630 -95.335510
Twin Lakes S.P.	72	B4	42.480180 -94.629860
Viking Lake S.P.	86	B3	40.973170 -95.053710
Wanata S.P.	72	A3	42.911340 -95.338080
Waubonsie S.P.	86	A3	40.677770 -95.683680
Wildcat Den S.P.	87	F2	41.467700 -90.869330

KANSAS

KANSAS	PAGE	GRID	LATITUDE LONGITUDE
National Park & Rec. Areas			
Fort Larned N.H.S.	43	D3	38.188740 -99.220620
Fort Scott N.H.S.	106	B1	37.843350 -94.704840
Monument Rocks Natl. Landmark	42	B2	38.790569 -100.762366
Nicodemus N.H.S.	42	C2	39.390833 -99.617500
State Park & Rec. Areas			
Atchison State Fishing Lake	96	B1	39.639010 -95.171830
Black Kettle State Fishing Lake	43	E3	38.229240 -97.509390
Bourbon State Fishing Lake	106	B1	37.793450 -95.069690
Brown State Fishing Lake	96	A1	39.847030 -95.373860
Cedar Bluff S.P.	42	C2	38.798230 -99.715060
Chase State Fishing Lake	43	F3	38.368480 -96.588000
Cheney S.P.	43	E4	37.732700 -97.844350
Clark State Fishing Lake	42	C4	37.391670 -99.784720
Clinton S.P.	96	A3	38.941970 -95.353960
Cowley State Fishing Lake	51	F1	37.104040 -96.795000
Crawford S.P.	106	B1	37.634320 -94.809820
Cross Timbers S.P.	106	A1	37.774514 -95.943431
Douglas State Fishing Lake	96	B3	38.796030 -95.165150
Eisenhower S.P.	96	A3	38.535720 -95.744270
El Dorado S.P.	43	F4	37.861420 -96.749460
Elk City S.P.	106	A2	37.251130 -95.774090
Fallriver S.P.	43	F4	37.653550 -96.043600
Glen Elder S.P.	43	D1	39.512160 -98.339140
Hain State Fishing Lake	42	C4	37.854250 -99.858020
Hamilton State Fishing Lake	42	B3	38.039090 -101.816940
Hillsdale S.P.	96	B3	38.660700 -94.894000
Kanopolis S.P.	43	E3	38.600340 -97.979500
Kingman State Fishing Lake	43	E4	37.651390 -98.306940
Kiowa State Fishing Lake	43	D4	37.612570 -99.299000
Leavenworth State Fishing Lake	96	B2	39.126970 -95.141700
Logan State Fishing Lake	42	B2	38.940280 -101.236940
Lovewell S.P.	43	E1	39.903310 -98.043090
Lyon State Fishing Lake	43	F3	38.546520 -96.058050
McPherson State Fishing Lake	43	E3	38.478667 -97.468267
Meade S.P.	42	C4	37.172220 -100.450000

Park	Page	Grid	Latitude Longitude
Miami State Fishing Lake	96	B3	38.422220 -94.785280
Milford S.P.	43	F2	39.104290 -96.895520
Mushroom Rock S.P.	43	E2	38.722222 -98.032222
Nebo State Fishing Lake	96	A2	39.447220 -95.595830
Neosho State Fishing Lake	106	B1	37.430570 -95.202550
Ottawa State Fishing Lake	43	E2	39.103040 -97.573060
Perry S.P.	96	A2	39.140210 -95.492480
Pomona S.P.	96	A3	38.652400 -95.600800
Pottawatomie State Fishing Lake No. 1	43	F1	39.470370 -96.407510
Pottawatomie State Fishing Lake No. 2	43	F2	39.228100 -96.533660
Prairie Dog S.P.	42	C1	39.811810 -99.963920
Prairie Spirit Trail S.P.	96	A4	38.280278 -95.242222
Rooks State Fishing Lake	43	D2	39.398290 -99.315020
Saline State Fishing Lake	43	E2	38.903159 -97.657510
Sand Hills S.P.	43	E3	38.116667 -97.833333
Scott S.P.	42	B2	38.684867 -100.922500
Shawnee State Fishing Lake	96	A2	39.206940 -95.804170
Tuttle Creek S.P.	43	F2	39.255560 -96.583330
Washington State Fishing Lake	43	E1	39.929780 -97.118830
Webster S.P.	43	D2	39.407840 -99.454550
Wilson State Fishing Lake	106	A1	38.910450 -98.497950
Wilson S.P.	43	D2	38.915000 -98.500000

KENTUCKY	PAGE	GRID	LATITUDE LONGITUDE
National Park & Rec. Areas			
Abraham Lincoln Birthplace N.H.P.	110	A1	37.532280 -85.733570
Land Between the Lakes N.R.A.	109	D2	36.776912 -88.059988
Mammoth Cave Natl. Park-Vis. Ctr.	109	F2	37.186800 -86.101300
State Park & Rec. Areas			
Barren River Lake State Resort Park	110	A2	36.853220 -86.053850
Ben Hawes S.P.	109	E1	37.797034 -87.188186
Blue Licks Bfld. State Resort Park	100	C3	38.434960 -83.991340
Buckhorn Lake State Resort Park	111	D1	37.312890 -83.423040
Carter Caves State Resort Park	101	D4	38.371470 -83.108510
Columbus-Belmont S.P.	108	C2	36.761990 -89.107000
Cumberland Falls State Resort Park	110	C2	36.834390 -84.350170
Fishtrap Lake S.P.	111	E1	37.432048 -82.417926
Fort Boonesborough S.P.	110	C1	37.899345 -84.270040
General Butler State Resort Park	100	A3	38.669950 -85.146050
Grayson Lake S.P.	101	D4	38.208630 -83.014910
Greenbo Lake State Resort Park	101	D3	38.479130 -82.867630
Green River Lake S.P.	110	A2	37.277440 -85.338730
Jenny Wiley State Resort Park-East Ent.	111	E1	37.730120 -82.740990
Jenny Wiley State Resort Park-South Ent.	111	E1	37.687680 -82.725690
Jenny Wiley State Resort Park-West Ent.	111	E1	37.727250 -82.745880
John James Audubon S.P.	99	D4	37.889250 -87.556510
Kentucky Dam Village State Resort Park	109	D2	36.996880 -88.285716
Kingdom Come S.P.	111	D2	36.981850 -82.982210
Lake Barkley State Resort Park	109	D2	36.809190 -87.928310
Lake Cumberland State Resort Park	110	B2	36.930320 -85.040960
Levi Jackson S.P.	110	C2	37.085250 -84.059250
Lincoln Homestead S.P.	110	B1	37.760080 -85.215930
My Old Kentucky Home S.P.	110	A1	37.808140 -85.458840
Natural Bridge State Resort Park	110	C1	37.777470 -83.676310
Nolin Lake S.P.	109	F1	37.297641 -86.212624
Old Fort Harrod S.P.	110	B1	37.762130 -84.845670
Pennyrile Forest State Resort Park	109	E2	37.057410 -87.649390
Pine Mtn. State Resort Park	110	C3	36.735270 -83.700790
Rough River State Resort Park	109	F1	37.615410 -86.504410
Taylorsville Lake S.P.	100	A4	37.993990 -85.227813
Yatesville Lake S.P.	101	D4	38.093300 -82.617800

LOUISIANA	PAGE	GRID	LATITUDE LONGITUDE
National Park & Rec. Areas			
Cane River Creole N.H.P.	125	D4	31.739690 -93.083080
Jean Lafitte N.H.P. & Pres.-Chalmette Vis. Ctr.	134	A3	29.942100 -89.994400
Jean Lafitte N.H.P. & Pres.-French Quarter Vis. Ctr.	134	A3	29.954600 -90.065100
Jean Lafitte N.H.P.-Wetlands Acadian Cultural Center	134	A3	29.795969 -90.824480
Poverty Point Natl. Mon. & S.H.S.	125	F2	32.633370 -91.403880
State Park & Rec. Areas			
Bayou Segnette S.P.	134	B3	29.902720 -90.153800
Chemin-A-Haut S.P.	125	F1	32.913460 -91.847550
Chicot S.P.	133	E1	30.829870 -92.276180
Cypremort Point S.P.	133	F3	29.731960 -91.840740
Fairview-Riverside S.P.	134	B2	30.408730 -90.140360
Fontainebleau S.P.	134	B2	30.345470 -90.022850
Grand Isle S.P.-Temp. Closed	134	B4	29.256640 -89.958480
Hodges Gardens S.P.	125	D4	31.369280 -93.424860
Jimmie Davis S.P.	125	E3	32.265000 -92.540300
Lake Bistineau S.P.	125	D2	32.440250 -93.395910
Lake Bruin S.P.	126	A3	31.955370 -91.198080
Lake Claiborne S.P.	125	D2	32.713000 -92.923360
Lake D'Arbonne S.P.	125	E2	32.784850 -92.490310
Lake Fausse Pointe S.P.	133	F3	30.067820 -91.615790
North Toledo Bend S.P.	124	C4	31.558910 -93.732060
Palmetto Island S.P.	133	F3	29.862877 -92.144165
Poverty Point Reservoir S.P.	125	F2	32.540446 -91.421356
Saint Bernard S.P.	134	C3	29.864460 -89.899190
South Toledo Bend S.P.	125	D4	31.213889 -93.575000
Tickfaw S.P.	134	B2	30.382180 -90.631150

MAINE	PAGE	GRID	LATITUDE LONGITUDE
National Park & Rec. Areas			
Acadia Natl. Park-Park Loop Road	83	D2	44.338700 -68.183200
Acadia Natl. Park-Sieur de Monts Ent.	83	D2	44.360000 -68.205200
Acadia Natl. Park-Stanley Brook Ent.	83	D2	44.296300 -68.242000
Katahdin Woods & Waters Natl. Mon.	85	D3	45.883549 -68.737849
State Park & Rec. Areas			
Aroostook S.P.	85	E2	46.612720 -68.005840
Baxter S.P.	84	C3	45.950290 -69.049080
Camden Hills S.P.	82	C2	44.232050 -69.046530
Cobscook Bay S.P.	83	E1	44.855290 -67.171680
Damariscotta Lake S.P.	82	C2	44.200070 -69.452900
Ferry Beach S.P.	82	B4	43.482410 -70.391520
Lake Saint George S.P.	82	C2	44.398950 -69.345710
Lamoine S.P.	83	D2	44.456000 -68.298520
Mount Blue S.P.	82	B1	44.721780 -70.417080
Peaks-Kenny S.P.	84	C4	45.256680 -69.254600
Popham Beach S.P.	82	C3	43.738740 -69.795830
Rangeley Lake S.P.	82	B1	44.919550 -70.696950
Range Ponds S.P.	82	B3	44.033540 -70.345080
Roque Bluffs S.P.	83	E2	44.614680 -67.479300
Saint Croix Island International Hist. Site	83	E1	45.128333 -67.133333
Sebago Lake S.P.	82	B3	43.916590 -70.570190
Shackford Head S.P.	83	F1	44.906191 -66.989979
Swan Lake S.P.	82	C2	44.568860 -68.981070
Vaughan Woods S.P.	82	A4	43.212680 -70.809320
Warren Island S.P.	82	C2	44.260445 -68.952255
Wolfe's Neck Woods S.P.	82	B3	43.827190 -70.084460

MARYLAND	PAGE	GRID	LATITUDE LONGITUDE
National Park & Rec. Areas			
Assateague Island Natl. Seashore	114	C2	38.239580 -75.140410
Harriet Tubman Underground RR N.H.P.	103	F3	38.322307 -76.176243
Thomas Stone N.H.S.	144	B4	38.529700 -77.032370
State Park & Rec. Areas			
Assateague S.P.	114	C2	38.250170 -75.156270
Big Run S.P.	102	B1	39.545090 -79.137254
Catoctin Mtn. Park-Vis. Ctr.	144	A1	39.633100 -77.449700
Cunningham Falls S.P.	144	A1	39.625040 -77.458130
Deep Creek Lake S.P.	102	B1	39.512110 -79.300150
Elk Neck S.P.	145	D1	39.482890 -75.983630
Fort Frederick S.P.	103	D1	39.616050 -78.007060
Gambrill S.P.	144	A1	39.468330 -77.495730
Greenwell S.P.	103	E4	38.364930 -76.525260
Gunpowder Falls S.P.	144	C1	39.536710 -76.502800
Hart-Miller Island S.P.	144	C2	39.251219 -76.376903
Janes Island S.P.	103	F4	38.009810 -75.846380
Martinak S.P.	145	E3	38.862920 -75.837790
North Point S.P.	144	C2	39.221910 -76.431600
Patapsco Valley S.P.	144	B2	39.296580 -76.781500
Patuxent River S.P.	144	B2	39.280790 -77.129620
Pocomoke River S.P.	114	C2	38.135410 -75.494870
Point Lookout S.P.	103	F4	38.066190 -76.336550
Rocks S.P.	144	C1	39.630140 -76.418120
Rocky Gap S.P.	102	C1	39.698430 -78.651150
Rosaryville S.P.	144	C3	38.778450 -76.799260
Saint Clement's Island S.P.	103	E4	38.225200 -76.749690
Saint Mary's River S.P.	103	E4	38.262940 -76.525640
Sandy Point S.P.	144	C3	39.021750 -76.420280
Seneca Creek S.P.	144	A2	39.152200 -77.247710
Smallwood S.P.	144	B4	38.556509 -77.185257
South Mtn. S.P.	144	A1	39.540058 -77.607422
Susquehanna S.P.	145	D1	39.599840 -76.154590
Swallow Falls S.P.	102	B1	39.506550 -79.448750
Tuckahoe S.P.	145	D3	38.967120 -75.943410
Washington Mon. S.P.	144	A1	39.499810 -77.631890
Wye Oak S.P.	145	D3	38.939150 -76.080230

MASSACHUSETTS	PAGE	GRID	LATITUDE LONGITUDE
National Park & Rec. Areas			
Adams N.H.P.-Vis. Ctr.	151	D1	42.257000 -71.011200
Boston Harbor Island N.R.A.	151	D1	42.319705 -70.928555
Cape Cod Natl. Seashore	151	F2	41.835890 -69.973730
Lowell N.H.P.-Market Mills Vis. Ctr.	95	E1	42.644400 -71.312800
Minute Man N.H.P.-Minute Man Vis. Ctr.	151	D1	42.449000 -71.268700
Minute Man N.H.P.-North Bridge Vis. Ctr.	151	D1	42.470800 -71.352600
New Bedford Whaling N.H.P.	151	D4	41.635570 -70.924250
Salem Maritime N.H.S.	151	D1	42.521490 -70.886980
Saugus Iron Works N.H.S.	151	D1	42.468230 -71.009110
Waquoit Bay Natl. Estuarine Research Res.	151	E4	41.581300 -70.524800
State Park & Rec. Areas			
Ames-Nowell S.P.	151	D2	42.113140 -70.975230
Ashland S.P.	150	C2	42.246380 -71.475560
Blackstone River & Canal Heritage S.P.	150	C2	42.099500 -71.618780
Borderland S.P.	151	D2	42.058560 -71.166330
Bradley Palmer S.P.	151	F1	42.652180 -70.911000
Callahan S.P.	150	C1	42.315140 -71.367710
Demarest Lloyd S.P.	151	D4	41.525790 -70.990530
Dighton Rock S.P.	151	D3	41.811230 -71.098440
Halibut Point S.P.	151	F1	42.686100 -70.631070
Hampton Ponds S.P.	150	A2	42.178350 -72.690030
Holyoke Range S.P.	150	A1	42.297270 -72.5308
Joseph Sylvia State Beach	151	E4	41.424140 -70.5538
Lake Wyola S.P.-Carroll Holmes Rec. Area	150	A1	42.500366 -72.4306
Moore S.P.	150	B1	42.312354 -71.9542
Nickerson S.P.	151	F3	41.775550 -70.0282
Pilgrim Mem. (Plymouth Rock) S.P.	151	E2	41.958850 -70.6628
Red Bridge S.P.	150	A2	42.175500 -72.4066
Robinson S.P.	150	A2	42.081680 -72.6586
Rutland S.P.	150	B1	42.371470 -71.9976
Savoy Mtn. State Forest	94	C1	42.626540 -73.0155
Skinner S.P.	150	A1	42.304220 -72.5987
South Cape Beach S.P.	151	E4	41.554582 -70.5081
Wahconah Falls S.P.	94	C1	42.491430 -73.1207
Watson Pond S.P.	151	D2	41.956260 -71.1160
Wells S.P.	150	B2	42.142290 -72.0424
Whitehall S.P.	150	C2	42.227210 -71.5843
Wompatuck S.P.	151	D2	42.218770 -70.8666

MICHIGAN	PAGE	GRID	LATITUDE LONGITUDE
National Park & Rec. Areas			
Father Marquette Natl. Mem.	70	C2	45.853912 -84.7288
Grand Island N.R.A.	70	A1	46.500405 -86.6576
Isle Royale Natl. Park-Rock Harbor Vis. Ctr.	65	F2	48.145530 -88.4822
Isle Royale Natl. Park-Windigo Vis. Ctr.	65	F2	47.912700 -89.1569
Keweenaw N.H.P.	65	F3	47.242160 -88.4480
Pictured Rocks Natl. Lakeshore-East Ent.	70	A1	46.657450 -86.0211
Pictured Rocks Natl. Lakeshore-West Ent.	70	A1	46.474000 -86.5530
Sleeping Bear Dunes Natl. Lakeshore	70	A4	44.785210 -86.0496
State Park & Rec. Areas			
Albert E. Sleeper S.P.	76	C2	43.972880 -83.2055
Algonac S.P.	76	C4	42.654760 -82.5145
Aloha S.P.	70	C3	45.525850 -84.4643
Baraga S.P.	65	F4	46.762070 -88.4993
Bewabic S.P.	68	C2	46.094260 -88.4222
Brimley S.P.	70	C1	46.412970 -84.5550
Burt Lake S.P.	70	C3	45.401305 -84.6195
Cambridge Junction Hist. S.P.	90	B1	42.066990 -84.2255
Charles Mears S.P.	75	E2	43.781980 -86.4396
Cheboygan S.P.	70	C2	45.644860 -84.4204
Clear Lake S.P.	70	C3	45.127390 -84.1739
Coldwater Lake S.P.	90	A1	43.665975 -84.9487
Craig Lake S.P.	68	C1	46.538810 -88.1277
Duck Lake S.P.	75	E3	43.354880 -86.3975
F.J. Mclain S.P.	65	F3	47.239400 -88.5871
Fayette Hist. S.P.	70	A2	45.717200 -86.6646
Fisherman's Island S.P.	70	B3	45.307550 -85.3015
Fort Wilkins Hist. S.P.	65	F3	47.466780 -87.8782
Grand Haven S.P.	75	E3	43.056100 -86.2459
Grand Mere S.P.	89	E1	41.995190 -86.53879
Harrisville S.P.	71	D4	44.649800 -83.29392
Hart-Montague Trail S.P.	75	E2	43.688800 -86.3719
Hartwick Pines S.P.	70	C4	44.744180 -84.64834
Holland S.P.	75	E4	42.780310 -86.20141
Indian Lake S.P.	70	A2	45.960420 -86.3644
Interlochen S.P.	70	B4	44.631370 -85.76663
J.W. Wells S.P.	69	D3	45.389070 -87.37136
Kal-Haven Trail S.P.	75	E4	42.324698 -85.66773
Lake Gogebic S.P.	68	B1	46.459950 -89.57311
Lakelands Trail S.P.	76	B4	42.408249 -83.96404
Lakeport S.P.	76	C3	43.129120 -82.50182
Leelanau S.P.	70	B3	45.209320 -85.54622
Ludington S.P.	75	E1	44.031100 -86.50546
Mackinac Island S.P.	70	C2	45.849880 -84.61765
Muskallonge Lake S.P.	70	B1	46.677100 -85.62521
Muskegon S.P.	75	E3	43.247900 -86.34148
Negwegon S.P.	71	D4	44.855020 -83.32924
Newaygo S.P.	75	F2	43.500600 -85.58226
North Higgins Lake S.P.	70	C4	44.515030 -84.75398
Onaway S.P.	70	C3	45.430530 -84.22902
Orchard Beach S.P.	75	E1	44.278860 -86.31448
Otsego Lake S.P.	70	C4	44.927770 -84.68898
P.H. Hoeft S.P.	70	C3	45.463700 -83.88356
P.J. Hoffmaster S.P.	75	E3	43.132870 -86.26546
Palms Book S.P.	70	A2	46.003280 -86.38513
Petoskey S.P.	70	B3	45.407950 -84.90216
Porcupine Mts. Wilderness S.P.	65	E4	46.816070 -89.62185
Port Crescent S.P.	76	C1	44.007570 -83.05129
Sanilac Petroglyphs Hist. S.P.	76	C2	43.649367 -83.01801
Saugatuck Dunes S.P.	75	E4	42.695990 -86.18684
Seven Lakes S.P.	76	B3	42.816750 -83.64812
Silver Lake S.P.	75	E2	43.663650 -86.49266
Sleepy Hollow S.P.	76	A3	42.925020 -84.40862
South Higgins Lake S.P.	76	A1	44.432818 -84.67029
Sterling S.P.	90	C1	41.921490 -83.34268
Straits S.P.	70	C2	45.858090 -84.72020
Tahquamenon Falls S.P.-East Ent.	70	B1	46.598030 -85.14789
Tahquamenon Falls S.P.-West Ent.	70	B1	46.564190 -85.29253
Tawas Point S.P.	76	B1	44.255820 -83.44305
Thompson's Harbor S.P.	71	D3	45.346705 -83.56743
Traverse City S.P.	70	B4	44.748050 -85.55380
Twin Lakes S.P.	65	E4	46.892210 -88.85656
Van Buren S.P.	75	E4	42.333830 -86.30483

Buren Trail S.P.	89	F1	42.211405 -86.171105
Riper S.P.	68	C1	46.525260 -87.991150
er J. Hayes S.P.	90	B1	42.072830 -84.137820
ren Dunes S.P.	89	E1	41.900980 -86.595260
ren Woods S.P.	89	E1	41.840680 -86.631290
el Rec. Area	76	C4	42.596720 -82.825140
e Pine Trail S.P.	75	F2	44.222900 -85.426700
erness S.P.-East Ent.	70	B2	45.748160 -84.853500
erness S.P.-West Ent.	70	B2	45.679360 -84.964170
am Mitchell S.P.	75	F1	44.236880 -85.453990
son S.P.	76	A1	44.029620 -84.806070
ng S.P.	70	B3	45.235240 -85.041450

MINNESOTA

	PAGE	GRID	LATITUDE LONGITUDE
ional Park & Rec. Areas			
nd Portage Natl. Mon.	65	E2	47.996274 -89.734256
estone Natl. Mon.	27	F3	44.013150 -96.325360
ageurs Natl. Park-Ash River Vis. Ctr.	64	C2	48.435600 -92.850300
ageurs Natl. Park-Kabetogama Lake Vis. Ctr.	64	C2	48.446100 -93.030100
ageurs Natl. Park-Rainy Lake Vis. Ctr.	64	C2	48.584400 -93.161500
te Park & Rec. Areas			
n S.P.	67	D4	44.847930 -92.791020
ning S.P.	67	D2	46.179730 -92.855170
r Head Lake S.P.	64	C3	47.792720 -92.083720
ver Creek Valley S.P.	73	E2	43.636790 -91.573190
e Mounds S.P.	27	F4	43.714340 -96.183100
alo River S.P.	19	F4	46.866260 -96.469980
nden S.P.	27	F3	44.362880 -95.917480
ibou Falls State Wayside	65	D3	47.463890 -91.030660
ley S.P.	73	E1	44.116790 -92.169320
cade River S.P.	65	D3	47.712950 -90.497930
arles A. Lindbergh S.P.	66	C2	45.959410 -94.387640
ss River State Wayside	65	D3	47.543420 -90.897770
w Wing S.P.	66	C1	46.272630 -94.316400
her Hennepin S.P.	66	C1	46.144520 -93.484260
ndrau S.P.	72	B1	44.294360 -94.482020
od Bay State Wayside	64	C4	47.038500 -91.642540
estville Mystery Cave S.P.	73	E2	43.637520 -92.220270
t Ridgely S.P.	72	B1	44.454810 -94.718310
nz Jevne S.P.	64	B2	48.641140 -94.058260
ntenac S.P.	67	E4	44.525200 -92.338730
orge H. Crosby Manitou S.P.	65	D3	47.478990 -91.123070
acial Lakes S.P.	66	A3	45.540550 -95.529600
ndalough S.P.	19	F4	46.313314 -95.679290
oseberry Falls S.P.	65	D3	47.145430 -91.462380
and Portage S.P.	65	E2	47.999150 -89.598690
eat River Bluffs S.P.	73	E1	43.939100 -91.430050
yes Lake S.P.	19	F1	48.641070 -95.570600
l Annex Mine S.P.	64	B3	47.327490 -93.277520
piration Peak State Wayside	66	A1	46.136880 -95.578650
sca S.P.	64	A3	47.194490 -95.166740
y Cooke S.P.	64	C4	46.658790 -92.349200
hn A. Latsch S.P.	73	E1	44.164720 -91.823860
seph R. Brown State Wayside	66	B4	44.750328 -95.324425
dge C.R. Magney S.P.	65	E3	47.818090 -90.051230
en Woods S.P.	72	B2	43.732140 -95.072220
donce River State Wayside	65	E3	47.793930 -90.154140
c Qui Parle S.P.	27	F2	45.024680 -95.896580
ke Bemidji S.P.	64	A3	47.536890 -94.832320
ke Bronson S.P.	19	F1	48.730940 -96.630720
ke Carlos S.P.	66	B2	46.000540 -95.334430
ke Louise S.P.	73	D2	43.532620 -92.509250
ke Maria S.P.	66	C3	45.304810 -93.935570
ke Shetek S.P.	72	A1	44.105740 -95.699730
aplewood S.P.	19	F4	46.549910 -95.966720
cCarthy Beach S.P.	64	B3	47.674110 -93.027350
ille Lacs Kathio S.P.	66	C2	46.160740 -93.758020
inneopa S.P.	72	C1	44.162190 -94.110310
onson Lake S.P.	66	B3	45.321300 -95.270470
oose Lake S.P.	64	C4	46.436360 -92.743090
yre-Big Island S.P.	73	D2	43.623847 -93.289096
erstrand Big Woods S.P.	73	D1	44.327040 -93.111210
d Mill S.P.	19	F2	48.369790 -96.569420
ay Berglund State Wayside	65	D3	47.608200 -90.771930
ce Lake S.P.	73	D1	44.095380 -93.063940
ush River State Wayside	66	C4	44.507240 -93.931409
aint Croix S.P.	67	D2	45.960615 -92.611630
akatah Lake S.P.	72	C1	44.218000 -93.509970
am Brown Mem. State Wayside	27	F1	45.596160 -96.841410
avanna Portage S.P.	64	B4	46.819130 -93.176040
cenic S.P.	64	B3	47.702450 -93.564710
choolcraft S.P.	64	B3	47.223040 -93.805320
ibley S.P.	66	B3	45.318990 -95.011930
oudan Underground Mine S.P.	64	C2	47.818130 -92.246090
plit Rock Creek S.P.	27	F4	43.907240 -96.367970
plit Rock Lighthouse S.P.	65	D3	47.189800 -91.395010
emperance River S.P.	65	D3	47.558780 -90.867930
ettegouche S.P.	65	D3	47.337210 -91.200670
pper Sioux Agency S.P.	66	B4	44.734540 -95.456460
hitewater S.P.	73	E1	44.068880 -92.040100
ild River S.P.	67	D3	45.524100 -92.754500
William O'Brien S.P.	67	D3	45.223900 -92.763500
Zippel Bay S.P.	64	A1	48.840630 -94.849950

MISSISSIPPI

	PAGE	GRID	LATITUDE LONGITUDE
National Park & Rec. Areas			
Gulf Islands Natl. Seashore	135	D2	30.407200 -88.749220
Natchez N.H.P.-Vis. Reception Ctr.	125	F4	31.553900 -91.412400
State Park & Rec. Areas			
Bogue Homa State Fishing Lake	127	D4	31.703200 -89.026400
Calling Panther State Fishing Lake	126	B3	32.197100 -90.265100
Clarkco S.P.	127	D3	32.108500 -88.693970
Columbia State Fishing Lake	134	C1	31.183500 -89.738400
Florewood S.P.	118	B4	33.525120 -90.250362
George Payne Cossar S.P.	118	B3	34.122710 -89.882100
Golden Mem. S.P.	126	C2	32.568560 -89.407640
Great River Road S.P.	118	A4	33.851733 -91.027574
Hugh White S.P.	118	B4	33.796080 -89.743010
J.P. Coleman S.P.	119	D2	34.924254 -88.171706
Jeff Davis State Fishing Lake	126	B4	31.567700 -89.839800
Kemper County State Fishing Lake	127	D2	32.804167 -88.730556
Lake Lincoln S.P.	126	B4	31.684354 -90.337142
Legion S.P.	127	D1	33.148690 -89.042460
Leroy Percy S.P.	126	A1	33.160500 -90.938250
Mary Crawford State Fishing Lake	126	B4	31.574900 -90.154000
Monroe State Fishing Lake	119	D4	33.941500 -88.568700
Natchez S.P.	126	A4	31.589580 -91.220350
Neshoba County State Fishing Lake	126	C2	32.706200 -89.010500
Oktibbeha County State Fishing Lake	118	C4	33.505700 -88.933400
Paul B. Johnson S.P.	134	C1	31.133800 -89.233910
Percy Quin S.P.	134	B1	31.189020 -90.510660
Perry State Fishing Lake	135	D1	31.132400 -88.899800
Prentiss Walker State Fishing Lake	126	C3	31.833200 -89.589500
Roosevelt S.P.	126	C2	32.321920 -89.664980
Simpson County State Fishing Lake	126	C3	31.913500 -89.794500
Tippah County State Fishing Lake	118	C2	34.794290 -88.950660
Tishomingo S.P.	119	D2	34.615670 -88.183390
Tom Bailey State Fishing Lake	127	D2	32.425030 -88.523069
Tombigbee S.P.	119	D3	34.231870 -88.628870
Trace S.P.	118	C3	34.260020 -88.886560
Wall Doxey S.P.	118	C2	34.660270 -89.459290
Walthall State Fishing Lake	134	B1	31.059184 -90.133939

MISSOURI

	PAGE	GRID	LATITUDE LONGITUDE
National Park & Rec. Areas			
George Washington Carver Natl. Mon.	106	C2	36.986160 -94.351890
Ozark Natl. Scenic Riverways	107	F2	37.281400 -91.408000
State Park & Rec. Areas			
Bennett Spring S.P.	107	D1	37.725440 -92.856390
Big Lake S.P.	86	A4	40.092090 -95.347300
Big Oak Tree S.P.	108	C3	36.641990 -89.290180
Big Sugar Creek S.P.	106	C3	36.584106 -93.819122
Crowder S.P.	86	C4	40.082140 -93.669310
Cuivre River S.P.	97	F2	39.062380 -90.938640
Echo Bluff S.P.	107	F1	37.315893 -91.411322
Elephant Rocks S.P.	108	A1	37.652150 -90.690810
Finger Lakes S.P.	97	E2	39.075400 -92.314750
Graham Cave S.P.	97	F3	38.908850 -91.576090
Grand Gulf S.P.	107	F3	36.544100 -91.636370
Ha Ha Tonka S.P.	97	D4	37.975410 -92.762230
Harry S. Truman S.P.	97	D4	38.274650 -93.442390
Hawn S.P.	108	B1	37.833660 -90.241610
Johnson's Shut-Ins S.P.	108	A1	37.547920 -90.853020
Katy Trail S.P.	97	E3	38.975190 -92.750160
Knob Noster S.P.	96	C3	38.753020 -93.577440
Lake of the Ozarks S.P.	97	E4	38.133990 -92.564260
Lake Wappapello S.P.	108	A2	36.942210 -90.344400
Lewis & Clark S.P.	96	B1	39.538900 -95.052900
Long Branch S.P.	97	E1	39.767610 -92.526480
Mark Twain S.P.	97	E2	39.485270 -91.795340
Meramec S.P.	97	F4	38.215350 -91.123070
Montauk S.P.	107	F1	37.454710 -91.690970
Morris S.P.	108	B3	36.554166 -90.043220
Onondaga Cave S.P.	97	F4	38.064310 -91.230140
Pershing S.P.	97	D1	39.776270 -93.211130
Pomme de Terre S.P.	107	D1	37.874380 -93.318700
Roaring River S.P.	106	C3	36.590110 -93.834420
Robertsville S.P.	98	A3	38.429120 -90.818110
Rock Bridge Mem. S.P.	97	E3	38.883350 -92.331890
Saint Francois S.P.	98	A4	37.972900 -90.536210
Saint Joe S.P.	108	A1	37.824990 -90.537480
Sam A. Baker S.P.	108	A2	37.254530 -90.505080
Stockton S.P.	106	C1	37.622470 -93.753070
Table Rock S.P.	107	D3	36.583440 -93.309150
Taum Sauk Mtn. S.P.	108	A1	37.669500 -90.673400
Thousand Hills S.P.	87	D4	40.185160 -92.643070
Trail of Tears S.P.	108	B1	37.452880 -89.490760
Van Meter S.P.	97	D2	39.262590 -93.267210
Wakonda S.P.	97	F1	40.004250 -91.526060
Wallace S.P.	96	C1	39.660760 -94.213290
Washington S.P.	98	A4	38.085600 -90.685650
Watkins Mill S.P.	96	C2	39.383920 -94.265130
Weston Bend S.P.	96	B2	39.392960 -94.863430

MONTANA

	PAGE	GRID	LATITUDE LONGITUDE
National Park & Rec. Areas			
Bighorn Canyon N.R.A.	24	C2	45.330090 -107.871650
Fort Benton Natl. Hist. Landmark	16	A2	47.823210 -110.661910
Glacier Natl. Park-Many Glacier Ent.	15	D1	48.827150 -113.551540
Glacier Natl. Park-St Mary Ent.	15	D1	48.747120 -113.439650
Glacier Natl. Park-Two Medicine Ent.	15	D1	48.494210 -113.262250
Glacier Natl. Park-West Ent.	15	D1	48.499890 -113.987190
Grant-Kohrs Ranch N.H.S.	15	E4	46.398900 -112.736680
Little Bighorn Bfld. Natl. Mon.	24	C1	45.570080 -107.434710
Natl. Bison Range	15	D3	47.371674 -114.262066
Rattlesnake N.R.A.	15	D4	47.040775 -113.933333
State Park & Rec. Areas			
Ackley Lake S.P.	16	B4	46.947220 -109.936110
Anaconda Smoke Stack S.P.	23	D1	46.111037 -112.969599
Bannack S.P.	23	D2	45.159170 -112.997780
Beaverhead Rock S.P.	23	E2	45.383330 -112.458330
Beavertail Hill S.P.	15	D4	46.721660 -113.576420
Big Arm S.P.	15	D3	47.815360 -114.307930
Black Sandy S.P.	15	E4	46.756940 -111.888890
Chief Plenty Coups S.P.	24	B2	45.429700 -108.532500
Clark's Lookout S.P.	23	E2	45.236110 -112.630560
Cooney S.P.	24	B2	45.435050 -109.225330
Council Grove S.P.	15	D4	46.912500 -114.150000
Finley Point S.P.	15	D3	47.763830 -114.078723
First Peoples Buffalo Jump S.P.	16	A3	47.494887 -111.525201
Fish Creek S.P.	14	C4	46.990214 -114.715914
Fort Owen S.P.	15	D4	46.519440 -114.095830
Frenchtown Pond S.P.	15	D3	47.039530 -114.259220
Granite Ghost Town S.P.	23	D1	46.319000 -113.257000
Greycliff Prairie Dog Town S.P.	24	B1	45.767600 -109.794180
Hell Creek S.P.	17	D3	47.620290 -106.884510
Lake Elmo S.P.	24	C1	45.845280 -108.481310
Lake Mary Ronan S.P.	15	D2	48.204020 -114.330340
Lewis & Clark Caverns S.P.	23	E1	45.821840 -111.848510
Logan S.P.	14	C2	48.204020 -114.330340
Lone Pine S.P.	15	D2	48.175580 -114.339560
Lost Creek S.P.	23	D1	46.203020 -112.993810
Madison Buffalo Jump S.P.	23	F1	45.665140 -111.062770
Makoshika S.P.	17	F4	47.090240 -104.709970
Medicine Rocks S.P.	25	F1	46.046460 -104.456740
Missouri Headwaters S.P.	23	F1	45.909129 -111.497411
Painted Rocks S.P.	22	C1	45.706650 -114.282530
Pictograph Cave S.P.	24	C1	45.737500 -108.430830
Pirogue Island S.P.	17	E4	46.440560 -105.816670
Placid Lake S.P.	15	D3	47.138040 -113.524960
Rosebud Bfld. S.P.	25	D2	45.208270 -106.944460
Salmon Lake S.P.	15	D4	47.042270 -113.390390
Sluice Boxes S.P.	16	A3	47.211400 -110.939660
Smith River S.P.	16	A4	46.721219 -111.173819
Spring Meadow Lake S.P.	15	E4	46.612220 -112.075000
Thompson Falls S.P.	14	C3	47.618060 -115.387500
Tongue River Reservoir S.P.	25	D2	45.093520 -106.804670
Tower Rock S.P.	15	E3	47.181000 -111.816000
Travelers' Rest S.P.	15	D4	46.751000 -114.089000
Wayfarers S.P.	15	D2	48.057400 -114.079550
West Shore S.P.	15	D2	47.948780 -114.189160
Whitefish Lake S.P.	15	D2	48.204020 -114.330340
Wild Horse Island S.P.	15	D3	47.844640 -114.279970
Yellow Bay S.P.	15	D2	47.874500 -114.027080

NEBRASKA

	PAGE	GRID	LATITUDE LONGITUDE
National Park & Rec. Areas			
Agate Fossil Beds Natl. Mon.	33	F2	42.423860 -103.791120
Chimney Rock N.H.S.	33	F3	41.719650 -103.336070
Pine Ridge N.R.A.	33	F1	42.625880 -103.205570
Scotts Bluff Natl. Mon.	33	F2	41.832380 -103.717550
State Park & Rec. Areas			
Chadron S.P.	34	A1	42.711540 -103.008500
Eugene T. Mahoney S.P.	35	F3	41.026387 -96.314180
Fort Robinson S.P.	33	F1	42.654050 -103.492100
Indian Cave S.P.	86	A4	40.263280 -95.586630
Niobrara S.P.	35	E1	42.747450 -98.051850
Platte River S.P.	35	F3	40.986840 -96.219290
Ponca S.P.	35	F1	42.600360 -96.714940
Smith Falls S.P.	34	C1	42.891670 -100.316670

NEVADA

	PAGE	GRID	LATITUDE LONGITUDE
National Park & Rec. Areas			
Basin & Range Natl. Mon.	38	B3	37.931620 -115.350935
Devils Hole (Death Valley Natl. Park)	45	F3	36.423889 -116.305833
Gold Butte Natl. Mon.	46	B1	36.390553 -114.170000
Great Basin Natl. Park-Vis. Ctr.	38	C2	39.005600 -114.220000
Lake Mead N.R.A.-North Ent.	46	B2	36.161180 -114.905200
Lake Mead N.R.A.-South Ent.	46	B2	36.021230 -114.796340
Lake Mead N.R.A.-West Ent.	46	B2	36.105980 -114.900940
Spring Mts. N.R.A.	46	A1	36.245200 -115.233910
Tule Springs Fossil Beds Natl. Mon.	46	A1	36.324457 -115.293643
State Park & Rec. Areas			
Berlin-Ichthyosaur S.P.	37	F2	38.880300 -117.607930
Big Bend of the Colorado State Rec. Area	53	F1	35.116730 -114.640820

Cathedral Gorge S.P.	38	C4	37.820280 -114.407890
Dayton S.P.-North Ent.	37	D2	39.253540 -119.587190
Echo Canyon S.P.	38	C4	38.195000 -114.512900
Kershaw-Ryan S.P.	38	C4	37.586380 -114.533260
Lake Tahoe-Nevada S.P.	37	D2	39.213670 -119.928300
Spring Mtn. Ranch S.P.	46	A2	36.073830 -115.443710
Spring Valley S.P.	38	C3	38.003920 -114.207570
Valley of Fire S.P.	46	B1	36.429710 -114.513590
Wild Horse State Rec. Area	30	B3	41.670739 -115.799805

NEW HAMPSHIRE	PAGE	GRID	LATITUDE LONGITUDE
National Park & Rec. Areas			
Saint-Gaudens N.H.S.	81	E4	43.501570 -72.362510
State Park & Rec. Areas			
Bear Brook S.P.	81	F4	43.133800 -71.366040
Cardigan S.P.	81	E3	43.647990 -71.949570
Crawford Notch S.P.	81	F2	44.181760 -71.398780
Echo Lake S.P.	81	F3	44.067430 -71.166000
Forest Lake S.P.	81	F2	44.354490 -71.673180
Hampton Beach S.P.	95	E1	42.898333 -70.812778
Kingston S.P.	95	E1	42.929020 -71.054680
Lake Tarleton S.P.	81	E3	43.975833 -71.963333
Miller S.P.	95	D1	42.861630 -71.878750
Monadnock S.P.	95	D1	42.845440 -72.086590
Mount Sunapee S.P.	81	E4	43.332120 -72.079800
Pawtuckaway S.P.	81	F4	43.082150 -71.152130
Pillsbury S.P.	81	E4	43.236860 -72.122830
Pisgah S.P.	94	C1	42.810310 -72.408340
Umbagog Lake S.P.	81	F1	44.712990 -71.072700
Wellington S.P.	81	F3	43.641280 -71.782980
Wentworth S.P.	81	F3	43.603056 -71.136389
White Lake S.P.	81	F3	43.830880 -71.218220
Winslow S.P.	81	E4	43.391730 -71.869540

NEW JERSEY	PAGE	GRID	LATITUDE LONGITUDE
National Park & Rec. Areas			
Delaware Water Gap N.R.A.	94	A4	40.970390 -75.128100
Gateway N.R.A.	147	F1	40.396420 -73.981160
Morristown N.H.P.	148	A4	40.744670 -74.565290
Thomas Edison N.H.P.	148	A4	40.787188 -74.256497
State Park & Rec. Areas			
Allaire S.P.	147	E2	40.153470 -74.111390
Allamuchy Mtn. S.P.	104	C1	40.921244 -74.782222
Barnegat Lighthouse S.P.	147	E4	39.762750 -74.107950
Cape May Point S.P.	104	C4	38.932950 -74.961010
Corson's Inlet S.P.	105	D4	39.216340 -74.647070
Delaware & Raritan Canal S.P.	147	D1	40.473230 -74.571100
Double Trouble S.P.	147	E3	39.900550 -74.225120
Farny S.P.	148	A3	40.997170 -74.459060
Fortescue State Marina	145	F2	39.243178 -75.176636
Fort Mott S.P.	146	B4	39.612100 -75.543430
Hacklebarney S.P.	105	D1	40.751170 -74.736590
High Point S.P.	148	A2	41.304800 -74.669650
Hopatcong S.P.	148	A3	40.911780 -74.667000
Island Beach S.P.	147	E3	39.905240 -74.081510
Liberty S.P.	148	B4	40.697330 -74.063870
Long Pond Ironworks S.P.	148	A2	41.140986 -74.309228
Monmouth Bfld. S.P.	147	E2	40.269340 -74.302800
Parvin S.P.	146	C4	39.524490 -75.160460
Pigeon Swamp S.P.	147	E1	40.394420 -74.487150
Princeton Bfld. S.P.	147	D2	40.332490 -74.675650
Rancocas S.P.	147	D3	39.990420 -74.837480
Ringwood S.P.	148	A2	41.127600 -74.260130
Swartswood S.P.	94	A4	41.081680 -74.813620
Voorhees S.P.	104	C1	40.695060 -74.887030
Washington Crossing S.P.	147	D2	40.296920 -74.866420
Washington Rock S.P.	148	A4	40.613580 -74.472860
Wawayanda S.P.	148	A2	41.199240 -74.392440

NEW MEXICO	PAGE	GRID	LATITUDE LONGITUDE
National Park & Rec. Areas			
Aztec Ruins Natl. Mon.	48	B1	36.833920 -108.000570
Bandelier Natl. Mon.	48	C2	35.780130 -106.264830
Capulin Mtn. Natl. Mon.	49	E1	36.781990 -103.986110
Carlsbad Caverns Natl. Park-Vis. Ctr.	57	E3	32.175400 -104.444000
Chaco Culture N.H.P.	48	B2	36.016190 -107.924060
Datil Well N.R.A.	48	B4	34.154130 -107.852610
El Malpais Natl. Cons. Area	48	B4	35.059720 -107.876400
El Morro Natl. Mon.	48	B3	35.043480 -108.346250
Fort Union Natl. Mon.	49	D2	35.904230 -105.010740
Gila Cliff Dwellings Natl. Mon.	56	A2	33.229540 -108.264630
Kasha-Katuwe Tent Rocks Natl. Mon.	48	C2	35.663200 -106.410800
Manhattan Project N.H.P.	48	C2	35.882455 -106.304212
Pecos N.H.P.	49	D3	35.578750 -105.762400
Petroglyph Natl. Mon.	48	C3	35.139490 -106.709670
Río Grande Del Norte Natl. Mon.	49	D1	36.640260 -105.877033
Salinas Pueblo Missions Natl. Mon.	48	C4	34.520370 -106.241250
Salinas Pueblo Missions Natl. Mon.-Gran Quivira	49	D4	34.260000 -106.091000
White Sands Natl. Mon.	56	C2	32.820130 -106.272980
State Park & Rec. Areas			
Bluewater Lake S.P.	48	B3	35.302730 -108.106930
Bottomless Lakes S.P.	57	E2	33.316630 -104.332880
Brantley Lake S.P.	57	E3	32.571390 -104.366210
Caballo Lake S.P.	56	B2	32.911370 -107.313580
Cimarron Canyon S.P.	49	D1	36.537600 -105.221130
City of Rocks S.P.	56	A2	32.594860 -107.973850
Clayton Lake S.P.	49	F1	36.573070 -103.300690
Conchas Lake S.P.	49	E3	35.394760 -104.181790
Coronado S.P.	48	C3	35.329130 -106.557870
Coyote Creek S.P.	49	D2	36.188020 -105.233260
Eagle Nest S.P.	49	D1	36.542100 -105.261300
Elephant Butte Res. S.P.-South Ent.	56	B1	33.176180 -107.207460
El Vado Lake S.P.	48	C1	36.593710 -106.735790
Fenton Lake S.P.	48	C2	35.887230 -106.723170
Heron Lake S.P.	48	C1	36.693840 -106.654230
Hyde Mem. S.P.	49	D2	35.737890 -105.836540
Leasburg Dam S.P.	56	B3	32.492680 -106.922380
Living Desert Zoo & Gardens S.P.	57	E3	32.449839 -104.286341
Manzano Mtn. S.P.	48	C4	34.603880 -106.360960
Morphy Lake S.P.	49	D2	35.968660 -105.366600
Navajo Lake S.P.	48	B1	36.831950 -107.586950
Oasis S.P.	49	F4	34.259740 -103.334280
Oliver Lee Mem. S.P.	56	C2	32.744640 -105.934520
Pancho Villa S.P.	56	B4	31.828050 -107.641200
Percha Dam S.P.	56	B2	32.873610 -107.308100
Red Rock S.P.	48	A3	35.537910 -108.605900
Rockhound S.P.	56	B3	32.185550 -107.613090
Santa Rosa Lake S.P.	49	E3	34.987930 -104.658750
Smokey Bear Hist. S.P.	57	D1	33.545620 -105.573170
Storrie Lake S.P.	49	D2	35.655720 -105.231840
Sugarite Canyon S.P.	49	E1	36.944191 -104.381651
Sumner Lake S.P.	49	E4	34.607520 -104.389050
Ute Lake S.P.	49	F3	35.340630 -103.442500
Villanueva S.P.	49	D3	35.259530 -105.368970

NEW YORK	PAGE	GRID	LATITUDE LONGITUDE
National Park & Rec. Areas			
Eleanor Roosevelt N.H.S.	94	B3	41.763170 -73.902960
Fire Island Natl. Seashore	149	D4	40.735320 -72.866620
Fort Stanwix Natl. Mon.	79	E3	43.211930 -75.454740
Gateway N.R.A.	148	B4	40.581100 -73.887790
Home of F.D.R. N.H.S.	94	B3	41.767038 -73.938193
Sagamore Hill N.H.S.	148	C3	40.882480 -73.505550
Saratoga N.H.P.	81	D4	43.002690 -73.612110
Statue of Liberty Natl. Mon.	148	B4	40.689547 -74.044029
Thomas Cole N.H.S.	94	B2	42.225900 -73.861600
Van Buren N.H.S.	94	B2	42.370610 -73.701010
Vanderbilt Mansion N.H.S.	94	B3	41.796482 -73.942359
Women's Rights N.H.P.	79	D3	42.910580 -76.800260
State Park & Rec. Areas			
Adirondack Park	80	C2	43.455590 -73.695930
Allegany S.P.	92	B1	42.106480 -78.765940
Battle Island S.P.	79	D3	43.362780 -76.442150
Bear Mtn. S.P.	148	B2	41.278350 -73.970290
Beaver Island S.P.	78	A3	42.968170 -78.969560
Bowman Lake S.P.	79	E4	42.516970 -75.670400
Buttermilk Falls S.P.	79	D4	42.347410 -76.489130
Caleb Smith S.P. Pres.	149	D3	40.854190 -73.221190
Canandaigua Lake State Marine Park	78	C3	42.875964 -77.275600
Captree S.P.	149	D4	40.636640 -73.263210
Catskill Park	94	A2	42.050290 -74.288840
Cedar Point S.P.	79	D1	44.200670 -76.191000
Chenango Valley S.P.	93	E1	42.215040 -75.818020
Chittenango Falls S.P.	79	E3	42.981520 -75.845030
Clarence Fahnestock S.P.	148	B1	41.423620 -73.799560
Cold Spring Harbor S.P.	148	C3	40.867450 -73.461900
Connetquot River S.P. Pres.	149	D4	40.748070 -73.153510
Cumberland Bay S.P.	81	D1	44.725090 -73.421450
Darien Lakes S.P.	78	B3	42.908460 -78.433300
Delta Lake S.P.	79	E3	43.290030 -75.414910
Evangola S.P.	78	A4	42.604460 -79.105610
Fair Haven Beach S.P.	79	D3	43.320570 -76.696210
Fort Niagara S.P.	78	A3	43.261790 -79.061460
Four Mile Creek S.P.	78	A3	43.272530 -78.996270
Franny Reese S.P.	148	B1	41.704118 -73.956553
Golden Hill S.P.	78	B2	43.365250 -78.489310
Goosepond Mtn. S.P.	148	A2	41.354460 -74.254470
Gov. Alfred E. Smith/Sunken Meadow S.P.	149	D3	40.911970 -73.262940
Green Lakes S.P.	79	E3	43.060000 -75.969030
Hamlin Beach S.P.	78	C2	43.361130 -77.944460
Harriman S.P.	148	B2	41.293010 -74.026560
Heckscher S.P.	149	D4	40.712860 -73.168480
Highland Lakes S.P.	148	A1	41.489806 -74.325085
Hither Hills S.P.	149	F3	41.007700 -72.014500
Hudson Highlands S.P.	148	B2	41.428060 -73.966740
Hudson River Islands S.P.	94	B2	42.318574 -73.778343
Hunt's Pond S.P.	79	E4	42.594020 -75.378140
James Baird S.P.	148	B1	41.689100 -73.799390
Jones Beach S.P.	148	C4	40.595000 -73.521070
Keewaydin S.P.	79	E1	44.322390 -75.925740
Keuka Lake S.P.	78	C4	42.594280 -77.130360
Lake Erie S.P.	78	A4	42.419070 -79.434430
Lakeside Beach S.P.	78	B2	43.367090 -78.236040
Lake Superior S.P.	94	A3	41.658590 -74.869
Letchworth S.P.	78	B4	42.693530 -77.961
Lodi Point S.P.	79	D4	42.619210 -76.863
Long Point S.P.	79	D1	44.026130 -76.219
Mark Twain S.P.	93	D1	42.205200 -76.823
Mary Island S.P.	79	E1	44.350460 -75.930
Max V. Shaul S.P.	79	F4	42.546790 -74.410
Minnewaska S.P. Pres.	148	A1	41.745910 -74.268
Montauk Point S.P.	149	F3	41.065020 -71.886
Moreau Lake S.P.	80	C4	43.226370 -73.707
Oquaga Creek S.P.	93	F1	42.172320 -75.442
Orient Beach S.P.	149	F2	41.154580 -72.245
Pinnacle S.P.	93	D1	42.098100 -77.220
Pixley Falls S.P.	79	E2	43.401100 -75.345
Point Au Roche S.P.	81	D1	44.779990 -73.411
Robert Moses S.P.	148	C4	40.624930 -73.261
Saratoga Spa S.P.	80	C4	43.056950 -73.801
Selkirk Shores S.P.	79	D2	43.544300 -76.191
Seneca Lake S.P.	79	D3	42.873410 -76.960
Southwick Beach S.P.	79	D2	43.767270 -76.196
Sterling Forest S.P.	148	A2	41.220200 -74.187
Storm King S.P.	148	B2	41.432560 -73.987
Taconic S.P.	94	B2	42.007680 -73.508
Tallman Mtn. S.P.	148	B3	41.037270 -73.915
Verona Beach S.P.	79	E3	43.179070 -75.725
Waterson Point S.P.	79	E1	44.339030 -76.010
Wellesley Island S.P.	79	E1	44.315970 -76.019
Whetstone Gulf S.P.	79	E2	43.702310 -75.459
Wildwood S.P.	149	D3	40.954230 -72.788
Wilson-Tuscarora S.P.	78	B3	43.307080 -78.854

NORTH CAROLINA	PAGE	GRID	LATITUDE LONGITUDE
National Park & Rec. Areas			
Cape Hatteras Natl. Seashore	115	F3	35.766700 -75.526
Cape Lookout Natl. Seashore	115	E4	34.886110 -76.331
Carl Sandburg Home N.H.S.	121	E1	35.270000 -82.4500
Fort Raleigh N.H.S.	115	F2	35.932360 -75.7085
Great Smoky Mts. Natl. Park-Cades Cove Vis. Ctr.	121	D1	35.585300 -83.8429
Great Smoky Mts. Natl. Park-Oconaluftee Vis. Ctr.	121	D1	35.515300 -83.3053
Great Smoky Mts. Natl. Park-Sugarlands Vis. Ctr.	121	D1	35.685600 -83.5367
State Park & Rec. Areas			
Carolina Beach S.P.	123	E3	34.045240 -77.9034
Cliffs of the Neuse S.P.	123	E1	35.232900 -77.8983
Crowders Mtn. S.P.	122	A1	35.212350 -81.2929
Dismal Swamp S.P.	113	F3	36.517470 -76.3607
Fort Macon S.P.	115	E4	34.697750 -76.6995
Goose Creek S.P.	123	F1	35.483140 -76.9022
Gorges S.P.	121	E1	35.108400 -82.9439
Hammocks Beach S.P.	123	F2	34.671810 -77.1387
Hanging Rock S.P.	112	B3	36.413030 -80.2539
Haw River S.P.	112	B3	36.249719 -79.7559
Jockey's Ridge S.P.	115	F2	35.961820 -75.6269
Jones Lake S.P.	123	D2	34.698900 -78.6249
Lake James S.P.	111	F4	35.728064 -81.9019
Lake Norman S.P.	112	A4	35.665780 -80.9384
Lake Waccamaw S.P.	123	D3	34.272650 -78.4660
Lumber River S.P.	123	D3	34.390831 -79.0041
Medoc Mtn. S.P.	113	D3	36.280410 -77.8778
Merchants Millpond S.P.	113	F3	36.450601 -76.6929
Morrow Mtn. S.P.	122	B1	35.370390 -80.1024
Mount Mitchell S.P.	111	E4	35.814600 -82.1461
Pettigrew S.P.	113	F4	35.789580 -76.4069
Pilot Mtn. S.P.	112	A3	36.345530 -80.4783
Raven Rock S.P.	123	D1	35.461520 -78.9126
Singletary Lake S.P.	123	D2	34.581570 -78.4520
South Mts. S.P.	121	F1	35.601190 -81.6267
Stone Mtn. S.P.	112	A3	36.374390 -81.0180

NORTH DAKOTA	PAGE	GRID	LATITUDE LONGITUDE
National Park & Rec. Areas			
Fort Union N.H.S.	17	F2	48.002390 -104.0435
Knife River N.H.S.	18	B3	47.336680 -101.3874
Theodore Roosevelt Natl. Park-Elkhorn Site	17	F3	47.226950 -103.6223
Theodore Roosevelt Natl. Park-North Unit	18	A3	47.600300 -103.2610
Theodore Roosevelt Natl. Park-South Unit	18	A4	46.915500 -103.5270
State Park & Rec. Areas			
Beaver Lake S.P.	18	C4	46.401260 -99.6158
Cross Ranch S.P.	18	B3	47.213530 -101.0001
Doyle Mem. S.P.	27	D1	46.204880 -99.48215
Fort Abercrombie S.P.	19	F4	46.444530 -96.71880
Fort Lincoln S.P.	18	B4	46.769420 -100.8478
Fort Ransom S.P.	19	E4	46.544100 -97.92557
Fort Stevenson S.P.	18	B3	47.596890 -101.4205
Grahams Island S.P.	19	D2	48.052500 -99.06830
Icelandic S.P.	19	E1	48.772620 -97.73699
Lake Metigoshe S.P.	18	C1	48.980640 -100.3267
Lake Sakakawea S.P.	18	B3	47.511020 -101.4493
Lewis & Clark S.P.	18	A2	48.115350 -103.2414
Little Missouri Bay S.P.	18	A3	47.550030 -102.7382
Pembina S.P.	19	E1	48.964720 -97.24050

	PAGE	GRID	LATITUDE LONGITUDE
e River S.P.	19	E2	47.931660 -97.505390
estone Bfld. S.P.	27	D1	46.169190 -98.857330

OHIO

OHIO	PAGE	GRID	LATITUDE LONGITUDE
ional Park & Rec. Areas			
les Young Buffalo Soldiers Natl. Mon.	100	C1	39.689722,-83.891111
hoga Valley Natl. Park-Canal Vis. Ctr.	91	E2	41.372600 -81.613700
hoga Valley Natl. Park-nt Farm Vis. Info. Ctr.	91	E2	41.200900 -81.573100
ewell Culture N.H.P.	101	D2	39.298360 -82.917810
es A. Garfield N.H.S.	91	E2	41.663600 -81.351260
e Park & Rec. Areas			
Marion S.P.	101	D1	39.633730 -82.885720
ns Lake S.P.	100	C3	38.812900 -83.519400
n Creek S.P.	90	C4	40.226870 -82.981320
camp S.P.	101	F1	40.047030 -81.031710
ver Creek S.P.	91	F3	40.726220 -80.613590
Rock S.P.	101	E1	39.832780 -81.858370
k Creek S.P.	100	C1	39.946410 -83.729550
keye Lake S.P.	101	D1	39.906540 -82.526270
Oak S.P.	101	E1	39.527740 -82.023260
sar Creek S.P.	100	C1	39.515730 -84.041070
wba Island S.P.	91	D2	41.573530 -82.855780
van Lake S.P.	100	C2	39.387600 -83.882970
ne Creek S.P.	90	C2	41.603770 -83.192910
r Creek S.P.	101	D1	39.649260 -83.246340
aware S.P.	90	C4	40.377690 -83.071590
on S.P.	101	E1	40.023600 -82.111910
Fork S.P.	100	C2	39.002050 -84.151210
t Harbor S.P.	91	D2	41.540930 -82.820830
dley S.P.	91	D3	41.122990 -82.219390
ked Run S.P.	101	E2	39.085000 -81.770460
eva S.P.	91	F1	41.852760 -80.963280
nd Lake Saint Marys S.P.	90	B4	40.549240 -84.436500
ford Lake S.P.	91	F3	40.796100 -80.893760
rison Lake S.P.	90	B2	41.637190 -84.361760
dlands Beach S.P.	91	E1	41.752140 -81.294480
cking Hills S.P.	101	D2	39.494180 -82.611910
eston Woods S.P.	100	B1	39.573820 -84.715380
ependence Dam S.P.	90	B2	41.282470 -84.313500
an Lake S.P.	90	B4	40.510360 -83.842980
kson Lake S.P.	101	D3	38.902850 -82.596780
erson Lake S.P.	91	F4	40.472050 -80.808930
n Bryan S.P.	100	C1	39.791020 -83.867790
eys Island S.P.	91	D2	41.614080 -82.712110
er Lake S.P.	90	B4	40.197650 -83.981740
e Alma S.P.	101	D2	39.153450 -82.516810
e Hope S.P.	101	E2	39.318500 -82.354920
e Logan S.P.	101	D1	39.536400 -82.460590
e Loramie S.P.	90	B4	40.359750 -84.359730
e White S.P.	101	D2	39.109160 -83.040330
dison Lake S.P.	100	C1	39.866250 -83.374930
labar Farm S.P.	91	D3	40.649590 -82.398390
ry Jane Thurston S.P.	90	B2	41.409630 -83.881320
umee Bay S.P.	90	C2	41.678020 -83.353360
hican S.P.	91	D4	40.609510 -82.257600
squito Lake S.P.	91	F2	41.301940 -80.767990
unt Gilead S.P.	91	D4	40.547820 -82.816770
skingum River S.P.	101	E1	40.044140 -81.978260
son-Kennedy Ledges S.P.	91	F2	41.330090 -81.040190
nt Creek S.P.	100	C2	39.228360 -83.374450
e Lake S.P.	101	D2	39.158270 -83.220950
rtage Lakes S.P.	91	E3	40.966260 -81.565190
nderson S.P.	91	E2	41.461540 -81.219590
matuning S.P.	91	F2	41.580110 -80.541530
ail Hollow S.P.	91	E3	40.970200 -81.325100
cky Fork S.P.	100	C2	39.188310 -83.529730
lt Fork S.P.	91	E4	40.081830 -81.460400
oto Trail S.P.	101	D2	39.223620 -82.931210
awnee S.P.	101	D3	38.747670 -83.211220
uth Bass Island S.P.	91	D2	41.644690 -82.835950
onelick S.P.	100	C2	39.226160 -84.057210
ouds Run S.P.	101	E2	39.334320 -82.017690
camore S.P.	100	B1	39.803410 -84.373470
Hollow S.P.	101	D2	39.353790 -82.780200
nker's Creek S.P.	91	E2	41.276180 -81.368910
n Buren S.P.	90	C3	41.138290 -83.644940
est Branch S.P.	91	E3	41.133310 -81.189660
olf Run S.P.	101	F1	39.789770 -81.540180

OKLAHOMA

OKLAHOMA	PAGE	GRID	LATITUDE LONGITUDE
ational Park & Rec. Areas			
ickasaw N.R.A.	51	F4	34.497390 -96.970110
inding Stair Mtn. N.R.A.	116	B2	34.749705 -94.793055
ate Park & Rec. Areas			
dair S.P.	106	B4	35.832230 -94.624100
abaster Caverns S.P.	51	D1	36.697490 -99.149430
rowhead S.P.	116	A1	35.168240 -95.639970
eaver Dunes S.P.	50	B2	36.841129 -100.514988
ernice S.P.	106	B3	36.626670 -94.901670
ack Mesa S.P.	49	F1	36.855620 -102.885680
oggy Depot S.P.	51	F4	34.321747 -96.311302
Boiling Springs S.P.	51	D1	36.452950 -99.298900
Brushy Lake S.P.	116	B1	35.543680 -94.817676
Cherokee Landing S.P.	106	B4	35.758890 -94.908610
Cherokee S.P.	106	B3	36.480280 -95.050560
Clayton Lake S.P.	116	A2	34.549420 -95.308330
Dripping Springs S.P.	51	F3	35.611437 -96.068911
Fort Cobb S.P.	51	D3	35.203720 -98.464990
Foss S.P.	51	D3	35.578510 -99.186830
Gloss Mtn. S.P.	51	D2	36.367190 -98.576460
Great Plains S.P.	51	D4	34.730340 -98.985690
Great Salt Plains S.P.	51	E1	36.753170 -98.149930
Greenleaf S.P.	106	A4	35.623260 -95.180950
Hochatown S.P.	116	B3	34.197390 -94.766300
Honey Creek S.P.	106	B3	36.574060 -94.784370
Hugo Lake S.P.	116	A3	34.016384 -95.375061
Keystone S.P.	51	F2	36.137440 -96.264340
Lake Eucha S.P.	106	B3	36.353930 -94.824000
Lake Eufaula S.P.	116	A1	35.427900 -95.546100
Lake Murray S.P.	51	F4	34.154880 -97.120950
Lake Texoma S.P.	59	F1	33.997590 -96.651310
Lake Thunderbird S.P.	51	E3	35.232320 -97.247550
Lake Wister S.P.	116	B2	34.948700 -94.710400
Little Blue-Disney S.P.	106	B3	36.480260 -95.009130
Little Sahara S.P.	51	D1	36.532900 -98.890870
McGee Creek S.P.	116	A3	34.302927 -95.875467
Natural Falls S.P.	106	B4	36.151900 -94.673300
Okmulgee S.P.	51	F2	35.621900 -96.067700
Osage Hills S.P.	51	F1	36.757360 -96.176220
Raymond Gary S.P.	116	A3	33.997580 -95.253860
Red Rock Canyon S.P.	51	D3	35.456350 -98.358310
Sequoyah Bay S.P.	106	A4	35.886000 -95.276000
Sequoyah S.P.	106	A4	35.932960 -95.230650
Snowdale S.P.	106	A3	36.307710 -95.199040
Spavinaw S.P.	106	B3	36.385890 -95.053290
Talimena S.P.	116	B2	34.788290 -94.950690
Tenkiller S.P.	116	B1	35.598000 -95.031100
Twin Bridges S.P.	106	B2	36.804320 -94.757920
Wah-Sha-She S.P.	51	F1	36.926000 -96.091000
Walnut Creek S.P.	51	F2	36.251210 -96.280130

OREGON

OREGON	PAGE	GRID	LATITUDE LONGITUDE
National Park & Rec. Areas			
Cascade-Siskiyou Natl. Mon.	28	C2	42.068300 -122.399940
Crater Lake Natl. Park-Annie Spring Ent. Sta.	28	C1	42.868700 -122.169000
Crater Lake Natl. Park-North Ent. Sta.	28	C1	43.086900 -122.116000
Hells Canyon N.R.A.-East Ent.	22	B1	45.500680 -116.806560
Hells Canyon N.R.A.-South Ent.	22	B1	44.903300 -116.957080
Hells Canyon N.R.A.-West Ent.	22	B1	45.176360 -117.040740
John Day Fossil Beds Natl. Mon.-Clarno Unit	21	D2	44.911250 -120.431780
John Day Fossil Beds Natl. Mon.-Painted Hills Unit	21	D3	44.661170 -120.254750
John Day Fossil Beds Natl. Mon.-Sheep Rock Unit	21	E3	44.555480 -119.645010
Lewis & Clark N.H.P.-Fort Clatsop	20	B1	46.138260 -123.876670
Lewis & Clark N.H.P.-Salt Works	20	B1	46.134551 -123.880420
Lewis & Clark N.H.P.-Sunset Beach	20	B1	46.099430 -123.936390
Newberry Natl. Volcanic Mon.	21	D4	43.716800 -121.376960
Oregon Caves Natl. Mon. & Pres.	28	B2	42.103910 -123.414300
Oregon Dunes N.R.A.-North Ent.	20	A4	43.885610 -124.120860
Oregon Dunes N.R.A.-South Ent.	20	A4	43.579470 -124.186490
State Park & Rec. Areas			
Ainsworth S.P.	20	C2	45.595720 -122.052980
Alfred A. Loeb S.P.	28	A2	42.113180 -124.188520
Beverly Beach S.P.	20	B3	44.726250 -124.057290
Bullards Beach S.P.	28	A1	43.150990 -124.395480
Cape Arago S.P.	20	A4	43.326140 -124.381770
Cape Blanco S.P.	28	A1	42.826660 -124.524640
Cape Lookout S.P.	20	B2	45.367667 -123.961127
Carl G. Washburne Mem. S.P.	20	A3	44.141990 -124.117490
Cascadia S.P.	20	C3	44.397100 -122.477480
Catherine Creek S.P.	22	A2	45.148890 -117.733990
Collier Mem. S.P.	28	C1	42.641810 -121.880630
Ecola S.P.	20	B1	45.916550 -123.967430
Elijah Bristow S.P.	20	C4	43.935470 -122.844270
Fort Columbia S.P.	20	B1	46.252580 -123.921500
Fort Stevens S.P.	20	B1	46.183200 -123.959940
Harris Beach S.P.	28	A2	42.067930 -124.305860
Hat Rock S.P.	21	E1	45.908260 -119.164510
Hilgard Junction S.P.	21	F2	45.342060 -118.236470
Humbug Mtn. S.P.	28	A1	42.686870 -124.445970
Illinois River Forks S.P.	28	B2	42.154870 -123.649870
Jessie M. Honeyman Mem. S.P.	20	A4	43.933440 -124.106440
Lake Owyhee S.P.	22	A4	43.638380 -117.229090
Lapine S.P.	21	D4	43.768452 -121.513399
Maryhill S.P.	21	D1	45.683060 -120.825830
Mayer S.P.	21	D1	45.682780 -121.301080
Milo Mciver S.P.	20	C2	45.306110 -122.372220
Molalla River S.P.	20	C2	45.294840 -122.696400
Nehalem Bay S.P.	20	B1	45.710000 -123.931470
Ona Beach S.P.	20	B3	44.518060 -124.075960
Oswald West S.P.	20	B1	45.770000 -123.958610
Port Orford Heads S.P.	28	A1	42.739470 -124.509730
Prineville Reservoir S.P.	21	D3	44.144660 -120.737770
Robert Straub S.P.	20	B2	45.183160 -123.965116
Rooster Rock S.P.	20	C2	45.546320 -122.236500
Shore Acres S.P.	20	A4	43.329940 -124.376510
Silver Falls S.P.	20	C2	44.853752 -122.662258
Smith Rock S.P.	21	D3	44.360540 -121.138400
South Beach S.P.	20	B3	44.598450 -124.059350
Starvation Creek S.P.	20	C1	45.688550 -121.690180
Stub Stewart S.P.	20	B1	45.739050 -123.199461
Sunset Bay S.P.	20	A4	43.339010 -124.353990
The Cove Palisades S.P.	21	D3	44.557460 -121.262110
Tumalo S.P.	21	D3	44.086760 -121.308730
Umpqua Lighthouse S.P.	20	A4	43.669610 -124.182830
Valley of the Rogue S.P.	28	B1	42.410770 -123.129310
Viento S.P.	20	C1	45.697240 -121.668310
Wallowa Lake S.P.	22	A2	45.280690 -117.208230
White River Falls S.P.	21	D2	45.166870 -121.087420
Willamette Mission S.P.	20	B2	45.080740 -123.031510
William M. Tugman S.P.	20	A4	43.623640 -124.181910

PENNSYLVANIA

PENNSYLVANIA	PAGE	GRID	LATITUDE LONGITUDE
National Park & Rec. Areas			
Allegheny N.R.A	92	B1	41.943055 -78.867025
Allegheny Portage Railroad N.H.S.	92	B4	40.377020 -78.835870
Eisenhower N.H.S.	103	E1	39.818000 -77.232610
Flight 93 Natl. Mem.	92	B4	40.055200 -78.900900
Fort Necessity Natl. Bfld.	102	B1	39.816340 -79.584310
Friendship Hill N.H.S.	102	B1	39.777778 -79.929167
Gettysburg N.M.P.	103	E1	39.811600 -77.226100
Grey Towers N.H.S.	94	A3	41.325224 -74.871113
Hopewell Furnace N.H.S.	146	B2	40.206760 -75.773570
Johnstown Flood Natl. Mem.	92	B4	40.350710 -78.772480
Valley Forge N.H.P.	146	C2	40.102240 -75.422960
State Park & Rec. Areas			
Bald Eagle S.P.	92	C3	41.041960 -77.642780
Big Spring S.P.	92	C4	40.266850 -77.654410
Black Moshannon S.P.	92	C3	40.915190 -78.058570
Blue Knob S.P.	92	B4	40.265800 -78.584480
Buchanan's Birthplace S.P.	103	D1	39.872660 -77.953190
Caledonia S.P.	103	D1	39.905610 -77.478880
Chapman S.P.	92	B1	41.757850 -79.170350
Cherry Springs S.P.	92	C2	41.662778 -77.823056
Codorus S.P.	103	E1	39.783180 -76.908920
Colonel Denning S.P.	93	D4	40.281820 -77.416630
Colton Point S.P.	93	D2	41.711180 -77.465430
Cook Forest S.P.	92	B2	41.333790 -79.210440
Cowans Gap S.P.	103	D1	39.997980 -77.921530
Delaware Canal S.P.	146	C1	40.545565 -75.087831
Elk S.P.	92	B2	41.606100 -78.564780
Erie Bluffs S.P.	91	F1	42.008333 -80.410833
Evansburg S.P.	146	C2	40.197510 -75.407080
Frances Slocum S.P.	93	E2	41.347380 -75.893760
French Creek S.P.	146	B2	40.236580 -75.795660
Gouldsboro S.P.	93	F2	41.232250 -75.495730
Greenwood Furnace S.P.	92	C3	40.649610 -77.756090
Hickory Run S.P.	93	F3	41.035170 -75.736220
Hills Creek S.P.	93	D1	41.805190 -77.187600
Hyner Run S.P.	92	C2	41.359150 -77.623850
Kettle Creek S.P.	92	C2	41.377120 -77.930130
Keystone S.P.	92	A4	40.374250 -79.377830
Lackawanna S.P.	93	F2	41.575030 -75.711520
Laurel Hill S.P.	102	B1	39.984470 -79.234840
Laurel Mtn. S.P.	92	B4	40.179670 -79.131530
Laurel Ridge S.P.	92	B4	39.958400 -79.360160
Lehigh Gorge S.P.	93	F3	40.971900 -75.761840
Leonard Harrison S.P.	93	D2	41.698420 -77.450810
Little Buffalo S.P.	93	D4	40.454420 -77.169170
Little Pine S.P.	93	D2	41.371240 -77.360310
Lyman Run S.P.	92	C1	41.723650 -77.768470
Marsh Creek S.P.	146	B3	40.069360 -75.717320
Maurice K. Goddard S.P.	92	A2	41.428380 -80.145140
McConnells Mill S.P.	92	A3	40.963530 -80.168810
Memorial Lake S.P.	93	E4	40.424760 -76.590540
Mont Alto S.P.	103	D1	39.839130 -77.540630
Moraine S.P.	92	A3	40.940280 -80.098520
Nescopeck S.P.	93	E3	41.067100 -75.925300
Nockamixon S.P.	146	C1	40.463630 -75.242010
Ohiopyle S.P.	102	B1	39.865030 -79.504310
Oil Creek S.P.-East Ent.	92	A2	41.512130 -79.661810
Ole Bull S.P.	92	C2	41.543590 -77.709430
Parker Dam S.P.	92	C2	41.205140 -78.504310
Penn-Roosevelt S.P.	92	C3	40.726389 -77.702500
Pine Grove Furnace S.P.	103	D1	40.032910 -77.305070
Poe Paddy S.P.	93	D3	40.834150 -77.417380
Presque Isle S.P.	92	A1	42.114200 -80.153590
Prince Gallitzin S.P.	92	B3	40.669760 -78.575650
Promised Land S.P.	93	F2	41.313560 -75.210370
Pymatuning S.P.	91	F2	41.605440 -80.387840
Raccoon Creek S.P.	91	F4	40.503160 -80.424460
Ralph Stover S.P.	146	C1	40.440420 -75.106050
Raymond B. Winter S.P.	93	D3	40.992340 -77.200450

PENNSYLVANIA (cont.)	PAGE	GRID	LATITUDE LONGITUDE
Ricketts Glen S.P.	93	E2	41.336190 -76.300420
Ryerson Station S.P.	102	A1	39.892310 -80.450030
S.B. Elliott S.P.	92	C3	41.112740 -78.526100
Salt Springs S.P.	93	E1	41.911090 -75.868720
Samuel S. Lewis S.P.	103	E1	39.996580 -76.550410
Shawnee S.P.	102	C1	40.038060 -78.645850
Shikellamy S.P.	93	D3	40.879390 -76.802950
Sinnemahoning S.P.	92	C2	41.450650 -78.055090
Susquehannock S.P.	146	A3	39.805770 -76.283410
Swatara S.P.	93	E4	40.481480 -76.551350
Tobyhanna S.P.	93	F2	41.214130 -75.384030
Trough Creek S.P.	92	C4	40.311620 -78.131820
Tyler S.P.	146	C2	40.233330 -74.951170
Warriors Path S.P.	92	C4	40.193330 -78.249880
Washington Crossing Hist. Park	104	C2	40.312256 -74.859711
Whipple Dam S.P.	92	C3	40.682250 -77.868410
Worlds End S.P.	93	E2	41.471880 -76.587060
Yellow Creek S.P.	92	B4	40.575830 -79.004420

RHODE ISLAND	PAGE	GRID	LATITUDE LONGITUDE
State Park & Rec. Areas			
Beavertail S.P.	150	C4	41.457030 -71.396950
Block Island State Beach	95	D4	41.180850 -71.566460
Brenton Point S.P.	150	C4	41.450430 -71.355870
Burlingame S.P.	150	C4	41.361610 -71.701370
Casimir Pulaski Mem. S.P.	150	C3	41.950000 -71.766670
Colt S.P.	151	D3	41.684590 -71.288860
East Matunuck State Beach	150	C4	41.378350 -71.525630
Fishermen's Mem. S.P.	150	C4	41.380630 -71.488000
Fort Adams S.P.	150	C4	41.469150 -71.339990
Goddard Mem. S.P.	150	C3	41.651030 -71.442040
Haines Mem. S.P.	150	C3	41.752960 -71.348600
Misquamicut State Beach	95	D4	41.324510 -71.800670
Rocky Point S.P.	150	C3	41.691482 -71.363654
R.W. Wheeler State Beach	150	C4	41.372620 -71.495530
Scarborough State Beach	150	C4	41.389770 -71.474260

SOUTH CAROLINA	PAGE	GRID	LATITUDE LONGITUDE
National Park & Rec. Areas			
Charles Pinckney N.H.S.	131	D2	32.847150 -79.824090
Congaree Natl. Park	122	A4	33.836100 -80.827660
Kings Mtn. N.M.P.	122	A1	35.140120 -81.386890
Ninety Six N.H.S.	121	F3	34.162740 -82.010980
Reconstruction Era Natl. Mon.	130	C2	32.432790 -80.670458
State Park & Rec. Areas			
Andrew Jackson S.P.	122	B2	34.839560 -80.810110
Barnwell S.P.	130	B1	33.329250 -81.300400
Calhoun Falls S.P.	121	E3	34.106792 -82.604200
Cheraw S.P.	122	C2	34.642370 -79.927640
Devils Fork S.P.	121	E2	34.952527 -82.946085
Edisto Beach S.P.	130	C2	32.505410 -80.310310
Givhans Ferry S.P.	130	C1	33.031640 -80.382150
Hickory Knob State Resort Park	121	E4	33.884250 -82.416010
Huntington Beach S.P.	123	D4	33.502650 -79.081200
Jones Gap S.P.	121	E1	35.126360 -82.558350
Kings Mtn. S.P.	122	A1	35.113030 -81.394040
Lake Warren S.P.	130	B2	32.844830 -81.165070
Little Pee Dee S.P.	122	C3	34.331020 -79.282170
Myrtle Beach S.P.	123	D4	33.649210 -78.938600
N.R. Goodale S.P.	122	B3	34.281580 -80.525150
Oconee S.P.	121	E2	34.867297 -83.106098
Paris Mtn. S.P.	121	E2	34.924970 -82.365540
Poinsett S.P.	122	B4	33.804360 -80.544920
Santee S.P.	122	B4	33.500200 -80.489820
Table Rock S.P.	121	E2	35.022050 -82.710700

SOUTH DAKOTA	PAGE	GRID	LATITUDE LONGITUDE
National Park & Rec. Areas			
Badlands Natl. Park-Interior Ent.	26	B4	43.741900 -101.957000
Badlands Natl. Park-Northeast Ent.	26	B4	43.792400 -101.906000
Badlands Natl. Park-Pinnacles Ent.	26	B4	43.885500 -102.238000
Jewel Cave Natl. Mon.	25	F4	43.736500 -103.819940
Minuteman Missile N.H.S.	26	B4	43.833931 -101.899685
Mount Rushmore Natl. Mem.	26	A4	43.886730 -103.440610
Wind Cave Natl. Park-Vis. Ctr.	26	A4	43.556100 -103.478000
State Park & Rec. Areas			
Bear Butte S.P.	26	A3	44.460580 -103.433750
Custer S.P.	26	A4	43.770310 -103.440130
Fisher Grove S.P.	27	E2	44.883340 -98.356640
Hartford Beach S.P.	27	F2	45.398870 -96.665260
Lake Herman S.P.	27	F4	43.993120 -97.159790
Newton Hills S.P.	35	F1	43.218860 -96.569700
Oakwood Lakes S.P.	27	F3	44.454310 -96.989490
Palisades S.P.	27	F4	43.687970 -96.511470
Roy Lake S.P.	27	E1	45.703360 -97.419650
Sica Hollow S.P.	27	E1	45.740690 -97.229150
Union Grove S.P.	35	F1	42.922630 -96.785530

TENNESSEE	PAGE	GRID	LATITUDE LONGITUDE
National Park & Rec. Areas			
Andrew Johnson N.H.S.	111	D4	36.157710 -82.836880
Big South Fork Natl. River & Rec. Area	110	B3	36.475400 -84.752100
Manhattan Project N.H.P.	37	D2	35.928419 -85.350923
State Park & Rec. Areas			
Big Hill Pond S.P.	119	D1	35.078890 -88.718860
Big Ridge S.P.	110	C3	36.241600 -83.929280
Bledsoe Creek S.P.	109	F3	36.378050 -86.356660
Cedars of Lebanon S.P. & Forest	109	F4	36.093930 -86.335620
Chickasaw S.P.	119	D1	35.393241 -88.772298
Cove Lake S.P.	110	C3	36.305830 -84.210750
Cumberland Mtn. S.P.	110	B4	35.898460 -84.995130
David Crockett S.P.	119	E1	35.242690 -87.354850
Davy Crockett Birthplace S.P.	111	E3	36.221980 -82.662770
Edgar Evins S.P.	110	A4	36.086050 -85.812460
Fall Creek Falls S.P.	120	B1	35.622200 -85.208000
Frozen Head S.P. & Nat. Area-North Ent.	110	B4	36.122550 -84.433320
Frozen Head S.P. & Nat. Area-South Ent.	110	B4	36.102180 -84.446970
Harpeth River S.P.	109	E4	36.079240 -86.956920
Harrison Bay S.P.	120	B1	35.175850 -85.115350
Henry Horton S.P.	119	F1	35.596510 -86.698690
Hiwassee–Ocoee Scenic Rivers S.P.	120	C1	35.224557 -84.504269
Indian Mtn. S.P.	110	C3	36.583050 -84.139900
Long Hunter S.P.	109	F4	36.094340 -86.557330
Meeman-Shelby Forest S.P.	118	B1	35.336800 -90.029010
Montgomery Bell S.P.	109	E4	36.106750 -87.268690
Mousetail Landing S.P.	109	D4	35.581900 -87.859100
Natchez Trace S.P.	109	D4	35.839580 -88.252820
Nathan Bedford Forrest S.P.	109	D4	36.087900 -87.979750
Norris Dam S.P.	110	C3	36.234560 -84.127020
Old Stone Fort State Arch. Park	120	A1	35.487270 -86.101330
Panther Creek S.P.	111	D3	36.212760 -83.412420
Paris Landing State Resort Park	109	D3	36.441760 -88.090180
Pickett S.P.	110	B3	36.537374 -84.802126
Pickwick Landing S.P.	119	D2	35.051790 -88.242650
Pinson Mounds State Arch. Park	119	D1	35.504130 -88.683020
Reelfoot Lake S.P.	108	B3	36.414410 -89.426880
Roan Mtn. S.P.	111	E4	36.161110 -82.097000
Rock Island S.P.	110	A4	35.810000 -85.641550
Standing Stone S.P.	110	A3	36.458910 -85.437690
T.O. Fuller S.P.	118	B2	35.057810 -90.113650
Tims Ford S.P.	120	A1	35.220999 -86.255889
Warriors Path S.P.	111	E5	36.504610 -82.481090

TEXAS	PAGE	GRID	LATITUDE LONGITUDE
National Park & Rec. Areas			
Alibates Flint Quarries Natl. Mon.	50	A3	35.571900 -101.633880
Amistad N.R.A.	60	B2	29.449920 -101.053170
Big Bend Natl. Park-North Ent.	62	C4	29.680900 -103.167000
Big Bend Natl. Park-West Ent.	62	C4	29.306600 -103.523000
Fort Davis N.H.S.	62	B2	30.604120 -103.886010
Guadalupe Mts. Natl. Park-Vis. Ctr.	57	D3	31.894300 -104.822000
Lyndon B. Johnson N.H.P.	61	D2	30.276020 -98.411990
Padre Island Natl. Seashore	63	F3	27.553470 -97.248370
Palo Alto Btfd. N.H.P.	63	F4	26.011630 -97.481570
State Park & Rec. Areas			
Abilene S.P.	58	C3	32.241360 -99.879230
Atlanta S.P.	124	C1	33.229500 -94.249300
Balmorhea S.P.	62	B2	30.946270 -103.784890
Bastrop S.P.	61	E2	30.098960 -97.229090
Bentsen-Rio Grande Valley S.P.	63	E4	26.182530 -98.382360
Big Bend Ranch S.P.	62	B4	29.265070 -103.791910
Big Spring S.P.	58	A3	32.229650 -101.483090
Blanco S.P.	61	D2	30.093240 -98.423420
Bonham S.P.	59	F1	33.543100 -96.149640
Brazos Bend S.P.	132	A4	29.371480 -95.631890
Buescher S.P.	61	E2	30.073570 -97.176140
Caddo Lake S.P.	124	C2	32.684230 -94.177070
Caprock Canyons S.P. & Trailway	50	B4	34.406440 -101.048830
Choke Canyon S.P.-Calliham Unit	61	D4	28.460970 -98.356380
Choke Canyon S.P.-South Shore Unit	61	D4	28.467610 -98.239550
Cleburne S.P.	59	E3	32.265180 -97.560680
Colorado Bend S.P.	61	D1	31.062510 -98.504250
Cooper Lake S.P.	124	A1	33.305282 -95.648346
Copper Breaks S.P.	50	C4	34.113660 -99.747800
Daingerfield S.P.	124	B1	33.028720 -94.714510
Davis Mts. S.P.	62	B2	30.599520 -103.929220
Dinosaur Valley S.P.	59	E3	32.250020 -97.814620
Eisenhower S.P.	59	F1	33.822670 -96.616120
Fairfield Lake S.P.	59	F3	31.765910 -96.076220
Falcon S.P.	63	D3	26.583500 -99.144790
Fort Boggy S.P.	124	A4	31.189627 -95.986069
Fort Griffin S.H.S.	58	C2	32.924690 -99.219370
Fort Parker S.P.	59	F4	31.592650 -96.524370
Fort Richardson S.P. & Hist. Site	59	D2	33.206060 -98.164810
Franklin Mts. S.P.	56	C3	31.912060 -106.517140
Galveston Island S.P.	132	B4	29.196240 -94.956210
Garner S.P.	60	C2	29.600900 -99.744220
Goliad S.P.	61	E4	28.655190 -97.383580
Goose Island S.P.	61	F4	28.134060 -96.984350
Guadalupe River S.P.	61	D2	29.849890 -98.509590
Huntsville S.P.	132	A2	30.638130 -95.511370
Inks Lake S.P.	61	D1	30.738290 -98.366450
Kerrville-Schreiner S.P.	60	C2	30.007930 -99.117640
Lake Arrowhead S.P.	59	D1	33.759300 -98.396610
Lake Bob Sandlin S.P.	124	B1	33.054090 -95.10
Lake Brownwood S.P.	59	D3	31.857370 -99.02
Lake Casa Blanca International S.P.	63	D2	27.536739 -99.43
Lake Colorado City S.P.	58	B3	32.313460 -100.9
Lake Corpus Christi S.P.	61	E4	28.060360 -97.86
Lake Livingston S.P.	132	B1	30.671300 -95.00
Lake Mineral Wells S.P.	59	E2	32.814570 -98.04
Lake Somerville S.P. & Trailway	61	F1	30.315760 -96.62
Lake Tawakoni S.P.	59	F2	32.841610 -95.99
Lake Texana S.P.	61	F3	28.953610 -96.56
Lake Whitney S.P.	59	E3	31.924780 -97.35
Lockhart S.P.	61	E2	29.857610 -97.69
Longhorn Cavern S.P.	61	D1	30.686610 -98.35
Lyndon B. Johnson S.P. & Hist. Site-Ranch Unit	61	D2	30.235180 -98.62
Martin Creek Lake S.P.	124	B3	32.283090 -94.58
Martin Dies Junior S.P.	132	C1	30.848980 -94.16
Meridian S.P.	59	E3	31.892440 -97.69
Mission Tejas S.P.	124	A4	31.546110 -95.23
Monahans Sandhills S.P.	57	F4	31.634940 -102.81
Mother Neff S.P.	59	E4	31.319150 -97.47
Mustang Island S.P.	63	F2	27.677020 -97.17
Palmetto S.P.	61	E2	29.597280 -97.58
Palo Duro Canyon S.P.	50	B3	34.985710 -101.70
Pedernales Falls S.P.	61	D1	30.273110 -98.25
Possum Kingdom S.P.	59	D2	32.878970 -98.56
Purtis Creek S.P.	124	A2	32.373340 -95.97
Ray Roberts Lake S.P.	59	F1	33.444050 -96.92
Rusk–Palestine S.P.-East	124	B3	31.803560 -95.19
Rusk–Palestine S.P.-West	124	A4	31.739260 -95.57
Sabine Pass Battleground S.H.S.	132	C3	29.726520 -93.87
San Angelo S.P.	58	B4	31.491919 -100.54
Sea Rim S.P.	132	C3	29.677900 -94.03
Seminole Canyon S.P. & Hist. Site	60	A2	29.709000 -101.29
South Llano River S.P.	60	C1	30.445430 -99.80
Stephen F. Austin S.P.	61	F2	29.812030 -96.10
Tyler S.P.	124	A2	32.481750 -95.28

UTAH	PAGE	GRID	LATITUDE LONGITUDE
National Park & Rec. Areas			
Arches Natl. Park	40	A2	38.615570 -109.61
Bears Ears Natl. Mon.	41	A3	37.703318 -109.91
Bryce Canyon Natl. Park	39	E4	37.641700 -112.16
Canyonlands Natl. Park-East Ent.	40	A3	38.168510 -109.75
Canyonlands Natl. Park-Horseshoe Canyon Unit	39	F3	38.497740 -110.20
Canyonlands Natl. Park-North Ent.	40	A3	38.490150 -109.80
Canyonlands Natl. Park-West Ent.	40	A3	38.255440 -110.18
Capitol Reef Natl. Park	39	E3	38.291020 -111.26
Cedar Breaks Natl. Mon.-East Ent.	39	D4	37.655230 -112.81
Cedar Breaks Natl. Mon.-North Ent.	39	D4	37.665730 -112.83
Cedar Breaks Natl. Mon.-South Ent.	39	D4	37.598730 -112.85
Glen Canyon N.R.A.	39	F4	38.255440 -110.18
Golden Spike N.H.S.	31	E3	41.620482 -112.54
Grand Staircase-Escalante Natl. Mon.	39	E4	37.420000 -111.55
Natural Bridges Natl. Mon.	39	F4	37.608120 -109.96
Rainbow Bridge Natl. Mon.	47	E1	37.110810 -110.40
Zion Natl. Park-East Ent.	39	D4	37.235370 -112.86
Zion Natl. Park-Main Ent.	39	D4	37.201970 -112.98
State Park & Rec. Areas			
Anasazi S.P. Mus.	39	E3	37.922399 -111.42
Antelope Island S.P.	31	E4	41.089290 -112.11
Bear Lake (Rendezvous Beach) S.P.	31	F2	41.962200 -111.40
Bear Lake S.P.	31	F2	41.965360 -111.39
Camp Floyd– Stagecoach Inn S.P.	31	E4	40.258360 -112.097
Coral Pink Sand Dunes S.P.	47	D1	37.036964 -112.731
Dead Horse Point S.P.	40	A3	38.510220 -109.729
Deer Creek S.P.	31	F4	40.452620 -111.477
Edge of the Cedars S.P.	40	A4	37.629760 -109.491
Escalante Petrified Forest S.P.	39	E4	37.783820 -111.630
Fremont Indian S.P.	39	D3	38.579537 -112.314
Goblin Valley S.P.	39	F3	38.580620 -110.712
Goosenecks S.P.	40	A4	37.174730 -109.926
Green River S.P.	39	F2	38.995500 -110.156
Gunlock S.P.-North Ent.	38	C4	37.275970 -113.768
Gunlock S.P.-South Ent.	38	C4	37.251490 -113.772
Huntington S.P.	39	F2	39.315200 -110.977
Hyrum S.P.	31	E3	41.626220 -111.872
Iron Mission S.P.	39	D4	37.688349 -113.061
Kodachrome Basin S.P.	39	E4	37.501670 -111.993
Millsite S.P.	39	E2	39.099020 -111.184
Otter Creek S.P.	39	E3	38.167430 -112.021
Palisade S.P.	39	E2	39.195800 -111.691
Piute S.P.	39	E3	38.322530 -112.204
Quail Creek S.P.	39	D4	37.105000 -113.576
Red Fleet S.P.	32	B4	40.553300 -109.518
Rockport S.P.	31	F4	40.751890 -111.367
Sand Hollow S.P.	46	C1	37.144830 -113.382
Scofield S.P.	39	E1	39.708600 -110.921
Snow Canyon S.P.-East Ent.	38	C4	37.212120 -113.630
Snow Canyon S.P.-North Ent.	38	C4	37.256790 -113.632
Snow Canyon S.P.-South Ent.	38	C4	37.183380 -113.645
Starvation S.P.	32	A4	40.104100 -110.330

aker S.P.-North Ent.	32	A4	40.534870 -109.522440
aker S.P.-South Ent.	32	A4	40.504850 -109.528870
orial Statehouse S.P.	39	D2	38.985880 -112.353530
tch Mtn. S.P.	31	F4	40.477770 -111.519990
rd Bay S.P.-North Ent.	31	E3	41.418810 -112.052390
rd Bay S.P.-South Ent.	31	E3	41.350610 -112.069060
S.P.	39	E2	39.381240 -112.028360

VERMONT	PAGE	GRID	LATITUDE LONGITUDE
onal Park & Rec. Areas			
h-Billings-Rockefeller N.H.P.	81	E3	43.635833 -72.538333
salamoo Natl. Rec. Area	81	D3	43.879457 -73.098532
e Park & Rec. Areas			
S.P.	81	E3	44.051150 -72.626440
bury S.P.	81	D3	43.904250 -73.065370
on Island S.P.	81	D1	44.779660 -73.180050
p Plymouth S.P.	81	E4	43.475810 -72.694987
R. S.P.	81	D3	44.058850 -73.409210
rald Lake S.P.	81	D4	43.283790 -73.002250
Moon S.P.	81	D3	43.699720 -73.223220
sland Bay S.P.	81	D2	44.226230 -73.277660
Saint Catherine S.P.	81	D4	43.483000 -73.202580
River S.P.	81	D2	44.388940 -72.768360
y Stark S.P.	94	C1	42.854920 -72.813790
h Hero S.P.	81	D1	44.908210 -73.235110
er Pond S.P.	81	E2	44.251467 -72.247550
water S.P.	81	E2	44.280200 -72.275060
nshend S.P.	81	E4	43.041920 -72.691600
erhill S.P.	81	D2	44.528880 -72.843920
dford S.P.	94	C1	42.894450 -73.037790
ds Island S.P.	81	D1	44.802500 -73.209283

VIRGINIA	PAGE	GRID	LATITUDE LONGITUDE
onal Park & Rec. Areas			
omattox Court House N.H.P.	112	C1	37.377367 -78.795290
ker T. Washington Natl. Mon.	112	B2	37.120500 -79.733340
ar Creek & Belle Grove N.H.P.	102	C2	39.023500 -78.289000
onial N.H.P.	114	A4	37.211390 -76.776730
nberland Gap N.H.P.-Vis. Ctr.	111	D3	36.602600 -83.695400
ericksburg & Spotsylvania Co. ds. Mem. N.M.P.	103	D4	38.254300 -77.451890
rge Washington Birthplace Natl. Mon.	114	A2	38.192353 -76.927192
assas Natl. Bfld. Park	144	A3	38.806030 -77.572810
unt Rogers N.R.A.	111	F2	36.811360 -81.420130
nandoah Natl. Park- ont Royal North Ent.	102	C3	38.903300 -78.192400
nandoah Natl. Park- ckfish Gap South Ent.	102	C3	38.033900 -78.858900
nandoah Natl. Park-Swift Run Gap Ent.	102	C3	38.359100 -78.546700
nandoah Natl. Park-Thornton Gap Ent.	102	C3	38.662300 -78.320600
te Park & Rec. Areas			
r Creek Lake S.P.	113	D1	37.532970 -78.274890
e Isle S.P.	114	B2	37.774526 -76.599222
opokes Plantation S.P.	114	A4	37.140400 -76.748590
ytor Lake S.P.	112	A2	37.057620 -80.622140
ithat S.P.	102	B4	37.914520 -79.796740
y Stone S.P.	112	B2	36.791790 -80.117890
se Cape S.P.	115	F1	36.691370 -75.924410
t Landing S.P.	114	B4	36.915601 -76.057000
yson Highlands S.P.	111	F3	36.611920 -81.489900
liday Lake S.P.	113	D1	37.404610 -78.644920
ngry Mother S.P.	111	F2	36.880860 -81.525750
nes River S.P.	112	C1	37.540400 -78.839300
topeke S.P.	114	B4	37.169292 -75.982919
e Anna S.P.	103	D4	38.125850 -77.821690
son Neck S.P.	103	E3	38.640740 -77.194400
ural Bridge S.P.	112	C1	37.633038 -79.543034
ural Tunnel S.P.	111	E3	36.707520 -82.744090
v River Trail S.P.	112	A2	36.870180 -80.868550
oneechee S.P.	113	D3	36.633330 -78.525420
ahontas S.P.	113	E1	37.366240 -77.573870
whatan S.P.	113	D1	37.678066 -77.925997
lor's Creek Bfld. Hist. S.P.	113	D1	37.298470 -78.229470
Meadows S.P.	103	D2	38.988703 -77.968913
ith Mtn. Lake S.P.	112	B2	37.091110 -79.592110
n Lakes S.P.	113	D2	37.336900 -77.934100
stmoreland S.P.	103	E4	38.158690 -76.870120
k River S.P.	113	F1	37.414190 -76.713650

WASHINGTON	PAGE	GRID	LATITUDE LONGITUDE
tional Park & Rec. Areas			
umbia River Gorge Natl. Scenic Area	21	D1	45.715322 -121.818667
t Vancouver N.H.S.	20	C1	45.626940 -122.656310
nford Reach Natl. Mon.	13	E4	46.483333 -119.533333
ke Chelan N.R.A.	13	D2	48.309080 -120.657730
ke Roosevelt N.R.A.	13	F2	47.972680 -118.970580
wis & Clark N.H.P.-Discovery Trail	12	B4	46.370033 -124.053503
wis & Clark N.H.P.-Dismal Nitch	20	B1	46.249033 -123.862903
wis & Clark N.H.P.-Sta. Camp	20	B1	46.263111 -123.932571
nhattan Project N. H.P.	13	E4	46.316332 -119.301848
unt Baker N.R.A.	12	C1	48.714167 -121.805900
unt Rainier Natl. Park-Nisqually Ent.	12	C5	46.741400 -121.919040
unt Rainier Natl. Park-Stevens Can. Ent.	12	C7	46.754730 -121.557010
Mount Rainier Natl. Park-White River Ent.	12	C8	46.902040 -121.554340
Mount Saint Helens Natl. Mon.	12	C4	46.277590 -122.218820
North Cascades Natl. Park-Golden West	13	D1	48.308200 -120.655000
North Cascades Natl. Park- Northern Cascades Vis. Ctr.	13	D1	48.666100 -121.264000
Olympic Natl. Park-Vis. Ctr.	12	B2	48.096700 -123.428000
Olympic Natl. Park-Vis. Ctr.- Hoh Rain Forest	12	B2	47.860700 -123.935000
Olympic Natl. Park-Vis. Ctr.- Hurricane Ridge	12	B2	47.969200 -123.498000
Ross Lake N.R.A.	13	D1	48.674250 -121.244730
San Juan Island N.H.P.	12	B2	48.534580 -123.016250
San Juan Islands Natl. Mon.	12	C2	48.531944,-123.029167
Whitman Mission N.H.S.	21	F1	46.040910 -118.468110
State Park & Rec. Areas			
Alta Lake S.P.	13	E2	48.031990 -119.934710
Anderson Lake S.P.	12	C2	48.014590 -122.810680
Belfair S.P.	12	C3	47.430630 -122.881400
Birch Bay S.P.	12	C1	48.903210 -122.757880
Bogachiel S.P.	12	A2	47.894790 -124.362820
Brooks Mem. S.P.	21	D1	45.950590 -120.664200
Camano Island S.P.	12	C2	48.131680 -122.503240
Cape Disappointment S.P.	20	B1	46.294210 -124.053610
Columbia Hills S.P.	21	D1	45.643030 -121.106410
Crawford S.P.	14	A1	48.992070 -117.370370
Curlew Lake S.P.	13	F1	48.719280 -118.661740
Damon Point S.P.	12	B4	46.945300 -124.132100
Deception Pass S.P.	12	C2	48.390970 -122.646880
Dosewallips S.P.	12	C3	47.687570 -122.899860
Fields Spring S.P.	22	A1	46.087520 -117.173650
Flaming Geyser S.P.	12	C3	47.280230 -122.041870
Fort Casey S.P.	12	C2	48.159760 -122.672410
Fort Okanogan S.P.	13	E2	48.102370 -119.678720
Fort Simcoe S.P.	13	D4	46.345340 -120.823460
Fort Townsend S.P.	12	C2	48.078260 -122.805690
Ginkgo Petrified Forest S.P.	13	E4	46.949010 -119.997490
Goldendale Observatory S.P.	21	D1	45.837090 -120.815890
Ike Kinswa S.P.	12	C4	46.555780 -122.536570
Jarrell Cove S.P.	12	B3	47.285940 -122.881080
Joseph Whidbey S.P.	12	C2	48.308370 -122.713170
Kitsap Mem. S.P.	12	C3	47.816580 -122.646840
Lake Chelan S.P.	13	D2	47.869430 -120.191110
Lake Easton S.P.	13	D3	47.249380 -121.190920
Lake Wenatchee S.P.	13	D3	47.816340 -120.729780
Larrabee S.P.	12	C2	48.650620 -122.489810
Lewis & Clark S.P.	12	C4	46.525850 -122.817910
Lewis & Clark Trail S.P.	13	F4	46.287600 -118.073340
Lincoln Rock S.P.	13	D3	47.535490 -120.282280
Millersylvania S.P.	12	B4	46.909610 -122.905950
Moran S.P.	12	C1	48.657700 -122.859630
Mount Spokane S.P.	14	B2	47.899290 -117.124350
Nolte S.P.	12	C3	47.267320 -121.943420
Ocean City S.P.	12	B4	47.038520 -124.158130
Osoyoos S.P.	13	E1	48.950060 -119.434350
Pacific Beach S.P.	12	A3	47.205980 -124.202220
Pacific Pines S.P.	12	B4	46.507610 -124.049150
Palouse Falls S.P.	13	F4	46.664030 -118.228660
Peace Arch S.P.	12	C1	49.000980 -122.751580
Pearrygin Lake S.P.	13	E2	48.496720 -120.146950
Peshastin Pinnacles S.P.	13	D3	47.578810 -120.613860
Potholes S.P.	13	E4	46.970780 -119.351180
Potlatch S.P.	12	B3	47.363000 -123.158140
Rainbow Falls S.P.	12	B4	46.631010 -123.237350
Rockport S.P.	12	C2	48.487920 -121.601870
Sacajawea S.P.	21	F1	46.210140 -119.046050
Scenic Beach S.P.	12	C3	47.649250 -122.845470
Seaquest S.P.	12	C4	46.295880 -122.820860
Sequim Bay S.P.	12	B2	48.040750 -123.030920
Shine Tidelands S.P.	12	C2	47.867990 -122.638700
Steamboat Rock S.P.	13	E2	47.828650 -119.134340
Sun Lakes S.P.	13	E3	47.596540 -119.387760
Triton Cove S.P.	12	B3	47.609112 -122.986526
Twenty-Five Mile Creek S.P.	13	D2	47.992520 -120.263610
Twin Harbors S.P.	12	B4	46.858850 -124.104210
Wallace Falls S.P.	12	C2	47.865610 -121.680050
Wanapum S.P.	13	E4	46.924760 -119.991690
Westport Light S.P.	12	B4	46.891700 -124.111630

WEST VIRGINIA	PAGE	GRID	LATITUDE LONGITUDE
National Park & Rec. Areas			
Bluestone Natl. Scenic River	112	A1	37.584300 -80.957900
Gauley River N.R.A.	101	F4	38.191800 -81.001920
Harpers Ferry N.H.P.	103	D2	39.318820 -77.759060
New River Gorge Natl. River	101	F4	37.875670 -81.077598
Spruce Knob Seneca Rocks N.R.A.	102	B3	38.681180 -79.544480
State Park & Rec. Areas			
Audra S.P.	102	A2	39.041110 -80.067500
Beartown S.P.	102	A4	38.051750 -80.275420
Blennerhassett Island Hist. S.P.	101	E2	39.273300 -81.644800
Bluestone S.P.	112	A1	37.623050 -80.934710
Cacapon Resort S.P.	102	C1	39.502980 -78.291330
Camp Creek S.P.	111	F1	37.508173 -81.132873
Carnifex Ferry Bfld. S.P.	101	F4	38.211290 -80.941850
Cass Scenic Railroad S.P.	102	A3	38.396520 -79.914280
Cedar Creek S.P.	101	F3	38.880780 -80.849420
Droop Mtn. Bfld. S.P.	102	A4	38.113200 -80.271670
Holly River S.P.	102	A3	38.653140 -80.382620
Little Beaver S.P.	112	A1	37.756570 -81.079780
Moncove Lake S.P.	112	B1	37.616950 -80.354730
Pinnacle Rock S.P.	111	F1	37.308190 -81.291430
Prickett's Fort S.P.	102	A1	39.514090 -80.099960
Tomlinson Run S.P.	91	F4	40.550660 -80.595950
Tygart Lake S.P.	102	A2	39.248160 -80.021060
Valley Falls S.P.	102	A2	39.392900 -80.070480
Watoga S.P.	102	A4	38.122510 -80.155660
Watters Smith Mem. S.P.	102	A2	39.174520 -80.414260

WISCONSIN	PAGE	GRID	LATITUDE LONGITUDE
National Park & Rec. Areas			
Apostle Islands Natl. Lakeshore	65	D4	46.812210 -90.820780
Saint Croix Natl. Scenic Riverway	67	E2	45.415700 -92.646270
State Park & Rec. Areas			
Amnicon Falls S.P.	64	C4	46.608210 -91.887850
Aztalan S.P.	74	B3	43.068310 -88.863750
Belmont Mound S.P.	74	A4	42.768611 -90.349444
Big Bay S.P.	65	D4	46.811030 -90.696960
Big Foot Beach S.P.	74	C4	42.567330 -88.436790
Blue Mound S.P.	74	A3	43.026990 -89.840740
Brunet Island S.P.	67	F3	45.176220 -91.161610
Buckhorn S.P.	74	A1	43.948280 -90.002130
Copper Culture S.P.	68	C4	44.887440 -87.897940
Copper Falls S.P.	65	D4	46.351710 -90.643670
Council Grounds S.P.	68	A3	45.184840 -89.734290
Devil's Lake S.P.	74	A2	43.429010 -89.734900
Governor Dodge S.P.	74	A3	43.019560 -90.141950
Governor Thompson S.P.	68	C3	45.326309 -88.219205
Harrington Beach S.P.	75	D2	43.499430 -87.811890
Hartman Creek S.P.	74	B1	44.318070 -89.194320
High Cliff S.P.	74	C1	44.166680 -88.291760
Interstate S.P.	67	D3	45.396410 -92.636580
Kinnickinnic S.P.	67	D4	44.837280 -92.733190
Kohler-Andrae S.P.	75	D2	43.672740 -87.719320
Lake Kegonsa S.P.	74	B3	42.978005 -89.230300
Lake Wissota S.P.	67	F4	44.980950 -91.313740
Merrick S.P.	73	E1	44.152740 -91.744120
Mill Bluff S.P.	74	A1	43.961610 -90.317980
Mirror Lake S.P.	74	A2	43.568770 -89.834930
Natural Bridge S.P.	74	A2	43.344930 -89.928290
Nelson Dewey S.P.	73	F4	42.743740 -91.037860
New Glarus Woods S.P.	74	B4	42.786830 -89.631980
Newport S.P.	69	D3	45.241470 -86.998830
Pattison S.P.	64	C4	46.535290 -92.121410
Peninsula S.P.	69	D3	45.133080 -87.213280
Perrot S.P.	73	F1	44.016350 -91.479670
Potawatomi S.P.	69	D4	44.849990 -87.407640
Rib Mtn. S.P.	68	B4	44.915800 -89.669360
Roche-A-Cri S.P.	74	A1	43.996120 -89.812370
Rock Island S.P.	69	E3	45.398990 -86.855970
Rocky Arbor S.P.	74	A2	43.647890 -89.808240
Straight Lake S.P.	67	E2	45.597399 -92.406609
Tower Hill S.P.	74	A3	43.147090 -90.043750
Whitefish Dunes S.P.	69	D4	44.928910 -87.182150
Wildcat Mtn. S.P.	74	A2	43.688870 -90.566800
Willow River S.P.	67	D3	45.017610 -92.672610
Wyalusing S.P.	73	F3	42.978770 -91.118560
Yellowstone Lake S.P.	74	A4	42.777360 -89.993540

WYOMING	PAGE	GRID	LATITUDE LONGITUDE
National Park & Rec. Areas			
Devils Tower Natl. Mon.	25	E3	44.586870 -104.706710
Flaming Gorge N.R.A.	32	A3	41.254860 -109.611400
Fort Laramie N.H.S.	33	E2	42.202530 -104.558590
Fossil Butte Natl. Mon.	31	F2	41.855370 -110.782340
Grand Teton Natl. Park-Granite Canyon Ent.	23	F4	43.597990 -110.801640
Grand Teton Natl. Park-Moose Ent.	23	F4	43.655860 -110.718350
Grand Teton Natl. Park-Moran Ent.	23	F4	43.843640 -110.511950
John D. Rockefeller Jr. Mem. Parkway	24	A3	44.108800 -110.685508
Medicine Wheel Natl. Hist. Landmark	24	C2	44.826200 -107.921717
Yellowstone Natl. Park-East Ent.	23	F3	44.489540 -110.001560
Yellowstone Natl. Park-North East Ent.	23	F3	45.006120 -109.991550
Yellowstone Natl. Park-North Ent.	23	F3	45.030110 -110.705460
Yellowstone Natl. Park-South Ent.	23	F3	44.134730 -110.666170
Yellowstone Natl. Park-West Ent.	23	F3	44.658720 -111.098970
State Park & Rec. Areas			
Bear River S.P.	31	F3	41.267257 -110.938030
Boysen S.P.	32	C1	43.270160 -108.115260
Buffalo Bill S.P.	24	B3	44.505020 -109.249540
Curt Gowdy S.P.	33	E3	41.175380 -105.243640
Edness K. Wilkins S.P.	33	D1	42.857220 -106.177370
Glendo S.P.	33	E1	42.476060 -104.998910
Guernsey S.P.	33	E2	42.287400 -104.763460
Hot Springs S.P.	24	C4	43.653980 -108.201790
Keyhole S.P.	25	E3	44.356490 -104.825810
Seminoe S.P.	33	D2	42.150350 -106.905870
Sinks Canyon S.P.	32	B1	42.752600 -108.804770

CANADA

ALBERTA	PAGE	GRID	LATITUDE LONGITUDE
National Park & Rec. Areas			
Banff Natl. Park-Banff Vis. Ctr.	164	B2	51.177400 -115.570900
Banff Natl. Park-Lake Louise Vis. Ctr.	164	B2	51.425200 -116.178400
Banff Park Mus. N.H.S.	164	B3	51.174300 -115.571100
Bar U Ranch N.H.S.	164	C3	50.420300 -114.244400
Cave and Basin N.H.S.	164	B3	51.168300 -115.591400
Elk Island Natl. Park	159	D4	53.572500 -112.841900
Jasper Natl. Park-Icefield Center	164	A1	52.233500 -117.234800
Jasper Natl. Park-Jasper Information Center	164	A1	52.877300 -118.080900
Rocky Mtn. House N.H.S.	164	C2	52.377590 -114.931237
Waterton Lakes Natl. Park-Waterton Vis. Ctr.	164	C4	49.051400 -113.906300
Wood Buffalo Natl. Park-Fort Chipewyan Vis. Ctr.	155	F2	48.714100 -111.154300
Provincial Park & Rec. Areas			
Aspen Beach Prov. Park	164	C2	52.454530 -113.975750
Beauvais Lake Prov. Park	164	C4	49.409500 -114.117000
Big Hill Springs Prov. Park	164	C3	51.251670 -114.386940
Big Knife Prov. Park	165	D2	52.489720 -112.210560
Birch Mts. Wildland Prov. Park	159	D1	57.509400 -112.957000
Bluerock Wildland Prov. Park	164	C3	50.642300 -114.654000
Bob Creek Wildland Prov. Park	164	C4	49.973700 -114.286000
Bow Valley Prov. Park	164	C3	51.040400 -115.077000
Bow Valley Wildland Prov. Park	164	B3	51.032600 -115.259000
Brown-Lowery Prov. Park	164	C3	50.813900 -114.430600
Calling Lake Prov. Park	159	D3	55.179720 -113.272500
Caribou Mts. Wildland Prov. Park	155	F3	59.205600 -114.897000
Carson-Pegasus Prov. Park	158	C3	54.295800 -115.645000
Castle Wildland Prov. Park	164	C4	49.306456 -114.299287
Chain Lakes Prov. Park	164	C3	50.200000 -114.183330
Chinchaga Wildland Prov. Park	158	B1	57.163400 -119.582000
Cold Lake Prov. Park	159	E3	54.602400 -110.072000
Cold Lake Prov. Park-North Shore	159	E3	54.644800 -110.103600
Crimson Lake Prov. Park	164	C2	52.466900 -115.048000
Cross Lake Prov. Park	159	D3	54.649300 -113.791000
Crow Lake Prov. Park	159	D2	55.800456 -112.152014
Dillberry Lake Prov. Park	165	E1	52.570200 -110.030000
Dinosaur Prov. Park	165	D3	50.770100 -111.480000
Don Getty Wildland Prov. Park	164	B2	50.893000 -114.993000
Dry Island Buffalo Jump Prov. Park	164	C2	51.929500 -112.975000
Dunvegan Prov. Park	158	B2	55.923600 -118.594400
Dunvegan West Wildland Prov. Park	158	B2	56.088900 -119.297000
Elbow Sheep Wildland Prov. Park	164	C3	50.703500 -114.939000
Fort Assiniboine Sandhills Wildland Prov. Park	158	C3	54.387100 -114.608000
Garner Lake Prov. Park	159	D3	54.183420 -111.741000
Gipsy Lake Wildland Prov. Park	159	E2	56.493500 -110.386000
Gooseberry Lake Prov. Park	165	D2	52.116940 -110.759170
Grand Rapids Wildland Prov. Park	159	D1	56.484200 -112.343000
Greene Valley Prov. Park	158	B2	56.140900 -117.242000
Gregoire Lake Prov. Park	159	E1	56.485000 -111.182780
Grizzly Ridge Wildland Prov. Park	158	C3	55.137700 -115.049000
Hay-Zama Lakes Wildland Prov. Park	155	F3	58.774100 -119.016000
Hilliard's Bay Prov. Park	158	C2	55.502900 -116.001000
Hubert Lake Wildland Prov. Park	158	C3	54.554100 -114.244000
Kakwa Wildland Prov. Park	158	A3	54.034600 -119.810000
Kinbrook Island Prov. Park	165	D3	50.437189 -111.910595
La Biche River Wildland Prov. Park	159	D3	54.987000 -112.626000
Lakeland Prov. Park	159	E3	54.759300 -111.557000
Lakeland Prov. Rec. Area	159	E3	54.721800 -111.398000
Lesser Slave Lake Prov. Park	158	C2	55.448000 -114.817000
Lesser Slave Lake Wildland Prov. Park	158	C2	55.497700 -115.567000
Little Bow Prov. Park	164	C3	50.227930 -112.926590
Little Fish Lake Prov. Park	165	D2	51.374246 -112.200944
Long Lake Prov. Park	159	D3	54.439986 -112.763465
Marguerite River Wildland Prov. Park	159	E1	57.638400 -110.266000
Midland Prov. Park	165	D2	51.478295 -112.771085
Miquelon Lake Prov. Park	159	D4	53.246900 -112.874000
Moonshine Lake Prov. Park	158	B2	55.883800 -119.216000
Moose Lake Prov. Park	159	E3	54.272986 -110.931143
Notikewin Prov. Park	158	C1	57.218300 -117.148000
Obed Lake Prov. Park	158	B4	53.558200 -117.101000
O'Brien Prov. Park	158	B3	55.065242 -118.822285
Otter-Orloff Lakes Wildland Prov. Park	159	D2	55.364200 -113.551000
Park Lake Prov. Park	164	C4	49.806621 -112.924681
Peace River Wildland Prov. Park	158	B2	55.983200 -117.765000
Pembina River Prov. Park	158	C4	53.611859 -114.985313
Peter Lougheed Prov. Park	164	B3	50.684100 -115.184000
Pigeon Lake Prov. Park	164	C1	53.029547 -114.150507
Police Outpost Prov. Park	164	C4	49.004503 -113.464980
Queen Elizabeth Prov. Park	158	B2	56.219128 -117.693540
Red Lodge Prov. Park	164	C2	51.947917 -114.243862
Rochon Sands Prov. Park	165	D2	52.461755 -112.892373
Rock Lake Solomon Creek Wildland Prov. Park	158	B4	53.413700 -118.118000
Saskatoon Island Prov. Park	158	B2	55.205201 -119.085401
Sheep River Prov. Park	164	C3	50.647300 -114.660000
Sir Winston Churchill Prov. Park	159	D3	54.832050 -111.976109
Spray Valley Prov. Park	164	B3	50.888700 -115.293000
Stony Mtn. Wildland Prov. Park	159	E2	56.211500 -111.244000
Sundance Prov. Park	158	B4	53.668700 -116.926000
Sylvan Lake Prov. Park	164	C2	52.315760 -114.092272
Thunder Lake Prov. Park	158	C3	54.131941 -114.725882
Tillebrook Prov. Park	165	D3	50.538593 -111.812268
Vermilion Prov. Park	159	E4	53.367679 -110.909771
Wabamun Lake Prov. Park	158	C4	53.565029 -114.441575
Whitehorse Wildland Prov. Park	164	B1	52.957900 -117.395000
Whitemud Falls Wildland Prov. Park	159	E1	56.703400 -110.084000
Whitney Lakes Prov. Park	159	E4	53.847100 -110.537000
William A. Switzer Prov. Park	158	B4	53.492000 -117.804000
Williamson Prov. Park	158	B3	55.081821 -117.560174
Willow Creek Prov. Park	164	C3	50.118067 -113.776021
Winagami Lake Prov. Park	158	C2	55.627500 -116.738000
Winagami Wildland Prov. Park	158	C2	55.611900 -116.635000
Woolford Prov. Park	164	C4	49.178498 -113.190438
Writing-On-Stone Prov. Park	165	D4	49.061400 -111.639000
Wyndham-Carseland Prov. Park	164	C3	50.827750 -113.436542
Young's Point Prov. Park	158	B3	55.148000 -117.572000

BRITISH COLUMBIA	PAGE	GRID	LATITUDE LONGITUDE
National Park & Rec. Areas			
Chilkoot Trail N.H.S.	155	D3	59.756667 -134.960833
Fort Langley N.H.S.	163	D3	49.168056 -122.569167
Fort McLeod N.H.S.	157	E1	54.992384 -123.039629
Fort Saint James N.H.S.	157	D2	54.440278 -124.255556
Gitwangak Battle Hill N.H.S.	156	C1	55.119444 -128.018056
Glacier Natl. Park-Eastern Welcome Sta.	164	A2	51.511700 -117.442000
Glacier Natl. Park-Rogers Pass Discovery Center	164	A2	51.300600 -117.521500
Gulf Islands Natl. Park Res.	163	D4	48.769400 -123.210000
Gulf of Georgia Cannery N.H.S.	163	D3	49.124722 -123.199722
Gwaii Haanas Natl. Park Res. & Haida Heritage Site	156	A3	52.349722 -131.433056
Kootenay Natl. Park-Radium Hot Springs Vis. Ctr.	164	B3	50.619500 -116.069800
Kootenay Natl. Park-Vermilion Crossing Vis. Ctr.	164	B3	51.000000 -115.966000
Mount Revelstoke Natl. Park-Western Welcome Sta.	164	A2	51.042000 -117.983900
Pacific Rim Natl. Park Res.-Broken Group Islands	162	B3	48.891100 -125.300800
Pacific Rim Natl. Park Res.-Pacific Rim Vis. Ctr.	162	B3	48.992000 -125.587200
Pacific Rim Natl. Park Res.-West Coast Trail	162	C4	48.704800 -124.866100
Pacific Rim Natl. Park Res.-Wickaninnish Interpretive Center	162	B3	49.012700 -125.674200
Yoho Natl. Park-Field Vis. Ctr.	164	B2	51.397800 -116.492000
Provincial Park & Rec. Areas			
Akamina-Kishinena Prov. Park	164	C4	49.032700 -114.178000
Alexandra Bridge Prov. Park	163	E2	49.700000 -121.399722
Alice Lake Prov. Park	163	D2	49.783056 -123.116667
Allison Lake Prov. Park	163	F2	49.683056 -120.599722
Anstey Hunakwa Prov. Park	164	A2	51.140600 -118.924300
Arctic Pacific Lakes Prov. Park	157	E2	54.384400 -121.553000
Arrow Lakes Prov. Park	164	A3	49.883056 -118.065667
Arrowstone Prov. Park	163	E1	50.879900 -121.273000
Atlin Prov. Park	155	E3	59.165400 -133.914000
Babine Lake-Pendleton Bay Marine Prov. Park	157	D2	54.533000 -125.724800
Babine Lake-Smithers Landing Marine Prov. Park	156	C1	55.098400 -126.600000
Babine Mountains Prov. Park	156	C1	54.913100 -126.928000
Babine River Corridor Prov. Park	156	C1	55.577400 -127.032000
Barkerville Prov. Park	157	E3	53.088889 -121.510833
Bear Creek Prov. Park	163	F2	49.930556 -119.520556
Bearhole Lake Prov. Park	158	A3	55.043400 -120.568000
Beatton Prov. Park	158	A1	56.333056 -120.933056
Beaumont Prov. Park	157	D2	54.050000 -124.616667
Beaver Creek Prov. Park	164	A4	49.066667 -117.600000
Big Bar Lake Prov. Park	157	E4	51.316667 -121.816667
Big Bunsby Marine Prov. Park	162	A2	50.120800 -127.504200
Big Creek Prov. Park	157	E4	51.301500 -123.158000
Bijoux Falls Prov. Park	157	E1	55.300000 -122.666667
Birkenhead Lake Prov. Park	163	D1	50.577900 -122.737000
Bishop River Prov. Park	162	C1	50.912500 -124.038000
Blanket Creek Prov. Park	164	A3	50.833056 -118.083056
Bligh Island Marine Prov. Park	162	A2	49.633300 -126.553000
Bowron Lake Prov. Park	157	F3	53.174100 -121.012000
Boya Lake Prov. Park	155	E3	59.380500 -129.090000
Brandywine Falls Prov. Park	163	D2	50.033056 -123.116667
Bridal Veil Falls Prov. Park	163	E3	49.183056 -121.733056
Bridge Lake Prov. Park	157	F4	51.483056 -120.700000
Bromley Rock Prov. Park	163	F3	49.416667 -120.258056
Brooks Peninsula Prov. Park	162	A2	50.180300 -127.657000
Broughton Archipelago Marine Prov. Park	162	A1	50.687100 -126.663000
Bugaboo Prov. Park	164	B3	50.794700 -116.808000
Callaghan Lake Prov. Park	163	D2	50.206900 -123.189000
Bull Canyon Prov. Park	157	E4	52.091667 -123.374722
Canal Flats Prov. Park	164	B3	50.183056 -115.816667
Canim Beach Prov. Park	157	F4	51.816667 -120.872667
Cape Scott Prov. Park	162	A1	50.765900 -128.246000
Cariboo Mts. Prov. Park	157	F3	52.852600 -120.538000
Cariboo River Prov. Park	157	F3	52.873600 -121.22
Carmanah Walbran Prov. Park	162	C4	48.654500 -124.62
Carp Lake Prov. Park	157	E2	54.769400 -123.38
Catala Island Marine Prov. Park	162	A2	49.835833 -127.05
Cathedral Prov. Park	163	F3	49.069800 -120.17
Champion Lakes Prov. Park	164	A4	49.184100 -117.62
Charlie Lake Prov. Park	158	A1	56.316667 -120.99
Chasm Prov. Park	157	F4	51.178900 -121.43
Chilliwack Lake Prov. Park	163	E3	49.072200 -121.43
Clayoquot Arm Prov. Park	162	B3	49.172800 -125.56
Clayoquot Plateau Prov. Park	162	B3	49.225100 -125.42
Clendinning Prov. Park	162	C1	50.429700 -123.73
Codville Lagoon Marine Prov. Park	156	C4	52.060833 -127.85
Conkle Lake Prov. Park	164	A4	49.166667 -119.10
Coquihalla Canyon Prov. Park	163	E3	49.371944 -121.36
Cormorant Channel Marine Prov. Park	162	A1	50.593500 -126.85
Cowichan River Prov. Park	162	C4	48.780800 -123.92
Crooked River Prov. Park	157	E2	54.466667 -122.66
Crowsnest Prov. Park	164	C4	49.649722 -114.69
Cummins Lakes Prov. Park	164	A2	52.104100 -118.06
Cypress Prov. Park	163	D3	49.425800 -123.209
Dahl Lake Prov. Park	157	E2	53.769900 -123.293
Desolation Sound Marine Prov. Park	162	C2	50.101100 -124.71
Diana Lake Prov. Park	156	B2	54.216667 -130.166
Downing Prov. Park	163	E1	51.000000 -121.783
Dry Gulch Prov. Park	164	B3	50.583056 -116.033
Duffey Lake Prov. Park	163	D1	50.407500 -122.337
Dune Za Keyih Prov. Park	155	E3	58.323000 -126.355
Echo Lake Prov. Park	164	A3	50.199722 -118.700
Edge Hills Prov. Park	163	E1	51.035900 -121.871
Elk Falls Prov. Park	162	B2	50.041000 -125.324
Elk Lakes Prov. Park	164	C3	50.480800 -115.088
Ellison Prov. Park	164	A3	50.173333 -119.433
Emory Creek Prov. Park	163	E3	49.516667 -121.416
Eneas Lakes Prov. Park	163	F2	49.752400 -119.936
Entiako Prov. Park	157	D3	53.221500 -125.443
Epper Passage Prov. Park	162	B3	49.219167 -125.949
Eskers Prov. Park	157	E2	54.081300 -123.205
Ethel F. Wilson Mem. Prov. Park	157	D2	54.416667 -125.683
Fillongley Prov. Park	162	C3	49.534100 -124.755
Finger-Tatuk Prov. Park	157	D2	53.515600 -124.226
Flat Lake Prov. Park	157	F4	51.499400 -121.521
Flores Island Prov. Park	162	B3	49.291000 -126.173
Francois Lake Prov. Park	157	D2	53.966667 -125.166
French Beach Prov. Park	162	C4	48.383056 -123.933
Garibaldi Prov. Park	163	D2	49.943200 -122.751
Gibson Marine Prov. Park	162	B3	49.266667 -126.066
Gitnadoiks River Prov. Park	156	B2	54.161700 -129.162
Gladstone Prov. Park	164	A4	49.268900 -118.269
God's Pocket Marine Prov. Park	162	A1	50.837200 -127.562
Goldpan Prov. Park	163	E2	50.350000 -121.383
Gordon Bay Prov. Park	162	C4	48.833056 -124.199
Graham-Laurier Prov. Park	155	F4	56.594900 -123.466
Graystokes Prov. Park	164	A3	49.986200 -118.850
Green Inlet Marine Prov. Park	156	C3	52.918167 -128.485
Green Lake Prov. Park	157	F4	51.400000 -121.199
Hamber Prov. Park	164	A2	52.380300 -117.882
Harmony Islands Marine Prov. Park	162	C2	49.862222 -124.012
Ha'thayim Marine Prov. Park	162	C2	50.169400 -124.955
Heather-Dina Lakes Prov. Park	157	E1	55.508300 -123.285
Height of the Rockies Prov. Park	164	B3	50.488900 -115.228
Herald Prov. Park	164	A3	50.788056 -119.201
Hesquiat Lake Prov. Park	162	B3	49.500000 -126.385
Hitchie Creek Prov. Park	162	C4	48.795556 -124.737
Horne Lake Caves Prov. Park	162	C3	49.344167 -124.755
Horsefly Lake Prov. Park	157	F3	52.383056 -121.300
Inkaneep Prov. Park	163	F3	49.233056 -119.533
Inland Lake Prov. Park	162	C2	49.953800 -124.481
Itcha Ilgachuz Prov. Park	157	D3	52.711500 -124.9740
Jackman Flats Prov. Park	164	A1	52.950000 -119.4166
Jedediah Island Marine Prov. Park	162	C3	49.500000 -124.1997
Jewel Lake Prov. Park	164	A4	49.183056 -118.5997
Jimsmith Lake Prov. Park	164	B4	49.483056 -115.833
Joffre Lakes Prov. Park	163	D2	50.344100 -122.477
Johnstone Creek Prov. Park	164	A4	49.050000 -119.0497
Juan De Fuca Prov. Park	162	C4	48.489800 -124.2900
Junction Sheep Range Prov. Park	157	E4	51.801000 -122.4350
Juniper Beach Prov. Park	163	E1	50.785833 -121.0830
Kakwa Prov. Park & Protected Area	158	A3	54.057200 -120.2960
Kekuli Bay Prov. Park	164	A3	50.183056 -119.3402
Kentucky-Alleyne Prov. Park	163	F2	49.916667 -120.5666
Kianuko Prov. Park	164	B4	49.421600 -116.4560
Kikomun Creek Prov. Park	164	B4	49.233056 -115.2500
Kilby Prov. Park	163	E3	49.237500 -121.9608
Kinaskan Lake Prov. Park	155	E4	57.496100 -130.2340
Kiskatinaw Prov. Park	158	A2	55.950000 -120.5666
Kleanza Creek Prov. Park	156	C2	54.599722 -128.3997
Klewnuggit Inlet Marine Prov. Park	156	B2	53.688500 -129.6970
Kluskoil Lake Prov. Park	157	D3	53.202900 -123.8920
Kokanee Creek Prov. Park	164	B4	49.605722 -117.1330
Kokanee Glacier Prov. Park	164	B4	49.781800 -117.1360
Kootenay Lake Prov. Park	164	B3	50.085000 -116.9311

›dacha Wilderness Prov. Park	155	E3	57.820400 -125.058000
›e Jeune Prov. Park	163	F1	50.483056 -120.483056
›lse Lake Prov. Park	156	C2	54.398900 -128.533000
› Point Prov. Park	162	A1	50.333056 -127.966667
›hart Beach Prov. Park	164	B4	49.516667 -116.783056
›hart Creek Prov. Park	164	B4	49.497300 -116.705000
›land Bay Prov. Park	162	B2	50.049722 -125.450000
›e Inlet Marine Prov. Park	156	B2	53.555556 -129.580278
›Millan Prov. Park	162	C3	49.283056 -124.666667
› Lake Prov. Park	162	B2	50.210000 -125.215000
›sons Landing Prov. Park	162	C2	50.121500 -124.928300
›uinna Marine Prov. Park	162	B3	49.390500 -126.342000
›ble River Prov. Park	162	A1	50.544300 -127.526000
›ha Creek Prov. Park	164	A3	51.141667 -118.198122
›onnell Lake Prov. Park	163	F1	50.521944 -120.456667
›onald Creek Prov. Park	164	A3	50.131056 -117.813667
›atl Creek Prov. Park	163	E2	50.036100 -122.054000
›erly Lake Prov. Park	158	A2	55.800000 -121.700000
›nich Lakes Prov. Park	164	A2	51.327200 -119.353000
›ck Prov. Park	163	F2	50.178667 -120.533056
›se Valley Prov. Park	157	E4	51.649800 -121.648000
›ton Lake Prov. Park	162	B2	50.116667 -125.483056
›nt Assiniboine Prov. Park	164	B3	50.937400 -115.761000
›nt Blanchet Prov. Park	157	D1	55.275500 -125.863000
›nt Fernie Prov. Park	164	C4	49.483056 -115.099722
›nt Pope Prov. Park	157	D2	54.490700 -124.331000
›nt Robson Prov. Park	164	A1	52.927000 -118.831000
›nt Seymour Prov. Park	163	D3	49.392400 -122.926000
›nt Terry Fox Prov. Park	164	A1	52.940800 -119.254000
›ie Lake Prov. Park	164	B4	49.373333 -115.837222
›a-Bellevue Prov. Park	164	A4	49.752100 -119.374000
›atlatch Prov. Park	163	E2	49.980200 -121.780000
›oon Prov. Park	156	A2	53.863400 -131.889000
›n Falls Prov. Park	163	D2	50.283056 -122.833056
›cy Greene Prov. Park	164	A4	49.250000 -117.933056
›el Plate Prov. Park	163	F3	49.399722 -119.949722
›olum River Prov. Park	163	E3	49.366667 -121.341667
›pkish Lake Prov. Park	162	A2	50.337700 -127.005000
›onlith Lake Prov. Park	163	F1	50.795556 -119.777778
›bury Lake Prov. Park	164	B4	49.533056 -115.483056
›hatlitz Prov. Park	162	A2	49.815700 -126.981000
›opus Island Marine Prov. Park	162	B2	50.278400 -125.242100
›nagan Lake Prov. Park	163	F2	49.683056 -119.719867
›nagan Mtn. Prov. Park	163	F2	49.724600 -119.629000
›over Arm Prov. Park	162	C2	49.999722 -124.726667
› Island Lake Prov. Park	158	A2	55.300000 -120.266667
›ens Beach Prov. Park	157	D2	54.416667 -124.399722
› Lake Prov. Park	163	F1	50.741667 -120.120556
›econe Burke Prov. Park	163	D3	49.526200 -122.721000
›boise Bay Prov. Park	162	C3	49.516667 -123.749722
›eau Cove Prov. Park	163	D3	49.549722 -123.233056
›nier Lake Prov. Park	164	B4	49.900000 -115.650000
›cess Louisa Marine Prov. Park	162	C2	50.203722 -123.766667
›migan Creek Prov. Park	157	F2	53.487600 -120.880000
›tchesakut Lake Prov. Park	157	E3	52.983056 -122.933056
›den Lake Prov. Park	157	E2	53.928000 -121.912000
›tsino Prov. Park	162	A1	50.491667 -127.816667
›rguard Falls Prov. Park	157	F3	52.973333 -119.366667
›fern-Keily Prov. Park	155	F3	57.405600 -123.878000
›berts Creek Prov. Park	162	C3	49.433056 -123.666667
›ley Lake Prov. Park	163	D3	49.250000 -122.400000
›sebery Prov. Park	164	B3	50.033056 -117.400000
›yrock Lake Prov. Park	157	D2	54.677100 -125.348000
›kle Prov. Park	163	D4	48.766667 -123.383056
›gged Point Marine Prov. Park	162	A2	49.963889 -127.238889
›nt Mary's Alpine Prov. Park	164	B4	49.877000 -116.348000
›dy Island Marine Prov. Park	162	C3	49.616667 -124.849722
›oen Lake Prov. Park	162	B2	50.176500 -126.245000
›oolhouse Lake Prov. Park	157	F4	51.883600 -120.993000
›eley Lake Prov. Park	156	C1	55.199722 -127.683056
›ven Sisters Prov. Park	156	C1	54.946900 -128.150000
›ver Beach Prov. Park	164	A2	51.240278 -118.955556
›ver Lake Prov. Park	163	E3	49.316667 -121.399722
›ver Star Prov. Park	164	A3	50.376900 -119.082000
›nson Prov. Park	162	C3	49.479700 -123.962900
›hist Prov. Park	163	E2	50.249722 -121.500000
›ookumchuck Narrows Prov. Park	162	C2	49.744700 -123.915500
›elt Bay Prov. Park	162	C2	50.033056 -124.983056
›vchea Bay Prov. Park	157	D2	54.419167 -124.448333
›oat Lake Prov. Park	162	C3	49.300000 -124.916667
›uitty Bay Prov. Park	162	C3	49.454167 -124.166667
›gleap Prov. Park	164	B4	49.058700 -117.048000
›elhead Prov. Park	163	E1	50.752778 -120.868056
›mwinder Prov. Park	163	F3	49.366667 -120.133056
›ne Mtn. Prov. Park	155	E3	58.588600 -124.757000
›athcona Prov. Park	162	B2	49.629300 -125.710000
›art Lake Marine Prov. Park	157	D2	54.650000 -125.000000
›garbowl Prov. Park	157	E2	53.828000 -121.589000
›kunka Falls Prov. Park	157	E1	55.316667 -121.700000
›phur Passage Prov. Park	162	B3	49.412000 -126.094000
›mmit Lake Prov. Park	164	A3	50.150000 -117.666667
›rge Narrows Prov. Park	162	B2	50.233056 -125.149722
Sutherland River Prov. Park	157	D2	54.338300 -124.818000
Sydney Inlet Prov. Park	162	B3	49.480000 -126.283000
Syringa Prov. Park	164	A4	49.378000 -117.906000
Tahsish-Kwois Prov. Park	162	A2	50.189100 -127.161000
Tatlatui Prov. Park	155	E4	56.996200 -127.386000
Tatshenshini-Alsek Prov. Park	155	D3	59.595900 -137.443000
Taylor Arm Prov. Park	162	B3	49.283056 -125.049722
Ten Mile Lake Prov. Park	157	E3	53.066667 -122.450000
Thurston Bay Marine Prov. Park	162	B2	50.383056 -125.316667
Ts'il-os Prov. Park	157	D4	51.191700 -123.971000
Tudyah Lake Prov. Park	157	E1	55.066667 -123.033056
Tunkwa Prov. Park	163	E1	50.615200 -120.887000
Tyhee Lake Prov. Park	156	C2	54.700000 -127.033056
Union Passage Marine Prov. Park	156	B3	53.410900 -129.436000
Upper Adams River Prov. Park	164	A2	51.682700 -119.228000
Valhalla Prov. Park	164	A4	49.873700 -117.567000
Vargas Island Prov. Park	162	B3	49.174000 -126.031000
Vaseux Lake Prov. Park	164	A4	49.268200 -119.474000
Walsh Cove Prov. Park	162	C2	50.268056 -124.800000
Wasa Lake Prov. Park	164	B4	49.793056 -115.738056
West Arm Prov. Park	164	B4	49.507000 -117.118000
West Lake Prov. Park	157	E2	53.733056 -122.866667
Whiskers Point Prov. Park	157	E1	54.900000 -122.933056
White Pelican Prov. Park	157	E3	52.284000 -123.031000
Whiteswan Lake Prov. Park	164	B3	50.145300 -115.487000
Woss Lake Prov. Park	162	A2	50.060400 -126.626000
Yahk Provincial Park	164	B4	49.083056 -116.083056
Yard Creek Prov. Park	164	A3	50.899722 -118.799722

MANITOBA	PAGE	GRID	LATITUDE LONGITUDE
National Park & Rec. Areas			
Lower Fort Garry N.H.S.	167	E3	50.136850 -96.940569
Riding Mtn. Natl. Park-Deep Lake Ranger Sta.	167	D3	50.860300 -100.836600
Riding Mtn. Natl. Park-Lake Audy Ranger Sta.	167	D3	50.712900 -100.230600
Riding Mtn. Natl. Park-McKinnon Creek Ranger Sta.	167	D3	50.787100 -99.579500
Riding Mtn. Natl. Park-Moon Lake Ranger Sta.	167	D3	50.995900 -100.067200
Riding Mtn. Natl. Park-South Lake Ranger Sta.	167	D3	50.655200 -100.061600
Riding Mtn. Natl. Park-Sugarloaf Ranger Sta.	167	D3	50.985300 -100.742100
Riding Mtn. Natl. Park-Whirlpool Ranger Sta.	167	D3	50.683300 -99.553500
Provincial Park & Rec. Areas			
Asessippi Prov. Park	166	C3	50.966400 -101.379700
Atikaki Prov. Wilderness Park	167	F2	51.532200 -95.547000
Bakers Narrows Prov. Park	161	D3	54.671100 -101.675000
Beaudry Prov. Park	167	E4	49.853900 -97.473300
Bell Lake Prov. Park	166	C1	52.541700 -101.241400
Birds Hill Prov. Park	167	E3	50.028800 -96.893200
Camp Morton Prov. Park	167	E3	50.710000 -96.990300
Clearwater Lake Prov. Park	161	D3	54.096200 -101.162000
Criddle–Vane Homestead Prov. Park	167	D4	49.707600 -99.596600
Duck Mtn. Prov. Park	167	D2	51.715600 -101.112000
Elk Island Prov. Park	167	E3	50.758300 -96.536500
Grand Beach Prov. Park	167	E3	50.567900 -96.554900
Grass River Prov. Park	161	D3	54.655500 -101.092000
Hecla–Grindstone Prov. Park	167	E2	51.198300 -96.660200
Hnausa Beach Prov. Park	167	E3	50.900300 -96.992200
Kettle Stones Prov. Park	167	D2	52.359200 -100.595300
Lake Saint George Prov. Park	167	E2	51.719703 -97.406772
Lundar Beach Prov. Park	167	E3	50.724000 -98.273000
Manipogo Prov. Park	167	D2	51.517000 -99.550000
Nopiming Prov. Park	167	F3	50.665200 -95.305600
North Steeprock Lake Prov. Park	166	C1	52.611800 -101.380000
Paint Lake Prov. Park	161	E2	55.492100 -98.018000
Patricia Beach Prov. Park	167	E3	50.467300 -96.575300
Pembina Valley Prov. Park	167	E4	49.038500 -98.296400
Pinawa Dam Prov. Park	167	F3	50.145200 -95.945700
Rainbow Beach Prov. Park	167	D3	51.099400 -99.718400
Saint Ambroise Beach Prov. Park	167	E3	50.275500 -98.074300
Saint Malo Prov. Park	167	E4	49.321400 -96.930490
South Atikaki Prov. Park	167	F3	51.041400 -95.417600
Spruce Woods Prov. Park	167	D4	49.703100 -99.141900
Stephenfield Prov. Park	167	E4	49.523400 -98.300500
Turtle Mtn. Prov. Park	167	D4	49.041500 -100.216000
Watchorn Prov. Park	167	E2	51.293100 -98.598500
Whitefish Lake Prov. Park	166	C2	52.333900 -101.587100
Whiteshell Prov. Park	167	F3	50.140900 -95.584400
William Lake Prov. Park	167	D4	49.055000 -100.038800
Winnipeg Beach Prov. Park	167	E3	50.512300 -96.967000

NEW BRUNSWICK	PAGE	GRID	LATITUDE LONGITUDE
National Park & Rec. Areas			
Beaubears Island N.H.S.	179	D3	46.972778 -65.569444
Fort Beauséjour N.H.S.	180	C1	45.865278 -64.290278
Fort Gaspareaux N.H.S.	180	C1	46.040833 -64.072778
Fundy Natl. Park-Vis. Ctr.	180	C1	45.659500 -65.132600
Kouchibouguac Natl. Park-Vis. Ctr.	179	D3	46.773200 -65.004900
Monument Lefebvre N.H.S.	180	C1	45.979167 -64.567222
Roosevelt Campobello International Park	180	A2	44.849722 -66.949722
Saint Andrews Blockhouse N.H.S.	180	A2	45.076389 -67.063889
Saint Croix Island International Hist. Site	180	A2	45.127778 -67.133333
Provincial Park & Rec. Areas			
De la République Prov. Park	178	B3	47.442778 -68.395556
Herring Cove Prov. Park	180	A2	44.866667 -66.933056
Mactaquac Prov. Park	180	A1	45.959025 -66.892556
Mount Carleton Prov. Park	178	C3	47.392300 -66.835500
Murray Beach Prov. Park	180	C1	46.016667 -63.983056
New River Beach Prov. Park	180	A2	45.133056 -66.533056
Parlee Beach Prov. Park	180	C1	46.233056 -64.499722
Sugarloaf Prov. Park	178	C2	47.974000 -66.671900
The Anchorage Prov. Park	180	A3	44.649722 -66.800000

NEWFOUNDLAND & LABRADOR	PAGE	GRID	LATITUDE LONGITUDE
National Park & Rec. Areas			
Castle Hill N.H.S.	183	E4	47.251389 -53.971111
Gros Morne Natl. Park-Vis. Ctr.	182	C2	49.571500 -57.877900
Hawthorne Cottage N.H.S.	183	E4	47.543333 -53.210833
L'Anse aux Meadows N.H.S.	183	F1	51.595000 -55.532778
Port au Choix N.H.S.	182	C1	50.712222 -57.375278
Red Bay N.H.S.	183	F1	51.733056 -56.415556
Ryan Premises N.H.S.	183	E3	48.648056 -53.112500
Terra Nova Natl. Park-Information Center	183	E3	48.394900 -54.204000
Terra Nova Natl. Park-Saltons Vis. Ctr.	183	E3	48.580600 -53.958900
Provincial Park & Rec. Areas			
Barachois Pond Prov. Park	182	C3	48.477100 -58.256600
Blow Me Down Prov. Park	182	C2	49.090833 -58.364444
Butter Pot Prov. Park	183	F4	47.390900 -53.071300
Chance Cove Prov. Park	183	F4	46.776900 -53.045400
Codroy Valley Prov. Park	182	C4	47.833333 -59.337778
Deadman's Bay Prov. Park	183	E2	49.331389 -53.692500
Dildo Run Prov. Park	183	E2	49.535556 -54.721667
Dungeon Prov. Park	183	E3	48.666667 -53.083611
Frenchman's Cove Prov. Park	183	D4	47.209444 -55.401667
Gooseberry Cove Prov. Park	183	E4	47.068056 -54.087778
J.T. Cheeseman Prov. Park	182	C4	47.631111 -59.249444
La Manche Prov. Park	183	F4	47.175200 -52.901200
Lockston Path Prov. Park	183	E3	48.437778 -53.379722
Notre Dame Prov. Park	183	E2	49.115833 -55.086389
Pinware River Prov. Park	183	F1	51.631667 -56.704167
Sandbanks Prov. Park	182	C4	47.607222 -57.646944
Sir Richard Squires Mem. Prov. Park	183	D2	49.354000 -57.213400
The Arches Prov. Park	182	C2	50.113333 -57.663056

NORTHWEST TERRITORIES	PAGE	GRID	LATITUDE LONGITUDE
National Park & Rec. Areas			
Nááts'ihch'oh Natl. Park Res.	155	E2	62.617399 -128.787113
Nahanni Natl. Park Res.	155	E3	61.083333 -123.600000
Tuktut Nogait Natl. Park	155	E1	69.283333 -123.016667

NOVA SCOTIA	PAGE	GRID	LATITUDE LONGITUDE
National Park & Rec. Areas			
Alexander Graham Bell N.H.S.	181	F1	46.102778 -60.745556
Cape Breton Highlands Natl. Park-East Ent.	182	B4	46.642800 -60.404200
Cape Breton Highlands Natl. Park-West Ent.	182	B4	46.647300 -60.950200
Fort Anne N.H.S.	180	B3	44.741667 -65.519167
Fort Edward N.H.S.	180	C2	44.995556 -64.135278
Fortress of Louisbourg N.H.S.	181	F1	45.900300 -59.995100
Grand-Pré N.H.S.	180	C2	45.108889 -64.311944
Grassy Island N.H.S.	181	F2	45.336667 -60.973611
Kejimkujik Natl. Park (Seaside Adjunct)	180	C4	43.865800 -64.836900
Kejimkujik Natl. Park and N.H.S.	180	B3	44.336700 -65.268200
Marconi N.H.S.	181	F4	46.211111 -59.952778
Port-Royal N.H.S.	180	B3	44.712500 -65.610556
Saint Peters Canal N.H.S.	181	F1	45.655556 -60.870556
York Redoubt N.H.S.	181	D3	44.596583 -63.552439
Provincial Park & Rec. Areas			
Amherst Shore Prov. Park	180	C1	45.961181 -63.879025
Battery Prov. Park	181	F1	45.657022 -60.866764
Beaver Mtn. Prov. Park	181	E2	45.567556 -62.153583
Blomidon Prov. Park	180	C2	45.255869 -64.352056
Boylston Prov. Park	181	E2	45.426839 -61.510603
Cape Chignecto Prov. Park	180	C2	45.375800 -64.891300
Caribou–Munroes Island Prov. Park	181	D1	45.721800 -62.656914
Ellenwood Lake Prov. Park	180	B4	43.929481 -66.005700
Five Islands Prov. Park	180	C2	45.407781 -64.021500
Graves Island Prov. Park	180	C3	44.565550 -64.218642
Laurie Prov. Park	181	D2	44.878175 -63.602194
Martinique Beach Prov. Park	181	D3	44.689911 -63.147567
Mira River Prov. Park	181	F1	46.026006 -60.037433
Porters Prov. Park	181	D3	44.691106 -63.308892
Rissers Beach Prov. Park	180	C3	44.232397 -64.423919
Salsman Prov. Park	181	E2	45.236856 -61.767150
Salt Springs Prov. Park	181	D2	45.545280 -62.878890
Shubenacadie Prov. Wildlife Park	181	D2	45.087222 -63.387500
Smileys Prov. Park	180	C2	45.013925 -63.961247
The Islands Prov. Park	180	B4	43.765503 -65.340347
Thomas Raddall Prov. Park	180	C4	43.844783 -64.919694
Valleyview Prov. Park	180	B2	44.875200 -65.316064
Wentworth Prov. Park	181	D2	45.627222 -63.567222
Whycocomagh Prov. Park	181	F1	45.968094 -61.109908

ONTARIO	PAGE	GRID	LATITUDE LONGITUDE
National Park & Rec. Areas			
Battle of the Windmill N.H.S.	174	B4	44.722778 -75.486944
Bell Homestead N.H.P.	172	C3	43.107946 -80.273060
Bellevue House N.H.S.	173	F1	44.220556 -76.506667
Bruce Peninsula Natl. Park	170	C4	45.189100 -81.485500
Fathom Five Natl. Marine Park	170	C4	45.304800 -81.727600
Fort George N.H.S.	173	D3	43.252778 -79.051111
Fort Henry N.H.S.	173	F1	44.230833 -76.459444
Fort Malden N.H.S.	172	A4	42.108056 -83.113889
Fort Mississauga N.H.S.	173	D3	43.260833 -79.076667
Fort Saint Joseph N.H.S.	170	B3	46.063889 -83.944167
Fort Wellington N.H.S.	174	B4	44.713889 -75.510833
Georgian Bay Islands Natl. Park-Welcome Center	171	D4	44.803900 -79.720400
Glengarry Cairn N.H.S.	174	C3	45.121667 -74.490278
Merrickville Blockhouse N.H.S.	174	B4	44.916667 -75.837500
Peterborough Lift Lock N.H.S.	173	E1	44.308056 -78.300556
Point Clark Lighthouse N.H.S.	172	B2	44.073056 -81.756667
Point Pelee Natl. Park-Park Ent. Kiosk	172	A4	41.987700 -82.549900
Point Pelee Natl. Park-Vis. Ctr.	172	A4	41.931700 -82.513500
Pukaskwa Natl. Park-Information Center	170	A2	48.700400 -86.197200
Queenston Heights N.H.S.	173	D3	43.158056 -79.052778
Sault Ste. Marie Canal N.H.S.	170	B3	46.511667 -84.355556
Sir John Johnson House N.H.S.	174	C4	45.144444 -74.580000
Southwold Earthworks N.H.S.	172	B3	42.677778 -81.351389
Thousand Islands Natl. Park-Vis. Ctr.	174	A4	44.452300 -75.860300
Trent-Severn Waterway N.H.S.	173	E1	44.137500 -77.590100
Woodside N.H.S.	172	C2	43.466667 -80.499722
Provincial Park & Rec. Areas			
Abitibi-De-Troyes Prov. Park	171	D1	48.786500 -80.066300
Albany River Prov. Park	169	E1	51.358200 -88.134000
Algonquin Prov. Park	171	E4	45.605300 -78.323900
Arrowhead Prov. Park	171	D4	45.391700 -79.197200
Awenda Prov. Park	172	C1	44.854400 -79.989800
Balsam Lake Prov. Park	173	D1	44.642000 -78.864000
Bass Lake Prov. Park	173	D1	44.602000 -79.475000
Batchawana Prov. Park	170	B3	46.941900 -84.587010
Blue Lake Prov. Park	168	B3	49.904200 -93.525600
Bon Echo Prov. Park	171	E4	44.905600 -77.246600
Bonnechere Prov. Park	171	E4	45.658400 -77.570800
Bonnechere River Prov. Park	171	E4	45.674400 -77.661500
Brightsand River Prov. Park	169	D3	49.936700 -90.265400
Bronte Creek Prov. Park	173	D2	43.410490 -79.767830
Caliper Lake Prov. Park	168	B3	49.061670 -93.912780
Carson Lake Prov. Park	171	E4	45.502780 -77.746390
Chapleau-Nemegosenda River Prov. Park	170	B2	48.262300 -83.035300
Charleston Lake Prov. Park	174	A4	44.515400 -76.013600
Chutes Prov. Park	170	C3	46.219510 -82.071480
Craigleith Prov. Park	172	C1	44.535000 -80.367000
Darlington Prov. Park	173	D2	43.875480 -78.778300
Devil's Glen Prov. Park	172	C1	44.361000 -80.207800
Driftwood Prov. Park	171	E3	46.179000 -77.843000
Earl Rowe Prov. Park	172	C1	44.150000 -79.898000
Emily Prov. Park	173	D1	44.340530 -78.532860
Esker Lakes Prov. Park	171	D2	48.290100 -79.906100
Fairbank Prov. Park	170	C3	46.468070 -81.440410
Ferris Prov. Park	173	E1	44.293000 -77.788000
Finlayson Point Prov. Park	171	D3	47.055000 -79.797000
Fitzroy Prov. Park	174	A3	45.482680 -76.209400
French River Prov. Park	171	D3	46.008600 -80.620900
Frontenac Prov. Park	174	A4	44.540500 -76.512700
Fushimi Lake Prov. Park	169	F3	49.824800 -83.913800
Greenwater Prov. Park	170	C1	49.215900 -81.291000
Grundy Lake Prov. Park	171	D4	45.939800 -80.530400
Halfway Lake Prov. Park	170	C3	46.905700 -81.650500
Inverhuron Prov. Park	172	B1	44.298000 -81.580000
Ivanhoe Lake Prov. Park	170	C2	47.957600 -82.742600
John E. Pearce Prov. Park	172	B4	42.617000 -81.444000
Kakabeka Falls Prov. Park	169	D4	48.403290 -89.624130
Kap-Kig-Iwan Prov. Park	171	D2	47.789960 -79.884990
Kettle Lakes Prov. Park	170	C1	48.569400 -80.865400
Killarney Prov. Park	170	C3	46.099400 -81.386900
Killbear Prov. Park	171	D4	45.346200 -80.191200
Kopka River Prov. Park	169	D2	50.006300 -89.493000
Lady Evelyn-Smoothwater Prov. Park	171	D2	47.368500 -80.489300
Lake of the Woods Prov. Park	168	B3	49.221200 -94.606000
Lake on the Mtn. Prov. Park	173	F1	44.039940 -77.056080
Lake Saint Peter Prov. Park	171	E4	45.322000 -78.024000
Lake Superior Prov. Park	170	A2	47.595200 -84.756500
Larder River Prov. Park	171	D2	47.936300 -79.642800
La Verendrye Prov. Park	169	D4	48.138300 -90.431300
Little Abitibi Prov. Park	170	C1	49.637900 -80.922900
Little Current River Prov. Park	169	E2	50.724100 -86.211000
Long Point Prov. Park	172	C4	42.565000 -80.306000
Lower Madawaska River Prov. Park	171	E4	45.236200 -77.289300
MacGregor Point Prov. Park	172	B1	44.403700 -81.465600
Macleod Prov. Park	169	E3	49.676190 -86.931000
Makobe-Grays River Prov. Park	171	D2	47.617200 -80.376300
Mara Prov. Park	173	D1	44.589000 -79.349000
Mark S. Burnham Prov. Park	173	E1	44.299900 -78.257000
Marten River Prov. Park	171	D3	46.729000 -79.807000
Mattawa River Prov. Park	171	D3	46.315000 -79.108400
McRae Point Prov. Park	173	D1	44.569000 -79.320000
Mikisew Prov. Park	171	D4	45.820000 -79.512000
Missinaibi River Prov. Park	170	B1	49.101400 -83.234700
Mississagi Prov. Park	170	C3	46.596500 -82.682500
Mississagi River Prov. Park	170	C3	47.012600 -82.632700
Murphys Point Prov. Park	174	A4	44.774300 -76.240700
Nagagamisis Prov. Park	169	F3	49.475700 -84.771000
Neys Prov. Park	169	E4	48.750500 -86.591900
North Beach Prov. Park	173	E2	43.951050 -77.522660
Oastler Lake Prov. Park	171	D4	45.309000 -79.964800
Obabika River Prov. Park	171	D3	47.221200 -80.262600
Obatanga Prov. Park	170	A2	48.323000 -85.093700
Ojibway Prov. Park	168	C3	49.990900 -92.144400
Opeongo River Prov. Park	171	E4	45.576256 -77.887363
Otoskwin-Attawapiskat River Prov. Park	169	D1	52.235700 -87.491300
Ottawa River Prov. Park	174	A3	45.741700 -76.779800
Ouimet Canyon Prov. Park	169	D4	48.773350 -88.667400
Oxtongue River-Ragged Falls Prov. Park	171	D4	45.366900 -78.914100
Pakwash Prov. Park	168	B2	50.749800 -93.551400
Pancake Bay Prov. Park	170	B3	46.967200 -84.661100
Petroglyphs Prov. Park	173	E1	44.618300 -78.041700
Pigeon River Prov. Park	169	D4	48.025041 -89.572294
Pinery Prov. Park	172	B3	43.257200 -81.834000
Pipestone River Prov. Park	169	D1	52.244300 -90.313500
Point Farms Prov. Park	172	B2	43.804000 -81.700000
Port Bruce Prov. Park	172	B3	42.664000 -81.027000
Port Burwell Prov. Park	172	C3	42.646000 -80.816000
Potholes Prov. Park	170	B2	47.958700 -84.294020
Presqu'Ile Prov. Park	173	E2	44.007000 -77.735000
Quetico Prov. Park	168	C4	48.404500 -91.498700
Rainbow Falls Prov. Park	169	E4	48.830090 -87.389580
Renè Brunelle Prov. Park	170	C1	49.453700 -82.147900
Restoule Prov. Park	171	D3	46.080400 -79.839800
Rideau River Prov. Park	174	B4	45.060000 -75.672000
Rock Point Prov. Park	173	D3	42.854000 -79.552000
Rondeau Prov. Park	172	B4	42.278200 -81.865100
Rushing River Prov. Park	168	B3	49.681850 -94.234890
Samuel de Champlain Prov. Park	171	D3	46.301900 -78.864100
Sandbanks Prov. Park	173	F2	43.910200 -77.267200
Sandbar Lake Prov. Park	168	C3	49.491000 -91.555700
Sauble Falls Prov. Park	172	B1	44.673170 -81.257350
Selkirk Prov. Park	172	C3	42.824000 -79.961000
Sharbot Lake Prov. Park	174	A4	44.775500 -76.724600
Sibbald Point Prov. Park	173	D1	44.322160 -79.325570
Silent Lake Prov. Park	171	E4	44.907500 -78.047200
Silver Lake Prov. Park	174	A4	44.829770 -76.574680
Sioux Narrows Prov. Park	168	B3	49.429570 -94.037260
Six Mile Lake Prov. Park	171	D4	44.819500 -79.733500
Sleeping Giant Prov. Park	169	D4	48.419300 -88.795500
Solace Prov. Park	170	C3	47.189200 -80.683500
Springwater Prov. Park	173	D1	44.443500 -79.748500
Steel River Prov. Park	169	E3	49.161900 -86.812600
Sturgeon Bay Prov. Park	171	D4	45.623400 -80.414100
Sturgeon River Prov. Park	170	C3	46.949800 -80.523900
The Massasauga Prov. Park	171	D4	45.203400 -80.044300
The Shoals Prov. Park	170	B2	47.884800 -83.808000
Turkey Point Prov. Park	172	C3	42.694000 -80.333150
Turtle River-White Otter Lake Prov. Park	168	C3	49.129700 -92.042300
Upper Madawaska River Prov. Park	171	E4	45.513700 -78.078700
Wabakimi Prov. Park	169	D2	50.719100 -89.448500
Wakami Lake Prov. Park	170	C2	47.489700 -82.842000
Wasaga Beach Prov. Park	172	C1	44.494000 -80.027100
Wheatley Prov. Park	172	A4	42.098000 -82.448800
White Lake Prov. Park	170	A1	48.603500 -85.880900
Windy Lake Prov. Park	170	C3	46.619820 -81.455980
Woodland Caribou Prov. Park	168	B2	51.096900 -94.749000

PRINCE EDWARD ISLAND	PAGE	GRID	LATITUDE LONGITUDE
National Park & Rec. Areas			
Port-la-Joye–Fort Amherst N.H.S.	179	E4	46.195278 -63.133611
Prince Edward Island Natl. Park-Brackley Vis. Ctr.	179	E4	46.406200 -63.196600
Prince Edward Island Natl. Park-Cavendish Vis. Ctr.	179	E4	46.492300 -63.379700
Provincial Park & Rec. Areas			
Brudenell River Prov. Park	179	F4	46.209583 -62.588556
Buffaloland Prov. Park	179	F4	46.092500 -62.617778
Cabot Beach Prov. Park	179	E4	46.557250 -63.704250
Cedar Dunes Prov. Park	177	F4	46.622222 -64.381944
Chelton Beach Prov. Park	179	E4	46.303944 -63.747167
Green Park Prov. Park	177	F4	46.590972 -63.890333
Jacques Cartier Prov. Park	177	F4	46.851222 -64.013000
Kings Castle Prov. Park	179	F4	46.019167 -62.567389
Linkletter Prov. Park	179	E4	46.402694 -63.850361
Lord Selkirk Prov. Park	179	F4	46.091889 -62.906000
Mill River Prov. Park	177	F4	46.749722 -64.166667
Northumberland Prov. Park	179	F4	45.966667 -62.716667
Panmure Island Prov. Park	179	F4	46.133056 -62.466667
Red Point Prov. Park	179	F4	46.366667 -62.133056
Wood Islands Prov. Park	181	D1	45.949722 -62.749722

QUÉBEC	PAGE	GRID	LATITUDE LONGITUDE
National Park & Rec. Areas			
Lieu Historique Natl. du Fort-Lennox	175	D4	45.120556 -73.268
Lieu Historique Natl. du Fort-Témiscamingue	171	D2	47.295000 -79.456
Parc Natl. de Forillon	179	D1	48.854300 -64.396
Parc Natl. de la Mauricie-East Ent.	175	D1	46.752600 -72.792
Parc Natl. de la Mauricie-South Ent.	175	D1	46.650000 -72.969
Parc Natl. d'Opémican	171	D3	46.884041 -79.096
Réserve de Parc Natl. de l'Archipel-de-Mingan	177	F1	50.237100 -63.606
Provincial Park & Rec. Areas			
Parc d'Aiguebelle	171	D1	48.510300 -78.745
Parc d'Anticosti	182	A2	49.463200 -62.819
Parc de Frontenac	175	E3	45.848600 -71.184
Parc de la Gaspésie	178	C1	48.941500 -66.214
Parc de la Gatineau	174	A3	45.566667 -75.949
Parc de la Jacques-Cartier	175	E1	47.317300 -71.347
Parc de la Pointe-Taillon	176	C3	48.717300 -71.993
Parc de la Yamaska	175	D3	45.429400 -72.601
Parc de l'Île-Bonaventure-et-du-Rocher-Percé	179	E1	48.496389 -64.161
Parc de Miguasha	178	C2	48.110556 -66.369
Parc de Plaisance	174	B3	45.597900 -75.123
Parc de Récréation du Mont-Orford	175	D3	45.344700 -72.212
Parc des Grands-Jardins	176	C4	47.681300 -70.836
Parc des Hautes-Gorges-de-la-Rivière-Malbaie	176	C3	47.918700 -70.498
Parc des Monts-Valin	176	C3	48.598600 -70.825
Parc du Bic	178	A1	48.355300 -68.797
Parc du Mont-Mégantic	175	E3	45.450700 -71.167
Parc du Mont-Saint-Bruno	175	D3	45.555278 -73.309
Parc du Mont-Tremblant	174	C2	46.443000 -74.344
Parc du Saguenay	176	C3	48.289900 -70.243
Parc Marin du Saguenay-Saint-Laurent	178	A2	48.133056 -69.733
Parc Régional du Massif du Sud	175	F2	46.581389 -70.467

SASKATCHEWAN	PAGE	GRID	LATITUDE LONGITUDE
National Park & Rec. Areas			
Batoche N.H.S.	165	F1	52.752800 -106.116
Battle of Fish Creek N.H.S.	165	F1	52.550000 -106.180
Fort Battleford N.H.S.	165	E1	52.713800 -108.259
Fort Espèrance N.H.S.	166	C3	50.451400 -101.712
Fort Livingstone N.H.S.	166	C2	51.903880 -101.960
Fort Pelly N.H.S.	166	C2	51.795900 -101.951
Fort Walsh N.H.S.	165	E4	49.559100 -109.901
Grasslands Natl. Park-East Block Vis. Ctr.	166	A4	49.370800 -106.384
Grasslands Natl. Park-West Block Vis. Reception Ctr.	166	A4	49.203800 -107.732
Prince Albert Natl. Park-Waskesiu Vis. Ctr.	160	B3	53.922500 -106.081
Provincial Park & Rec. Areas			
Blackstrap Prov. Park	166	A2	51.755600 -106.458
Buffalo Pound Prov. Park	166	B3	50.576200 -105.361
Candle Lake Prov. Park	160	B4	53.845000 -105.252
Cannington Manor Prov. Hist. Park	166	C4	49.712900 -102.027
Clearwater River Prov. Park	159	E1	56.929300 -109.043
Crooked Lake Prov. Park	166	C3	50.592200 -102.741
Cumberland House Prov. Hist. Park	160	C4	53.948000 -102.421
Cypress Hills Interprovincial Park	165	E4	49.632400 -109.809
Danielson Prov. Park	166	A2	51.252200 -106.866
Douglas Prov. Park	166	A3	51.025300 -106.480
Echo Valley Prov. Park	166	B3	50.808500 -103.891
Fort Carlton Prov. Park	166	A1	52.867100 -106.542
Fort Pitt Prov. Park	165	E1	53.577000 -109.806
Good Spirit Lake Prov. Park	166	C2	51.543500 -102.707
Greenwater Lake Prov. Park	166	C1	52.532000 -103.448
Katepwa Point Prov. Park	166	B3	50.693165 -103.626
Lac La Ronge Prov. Park	160	C3	55.249200 -104.769
Last Mtn. House Prov. Park	166	B3	50.722800 -104.823
Makwa Lake Prov. Park	159	E3	54.016800 -109.234
Meadow Lake Prov. Park	159	E3	54.501400 -109.076
Moose Mtn. Prov. Park	166	C4	49.821300 -102.424
Narrow Hills Prov. Park	160	C3	54.091300 -104.643
Pike Lake Prov. Park	166	A2	51.893200 -106.819
Rowan's Ravine Prov. Park	166	B3	50.995600 -105.179
Saint Victor Prov. Park	166	A4	49.395300 -105.873
Saskatchewan Landing Prov. Park	165	F3	50.664600 -107.997
Steele Narrows Prov. Park	159	E3	54.025900 -109.318
The Battlefords Prov. Park	165	E1	53.132500 -108.381
Touchwood Hills Prov. Park	166	B2	51.306400 -104.014
Wildcat Hill Prov. Park	166	C1	53.273946 -102.492
Wood Mtn. Post Prov. Hist. Park	166	A4	49.320833 -106.379

YUKON	PAGE	GRID	LATITUDE LONGITUDE
National Park & Rec. Areas			
Dawson Hist. Complex N.H.S.	155	D2	64.050000 -139.433
Ivvavik Natl. Park	155	D1	69.519722 -139.525
Kluane Natl. Park and Res.-North Vis. Ctr.	155	D3	60.991800 -138.520
Kluane Natl. Park and Res.-South Vis. Ctr.	155	D3	60.752900 -137.5101
Vuntut Natl. Park	155	D1	68.306944 -140.047
Provincial Park & Rec. Areas			
Herschel Island-Qikiqtaruk Territorial Park	155	D1	69.592100 -139.092

Continued from page 11

SOUTHEAST

Blue Ridge Parkway★★
574 miles/924 kilometers
Maps 102, 112, 111, 190, 121
From **Front Royal**, take US-340 S to begin **Skyline Drive★★**, the best-known feature of **Shenandoah NP★★**. The drive follows former Indian trails along the **Blue Ridge Parkway★★. Marys Rock Tunnel to Rockfish Entrance Station★★** passes the oldest rock in the park and **Big Meadows★**. The Drive ends at **Rockfish Gap** at I-64, but continue S on the Parkway. From Terrapin Hill Overlook, detour 16mi W on Rte. 130 to see **Natural Bridge★★**. Enter NC at **Cumberland Knob**, then pass **Blowing Rock★**, **Grandfather Mountain★★** and **Linville Falls★★**. Detour 4.8mi to **Mount Mitchell SP★** to drive to the top of the tallest mountain (6,684ft) E of the Mississippi.
At mile 382, the **Folk Art Center** stocks high-quality regional crafts. Popular **Biltmore Estate★★** in **Asheville★** (North Exit of US-25, then 4mi N) includes formal **gardens★★**.
The rugged stretch from **French Broad River to Cherokee** courses 17 tunnels within two national forests. **Looking Glass Rock★★** is breathtaking. The Parkway ends at **Cherokee**, gateway to **Great Smoky Mountains NP★★★** and home of Cherokee tribe members.

Skyline Drive, Shenandoah NP, Blue Ridge Parkway
© zrfphoto/iStockphoto.com

Central Kentucky★★
379 miles/610 kilometers
Maps 230, 100, 214, 2 27, 110
From **Louisville★★**, home of the **Kentucky Derby★★★**, take I-64 E to **Frankfort**, the state capital. Continue E to **Lexington★★**, heart of **Bluegrass Country★★** with its rolling meadows and white-fenced horse farms.
Stop at the **Kentucky Horse Park★★★** (4089 Iron Works Pkwy.) for the daily **Parade of Breeds**. Then head S on I-75 through Richmond to the craft center/college town of **Berea**. Return to Lexington and follow the Blue Grass Parkway SW to Exit 25. There, US-150 W leads to Bardstown, site of **My Old Kentucky Home SP★**, immortalized by Stephen Foster in what is now the state song. Drive S from Bardstown on US-31E past **Abraham Lincoln Birthplace NHS★**. Turn right onto Rte. 70 to Cave City, then take US-31W to Park City, gateway to **Mammoth Cave NP★★★**, which features the world's longest cave system. Return to Louisville via I-65 to end the tour.

Florida's Northeast Coast★★
174 miles/280 kilometers
Maps 222, 139, 141, 232
From **Jacksonville★**, drive E on Rte. 10 to **Atlantic Beach**, the most affluent of Jacksonville's beach towns. Head S on Rte. A1A through residential **Neptune Beach**, blue-collar **Jacksonville Beach** and upscale **Ponte Vedra Beach** to reach **St. Augustine★★★**, the oldest city in the US and former capital of Spanish Florida. Farther S, car-racing mecca **Daytona Beach** is known for its **international speedway**. Take US-92 across the Intracoastal Waterway to US-1, heading S to **Titusville**. Take Rte. 402 across the Indian River to **Merritt Island NWR★★** to begin **Black Point Wildlife Drive★**. Return to Titusville and follow Rte. 405 to **Kennedy Space Center★★★**, one of Florida's top attractions, to end the tour.

Castillo de San Marcos, St. Augustine, Florida's Northeast Coast
© S. Greg Panosian/iStockphoto.com

Florida Keys★★
168 miles/270 kilometers
Maps 143, 142
*Note: Green **mile-marker** (MM) posts, sometimes difficult to see, line US-1 (Overseas Hwy.), showing distances from Key West (MM 0). Much of the route is two-lane, and traffic can be heavy in December to April and on weekends. Allow 3hrs for the drive. Crossing 43 bridges and causeways (only one over land), the highway offers fine views of the Atlantic Ocean (E) and Florida Bay (W).*
Drive S from **Miami★★★** on US-1. Near **Key Largo★**, **John Pennekamp Coral Reef SP★★** habors tropical fish, coral and fine snorkeling waters. To the SW, **Islamorada** is known for **charter fishing**. At **Marathon** (MM 50), **Sombrero Beach** is a good swimming spot, but

Bahia Honda SP, Florida Keys
© fotoVoyager/iStockphoto.com

Bahia Honda SP★★ (MM 36.8) is considered the best **beach★★** in the Keys. Pass **National Key Deer Refuge★** (MM 30.5), haven to the 2ft-tall deer unique to the lower Keys. End at **Key West★★★**, joining others at **Mallory Square Dock** to view the **sunset★★**.

The Ozarks★
343 miles/552 kilometers
Maps 227, 117, 219, 107, 106
From the state capital of **Little Rock**, take I-30 SW to Exit 111, then US-70 W to Hot Springs. Drive N on Rte. 7/Central Ave. to **Hot Springs NP★★**to enjoy the therapeutic waters. Travel N on Rte. 7 across the Arkansas River to Russellville. Continue on **Scenic Highway 7★** N through **Ozark National Forest** and across the **Buffalo National River** to Harrison. Take US-62/65 NW to Bear Creek Springs, continuing W on US-62 through **Eureka Springs★**, with its historic district, to **Pea Ridge NMP★**, a Civil War site. Return E on US-62 to the junction of Rte. 21 at Berryville. Travel N on Rte. 21 to Blue Eye, taking Rte. 86 E to US-65, which leads N to the entertainment hub of **Branson**, Missouri, to end the tour.

River Road Plantations★★
200 miles/323 kilometers
Maps 239, 134, 194
From **New Orleans★★★**, take US-90 W to Rte. 48 along the Mississippi River to Destrehan. At no. 13034, **Destrehan★★** is considered the oldest plantation house in the Mississippi Valley. Continue NW on Rte. 48 to US-61 to Laplace to connect to Rte. 44. Head N past **San Francisco Plantation★**, built in 1856. At Burnside, take Rte. 75 N to St. Gabriel. En route, watch for **Houmas House★** (40136 Hwy. 942). Take Rte. 30 to **Baton Rouge★**, the state capital. Then drive S along the **West Bank★★** on Rte. 1 to White Castle, site of **Nottoway★**, the largest plantation home in the South. Continue to Donaldsonville, then turn onto Rte. 18. Travel E to Gretna, passing **Oak Alley★** (no. 3645) and **Laura Plantation★★** (no. 2247) along the way. From Gretna, take US-90 to New Orleans, where the tour ends.

CANADA

Gaspésie, Québec★★★
933 kilometers/578 miles
Maps 178, 179
Leave **Sainte-Flavie** via Rte. 132 NE, stopping to visit **Reford Gardens★★★** en route to **Matane**. After Cap-Chat, take Rte. 299 S to **Gaspésie Park★** for expansive **views★★**. Back on Rte. 132, follow the **Scenic Route from**

Percé Rock, Gaspésie, Québec
© Sime/Photononstop

La Martre to Rivière-au-Renard★★. Continue to **Cap-des-Rosiers**, entrance to majestic **Forillon NP**★★. Follow Rte. 132 along the coast through **Gaspé**★, the administrative center of the peninsula, to **Percé**★★★, a coastal village known for **Percé Rock**★★, a mammoth offshore rock wall. Drive SW on Rt. 132 through **Paspébiac** to **Carleton**, which offers a **panorama**★★ from the summit of **Mont Saint-Joseph**. Farther SW, detour 6km/4mi S to see an array of fossils at **Parc de Miguasha**★. Back on Rte. 132, travel W to **Matapédia**, then follow Rte. 132 N, passing **Causapscal**—a departure point for salmon fishing expeditions—to end the tour at Sainte-Flavie.

North Shore Lake Superior★★

275 kilometers/171 miles
Map 169
From the port city of **Thunder Bay**★★—and nearby **Old Fort William**★★—drive the Trans-Canada Hwy. (Rte. 11/17) E to Rte. 587. Detour to **Sleeping Giant PP**★, which offers fine **views**★ of the lake. Back along the Trans-Canada Hwy., **Amethyst Mine** (take E. Loon Rd.) is a rock hound's delight (fee). Farther NE, located 12km/8mi off the highway, **Ouimet Canyon**★★ is a startling environment for the area. Just after the highway's Red Rock turnoff, watch for **Red Rock Cuesta**, a natural formation 210m/690ft high. Cross the Nipigon River and continue along **Nipigon Bay**★★, enjoying **views**★★ of the rocky, conifer-covered islands. The **view**★★ of **Kama Bay** through **Kama Rock Cut** is striking. Continue to **Schreiber** to end the tour.

Nova Scotia's Cabot Trail★★

338 kilometers/210 miles
Map 181
From **Baddeck**★, follow Hwy. 105 S to the junction with **Cabot Trail** to **North East Margaree**★ in salmon-fishing country. Take this road NW to Margaree Harbour, then N to **Chéticamp**, an enclave of Acadian culture. Heading inland, the route enters **Cape Breton Highlands NP**★★, combining seashore and mountains. At Cape North, detour N around Aspy Bay to **Bay St. Lawrence**★★. Then head W to tiny **Capstick** for shoreline **views**★. Return S to Cape North, then drive E to South Harbour. Take the coast road, traveling S through the fishing villages of **New Haven** and **Neils Harbour**★. Rejoin Cabot Trail S, passing the resort area of the **Ingonishs**. Take the right fork after Indian Brook to reach St. Ann's, home of **Gaelic College**★, specializing in bagpipe and Highland dance classes. Rejoin Hwy. 105 to return to Baddeck.

Cabot Trail, Cape Breton Highlands NP
© Jerry Whaley/age fotostock

Canadian Rockies★★★

467 kilometers/290 miles
Map 164
Leave Banff★★ by Hwy. 1, traveling W. After 5.5km/3.5mi, take **Bow Valley Parkway**★ (Hwy. 1A) NW within **Banff NP**★★★. At Lake Louise Village, detour W to find **Lake Louise**★★★. Back on Hwy. 1, head N to the junction of Hwy. 93, turn W and follow Hwy. 1 past Kicking Horse Pass into **Yoho NP**★★.

Moraine Lake, Banff NP, Canadian Rockies
© Robert Harding/hemis.fr

Continue through Field, and turn right onto the road N to **Emerald Lake**★★★. Return to the junction of Rte. 93 and Hwy. 1, heading N on Rte. 93 along the Icefields **Parkway**★★★. Pass **Crowfoot Glacier**★★ and **Bow Lake**★★ on the left. **Peyto Lake**★★★ is reached by spur road. After **Parker Ridge**★★, massive **Athabasca Glacier**★★★ looms on the left. Continue to **Jasper**★ and **Jasper NP**★★★. From Jasper, turn left onto Hwy. 16 and head into **Mount Robson PP**★★, home to **Mount Robson**★★★ (3,954m/12,972ft.). End the tour at Tête Jaune Cache.

Vancouver Island★★★

337 kilometers/209 miles
Maps 282, 163, 162
To enjoy a scenic drive that begins 11mi N of **Victoria**★★★, take Douglas St. N from Victoria to the Trans-Canada Highway (Hwy. 1) and follow **Malahat Drive**★ (between Goldstream PP and Mill Bay Rd.) for 12mi. Continue N on Hwy. 1 past Duncan, **Chemainus**★—known for its murals—and Nanaimo to Parksville. Take winding Rte. 4 W (Pacific Rim Hwy.) passing **Englishman River Falls PP**★ and **Cameron Lake**. Just beyond the lake, **Cathedral Grove**★★ holds 800-year-old Douglas firs. The road descends to **Port Alberni**, departure point for cruises on Barkley Sound, and follows Sproat Lake before climbing Klitsa Mountain. The route leads to the Pacific along the Kennedy River. At the coast, turn left and drive SE to Ucluelet. Then head N to enter **Pacific Rim NPR**★★★. Continue to road's end at **Tofino**★ to end the tour.

Tofino harbor, Vancouver Island

Yukon Circuit★★

1,485 kilometers/921 miles
Map 155
From **Whitehorse**★, capital of Yukon Territory, drive N on the **Klondike Hwy.** (Rte. 2), crossing the Yukon River at **Carmacks**. After 196km/122mi, small islands divide the river into fast-flowing channels at **Five Finger Rapids**★. From Stewart Crossing, continue NW on Rte. 2 to **Dawson**★★, a historic frontier town. Ferry across the river and drive the **Top of the World Hwy.**★★ (Rte. 9), with its **views**★★★, to the Alaska border. Rte. 9 joins Rte. 5, passing tiny **Chicken**, Alaska. At Tetlin Junction, head SE on Rte. 2, paralleling **Tetlin NWR**. Enter Canada and follow the **Alaska Highway**★★ (Rte. 1) SE along **Kluane Lake**★★ to **Haines Junction**, gateway to **Kluane NPR**★★, home of **Mount Logan**, Canada's highest peak (5,959m/19,550ft). Continue E to Rte. 2 to return to Whitehorse.

Kluane NPR, Yukon Circuit

Notes

Notes

Developed using Globe Turner, LLC data. The information contained herein is for informational purposes only. No representation is made or warranty given as to its content, road conditions or route usability or expeditiousness. User assumes all risk of use. Globe Turner, LLC, its parents and affiliates, and Michelin North America, Inc. and their respective suppliers assume no responsibility for any loss or delay resulting from such use.

MICHELIN NORTH AMERICA, INC.

Michelin Travel & Lifestyle North America

One Parkway South

Greenville, SC 29615 U.S.A.